ANTHROPOLOGY

To the memory of my mother,
Mariana Kottak Roberts

Higher Education

ANTHROPOLOGY: THE EXPLORATION OF HUMAN DIVERSITY

1 2 3 4 5 6 7 8 9 0 **DOW/DOW** 0 9 8 7 6

ISBN-13: 978-0-07-353094-9
ISBN-10: 0-07-353094-8

Vice President and Editor-in-Chief: *Emily Barrosse*
Publisher: *Phillip A. Butcher*
Sponsoring Editor: *Monica N. Eckman*
Senior Developmental Editor: *Thomas B. Holmes*
Editorial Assistant: *Teresa C. Treacy*
Senior Marketing Manager: *Daniel M. Loch*
Managing Editor: *Jean Dal Porto*
Project Manager: *Jean R. Starr*
Art Director: *Jeanne Schreiber*
Art Editor: *Katherine McNab*
Map Preparation: *Mapping Specialists*
Design Manager: *Robin Mouat*
Senior Designer: *Preston Thomas III*
Interior Design: *Linda Robertson*
Senior Photo Research Coordinator: *Alexandra Ambrose*
Photo Researcher: *Barbara Salz*
Cover photo: *© Dennis Cox/ChinaStock*
Media Project Manager: *Ron Nelms*
Media Producer: *Michele Borelli*
Production Supervisor: *Jason I. Huls*
Copyeditor: *Sharon O'Donnell*
Proofreader: *David M. Shapiro*
Permissions: *Wesley Hall*
Composition: *9.5/11 Palatino, by Precision Graphics*
Printing: **45# *New Era Matte, R. R. Donnelley & Sons***

Credits: The credits section for this book begins on page C1 and is considered an extension of the copyright page.

Library of Congress Cataloging-in-Publication Data
Kottak, Conrad Phillip.
    Anthropology : the exploration of human diversity / Conrad Phillip Kottak.-- 12th ed.
        p. cm.
    Includes bibliographical references and index.
    ISBN-13: 978-0-07-353094-9 (pbk. alk. paper)
    ISBN-10: 0-07-353094-8 (pbk. : alk. paper)
    1. Anthropology. I. Title.
GN25.K67 2008
301--dc22
                                                            2006046622

ANTHROPOLOGY

The Exploration of Human Diversity

Twelfth Edition

Conrad Phillip Kottak

University of Michigan

Boston   Burr Ridge, IL   Dubuque, IA   New York   San Francisco   St. Louis
Bangkok   Bogotá   Caracas   Kuala Lumpur   Lisbon   London   Madrid   Mexico City
Milan   Montreal   New Delhi   Santiago   Seoul   Singapore   Sydney   Taipei   Toronto

Brief Contents

v

Contents

About the Author

Conrad Phillip Kottak (A.B. Columbia College, 1963; Ph.D. Columbia University, 1966) is a professor of Anthropology at the University of Michigan, where he has taught since 1968. He served as Anthropology Department chair from 1996 to 2006. In 1991 he was honored for his teaching by the university and the state of Michigan. In 1992 he received an excellence in teaching award from the College of Literature, Sciences, and the Arts of the University of Michigan. In 1999 the American Anthropological Association (AAA) awarded Professor Kottak the AAA/Mayfield Award for Excellence in the Undergraduate Teaching of Anthropology. In 2005 he was elected to the American Academy of Arts and Sciences.

Professor Kottak has done ethnographic fieldwork in Brazil (since 1962), Madagascar (since 1966), and the United States. His general interests are in the processes by which local cultures are incorporated—and resist incorporation—into larger systems. This interest links his earlier work on ecology and state formation in Africa and Madagascar to his more recent research on global change, national and international culture, and the mass media.

The fourth edition of Kottak's popular case study *Assault on Paradise,* based on his continuing field work in Arembepe, Bahia, Brazil, was published in 2006 by McGraw-Hill. In a research project during the 1980s, Kottak blended ethnography and survey research in studying "Television's Behavioral Effects in Brazil." That research is the basis of Kottak's book *Prime-Time Society: An Anthropological Analysis of Television and Culture* (Wadsworth 1990)—a comparative study of the nature and impact of television in Brazil and the United States.

Kottak's other books include *The Past in the Present: History, Ecology and Cultural Variation in Highland Madagascar* (1980), *Researching American Culture: A Guide for Student Anthropologists* (1982) (both University of Michigan Press), and *Madagascar: Society and History* (1986) (Carolina Academic Press). The most recent editions (twelfth) of his texts *Anthropology: The Exploration of Human Diversity* (this book) and *Cultural Anthropology* are being published by McGraw-Hill in 2007. He is also the author of *Mirror for Humanity: A Concise Introduction to Cultural Anthropology* (5th ed., McGraw-Hill, 2007) and *Window on Humanity: A Concise Introduction to Anthropology* (2nd ed., McGraw-Hill, 2007). With Kathryn A. Kozaitis, he wrote *On Being Different: Diversity and Multiculturalism in the North American Mainstream* (2nd ed., McGraw-Hill, 2003).

Conrad Kottak's articles have appeared in academic journals, including *American Anthropologist, Journal of Anthropological Research, American Ethnologist, Ethnology, Human Organization,* and *Luso-Brazilian Review.* He also has written for more popular journals, including *Transaction/SOCIETY, Natural History, Psychology Today,* and *General Anthropology.*

In recent research projects, Kottak and his colleagues have investigated the emergence of ecological awareness in Brazil, the social context of deforestation and biodiversity conservation in Madagascar, and popular participation in economic development planning in northeastern Brazil. Since 1999 Professor Kottak has been active in the University of Michigan's Center for the Ethnography of Everyday Life, supported by the Alfred P. Sloan Foundation. In that capacity, for a research project titled "Media, Family, and Work in a Middle-Class Midwestern Town," Kottak has investigated how middle-class families draw on various media in planning, managing, and evaluating their choices and solutions with respect to the competing demands of work and family.

Conrad Kottak appreciates comments about his books from professors and students. He can be readily reached by e-mail at the following Internet address:

ckottak@bellsouth.net

Preface

Since 1968, I've regularly taught Anthropology 101 ("Introduction to Anthropology") to a class of 375 to 550 students. Feedback from students, teaching assistants, and my fellow instructors keeps me up to date on the interests, needs, and views of the people for whom this text is written. I continue to believe that effective textbooks are rooted in enthusiasm and enjoyment of one's own teaching experience.

As a college student, I was drawn to anthropology by its breadth and because of what it could tell me about the human condition, present and past. Since then, I've been fortunate in spending my teaching career at a university (Michigan) that values and unites anthropology's four subdisciplines. I have daily contact with members of all the subfields, and as a regular teacher of the four-field introductory anthropology course, I'm happy to keep up with those subfields. I love anthropology's breadth. I believe that anthropology has compiled an impressive body of knowledge about human diversity in time and space, and I'm eager to introduce that knowledge in the pages that follow. I believe strongly in anthropology's capacity to enlighten and inform. Anthropology's subject matter is intrinsically fascinating, and its focus on diversity helps students understand and interact with their fellow human beings in an increasingly interconnected world and an increasingly diverse North America.

I decided to write this book back in 1972, when there were far fewer introductory anthropology texts than there are today. The texts back then tended to be overly encyclopedic. I found them too long and too unfocused to fit my course and my image of contemporary anthropology. The field of anthropology was changing rapidly. Anthropologists were writing about a "new archaeology" and a "new ethnography." Fresh fossil finds and biochemical studies were challenging our understanding of human and primate evolution. Studies of monkeys and apes in their natural settings were contradicting conclusions that were based on observations in zoos. Studies of language as actually used in society were revolutionizing formal and static linguistic models. In cultural anthropology, symbolic and interpretive approaches were joining ecological and materialist ones.

Today there are new issues and approaches, such as molecular anthropology and new forms of spatial analysis. The fossil and archaeological records expand every day. Profound changes have affected the people and societies ethnographers traditionally have studied. In cultural anthropology it's increasingly difficult to know when to write in the present and when to write in the past tense. Anthropology hasn't lost its excitement. Yet many texts ignore change—except maybe with a chapter tacked on at the end—and write as though anthropology and the people it studies were the same as they were a generation ago. While any competent anthropology text must present anthropology's core, it also should demonstrate anthropology's relevance to today's world. *Anthropology: The Exploration of Human Diversity*, 12th edition, has a unique set of goals and themes.

GOALS

This book has three main goals. My first goal is to offer a thorough, up-to-date, and holistic introduction to anthropology that systematically approaches the course from a four-field perspective. Anthropology is a *science*—a "systematic field of study or body of knowledge that aims, through experiment, observation, and deduction, to produce reliable explanations of phenomena, with reference to the material and physical world" (*Webster's New World Encyclopedia* 1993, p. 937). Anthropology is a humanistic science devoted to discovering, describing, and explaining similarities and differences in time and space. In *Mirror for Man*, one of the first books I ever read in anthropology, I was impressed by Clyde Kluckhohn's (1944) description of anthropology as "the science of human similarities and differences" (p. 9). Kluckhohn's statement of the need for such a field still stands: "Anthropology provides a scientific basis for dealing with the crucial dilemma of the world today: how can peoples of different appearance, mutually unintelligible languages, and dissimilar ways of life get along peaceably together?" (p. 9).

Anthropology is a science with clear links to the humanities, as it brings a comparative and cross-cultural perspective to forms of creative expression. One might say that anthropology is among the most humanistic academic fields because of its fundamental respect for human diversity. Anthropologists routinely listen to, record, and attempt to represent voices and perspectives from a multitude of times, places, nations, and cultures. Through its four subfields, anthropology brings together biological, social, cultural, linguistic, and historical approaches. Multiple and diverse perspectives offer a fuller understanding of what it means to be human than is provided by academic fields that lack anthropology's broad vision.

My second goal was to write a book that would be good for students. This book would be user-friendly in approach and pedagogy. It would stress to students why anthropology should matter to them and how it can be used to understand themselves. By discussing current events in relation to anthropology's core, it would show how anthropology affects their lives. Through the unique "Beyond the Classroom" boxes (see below), the book also would highlight the work that students just like them are doing in anthropology.

It's been my aim throughout my 12 editions to write the most current, timely, and up-to-date textbook available. I try to be fair and objective in covering various and sometimes diverging approaches, but I make my own views known and write in the first person when it seems appropriate. I've heard colleagues who have used other textbooks complain that some authors seem so intent on presenting every conceivable theory about an issue—the origin of agriculture, for example—that students are bewildered by the array of possibilities. Anthropology should not be made so complicated that it is impossible for beginning students to appreciate and understand. Thus, the textbook author, like the instructor, must be able to guide the student.

My third goal was to write a book that professors, as well as students, would appreciate. The organization of this text is intended to cover core concepts and basics while also discussing prominent current issues and interests. I sought to create a text that is readable, attractive, amply illustrated, and up to date and that features an extraordinary support package, including supplements that benefit both student and professor.

THEMES

This 12th edition has two themes that mirror the three goals just discussed. These themes are "Bringing It All Together" and "Understanding Ourselves."

Bringing It All Together Most texts give lip service to the fact that anthropology is an integrated, comparative, four-field approach to human similarities and differences. This book, however, takes a truly holistic approach through the "Bringing It All Together" essays that come after Chapters 6, 9, 11, 15, 20, and 25. These essays show how anthropology's subfields and dimensions combine to interpret and explain a common topic. The topics that are "brought together" are (1) deforestation, as a threat to biological and cultural diversity, which applied anthropologists have attempted to mitigate; (2) the matter of when *Homo sapiens* became fully human, behaviorally as well as biologically, and the kinds of cultural (archaeological) evidence we have for this emergence; (3) the biological and cultural dimensions of the peopling of Polynesia, one of the last major areas to be settled by humans; (4) issues involving unity and diversity, in terms of ethnicity, "race," culture, and language in Canada; (5) archaeological, physical, linguistic, and cultural features of the Basques, including their place in Europe and Basque migration to the United States; and (6) the use of cultural and linguistic symbols in the proliferation of fast food, and the biological implications of this spread, in terms of increasing obesity. Marginal icons in each chapter direct the reader to a "Bringing It All Together" essay that complements the topic at hand.

In this 12th edition, in the "Bringing It All Together" essays as well as in each chapter, I've made a special effort to highlight anthropology as a **biocultural** field. Anthropology combines biological and cultural approaches in commenting on and solving a host of issues and problems. Anthropology's comparative, biocultural perspective also recognizes that cultural forces constantly mold human biology.

Understanding Ourselves It's common and proper for texts to present facts and theories prominent in the field of study, but often such material seems irrelevant to the student. In anthropology particularly, facts and theories should be presented not just to be read and remembered, but because they help us understand ourselves. "Understanding Ourselves" paragraphs, found in each chapter, answer the question "So what?" For example, we see how the unique human combination of upright bipedalism and large brain size affects the birthing, maturation, and socialization of our children. Many of these discussions also "bring together" the biological and cultural dimensions of anthropology, and so the overall theme of this book may be stated as "Understanding Ourselves by Bringing It All Together through Anthropology's Unique Four-Field Approach."

ORGANIZATION

The 12th edition of *Anthropology: The Exploration of Human Diversity,* guided by very thoughtful reviewers, covers the core and basics of all four subfields, as well as prominent current issues and approaches.

Part I ("The Dimensions of Anthropology") introduces anthropology as a four-field, integrated discipline, with academic and applied dimensions, that examines human biological and cultural diversity in time and space. Anthropology is discussed as a comparative, holistic, and biocultural science, featuring biological, social, cultural, linguistic, and historical approaches. Part I explores links between anthropology and other fields—other natural sciences as well as social sciences and the humanities. Examples of applied anthropology from the various subfields are provided. This part was designed with one of my goals (as mentioned previously) for the text in mind—introducing a holistic, biocultural field consisting of four subfields and two dimensions.

Part II ("Physical Anthropology and Archaeology") begins with a chapter (Chapter 3) devoted to ethics and methods in the two subfields. (Ethics are considered further in Appendix 2.) Part II poses and answers several key questions. When did we originate, and how did we become what we are? What role do genes, the environment, society, and culture play in human variation and diversity? How do we explain biological diversity in the species *Homo sapiens?* How does such diversity relate to the idea of race? What can we tell about our origins and nature from the study of our nearest relatives—nonhuman primates? When and how did the primates originate? What key features of their early adaptations are still basic to our abilities, behavior, and perceptions? How did hominids develop from our primate ancestors? When, where, and how did the first hominids emerge and expand? What about the earliest real humans? What major transitions have taken place since the emergence of *Homo sapiens?* The origin of food production (the domestication of plants and animals) was a major change in human adaptation, with profound implications for society and culture. The spread and intensification of food production are tied to the appearance of the first towns, cities, and states, and the emergence of social stratification and major inequalities.

Part III ("Cultural Diversity") begins with a discussion of the culture concept, and the related topic of ethnicity, in relation to race and its social construction. Culture and language are linked through learning, sharing, and reliance on symbolic thought. Throughout Part III, discussions of relevant concepts, theory, and explanations are combined with rich ethnographic examples and case studies. Part III examines how sociocultural diversity is manifest and expressed in such domains as language, economic and political systems, family and kinship, marriage, gender, religion, and the arts.

Having explored diversity in the major domains of cultural life in Part III, we examine their transformations and expressions in the modern world in Part IV ("The Changing World"). Part IV is one of the key differences between this anthropology text and others. Several important questions are addressed in Part IV: How and why did the modern world system emerge? How has world capitalism affected patterns of stratification and inequality within and among nations? What were colonialism and imperialism and their legacies? What was Communism, and what has happened since its fall? How do economic development and globalization affect the peoples, societies, and communities among which anthropologists have traditionally worked? How do people actively interpret and confront the world system and the products of globalization? What factors threaten continued human diversity? How can anthropologists work to ensure the preservation of that diversity?

SPECIAL FEATURES

Working closely together, the author, editors, designer, and photo researcher have developed a format for this text that supports the goal of a readable, practical, up-to-date, and attractive book. I tried to follow through with my goal of making the book student-friendly.

The text, its accompanying student CD-ROM, and the Online Learning Center website work together as an integrated learning system to bring the theories, research findings, and basic concepts of anthropology to life for students. Offering a combination of print, multimedia, and web-based materials, this comprehensive system meets the needs of instructors and students with a variety of teaching and learning styles. The material that follows describes the many features of the text, student CD-ROM, and Online Learning Center, as well as the supplementary materials that support those resources.

Chapter Opener and Overview

The opening of each chapter is designed to engage the reader immediately in the chapter content. Each chapter begins with an outline of key points. The Overview is located in a box on the second page. Both of these elements help students organize their reading and concentrate on the chapter's critical concepts and main points.

News Briefs

A news story begins on the fourth page of each chapter. These stories serve as a bridge between the world we live in and the chapter content. They convey the excitement and relevance of anthropological inquiry and demonstrate that topics raised in every chapter can be found in today's headlines.

Living Anthropology Videos

This **feature**, indicated on the page margin in each chapter, directs students to video clips on the **student CD-ROM** that accompanies each copy of this book. These clips bring anthropological practices to life, showing practitioners at work and providing an intimate view of their research and subjects. The CD-ROM has 25 clips, each corresponding to a chapter in the textbook. Ranging in length from about 1.5 to 5 minutes, the clips can be used for assignments, discussion groups, or in-class activities. These clips were chosen because they are especially informative and contain visual content that can be difficult to present in a lecture format. Examples range from glimpses at the lives of different cultures to animated sequences depicting hominid ancestors in motion. Other clips were chosen because they provide a provocative look at a topic and can be useful for sparking students' interest and for starting a lecture or a discussion. A videotape version of the clips is also offered for instructor use as an in-class lecture launcher.

Every clip has been selected from a video published by *Films for the Humanities and Sciences*. The video programs from which these clips were excerpted are detailed on the student CD-ROM for those who would like to obtain a complete version on videotape.

Anthropology Atlas

The *Anthropology Atlas*, designed as an insert in the text, includes 17 maps covering topics impor-

tant to all four fields in anthropology. This feature allows students to explore the geographic and visual dimensions of anthropology through a series of annotated maps and exercises associated with each one. Cross-references to individual maps are found in the margins of most chapters. Maps also include interpretive questions to test a student's skill with map usage. The atlas is located before the appendices in the back of the book.

Bringing It All Together Cross-References

Callouts appear in the text to direct students to one of the six essays that complement the topic being discussed in the chapter (see "Themes" above). These provide ready access to the "Bringing It All Together" essays at related points within the chapters.

Beyond the Classroom Boxes

These thematic boxes, which are found in most chapters, report on student-based research. They enable students to read about the work of their peers, further highlighting the relevance of anthropology in the real world and suggesting possible research and academic options as well.

Interesting Issues Boxes

Coverage of current issues in anthropology, often with maps and photos, raises students' awareness of some of the more provocative aspects of anthropology today. These boxes are located in each chapter.

Chapter Summaries

Each chapter includes a clearly written, concise numbered summary to aid the student in reviewing key themes and concepts.

Key Terms

Care has been taken to present understandable and accurate definitions of each key term found in a chapter. These terms are highlighted in bold type when they are introduced. A list of key terms and definitions in each chapter is found at the end of the chapter. In addition, the glossary at the end of the book includes a complete list of key terms and definitions for the entire text.

Critical Thinking Exercises

After the summary and key terms, each chapter includes critical thinking questions that will challenge students to apply what they have read about in the chapter.

Suggested Additional Readings

An up-to-date list of additional reading materials, briefly annotated, comes at the end of each chapter to help guide student research.

Linkages

At the end of each chapter are comments and questions that link a text chapter to information in three other McGraw-Hill books: *Assault on Paradise*, 4th ed., by Conrad Phillip Kottak; *Culture Sketches*, 4th ed., by Holly Peters-Golden; and *The Gebusi*, a new case study by Bruce Knauft. Instructors may want to use one or more of these books to supplement the main text.

Internet Exercises

Included here are suggested exercises for the student to explore on the World Wide Web. Internet Exercises take students online to analyze anthropological issues relevant to chapter topics.

Appendixes

Appendix 1: A History of Theories in Anthropology This essay provides an overview of anthropological theories and their evolution and relevance to contemporary thought.

Appendix 2: Ethics and Anthropology This essay provides an overview of ethical issues faced by practitioners in the field of anthropology.

Appendix 3: American Popular Culture This essay explores the nature of popular culture from an anthropological point of view.

Inside Covers

This edition includes two informative visual guides. The first, located on the inside front cover, highlights the coverage and chapter locations of anthropological theories in the text. The inside back cover features a similar guide to the coverage and chapter locations of race, ethnicity, class, and gender topics.

IMPORTANT FEATURES OF THE TWELFTH EDITION

Design

The large page size and contemporary design enhance the readability of the text and the clarity of its pedagogical features.

Content

- Besides the thorough updating I do with all editions, I've added new content to most chapters. To avoid increasing the length of the book, I've made cuts as well.

- I believe that systematic consideration of race, ethnicity, and gender is vital in an introductory anthropology text. Two chapters present here are not found consistently in other anthropology texts: "Ethnicity and Race" (Chapter 14) and "Gender" (Chapter 20). Race, as a discredited term in biology, is also discussed at length in Chapter 5 ("Human Variation and Adaptation"). Anthropology's distinctive four-field and biocultural approaches can shed special light on these topics. Race and gender studies are fields in which anthropology has always taken the lead. I'm convinced that anthropology's special contributions to understanding the biological, social, cultural, and linguistic dimensions of race, ethnicity, and gender should be highlighted in any introductory text. They certainly are highlighted in this one—not just in their special chapters, but throughout the text, starting in Chapter 1. So important are these topics in this textbook that there is an *Inside Back Cover Guide to Race and Ethnicity, Gender, and Social Class/Stratification.* That table locates by chapter discussions of specific topics involving race and ethnicity, gender, and social class/stratification.

- The history of anthropological theory is a field I teach regularly and enjoy reading and writing about, but reviewers have been mixed about the need for a formal chapter on this topic in the book. Some say they would never have time to assign it; others think it's needed in an introductory text. I believe that Appendix 1, "A History of Theories in Anthropology," is substantial enough for instructors who want a chapter on theory. For those who don't see the need for such a chapter, its placement as an appendix doesn't interfere with the flow of the book. Furthermore, an *Inside Front Cover Theory Guide* highlights by chapter the major theoretical approaches discussed in the book.

- The color *Anthropology Atlas* insert includes 17 maps covering topics important to all four fields in anthropology.

- *Linkages* sections at the end of each chapter integrate the text through comments and questions to three ethnographic studies also published by McGraw-Hill: *Assault on Paradise*, 4th ed., by Conrad Phillip Kottak;

Culture Sketches, 4th ed., by Holly Peters-Golden; and *The Gebusi,* a recent case study by Bruce Knauft.

- *News Briefs,* including several from 2005 and 2006, introduce each chapter and show how anthropology attracts public attention and how it relates to contemporary events, issues, and world affairs.

- *Interesting Issues* boxes have been updated and revised, with a timely new one titled "Intelligent Design versus Evolutionary Theory." These features, which offer unique coverage of current issues in anthropology, many with maps and photos, raise students' awareness of some of the more provocative aspects of anthropology today.

- *Critical Thinking Questions* and *Suggested Additional Readings,* found at the end of each chapter, have been updated. There are five critical thinking questions per chapter. These questions allow the student to extend and apply information in that chapter beyond the context in which it was presented originally. The readings direct students to additional work related to the theme of the chapter. This is useful when papers have been assigned on particular topics.

Pedagogy

- *Chapter Overviews* are presented in a concise box on the second page of each chapter.

- *Living Anthropology entries* are textual callouts directing the student to related video content and exercises on the new student CD-ROM.

- *Internet Connection icons* appear throughout the text signaling where more information on a particular topic is available for the student to explore online. These links connect with websites that I have chosen for their quality and relevance to the topic of a given chapter.

- *Understanding Ourselves* paragraphs, providing valuable context for anthropology concepts (see "Themes" above), are designed as callouts within the text for easier reading.

- *Atlas icons* appear in the text margins to direct students to related map activities in the atlas. *Interpret the world questions* are critical thinking questions about the maps and geography, and appear on the map pages of the *Anthropology Atlas.*

- *Kinship diagrams* have been designed for added clarity.

SUPPORT FOR STUDENTS AND INSTRUCTORS

For the Student

Kottak Living Anthropology Student CD-ROM This supplement features a powerful marriage of anthropological video clips and pedagogy to reinforce concepts from each chapter of the text. There are 25 succinct video clips, each corresponding to a chapter in the textbook. Selected from full-length anthropology-related films distributed by *Films for the Humanities and Sciences,* these clips can be used for assignments, discussion groups, or in-class activities. Each clip is accompanied by a text overview and probing questions to exercise the student's critical thinking skills. These clips also correspond to the clips provided on the Lecture Launcher VHS tape provided to instructors.

Student's Online Learning Center, www.mhhe.com/kottak (originated by Chris Glew and Patrick Livingood and revised by Jennifer Winslow) This free web-based student supplement features a large number of helpful tools, interactive exercises and activities, links, and useful information. Students will need a new copy of the textbook to access the areas of the site that are password-protected. Designed specifically to complement the individual chapters of the text, the Kottak Online Learning Center gives students access to material such as the following:

- *Internet Exercises:* Offer chapter-related links to the World Wide Web and activities for students to complete based on the sites.

- *Student Self-Quizzes:* Offer students the chance to reinforce their learning through multiple choice, true and false, and essay questions.

- *Virtual Explorations:* These activities are based on anthropology-related film clips, animations, and simulations. They are excellent tools for improving one's understanding of complex processes and phenomena related to anthropology.

- *Interactive Exercises:* Available for many chapters of the text, they allow students to work interactively with visuals, maps, and line drawings to review chapter content.

- *Chapter Objectives, Outlines, and Overviews:* Provide guidance for understanding key chapter content.

- *PowerPoint Lecture Notes:* Offer point-by-point synopses of critical ideas for each chapter.

- *Glossary* of key terms, including audible pronunciation guide to select terms.

- *Vocabulary Flash Cards:* Allow students to test their mastery of key terms.

- *FAQs:* Give students answers to common chapter-related questions.

- *Career Opportunities:* Offer students links to information about careers in anthropology.

- Helpful *web links* are provided to the following:

  General anthropology web links for each chapter of the text.

  Bringing It All Together links that offer students the opportunity to further explore background related to the Bringing It All Together sections in the text.

PowerWeb PowerWeb is a resource for the introductory course that is fully integrated with the Online Learning Center website. PowerWeb content is password-protected and includes referenced course-specific web links, articles, and news briefs about anthropology. It also provides study tools and other resources for the student.

Linkages Case Studies Where appropriate, chapters end with a section titled "Linkages," in which the content of that chapter is linked to three other McGraw-Hill titles: *Assault on Paradise*, 4th ed., by Conrad Phillip Kottak; *Culture Sketches*, 4th ed., by Holly Peters-Golden; and *The Gebusi* by Bruce Knauft. Instructors may wish to use one or more of these short books as a supplement to the main text. Based on more than 40 years of longitudinal field work, *Assault on Paradise* tells the story of how globalization has affected a small but rapidly growing community in northeastern Brazil. *Culture Sketches* provides short and very up-to-date case studies of 13 different societies, several of which are classic ethnographic examples. *The Gebusi* is a new and highly readable book by the eminent anthropologist Bruce Knauft, based on his field work among the people of that name in Papua New Guinea.

For the Instructor

The Instructor Online Learning Center (originated by Chris Glew and Patrick Livingood, with revisions to the Instructor's Manual by Britt Halvorson and an updated Test Bank by Maria Perez) This easy-to-use Web site provides:

- *Instructor's Manual:* The definitive guide for teaching with Kottak *Anthropology.*

- *PowerPoint Lecture Slides:* Provide instructors with a ready-made resource to organize their lectures.

- *Computerized Test Bank:* Offers numerous multiple choice, true and false, and essay questions in an easy-to-use program that is compatible with Windows and Macintosh computers. A printed version of the test bank is also provided in a Word-compatible format. McGraw-Hill's EZ Test is a flexible and easy-to-use electronic testing program. The program allows instructors to create tests from book specific items. It accomodates a wide range of question types and instructors may add their own questions. Multiple versions of the test can be created and any test can be exported for use with course management systems such as WebCT, BlackBoard, or PageOut. EZ Test Online is a new service and gives you a place to easily administer your EZ Test created exams and quizzes online. The program is available for Windows and Macintosh environments.

- *A Question Bank for the Classroom Performance System (CPS):* CPS is a revolutionary wireless response system that gives instructors immediate feedback from every student in the class. CPS units include easy-to-use software and hardware for creating and delivering questions and assessments to your class. Every student simply responds with his or her individual wireless response pad, providing instant results. CPS questions for classroom use are included on the Instructor's OLC for instructors who choose to adopt this technology, which is available from your school's McGraw-Hill service representative.

- Information previously included in the printed Instructor's Resource Binder is now provided electronically on the Instructor's OLC. These useful guides include:

  Chapter outlines

  Suggested lecture topics

  Suggested films for classroom use

  Guide to the Lecture Launcher video supplement

  Correlation guide to popular anthologies and supplements, offering chapter-by-chapter suggestions for integrating other materials into the course.

- *An Image Bank:* Offers professors the opportunity to create custom-made, professional-looking presentations and handouts by providing electronic versions of many of the maps, charts, line art, and photos in the text along with additional relevant images not included in the text. All the images are ready to be used in any applicable teaching tools, including PowerPoint slides.

- *Links to Professional Resources:* Provide useful links to professional anthropological websites and organizations on the Internet.

Lecture Launcher VHS Tape This supplement offers professors a dynamic way to kick off lectures or illustrate key concepts by providing short (two- to four-minute) film clips pulled from the collection of *Films for the Humanities and Sciences.* Each clip is tied to a chapter in the text. A complete guide to correlating and using these clips with the text is provided on the Instructor's OLC. Most of these clips are also available on the student CD-ROM and have been incorporated into the Living Anthropology feature highlighted in the chapters. This allows the videos to be used in a variety of ways—from in-class viewing to homework assignments or independent study. The Living Anthropology feature in the text effectively links the videos to specific topics discussed by the author.

Faces of Culture Video Correlation Guide For instructors using the *Faces of Culture* video series, this guide correlates each video to the appropriate chapter in the text and recommends chapter-by-chapter uses of the video series.

WHAT'S NEW IN EACH CHAPTER?

Chapter 1: What Is Anthropology?

Chapter 1 introduces anthropology as a four-field, integrated, biocultural discipline that focuses on human biological and cultural diversity in time and space. Anthropology is discussed as a comparative and holistic science, with links to the natural and social sciences and the humanities. Chapter 1 concludes with a section titled "Science, Explanation, and Hypothesis Testing." A new "News Brief" on anthropological field work in northern Kenya begins the chapter. The section "Cultural Forces Shape Human Biology" has been revised. A redundant section on applied anthropology has been incorporated into Chapter 2. There is new information on early American anthropology, garbology, and the Trobriand Islands.

Chapter 2: Applying Anthropology

In Chapter 2, applied anthropology is presented as a second dimension, rather than a fifth subfield, of anthropology. Examples of applied anthropology from the various subfields are provided. A new "News Brief" on an anthropologist's role in

New Orleans after Hurricane Katrina begins the chapter. The chapter introduction has been totally rewritten. There is an expanded discussion of ethical dilemmas in applied anthropology.

Chapter 3: Ethics and Methods in Physical Anthropology and Archaeology

Chapter 3 focuses on ethical issues, research methods, and dating techniques. The ethical issues anthropologists increasingly confront are highlighted. Students learn how anthropologists do their work and how that work is relevant in understanding ourselves. The "News Brief" on forensic anthropology, formerly in Chapter 2, now starts Chapter 3, which has been updated throughout.

Chapter 4: Evolution and Genetics

Chapter 4 discusses natural selection and other evolutionary principles, along with genetics. I try to provide a gentle, yet complete, introduction to these difficult topics. This chapter has been revised substantially, with a new "Interesting Issues" box on evolution versus intelligent design. The discussion of natural selection has been revised and includes a new section on peppered moths. The chapter contains a new discussion of evolution as theory and fact and a new "News Brief" on chromosomes and disease. There is an expanded discussion of prevailing theories of inheritance when Mendel did his experiments. The discussion of mutations has been revised and made more concise, with new material on mutation through chromosome rearrangements. The discussions of drift, microevolution, and macroevolution have been revised.

Chapter 5: Human Variation and Adaptation

Chapter 5 surveys ways of understanding human biological adaptation and diversity, including a discussion of race as a discredited biological concept. Recent research on high-altitude adaptation is highlighted. A new introduction discusses biological diversity and problems with racial classification. The discussion of disease and evolution has been updated.

Chapter 6: The Primates

Chapter 6 describes primate traits, trends in primate evolution, and the major primate groups. Also included is information on endangered primates and on hunting by chimpanzees. Again, I've tried to cover the basics—what's interesting and relevant about primates—while avoiding the more confusing classificatory terminology that some other texts provide. A new "News Brief" begins the chapter with a discussion of ape (orangutan) tool use based on learning and its relevance to the origins of human culture. In this chapter and throughout the 12th edition, hominins (the human line and its ancestors after the split from the African apes) are now distinguished from hominids, which include humans, chimps, and gorillas. The section on gorillas has been expanded to include recent research on western lowland gorillas. Additional photos illustrate primate diversity.

Chapter 7: Primate Evolution

Chapter 7 explores primate evolution, including recent models of how and when the primates emerged. Its photos compare fossil primates with their most similar living relatives. There is a new discussion of the role of angiosperms (flowering plants) in primate evolution. An expanded discussion of Miocene apes, including a new section on Eurasian apes, examines several possible common ancestors for humans and the apes, including *Pierolapithecus* from Spain. Also discussed are the Toumai discovery from Chad and *Orrorin tugenensis* from Kenya—possible early hominins.

Chapter 8: Early Hominins

Chapter 8, which has been rewritten substantially, considers early hominins—their fossils and tool making—from *Ardipithecus* and the australopithecines to the advent of *Homo*. The latest finds and interpretations are covered. A new section titled "What Makes Us Human?" begins the chapter by examining bipedalism, the brain, childhood dependency, tools, and teeth as human features and their importance at various stages of human evolution. All charts and tables have been updated. The discussions of *Ardipithecus* and *Kenyanthropus* have been separated. New photos have been added to illustrate diversity among early hominins.

Chapter 9: The Genus *Homo*

This chapter has been rewritten substantially. The discussions of *H. habilis, H. rudolfensis,* and early *H. erectus,* formerly in Chapter 8, now, more appropriately, begin Chapter 9. Based on discoveries confirming the expansion of early *H. erectus* (sometimes called *H. ergaster*) out of Africa, Chapter 9 describes recent fossil finds in Europe. There is new material on archaic *H. sapiens,* including archaeological evidence for a human presence in England 700,000 years ago. A new "News Brief" argues that anatomically modern humans arrived in Europe earlier—but overlapped with Neandertals less—than previously thought. New illustrations have been added. A discussion of *H. floresiensis* concludes the chapter.

Chapter 10: The First Farmers

An updated Chapter 10 examines the origin and implications, and the costs and benefits, of food production (the domestication of plants and animals). The seven world centers of domestication are identified and discussed, with a focus on the first farmers and herders in the Middle East and the first farmers in Mexico and adjacent areas. A section titled "Explaining the Neolithic" focuses on the factors that influenced the origin and spread of Neolithic economies in various world areas.

Chapter 11: The First Cities and States

Chapter 11 examines the emergence of towns, cities, chiefdoms, and states. Its examples include the Middle East, India/Pakistan, China, Mesoamerica, Peru, and Africa. Students learn how archaeologists make inferences about ancient societies from contemporary ethnographic studies. This illustrates the text's overall focus on anthropology as a four-field discipline in which findings from one subfield are integral to the others. Chapter 11 parallels the structure of Chapter 10, which begins with theory and explanation and then discusses cases.

Chapter 12: Methods in Cultural Anthropology

Chapter 12 focuses on methods in cultural anthropology, beginning with a new section titled "Ethical Considerations: Networking and Reciprocation." Ethnography and survey research are among the methods considered. A new "News Brief" on restoring lost languages, with a focus on Native American languages, begins this chapter.

Chapter 13: Culture

Chapter 13, which examines the anthropological concept of culture including its symbolic and adaptive features, has been updated based on recent writing and statistics. A new "News Brief" updates efforts by the Makah Indians to return to their whaling past. A new discussion distinguishes between the moral and methodological meanings of cultural relativism.

Chapter 14: Ethnicity and Race

Chapter 14, which discusses the social construction of race and ethnicity, offers cross-cultural examples of variation in racial classification and ethnic relations. This chapter has been thoroughly updated, with the most recent sources and census data for the United States and Canada available in several key tables. A new "News Brief" describes dilemmas in racial classification that African Americans face when they visit Ghana.

Chapter 15: Language and Communication

Chapter 15 introduces methods and topics in linguistic anthropology, including descriptive and historical linguistics, sociolinguistics, and language and culture. A new "News Brief" begins the chapter with a discussion of sociolinguistic discrimination in the American Midwest.

Chapter 16: Making a Living

Chapter 16 surveys economic anthropology, including adaptive strategies (systems of food production) and exchange systems. The idea of industrial alienation is now illustrated here by Ong's study of Malaysian factory women, formerly in Chapter 23. The discussion of potlatching has been revised. The "Interesting Issues" box on scarcity has been updated based on a revisit to Madagascar.

Chapter 17: Political Systems

Using case material from various societies, Chapter 17 discusses political systems in terms of scale and types of conflict resolution. The section on "Foraging Bands" has been revised. Sections titled "Hegemony" and "Weapons of the Weak," formerly in Chapter 25, have been moved here, where they are discussed as forms of social control, along with "Politics, Shame, and Sorcery."

Chapter 18: Families, Kinship, and Descent

Chapter 18 discusses families, households, and descent groups cross-culturally, and also with reference to updated U.S. and Canadian census data. There is new material, including a new table, on changes in the divorce rate in the United States.

Chapter 19: Marriage

Chapter 19 examines exogamy, endogamy, the incest taboo, caste, postmarital residence rules, marital prestations, replacement marriage, and plural marriage cross-culturally. Also covered are divorce and same-sex marriage, updated to reflect recent events and legal decisions in the United States and Canada. There is a new section titled "Although Tabooed, Incest Does Happen." The section on royal endogamy has been revised.

Chapter 20: Gender

A thoroughly updated Chapter 20 examines cross-cultural similarities and differences in male and female roles, rights, and responsibilities. Systems of gender stratification and multiple genders are examined. There is information on contemporary gender roles and issues, including the feminization of poverty. The latest relevant census data is included.

Chapter 21: Religion

Chapter 21 surveys time-honored anthropological approaches to religion, while also discussing contemporary world religions and religious movements. This chapter features a "News Brief" on Islam's expansion, along with revisions of the sections titled "Antimodernism and Fundamentalism" and "A New Age." The section on contemporary world religions has been revised and updated, with a new table and figure illustrating number of adherents.

Chapter 22: The Arts

Chapter 22 explores major themes across various arts and cultures, from the definition and nature of art to links between art and religion, art as work, and art in its social context and transmission across the generations. New Sections are titled "Ethnomusicology," "Representations of Art and Culture," "Art and Communication," and "Art and Politics." A new "News Brief," "Narratives of Social Class and the Social Gap," focusing on film and print narratives, begins the chapter. The discussion of music has been expanded.

Chapter 23: The Modern World System

Chapter 23 examines the emergence and nature of the modern world system, including industrial and postindustrial systems of socioeconomic stratification and their impact on nonindustrial societies. The chapter has been revised and updated, particularly with discussions of outsourcing and global energy consumption.

Chapter 24: Colonialism and Development

Chapter 24 discusses the colonial systems and development policies that have impinged on the people and societies anthropology traditionally has studied. Major sections examine neoliberalism, Communism and its fall, and postsocialist transitions.

Chapter 25: Cultural Exchange and Survival

Chapter 25 continues the examination of how development and globalization affect the peoples, societies, and communities in which anthropologists traditionally have worked. Using recent examples, it shows how local people actively confront the world system and the products of globalization. There is a major new section titled "Indigenous Peoples," including a new "Beyond the Classroom" box. The chapter concludes with a final consideration of the role of the anthropologist in ensuring the continuance and preservation of cultural diversity.

Appendix 1: A History of Theories in Anthropology

Appendix 1 surveys theories in anthropology from 19th-century evolutionism, through Boasian anthropology, functionalism, structural functionalism, neoevolutionism, cultural materialism, structuralism, symbolic and interpretive anthropology, practice theory, world-system theory and political economy, to anthropology today.

Appendix 2: Ethics and Anthropology

Appendix 2 is a general treatment of ethics in anthropology, including the AAA Code of Ethics.

Appendix 3: American Popular Culture

Appendix 3 illustrates how culture is shared in contemporary society through case studies of American popular culture.

ACKNOWLEDGMENTS

As always, I'm grateful to many colleagues at McGraw-Hill. Thom Holmes once again has done an outstanding job as developmental editor. His ideas about design have been implemented to give this book a clean, modern look. I also appreciate Thom's suggestions for content revision and his guidance and substantial help as we've worked on this edition. Thanks, too, to Dan Loch, a knowledgeable, creative, and enthusiastic marketing manager. I'm also pleased to continue my association with my friend Phil Butcher, McGraw-Hill's editorial director for social sciences and humanities. Phil has provided support and encouragement for well over a decade.

I thank Jean Starr once again for her work as project manager, guiding the manuscript through production and keeping everything moving on schedule. Jason Huls, production supervisor, worked with the printer to make sure everything came out right. It's always a pleasure to plan and choose photos with Barbara Salz, freelance photo researcher, with whom I've worked for almost 20 years. Thanks, too, to Susan Mansfield, Barbara's assistant, who also worked on the photo program for this edition. I thank Britt Halvorson and Maria Perez for their work on the Instructor Manual and Test Bank for this book. Jennifer Winslow did an outstanding job updating the online components for the student and instructor websites for the book. Gerry Williams updated the instructor PowerPoint files, and Mark Stephens provided editing help on all the Internet links and bibliographic references found in the book. Sincere thanks to Sharon O'Donnell for another excellent job of copyediting; and David Shapiro for proofreading. Preston Thomas worked with Thom Holmes to conceive and execute the design.

Robin Mouat, design manager, and Alex Ambrose, photo research coordinator, also deserve thanks along with Jeanne Schreiber, art director, and Katherine McNab, art editor. Teresa Treacy, McGraw-Hill's editorial assistant for anthropology, helped tremendously with reviews and all phases of manuscript preparation. Tara Maldonado worked with Thom and Teresa to assemble the visual arts manuscript, relieving me of that time-consuming responsibility. For the creation of the attractive maps, I would like to acknowledge the work of Mapping Specialists.

Thanks, too, to Michele Borrelli, media producer, for creating the OLC and student CD-ROM with video clips, and all the other supplements. Once again I thank Wesley Hall, who has handled the literary permissions.

I'm especially indebted to the professors who reviewed the eleventh edition of this book and of my *Cultural Anthropology*. They suggested many of the changes I have implemented here. Their names and schools are as follows:

Reviewers of the Eleventh Edition

E. F. Aranyosi
University of Washington

Lisa Kaye Brandt
North Dakota State University

Margaret S. Bruchez
Blinn College

Andrew Buckser
Purdue University

Darryl de Ruiter
Texas A&M University

William W. Donner
Kutztown University

Todd Jeffrey French
University of New Hampshire, Durham

Vance Geiger
University of Central Florida

Dr. Stevan R. Jackson
Radford University

Brian Malley
University of Michigan

De Ann Pendry
University of Tennessee–Knoxville

Mary S. Willis
University of Nebraska–Lincoln

I'm also grateful to the reviewers of the seventh, eighth, ninth, and tenth editions of this book and my *Cultural Anthropology* text. Their comments also helped me plan this twelfth edition. Their names are as follows:

Other Reviewers

Julianna Acheson
Green Mountain College

Mohamad Al-Madani
Seattle Central Community College

Robert Bee
University of Connecticut

Kathleen T. Blue
Minnesota State University

Daniel Boxberger
Western Washington University

Vicki Bradley
University of Houston

Ethan M. Braunstein
Northern Arizona University

Ned Breschel
Morehead State University

Peter J. Brown
Emory University

Andrew Buckser
Purdue University

Karen Burns
University of Georgia

Richard Burns
Arkansas State University

Mary Cameron
Auburn University

Joseph L. Chartkoff
Michigan State University

Dianne Chidester
University of South Dakota

Inne Choi
California Polytechnic State University–San Luis Obispo

Jeffrey Cohen
Penn State University

Fred Conquest
Community College of Southern Nevada

Barbara Cook
California Polytechnic State University–San Luis Obispo

Norbert Dannhaeuser
Texas A&M University

Michael Davis
Truman State University

Robert Dirks
Illinois State University

Bill Donner
Kutztown University of Pennsylvania

Paul Durrenberger
Pennsylvania State University

George Esber
Miami University of Ohio

Grace Fraser
Plymouth State College

Laurie Godfrey
University of Massachusetts–Amherst

Bob Goodby
Franklin Pierce College

Tom Greaves
Bucknell University

Mark Grey
University of Northern Iowa

Homes Hogue
Mississippi State University

Kara C. Hoover
Georgia State University

Alice James
Shippensburg University of Pennsylvania

Richard King
Drake University

Eric Lassiter
Ball State University

Jill Leonard
University of Illinois–Urbana–Champaign

Kenneth Lewis
Michigan State University

David Lipset
University of Minnesota

Jonathan Marks
University of North Carolina–Charlotte

H. Lyn Miles
University of Tennessee at Chattanooga

Barbara Miller
George Washington University

Richard G. Milo
Chicago State University

John Nass, Jr.
California University of Pennsylvania

Frank Ng
California State University–Fresno

Martin Ottenheimer
Kansas State University

Leonard Plotnicov
University of Pittsburgh

Janet Pollak
William Patterson College

Howard Prince
CUNY–Borough of Manhattan Community College

Frances E. Purifoy
University of Louisville

Steven Rubenstein
Ohio University

Mary Scott
San Francisco State University

Brian Siegel
Furman University

Megan Sinnott
University of Colorado–Boulder

Esther Skirboll
Slippery Rock University of Pennsylvania

Gregory Starrett
University of North Carolina–Charlotte

Karl Steinen
State University of West Georgia

Noelle Stout
Foothill and Skyline Colleges

Susan Trencher
George Mason University

Mark Tromans
Broward Community College

Christina Turner
Virginia Commonwealth University

Donald Tyler
University of Idaho

Daniel Varisco
Hofstra University

Albert Wahrhaftig
Sonoma State University

David Webb
Kutztown University of Pennsylvania

George Westermark
Santa Clara University

Donald A. Whatley
Blinn College

Nancy White
University of South Florida

I was delighted by the enthusiasm expressed in their comments.

Students, too, regularly share their insights about this and my other texts via e-mail and so have contributed to this book. Anyone—student or instructor—with access to e-mail can reach me at the following Internet address: **ckottak@bellsouth.net.**

As usual, my family has offered me understanding, support, and inspiration during the preparation of this book. Dr. Nicholas Kottak, who received his doctorate in anthropology in 2002, regularly shares his insights with me, as does Isabel (Betty) Wagley Kottak, my companion in the field and in life for four decades. I renew my dedication of this book to my mother, Mariana Kottak Roberts, for kindling my interest in the human condition, for reading and commenting on what I write, and for the insights about people and society she provided. For the first time, sadly, this edition must be dedicated to her memory, as she died in the fall of 2005.

After almost four decades of teaching, I've benefited from the knowledge, help, and advice of so many friends, colleagues, teaching assistants, and students that I can no longer fit their names into a short preface. I hope they know who they are and accept my thanks.

I'm especially grateful to my many colleagues at Michigan who regularly share their insights and suggest ways of making my books better. Thanks especially to my fellow 101ers: Kelly Askew, Tom Fricke, Stuart Kirsch, Holly Peters-Golden, Elisha Renne, and Andrew Shryock. Their questions and suggestions help me keep this book current. Special thanks to Joyce Marcus and Kent Flannery for providing me with the domestication dates included in the map on the spread of agriculture. I renew my thanks to Joyce for her guidance on Chapter 11 of previous editions. Throughout my career at Michigan, I've been privileged to work with scholars such as Kent, Joyce, Jeff Parsons, and Henry Wright, who share my interest in state formation. I also thank Roberto Frisancho, John Mitani, and Milford Wolpoff, who are always willing to answer my questions about biological anthropology.

Since 1968 I've taught Anthropology 101 ("Introduction to Anthropology"), with the help of several teaching assistants (graduate student instructors) each time. Feedback from students and graduate student instructors keeps me up to date on the interests, needs, and views of the people for whom this book is written. I continue to believe that effective textbooks are based in enthusiasm and in practice—in the enjoyment of teaching. I hope this product of my experience will be helpful to others.

Conrad Phillip Kottak
Ann Arbor, Michigan
ckottak@bellsouth.net

Walkthrough

Chapter Openers

Each chapter begins with an outline of key points.

15
Language and Communication

CHAPTER OUTLINE

What Is Language?
Nonhuman Primate Communication
  Call Systems
  Sign Language
  The Origin of Language
Nonverbal Communication
The Structure of Language
  Speech Sounds
Language, Thought, and Culture
  The Sapir-Whorf Hypothesis
  Focal Vocabulary
  Meaning
Sociolinguistics
  Linguistic Diversity
  Gender Speech Contrasts
  Language and Status Position
  Stratification
  Black English Vernacular (BEV)
Historical Linguistics

WHAT IS LANGUAGE?

Language, which may be spoken (*speech*) or written (*writing*), is [the] primary means of communication. Writing has existed for ab[out] 6,000 years. Language originated thousands of years before that, [but] no one can say exactly when. Like culture in general, of which l[an]guage is a part, language is transmitted through learning, as par[t of] enculturation. Language is based on arbitrary, learned associati[ons] between words and the things for which they stand. The complex[ity]

A concise **Overview** helps students organize their reading and focus on critical concepts.

Ethnographers (field workers in cultural anthropology) typically have done field work outside their nations of origin. In the host country, the ethnographer seeks permission, cooperation, and knowledge from government officials, scholars, and many others, most importantly the people of the community being studied. Cultural sensitivity is paramount when the research subjects are living people into whose lives the anthropologist intrudes. Anthropologists need to establish and maintain appropriate, collaborative, and nonexploitative relationships with colleagues and communities in the host country.

To work in a host country and community, researchers must inform officials and colleagues there about the purpose and funding, and the anticipated results and impacts, of the research. Researchers have to gain the informed consent of all affected parties—from the authorities who control access to the field site to the members of the community to be studied. Before the research begins, people should be informed about the purpose, nature, and procedures of the research and its potential costs and benefits to them. *Informed consent* (agreement to take part in the research) should be obtained from anyone who provides information or who might be affected by the research.

A process of culturally appropriate networking, which will vary from country to country, is necessary before field work can begin. As one illustration, consider how I prepared for my first field work in Madagascar, which began in 1966. Before arriving in Madagascar I obtained a visa to

do research there from Madagascar's embassy in France, where I spent six months on language preparation. I needed to learn Malagasy, the language of Madagascar, a former colony of France. Once I reached Antananarivo, Madagascar's capital, I visited university anthropologists there to draw on their expertise and get their advice about my plans. Later, when I arrived in the territory of the ethnic group (Betsileo—Figure 12.1) I planned to study, I met with the province chief. Eventually I met with the heads of all the lower-level administrative units where I would be working. Next, I became friendly with knowledgeable people in the small town where I first settled. Townfolk have social networks that extend to rural areas—where I would be doing the bulk of my ethnographic field work. Through personal contacts, I created a network that eventually enabled me to work in several rural villages, one of which was my primary field site. Throughout my stay in Madagascar, I tried to stay in touch with the scholars and officials who had helped me at the outset. When I later applied for grants to return to Madagascar, I included two of those scholars as funded participants in the research. Such networking is an important part of any field research project in cultural or linguistic anthropology.

OVERVIEW

The anthropologist's deepest ethical commitment is to the people he or she studies. Ethnography refers to the firsthand study of local cultural settings—field sites. Observing and working closely with local people, ethnographers learn the details of their lives. Life histories reveal personal experiences with culture. Genealogical information is important in societies in which kinship, descent, and marriage organize social life. Longitudinal research is the systematic study of an area or field site over time. Multisited ethnography, involving more than one field site, by a team or individual, is increasingly common.

Traditionally, cultural anthropologists worked in small-scale societies; sociologists, in modern nations. How does survey research, which typifies sociology, differ from ethnography? With more literate respondents, survey researchers use questionnaires, which research subjects fill out. Sociologists study samples to make inferences about a larger population. Given the diversity that exists in modern nations, even anthropologists may adopt some survey procedures. However, anthropologists also retain the firsthand investigation characteristic of ethnography.

FIGURE 12.1 Location of the Betsileo in Madagascar.

260 PART 2 Cultural Diversity

News Briefs

A news story, beginning on the fourth page of each chapter, conveys the excitement and relevance of anthropological inquiry, even to today's headlines.

* NEWS BRIEF *

Restoring Lost Languages: A Form of Cultural Heritage Management

NEW YORK TIMES NEWS BRIEF
by John Noble Wilford
March 7, 2006

Language is a key ingredient in being human. Language and culture go together. Cultural transmission depends on language, and language is a vital part of culture. Contemporary Native Americans display a renewed pride in cultural heritage, accompanied by an interest in the languages spoken by their ancestors. As we'll see in Chapter 15, "Language and Communication," any language helps organize and express modes of thought, systems of meaning, worldviews, and cultural understandings. When languages die, so do meaning systems; cultural diversity is reduced. This story describes one form of cultural heritage management—the science of reconstructing lost languages, known as language revitalization.

In the new movie about Jamestown, the first permanent English settlement in North America, founded in 1607, the paramount Indian chief Powhatan asks Capt. John Smith where his people came from. The sky?

Responding to the question, translated by an Indian whose smattering of English probably came indirectly from the earlier failed Roanoke colony in North Carolina, Smith replies: "The sky? No. We come from England, an island on the other side of the sea."

The dialogue continues as the interpreter puts Smith's reply in Powhatan's own words, Virginia Algonquian, a language not spoken for more than two centuries. Like most of the 800 or more indigenous languages of North America when Europeans first arrived, Powhatan's became extinct as Indians declined in number, dispersed and lost their cultural identity.

But a small yet growing number of linguists and anthropologists has been busy in recent years recreating such dead or dying Indian speech.

Their field is language revitalization, the science of reconstructing lost languages. One byproduct of the scholarship is the dialogue in Virginia Algonquian for the movie "The New World."

More than moviemaking is behind the research. A revival of ethnic pride and cultural studies among Indians has stimulated Indians' interest in their languages, some long dead. Of the more than 15 original Algonquian languages in eastern North America, the two still spoken are Passamaquoddy-Malecite in Maine and Mikmaq in New Brunswick . . .

The passing of a language diminishes cultural diversity, anthropologists say, and the restoration of at least some part of a language is an act of reclaiming a people's heritage.

Blair A. Rudes, a linguist at the University of North Carolina, Charlotte, who specializes in reconstructing Indian languages, said several Algonquian communities in the East had efforts under way to recover their lost languages and return them to daily use . . .

When the director of "The New World," Terrence Malick, decided that for authenticity Powhatan should speak in his own language, he called in Dr. Rudes, who has worked with Dr. Goddard in reconstructing the defunct Algonquian language of the Pequot of Connecticut. He is also engaged in language restoration for the Catawba of North Carolina and is collaborating with Helen Rountree, emeritus professor of anthropology at Old Dominion University, on a dictionary of Virginia Algonquian.

Dr. Rudes was asked what Powhatan and his daughter Pocahontas would say and how they would say it. It was a daunting assignment.

The related Algonquian languages were among the first in America to die out, and no one is known to have spoken Virginia Algonquian since 1785 . . . Just two contemporary accounts—one by Captain Smith and the other by the Jamestown colony secretary, William Strachey—preserved some Virginia Algonquian words, including ones

In recent years linguists and anthropologists have worked to recreate dead and dying Native American speech. This field is known as language revitalization. One byproduct of the scholarship is the dialogue in Virginia Algonquian for the movie The New World. Shown here, from that 2006 film, are Colin Farrell and Q'orianka Kilcher, who play Captain Smith and Pocahontas.

Chapter 12 Ethics and Methods in Cultural Anthropology **261**

xxxiii

Interesting Issues Boxes

These boxes feature discussions of provocative aspects of anthropology today and promote critical thinking.

INTERESTING ISSUES

Ethnic Nationalism Runs Wild

The Socialist Federal Republic of Yugoslavia was a nonaligned country outside the former Soviet Union (U.S.S.R.). Like the U.S.S.R., Yugoslavia fell apart, mainly along ethnic and religious lines, in the early 1990s. Among Yugoslavia's ethnic groups were Roman Catholic Croats, Eastern Orthodox Serbs, Muslim Slavs, and ethnic Albanians. Citing ethnic and religious differences, several republics broke away from Yugoslavia in 1991–1992. These republics included Slovenia, Croatia, and Bosnia-Herzegovina (see Figure 14.3). Serbia and Montenegro are the two remaining republics within Yugoslavia. In Kosovo, which is a province in Serbia, but one whose population is 90 percent ethnic Albanian, there has been a strong movement for independence, led by the Kosovo Liberation Army.

Much of the ethnic differentiation in Yugoslavia has been based on religion, culture, political and military history, and some differences involving language. Serbo-Croatian is a Slavic language spoken, with dialect variation, by Serbs, Croats, and Muslim Slavs alike. (Albanian is a separate language.) Croats and Serbs use different alphabets. The Croats have adopted the Roman alphabet, but the Serbs use the Cyrillic alphabet, which they share with Russia and Bulgaria. The two alphabets help promote ethnic differentiation and nationalism. Serbs and Croats, who share speech, are divided by writing—by literature, newsprint, and political manifestos.

The Yugoslav Serbs reacted violently—with military intervention—after a 1992 vote for the independence of Muslim-led Bosnia-Herzegovina, whose population is one-third Serbian. In Bosnia, the Serbs initiated a policy of forced expulsion—"ethnic purification"—against Croats, but mainly against Muslim Slavs. Serbs in Yugoslavia, who controlled the national army, lent their support to the Bosnian Serbs in their "ethnic-cleansing" campaign.

Backed by the Yugoslav army, Bosnian Serb militias rounded up Bosnian Muslims, killed groups of them, and burned and looted their homes. Thousands of Slavs fled. Hundreds of thousands of Muslims became involuntary refugees in tent camps, school gyms, and parks.

The Serbs had no use for the ethnic coexistence that the previous Yugoslav socialist government had encouraged. The Serbs also wished to avenge historic affronts by Muslims and Croats. In the 15th century, Muslim Turks had overthrown a Serbian ruler, persecuted the Serbs, and—eventually—converted

For more on Bosnia see the Virtual Exploration and the Internet Exercises at your OLC.

mhhe.com/kottak

FIGURE 14.3 Former Yugoslavia, with Province and Republics.
The former Yugoslavia, although a socialist nation, was a nonaligned country outside the former Soviet Union. Like the U.S.S.R., Yugoslavia disintegrated in the early 1990s. The breakaway portions included Slovenia, Croatia, and Bosnia-Herzegovina.

In creating multiethnic states, former colonial powers such as France and England often erected boundaries that corresponded poorly with preexisting cultural divisions. But colonial institutions also helped create new "imagined communities" beyond nations. One example is the idea of *négritude* ("black association and identity"). This concept was developed by dark-skinned intellectuals from the Francophone (French-speaking) colonies of West Africa and the Caribbean. (Günther Schlee, ed. [2002] provides cases illustrating the role of "imagined differences" in ethnic conflict—the dark side of imagining communities.)

314 PART 3 Cultural Diversity

Unique Beyond the Classroom Boxes

These boxes highlight undergraduate student research in anthropology and enable students to read about the work that students just like them are doing in anthropology.

BEYOND THE CLASSROOM

Stories from Women Domestics of the Yucatán

BACKGROUND INFORMATION

STUDENT:
Angela C. Stuesse

SUPERVISING PROFESSOR:
Allan F. Burns

SCHOOL:
University of Florida

YEAR IN SCHOOL/MAJOR:
Senior/Anthropology

FUTURE PLANS:
Master's in Latin American Studies

PROJECT TITLE:
The Patrona-Empleada* Relationship Revealed: Stories from Women Domestics of the Yucatán

What research techniques are illustrated in this account of undergraduate research? Think about this student's approach in terms of the issues raised in the section on the evolution of ethnography.

My fascination with anthropology sprang to life in early 1996, during a semester of study abroad in the Yucatán of Mexico. It was also there that I first came into contact with domestic workers of Latin America. Witness to the daily interactions between my host-family and their servant, I became intrigued by the complex nature of their relationship and decided to return the following year to do research for my honors thesis.

The testimonial of a domestic worker is often the story of both her personal and professional life. This is because she works not in an office, but rather in her *patrona's* home. Over time, the distinction between employee and family member blurs. The indefinite relationship that results gives rise to many questions: To what extent is the servant influenced by the values and attitudes of her *patrona?* How does the way she perceives her own life compare with the way her *patrona* sees her? Under what conditions does their bond become less work-related and more analogous to family? What causes their association to be hierarchical in nature, and in what ways is this verticality expressed and/or mediated? These themes were the driving force of my investigations.

Through personal contacts, I met four domestic workers who agreed to participate in my research. They ranged in age from 17 to 70 years old, and had between 5 and 50 years of experience. Research methods included auto-photography, unstructured and semi-structured interviews, and participant observation. Our conversations were sometimes light-hearted, sometimes very serious, and always key to a deeper understanding of each individual. Apart from listening and discussing, I also learned from these women by watching and doing. I helped them hang the laundry, set the table, sweep the patio, and fill the swimming pool. I visited their pueblos and met their families. We spent hours exchanging thoughts and discussing life. I laughed along with many and I held a hand as one woman cried. It was by participating in simple events like these that I began to understand

the profundity and strength of these unique women. By interviewing and getting to know their *patronas* as well, I was able to analyze the nature of their relationships and place them within the context of existing ethnographic literature and theory.

The resulting thesis gives identity to the faceless numbers common in survey and demographic research. Through my writing I have attempted to let these women speak, to give them decision, control, and value. I also have explored the genre known as "narrative ethnography," which, by including first-person experiences, rejects the idea that a valid, professional study must be "objective" and "scientific." My research adds to the growing body of narrative ethnographic, testimonial, and introspective literature about women domestics and change in the Yucatán and Latin America. With each new study we are a few steps closer to a greater cultural understanding.

*Patrona literally means patron or boss, referring to the female head of the household who oversees the domestic servants.

Empleada literally means employee, here referring to the female domestic servant.

cal analysis can support and round out an ethnographic account of local social life.

However, in the best studies, the hallmark of ethnography remains: Anthropologists enter the community and get to know the people. They participate in local activities, networks, and associations, in the city or in the countryside. They observe and experience social conditions and problems. They watch the effects of national policies and programs on local life. I believe that the ethnographic method and the emphasis on personal relationships in social research are valuable gifts that cultural anthropology brings to the study of a complex society.

Chapter 12 Ethics and Methods in Cultural Anthropology **273**

End-of-Chapter Features For Easy Review

Clear, numbered chapter **Summaries**

Critical Thinking Questions challenge one's understanding of key chapter concepts.

Key Terms for quick review

Suggested Additional Readings guide student research

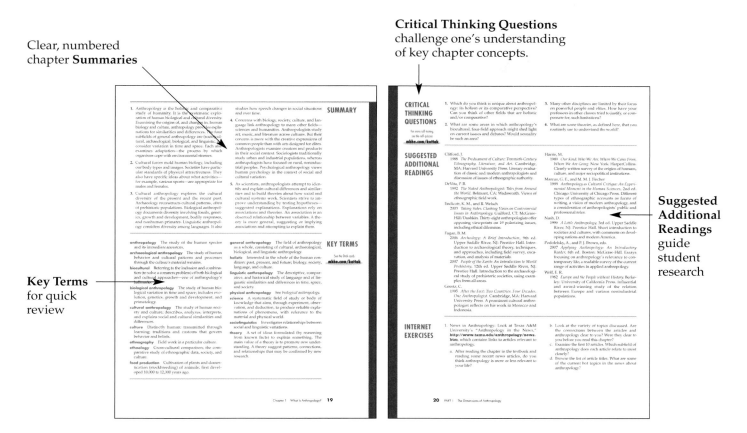

Internet Exercises take students online to analyze issues relevant to the chapter.

The **Linkages** feature encourages additional exploration of key chapter topics by linking the student to information in three other McGraw-Hill books: *Assault on Paradise*, 4th ed., by Conrad Phillip Kottak; *Culture Sketches: Case Studies in Anthropology*, 4th ed., by Holly Peters-Golden; and *The Gebusi*, a new case study by Bruce Knauft.

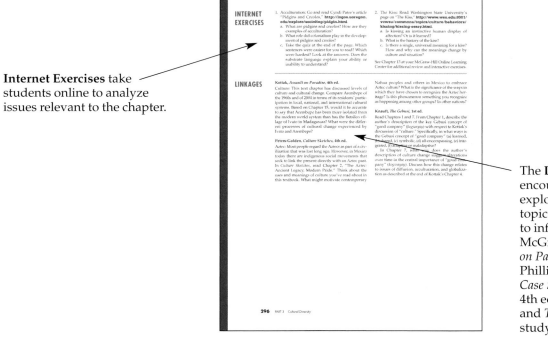

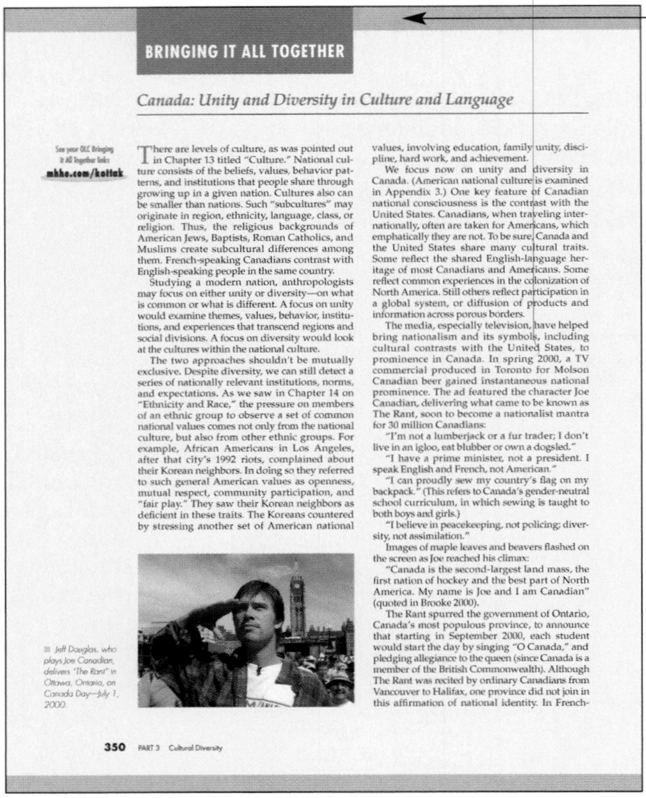

Bringing It All Together Essays

Unique thematic essays—appearing after groups of related chapters—show how anthropology's subfields combine to interpret and to explain a common topic. The essays offer a truly integrated, comparative, and holistic approach to anthropology. Through multiple and diverse perspectives, they offer students a fuller understanding of what it means to be human.

BRINGING IT ALL TOGETHER

Canada: Unity and Diversity in Culture and Language

See your OLC Bringing It All Together links
mhhe.com/kottak

There are levels of culture, as was pointed out in Chapter 13 titled "Culture." National culture consists of the beliefs, values, behavior patterns, and institutions that people share through growing up in a given nation. Cultures also can be smaller than nations. Such "subcultures" may originate in region, ethnicity, language, class, or religion. Thus, the religious backgrounds of American Jews, Baptists, Roman Catholics, and Muslims create subcultural differences among them. French-speaking Canadians contrast with English-speaking people in the same country.

Studying a modern nation, anthropologists may focus on either unity or diversity—on what is common or what is different. A focus on unity would examine themes, values, behavior, institutions, and experiences that transcend regions and social divisions. A focus on diversity would look at the cultures within the national culture.

The two approaches shouldn't be mutually exclusive. Despite diversity, we can still detect a series of nationally relevant institutions, norms, and expectations. As we saw in Chapter 14 on "Ethnicity and Race," the pressure on members of an ethnic group to observe a set of common national values comes not only from the national culture, but also from other ethnic groups. For example, African Americans in Los Angeles, after that city's 1992 riots, complained about their Korean neighbors. In doing so they referred to such general American values as openness, mutual respect, community participation, and "fair play." They saw their Korean neighbors as deficient in these traits. The Koreans countered by stressing another set of American national values, involving education, family unity, discipline, hard work, and achievement.

We focus now on unity and diversity in Canada. (American national culture is examined in Appendix 3.) One key feature of Canadian national consciousness is the contrast with the United States. Canadians, when traveling internationally, often are taken for Americans, which emphatically they are not. To be sure, Canada and the United States share many cultural traits. Some reflect the shared English-language heritage of most Canadians and Americans. Some reflect common experiences in the colonization of North America. Still others reflect participation in a global system, or diffusion of products and information across porous borders.

The media, especially television, have helped bring nationalism and its symbols, including cultural contrasts with the United States, to prominence in Canada. In spring 2000, a TV commercial produced in Toronto for Molson Canadian beer gained instantaneous national prominence. The ad featured the character Joe Canadian, delivering what came to be known as The Rant, soon to become a nationalist mantra for 30 million Canadians:

"I'm not a lumberjack or a fur trader; I don't live in an igloo, eat blubber or own a dogsled."

"I have a prime minister, not a president. I speak English and French, not American."

"I can proudly sew my country's flag on my backpack." (This refers to Canada's gender-neutral school curriculum, in which sewing is taught to both boys and girls.)

"I believe in peacekeeping, not policing; diversity, not assimilation."

Images of maple leaves and beavers flashed on the screen as Joe reached his climax:

"Canada is the second-largest land mass, the first nation of hockey and the best part of North America. My name is Joe and I am Canadian" (quoted in Brooke 2000).

The Rant spurred the government of Ontario, Canada's most populous province, to announce that starting in September 2000, each student would start the day by singing "O Canada," and pledging allegiance to the queen (since Canada is a member of the British Commonwealth). Although The Rant was recited by ordinary Canadians from Vancouver to Halifax, one province did not join in this affirmation of national identity. In French-

Jeff Douglas, who plays Joe Canadian, delivers "The Rant" in Ottawa, Ontario, on Canada Day—July 1, 2000.

350   PART 3   Cultural Diversity

Understanding Ourselves

Understanding Ourselves paragraphs point out the relevance of anthropology to the student's life.

UNDERSTANDING OURSELVES

How does the emic-etic distinction help us understand ourselves? To exemplify an emic versus an etic perspective, consider that laypeople (including many Americans) may believe that chills and drafts cause colds, which scientists know are caused by germs. In cultures that lack the germ theory of disease, illnesses are emically explained by various causes, ranging from spirits, to ancestors, to witches. *Illness* refers to a culture's (emic) perception and explanation of bad health, whereas *disease* refers to the scientific—etic—explanation of poor health, involving known pathogens. Like people raised in any culture, we suffer both from illness (what we think we have) and from disease (what we really have), which may not be the same. Bad health has both emic and etic roots.

Another example is the emics and etics of color terminology, to which we return in the chapter on language. In different cultures, people label colors differently. Some cultures have only 2 basic color terms—for light and dark—whereas others have all 11 primary color terms, plus a series of additional ones that recognize finer discriminations of shade and hue. Etically, the color spectrum exists everywhere, but emically, people interpret and classify it differently in different societies.

classic *Argonauts of the Western Pacific* (1922/1961), were similar to earlier traveler and explorer accounts in describing the writer's discovery of unknown people and places. However, the scientific aims of ethnographies set them apart from books by explorers and amateurs.

More recently, the style that dominated "classic" ethnographies has been characterized as *ethnographic realism.* The writer's goal was to present an accurate, objective, scientific account of a different way of life, written by someone who knew it firsthand. This knowledge came from immersion in an alien language and culture. Ethnographers derived their authority—both as scientists and as voices of "the native" or "the other"—from this personal research experience.

Malinowski's ethnographies were guided by the assumption that aspects of culture are linked and intertwined. Beginning by describing a Trobriand sailing expedition, the ethnographer then follows the links between that entry point and other areas of the culture, such as magic, religion, myths, kinship, and trade. Compared with Malinowski, today's ethnographies tend to be less inclusive and holistic, focusing on particular topics, such as kinship or religion.

According to Malinowski, a primary task of the ethnographer is "to grasp the native's point of view, his relation to life, to realize *his* vision of *his* world" (1922/1961, p. 25—Malinowski's italics). This is a good statement of the need for the emic perspective, as was discussed earlier. Since the 1970s, *interpretive anthropology* has considered the task of describing and interpreting that which is meaningful to natives. Interpretivists such as Clifford Geertz (1973) view cultures as meaningful texts that natives constantly "read" and ethnographers must decipher. According to Geertz, anthropologists may choose anything in a culture that interests them, fill in details, and elaborate to inform their readers about meanings in that culture. Meanings are carried by public symbolic forms, including words, rituals, and customs. (For more on Malinowski and Geertz, see Appendix 1.)

One trend in ethnographic writing since the 1980s has been to question traditional goals, methods, and styles, including ethnographic realism and salvage ethnography (Clifford 1982, 1988; Marcus and Cushman 1982). Marcus and Fischer argue that experimentation in ethnographic writing is necessary because all peoples and cultures have already been "discovered" and must now be "rediscovered . . . in changing historical circumstances" (1986, p. 24).

In general, experimental anthropologists see ethnographies as works of art as well as works of science. Ethnographic texts may be viewed as literary creations in which the ethnographer, as mediator, communicates information from the "natives" to readers. Some experimental ethnographies are "dialogic," presenting ethnography as a dialogue between the anthropologist and one or more native informants (e.g., Behar 1993;

Bronislaw Malinowski (1884–1942) learned with villagers in the Trobriand Islands. A Polish anthropologist who spent most of his professional life in England, Malinowski is generally considered the father of ethnography. Does this photo suggest anything about Malinowski's relationship with the villagers?

Chapter 12   Ethics and Methods in Cultural Anthropology   267

Internet Connection Icons

Internet Connection Icons denote where more information on a particular topic is available for the student to explore online.

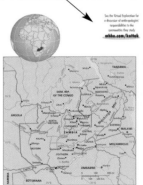

See the Virtual Exploration for a discussion of anthropologists' responsibilities to the communities they study.
mhhe.com/kottak

been followed for five decades. Periodic village censuses provide basic data on population, economy, kinship, and religious behavior. Censused people who have moved are traced and interviewed to see how their lives compare with those of people who have stayed in the villages.

A series of different research questions have emerged, while basic data on communities and individuals continue to be collected. The first focus of study was the impact of a large hydroelectric dam, which subjected the Gwembe people to forced resettlement. The dam also spurred road building and other activities that brought the people of Gwembe more closely in touch with the rest of Zambia (Colson 1971; Scudder 1982; Scudder and Habarad 1991).

Later on, education became the research focus. Scudder and Colson (1980) examined how education provided access to new opportunities as it also widened a social gap between people with different educational levels. A third major study then examined a change in brewing and drinking patterns, including a rise in alcoholism, in relation to changing markets, transportation, and exposure to town values (Colson and Scudder 1988).

Team Research

As mentioned, longitudinal research is often team research. My own field site of Arembepe, Brazil, for example, first entered the world of anthropology as a field-team village in the 1960s. It was one of four sites for the now-defunct Columbia-Cornell-Harvard-Illinois Summer Field Studies Program in Anthropology. For at least three years, that program sent a total of about 20 undergraduates annually, the author included, to do brief summer research abroad. We were stationed in rural communities in four countries: Brazil, Ecuador, Mexico, and Peru. Since my wife, Isabel Wagley Kottak, and I began studying it in 1962, Arembepe has become a longitudinal field site. Three generations of researchers have monitored various aspects of change and development. The community has changed from a village into a town. Its economy, religion, and social life have been transformed.

Brazilian and American researchers worked with us on team research projects during the 1980s (on television's impact) and the 1990s (on ecological awareness and environmental risk perception). Graduate students from the University of Michigan have drawn on our baseline information from the 1960s as they have studied various topics in Arembepe. In 1990, Doug Jones, a Michigan student doing biocultural research, used Arembepe as a field site to investigate standards of physical attractiveness. In 1996–1997, Janet Dunn studied family planning and changing female reproductive strategies (Dunn 2000). Chris O'Leary, who first visited Arembepe in summer 1997, has investigated a

FIGURE 12.2   Location of Gwembe in Zambia.

striking aspect of religious change in Arembepe—the arrival of Protestantism. Later he did a study of changing food preferences (O'Leary 2002).

Arembepe is thus a site where various field workers have worked as members of a longitudinal team. The more recent researchers have built on prior contacts and findings to increase knowledge about how local people meet and manage new circumstances. I think that scholarship should be a community enterprise. The information we gathered in the past is there for new generations to use. To monitor changing attitudes and to understand the relation between television and family planning, Janet Dunn reinterviewed many of the women we had interviewed in the 1980s. Similarly, Chris O'Leary, who compared food habits and nutritional status in Arembepe and another Brazilian town, had access to dietary information from our 1964 interviews.

Contemporary forces of change are too pervasive and complex to be understood fully by a "lone ethnographer"—a researcher who starts

Chapter 12   Ethics and Methods in Cultural Anthropology   269

Living Anthropology Videos

Notes within each chapter direct students to video clips on the **Living Anthropology student CD-ROM.** These clips provide an intimate inside look at anthropological practices.

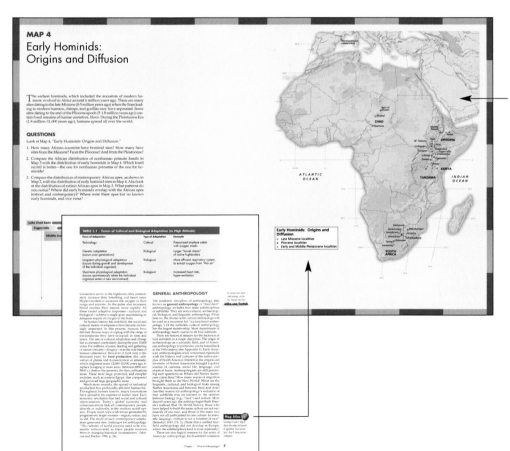

Anthropology Atlas

The in-text Atlas includes 17 maps covering topics important to all four fields of anthropology. Cross-references to individual maps are found in the chapter margins. Maps also include interpretive questions to test a student's skill with map usage.

Appendix 1

A History of Theories in Anthropology

Anthropology has various fathers and mothers. The fathers include Lewis Henry Morgan, Sir Edward Burnett Tylor, Franz Boas, and Bronislaw Malinowski. The mothers include Ruth Benedict and especially Margaret Mead. Some of the fathers might be classified better as grandfathers, since one, Franz Boas, was the intellectual father of Mead and Benedict, and since what is known now as Boasian anthropology arose mainly in opposition to the 19th-century evolutionism of Morgan and Tylor.

My goal here is to survey the major theoretical perspectives that have characterized anthropology since its emergence in the second half of the nineteenth century. Evolutionary perspectives, especially those associated with Morgan and Tylor, dominated early anthropology. The early 20th century witnessed various reactions to 19th-century evolutionism. In Great Britain, functionalists such as Malinowski and Alfred Reginald Radcliffe-Brown abandoned the speculative historicism of the evolutionists in favor of studies of present-day living societies. In the United States, Boas and his followers rejected the search for evolutionary stages in favor of a historical approach that traced borrowing between cultures and the spread of culture traits across geographic areas. Functionalists

and Boasians alike saw cultures as integrated and patterned. The functionalists especially viewed societies as systems in which various parts worked together to maintain the whole.

By the mid-20th century, following World War II and the collapse of colonialism, there was a revived interest in change, including new evolutionary approaches. Other anthropologists concentrated on the symbolic basis and nature of culture, using symbolic and interpretive approaches to uncover patterned symbols and meanings. By the 1980s anthropologists had grown more interested in the relation between culture and the individual, and the role of human action (agency) in transforming culture. There was also a resurgence of historical approaches, including those that viewed local cultures in relation to colonialism and the world system. Contemporary anthropology is marked by increasing specialization, based on special topics and identities. Reflecting this specialization, some anthropologists have moved away from the holistic, bicultural view of anthropology that is reflected in this book. However, the Boasian view of anthropology as a four-subfield discipline—including biological, archaeological, cultural, and linguistic anthropology—continues to thrive at many universities as well.

EVOLUTIONISM

Both Tylor and Morgan wrote classic books during the 19th century. Tylor (1871/1958) offered a classic definition of culture and proposed it as a topic that could be studied scientifically. Morgan's influential books included *Ancient Society* (1877/1963), *The League of the Ho-dé-no-sau-nee or Iroquois* (1851/1966), and *Systems of Consanguinity and Affinity of the Human Family* (1870/1997). The first was a key work in cultural evolution. The

second was an early ethnography. The third was the first systematic compendium of cross-cultural data on systems of kinship terminology.

Ancient Society is a key example of 19th-century evolutionism applied to society. Morgan assumed that human society had evolved through a series of stages, which he called savagery, barbarism, and civilization. He subdivided savagery and barbarism into three substages each: lower, middle, and upper savagery and lower, middle, and upper barbarism. In Morgan's scheme, the earliest

A1

Appendix: "A History of Theories in Anthropology"

This essay provides a thought-provoking overview of anthropological theory, its evolution, and relevance to contemporary thought.

Kottak Living Anthropology Student CD-ROM

This CD-ROM combines selected anthropological video clips and review questions to reinforce concepts from each chapter of the text. Each of the clips is accompanied by a text overview and probing questions to exercise the student's critical thinking skills.

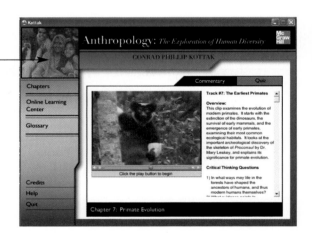

Online Learning Center

A fully updated Kottak Online Learning Center offers a rich assortment of media and content to accompany the text. The website provides professors with an Image Bank and other valuable resources, and gives students all of their book-specific, technology-based resources and activities in one convenient place.

Lecture Launcher VHS Videotape

This supplement offers professors a dynamic way to begin lectures or illustrate key concepts, by providing short (two- to four-minute) video segments taken from full-length, anthropology-related films from *Films from the Humanities and Sciences*. Video segments are tied to specific text chapters.

MAURITANIA

SENEGAL

MALI

NIGER

GAMBIA

GUINEA-
BISSAU

BURKINA FASO

GUINEA

BENIN

SIERRA
LEONE

IVORY
COAST

GHANA

NIGERIA

ATLANTIC
OCEAN

10°

LIBERIA

TOGO

0   150   300 Miles

0   150   300 Kilometers

10°

GREENLAND
(DENMARK)

U.S.

80°   60°   40°

UNITED KI

CANADA

NORTH
PACIFIC
OCEAN

60°

IREl

A

UNITED STATES

NORTH
ATLANTIC
OCEAN

PORT

MOR

40°

MEXICO

Tropic of Cancer

U.S.

20°

MAURITANI

CAPE
VERDE

COLOMBIA

GUYANA
SURINAME
FRENCH
GUIANA
(FR)

CENTRAL AF

SÃO TOMÉ

Equator

ECUADOR

VENEZUELA

EQUAT

0°

CO

P
E
R
U

B R A Z I L

WESTERN
SAMOA

BOLIVIA

TONGA

PARAGUAY

20°

Tropic of Capricorn

CHILE

A
R
G
E
N
T
I
N
A

URUGUAY

SOUTH
PACIFIC
OCEAN

SOUTH
ATLANTIC
OCEAN

Antarctic Circle

90°

U.S.

80°

70°

THE
BAHAMAS

0   300 Miles

0   300 Kilometers

CUBA

20°

MEXICO

DOMINICAN
REPUBLIC

PUERTO RICO

JAMAICA

HAITI

BELIZE

ST. KITTS AND NEVIS
ANTIGUA AND BARBUDA
DOMINICA

GUATEMALA

HONDURAS

CARIBBEAN
SEA

MARTINIQUE

ST. LUCIA

EL
SALVADOR

NICARAGUA

ST. VINCENT AND THE GRENADINES

BARBADOS
GRENADA

10°

COSTA RICA

PANAMA

TRINIDAD AND TOBAGO

COLOMBIA

VENEZUELA

0   1000   2000 Miles

Scale: 1 to 125,000,000

0   1000   2000   3000 Kilometers

Note: All world maps are Robinson projection.

ANTHROPOLOGY

1

What Is Anthropology?

CHAPTER OUTLINE

Human Adaptability
    Adaptation, Variation, and Change
General Anthropology
    Cultural Forces Shape Human Biology
The Subdisciplines of Anthropology
    Cultural Anthropology
    Archaeological Anthropology
    Biological, or Physical, Anthropology
    Linguistic Anthropology
Anthropology and Other Academic Fields
    Cultural Anthropology and Sociology
    Anthropology and Psychology
Science, Explanation, and Hypothesis Testing

HUMAN ADAPTABILITY

Anthropologists study human beings wherever and whenever they find them—in northern Kenya (see the "News Brief"), a Turkish café, a Mesopotamian tomb, or a North American shopping mall. Anthropology is the exploration of human diversity in time and space. Anthropology studies the whole of the human condition: past, present, and future; biology, society, language, and culture. Of particular interest is the diversity that comes through human adaptability.

Humans are among the world's most adaptable animals. In the Andes of South America, people wake up in villages 16,000 feet above sea level and then trek 1,500 feet higher to work in tin mines. Tribes in the Australian desert worship animals and discuss philosophy. People survive malaria in the tropics. Men have walked on the moon. The model of the *Starship Enterprise* in Washington's Smithsonian Institution symbolizes the desire to "seek out new life and civilizations, to boldly go where no one has gone before." Wishes to know the unknown, control the uncontrollable, and create order out

3

of chaos find expression among all peoples. Creativity, adaptability, and flexibility are basic human attributes, and human diversity is the subject matter of anthropology.

Students are often surprised by the breadth of **anthropology,** which is the study of the human species and its immediate ancestors. Anthropology is a uniquely comparative and **holistic** science. Holism refers to the study of the whole of the human condition: past, present, and future; biology, society, language, and culture. (See the "News Brief" for an account of the varied techniques that anthropologists have used to study the Ariaal people of northern Kenya since the 1970s.) Most people think that anthropologists study fossils and nonindustrial, non-Western cultures, such as the Ariaal, and many of them do. But anthropology is much more than the study of nonindustrial peoples: It is a comparative field that examines all societies, ancient and modern, simple and complex. The other social sciences tend to focus on a single society, usually an industrial nation like the United States or Canada. Anthropology, however, offers a unique cross-cultural perspective by constantly comparing the customs of one society with those of others.

People share society—organized life in groups—with other animals, including baboons, wolves, and even ants. Culture, however, is distinctly human. **Cultures** are traditions and customs, transmitted through learning, that form and guide the beliefs and behavior of the people exposed to them. Children learn such a tradition by growing up in a particular society, through a process called enculturation. Cultural traditions include customs and opinions, developed over the generations, about proper and improper behavior. These traditions answer such questions as: How should we do things? How do we make sense of the world? How do we tell right from wrong? What is right, and what is wrong? A culture produces a degree of consistency in behavior and thought among the people who live in a particular society.

The most critical element of cultural traditions is their transmission through learning rather than through biological inheritance. Culture is not itself biological, but it rests on certain features of human biology. For more than a million years, humans have had at least some of the biological capacities on which culture depends. These abilities are to learn, to think symbolically, to use language, and to employ tools and other products in organizing their lives and adapting to their environments.

Anthropology confronts and ponders major questions of human existence as it explores human biological and cultural diversity in time and space. By examining ancient bones and tools, we unravel the mysteries of human origins. When did our ancestors separate from those remote great-aunts and great-uncles whose descendants are the apes? Where and when did *Homo sapiens* originate? How has our species changed? What are we now, and where are we going? How have changes in culture and society influenced biological change? Our genus, *Homo,* has been changing for more than one million years. Humans continue to adapt and change both biologically and culturally.

OVERVIEW

Exploring human biological and cultural diversity in time and space, anthropology confronts basic questions of human existence and survival: how we originated, how we have changed, and how we are still changing. Anthropology is holistic, studying the whole of the human condition: past, present, and future; biology, society, language, and culture. Anthropology's four subfields are cultural, archaeological, biological, and linguistic anthropology.

Culture is a key aspect of human adaptability and success. Cultures are traditions and customs, transmitted through learning, that guide the beliefs and behavior of the people exposed to them. Cultural forces constantly mold and shape human biology and behavior. Cultural anthropology examines cultural diversity of the present and recent past. Archaeology reconstructs behavior by studying material remains. Biological anthropologists study human fossils, genetics, and bodily growth. They also study nonhuman primates (monkeys and apes). Linguistic anthropology considers how speech varies with social factors and over time. Anthropology is related to many other fields: both natural sciences (e.g., biology) and social sciences (e.g., sociology).

ADAPTATION, VARIATION, AND CHANGE

Adaptation refers to the processes by which organisms cope with environmental forces and stresses, such as those posed by climate and *topography* or terrains, also called landforms. How do organisms change to fit their environments, such as dry climates or high mountain altitudes? Like other animals, humans use biological means of adaptation. But humans are unique in also having cultural means of adaptation. Table 1.1 summarizes the cultural and biological means that humans use to adapt to high altitudes.

Mountainous terrains pose particular challenges, those associated with high altitude and oxygen deprivation. Consider four ways (one cultural and three biological) in which humans may cope with low oxygen pressure at high altitudes. Illustrating cultural (technological) adaptation would be a pressurized airplane cabin equipped with oxygen masks. There are three ways of adapting biologically to high altitudes: genetic

Remote and Poked, Anthropology's Dream Tribe

NEW YORK TIMES NEWS BRIEF

by Marc Lacey
December 18, 2005

"Been on any digs lately?" Anthropologists are accustomed to that question, after announcing their profession. Often people confuse anthropology with archaeology, which is one—but just one—of anthropology's four subfields. Many anthropologists do dig in the ground, but others dig into the intricacies of human biology and living cultural expression. Anthropologists are known for their close observation of human behavior in natural settings and their focus on diversity. It is typical of the anthropological approach to go right to—and live with—the local people, whether in northern Kenya, as described here, or in middle-class America.

Anthropologists study human biology and culture in varied times and places and in a rapidly changing world. This news story focuses on a remote population, the Ariaal of northern Kenya, whom anthropologists have been studying since the 1970s. This account previews the multifaceted research interests that anthropologists have. Among the Ariaal, anthropologists have studied a range of topics, including kinship and marriage customs, conflict, and even biomedical issues such as illness and body type and function. As you read this account, consider, too, what anthropologists get from the people being studied and vice versa.

Anthropologists and other researchers have long searched the globe for people isolated from the modern world. The Ariaal, a nomadic community of about 10,000 people in northern Kenya, have been seized on by researchers since the 1970's, after one anthropologist, Elliot Fratkin—stumbled upon them and began publishing his accounts of their lives . . . .

Other researchers have done studies on everything from their cultural practices to their testosterone levels. *National Geographic* focused on the Ariaal in 1999, in an article on vanishing cultures.

But over the years, more and more Ariaal—like the Masai and the Turkana in Kenya and the Tuaregs and Bedouins elsewhere in Africa—are settling down. Many have emigrated closer to Marsabit, the nearest town, which has cellphone reception and even sporadic Internet access.

The scientists continue to arrive in Ariaal country, with their notebooks, tents and bizarre queries, but now they document a semi-isolated people straddling modern life and more traditional ways.

"The era of finding isolated tribal groups is probably over," said Dr. Fratkin, a professor at Smith College who has lived with the Ariaal for long stretches and is regarded by some of them as a member of the tribe.

For Benjamin C. Campbell, a biological anthropologist at Boston University who was introduced to the Ariaal by Dr. Fratkin, their way of life, diet and cultural practices make them worthy of study.

Other academics agree. Local residents say they have been asked over the years how many livestock they own (many), how many times they have had diarrhea in the last month (often) and what they ate the day before yesterday (usually meat, milk or blood).

Ariaal women have been asked about the work they do, which seems to exceed that of the men, and about local marriage customs, which compel their prospective husbands to hand over livestock to their parents before the ceremony can take place . . .

The researchers may not know this, but the Ariaal have been studying them all these years as well.

The Ariaal note that foreigners slather white liquid on their very white skin to protect them from the sun, and that many favor short pants that show off their legs and the clunky boots on their feet. Foreigners often partake of the local food but drink water out of bottles and munch on strange food in wrappers between meals, the Ariaal observe.

■ *Koitaton Garawale (left) is amused by questions posed by researcher Daniel Lemoille in Songa, Kenya, on December 1, 2005. The Ariaal, a nomadic community of about 10,000 people in northern Kenya, have been studied since the 1970s by Eliot Fratkin and other anthropologists, representing various subfields.*

The scientists leave tracks as well as memories behind. For instance, it is not uncommon to see nomads in T-shirts bearing university logos, gifts from departing academics.

In Lewogoso Lukumai, a circle of makeshift huts near the Ndoto Mountains, nomads rushed up to a visitor and asked excitedly in the Samburu language, "Where's Elliot?"

They meant Dr. Fratkin, who describes in his book "Ariaal Pastoralists of Kenya" how in 1974 he stumbled upon the Ariaal, who had been little known until then. With money from the University of London and the Smithsonian Institution, he was traveling north from Nairobi in search of isolated agro-pastoralist groups in Ethiopia. But a coup toppled Haile Selassie, then the emperor, and the border between the countries was closed. So as he sat in a bar in Marsabit, a boy approached and, mistaking him for a tourist, asked if he wanted to see the elephants in a nearby forest. When the aspiring anthropologist declined, the boy asked if he wanted to see a traditional ceremony at a local village instead. That was Dr. Fratkin's introduction to the Ariaal, who share cultural traits with the Samburu and Rendille tribes of Kenya.

Soon after, he was living with the Ariaal, learning their language and customs while fighting off mosquitoes and fleas in his hut of sticks covered with grass.

The Ariaal wear sandals made from old tires and many still rely on their cows, camels and goats to survive. Drought is a regular feature of their world, coming in regular intervals and testing their durability.

"I was young when Elliot first arrived," recalled an Ariaal elder known as Lenampere in Lewogoso

Lukumai, a settlement that moves from time to time to a new patch of sand. "He came here and lived with us. He drank milk and blood with us. After him, so many others came." . . .

Not all African tribes are as welcoming to researchers, even those with the necessary permits from government bureaucrats. But the Ariaal have a reputation for cooperating—in exchange, that is, for pocket money. "They think I'm stupid for asking dumb questions," said Daniel Lemoille, headmaster of the school in Songa, a village outside of Marsabit for Ariaal nomads who have settled down, and a frequent research assistant for visiting professors. "You have to try to explain that these same questions are asked to people all over the world and that their answers will help advance science." . . .

The Ariaal have no major gripes about the studies, although the local chief in Songa, Stephen Lesseren, who wore a Boston University T-shirt the other day, said he wished their work would lead to more tangible benefits for his people.

"We don't mind helping people get their Ph.D.'s," he said. "But once they get their Ph.D.'s, many of them go away. They don't send us their reports . . . We want feedback. We want development."

Even when conflicts break out in the area, as happened this year as members of rival tribes slaughtered each other, victimizing the Ariaal, the research does not cease. With tensions still high, John G. Galaty, an anthropologist at McGill University in Montreal who studies ethnic conflicts, arrived in northern Kenya to question them.

In a study in *The International Journal of Impotence Research,* Dr.

Campbell found that Ariaal men with many wives showed less erectile dysfunction than did men of the same age with fewer spouses.

Dr. Campbell's body image study, published in the *Journal of Cross-Cultural Psychology* this year, also found that Ariaal men are much more consistent than men in other parts of the world in their views of the average man's body [one like their own] and what they think women want [one like their own].

Dr. Campbell came across no billboards or international magazines in Ariaal country and only one television in a local restaurant that played CNN, leading him to contend that Ariaal men's views of their bodies were less affected by media images of burly male models with six-pack stomachs and rippling chests.

To test his theories, a nonresearcher without a Ph.D. showed a group of Ariaal men a copy of *Men's Health* magazine full of pictures of impossibly well-sculpted men and women. The men looked on with rapt attention and admired the chiseled forms.

"That one, I like," said one nomad who was up in his years, pointing at a photo of a curvy woman who was clearly a regular at the gym. Another old-timer gazed at the bulging pectoral muscles of a male bodybuilder in the magazine and posed a question that got everybody talking. Was it a man, he asked, or a very, very strong woman?

———

SOURCE: Marc Lacey, "Remote and Poked, Anthropology's Dream Tribe," *New York Times,* December 18, 2005, Late Edition—Final, Section 1, p. 1.

adaptation, long-term physiological adaptation, and short-term physiological adaptation. First, native populations of high-altitude areas, such as the Andes of Peru and the Himalayas of Tibet and Nepal, seem to have acquired certain genetic advantages for life at very high altitudes. The Andean tendency to develop a voluminous chest and lungs probably has a genetic basis. Second,

regardless of their genes, people who grow up at a high altitude become physiologically more efficient there than genetically similar people who have grown up at sea level would be. This illustrates long-term physiological adaptation during the body's growth and development. Third, humans also have the capacity for short-term or immediate physiological adaptation. Thus, when

6 PART 1 The Dimensions of Anthropology

TABLE 1.1 Forms of Cultural and Biological Adaptation (to High Altitude)

Form of Adaptation	Type of Adaptation	Example
Technology	Cultural	Pressurized airplane cabin with oxygen masks
Genetic adaptation (occurs over generations)	Biological	Larger "barrel chests" of native highlanders
Long-term physiological adaptation (occurs during growth and development of the individual organism)	Biological	More efficient respiratory system, to extract oxygen from "thin air"
Short-term physiological adaptation (occurs spontaneously when the individual organism enters a new environment)	Biological	Increased heart rate, hyperventilation

lowlanders arrive in the highlands, they immediately increase their breathing and heart rates. Hyperventilation increases the oxygen in their lungs and arteries. As the pulse also increases, blood reaches their tissues more rapidly. All these varied adaptive responses—cultural and biological—achieve a single goal: maintaining an adequate supply of oxygen to the body.

As human history has unfolded, the social and cultural means of adaptation have become increasingly important. In this process, humans have devised diverse ways of coping with the range of environments they have occupied in time and space. The rate of cultural adaptation and change has accelerated, particularly during the past 10,000 years. For millions of years, hunting and gathering of nature's bounty—*foraging*—was the sole basis of human subsistence. However, it took only a few thousand years for **food production** (the cultivation of plants and domestication of animals), which originated some 12,000–10,000 years ago, to replace foraging in most areas. Between 6000 and 5000 B.P. (before the present), the first civilizations arose. These were large, powerful, and complex societies, such as ancient Egypt, that conquered and governed large geographic areas.

Much more recently, the spread of industrial production has profoundly affected human life. Throughout human history, major innovations have spread at the expense of earlier ones. Each economic revolution has had social and cultural repercussions. Today's global economy and communications link all contemporary people, directly or indirectly, in the modern world system. People must cope with forces generated by progressively larger systems—region, nation, and world. The study of such contemporary adaptations generates new challenges for anthropology: "The cultures of world peoples need to be constantly rediscovered as these people reinvent them in changing historical circumstances" (Marcus and Fischer 1986, p. 24).

GENERAL ANTHROPOLOGY

The academic discipline of anthropology, also known as **general anthropology** or "four-field" anthropology, includes four main subdisciplines or subfields. They are sociocultural, archaeological, biological, and linguistic anthropology. (From here on, the shorter term *cultural anthropology* will be used as a synonym for "sociocultural anthropology.") Of the subfields, cultural anthropology has the largest membership. Most departments of anthropology teach courses in all four subfields.

There are historical reasons for the inclusion of four subfields in a single discipline. The origin of anthropology as a scientific field, and of American anthropology in particular, can be traced back to the 19th century (see Appendix 1). Early American anthropologists were concerned especially with the history and cultures of the native peoples of North America. Interest in the origins and diversity of Native Americans brought together studies of customs, social life, language, and physical traits. Anthropologists are still pondering such questions as: Where did Native Americans come from? How many waves of migration brought them to the New World? What are the linguistic, cultural, and biological links among Native Americans and between them and Asia? Another reason for anthropology's inclusion of four subfields was an interest in the relation between biology (e.g., "race") and culture. More than 60 years ago, the anthropologist Ruth Benedict realized that "In World history, those who have helped to build the same culture are not necessarily of one race, and those of the same race have not all participated in one culture. In scientific language, culture is not a function of race" (Benedict 1940, Ch. 2). (Note that a unified four-field anthropology did not develop in Europe, where the subdisciplines tend to exist separately.)

There are also logical reasons for the unity of American anthropology. Each subfield considers

For current news about anthropology, see the OLC Internet Exercises

mhhe.com/kottak

Map Atlas

See Maps 8 and 9. Map 8 shows the origin and spread of agriculture (food production). Map 9 shows ancient civilizations.

Early American anthropology was especially concerned with the history and cultures of Native North Americans. Ely S. Parker, or Ha-sa-no-an-da, was a Seneca Indian who made important contributions to early anthropology. Parker also served as Commissioner of Indian Affairs for the United States.

For a quiz on the subdisciplines of anthropology, see the Interactive Exercise

mhhe.com/kottak

variation in time and space (that is, in different geographic areas). Cultural and archaeological anthropologists study (among many other topics) changes in social life and customs. Archaeologists have used studies of living societies and behavior patterns to imagine what life might have been like in the past. Biological anthropologists examine evolutionary changes in physical form, for example, anatomical changes that might have been associated with the origin of tool use or language. Linguistic anthropologists may reconstruct the basics of ancient languages by studying modern ones.

The subdisciplines influence each other as anthropologists talk to each other, read books and journals, and associate in professional organizations. General anthropology explores the basics of human biology, society, and culture and considers their interrelations. Anthropologists share certain key assumptions. Perhaps the most fundamental is the idea that sound conclusions about "human nature" cannot be derived from studying a single nation, society, or cultural tradition. A comparative, cross-cultural approach is essential.

Cultural Forces Shape Human Biology

For example, anthropology's comparative, biocultural perspective recognizes that cultural forces constantly mold human biology. (**Biocultural** refers to the inclusion and combination of both biological and cultural perspectives and approaches to comment on or solve a particular issue or problem.) Culture is a key environmental force in determining how human bodies grow and develop. Cultural traditions promote certain activities and abilities, discourage others, and set standards of physical well-being and attractiveness. Physical activities, including sports, which are influenced by culture, help build the body. For example, North American girls are encour-

aged to pursue, and therefore do well in competition involving figure skating, gymnastics, track and field, swimming, diving, and many other sports. Brazilian girls, although excelling in the team sports of basketball and volleyball, haven't fared nearly as well in individual sports as have their American and Canadian counterparts. Why are people encouraged to excel as athletes in some nations but not others? Why do people in some countries invest so much time and effort in competitive sports that their bodies change significantly as a result?

Cultural standards of attractiveness and propriety influence participation and achievement in sports. Americans run or swim not just to compete but to keep trim and fit. Brazil's beauty standards accept more fat, especially in female buttocks and hips. Brazilian men have had some international success in swimming and running, but Brazil rarely sends female swimmers or runners to the Olympics. One reason Brazilian women avoid competitive swimming in particular may be that sport's effects on the body. Years of swimming sculpt a distinctive physique: an enlarged upper torso, a massive neck, and powerful shoulders and back. Successful female swimmers tend to be big, strong, and bulky. The countries that produce them most consistently are the United States, Canada, Australia, Germany, the Scandinavian nations, the Netherlands, and the former Soviet Union, where this body type isn't as stigmatized as it is in Latin countries. Swimmers develop hard bodies, but Brazilian culture says that women

UNDERSTANDING OURSELVES

Our parents may tell us that drinking milk and eating vegetables promote healthy growth, but they don't as readily recognize the role that culture plays in shaping our bodies. Our genetic attributes provide a foundation for our growth and development, but human biology is fairly plastic. That is, it is malleable; the environment influences how we grow. Identical twins raised from birth in radically different environments (e.g., one in the high Andes and one at sea level) will not, as adults, be physically identical. Nutrition matters in growth; so do cultural guidelines about what is proper for boys and girls to do. Culture is an environmental force that affects our development as much as do nutrition, heat, cold, and altitude. One aspect of culture is how it provides opportunities for various activities. We get to be good at sports by practicing them. When you grew up, which was it easiest for you to engage in—baseball, golf, mountain climbing, fencing, or some other sport? Think about why.

Years of swimming sculpt a distinctive physique: an enlarged upper torso, a massive neck, and powerful shoulders and back. Shown here are members of the Stanford University swim team.

should be soft, with big hips and buttocks, not big shoulders. Many young female swimmers in Brazil choose to abandon the sport rather than the "feminine" body ideal.

THE SUBDISCIPLINES OF ANTHROPOLOGY

Cultural Anthropology

Cultural anthropology is the study of human society and culture, the subfield that describes, analyzes, interprets, and explains social and cultural similarities and differences. To study and interpret cultural diversity, cultural anthropologists engage in two kinds of activity: ethnography (based on field work) and ethnology (based on cross-cultural comparison). **Ethnography** provides an account of a particular community, society, or culture. During ethnographic field work, the ethnographer gathers data that he or she organizes, describes, analyzes, and interprets to build and present that account, which may be in the form of a book, article, or film. Traditionally, ethnographers have lived in small communities (such as Arembepe, Brazil—see "Interesting Issues" on pages 12–13) and studied local behavior, beliefs, customs, social life, economic activities, politics, and religion. What

kind of experience is ethnography for the ethnographer? The box offers some clues.

The anthropological perspective derived from ethnographic field work often differs radically from that of economics or political science. Those fields focus on national and official organizations and policies and often on elites. However, the groups that anthropologists have traditionally studied usually have been relatively poor and powerless, as are most people in the world today. Ethnographers often observe discriminatory practices directed toward such people, who experience food shortages, dietary deficiencies, and other aspects of poverty. Political scientists tend to study programs that national planners develop, while anthropologists discover how these programs work on the local level.

Cultures are not isolated. As noted by Franz Boas (1940/1966) many years ago, contact between neighboring tribes has always existed and has extended over enormous areas. "Human populations construct their cultures in interaction with one another, and not in isolation" (Wolf 1982, p. ix). Villagers increasingly participate in regional, national, and world events. Exposure to external forces comes through the mass media, migration, and modern transportation. City and nation increasingly invade local communities with the arrival of tourists, development agents, government and religious officials, and political candidates. Such linkages are prominent components of regional, national, and international systems of politics, economics, and information. These larger systems increasingly affect the people and places anthropology traditionally has studied. The study of such linkages and systems is part of the subject matter of modern anthropology.

Ethnology examines, interprets, analyzes, and compares the results of ethnography—the data gathered in different societies. It uses such data to compare and contrast and to make generalizations about society and culture. Looking beyond the particular to the more general, ethnologists attempt to identify and explain cultural differences and similarities, to test hypotheses, and to build theory to enhance our understanding of how social and cultural systems work. (See the section "Science, Explanation, and Hypothesis Testing" at the end of this chapter.) Ethnology gets its data for comparison not just from ethnography but also from the other subfields, particularly from archaeological anthropology, which reconstructs social systems of the past. (Table 1.2 summarizes the main contrasts between ethnography and ethnology.)

Archaeological Anthropology

Archaeological anthropology (more simply, "archaeology") reconstructs, describes, and interprets human behavior and cultural patterns through material remains. At sites where people live or have lived, archaeologists find artifacts, material items that humans have made, used, or modified, such as tools, weapons, camp sites, buildings, and garbage. Plant and animal remains and ancient garbage tell stories about consumption and activities. Wild and domesticated grains have different characteristics, which allow archaeologists to distinguish between gathering and cultivation. Examination of animal bones reveals the ages of slaughtered animals and provides other information useful in determining whether species were wild or domesticated.

Analyzing such data, archaeologists answer several questions about ancient economies. Did the group get its meat from hunting, or did it domesticate and breed animals, killing only those of a certain age and sex? Did plant food come from wild plants or from sowing, tending, and harvest-

 STUDENT CD-ROM LIVING ANTHROPOLOGY

"New" Knowledge among the Batak
Track 1

This clip shows Batak women, men, and children at work, making a living. It describes how they grow rice in an environmentally friendly way, unlike the destructive farming techniques of the lowlanders who have invaded their homeland. How have the Batak and conservation agencies worked together to reduce deforestation? Based on the clip, name several ways in which the Batak are influenced by forces beyond their homeland.

ing crops? Did the residents make, trade for, or buy particular items? Were raw materials available locally? If not, where did they come from? From such information, archaeologists reconstruct patterns of production, trade, and consumption.

Archaeologists have spent much time studying potsherds, fragments of earthenware. Potsherds are more durable than many other artifacts, such as textiles and wood. The quantity of pottery fragments allows estimates of population size and density. The discovery that potters used materials that were not locally available suggests systems of trade. Similarities in manufacture and decoration at different sites may be proof of cultural connections. Groups with similar pots may be historically related. Perhaps they shared common cultural ancestors, traded with each other, or belonged to the same political system.

Many archaeologists examine paleoecology. *Ecology* is the study of interrelations among living things in an environment. The organisms and environment together constitute an ecosystem, a patterned arrangement of energy flows and exchanges. Human ecology studies ecosystems that include people, focusing on the ways in which human use "of nature influences and is influenced by social organization and cultural values" (Bennett 1969, pp. 10–11). *Paleoecology* looks at the ecosystems of the past.

In addition to reconstructing ecological patterns, archaeologists may infer cultural transformations, for example, by observing changes in the size and type of sites and the distance between them. A city develops in a region where only towns, villages, and hamlets existed a few

TABLE 1.2 Ethnography and Ethnology—Two Dimensions of Cultural Anthropology	
Ethnography	**Ethnology**
Requires fieldwork to collect data	Uses data collected by a series of researchers
Often descriptive	Usually synthetic
Group/community specific	Comparative/cross-cultural

An archaeological team works at Harappa, one site from an ancient Indus River civilization dating back some 4,800 years.

centuries earlier. The number of settlement levels (city, town, village, hamlet) in a society is a measure of social complexity. Buildings offer clues about political and religious features. Temples and pyramids suggest that an ancient society had an authority structure capable of marshaling the labor needed to build such monuments. The presence or absence of certain structures, like the pyramids of ancient Egypt and Mexico, reveals differences in function between settlements. For example, some towns were places where people came to attend ceremonies. Others were burial sites; still others were farming communities.

Archaeologists also reconstruct behavior patterns and lifestyles of the past by excavating. This involves digging through a succession of levels at a particular site. In a given area, through time, settlements may change in form and purpose, as may the connections between settlements. Excavation can document changes in economic, social, and political activities.

Although archaeologists are best known for studying prehistory, that is, the period before the invention of writing, they also study the cultures of historical and even living peoples. Studying sunken ships off the Florida coast, underwater archaeologists have been able to verify the living conditions on the vessels that brought ancestral African Americans to the New World as enslaved people. In a research project begun in 1973 in Tucson, Arizona, archaeologist William Rathje has learned about contemporary life by studying modern garbage. The value of "garbology," as

Rathje calls it, is that it provides "evidence of what people did, not what they think they did, what they think they should have done, or what the interviewer thinks they should have done" (Harrison, Rathje, and Hughes 1994, p. 108). What people report may contrast strongly with their real behavior as revealed by garbology. For example, the garbologists discovered that the three Tucson neighborhoods that reported the lowest beer consumption actually had the highest number of discarded beer cans per household (Podolefsky and Brown 1992, p. 100)! Rathje's garbology also has exposed misconceptions about how much of different kinds of trash are in landfills: While most people thought that fast-food containers and disposable diapers were major waste problems, in fact they were relatively insignificant compared with paper, including environmentally friendly, recyclable paper (Rathje and Murphy 2001).

Biological, or Physical, Anthropology

The subject matter of **biological,** or **physical, anthropology** is human biological diversity in time and space. The focus on biological variation unites five special interests within biological anthropology:

1. Human evolution as revealed by the fossil record (paleoanthropology).

2. Human genetics.

Even Anthropologists Get Culture Shock

I first lived in Arembepe (Brazil) during the (North American) summer of 1962. That was between my junior and senior years at New York City's Columbia College, where I was majoring in anthropology. I went to Arembepe as a participant in a now defunct program designed to provide undergraduates with experience doing ethnography—firsthand study of an alien society's culture and social life.

Brought up in one culture, intensely curious about others, anthropologists nevertheless experience culture shock, particularly on their first field trip. Culture shock refers to the whole set of feelings about being in an alien setting, and the ensuing reactions. It is a chilly, creepy feeling of alienation, of being without some of the most ordinary, trivial (and therefore basic) cues of one's culture of origin.

As I planned my departure for Brazil in 1962, I could not know just how naked I would feel without the cloak of my own language and culture. My sojourn in Arembepe would be my first trip outside the United States. I was an urban boy who had grown up in Atlanta, Georgia, and New York City. I had little experience with rural life in my own country, none with Latin America, and I had received only minimal training in the Portuguese language.

New York City direct to Salvador, Bahia, Brazil. Just a brief stopover in Rio de Janeiro; a longer visit would be a reward at the end of field work. As our prop jet approached tropical Salvador, I couldn't believe the whiteness of the sand. "That's not snow, is it?" I remarked to a fellow field team member . . .

My first impressions of Bahia were of smells—alien odors of ripe and decaying mangoes, bananas, and passion fruit—and of swatting the ubiquitous fruit flies I had never seen before, although I had read extensively about their reproductive behavior in genetics classes. There were strange concoctions of rice, black beans, and

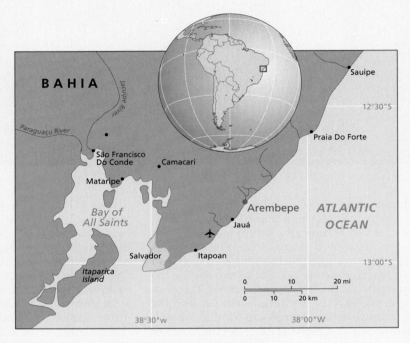

FIGURE 1.1   Location of Arembepe, Bahia, Brazil.

3. Human growth and development.

4. Human biological plasticity (the body's ability to change as it copes with stresses, such as heat, cold, and altitude).

5. The biology, evolution, behavior, and social life of monkeys, apes, and other nonhuman primates.

These interests link physical anthropology to other fields: biology, zoology, geology, anatomy, physiology, medicine, and public health. Osteology—the study of bones—helps paleoanthropologists, who examine skulls, teeth, and bones, to identify human ancestors and to chart changes in anatomy over time. A paleontologist is a scientist who studies fossils. A paleoanthro-

pologist is one sort of paleontologist, one who studies the fossil record of human evolution. Paleoanthropologists often collaborate with archaeologists, who study artifacts, in reconstructing biological and cultural aspects of human evolution. Fossils and tools are often found together. Different types of tools provide information about the habits, customs, and lifestyles of the ancestral humans who used them.

More than a century ago, Charles Darwin noticed that the variety that exists within any population permits some individuals (those with the favored characteristics) to do better than others at surviving and reproducing. Genetics, which developed later, enlightens us about the causes and transmission of this variety. However, it isn't just genes that cause variety. During any

Conrad Kottak, with his Brazilian nephew Guilherme Roxo, on a revisit to Arembepe in 2004.

our car through the village streets until we parked in front of our house, near the central square. Our first few days in Arembepe were spent with children following us everywhere. For weeks we had few moments of privacy. Children watched our every move through our living room window. Occasionally one made an incomprehensible remark. Usually they just stood there . . .

The sounds, sensations, sights, smells, and tastes of life in northeastern Brazil, and in Arembepe, slowly grew familiar . . . I grew accustomed to this world without Kleenex, in which globs of mucus habitually drooped from the noses of village children whenever a cold passed through Arembepe. A world where, seemingly without effort, women . . . carried 18-liter kerosene cans of water on their heads, where boys sailed kites and sported at catching houseflies in their bare hands, where old women smoked pipes, storekeepers offered cachaça (common rum) at nine in the morning, and men played dominoes on lazy afternoons when there was no fishing. I was visiting a world where human life was oriented toward water—the sea, where men fished, and the lagoon, where women communally washed clothing, dishes, and their own bodies.

gelatinous gobs of unidentifiable meats and floating pieces of skin. Coffee was strong and sugar crude, and every tabletop had containers for toothpicks and for manioc (cassava) flour to sprinkle, like Parmesan cheese, on anything one might eat. I remember oatmeal soup and a slimy stew of beef tongue in tomatoes. At one meal a disintegrating fish head, eyes still attached, but barely, stared up at me as the rest of its body floated in a bowl of bright orange palm oil . . .

I only vaguely remember my first day in Arembepe (Figure 1.1). Unlike ethnographers who have studied remote tribes in the tropical forests of interior South America or the highlands of Papua New Guinea, I did not have to hike or ride a canoe for days to arrive at my field site. Arembepe was not isolated relative to such places, only relative to every other place I had ever been . . .

I do recall what happened when we arrived. There was no formal road into the village. Entering through southern Arembepe, vehicles simply threaded their way around coconut trees, following tracks left by automobiles that had passed previously. A crowd of children had heard us coming, and they pursued

This description is adapted from my ethnographic study *Assault on Paradise: The Globalization of a Little Community in Brazil*, 4th ed. (New York: McGraw-Hill, 2006).

individual's lifetime, the environment works along with heredity to determine biological features. For example, people with a genetic tendency to be tall will be shorter if they are poorly nourished during childhood. Thus, biological anthropology also investigates the influence of environment on the body as it grows and matures. Among the environmental factors that influence the body as it develops are nutrition, altitude, temperature, and disease, as well as cultural factors, such as the standards of attractiveness we considered previously.

Biological anthropology (along with zoology) also includes primatology. The primates include our closest relatives—apes and monkeys. Primatologists study their biology, evolution, behavior, and social life, often in their natural environments. Primatology assists paleoanthropology, because primate behavior may shed light on early human behavior and human nature.

Linguistic Anthropology

We don't know (and probably never will) when our ancestors acquired the ability to speak, although biological anthropologists have looked to the anatomy of the face and the skull to speculate about the origin of language. And primatologists have described the communication systems of monkeys and apes. We do know that well-developed, grammatically complex languages have existed for thousands of years. Linguistic anthropology offers further illustration of anthropology's interest in comparison, variation, and

The Utility of Hand and Foot Bones for Problems in Biological Anthropology

BACKGROUND INFORMATION

STUDENT:
Alicia Wilbur

SUPERVISING PROFESSOR:
Della Collins Cook

SCHOOL:
Indiana University

YEAR IN SCHOOL/MAJOR:
Junior and Senior/Anthropology

FUTURE PLANS:
Ph.D. in Biological Anthropology

PROJECT TITLE:
The Utility of Hand and Foot Bones for Problems in Bioanthropology

How does this account suggest common problems of interest to more than one subfield of anthropology? Does the research have implications for cultural as well as for biological and archaeological anthropology?

The large, well-preserved skeletal series from west-central Illinois, housed in the Department of Anthropology at Indiana University, has been the focus of many archaeological and bioanthropological research projects over the years. I became interested in the use of hand and foot bones to determine the stature and sex of the individuals buried in those mounds. This information is important for both archaeological and biological studies of past peoples and their cultures, but is also relevant to modern forensic and mass disaster situations. In both archaeological and modern situations, the human remains recovered may be extremely fragmentary. A single hand or foot can play an important role in identifying modern victims of crime or mass disasters.

Most equations used for estimating adult stature or determining sex from skeletal material are constructed from data on modern Europeans or modern Americans of European or African extraction. Because body proportions differ between populations, applying these equations to skeletal remains of other groups may give inaccurate results. A benefit of my study was that it was constructed on Native American remains and thus could be used for modern Native Americans' remains in forensic cases or mass disasters.

I measured femurs (the thigh bone) and hand and foot bones for 410 adult skeletons and used statistical methods to predict the sex of the individuals, with accuracies exceeding 87 percent. Stature estimation also was found to be possible with hand and foot bones, although the range given was too large to be useful in a court of law. Still, estimates resulting from these equations may be useful for delimiting a range of possible heights for preliminary identification purposes.

The project was published in the *International Journal of Osteoarchaeology* in 1998. While running statistical analyses on the hand and foot data, I noticed a discrepancy in the body proportions of one female adult. Upon carefully examining the rest of her skeleton, I discovered a suite of skeletal anomalies that suggest a rare genetic syndrome called Rubinstein-Taybi Syndrome that affects many organs. Symptoms include delayed growth, mental retardation, and abnormalities of the head and face, including widely spaced eyes and an abnormally large nose. Affected individuals also may have abnormally large big toes and thumbs. There also may be breathing and swallowing difficulties.

It may yet prove possible to analyze DNA from this sample to determine if my diagnosis is correct. If so, it would be the earliest known case of this syndrome. Knowing that this individual lived to mid- to late adulthood with several physical and mental disabilities tells us something about her culture.

These types of studies on skeletal material are important for the information they give us about the past and also for their relevance to modern problems. Future research will focus on genetic and infectious diseases that beset ancient peoples as well as application of this work to modern problems.

change. **Linguistic anthropology** studies language in its social and cultural context, across space and over time. Some linguistic anthropologists make inferences about universal features of language, linked perhaps to uniformities in the human brain. Others reconstruct ancient languages by comparing their contemporary descendants and in so doing make discoveries about history. Still others study linguistic differences to discover varied perceptions and patterns of thought in different cultures.

Historical linguistics considers variation in time, such as the changes in sounds, grammar, and vocabulary between Middle English (spoken from approximately A.D. 1050 to 1550) and modern English. **Sociolinguistics** investigates relationships between social and linguistic variation. No language is a homogeneous system in which everyone speaks just like everyone else. How do different speakers use a given language? How do linguistic features correlate with social factors, including class and gender differences (Tannen 1990)? One reason for variation is geography, as in regional dialects and accents. Linguistic variation also is expressed in the bilingualism of ethnic groups. Linguistic and cultural anthropologists collaborate in studying links between language and many other aspects of culture, such as how people reckon kinship and how they perceive and classify colors.

ANTHROPOLOGY AND OTHER ACADEMIC FIELDS

As mentioned previously, one of the main differences between anthropology and the other fields that study people is holism, anthropology's unique blend of biological, social, cultural, linguistic, historical, and contemporary perspectives. Paradoxically, while distinguishing anthropology, this breadth is what also links it to many other disciplines. Techniques used to date fossils and artifacts have come to anthropology from physics, chemistry, and geology. Because plant and animal remains often are found with human bones and artifacts, anthropologists collaborate with botanists, zoologists, and paleontologists.

As a discipline that is both scientific and humanistic, anthropology has links with many other academic fields. Anthropology is a **science**—a "systematic field of study or body of knowledge that aims, through experiment, observation, and deduction, to produce reliable explanations of phenomena, with reference to the material and physical world" (*Webster's New World Encyclopedia* 1993, p. 937). The following chapters present anthropology as a humanistic science devoted to discovering, describing, understanding, and explaining similarities and differences in time and space among humans and our ancestors. Clyde Kluckhohn (1944) described anthropology as "the science of human similarities and differences" (p. 9). His statement of the need for such a field still stands: "Anthropology provides a scientific basis for dealing with the crucial dilemma of the world today: how can peoples of different appearance, mutually unintelligible languages, and dissimilar ways of life get along peaceably together?" (p. 9). Anthropology has compiled an impressive body of knowledge that this textbook attempts to encapsulate.

Besides its links to the natural sciences (e.g., geology, zoology), and social sciences (e.g., sociology, psychology), Anthropology also has strong links to the humanities. The humanities include English, comparative literature, classics, folklore, philosophy, and the arts. These fields study languages, texts, philosophies, arts, music, performances, and other forms of creative expression. Ethnomusicology, which studies forms of musical expression on a worldwide basis, is especially closely related to anthropology. Also linked is folklore, the systematic study of tales, myths, and legends from a variety of cultures. One might well argue that anthropology is among the most humanistic of all academic fields because of its fundamental respect for human diversity. Anthropologists listen to, record, and represent voices from a multitude of nations and cultures. Anthropology values local knowledge, diverse worldviews, and alternative philosophies. Cultural anthropology and linguistic anthropology in particular bring a comparative and nonelitist perspective to forms of creative expression, including language, art, narratives, music, and dance, viewed in their social and cultural context.

Cultural Anthropology and Sociology

Cultural anthropology and sociology share an interest in social relations, organization, and behavior. However, important differences between these disciplines arose from the kinds of societies each traditionally studied. Initially sociologists focused on the industrial West; anthropologists, on nonindustrial societies. Different methods of data collection and analysis emerged to deal with those different kinds of societies. To study large-scale, complex nations, sociologists came to rely on questionnaires and other means of gathering masses of quantifiable data. For many years, sampling and statistical techniques have been basic to sociology, whereas statistical training has been less common in anthropology (although this is changing as anthropologists increasingly work in modern nations).

Traditional ethnographers studied small and nonliterate (without writing) populations and relied on methods appropriate to that context. "Ethnography is a research process in which the anthropologist closely observes, records, and engages in the daily life of another culture—an experience labeled as the fieldwork method—and then writes accounts of this culture, emphasizing descriptive detail" (Marcus and Fischer 1986, p. 18). One key method described in this quote is participant observation—taking part in the events one is observing, describing, and analyzing.

In many areas and topics, anthropology and sociology now are converging. As the modern world system grows, sociologists now do research in developing countries and in other places that were once mainly within the anthropological orbit. As industrialization spreads, many anthropologists now work in industrial nations, where they study diverse topics, including rural decline, inner-city life, and the role of the mass media in creating national cultural patterns.

Anthropology and Psychology

Like sociologists, most psychologists do research in their own society. But statements about "human" psychology cannot be based solely on observations made in one society or in a single type of society. The area of cultural anthropology known as psychological anthropology studies cross-cultural variation in psychological traits. Societies instill different values by training children differently. Adult personalities reflect a culture's child-rearing practices.

Bronislaw Malinowski, an early contributor to the cross-cultural study of human psychology, is famous for his field work among the Trobriand Islanders of the South Pacific (Figure 1.2). The Trobrianders reckon kinship matrilineally. They consider themselves related to the mother and her relatives, but not to the father. The relative who disciplines the child is not the father but the mother's brother, the maternal uncle. Trobrianders show a marked respect for the uncle, with whom a boy usually has a cool and distant relationship. In contrast, the Trobriand father–son relationship is friendly and affectionate.

Malinowski's work among the Trobrianders suggested modifications in Sigmund Freud's famous theory of the universality of the Oedipus complex (Malinowski 1927). According to Freud (1918/1950), boys around the age of five become sexually attracted to their mothers. The Oedipus complex is resolved, in Freud's view, when the boy overcomes his sexual jealousy of, and identifies with, his father. Freud lived in patriarchal Austria during the late 19th and early 20th centuries—a social milieu in which the father was a strong authoritarian figure. The Austrian father was the child's primary authority figure and the mother's sexual partner. In the Trobriands, the father had only the sexual role.

If, as Freud contended, the Oedipus complex always creates social distance based on jealousy toward the mother's sexual partner, this would have shown up in Trobriand society. It did not. Malinowski concluded that the authority structure did more to influence the father–son relationship than did sexual jealousy. Although Melford Spiro (1993) has critiqued Malinowski's conclusions (see also Weiner 1988), no contemporary anthropologist would dispute Malinowski's contention that individual psychology is molded in a specific cultural context. Anthropologists continue to provide cross-cultural perspectives on psychoanalytic propositions (Paul 1989) as well as on issues of developmental and cognitive psychology (Shore 1996).

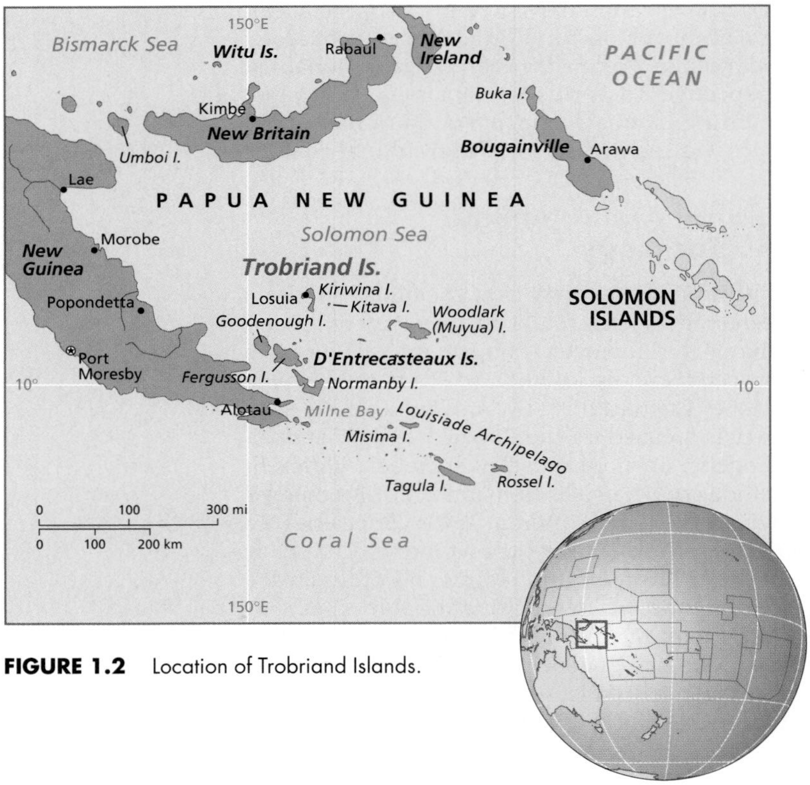

SCIENCE, EXPLANATION, AND HYPOTHESIS TESTING

A key feature of anthropology is its comparative, cross-cultural dimension. As was stated previously (see p. 10), *ethnology* draws on ethnographic, as well as archaeological, data to compare and contrast, and to make generalizations about, societies and cultures. As a scientific pursuit, ethnology attempts to identify and explain cultural

FIGURE 1.2 Location of Trobriand Islands.

How much would we know about human behavior, thought, and feeling if we studied only our own kind? What if our entire understanding of human behavior were based on analysis of questionnaires filled out by college students in Oregon? A radical question but one that should make you think about the basis for statements about what humans are like. A primary reason why anthropology helps us understand ourselves is the cross-cultural perspective. One culture can't tell us everything we need to know about what it means to be human. Earlier we saw how cultural forces influence our physical growth. Culture also guides our emotional and cognitive growth and helps determine the kinds of personalities we have as adults. Among scholarly disciplines, anthropology stands out as the field that provides the cross-cultural test. How does television affect us? To answer that question, study not just North America in 2006 but some other place—and perhaps also some other time (such as Brazil in the 1980s; see Kottak 1990b). Anthropology specializes in the study of human variation in space and time.

■ *Bronislaw Malinowski is famous for his fieldwork among the matrilineal Trobriand Islanders of the South Pacific. Does this Trobriand market scene suggest anything about the status of Trobriand women?*

differences and similarities, test hypotheses, and build theory to enhance our understanding of how social and cultural systems work.

In their 1997 article "Science in Anthropology," Melvin Ember and Carol R. Ember stress a key feature of science as a way of viewing the world: Science recognizes the tentativeness and uncertainty of our knowledge and understanding. Scientists strive to improve understanding by testing *hypotheses*—suggested explanations of things and events. In science, understanding means *explaining*—showing how and why the thing to be understood (the explicandum) is related to other things in some known way. Explanations rely on associations and theories. An association is an observed relationship between two or more variables. A theory is more general, suggesting or implying associations and attempting to explain them (Ember and Ember 1997).

A thing or event, for example, the freezing of water, is explained if it illustrates a general principle or association. "Water solidifies at 32 degrees" states an association between two variables: the state of the water and the air temperature. The truth of the statement is confirmed by repeated observations. In the physical sciences, such relationships are called "laws." Explanations based on such laws allow us to understand the past and predict the future.

In the social sciences, associations usually are stated probabilistically: Two or more variables *tend to be* related in a predictable way, but there are exceptions (Ember and Ember 1997). For example, in a worldwide sample of societies, the anthropologist John Whiting (1964) found a strong (but not 100 percent) association or correlation between a low-protein diet and a long postpartum sex taboo—a prohibition against sexual intercourse between husband and wife for a year or more after the birth of a child.

Laws and statistical associations explain by relating the explicandum (e.g., the postpartum sex taboo) to one or more other variables (e.g., a low-protein diet). We also want to know why such associations exist. Why do societies with low-protein diets have long postpartum sex taboos? Scientists formulate theories to explain the correlations they observe.

A **theory** is a set of ideas formulated (by reasoning from known facts) to explain something. A theory provides a framework that helps us understand *why* (something exists). Returning to the postpartum sex taboo, why might societies with low-protein diets develop this taboo? Whiting's theory is that the taboo is adaptive; it helps people survive and reproduce in certain environments. With too little protein in their diets, babies may develop a protein-deficiency disease called kwashiorkor. But if the mother delays her next pregnancy, her current baby, by breast-feeding longer, has a better chance to survive. Whiting suggests that parents may be unconsciously or consciously aware that having another baby too soon might jeopardize the survival of the first one. Thus, they avoid sex for more than a year after the birth of the first baby.

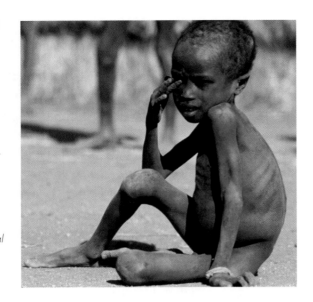

This child's bloated body is due to protein malnutrition. This condition, known as kwashiorkor, comes from a West African word meaning "one-two." This refers to the practice in some societies of abruptly weaning one infant when a second one is born. With no mother's milk, the first baby may get no protein at all. What are some cultural ways of fending off kwashiorkor?

When such abstinence becomes institutionalized, everyone is expected to respect the taboo.

A theory is an explanatory framework containing a series of statements. An association simply states an observed relationship between two or more known variables. Parts of a theory, by contrast, may be difficult or impossible to observe or to know directly. With Whiting's theory, for example, it would be hard to determine whether people developed the sex taboo because they recognized that it would give babies a better chance to survive. Typically, some elements of a theory are unobservable (at least at present). In contrast, statistical associations are based entirely on observations (Ember and Ember 1997).

If an association is tested and found to recur again and again, we may consider it proved. Theories, by contrast, are unprovable. Although much evidence may support them, their truth isn't established with certainty. Many of the concepts and ideas in theories aren't directly observable or verifiable. Thus, scientists may try to explain how light behaves by postulating that it consists of "photons," which can't be observed even with the most powerful microscope. The photon is a "theoretical construct," something that can't be seen or verified directly (Ember and Ember 1997).

Why should we bother with theories if we can't prove them? According to the Embers, the main value of a theory is to promote new understanding. A theory can suggest patterns, connections, or relationships that may be confirmed by new research. Whiting's theory, for example, suggests hypotheses for future researchers to test. Because the theory proposes that the postpartum taboo is adaptive under certain conditions, one might hypothesize that certain changes would lead the taboo to disappear. By adopting birth control, for instance, families could space births without avoiding intercourse. So, too, might the

taboo disappear if babies started receiving protein supplements, which would reduce the threat of kwashiorkor.

Although theories can't be proved, they can be rejected. The method of *falsification* (showing a theory to be wrong) is our main way of evaluating theories. If a theory is true, certain predictions should stand up to tests designed to disprove them. Theories that haven't been disproved are accepted (for the time being at least) because the available evidence seems to support them.

What is acceptable evidence that an explanation is probably right? Cases that have been personally selected by a researcher don't provide an acceptable test of a hypothesis or theory. (Imagine that Whiting had combed the ethnographic literature and chosen to cite only those societies that supported his theory.) Ideally, hypothesis testing should be done using a sample of cases that have been selected randomly from some statistical universe. (Whiting did this in choosing his cross-cultural sample.) The relevant variables should be measured reliably, and the strength and significance of the results should be evaluated by using legitimate statistical methods (Bernard 1994).

UNDERSTANDING OURSELVES

Science is a powerful tool for understanding ourselves. Properly, science isn't rigid or dogmatic; scientists recognize the tentativeness and uncertainty of knowledge and understanding, which they try to improve and enhance. Working to confirm laws, refine theories, and provide accurate explanations, scientists strive to be objective. Science relies on unbiased methods, such as random sampling, impartial analytic techniques, and standard statistical tests. But complete objectivity is impossible. There is always observer bias—that is, the presence of the scientist and his or her tools and methods always affects the outcome of an experiment, observation, or analysis. Through their very presence, anthropologists influence the living people and social conditions they study, as do survey researchers when they phrase questions in certain ways. Statisticians have designed techniques to measure and control for observer bias, but observer bias can't be eliminated totally. As scientists, we can only strive for objectivity and impartiality. Science, which has many limitations, certainly is not the only way we have to understand ourselves. Nevertheless, its goals of objectivity and impartiality help distinguish science from ways of knowing that are more biased, more rigid, and more dogmatic.

1. Anthropology is the holistic and comparative study of humanity. It is the systematic exploration of human biological and cultural diversity. Examining the origins of, and changes in, human biology and culture, anthropology provides explanations for similarities and differences. The four subfields of general anthropology are (socio)cultural, archaeological, biological, and linguistic. All consider variation in time and space. Each also examines adaptation—the process by which organisms cope with environmental stresses.

2. Cultural forces mold human biology, including our body types and images. Societies have particular standards of physical attractiveness. They also have specific ideas about what activities—for example, various sports—are appropriate for males and females.

3. Cultural anthropology explores the cultural diversity of the present and the recent past. Archaeology reconstructs cultural patterns, often of prehistoric populations. Biological anthropology documents diversity involving fossils, genetics, growth and development, bodily responses, and nonhuman primates. Linguistic anthropology considers diversity among languages. It also studies how speech changes in social situations and over time.

4. Concerns with biology, society, culture, and language link anthropology to many other fields—sciences and humanities. Anthropologists study art, music, and literature across cultures. But their concern is more with the creative expressions of common people than with arts designed for elites. Anthropologists examine creators and products in their social context. Sociologists traditionally study urban and industrial populations, whereas anthropologists have focused on rural, nonindustrial peoples. Psychological anthropology views human psychology in the context of social and cultural variation.

5. As scientists, anthropologists attempt to identify and explain cultural differences and similarities and to build theories about how social and cultural systems work. Scientists strive to improve understanding by testing hypotheses—suggested explanations. Explanations rely on associations and theories. An association is an observed relationship between variables. A theory is more general, suggesting or implying associations and attempting to explain them.

anthropology   The study of the human species and its immediate ancestors.

archaeological anthropology   The study of human behavior and cultural patterns and processes through the culture's material remains.

biocultural   Referring to the inclusion and combination (to solve a common problem) of both biological and cultural approaches—one of anthropology's hallmarks.

biological anthropology   The study of human biological variation in time and space; includes evolution, genetics, growth and development, and primatology.

cultural anthropology   The study of human society and culture; describes, analyzes, interprets, and explains social and cultural similarities and differences.

culture   Distinctly human; transmitted through learning; traditions and customs that govern behavior and beliefs.

ethnography   Fieldwork in a particular culture.

ethnology   Cross-cultural comparison; the comparative study of ethnographic data, society, and culture.

food production   Cultivation of plants and domestication (stockbreeding) of animals; first developed 10,000 to 12,000 years ago.

general anthropology   The field of anthropology as a whole, consisting of cultural, archaeological, biological, and linguistic anthropology.

holistic   Interested in the whole of the human condition: past, present, and future; biology, society, language, and culture.

linguistic anthropology   The descriptive, comparative, and historical study of language and of linguistic similarities and differences in time, space, and society.

physical anthropology   See *biological anthropology.*

science   A systematic field of study or body of knowledge that aims, through experiment, observation, and deduction, to produce reliable explanations of phenomena, with reference to the material and physical world.

sociolinguistics   Investigates relationships between social and linguistic variations.

theory   A set of ideas formulated (by reasoning from known facts) to explain something. The main value of a theory is to promote new understanding. A theory suggest patterns, connections, and relationships that may be confirmed by new research.

CRITICAL THINKING QUESTIONS

For more self-testing,
see the self-quizzes

mhhe.com/kottak

1. Which do you think is unique about anthropology: its holism or its comparative perspective? Can you think of other fields that are holistic and/or comparative?

2. What are some areas in which anthropology's biocultural, four-field approach might shed light on current issues and debates? Would sexuality be such an area?

3. Many other disciplines are limited by their focus on powerful people and elites. How have your professors in other classes tried to justify, or compensate for, such limitations?

4. What are some theories, as defined here, that you routinely use to understand the world?

SUGGESTED ADDITIONAL READINGS

Clifford, J.
  1988 *The Predicament of Culture: Twentieth-Century Ethnography, Literature, and Art.* Cambridge, MA: Harvard University Press. Literary evaluation of classic and modern anthropologists and discussion of issues of ethnographic authority.

DeVita, P. R.
  1992 *The Naked Anthropologist: Tales from Around the World.* Belmont, CA: Wadsworth. Views of ethnographic field work.

Endicott, K. M., and R. Welsch
  2003 *Taking Sides: Clashing Views on Controversial Issues in Anthropology.* Guilford, CT: McGraw-Hill/Dushkin. Thirty-eight anthropologists offer opposing viewpoints on 19 polarizing issues, including ethical dilemmas.

Fagan, B. M.
  2006 *Archeology: A Brief Introduction,* 9th ed. Upper Saddle River, NJ: Prentice Hall. Introduction to archaeological theory, techniques, and approaches, including field survey, excavation, and analysis of materials.
  2007 *People of the Earth: An Introduction to World Prehistory,* 12th ed. Upper Saddle River, NJ: Prentice Hall. Introduction to the archaeological study of prehistoric societies, using examples from all areas.

Geertz, C.
  1995 *After the Fact: Two Countries, Four Decades, One Anthropologist.* Cambridge, MA: Harvard University Press. A prominent cultural anthropologist reflects on his work in Morocco and Indonesia.

Harris, M.
  1989 *Our Kind: Who We Are, Where We Came From, Where We Are Going.* New York: HarperCollins. Clearly written survey of the origins of humans, culture, and major sociopolitical institutions.

Marcus, G. E., and M. M. J. Fischer
  1999 *Anthropology as Cultural Critique: An Experimental Moment in the Human Sciences,* 2nd ed. Chicago: University of Chicago Press. Different types of ethnographic accounts as forms of writing, a vision of modern anthropology, and a consideration of anthropologists' public and professional roles.

Nash, D.
  1999 *A Little Anthropology,* 3rd ed. Upper Saddle River, NJ: Prentice Hall. Short introduction to societies and cultures, with comments on developing nations and modern America.

Podolefsky, A., and P. J. Brown, eds.
  2007 *Applying Anthropology: An Introductory Reader,* 8th ed. Boston: McGraw-Hill. Essays focusing on anthropology's relevance to contemporary life; a readable survey of the current range of activities in applied anthropology.

Wolf, E. R.
  1982 *Europe and the People without History.* Berkeley: University of California Press. Influential and award-winning study of the relation between Europe and various nonindustrial populations.

INTERNET EXERCISES

1. News in Anthropology: Look at Texas A&M University's "Anthropology in the News," **http://www.tamu.edu/anthropology/news.htm**, which contains links to articles relevant to anthropology.

   a. After reading the chapter in the textbook and reading some recent news articles, do you think anthropology is more or less relevant to your life?

   b. Look at the variety of topics discussed. Are the connections between the articles and anthropology clear to you? Were they clear to you before you read this chapter?

   c. Examine the first 10 articles. Which subfield of anthropology does each article relate to most closely?

   d. Browse the list of article titles. What are some of the current hot topics in the news about anthropology?

2. Careers in Anthropology: Go to the American Anthropological Association's Jobs Page (**http://aaanet.jobcontrolcenter.com/search/results/**) and Northern Kentucky University's list of organizations in their area hiring anthropologists (**http://www.nku.edu/~anthro/careers.html**).

   a. What kinds of organizations are hiring anthropologists?
   b. What kinds of qualifications are these employers looking for? Do they require a graduate degree, or are they seeking people with an undergraduate degree in anthropology?
   c. What subfields are being sought by employers?

Note that these are just two job listing pages on the Web, and there are many others. If you have an interest in a field of anthropology that is not listed on these pages, use a Web search engine to research what kinds of jobs are available. A good place to start is **http://www.aaanet.org/careers.htm** for more information on careers in anthropology.

See Chapter 1 at your McGraw-Hill Online Learning Center for additional review and interactive exercises.

LINKAGES

Assault on Paradise

Read Chapter 1 of *Assault on Paradise,* 4th edition, by Conrad Phillip Kottak. How does the anthropological research experience described in this chapter differ from sociological research? Based on this account, does ethnography appeal to you? Do you know of, or have you ever visited, places comparable to Arembepe in the 1960s?

Culture Sketches

In *Culture Sketches,* 4th edition, by Peters-Golden, read Chapter 12, "The Samoans: Matai and Migration." Using what you've learned about the four subfields of anthropology and about holistic and comparative perspectives of anthropology, how would you address the Mead–Freeman debate? What might be the consequences, positive or negative, of such a controversy to the field of anthropology? How might the potential for such disagreement influence future field work?

2

Applying Anthropology

WHAT IS APPLIED ANTHROPOLOGY?

Anthropology is not a science of the exotic carried on by quaint scholars in ivory towers. Rather, it is a holistic, comparative, biocultural field with a lot to tell the public. Anthropology's foremost professional organization, the American Anthropological Association (AAA), has formally acknowledged a public service role by recognizing that anthropology has two dimensions: (1) academic anthropology and (2) practicing or **applied anthropology.** The latter refers to the application of anthropological data, perspectives, theory, and methods to identify, assess, and solve contemporary social problems. As Erve Chambers (1987, p. 309) states it, applied anthropology is the "field of inquiry concerned with the relationships between anthropological knowledge and the uses of that knowledge in the world beyond anthropology." More and more anthropologists from the four subfields now work in such "applied" areas as public health, family planning, business, economic development, and cultural resource management (see the "News Brief").

Applied anthropology encompasses any use of the knowledge and/or techniques of the four subfields to identify, assess, and solve practical problems. Because of anthropology's breadth, it has many

See the OLC Internet Exercises
mhhe.com/kottak

23

applications. For example, applied medical anthropologists consider both the sociocultural and the biological contexts and implications of disease and illness. Perceptions of good and bad health, along with actual health threats and problems, differ among cultures. Various societies and ethnic groups recognize different illnesses, symptoms, and causes and have developed different health-care systems and treatment strategies. Medical anthropologists are both biological and cultural, and both academic and applied. Applied medical anthropologists, for example, have served as cultural interpreters in public health programs, which must fit into local culture and be accepted by local people.

Other applied anthropologists work for international development agencies, such as the World Bank and the United States Agency for International Development (USAID). The job of such development anthropologists is to assess the social and cultural dimensions of economic development. Anthropologists are experts on local cultures. Working with and drawing on the knowledge of local people, anthropologists can identify specific social conditions and needs that must be addressed and that influence the failure or success of development schemes. Planners in Washington or Paris often know little about, say, the labor necessary for crop cultivation in rural Africa. Development funds are often wasted if an

 STUDENT CD-ROM LIVING ANTHROPOLOGY

Unearthing Evil: Archaeology in the Cause of Justice
Track 2

This clip features archaeologist Richard Wright and his team of 15 forensic archaeologists and anthropologists working "in the cause of justice" in Bosnia-Herzegovina in 1998. The focus of the clip is the excavation of a site of mass burial or reburial of the bodies of some 660 civilians who were murdered during the conflict that followed the dissolution of Yugoslavia. Wright and his colleagues worked with the international community to provide evidence of war crimes. This evidence has led to the convictions of war criminals. Why was Wright nervous about this work? Compare the forensic work shown here with the discussion of forensic anthropology in this chapter.

anthropologist is not asked to work with the local people to identify local needs, demands, priorities, and constraints.

Projects routinely fail when planners ignore the cultural dimension of development. Problems arise from lack of attention to, and consequent lack of fit with, existing sociocultural conditions. One example is a very naive and culturally incompatible project in East Africa. The major fallacy was to attempt to convert nomadic herders into farmers. The planners had absolutely no evidence that the herders, on whose land the project was to be implemented, wanted to change their economy. The herders' territory was to be used for new commercial farms, and the herders were to be converted into small farmers and sharecroppers. The project, whose planners included no anthropologists, totally neglected social issues. The obstacles would have been evident to any anthropologist. The herders were expected to give up a generations-old way of life in order to work three times harder growing rice and picking cotton. What possibly could motivate them to give up their freedom and mobility to work as sharecroppers for commercial farmers? Certainly not the meager financial return the project planners estimated for the herders—an average of $300 annually versus more than $10,000 for their new bosses, the commercial farmers.

To avoid such unrealistic projects, and to make development schemes more socially sensitive and culturally appropriate, development organizations now regularly include anthropologists on planning teams. Their team colleagues may include agronomists, economists, veterinarians, geologists, engineers, and health specialists. Applied anthropologists also apply their skills in studying the human dimension of environmental degradation (e.g., deforestation, pollution). Anthropologists examine how the environment influences humans and how human activities affect the biosphere and the earth itself.

OVERVIEW

Anthropology has two dimensions: academic and applied. In varied settings anthropology regularly is "applied"—used to identify and solve problems involving human behavior, social conditions, and public health. Applied, aka "practicing," anthropologists work for various groups and organizations, including governments, agencies, and businesses. Many applied anthropologists work with local people to identify and realize their perceived needs and to plan and implement culturally appropriate change, while also attempting to protect those people from harmful policies.

Anthropology is applied in educational, urban, rural, medical, and business settings. Such domains may have theoretical as well as applied, and biological as well as sociocultural, dimensions. Educational anthropologists work in classrooms, homes, neighborhoods, and other settings relevant to education. Urban anthropologists study problems and policies involving migration, city life, and urbanization. Medical anthropologists examine disease and health-care systems cross-culturally. For business, key aspects of anthropology include ethnography and observation as ways of gathering data, cross-cultural expertise, and a focus on diversity. Anthropology's comparative outlook provides a valuable background for overseas work. A focus on culture and diversity is also highly relevant to work in contemporary North America.

Archaeologist in New Orleans Finds a Way to Help the Living

NEW YORK TIMES NEWS BRIEF

by John Schwartz
January 3, 2006

Anthropology is applied in identifying and solving various kinds of problems involving social conditions and human behavior, such as helping a community preserve its culture in the face of threat or disaster. Among the clients of applied anthropologists are governments, agencies, local communities, and businesses. This news story describes the work of an anthropologist doing public archaeology in New Orleans in the wake of Hurricane Katrina. Cultural resource management, as discussed here, is one form of applied anthropology: the application of anthropological perspectives, theory, methods, and data to identify, assess, and solve social problems.

"That's a finger bone."

Shannon Lee Dawdy kneeled in the forlorn Holt graveyard to touch a thimble-size bone poking up out of the cracked dirt. She examined it without revulsion, with the fascination of a scientist and with the sadness of someone who loves New Orleans.

Dr. Dawdy, a 38-year-old assistant professor of anthropology at the University of Chicago, is one of the more unusual relief workers among the thousands who have come to the devastated expanses of Louisiana, Mississippi and Texas in the aftermath of Hurricanes Katrina and Rita. She is officially embedded with the Federal Emergency Management Agency [FEMA] as a liaison to the state's historic preservation office.

Her mission is to try to keep the rebuilding of New Orleans from destroying what is left of its past treasures and current culture.

While much of the restoration of the battered Gulf Coast is the effort of engineers and machines, the work of Dr. Dawdy, trained as an archaeologist, an anthropologist and a historian, shows that the social sciences have a role to play as well. "It's a way that archaeology can contribute back to the living," she said, "which it doesn't often get to do."

Holt cemetery, a final resting place for the city's poor, is just one example of what she wants to preserve and protect.

Other New Orleans graveyards have gleaming mausoleums that keep the coffins above the marshy soil. But the coffins of Holt are buried, and the ground covering many of them is bordered with wooden frames marked with makeshift headstones.

Mourners decorate the graves with votive objects: teddy bears for children and an agglomeration of objects, including ice chests, plastic jack-o'-lanterns and chairs, on the graves of adults. There is the occasional liquor bottle . . .

Many of the objects on the graves were washed away by the storm, or shifted from one part of the graveyard to another. Dr. Dawdy has proposed treating the site as archaeologists would an ancient site in which objects have been exposed on the surface by erosion.

Before the hurricanes, the cemetery was often busy, a hub of activity on All Soul's Day, when people came to freshen the grave decorations.

"The saddest thing to me now was how few people we see," she said, looking at the empty expanse and the scarred live oaks. "I realize we're having enough trouble taking care of the living," she added, but the lack of activity in a city normally so close to the spirits of the past "drove home how far out of whack things are." . . .

Treating Holt as an archaeological site means the government should not treat the votive artifacts as debris, she said, but as the religious artifacts that they are, with some effort to restore the damaged site, to find the objects and at least record where they came from.

FEMA simply tries to clean up damaged areas, and its Disaster Mortuary Operational Response Teams—called Dmort—deal with the bodies of the dead and address problems in cemeteries that might lead to disease.

■ *Archaeologist Shannon Dawdy of the University of Chicago at work in New Orleans, post-Katrina.*

If such places are destroyed, Dr. Dawdy said, "then people don't feel as connected here." She added that they might be more willing to come back to a damaged city if they felt they were returning to a recognizable home.

Though she has deep emotional ties to New Orleans, Dr. Dawdy was born in Northern California. She came here in 1994 to write her master's thesis for the College of William & Mary, and, "I wrote it all day," she said. "If I had written a minimum of five pages, I could come out for a parade at night." Over the eight weeks it took to finish the project, she said: "I fell in love with New Orleans. I really consider it the home of my heart."

She started a pilot program at the University of New Orleans, working with city planners and grants for research projects that involved excavation, oral history and hands-on work with the city to safeguard its buried treasures.

She left that job to earn a double doctorate at the University of Michigan in anthropology and history that focused on French colonial times in New Orleans, then landed a coveted faculty position at the University of Chicago . . .

Even before Hurricane Katrina, Dr. Dawdy had found ways to return to New Orleans. In 2004, she made an intriguing discovery while researching a possible archaeological site under an old French Quarter parking garage slated for demolition. Property records and advertisements from the 1820's said that the site had been the location of a hotel with an enticing name: the Rising Sun Hotel.

Dr. Dawdy found a January 1821 newspaper advertisement for the hotel in which its owners promised to "maintain the character of giving the best entertainment, which this house has enjoyed for twenty years past."

It went on: "Gentlemen may here rely upon finding attentive Servants. The bar will be supplied with genuine good Liquors; and at the Table, the fare will be of the best the market or the season will afford." . . .

New Orleans, she noted, has always been known for its libertine lifestyle. The French all but abandoned the city as its colony around 1735 as being unworthy of the nation's support as a colony. Novels like "Manon Lescaut" portrayed the city as a den of iniquity and corruption, and across Europe, "they thought the locals were basically a bunch of rogues, immoral and corrupt," Dr. Dawdy said.

She added that she saw parallels to today, as some skepticism emerges about rebuilding the city. Dr. Dawdy characterized that posture as, "Those people in New Orleans aren't worth saving, because they're all criminals anyway." But even if the devastation makes it hard to envision the road back, the city, she said, is worth fighting for.

"The thing about New Orleans that gives me hope is they are so tied to family, place, history," Dr. Dawdy said. "If anyone is going to stick it out, out of a sense of history, out of a sense of tradition, it is New Orleans."

SOURCE: John Schwartz, "Archaeologist in New Orleans Finds a Way to Help the Living," *New York Times*, January 3, 2006, pp. F1, F4.

Applied anthropologists also work in North America. Garbologists help the Environmental Protection Agency, the paper industry, and packaging and trade associations. Applied archaeology, usually called *public archaeology,* includes such activities as cultural resource management, contract archaeology, public educational programs, and historic preservation. (This chapter's "News Brief" illustrates a form of public archaeology, involving cultural preservation in the wake of Hurricane Katrina.) An important role for public archaeology has been created by legislation requiring evaluation of sites threatened by dams, highways, and other construction activities. To decide what needs saving, and to preserve significant information about the past when sites cannot be saved, is the work of **cultural resource management (CRM).** CRM involves not only preserving sites but allowing their destruction if they are not significant. The "management" part of the term refers to the evaluation and decision-making process. If additional information is needed to make decisions, then survey or excavation may be done. CRM funding comes from federal, state, and local governments and from developers who must comply with preservation regulations. Cultural resource managers work for federal, state, and county agencies and other clients. Applied cultural anthropologists sometimes work with the public archaeologists, assessing the human problems generated by the proposed change and determining how they can be reduced.

Remember that applied anthropologists come from all four subfields. Biological anthropologists work in public health, nutrition, genetic counseling, substance abuse, epidemiology, aging, and mental illness. They apply their knowledge of human anatomy and physiology to the improvement of automobile safety standards and to the design of airplanes and spacecraft. Forensic (physical) anthropologists work with the police, medical examiners, the courts, and international organizations to identify victims of crimes, accidents, wars, and terrorism. From skeletal remains they may determine age, sex, size, ethnic origin, and number of victims. Applied physical anthropologists link injury patterns to design flaws in aircraft and vehicles.

Cultural anthropologists have influenced social policy by showing that strong kin ties exist in city neighborhoods whose social organization previously was considered "fragmented" or "pathological." Suggestions for improving education emerge from ethnographic studies of classrooms and surrounding communities. Linguistic anthropologists show the influence of dialect differences on classroom learning. In general, applied anthropology aims to find humane and effective ways of helping the people whom anthropologists have traditionally studied. Table 2.1 shows the four subfields and two dimensions of anthropology.

There are two important professional groups of applied anthropologists (also called **practicing anthropologists**). The older is the independent Society for Applied Anthropology (SfAA), founded in 1941. The second, the National Association for the Practice of Anthropology (NAPA), was established as a unit of the American Anthropological Association in 1983. (Many people belong to both groups.) Practicing anthropologists work (regularly or occasionally, full or part time) for nonacademic clients. These clients include governments, development agencies, nongovernmental organizations (NGOs), tribal and ethnic associations, interest groups, businesses, and social-service and educational agencies. Applied anthropologists work for groups that promote, manage, and assess programs and policies aimed at influencing human behavior and social conditions. The scope of applied anthropology includes change and development abroad as well as in North America (see Ervin 2005.)

THE ROLE OF THE APPLIED ANTHROPOLOGIST

By instilling an appreciation for human diversity, anthropology combats *ethnocentrism*—the tendency to view one's own culture as superior and to apply one's own cultural values in judging the

Supervised by archaeologists from India, with funding from the United Nations, these workers are cleaning and restoring the front facade of Cambodia's historic Angkor Wat temple. To decide what needs saving, and to preserve significant information about the past even when sites cannot be saved, is the work of cultural resource management (CRM).

behavior and beliefs of people raised in other cultures. This broadening, educational role affects the knowledge, values, and attitudes of people exposed to anthropology. Now we focus on the question: What specific contributions can anthropology make in identifying and solving problems stirred up by contemporary currents of economic, social, and cultural change?

Because anthropologists are experts on human problems and social change and because they study, understand, and respect cultural values, they are highly qualified to suggest, plan, and implement policy affecting people. Proper roles for applied anthropologists include (1) identifying needs for change that local people perceive, (2) working with those people to design culturally appropriate and socially sensitive change, and (3) protecting local people from harmful policies and projects that threaten them.

There was a time—the 1940s in particular—when most anthropologists focused on the application of their knowledge. During World War II, American anthropologists studied Japanese and German "culture at a distance" in an attempt to

TABLE 2.1 The Four Subfields and Two Dimensions of Anthropology	
Anthropology's Subfields (General Anthropology)	**Examples of Application (Applied Anthropology)**
Cultural anthropology	Development anthropology
Archaeological anthropology	Cultural resource management (CRM)
Biological or physical anthropology	Forensic anthropology
Linguistic anthropology	Study of linguistic diversity in classrooms

■ Like other forensic anthropologists, Dr. Kathy Reichs (shown here) and her alter ego, Temperance Brennan, work with the police, medical examiners, the courts, and international organizations to identify victims of crimes, accidents, wars, and terrorism. Brennan is the heroine of several novels by Reichs, as well as of the TV series Bones, which debuted on Fox in 2005.

powerless. Applied anthropologists working for businesses try to solve the problem of expanding profits for their employer or client. In market research, ethical issues may arise as anthropologists attempt to help companies operate more efficiently and profitably. Ethical ambiguities are present as well in cultural resource management. A CRM firm typically is hired by someone seeking to build a road or a factory. In such cases, the client may have a strong interest in an outcome in which no sites are found that need protecting. To whom does the researcher owe loyalty, and what problems might be involved in holding firm to the truth?

Like the colonial anthropologists, applied anthropologists still face ethical dilemmas because they do not set the policies they have to implement, and because it is difficult to criticize programs in which they have participated (see Escobar 1991, 1994). Anthropology's professional organizations have addressed these problems by establishing codes of ethics and ethics committees. See Appendix 2 and http://www.aaanet.org for the code of ethics of the AAA. As Tice (1997) notes, attention to ethical issues is paramount in the teaching of applied anthropology today.

ACADEMIC AND APPLIED ANTHROPOLOGY

Applied anthropology did not disappear during the 1950s and 1960s, but academic anthropology did most of the growing after World War II. The baby boom, which began in 1946 and peaked in 1957, fueled expansion of the American educational system and thus of academic jobs. New junior, community, and four-year colleges opened, and anthropology became a standard part of the college curriculum. During the 1950s and 1960s, most American anthropologists were college professors, although some still worked in agencies and museums.

This era of academic anthropology continued through the early 1970s. Especially during the Vietnam War, undergraduates flocked to anthropology classes to learn about other cultures. Students were especially interested in Southeast Asia, whose indigenous societies were being disrupted by war. Many anthropologists protested the superpowers' apparent disregard for non-Western lives, values, customs, and social systems.

During the 1970s, and increasingly thereafter, although most anthropologists still worked in academia, others found jobs with international organizations, government, businesses, hospitals, and schools. About half of students graduating with Ph.D.s in anthropology today will have careers outside academia. This shift toward appli-

predict the behavior of the enemies of the United States. After the war, Americans did applied anthropology in the Pacific, working to gain native cooperation with American policies in various trust territories.

Modern applied anthropology differs from an earlier version that mainly served the goals of colonial regimes. Application was a central concern of early anthropology in Great Britain (in the context of colonialism) and the United States (in the context of Native American policy). Before turning to the new, we should consider some dangers of the old.

In the context of the British empire, specifically its African colonies, Malinowski (1929a) proposed that "practical anthropology" (his term for colonial applied anthropology) should focus on Westernization, the diffusion of European culture into tribal societies. Malinowski questioned neither the legitimacy of colonialism nor the anthropologist's role in making it work. He saw nothing wrong with aiding colonial regimes by studying land tenure and land use, to decide how much of their land natives should keep and how much Europeans should get. Malinowski's views exemplify a historical association between anthropology, particularly in Europe, and colonialism (Maquet 1964).

Today, many applied anthropologists see their work as a helping profession, devoted to assisting local people, as anthropologists speak up for the disenfranchised in the international political arena. But applied anthropologists also solve problems for clients who are neither poor nor

cation has benefited the profession. It has forced anthropologists to consider the wider social value and implications of their research.

Theory and Practice

One of the most valuable tools in applying anthropology is the ethnographic method. Ethnographers study societies firsthand, living with and learning from ordinary people. Ethnographers are participant-observers, taking part in the events they study in order to understand local thought and behavior. Applied anthropologists use ethnographic techniques in both foreign and domestic settings. Other "expert" participants in social-change programs may be content to converse with officials, read reports, and copy statistics. However, the applied anthropologist's likely early request is some variant of "take me to the local people." We know that people must play an active role in the changes that affect them and that "the people" have information that "the experts" lack.

Anthropological theory—the body of findings and generalizations of the subdisciplines—also guides applied anthropology (see Appendix 1). Anthropology's holistic and biocultural perspectives—its interest in biology, society, culture, and language—permit the evaluation of many issues that affect people. Theory aids practice, and application fuels theory. As we compare social-change policy and programs, our understanding of cause and effect increases. We add new generalizations about culture change to those discovered in traditional and ancient cultures.

Anthropology's systemic perspective recognizes that changes don't occur in a vacuum. A program or project always has multiple effects, some of which are unforeseen. For example, dozens of economic development projects intended to increase productivity through irrigation have worsened public health by creating waterways where diseases thrive. In an American example of unintended consequences, a program aimed at enhancing teachers' appreciation of cultural differences led to ethnic stereotyping (Kleinfeld 1975). Specifically, Native American students did not welcome teachers' frequent comments about their Indian heritage. The students felt set apart from their classmates and saw this attention to their ethnicity as patronizing and demeaning.

ANTHROPOLOGY AND EDUCATION

Anthropology and education refers to anthropological research in classrooms, homes, and neighborhoods (see Spindler 2000, 2005). Some of the most interesting research has been done in class-

UNDERSTANDING OURSELVES

Is change good? American culture seems to think so. "New and improved" is a slogan we hear all the time—a lot more often than "old reliable." But new isn't always improved. People often resist change, as the Coca Cola Company (TCCC) discovered in 1985 when it changed the formula of its premium soft drink and introduced "New Coke." When hordes of customers protested, TCCC brought back old, familiar, reliable Coke under the name "Coca Cola Classic," which thrives today. New Coke is history.

TCCC tried a *top-down change* (a change decided and initiated at the top of a hierarchy rather than by the communities affected by the change). The people, that is, customers, didn't ask TCCC to change its product; executives made the decision to change Coke's taste. Executives are to business decisions as policy makers are to social change programs; both stand at the top of organizations that provide goods and services to people. Smart executives and policy makers listen to people to try to determine *locally based demand*—what the people want. What's working well (assuming it's not discriminatory or illegal) should be maintained, encouraged, and strengthened. What's wrong, and how can it be fixed? What changes do the people—and which people—want? How can conflicting wishes and needs be accommodated? Applied anthropologists help answer these questions, which are crucial in understanding whether change is needed, and how it will work.

rooms, where anthropologists observe interactions among teachers, students, parents, and visitors. Jules Henry's classic account of the American elementary school classroom (1955) shows how students learn to conform to and compete with their peers. Anthropologists also follow students from classrooms into their homes and neighborhoods, viewing children as total cultural creatures whose enculturation and attitudes toward education belong to a context that includes family and peers (Zou and Trueba 2002).

Sociolinguists and cultural anthropologists work side by side in education research, for example, in a study of Puerto Rican seventh-graders in the urban Midwest (Hill-Burnett 1978). In classrooms, neighborhoods, and homes, anthropologists uncovered some misconceptions by teachers. For example, the teachers had mistakenly assumed that Puerto Rican parents valued education less

In this bilingual class, kids point as their teacher holds up cards that say "point" in English and Spanish. In such classrooms, and extending out into the community, anthropologists of education study the backgrounds, behavior, beliefs, and attitudes of teachers, students, parents, and families in their (multi)cultural context.

than did non-Hispanics. However, in-depth interviews revealed that the Puerto Rican parents valued it more.

Researchers also found that certain practices were preventing Hispanics from being adequately educated. For example, the teachers' union and the board of education had agreed to teach "English as a foreign language." However, they had not provided bilingual teachers to work with Spanish-speaking students. The school started assigning all students (including non-Hispanics) with low reading scores and behavior problems to the English-as-a-foreign-language classroom.

This educational disaster brought together a teacher who spoke no Spanish, children who barely spoke English, and a group of English-speaking students with reading and behavior problems. The Spanish speakers were falling behind not just in reading but in all subjects. They could at least have kept up in the other subjects if a Spanish speaker had been teaching them science, social studies, and math until they were ready for English-language instruction in those areas.

A dramatic illustration of the relevance of applied sociolinguistics to education comes from Ann Arbor, Michigan. In 1979, the parents of several black students at the predominantly white Dr. Martin Luther King Jr. Elementary School sued the board of education. They claimed that their children faced linguistic discrimination in the classroom.

The children, who lived in a neighborhood housing project, spoke Black English Vernacular (BEV) at home. At school, most had encountered problems with their classwork. Some had been labeled "learning-impaired" and placed in remedial reading courses. (Consider the embarrassment that children suffer and the effect on self-image of such labeling.)

The African American parents and their attorney contended that the children had no intrinsic learning disabilities but simply did not understand everything their teachers said. Nor did their teachers always understand them. The lawyer argued that because BEV and Standard English (SE) are so similar, teachers often misinterpreted a child's correct pronunciation (in BEV) of an SE word as a reading error.

The children's attorney recruited several sociolinguists to testify on their behalf. The school board, by contrast, could not find a single qualified linguist to support its argument that there was no linguistic discrimination.

The judge ruled in favor of the children and ordered the following solution: Teachers at the King School had to attend a full-year course designed to improve their knowledge of nonstandard dialects, particularly BEV. The judge did not advocate that the teachers learn to speak BEV or that the children do their assignments in BEV. The school's goal remained to teach the children to use SE, the standard dialect, correctly. Before this could be accomplished, however, teachers and students alike had to learn how to recognize the differences between these similar dialects. At the end of the year, most of the teachers interviewed in the local newspaper said the course had helped them.

In a diverse, multicultural populace, teachers should be sensitive to and knowledgeable about linguistic and cultural differences. Children need to be protected so that their ethnic or linguistic background is not used against them. That is what happens when a social variation is regarded as a learning disability.

URBAN ANTHROPOLOGY

By 2025, the developing nations will account for 85 percent of the world's population, compared with 77 percent in 1992 (Stevens 1992). Solutions to future problems will depend increasingly on understanding non-Western cultural backgrounds. The fastest population growth rates are in the less developed countries, especially in urban areas. The world had only 16 cities with more than a million people in 1900, but there are more than 300 such cities today. By 2025, 60 percent of the global population will be urban, compared with 37 percent in 1990 (Stevens 1992). Rural migrants often move to slums, where they live in hovels without utilities and public sanitation facilities.

In 2003 the United Nations (UN) estimated that some 940 million people, about a sixth of earth's population, were living in urban slums, mostly without water, sanitation, public services, and legal security (Vidal 2003). The UN estimates that in three decades the urban population of the developing world will double—to 4 billion people. Rural populations will barely increase and will start declining after 2020 (Vidal 2003). The concentration of people in slums will be accompanied by rising rates of crime and water, air, and noise pollution. These problems will be most severe in the less-developed countries. Almost all (97 percent) of the projected world population increase will occur in developing countries, 34 percent in Africa alone (Lewis 1992). Although the rate of population increase is low in northern countries, such as the United States, Canada, and most European nations, global population growth will continue to affect the Northern Hemisphere, especially through international migration. There has been substantial recent migration to the United States and Canada from developing countries with high growth rates, such as India and Mexico.

As industrialization and urbanization spread globally, anthropologists increasingly study these processes and the social and health problems they create. Urban anthropology, which has theoretical (basic research) and applied dimensions, is the cross-cultural, ethnographic, and biocultural

■ *During the Vietnam War, many anthropologists protested the superpowers' disregard for the values, customs, social systems, and lives of Third World peoples. Several anthropologists (including the author) attended this all-night Columbia University "teach-in" against the war in 1965.*

study of global urbanization and life in cities (see Aoyagi, Nas, and Traphagan, eds. 1998; Gmelch and Zenner 2002; Stevenson 2003). The United States and Canada also have become popular arenas for urban anthropological research on topics such as ethnicity, poverty, class, and subcultural variations (Mullings 1987).

Urban versus Rural

Recognizing that a city is a social context that is very different from a rural community, an early student of Third World urbanization, the anthropologist Robert Redfield, focused on contrasts between rural and urban life. He contrasted rural communities, whose social relations are on a face-to-face basis, with cities, where impersonality characterizes many aspects of life. Redfield (1941) proposed that urbanization be studied along a rural–urban continuum. He described differences in values and social relations in four sites that spanned such a continuum. In Mexico's Yucatán peninsula, Redfield compared an isolated Maya-speaking Indian community, a rural peasant village, a small provincial city, and a large capital. Several studies in Africa (Little 1971) and Asia were influenced by Redfield's view that cities are centers through which cultural innovations spread to rural and tribal areas.

In any nation, urban and rural represent different social systems. However, migrants bring rural social forms, practices, and beliefs to town. They also take back urban and national patterns when they visit, or move back permanently to, their villages of origin. Inevitably, the experiences and social units of rural areas affect adaptation to city life. City folk also develop new institutions to meet specific urban needs (Mitchell 1966).

See the OLC Internet Exercises
mhhe.com/kottak

In Peshawar, Pakistan, young boys receive instruction. What do you see here that differs from classrooms in your country?

Applying anthropology to urban planning starts by identifying the key social groups in the urban context. After identifying those groups, the anthropologist elicits their wishes for change and helps translate those needs to funding agencies. The next step is to work with the agencies and the people to ensure that changes are implemented correctly and that they correspond to what the people said they wanted at the outset. African urban groups that an applied anthropologist would consult include ethnic associations, occupational groups, social clubs, religious groups, and burial societies. Through membership in these groups, urban Africans have wide networks of personal contacts and support. Ethnic or "tribal" associations are common in both West and East Africa (Banton 1957; Little 1965). These groups maintain links with, and provide cash support and urban lodging for, their rural relatives.

The ideology of such associations is that of a gigantic kin group. The members call one another "brother" and "sister." As in an extended family, rich members help their poor relatives. When members fight among themselves, the group acts as judge. A member's improper behavior can lead to expulsion—an unhappy fate for a migrant in a large ethnically heterogeneous city.

Modern North American cities also have kin-based ethnic associations. One example comes from Los Angeles, which has the largest Samoan immigrant community (over 12,000 people) in the United States. Samoans in Los Angeles draw on their traditional system of *matai* (*matai* means chief; the *matai* system now refers to respect for elders) to deal with modern urban problems. One example: In 1992, a white police officer shot and killed two unarmed Samoan brothers. When a

See the Virtual Exploration
mhhe.com/kottak

judge dismissed charges against the officer, local leaders used the *matai* system to calm angry youths (who have formed gangs, like other ethnic groups in the Los Angeles area). Clan leaders and elders organized a well-attended community meeting, in which they urged young members to be patient.

Los Angeles Samoans also used the American judicial system. They brought a civil case against the officer in question and pressed the U.S. Justice Department to initiate a civil-rights case in the matter (Mydans 1992b). One role for the urban applied anthropologist is to help relevant social groups deal with larger urban institutions, such as legal and social-service agencies with which recent migrants, in particular, may be unfamiliar (see Holtzman 2000).

MEDICAL ANTHROPOLOGY

Medical anthropology is both academic/theoretical and applied/practical. It is a field that includes both biological and sociocultural anthropologists (see Anderson 1996; Brown 1998; Joralemon 1999). Medical anthropology is discussed in this chapter because of its many applications. Medical anthropologists examine such questions as: Which diseases affect different populations? How is illness socially constructed? How does one treat illness in effective and culturally appropriate ways?

This growing field considers the biocultural context and implications of disease and illness (Helman 2001; Strathern and Stewart 1999). **Disease** refers to a scientifically identified health threat caused by a bacterium, virus, fungus, para-

In Ghana, a police officer talks to street children about their rights. In cities around the world, applied anthropologists work with formal and informal associations, including gangs, clubs, and youth groups.

site, or other pathogen. **Illness** is a condition of poor health perceived or felt by an individual (Inhorn and Brown 1990). Cross-cultural research shows that perceptions of good and bad health, along with health threats and problems, are culturally constructed. Different ethnic groups and cultures recognize different illnesses, symptoms, and causes and have developed different health-care systems and treatment strategies.

Disease also varies among cultures (Baer, Singer, and Susser 2003). Traditional and ancient hunter-gatherers, because of their small numbers, mobility, and relative isolation from other groups, were not subject to most of the epidemic infectious diseases that affect agrarian and urban societies (Cohen and Armelagos 1984; Inhorn and Brown 1990). Epidemic diseases such as cholera, typhoid, and bubonic plague thrive in dense populations, and thus among farmers and city dwellers. The spread of malaria has been linked to population growth and deforestation associated with food production.

Certain diseases have spread with economic development. *Schistosomiasis* or bilharzia (liver flukes) is probably the fastest-spreading and most dangerous parasitic infection now known (Heyneman 1984). It is propagated by snails that live in ponds, lakes, and waterways, usually ones created by irrigation projects. A study done in a Nile Delta village in Egypt (Farooq 1966) illustrated the role of culture (religion) in the spread of schistosomiasis. The disease was more common among Muslims than among Christians because of an Islamic practice called *wudu*, ritual ablution (bathing) before prayer. The applied anthropology approach to reducing such diseases is to see if natives perceive a connection between the vector (e.g., snails in the water) and the disease, which can take years to develop. If they do not, such information may be spread by enlisting active local groups and schools. With the worldwide diffusion of the electronic mass media, culturally appropriate public information campaigns have increased awareness and modified behavior that has public health consequences.

In eastern Africa, AIDS and other sexually transmitted diseases (STDs) have spread along highways, via encounters between male truckers and female prostitutes. STDs also are spread through prostitution, as young men from rural

■ *Schistosomiasis is among the fastest spreading and most dangerous parasitic infections now known. It is propagated by snails that live in ponds, lakes, and waterways (often ones created by irrigation projects) such as this one in Luxor, Egypt. As an applied anthropologist, what would you do to cut the rate of infection?*

areas seek wage work in cities, labor camps, and mines. When the men return to their natal villages, they infect their wives (Larson 1989; Miller and Rockwell 1988). Cities are also prime sites of STD transmission in Europe, Asia, and North and South America (Baer, Singer, and Susser 2003; French 2002).

The kind and incidence of disease vary among societies, and cultures interpret and treat illness differently. Standards for sick and healthy bodies are cultural constructions that vary in time and space (Martin 1992). Still, all societies have what George Foster and Barbara Anderson (1978) call "disease-theory systems" to identify, classify, and explain illness. According to Foster and Anderson (1978), there are three basic theories about the causes of illness: personalistic, naturalistic, and emotionalistic. *Personalistic disease theories* blame illness on agents (often malicious), such as sorcerers, witches, ghosts, or ancestral spirits. *Naturalistic disease theories* explain illness in impersonal terms. One example is Western medicine or *biomedicine,* which aims to link illness to scientifically demonstrated agents that bear no personal malice toward their victims. Thus, Western medicine attributes illness to organisms (e.g., bacteria, viruses, fungi, or parasites), accidents, or toxic materials. Other naturalistic ethnomedical systems blame poor health on unbalanced body fluids. Many Latin cultures classify food, drink, and environmental conditions as "hot" or "cold." People believe their health suffers when they eat or drink hot or cold substances together or under

inappropriate conditions. For example, one shouldn't drink something cold after a hot bath or eat a pineapple (a "cold" fruit) when one is menstruating (a "hot" condition).

Emotionalistic disease theories assume that emotional experiences cause illness. For example, Latin Americans may develop *susto,* or soul loss, an illness caused by anxiety or fright (Bolton 1981; Finkler 1985). Its symptoms include lethargy, vagueness, and distraction. Of course, modern psychoanalysis also focuses on the role of the emotions in physical and psychological well-being.

All societies have **health-care systems.** These consist of beliefs, customs, specialists, and techniques aimed at ensuring health and preventing, diagnosing, and curing illness. A society's illness-causation theory is important for treatment. When illness has a personalistic cause, shamans and other magico-religious specialists may be good curers. They draw on varied techniques (occult and practical) that comprise their special expertise. A shaman (magico-religious specialist) may cure soul loss by enticing the spirit back into the body. Shamans may ease difficult childbirths by asking spirits to travel up the birth canal to guide the baby out (Lévi-Strauss 1967). A shaman may cure a cough by counteracting a curse or removing a substance introduced by a sorcerer.

All cultures have health-care specialists. If there is a "world's oldest profession" besides hunter and gatherer, it is **curer,** often a shaman. The curer's role has some universal features (Foster and Anderson 1978). Thus, curers emerge through a culturally defined process of selection (parental prodding, inheritance, visions, dream instructions) and training (apprentice shamanship, medical school). Eventually, the curer is certified by older practitioners and acquires a professional image. Patients believe in the skills of the curer, whom they consult and compensate.

We should not lose sight, ethnocentrically, of the difference between **scientific medicine** and Western medicine per se (Lieban 1977). Despite advances in pathology, microbiology, biochemistry, surgery, diagnostic technology, and applications, many Western medical procedures have little justification in logic or fact. Overprescription of tranquilizers and drugs, unnecessary surgery, and the impersonality and inequality of the physician–patient relationship are questionable features of Western medical systems. Also, overuse of antibiotics, not just for people, but also in animal feed and antibacterial soaps, seems to be triggering an explosion of resistant microorganisms, which may pose a long-term global public health hazard.

Still, Western medicine surpasses tribal treatment in many ways. Although medicines like quinine, coca, opium, ephedrine, and rauwolfia were discovered in nonindustrial societies, thousands of effective drugs are available today to treat myriad diseases. Preventive health care improved during the 20th century. Today's surgical procedures are safer and more effective than those of traditional societies.

But industrialization has spawned its own health problems. Modern stressors include noise, air, and water pollution; poor nutrition; dangerous machinery; impersonal work; isolation; poverty; homelessness; and substance abuse. Health problems in industrial nations are due as much to economic, social, political, and cultural factors as to pathogens. In modern North America, for example, poverty contributes to many illnesses. These include arthritis, heart conditions, back problems, and hearing and vision impairment (see Bailey 2000). Poverty is also a factor in the differential spread of infectious diseases.

Medical anthropologists have served as cultural interpreters in public health programs, which must pay attention to native theories about the nature, causes, and treatment of illness. Successful health interventions cannot simply be forced on communities. They must fit into local cultures and be accepted by local people. When Western medicine is introduced, people usually retain many of their old methods while also accepting new ones (see Green 1987/1992). Native curers may go on treating certain conditions (like spirit possession), whereas M.D.s may deal with others. If both modern and traditional specialists are consulted and the patient is cured, the native curer may get as much credit as or more credit than the physician.

A more personal treatment of illness that emulates the non-Western curer-patient-community

A traditional healer at work in Malaysia. Shown here, mugwort, a small, spongy herb, is burned to facilitate healing. The healer lights one end of a moxa stick, roughly the shape and size of a cigar, and attaches it, or holds it close, to the area being treated for several minutes until the area turns red. The purpose of moxibustion is to strengthen the blood, stimulate spiritual energy, and maintain general health.

relationship could probably benefit Western systems. Western medicine has tended to draw a rigid line between biological and psychological causation. Non-Western theories usually lack this sharp distinction, recognizing that poor health has intertwined physical, emotional, and social causes. The mind-body opposition is part of Western folk taxonomy, not of science.

ANTHROPOLOGY AND BUSINESS

Carol Taylor (1987) discusses the value of an "anthropologist-in-residence" in a large, complex organization such as a hospital or a business. A free-ranging ethnographer can be a perceptive oddball when information and decisions usually move through a rigid hierarchy. If allowed to observe and converse freely with all types and levels of personnel, the anthropologist may acquire a unique perspective on organizational conditions and problems. For many years, anthropologists have used ethnography to study business settings (Arensberg 1987; Jordan 2003). For example, ethnographic research in an auto factory may view workers, managers, and executives as different social categories participating in a common social system. Each group has characteristic attitudes, values, and behavior patterns. These are transmitted through *microenculturation*, the process by which people learn particular roles in a limited social system. The free-ranging nature of ethnography takes the anthropologist from worker to executive. Each of these people is both an individual with a personal viewpoint and a cultural creature whose perspective is, to some extent, shared with other members of a group. Applied anthropologists have acted as "cultural

UNDERSTANDING OURSELVES

If we're feeling sick, we often feel better once a label (diagnosis) is attached to our illness. In contemporary society, it's usually a physician who provides us with such a label—and maybe with a medicine that cures it or alleviates our suffering. In other contexts, a shaman or magico-religious specialist provides the diagnosis and treatment plan. We live in a world where alternative health-care systems coexist, sometimes competing with, sometimes complementing, one another. Never have people had access to such a wide range of choices in health care. In seeking good health and survival, it may be only natural for people to draw on alternative systems—acupuncture for one problem, chiropractic for another, medicine for a third, psychotherapy for a fourth, spiritual healing for a fifth. Think about the alternative treatment systems you may have used in the last year.

New Life, Good Health

BACKGROUND INFORMATION

STUDENT:
Ann L. Bretnall

SUPERVISING PROFESSOR:
David Himmelgreen

SCHOOL:
University of South Florida

YEAR IN SCHOOL/MAJOR:
Senior/Anthropology

FUTURE PLANS:
After completion of master's in applied anthropology, work with the local social-service agencies in community outreach projects

PROJECT TITLE:
Establishing a Farmers Market for the Local Hispanic Community

Note how this essay links the worlds of commerce, nutrition, health, and social interaction. The comfortable and convivial atmosphere of the local farmers' market is an appropriate setting for applying anthropology—aimed at culturally appropriate education and innovation. As immigration has increased, work demands and ready access to fast foods have changed the nature of meals and diet among Latinos and Latinas in the Tampa area. Ann Bretnall discusses her work organizing educational events and the participation of local community members in the farmer's market.

The Applied Anthropology program at the University of South Florida, in Tampa, gives students practical experience with community projects. The Project New Life-Good Health (Nueva Vida-Buena Salud) is one of many projects the Anthropology Department is currently working on. This project is designed to develop and implement a community-engaged nutrition and health education program targeting recently arrived Latino immigrant families. My project is to develop a church-based farmer's market for the local Hispanic community.

In recent years the Hispanic population of Hillsborough County, which includes Tampa, has significantly increased. Immigrants have arrived from Central and South America and from the Caribbean. According to U.S. Census Bureau data, the 1990 Hispanic population of Hillsborough County was 106,908, rising to 179,692 in 2000.

Project New Life-Good Health rests on two previous projects focusing on the local Hispanic community. Those projects were called "Acculturation and Nutritional Needs Assessment of Tampa" (ANNA-T) and "Promoting Adequate Nutrition" (PAN). The ANNA-T project investigated food consumption and physical activity patterns of recently arrived Latino immigrants. The research of ANNA-T helped to develop project PAN. PAN was a series of culturally tailored nutrition-education and disease-prevention seminars targeting low-income Latino families. Projects ANNA-T and PAN found there had been a significant change in diet, with a new emphasis on fast food and sodas and a reduced consumption of fresh fruits and vegetables. ANNA-T also discovered that lack of time and of social support were barriers to traditional family meals.

The goals of project New Life-Good Health are to: 1) develop a culturally appropriate nutrition-education and disease-prevention curriculum, 2) conduct a series of healthy-eating and disease-prevention seminars, and 3) develop a church-based farmers' market that includes nutrition-education and health-promotion activities for the larger community. Local farmers' markets have an open and informal setting, which provides a unique ambiance to the shopping experience. This social setting allows customers to converse easily with vendors, unlike the sometimes uncomfortable interactions with employees in a grocery store.

My work with the Project New Life-Good Health farmers' market involves organizing the resources necessary to implement farmers' market events. In interviews and observations, I have found genuine interest among community members and vendors. The literature I reviewed also confirms advantages to individuals involved in local farmers' markets. Efforts by community members to organize and establish the farmers' market as their own will be crucial to the success of the market as a permanent institution in their community.

To summarize, the goal of the farmers' market is to provide a venue to understand community needs, to educate, and to improve the nutrition and health of the local Hispanic community. This can be accomplished by ensuring the availability of some culturally specific foods and by introducing other healthful foods into the Hispanic diet. Our ongoing research will provide the local community with the resources to continue and manage the farmers' market as a positive and sustainable alternative within their local economy.

brokers," translating managers' goals or workers' concerns to the other group.

Closely observing how people actually use products, anthropologists work with engineers to design products that are more user-friendly. Increasingly, anthropologists are working with high-tech companies, where they use their observational skills to study how people work, live, and use technology. Such studies can be traced to 1979, when the Xerox Palo Alto (California) Research Center (PARC) hired the anthropologist Lucy Suchman. She worked in a laboratory where researchers were trying to build artificial intelligence to help people use complicated copiers. Suchman observed and filmed people having trouble with a copying job. From her research came the realization that simplicity is more important than fancy features. That's why all Xerox copiers, no matter how complex, now include a single green copy button for when someone wants an uncomplicated copy.

"[Our] graduate students keep getting snatched up by companies," says Marietta Baba (dean of social science at Michigan State University), former chair of the anthropology department at Wayne State University (WSU) in Detroit (quoted in Weise 1999). WSU trains anthropology students to observe social interactions to understand the underlying structures of a culture, and to apply those methods to industry. Baba estimates that about 9,000 American anthropologists work in academia and that about 2,200 hold applied anthropology positions in industry. "But the proportions are shifting, so you're getting more and more applied ones," she says (quoted in Weise 1999). Companies hire anthropologists to gain a better understanding of their customers and to find new products and markets that engineers and marketers might never imagine (see "Interesting Issues" on p. 38). Andrea Saveri, a director at the Institute for the Future in Menlo Park, California, contends that traditional market research is limited by its question-and-answer format. "In the case of surveys, you're telling the respondent how to answer and you're not giving them any room for anything else" (quoted in Weise 1999). Saveri, who thinks ethnography is more precise and powerful than surveys, employs anthropologists to investigate the consequences of technology (Weise 1999).

For business, key features of anthropology include (1) ethnography and observation as ways of gathering data, (2) cross-cultural expertise, and (3) a focus on cultural diversity. The cross-cultural perspective enters the picture when businesses seek to know why other nations have higher (or lower) productivity than we do (Ferraro 2006). Reasons for differential productivity are cultural, social, and economic. To find them, anthropologists must focus on key features in the organization of production. Subtle but potentially important differences can emerge from workplace ethnography—close observation of workers and managers in their natural (workplace) setting.

CAREERS AND ANTHROPOLOGY

Many college students find anthropology interesting and consider majoring in it. However, their parents or friends may discourage them by asking, "What kind of job are you going to get with an anthropology major?" The first step in answering this question is to consider the more general question "What do you do with any college major?" The answer is "Not much, without a good bit of effort, thought, and planning." A survey of graduates of the literary college of the University of Michigan showed that few had jobs that were clearly linked to their majors. Medicine, law, and many other professions require advanced degrees. Although many colleges offer bachelor's degrees in engineering, business, accounting, and social work, master's degrees are often needed to get the best jobs in those fields. Anthropologists, too, need an advanced degree, most typically a Ph.D., to find gainful employment in academic, museum, or applied anthropology.

A broad college education, and even a major in anthropology, can be an excellent foundation for success in many fields. Many University of Michigan undergraduates who are planning careers in medicine, public health, or dentistry

At a major information technology company, Marietta Baba examines one of the world's fastest supercomputers. She is studying that firm's adaptation to the rise of the service economy. Professor Baba, a prominent applied anthropologist and Dean of the College of Social Science at Michigan State University, also has studied Michigan's automobile industry.

Hot Asset in Corporate: Anthropology Degrees

More and more businesses are hiring anthropologists because they like anthropology's characteristic observation of behavior in natural settings and its focus on cultural diversity. Thus, as we see in this article, Hallmark Cards has hired anthropologists to observe parties, holidays, and celebrations of ethnic groups to improve its ability to design cards for targeted audiences. Anthropologists go into people's homes to see how they actually use products. This permits better product design and more effective advertising.

Don't throw away the MBA degree yet.

But as companies go global and crave leaders for a diverse workforce, a new hot degree is emerging for aspiring executives: anthropology.

The study of man is no longer a degree for museum directors. Citicorp created a vice presidency for anthropologist Steve Barnett, who discovered early warning signs to identify people who don't pay credit card bills.

Not satisfied with consumer surveys, Hallmark is sending anthropologists into the homes of immigrants, attending holidays and birthday parties to design cards they'll want.

No survey can tell engineers what women really want in a razor, so marketing consultant Hauser Design sends anthropologists into bathrooms to watch them shave their legs.

Unlike MBAs, anthropology degrees are rare: one undergraduate degree for every 26 in business and one anthropology Ph.D. for every 235 MBAs.

Textbooks now have chapters on business applications. The University of South Florida has created a course of study for anthropologists headed for commerce.

Motorola corporate lawyer Robert Faulkner got his anthropology degree before going to law school. He says it becomes increasingly valuable.

"When you go into business, the only problems you'll have are people problems," was the advice given to teenager Michael Koss by his father in the early 1970s.

Koss, now 44, heeded the advice, earned an anthropology degree from Beloit College in 1976, and is today CEO of the Koss headphone manufacturer.

Katherine Burr, CEO of The Hanseatic Group, has masters in both anthropology and business from the University of New Mexico. Hanseatic was among the first money management programs to predict the Asian crisis and last year produced a total return of 315% for investors.

"My competitive edge came completely out of anthropology," she says. "The world is so unknown, changes so rapidly. Preconceptions can kill you."

Companies are starving to know how people use the Internet or why some pickups, even though they are more powerful, are perceived by consumers as less powerful, says Ken Erickson, of the Center for Ethnographic Research.

It takes trained observation, Erickson says. Observation is what anthropologists are trained to do.

SOURCE: Del Jones, "Hot Asset in Corporate: Anthropology Degrees," *USA Today,* February 18, 1999, p. B1.

choose a joint major in anthropology and zoology. A recent survey of women executives showed that most had not majored in business but in the social sciences or humanities. Only after graduating did they study business, obtaining a master's degree in business administration. These executives felt that the breadth of their college educations had contributed to their business careers. Anthropology majors go on to medical, law, and business schools and find success in many professions that often have little explicit connection to anthropology.

Anthropology's breadth provides knowledge and an outlook on the world that are useful in many kinds of work. For example, an anthropology major combined with a master's degree in business is excellent preparation for work in international business. However, job seekers must always convince employers that they have a special and valuable "skillset."

Breadth is anthropology's hallmark. Anthropologists study people biologically, culturally, socially, and linguistically, in time and space, in developed and underdeveloped nations, in simple and complex settings. Physical anthropologists teach about human biology in time and space, including our origins and evolution. Most colleges have cultural anthropology courses that compare cultures and others that focus on particular world areas, such as Latin America, Asia, and Native North America. The knowledge of geographic areas acquired in such courses can be useful in many jobs. Anthropology's comparative outlook, its long-standing Third World focus, and its appreciation of diverse lifestyles combine to provide an excellent foundation for overseas employment (see Omohundro 2001).

Even for work in North America, the focus on culture is valuable. Every day we hear about cultural differences and about social problems whose solutions require a multicultural viewpoint—an ability to recognize and reconcile ethnic differences. Government, schools, and private firms constantly deal with people from different social classes, ethnic groups, and tribal backgrounds. Physicians, attorneys, social workers, police officers, judges, teachers, and students can all do a better job if they understand social differences in a part of the world that is one of the most ethnically diverse in history.

Knowledge about the traditions and beliefs of the many social groups within a modern nation is important in planning and carrying out programs that affect those groups. Attention to social background and cultural categories helps ensure the welfare of affected ethnic groups, communities, and neighborhoods. Experience in planned social change—whether community organization in North America or economic development overseas—shows that a proper social study should be done before a project or policy is implemented. When local people want the change and it fits their lifestyle and traditions, it will be more successful, beneficial, and cost effective. There will be not only a more humane but a more economical solution to a real social problem.

People with anthropology backgrounds are doing well in many fields. Furthermore, even if the job has little or nothing to do with anthropology in a formal or obvious sense, anthropology is always useful when we work with fellow human beings. For most of us, this means every day of our lives.

1. Anthropology has two dimensions: academic and applied. Applied anthropology uses anthropological perspectives, theory, methods, and data to identify, assess, and solve problems. Applied anthropologists have a range of employers. Examples: government agencies; development organizations; NGOs; tribal, ethnic, and interest groups; businesses; social services and educational agencies. Applied anthropologists come from all four subfields. Ethnography is one of applied anthropology's most valuable research tools. Another is the comparative, cross-cultural, biocultural perspective. A systemic perspective recognizes that changes have multiple consequences, some unintended.

2. Anthropology and education researchers work in classrooms, homes, and other settings relevant to education. Such studies may lead to policy recommendations. Both academic and applied anthropologists study migration from rural areas to cities and across national boundaries. North America has become a popular arena for urban anthropological research on migration, ethnicity, poverty, and related topics. Although rural and urban are different social systems, there is cultural diffusion from one to the other. Rural and tribal social forms affect adjustment to the city.

3. Medical anthropology is the cross-cultural, biocultural study of health problems and conditions, disease, illness, disease theories, and health-care systems. Medical anthropology includes biological and cultural anthropologists and has theoretical (academic) and applied dimensions. In a given setting, the characteristic diseases reflect diet, population density, economy, and social complexity. Native theories of illness may be personalistic, naturalistic, or emotionalistic. In applying anthropology to business, the key features are (1) ethnography and observation as ways of gathering data, (2) cross-cultural expertise, and (3) a focus on cultural diversity.

4. A broad college education, including anthropology and foreign-area courses, offers excellent background for many fields. Anthropology's comparative outlook and cultural relativism provide an excellent basis for overseas employment. Even for work in North America, a focus on culture and cultural diversity is valuable. Anthropology majors attend medical, law, and business schools and succeed in many fields, some of which have little explicit connection with anthropology.

anthropology and education Anthropological research in classrooms, homes, and neighborhoods, viewing students as total cultural creatures whose enculturation and attitudes toward education belong to a larger context that includes family, peers, and society.

applied anthropology The application of anthropological data, perspectives, theory, and methods to identify, assess, and solve contemporary social problems.

cultural resource management (CRM) The branch of applied archaeology aimed at preserving sites threatened by dams, highways, and other projects.

curer Specialized role acquired through a culturally appropriate process of selection, training, certification, and acquisition of a professional image; the curer is consulted by patients, who believe in his or her special powers, and receives some form of special consideration; a cultural universal.

disease A scientifically identified health threat caused by a bacterium, virus, fungus, parasite, or other pathogen.

health-care systems Beliefs, customs, and specialists concerned with ensuring health and preventing and curing illness; a cultural universal.

illness A condition of poor health perceived or felt by an individual.

medical anthropology Unites biological and cultural anthropologists in the study of disease, health problems, health-care systems, and theories about illness in different cultures and ethnic groups.

practicing anthropologists Used as a synonym for applied anthropology; anthropologists who practice their profession outside academia.

scientific medicine As distinguished from Western medicine, a health-care system based on scientific knowledge and procedures, encompassing such fields as pathology, microbiology, biochemistry, surgery, diagnostic technology, and applications.

CRITICAL THINKING QUESTIONS

For more self-testing, see the self-quizzes

mhhe.com/kottak

1. What else are you studying this semester? Do those fields have an applied dimension, too? Are they more or less useful than anthropology is?

2. Describe a setting in which you might use ethnography and observation to do applied anthropology. What other research methods might you also use in that setting?

3. Think back to your grade school or high school classroom. Were there any social issues that might have interested an anthropologist? Were there any problems that an applied anthropologist might have been able to solve? How so?

4. What do you see as the costs and benefits of Western medicine compared with tribal medicine? Are there any conditions for which you'd prefer treatment by a tribal curer than a Western curer?

5. Think of a business context you know well. How might applied anthropology help that business function better? How would the applied anthropologist gather the information to suggest improvements?

6. Besides the examples given in this chapter, think of some other problems or issues in the modern world to which applied anthropology might contribute.

SUGGESTED ADDITIONAL READINGS

Anderson, R.
  1996 *Magic, Science, and Health: The Aims and Achievements of Medical Anthropology.* Fort Worth: Harcourt Brace. Up-to-date text, focusing on variation associated with race, gender, ethnicity, age, and ableness.

Bailey, E. J.
  2000 *Medical Anthropology and African American Health.* Westport, CT: Bergin and Garvey. Medical issues affecting, and anthropological research involving, African Americans.

Brown, P. J.
  1998 *Understanding and Applying Medical Anthropology.* Boston: McGraw-Hill. Medical anthropology, basic and applied.

Chambers, E.
  1985 *Applied Anthropology: A Practical Guide.* Upper Saddle River, NJ: Prentice Hall. How to do applied anthropology, by a leader in the field.
  2000 *Native Tours: The Anthropology of Travel and Tourism.* Prospect Heights, IL: Waveland. How anthropologists study the world's number one business—travel and tourism.

Eddy, E. M., and W. L. Partridge, eds.
  1987 *Applied Anthropology in America,* 2nd ed. New York: Columbia University Press. Historical review of applications of anthropological knowledge in the United States.

Ervin, A. M.
  2005 *Applied Anthropology: Tools and Perspectives for Contemporary Practice,* 2nd ed. Boston: Pearson/Allyn & Bacon. Up-to-date treatment of applied anthropology.

Ferraro, G. P.
  2006 *The Cultural Dimension of International Business,* 5th ed. Upper Saddle River, NJ: Prentice Hall. How the theory and insights of cultural anthropology can influence the conduct of international business.

Gmelch, G., and W. Zenner
  2002 *Urban Life: Readings in the Anthropology of the City.* Prospect Heights, IL: Waveland. Up-to-date anthology.

Gwynne, M. A.
  2003 *Applied Anthropology: A Career-Oriented Approach.* Boston: Allyn & Bacon. Various applied opportunities in anthropological careers.

Holtzman, J.
  2000 *Nuer Journeys, Nuer Lives.* Boston: Allyn & Bacon. How immigrants from Sudan adapt to Minnesota's Twin Cities and to the American social-service system.

Human Organization
  The quarterly journal of the Society for Applied Anthropology. An excellent source for articles on applied anthropology and development.

Joralemon, D.
  1999 *Exploring Medical Anthropology.* Boston: Allyn & Bacon. Recent introduction to a growing field.
McDonald, J. H., ed.
  2002 *The Applied Anthropology Reader.* Boston: Allyn & Bacon. Recent descriptions of case experiences and approaches.
Omohundro, J. T.
  2001 *Careers in Anthropology,* 2nd ed. Boston: McGraw-Hill. Offers some vocational guidance.
Sargent, C. F., and C. B. Brettell
  1996 *Gender and Health: An International Perspective.* Upper Saddle River, NJ: Prentice Hall. How culture affects the relation among gender, health-care organization, and health policy.
Spindler, G. D., ed.
  2000 *Fifty Years of Anthropology and Education, 1950–2000: A Spindler Anthology.* Mahwah, NJ: Erlbaum. Survey of the field of educational anthropology by two prominent contributors, George and Louise Spindler.

Stephens, W. R.
  2002 *Careers in Anthropology: What an Anthropology Degree Can Do for You.* Boston: Allyn & Bacon. Making the most of an anthropology degree.
Stevenson, D.
  2003 *Cities and Urban Cultures.* Philadelphia: Open University Press. A cross-cultural consideration.
Strathern, A., and P. J. Stewart
  1999 *Curing and Healing: Medical Anthropology in Global Perspective.* Durham, NC: Carolina Academic Press. Cross-cultural examples of medical anthropology.
Van Willigen, J.
  2002 *Applied Anthropology: An Introduction,* 3rd ed. Westport, CT: Bergin and Garvey. Excellent review of the growth of applied anthropology and its links to general anthropology.

INTERNET EXERCISES

1. Go to the website for the Central Identification Laboratory, Hawaii (CILHI), **http://www.qmmuseum.lee.army.mil/mortuary/worldwide_cilhi_mission.htm** and read about what this organization does.
   a. What does the CILHI do?
   b. The CILHI is one of the largest employers of forensic anthropologists in the world. How are forensic anthropologists important for its mission?
   c. What kind of educational background do many of the staff members have? Where are some of the institutions they attended?

2. Go to the publication from the United States Agency for International Development (USAID) titled "Population and the Environment: A Delicate Balance" (**http://pdf.dec.org/pdf_docs/PNACP195.pdf**).
   a. What are some of the major environmental threats due to population growth the world faces?
   b. What can groups like USAID do in the face of these threats?
   c. What contributions does anthropology have to offer? Should organizations like USAID employ anthropologists?
   d. What is the role of applied anthropology for environmental issues?

See Chapter 2 at your McGraw-Hill Online Learning Center for additional review and interactive exercises.

LINKAGES

Assault on Paradise

In Kottak's *Assault on Paradise,* 4th edition, read the sections of Chapter 9 titled "Welfare and Education" and "Public Health," which describe improvements in public health, education, and welfare between the 1960s and the 1980s. For background information on health and education during the 1960s, see Chapter 2. In the 1960s what problems might an applied anthropologist have identified as ones with which Arembepeiros most needed help? Had those problems been solved, or at least addressed, by the 1980s? Pay particular attention to health and education.

Culture Sketches

In *Culture Sketches,* 4th edition, by Peters-Golden, read Chapter 11 on "The Ojibwa: The People Endure." Urban anthropology is one applied field presented in this text chapter, which discusses differences between rural and urban life, and the process of change through urbanization. What sorts of changes have occurred in Ojibwa life through urbanization? Might the move from reservation to city, for Native Americans, be different from urbanization experienced by other social groups? Why or why not?

3

Ethics and Methods in Physical Anthropology and Archaeology

ETHICS

Science exists in society and also in the context of law, values, and ethics. Anthropologists can't study things simply because they happen to be interesting or of value to science. Anthropologists are increasingly aware of the ethical and legal contexts in which their work unfolds. Problems involving contrasting systems of ethics and values are especially likely to occur when anthropologists work outside their country or culture of origin.

Anthropologists frequently do research outside their own nations. Physical anthropologists and archaeologists often work as members of international teams. These teams include researchers from several countries, including the *host country*—the place (e.g., Guatemala—see the "News Brief") where the research takes place. In **paleoanthropology** (aka *human paleontology*)—the study of human evolution through the fossil record—physical anthropologists and archaeologists often work together, as they do in forensic anthropology, as described in the news story. Although physical anthropologists are more interested in bones and archaeologists in artifacts, their work may proceed jointly, as they try to infer the relation between the physical and cultural features of the remains they are examining. Much of our knowledge of early human evolution comes from Africa, where international collaboration is common (see Dalton 2006).

International work exposes physical anthropologists and archaeologists to varying national and cultural procedures, value systems, and ethical and legal codes. In such contexts, the American Anthropological Association (AAA) advises anthropologists to be guided by its Code of Ethics (see Appendix 2). To gain permission and collaboration in the host country, anthropologists need to inform officials and colleagues there about the purpose, funding, and likely results of their research. They need to negotiate the matter of where the materials produced by the research will be analyzed and stored—in the host country or in the anthropologists' country—and for how long. To whom do research materials, such as bones, artifacts, and blood samples, belong? What kinds of restrictions will apply to their use?

It's crucial for anthropologists to establish and maintain proper relations between themselves as guests and the host nations and communities where they work. The anthropologist's primary ethical obligation is to the people, species, and materials he or she studies. Although nonhuman primates can't give informed consent, primatologists still must take steps to ensure that their research doesn't endanger the animals. Either government agencies or nongovernmental organizations (NGOs) may be entrusted with protecting primates. If this is the case, the anthropologist will need their permission and informed consent to conduct research. (**Informed consent** refers to people's agreement to take part in research after they have been fully informed about its purpose, nature, procedures, and potential impact on them.)

With living humans, informed consent is a necessity—for example, in obtaining biological samples, such as blood or urine. The research subjects must be told how the samples will be collected, used, and identified, and about the potential costs and benefits to them. Informed consent is needed from anyone providing data or information, owning materials being studied, or otherwise having an interest that might be affected by the research.

The AAA Code says that anthropologists should not exploit individuals, groups, animals, or cultural or biological materials. They should recognize their debt to the people with whom they work and should reciprocate in appropriate ways. For example, it is highly appropriate for North American anthropologists working in another country to (1) include host country colleagues in their research planning and requests for funding, (2) establish truly collaborative relationships with those colleagues and their institutions before, during, and after field work, (3) include host country colleagues in dissemination, including publication, of the research results, and (4) ensure that something is "given back" to host country colleagues. For example, research equipment and technology are allowed to remain in the host country. Or funding is provided for host country colleagues to do research, attend international meetings, or visit foreign institutions—especially those where their international collaborators work.

Physical anthropologists and archaeologists, more often than cultural anthropologists, work as members of teams. Teams include host country collaborators; typically, they also include students—graduate and undergraduate. Training students in

---

OVERVIEW

Because science exists in society and also in the context of law and ethics, anthropologists can't study things simply because they have potential scientific value. The anthropologist's foremost ethical obligation is to the people, species, and materials he or she studies.

Physical anthropologists and archaeologists pursue diverse research topics, using varied methods and often working together. At an archaeological site, a physical anthropologist may complement the picture of ancient life by examining skeletons to reconstruct their diet and health status. Primate studies suggest hypotheses based on behavior that humans do or don't share with our nearest relatives. Another topic within physical anthropology is bone biology, involving genetics, cell structure, growth and decay, and patterns of movement. Paleopathologists examine disease and injury in ancient skeletons. Molecular anthropologists use genetic analysis (of DNA sequences) to assess evolutionary relationships.

Like paleoanthropologists and paleontologists, archaeologists combine local (excavation) and regional (systematic survey) perspectives. Sites are excavated because they are in danger of being destroyed or because they can answer specific research questions. Anthropologists and paleontologists use various methods, including stratigraphy and radiometry, to date fossils.

The Bones Tell the Story

NEW YORK TIMES NEWS BRIEF

by Claudia Dreifus
March 30, 2004

Some of anthropology's applications, while useful, can be grim. Fredy Peccerelli's work as a forensic anthropologist combines elements of pathology, archaeology, and anthropology to solve crimes. Forensic anthropologists include both archaeologists such as Peccerelli, and physical anthropologists, such as Kathy Reichs, whose work inspired the TV series Bones *and several popular mystery novels. Forensic anthropology illustrates anthropology's holistic approach, as anthropologists with varied backgrounds work with community residents to locate and reconstruct crimes, and to give closure to people whose relatives are missing and presumed to be dead. Forensic anthropology applies the techniques of physical anthropology, archaeology, and osteology, a branch of anatomy that deals with bones, to identify the missing and establish how they died. The skeleton provides a profile allowing estimates of age, ancestry, sex, stature, and other details about how the person lived. For more on forensic anthropology (in Bosnia), see Track 2 of the Living Anthropology CD-ROM.*

Fredy A. Peccerelli spends his days exhuming mass graves and examining the bones of murder vic-

tims, hoping that the dead will speak to him. A forensic anthropologist, Mr. Peccerelli, 33, combines elements of pathology, archaeology and anthropology to solve crimes. Human rights organizations employ forensic anthropologists to document war crimes and human rights abuses. Mr. Peccerelli, director of the Guatemalan Forensic Anthropology Foundation, has investigated the deaths of thousands of civilians killed in the civil war in Guatemala from 1960 to 1996. ''What we do is all about life,'' he said here last month on a break at the annual meeting of the American Association for the Advancement of Science. ''It's about people. This is about applying scientific knowledge for everyday human issues.'' The association awarded its science and human rights prize for 2004 to Mr. Peccerelli and his colleagues at the foundation for promoting ''human rights at great personal risk.''

Q. What is the job definition of forensic anthropologist?

A. We use the tools of science to answer important historical questions. For instance, what was the fate of thousands of people who disappeared in the 1970's ''dirty war'' in Argentina? Or what happened to approximately 7,000

or 8,000 Muslim men in Srebrenica in 1995, after United Nations troops left that Bosnian village? Or who were some of the estimated 200,000 Guatemalans killed during 36 years of internal armed conflict? To answer these sorts of questions, forensic anthropologists locate graves and exhume remains. We then apply the techniques of physical anthropology, archaeology and osteology, a branch of anatomy that deals with bones, to identify the missing and establish how they died. A forensic anthropologist tries to identify an individual victim by establishing a profile from the skeleton. It has clues to age, ancestry, sex, stature, how this person lived and how that lifestyle is reflected on the skeleton. We always say, ''The bones tell the story.''

Q. How do you get the bones to speak, to tell the story of a victim?

A. We learn all we can about the victims and the incident where they died. From the reports of eyewitnesses and family members, we get information that helps us locate the graves. We then take everything out of the ground and document what we've found. We next send the bones to an anthropologist in Guatemala City, who analyzes the remains. You look for obvious things in the bones, bullet holes, crushed skulls, breaks, gashes. We are looking for evidence of trauma that will lead us to make an interpretation on whether or not this was a wrongful death. After we've identified the person and determined the cause of death, our findings are handed

■ *Fredy Peccerelli and Rosalina Tuyuc, director of the National Coordination of Guatemalan Widows (CONAVIGUA), speak to reporters during a news conference in Guatemala City on August 25, 2003. Forensic experts were planning exhumations in an area where there are believed to be hundreds of people killed by the Guatemalan military during that country's civil war.*

over to the authorities, because we want to create the possibility of justice. With Guatemala, I say "possibility," because the organization has conducted over 400 investigations, found the remains of about 3,000 people. We've seen three cases go to trial.

Q. You grew up in Brooklyn, though you are Guatemalan. Why did your family immigrate?

A. We moved in 1980, one of the heaviest years in the civil war in Guatemala, at a time when the death squads were most active. My father was a lawyer who headed the Guatemalan weight-lifting team at the Moscow Olympics. When he returned home from it, someone denounced my father, "He's a Red!" They wanted my father's job. In those days, just pointing the finger was enough to get a person killed. Then, my father started getting letters from the death squads. He went into hiding in Guatemala City and then later he fled to New York City. Soon, my mother got a letter saying they knew my father was gone, but if he ever set foot in Guatemala again they would kill him that day. With that, my grandparents took us all to New York. I was 9.

Q. Was Brooklyn a different world for you?

A. Oh, yes. As a kid, my worries were are the Yankees going to make the playoffs, and not how many people are dying in Guatemala. I spent my teen years wanting to be normal and to fit in. Some of that changed when I got to Brooklyn College in 1991 and began feeling the need to reconnect to my heritage. I studied anthropology and archaeology, because these were disciplines that I hoped might take me back to Guatemala. In 1994, Brooklyn College sent me to the annual meeting of the American Anthropological Association, where Dr. Clyde Snow and Dr. Karen Burns, two leaders of this emerging discipline, forensic anthropology, spoke about their work. They talked about exhuming mass graves in Guatemala and about how forensic anthropology was an important tool in winning justice for the dead. Afterward, I went up to Dr. Burns and offered my help.

Q. In your work, are you able to use the new DNA technologies to make identifications?

A. Not all that much. DNA testing can be a great thing. But it's very expensive, and right now there are no labs in Guatemala that can do it.

Q. Do you find it difficult to be around cadavers?

A. In Guatemala, most of the massacres took place in the 1980's, and a lot of time has gone by. So most of what you work with is bones, and the bones are dry. Now, that's very different from working in Bosnia, in Srebrenica, where we went for the International War Crimes Tribunal to identify the remains of that massacre there. The ground had frozen, and when we opened the graves, the bodies were still fresh and the smell was terrible. At a certain moment, I had to decide whether I was cut out for this.

Q. Considering your family history, do you ever do exhumations and think that could have been my father down there?

A. Sure. And that's part of what motivates me. The other part is that once you've heard a relative tell of their search for a missing loved one, then you want to do everything possible to help them. By identifying the remains, it helps satisfy the natural needs of the family for closure. After our investigations, the remains are returned to the families, and they can have their ceremonies.

Q. Have you been threatened for your work?

A. Two years ago, a forensic anthropologist in Guatemala received a letter with a list of 11 people they said they were going to kill. My name was No. 2. We started getting phone calls at the office, "Tell Fredy, we're going to kill him." The threats were very specific, saying that none of the exhumations were going to lead to prosecutions and that the foundation's work was to stop. The American Embassy and the United Nations let the government know they supported us. The work, of course, continued. Right now, I'm on sabbatical to pursue my own studies in England, but my colleagues certainly have not stopped.

───────
SOURCE: Claudia Dreifus, "A Conversation With: Fredy Peccerelli; 'The Bones Tell the Story': Revealing History's Darker Days," *New York Times,* March 30, 2004. http://query.nytimes.com/search/restricted/article?res=F00A12FC34540C738FDDAA0894DC404482.

the value of long-term collaboration is one way of preserving opportunities for future field workers to follow current researchers to the field.

METHODS

There are all sorts of specialized research interests, topics, and methods within both physical anthropology and archaeology. (Given space limitations, only some of them can be covered here.)

Remember that physical anthropologists and archaeologists often collaborate. In the study of human evolution, the physical anthropologists focus on the fossil remains—and what they tell us about ancient human biology. The archaeologists focus on the artifacts—and what they tell us about past cultures. Often their work proceeds jointly as they try to infer the relation between the physical features and cultural features of the remains they are examining. What are some of the methods and techniques used by physical anthropologists and archaeologists?

Multidisciplinary Approaches

Scientists from diverse fields, for example, soil science and **paleontology** (the study of ancient life through the fossil record), using varied techniques, collaborate with physical anthropologists and archaeologists in the study of sites where fossils and/or artifacts have been found. **Palynology,** the study of ancient plants through pollen samples taken from such sites, is used to determine a site's environment at the time of occupation. Physical anthropologists and archaeologists turn to physicists and chemists for help with dating techniques. Physical anthropologists representing a subspecialty known as *bioarchaeology* may complement the picture of ancient life at a particular site by examining human skeletons to reconstruct their physical traits, health status, and diet (Larsen 2000). Evidence for social status may endure in hard materials—bones, jewels, buildings—through the ages. During life, bone growth and stature are influenced by diet. Genetic differences aside, taller people are often that way because they eat better than shorter people do. Differences in the chemical composition of groups of bones at a site may help distinguish privileged nobles from less fortunate commoners. To reconstruct ancient biology and ways of life, physical anthropologists, archaeologists, and their collaborators analyze the remains of humans, plants, and animals, as well as such artifacts (manufactured items) as ceramics, tiles, casts, and metals.

Physical anthropologists and archaeologists draw on low-tech as well as high-tech tools and methods. Small hand-held tools are used at excavation sites, where photos, maps, drawings, and measurements record where every find stands in relation to the site as a whole. Data are entered in field notebooks and computers.

Illustrating more sophisticated technology, sites, such as a system of ancient canals, may be located and defined from the air. Aerial photos (taken from airplanes) and satellite images are forms of **remote sensing** used in site location. For example, ancient buried footpaths visible not to the naked eye but only in satellite imagery have been studied in Costa Rica by University of Colorado and National Aeronautics and Space Administration (NASA) archaeologists (Scott 2002). Up to six feet of volcanic ash, sediment, and vegetation had covered and obscured the footpaths. Images of the paths, some dating to 2,500 years ago, were first made in 1984 by a NASA aircraft using instruments that could "see" in the electromagnetic spectrum invisible to humans. In 2001 a commercial satellite took additional images of the buried footpaths, which showed up as thin red lines, reflecting the dense vegetation growing over them. The footpaths were dated on the basis of the stratigraphy (layers of geological deposits) of the Arenal volcano, which has erupted 10 times in the last 4,000 years.

Village life was established around Arenal some 4,000 years ago, and endured through the Spanish Conquest some 500 years ago. Villagers periodically fled volcanic eruptions, returning when it was safe to resume farming of corn and beans in the nutrient-rich volcanic soil. According to team leader Payson Sheets of the University of Colorado, "they inhabited a very large region and seemed to avoid conflict, conquest and serious disease . . . They led comfortable lives, relying on an abundance of natural resources and a stable culture" (quoted in Scott 2002).

Excavation of the footpaths uncovered stone tools, pottery, and floors of ancient houses. The paths once linked a cemetery to a spring and quarries where construction stone was mined. A

Map 1 (in the insert) documents deforestation by showing annual changes in forest cover worldwide.

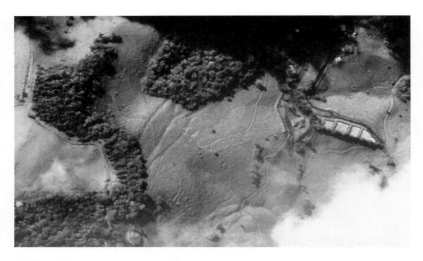

Biocultural Case Study

For more on deforestation and on how anthropology's subfields and dimensions unite around a particular problem, see the "Bringing It All Together" essay that immediately follows Chapter 6.

primary goal of a 2002 field team led by Sheets was to understand ancient activities at the cemetery, where bodies were laid to rest in stone coffins. Funerary ceramics and meal vessels, plus cooking stones, indicate that people camped, cooked, and feasted at the cemetery for long time periods (Scott 2002).

Anthropologists work with geologists, geographers, and other scientists in using satellite images to find not just ancient footpaths, roads, canals, and irrigation systems but also patterns and sites of, say, flooding or deforestation, which can then be investigated on the ground. Anthropologists have used satellite imagery to identify, and then investigate on the ground, regions where deforestation is especially severe and where people and biodiversity, including nonhuman primates, may be at risk (Green and Sussman 1990; Kottak 1999b; Kottak, Gezon, and Green 1994).

Primatology

Primatologists are like ethnographers in their close observation of a group of primates, in this case, nonhuman. Primate behavior has been observed in zoos (e.g., de Waal 2000) and through experimentation (e.g., Harlow 1966), but the most significant studies have been done in natural settings, among free-ranging apes, monkeys, and lemurs. You, as an anthropology student, may be given an assignment to observe primates in zoos. Try to avoid nocturnal primates, which probably will be sleeping when you visit the zoo, unless you visit the Hall of Night Animals at New York's Bronx Zoo—or a similar zoo habitat in which animals, through lighting, are fooled into switching night and day. Some primatologists have studied free-ranging nocturnal primates, such as tarsiers, owl monkeys, and the aye-aye of Madagascar. But most primates are active during the day (*diurnal*), as are humans, and are easier to study for that reason. It's also easier for humans to study

terrestrial than arboreal species. In Madagascar I've raced down hills following lemurs moving rapidly through the trees. As a college student I made the mistake of studying the slow loris in New York's Central Park Zoo. That loris, a prosimian, or lemur-like animal, catches insects by staying still, then suddenly snaring bugs that land nearby. Unless there are insects in the cage, observing the slow loris (like observing the South American sloth, which is *not* a primate) is only slightly more interesting than watching an egg.

Since the 1950s, when primatologists began their shift from zoos to natural settings, numerous studies have been done of apes (chimps, gorillas, orangutans, and gibbons), monkeys (e.g., baboons, macaques), and lemurs (e.g., Madagascar's indrii, sifaka, and ring-tailed lemurs). Arboreal primates (those which spend most of their time in the trees—e.g., howler monkeys and gibbons) may be difficult to see and follow, but they typically make a lot of noise. Their communication systems, including howls and calls, can be studied and teach us about how primates communicate. Studies of primate social systems and behavior, including their mating patterns, infant care, and patterns of contact and dispersal, suggest hypotheses about behavior that humans do or do not share with our nearest relatives—and also with our hominid ancestors.

Like ethnographers, primatologists have to establish rapport (a "friendly" working relationship) with the individuals they are studying. Since language can't be used with nonhuman primates, rapport involves gradual habituation; the animals have to get used to the researcher. Animals must be identified and observed over time. Often a fledgling primatologist will join a longitudinal team that has been observing a group of monkeys or apes for years, even decades. Identification of the animals and close attention to their behavior and interactions are necessary to understand primate behavior and social organization. Particular animals may be followed for set periods of time—with each episode of behavior and interaction systematically recorded on film or in a notebook. Or the researcher can focus on certain scenes, for example, a particular tree or water source where primates congregate at particular times. Or individuals and/or places can be chosen randomly for study at particular times.

Although *Homo sapiens*, unlike most other primates, is neither a "threatened" nor an "endangered" species, many humans live in areas of poverty and overpopulation. The pressure of human activities on scarce resources, such as forested lands, creates threats for primates and animals sharing their habitat. People hunt or buy primates for food and for their assumed medicinal properties. People also clear land from, and build roads through, forested habitats where primates once thrived. Deforestation is a major threat to primates. Many cultural anthropologists work with people whose activities pose threats to primates. Working in the same areas, primatologists are experts on the precise habitat, needs, and behavior patterns of the nonhuman primates. Working together and with conservation groups and governments, cultural and physical anthropologists can apply their knowledge in devising plans to conserve forests and their animal dwellers, while also allowing people to meet their basic needs.

Anthropometry

Physical anthropologists use various techniques to study nutrition, growth, and development. **Anthropometry** is the measurement of human body parts and dimensions, including skeletal parts (*osteometry*). Anthropometry is done on living people as well as on skeletal remains from sites. Body mass and composition provide measures of nutritional status in living people. Body mass is calculated from height and weight. The *body mass index* (kg/m^2) is the ratio of weight in kilograms divided by height in meters squared. An adult body mass above 30 is considered at risk of overweight, while one below 18 is at risk of underweight or malnutrition. To assess body composition, subcutaneous (below the surface) fat is estimated from skin fold thickness (measured with calipers) and body circumference. These values are compared to anthropometric standards (Frisancho 1990). For a given gender and age group, values above the 85th percentile are associated with excess fat, and values below the 15th percentile are associated with leanness.

A machine called a *calorimeter* is used to measure resting metabolic rates, based on the amount of oxygen consumed and carbon dioxide produced when an individual rests for 30 minutes. The instrument calculates the body's minimum energy needs (in calories) at rest. Based on daily calories consumed, used at rest, and used in activities, scientists can determine whether conditions favor weight gain or loss. Measurement of the resting metabolic rate also reveals the extent to which weight gains or losses may reflect metabolism versus eating patterns.

Knowledge about how contemporary humans adapt (e.g., to heat and cold) and use energy (e.g., in metabolism) can be used to understand human evolution. For example, during hominid evolution brain size has increased. In contemporary humans, the brain represents just 5 percent of body weight, yet brain activity consumes 20 percent of the resting metabolic rate. During human evolution, the adaptive advantages of having a large brain must have outweighed the high cost in energy. However, increased activity would have been necessary to feed growing human bodies and brains.

Joe Zias, a curator at Rockefeller Museum, measures an ancient skull. Anthropometry is done on skeletal remains from sites as well as on living people. Has anyone ever done anthropometry on you?

Bone Biology

Central to physical anthropology is **bone biology** (or skeletal biology)—the study of bone as a biological tissue, including its genetics; cell structure; growth, development, and decay; and patterns of movement (*biomechanics*) (Katzenberg and Saunders, eds. 2000). Within bone biology, *osteology* is the study of skeletal variation and its biological and social causes. Osteologists study such variables as stature in living and ancient populations (White and Folkens 2000). The interpretation of fossil remains relies on understanding the structure and function of the skeleton. **Paleopathology** is the study of disease and injury in skeletons from archaeological sites. Some forms of cancer leave evidence in the bone. Breast cancer, for example, may spread (metastasize) skeletally, leaving holes or lesions in bones and skulls. Certain infectious diseases (e.g., syphilis and tuberculosis) also mark bone, as do injuries and nutritional deficiencies (e.g., rickets, a vitamin D deficiency that deforms the bones).

In forensic anthropology, as discussed in Chapter 2 and in this chapter's "News Brief," physical anthropologists and archaeologists work in a legal context, assisting coroners, medical examiners, and law enforcement agencies in recovering, analyzing,

A Novel Method of Assessing Why People Cooperate

Using a novel method of scanning neural activity in people playing games, scientists have discovered that cooperation triggers pleasure in the brain. Anthropologist James Rilling and five other scientists monitored brain activity in young women playing a laboratory game called Prisoner's Dilemma. Players select greedy or cooperative strategies as they pursue financial gain. The researchers found that the choice to cooperate stimulated areas of the brain associated with pleasure and reward-seeking behavior—the same areas that respond to desserts, pictures of pretty faces, money, and cocaine (Angier 2002; Rilling et al. 2002). According to coauthor Gregory S. Berns, "In some ways, it says that we're wired to cooperate with each other" (quoted in Angier 2002).

The researchers studied 36 women age 20 to 60. Why women? Some previous studies had found male–male pairs to be more cooperative than female–female pairs, and others had found the opposite. Rilling and his colleagues didn't want to mix more cooperative and less cooperative pairs, and so they restricted their sample to one gender to control for possible differences in tendencies toward cooperation. The choice to use women rather than men was an arbitrary one.

In the experiment two women would meet each other briefly ahead of time. One was then placed in the scanner, while the other remained outside the scanning room. The two interacted by computer, playing about 20 rounds of the game. In every round, each player pressed a button to indicate whether she would "cooperate" or "defect." Her answer would be shown on-screen to the other player. Money was awarded after each round. When one player defected and the other cooperated, the defector earned $3, and the cooperator earned nothing. When both cooperated, each earned $2. If both defected, each earned $1. Mutual cooperation from start to finish was a more profitable strategy, at $40 a woman, than complete mutual defection, which yielded only $20 to each woman.

If one woman got greedy, she took the risk that the cooperative strategy might fall apart and that both players would lose money as a result. Most of the time, the women cooperated. Even occasional defections weren't always fatal to an alliance, although the woman who had been "betrayed' once might be suspicious after that. Because of occasional defections, the average per-experiment take for the participants was in the range of $30.

The scans showed that two broad areas of the brain were activated by cooperation. Both areas are rich in neurons that respond to dopamine, a brain chemical that plays a well-known role in addictive behaviors. One is the anteroventral striatum in the midbrain, just above the spinal cord. Experiments have shown that when electrodes are placed in this area, rats will repeatedly press a bar to stimulate the electrodes. They apparently receive such pleasurable feedback that they will starve to death rather than stop pressing the bar (Angier 2002).

Another brain region activated during cooperation was the orbitofrontal cortex, just above the eyes. Besides being part of the reward-processing system, this area is involved in impulse control. According to Rilling, "Every round, you're confronted with the possibility of getting an extra dollar by defecting. The choice to cooperate requires impulse control" (quoted in Angier 2002).

In some cases, the woman in the scanner played a computer and knew her partner was a machine. In other tests, women played a computer but thought it was a human. The reward circuitry of the women was considerably less responsive when they knew they were playing against a computer. The thought of a human bond, not mere monetary gain, was the source of contentment. Also, the women were asked afterward to summarize their feelings during the games. They often described feeling good when they cooperated and expressed feelings of camaraderie toward their playing partners.

Assuming the urge to cooperate is to some extent innate among humans, and is reinforced by our neural circuitry, why did it arise? Anthropologists generally assume that it took teamwork and altruism for our ancestors to hunt large game, share food, and engage in other social activities, including raising children. A neural tendency to cooperate and to share would have conferred a survival advantage on our ancestors. Instead of "Why can't we all get along," these researchers were exploring why we get along so well.

SOURCES: Information from N. Angier, "Why We're So Nice: We're Wired to Cooperate," *New York Times*, July 23, 2002. http://www.nytimes.com/2002/07/23/health/psychology/23COOP.html; J. K. Rilling et al., "A Neural Basis for Social Cooperation," *Neuron* 35:395–405; J. K. Rilling, personal communication.

and identifying human remains and determining the cause of death (Nafte 2000; Prag and Neave 1997). For example, when unknown skeletal remains are found, the police and the Delaware Medical Examiner's Office call on University of Delaware physical anthropologist Karen Rosenberg to help identify the body. By examining the bones, Rosenberg can determine characteristics, such as the height, age, and sex of the person. She notes that "the police authorities always ask for the race of an unidentified person. But racial categories are, in part, culturally defined and in any case are not closed biological 'types.' Recently I identified a skeleton as possibly being Caucasian, then on subsequent examinations thought he might be African American. In actuality, when the identification was made, he turned out to be Hispanic" (Rosenberg, quoted in Moncure 1998).

Humans are really social compared with our primate relatives. Even chimps, our closest relatives, don't cooperate nearly to the extent that we do. Apparently apes aren't wired for cooperation and altruism as we are (see "Interesting Issues," p. 50). We'll never know all the causes of human sociality, but some are based in human anatomy—from the brain to the pelvis. Consider the female pelvis, whose evolution has been guided by these facts: (1) Humans walk upright, (2) babies are born with big brains, and (3) babies have to negotiate a complicated birth canal during childbirth.

There are striking and significant contrasts between primates and humans in anatomy and in the birthing process. Nonhuman primates aren't bipedal; compared with humans, they have smaller brains, simpler birth canals, and more independent infants. As they move through the birth canal, human babies must make several turns, so that their heads and shoulders, the two body parts with the largest dimensions, are consistently aligned with the widest parts of the birth canal. Monkeys and apes don't have this problem. Unlike those of humans, primate birth canals have a constant shape.

Also, the primate infant emerges facing forward. The mother can grasp it, even pull it straight to her nipple. Human babies are born facing backward, away from the mother, and so she has trouble assisting in the birth. The presence of someone else (e.g., a midwife) to help with delivery reduces the mortality risk for human infants and their mothers.

Birthing assistance is almost universal among human societies. According to Karen Rosenberg and Wenda Trevathan (2001), our wish to have supportive, familiar people around at childbirth goes way back. On the basis of pelvic openings, and estimated infant skull sizes, of extinct hominids, Rosenberg and Trevathan (2001) conclude that such assistance may date back millions of years. Nonhuman primate mothers seek seclusion when they give birth, and act as their own midwives in the birthing process. Not so humans—social as ever. Midwives, obstetricians, baby showers—all are expressions of human sociality with deep evolutionary roots.

■ Birthing assistance is almost universal in human societies. Shown here, an Uzbeki midwife uses a traditional instrument to listen to a baby's heartbeat.

Molecular Anthropology

Molecular anthropology uses genetic analysis (of DNA sequences) to assess evolutionary links. Through molecular comparison, evolutionary distance among living species, along with dates of most recent common ancestry, can be estimated. Molecular studies also have been used to assess and date the origins of modern humans and examine their relation to extinct human groups such as the Neandertals, which thrived in Europe between 130,000 and 28,000 years ago.

In 1997, ancient DNA was extracted from a Neanderthal bone originally found in Germany's Neander Valley in 1856. This was the first time the DNA of a premodern human had been recovered. This DNA, from an upper arm bone (humerus), was compared with the DNA of modern humans. There were 27 differences between the Neandertal DNA and modern DNA; by contrast, samples of modern DNA show only 5 to 8 differences among the samples.

Molecular anthropologists examine relationships among ancient and contemporary populations and among species. It's well established, for example, that humans and chimpanzees have more than 98 percent of their DNA in common. Molecular anthropologists also reconstruct waves and patterns of migration and settlement. A *haplogroup* is a biological lineage (a large group of related people) defined by a specific cluster of genetic traits that occur together. Native Americans have four major haplogroups, which are also linked to East Asia. Among the many sorts of questions that molecular anthropology may answer: How can DNA sequences be used to trace migration routes during the peopling of North America or the Pacific?

For nonhuman primates, molecular anthropologists use DNA sequences to identify parentage, and to calculate kinship and degree of inbreeding within primate colonies. We'll see

Biocultural Case Study

For more on the peopling of the Pacific and on how anthropology's subfields unite to solve a particular problem, see the "Bringing It All Together" essay that immediately follows Chapter 11.

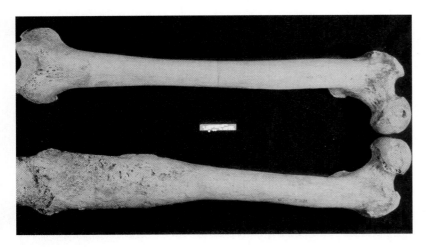

Two adult femora. The top one is normal in size and shape. The bottom one shows swelling and a ragged surface resulting from the chronic bacterial infection called osteomyelitis. These thigh bones are from the Mississippian period Hazel site in Arkansas.

later that molecular anthropologists also use "genetic clocks" to estimate divergence time (date of most recent common ancestry) among species (e.g., humans, chimps, and gorillas—5 million to 8 million years ago) and of various human groups (e.g., Neanderthals and modern humans).

Paleoanthropology

Paleoanthropologists study early hominids through fossil remains. **Fossils** are remains (e.g., bones), traces, or impressions (e.g., footprints) of ancient life. Typically, a team composed of scientists, students, and local workers, representing diverse backgrounds and academic fields, participates in a paleoanthropological study. Such teams may include physical anthropologists, archaeologists, paleontologists, geologists, palynologists, paleoecologists, physicists, and chemists. Their common goal is to date and reconstruct the structure, behavior, and ecology of early hominids. The geologists and paleontologists may be called in during early surveying—perhaps using remote sensing—to locate potential early hominid sites. Paleontologists help locate fossil beds containing remains of animals that can be dated and that are known to have coexisted with hominids at various time periods. Good preservation of faunal remains may suggest that hominid fossils have survived as well. Sometimes it's impossible to date the hominid fossils and artifacts found at a given site by using the most accurate and direct (radiometric) methods. In this case, comparison of the faunal remains at that site with similar, but more securely dated, fauna at another site may suggest a date for those animal fossils and the hominids and artifacts associated with them (see Gugliotta 2005).

Once potential sites have been identified, more intensive surveying begins. Archaeologists take over and search for hominid traces—bones or tools. Only hominids work rock to make tools and move rock fragments over long distances (see Watzman 2006). Some early hominid sites are strewn with thousands of tools. If a site is shown to be a hominid site, much more concentrated work begins. Financial support may come from private donations and government agencies. The research project usually is headed by an archaeologist or a physical anthropologist. The field crew will continue to survey and map the area and start searching carefully for bones and artifacts eroding out of the soil. Also, they will take pollen and soil samples for ecological analysis and rock samples for use in various dating techniques. Analysis is done in laboratories, where specimens are cleaned, sorted, labeled, and identified.

Consideration of the animal habitats suggested by the site (e.g., forest, woodland, or open country) will assist in the reconstruction of the paleoecological settings in which early hominids lived. Pollen samples help reveal diet. Sediments and other geological samples will suggest climatic conditions at the time of deposition. Sometimes fossils are embedded in rock, from which they must be extracted carefully. Once recovered and cleaned, fossils may be made into casts to permit wider study.

SURVEY AND EXCAVATION

Archaeologists and paleoanthropologists typically work in teams and across time and space. Typically, archaeologists, paleoanthropologists, and paleontologists combine both local and regional perspectives. The most common local approach is to excavate, or dig, through layers in a site. Regional approaches include remote sensing, for example, the discovery of ancient Costa Rican footpaths from space that was described earlier, and systematic survey on the ground. Archaeologists recognize that sites aren't usually discrete and isolated, but are parts of larger (regional) social systems, such as a series of villages that offered tribute to the same chief, or bands of hunter-gatherers who once got together for annual ceremonies at a particular place.

Let's examine some of the main techniques that anthropologists use to study patterns of behavior in ancient societies, based on their material remains. Archaeologists recover remains from a series of contexts, such as pits, sites, and regions. The archaeologist also integrates data about different social units of the past, such as the household, the band, the village, and the regional system.

Systematic Survey

Archaeologists and paleoanthropologists have two basic fieldwork strategies: systematic survey and excavation. **Systematic survey** provides a regional perspective by gathering information on settlement patterns over a large area. *Settlement pattern* refers to the distribution of sites within a particular region. Regional surveys reconstruct settlement patterns by addressing several questions: Where were sites located? How big were they? What kinds of buildings did they have? How old are the sites? Ideally, a systematic survey involves walking over the entire survey area and recording the location and size of all sites. From artifacts found on the surface, the surveyor estimates when each site was occupied. A full-coverage survey isn't always possible. The ground cover may be impenetrable (e.g., thick jungle), or certain parts of the survey area may be inaccessible. Permission to survey may be denied by landowners. Surveyors may have to rely on remote sensing to help locate and map sites.

With regional data, scientists can address many questions about the prehistoric communities that lived in a given area. Archaeologists use settlement pattern information to make population estimates and to assess levels of social complexity. Among hunter-gatherers and simple farmers, there are generally low numbers of people living in small camp sites or hamlets with little variation in the architecture. Such sites are scattered fairly evenly across the landscape. With increasing social complexity, the settlement patterns become more elaborate. Population levels rise. Such social factors as trade and warfare have played a more important role in determining the location of sites (on hilltops, waterways, trade routes). In complex societies, a settlement hierarchy of sites emerges. Certain sites are larger, with greater architectural differentiation, than others. Large sites with specialized architecture (elite residences, temples, administrative buildings, meeting places) are generally interpreted as regional centers that exerted control over the smaller sites with less architectural differentiation.

Excavation

Archaeologists also gather information about the past by excavating sites. During an **excavation,** scientists recover remains by digging through the cultural and natural stratigraphy—the layers of deposits that make up a site. These layers or strata are used to establish the relative time order of the materials encountered during the dig. This relative chronology is based on the principle of *superposition:* In an undisturbed sequence of strata, the oldest layer is on the bottom. Each successive layer above is younger than the one below. Thus, artifacts and fossils from lower strata are older than those recovered from higher strata in the same deposit. This relative time ordering of material remains lies at the heart of archaeological, paleoanthropological, and paleontological research.

The archaeological and fossil records are so rich, and excavation is so labor-intensive and expensive, that nobody digs a site without a good reason. Sites are excavated because they are endangered, or because they answer specific research questions. Cultural resource management (CRM), as discussed in Chapter 2, focuses on managing the preservation of archaeological sites that are threatened by modern development. Many countries require archaeological impact studies before construction can take place. If a site is at risk and the development cannot be stopped, CRM archaeologists are called in to salvage what information they can from the site. Another reason a site may be chosen for excavation is that it is well suited to answer specific research questions. For example, an archaeologist studying the origins of agriculture wouldn't want to excavate a large, fortified hilltop city with a series of buildings dating to a period well after the first appearance of farming communities. Rather, he or she would look for a small hamlet-size site located on or near good farmland and near a water source. Such a site would have evidence of an early occupation dating to the period when farming communities first appeared in that region.

Before a site is excavated, it is mapped and surface collected so that the researchers can make an informed decision about where exactly to dig. The collecting of surface materials at a given site is similar to what is done over a much larger area in a regional survey. A grid is drawn to represent and subdivide the site. Then collection units, which are equal-size sections of the grid, are marked off on the actual site. This grid enables the researchers to record the exact location of any artifact, fossil, or feature found at the site. By examining all the materials on the surface of the site, archaeologists can direct their excavations toward the areas of the site that are most likely to yield information that will address their research interests. Once an area is selected, digging begins, and the location of every artifact or feature is recorded in three dimensions.

Digging may be done according to arbitrary levels. Thus, starting from the surface, consistent amounts of soil (usually 4 to 8 feet [1.2 to 2.4 meters]) are systematically removed from the excavation unit. This technique of excavation is a quick way of digging, since everything within a certain depth is removed at once. This kind of excavation usually is done in test pits, which are used to determine how deep the deposits of a site go and to establish a rough chronology for that site.

A more labor-intensive and refined way of excavating is to dig through the stratigraphy one layer at a time. The strata, which are separated by differences in color and texture, are studied one by one. This technique provides more information about the context of the artifacts, fossils, or

See the OLC Internet Exercises
mhhe.com/kottak

■ *An archaeologist drives in another stake for a large grid at an excavation site in Teotihuacan, Mexico. Such a grid enables the researchers to record the exact location of any artifact or feature found at the site.*

features because the scientist works more slowly and in meaningful layers. A given 4-foot (1.2-meter) level may include within it a series of successive house floors, each with artifacts. If this deposit is excavated according to arbitrary levels, all the artifacts are mixed together. But if it is excavated according to the natural stratigraphy, with each house floor excavated separately, the resulting picture is much more detailed. The procedure here is for the archaeologist to remove and bag all the artifacts from each house floor before proceeding to the level below that one.

Any excavation recovers varied material remains, such as ceramics, stone artifacts (lithics), human and animal bones, and plant remains. Such remains may be small and fragmented. To increase the likelihood that small remains will be recovered, the soil is passed through screens. To recover very small remains, such as fish bones and carbonized plant remains, archaeologists use a technique called *flotation.* Soil samples are sorted using water and a series of very fine meshes. When the water dissolves the soil, the carbonized plant remains float to the top. The fish bones and other heavier remains sink to the bottom. Flotation requires considerable time and labor. This makes it inappropriate to use on all the soil that is excavated from a site. Flotation samples are taken from a limited number of deposits, such as house floors, trash pits, and hearths.

KINDS OF ARCHAEOLOGY

Archaeologists pursue diverse research topics, using a wide variety of methods. Experimental archaeologists try to replicate ancient techniques and processes (e.g., tool making) under controlled conditions. Historical archaeologists use written records as guides and supplements to archaeological research. They work with remains more recent—often much more recent—than the advent of writing. Colonial archaeologists, for instance, use historical records as guides to locate and excavate postcontact sites in North and South America, and to verify or question written accounts. Classical archaeologists usually are affiliated with university departments of classics or the history of art, rather than with anthropology departments. These classical scholars focus on the literate civilizations of the Old World, such as Greece, Rome, and Egypt. Classical archaeologists are often as (or more) interested in art—styles of architecture and sculpture—as in the social, political, and economic variables that typically interest the anthropologist. Underwater archaeology is a growing field that investigates submerged sites, most often shipwrecks. Special techniques, including remotely operated vehicles like the one shown in the movie *Titanic,* are used, but divers also do underwater survey and excavation.

In Chapter 2, cultural resource management was discussed as a form of applied (or public) anthropology, as archaeologists apply their techniques of data gathering and analysis to manage sites that are threatened by development, public works, and road building. Some CRM archaeologists are *contract archaeologists,* who typically negotiate specific contracts (rather than applying for research grants) for their studies, which often must be done rapidly, for example, when an immediate threat to archaeological materials becomes known. Based on a membership study done for the Society of American Archaeology, Melinda Zeder (1997) found that 40 percent of the respondents worked as contract archaeologists—for firms in the private sector, state and federal agencies, and educational institutions. An equivalent 40 percent held academic positions.

DATING THE PAST

The archaeological record hasn't revealed every ancient society that has existed on earth; nor is the fossil record a representative sample of all the plants and animals that have ever lived. Some species and body parts are better represented than others are, for many reasons. Hard parts, such as bones and teeth, preserve better than do soft parts, such as flesh and skin. The chances of fossilization increase when remains are buried in a newly forming sediment, such as silt, gravel, or sand. Good places for bones to be buried in sediments include swamps, floodplains, river deltas, lakes, and caves. The species that inhabit such areas have a better chance to be preserved than do animals that live in other habitats. Fossilization is also favored in areas with volcanic ash, or in areas where rock fragments eroding from rising highlands are accumulating in valleys or lake basins. Once remains do get buried, chemical conditions must be right for fossilization to occur. If the sediment is too acidic, even bone and teeth will dissolve. The study of the processes that affect the remains of dead animals is called **taphonomy**, from the Greek *taphos*, which means "tomb." Such processes include scattering by carnivores and scavengers, distortion by various forces, and the possible fossilization of the remains.

The conditions under which fossils are found also influence the fossil record. For example, fossils are more likely to be uncovered through erosion in arid areas than in wet areas. Sparse vegetation allows wind to scour the landscape and uncover fossils. The fossil record has been accumulating longer and is more extensive in Europe than in Africa because civil engineering projects and fossil hunting have been going on longer in Europe than in Africa.

A world map showing where fossils have been found does not indicate the true range of ancient animals. Such a map tells us more about ancient geological activity, modern erosion, or recent human activity—such as paleontological research or road building. In considering the primate and hominid fossil records in later chapters, we'll see that different areas provide more abundant fossil evidence for particular time periods. This doesn't necessarily mean that primates or hominids were not living elsewhere at the same time. Nor does failure to find a fossil species in a particular place always mean that species did not live there. In the words of paleoanthropologist Christopher Stringer, "absence of evidence does not necessarily prove evidence of absence" (quoted in Gugliotta 2005). What dating techniques are used to determine *when* animals that have been fossilized actually lived?

We've seen that *paleontology* is the study of ancient life through the fossil record and that

This diver holds a ceramic vessel uncovered from a ship wrecked in 1025 A.D., in Turkey's Serce Liman Bay, Mugla province. Graduate degrees in underwater, or nautical, archaeology are available at East Carolina University, Florida State University, and Texas A&M University. This growing field of study investigates submerged sites, most often shipwrecks.

paleoanthropology is the study of ancient humans and their immediate ancestors. These fields have established a time frame, or *chronology*, for the evolution of life. Scientists use several techniques to date fossils. These methods offer different degrees of precision and are applicable to different periods of the past.

Relative Dating

Chronology is established by assigning dates to geologic layers (strata) and to the material remains, such as fossils and artifacts, within them. Dating may be relative or absolute. **Relative dating** establishes a time frame in relation to other strata or materials rather than absolute dates in numbers. Many dating methods are based on the geological study of **stratigraphy**, the science that examines the ways in which earth sediments accumulate in layers known as *strata* (singular, *stratum*). As was noted previously, in an undisturbed sequence of strata, age increases with depth. Soil that erodes from a hillside into a valley covers, and is younger than, the soil deposited there previously. Stratigraphy permits relative dating. That is, the fossils in a given stratum are younger than those in the layers below and older than those in the layers above. We may not know the exact or absolute dates of the fossils, but we can place them in time relative to remains in other layers. Changing environmental forces, such as lava flows and the alternation of land and sea, cause different materials to be deposited in a given sequence of strata; this allows scientists to distinguish between the strata.

Remains of animals and plants that lived at the same time are found in the same stratum. When fossils are found within a stratigraphic sequence, scientists know their dates relative to fossils in other strata; this is relative dating. When fossils

■ A swamp is a good place for bones to be buried in sediments. Here a female mammoth is represented sinking into the La Brea Tarpits in Los Angeles, California. What other locales and conditions favor fossilization?

absorb carbon dioxide. ^{14}C moves up the food chain as animals eat plants and as predators eat other animals.

With death, the absorption of ^{14}C stops. This unstable isotope starts to break down into nitrogen (^{14}N). It takes 5,730 years for half the ^{14}C to change to nitrogen; this is the half-life of ^{14}C. After another 5,730 years only one-quarter of the original ^{14}C will remain. After yet another 5,730 years only one-eighth will be left. By measuring the proportion of ^{14}C in organic material, scientists can determine a fossil's date of death, or the date of an ancient campfire. However, because the half-life of ^{14}C is short, this dating technique is less dependable for specimens older than 40,000 years than it is for more recent remains.

Fortunately, other radiometric dating techniques are available for earlier periods. One of the most widely used is the potassium-argon (K/A) technique. ^{40}K is a radioactive isotope of potassium that breaks down into argon-40, a gas. The half-life of ^{40}K is far longer than that of ^{14}C—1.3 *billion* years. With this method, the *older* the specimen, the more reliable the dating. Furthermore, whereas ^{14}C dating can be done only on organic remains, K/A dating can be used only for inorganic substances: rocks and minerals.

^{40}K in rocks gradually breaks down into argon-40. That gas is trapped in the rock until the rock is heated intensely (as with volcanic activity), at which point it may escape. When the rock cools, the breakdown of potassium into argon resumes. Dating is done by reheating the rock and measuring the escaping gas.

In Africa's Great Rift Valley, which runs down eastern Africa and in which early hominid fossils abound, past volcanic activity permits K/A dating. In studies of strata containing fossils, scientists find out how much argon has accumulated in rocks since they were last heated. They then determine, using the standard ^{40}K half-life, the date of that heating. Considering volcanic rocks at the top of a stratum with fossil remains, scientists establish that the fossils are *older than*, say, 1.8 million years. By dating the volcanic rocks below the fossil remains, they determine that the fossils are *younger than*, say, 2 million years. Thus, the age of the fossils and of associated material is set at between 2 million and 1.8 million years. Note that absolute dating is that in name only; it may give ranges of numbers rather than exact dates.

Many fossils were discovered before the advent of modern stratigraphy. Often we can no longer determine their original stratigraphic placement. Furthermore, fossils aren't always discovered in volcanic layers. Like ^{14}C dating, the K/A technique applies to a limited period of the fossil record. Because the half-life of ^{40}K is so long, the technique cannot be used with materials less than 500,000 years old.

are found in a particular stratum, the associated geological features (such as frost patterning) and remains of particular plants and animals offer clues about the climate at the time of deposition.

Besides stratigraphic placement, another technique of relative dating is fluorine absorption analysis. Bones fossilizing in the same ground for the same length of time absorb the same proportion of fluorine from the local groundwater. Fluorine analysis uncovered a famous hoax involving the so-called Piltdown man, once considered an unusual and perplexing human ancestor (Winslow and Meyer 1983). The Piltdown "find," from England, turned out to be the jaw of a young orangutan attached to a *Homo sapiens* skull. Fluorine analysis showed the association to be false. The skull had much more fluorine than the jaw—impossible if they had come from the same individual and had been deposited in the same place at the same time. Someone had fabricated Piltdown man in an attempt to muddle the interpretation of the fossil record. (The attempt was partially successful—it did fool some scientists.)

Absolute Dating: Radiometric Techniques

The previous section reviewed relative dating based on stratigraphy and fluorine absorption analysis. Fossils also can be dated more precisely, with dates in numbers (**absolute dating**), by using several methods. For example, the ^{14}C, or carbon-14, technique is used to date organic remains. This is a *radiometric* technique (so called because it measures radioactive decay). ^{14}C is an unstable radioactive isotope of normal carbon, ^{12}C. Cosmic radiation entering the earth's atmosphere produces ^{14}C, and plants take in ^{14}C as they

For more information on radiocarbon dating, see the Virtual Exploration

mhhe.com/kottak

Looking down on the Great Rift Valley, which runs through Ethiopia, Kenya (shown here), and Tanzania. What dating techniques can be used in this volcanic region?

Other radiometric dating techniques can be used to cross-check K/A dates, again by using minerals surrounding the fossils. One such method, *uranium series dating*, measures fission tracks produced during the decay of radioactive uranium (^{238}U) into lead. Two other radiometric techniques are especially useful for fossils that cannot be dated by ^{14}C (up to 40,000 BP) or ^{40}K (more than 500,000 BP). These methods are *thermoluminescence (TL)* and *electron spin resonance (ESR)*. Both TL and ESR measure the electrons that are constantly being trapped in rocks and minerals (Shreeve 1992). Once a date is obtained for a rock found associated with a fossil, that date also can

be applied to that fossil. The time spans for which the various absolute dating techniques are applicable are summarized in Table 3.1.

Absolute Dating: Dendrochronology

Dendrochronology, or tree-ring dating, is a method of absolute dating that is based on the study and comparison of patterns of tree-ring growth. Such dating is based on the fact that trees grow by adding one ring every year. Counting the rings reveals the age of a tree. Around 1920, A. E. Douglass of the University of Arizona noticed that wide rings grew during wet years, while narrow

TABLE 3.1 Absolute Dating Techniques

Technique	Abbreviation	Materials Dated	Effective Time Range
Carbon-14	^{14}C	Organic materials	Up to 40,000 years
Potassium-argon	K/A and ^{40}K	Volcanic rock	Older than 500,000 years
Uranium series	^{238}U	Minerals	Between 1,000 and 1,000,000 years
Thermoluminescence	TL	Rocks and minerals	Between 5,000 and 1,000,000 years
Electron spin resonance	ESR	Rocks and minerals	Between 1,000 and 1,000,000 years
Dendrochronology	Dendro	Wood and charcoal	Up to 11,000 years

■ *Dr. Tom Sweatnam of the University of Arizona displays tree samples from a Giant Sequoia. What kinds of information can you get from studying tree rings?*

rings grew during dry years. Climatic variation, for example, moisture, cold, or drought, produces a distinctive year-by-year ring pattern—observable in all the trees that have grown over the same time period in a given region. Ring patterns of trees can be compared and matched ring for ring. Charting such patterns back through time, scientists can compare wood from ancient buildings to known tree-ring chronologies, match the ring patterns, and determine precisely—to the year—the age of the wood used by the historic or prehistoric builder (see Kuniholm 1995; Miller 2004; Schweingruber 1988).

Crossdating is the process of matching ring patterns among trees and assigning rings to specific calendar years. Both visual and statistical techniques are used to make the matches. Wood or charcoal samples from buildings and archaeological sites are crossdated with each other and with wood from living trees to extend the tree-ring chronology beyond the date of the oldest ring of the oldest living tree in the region (Kuniholm 1995).

Tree-ring dating was first used in the southwestern United States for Native American communities and historical settlements. The bristlecone pine chronology of the American Southwest now exceeds 8,500 years (see Miller 2004). A northern European chronology based on the study of oak and pine is over 11,000 years long. The objective of Cornell University's Aegean dendrochronology project (http://www.arts.cornell.edu/dendro/), directed by Peter Kuniholm, is to build a master chronology for the region of the Aegean Sea and the Middle East. So far this project has established over 6,000 years of tree-ring chronologies covering much of the period back to about 9,500 years ago for portions of the Aegean, the Balkans, and the

Map Atlas

Map 8 in the insert shows the spread of agriculture during and after the Neolithic, in the Aegean region and elsewhere.

Middle East, including Turkey, Cyprus, Greece, parts of Bulgaria and the former Yugoslavia, and some of Italy. (There is one major gap, for which matches have not yet been made, between about 1,500 and 2,500 years ago.) The goal is to extend the chronology back to the period in which prehistoric peoples first started using significant amounts of wood in construction (Kuniholm 1995, 2004).

Dendrochronology is limited to certain tree species—those growing in a climate with marked seasons. The technique works with oak, pine, juniper, fir, boxwood, yew, spruce, and occasionally chestnut. Trees that can't be used include olive, willow, poplar, fruit trees, and cypress. The trees must come from the same region—thus having been exposed to the same environmental patterns—and long ring sequences are needed. Some junipers have as many as 918 rings. Some charcoal fragments from the Neolithic site of Çatal Hüyük in Turkey (see Chapter 10), where dendrochronology has established a 700-year sequence, have as many as 250 rings preserved (Kuniholm 1995). Not only do tree rings permit absolute dating; they also provide information about climatic patterns in specific regions.

Molecular Dating

In 1987, in a very influential study, researchers at the University of California at Berkeley used DNA analysis to advance the idea that anatomically modern humans (AMHs) arose fairly recently (around 130,000 years ago) in Africa. Rebecca Cann, Mark Stoneking, and Allan C. Wilson (1987) analyzed genetic traits in placentas donated by 147 women whose ancestors came from various parts of the world. The researchers focused on mitochondrial DNA (mtDNA), which only the mother contributes to the fertilized egg, and thus to the child. To establish a "genetic clock," the researchers measured the variation in mtDNA in their 147 tissue samples. They cut each sample into segments to compare with the others. By estimating the number of mutations (spontaneous changes in DNA) that had taken place in each sample since its common origin with the 146 others, the researchers drew an evolutionary tree with the help of a computer. That tree started in Africa, then branched in two. One group stayed in Africa. The other one left Africa and carried its mtDNA to the rest of the world. Assuming a constant mutation rate (e.g., one mutation per 25,000 years), and counting the number of mutations in each sample, molecular anthropologists estimate the time period of the most recent common ancestor. Note that such estimates of divergence dates based on a constant mutation rate are not as widely accepted as are radiometric dating and dendrochronology.

1. Because science exists in society and also in the context of law and ethics, anthropologists can't study things simply because they happen to be interesting or of scientific value. Anthropologists have obligations to their scholarly field, to the wider society and culture (including that of the host country), and to the human species, other species, and the environment. The anthropologist's primary ethical obligation is to the people, species, and materials he or she studies.

2. Physical anthropologists and archaeologists pursue diverse research topics, using varied methods and often working together. At an archaeological site, physical anthropologists may complement the picture of ancient life by examining skeletons to reconstruct their physical traits, health status, and diet. Remote sensing may be used to locate ancient footpaths, roads, canals, and irrigation systems, which can then be investigated on the ground.

3. Studies of primates suggest hypotheses about behavior that humans do or do not share with our nearest relatives—and also with our hominid ancestors. Anthropometry, the measurement of human body parts and dimensions, is done on living people and on skeletal remains from sites. Central to physical anthropology is bone biology—the study of bone genetics; cell structure; growth, development, and decay; and patterns of movement. Osteologists study skeletal variation and its biological and social causes. Paleopathology is the study of disease and injury in skeletons from archaeological sites. Molecular anthropology uses genetic analysis (of DNA sequences) to assess evolutionary relationships among ancient and contemporary populations and among species.

4. Archaeologists, who typically work in teams and across time and space, combine both local (excavation) and regional (systematic survey) perspectives. Archaeologists use settlement pattern information to make population estimates and to assess levels of social complexity. Sites are excavated because they are in danger of being destroyed or because they address specific research interests. There are many kinds of archaeology, such as historical, classical, and underwater archaeology.

5. The fossil record is not a representative sample of all the plants and animals that ever lived. Hard parts, such as bones and teeth, preserve better than soft parts, such as flesh and skin, do. Anthropologists and paleontologists use stratigraphy and radiometric techniques to date fossils. Carbon-14 (^{14}C) dating is most effective with fossils less than 40,000 years old. Potassium-argon (K/A) dating can be used for fossils older than 500,000 years. ^{14}C dating is done on organic matter, whereas the K/A, ^{238}U, TL, and ESR dating techniques are used to analyze minerals that lie below and above fossils. Dendrochronology, or tree-ring dating, is a method of absolute dating based on the study and comparison of patterns of tree-ring growth. Molecular anthropology has also been used as a dating technique, based on the assumption of a constant mutation rate.

absolute dating   Dating techniques that establish dates in numbers or ranges of numbers; examples include the radiometric methods of ^{14}C, K/A, ^{238}U, TL, and ESR dating.

anthropometry   The measurement of human body parts and dimensions, including skeletal parts *(osteometry)*.

bone biology   The study of bone as a biological tissue, including its genetics; cell structure; growth, development, and decay; and patterns of movement *(biomechanics)*.

dendrochronology   Or tree-ring dating: a method of absolute dating based on the study and comparison of patterns of tree-ring growth.

excavation   Digging through the layers of deposits that make up an archaeological or fossil site.

fossils   Remains (e.g., bones), traces, or impressions (e.g., footprints) of ancient life.

informed consent   Agreement to take part in research, after the people being studied have been told about that research's purpose, nature, procedures, and potential impact on them.

molecular anthropology   Genetic analysis, involving comparison of DNA sequences, to determine evolutionary links and distances among species and among ancient and modern populations.

paleoanthropology   Study of hominid and human life through the fossil record.

paleontology   Study of ancient life through the fossil record.

paleopathology   Study of disease and injury in skeletons from archaeological sites.

palynology   Study of ancient plants through pollen samples from archaeological or fossil sites in order to determine a site's environment at the time of occupation.

relative dating   Dating technique, for example, stratigraphy, that establishes a time frame in relation to other strata or materials, rather than absolute dates in numbers.

remote sensing   Use of aerial photos and satellite images to locate sites on the ground.

stratigraphy   Science that examines the ways in which earth sediments are deposited in demarcated layers known as strata (singular, stratum).

systematic survey Information gathered on patterns of settlement over a large area; provides a regional perspective on the archaeological record.

taphonomy The study of the processes that affect the remains of dead animals, such as their scattering by carnivores and scavengers, their distortion by various forces, and their possible fossilization.

CRITICAL THINKING QUESTIONS

1. Imagine yourself to be a physical anthropologist working as part of an international team at an African site where early human fossils have been discovered. What other academic disciplines might be represented on your team? What kinds of jobs would there be for team members, and where would the members be recruited? What might happen to the fossils and other materials that were recovered? Who would be the authors of the scientific papers describing any discovery made by the team?

2. Are humans more sociable than other primates are? What kinds of evidence for human sociality have been discussed in this chapter?

3. What are some of the main similarities and differences between ethnography and the study of primate behavior?

4. Give some examples of ways in which remote sensing is useful to anthropologists.

5. How can fossils be dated when radiometric dating is impossible?

SUGGESTED ADDITIONAL READINGS

Boaz, N. T., and A. J. Almquist
    2002 *Biological Anthropology: A Synthetic Approach to Human Evolution*, 2nd ed. Upper Saddle River, NJ: Prentice Hall. Basic text in physical anthropology; includes discussion of methods.

Feder, K. L.
    2004 *Linking to the Past: A Brief Introduction to Archaeology.* New York: Oxford University Press. Includes a discussion of field methods in archaeology.

Goldberg, P., V. T. Holliday, and C. R. Ferring
    2000 *Earth Sciences and Archaeology.* New York: Kluwer Academic/Plenum Press. Links between archaeology and geology.

Katzenberg, M. A., and S. R. Saunders, eds.
    2000 *Biological Anthropology of the Human Skeleton.* New York: Wiley. Analysis of skeletal and dental remains, including use of new technology.

Larsen, C. S.
    2000 *Skeletons in Our Closet: Revealing Our Past through Bioarchaeology.* Princeton, NJ: Princeton University Press. How human remains from archaeological sites help us interpret lifetime events such as disease, injury, tool use, and diet.

Nafte, M.
    2000 *Flesh and Bone: An Introduction to Forensic Anthropology.* Durham, NC: Carolina Academic Press. Methods and procedures, avoiding technical terminology.

Park, M. A.
    2005 *Biological Anthropology,* 4th ed. Boston: McGraw-Hill. A concise introduction, with a focus on scientific inquiry.

Prag, J., and R. Neave
    1997 *Making Faces: Using Forensic and Archaeological Evidence.* College Station: Texas A&M University Press. How ancient faces are reconstructed.

Renfrew, C., and P. Bahn
    2004 *Archaeology: Theories, Methods, and Practice,* 4th ed. London: Thames and Hudson. Most useful treatment of methods in archaeological anthropology.

Turnbaugh, W. A., R. Jurmain, L. Kilgore, and H. Nelson
    2002 *Understanding Physical Anthropology and Archaeology,* 8th ed. Belmont, CA: Wadsworth. Introduction to these two subfields, with a discussion of methods in each.

White, T. D., and P. A. Folkens
    2000 *Human Osteology,* 2nd ed. San Diego: Academic Press. Includes case studies and discussion of molecular osteology, with life-size photos of skeletal parts.

1. Dating Techniques: Go to the U.S. Geological Survey website on Fossils, Rocks, and Time (**http://pubs.usgs.gov/gip/fossils/contents. html**) and read through all the sections.
   a. How do researchers use the law of superposition to date fossils?
   b. What are isotopes? How are they used by researchers to calculate numeric dates for fossils?
   c. How do relative and absolute/numeric dating techniques complement each other?

2. Go to the online field journal for the 2002 Warren Wilson College Field School (**http://www. warren-wilson.edu/~arch/fs2002/main.html**). Read the introduction and then click on Day 1. Browse through each day of the field school to get a sense of what the archaeological research was like.
   a. What are some of the investigative techniques that the archaeologists used?
   b. What were some of the significant discoveries? Why were they important?

See Chapter 3 at your McGraw-Hill Online Learning Center for additional review and interactive exercises.

INTERNET EXERCISES

Assault on Paradise

This chapter points out that physical anthropologists and archaeologists typically work as members of teams, including international teams. Arembepe, as described in Kottak's *Assault on Paradise,* 4th edition, is described as a "field team village." Read Chapters 1 and 12 through 14 for information about early and later field team research in Arembepe. What models did Arembepeiros use to interpret and deal with the outsiders who visited them?

LINKAGES

4

Evolution and Genetics

EVOLUTION

Compared with other animals, humans have uniquely varied ways—cultural and biological—of adapting to environmental stresses. Exemplifying cultural adaptation, we manipulate our artifacts and behavior in response to environmental conditions. Contemporary North Americans turn up thermostats or travel to Florida in the winter. We turn on fire hydrants, swim, or ride in air-conditioned cars from New York City to Maine to escape the summer's heat. Although such reliance on culture has increased in the course of human evolution, people haven't stopped adapting biologically. As in other species, human populations adapt genetically in response to environmental forces, and individuals react physiologically to stresses. Thus, when we work in the midday sun, sweating occurs spontaneously, cooling the skin and reducing the temperature of subsurface blood vessels.

According to creationism, all life originated during the six days of Creation described in the Bible. Catastrophism proposed that fires and floods, including the biblical deluge involving Noah's ark (depicted in this painting by the American artist Edward Hicks), destroyed certain species. Note that creationism is not a scientific theory (see pp. 17–18, Chapter 1).

OVERVIEW

Charles Darwin and Alfred Russel Wallace proposed that natural selection could explain the origin and evolution of species, as well as biological diversity among life forms. The *fact* of evolution was known prior to Darwin. The *theory* of evolution, through natural selection (*how* evolution occurred), was Darwin's major contribution. Darwin didn't know about the genetic mechanisms that allow natural selection to work. His contemporary Gregor Mendel made the pioneering discovery that genetic traits are inherited as discrete units, now called chromosomes and genes. Mendel also discovered that hereditary units may be inherited independently of each other and then reunite in new combinations, supplying some of the variety on which natural selection depends.

The adaptive value of particular traits depends on the environment. When the environment changes, selection works with traits that already are present in the population. If there isn't enough variety to permit adaptation to the environmental change, extinction is likely. Other evolutionary mechanisms work along with natural selection. Genetic drift operates most obviously in small populations, where pure chance can easily change gene frequencies. Gene flow and interbreeding keep subgroups of the same species connected genetically and thus work against speciation—the formation of new species.

We are ready now for a more detailed look at the principles that determine human biological adaptation, variation, and change.

During the 18th century, many scholars became interested in biological diversity, human origins, and our position within the classification of plants and animals. At that time, the commonly accepted explanation for the origin of species came from Genesis, the first book of the Bible: God had created all life during six days of Creation. According to **creationism,** biological similarities and differences originated at the Creation. Characteristics of life forms were seen as immutable; they could not change. Through calculations based on genealogies in the Bible, the biblical scholars James Ussher and John Lightfoot even claimed to trace the Creation to a very specific time: October 23, 4004 B.C. at 9 A.M.

Carolus Linnaeus (1707–1778) developed the first comprehensive and still influential classification, or taxonomy, of plants and animals. He grouped life forms on the basis of similarities and differences in their physical characteristics. He used traits such as the presence of a backbone to distinguish vertebrates from invertebrates and the presence of mammary glands to distinguish mammals from birds. Linnaeus viewed the differences between life forms as part of the Creator's orderly plan. Biological similarities and differences, he thought, had been established at the time of Creation and had not changed.

Fossil discoveries during the 18th and 19th centuries raised doubts about creationism. Fossils showed that different kinds of life had once existed. If all life had originated at the same time, why weren't ancient species still around? Why weren't contemporary plants and animals found in the fossil record? A modified explanation combining creationism with **catastrophism** arose to replace the original doctrine. In this view, fires, floods, and other catastrophes, including the biblical flood involving Noah's ark, had destroyed ancient species. After each destructive event, God had created again, leading to contemporary species. How did the catastrophists explain certain clear similarities between fossils and modern animals? They argued that some ancient species had managed to survive in isolated areas. For example, after the biblical flood, the progeny of the animals saved on Noah's ark spread throughout the world.

Theory and Fact

The alternative to creationism and catastrophism was *transformism,* also called **evolution.** Evolutionists believe that species arise from others through a long and gradual process of transformation, or descent with modification. Charles Darwin became the best known of the evolutionists. However, he was influenced by earlier scholars, including his own grandfather. In a book

The History of Chromosomes May Shape the Future of Diseases

NEW YORK TIMES NEWS BRIEF

by Carl Zimmer
August 30, 2005

The study of chromosomes, of which humans have 23 pairs, offers clues about evolutionary history and the origin of diseases—potentially leading to more effective treatment strategies. Described here is one category of mutation–chromosomal rearrangement—that can produce speciation, the formation of new species. This "News Brief" mentions two ways in which chromosomes are rearranged. One is inversion: A piece of the chromosome hives off, turns around, and is reattached. Another occurs when a piece splits off and migrates to a different part of the chromosome, where it reattaches. Such chromosomal rearrangements differ from single gene mutations that also are discussed in this chapter. As described in this news story, chromosomes have certain "hot spots" where breaks are most likely to occur, leading to rearrangements that sometimes influence speciation and at other times lead to diseases such as cancer.

The common ancestor of humans and the rhesus macaque monkey lived about 25 million years ago. But despite that vast gulf of time, our chromosomes still retain plenty of evidence of our shared heritage.

A team of scientists at the National Cancer Institute recently documented this evidence by constructing a map of the rhesus macaque's DNA, noting the location of 802 genetic markers in its genome. Then they compared the macaque map to a corresponding map of the human genome. The order of thousands of genes was the same.

"About half of the chromosomes are pretty much intact," said William Murphy, a member of the team, now at Texas A&M University.

The other chromosomes had become rearranged over the past 25 million years, but Dr. Murphy and his colleagues were able to reconstruct their evolution. Periodically, a chunk of chromosome was accidentally

sliced out of the genome, flipped around and inserted backward.

In other cases, the chunk was ferried to a different part of the chromosome. All told, 23 of these transformations took place, and within these blocks of DNA, the order of the genes remained intact.

"It's fairly easy to see how you can convert the chromosomes from the macaque to the human," Dr. Murphy said.

This new macaque study, which is set to appear in a future issue of the journal *Genomics*, is just one of many new papers charting the history of chromosomes—in humans and other species. While scientists have been studying chromosomes for nearly a century, only in the last few years have large genome databases, powerful computers and new mathematical methods allowed scientists to trace these evolutionary steps.

Scientists hope that uncovering the history of chromosomes will have practical applications to diseases like cancer, in which rearranged chromosomes play a major part.

Scientists have known for over 70 years that chromosomes can be rearranged. With a microscope, it is possible to make out the banded patterns on chromosomes and to compare the pattern in different species.

Scientists discovered that different populations of fruit fly species could be distinguished by inverted segments in their chromosomes.

Later, molecular biologists discovered how cells accidentally rearranged large chunks of genetic material as they made new copies of their chromosomes. By the 1980's, scientists were able to identify some major events in chromosome evolution. Humans have 23 pairs of chromosomes, for example, while chimpanzees and other apes have 24. Scientists determined that two ancestral chromosomes fused together after the ancestors of humans split off from other apes some six million years ago.

But a more detailed understanding of how chromosomes had changed would have to wait until scientists had amassed more information. In the mid-1990's, Dr. Pevzner and Sridhar Hannenhalli of the University of Pennsylvania invented a fast method for comparing chromosomes from two different species and determining the fewest number of rearrangements . . . that separate them.

They introduced the method with a series of talks with titles like "Transforming Cabbage Into Turnips" and "Transforming Mice Into Men." . . .

Dr. Pevzner himself joined with Dr. Murphy and 23 other scientists to analyze the last 100 million years of mammal evolution. They compared the genomes of humans to cats, dogs, mice, rats, pigs, cows and horses, using a program developed by Harris A. Lewin and his colleagues at the University of Illinois, called the Evolution Highway.

The program allowed them to trace how each lineage's chromosomes had become rearranged over time. They published their results in the July 22 [2005] issue of *Science.*

The scientists found some chromosomes barely altered and others heavily reworked. They also discovered that the rate for rearrangements was far from steady. After the end of the Cretaceous Period, when large dinosaurs became extinct, the chromosomes of mammals began rearranging two to five times as fast as before. That may reflect the evolutionary explosion of mammals that followed the dinosaur extinctions, as mammals rapidly occupied new ecological niches as predators and grazers, fliers and swimmers . . .

The new results raise questions about how evolution makes chromosome rearrangements part of a species' genome. In many cases, these mutations cause diseases, so natural selection should make them disappear quickly from a population.

But scientists have also documented some rearrangements

Chromosomal rearrangement is an important form of mutation, as described in this news story. Mutation rates vary among species. Based on the reconstruction diagrammed here, the order of genes on the X chromosome of humans, cats, dogs, pigs, and horses has not altered during 100 million years of mammalian evolution. By contrast, segments of the X chromosome have been rearranged many times in mice and rats.

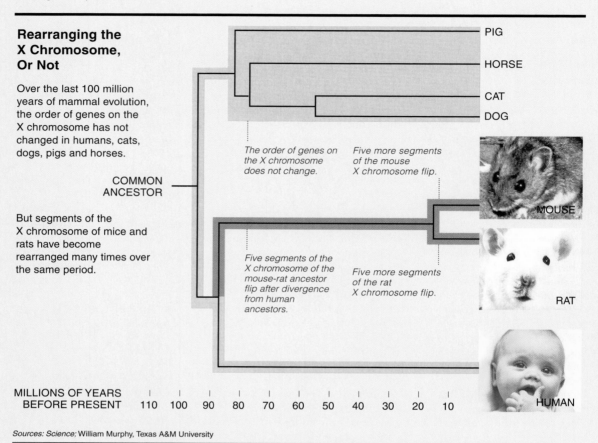

Rearranging the X Chromosome, Or Not

Over the last 100 million years of mammal evolution, the order of genes on the X chromosome has not changed in humans, cats, dogs, pigs and horses.

COMMON ANCESTOR

But segments of the X chromosome of mice and rats have become rearranged many times over the same period.

PIG

HORSE

CAT

DOG

The order of genes on the X chromosome does not change.

Five more segments of the mouse X chromosome flip.

MOUSE

Five segments of the X chromosome of the mouse-rat ancestor flip after divergence from human ancestors.

Five more segments of the rat X chromosome flip.

RAT

HUMAN

MILLIONS OF YEARS BEFORE PRESENT   110   100   90   80   70   60   50   40   30   20   10

Sources: Science; William Murphy, Texas A&M University

that are not hazardous or that are even beneficial. This year, for example, scientists discovered that some Northern Europeans carry a large inverted segment on one of their chromosomes. This inversion boosts the fertility of women who carry it. Chromosome rearrangements may also play a role in the origin of new species. Scientists often find that closely related species living in overlapping ranges have rearranged chromosomes. The mismatch of chromosomes may make it impossible for the two species to hybridize . . .

The *Science* study and the newer study on macaques suggest that chromosomes tend to break in certain places, a hypothesis first offered by Dr. Pevzner in 2003 . . . "Certain regions of the genome are being broken over and over again."

It is too early to say why these regions have become break points, said Evan Eichler of the University of Washington, who was not involved in the mammal study. "There's something about these regions that makes them hot, and we have to figure out what that hot factor is," he said.

Dr. Eichler argues that it is important to figure out what that is because a number of human congenital diseases are associated with chromosome rearrangements at these same break points.

"Here you have a beautiful connection," he said. "The same thing that causes big-scale rearrangement between a human and chimp or a gorilla, these same sites are often the site of deletion associated with diseases."

Some of these diseases involve chromosome rearrangements in a fertilized egg, leading to congenital disorders. Cancer cells also undergo large-scale chromosome rearrangements, often at the same break points identified in the recent evolution study.

"We could have inherited some weaknesses in our genome that we have to understand and deal with medically," said David Haussler of the University of California, Santa Cruz. "And that has to do with the history of how our genome is built."

SOURCE: Carl Zimmer, "The History of Chromosomes May Shape the Future of Diseases," *New York Times*, August 30, 2005. http://www.nytimes.com/2005/08/30/science/30gene.html?ei=5070&en=672b16463342c995&ex=1138165200&pagewanted=print.

called *Zoonomia* published in 1794, Erasmus Darwin had proclaimed the common ancestry of all animal species.

Charles Darwin also was influenced by Sir Charles Lyell, the father of geology. During Darwin's famous voyage to South America aboard the *Beagle,* he read Lyell's influential book *Principles of Geology* (1837/1969), which exposed him to Lyell's principle of **uniformitarianism.** Uniformitarianism states that the present is the key to the past. Explanations for past events should be sought in the long-term action of ordinary forces that still operate today. Thus, natural forces (rainfall, soil deposition, earthquakes, and volcanic action) gradually have built and modified geological features such as mountain ranges. The earth's structure has been transformed gradually through natural forces operating for millions of years (see Weiner 1994).

Uniformitarianism was a necessary building block for evolutionary theory. It cast serious doubt on the belief that the world was only 6,000 years old. It would take much longer for such ordinary forces as rain and wind to produce major geological changes. The longer time span also allowed enough time for the biological changes that fossil discoveries were revealing. Darwin applied the ideas of uniformitarianism and long-term transformation to living things. He argued that all life forms are ultimately related and that the number of species has increased over time. (For more on science, evolution, and creationism, see Futuyma 1995; Gould 1999; Wilson 2002.)

Charles Darwin provided a theoretical framework for understanding evolution. He offered natural selection as a powerful evolutionary mechanism that could explain the origin of species, biological diversity, and similarities among related life forms. Darwin proposed a *theory of evolution* in the strict sense. A **theory** is a set of ideas formulated (by reasoning from known facts) to explain something. The main value of a

---

 STUDENT CD-ROM LIVING ANTHROPOLOGY

Natural Selection
Track 4

This clip demonstrates the results of pigeon breeding in England, pointing out that more than 200 breeds of pigeons are known. The variety he observed among domestic birds (English pigeons) and wild birds (finches in the Galápagos Islands) led Charles Darwin to believe that comparable processes of selection were at work. In the first case the selection was artificial, the result of animal domestication and breeding experiments. In the second case the selection was natural, having to do with impersonal environmental forces. Are breeding experiments always useful to the animals in question? Which takes longer—artificial selection or natural selection?

■ *Charles Darwin at his home at Down House, Kent, England, around 1880.*

theory is to promote new understanding. A theory suggests patterns, connections, and relationships that may be confirmed by new research. The *fact* of evolution (that evolution has occurred) was known earlier, for example by Erasmus Darwin. The *theory* of evolution, through natural selection (*how* evolution occurred), was Darwin's major contribution. Actually, natural selection wasn't Darwin's unique discovery. Working independently, the naturalist Alfred Russel Wallace had reached a similar conclusion (Shermer 2002). In a joint paper read to London's Linnaean Society in 1858, Darwin and Wallace made their discovery public. Darwin's book *On the Origin of Species* (1859/1958) offered much fuller documentation.

Natural selection is the process by which the forms most fit to survive and reproduce in a given environment do so in greater numbers than others in the same population. More than survival of the fittest, natural selection is differential reproductive success. Natural selection is a natural process that leads to a result. Natural selection operates when there is competition for strategic resources (those necessary for life) such as food and space between members of the population. There is also the matter of finding mates. You can win the competition for food and space and have no mate and thus have no impact on the future of the species. For natural selection to work on a particular population, there must be variety within that population, as there always is.

For information on common misconceptions about evolution, see your OLC Internet Exercises

mhhe.com/kottak

Intelligent Design versus Evolutionary Theory

"Intelligent design" (ID) no longer can be mentioned in biology classes in a Pennsylvania public school district, a federal district judge ruled on December 20, 2005. Dover Area School Board members had violated the Constitution when they ordered that its biology curriculum had to include the notion that life on earth was produced by an unspecified intelligent designer. Administrators had been required to read a statement in biology classes asserting that evolution was a theory, not a fact; that the evidence for evolution had gaps; and that ID offered an alternative explanation laid out in a book (purchased by church funds) in the school library. According to the judge (a Republican appointed by President George W. Bush), that statement amounted to an endorsement of religion. It could cause students to doubt a generally accepted scientific theory by presenting a religious alternative masquerading as a scientific theory (see *New York Times* 2005, p. A32).

The Dover school board policy, adopted in October 2004, was believed to have been the first of its kind in the United States. Their attorneys claimed that school board members were seeking to improve science education by exposing students to alternatives to Charles Darwin's theory that evolution occurs through natural selection. ID proponents argued that evolutionary theory can't fully explain complex life forms. Their opponents contended that ID amounts to a secular repackaging of creationism, which courts have ruled cannot be taught in public schools. The Pennsylvania judge agreed: The secular purposes claimed by the board were a pretext for the board's real purpose—to promote religion in public schools.

ID advocates have since been voted off the Dover school board. The new board plans to remove ID from science classes, but interested students may be able to learn about ID in an elective course on comparative reli-

gion. ID did not belong in the *science* curriculum, the judge ruled, because it is "a religious view, a mere relabeling of creationism and not a scientific theory"(*New York Times* 2005, p. A32).

The ID movement asserts that life forms are too complex to have been formed by natural processes and must have been created by a higher intelligence. The fundamental claim of intelligent design proponents, such as William A. Dembski, is that "there are natural systems that cannot be adequately explained in terms of undirected natural forces and that exhibit features which in any other circumstance we would attribute to intelligence" (Demski 2004). The source of this intelligence never is identified officially. But since the naturalness of the design is denied, its supernaturalness would seem to be assumed. By injecting ID into the science curriculum, the judge ruled, Dover's board was unconstitutionally endorsing a religious view that advances "a particular version of Christianity" (*New York Times* 2005, p. A32). Attempts, of variable success and spurring ongoing legal challenges, have been made to teach ID in biology classes in several other states. ID's greatest success has been in Kansas, where the State Board of Education has changed the definition of science so it is not limited to natural explanations. This opens the way for including ID and other forms of creationism.

The Pennsylvania court case thoroughly examined the claim that ID was science. After a six-week trial featuring hours of expert testimony, that claim was rejected. The judge found that ID violated the ground rules of science by invoking supernatural causation and by making assertions that could not be tested or proved wrong (falsified). Nor has ID gained acceptance in the scientific community. It lacks a research and testing program and is unsupported by peer-reviewed research (*New York Times* 2005).

Evolution as a *scientific theory* (as defined in the text) is a central orga-

nizing principle of modern biology and anthropology. Evolution also is a *fact*. There is absolutely no doubt that biological evolution has occurred and is occurring still. What is at issue in biology are questions of details of the process and the relative importance of different evolutionary mechanisms. "It is a *fact* that the earth with liquid water, is more than 3.6 billion years old. It is a *fact* that cellular life has been around for at least half of that period and that organized multicellular life is at least 800 million years old. It is a *fact* that major life forms now on earth were not at all represented in the past. There were no birds or mammals 250 million years ago. It is a *fact* that major life forms of the past are no longer living. There used to be dinosaurs . . . and there are none now. It is a *fact* that all living forms come from previous living forms. Therefore, all present forms of life arose from ancestral forms that were different. Birds arose from nonbirds and humans from nonhumans. No person who pretends to any understanding of the natural world can deny these facts any more than she or he can deny that the earth is round, rotates on its axis, and revolves around the sun" (Lewontin 1981, quoted in Moran 1993).

One key feature of science, as we saw in Chapter 1 (pp. 16–18), is to recognize the tentativeness and uncertainty of knowledge and understanding, which scientists try to improve. As they work to refine theories and to provide accurate explanations, scientists strive for objectivity and impartiality (trying to reduce the influence of the scientist, including his or her personal beliefs and actions). Science has many limitations and is not the only way we have of understanding. Certainly, the study of religion is another path to understanding. But the goals of objectivity and impartiality do help distinguish science from ways of knowing that are more biased, more rigid, and more dogmatic.

The giraffe's neck can illustrate how natural selection works on variety within a population. In any group of giraffes, there is always variation in neck length. When food is adequate, the animals have no problem feeding themselves. But when there is pressure on strategic resources, so that dietary foliage is not as abundant as usual, giraffes with longer necks have an advantage. They can feed off the higher branches. If this feeding advantage permits longer-necked giraffes to survive and reproduce even slightly more effectively than shorter-necked ones, giraffes with longer necks will transmit more of their genetic material to future generations than will giraffes with shorter necks.

An incorrect alternative to this (Darwinian) explanation would be the inheritance of acquired characteristics. That is the idea that in each generation, individual giraffes strain their necks to reach just a bit higher. This straining somehow modifies their genetic material. Over generations of strain, the average neck gradually gets longer through the accumulation of small increments of neck length acquired during the lifetime of each generation of giraffes. This is not how evolution works. If it did work in this way, weight lifters could expect to produce especially muscular babies. Workouts that promise no gain without the pain apply to the physical development of individuals, not species. Instead, evolution works as the process of natural selection takes advantage of the variety that is already present in a population. That's how giraffes got their necks.

Evolution through natural selection continues today. For example, in human populations there is differential resistance to disease, as we'll see in the discussion of sickle-cell anemia below. One classic recent example of natural selection is the peppered moth, which can be light or dark (in either case with black speckles, thus the name "peppered"). A change in this species illustrates recent natural selection (in our own industrial age) through what has been called *industrial melanism*. Great Britain's industrialization changed the environment to favor darker moths (those with more melanin) rather than the lighter-colored ones that were favored previously. During the 1800s industrial pollution increased; soot coated buildings and trees, turning them a darker color. The previously typical peppered moth, which had a light color, now stood out against the dark backgrounds of sooty buildings and trees. Such light-colored moths were easily visible to their predators. Through mutations (see below), a new strain of peppered moth, with a darker phenotype, was favored. Because these darker moths were fitter—that is harder to detect—in polluted environments, they survived and reproduced in greater numbers than lighter moths did. We see how natural selection may favor darker moths in polluted

environments and lighter-colored moths in non-industrial or less polluted environments because of their variant abilities to merge in with their environmental colors and thus avoid predators.

A speckled peppered moth and a black one alight on a soot-blackened tree. Which phenotype is favored in this environment? How could this adaptive advantage change?

Evolutionary theory is used to explain. Remember from Chapter 1 that the goal of science is to increase understanding through explanation: showing how and why the thing (or class of things) to be understood (e.g., the variation within species, the geographic distribution of species, the fossil record) depends on other things. Explanations rely on associations and theories. An association is an observed relationship between two or more variables, such as the length of a giraffe's neck and the number of its offspring, or an increase in the frequency of dark moths as industrial pollution spreads. A theory is more general, suggesting or implying associations and attempting to explain them. A thing or event—for example, the giraffe's long neck—is explained if it illustrates a general principle or association, such as the concept of adaptive advantage. The truth of a scientific statement (e.g., evolution occurs because of differential reproductive success due to variation within the population) is confirmed by repeated observations. (See "Interesting Issues" for a discussion of differences between evolutionary theory and intelligent design.)

GENETICS

Charles Darwin recognized that for natural selection to operate, there must be variety in the population undergoing selection. Documenting and explaining such variety among humans—human biological diversity—is one of anthropology's

major concerns. Genetics, a science that emerged after Darwin, helps us understand the causes of biological variation. We now know that DNA (deoxyribonucleic acid) molecules make up genes and chromosomes, which are the basic hereditary units. Biochemical changes (mutations) in DNA provide much of the variety on which natural selection operates. Through sexual reproduction, recombination of the genetic traits of mother and father in each generation leads to new arrangements of the hereditary units received from each parent. Such genetic recombination also adds variety on which natural selection may operate.

Mendelian genetics studies the ways in which chromosomes transmit genes across the generations. **Biochemical genetics** examines structure, function, and changes in DNA. **Population genetics** investigates natural selection and other causes of genetic variation, stability, and change in breeding populations.

Mendel's Experiments

In 1856, in a monastery garden, the Austrian monk Gregor Mendel began a series of experiments that were to reveal the basic principles of genetics. Mendel studied the inheritance of seven contrasting traits in pea plants. For each trait there were only two forms. For example, plants were either tall (6 to 7 feet [1.8 to 2.1 meters]) or short (9 to 18 inches [23 to 46 centimeters]), with no intermediate forms. The ripe seeds could be either smooth and round or wrinkled. The peas could be either yellow or green, again with no intermediate colors.

When Mendel began his experiments, one of the prevailing beliefs about heredity was what has been called the "paint-pot" theory. According to this theory, the traits of the two parents blended in their children much as two pigments are blended in a can of paint. Children were therefore a unique mixture of their parents, and when these children married and reproduced, their traits would inextricably blend with those of their spouses. However, prevailing notions about heredity also recognized that occasionally the traits of one parent might swamp those of the other. If children looked far more like their mother than their father, people might say that her "blood" was stronger than his. Occasionally, too, there would be a "throwback," a child who was the image of his or her grandparent or who possessed a distinctive chin or nose characteristic of a whole line of descent.

Through his experiments with pea plants, Mendel discovered that heredity is determined by discrete particles or units. Although traits could disappear in one generation, they reemerged in their original form in later generations. For example, Mendel crossbred pure strains of tall and short plants. Their offspring were all tall. This was the first descending, or first filial, generation, designated F_1. Mendel then interbred the plants of the F_1 generation to produce a generation of grandchildren, the F_2 generation (Figure 4.1). In this generation, short plants reappeared. Among thousands of plants in the F_2 generation, there was approximately one short plant for every three tall ones.

From similar results with the other six traits, Mendel concluded that although a **dominant** form could mask the other form in *hybrid,* or mixed, individuals, the dominated trait—the **recessive**—was not destroyed; it wasn't even changed. Recessive traits would appear in unaltered form in later generations because genetic traits were inherited as discrete units.

These basic genetic units that Mendel described were factors (now called genes or alleles) located on **chromosomes.** Chromosomes are arranged in matching (homologous) pairs. Humans have 46 chromosomes, arranged in 23 pairs, one in each pair from the father and the other from the mother.

For simplicity, a chromosome may be pictured as a surface (see Figure 4.2) with several positions, to each of which we assign a lowercase letter. Each position is a **gene.** Each gene determines, wholly or partially, a particular biological trait, such as whether one's blood is A, B, or O. **Alleles** (for example, b^1 and b^2 in Figure 4.2) are biochemically different forms of a given gene. In humans, A, B, AB, and O blood types reflect different combinations of alleles of a particular gene.

In Mendel's experiments, the seven contrasting traits were determined by genes on seven different pairs of chromosomes. The gene for height occurred in one of the seven pairs. When Mendel crossbred pure tall and pure short plants to produce his F₁ generation, each of the offspring received an allele for tallness (T) from one parent and one for shortness (t) from the other. These offspring were mixed, or **heterozygous**, with respect to height; each had two dissimilar alleles of that gene. Their parents, in contrast, had been **homozygous**, possessing two identical alleles of that gene (see Hartl and Jones 2002).

In the next generation (F₂), after the mixed plants were interbred, short plants reappeared in the ratio of one short to three talls. Knowing that shorts only produced shorts, Mendel could assume that they were genetically pure. Another fourth of the F₂ plants produced only talls. The remaining half, like the F₁ generation, were heterozygous; when interbred, they produced three talls for each short. (See Figure 4.3.)

Dominance produces a distinction between **genotype**, or hereditary makeup, and **phenotype**, or expressed physical characteristics. Genotype is what you really are genetically; phenotype is what you appear as. Mendel's peas had three genotypes—TT, Tt, and tt—but only two phenotypes—tall and short. Because of dominance, the heterozygous plants were just as tall as the genetically pure tall ones. How do Mendel's discoveries apply to humans? Although some of our genetic traits follow Mendelian laws, with only two forms—dominant and recessive—other traits are determined differently. For instance, three alleles determine whether our blood type is A, B, AB, or O. People with two alleles for type O have that blood type. However, if they received a gene for either A or B from one parent and one for O from the other, they will have blood type A or B. In other words, A and B are both dominant over O. A and B are said to be *codominant*. If people inherit a gene for A from one parent and one for B from the other, they will have type AB blood, which is chemically different from the other varieties, A, B, and O.

These three alleles produce four phenotypes—A, B, AB, and O—and six different genotypes—OO, AO, BO, AA, BB, and AB (Figure 4.4). There are fewer phenotypes than genotypes because O is recessive to both A and B.

Independent Assortment and Recombination

Through additional experiments, Mendel also formulated his law of **independent assortment**. He discovered that traits are inherited indepen-

Trait Exhibited by F₁ Hybrids	F₂ Generation (produced by crossbreeding F₁ hybrids)	
	Exhibit Dominant Trait	Exhibit Recessive Trait
Smooth seed shape	Smooth 3	Wrinkled 1
Yellow seed interior	Yellow 3	Green 1
Gray seed coat	Gray 3	White 1
Inflated pod	Inflated 3	Pinched 1
Green pod	Green 3	Yellow 1
Axial pod	Axial 3	Terminal 1
Tall stem	Tall 3	Short 1

Offspring exhibit dominant or recessive traits in ratio of 3:1.

FIGURE 4.1 Mendel's Second Set of Experiments with Pea Plants.
Dominant colors are shown unless otherwise indicated.

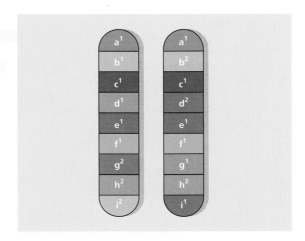

FIGURE 4.2 Simplified Representation of a Normal Chromosome Pair.
Letters indicate genes; superscripts indicate alleles.

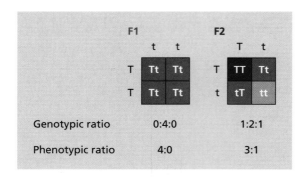

FIGURE 4.3 Punnett Squares of a Homozygous Cross and a Heterozygous Cross.

These squares show how phenotypic ratios of the F₁ and F₂ generation are generated. Colors show genotypes.

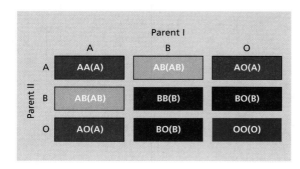

FIGURE 4.4 Determinants of Phenotypes (Blood Groups) in the ABO System.

The four phenotypes—A, B, AB, and O—are indicated in parentheses and by color.

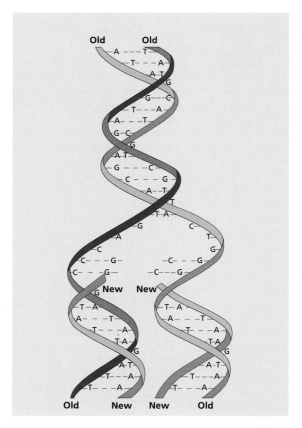

FIGURE 4.5 A double-stranded DNA molecule "unzips," and a new strand forms on each of the old ones, producing two molecules, and eventually two cells, each identical to the first.

dently of one another. For example, he bred pure round yellow peas with pure wrinkled green ones. All the F₁ generation peas were round and yellow, the dominant forms. But when Mendel interbred the F₁ generation to produce the F₂, four phenotypes turned up. Round greens and wrinkled yellows had been added to the original round yellows and wrinkled greens.

The independent assortment and recombination of genetic traits provide one of the main ways by which variety is produced in any population. **Recombination** is important in biological evolution because it creates new types on which natural selection can operate.

BIOCHEMICAL, OR MOLECULAR, GENETICS

If, as in Mendel's experiments, the same genetic traits always appeared in predictable ratios across the generations, there would be continuity rather than change. There would be no evolution. Various kinds of mutations produce the variety

on which natural selection depends. Since Mendel's time, scientists have learned about **mutations**—changes in the DNA molecules of which genes and chromosomes are built. Mendel demonstrated that variety is produced by genetic recombination. Mutation, however, is even more important as a source of new biochemical forms on which natural selection may operate.

DNA does several things basic to life. DNA can copy itself, forming new cells, replacing old ones, and producing the sex cells, or *gametes,* that make new generations. DNA's chemical structure also guides the body's production of proteins—enzymes, antigens, antibodies, hormones, and hundreds of others.

The DNA molecule is a double helix (Crick 1962/1968; Watson 1970). Imagine it as a small rubber ladder that you can twist into a spiral. Its sides are held together by chemical bonds between four bases: thymine (T), adenine (A), cytosine (C), and guanine (G). DNA's duplication leads to ordinary cell division, as shown in Figure 4.5.

In protein building, another molecule, RNA, carries DNA's message from the cell's nucleus to its *cytoplasm* (outer area). The structure of RNA, with paired bases, matches that of DNA. This permits RNA to carry a message from DNA in the cell nucleus to guide the construction of proteins in the cytoplasm. A protein, which is a chain of amino acids, is constructed by "reading" a length of RNA. RNA's bases are read as three-letter "words," called *triplets*—for example, AAG. (Because DNA and RNA have four bases, which can occur anywhere in the "word," there are $4 \times 4 \times 4 = 64$ possible triplets.) Each triplet "calls" a particular amino acid, although there is some redundancy; for example, AAA and AAG both call for the amino acid lysine. A protein is made as amino acids are assembled in the proper sequence.

Thus proteins are built following instructions sent by DNA, with RNA's assistance. In this way, DNA, the basic *hereditary* material, also initiates and guides the construction of hundreds of proteins necessary for bodily growth, maintenance, and repair.

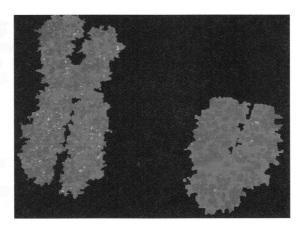

The chromosomes that determine sex in humans. The X chromosome (left) is clearly larger than the Y chromosome (right). What are the genotypes of males and females in terms of these chromosomes?

Cell Division

An organism develops from a fertilized egg, or *zygote*, created by the union of two sex cells (gametes), a sperm from the father and an egg (ovum) from the mother. The zygote grows rapidly through **mitosis,** or ordinary cell division, which continues as the organism grows. Mistakes in this process of cell division, like the chromosomal breaks and rearrangements described in the news story, can cause diseases such as cancer.

The special process by which sex cells are produced is called **meiosis.** Unlike ordinary cell division, in which two cells emerge from one, in meiosis four cells are produced from one. Each has half the genetic material of the original cell. In human meiosis, four cells, each with 23 individual chromosomes, are produced from an original cell with 23 pairs.

With fertilization of egg by sperm, the father's 23 chromosomes combine with the mother's 23 to re-create the pairs in every generation. However, the chromosomes sort independently, so that a child's genotype is a random combination of the DNA of its four grandparents. It is conceivable that one grandparent will contribute very little to its grandchild's heredity. Independent assortment of chromosomes is a major source of variety, because the parents' genotypes can be assorted in 2^{23}, or more than 8 million, different ways.

Crossing Over

Another source of variety is **crossing over.** Before fertilization, early in meiosis, as a sperm or egg is being formed, paired chromosomes temporarily intertwine as they duplicate themselves. As they do this, they often exchange lengths of their DNA (Figure 4.6). Crossovers are the sites where homologous chromosomes have exchanged segments by breakage and recombination.

Because of crossing over, each new chromosome is partially different from either member of the original pair. As a person produces sex cells, replacing, say, part of a chromosome one has received from one's mother with a corresponding section of the homologous chromosome from one's father, crossing over partially contradicts Mendel's law of independent assortment and makes a new combination of genetic material available to the offspring. Because crossing over can occur with any chromosome pair, it is an important source of variety.

Mutation

Mutations are the most important source of variety on which natural selection depends and operates. The simplest mutation results from substitution of just one base in a triplet by another. (This is called a *base substitution mutation.*) If such a mutation occurs in a sex cell that joins with another in a fertilized egg, the new organism will carry the mutation in every cell. As DNA directs protein building, a protein different from that produced by the nonmutant parent *may* be produced in the child. The child's protein building will differ from the parent's only if the new base codes for a different amino acid. Because the same amino acid can be coded by more than one triplet, a base substitution mutation doesn't always produce a different protein. However, the abnormal protein associated with the hereditary disease sickle-cell anemia, described below, is caused by just such a difference in a single base between normal individuals and those afflicted with the disease.

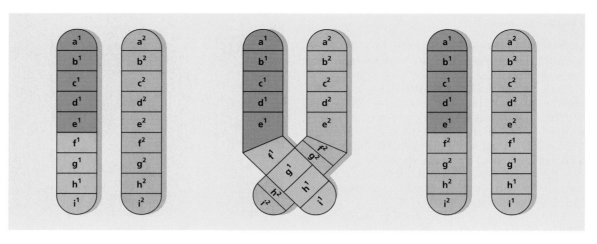

FIGURE 4.6 Crossing Over.

In the first phase of meiosis, homologous chromosomes intertwine as they duplicate themselves. As they do this, they often exchange lengths of their DNA, as shown here. This is known as crossing over. Note that the lower lengths of the original pair now differ. Each chromosome is therefore chemically different from either member of the original pair.

Another form of mutation—*chromosomal rearrangement*—was described in the "News Brief" at the beginning of the chapter. Pieces of a chromosome can break off, turn around and reattach, or migrate someplace else on that chromosome. This can occur in the sex cell, or in the fertilized egg or the growing organism, during mitosis. A mismatch of chromosomes resulting from rearrangement can lead to speciation (the formation of new species). Scientists often find that separate but closely related species living in overlapping ranges cannot interbreed because their chromosomes, due to rearrangement, no longer match. Chromosome rearrangements in a fertilized egg can lead to congenital disorders. Cancer cells undergo large-scale chromosome rearrangements. Chromosomes also may fuse. When the ancestors of humans split off from those of chimpanzees around six million years ago, two ancestral chromosomes fused together in the human line. Humans have 23 chromosome pairs, versus 24 for chimps.

Mutation rates vary, but for base substitution mutations, the likely average is 10^{-9} mutations per DNA base per generation. This means that approximately three mutations will occur in every sex cell (Strachan and Read 2004). Many geneticists believe that most mutations are neutral, conferring neither advantage nor disadvantage. Others argue that most mutations are harmful and will be weeded out because they deviate from types that have been selected over the generations. However, if the selective forces affecting a population change, mutations in its gene pool may acquire an adaptive advantage they lacked in the old environment.

Evolution depends on mutations as a major source of genetically transmitted variety, raw material on which natural selection can work. (Crossing over, independent assortment, and chromosomal recombination are other sources.) Alterations in genes and chromosomes may result in entirely new types of organisms, which may demonstrate some new selective advantage. Variants produced through mutation can be especially significant if there is a change in the environment. They may prove to have an advantage they lacked in the old environment. The spread of the allele that determines sickle-cell anemia, to be examined below, provides one example.

POPULATION GENETICS AND MECHANISMS OF GENETIC EVOLUTION

Population genetics studies the stable and changing populations in which most breeding normally takes place (see Gillespie 2004; Hartl 2000). The term **gene pool** refers to all the alleles, genes, chromosomes, and genotypes within a breeding population—the "pool" of genetic material available. When population geneticists use the term *evolution,* they have a more specific definition in mind than the one given earlier ("descent with modification over the generations"). For geneticists, **genetic evolution** is defined as a change in gene frequency, that is, in the frequency of alleles in a breeding population from generation to generation. Any factor that contributes to such a change can be considered a mechanism of genetic evolution. Those mechanisms include natural selection, mutation (already examined), random genetic drift, and gene flow (see Mayr 2001).

Natural Selection

Natural selection remains the best explanation for (genetic) evolution. Essential to understanding evolution through natural selection is the distinction between genotype and phenotype. Genotype refers just to hereditary factors—genes and chromosomes. Phenotype—the organism's evident biological characteristics—develops over the years as the organism is influenced by particular environmental forces. (See the photo of the identical twins. Identical twins have exactly the same genotype, but their actual biology, their phenotypes, may differ as a result of variation in the environments in which they have been raised.) Also, because of dominance, individuals with different genotypes may have identical phenotypes (like Mendel's tall pea plants). Natural selection can operate only on phenotype—on what is exposed, not on what is hidden. For example, a harmful recessive gene can't be eliminated from the gene pool if it is masked by a favored dominant.

Phenotype includes not only outward physical appearance, but also internal organs, tissues, and cells and physiological processes and systems. Many biological reactions to foods, disease, heat, cold, sunlight, and other environmental factors are not automatic, genetically programmed responses but the product of years of exposure to particular environmental stresses. Human biology is not set at birth but has considerable *plasticity*. That is, it is changeable, being affected by the environmental forces, such as diet and altitude, that we experience as we grow up (see Bogin 2001).

The environment works on the genotype to build the phenotype, and certain phenotypes do better in some environments than other phenotypes do. However, remember that favored phenotypes can be produced by different genotypes. Because natural selection works only on genes that are expressed, maladaptive recessives can be removed only when they occur in homozygous form. When a heterozygote carries a maladaptive recessive, its effects are masked by the favored dominant. The process of perfecting the fit between organisms and their environment is gradual.

Directional Selection

After several generations of selection, gene frequencies will change. Adaptation through natural selection will have occurred. Once that happens, those traits that have proved to be the most **adaptive** (favored by natural selection) in that environment will be selected again and again from generation to generation. Given such *directional selection,* or long-term selection of the same trait(s), maladaptive recessive alleles will be removed from the gene pool.

Directional selection will continue as long as environmental forces stay the same. However, if the environment changes, new selective forces

Identical twins, such as Daniel and Henrik Sedin, have exactly the same genotype. Such twins can vary in phenotype (e.g., in height or weight) depending on their environment and events during growth and development.

start working, favoring different phenotypes. This also happens when part of the population colonizes a new environment. Selection in the changed, or new, environment continues until a new equilibrium is reached. Then there is directional selection until another environmental change or migration takes place. Over millions of years, such a process of successive adaptation to a series of environments has led to biological modification and branching. The process of natural selection has led to the tremendous array of plant and animal forms found in the world today.

Selection operates *only* on traits that are present in a population. A favorable mutation *may* occur, but a population doesn't normally come up with a new genotype or phenotype just because one is needed or desirable. Many species have become extinct because they weren't sufficiently varied to adapt to environmental shifts.

There are also differences in the amount of environmental stress that organisms' genetic potential enables them to tolerate. Some species are adapted to a narrow range of environments. They are especially endangered by environmental fluctuation. Others—*Homo sapiens* among them—tolerate much more environmental variation because their genetic potential permits many adaptive possibilities. Humans can adapt rapidly to changing conditions by modifying both biological responses and learned behavior. We don't have to delay adaptation until a favorable mutation appears.

Sexual Selection

Selection also operates through competition for mates in a breeding population. Males may openly compete for females, or females may choose to mate with particular males because they have desirable traits. Obviously, such traits vary from species to species. Familiar examples include color in birds; male birds, such as cardinals, tend to be more brightly colored than females are. Colorful males have a selective advantage because females

For an example of natural selection, see your OLC Internet Exercises
mhhe.com/kottak

For an introduction
to evolution, see the
Virtual Exploration

mhhe.com/kottak

■ *Sexual selection:
In many bird species,
colorful males have a
selective advantage
because females are
more likely to mate with
them than with less colorful males. Observe the
difference between male
and female peacocks.
What other peacock
feature might aid in
attracting a mate?*

like them better. As, over the generations, females have opted for colorful mates, the alleles responsible for color have built up in the species. **Sexual selection,** based on differential success in mating, is the term for this process in which certain traits of one sex are selected because of advantages they confer in winning mates.

Stabilizing Selection

We have seen that natural selection reduces variety in a population through directional selection—by favoring one trait or allele over another. Selective forces can also work to *maintain* variety through *stabilizing selection*, by favoring a **balanced polymorphism,** in which the frequencies of two or more alleles of a gene remain constant from generation to generation. This may be because the

phenotypes they produce are neutral, or equally favored, or equally opposed by selective forces. Sometimes a particular force favors (or opposes) one allele while a different but equally effective force favors (or opposes) the other allele.

One well-studied example of a balanced polymorphism involves two alleles, Hb^A and Hb^S, that affect the production of the beta strain (Hb) of human hemoglobin. Hemoglobin, which is located in our red blood cells, carries oxygen from the lungs to the rest of the body via the circulatory system. The allele that produces normal hemoglobin is Hb^A. Another allele, Hb^S, produces a different hemoglobin. Individuals who are homozygous for Hb^S suffer from *sickle-cell anemia*. Such anemia, in which the red blood cells are shaped like crescents or sickles, is associated with a disease that is usually fatal. This condition interferes with the blood's ability to store oxygen. It increases the heart's burden by clogging the small blood vessels.

Given the fatal disease associated with Hb^S, geneticists were surprised to discover that certain populations in Africa, India, and the Mediterranean had very high frequencies of Hb^S (Figure 4.7). In some West African populations, that frequency is around 20 percent. Researchers eventually discovered that both Hb^A and Hb^S are maintained because selective forces in certain environments favor the heterozygote over either homozygote.

Initially, scientists wondered why, if most Hb^S homozygotes died before they reached reproductive age, the harmful allele hadn't been eliminated. Why was its frequency so high? The answer turned out to lie in the *heterozygote's* greater fitness. Only people who were homozygous for Hb^S died from sickle-cell anemia. Heterozygotes suffered very mild anemia, if any. On the other hand, although people homozygous for Hb^A did not suffer from anemia, they were much more susceptible to *malaria*—a killer disease that continues to plague *Homo sapiens* in the tropics.

The heterozygote, with one sickle-cell allele and one normal one, was the fittest phenotype for a malarial environment. Heterozygotes have enough abnormal hemoglobin, in which malaria parasites cannot thrive, to protect against malaria. They also have enough normal hemoglobin to fend off sickle-cell anemia. The Hb^S allele has been maintained in these populations because the heterozygotes survived and reproduced in greater numbers than did people with any other phenotype.

The example of the sickle-cell allele demonstrates the relativity of evolution through natural selection: Adaptation and fitness are in relation to specific environments. Traits are not adaptive or maladaptive for all times and places. Even harmful alleles can be selected if heterozygotes have an advantage. Moreover, as the environment

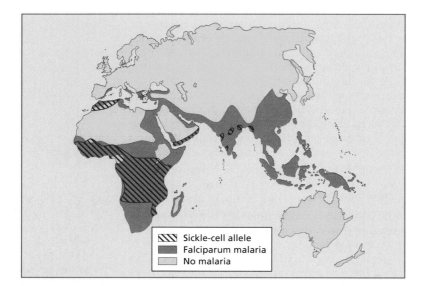

FIGURE 4.7 Distribution of Sickle-Cell Allele and Falciparum Malaria in the Old World. SOURCE: Adapted from Joseph B. Birdsell, *Human Evolution: An Introduction to the New Physical Anthropology,* 3rd ed. (Boston: Houghton Mifflin, 1981).

"Hey, it's all in the genes." When did you last hear a statement like that? We routinely use assumptions about genetic determination to explain, say, why tall parents have tall kids or why obesity runs in families. But how true is the statement? How much do our genes influence our bodies? The genetic causes of some of our physical traits are clear. This is true with the ABO blood group system, and with other blood factors, such as whether we are Rh positive or negative and whether we are sickle-cell carriers. But the genetic roots of other physical traits aren't so clear. For example, can you crease or fold your tongue by raising its sides? Some people can; some people never can; some people who never thought they could can after practicing. An apparent genetic limitation turns out to be more plastic.

Human biology is plastic, but only to a degree. If you're born with blood group O, you've got it for the rest of your life. The same applies to disorders due to harmful genes, such as those that cause hemophilia (transmitted on the X chromosome) and sickle-cell anemia. Still, if there's no genetic solution, there may be a cultural one. Modern medicine now treats effectively a variety of genetic disorders that once would have been much more life threatening. Fortunately for us, plasticity through culture steps in to complement human biological plasticity.

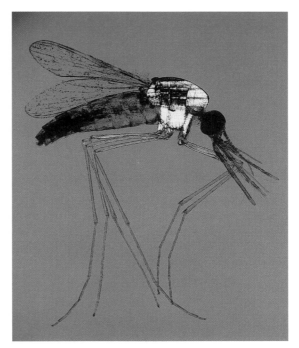

■ Beware the Anopheles *mosquito*, vector of malaria. An adult female is shown here.

those of getting four of one color and two of the other. Step 2 is to fill a new bag with 12 marbles on the basis of the ratio of marbles you drew in step 1. Assume that you drew four reds and two blues: The new bag will have eight red marbles and four blue ones. Step 3 is to draw six marbles from the new bag. Your chances of drawing blues in step 3 are lower than they were in step 1, and the probability of drawing all reds increases. If you do draw all reds, the next bag (step 4) will have only red marbles.

This game is analogous to random genetic drift operating over the generations. The blue marbles were lost purely by chance. Alleles, too, can be lost by chance rather than because of any disadvantage they confer. Lost alleles can reappear in a gene pool only through mutation.

Although genetic drift can operate in any population, large or small, *fixation* due to drift is more rapid in small populations. Fixation refers to the total replacement of blue marbles by red marbles—or, to use a human example, of blue eyes by brown eyes. The history of the human line is characterized by a series of small populations, migrations, and fixation due to genetic drift. One cannot understand human origins, human genetic variation, and a host of other important anthropological topics without recognizing the importance of genetic drift.

Gene Flow

A third mechanism of genetic evolution is **gene flow,** the exchange of genetic material between populations of the same species. Gene flow, like

changes, favored phenotypes and gene frequencies can change. In malaria-free environments, normal-hemoglobin homozygotes reproduce more effectively than heterozygotes do. With no malaria, the frequency of Hb^S declines because Hb^S homozygotes can't compete in survival and reproduction with the other types. This has happened in areas of West Africa where malaria has been reduced through drainage programs and insecticides. Selection against Hb^S also has occurred in the United States among Americans descended from West Africans (Diamond 1997).

Random Genetic Drift

A second mechanism of genetic evolution is **random genetic drift.** This is a change in allele frequency that results not from natural selection but from chance. To understand why, compare the sorting of alleles to a game involving a bag of 12 marbles, 6 red and 6 blue. In step 1, you draw six marbles from the bag. Statistically, your chances of drawing three reds and three blues are less than

Biocultural Case Study

For more on the peopling of the Pacific and on how anthropology's subfields unite to solve a particular problem, see the "Bringing It All Together" essay that immediately follows Chapter 11.

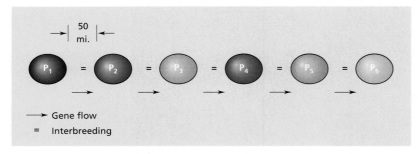

FIGURE 4.8   Gene Flow between Local Populations.

P₁–P₆ are six local populations of the same species. Each interbreeds (=) only with its neighbor(s). Although members of P₆ never interbreed with P₁, P₆ and P₁ are linked through gene flow. Genetic material that originates in P₁ eventually will reach P₆, and vice versa, as it is passed from one neighboring population to the next. Because they share genetic material in this way, P₁–P₆ remain members of the same species. In many species, local populations distributed throughout a larger territory than the 250 miles depicted here are linked through gene flow.

mutation, works in conjunction with natural selection by providing variety on which selection can work. Gene flow may consist of direct interbreeding between formerly separated populations of the same species (e.g., Europeans, Africans, and Native Americans in the United States), or it may be indirect.

Consider the following hypothetical case (Figure 4.8). In a certain part of the world live six local populations of a certain species. P₁ is the westernmost of these populations. P₂, which interbreeds with P₁, is located 50 miles to the east. P₂ also interbreeds with P₃, located 50 miles east of P₂. Assume that each population interbreeds with, and only with, the adjacent populations. P₆ is located 250 miles from P₁ and does not directly interbreed with P₁, but it is tied to P₁ through the chain of interbreeding that ultimately links all six populations.

Assume further that some allele exists in P₁ that isn't particularly advantageous in its environment. Because of gene flow, this allele may be passed on to P₂, by it to P₃, and so on, until it eventually reaches P₆. In P₆ or along the way, the allele may encounter an environment in which it does have a selective advantage. If this happens, it may serve, like a new mutation, as raw material on which natural selection can operate.

Alleles are spread through gene flow even when selection is not operating on the allele. In the long run, natural selection works on the variety within a population, whatever its source. Selection and gene flow have worked together to spread the Hbˢ allele in Central Africa. Frequencies of Hbˢ in Africa reflect not only the intensity of malaria but also the length of time gene flow has been going on (Livingstone 1969).

Gene flow is important in the study of the origin of species. A **species** is a group of related organisms whose members can interbreed to produce offspring that can live and reproduce. A species has to be able to reproduce itself through time. We know that horses and donkeys belong to different species because their offspring cannot meet the test of long-term survival. A horse and a donkey may breed to produce a mule, but mules are sterile. So are the offspring of lions with tigers. Gene flow tends to prevent **speciation**—the formation of new species—unless subgroups of the same species are separated for a sufficient length of time.

When gene flow is interrupted, and isolated subgroups are maintained, new species may arise. Imagine that an environmental barrier arises between P₃ and P₄, so that they no longer interbreed. If over time, as a result of isolation, P₁, P₂, and P₃ become incapable of interbreeding with the other three populations, speciation will have occurred.

THE MODERN SYNTHESIS

The currently accepted view of evolution is known as the "modern synthesis." This refers to the synthesis or combination of Darwin's theory of evolution by natural selection and Mendel's genetic discoveries. The modern synthesis also explains what Mendel could not—the inheritance of multifactorial or complex traits (e.g., height; see the next chapter). According to the modern synthesis, speciation (the formation of new species) occurs when they become reproductively isolated from one another. How does genetic evolution lead, or not, to new species?

Microevolution refers to genetic changes in a population or species over a few, several, or many generations, but without speciation. **Macroevolution** refers to larger-scale or more significant genetic changes in a population or species, usually over a longer time period, which result in speciation. Indeed, macroevolution is defined as speciation, the divergence of one ancestral species into two (or more) descendant species. Most biologists assume that species develop gradually as successive mutations accumulate in isolated populations, so that eventually the populations are too different to interbreed. But the time and the number of generations required for microevolution to become macroevolution are highly variable.

Modern-day creationists sometimes use a misunderstanding of the contrast between microevolution and macroevolution to comment on evolution. They may say they accept microevolution, such as a change in a species' size or coloring, or as demonstrated in the laboratory or through studies of such traits as the sickle-cell allele. Macroevolution, they claim, by contrast, can't be demonstrated, only inferred from the fossil record.

Tongue rolling—a genetic trait, at least partially. Some members of this family seem to be better at it than others are.

Note, however, that no degree of phenotypical difference is implied by the term *macroevolution*. In the "News Brief" at the beginning of this chapter, we saw that a simple chromosomal rearrangement can be sufficient to separate two closely related species whose ranges overlap. They belong to different species not because they are isolated from each other in space, but because they cannot hybridize. Although no phenotypic difference is visible between these reproductively isolated species, this is a case of macroevolution rather than microevolution.

To exaggerate the contrast between microevolution and macroevolution would imply, incorrectly, that there are two fundamentally distinct evolutionary processes. Scientists see no such contrast: Microevolution and macroevolution happen in the same way and for the same reasons, reflecting the mechanisms of genetic evolution discussed in this chapter. The modern synthesis recognizes that microevolutionary processes are sufficient to explain macroevolution.

Punctuated Equilibrium

Charles Darwin saw species as arising from others over time, in a gradual and orderly fashion. Microevolutionary changes would accumulate over the generations to eventually produce macroevolution. In other words, minor alterations in the gene pool, accumulating generation after generation, would add up to major changes, including speciation, after thousands of years.

The **punctuated equilibrium** model of evolution (see Eldredge 1985; Gould 2002) points to the fact that long periods of stasis (stability), during which species change little, may be interrupted (punctuated) by evolutionary leaps. One reason for such apparent jumps (which are revealed by the fossil record) may be extinction of one species followed by invasion by a closely related species. For example, a sea species may die out when a shallow body of water dries up, while a closely related species survives in deeper waters. Later, when the sea reinvades the first locale, the protected species will extend its range to the first area. Another possibility is that when barriers are removed, a group may replace, rather than succeed, a related one because it has a trait that makes it adaptively fitter in the environment they now share.

When there is a sudden environmental change, rather than such extinction and replacement, another possibility is for the pace of evolution to speed up. Some highly significant mutation(s) or combination of genetic changes may permit the survival of a radically altered species in a new and very different environmental niche. Many scientists believe that the evolution of our hominid ancestors was marked by one or more such evolutionary leaps.

Although species can survive radical environmental shifts, a more common fate is extinction. The earth has witnessed several mass extinctions—worldwide catastrophes affecting multiple species. The biggest one divided the era of "ancient life" (the Paleozoic) from the era of "middle life" (the Mesozoic). This mass extinction occurred 245 million years ago, when 4.5 million of the earth's estimated 5 million species (mostly invertebrates) were wiped out. The second biggest extinction, around 65 million years ago, destroyed the dinosaurs. One explanation for the extinction of the dinosaurs is that a massive, long-lasting cloud of gas and dust arose from the impact of a giant meteorite at the end of the Mesozoic. The cloud blocked solar radiation and therefore photosynthesis, ultimately destroying most plants and the chain of animals that fed on them.

From the fossil record, including the hominid fossil record to be discussed in Chapters 8 and 9, we know there are periods of more intense evolutionary change. The news story at the beginning of this chapter describes variable mutation rates among species. At the end of the Mesozoic, the extinction of the dinosaurs was accompanied by the rapid spread and speciation of mammals and birds. Speciation responds to many factors, including the rate of environmental change, the speed with which geographic barriers rise or fall, the degree of competition with other species, and the effectiveness of the group's adaptive response. (See Appendix 1 for evolutionary theories applied to cultural change.)

SUMMARY

1. In the 18th century, Carolus Linnaeus developed biological taxonomy. He viewed differences and similarities among organisms as part of God's orderly plan rather than as evidence for evolution. Charles Darwin and Alfred Russel Wallace proposed that natural selection could explain the origin of species, biological diversity, and similarities among related life forms. Natural selection requires variety in the population undergoing selection.

2. Through breeding experiments with peas in 1856, Gregor Mendel discovered that genetic traits pass on as units. These are now known to be chromosomes, which occur in homologous pairs. Alleles, some dominant, some recessive, are the chemically different forms that occur at a given genetic locus. Mendel also formulated the law of independent assortment. Each of the seven traits he studied in peas was inherited independently of all the others. Independent assortment of chromosomes and their recombination provide some of the variety needed for natural selection. But the major source of such variety is mutation, an alteration in the DNA molecules of which genes are made.

3. Biochemical, or molecular, genetics studies structure, function, and changes in genetic material—DNA. Genetic changes that provide variety within a population include base substitution mutations, chromosomal rearrangements, and genetic recombination. Population genetics studies gene frequencies in stable and changing populations. Natural selection is the most important mechanism of evolutionary change. Others include random genetic drift and gene flow. Natural selection works with traits already present in the population. If variety is insufficient to permit adaptation to environmental change, extinction is likely. New types don't appear just because they are needed.

4. One well-documented case of natural selection in contemporary human populations is that of the sickle-cell allele. In homozygous form, the sickle-cell allele, Hb^S, produces an abnormal hemoglobin. This clogs the small blood vessels, impairing the blood's capacity to store oxygen. The result is sickle-cell anemia, which is usually fatal. The distribution of Hb^S has been linked to that of malaria. Homozygotes for normal hemoglobin are susceptible to malaria and die in great numbers. Homozygotes for the sickle-cell allele die from anemia. Heterozygotes get only mild anemia and are resistant to malaria. In a malarial environment, the heterozygote has the advantage. This explains why an apparently maladaptive allele is preserved. The preservation of Hb^A and Hb^S alleles within a breeding population is an example of a balanced polymorphism, in which the heterozygote has greater fitness than does either homozygote.

5. Other mechanisms of genetic evolution complement natural selection. Random genetic drift operates most obviously in small populations, where pure chance can easily change allele frequencies. Gene flow and interbreeding keep subgroups of the same species genetically connected and thus impede speciation.

6. The modern synthetic theory of evolution (the modern synthesis) blends the Darwin and Wallace theory of evolution through natural selection with Mendel's discovery of the gene. Microevolution and macroevolution are two ends (short-term and long-term) of a continuum of evolutionary change in which gradually changing allele frequencies in a population eventually can lead to the formation of new species. Punctuated equilibrium theory states that long periods of stasis (stability), during which species change little, are interrupted (punctuated) by evolutionary leaps.

adaptive   Favored by natural selection in a particular environment.

allele   A biochemical variant of a particular gene.

balanced polymorphism   Two or more forms, such as alleles of the same gene, that maintain a constant frequency in a population from generation to generation.

biochemical genetics   Field that studies structure, function, and changes in genetic material—aka molecular genetics.

catastrophism   View that extinct species were destroyed by fires, floods, and other catastrophes. After each destructive event, God created again, leading to contemporary species.

chromosomes   Basic genetic units, occurring in matching (homologous) pairs; lengths of DNA made up of multiple genes.

creationism   Explanation for the origin of species given in Genesis: God created the species during the original six days of Creation.

crossing over   During meiosis, the process by which homologous chromosomes intertwine and exchange segments of their DNA.

dominant   Allele that masks another allele in a heterozygote.

evolution   Belief that species arose from others through a long and gradual process of transformation, or descent with modification.

gene   Area in a chromosome pair that determines, wholly or partially, a particular biological trait, such as whether one's blood type is A, B, or O.

gene flow   Exchange of genetic material between populations of the same species through direct or indirect interbreeding.

gene pool   All the alleles, genes, chromosomes, and genotypes within a breeding population—the "pool" of genetic material available.

genetic evolution   Change in gene frequency within a breeding population.

genotype   An organism's hereditary makeup.

heterozygous   Having dissimilar alleles of a given gene.

homozygous   Possessing identical alleles of a particular gene.

independent assortment   Mendel's law of; chromosomes are inherited independently of one another.

macroevolution   Large-scale changes in allele frequencies in a population, usually over a longer time period (than microevolution)—changes that culminate in the evolution of new species.

meiosis   Special process by which sex cells are produced; four cells are produced from one, each with half the genetic material of the original cell.

Mendelian genetics   Studies ways in which chromosomes transmit genes across the generations.

microevolution   Small-scale changes in allele frequencies over generations without speciation.

mitosis   Ordinary cell division; DNA molecules copy themselves, creating two identical cells out of one.

mutation   Change in the DNA molecules of which genes and chromosomes are built.

natural selection   The process by which the forms most fit to survive and reproduce in a given environment do so in greater numbers than others in the same population; more than survival of the fittest, natural selection is differential reproductive success.

phenotype   An organism's evident traits, its "manifest biology"—anatomy and physiology.

population genetics   Field that studies causes of genetic variation, maintenance, and change in breeding populations.

punctuated equilibrium   Evolutionary theory that long periods of stasis (stability), during which species change little, are interrupted (punctuated) by evolutionary leaps.

random genetic drift   Change in gene frequency that results not from natural selection but from chance; most evident in small populations.

recessive   Genetic trait masked by a dominant trait.

recombination   Following independent assortment of chromosomes, new arrangements of hereditary units produced through bisexual reproduction.

sexual selection   Based on differential success in mating, the process in which certain traits of one sex (e.g., color in male birds) are selected because of advantages they confer in winning mates.

speciation   Formation of new species; occurs when subgroups of the same species are separated for a sufficient length of time.

species   Population whose members can interbreed to produce offspring that can live and reproduce.

theory   A set of ideas formulated (by reasoning from known facts) to explain something. The main value of a theory is to promote new understanding. A theory suggests patterns, connections, and relationships that may be confirmed by new research.

uniformitarianism   Belief that explanations for past events should be sought in ordinary forces that continue to work today.

CRITICAL THINKING QUESTIONS

1. If you are (or are pretending you are) a creationist, what do you see as the most convincing evidence for evolution?

2. If you are (or are pretending you are) an evolutionist, what do you see as the least convincing evidence for evolution?

3. Imagine that some of the seven traits that Mendel studied in pea plants were determined by genes on the same chromosome. How might his results have differed?

4. Is *Homo sapiens* more or less adaptable than other species? What makes us so adaptable? Can you think of some species that are more adaptable than we are?

5. Which of the mechanisms of genetic evolution acts to prevent speciation?

SUGGESTED ADDITIONAL READINGS

Cavalli-Sforza, L. L., P. Menozzi, and A. Piazza
  1994   *The History and Geography of Human Genes.* Princeton, NJ: Princeton University Press. Comprehensive look at the geographic spread of human genes.

Cavalli-Sforza, L. L., and W. F. Bodmer
  1999   *The Genetics of Human Populations.* Mineola, NY: Dover. Principles and cases in population genetics, applied to humans.

Conner, J. K., and D. L. Hartl
  2004   *A Primer of Population Genetics.* Sunderland, MA: Sinauer Associates. Short introduction to the field.

Eiseley, L.
  1961   *Darwin's Century.* Garden City, NY: Doubleday, Anchor Books. Discussion of Lyell, Darwin, Wallace, and other major contributors to natural selection and transformation.

Futuyma, D. J.
  1995   *Science on Trial,* updated ed. Sunderland, MA: Sinauer Associates. The case of evolution versus creationism—favoring the former.
  1998   *Evolutionary Biology.* Sunderland, MA: Sinauer Associates. Basic text.

Gillespie, J. H.
  2004   *Population Genetics: A Concise Guide,* 2nd ed. Baltimore: Johns Hopkins University Press. Good introduction to population genetics.

Gould, S. J.
  1999   *Rock of Ages: Science and Religion in the Fullness of Life.* New York: Ballantine Books. Evolution, science, and religion by the well-known naturalist and science writer.
  2002   *The Structure of Evolutionary Theory.* Cambridge, MA: Belknap Press of Harvard University Press. Explores the punctuated equilibrium model and other aspects of evolutionary theory.

Hartl, D. L., and E. W. Jones
  2006   *Essential Genetics,* 4th ed. Boston: Jones and Bartlett. Basic introduction to genetics.

Lewontin, R.
  2000   *It Ain't Necessarily So: The Dream of the Human Genome and Other Illusions.* New York: New York Review of Books. Questions about nature, nurture, and contemporary genetic research.

Mayr, E.
  2001   *What Evolution Is.* New York: Basic Books. A master scholar sums it all up.

O'Rourke, D. H.
  2003   "Anthropological Genetics in the Genomic Era: A Look Back and Ahead." *American Anthropologist* 105(1):101–109. How the human genome project relates to anthropology.

Shermer, M.
  2002   *In Darwin's Shadow: The Life and Science of Alfred Russel Wallace.* New York: Oxford University Press. The other inventor of natural selection.

Weiner, J.
  1994   *The Beak of the Finch: A Story of Evolution in Our Time.* New York: Alfred A. Knopf. An excellent introduction to Darwin and to evolutionary theory.

Wilson, D. S.
  2002   *Darwin's Cathedral: Evolution, Religion, and the Nature of Society.* Chicago: University of Chicago Press. Religion, sociology, and evolution.

1. Creationism: Look at the CreationWise cartoon website, **http://members.aol.com/dwr51055/humor.htm**. This site uses cartoons to express the concerns creationists have about evolution.
   a. What is the creationist version of the origin of life? What evidence do creationists use to support their claims? According to these cartoons, what are some of the problems that creationists have with evolution?
   b. What would be the response to these questions from a scientist who studies evolution?

2. Human Blood Groups: Visit the following website of SCARF (Serum, Cells and Rare Fluid Exchange): **http://jove.prohosting.com/~scarfex/blood/groups.html**. The SCARF Exchange is an international group of scientists, physicians, and other individuals interested in human blood groups and transfusion medicine.

   a. How many human blood group systems are listed? Click on ISBT number 004-RH. From what animal is the name RH derived? Do humans share the RH factor with that animal? What are the genetics of the RH factor? How can the RH factor affect fetal development? Where is the RH factor found, just in the blood or in other bodily fluids as well?
   b. Click on ISBT number 001-ABO. Why is blood group testing important in giving and receiving blood? What are the genetics of the ABO system? On what chromosome are the ABO genes located? Where are the ABO antigens found, just in the blood or in other bodily fluids as well?

See Chapter 4 at your McGraw-Hill Online Learning Center for additional review and interactive exercises.

5

Human Variation
and Adaptation

RACE: A DISCREDITED CONCEPT IN BIOLOGY

Contemporary North America is strikingly rich in human biological diversity. The photos here (in this chapter and this book) illustrate just a fraction of the world's biological variation. Additional illustration comes from your own experience. Look around you in your classroom or at the mall or multiplex. Inevitably you'll see people whose ancestors lived in many lands. The first (Native) Americans had to cross a land bridge that once linked Siberia to North America. For later immigrants, perhaps including your own parents or grandparents, the voyage may have been across the sea, or overland from nations to the south. They came for many reasons; some came voluntarily, while others were brought in chains. The scale of migration in today's world is so vast that millions of people routinely cross national borders or live far from the homelands of their grandparents. Now meeting every day are diverse human beings whose biological features reflect adaptation to a wide range of environments other than the ones they now inhabit. Physical contrasts, such as the different ways of adapting to high altitudes described in the "News Brief," are evident to anyone. Anthropology's job is to explain them.

Historically, scientists have approached the study of human biological diversity in two main ways: (1) racial classification (now largely

The photos in this chapter illustrate only a small part of the range of human biological diversity. Shown here is a Bai minority woman, from Shapin, in China's Yunnan province.

 STUDENT CD-ROM LIVING ANTHROPOLOGY

Origins of the Modern Concepts of Race
Track 5

This clip features Dr. Jonathan Marks, a prominent biological anthropologist, discussing the origin and development of the problematic concept of race. As Marks points out, racial classification rests on the universal human tendency to classify. According to the clip, what historical political development also contributed to the race concept? Besides arbitrary physical characteristics, what are other ways of classifying human beings? How many human races did Linnaeus recognize? What, according to the clip, is the proper number of races into which humans should be categorized?

abandoned), versus (2) the current explanatory approach, which focuses on understanding specific differences. First we'll consider problems with **racial classification** (the attempt to assign humans to discrete categories [purportedly] based on common ancestry). Then we'll offer some explanations for specific aspects of human biological diversity. *Biological differences are real, important, and apparent to us all.* Modern scientists find it most productive to seek *explanations* for this diversity, rather than trying to pigeonhole people into categories called races. Certainly, human groups do vary biologically—for example, in their genetic attributes. But often we observe gradual, rather than abrupt, shifts in gene frequencies between neighboring groups. Such gradual genetic shifts are called **clines,** and they are incompatible with discrete and separate races.

What is race anyway? In theory, a biological race would be a geographically isolated subdivision of a species. Such a *subspecies* would be capable of interbreeding with other subspecies of the same species, but it would not actually do so because of its geographic isolation. Some biologists also use "race" to refer to "breeds," as of dogs or roses. Thus, a pit bull and a chihuahua would be different races of dogs. Such domesticated "races" have been bred by humans for generations. Humanity (*Homo sapiens*) lacks such races because human populations have not been isolated enough from one another to develop into such discrete groups. Nor have humans experienced controlled breeding like that which has created the various kinds of dogs and roses.

A race is supposed to reflect shared *genetic* material (inherited from a common ancestor), but early scholars instead used *phenotypical* traits (usually skin color) for racial classification. *Phenotype* refers to an organism's evident traits, its "manifest biology"—anatomy and physiology. Humans display hundreds of evident (detectable) physical traits. They range from skin color, hair form, eye color, and facial features (which are visible) to blood groups, color blindness, and enzyme production (which become evident through testing).

Racial classifications based on phenotype raise the problem of deciding which trait(s) should be primary. Should races be defined by height, weight, body shape, facial features, teeth, skull form, or skin color? Like their fellow citizens, early European and American scientists gave priority to

OVERVIEW

Scientists have approached the study of human biological diversity in two main ways: racial classification, an approach that has been rejected, and the current explanatory approach. It isn't possible to define human races biologically. Because of the many problems involved in placing human beings within discrete racial categories, biologists now focus on specific biological traits and conditions, and attempt to explain them. Biological similarities between groups may reflect—rather than common ancestry—similar but independent adaptations to similar natural selective forces.

Links have been established between genetically determined traits, such as hemoglobins in the blood, and selective forces, such as malaria. Selection through differential resistance to disease has influenced the distribution of human blood groups. Natural selective forces also have influenced the distribution of human skin color; facial features; and body size, form, and shape.

Phenotypical adaptation refers to adaptive changes that occur during the individual's lifetime, reflecting the environment the organism encounters as it grows. Biological similarities between geographically distant populations may be due to similar but independent genetic changes, rather than to common ancestry, or they may reflect similar physiological responses to common stresses during growth.

Three Adaptations to Thin Air

NATIONAL GEOGRAPHIC NEWS BRIEF

by Hillary Mayell
February 25, 2004

We've seen, especially in the last chapter, that humans have access to varied ways—biological and cultural—of adapting to environmental stresses, such as disease, heat, cold, humidity, sunlight, and altitude, as described in this news story. In this chapter and the last one, we see how humans have adapted and evolved in the short term. In Chapters 7 through 9, which deal with primate and human evolution, we shall see how humans adapt over much longer time periods, such that speciation occurs. This contrast between short-term and long-term adaptation and evolution illustrates the discussion of microevolution and macroevolution at the end of the last chapter.

Not only do humans evolve and adapt genetically over the generations, they also have the ability to use culture (e.g., tools) to adapt. Remember, too, the discussion in the last chapter of human biological plasticity: our ability to respond adaptively as we grow and develop biologically from childhood to adulthood. Pay attention in this news story to the dramatically different ways in which three populations adapt to high altitudes. The biological diversity we observe among contemporary and prehis-

toric humans has many causes. This chapter examines those causes, while rejecting attempts to pigeonhole humans into discrete biological categories called races.

Prehistoric and contemporary human populations living at altitudes of at least 8,000 feet (2,500 meters) above sea level may provide unique insights into human evolution, reports an interdisciplinary group of scientists.

Indigenous highlanders living in the Andean Altiplano in South America, in the Tibetan Plateau in Asia, and at the highest elevations of the Ethiopian Highlands in east Africa have evolved three distinctly different biological adaptations for surviving in the oxygen-thin air found at high altitude.

"To have examples of three geographically dispersed populations adapting in different ways to the same stress is very unusual," said Cynthia Beall, a physical anthropologist at Case Western Reserve University in Cleveland, Ohio. "From an evolutionary standpoint the question becomes, Why do these differences exist? . . ."

"High-altitude populations offer a unique natural lab that allows us to follow [many] lines

of evidence—archaeological, biological, climatological—to answer intriguing questions about social, cultural, and biological adaptations," said Mark Aldenderfer, an archaeologist at the University of California, Santa Barbara . . .

The Andean and Tibetan plateaus rise some 13,000 feet (4 kilometers) above sea level. As prehistoric hunter-gatherers moved into these environments, they . . . likely suffered acute hypoxia, a condition created by a diminished supply of oxygen to body tissues. At high altitudes the air is much thinner than at sea level. As a result, a person inhales fewer oxygen molecules with each breath. Symptoms of hypoxia, sometimes known as mountain sickness, include headaches, vomiting, sleeplessness, impaired thinking, and an inability to sustain long periods of physical activity. At elevations above 25,000 feet (7,600 meters), hypoxia can kill.

The Andeans adapted to the thin air by developing an ability to carry more oxygen in each red blood cell. That is: They breathe at the same rate as people who live at sea level, but the Andeans have the ability to deliver oxygen throughout their bodies more effectively than people at sea level do.

"Andeans counter having less oxygen in every breath by having higher hemoglobin concentrations in their blood," Beall said. Hemoglobin is the protein in red blood cells that ferries oxygen through the blood system. Having more hemoglobin to

High-altitude adaptation: People of the Himalayas, such as this Sherpa man in Solu Khumbu, Nepal, increase their oxygen intake by taking more breaths per minute than do people who live at sea level. Also, their lungs synthesize large amounts of nitric oxide from the air. Nitric oxide expands their blood vessels, enabling them to offset low oxygen content in their blood with increased blood flow.

carry oxygen through the blood system than people at sea level counterbalances the effects of hypoxia.

Tibetans compensate for low oxygen content much differently. They increase their oxygen intake by taking more breaths per minute than people who live at sea level.

"Andeans go the hematological route, Tibetans the respiratory route," Beall said.

In addition, Tibetans may have a second biological adaptation, which expands their blood vessels, allowing them to deliver oxygen throughout their bodies more effectively than sea-level people do.

Tibetans' lungs synthesize larger amounts of a gas called nitric oxide from the air they breathe. "One effect of nitric oxide is to increase the diameter of blood vessels, which suggests that Tibetans may offset low oxygen content in their blood with increased blood flow," Beall said.

A pilot study Beall conducted of Ethiopian highlanders living at 11,580 feet (3,530 meters) suggests that—unlike the Tibetans—they don't breathe more rapidly than people at sea level and aren't able to more effectively synthesize nitric oxide. Nor do the Ethiopians have higher hemoglobin counts than sea-level people, as the Andeans do.

Yet despite living at elevations with low oxygen content, "the Ethiopian highlanders were hardly hypoxic at all," Beall said. "I was genuinely surprised."

So what adaptation have the Ethiopian highlanders' bodies evolved to survive at high altitude? "Right now we have no clue how they do it," Beall said . . .

Knowing how long the populations have been living at the top of the world is crucial to answering the evolutionary question of whether these adaptations are the result of differences in the founding populations, random genetic mutations, or the passage of time.

Archaeologists, paleontologists, and climatologists are pooling their knowledge to pinpoint when some of these early migrations to the high plateaus occurred.

Aldenderfer . . . says cultural adaptations would have to occur first.

"The ability to survive in such harsh environments required control of fire, an expanded tool kit that included bone needles to make complicated clothing that protected the body in a significant way, and the cultural flexibility to change subsistence practices," he said.

Climatologists' changing understanding of the nature of the last ice age is contributing to archaeological efforts.

Ice-core and other evidence show that, rather than being a monolithic period lasting 100,000 years with frigid temperatures and glacial landscapes, the Ice Age included long periods of relatively mild weather.

"Through most of the 20th century it was thought that the Tibetan Plateau was covered by a monstrous ice sheet during the last glacial maximum, about 21,000 years ago," Aldenderfer said. "People couldn't live on an ice sheet. So archaeologists wouldn't even bother to look for sites from that time period."

[Now] knowing the Tibetan Plateau more closely resembled Arctic tundra has led to the discovery of new sites. Archaeological evidence suggests hunter-gatherers occupied the Tibetan Plateau some 25,000 to 20,000 years ago. People began moving into the Andean Altiplano around 11,500 to 11,000 years ago.

What motivated prehistoric people to move into the harsh and challenging conditions presented by high altitude?

"The highlands offered an attractive option with a landscape that was open and pristine," Aldenderfer said. "People probably started out moving up and down for short terms, and then gradually settled at the higher elevations."

Changing environmental conditions also created "new opportunities and new constraints," he said.

In South America, for example, the maritime environment began transforming as temperatures warmed, glaciers retreated, and sea levels rose. Large mammals such as mammoths and mastodons gradually went extinct, as did other herbivores. Warmer temperatures allowed plants and animals to move to higher elevations, creating resource-rich patches of habitat in highland areas . . .

Similar processes likely occurred in Tibet. Prehistoric people occupied the landscape during the interglacial process, when conditions were relatively benign and hunting was plentiful, Aldenderfer said.

"Suddenly [thereafter] it gets really cold. Biomass declined precipitously. It becomes very arid because of wind-flow patterns. The landscape becomes one of very patchy vegetation, rocky. And the huge herds of gazelle, antelope, and sheep wax and wane," Aldenderfer said. "What happens? . . . Finding biological differences suggests they toughed it out and adapted."

SOURCE: Hillary Mayell, "Three High-Altitude Peoples, Three Adaptations to Thin Air," *National Geographic News*, February 25, 2004. http://news.nationalgeographic.com/news/2004/02/0224_040225_evolution.html.

skin color. Many school books and encyclopedias still proclaim the existence of three great races: the white, the black, and the yellow. This overly simplistic classification was compatible with the political use of race during the colonial period of the late 19th and early 20th centuries. Such a tripartite scheme kept white Europeans neatly separate from their African, Asian, and Native American subjects. (See "Interesting Issues" for the American Anthropological Association's statement on race.)

Colonial empires began to break up, and scientists began to question established racial categories, after World War II.

Races Are Not Biologically Distinct

History and politics aside, one obvious problem with "color-based" racial labels is that the terms don't accurately describe skin color. "White" people are more pink, beige, or tan than white. "Black" people are various shades of brown, and "yellow" people are tan or beige. But these terms have also been dignified by more scientific-*sounding* synonyms: Caucasoid, Negroid, and Mongoloid.

Another problem with the tripartite scheme is that many populations don't fit neatly into any one of the three "great races." For example, where would one put the Polynesians? *Polynesia* is a triangle of South Pacific islands formed by Hawaii to the north, Easter Island to the east, and New Zealand to the southwest. Does the "bronze" skin color of Polynesians connect them to the Caucasoids or to the Mongoloids? Some scientists, recognizing this problem, enlarged the original tripartite scheme to include the Polynesian "race." Native Americans presented a similar problem. Were they red or yellow? Some scientists added a fifth race—the "red," or Amerindian—to the major racial groups.

Many people in southern India have dark skins, but scientists have been reluctant to classify them with "black" Africans because of their Caucasoid facial features and hair form. Some, therefore, have created a separate race for these people. What about the Australian aborigines, hunters and gatherers native to what has been, throughout human history, the most isolated continent? By skin color, one might place some Native Australians in the same race as tropical Africans. However, similarities to Europeans in hair color (light or reddish) and facial features have led some scientists to classify them as Caucasoids. But there is no evidence that Australians are closer genetically or historically to either of these groups than they are to Asians. Recognizing this problem, scientists often regard Native Australians as a separate race.

Finally, consider the San ("Bushmen") of the Kalahari Desert in southern Africa. Scientists have perceived their skin color as varying from brown to yellow. Some who regard San skin as "yellow" have placed them in the same category as Asians. In theory, people of the same race share more recent common ancestry with each other than they do with any others. But there is no evidence for recent common ancestry between San and Asians. Somewhat more reasonably, some scholars assign the San to the Capoid race (from the Cape of Good Hope), which is seen as being different from other groups inhabiting tropical Africa.

A Native American: a Chiquitanos Indian woman from Bolivia.

A young man from the Marquesas Islands in Polynesia.

A Native Australian.

Biocultural Case Study

For information on physical diversity among Pacific Islanders, see the "Bringing It All Together" essay that immediately follows Chapter 11.

American Anthropological Association (AAA) Statement on "Race"

As a result of public confusion about the meaning of "race," claims as to major biological differences among "races" continue to be advanced. Stemming from past AAA actions designed to address public misconceptions on race and intelligence, the need was apparent for a clear AAA statement on the biology and politics of race that would be educational and informational.

The following statement was adopted by the Executive Board of the American Anthropological Association in May 1998, based on a draft prepared by a committee of representative anthropologists. The Association believes that this statement represents the thinking and scholarly positions of most anthropologists.

In the United States both scholars and the general public have been conditioned to viewing human races as natural and separate divisions within the human species based on visible physical differences. With the vast expansion of scientific knowledge in this century, however, it has become clear that human populations are not unambiguous, clearly demarcated, biologically distinct groups. Evidence from the analysis of genetics (e.g., DNA) indicates that most physical variation, about 94%, lies within so-called racial groups. Conventional geographic "racial" groupings differ from one another only in about 6% of their genes. This means that there is greater variation within "racial" groups than between them. In neighboring populations there is much overlapping of genes and their phenotypic (physical) expressions. Throughout history whenever different groups have come into contact, they have interbred. The continued sharing of genetic materials has maintained all of humankind as a single species.

Physical variations in any given trait tend to occur gradually rather than abruptly over geographic areas. And because physical traits are inherited independently of one another, knowing the range of one trait does not predict the presence of others. For example, skin color varies largely from light in the temperate areas in the north to dark in the tropical areas in the south; its intensity is not related to nose shape or hair texture. Dark skin may be associated with frizzy or kinky hair or curly or wavy or straight hair, all of which are found among different indigenous peoples in tropical regions. These facts render any attempt to establish lines of division among biological populations both arbitrary and subjective.

Historical research has shown that the idea of "race" has always carried more meanings than mere physical differences; indeed, physical variations in the human species have no meaning except the social ones that humans put on them. Today scholars in many fields argue that "race" as it is understood in the United States of America was a social mechanism invented during the 18th century to refer to those populations brought together in colonial America: the English and other European settlers, the conquered Indian peoples, and those peoples of Africa brought in to provide slave labor.

From its inception, this modern concept of "race" was modeled after an ancient theorem of the Great Chain of Being, which posited natural categories on a hierarchy established by God or nature. Thus "race" was a mode of classification linked specifically to peoples in the colonial situation. It subsumed a growing ideology of inequality devised to rationalize European attitudes and treatment of the conquered and enslaved peoples. Proponents of slavery in particular during the 19th century used "race" to justify the retention of slavery. The ideology magnified the differences among Europeans, Africans, and Indians, established a rigid hierarchy of socially exclusive categories, underscored and bolstered unequal rank and status differences, and provided the rationalization that the inequality was natural or God-given. The different physical traits of African-Americans and Indians became markers or symbols of their status differences.

Similar problems arise when any single trait is used as a basis for racial classification. An attempt to use facial features, height, weight, or any other phenotypical trait is fraught with difficulties. For example, consider the *Nilotes*, natives of the upper Nile region of Uganda and Sudan. Nilotes tend to be tall and to have long, narrow noses. Certain Scandinavians are also tall, with similar noses. Given the distance between their homelands, to classify them as members of the same race makes little sense. There is no reason to assume that Nilotes and Scandinavians are more closely related to each other than either is to shorter and nearer populations with different kinds of noses.

Would it be better to base racial classifications on a combination of physical traits? This would avoid some of the problems mentioned above, but others would arise. First, skin color, stature, skull form, and facial features (nose form, eye shape, lip thickness) don't go together as a unit. For example, people with dark skin may be tall or short and have hair ranging from straight to very

As they were constructing US society, leaders among European-Americans fabricated the cultural/behavioral characteristics associated with each "race," linking superior traits with Europeans and negative and inferior ones to blacks and Indians. Numerous arbitrary and fictitious beliefs about the different peoples were institutionalized and deeply embedded in American thought . . .

Ultimately "race" as an ideology about human differences was subsequently spread to other areas of the world. It became a strategy for dividing, ranking, and controlling colonized people used by colonial powers everywhere. But it was not limited to the colonial situation. In the latter part of the 19th century it was employed by Europeans to rank one another and to justify social, economic, and political inequalities among their peoples. During World War II, the Nazis under Adolf Hitler enjoined the expanded ideology of "race" and "racial" differences and took them to a logical end: the extermination of 11 million people of "inferior races" (e.g., Jews, Gypsies, Africans, homosexuals, and so forth) and other unspeakable brutalities of the Holocaust.

"Race" thus evolved as a world view, a body of prejudgments that distorts our ideas about human differences and group behavior. Racial beliefs constitute myths about the diversity in the human species and about the abilities and behavior of people homogenized into "racial" categories. The myths fused behavior and physical features together in the public mind, impeding our com-

In Saint Petersburg, Russia, a police officer checks the identities of a group of Roma (Gypsies). Roma have faced discrimination in many nations. During World War II, the Nazis led by Adolf Hitler murdered eleven million Jews, Gypsies, Africans, homosexuals, and others.

prehension of both biological variations and cultural behavior, implying that both are genetically determined. Racial myths bear no relationship to the reality of human capabilities or behavior . . .

We now understand that human cultural behavior is learned, conditioned into infants beginning at birth, and always subject to modification. No human is born with a built-in culture or language. Our temperaments, dispositions, and personalities, regardless of genetic propensities, are developed within sets of meanings and values that we call "culture" . . .

It is a basic tenet of anthropological knowledge that all normal human beings have the capacity to learn any cultural behavior. The American experience with immigrants from hundreds of different language and cultural backgrounds who have acquired some version of American culture traits and behavior is the clearest evidence of this fact. Moreover, people of all physical variations have learned different cultural behaviors and continue to do so as modern transportation moves millions of immigrants around the world.

How people have been accepted and treated within the context of a given society or culture has a direct impact on how they perform in that society. The "racial" world view was invented to assign some groups to perpetual low status, while others were permitted access to privilege, power, and wealth. The tragedy in the United States has been that the policies and practices stemming from this world view succeeded all too well in constructing unequal populations among Europeans, Native Americans, and peoples of African descent. Given what we know about the capacity of normal humans to achieve and function within any culture, we conclude that present-day inequalities between so-called "racial" groups are not consequences of their biological inheritance but products of historical and contemporary social, economic, educational, and political circumstances.

NOTE: For further information on human biological variations, see the statement prepared and issued by the American Association of Physical Anthropologists, 1996 (American Journal of Physical Anthropology 101, pp. 569–70).

curly. Dark-haired populations may have light or dark skin, along with various skull forms, facial features, and body sizes and shapes. The number of combinations is very large, and the amount that heredity (versus environment) contributes to such phenotypical traits is often unclear.

There is a final objection to racial classification based on phenotype. The phenotypical characteristics on which races are based supposedly reflect genetic material that is shared and that has stayed the same for long time periods. But phenotypical similarities and differences don't necessarily have a genetic basis. Because of changes in the environment that affect individuals during growth and development, the range of phenotypes characteristic of a population may change without any genetic change. There are several examples. In the early 20th century, the anthropologist Franz Boas (1940/1966) described changes in skull form (e.g., toward rounder heads) among the children of Europeans who had migrated to North America. The reason for this was not a change in genes, for

An Afghan woman.

See Map 7 in the insert, which plots the distribution of human skin color in relation to ultraviolet variation from the sun.

survive by producing more offspring. The role of natural selection in producing variation in skin color will illustrate the explanatory approach to human biological diversity. Comparable explanations have been provided for many other aspects of human biological variation, as we'll see later in this chapter.

Skin color is a complex biological trait. That means it is influenced by several genes. Just how many isn't known. **Melanin,** the primary determinant of human skin color, is a chemical substance manufactured in the epidermis, or outer skin layer. The melanin cells of darker-skinned people produce more and larger granules of melanin than do those of lighter-skinned people. By screening out ultraviolet radiation from the sun, melanin offers protection against a variety of maladies, including sunburn and skin cancer.

Prior to the 16th century, most of the world's very dark-skinned peoples lived in the **tropics,** a belt extending about 23 degrees north and south of the equator, between the Tropic of Cancer and the Tropic of Capricorn. The association between dark skin color and a tropical habitat existed throughout the Old World, where humans and their ancestors have lived for millions of years. The darkest populations of Africa evolved not in shady equatorial forests but in sunny open grassland, or savanna, country.

Outside the tropics, skin color tends to be lighter. Moving north in Africa, for example, there is a gradual transition from dark brown to medium brown. Average skin color continues to lighten as one moves through the Middle East, into southern Europe, through central Europe, and to the north. South of the tropics skin color is also lighter. In the Americas, by contrast, tropical populations do not have very dark skin. This is the case because the settlement of the New World, by light-skinned Asian ancestors of Native Americans, was relatively recent, probably dating back no more than 20,000 years.

How, aside from migrations, can we explain the geographic distribution of skin color? Natural selection provides an answer. In the tropics, there is intense ultraviolet radiation from the sun. Unprotected humans there face the threat of severe sunburn, which can increase susceptibility to disease. This confers a selective *dis*advantage (i.e., less success in surviving and reproducing) on lighter-skinned people in the tropics (unless they stay indoors or use cultural products, like umbrellas or lotions, to screen sunlight). Sunburn also impairs the body's ability to sweat. This is a second reason why light skin color, given tropical heat, can diminish the human ability to live and work in equatorial climates. A third disadvantage of having light skin color in the tropics is that exposure to ultraviolet radiation can cause skin cancer (Blum 1961).

the European immigrants tended to marry among themselves. Also, some of their children had been born in Europe and merely raised in the United States. Something in the environment, probably in the diet, was producing this change. We know now that changes in average height and weight produced by dietary differences in a few generations are common and may have nothing to do with race or genetics. (See Appendix 1 for more on Franz Boas.)

Explaining Skin Color

Traditional racial classification assumed that biological characteristics were determined by heredity and that they were stable (immutable) over long periods of time. We now know that a biological similarity doesn't necessarily indicate recent common ancestry. Dark skin color, for example, can be shared by tropical Africans and Native Australians for reasons other than common ancestry. It is not possible to *define races* biologically. Still, scientists have made much progress in *explaining* variation in human skin color, along with many other expressions of human biological diversity. We shift now from classification to *explanation,* in which natural selection plays a key role.

As recognized by Charles Darwin and Alfred Russel Wallace, *natural selection* is the process by which the forms most fit to survive and reproduce in a given environment do so. Over the years, the less fit organisms die out, and the favored types

A fourth factor affecting the geographic distribution of skin color is vitamin D production by the body. W. F. Loomis (1967) focused on the role of ultraviolet radiation in stimulating the manufacture of vitamin D by the human body. The unclothed human body can produce its own vitamin D when exposed to sufficient sunlight. But in a cloudy environment that is also so cold that people have to dress themselves much of the year (such as northern Europe, where very light skin color evolved), clothing interferes with the body's manufacture of vitamin D. The ensuing shortage of vitamin D diminishes the absorption of calcium in the intestines. A nutritional disease known as **rickets,** which softens and deforms the bones, may develop. In women, deformation of the pelvic bones from rickets can interfere with childbirth. During northern winters, light skin color maximizes the absorption of ultraviolet radiation and the manufacture of vitamin D by the few parts of the body that are exposed to direct sunlight. There has been selection against dark skin color in northern areas because melanin screens out ultraviolet radiation.

Considering vitamin D production, light skin is an advantage in the cloudy north, but a disadvantage in the sunny tropics. Loomis suggested that in the tropics, dark skin color protects the body against an *overproduction* of vitamin D by screening out ultraviolet radiation. Too much vitamin D can lead to a potentially fatal condition **(hypervitaminosis D),** in which calcium deposits build up in the body's soft tissues. The kidneys may fail. Gallstones, joint problems, and circulation problems are other symptoms of hypervitaminosis D.

This discussion of skin color shows that common ancestry, the presumed basis of race, is not the only reason for biological similarities. We see that natural selection has made a major contribution to our understanding of variation in skin color, as well as many other human biological differences and similarities.

HUMAN BIOLOGICAL ADAPTATION

This section considers several additional examples of human biological diversity that reflect adaptation to environmental stresses, such as disease, diet, and climate. There is abundant evidence for human genetic adaptation and thus for evolution (change in gene frequency) through selection working in specific environments. One example is the adaptive value of the Hb^S heterozygote and its spread in malarial environments, which was discussed in Chapter 4. Adaptation and evolution go on in specific environments.

Before the 16th century, almost all the very dark-skinned populations of the world lived in the tropics, as does this Samburu woman from Kenya.

Very light skin color, illustrated in this photo of a blond, blue-eyed North Sea German fisherman, maximizes absorption of ultraviolet radiation by those few parts of the body exposed to direct sunlight during northern winters. This helps prevent rickets.

There is no generally or ideally adaptive allele and no perfect phenotype. Nor can an allele be assumed to be maladaptive for all times and all places. We have seen that even Hb^S, which produces a lethal anemia, has a selective advantage in the heterozygous form in malarial environments.

Also, alleles that were once maladaptive may lose their disadvantage if the environment shifts. Color blindness (disadvantageous for hunters and forest dwellers) and a form of genetically determined diabetes are examples. Today's environment contains medical techniques that allow people with such conditions to live fairly normal lives. Formerly maladaptive alleles have thus become neutral with respect to selection. With thousands of human genes now known, new genetic traits are discovered almost every day. Such studies tend to focus on genetic abnormalities, because of their medical and treatment implications.

Skin Pigmentation in Papua New Guinea

BACKGROUND INFORMATION

STUDENT:
Heather Norton

SUPERVISING PROFESSOR:
Jonathan Friedlaender, Temple University; Andy Merriwether, University of Michigan; and Mark Shriver, Pennsylvania State University

SCHOOL:
Pennsylvania State University

YEAR IN SCHOOL/MAJOR:
Graduated in spring 2000/ Anthropology

FUTURE PLANS:
Field work in Melanesia (the Solomon Islands).

PROJECT TITLE:
Skin Pigmentation in Papua New Guinea.

What aspects of human biological variation are addressed in this study? Are they genotypic or phenotypic?

Following my senior year at Penn State, I spent five weeks in Papua New Guinea studying variation in skin pigmentation. I was part of a larger research effort led by Dr. Jonathan Friedlaender and Dr. Andy Merriwether. The goal was to examine variation in mitochondrial and Y-chromosome DNA sequences in an attempt to identify patterns of migration to the islands of Melanesia. Skin pigmentation is a phenotypic trait that shows extensive variation around the world.

Skin color is primarily determined by the pigment melanin, although others, such as hemoglobin, may also contribute. One way to measure skin pigmentation is to use reflectometry, the controlled illumination of an object and the precise measurement of the light that is reflected from it. The narrow-band spectrophotometer that I used estimates the concentration of hemoglobin and melanin by taking reflectance readings. The resulting measurements are known as the melanin index (M), and the erythema index (E). The more darkly pigmented an individual, the greater their M-index measurement. I took multiple

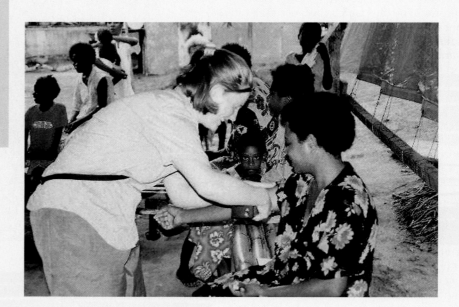

Genes and Disease

According to the *World Health Report,* published by the World Health Organization (WHO) in Geneva, Switzerland, tropical diseases affect more than 10 percent of the world's population. Malaria, the most widespread of these diseases, afflicts between 350 million and 500 million people annually (World Malaria Report 2005). Schistosomiasis (snail fever), a waterborne parasitic disease, affects more than 200 million. Some 120 million people have filariasis, which causes elephantiasis—lymphatic obstruction leading to the enlargement of body parts, par-

ticularly the legs and scrotum (check out the website of the World Health Organization at http://www.who.int/home/).

The malaria threat has been spreading. Brazil had 560,000 cases in 1988, versus 100,000 in 1977. Worldwide, the number of malaria cases rose from 270 million in 1990 to over 350 million today. Contributing to this rise is the increasing resistance of parasites to drugs used to treat malaria (World Malaria Report 2005). However, hundreds of millions of people are genetically resistant. Sickle-cell hemoglobin is the best known of the genetic antimalarials (Diamond 1997).

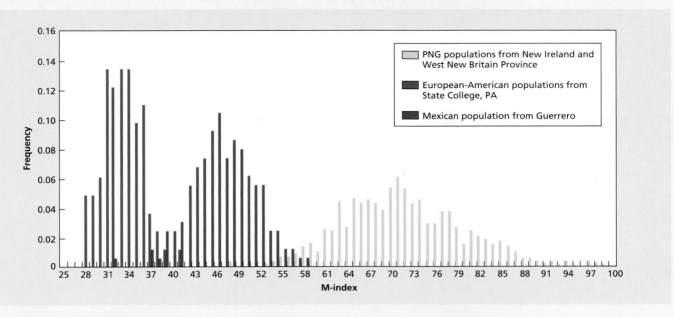

Skin Pigmentation among Various Human Groups.
M = Index of PNG, European-American, and Mexican Populations

measurements on both of the inner arms of each subject, as well as measurements of their hair color.

I chose to study pigmentation in Melanesia because of its variability among individuals there. In two weeks I was able to obtain samples from Bougainvillians, whose skin contains large amounts of melanin, as well as from lighter-skinned individuals from the Sepik region of Papua New Guinea. This area of the world is also interesting from a pigmentation perspective in terms of hair color. Individuals from Papua New Guinea and other Melanesian islands, as well as Australian aborigines, display a trait known as blondism. This refers to very blond hair, similar to someone of European descent, with darkly pigmented skin. This histogram shows the wide range of pigmentation found on the two islands—individuals at the upper end of the scale are from Bougainville, while those at the lower end are from areas such as the Sepik.

I am currently doing statistical analyses to see if differences in skin color are associated in any way with language. Although close to 1,000 languages are spoken in Papua New Guinea, they belong to two main groups, Austronesian and non-Austronesian. The non-Austronesian speakers appear to have migrated to New Guinea first, followed by a second wave of Austronesian-speaking groups. Current mitochondrial DNA evidence supports this theory. If significant skin color differences between the two groups can be shown, it may help lend support to that argument. I hope to return to Melanesia to continue my study of pigmentation variation, this time in the neighboring Solomon Islands.

Microbes have been major selective agents for humans, particularly before the arrival of modern medicine. Some people are genetically more susceptible to certain diseases than others are, and the distribution of human blood types continues to change in response to natural selection.

After food production emerged around 10,000 years ago, infectious diseases posed a mounting risk and eventually became the foremost cause of human mortality. Food production favors infection for several reasons. Cultivation sustains larger, denser populations and a more sedentary life style than does hunting and gathering. People live closer to each other and to their own wastes, making it easier for microbes to survive and to find hosts. Domesticated animals also transmit diseases to people.

Until 1977, when the last case of smallpox was reported, smallpox had been a major threat to humans and a determinant of blood group frequencies (Diamond 1990, 1997). The smallpox virus is a mutation from one of the pox viruses that plague such domesticated animals as cows, sheep, goats, horses, and pigs. Smallpox appeared in human beings after people and animals started living together. Smallpox epidemics have played

In New York City in 1947, the appearance of nine cases of smallpox, including two deaths, spurred a very successful mass vaccination program. Shown here, lines of people wait to be vaccinated at the New York Health Department on April 14, 1947. The threat made the cover of Cosmopolitan magazine.

important roles in world history, often killing one-fourth to one-half of the affected populations. Smallpox contributed to Sparta's defeat of Athens in 430 B.C. and to the decline of the Roman empire after A.D. 160.

The ABO blood groups have figured in human resistance to smallpox. Blood is typed according to the protein and sugar compounds on the surface of the red blood cells. Different substances (compounds) distinguish between type A and type B blood. Type A cells trigger the production of *antibodies* in B blood, so that A cells clot in B blood. The different substances work like chemical passwords; they help us distinguish our own cells from invading cells, including microbes, we ought to destroy. The surfaces of some microbes have substances similar to ABO blood group substances. We don't produce antibodies to substances similar to those on our own blood cells. We can think of this as a clever evolutionary trick by the microbes to deceive their hosts, because we don't normally develop antibodies against our own biochemistry.

People with A or AB blood are more susceptible to smallpox than are people with type B or type O. Presumably this is because a substance on the smallpox virus mimics the type A substance, permitting the virus to slip by the defenses of the type A individual. By contrast, type B and type O individuals produce antibodies against smallpox because they recognize it as a foreign substance.

The relation between type A blood and susceptibility to smallpox was first suggested by the low frequencies of the A allele in areas of India and Africa where smallpox had been endemic. A comparative study done in rural India in 1965–1966, during a virulent smallpox epidemic, did much to confirm this relationship. Drs. F. Vogel and M. R. Chakravartti analyzed blood samples from smallpox victims and their uninfected siblings (Diamond 1990). The researchers found 415 infected children, none ever vaccinated against smallpox. All but eight of the infected children had an uninfected (also unvaccinated) sibling.

The results of the study were clear: Susceptibility to smallpox varied with ABO type. Of the 415 infected children, 261 had the A allele; 154 lacked it. Among their 407 uninfected siblings, the ratio was reversed. Only 80 had the A allele; 327 lacked it. The researchers calculated that a type A or type AB person had a seven times greater chance of getting smallpox than did an O or B person.

In most human populations, the O allele is more common than A and B combined. A is most common in Europe; B frequencies are highest in Asia. Since smallpox was once widespread in the Old World, we might wonder why natural selection didn't eliminate the A allele entirely. The answer appears to be this: Other diseases spared the type A people and penalized those with other blood groups.

For example, type O people seem to be especially susceptible to the bubonic plague—the

"Black Death" that killed a third of the population of medieval Europe. Type O people are also more likely to get cholera, which has killed as many people in India as smallpox has. On the other hand, blood group O may increase resistance to syphilis. The ravages of that sexually transmitted disease, which may have originated in the New World, may explain the very high frequency of type O blood among the native populations of Central and South America. The distribution of human blood groups appears to represent a compromise among the selective effects of many diseases.

Associations between ABO blood type and noninfectious disorders also have been noted. Type O individuals are most susceptible to duodenal and gastric ulcers. Type A individuals seem most prone to stomach and cervical cancer and ovarian tumors. However, since these noninfectious disorders tend to occur after reproduction has ended, their relevance to adaptation and evolution through natural selection is doubtful (see also Weiss 1993).

In the case of diseases for which there are no cures, genetic resistance maintains its significance. There is genetic variation in susceptibility to the HIV virus, for example. We know that people exposed to HIV vary in their risk of developing AIDS and in the rate at which the disease progresses. AIDS is widespread in many African nations (and in the United States, France, and Brazil). Particularly in Africa, where treatment strategies now used in the industrial nations are not widely available, the death rate from AIDS could eventually (let us hope it does not) rival that of past epidemics of smallpox and plague. If so, AIDS could cause large shifts in human gene frequencies—again illustrating the ongoing operation of natural selection.

Facial Features

Natural selection also affects facial features. For instance, long noses seem to be adaptive in arid areas (Brace 1964; Weiner 1954), because membranes and blood vessels inside the nose moisten the air as it is breathed in. Long noses are also adaptive in cold environments, because blood vessels warm the air as it is breathed in. This nose form distances the brain, which is sensitive to bitter cold, from raw outer air. These were adaptive biological features for humans who lived in cold climates before the invention of central heating.

The association between nose form and temperature is recognized as **Thomson's nose rule** (Thomson and Buxton 1923), which shows up statistically. In plotting the geographic distribution of nose length among human populations who have lived for many generations in the areas they now inhabit, the average nose does tend to be longer in areas with lower mean annual temperatures.

This Nilotic man, a Nuer herder from Sudan, has a tall linear body with elongated extremities (note his fingers). Such proportioning increases the surface area relative to mass and thus dissipates heat (Allen's rule). What other body form can achieve the same result?

Other facial features also illustrate adaptation to selective forces. Among contemporary humans, average tooth size is largest among Native Australian hunters and gatherers, for whom large teeth had an adaptive advantage, given a diet based on foods with a considerable amount of sand and grit. People with small teeth—if false teeth and sand-free foods are unavailable—can't feed themselves as effectively as people with more massive dentition can (see Brace 2000).

Size and Body Build

Certain body builds have adaptive advantages for particular environments. In 1847, the German biologist Karl Christian Bergmann observed that within the same species of warm-blooded animals, populations with smaller individuals are more often found in warm climates, while those with greater bulk, or mass, are found in colder regions. The relation between body weight and temperature is summarized in **Bergmann's rule:** The smaller of two bodies similar in shape has more surface area per unit of weight. Therefore, it sheds heat more efficiently. (Heat loss occurs on the body's surface—the skin perspires.) Average body size tends to increase in cold areas and to decrease in hot ones because big bodies hold heat better than small ones do. To be more precise, in a large sample of native populations, average adult

male weight increased by 0.66 pound (0.3 kilogram) for every 1 degree Fahrenheit fall in mean annual temperature (Roberts 1953; Steegman 1975). The "pygmies" and the San, who live in hot climates and weigh only 90 pounds on the average, illustrate this relation in reverse.

Body shape differences also reflect adaptation to temperature through natural selection. The relationship between temperature and body shape in animals and birds was first recognized in 1877 by the zoologist J. A. Allen. **Allen's rule** states that the relative size of protruding body parts—ears, tails, bills, fingers, toes, limbs, and so on—increases with temperature. Among humans, slender bodies with long digits and limbs are advantageous in tropical climates. Such bodies increase body surface relative to mass and allow for more efficient heat dissipation. Among the cold-adapted Eskimos, the opposite phenotype is found. Short limbs and stocky bodies serve to conserve heat. Cold area populations tend to have larger chests and shorter arms than do people from warm areas (Roberts 1953).

This discussion of adaptive relationships between climate and body size and shape illustrates that natural selection may achieve the same effect in different ways. East African Nilotes, who live in a hot area, have tall, linear bodies with elongated extremities that increase surface area relative to mass and thus maximize heat dissipation (illustrating Allen's rule). Among the "pygmies," the reduction of body size achieves the same result (illustrating Bergmann's rule). Similarly, the large bodies of northern Europeans and the compact stockiness of the Eskimos serve the same function of heat conservation.

Similarly, as spelled out in the news story at the beginning of this chapter, human populations use different, but equally effective, biological means of adapting to the environmental stresses associated with high altitudes. Andeans have adapted to thin air by developing the ability to carry more oxygen in each red blood cell, compared with people who live at sea level. Having more hemoglobin to carry oxygen counterbalances the effects of hypoxia. Tibetans, in contrast, increase their oxygen intake by taking more breaths per minute than do people who live at sea level. Also, their lungs synthesize large amounts of nitric oxide from the air they breathe. The nitric oxide works to expand the diameter of their blood vessels, so that Tibetans offset low oxygen content in their blood with increased blood flow. Ethiopian highlanders, by contrast, use none of these mechanisms. Compared with sea-level peoples, they don't breathe more rapidly, synthesize nitric oxide more effectively, or have a higher hemoglobin count. The exact biological mechanisms that enable Ethiopians to survive at high altitudes are being investigated.

Lactose Tolerance

Many biological traits that illustrate human adaptation are not under simple genetic control. Genetic determination of such traits may be likely but unconfirmed, or several genes may interact to influence the trait in question. Sometimes there is a genetic component, but the trait also responds to stresses encountered during growth. We speak of **phenotypical adaptation** when adaptive changes occur during an individual's lifetime. Phenotypical adaptation is made possible by biological plasticity—our ability to change in response to the environments we encounter as we grow (see Bogin 2001; Frisancho 1993). Recall the discussion of physiological adaptation to high altitude in Chapter 1 and in the "News Brief" at the beginning of this chapter.

Genes and phenotypical adaptation work together to produce a biochemical difference between human groups in the ability to digest large amounts of milk—an adaptive advantage when other foods are scarce and milk is available, as it is in dairying societies. All milk, whatever its source, contains a complex sugar called *lactose*. The digestion of milk depends on an enzyme called *lactase*, which works in the small intestine. Among all mammals except humans and some of their pets, lactase production ceases after weaning, so that these animals can no longer digest milk.

Lactase production and the ability to tolerate milk vary between populations. About 90 percent of northern Europeans and their descendants are lactose tolerant; they can digest several glasses of milk with no difficulty. Similarly, about 80 percent of two African populations, the Tutsi of Rwanda and Burundi in East Africa and the Fulani of Nigeria in West Africa, produce lactase and digest milk easily. Both of these groups traditionally have been herders. However, such nonherders as the Yoruba and Igbo in Nigeria, the Baganda in Uganda, the Japanese and other Asians, Eskimos, South American Indians, and many Israelis cannot digest lactose (Kretchmer 1972/1975).

However, the variable human ability to digest milk seems to be a difference of degree. Some populations can tolerate very little or no milk, but

In Canada's Northwest Territories, this Inuit father and son are dressed in caribou fur clothing. Compact stockiness and fur coats are adaptively advantageous in a very cold environment.

others are able to metabolize much greater quantities. Studies show that people who move from no-milk or low-milk diets to high-milk diets increase their lactose tolerance; this suggests some phenotypical adaptation. We can conclude that no simple genetic trait accounts for the ability to digest milk. Lactose tolerance appears to be one of many aspects of human biology governed both by genes and by phenotypical adaptation to environmental conditions.

We see that human biology changes constantly, even without genetic change. In this chapter we've considered ways in which humans adapt biologically to their environments, and the effects of such adaptation on human biological diversity. Modern biological anthropology seeks to *explain* specific aspects of human biological variation. The explanatory framework encompasses the same mechanisms—selection, mutation, drift, gene flow, and plasticity—that govern adaptation, variation, and evolution among other life forms (see Futuyma 1998; Mayr 2001).

SUMMARY

1. Humans have access to varied ways—biological and cultural—of adapting to environmental stresses, such as disease, heat, cold, humidity, sunlight, and altitude. Biological diversity among contemporary and prehistoric humans has many causes. This chapter examines those causes, while rejecting attempts to pigeonhole humans into discrete biological categories called races.

2. How do scientists approach the study of human biological diversity? Because of a range of problems involved in classifying humans into racial categories, contemporary biologists focus on specific differences and try to explain them. Because of extensive gene flow and interbreeding, *Homo sapiens* has not evolved subspecies or distinct races. The genetic breaks that do exist among human populations have not led to the formation of discrete races.

3. Biological similarities between groups may reflect—rather than common ancestry—similar but independent adaptations to similar natural selective forces, such as degrees of ultraviolet radiation from the sun in the case of skin color.

4. Differential resistance to infectious diseases such as smallpox has influenced the distribution of human blood groups. There are genetic anti-malarials, such as the sickle-cell allele discussed in Chapter 4. Natural selection also has operated on facial features and body size and shape.

5. Phenotypical adaptation refers to adaptive changes that occur in an individual's lifetime in response to the environment the organism encounters as it grows. Lactose tolerance is due partly to phenotypical adaptation. Biological similarities between geographically distant populations may be due to similar but independent genetic changes, rather than to common ancestry. Or they may reflect similar physiological responses to common stresses during growth. Also, human populations have developed different but equally effective ways of adapting to environmental conditions such as heat, cold, and high altitudes.

KEY TERMS

See the flash cards
mhhe.com/kottak

Allen's rule   Rule stating that the relative size of protruding body parts (such as ears, tails, bills, fingers, toes, and limbs) tends to increase in warmer climates.

Bergmann's rule   Rule stating that the smaller of two bodies similar in shape has more surface area per unit of weight and therefore can dissipate heat more efficiently; hence, large bodies tend to be found in colder areas and small bodies in warmer ones.

cline   A gradual shift in gene frequencies between neighboring populations.

hypervitaminosis D   Condition caused by an excess of vitamin D; calcium deposits build up in the body's soft tissues, and the kidneys may fail; symptoms include gallstones and joint and circulation problems; may affect unprotected light-skinned individuals in the tropics.

melanin   Substance manufactured in specialized cells in the lower layers of the epidermis (outer skin layer); melanin cells in dark skin produce more melanin than do those in light skin.

phenotypical adaptation   Adaptive biological changes that occur during the individual's lifetime, made possible by biological plasticity.

racial classification   The attempt to assign humans to discrete categories (purportedly) based on common ancestry.

rickets   Nutritional disease caused by a shortage of vitamin D; interferes with the absorption of calcium and causes softening and deformation of the bones.

Thomson's nose rule   Rule stating that the average nose tends to be longer in areas with lower mean annual temperatures; based on the geographic distribution of nose length among human populations.

tropics   Geographic belt extending about 23 degrees north and south of the equator, between the Tropic of Cancer (north) and the Tropic of Capricorn (south).

CRITICAL THINKING QUESTIONS

For more self-testing,
see the self-quizzes
mhhe.com/kottak

1. If *race* is a discredited term in biology, what has replaced it?

2. What are the main problems with racial classification based on phenotype?

3. Choose five people in your classroom who illustrate a range of phenotypical diversity. Which of their features vary most evidently? How do you explain this variation? Is some of the variation due to culture rather than to biology?

4. Did anything stated in this chapter about your ABO blood type give you cause for alarm? Why?

5. How would you design the ideal body for a very cold climate? How about for a very hot one?

SUGGESTED ADDITIONAL READINGS

Bogin, B.
   2001   *The Growth of Humanity.* New York: Wiley-Liss. Up-to-date perspective on human growth and development.

Diamond, J. M.
   1997   *Guns, Germs, and Steel: The Fates of Human Societies.* New York: W.W. Norton. An ecological approach to expansion and conquest in world history by a nonanthropologist.

Frisancho, A. R.

    1993   *Human Adaptation and Accommodation.* Ann Arbor: University of Michigan Press. Influence of the environment on phenotype, particularly during growth and development; a basic text.

Marks, J. M.

    1995   *Human Biodiversity: Genes, Race, and History.* New York: Aldine de Gruyter. See the "Living Anthropology CD-ROM" feature for this chapter for comments by the author of this insightful book.

Molnar, S.

    2005   *Human Variation: Races, Types, and Ethnic Groups,* 6th ed. Upper Saddle River, NJ: Prentice Hall. Links between biological and social diversity.

Montagu, A.

    1981   *Statement on Race: An Annotated Elaboration and Exposition of the Four Statements on Race Issued by the United Nations Educational, Scientific, and Cultural Organization.* Westport, CT: Greenwood. United Nations positions on race analyzed.

Montagu, A., ed.

    1997   *Man's Most Dangerous Myth: The Fallacy of Race,* 6th ed. Walnut Creek, CA: AltaMira. Revision of classic book.

Roberts, D. F.

    1986   *Genetic Variation and Its Maintenance: With Particular Reference to Tropical Populations.* New York: Cambridge University Press. Evidence for human genetic evolution, with a focus on tropical populations.

Shanklin, E.

    1994   *Anthropology and Race.* Belmont, CA: Wadsworth. A concise introduction to the race concept from the perspective of anthropology.

Wade, P.

    2002   *Race, Nature, and Culture: An Anthropological Perspective.* Sterling, VA: Pluto Press. A processual approach to human biology and race.

Weiss, K. M.

    1993   *Genetic Variation and Human Disease: Principles and Evolutionary Approaches.* New York: Cambridge University Press. Selection connected with human diseases.

INTERNET EXERCISES

1. Go to the website **http://anthro.palomar.edu/vary/vary_2.htm** and read the essay titled "Models of Classification."
   a. What are the three basic ways in which anthropologists have tried to classify people on the basis of biological differences?
   b. How does the populational model differ from the typological model? Which of those two models is preferable? What's the main problem with the populational model?
   c. Does the clinal model lead to the identification of human races? Is there any problem with the clinal model? Which model comes closest to grasping the real nature of human variation? Is there more genetic variation among chimpanzees than among humans?

2. Adaptation to Environment: Read Dennis O'Neil's page on "Adapting to Climate Extremes" (**http://anthro.palomar.edu/adapt/adapt_2.htm**).
   a. What is Bergmann's rule? What is Allen's rule?
   b. How do the !Kung and Australian Aborigines respond to cold differently from the Inuit and groups from Tierra del Fuego? Is there an adaptive reason why these groups have different responses to cold?
   c. What are the advantages of evaporative cooling? What are the disadvantages?

See Chapter 5 at your McGraw-Hill Online Learning Center for additional review and interactive exercises.

6

The Primates

OUR PLACE AMONG PRIMATES

Primatology is the study of nonhuman primates—fossil and living apes, monkeys, and prosimians—including their behavior and social life. Primatology is fascinating in itself, but it also helps anthropologists make inferences about the early social organization of

■ *Compare the human and the gorilla. What similarities do you notice? What differences? Humans, gorillas, and chimps have more than 98 percent of their DNA in common.*

hominids (members of the zoological family that includes fossil and living humans) and untangle issues of human nature and the origins of culture, such as early tool making—its nature and value. (Focusing on one of the great apes, the orangutan, the "News Brief" describes tool use based on learning and its relevance to the origins of human culture.) Of particular relevance to humans are two kinds of primates:

1. Those whose ecological adaptations are similar to our own: **terrestrial** monkeys and apes—that is, primates that live on the ground rather than in the trees.

2. Those that are most closely related to us: the great apes, specifically the chimpanzees and gorillas.

Similarities between humans and apes are evident in anatomy, brain structure, genetics, and biochemistry. The physical similarities between humans and apes are recognized in zoological taxonomy—the assignment of organisms to categories (*taxa;* singular, *taxon*) according to their relationship and resemblance. Many similarities between organisms reflect their common *phylogeny*—their genetic relatedness based on common ancestry. In other words, organisms share features they have inherited from the same ancestor. Humans and apes belong to the same taxonomic superfamily, *Hominoidea* (**hominoids**). Monkeys are placed in two others (Ceboidea and Cercopithecoidea). This means that humans and apes are more closely related to each other than either is to monkeys.

Figure 6.1 summarizes the various levels of classification used in zoological **taxonomy.** Each lower-level unit belongs to the higher-level unit above it. Thus, looking toward the bottom of Figure 6.1, similar species belong to the same genus (plural, *genera*). Similar genera make up the same family, and so on through the top of Figure 6.1, where similar phyla (plural of *phylum*) are included in the same kingdom.

We see that the highest (most inclusive) taxonomic level is the *kingdom.* At that level, animals are distinguished from plants. The lowest-level taxa are species and subspecies. A *species* is a group of organisms that can mate and give birth to *viable* (capable of living) and *fertile* (capable of

OVERVIEW

Humans, apes, monkeys, and prosimians belong to the zoological order known as primates. The apes are our closest relatives. Humans share more than 98 percent of their DNA with chimpanzees and gorillas.

Early primates, like many contemporary ones, lived in the trees. Reflecting our arboreal heritage, primates share certain anatomical features. These features include grasping hands with opposable thumbs, depth vision, and the use of the fingertip pads as the main organs of touch. With large and complex brains, humans, apes, and monkeys rely extensively on learning. Primates live in social groups and invest considerable time and energy in their offspring and kin.

Gorillas, the least arboreal apes, are vegetarians that are confined to equatorial Africa. Chimpanzees live in the forests and woodlands of tropical Africa. All the apes and many other primate species are endangered, mainly by deforestation and human hunting. Some important developments in human evolution, such as hunting and tool making, are foreshadowed in other primates, particularly chimpanzees.

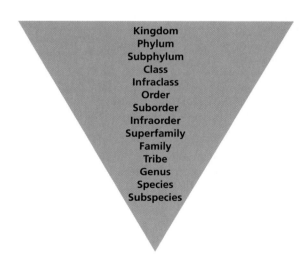

FIGURE 6.1 The Principal Classificatory Units of Zoological Taxonomy.

Moving down the figure, the classificatory units become more exclusive, so that "Kingdom" at the top is the most inclusive unit and "Subspecies" at the bottom is the most exclusive.

A Revealing Behavior in "Orangutan Heaven and Human Hell"

NEW YORK TIMES NEWS BRIEF

by Connie Rogers
November 15, 2005

Primatologists study nonhuman primates, such as apes, monkeys, and lemurs. The study of monkeys, and particularly that of apes, is of particular interest to anthropology because their attributes and behavior can suggest things about human nature and origins. Of particular relevance to humans are two kinds of primates: (1) those that spend much of their time on the ground, including baboons, gorillas, chimpanzees, and, to some extent the orangutans described here, and (2) those that are most closely related to us: the great apes, which include the orangs (although chimps and gorillas are much closer relatives). Heralded in this "News Brief," based on a conversation with the Dutch primatologist Carel von Schaik, is his book Among Orangutans: Red Apes and the Rise of Human Culture *(Schaik 2004).*

Humans share many features of anatomy, temperament, and behavior, including the sociability described here, with our primate relatives. This news story reports on a learned ability—reliance on tools—that the great apes share with humans. The use and even the manufacture of crude tools by chimpanzees has been known for many years. Observation of tool use by gorillas and orangs is more recent. Schaik's book reports more fully on the studies described here. Knowing now that all the great apes can learn how to use tools, we can speculate that the common ancestor of apes and humans also had at least a rudimentary capacity for cultural learning.

People keep asking Carel van Schaik if there is anything left to discover in fieldwork.

"I tell them, 'A lot,'" said Dr. van Schaik, the Dutch primatologist. "Look at gorillas. We've been studying them for decades, and we just now have discovered that they use tools. The same is true for orangutans."

In 1992, when Dr. van Schaik began his research in Suaq, a swamp forest in northern Sumatra, orangutans were believed to be the only great ape that lived a largely solitary life foraging for hard-to-find fruit thinly distributed over a large area.

Researchers thought they were slow-moving creatures—some even called them boring—that didn't have time to do much but eat.

But the orangutans Dr. van Schaik found in Suaq turned all that on its head. More than 100 were gathered together doing things the researchers had never seen in the wild.

Dr. van Schaik worked there for seven years and came to the radical conclusion that orangutans were "every bit as sociable, as technically adept and as culturally capable" as chimpanzees.

His new conclusions about how apes—and humans—got to be so smart are detailed in his latest book, "Among Orangutans: Red Apes and the Rise of Human Culture."

Now a professor of anthropology at the University of Zurich and the director of its Anthropological Institute and Museum, Dr. van Schaik discussed his findings in a recent telephone interview from his office there.

Q. What were you looking for in the Suaq swamp?

A. We'd been working in a mountainous area in northern Sumatra, and it felt as if we were missing the full picture of orangutan social organization. All higher primates—all of them—live in distinct social units except for the orangutan. That's a strong anomaly, and I wanted to solve it.

Q. How was Suaq different from other orangutan habitats?

A. It was an extraordinarily productive swamp forest with by far the highest density of orangutans—over twice the record number. The animals were the most sociable we'd ever seen: they hang out together,

they're nice to each other, they even share food.

Q. But you almost left this orangutan habitat after a year?

A. We'd never worked in a place like this, and it was exhausting. To get into the swamp where they were we would wade through water—sometimes chest deep, two hours in, two hours out every day. There were countless species of mosquitoes.

It was what I call orangutan heaven and human hell. But then someone noticed that they were poking sticks into tree holes. It sounded like tool use, so we decided to build boardwalks in the swamp, and things got a lot easier.

Q. Were orangutans using tools?

A. It turned out Suaq had an amazing repertoire of tool use. They shape sticks to get at honey and insects. Then they pick another kind of stick to go after the scrumptious fat-packed seeds of the neesia fruit. One of them figured out that you could unleash the seeds with a stick and that was a big improvement in their diet.

Lean times are rare at Suaq, not only because the forest is productive, but because the orangutans can get to

■ *The cover of Carel van Schaik's 2004 book,* Among Orangutans: Red Apes and the Rise of Human Culture, *which is described in this account.*

so much more food by using tools. So they can afford to be more sociable.

Q. How did you discover that the tool use is socially transmitted?

A. Well, one way to prove it is to see if the orangutans use tools everywhere the neesia tree exists. This was in the late 90's. Swamps were being clear-cut and drained everywhere, and the civil war in Aceh was spreading.

I felt like an anthropologist trying to document a vanishing tribe. It turned out that in the big swamps on one side of a river, the orangutans do use tools, and in the small swamp on the other side, they don't. Neesia trees and orangutans exist in both places. But the animals can't cross the river, so the knowledge hadn't spread. At that point, the penny dropped and I realized their tool use was cultural.

Q. So your discovery that the orangutans learned tool use from one another explains "the rise of

human culture" part of your book's subtitle?

A. Well, yes. Orangutans split off from the African lineage some 14 million years ago. If both chimps and orangutans make tools, our common great ape ancestor probably had the capacity for culture.

Q. I always thought we got smart after we came down from the trees.

A. Actually orangutans are the largest arboreal mammal and have no predators up in the trees so they live a very long time—up to 60 years in the wild—and have the slowest life history of any nonhuman mammal including elephants and whales.

A slow life history is key to growing a large brain. The other key to intelligence is sociability.

Q. Were orangutans more social in the past?

A. I guess the rich forest areas that allowed them to live in groups were much more common in the past—they're the ones that are best for rice

growing and farming—but there's no way of knowing for sure. . .

Q. You end your book with a bleak picture of the future of orangutans because of habitat conversion and illegal logging. Since then there's been a devastating tsunami and people need to cut down even more trees to put roofs over their heads. What does the future look like now?

A. One way to help people in Sumatra would be to donate wood on a large scale. But things may be better in Borneo.

There's a new Indonesian president, and in the last few months it looks as if the government is serious about cracking down on illegal logging. That leaves me more hopeful.

SOURCE: Connie Rogers, "Revealing Behavior in 'Orangutan Heaven and Human Hell': A Conversation with Carel van Schaik," *New York Times*, November 15, 2005, p. F2.

reproducing) offspring whose own offspring are viable and fertile. *Speciation* (the formation of a new species) occurs when groups that once belonged to the same species can no longer interbreed. After a sufficiently long period of reproductive isolation, two closely related species assigned to the same genus will have evolved out of one.

At the lowest level of taxonomy, a species may have subspecies. These are its more or less, but not yet totally, isolated subgroups. Subspecies can coexist in time and space. For example, the Neandertals, who thrived between 130,000 and 28,000 years ago, often are assigned not to a separate species but merely to a different subspecies of *Homo sapiens*. Just one subspecies of *Homo sapiens* survives today.

The similarities used to assign organisms to the same taxon are called **homologies,** similarities they have jointly inherited from a common ancestor. Table 6.1 summarizes the place of humans in zoological taxonomy. We see in Table 6.1 that we are mammals, members of the class Mammalia. This is a major subdivision of the kingdom Animalia. Mammals share certain traits, including mammary glands, that set them apart from other taxa, such as birds, reptiles, amphibians, and insects. Mammalian homologies indicate that all mammals share more recent common ancestry

with each other than they do with any bird, reptile, or insect.

Humans are mammals that, at a lower taxonomic level, belong to the *order* Primates. Another mammalian order is Carnivora: the carnivores (dogs, cats, foxes, wolves, badgers, weasels). Rodentia (rats, mice, beavers, squirrels) form yet another mammalian order. The primates share structural and biochemical homologies that distinguish them from other mammals. These resemblances were inherited from their common early primate ancestors after those early primates became reproductively isolated from the ancestors of the other mammals.

HOMOLOGIES AND ANALOGIES

Organisms should be assigned to the same taxon on the basis of homologies. The extensive biochemical homologies between apes and humans confirm our common ancestry and support our traditional joint classification as hominoids. For example, it is estimated that humans, chimpanzees, and gorillas have more than 98 percent of their DNA in common.

TABLE 6.1 The Place of Humans (*Homo sapiens*) in Zoological Taxonomy

Homo sapiens is an Animal, Chordate, Vertebrate, Mammal, Primate, Anthropoid, Catarrhine, Hominoid, and Hominin. (Table 6.2 shows the taxonomic placement of the other primates.)

Taxon	Scientific (Latin) Name	Common (English) Name
Kingdom	Animalia	Animals
Phylum	Chordata	Chordates
Subphylum	Vertebrata	Vertebrates
Class	Mammalia	Mammals
Infraclass	Eutheria	Eutherians
Order	Primates	Primates
Suborder	Anthropoidea	Anthropoids
Infraorder	Catarrhini	Catarrhines
Superfamily	Hominoidea	Hominoids
Family	Hominidae	Hominids
Tribe	Hominini	Hominins
Genus	*Homo*	Humans
Species	*Homo sapiens*	Recent humans
Subspecies	*Homo sapiens sapiens*	Anatomically modern humans

However, common ancestry isn't the only reason for similarities between species. Similar traits also can arise if species experience similar selective forces and adapt to them in similar ways. We call such similarities **analogies.** The process by which analogies are produced is called **convergent evolution.** For example, fish and porpoises share many analogies resulting from convergent evolution to life in the water. Like fish, porpoises, which are mammals, have fins. They are also hairless and streamlined for efficient locomotion. Analogies between birds and bats (wings, small size, light bones) illustrate convergent evolution to flying (see Angier 1998).

In theory, only homologies should be used in taxonomy. With reference to the hominoids, there is no doubt that humans, gorillas, and chimpanzees are more closely related to each other than any of the three is to orangutans, which are Asiatic apes (Ciochon 1983). *Hominidae* is the name of the zoological family that includes hominids—fossil and living humans. Because chimps and gorillas share a more recent common ancestor with humans than they do with the orangutan, many scientists now also place gorillas and chimps in the hominid family. **Hominid** would then refer to the zoological family that includes fossil and living humans, chimpanzees,

gorillas, and their common ancestors. This leaves the orangutan (genus *Pongo*) as the only member of the pongid family (*Pongidae*). If chimps and gorillas are classified as hominids, what do we call the group that leads to humans but not to chimps and gorillas? For that, some scientists insert a taxonomic level called *tribe* between family and genus. The tribe *hominini* describes all the human species that ever have existed (including the extinct ones) and excludes chimps and gorillas. When scientists use the word *hominin* today, they mean pretty much the same thing as when they used the word *hominid* 20 years ago (Greiner 2003). Table 6.2 and Figure 6.2 illustrate our degree of relatedness to other primates.

PRIMATE TENDENCIES

Primates are varied because they have adapted to diverse ecological niches. Some primates are active during the day; others, at night. Some eat insects; others, fruits; others, shoots, leaves, and bulk vegetation; and others, seeds or roots. Some primates live on the ground, others live in trees, and there are intermediate adaptations. However, because the earliest primates were tree dwellers,

See the Virtual Exploration
mhhe.com/kottak

TABLE 6.2 Primate Taxonomy

The subdivisions of the two primate suborders: Prosimii (Prosimians) and Anthropoidea (Anthropoids). Humans (see also Table 6.1) are anthropoids who belong to the superfamily Hominoidea (the hominoids), along with the apes.

Suborder	Infraorder	Superfamily	Family	Subfamily
Prosimii (Prosimians)	Lemuriformes (Lemurs)	Lemuroidea	Daubentoniidae (Aye-aye)	
			Indridae (Indri)	
			Lemuridae (Lemurs)	
	Lorisiformes (Lorises)	Lorisoidea	Lorisidae	Galaginae (Bushbabies)
				Lorisinae
	Tarsiiformes (Tarsiers)	Tarsioidea	Tarsiidae	
Anthropoidea (Anthropoids)	Platyrrhini (New World monkeys)	Ceboidea	Callitrichidae (Tamarins and marmosets)	
			Cebidae	Atelinae (Spider monkeys and woolly monkeys)
	Catarrhini (Catarrhines)	Cercopithecoidea (Old World monkeys)	Cercopithecidae	Cercopithecinae (Macaques, guenons, and baboons)
				Colobinae (Colobines)
		Hominoidea (Hominoids)	Hylobatidae (Gibbons and siamangs)	
			Pongidae (Orangutans)	
			Hominidae (Gorillas, chimpanzees, and humans)	

SOURCE: Adapted from R. Martin, "Classification of Primates," in S. Jones, R. Martin, and D. Pilbeam, eds., *The Cambridge Encyclopedia of Human Evolution* (Cambridge, England: Cambridge University Press, 1992), pp. 20–21.

modern primates share homologies reflecting their common **arboreal** heritage.

Many trends in primate evolution are best exemplified by the **anthropoids**: monkeys, apes, and humans, which constitute the suborder *Anthropoidea*. The other primate suborder, Prosimii, includes lemurs, lorises, and tarsiers. These prosimians are more distant relatives of humans than are monkeys and apes. The primate trends—most developed in the anthropoids—can be summarized briefly. Together they constitute an anthropoid heritage that humans share with monkeys and apes.

1. **Grasping.** Primates have five-digited feet and hands that are suited for grasping. Certain features of hands and feet that were originally adaptive for arboreal life have been transmitted across the generations to contemporary primates. Flexible hands and feet that could encircle branches were important features in the early primates' arboreal life. Thumb opposability might have been favored by the inclusion of insects in the early primate diet. Manual dexterity makes it easier to catch insects attracted to abundant arboreal flowers and

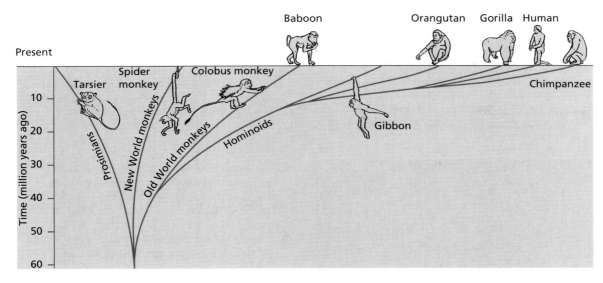

FIGURE 6.2 Primate Family Tree.

When did the common ancestors of all the primates live? SOURCE: From Roger Lewin, *Human Evolution: An Illustrated Introduction*, 3rd ed. (Boston: Blackwell Scientific Publications, 1993), p. 44.

fruits. Humans and many other primates have **opposable thumbs:** The thumb can touch the other fingers. Some primates also have grasping feet. However, in adapting to **bipedal (two-footed)** locomotion, humans eliminated most of the foot's grasping ability.

2. **Smell to Sight.** Several anatomical changes reflect the shift from smell to sight as the primates' most important means of obtaining information. Monkeys, apes, and humans have excellent *stereoscopic* (able to see in depth) and color vision. The portion of the brain devoted to vision expanded, while the area concerned with smell shrank.

3. **Nose to Hand.** Sensations of touch, conveyed by *tactile organs,* also provide information. The tactile skin on a dog's or cat's nose transmits information. Cats' tactile hairs, or whiskers, also serve this function. In primates, however, the main touch organ is the hand, specifically the sensitive pads of the "fingerprint" region.

4. **Brain Complexity.** The proportion of brain tissue concerned with memory, thought, and association has increased in primates. The primate ratio of brain size to body size exceeds that of most mammals.

5. **Parental Investment.** Most primates give birth to a single offspring rather than a litter. Because of this, growing primates receive more attention and have more learning opportunities than do other mammals. Learned behavior is an important part of primate adaptation.

▪ Primates have five-digited feet and hands, well suited for grasping. Flexible hands and feet that could encircle branches were important features in the early primates' arboreal life. In adapting to bipedal (two-footed) locomotion, hominids eliminated most of the foot's grasping ability—illustrated here by the chimpanzee.

6. **Sociality.** Primates tend to be social animals that live with others of their species (see the "News Brief"). The need for longer and more attentive care of offspring places a selective value on support by a social group.

PROSIMIANS

The primate order has two suborders: **prosimians** and **anthropoids**. The early history of the primates is limited to prosimian-like animals known through the fossil record. (See Chapter 7.) The first anthropoids, ancestral to monkeys, apes, and humans, appeared more than 40 million years

A slender loris with Trumpet Creeper flowers at Duke University's impressive Primate Center in North Carolina. The slender loris is a small nocturnal primate found (in the wild) only in the tropical rainforests of southern India and Sri Lanka.

Crowned lemurs (Eulemur coronatus) in Ankarana, northern Madagascar. Among crown lemurs, the males are reddish and females are grey.

Think about our senses—vision, hearing, touch, smell, and taste. Where have we suffered sensory loss during our evolutionary history? Like almost all the anthropoids, humans are diurnal, active during the day. If we were night animals, we'd sense things differently. Maybe our eyes would be bigger, like those of an owl or a tarsier. Maybe we'd have biological radar systems, as bats do. Perhaps we'd develop a more acute sense of hearing or smell to penetrate the shield of the dark. As animals, humans are programmed to rise at dawn and to sleep when the sun disappears. As cultural creatures, we venture into the night with torches, lanterns, and flashlights, and we shut the dark out of our dwellings by using artificial light.

Which is most debilitating—loss of vision, hearing, or smell? Among our senses, we seem to value hearing, and above all vision, most. The anthropoids as a group are preeminently visual animals. Whole industries exist to improve our sight and hearing. But how often do you hear of a product designed to improve your ability to smell, taste, or touch things? Other animals can detect all kinds of scents and odors that help them interpret the world. Humans, by contrast, use an array of products designed *not* to improve our sense of smell, but to eliminate even the faint odors our limited olfactory apparatus permits us to smell. *Blindness* and *deafness* are common words that indicate the senses whose loss we deem most significant. The rarity of the word *anosmia*, the inability to smell, tells us something about our senses and our values. The sensory shifts that occurred in primate evolution, especially the one from smell to sight, explain something fundamental about ourselves.

ago. Some prosimians managed to survive in Africa and Asia because they were adapted to nocturnal life. As such, they did not compete with anthropoids, which are active during the day. Prosimians (lemurs) in Madagascar had no anthropoid competitors until people colonized that island some 1,500 years ago.

In their behavior and biology, Madagascar's *lemurs,* with 33 species, show adaptations to an array of environments or ecological niches. Their diets and times of activity differ. Lemurs eat fruits, other plant foods, eggs, and insects. Some are nocturnal; others are active during the day. Some are totally arboreal; others spend some time in the trees and some on the ground. Another kind of prosimian is the *tarsier,* today confined to

Providing Apes Refuge: A Cultural Study of the Great Ape Sanctuary Community

BACKGROUND INFORMATION

STUDENT:
Stephen Ham

SUPERVISING PROFESSOR:
Dorothy Holland

SCHOOL:
University of North Carolina at Chapel Hill

YEAR IN SCHOOL/MAJOR:
Graduated in 2004/Anthropology

FUTURE PLANS:
Peace Corps volunteer in Ghana; doctorate after two-year service in Peace Corps

PROJECT TITLE:
Providing Apes Refuge:
A Cultural Study of the Great Ape Sanctuary Community

For his senior honors thesis, Stephen Ham turned his attention to ape sanctuaries and the community of scientists, veterinarians, and concerned individuals who work in them. His project combined his interests in cultural anthropology and primatology—specifically his concern with safeguarding the endangered primates that are our closest relatives.

Fusing my interests in wildlife conservation and cultural anthropology, as an undergraduate I began a research project focusing on people involved in the operation of great ape sanctuaries. Through my honors thesis research, my hope was to capture the perspective of a community of highly dedicated individuals who have devoted their lives to protecting humans' closest living relatives.

Sanctuaries are unique facilities where great apes are given haven from human intrusion. Apes are confiscated from the bushmeat trade, entertainment industry, and other captive settings, and sanctuaries are the institutions that offer them solace. My goal was to explore not only why individuals became involved with great ape conservation through sanctuaries but also how these people viewed their relationship and responsibility to these sentient nonhuman beings. I then investigated how these understandings were reflected in the actual creation and operation of the sanctuaries.

My work led me to Uganda to attend the Pan African Sanctuary Alliance Conference, which was a gathering of great ape sanctuary managers from across the continent and included a visit to a local sanctuary. I then volunteered for several weeks at one of the world's largest chimpanzee sanctuaries, Chimfunshi Wildlife Orphanage in Northern Zambia. These research experiences allowed me to interview a variety of individuals from the sanctuary community and to experience all aspects of day-to-day sanctuary operation. While at Chimfunshi, I became a member of this community as I rehabilitated young chimps confiscated from poachers, shadowed veterinarians during their routine checkups, and implemented educational curricula, which taught the local community about the plight of Africa's ape populations. By becoming a participant, I was better equipped to write about the culture created by sanctuary workers and operators.

After my work in Africa, I returned to the United States to travel with famed anthropologist, Dr. Jane Goodall, as she lectured on chimpanzee behavior and ape conservation. (This opportunity arose from my previous work with the Jane Goodall Institute.) I traveled to several great ape sanctuaries around the United States and interviewed experts in the primate conservation field, including extensive discussions with Dr. Goodall. I began to compare and contrast the sanctuary community in America with that of Africa.

To further this line of inquiry, I was a guest of the Gorilla Foundation in California, home of Koko the signing gorilla. My time with the staff of the Gorilla Foundation allowed me to explore the sanctuary creation process, as Koko is being relocated to a sanctuary in Hawaii. In the end, my thesis captured the sanctuary community's perspective and became the first such project academically to examine this unique group of people. I examined how a facility can create and enforce people's perceptions. This project also let me to exercise various skills learned from my anthropology classes. There is no educational substitute for field experience. Overall my thesis has provided a framework from which my future research projects will stem.

Indonesia, Malaysia, and the Philippines. From the fossil record, we know that 50 million years ago, several genera of tarsier-like prosimians lived in North America and Europe, which were much warmer then than they are now (Boaz 1997). The one genus of tarsier that survived is totally nocturnal. Active at night, tarsiers don't directly compete with anthropoids, which are active during the day. Lorises are other nocturnal prosimians found in Africa and Asia.

ANTHROPOIDS

All anthropoids share resemblances that can be considered trends in primate evolution in the sense that these traits are fully developed neither in the fossils of primates that lived prior to 45 million years ago nor among contemporary prosimians.

Anthropoids have overlapping fields of vision, permitting them to see things in depth. With reduction of the snout, anthropoid eyes are placed forward in the skull and look directly ahead. The fields of vision of our eyes overlap. Depth perception, impossible without overlapping visual fields, proved adaptive in the trees. Tree-dwelling primates that could judge distance better because of depth perception survived and reproduced in greater numbers than did those that could not.

The abilities to see in depth and in color may have developed together. Both helped early anthropoids interpret their arboreal world. Superior vision made it easier to distinguish edible insects, fruits, berries, and leaves. Furthermore, having color and depth vision makes it easier to groom—to remove burrs, insects, and other small objects from other primates' hair. Grooming is one way of forming and maintaining social bonds.

Visual and tactile changes have been interrelated. Monkeys, apes, and humans have neither tactile muzzle skin nor "cat's whiskers." Instead, fingers are the main touch organs. The ends of the fingers and toes are sensitive tactile pads. Forward placement of the eyes and depth vision allow anthropoids to pick up small objects, hold them in front of their eyes, and appraise them. Our ability to thread a needle reflects an intricate interplay of hands and eyes that took millions of years to achieve. Manual dexterity, including the opposable thumb, confers a tremendous advantage in examining and manipulating objects and is essential to a major human adaptive capacity: tool making. Among monkeys, thumb opposability is indispensable for feeding and grooming.

Another trend is increased size of the *cranium* (skull) to fit a larger brain. The brain-to-body size ratio is greater among anthropoids than among prosimians. Even more important, the brain's outer layer—concerned with memory, associa-tion, and integration—is relatively larger. Monkeys, apes, and humans store an array of visual images in their memories, which permits them to learn more. The ability to learn from experience and from other group members is a major reason for the success of the anthropoids compared to most other mammals.

MONKEYS

The anthropoid suborder has two infraorders: *platyrrhines* (New World monkeys) and *catarrhines* (Old World monkeys, apes, and humans). The catarrhines (sharp-nosed) and platyrrhines (flat-nosed) take their names from Latin terms that describe the placement of the nostrils (Figure 6.3). Old World monkeys, apes, and humans are all catarrhines. Being placed in the same taxon

FIGURE 6.3 Nostril Structure of Catarrhines and Platyrrhines.
Above: narrow septum and "sharp nose" of a guenon, a catarrhine (Old World monkey). Below: broad septum and "flat nose" of Humboldt's woolly monkey, a platyrrhine (New World monkey). Which nose is more like your own? What does that similarity suggest?

(infraorder in this case) means that Old World monkeys, apes, and humans are more closely related to each other than to New World monkeys. In other words, one kind of monkey (Old World) is more like a human than it is like another kind of monkey (New World). The New World monkeys were reproductively isolated from the catarrhines before the latter diverged into the Old World monkeys, apes, and humans. This is why New World monkeys are assigned to a different infraorder.

All New World monkeys and many Old World monkeys are arboreal. Whether in the trees or on the ground, however, monkeys move differently from apes and humans. Their arms and legs move parallel to one another, as dogs' legs do. This contrasts with the tendency toward *orthograde posture*, the straight and upright stance of apes and humans. Unlike apes, which have longer arms than legs, and humans, who have longer legs than arms, monkeys have arms and legs of about the same length. Most monkeys also have tails, which help them maintain balance in the trees. Apes and humans lack tails. The apes' tendency toward orthograde posture is most evident when they sit

down. When they move about, chimps, gorillas, and orangutans habitually use all four limbs.

New World Monkeys

New World monkeys live in the forests of Central and South America. There are interesting parallels between New World monkeys and some arboreal primates of the Old World. These analogies exhibit convergent evolution—that is, they have developed as a result of adaptation to a similar arboreal niche. Like the gibbon, a small Asiatic ape, some New World monkeys have developed a form of **brachiation**—under-the-branch swinging. Most monkeys run and jump from branch to branch, but gibbons and some New World monkeys swing through the trees, using their hands as hooks. Hand over hand, they move from branch to branch, propelled onward by the thrust of their bodies.

The tails of Old World monkeys (see below) are used solely for balance. By contrast, many New World monkeys have *prehensile*, or grasping, tails, that are useful not only for balance but also to hang on and even pick up objects (Figure 6.4). The prehensile tail's tactile skin permits it to work like a hand, for instance, in conveying food to the mouth. Old World monkeys, however, have developed their own characteristic anatomical specializations. They have rough patches of skin on the buttocks, adapted to sitting on hard rocky ground and rough branches. If the primate you see in the zoo has such patches, it's from the Old

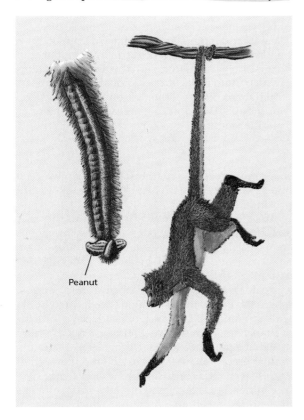

FIGURE 6.4 The Prehensile Tail of the Spider Monkey, a New World Monkey.

Such a tail can be used to grasp a branch, or to pick up small objects, such as the peanut. Do any of the apes have grasping tails?

A wooly spider monkey, a.k.a. muriqui, from Monte Clares, Brazil. The long arms and elongated prehensile tail create a spider-like image for this New World monkey.

■ A red colobus monkey in Zanzibar's Jozani forest. On the Tanzanian mainland this arboreal Old World monkey is the favored prey of chimpanzee hunters in certain locales.

World. If it has a prehensile tail, it's a New World monkey. With one exception, all monkeys and apes, and humans, too, of course, are diurnal—active during the day. Among the anthropoids, there's only one nocturnal animal, a New World monkey called the night monkey or owl monkey.

Old World Monkeys

Like apes and hominids, Old World monkeys have full color vision, which prosimians and most New World monkeys lack. In our *trichromatic color vision*, three retinal protein pigments called *opsins* absorb wavelengths of light, which the brain processes to produce full-color images. Humans, apes, and Old World monkeys have three opsin genes, while most New World monkeys have just two. Howler monkeys are the only New World monkeys with all three genes and thus with full color vision. Full color vision apparently evolved twice among the primates—once in the common ancestor of apes and Old World monkeys and again among ancestral howler monkeys (see Gilad et al. 2004).

Paralleling the difference in vision is one in dental formulas, which are 2:1:2:3 in Old World monkeys, apes, and humans, versus 2:1:3:3 in New World monkeys and prosimians. (The dental formula describes one-quarter of the mouth, either upper or lower left or right. It refers to the number of incisors [2], canines [1], premolars [2], and molars [3]. Humans have the numbers in brackets.) Old World monkeys, apes, and humans have lost the third premolar, which New World monkeys and prosimians retain. Yet another feature sets New World monkeys and prosimians off from hominids, apes, and Old World monkeys. This is the *rhinarium*, the moist, hairless area that surrounds the nostrils in most mammals, such as cats, dogs, prosimians, and New World monkeys. All the features that Old World monkeys, apes, and humans have in common confirm that they share more recently common ancestry with each other than they do with New World monkeys and prosimians.

The Old World monkeys have both terrestrial and arboreal species. Baboons and many macaques are terrestrial monkeys. Certain traits differentiate terrestrial and arboreal primates. Arboreal primates tend to be smaller. Smaller animals can reach a greater variety of foods in trees and shrubs, where the most abundant foods are located at the ends of branches. Low weight is adaptive for end-of-branch feeding. Arboreal monkeys are typically lithe and agile. They escape from the few predators in their environment—snakes and monkey-eating eagles—through alertness and speed. Large size, by contrast, is advantageous for terrestrial primates in dealing with their predators, which are more numerous on the ground.

Another contrast between arboreal and terrestrial primates is in **sexual dimorphism**—marked differences in male and female anatomy and temperament (see Fedigan 1992). Sexual dimorphism tends to be more marked in terrestrial than in arboreal species. Baboon and macaque males are larger and fiercer than are females of the same species. However, it's hard to tell, without close inspection, the sex of an arboreal monkey.

Of the terrestrial monkeys, the baboons of Africa and the (mainly Asiatic) macaques have been the subjects of many studies. Terrestrial monkeys have specializations in anatomy, psychology, and social behavior that enable them to cope with terrestrial life. Adult male baboons, for example, are fierce-looking animals that can weigh 100 pounds (45 kilograms). They display their long, projecting canines to intimidate predators and when confronting other baboons. Faced with a predator, a male baboon can puff up his ample mane of shoulder hair, so that the would-be aggressor perceives the baboon as larger than he actually is.

Longitudinal field research shows that, near the time of puberty, baboon and macaque males typically leave their home troop for another. Because males move in and out, females form the stable core of the terrestrial monkey troop (Cheney and Seyfarth 1990; Hinde 1983). By contrast, among chimpanzees and gorillas, females are more likely to emigrate and seek mates outside their natal social groups (Bradley et al. 2004; Rodseth et al. 1991; Wilson and Wrangham 2003). Among terrestrial monkeys, then, the core group consists of females. Among apes it is made up of males.

APES

The Old World monkeys have their own separate superfamily (Cercopithecoidea), while humans and the apes together compose the hominoid superfamily (Hominoidea). Among the hominoids, the so-called great apes are orangutans,

This mandrill (Papio sphinx) is a brightly-colored terrestrial Old World (African) monkey. Related to the baboon, which shares the same genus name (Papio), mandrills live in family groups consisting of an adult male, several females, and their young. Illustrating sexual dimorphism, female color is drabber and size smaller than in the male.

gorillas, and chimpanzees. Humans could be included here, too; we are sometimes called "the third African ape." The lesser (smaller) apes are the gibbons and siamangs of Southeast Asia and Indonesia.

Apes live in forests and woodlands. The light and agile gibbons, which are skilled brachiators, are completely arboreal. The heavier gorillas, chimpanzees, and adult male orangutans spend considerable time on the ground. Nevertheless, ape behavior and anatomy reveal past and present adaptation to arboreal life. For example, apes still build nests to sleep in trees. Apes have longer arms than legs, which is adaptive for brachiation (see Figure 6.5). The structure of the shoulder and

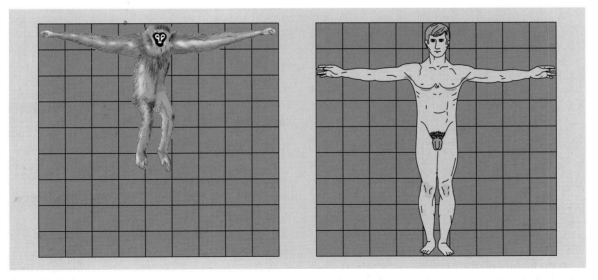

FIGURE 6.5 The Limb Ratio of the Arboreal Gibbon and Terrestrial *Homo*.
How does this anatomical difference fit the modes of locomotion used by gibbons and humans?

The terrestrial loco-
motion of chimps and
gorillas is called
knuckle-walking. In it,
long arms and callused
knuckles support the
trunk as the apes amble
around, leaning
forward, like this west-
ern lowland gorilla
male at Washington's
National Zoo.

With long arms
and fingers, the
gibbon is the most
agile of the apes.
Gibbons occasionally
walk upright on the
ground, using their
long arms as
balancers. Shown
here, a white-handed
gibbon strolls through
the forest.

clavicle (collarbone) of the apes and humans suggests that we had a brachiating ancestor. In fact,
young apes still do brachiate. Adult apes tend to
be too heavy to brachiate safely. Their weight is
more than many branches can withstand. Gorillas
and chimps now use the long arms they have
inherited from their more arboreal ancestors for
life on the ground. The terrestrial locomotion of
chimps and gorillas is called *knuckle-walking*. In it,
long arms and callused knuckles support the
trunk as the apes amble around, leaning forward.

Gibbons

Gibbons are widespread in the forests of Southeast Asia, especially in Malaysia. Smallest of the
apes, male and female **gibbons** have about the
same average height (3 feet, or 1 meter) and
weight (12 to 25 pounds, or 5 to 10 kilograms).
Gibbons spend most of their time just below the
forest canopy (treetops). For efficient brachiation,
gibbons have long arms and fingers, with short
thumbs. Slenderly built, gibbons are the most
agile apes. Unlike knuckle-walkers, they use their
long arms for balance when they occasionally
walk erect on the ground or along a branch. Gibbons are the preeminent arboreal specialists
among the apes. They subsist on a diet mainly of
fruits, with occasional insects and small animals.
Gibbons and siamangs, their slightly larger rela-

tives, tend to live in *primary groups,* which are composed of a permanently bonded male and female and their preadolescent offspring. Gibbons' evolutionary success is confirmed by their numbers and range. Hundreds of thousands of gibbons span a wide area of Southeast Asia.

Orangutans

There are two existing species of orangutan, Asiatic apes that belong to the genus *Pongo.* The range of the orangutan once extended into China, but contemporary orangs are confined to two Indonesian islands. Sexual dimorphism is marked, with the adult male weighing more than twice as much as the female. The orangutan male, like his human counterpart, is intermediate in size between chimps and gorillas. Some orang males exceed 200 pounds (90 kilograms). With only half the gorilla's bulk, male orangs can be more arboreal, although they typically climb, rather than swing through, the trees. The smaller size of females and young permits them to make fuller use of the trees. Orangutans have a varied diet of fruit, bark, leaves, and insects. Because orangutans live in jungles and feed in trees, they are especially difficult to study. However, field reports about orangutans in natural settings (MacKinnon 1974; Schaik 2004) have clarified their behavior and social organization. The studies of Carel van Schaik and his associates, as described in the "News Brief" at the start of this chapter, have challenged the idea that orangs by nature are solitary animals. Previous studies had found the tightest orang social units to consist of females and preadolescent young, with males foraging alone. More recent research has demonstrated orang sociability (Schaik 2004).

Gorillas

With just one species, *Gorilla gorilla,* there are three subspecies of gorillas. The western lowland gorilla, the smallest of the three in size, is the animal you normally see in zoos. Western lowland gorillas live in the forests and swamps of the Central African Republic, Congo, Cameroon, Gabon, Equatorial Guinea, and Nigeria. As many as 100,000 of these animals are thought to inhabit central Africa. The eastern lowland gorilla, of which there are only four in captivity, is slightly larger and lives in eastern Congo. There are no mountain gorillas, the third subspecies, in captivity. It's estimated that a mere 650 of these animals survive in the wild. In physical size, these are the largest gorillas, with the longest hair (to keep them warm in their mountainous habitat). They are also the rarest gorillas, which Dian Fossey and other scientists have studied in Rwanda, Uganda, and eastern Congo.

Full-grown male gorillas may weigh 400 pounds (180 kilograms) and stand 6 feet tall (1.8 meters). Like most terrestrial primates, gorillas show marked sexual dimorphism. The average adult female weighs half as much as the male. Gorillas spend little time in the trees. It's particularly cumbersome for an adult male to move his bulk about in a tree. When gorillas sleep in trees, they build nests, which are usually no more than 10 feet (3 meters) off the ground. By contrast, the nests of chimps and female orangs may be 100 feet (30 meters) above the ground.

Most of the gorilla's day is spent feeding. Gorillas move through jungle undergrowth eating ground plants, leaves, bark, fruits, and other vegetation. Like most primates, gorillas live in social groups. The troop is a common unit of primate social organization, consisting of multiple males and females and their offspring. Although troops with up to 30 gorillas have been observed, most gorillas live in groups of 10 to 20. Gorilla troops tend to have fairly stable memberships, with little shifting between troops (Fossey 1983). Each troop has a silver-back male, so designated because of the strip of white hair that extends down his back. This is the physical sign of full maturity among the male gorillas. The silverback is usually the only breeding male in the troop, which is why gorilla troops are sometimes called "one-male groups." However, a few younger, subordinate males may also adhere to such a one-male group (Harcourt, Fossey, and Sabater-Pi 1981; Schaller 1963).

Most of our knowledge of gorilla behavior comes from studies of the eastern mountain gorilla. Mountain gorilla males who grow up to become dominant silverbacks may stay in their natal group for life, but females migrate when they mature. Fierce competition among mountain gorilla males for females is common. Silverbacks usually act very aggressively when neighboring groups approach one another. Spectacular male-to-male displays may feature chest beating, charging, and hooting. About one in five displays ends in physical violence (Pickrell 2004).

By contrast, recent studies of western lowland gorillas reveal a very different—and nonaggressive—pattern of behavior and social organization. Members of neighboring groups feed together peacefully in swamps and other habitats. Females from one group may sit right by the silverback from another. One study of western lowland gorillas combined observation of behavior with DNA analysis, which showed kinship ties among neighboring groups (Bradley et al. 2004; Pickrell 2004). Brenda Bradley and her colleagues collected hair and dung left in night nests of 12 western gorilla groups. Paternity tests on DNA from silverback hair and dung samples showed that many western gorillas (especially those in directly neighboring groups) are related as half or full brothers or as fathers and sons.

Western gorilla groups are small. Each is led by one reproductively active silverback. Other

For a quiz on primate types, see the Interactive Exercises

mhhe.com/kottak

mature males appear to leave home but remain nearby. It makes sense for related western silverbacks to be friendly toward one another. Peaceful interactions may help sons and brothers to establish neighboring territories and attract females, and thus to pass their common genes on to the next generation. Some anthropologists have speculated that the kinship patterns of early humans would have been similar to those of chimps and gorillas, which emphasize kin ties through males (Pickrell 2004).

Chimpanzees

Chimpanzees belong to the genus *Pan*, which has two species: *Pan troglodytes* (the common chimpanzee) and *Pan paniscus* (the bonobo or "pygmy" chimpanzee) (de Waal 1997; Susman 1987). Like humans, chimps are closely related to the gorilla, although there are some obvious differences. Like gorillas, chimps live in tropical Africa, but they range over a larger area and more varied environments than gorillas do (Figure 6.6). The common chimp, *Pan troglodytes*, lives in western central Africa (Gabon, Congo, Cameroon), as well as in western Africa (Sierra Leone, Liberia, The Gambia) and eastern Africa

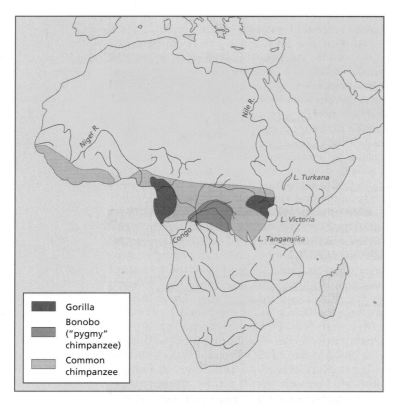

FIGURE 6.6 Geographic Distribution of African Apes. *Chimpanzees and gorillas are primarily rain forest dwellers. However, some chimpanzee populations live in woodland environments. This map shows the ranges of the three species of African apes.* SOURCE: From C. J. Jolly and F. Plog, *Physical Anthropology and Archeology*, 4th ed. (New York: McGraw-Hill, 1986), p. 115.

(Congo, Uganda, and Tanzania). Bonobos live in remote and densely forested areas of just one country—the Democratic Republic of Congo. Common chimps live mainly in tropical rain forests but also in woodlands and mixed forest-woodland-grassland areas, such as the Gombe Stream National Park, Tanzania, where Jane Goodall (1996) and other researchers began to study them in 1960.

There are dietary differences between chimps and gorillas. Gorillas eat large quantities of green bulk vegetation, but chimps, like orangutans and gibbons, prefer fruits. Chimps are actually omnivorous, adding animal protein to their diet by capturing small mammals, birds' eggs, and insects.

Chimps are lighter and more arboreal than gorillas are. The adult male's weight—between 100 and 200 pounds (45 to 90 kilograms)—is about a third that of the male gorilla. There is much less sexual dimorphism among chimps than among gorillas. Females approximate 88 percent of the average male height. This is similar to the ratio of sexual dimorphism in *Homo sapiens*.

Several scientists have studied wild chimps, and we know more about the full range of their behavior and social organization than we do about the other apes (see Wilson and Wrangham 2003; Wrangham et al., eds. 1994). The long-term research of Jane Goodall and others at Gombe provides especially useful information. Approximately 150 chimpanzees range over Gombe's 30 square miles (80 square kilometers). Goodall (1986, 1996) has described communities of about 50 chimps, all of which know one another and interact from time to time. Communities regularly split up into smaller groups: a mother and her offspring; a few males; males, females, and young; and occasionally solitary animals. Chimp communities are semiclosed. The social networks of males are more closed than are those of females, which are more likely to migrate and mate outside their natal group than males are (Wrangham, ed. 1994).

When chimps, which are very vocal, meet, they greet one another with gestures, facial expressions, and calls. They hoot to maintain contact during their daily rounds. Like baboons and macaques, chimps exhibit dominance relationships through attacks and displacement. Some adult females outrank younger males, although females do not display as strong dominance relationships among themselves as males do. Males occasionally cooperate in hunting parties.

Bonobos

Ancestral chimps, and especially humans, eventually spread out of the forests and into woodlands and more open habitats. Bonobos, which belong to the species *Pan paniscus*, apparently never left the protection of the trees. Up to 10,000 bonobos survive in the humid forests south of the Zaire River, in the Democratic Republic of Congo (DRC). Despite their common name—the pygmy chimpanzee—bonobos can't be distinguished from chimpanzees by size. Adult males of the smallest subspecies of chimpanzee average 95 pounds (43 kilograms), and females average 73 pounds (33 kilograms). These figures are about the same for bonobos (de Waal 1995, 1997).

Although much smaller than the males, female bonobos seem to rule. De Waal (1995, 1997) characterizes bonobo communities as female-centered, peace-loving, and egalitarian. The strongest social bonds are among females, although females also bond with males. The male bonobo's status reflects that of his mother, to whom he remains closely bonded for life.

The frequency with which bonobos have sex— and use it to avoid conflict—makes them exceptional among the primates. Despite frequent sex, the bonobo reproductive rate doesn't exceed that of the chimpanzee. A female bonobo gives birth every five or six years. Then, like chimps, female bonobos nurse and carry around their young for up to five years. Bonobos reach adolescence around seven years of age. Females, which first give birth at age 13 or 14, are full-grown by 15 years.

How do we know that bonobos use sexual activity to avoid conflict? According to de Waal:

> First, anything, including food, that arouses the interest of more than one bonobo at a time tends to result in sexual contact. If two bonobos approach a cardboard box thrown into their enclosure, they will briefly mount each other before playing with the box. Such situations lead to squabbles in most other species. But bonobos are quite tolerant, perhaps because they use sex to divert attention and to diffuse tension. Second, bonobo sex often occurs in aggressive contexts totally unrelated to food. A jealous male might chase another away from a female, after which the two males reunite and engage in scrotal rubbing. Or after a female hits a juvenile, the latter's mother may lunge at the aggressor, an action that is immediately followed by genital rubbing between the two adults (de Waal 1995, p. 87).

ENDANGERED PRIMATES

Deforestation poses a special risk for the primates, because 90 percent of the 190 living primate species live in tropical forests—in Africa, Asia, South America, and Central America. As the earth's human population swells, the populations of the nonhuman primates are shrinking. According to the Convention on International Trade in Endangered Species (ratified in 1973), all nonhuman primates are now endangered or

For more information on bonobos, see the Internet Exercise at your OLC

mhhe.com/kottak

Map 1 in the insert documents deforestation by showing annual changes in forest cover worldwide.

soon to be endangered. The apes (gibbons, gorillas, orangutans, and chimps) are in the "most endangered" category. Mountain gorillas, which once ranged widely in the forested mountains of East Africa, are now limited to a small area near the war-ravaged borders of Rwanda, the DRC, and Uganda. Other severely threatened species include the golden lion tamarin monkey of southeastern Brazil, the cotton-top tamarin of Colombia, the lion-tailed macaque of southern India, the woolly monkeys of Amazonia, and the orangutan of Southeast Asia (Mayell 2004a).

A combination of forestry and forest fires has been deadly to orangutans in Sumatra and Borneo in Indonesia. Sumatra, which is losing 1,000 orangs a year, has an estimated population of 6,000 left. A road for loggers and miners that penetrated the orangutan range in Sumatra led to contact with humans that proved fatal to hundreds of the animals. Borneo was devastated by fires in 1997–1998, leaving some 10,000–15,000 orangs, compared with 60,000 in 1980. Habitat destruction and fragmentation can isolate small groups of animals, leaving them vulnerable to extinction due to loss of genetic diversity. Primate populations are slow to recover from such threats. Ape species, for example, are slow reproducers, rarely having more than three to four offspring over a lifetime (Stern 2000).

Map 2 in the insert shows the world geographic distribution of nonhuman primates. Both surviving and extinct primate species are displayed.

A male bonobo (pygmy chimpanzee) from the Democratic Republic of Congo. Are bonobos smaller than chimps?

These include prosimians, New World monkeys, Old World monkeys, gibbons and siamangs, and the great apes. Note that primates once thrived in North America, when that continent was warmer and more forested than it is now.

Although the destruction of their forest habitats is the main reason the primates are disappearing, it isn't the only reason. Another threat is human hunting of primates for bush meat (Viegas 2000). In Amazonia, West Africa, and Central Africa, primates are a major source of food. People kill thousands of monkeys each year. Human hunting is less of a threat to primates in Asia. In India, Hindus avoid monkey meat because the monkey is sacred, while Moslems avoid it because monkeys are considered unclean and not fit for human consumption.

People also hunt primates for their skins and pelts; poachers sell their body parts as trophies and ornaments. Africans use the skins of black-and-white colobus monkeys for cloaks and head-dresses, and American and European tourists buy coats and rugs made from colobus pelts. In Amazonia, ocelot and jaguar hunters shoot monkeys to bait the traps they set for the cats.

Poachers pose the greatest threat to the mountain gorillas, of which there were as few as 250 left in the wild when Fossey started studying them (Fossey 1981, 1983). The poachers shoot the apes with high-powered rifles, then decapitate them and cut off their hands. They sell gorilla heads as trophies and turn their hands into grotesque ashtrays. Traps and snares set for antelope and buffalo also endanger gorillas, which sometimes get caught in the traps. Even if they manage to free themselves, they often die from infected wounds. The sad fate (murder and decapitation) of Dian Fossey's favorite gorilla, Digit, is familiar to those who have seen the 1988 film *Gorillas in the Mist*, the story of Fossey, her work with mountain gorillas, and her efforts to save them. Fossey herself was murdered in her cabin at her field site in Rwanda in 1985 (see Roberts 1995). The mystery of her death remains unsolved. The last entry in her diary reads: "When you realize the value of all life, you dwell less on what is past and concentrate on the preservation of the future." Through the efforts of the fund she established, the number of mountain gorillas has increased.

Primates also are killed when they are agricultural pests. In some areas of Africa and Asia, baboons and macaques raid the crops on which people depend for subsistence. Between 1947 and 1962, the government of Sierra Leone held annual drives to rid farm areas of monkeys, and between 15,000 and 20,000 primates perished each year.

A final reason for the demise of the primates is the capture of animals for use in labs or as pets. Although this threat is minor compared with deforestation and the hunting of primates for food, it does pose a serious risk to certain endangered species in heavy demand. One of the species most hurt by this trade is the chimpanzee, which has been widely used in biomedical research. One especially destructive way of capturing young primates is to shoot the mother and take her clinging infant.

SIMILARITIES BETWEEN HUMANS AND NONHUMAN PRIMATES

There is a substantial gap between primate society and fully developed human culture. However, studies of primates have revealed many similarities. Scholars used to contend that learned (versus instinctive) behavior separates humans from other animals. We know now that monkeys and apes also rely on learning. Many of the differences between humans and other primates are differences in degree rather than in kind. For example, monkeys learn from experiences, but humans learn much more. Another example: Apes make tools for specific tasks (see Mayell 2003), but human reliance on tools is much greater.

Learning

Common to monkeys, apes, and humans is the fact that behavior and social life are not rigidly programmed by the genes. All these animals learn throughout their lives. In several cases, an entire monkey troop has learned from the experiences of some of its members. In one group of Japanese macaques, a three-year-old female monkey started washing dirt off sweet potatoes before she ate them. First her mother, then her age peers, and finally the entire troop began washing sweet potatoes, too. The direction of learning was reversed when members of another macaque troop learned to eat wheat. After the dominant males had tried the new food, within four hours the practice had spread throughout the troop. Changes in learned behavior seem to spread more quickly from the top down than from the bottom up.

For monkeys as for people, the ability to learn, to profit from experience, confers a tremendous adaptive advantage, permitting them to avoid fatal mistakes. Faced with environmental change, primates don't have to wait for a genetic or physiological response. Learned behavior and social patterns can be modified instead.

Tools

Anthropologists used to distinguish humans from other animals as tool users, and there is no doubt that *Homo* does employ tools much more than any other animal does. However, tool use also turns up among several nonhuman species. For example, in the Galápagos Islands off western South America, there is a "woodpecker finch" that selects twigs to dig out insects and grubs from tree bark. Sea otters use rocks to break open mollusks, which are important in their diet. Beavers are famous for dam construction.

When it became obvious that people weren't the only tool users, anthropologists started contending that only humans make tools with foresight, that is, with a specific purpose in mind. Chimpanzees show that this, too, is debatable, as do the orangs described in the "News Brief" at the beginning of this chapter. Chimps living in the Tai forest of Ivory Coast make and use stone tools to break open hard, golfball-sized nuts (Mercader, Panger, and Boesch 2002). At specific sites, the chimps gather nuts, place them on trees which are used as anvils, and pound the nuts with heavy stones. Breaking open the nuts requires considerable force, which must be managed carefully. When too much force is applied, the nuts shatter into inedible pieces. The chimps also must select hammer stones suited to smashing the nuts and carry them to where the nut trees grow—sophisticated behavior for an animal. Nut

 STUDENT CD-ROM LIVING ANTHROPOLOGY

Bonobos and Language
Track 6

This clip presents the work of Dr. Sue Savage-Rumbaugh of Georgia State University, who has been working with chimpanzees and bonobos for more than 20 years. The clip focuses on her work with Kanzi, a male bonobo who has learned how to communicate through the manipulation of words and symbols. Like humans, but to a substantially lesser degree, apes can learn from observation, experience, and teaching. What did Kanzi learn that his mother could not learn? Why can't bonobos talk? Based on what you saw in the clip, would you say that Kanzi responds to spoken words or only to symbols?

cracking is a learned skill, with mothers showing their young how to do it.

In 1960, Jane Goodall (1996) began observing wild chimps—including their tool use and hunting behavior—at Gombe Stream National Park in Tanzania, East Africa. From the work of Goodall and many other researchers we know that wild chimps regularly make tools. To get water from places their mouths can't reach, thirsty chimps pick leaves, chew and crumple them, and then dip them into the water. Thus, with a specific purpose in mind, they devise primitive "sponges."

The most studied form of tool making by chimps involves "termiting." Chimps make tools to probe termite hills. They choose twigs, which they modify by removing leaves and peeling off bark to expose the sticky surface beneath. They carry the twigs to termite hills, dig holes with their fingers, and insert the twigs. Finally, they pull out the twigs and dine on termites that were attracted to the sticky surface.

Termiting isn't as easy as it might seem. Learning to termite takes time, and many Gombe chimps never master it. Twigs with certain characteristics must be chosen. Furthermore, once the twig is in the hill and the chimp judges that termites are crawling on its surface, the chimp must quickly flip the twig as it pulls it out so that the termites are on top. Otherwise they fall off as the twig comes out of the hole. This is an elaborate skill that neither all chimps nor all human observers have been able to master.

Chimps have other abilities essential to culture. When they are trained by humans, their skills flower, as anyone who has ever seen a movie, circus, or zoo chimp knows. Wild apes aim and throw objects. Humans have considerably elaborated the capacity to aim and throw, which is a homology passed down from the common ancestor of humans and apes. Without it we never would have developed projectile technology and weaponry—or baseball.

See the Internet Exercise at your OLC

mhhe.com/kottak

Tool use by chimps. These chimps are using stone tools to crack palm nuts in Liberia, as described in the text.

Predation and Hunting

Like tool making and language, hunting has been cited as a distinctive human activity that is not shared with our ape relatives. Again, however, primate research shows that what was previously thought to be a difference of kind is a difference of degree. The diets of other terrestrial primates are not exclusively vegetarian, as was once thought. Baboons kill and eat young antelopes, and researchers have repeatedly observed hunting by chimpanzees.

For several years John Mitani, David Watts, and other researchers have been observing chimpanzees at Ngogo in Uganda's Kibale National Park. This is the largest chimp community ever described in the wild. In 1998 it consisted of 26 adult males, 40 adult females, 16 adolescent males, 5 adolescent females, and 30 infants and juveniles (Mitani and Watts 1999). (Remember that chimp communities have a more stable male than female core membership—adolescent males tend to stay on while adolescent females tend to leave to join other troops.) The large community size permits the formation of large hunting parties, which contributes to hunting success. Hunting parties at Ngogo included an average of 26 individuals (almost always adult and adolescent males). Most hunts (78 percent) resulted in at least one prey item being caught—a much higher success rate than that among lions (26 percent), hyenas (34 percent), or cheetahs (30 percent). In most hunts (81 percent) the Ngogo chimps managed to catch multiple prey animals (three on average). The favored prey, at Ngogo as in other chimp communities, was the red colobus monkey.

As described by Mitani and Watts (1999), hunting by chimps is both opportunistic and planned. Opportunistic hunting took place when chimps encountered potential prey as they moved about during the day. Other hunts were organized patrols, in which the chimps became silent and moved together in a single file. They would stop, look up into the trees, scan, and change direction several times. Attentive to any arboreal movement, they would stop and search whenever they detected motion. After they spotted a monkey, the chase would begin. Encountering no prey, the chimps would go on patrolling, sometimes for several hours. The Ngogo chimps also collaborate by encircling red colobus groups, blocking potential escape routes, and driving their prey down hill slopes from taller to shorter trees. Chimps may give a specific call, the hunting call, at the start of a hunt, mobilizing hunters into action. Sometimes isolated chimps that encountered a red colobus monkey would give this call, after which other chimps would rush to the site and begin to hunt.

It turns out that chimps eat meat almost as much as some human hunter-gatherers do (Kopytoff 1995; Stanford 1999; Stanford and Bunn, eds. 2001). According to University of Southern California anthropologist Craig Stanford (1999), chimps may consume a quarter pound of meat a day when they hit their hunting stride. This meat intake is comparable to that of some contemporary groups of human hunter-gatherers. According to Stanford, male chimps often hunt as a way to gain access to sexually receptive females. Stanford repeatedly observed male chimps dangling monkey meat in front of a sexually swollen female, sharing only after copulation. When in **estrus** ("heat," or heightened sexual receptivity), female chimps copulate with more than a dozen males each day. The presence of meat in the diet of a female chimpanzee may enhance her offspring's survival chances (Kopytoff 1995). Meat sharing also could increase male reproductive success by making it easier to mate. Stanford found hunting to be seasonal at Gombe—occurring during the dry summer months, precisely the season when females tend to be sexually receptive, and when fruits, leaves, and nuts are scarce.

There appear to be political as well as sexual reasons for meat sharing by chimps. In 1992 the Japanese zoologist Toshisada Nishida described how, in Tanzania's Mahale Mountains, a high-ranking chimp male gave out pieces of meat to allies, while denying them to his enemies (Kopytoff 1995). Stanford observed a similar use of meat to cement alliances at Gombe. Archeological evidence indicates that humans hunted by at least 2.5 million years ago, based on stone meat-cutting tools found at Olduvai Gorge in Tanzania. Given our current understanding of chimp hunting and tool making, we can infer that hominids may have been hunting much earlier than the first archaeological evidence attests. Since chimps seem to devour the monkeys they kill, leaving few remains after their meal, we may never find archaeological evidence for the first hominid hunt, especially if it was done without stone tools.

Aggression and Resources

The potential for predation and aggression may be generalized in monkeys and apes, but its expression seems to depend on the environment. Jane Goodall specifically linked chimpanzees' aggression and predation to human encroachment on their natural habitat. The Gombe chimps are divided into a northern group and a smaller group of southerners. Parties from the north have invaded the southern territory and killed southern chimps. Infant victims were partially eaten by the assailants (Goodall 1986; Wade 2003).

John MacKinnon's research (1974) among orangutans on the Indonesian islands of Kalimantan (Borneo) and Sumatra showed that orangutans also had suffered as a result of human encroachment, particularly farming and timbering. On Borneo, in response to nearby human activities, orangs had developed a pattern of extreme sexual antagonism. During MacKinnon's field work, Bornean orangs rarely had sex. Their limited sexual encounters were always brief forced copulations, often with screaming infants clinging to their mothers throughout the ordeal.

As MacKinnon did his field work, logging operations were forcing orangs whose territory was destroyed into his research area, swelling the population it had to support. The response to this sudden overpopulation was a drastic decline in the local orang birth rate. Primates respond in various ways to encroachment and to population pressure. A change in sexual relationships that reduces the birth rate is one way of easing population pressure on resources.

We see that primate behavior is not rigidly determined by the genes. It is plastic (flexible), capable of varying widely as environmental forces change. Among humans, too, aggression increases when resources are threatened or scarce. What we know about other primates makes it reasonable to assume that early hominids were neither uniformly aggressive nor consistently meek. Their aggression and predation reflected environmental variation (see Silverberg and Gray, eds. 1992; Wrangham and Peterson 1996).

DIFFERENCES BETWEEN HUMANS AND NONHUMAN PRIMATES

The preceding sections have emphasized similarities between humans and other primates. *Homo* has elaborated substantially on certain tendencies

Through millions of years of adaptation to an omnivorous diet, humans and their ancestors have relied on gathering, hunting, and food sharing. These three Batak women from Palawan Island, the Philippines, share wild honeycombs.

shared with the apes. A unique concentration and combination of characteristics make humans distinct. However, the savanna or open grassland niche in which early humans evolved also selected certain traits that are not so clearly foreshadowed by the apes.

Sharing and Cooperation

Early humans lived in small social groups called bands, with economies based on hunting and gathering (foraging). Until fairly recently (12,000 to 10,000 years ago), all humans based their subsistence on hunting and gathering and lived in bands. Some such societies even managed to survive into the modern world, and ethnographers have studied them. From those studies we can conclude that in such societies, the strongest and most aggressive members do not dominate, as they do in a troop of terrestrial monkeys. Sharing and curbing of aggression are as basic to technologically simple humans as dominance and threats are to baboons.

We've seen that bonobos use sex to curb aggression and reduce conflict, and that male chimps cooperate in hunting. But as we saw from the brain response study described in Chapter 3, humans appear to be the most cooperative of the primates—in the food quest and other social activities. Except for meat sharing by chimps, the ape tendency is to forage individually. Monkeys also fend for themselves in getting food. Among human foragers, men generally hunt and women gather. Men and women bring resources back to the camp and share them. Older people who did not engage in the food quest get food from younger adults. Everyone shares the meat from a large animal. Nourished and protected by younger band members, elders live past the reproductive age and are respected for their knowledge and experience. The amount of information stored in a human band is far greater than that in any other primate society. Sharing, cooperation, and language are intrinsic to information storage. Through millions of years of adaptation to an omnivorous diet, humans have come to rely, more than any other primate, on hunting, food sharing, and cooperative behavior. These are universal features in human adaptive strategies.

Mating and Kinship

Another difference between humans and other primates involves mating. Among baboons, chimpanzees, and bonobos, most mating occurs when females enter estrus, during which they ovulate. Receptive females form temporary bonds with, and mate with, males. Human females, by contrast, lack a visible estrus cycle, and their ovulation is concealed. Neither a woman's sexual receptivity nor her readiness to conceive is physically evident, as it is in chimps and bonobos. Not knowing when ovulation is occurring, humans maximize their reproductive success by mating throughout the year. Human pair bonds for mating tend to be more exclusive and more durable than are those of chimps or bonobos. Related to our more constant sexuality, all human societies have some form of marriage. Marriage gives mating a reliable basis and grants to each spouse special, though not always exclusive, sexual rights in the other.

Marriage creates another major contrast between humans and nonhumans: exogamy and kinship systems. Most cultures have rules of exogamy requiring marriage outside one's kin or local group. Coupled with the recognition of kinship, exogamy confers adaptive advantages. It creates ties between the spouses' groups of origin. Their children have relatives, and therefore allies, in two kin groups rather than just one. The key point here is that ties of affection and mutual support between members of different local groups tend to be absent among primates other than *Homo*. There is a tendency among primates to disperse at adolescence. Among chimps and gorillas, females tend to migrate, seeking mates in other groups. Both male and female gibbons leave home when they become sexually mature. Once they find mates and establish their own territories, ties with their natal groups cease. For an exception, in which ties with the natal group are maintained after dispersal, see the section "Gorillas."

Among terrestrial monkeys, males leave the troop at puberty, eventually finding places elsewhere. The troop's core members are females. They sometimes form uterine groups made up of mothers, sisters, daughters, and sons that have not yet emigrated. This dispersal of males reduces the incidence of incestuous matings. Females mate with males born elsewhere, which join the troop at adolescence. Although kin ties are maintained between female monkeys, no close lifelong links are preserved through males.

Humans choose mates from outside the natal group, and usually at least one spouse moves. However, *humans maintain lifelong ties with sons and daughters.* The systems of kinship and marriage that preserve these links provide a major contrast between humans and other primates.

BEHAVIORAL ECOLOGY AND FITNESS

According to evolutionary theory, when the environment changes, natural selection starts to modify the *population*'s pool of genetic material. Natural selection has another key feature: the differential reproductive success of *individuals* within the population. **Behavioral ecology** studies the evolutionary basis of social behavior. It assumes that the genetic features of any species reflect a long history of differential reproductive success (that is, natural selection). In other words, biological traits of contemporary organisms have been transmitted across the generations because those traits enabled their ancestors to survive and reproduce more effectively than their competition.

Natural selection is based on *differential* reproduction. Members of the same species may compete to maximize their reproductive fitness—their genetic contribution to future generations. *Individual fitness* is measured by the number of direct descendants an individual has. Illustrating a primate strategy that may enhance individual fitness are cases in which male monkeys kill infants after entering a new troop. Destroying the offspring of other males, they clear a place for their own progeny (Hausfater and Hrdy, eds. 1984).

Besides competition, one's genetic contribution to future generations also can be enhanced by cooperation, sharing, and other apparently unselfish behavior. This is because of *inclusive fitness*—reproductive success measured by the genes one shares with relatives. By sacrificing for their kin—even if this means limiting their own direct reproduction—individuals actually may increase their genetic contributions (their shared genes) to the future. Inclusive fitness helps us understand why a female might invest in her sister's offspring, or why a male might risk his life to defend his brothers. If self-sacrifice perpetuates more of their genes than direct reproduction does, it makes sense in terms of behavioral ecology. Such a view can help us understand aspects of primate behavior and social organization.

Maternal care always makes sense in terms of reproductive fitness theory because females know their offspring are their own. But it's harder for males to be sure about paternity. Inclusive fitness theory predicts that males will invest most in offspring when they are surest the offspring are theirs. Gibbons, for example, have strict male–female pair bonding, which makes it almost certain that the offspring are those of both members of the pair. Thus we expect male gibbons to offer care and protection to their young, and they do. However, among species and in situations in which a male can't be sure about his paternity, it may make more sense to invest in a sister's offspring than in a mate's because the niece or nephew definitely shares some of that male's genes.

SUMMARY

1. Humans, apes, monkeys, and prosimians are primates. The primate order is subdivided into suborders, superfamilies, families, genera, species, and subspecies. Organisms in any subdivision (taxon) of a taxonomy are assumed to share more recent ancestry with each other than they do with organisms in other taxa. But it's sometimes hard to tell the difference between homologies, which reflect common ancestry, and analogies, biological similarities that develop through convergent evolution.

2. Prosimians are the older of the two primate suborders. Some 40 million years ago, anthropoids displaced prosimians from niches their ancestors once occupied. Tarsiers and lorises are prosimians that survived by adapting to nocturnal life. Lemurs survived on the isolated island of Madagascar.

3. Anthropoids include humans, apes, and monkeys. All share fully developed primate trends, such as depth and at least partial color vision. Other anthropoid traits include a shift in tactile areas to the fingers. The New World monkeys are all arboreal. Old World monkeys include both terrestrial species (e.g., baboons and macaques) and arboreal ones. The great apes are orangutans, gorillas, and chimpanzees. The lesser apes are gibbons and siamangs.

4. Gibbons and siamangs live in Southeast Asian forests. These apes are slight, arboreal animals whose mode of locomotion is brachiation. Sexual dimorphism, slight among gibbons, is marked among orangutans, which are confined to two Indonesian islands. Sexually dimorphic gorillas, the most terrestrial apes, are vegetarians confined to equatorial Africa. Two species of chimpanzees live in the forests and woodlands of tropical Africa. Chimps are less sexually dimorphic, more numerous, and more omnivorous than gorillas are. Terrestrial monkeys (baboons and macaques) live in troops. Baboon males, the troop's main protectors, are twice the size of females.

5. Deforestation poses a special risk for the primates. Most of the 190 living primate species are in tropical forests—in Africa, Asia, South America, and Central America. Primates also are endangered as humans hunt them for food (bush meat) and capture them for zoos and research.

6. There are significant differences between humans and other primates. But similarities are also extensive, and many differences are of degree rather than of kind. A unique concentration and combination of ingredients make humans distinct. Some of our most important adaptive traits are foreshadowed in other primates, particularly in the African apes. Primate behavior and social organization aren't rigidly programmed by the genes. The ability to learn, which is the basis of culture, is an adaptive advantage available to many nonhuman primates. Chimpanzees make tools for several purposes. They also hunt and share meat.

7. Important differences between humans and other primates remain. Aggression and dominance are characteristic of terrestrial monkeys. Sharing and cooperation are equally significant in human bands. Only humans have systems of kinship and marriage that permit us to maintain lifelong ties with relatives in different local groups.

8. From the perspective of behavioral ecology, individuals in a population compete to increase their genetic contribution to future generations. Maternal care makes sense from this perspective because females can be sure their offspring are their own. Because it's harder for males to be sure about paternity, evolutionary theory predicts they will invest most in offspring when they are surest the offspring are theirs.

KEY TERMS

See the flash cards
mhhe.com/kottak

analogies Similarities arising as a result of similar selective forces; traits produced by convergent evolution.

anthropoids Members of Anthropoidea, one of the two suborders of primates; monkeys, apes, and humans are anthropoids.

arboreal Tree-dwelling; arboreal primates include gibbons, New World monkeys, and many Old World monkeys.

behavioral ecology Study of the evolutionary basis of social behavior.

bipedal Two-footed; upright bipedalism is the characteristic human mode of locomotion.

brachiation Under-the-branch swinging; characteristic of gibbons, siamangs, and some New World monkeys.

convergent evolution Independent operation of similar selective forces; the process by which analogies are produced.

estrus Period of maximum sexual receptivity in female baboons, chimpanzees, and other primates, signaled by vaginal area swelling and coloration.

gibbons The smallest apes, natives of Asia; arboreal.

hominids Members of the zoological family that includes fossil and living humans, chimpanzees, gorillas, and their common ancestors.

hominoids Members of the superfamily including humans and all the apes.

homologies Traits that organisms have jointly inherited from a common ancestor.

opposable thumb A thumb that can touch all the other fingers.

primatology The study of fossil and living apes, monkeys, and prosimians, including their behavior and social life.

prosimians The primate suborder that includes lemurs, lorises, and tarsiers.

sexual dimorphism Marked differences in male and female anatomy and temperament.

taxonomy Classification scheme; assignment to categories (*taxa*; singular, *taxon*).

terrestrial Ground-dwelling; baboons, macaques, and humans are terrestrial primates; gorillas spend most of their time on the ground.

CRITICAL THINKING QUESTIONS

For more self-testing, see the self-quizzes
mhhe.com/kottak

1. Among the primates, give an example of an analogy produced through convergent evolution. Can you think of analogies involving animals other than primates?

2. What are the main trends in primate evolution? Compare a cat or dog with a monkey, ape, or human. What are the main differences in the sensory organs—those that have to do with vision, smell, and touch, for example?

3. What are some examples of ways in which nonhuman primates rely on learning to adapt to their environment?

4. Why is it significant that among primates, only humans maintain ties of affection and mutual support between different local groups?

5. How do behavioral ecology and fitness theory help us understand differences between female and male parental investment strategies?

SUGGESTED ADDITIONAL READINGS

Burton, F. D., and M. Eaton
  1995 *The Multimedia Guide to Non-Human Primates.* Upper Saddle River, NJ: Prentice Hall. A CD-ROM combining photos, illustrations, video, sound, and text—presenting over 200 species of nonhuman primates.

De Waal, F. B. M.
  1997 *Bonobo: The Forgotten Ape.* Berkeley: University of California Press. Field-based study of rare and remote apes noted for their similarities to humans and their sexual behavior.
  2000 *Chimpanzee Politics: Power and Sex among Apes,* rev. ed. Baltimore: Johns Hopkins University Press. Hierarchy, sex, and alliance among apes, mainly based on zoo observations.
  2001 *The Ape and the Sushi Master: Cultural Reflections by a Primatologist.* New York: Basic Books. Behavior of humans and apes.

Fedigan, L. M.
  1992 *Primate Paradigms: Sex Roles and Social Bonds.* Chicago: University of Chicago Press. Focuses on sex roles in primate social organization.

Fossey, D.
  1983 *Gorillas in the Mist.* Boston: Houghton Mifflin. Social organization of the mountain gorilla; basis of the popular film.

Goodall, J.
  1996 *My Life with the Chimpanzees.* New York: Pocket Books. Popular account of the author's life among the chimps.

Montgomery, S.
  1991 *Walking with the Great Apes: Jane Goodall, Dian Fossey, Biruté Galdikas.* Boston: Houghton Mifflin. The stories of three primatologists who have worked with, and to preserve, chimpanzees, gorillas, and orangutans.

Morbeck, M. E., A. Galloway, and A. L. Zihlman, eds.
1997 *The Evolving Female: A Life-History Perspective*. Princeton, NJ: Princeton University Press. Primatology and human evolution from a female perspective.

Russon, A. E., K. A. Bard, and S. Taylor Parker, eds.
1996 *Reaching into Thought: The Minds of the Great Apes*. New York: Cambridge University Press. Papers examining the intelligence of the apes.

Small, M. F.
1993 *Female Choices: Sexual Behavior of Female Primates*. Ithaca, NY: Cornell University Press. Sexual behavior and characteristics of female apes and monkeys.

Smuts, B. B.
1999 *Sex and Friendship in Baboons*. Cambridge, MA: Harvard University Press. Pair bonding, mutual support, and parental investment in baboon social organization, with implications for early human evolution.

Stanford, C. B.
1999 *Hunting Apes: Meat Eating and the Origins of Human Behavior*. Princeton, NJ: Princeton University Press. The role of meat and hunting in sex and alliance among wild chimps.

Stanford, C. B., and H. T. Bunn, eds.
2001 *Meat-Eating and Human Evolution*. New York: Oxford University Press. Compendium of various recent studies.

Strier, K. B.
2003 "Primate Behavioral Ecology: From Ethnography to Ethology and Back." *American Anthropologist* 105(1):16–27. Biocultural essay.
2007 *Primate Behavioral Ecology*, 3rd ed. Boston: Allyn & Bacon. Behavior and reproductive strategies among primates.

Strum, S. C., and L. M. Fedigan, eds.
2000 *Primate Encounters: Models of Science, Gender, and Society*. Chicago: University of Chicago Press. The roles of males and females in primate social organization.

Swindler, D. R.
1998 *Introduction to the Primates*. Seattle: University of Washington Press. Up-to-date survey.

Wrangham, R. W., ed.
1994 *Chimpanzee Cultures*. Cambridge, MA: Harvard University Press.

1. Primate Conflict: Go to the Living Link's video collection at Emory University's Center for the Advanced Study of Ape and Human Evolution website, **http://www.emory.edu/LIVING_LINKS/AV/conflict_28k.ram**, and watch the Chimpanzee Conflict movie.
   a. What different kinds of aggression are presented in the movie?
   b. What are the different responses to aggression? Did these responses tend to escalate or terminate the aggressive behavior?
   c. Is aggressive behavior restricted to adults? Does it take on different forms in juveniles?
   d. Which of these aggressive behaviors and responses do humans share with the chimpanzees? For example, do humans use bluff display?

2. Primate Taxonomy: Go to the Primate Taxonomy section of the Emory University Living Links website: **http://www.emory.edu/LIVING_LINKS/Taxonomy.html**.
   a. What percentage of our DNA do we share with chimps and bonobos?
   b. Are baboons and macaques more closely related to each other than humans and orangutans are? About how long ago did the lines leading to humans and orangutans separate? When did the hominoids split off from other primates?
   c. What are the largest and the smallest primates? Which primates have cheek pouches for food storage? Which primates have a complex stomach for the processing of foliage? Other than humans, which primates can be said to sing?
   d. Which primate has the largest geographic distribution, the largest brain, and the least hair on its body?

See Chapter 6 at your McGraw-Hill Online Learning Center for additional review and interactive exercises.

INTERNET EXERCISES

Saving the Forests

See your OLC "Bringing It All Together" links
mhhe.com/kottak

This essay, like all the "Bringing It All Together" essays in this book, shows how anthropology's subfields and dimensions can unite to deal with a particular problem.

Deforestation, a problem that faces the world, also is a topic that has attracted the attention of anthropology's four subfields and two dimensions. Anthropology always has been concerned with how environmental forces influence humans and primates and how human activities affect the biosphere and the earth itself. As we saw in Chapter 4, biological anthropologists have examined the relation between farming, deforestation, and the spread of malaria and the gene that causes sickle-cell anemia. Other physical anthropologists—primatologists—see deforestation as a major threat to the animals they study. Paleoanthropologists have suggested a link between climate change, shrinking of forests, and the origin of the human lineage. Archaeologists have viewed deforestation in the context of resource use by ancient farmers and herders. Lin-

guistic anthropologists have studied how people name and classify plants and forest resources. Cultural anthropologists have documented the varied uses people make of the forest and its products. From the fairy tales of Western Europe (e.g., Hansel and Gretel) to recent Hollywood films, the forest plays a potent symbolic role as a place of mystery, danger, and enchantment. Today applied anthropologists are working to devise culturally appropriate and effective strategies to curb deforestation and preserve biodiversity.

Deforestation is a global concern. Forest loss contributes to greenhouse gas production (CO_2), which has been implicated in global warming. The destruction of tropical forests is also a major factor in the loss of global biodiversity. This is the case because of the many species, often of limited distribution, in forests, especially in the tropics. Tropical forests may contain more than half of earth's species while covering just 6 percent of the planet's land surface. Yet tropical forests are disappearing at the rate of 10 million to 20 million hectares per year (the size of New York state).

◼ *Applied anthropology uses anthropological perspectives to identify and solve contemporary problems that affect humans. Deforestation is one such problem. Here women take part in a reforestation project in coastal Tanzania near Dar es Salaam.*

Among the tropical animals whose natural habitats are threatened, primates, most of which are forest dwellers, are especially at risk. Consider the Democratic Republic of the Congo (DRC), the country that ranks fourth in the world in terms of greatest biodiversity. Its threatened species include gorillas and bonobos. The major threat to the bonobo, which is found only in the DRC, is forestry and loss of the hardwood forests where most bonobos live (Sengupta 2004). In Indonesia, deforestation threatens the orangutan (Mayell 2004*a*). Contact with humans after the opening of a road for loggers and miners proved fatal to hundreds of orangs. Recent Indonesian policy has promoted plantations rather than forest preservation. Government policy has shifted from selective logging, which permits some animals to survive, to clear-cutting of the forest, which destroys the habitat (Dreifus 2000). Forests also have suffered from ancient and modern forest fires.

Cultural factors, including politics, affect the use of the forest and its perceived value to humans. Some governments and administrations are more environment-friendly than others are. And even if a country has strict environmental laws, those laws require enforcement. Consider Brazil's Amazon rain forest, where dozens of primate species live. Brazilian national deforestation policy has to be implemented at the local level, but many local political systems are controlled by ranching and mining interests that oppose environmental regulation.

Physical, archaeological, and cultural anthropologists have all examined how human strategies of adaptation, including economic activities, affect the environment, including use of the forest. The historic shift from foraging (hunting and gathering) to food production (farming and herding) first took place in the Middle East some 10,000–12,000 years ago, and again in the Western Hemisphere 5,000 years later. With food production, the rate at which human beings degrade their environments increased. Population increase and the need to expand farming caused deforestation in many parts of the ancient Middle East and Mesoamerica (Mexico, Guatemala, Belize, and Honduras). People cut down trees to plant crops such as wheat in the Middle East and maize (corn) in Mesoamerica. Even today, many farmers think of trees as giant weeds to be removed and replaced with productive fields. Many farmers burn vegetation to remove weeds, then use the ashes for fertilizer. Herders burn to promote the growth of young tender shoots for their livestock. If done too often, as may happen when population grows, these activities result in deforestation. The use of fuel wood by early smelters also took its toll on the forests.

As we'll see in Chapter 11, located in what is now western Honduras, Copán was once a thriv-

ing Maya royal center. Its collapse some 1,400 years ago was linked to deforestation, erosion, and soil exhaustion due to overpopulation and overfarming. Studies of Copán's paleopathology reveal food stress and malnutrition. Most (80 percent) of the corpses buried there had anemia, due to iron deficiency. Even Copán's nobles were malnourished. One noble skull, known to be such from its carved teeth and cosmetic deformation, has telltale signs of anemia: spongy areas at its rear.

What about forests, their uses and value, and threats to them today? In many parts of the world, forests supply medicinal plants; food products such as honey, game, and fruits; and wood—used to build houses, fences, and animal pens. Forests are also vital parts of watersheds—regions drained by river systems: trees take up and conserve water. By conserving water, forests impede erosion and siltation (mineral deposits) in irrigation canals.

Glen Green (a geologist) and Robert Sussman (a biological anthropologist) (1990) used remote sensing (as discussed in Chapter 3) to study deforestation in the eastern rain forests of Madagascar. In this area are found several endangered species, including the lemurs discussed in "Beyond the Classroom" in Chapter 7. Green and Sussman found deforestation there to be correlated both with topographic relief (the slope or steepness of the land) and with human population density. Sparsely populated areas and very hilly areas had less forest loss than did densely populated and flat to moderately hilly areas. More than half the forest cover in the sparsely populated regions had survived, compared with just 19 percent in the high-density areas. The Green–Sussman study exposed an important fact for policy makers: Although low relief areas need protection the most, nearly all of Madagascar's forest reserves had been established in hilly areas. What recommendation would an

The causes of deforestation are diverse. In this example from Madagascar, the rain forest has been cut back to enlarge a cattle ranch. What are some other causes of deforestation?

Map 1 in the insert documents deforestation by showing annual changes in forest cover worldwide, and Map 2 shows the geographic distribution of primates—living and fossil.

■ *Forests supply medicinal plants, food products, and wood. This woman is collecting medicinal plants in Sarawak, Malaysia.*

applied anthropologist make for the location of future protected areas?

Often, as in eastern Madagascar, in the ancient Middle East, and at Copán, deforestation is demographically driven—caused by population pressure. Madagascar's population is growing at a rate of 3 percent annually, doubling every generation. Population pressure leads to migration, including rural–urban migration. Madagascar's capital, Antananarivo, had just 100,000 people in 1967, but over 1 million by 1990. Urban growth promotes deforestation if city dwellers rely on fuel wood from the countryside, as has been true in Madagascar.

As forested watersheds disappear, crop productivity declines. Madagascar is known as the "great red island," after the color of its soil. On that island, the effects of erosion and runoff are visible to the naked eye. Looking at its rivers, Madagascar appears to be bleeding to death. Increasing runoff of water no longer trapped by trees causes erosion of low-lying rice fields near swollen rivers, as well as siltation in irrigation canals (Kottak et al. 1994).

Besides population pressure, another prominent cause of deforestation is commercial logging, which can degrade forests in several ways. Obviously, logging deforests because it removes trees. Less evident are the destructive effects of road building, tree dragging, and other features of com-

mercial logging. A logging road may cut a swath for erosion. In one village in Madagascar, whose forest had recently been invaded by loggers from outside, villagers told an ethnographer that the loggers killed a dozen trees for every log they dragged out (Kottak et al. 1994).

The global scenarios of deforestation include demographic pressure (from births or immigration) on subsistence economies, commercial logging, road building, cash cropping, fuel wood needs associated with urban expansion, and clearing and burning associated with livestock and grazing. The fact that forest loss has several causes has a policy implication: Different deforestation scenarios require different conservation strategies.

What can be done? On this question applied anthropology weighs in (see Kottak and Costa 1993), spurring policy makers to think about new conservation strategies. The traditional approach has been to restrict access to forested areas designated as parks, then employ park guards and punish violators. Modern strategies are more likely to consider the needs, wishes, and abilities of the people (often impoverished) living in and near the forest. Since effective conservation depends on the cooperation of the local people, their concerns must be addressed in devising conservation strategy.

Typically, forests have substantial economic and cultural utility for the communities in and near them. Forests supply firewood and wood for house and granary construction, fences, and technology (e.g., oxcarts and mortars and pestles—for pounding grain). Some forests are used for food production, including slash-and-burn or shifting cultivation. Tree crops such as bananas, fruits, and coffee do well in the forest, where foraging for wild products also proceeds. Forests also contain vital cultural products. In Madagascar, for example, these products include medicinal plants and pastes considered essential for the proper growth of children. In one ethnic group rice from a forest field is part of the ceremony used to ensure a successful and fertile marriage. Another ethnic group has its most sacred tombs in the forests. Traditionally, these culturally vital areas of the forest have been tabooed for burning and wood cutting. They are part of a local conservation system that has been in place for generations.

What happens when activities are banned not by the traditional culture but by an external agency? Government-imposed conservation policies may require people to change the way they have been doing things for generations to meet the goals of outside planners rather than those of local people. When communities are asked to give up traditional activities on which they depend for their livelihood, they usually resist. To be successful, conservation schemes must involve local people in planning and implementing the policies and programs that will affect them.

Effective environmentalism requires culturally informed negotiation with political and economic interests at the local, regional, national, and international levels. Here is an arena in which anthropology is fruitfully applied. Conservationists must learn to recognize and build on diverse systems of environmental values—different "ethnoecologies." (An *ethnoecology* is any society's traditional set of environmental perceptions, its ideas about the environment in relation to people and society.) Effective conservation strategy requires extensive and ongoing knowledge of affected areas and the socioeconomic and cultural practices of the local people.

To curb the global deforestation threat, we need conservation strategies that work. Laws and enforcement may help reduce commercially driven deforestation caused by burning and clearcutting. But local people also use and abuse forested lands. A challenge for the environmentally oriented applied anthropologist is to find ways to make forest preservation attractive to local people and ensure their cooperation. Successful conservation must be based on culturally appropriate policies, which applied anthropologists can help devise for specific places. To provide locally meaningful incentives, we need good anthropological knowledge of each affected area. Governments and international agencies are likely to fail if they try to impose their goals without considering the practices, customs, rules, laws, beliefs, and values of the people to be affected. Applied anthropologists work to make "good for the globe" good for the people.

7

Primate Evolution

FOSSILS AND CHRONOLOGY

The fossil record, as the "News Brief" reports, provides evidence for only 5 percent of extinct primates. With such small numbers, the fossil record gives us the merest glimpse of the diverse bioforms—living beings—that have existed on earth. In Chapter 3, in the section "Dating the Past," we learned why some areas and times are better represented in the fossil record than others are. Conditions favoring fossilization open special "time windows" for certain places and times, such as western Kenya from 18 to 14 **m.y.a.**—million years ago. Because western Kenya was geologically active then, it has a substantial fossil record. Between 12 and 8 m.y.a., the area was quieter geologically, and there are few fossils. After 8 m.y.a., another time window opens in the Rift Valley area of eastern Kenya. The East African highlands were rising, volcanoes were active, and lake basins were forming and filling with sediments. This time window extends through the present and includes

133

many hominid fossils, many of which are hominins. The term **hominin** describes all the human species that ever have existed, including the extinct ones, and excludes chimps and gorillas. Compared with East Africa, West Africa has been more stable geologically and has had few time windows (Jolly and White 1995).

In considering the primate fossil record, we'll see that different geographic areas provide more abundant fossil evidence for different time periods. This doesn't necessarily mean that primates weren't living elsewhere at the same time. The discussions of primate and human evolution must be tentative, because the fossil record is limited and spotty. Much is subject to change as knowledge increases. Recall from Chapter 1 that a key feature of science is to recognize the tentativeness and uncertainty of knowledge. Scientists, including fossil hunters, constantly seek out new evidence, and devise new methods, such as DNA comparison, to improve their understanding, in this case of primate and human evolution.

We learned in Chapter 3 that the remains of animals and plants that lived at the same time are found in the same stratum. Based on fossils found in stratigraphic sequences, the history of vertebrate life has been divided into three main eras. The *Paleozoic* was the era of ancient life—fishes, amphibians, and primitive reptiles. The *Mesozoic* was the era of middle life—reptiles, including the dinosaurs. The *Cenozoic* is the era of recent life—birds and mammals. Each era is divided into periods, and the periods are divided into epochs. (See Figure 7.1.)

Anthropologists are concerned with the Cenozoic era, which includes two periods: Tertiary and

See your OLC Internet Exercises
mhhe.com/kottak

See the Virtual Exploration
mhhe.com/kottak

Era	Period	
Cenozoic	Quaternary	1.8 m.y.a.
	Tertiary	65 m.y.a.
Mesozoic	Cretaceous	146 m.y.a.
	Jurassic	208 m.y.a.
	Triassic	245 m.y.a.
Paleozoic	Permian	286 m.y.a.
	Carboniferous	360 m.y.a.
	Devonian	410 m.y.a.
	Silurian	440 m.y.a.
	Ordovician	505 m.y.a.
	Cambrian	544 m.y.a.
Proterozoic	Neoproterozoic	900 m.y.a.
	Mesoproterozoic	1,600 m.y.a.
	Paleoproterozoic	2,500 m.y.a.
Archaean		3,800 m.y.a.
Hadean		4,500 m.y.a.

FIGURE 7.1 Geological Time Scales.
The geological time scale, based on stratigraphy. Eras are subdivided into periods; and periods, into epochs. In what era, period, and epoch did Homo *originate?*

Quaternary. Each of these periods is subdivided into epochs. The Tertiary had five epochs: Paleocene, Eocene, Oligocene, Miocene, and Pliocene. The Quaternary includes just two epochs: Pleistocene and Holocene, or Recent. Figure 7.1 gives the approximate dates of these epochs. Sediments from the Paleocene epoch (65 to 54 m.y.a.) have yielded fossil remains of diverse small mammals, some possibly ancestral to the primates. Prosimian-like fossils abound in strata dating from the Eocene (54 to 36 m.y.a.). The first anthropoid fossils date to

OVERVIEW

The primate order evolved by exploiting new opportunities that arose at the end of the Mesozoic era, around 65 million years ago. Flowering plants proliferated, along with the insects attracted to them and the animals that preyed on those insects. Grasping hands and depth perception aided in the capture of insects and were adaptive in an arboreal environment.

The Eocene epoch was the age of prosimians. By the end of the Eocene, the anthropoids had emerged, eventually to displace the prosimians in most places. In the next epoch, the Oligocene, New World monkeys split off from the ancestors of Old World monkeys, apes, and humans.

The ensuing Miocene epoch witnessed a fluorescence of proto-apes. After Africa collided with Eurasia, apes spread into Europe and Asia. The lines leading to the orangutan, on the one hand, and the African apes, on the other, split during the middle Miocene. The common ancestor of humans, chimps, and gorillas—as yet unidentified—lived during the late Miocene, some five to eight million years ago.

Era	Period	Epoch		Climate and Life Forms
Cenozoic	Quaternary	Holocene 11,000 B.P.		Transition to agriculture; emergence of states
		Pleistocene 1.8 m.y.a.		Climatic fluctuations, glaciation; *Homo, A. boisei*
	Tertiary	Pliocene 5 m.y.a.		*A. robustus, A. africanus, A. afarensis, A. anamensis, Ardipithecus*
		Miocene 23 m.y.a.		Cooler and drier grasslands spread in middle latitudes; Africa collides with Eurasia (16 m.y.a.); *Afropithecus, Sivapithecus,* etc.
		Oligocene 38 m.y.a.		Cooler and drier in the north; anthropoids in Africa (Fayum); separation of catarrhines and platyrrhines; separation of hylobatids from pongids and hominids
		Eocene 54 m.y.a.		Warm tropical climates become widespread; modern orders of mammals appear; prosimianlike primates; anthropoids appear by late Eocene
		Paleocene 65 m.y.a.		First major mammal radiation

FIGURE 7.1   Geological Time Scales—Concluded.
Periods and Epochs of the Cenozoic Era.

the middle to late Eocene (54 to 38 m.y.a.) and the early Oligocene (38 to 23 m.y.a.). Hominoids became widespread during the Miocene (23 to 5 m.y.a.). Hominins first appeared in the late Miocene or early Pliocene (5 to 2 m.y.a.) (Figure 7.1).

EARLY PRIMATES

When the Mesozoic era ended, and the Cenozoic began, some 65 million years ago, North America was connected to Europe, but not to South America. (The Americas joined some 20 million years ago.) Over millions of years, the continents have "drifted" to their present locations, carried along by the gradually shifting plates of the earth's surface (Figure 7.2).

During the Cenozoic, most land masses had tropical or subtropical climates. The Mesozoic era had ended with a massive worldwide extinction of plants and animals, including the dinosaurs. Thereafter, mammals replaced reptiles as the dominant large land animals. Trees and flowering plants soon proliferated, supplying arboreal foods for the primates that eventually evolved to fill the new niches.

According to the **arboreal hypothesis,** primates became primates by adapting to arboreal life. The primate traits and trends discussed in Chapter 6 developed as adaptations to life high up in the trees. A key feature was the importance of sight over smell. Changes in the visual appara-

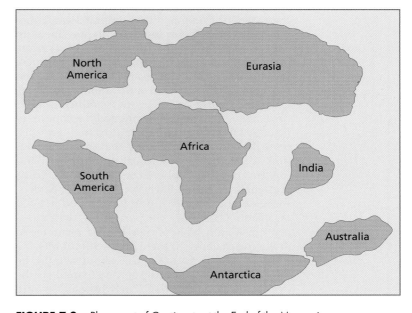

FIGURE 7.2   Placement of Continents at the End of the Mesozoic.
When the Mesozoic era ended, and the Cenozoic began, some 65 million years ago, North America was connected to Europe, but not to South America.

tus were adaptive in the trees, where depth perception facilitated leaping. Grasping hands and feet were used to crawl along slender branches. Grasping feet anchored the body as the primates reached for foods at the ends of branches. Early primates probably had omnivorous diets based

According to one theory, binocular vision and manipulative hands developed among primates because they facilitated the capture of insects. What is this theory called? Here a Colombian squirrel monkey uses its hands and eyes to eat a katydid.

Map Atlas

Map 3 indicates where various fossil primates lived during the Eocene, Oligocene, and Miocene epochs.

on foods available in the trees, such as flowers, fruits, berries, gums, and insects. The early Cenozoic era witnessed a proliferation of *angiosperms*—flowering plants. Their seeds, fruit, and the insects that were attracted to those flowering plants all figured prominently in the early primate diet.

Matt Cartmill (1974, 1992) observed that although primate traits work well in the trees, they aren't the only possible adaptations to arboreal life. Squirrels, for instance, do just fine with claws and snouts and without binocular vision. Something else must have figured in primate evolution, and Cartmill suggests a **visual predation hypothesis.** This is the idea that binocular vision, grasping hands and feet, and reduced claws developed because they facilitated the capture of insects, which were important in the early primate diet. Cartmill proposed that early primates first adapted to bushy forest undergrowth and low tree branches, where they foraged for fruits and insects. Particularly in pursuing insects, those early primates would have relied heavily on vision. Close-set eyes permitting depth perception would have allowed those primates to judge the distance to their prey without moving their heads. Eventually the snout would be reduced, with a less acute sense of smell, as the eyes came closer together. Early primates would have held on with their grasping feet as they snared their prey with their hands. Several living prosimians retain the small body size and insectivorous diet that may have characterized the first primates. Jurmain (1997) suggests that although key primate traits might have evolved first for life in the lower branches, such traits would have become even more adaptive when bug snatching was done higher up in the trees.

However, the anatomy and behavior of contemporary prosimians suggest a weakness in the visual predation hypothesis. Prosimians are considered to be more similar to the earliest primates than the anthropoids are. Yet prosimians, as they move about and feed themselves, rely less on vision than anthropoids do. Prosimians emphasize smell and hearing in their pursuit of food. Given this fact, primatologist Robert Sussman (2004) has proposed the **mixed diet hypothesis:** The increased use of angiosperms (flowering plants) led to modern primate characteristics. Early primates would have relied on vision as they sought fruits, seeds, and flowers as well as insects. The rapid spread of flowering plants in the Paleocene epoch roughly coincides with the emergence of the earliest primates.

Primatologists and paleontologists learn about the past through the discovery and analysis of material remains, such as bones and teeth. Often the fossil record provides clues about the ancient habitat. For example, if fossils of animals that live typically in forests today are found together in a given geological stratum, scientists can infer that the ancient environment was forested. The study of anatomically similar animals today also helps scientists understand the characteristics of past animals. Thus, to infer the adaptive characteristics, including the behavior patterns, of early primates, primatologists consider anatomically similar contemporary animals that live in similar habitats. An arboreal lemur, loris, or tarsier might be used, for example, to model the behavior of an anatomically similar fossil primate. The various hypotheses about the evolution of vision among early primates illustrate how the anatomy and behavior of contemporary animals can be used to infer the behavior of ancient life forms.

Early Cenozoic Primates

There is considerable fossil evidence that a diversified group of primates lived, mainly in Europe and North America, during the second epoch of the Cenozoic, the Eocene. On that basis it is likely that the earliest primates lived during the first epoch of the Cenozoic, the Paleocene (65–54 m.y.a.). The status of several fossils as possible Paleocene primates has been debated. As there is no consensus on this matter, such fossils are not discussed here.

A tiny primate skull found recently in China (Malkin 2004; Ni et al. 2004) confirms that early primates lived in Asia near the start of the Eocene. A team of Chinese paleontologists led by Xijun Ni found the new primate species, *Teilhardina asiatica,* in China's Hunan province. The 55-million-year-old skull, with most of its teeth intact, is the most complete skull ever found of a euprimate. (The term *euprimate* refers to the first mammals that shared characteristics such as forward-facing eyes and a relatively large brain

Suddenly, Primate Ancestors Pushed
Back to Time Dinosaurs Roamed

WASHINGTON POST NEWS BRIEF

by Guy Gugliotta
April 18, 2002

The fossil record confirms that a variety of primates lived, mainly in Europe and North America, during the geological epoch known as the Eocene (54–38 m.y.a.—million years ago). Based on such fossils, many paleontologists suspect that the earliest primates appeared during the previous epoch, the Paleocene (65–54 m.y.a.). The status of several Paleocene fossils as possible primates has been debated, but not resolved. It's estimated that we have fossil evidence for no more than 5 percent of extinct primate species. With such small numbers, the fossil record provides the merest glimpse of the diverse bioforms—living beings—that have existed on earth. But paleontology isn't the only scientific field that attempts to reconstruct phylogeny—relations of ancestry and descent. Remember molecular anthropology; evolutionary trees have been drawn on the basis of similarities and differences in DNA. Despite what we've seen in cartoons and movies, early humans did not coexist with dinosaurs. But maybe primates did. What analytic techniques described in this news brief support the unorthodox idea that primates may date back 85 million years?

Primates—the mammals from which humans evolved—emerged on Earth much earlier than had been thought, originating perhaps 85 million years ago during the age of the dinosaurs, according to a new analysis. The findings should add fuel to the debate between paleontologists, who place the origin of primates at 55 million years ago, and molecular biologists, who use DNA sequencing to suggest they may be as old as 90 million years.

Paleontologist Robert D. Martin, vice president of academic affairs at

Chicago's Field Museum, acknowledged that his team's new research supported the views of the "molecular clock" school, even though the method used by his team did not involve DNA analysis. Instead, the researchers developed a statistical model that builds an evolutionary tree based on the number of primate species alive today (235) and the number of recorded fossil species (396) and their ages. By assuming that each primate species would live approximately 2.5 million years, the team was able to estimate the length of time that elapsed between the oldest known fossil primate, which is 55 million years old, and a hypothetical "last common ancestor" of all primates, 80 million to 85 million years ago. The findings were reported in today's issue of the journal *Nature*. [See Figure 7.3.]

"I've been arguing for years that there's so many gaps in the fossil record that [primates are] probably much older than we thought," Martin said. "You look at how many species there are, and you can estimate the time of the original."

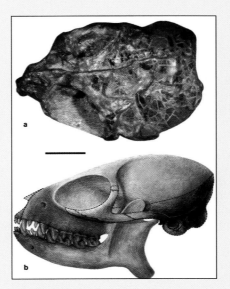

The implications of these findings, if shown to be accurate, could be profound. A primate ancestor 85 million years old would have shared the world with the dinosaurs, which went extinct 65 million years ago, probably in an ecological disaster caused by a meteor hitting the Earth . . . Martin said the earliest primate was probably a lemur-like tree dweller that weighed perhaps two pounds and dined on insects and fruit. Finally, an earlier date for primates would mean that continental drift (in which huge, ancient land masses broke up to form what are today's continents) had a significant effect in creating different primate species.

The new findings, however, drew criticism from several paleontologists, who noted that there is little fossil evidence from the dinosaur period that points to primates or indicates that mammals in general were flourishing.

"The primates are a successful group of animals," said K. Christopher Beard, curator of vertebrate paleontology at Pittsburgh's Carnegie Museum of Natural History . . . "If primates were around and doing well, I suspect we would have found their fossils," Beard continued. "What I would do is issue a challenge and ask them to say where these animals are hiding."

What the fossil record shows is that before the dinosaur extinction, mammals were neither particularly diverse, nor particularly large. Most were rodent-like creatures, and "the biggest was about the size of a beaver," said Johns Hopkins University paleontologist Kenneth Rose.

■ *The newly discovered skull of* Teilhardina asiatica *(top) and reconstruction (below) in China. Dated at 55 million years old, this find suggests an even earlier origin of the primates.*

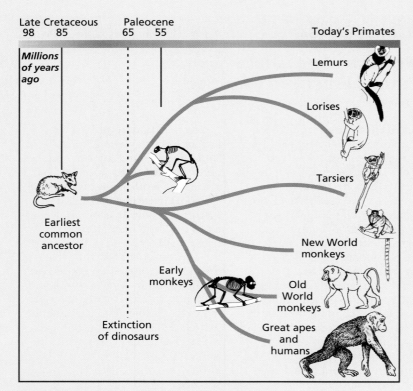

Late Cretaceous
98   85

Paleocene
65   55

Today's Primates

Millions
of years
ago

Lemurs

Lorises

Tarsiers

Earliest
common
ancestor

New World
monkeys

Early
monkeys

Old
World
monkeys

Extinction
of dinosaurs

Great apes
and
humans

FIGURE 7.3   A New Evolutionary Tree for Primates, Based on Calculations Reported in This Story.   SOURCE: BBC News, SCI/TECH, "Primate Ancestor Lived with Dinos," http://news.bbc.co.uk/hi/english/sci/tech/newsid_1935000/1935558.stm.

"There was an explosive radiation of mammals after [the dinosaur] extinction," Rose continued. "It took very little time before we get an animal the size of a steer, and soon we had some truly impressive creatures.

With no dinosaurs in the way, there was a lot of open ecological space."

But while everyone agrees that the first unequivocal fossil primate did not appear until 55 million years ago, Martin argues that the record is

too skimpy to conclude that the order began only a few million years prior to that.

"Primate paleontologists read the fossil record as if it told us everything," Martin said. "That's reasonable if you have a dense record, but our calculations show we have fossil evidence for only about 5 percent of the extinct primates."

By contrast, molecular biologists analyze DNA to calculate the amount of genetic difference in related species, creating an evolutionary tree that can be projected backward in time to the earliest common ancestor. "Our results actually fit the molecular trees, and they're always much earlier," Martin said. "Several people have generated the tree for mammals," and have come up with dates "around 90 million years." But "there are no fossils that say that," said Michael Novacek, provost and curator of paleontology at New York's American Museum of Natural History, even though "it could be that the record is incomplete." "So what's the truth?" Novacek asked. "I don't know."

SOURCE: *Washington Post* (http://www. washingtonpost.com), April 18, 2002, p. A03. http://www.washingtonpost. com/ac2/wp-dyn?pagename=article& node=&contentId=A4580-2002Apr17.

case with modern primates.) Fragments of euprimates, all dating to around 55 m.y.a., have been found in Europe and North America. The discovery of a euprimate in Asia means that primates were already widespread by then and that their common ancestor must have evolved even earlier. Some scientists place the earliest primates in Africa 65 million years ago, at the start of the Cenozoic. But as we see in the news story, recent genetic studies and phylogenetic models suggest an unorthodox date going as far back as 85 m.y.a. Ni and colleagues (2004) think that the relatively small eyes of the mouse-sized *Teilhardina asiatica* indicate that it was active during the day. This goes against another theory: that our earliest ancestors were nocturnal like tarsiers, with large round eyes for seeing in the dark.

The first fossil forms clearly identified as primates lived during the Eocene epoch (54–38 m.y.a.) in North America, Europe, Africa, and Asia. They reached Madagascar from Africa late in the Eocene. The ancestral lemurs must have traveled across the Mozambique Channel, which was narrower then than it is now, on thick mats of vegetation. Such naturally formed "rafts" have been observed forming in East African rivers, then floating out to sea.

In primate evolution, the Eocene was the age of the prosimians, with at least 60 genera in two main families (*Omomyidae* and *Adapidae*). The widely distributed **omomyid** family lived in North America, Europe, and Asia. The omomyids, such as *Shoshonius*, portrayed in the drawing on page 139, were squirrel-sized. But unlike squirrels

■ Compare this line drawing reconstruction of Shoshonius, a member of the Eocene omomyid family, with a modern tarsier from Mindanao in the Philippines. What similarities and differences do you notice?

they had grasping hands and feet, used to manipulate objects and to climb by encircling small branches. Early members of the omomyid family may be ancestral to all anthropoids. Later ones may be ancestral to tarsiers.

The **adapid** family was probably ancestral to the lemur–loris line. The only major difference between the Eocene adapids, such as *Smilodectes*, shown in the drawing on page 140, and today's lemurs and lorises is that the latter have a dental comb (see Figure 7.4). This structure is formed from the incisor and canine teeth of the lower jaw.

Sometime during the Eocene, ancestral anthropoids branched off from the prosimians by becoming more diurnal (active during the day)

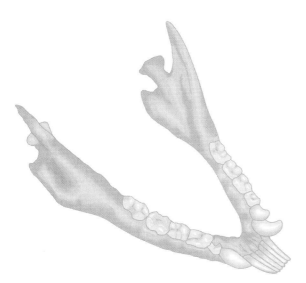

FIGURE 7.4 A Dental Comb.

A dental comb is a derived trait present among contemporary lemurs and lorises but absent in Eocene adapids such as Smilodectes. SOURCE: Robert Jurmain and Harry Nelson, *Introduction to Physical Anthropology*, 6th ed. (Minneapolis: West Publishing, 1994), p. 210.

and by strengthening the trend favoring vision over smell. Some Eocene prosimians had larger brains and eyes, and smaller snouts, than others did. These were the ancestors of the anthropoids. Anthropoid eyes are rotated more forward when compared with lemurs and lorises. Also, anthropoids have a fully enclosed bony eye socket, which lemurs and lorises lack. And unlike lemurs and lorises, anthropoids lack a rhinarium, a moist nose continuous with the upper lip. Anthropoids have a dry nose, separate from the upper lip. Another distinguishing anthropoid feature has to do with molar cusps—bumps on the teeth. The primitive number of cusps on mammalian lower molars is six. The anthropoids have lost one or two cusps on their lower molars, so as to have four or five.

The oldest probable anthropoid discovered so far is *Eosimias,* from the Eocene of China. The oldest definite anthropoid is *Catopithecus,* from the late Eocene of Egypt. By the end of the Eocene, many prosimian species had become extinct, reflecting competition from the first anthropoids.

Oligocene Anthropoids

During the Oligocene epoch (38–23 m.y.a.), anthropoids became the most numerous primates. Most of our knowledge of early anthropoids is based on fossils from Egypt's Fayum deposits. This area is a desert today, but 36–31 million years ago it was a tropical rain forest.

The anthropoids of the Fayum lived in trees and ate fruits and seeds. Compared with prosimians, they had fewer teeth, reduced snouts, larger brains, and increasingly forward-looking eyes. Of the Fayum anthropoid fossils, the *parapithecid* family is the more primitive and is perhaps ancestral to the New World monkeys. The parapithecids were very small (two to three pounds), with similarities to living marmosets and tamarins, small South American monkeys.

Smilodectes *was a member of the lemur-like adapid family, which lived during the Eocene. Compare this drawing reconstructing a* Smilodectes *from Wyoming with a modern black lemur (*Eulemur macaco*) from Madagascar.*

The *propliopithecid* family seems ancestral to the catarrhines—Old World monkeys, apes, and humans. This family includes *Aegyptopithecus*, which, at 13–18 pounds (6 to 8 kilograms), was the size of a large domestic cat. The propliopithecids share with the later catarrhines a distinctive dental formula: 2.1.2.3, meaning two incisors, one canine, two premolars, and three molars. The more primitive primate dental formula is 2.1.3.3. Most other primates, including prosimians and New World monkeys, have the second formula, with three premolars instead of two. Besides the Fayum, Oligocene deposits with primate bones have been found in North and West Africa, southern Arabia, China, Southeast Asia, and North and South America.

The Oligocene was a time of major geological and climatic change. North America and Europe separated and became distinct continents. The Great Rift Valley system of East Africa formed. India drifted into Asia. A cooling trend began, especially in the Northern Hemisphere, where primates disappeared.

EARLY MIOCENE HOMINOIDS

The earliest hominoid fossils date to the Miocene epoch (23–5 m.y.a.), which is divided into three parts: lower, middle, and upper or late. The early Miocene (23–16 m.y.a.) was a warm and wet period, when forests covered East Africa. Recall from the last chapter that *Hominoidea* is the superfamily that includes fossil and living apes and humans. For simplicity's sake, the earliest hominoids are here called proto-apes, or simply apes. Although some of these may be ancestral to living apes, none is identical, or often even very similar, to modern apes.

Modern apes are few in number and in kind. But the Miocene epoch saw perhaps 100 ape species. They dominated the primate world, ranging over the widely forested areas of the Old World, in Eurasia from France to China and in Africa from Kenya to southern Africa. The 40 or so known genera of Miocene apes represent eight times the number of ape genera that survive today. Some 14 ape genera are known just from Africa's early Miocene, the period between 23 million and 16 million years ago. Those ancient apes varied considerably in size. The smallest weighed hardly more than a small house cat, while the largest may have approached the size of a gorilla. Their diet was even more varied than that of modern apes. Some specialized in leaves, others, in fruits and nuts, but most subsisted on ripe fruits, as most apes still do. The biggest difference between the early apes and surviving apes involved posture and locomotion. Modern apes use varied modes of locomotion, ranging from brachiation to knuckle walking. Early apes,

A Behavioral Ecology Study of Two Lemur Species

BACKGROUND INFORMATION

STUDENT 1:
Jennifer Burns

YEAR IN SCHOOL/MAJOR:
Senior/Anthropology

FUTURE PLANS:
Field work/graduate school

STUDENT 2:
Chris Howard

YEAR IN SCHOOL/MAJOR:
Postundergraduate/Anthropology

FUTURE PLANS:
Graduate school

SUPERVISING PROFESSORS:
Dr. Deborah Overdorff,
Dr. Beth Erhart

DEPARTMENT:
Anthropology

SCHOOL:
University of Texas at Austin

PROJECT TITLE:
A Behavioral Ecology Study
of Two Lemur Species

Lemurs are endangered prosimians confined to the island of Madagascar. In this account, pay attention to the problems and pitfalls of primatological research. How would the logistics of studying a baboon or gorilla troop differ from the field methods described here?

Simply the word "Madagascar" conjures up brilliant images of an exotic land. Having broken off from Africa approximately 165 million years ago, this magical island mesmerizes the scientific community as 85–90 percent of its flora and fauna is endemic.

Within the heart of southeastern Madagascar, Ranomafana National Park protects 41,600 hectares of montane rain forest. The park was established at the close of the 1980s and has done a remarkable job of integrating the needs of the Malagasy people with this segment of rain forest's need for protection from further destruction. A developed infrastructure helps the park to balance local and foreign tourist groups as well as scientific research. With one main research site and two bush camp research sites, many fruitful studies are conducted over a wide variety of flora and fauna.

The aims of our project are to better understand the social dynamics and feeding ecology of two of the twelve species of lemurs living within Ranomafana National Park: the red-fronted lemur, *Eulemur fulvus rufus*, and sifaka species, *Propithecus diadema edwardsi*. For five days each week over a six-month period, behav-ioral and ecological data were collected on one group from each species. To aid with individual distinction and recognition, the members of each group were fitted with colored identification necklaces, with one collar of each group containing a radio transmitter. This radio-tracking device made it possible to locate the groups each morning. While these classic techniques are tremendously helpful, problems can often occur with the radio equipment. Heavy rainfall can waterlog the gear, and the rugged mountainous terrain adds strong echoes to the signal, making group location more difficult. When the radio fails, finding the groups can be nearly impossible, as they cover a tremendous area, and can easily take days, if they are found at all.

These two species are of particular interest because of their many contrasts both physically and socially. In trying to more fully define and understand the implications of terms like "dominance," "leadership," "competition," "reproductive stress," and "male versus female roles" within varying lemur species, this study hopes to not only provide new insights, but also open the door to new questions.

---

such as *Proconsul*, to which we now turn, had more restricted and monkeylike means of moving about (see Begun 2003).

Proconsul

The ***Proconsul*** group represents the most abundant and successful anthropoids of the early Miocene. This group lived in Africa and includes four species. Possibly descended from the Oligo-cene propliopithecids, these early Miocene proto-apes had teeth with similarities to those of living apes. But their skeleton below the neck was more monkeylike. Some *Proconsul* species were the size of a small monkey; others, the size of a chimpanzee, usually with marked sexual dimorphism. Their dentition suggests they ate fruits and leaves.

Their skulls were more delicate than those of modern apes, and their legs were longer than their arms—more like monkeys. *Proconsul* probably moved through the trees like a monkey—on four limbs—and lacked the capacity for suspension and brachiation displayed by modern apes. *Proconsul* probably contained the last common ancestor shared by the Old World monkeys and the apes. By the middle Miocene (16–10 m.y.a.), *Proconsul* had been replaced by Old World monkeys and apes.

Fossils of Miocene monkeys and prosimians are rare; ape fossils are much more common. Like many living apes, those of the Miocene were forest dwellers and fruit eaters. They lived in areas that, as the forests retreated, monkeys would eventually colonize. By the late Miocene (10–5 m.y.a.) the age of the apes had ended, and monkeys had become the most common anthropoid in the Old World (except for humans, eventually).

Why did the Old World monkeys thrive as the Miocene apes faded? The probable answer was the monkeys' superior ability to eat leaves. Leaves are easier to get than fruits, which are typical ape foods. As the forests retreated at the end of the Miocene, most apes were restricted to the remaining tropical rain forests in areas of (mainly West) Africa and Southeast Asia. Monkeys survived over a wider area. They did so because they could process leaves effectively. Monkey molars developed *lophs*: ridges of enamel that run from side to side between the cusps of the teeth. Old World monkeys have two such lophs, so their molars are called *bilophodont*. Such lophs slice past each other like scissor blades, a good way to shear a leaf.

Some species of *Proconsul* may have been ancestral to the living African apes. *Proconsul* also may be ancestral to the Old World monkeys. *Proconsul* had all the primitive traits shared by apes and Old World monkeys and none of the derived traits of either. *Primitive* traits are those passed on unchanged from an ancestor, such as the five-cusped molars of the apes, which are inherited from an old anthropoid ancestor. *Derived* traits are those that develop in a particular taxon after they split from their common ancestor with another taxon. Examples are bilophodont molars among Old World monkeys. The Old World monkeys have derived bilophodont molars and primitive quadrupedal bodies. The apes have primitive molars and derived brachiating bodies. *Proconsul* had both primitive teeth and a primitive quadrupedal body.

Afropithecus

During the early Miocene (23–16 m.y.a.), Africa was cut off by water from Europe and Asia. But by the middle Miocene (16–10 m.y.a.), global sea levels had fallen and Africa had drifted into Arabia, providing a land connection between Africa, Europe, and Asia. Migrating both ways—out of and into Africa—after 16.5 m.y.a. were various animals, including hominoids. Proto-apes were the most common primates of the middle Miocene. Over 20 species have been discovered. (See Figure 7.5.) Their teeth retain the primitive anthropoid five-cusped molar pattern.

During the middle Miocene, the hominoids spread widely, in Europe, Asia, and Africa. *Afropithecus* is a large Miocene hominoid from northern Kenya, dated to 18 to 16 m.y.a. (Leakey, Leakey, and Walker 1988). The *Afropithecus* remains consist of skull, jaw, and postcranial (below the head) fragments. *Afropithecus* seems to have been a slow-moving arboreal ape, with large projecting front teeth (similar to those of the modern African apes).

EURASIAN APES

Most of the early Miocene apes went extinct. But one of them, perhaps *Afropithecus,* was ancestral to the species that crossed over into Eurasia some 16 million years ago. The apes that entered Eurasia from Africa passed through Saudi Arabia, where the remains of *Heliopithecus,* an ape similar

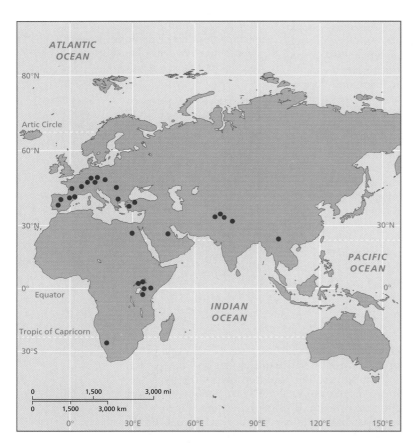

FIGURE 7.5 The Geographic Distribution of Known Miocene Apes.

SOURCE: Robert Jurmain and Harry Nelson, *Introduction to Physical Anthropology,* 6th ed. (Minneapolis: West Publishing, 1994), p. 302.

to *Afropithecus*, have been found. (Some scientists regard *Afropithecus* and *Heliopithecus* as members of a single genus.) Both had a thick covering of enamel on their teeth. This protective layer would have facilitated the processing of hard foods, such as nuts, and tough foods with durable husks. This dental innovation may have helped their descendants spread widely, since they could exploit food resources not available to *Proconsul* and most earlier apes (Begun 2003).

Evidence for great apes in Eurasia dates back roughly 13 million years. There were two main groups: *Dryopithecus* in Europe and *Sivapithecus* in Asia. Like living great apes, these animals had long, strongly built jaws, with large incisors, bladelike (as opposed to tusklike) canines, and long molars and premolars. This feeding apparatus suggests a diet of soft, ripe fruits. Studies of *Dryopithecus* and *Sivapithecus* teeth suggest that those apes grew fairly slowly, as living great apes do. Their life histories probably were like those of modern great apes: They matured slowly, lived long lives, and bore one large offspring at a time. Fossil braincases of *Dryopithecus* indicate a brain-to-body ratio comparable to that of chimps (Begun 2003)

The limb skeletons of these two ape groups also are like those of modern great apes. Both *Dryopithecus* and *Sivapithecus* were adapted to suspensory locomotion. The elbow joint was fully extendable and stable throughout the full range of motion. Among primates, this morphology is unique to apes, and it figures prominently in their ability to hang and swing below branches. *Dryopithecus* shows many other adaptations to suspension, both in its limb bones and in its hands and feet, which had powerful grasping capabilities. These features suggest that *Dryopithecus* moved through the trees much as living great apes do (Begun 2003).

Dryopithecus

Several species of *Dryopithecus* lived in Europe during the middle and late Miocene. The first fossil member of the **Dryopithecus** group (*Dryopithecus fontani*) was found in France in 1856. The five-cusped and fissure pattern of its molar teeth, known as the Y-5 arrangement, is typical of *Dryopithecus* and of hominoids in general. Several species of *Dryopithecus* eventually ranged from northwestern Spain to the Republic of Georgia. The evolutionary significance of *Dryopithecus* continues to be debated. Some studies link *Dryopithecus* to Asian apes; others see it as the ancestor of all living great apes. David Begun (2003) suggests that *Dryopithecus* is most closely related to an ape known as *Ouranopithecus* from Greece (see below). Begun sees either *Dryopithecus* or *Ouranopithecus* as the most likely ancestor of African apes and humans.

Sivapithecus

Representing the second of the two main groups of middle and late Miocene apes, *Sivapithecus* had a wide Eurasian distribution, including Turkey, Pakistan, India, Nepal, China, and Southeast Asia. **Sivapithecus** fossils were first found in the Siwalik Hills of Pakistan. A late Miocene find with an almost complete face from Pakistan's Potwar Plateau shows many similarities to the face of the modern orangutan. Because of facial and dental similarities, *Sivapithecus* of the late Miocene is now seen as ancestral to the modern orangutan. The orangutan line appears to have separated from the one leading to the African apes and humans by 11 million years ago.

The continental drift that helped create the land bridge between Africa and Eurasia as the middle Miocene began also triggered mountain

■ *Compare this* Sivapithecus *side view with a contemporary female orangutan.*

For information on contemporary deforestation see the "Bringing It All Together" essay that immediately follows Chapter 6.

See your OLC Internet Exercises

mhhe.com/kottak

building and climatic change. With a cooler, drier climate, forest patches, dry woodlands, and grasslands replaced extensive humid forests in East Africa and South Asia. Apes, such as ancestral orangutans, survived best deep in the tropics. The cooling trend continued through the late Miocene (10–5 m.y.a.). As grasslands spread, the stage was set for the divergence of the lines leading to humans, gorillas, and chimps.

Gigantopithecus

No discussion of ancient apes should neglect *Gigantopithecus*, almost certainly the largest primate that ever lived. Confined to Asia, it persisted for millions of years, from the late Miocene until 300,000 years ago, when it coexisted with members of our own genus, *Homo erectus* (Harder 2005). Some people think *Gigantopithecus* is not extinct yet, and that we know it today as the yeti and bigfoot (Sasquatch).

Gigantopithecus was discovered in an unlikely place. In China, druggists sell fossils known as "dragon's" teeth and bones, which are ground up to be used medicinally. In 1935 the anthropologist G. H. R. von Koenigswald recognized that a "dragon's tooth" being sold by a Hong Kong druggist was actually that of an extinct ape. Since then, three jaw bones and more than 1,000 teeth

■ A reconstruction of *Gigantopithecus* by Russell Ciochon and Bill Munns. Munns is shown here with "Giganto." What would be the likely environmental effects of a population of such large apes?

STUDENT CD-ROM LIVING ANTHROPOLOGY

The Earliest Primates
Track 7

This clip describes the environmental devastation that killed off the dinosaurs and paved the way for the emergence of the mammals, including early primates, which adapted to niches in tropical forests. The clip shows two kinds of living lemurs, as well as monkeys. Note their tails, their diversity, and their eating habits. The clip also features two fossil primates. What destroyed the dinosaurs, and when did that happen? Name an anatomical feature shared by *Purgatorius* and modern primates. When did *Proconsul* live? What was its mode of locomotion? Name three features of *Proconsul* that link it to chimpanzees and make it a possible human ancestor.

have been recovered, some in drugstores, some at geological sites in China and Vietnam (Pettifor 1995). Some such sites have *Gigantopithecus* remains associated with those of *Homo erectus* (Ciochon, Olsen, and James 1990), who may have hunted the ape into extinction.

With a fossil record consisting of nothing more than jaw bones and teeth, it is difficult to say for sure just how big *Gigantopithecus* was. Based on ratios of jaw and tooth size to body size in other apes, various reconstructions have been made. One has *Gigantopithecus* weighing 1,200 pounds (540 kilograms) and standing 10 feet (3 meters) tall (Ciochon et al. 1990). Another puts the height at 9 feet (2.7 meters) and cuts the weight in half (Simons and Ettel 1970). All agree, however, that *Gigantopithecus* was the largest ape that ever lived. There have been at least two species of *Gigantopithecus*: *G. blacki*, the one that coexisted with *H. erectus* in China and Vietnam, and the much earlier *G. giganteus*, from northern India.

Given its size, *Gigantopithecus* must have been a ground-dwelling ape rather than an arboreal brachiator. Based on its jaw and dental patterns, it probably ate grasses, fruits, seeds, and especially bamboo. Very large animals, including China's giant panda, need an abundant food source such as bamboo. *Gigantopithecus* molars were adapted to a diet demanding cutting, crushing, and grinding of tough, fibrous matter. The molars are massive and flat, with low crowns and thick enamel. The premolars are also broad and flat, resembling molars.

Could it be that *Gigantopithecus* did not go extinct, but survives today as the yeti ("abominable snowman" of the Himalayas) or Sasquatch (reportedly sighted in the Pacific Northwest)? Probably not. These creatures are based on legend, not fact. Survival of a species requires a sufficiently large breeding population. Given its dietary demands, *Gigantopithecus* would surely be detectable and have an observable environmental effect. Never have *Gigantopithecus* fossils or teeth been discovered in the Western Hemisphere. Nor are the areas of yeti and Sasquatch sightings ones in which *Gigantopithecus* would fit adaptively.

Oreopithecus

Is upright bipedalism unique to hominins? A recent reanalysis of the fossil remains of an ancient Italian ape suggests otherwise. *Oreopithecus bambolii,* which lived seven to nine million years ago, apparently spent much of its time standing upright and shuffling short distances to collect fruit and other foods. This mode of locomotion contrasts with those of other fossil and living apes, which climb, brachiate, or knuckle-walk. The first *Oreopithecus* fossils were found more than 100 years ago in central Italy. The taxonomic placement and evolutionary significance of *Oreopithecus* have been debated for decades. Similarities have been noted between this Italian ape and both the ramapithecid and the dryopithecid families.

Meike Kohler and Salvador Moyà-Solà (1997) have reanalyzed *Oreopithecus* remains in the Natural History Museum in Basel, Switzerland. These skeletal pieces represented the lower back, pelvis, leg, and foot. The scientists found the creature's lower body to be intermediate between those of apes and those of early hominins. Like early hominins, *Oreopithecus* had a lower back that arched forward, a vertically aligned knee joint, and a similar pelvis. All these features are significant for upright walking. However, *Oreopithecus* had a unique foot. Its big toe splayed out 90 degrees from the other toes, all of which were shorter and straighter than those of modern apes. The foot's birdlike, tripod design probably was associated with a short, shuffling stride. Considering the entire **postcranium** (the area behind or below the head—the skeleton), there are substantial similarities between *Oreopithecus, Dryopithecus,* and the living great apes and hominins.

Look at Map 3 in the insert. This map shows the world picture of primate evolution, indicating major sites with taxa and dates. Map 3 shows that the geographic distribution of primates has changed through time, with North America prominent during the Eocene, Eurasia during the Eocene and Miocene, and Africa from the Oligocene through the present.

A MISSING LINK?

The idea of "the missing link" goes back to an old notion called the "Great Chain of Being." This was the theological belief that various entities could be placed in a progressive chain. Among life forms,

The Great Chain of Being—a powerful visual metaphor for a divinely inspired universal hierarchy ranking all forms of higher and lower life. From Didacus Valades, Rhetorica Christiana (1579). What can you tell about the levels in the hierarchy?

humans were at the top of the chain. Above them stood only angels and divinity. Below them were the apes, most clearly the African apes. But humans seemed too exalted, too different from those apes, to be directly linked to them. Between humans and the apes, there needed to be some form more progressive than the apes—some sort of missing link in the Great Chain of Being. Although modern science does not endorse the Great Chain of Being, it does recognize that our ancestor was a life form that differed from contemporary gorillas and chimps. Humans are not descended from gorillas or chimps. Rather, humans and the African apes share a common ancestor—a creature that was like chimps and gorillas in some ways, like humans in others. Over time all three species have evolved and have diverged from one another. Is there reason to believe that a chimp ancestor living millions of years ago would look more like a hominin than a contemporary chimp does?

Human ancestors almost certainly diverged from those of chimps and gorillas late in the Miocene epoch, between eight and five million years ago. The evolutionary line leading to orangutans probably split from the one leading to humans, chimps, and gorillas around 11 m.y.a. Around eight million years ago, the common ancestors of humans, chimps, and gorillas started diverging (Fisher 1988*a*). They split up by occupying different environmental niches. Separated in

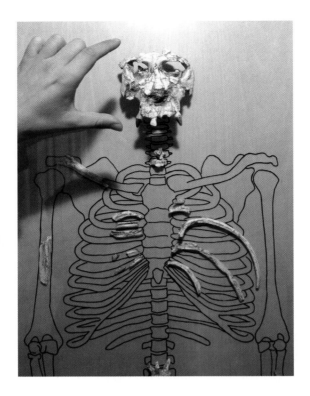

Pierolapithecus catalaunicus. *The Pierolapithecus bones discovered so far include much of the skull, hand, and foot bones, including toe and finger fragments, three vertebrae, two complete ribs, and large pieces of a dozen others. This Miocene ape, first described in 2004, may be the last common ancestor of all the world's living great apes, including the human family.*

The idea of a huge gap between humans and the apes persists—despite evidence that humans and chimps share about 98.7 percent of their DNA. There's no doubt that humans, chimps, and gorillas share a more recent common ancestor with each other than they do with other apes (e.g., the orangutan and the gibbon) or with any monkey. All the apes are more closely related to each other—and more physically alike—than they are to monkeys. So why is it that human parents at zoos go on saying to their kids "look at the monkey" when they are seeing a chimp, gorilla, or orang? It must be the old idea of our exalted status. We easily detect the monkey in the ape but not the ape in ourselves. Still, the apes fascinate us, to some degree because of their humanlike qualities. Gorillas are popular at zoos from San Diego to Atlanta, especially when they are displayed in "family" groups. The antics of orangutans and especially of chimps have been featured in movies and TV shows. The stories of Washoe the chimp and Koko the gorilla, apes that have been taught sign language, have been featured in magazines and on TV. Even the national tabloids on display in the grocery store often turn to apes for their animal stories. Invariably such stories continue the confusion with comments about "monkeying around" or "monkey see, monkey do." Apes aren't monkeys. Apes are a lot closer to humans than they are to monkeys. Imagine a live-action film called *Planet of the Monkeys.* Where could they find actors who could locomote on four legs for an entire movie?

space, they became reproductively isolated from one another—leading to speciation. Ancestral gorillas split off first. They eventually occupied forested zones of the mountains and lowlands of equatorial Africa. They developed a diet based on leaves, shoots, bulk vegetation, and fruits. Humans and chimps share a more recent common ancestor with each other than either does with the gorilla. Chimps evolved into frugivores (fruit eaters) in Africa's forests and woodlands. Ancestral hominins spent more time in Africa's open grasslands, or savannas. Ancestral chimps and humans, like their contemporary descendants, may well have added meat to their diet by hunting.

As we have seen, Miocene deposits in Africa, Asia, and Europe have yielded an abundance of hominoid fossils (see Figure 7.5). Some of these may have evolved into modern apes and humans, but others became extinct. Formerly, as was mentioned, certain Asian fossils such as *Sivapithecus* and "*Ramapithecus*" were analyzed as possible common ancestors of humans and the apes. Most scientists have now excluded these Miocene hominoids from the family tree of humans, chimps, and gorillas, considering *Sivapithecus* a probable ancestor of orangs. Discovered in Greece in 1989, the middle to late Miocene ape *Ouranopithecus* lived in Europe some 10–9 m.y.a. This find may be linked to the living African apes and even to hominins (Begun, Ward, and Rose 1997). One distinctive trait that *Ouranopithecus* shares with the modern African apes and humans is the *frontal sinus* (a cavity in the forehead, one of the areas where we get sinus infections and headaches).

On the basis of Miocene finds reported and analyzed during the last decade, some scientists have pondered a new scenario for ape and human evolution. As mentioned, during the middle Miocene, a land bridge connected Africa and Eurasia. This connection enabled hominoids to spread from Africa into Asia and Europe, where they diversified into the groups discussed previously. At the same time, the apes' forest habitat was shrinking in East Africa, and the number of ape species there shrank along with it. In the middle and late Miocene, there appears to have been much more ape diversity in Europe and Asia than there was in Africa. During the late Miocene, Old World monkeys took over from the dwindling African apes in many areas they once inhabited. The new hominoid evolutionary scenario, proposed but hardly established, is that the line leading to the African apes and hominins may have emerged in Europe, with a hominoid such as *Ouranopithecus* (see

Begun 2003). Then there would have been a return migration to Africa, where diversification of ancestral gorillas, chimps, and hominins started around 8 m.y.a. Continued work by fossil hunters, analysts, and taxonomists eventually may reconcile the main issues involving the Miocene apes in relation to their living successors.

Pierolapithecus catalaunicus

In November 2004, Spanish anthropologists announced their discovery of what may be the last common ancestor of all the world's living great apes, including the human family (Moyà-Solà et al. 2004). The new ape species, named *Pierolapithecus catalaunicus,* lived around 13 million years ago, during the Middle Miocene. This ancient ape could be the last common ancestor of humans, chimpanzees, gorillas, and orangutans. The find comes from a new and rich fossil site, near the village of Hostalets de Pierola in Catalonia, Spain. The name *Pierolapithecus* combines part of the village's name with the Greek word for ape, while *catalaunicus* commemorates Catalonia, the province where both the village and Barcelona are located.

The *Pierolapithecus* bones discovered so far include much of the skull, hand, and foot bones—including toe and finger fragments, three vertebrae, two complete ribs, and large pieces of a dozen others. The leader of the discovery team was Salvador Moyà-Solà of the Paleontology Institute in Barcelona. The find, consisting of 83 fossil fragments, appears to represent a single adult male that weighed about 75 pounds (34 kilograms). Like chimps and gorillas, *Pierolapithecus* was well adapted for tree climbing and knuckle-walking on the ground. Based on the shape of the single surviving tooth, it was probably a fruit-eater.

Several features distinguished *Pierolapithecus* from the lesser apes (gibbons and siamangs) and monkeys. Its rib cage, lower spine, and wrist suggest it climbed the way modern great apes do. The ape's chest, or thorax, is wider and flatter than that of monkeys. According to Moyà-Solà, "the thorax is the most important anatomical part of this fossil, because it is the first time that the modern apelike thorax has been found in the fossil record" (quoted in Perlman 2004, p. A-4).

In the current timetable of primate evolution, the lineage of monkeys split off some 25 m.y.a. from the hominin line, which developed toward apes and humans. The ancestors of the lesser apes separated from those of the great apes some 16–14 m.y.a. Then, around 11–10 m.y.a., the orangutans line diverged from the line leading to the African apes and humans. Yet another split took place when the gorilla line branched off from the line leading to chimpanzees and hominins. Around 7–6 m.y.a., another split in the lineage led to the various early hominins, to be examined in the next chapter. Some intriguing fossils dating from that critical time period have been discovered recently.

"Toumai"

Back to Africa for an important recent discovery. In July 2001 anthropologists working in Central Africa—in northern Chad's Djurab desert (Figure 7.6)—unearthed the 6–7-million-year-old skull of the oldest possible human ancestor yet found. This discovery consists of a nearly complete skull, two lower jaw fragments, and three teeth. Two additional jawbones and one more tooth were discovered subsequently (Wilford 2005). Toumai dates to the time period when humans and chimps would have been diverging from a common ancestor. "It takes us into another world, of creatures that include the common ancestor, the ancestral human and the ancestral chimp," George Washington University paleobiologist Bernard Wood said (quoted in Gugliotta 2002).

The discovery was made by a 40-member multinational team led by the French paleoanthropologist Michel Brunet. The actual discoverer

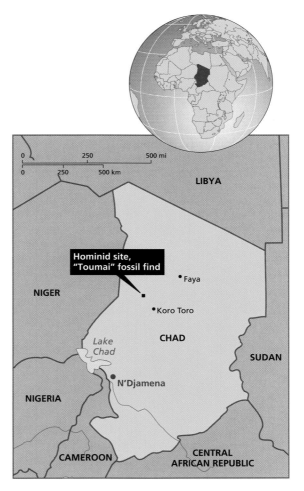

FIGURE 7.6   Location of Toumai Discovery.

French paleoanthropologist Michel Brunet holds Sahelanthropus tchadensis, *nicknamed "Toumai" (on the left), and a modern chimpanzee skull (on the right). If Toumai isn't a human ancestor, what else might it be?*

common ancestor. As we would expect in a fossil so close to the common ancestor, Toumai blends apelike and human characteristics (Wilford 2005). Although the brain was chimp-sized, the tooth enamel was thicker than a chimp's enamel, suggesting a diet that included not just fruits, but also tougher vegetation of a sort typically found in the savanna. Also, Toumai's snout did not protrude as far as a chimp's—making it more humanlike, and the canine tooth was shorter than those of other apes. "The fossil is showing the first glimmerings of evolution in our direction," according to University of California at Berkeley anthropologist Tim White (quoted in Gugliotta 2002).

Orrorin tugenensis

In January 2001 Brigitte Senut, Martin Pickford, and others reported the discovery, near the village of Tugen in Kenya's Baringo district, of possible early hominin fossils they called *Orrorin tugenensis* (Aiello and Collard 2001; Senut et al. 2001). The find consisted of 13 fossils from at least five individuals. The fossils include pieces of jaw with teeth, isolated upper and lower teeth, arm bones, and a finger bone. *Orrorin* appears to have been a chimp-sized creature that climbed easily and walked on two legs when on the ground. Its date of six million years ago is close to the time of the common ancestor of humans and chimps. The fossilized left femur (thigh bone) suggests upright bipedalism, while the thick right humerus (upper arm bone) suggests tree-climbing skills. Animal fossils found in the same rocks indicate that *Orrorin* lived in a wooded environment.

Orrorin's primitive (apelike) characteristics are seen in the upper incisor, upper canine, and lower premolar, which are more like the teeth of a female chimpanzee than like human teeth. But other dental and skeletal features, especially bipedalism, led the discoverers to assign *Orrorin* to the hominin lineage. *Orrorin* lived after Toumai but before *Ardipithecus kadabba*, discovered in Ethiopia, also in 2001, and dated to 5.8–5.5 m.y.a. The hominin status of *Ardipithecus*, to be considered at the beginning of the next chapter, is more generally accepted than is that of either Toumai or *Orrorin tugenensis*.

was the university undergraduate Ahounta Djimdoumalbaye, who spied the skull embedded in sandstone. The new fossil was dubbed *Sahelanthropus tchadensis*, referring to the northern Sahel region of Chad where it was found. The fossil is also known as "Toumai," a local name meaning "hope of life."

The discovery team identified the skull as that of an adult male with a chimp-sized brain (320–380 cubic centimeters), heavy brow ridges, and a relatively flat, humanlike face. Toumai's habitat included savanna, forests, rivers, and lakes—and abundant animal life: elephants, antelope, horses, giraffes, hyenas, hippopotamuses, wild boars, crocodiles, fish, and rodents. The animal species enabled the team to date the site where Toumai was found (by comparison with radiometrically dated sites with similar fauna).

Was Toumai the "missing link," a common ancestor, a gorilla ancestor (as Wolpoff, Senut, Pickford, and Hawks [2002] suggest), or the earliest hominin known to science? The discovery of Toumai moves scientists close to the time when humans and the African apes diverged from a

1. Primates have lived during the past 65 million years, the Cenozoic era, with seven epochs: Paleocene, Eocene, Oligocene, Miocene, Pliocene, Pleistocene, and Recent. The arboreal hypothesis states that primates evolved by adapting to life high up in the trees. The visual predation hypothesis suggests that key primate traits developed because they facilitated the capture of insects. The mixed diet hypothesis suggests that increased use of angiosperms (flowering plants) led to modern primate characteristics.

2. The first fossils clearly identified as primates lived during the Eocene (54–38 m.y.a.), mainly in North America and Europe. The omomyid family may be ancestral to the anthropoids and the tarsier. The adapid family was probably ancestral to the lemur–loris line.

3. During the Oligocene (38–23 m.y.a.), anthropoids became the most numerous primates. The parapithecid family may be ancestral to the New World monkeys. The propliopithecid family, including *Aegyptopithecus,* seems ancestral to the catarrhines—Old World monkeys, apes, and humans.

4. The earliest hominoid (ape or proto-ape) fossils are from the Miocene (23–5 m.y.a.). Africa's *Proconsul* group contained the last common ancestor shared by the Old World monkeys and the apes. At the start of the middle Miocene (16–10 m.y.a.), a land bridge formed connecting Africa and Eurasia. Proto-apes spread beyond Africa into Eurasia and became the most common primates

of the middle Miocene. There were two widespread groups of middle and late Miocene apes in Eurasia: *Dryopithecus* and *Sivapithecus. Sivapithecus* was ancestral to the modern orangutan. *Gigantopithecus,* the largest primate ever to live, persisted for millions of years in Asia, finally coexisting with *Homo erectus.*

5. *Dryopithecus,* whose species were widely distributed in Europe, may include the common ancestor of African apes and humans. *Ouranopithecus,* which lived in Europe some 10–9 m.y.a., is another possible hominid ancestor, through a reverse migration to Africa early in the late Miocene. *Oreopithecus bambolii,* which lived 9–7 m.y.a., was an ape that stood upright while collecting fruit and other foods. There are skeletal similarities between *Oreopithecus, Dryopithecus, Ouranopithecus,* and the living great apes and humans.

6. *Pierolapithecus catalaunicus,* which lived around 13 million years ago, could be the last common ancestor of humans, chimpanzees, gorillas, and orangutans. Anthropologists have yet to identify the fossils of the common ancestors of humans, gorillas, and chimps. However, biochemical evidence strongly suggests that the diversification into ancestral gorillas, chimps, and hominins began in Africa during the late Miocene. A skull found in 2001 in northern Chad, dated at 7–6 m.y.a., officially named *Sahelanthropus tchadensis,* more commonly called "Toumai," may or may not be the earliest hominin yet known, as may the somewhat less ancient *Orrorin tugenensis,* found in Kenya in 2001.

adapids Early (Eocene) primate family ancestral to lemurs and lorises.

arboreal hypothesis Idea that the primates evolved by adapting to life high up in the trees, where visual abilities would have been favored over the sense of smell, and grasping hands and feet would have been used for movement along branches.

Dryopithecus Zoological ape family living in Europe during the middle and late Miocene; probably includes the common ancestor of the lesser apes (gibbons and siamangs) and the great apes.

hominins Term used to describe all the human species that ever have existed, including the extinct ones, and excluding chimps and gorillas.

mixed diet hypothesis The idea that increased use of angiosperms (flowering plants) led to modern primate characteristics. Early primates would have relied on vision as they sought fruits, seeds, and flowers as well as insects.

m.y.a. Million years ago.

omomyids Early (Eocene) primate family found in North America, Europe, and Asia; early omomyids may be ancestral to all anthropoids; later ones may be ancestral to tarsiers.

postcranium The area behind or below the head; the skeleton.

Proconsul Early Miocene genus of the pliopithecoid superfamily; the most abundant and successful anthropoids of the early Miocene; the last common ancestor shared by the Old World monkeys and the apes.

Sivapithecus Widespread fossil group first found in Pakistan; includes specimens formerly called "*Ramapithecus*" and fossil apes from Turkey, China, and Kenya; early *Sivapithecus* may contain the common ancestor of the orangutan and the African apes; late *Sivapithecus* is now seen as ancestral to the modern orang.

visual predation hypothesis Idea that the primates evolved in lower branches and undergrowth by developing visual and tactile abilities to aid in hunting and snaring insects.

CRITICAL THINKING QUESTIONS

For more self-testing, see the self-quizzes

mhhe.com/kottak

1. What are the pluses and minuses of relying on the fossil record to reconstruct evolution? Besides fossils, what are other lines of evidence for primate and human evolution?

2. What are some unanswered questions about early primate evolution? What kinds of information would help provide answers?

3. Watch a squirrel move about. How do its movements compare with a monkey's movements? With a cat's movements? With your own? What do these observations suggest to you about that animal's ancestral habitat?

4. There have been reported sightings of "bigfoot" in the Pacific Northwest of North America and of the yeti (abominable snowman) in the Himalayas. What facts about apes lead you to question such reports?

5. What's the likelihood that Toumai, the 7–6-million-year-old skull found in 2001 in northern Chad, is a hominin? What else could it be? You might want to check the Internet for the latest on "Toumai."

SUGGESTED ADDITIONAL READINGS

Begun, D. R., C. V. Ward, and M. D. Rose
  1997 *Description: Function, Phylogeny, and Fossils: Miocene Hominoid Evolution and Adaptations.* New York: Plenum Press. A collection of very up-to-date scientific articles on the Miocene apes.

Ciochon, R. L., J. Olsen, and J. James
  1990 *Other Origins: The Search for the Giant Ape in Human Prehistory.* New York: Bantam Books. In search of *Gigantopithecus.*

Eldredge, N.
  1997 *Fossils: The Evolution and Extinction of Species.* Princeton, NJ: Princeton University Press. What fossils tell us about the natural history of species.

Fleagle, J. G.
  1999 *Primate Adaptation and Evolution,* 2nd ed. San Diego: Academic Press. Excellent introduction to adaptation of past and present primate species.

Hrdy, S. B.
  1999 *The Woman That Never Evolved,* rev. ed. Cambridge, MA: Harvard University Press. Revised edition of a well-known contribution to primate and human evolution.

Kemp, T. S.
  1999 *Fossils and Evolution.* New York: Oxford University Press. Interpreting the fossil record.

Kimbel, W. H., and L. B. Martin, eds.
  1993 *Species, Species Concepts, and Primate Evolution.* New York: Plenum Press. The evolution of primate species.

MacPhee, R. D. E., ed.
  1993 *Primates and Their Relatives in Phylogenetic Perspective.* New York: Plenum Press. Discussion of the primate family tree and its evolution.

Moyà-Solà, S., M. Köhler, D. M. Alba, I. Casanovas-Vilar, and J. Galindo
  2004 *Pierolapithecus catalaunicus,* a New Middle Miocene Great Ape from Spain. *Science* 306 (November 19): 1339–1344.

Perlman, D.
  2004 Fossil Find May Be the Father of Us All: It's Hailed as Last Common Kin of the Great Apes and Humans. *San Francisco Chronicle,* November 22, P. A–4. http://www.sfgate.com/cgi-bin/article.cgi?file=/chronicle/archive/2004/11/22/MNGIV9VF3G1.DTL.

Wade, N., ed.
  2001 *The New York Times Book of Fossils and Evolution,* rev. ed. New York: Lyons Press. Articles on fossils and evolution from the *New York Times.*

1. View Christopher R. Scotese's animation of continental drift (**http://www.scotese.com/pangeanim.htm**) or the website **http://www.clearlight.com/~mhieb/WVFossils/continents.html**. Both sites have both text and animation, which, after reading this chapter, should allow you to answer the following questions:
   a. When did primates first appear?
   b. At that time, which continents were connected? Which continents were isolated?
   c. The article that starts this chapter says that most of the discoveries of the earliest primates were in North America and Europe. Based on the map, does it make sense that similar specimens are being found in both places? Where else can we expect to find fossil evidence of early primates? Which continents are unlikely to have the earliest primates?

2. Bigfoot: Read Lorraine Ahearn's article "Bigfoot Theory: Reality Is What You Make of It," which is a report about a 1999 bigfoot conference (**http://groups.msn.com/NCBigfootInvestigations/inthenews.msnw**).
   a. This chapter states that some people (but few scientists) believe bigfoot is a living descendant of *Gigantopithecus blackei.* What are the arguments for and against this claim?
   b. What are some other bigfoot theories presented in this article? How could you go about testing them?
   c. What is your opinion about bigfoot? How would you go about testing it?

See Chapter 7 at your McGraw-Hill Online Learning Center for additional review and interactive exercises.

8

Early Hominins

WHAT MAKES US HUMAN?

In trying to determine whether a fossil is a human ancestor, should we look for traits that make us human today? Sometimes yes; sometimes no. We do look for similarities in DNA, including mutations shared by certain lineages but not others. But what about such key human attributes as bipedal locomotion, a long period of childhood dependency, big brains, and the use of tools and language? Some of these key markers of humanity are fairly recent—or have origins that are impossible to date. And ironically, some of the physical markers that have led scientists to identify certain fossils as early hominins rather than apes are features that have been lost during subsequent human evolution.

■ *Reconstruction of Australopithecus running bipedally with a pebble tool in hand. Along with tool use and manufacture, bipedalism is a key part of being human.*

Bipedalism

Postcranial material from *Ardipithecus* (5.8–4.4 m.y.a.), as described in this chapter's "News Brief," suggests a capacity for upright bipedal locomotion. Indeed, it was the shift toward this form of moving around that led to the distinctive

---

OVERVIEW

Although the first hominins appeared late in the Miocene, most hominin fossils have been dated to the Pliocene and Pleistocene epochs. Early hominin remains come mainly from eastern and southern Africa. The first hominins, discovered in Ethiopia, have been assigned to the genus *Ardipithecus* and date back almost six million years. The australopithecines, members of the genus *Australopithecus*, had evolved by four million years ago. *Ardipithecus* and the early australopithecines shared many features with the apes: small apelike skulls, slashing front teeth, and marked sexual dimorphism. Yet they walked on two legs. Upright bipedalism is a fundamental human characteristic that goes back more than five million years.

Remains of two groups, *A. africanus* and *A. robustus*, have been found in South Africa. Both had a powerful chewing apparatus, with large back teeth and robust faces, skulls, and muscle markings. The basis of their diet was savanna vegetation.

By two million years ago, there were two distinct hominin groups: early *Homo*—our ancestor—and *A. boisei*, the "hyperrobust" australopithecines, which became extinct a million years ago.

---

hominin way of life. **Bipedalism**—upright two-legged locomotion—is the key feature differentiating early hominins from the apes. African fossil discoveries suggest that hominin bipedalism is more than five million years old.

Bipedalism is considered to be an adaptation to an open grassland or savanna habitat. Scientists have suggested several advantages of bipedalism in such an environment: the ability to see over long grass, to carry items back to a home base, and to reduce the body's exposure to solar radiation. The fossil and archaeological records confirm that upright bipedal locomotion preceded stone tool manufacture and the expansion of the hominin brain. However, although the earliest hominins could move bipedally through open country during the day, they also preserved enough of an ape-like anatomy to make them good climbers. They could take to the trees to sleep at night and to escape terrestrial predators.

One explanation for bipedalism centers on environmental changes that swept Africa more than five million years ago. During the late Miocene, as the global climate became cooler and drier, grasslands in sub-Saharan Africa expanded. The rain forests contracted, shrinking the habitat available to arboreal primates (Wilford 1995). Also, at about the same time, a geological shift deepened the Rift Valley, which runs through Ethiopia, Kenya, and Tanzania. The sinking of the valley thrust up mountains. This left the land west of the valley more humid and arboreal, while the east became more arid and dominated by savanna. The common ancestors of hominins and chimpanzees were divided as a result. Those adapting to the humid west became the chimpanzee family. Those in the east had to forge a new life in an open environment (Coppens 1994).

At least one branch of the eastern primates—those that became hominins—ventured more and more into open country seeking food, but retreating to the trees to escape predators and to sleep at night. To move about more efficiently, and perhaps also to keep a lookout above the grasses for food or predators, these primates started standing up and walking on two legs. Presumably, this adaptation enhanced their chances of surviving and passing on genes that favored this stance and gait, leading eventually to bipedal hominins (Wilford 1995).

Yet another factor may have contributed to bipedalism. Early hominins might have found the intense tropical heat of the savanna very stressful. Most savanna-dwelling animals have built-in ways of protecting their brains from over-heating as their body temperatures rise during the day. This isn't true of humans, nor is it likely to have been true of early hominins. The only way we can protect our brains is by keeping our bodies cool. Could it be that early hominins stood up to cool off? Studies with scale models of primates suggest that quadrupedalism exposes the

■ N E W S   B R I E F ■

Another Branch of Early Human Ancestors Is Reported by Scientists

NEW YORK TIMES NEWS BRIEF

by John Noble Wilford
March 5, 2004

Based on molecular genetic calculations, scientists have surmised for decades that a lot was happening in hominid evolution between seven and five million years ago. Now the fossil record is bearing them out. Recent discoveries of possible hominin ancestors, such as Toumai (Sahelanthropus tchadensis) and Orrorin tugenensis, were discussed in Chapter 7. In the news here are fossils accepted more generally as hominins, assigned to the genus Ardipithecus, *found in 2001 in Ethiopia. Written in 2004, this news story reports a change in the designation of the* Ardipithecus *fossils. Originally they were considered to be an earlier subspecies of a previously known* Ardipithecus *species (Ardipithecus ramidus), which lived around 4.4 million years ago. Now they have been assigned to their own species,* Ardipithecus kadabba, *which is considered to be ancestral to the later* Ardipithecus. *Furthermore, the authors of the article on which this story is based make the controversial suggestion that these fossils, along with Toumai and Orrorin, may all belong to the same genus. These recent discoveries push the hominin lineage back to around six million years ago, near the time when the chimp–human split is assumed to have occurred based on molecular calculations. Note that the term* hominin *is used to refer to the human line after its split from ancestral chimps.* Hominid *is used when there is doubt about the hominin status of the fossil, for example, with Toumai.*

Another species has been added to the family tree of early human ancestors—and to controversies over how straight or tangled were the branches of that tree.

Long before *Homo erectus, Australopithecus afarensis* (Lucy, more than three million years ago) and several other distant kin, scientists are reporting today, there lived a primitive hominin species in what is

now Ethiopia about 5.5 million to 5.8 million years ago.

That would make the newly recognized species one of the earliest known human ancestors, perhaps one of the first to emerge after the chimpanzee and human lineages diverged from a common ancestor some six million to eight million years ago . . .

When its first fossil bones and teeth were described three years ago, paleoanthropologists tentatively identified it as a more apelike subspecies that they named *Ardipithecus ramidus kadabba.* The original ramidus species was found in 1994 in 4.4-million-year-old sediments, also in Ethiopia.

But with more discoveries and a closer study, especially of the teeth, the scientists decided that the kadabba fossils from five individuals were distinctive enough to qualify as a separate species, *Ardipithecus kadabba.* In that case, the scientists added, kadabba was not a subspecies, but the likely direct ancestor of ramidus. But there were too few skeletal bones yet to learn much about other aspects of kadabba.

The description and interpretation of the new hominin species appear

today in the journal *Science.* The authors of the report are Dr. Yohannes Haile-Selassie of the Cleveland Museum of Natural History, Dr. Gen Suwa of the University of Tokyo and Dr. Tim D. White of the University of California, Berkeley.

The kadabba fossils were found in the Middle Awash valley about 180 miles northeast of Addis Ababa, the Ethiopian capital. These are arid badlands now, but in the time of the early hominins the land was wooded and more hospitable.

Dr. Haile-Selassie said the shapes and wear patterns of six teeth in particular were "significant in understanding how the dentition evolved from an apelike common ancestor into the earliest hominins." They were also critical, he said, in differentiating the earlier and later species of the genus *Ardipithecus.*

Other scientists familiar with the research, but not involved in it, said they agreed or were at least inclined to agree with the authors' designation of a separate species for the fossils. But they were not so sure about the authors' proposal that the fossils were so similar to those of two other recently discovered early species that all three species might have actually belonged to a single genus of closely related hominids.

The other two hominid species are *Sahelanthropus tchadensis,* found in Chad and thought to be six million to seven million years old, and *Orrorin tugenensis,* a six-million-year-old specimen from Kenya. The two are primitive apelike creatures not much bigger than a modern chimp. Although the analysis of these remains is not complete, and still subject to debate, each has been classified as a separate genus and species. In their report on kadabba,

■ *Yohannes Haile-Selassie of the University of California at Berkeley holds the canine tooth of* Ardipithecus kadabba, *discovered in 1998.*

Dr. Haile-Selassie and his colleagues concluded, "Given the limited data currently available, it is possible that all of these remains represent specific or subspecific variation within a single genus."

Dr. White, one of the most experienced paleoanthropologists, emphasized this point in a telephone interview. "These earliest hominids are all very, very similar," he said. "When you look at these three snapshots we have, we are struck by the great biological similarity, not by pronounced differences, not by great lineage diversity."

But in an accompanying commentary in the journal, Dr. David R. Begun, a paleontologist at the University of Toronto,

questioned this interpretation. He said it was unlikely that all three of the early hominids belonged to a single genus, noting instead that the three exhibited evidence of striking diversity.

Dr. Begun conceded that "the level of uncertainty in the available direct evidence at this time renders irreconcilable differences of opinion inevitable."

The differences, broadly speaking, take the form of two images of what the hominin family tree looks like—a ladder or a bush. A growing number of scientists, finding multiple species of hominins that overlapped in time, contend that in response to new or changed circumstances hominins evolved

along many diverse lines—a bush with many branches.

Dr. Begun, in a telephone interview, emphasized that he was not disagreeing with the designation of the new species, but was "merely presenting an alternative" to the single-genus interpretation. "The material is so fragmentary," he said, "that we really can't know, and so our differences often are a reflection of different philosophies and experience in research." . . .

SOURCE: John Noble Wilford, "Another Branch of Early Human Ancestors Is Reported by Scientists," *New York Times*, March 5, 2004, late edition, final, Section A, p. 14, col. 1.

---

body to 60 percent more solar radiation than does bipedalism. The upright body could also catch the cooler breeze above the ground (Wilford 1995).

Brains, Skulls, and Childhood Dependency

Compared with contemporary humans, early hominins had very small brains. *Australopithecus afarensis,* a bipedal hominin that lived more than three million years ago, had a cranial capacity (430 cm^3—cubic centimeters) that barely surpassed the chimp average (390 cm^3). The form of the *afarensis* skull also is like that of the chimpanzee, although the brain-to-body size ratio may have been larger. Brain size has increased during hominin evolution, especially with the advent of the genus *Homo.* But this increase had to overcome some obstacles. Compared with the young of other primates, human children have a long period of childhood dependency, during which their brains and skulls grow dramatically. Larger skulls demand larger birth canals, but the requirements of upright bipedalism impose limits on the expansion of the human pelvic opening. If the opening is too large, the pelvis doesn't provide sufficient support for the trunk. Locomotion suffers, and posture problems develop. If, by contrast, the birth canal is too narrow, mother and child (without the modern option of Caesarean section) may die. Natural selection has struck a balance between the structural demands of upright posture and the tendency toward increased brain size—the birth of immature and dependent children whose brains and skulls grow dramatically after birth.

Biocultural Case Study

The "Bringing It All Together" essay that immediately follows Chapter 9 discusses the relation between biological and behavioral modernity—that is, when did people who looked like modern humans start acting like modern humans.

Tools

Given what is known (see Chapter 6) about tool use and manufacture by the great apes, it is likely that early hominins shared this ability as a homology with the apes. We'll see later that the first evidence for hominin stone tool manufacture is dated to 2.5 m.y.a. Upright bipedalism would have permitted the use of tools and weapons against predators and competitors in an open grassland habitat. Bipedal locomotion also allowed early hominins to carry things, perhaps including scavenged parts of carnivore kills. We know that primates have generalized abilities to adapt through learning. It would be amazing if early hominins, who are much more closely related to us than the apes are, didn't have even greater cultural abilities than contemporary apes have.

Teeth

One example of an early hominin trait that has been lost during subsequent human evolution is big back teeth. (Indeed a pattern of overall dental reduction has characterized human evolution.) As they adapted to the savanna, with its gritty, tough, and fibrous vegetation, it was adaptively advantageous for early hominins to have large back teeth and thick tooth enamel. This permitted thorough chewing of tough, fibrous vegetation and mixture with salivary enzymes to permit digestion of foods that otherwise would not have been digestible. The churning, rotary motion associated with such chewing also favored reduction of the canines and first premolars (bicuspids). These front teeth are much sharper and longer in the apes than in early hominins. The apes use their sharp self-honing teeth to pierce fruits. Males also flash their big sharp canines to intimidate and impress others, including potential mates. Although bipedalism seems to have characterized the human lineage since it split from the line leading to the African apes, many other "human" features came later. Yet other early hominin features, such as large back teeth and thick enamel—which we don't have now—offer clues about who was a human ancestor back then.

CHRONOLOGY OF HOMININ EVOLUTION

Recall that the term **hominin** is used to designate the human line after its split from ancestral chimps. **Hominid** refers to the taxonomic family that includes humans and the African apes and their immediate ancestors. In this book *hominid* is used when there is doubt about the hominin status of the fossil (e.g., with Toumai, as described in Chapter 7).

Although recent fossil discoveries have pushed the hominin lineage back to almost six million years (see the "News Brief"), humans actually haven't been around too long when the age of the earth is considered. If we compare earth's history to a 24-hour day (with one second equaling 50,000 years),

Earth originates at midnight.
The earliest fossils were deposited at 5:45 A.M.
The first vertebrates appeared at 9:02 P.M.
The earliest mammals, at 10:45 P.M.
The earliest primates, at 11:43 P.M.
The earliest hominins, at 11:57 P.M.
And *Homo sapiens* arrives 36 seconds before midnight. (Wolpoff, 1999, p. 10)

Although the first hominins appeared late in the Miocene epoch, for the study of hominin evolution, the Pliocene (5 to 2 m.y.a.), Pleistocene (2 m.y.a. to 10,000 B.P.), and Recent (10,000 B.P. to the present) epochs are most important. Until the end of the Pliocene, the main hominin genus was *Australopithecus*, which lived in sub-Saharan Africa. By the start of the Pleistocene, *Australopithecus* had evolved into *Homo*.

TABLE 8.1 Dates and Geographic Distribution of Major Hominoid, Hominid, and Hominin Fossil Groups

Fossil Group	Dates, m.y.a.	Known Distribution
Hominoid		
Pierolapithecus catalaunicus	13	Spain
Hominid		
Common ancestor of hominids	8?	East Africa
"Toumai"	7–6	Chad
Orrorin tugenensis	6	Kenya
Hominins		
Ardipithecus kadabba	5.8–5.5	Ethiopia
Ardipithecus ramidus	4.4	Ethiopia
Kenyanthropus platyops	3.5	Kenya
Australopithecines		
A. anamensis	4.2	Kenya
A. afarensis	3.8–3.0	East Africa (Laetoli, Hadar)
A. garhi	2.5	Ethiopia
Robusts	2.6–1.2	East and South Africa
A. robustus (aka *Paranthropus*)	2.0?–1.0?	South Africa
A. boisei	2.6?–1.0	East Africa
Graciles		
A. africanus	3.0–2.0?	South Africa
Homo		
H. habilis/H. rudolfensis	2.4?–1.7?	East Africa
H. ergaster/H. erectus	1.7?–0.3?	Africa, Asia, Europe
Homo sapiens	0.3–present	
Archaic H. sapiens	0.3–0.28 (300,000–28,000)	Africa, Asia, Europe
Neandertals	0.13–0.28 (130,000–28,000)	Europe, Middle East, North Africa
Anatomically Modern Humans (AMHs)	0.15?–present (150,000–present)	Worldwide (after 20,000 B.P.)

■ *Maeve Leakey
and Kenyanthropus
platyops, which she
discovered in 1999
by Lake Turkana
in northern Kenya.
What's the significance
of Kenyanthropus?*

THE EARLIEST HOMININS

Recent discoveries of fossils and tools have increased our knowledge of hominid and hominin evolution. The most significant recent discoveries have been made in Africa—Kenya, Tanzania, Ethiopia, and Chad. These finds come from different sites and may be the remains of individuals who lived hundreds of thousands of years apart. Furthermore, geological processes operating over thousands or millions of years inevitably distort fossil remains. Table 8.1 summarizes the major events in of hominid and hominin evolution. You should consult it throughout this chapter and the next one.

Ardipithecus

As we saw in the news story, early hominins assigned to *Ardipithecus kadabba* lived during the late Miocene, between 5.8 and 5.5 million years ago. Some Miocene hominins eventually evolved into a varied group of Pliocene–Pleistocene hominins known as the *australopithecines*—for which we have an abundant fossil record. This term reflects their one-time classification as members of a distinct taxonomic subfamily, the "Australopithecinae." We now know that the various species of *Australopithecus* discussed in this chapter do not form a distinct subfamily within the order Primates, but the name "australopithecine" has stuck to describe them. Today the distinction between the **australopithecines** and later hominins is made on the genus level. The australopithecines are assigned to the genus *Australopithecus (A.);* later humans, to *Homo (H.).*

Map 4 shows the sites where the earliest hominin fossils have been found, along with a timeline for hominin evolution.

Ardipithecus (ramidus) fossils were first discovered at Aramis in Ethiopia by Berhane Asfaw, Gen Suwa, and Tim White. Dating to 4.4 m.y.a., these *Ardipithecus ramidus* fossils consisted of the remains of some 17 individuals, with cranial, facial, dental, and upper limb bones. The news story discusses much older *Ardipithecus (kadabba)* fossils, dating back to 5.8 m.y.a., very near the time of the common ancestor of humans and the African apes. The *kadabba* find consists of 11 specimens, including a jaw bone with teeth, hand and foot bones, fragments of arm bones, and a piece of collarbone. At least five individuals are represented. These creatures were apelike in size, anatomy, and habitat. They lived in a wooded area rather than the open grassland or savanna habitat where later hominins proliferated. As of this writing, because of its probable bipedalism, *Ardipithecus kadabba* is recognized as the earliest known hominin, with the Toumai find from Chad, dated to 7–6 m.y.a., and *Orrorin tugenensis* from Kenya, dated to 6 m.y.a. (see Chapter 7), possibly even older hominins.

Kenyanthropus

Complicating the picture is another discovery, which Maeve Leakey has named *Kenyanthropus platyops,* or flat-faced "man" of Kenya. (Actually, the sex hasn't been determined.) This 1999 fossil find—of a nearly complete skull and partial jaw bone—was made by a research team led by Leakey, excavating on the western side of Lake Turkana in northern Kenya. They consider this 3.5-million-year-old find to represent an entirely new branch of the early human family tree.

Leakey views *Kenyanthropus* as showing that at least two hominin lineages existed as far back as 3.5 million years. One was the well-established fossil species *Australopithecus afarensis* (see below), best known from the celebrated Lucy skeleton. With the discovery of *Kenyanthropus* it would seem that Lucy and her kind weren't alone on the African plain. According to Leakey, Lucy may not be a direct human ancestor after all. The hominin family tree, once drawn with a straight trunk, is beginning to look more like a bush, with branches leading in many directions (Wilford 2001a).

Kenyanthropus has a flattened face and small molars that are strikingly different from those of *afarensis* (see below). Ever since its discovery in Ethiopia in 1974 by Donald Johanson, *afarensis* has been regarded as the most likely common ancestor of all subsequent hominins, including humans. With no other hominin fossils dated to the period between 3.8 million and 3.0 million years ago, this was the most reasonable conclusion scientists could draw. As a result of the *Kenyanthropus* discovery, however, the place of *afarensis* in human ancestry has been and will be debated. Taxonomic "splitters" (those who stress diversity and divergence) will focus on the differences between *afarensis* and *Kenyanthropus* and see it as representing a new taxon (genus and/or species), as Maeve Leakey has done. Taxonomic "lumpers" will focus on the similarities between *Kenyanthropus* and *afarensis* and may try to place them both in the same taxon—probably *Australopithecus*, which is well established.

THE VARIED AUSTRALOPITHECINES

In the scheme followed here, *Australopithecus* had at least six species:

1. *A. anamensis* (4.2 to 3.9 m.y.a.)

2. *A. afarensis* (3.8? to 3.0 m.y.a.)

3. *A. africanus* (3.0? to 2.0? m.y.a.)

4. *A. garhi* (2.5 m.y.a.)

5. *A. robustus* (2.0? to 1.0? m.y.a.)

6. *A. boisei* (2.6? to 1.0 m.y.a.)

The dates given for each species are approximate because an organism isn't a member of one species one day and a member of another species the next day. Nor could the same dating techniques be used for all the finds. The South African australopithecine fossils (*A. africanus* and *A. robustus*), for example, come from a nonvolcanic area where radiometric dating could not be done. Dating of those fossils has been based mainly on stratigraphy. The hominin fossils from the volcanic regions of East Africa usually have radiometric dates.

Australopithecus anamensis

Ardipithecus ramidus may (or may not) have evolved into *A. anamensis*, a bipedal hominin from northern Kenya, whose fossil remains were reported first by Maeve Leakey and Alan Walker in 1995 (Leakey et al. 1995; Rice 2002). *A. anamensis* consists of 78 fragments from two sites: Kanapoi and Allia Bay. The fossils include upper and lower jaws, cranial fragments, and the upper and lower parts of a leg bone (tibia). The Kanapoi fossils date to 4.2 m.y.a., and those at Allia Bay to 3.9 m.y.a. The molars have thick enamel, and the apelike canines are large. Based on the tibia, *anamensis* weighed about 110 pounds (50 kg.). This would have made it larger than either the earlier *Ardipithecus* or the later *A. afarensis*. Its anatomy implies that *anamensis* was bipedal. Because of its date and its location in the East African Rift valley, *A. anamensis* may be ancestral to *A. afarensis* (3.8–3.0 m.y.a.) which usually is considered ancestral to all the later australopithecines (*garhi, africanus, robustus,* and *boisei*) as well as to *Homo* (Figure 8.1).

Australopithecus afarensis

The hominin species known as **A. afarensis** includes fossils found at two sites, Laetoli in northern Tanzania and Hadar in the Afar region of Ethiopia. Laetoli is earlier (3.8 to 3.6 m.y.a.). The Hadar fossils probably date to between 3.3 and 3.0 m.y.a. Thus, based on the current evidence, *A. afarensis* lived between about 3.8 and 3.0 m.y.a. Research directed by Mary Leakey was responsible for the Laetoli finds. The Hadar discoveries resulted from an international expedition directed by D. C. Johanson and M. Taieb. The two sites have yielded significant samples of early hominin fossils. There are two dozen specimens from Laetoli, and the Hadar finds include the remains of between 35 and 65 individuals. The Laetoli remains are mainly teeth and jaw fragments, along with some very informative

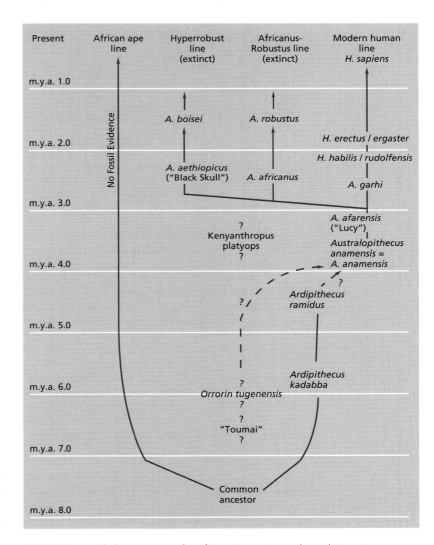

FIGURE 8.1 Phylogenetic Tree for African Apes, Hominids, and Hominins.
The presumed divergence date for ancestral chimps and hominins was between 6 and 8 m.y.a. Branching in later hominin evolution is also shown. For more exact dates, see the text and Table 8.1.

■ An ancient trail of
hominin footprints
fossilized in volcanic
ash. Mary Leakey found
this 230-foot (70-meter)
trail at Laetoli, Tanzania,
in 1979. It dates from
3.6 m.y.a. and confirms
that A. afarensis was a
striding biped.

three molars. Our dental formula is 2.1.2.3, for a total of 8 teeth on each side, upper and lower—32 teeth in all—if we have all our "wisdom teeth" (our third molars). Now back to the australopithecines. Like apes, and unlike modern humans, *A. afarensis* had sharp canine teeth that projected beyond the other teeth. Also like apes, their lower premolar was pointed and projecting to sharpen the upper canine. It had one long cusp and one tiny bump that hints at the bicuspid premolar that eventually developed in hominin evolution.

There is, however, evidence that powerful chewing associated with savanna vegetation was entering the *A. afarensis* feeding pattern. When the coarse, gritty, fibrous vegetation of grasslands and semidesert enters the diet, the back teeth change to accommodate heavy chewing stresses. Massive back teeth, jaws, and facial and cranial structures suggest a diet demanding extensive grinding and powerful crushing. *A. afarensis* molars are large (see Figure 8.2). The lower jaw (mandible) is thick and is buttressed with a bony ridge behind the front teeth. The cheekbones are large and flare out to the side for the attachment of powerful chewing muscles.

The skull of *A. afarensis* contrasts with those of later hominins. The cranial capacity of 430 cm^3 (cubic centimeters) barely surpasses the chimp average (390 cm^3). Below the neck, however—particularly in regard to locomotion—*A. afarensis* was unquestionably human. Early evidence of striding bipedalism comes from Laetoli, where volcanic ash, which can be directly dated by the K/A technique, covered a trail of footprints of two or three hominins walking to a water hole. These prints leave no doubt that a small striding biped lived in Tanzania by 3.6 m.y.a. The structure of the pelvic, hip, leg, and foot bones also confirms that upright bipedalism was *A. afarensis*'s mode of locomotion.

More recent finds show that bipedalism predated *A. afarensis*. *A. anamensis* (4.2 m.y.a.) was bipedal. Relevant postcranial material from the even older *Ardipithecus* (5.8–4.4 m.y.a.) also suggests a capacity for upright bipedal locomotion. Indeed, it was the shift toward this form of moving around that led to the distinctive hominin way of life. Bipedalism—upright two-legged locomotion—is the key feature differentiating early hominins from the apes.

Although bidepal, *A. afarensis* still contrasts in many ways with later hominins. Sexual dimorphism is especially marked. The male–female contrast in jaw size in *A. afarensis* was more marked than in the orangutan. There was a similar contrast in body size. *A. afarensis* females, such as Lucy, stood between 3 and 4 feet (.9 and 1.2 meters) tall; males might have reached 5 feet (1.5 meters). *A. afarensis* males weighed perhaps twice as much as the females did (Wolpoff 1999). Table 8.2 summarizes data on the various aus-

fossilized footprints. The Hadar sample includes skull fragments and postcranial material, most notably 40 percent of the complete skeleton of a tiny hominin female, dubbed "Lucy," who lived around 3 m.y.a.

Although the hominin remains at Laetoli and Hadar were deposited half a million years apart, their many resemblances explain their placement in the same species, *A. afarensis*. These fossils forced a reinterpretation of the early hominin fossil record. *A. afarensis,* although clearly a hominin, was so similar in many ways to chimps and gorillas that our common ancestry with the African apes must be very recent, certainly no more than 8 m.y.a. *Ardipithecus* and *A. anamensis* are even more apelike. These discoveries show that hominins are much closer to the apes than the previously known fossil record had suggested. Studies of the learning abilities and biochemistry of chimps and gorillas have taught a valuable lesson about homologies that the fossil record is now confirming.

The *A. afarensis* finds, which have been much more completely described than *Ardipithecus* and *A. anamensis*, make this clear. The many apelike features are surprising in definite hominins that lived as recently as 3 m.y.a. Discussion of hominin fossils requires a brief review of dentition. Moving from front to back, on either side of the upper or lower jaw, humans (and apes) have two incisors, one canine, two premolars, and

See the Internet Exercises
at your OLC

mhhe.com/kottak

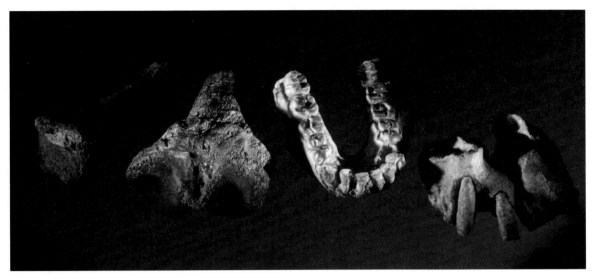

On the left, two sections of a tibia (dating back 4 million years) from A. anamensis, a bipedal hominin from northern Kenya. The tibia is the larger bone of the lower leg. Features of these bone fragments provide evidence that A. anamensis walked upright. To the right, an anamensis lower jaw and an upper jaw fragment. The molars have thick enamel, and the apelike canines are large.

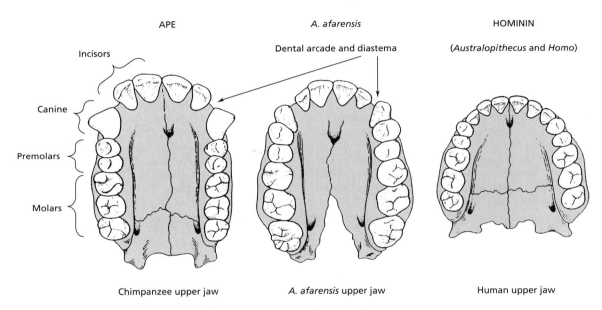

APE   A. afarensis   HOMININ

Dental arcade and diastema   (*Australopithecus* and *Homo*)

Incisors

Canine

Premolars

Molars

Chimpanzee upper jaw   *A. afarensis* upper jaw   Human upper jaw

FIGURE 8.2 Comparison of Dentition in Ape, Human, and *A. afarensis* Palates. SOURCE: © 1981 Luba Dmytryk Gudz/Brill Atlanta.

tralopithecines, including mid-sex body weight and brain size. Mid-sex means midway between the male average and the female average.

Lucy and her kind were far from dainty. Lucy's muscle-engraved bones are much more robust than ours are. With only rudimentary tools and weapons, early hominins needed powerful and resistant bones and muscles. Lucy's arms are longer relative to her legs than are those of later hominins. Here again her proportions are more apelike than ours are. Although Lucy neither brachiated nor knuckle-walked, she was probably a much better climber than modern people are, and she spent some of her day in the trees.

The *A. afarensis* fossils show that as recently as 3.0 m.y.a., our ancestors had a mixture of apelike and hominin features. Canines, premolars, and

skulls were much more apelike than most scholars had imagined would exist in such a recent ancestor. On the other hand, the molars, chewing apparatus, and cheekbones foreshadowed later hominin trends, and the pelvic and limb bones were indisputably hominin (Figure 8.3 on page 163). The hominin pattern was being built from the ground up.

Hominins walk with a striding gait that consists of alternating swing and stance phases for each leg and foot. As one leg is pushed off by the big toe and goes into the swing phase, the heel of the other leg is touching the ground and entering the stance phase. Four-footed locomotors such as Old World monkeys are always supported by two limbs. Bipeds, by contrast, are supported by one limb at a time.

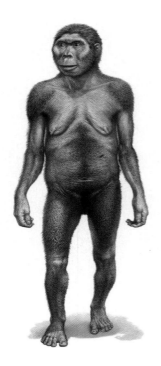

A reconstruction of Lucy, a member of A. afarensis, who lived at Hadar in Ethiopia more than 3 million years ago.

STUDENT CD-ROM LIVING ANTHROPOLOGY

Lucy
Track 8

This clip describes the discovery and characteristics of Lucy, the first member of *Australopithecus afarensis* to enter the fossil record. On her discovery in 1974, Lucy became the most ancient hominin and hominid in the fossil record at that time. Today that record includes several older probable or possible hominin ancestors, identified as such—like Lucy—by their upright bipedalism. The clip supplies answers to the following questions: Which of Lucy's anatomical traits were similar to those of chimpanzees? Which were similar to those of modern humans? How did Lucy's pelvis differ from an ape's pelvis? What is the explanation for this difference?

The pelvis, the lower spine, the hip joint, and the thigh bone change in accordance with the stresses of bipedal locomotion. Australopithecine pelvises are much more similar (although far from identical) to *Homo*'s than to apes' and show adaptation to bipedalism (Figure 8.4 on page 163). The blades of the australopithecine pelvis (iliac blades) are shorter and broader than are those of the ape.

The sacrum, which anchors the pelvis's two side bones, is larger, as in *Homo*. With bipedalism, the pelvis forms a sort of basket that balances the weight of the trunk and supports this weight with less stress. Fossilized spinal bones (vertebrae) show that the australopithecine spine had the lower spine (lumbar) curve characteristic of *Homo*. This curvature helps transmit the weight of the upper body to the pelvis and the legs. Placement of the *foramen magnum* (the "big hole" through which the spinal cord joins the brain) farther forward in *Australopithecus* and *Homo* than in the ape also represents an adaptation to upright bipedalism (Figure 8.5 on page 164).

TABLE 8.2   Facts about the Australopithecines Compared with Chimps and *Homo*

Species	Dates (m.y.a.)	Known Distribution	Important Sites	Body Weight (Mid-Sex)	Brain Size (Mid-Sex) (cm³)
Anatomically modern humans (AMHs)	150,000 to present			132 lb/60 kg	1,350
Pan troglodytes (chimpanzee)	Modern			93 lb/42 kg	390
A. boisei	2.6? to 1.2	E. Africa	Olduvai, East Turkana	86 lb/39 kg/	490
A. robustus	2.0? to 1.0?	S. Africa	Kromdraai, Swartkrans	81 lb/37 kg	540
A. africanus	3 to 2.0?	S. Africa	Taung, Sterkfontein, Makapansgat	79 lb/36 kg	490
A. afarensis	3.8 to 3.0	E. Africa	Hadar, Laetoli	77 lb/35 kg	430
A. anamensis	4.2 to 3.9	Kenya	Kanapoi Allia Bay	Insufficient data	No published skulls
Ardipithecus	5.8 to 4.4	Ethiopia	Aramis	Insufficient data	No published skulls

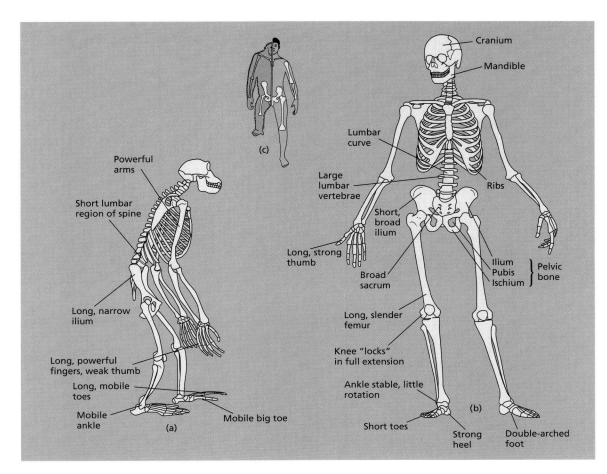

FIGURE 8.3 Comparison of *Homo sapiens* and *Pan troglodytes* (the Common Chimp).
(a) Skeleton of chimpanzee in bipedal position; (b) skeleton of modern human; (c) chimpanzee and human "bisected" and drawn to the same trunk length for comparison of limb proportions. The contrast in leg length is largely responsible for the proportional difference between humans and apes.

In apes, the thigh bone (femur) extends straight down from the hip to the knees. In *Australopithecus* and *Homo,* however, the thigh bone angles into the hip, permitting the space between the knees to be narrower than the pelvis during walking. The pelvises of the australopithecines were similar but not identical to those of *Homo.* The most significant contrast is a narrower australopithecine birth canal (Tague and Lovejoy 1986).

Expansion of the birth canal is a trend in hominin evolution. The width of the birth canal is related to the size of the skull and brain. *A. afarensis* had a small cranial capacity. Even in later australopithecines, brain size did not exceed 600 cubic centimeters. Undoubtedly, the australopithecine skull grew after birth to accommodate a growing brain, as it does (much more) in *Homo.* However, the brains of the australopithecines expanded less than ours do. In the australopithecines, the cranial sutures (the lines where the bones of the skull eventually come together) fused relatively earlier in life.

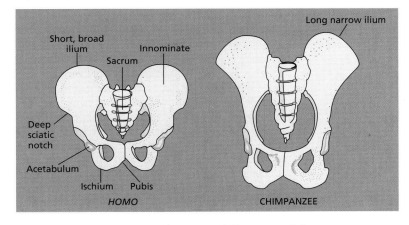

FIGURE 8.4 A Comparison of Human and Chimpanzee Pelvises.
The human pelvis has been modified to meet the demands of upright bipedalism. The blades (ilia; singular, ilium) of the human pelvis are shorter and broader than those of the ape. The sacrum, which anchors the side bones, is wider. The australopithecine pelvis is far more similar to that of Homo than to that of the chimpanzee, as we would expect in an upright biped.

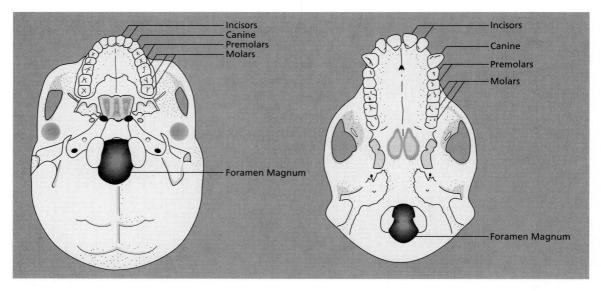

FIGURE 8.5 A Comparison of the Skull and Dentition (Upper Jaw) of *Homo* and the Chimpanzee.
The foramen magnum, *through which the spinal cord joins the brain, is located farther forward in Homo than in the ape. This permits the head to balance atop the spine with upright bipedalism. The molars and premolars of the ape form parallel rows. Human teeth, by contrast, are arranged in rounded, parabolic form. What differences do you note between human and ape canines? Canine reduction has been an important trend in hominin evolution.*

Young australopithecines must have depended on their parents and kin for nurturance and protection. Those years of childhood dependency would have provided time for observation, teaching, and learning. This may provide indirect evidence for a rudimentary cultural life.

Gracile and Robust Australopithecines

The fossils of *A. africanus* and *A. robustus* come from South Africa. In 1924, the anatomist Raymond Dart coined the term *Australopithecus africanus* to describe the first fossil representative of this species, the skull of a juvenile that was found accidentally in a quarry at Taung, South Africa. Radiometric dates are lacking for this nonvolcanic region, but the fossil hominins found at the five main South African sites appear (from stratigraphy) to have lived between 3 and 1 m.y.a.

There were two groups of South African australopithecines: **gracile** *(A. africanus)* and **robust** *(A. robustus)*. "Gracile" indicates that members of *A. africanus* were smaller and slighter, less robust, than were members of *A. robustus*. There were also very robust—*hyperrobust*—australopithecines in East Africa. In the classification scheme used here, these have been assigned to *A. boisei*. However, some scholars consider *A. robustus* and *A. boisei* to be regional variants of just one species, usually called *robustus* (sometimes given its own genus, *Paranthropus*).

The relationship between the graciles and the robusts has been debated for generations but has not been resolved. Graciles and robusts probably descend from *A. afarensis*, which itself was gracile in form, or from a South African version of *A. afarensis*. Some scholars have argued that the graciles lived before (3.0 to 2.0? m.y.a.) and were ancestral to the robusts (2.0? to 1.0? m.y.a.). Others contend that the graciles and the robusts were separate species that may have overlapped in time. (Classifying them as members of different species implies they were reproductively isolated from each other in time or space.) Other paleoanthropologists view the gracile and robust australopithecines as different ends of a continuum of variation in a single *polytypic species*—one with considerable phenotypic variation. The range of *Australopithecus* sites in East and South Africa is shown on Map 4 in the Map Atlas.

The trend toward enlarged back teeth, chewing muscles, and facial buttressing, which already is noticeable in *A. afarensis*, continues in the South African australopithecines. However, the canines are reduced, and the premolars are fully bicuspid. Dental form and function changed as dietary needs shifted from cutting and slashing to chewing and grinding.

The mainstay of the australopithecine diet was the vegetation of the savanna, although these early hominins also might have hunted small and slow-moving game. As well, they may have scavenged, bringing home parts of kills made by large

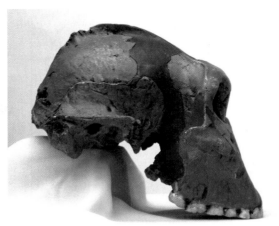

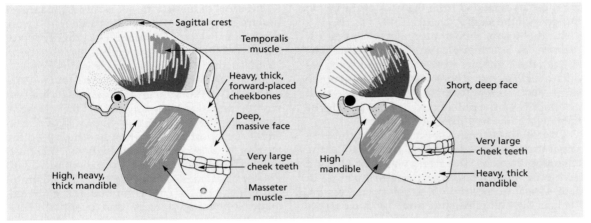

FIGURE 8.6 Skulls of Robust (Left) and Gracile (Right) Australopithecines, Showing Chewing Muscles.
Flaring cheek arches and, in some robusts, a sagittal crest supported this massive musculature. The early hominin diet—coarse, gritty vegetation of the savanna—demanded such structures. These features were most pronounced in A. boisei.

cats and other carnivores. The ability to hunt large animals was probably an achievement of *Homo* and is discussed later.

The skulls, jaws, and teeth of the australopithecines leave no doubt that their diet was mainly vegetarian. Natural selection modifies the teeth to conform to the stresses associated with a particular diet. Massive back teeth, jaws, and associated facial and cranial structures confirm that the australopithecine diet required extensive grinding and powerful crushing.

In the South African australopithecines, both deciduous ("baby") and permanent molars and premolars are massive, with multiple cusps. The later australopithecines had bigger back teeth than did the earlier ones. However, this evolutionary trend ended with early *Homo*, which had much smaller back teeth, reflecting a dietary change that will be described later.

Contrasts with *Homo* in the front teeth are less marked. But they are still of interest because of what they tell us about sexual dimorphism.

A. africanus's canines were more pointed, with larger roots, than *Homo*'s are. Still, the *A. africanus* canines were only 75 percent the size of the canines of *A. afarensis*. Despite this canine reduction, there was just as much canine sexual dimorphism in *A. africanus* as there had been in *A. afarensis* (Wolpoff 1999). Sexual dimorphism in general was much more pronounced among the early hominins than it is among *Homo sapiens*. *A. africanus* females were about 4 feet (1.2 meters), and males 5 feet (1.5 meters), tall. The average female probably had no more than 60 percent the weight of the average male (Wolpoff 1980a). (That figure contrasts with today's average female-to-male weight ratio of about 88 percent.)

Teeth, jaw, face, and skull changed to fit a diet based on tough, gritty, fibrous grasslands vegetation. A massive face housed large upper teeth and provided a base for the attachment of powerful chewing muscles. Australopithecine cheekbones were elongated and massive structures (Figure 8.6) that anchored large chewing muscles

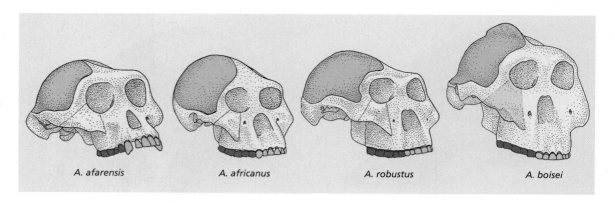

A. afarensis   A. africanus   A. robustus   A. boisei

running up the jaw. Another set of robust chewing muscles extended from the back of the jaw to the sides of the skull.

In the more robust australopithecines (*A. robustus* in South Africa and *A. boisei* in East Africa), these muscles were strong enough to produce a *sagittal crest,* a bony ridge on the top of the skull. Such a crest forms as the bone grows. It develops from the pull of the chewing muscles as they meet at the midline of the skull.

Overall robustness, especially in the chewing apparatus, increased through time among the australopithecines. This trend was most striking in *A. boisei,* which survived through 1.0 m.y.a in East Africa. Compared with their predecessors, the later australopithecines tended to have larger overall size, skulls, and back teeth. They also had thicker faces, more prominent crests, and more rugged muscle markings on the skeleton. By contrast, the front teeth stayed the same size.

Brain size (measured as cranial capacity, in cubic centimeters—cm^3) increased only slightly between *A. afarensis* (430 cm^3), *A. africanus* (490 cm^3), and *A. robustus* (540 cm^3) (Wolpoff 1999). These figures can be compared with an average cranial capacity of 1,350 cm^3 in *Homo sapiens.* The modern range goes from less than 1,000 cm^3 to more than 2,000 cm^3 in normal adults. The cranial capacity of chimps (*Pan troglodytes*) averages 390 cm^3 (see Table 8.2). The brains of gorillas (*Gorilla gorilla*) average around 500 cm^3, which is within the australopithecine range, but gorilla body weight is much greater.

THE AUSTRALOPITHECINES AND EARLY *HOMO*

Between 3 and 2 m.y.a., the ancestors of *Homo* split off and became reproductively isolated from the later australopithecines, such as *A. robustus* and *A. boisei,* which coexisted with *Homo* until around 1.0 m.y.a. The first evidence for speciation is dental. The fossil sample of hominin teeth from

East Africa dated to 2 m.y.a. has two clearly different sizes of teeth. One set is huge, the largest molars and premolars in hominin evolution; these teeth belong to *A. boisei.* The other group of (smaller) teeth belonged to our probable ancestor, *H. habilis,* the first exemplar of the genus *Homo.*

By 1.7 m.y.a., the difference was even more evident. Two hominin groups occupied different environmental niches in Africa. One of them, *Homo*—by then *Homo erectus*—had a larger brain and a reproportioned skull; it had increased the areas of the brain that regulate higher mental functions. These were our ancestors, hominins with greater capacities for culture than the australopithecines had. *H. erectus* hunted and gathered, made sophisticated tools, and eventually displaced its sole surviving cousin species, *A. boisei.*

A. boisei of East Africa, the hyperrobust australopithecines, had mammoth back teeth. *A. boisei* females had bigger back teeth than did earlier australopithecine males. *A. boisei* became ever more specialized with respect to one part of the traditional australopithecine diet, concentrating on coarse vegetation with a high grit content.

The separation that led to speciation between *A. boisei* and early *Homo* took time. And why, if two new *species* were forming, is one of them assigned to a new genus, *Homo*? This classification is done in retrospect, since we know that one species survived and evolved into a contemporary descendant whereas the other one became extinct. Hindsight shows us their very different lifeways, which suggest their placement in different genera.

We still don't know why, how, and exactly when the split between *Australopithecus* and *Homo* took place. Scholars have defended many different models, or theoretical schemes, to interpret the early hominin fossil record. Because new finds have so often forced reappraisals, most scientists are willing to modify their interpretation when given new evidence.

The model of Johanson and White (1979), who coined the term *A. afarensis,* proposes that *A. afarensis* split into two groups. One group, the

Palates of Homo sapiens (left) and A. boisei (right), a late, hyperrobust australopithecine. In comparing them, note the australopithecine's huge molars and premolars. What other contrasts do you notice? The large back teeth represent an extreme adaptation to a diet based on coarse, gritty savanna vegetation. Reduction in tooth size during human evolution applied to the back teeth much more than to the front.

ancestors of *Homo*, became reproductively isolated from other hominins between 3 and 2 m.y.a. This group appeared as **Homo habilis,** a term coined by L. S. B. and Mary Leakey for the first members of the genus *Homo. H. habilis* lived between 2 m.y.a. and about 1.7 m.y.a., by which time it had evolved into *H. erectus.* Other members of *A. afarensis* evolved into the various kinds of australopithecines (*A. africanus, A. robustus,* and hyperrobust *A. boisei,* the last member to become extinct).

In 1985, the paleoanthropologist Alan Walker made a significant find near Lake Turkana in northern Kenya. Called the "black skull" because of the blue-black sheen it bore from the minerals surrounding it, the fossil displayed a "baffling combination of features" (Fisher 1988*a*). The jaw was apelike and the brain was small (as in *A. afarensis*), but there was a massive bony crest atop the skull (as in *A. boisei*). Walker and Richard Leakey (Walker's associate on the 1985 expedition) view the black skull (dated to 2.6 m.y.a.) as a very early hyperrobust *A. boisei.* Others (e.g., Jolly and White 1995) assign the black skull to its own species, *A. aethiopicus.* The black skull shows that some of the anatomical features of the hyperrobust australopithecines (2.6? to 1.0 m.y.a.) did not change very much during well over one million years.

Regardless of when the split between *Homo* and *Australopithecus* occurred, there is good fossil evidence that *Homo* and *A. boisei* coexisted in East Africa. *A. boisei* seems to have lived in very arid areas, feeding on harder-to-chew vegetation than had any previous hominin. This diet would explain the hyperrobusts' huge back teeth, jaws, and associated areas of the face and skull.

OLDOWAN TOOLS

It may have been *Homo*'s increasing hunting proficiency that forced *A. boisei* into becoming an ever-more-specialized vegetarian. Tool making also might have had something to do with the split. The simplest obviously manufactured tools were discovered in 1931 by L. S. B. and Mary Leakey at Olduvai Gorge, Tanzania. This site gave the tools their name—Oldowan pebble tools. The oldest tools from Olduvai are about 1.8 million years old. Still older (2.5 to 2.0 m.y.a.) stone implements have been found in Ethiopia, Congo, and Malawi (Asfaw, White, and Lovejoy 1999; Lemonick and Dorfman 1999).

Stone tools consist of cores and flakes. The *core* is the piece of rock from which flakes are removed; the core can be worked to become a tool itself. A *chopper* is a tool made by flaking the edge of such a core on one side. **Oldowan** pebble tools represent the world's oldest formally recognized stone tools. With the use of cores about the size of a tennis ball, flakes were struck off one or both sides to form a chopping or cutting edge.

Core tools or choppers are the most common stone tools found at early African tool sites. Some may have been used for food processing—by pounding, breaking, or bashing. Other "choppers" may have been cores from which flakes, used for cutting or scraping, were removed. Flakes probably were used mainly as cutters, for example, to dismember game carcasses. Crushed fossil animal bones indicate that stones were used to break open marrow cavities. Also, Oldowan deposits include pieces of bone or horn with scratch marks suggesting they were used to dig up tubers or insects.

For more on early stone tools, see the Internet Exercises at your OLC
mhhe.com/kottak

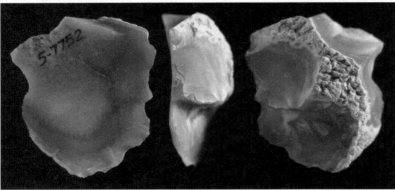

■ *Oldowan core tools or choppers are the most common stone tools found at early African tool sites. Some may have been used for food processing, by pounding, breaking, or bashing. Other "choppers" may only have been cores from which flakes, used for cutting or scraping, were removed. Above, a chopper core tool; below, a flake tool.*

Oldowan core and flake tools of the sort widely used between 1.5 and 2.0 m.y.a. are shown in the photos on this page. The flake tool in the lower photo is made of chert, whereas most Oldowan tools at Olduvai Gorge were made from basalt, which is locally more common and coarser.

For decades anthropologists have debated the identity of the earliest stone tool makers. The first *Homo habilis* find got its name (*habilis* is Latin for "able") for its presumed ability (and presumably first among hominins) to make tools. Recently the story has grown more complicated, with a discovery making it very likely that one kind of australopithecine also made and habitually used stone tools.

A. *garhi* and Early Stone Tools

In 1999 an international team reported the discovery, in Ethiopia, of a new species of hominin, along with the earliest traces of animal butchery (Asfaw, White, and Lovejoy 1999). These new fossils, dating to 2.5 m.y.a., may be the remains of a direct human ancestor and an evolutionary link between *Australopithecus* and the genus *Homo*. At the same site was evidence that antelopes and horses had been butchered with the world's earliest stone tools. When scientists excavated these hominin fossils, they were shocked to find a combination of unforeseen skeletal and dental features. They named the specimen *Australopithecus garhi*. The word *garhi* means "surprise" in the Afar language.

Tim White, coleader of the research team, viewed the discoveries as important for three reasons. First, they add a new potential ancestor to the human family tree. Second, they show that the thigh bone (femur) had elongated by 2.5 million years ago, a million years before the forearm shortened—to create our current human limb proportions. Third, evidence that large mammals were being butchered shows that early stone technologies were aimed at getting meat and marrow from big game. This signals a dietary revolution that eventually may have allowed an invasion of new habitats and continents (*Berkleyan* 1999).

In 1997 the Ethiopian archaeologist Sileshi Semaw announced he had found the world's earliest stone tools, dating to 2.5 m.y.a., at the nearby Ethiopian site of Gona. But which human ancestor had made these tools, he wondered, and what were they used for? The 1999 discoveries by Asfaw, White, and their colleagues provided answers, identifying *A. garhi* as the best candidate for toolmaker (*Berkleyan* 1999).

The association, in the same area at the same time, of *A. garhi*, animal butchery, and the earliest stone tools suggests that the australopithecines were toolmakers, with some capacity for culture. Nevertheless, cultural abilities developed exponentially with *Homo*'s appearance and expansion. With increasing reliance on hunting, tool making, and other cultural abilities, *Homo* eventually became the most efficient exploiter of the savanna niche. The last surviving members of *A. boisei* may have been forced into ever-more-marginal areas. They eventually became extinct. By 1 m.y.a., a single species of hominin, *H. erectus*, not only had rendered other hominin forms extinct but also had expanded the hominin range to Asia and Europe. An essentially human strategy of adaptation, incorporating hunting as a fundamental ingredient of a generalized foraging economy, had emerged. Despite regional variation, it was to be the basic economy for our genus until 11,000 years ago. We turn now to the fossils, tools, and life patterns of the various forms of *Homo*.

Hydrodynamic Sorting of Avian Skeletal Remains

BACKGROUND INFORMATION

STUDENT 1:
Josh Trapani

SUPERVISING PROFESSOR:
Peter Stahl

SCHOOL:
State University of New York
at Binghamton

YEAR IN SCHOOL/MAJOR:
Senior/Anthropology

FUTURE PLANS:
Graduate school

PROJECT TITLE:
Hydrodynamic Sorting
of Avian Skeletal Remains

People have dietary preferences for particular animal parts. Archaeologists typically encounter remains of animals that humans may have hunted and eaten. At a given site, certain kinds of bones may be more common than others are. How can we know whether humans choose some preferred parts to take away, while leaving others, or whether natural processes were responsible? This project examines the effects of water current in sorting avian (bird) bones. Some parts (e.g., skulls) are more likely than others are to have been moved by water, and this helps determine whether humans played a role in the selection of animal parts at the site.

Taphonomy is the study of the processes that affect preservation of organic remains. Specific taphonomic factors may bias (i.e., alter the preservation, condition, and identifiability of) archaeological and paleontological faunal assemblages in specific ways. It is necessary to understand the taphonomic biases an assemblage has been subjected to so that accurate interpretations about that assemblage can be made.

One important taphonomic agent is sorting by current. Many archaeological sites are located near water, and current action may alter their faunal assemblages. Currents sort bones in the same way they sort sediment: by selectively removing certain bones from a site while leaving others behind. Archaeologists often attribute relative frequencies of different skeletal elements at a site to human agency (e.g., dietary preference for certain parts of an animal over others). But if the assemblage has been subjected to sorting by current (or any of a number of other taphonomic factors), such interpretations may be erroneous.

Previous studies examined the way mammal and turtle bones sort in a current. However, a study with avian material had never been done before. Bird bones are structurally different from bones of other vertebrates and they often comprise an important component of human diet. I partially and completely skeletonized several domestic pigeons (*Columba livia*) and studied the way their bones sorted in a current.

I conducted the experiments in a flume, which is a large tank that simulates conditions inside a natural channel but allows for control of many variables. The bottom may be lined with sediment, and an adjustable current flows from one end to another. I examined the order that the bones moved in, how they moved, and how likely they were to be buried. I also examined transport of partially skeletonized birds to compare behavior of individual bones with articulated skeletal units. Repeated observations under a number of different flow conditions (e.g., current velocities, bedform types) allowed me to determine a general order in which bones were expected to move.

This "sorting sequence" is useful as a general guide to whether an avian assemblage has been sorted by a current. For example, an assemblage containing skulls (most likely to be moved) and scapulae or shoulder blades (least likely to be moved) was probably not subjected to sorting. However, if an assemblage contains many easily-moved bones and few "lag" bones (or vice versa), it becomes necessary to rule out current sorting before attributing observed relative frequencies to human (or other) agency.

I also attempted to establish correlations between sorting behavior and bone size, shape, and density. Finally, I noted similarities and differences between sorting sequences for the pigeon and already-published sequences for other vertebrates.

Hopefully, this research constitutes a small step in the direction of understanding how current sorting operates as a taphonomic bias. This knowledge may aid our interpretations of site formation and thus allow greater insight into past human behavior and practices.

1. Hominins lived during the late Miocene, Pliocene (5.0 to 2 m.y.a.), and Pleistocene (2 m.y.a. to 10,000 B.P.) epochs. The australopithecines had appeared by 4.2 m.y.a. The six species of *Australopithecus* were *A. anamensis* (4.2 m.y.a.), *A. afarensis* (3.8 to 3.0 m.y.a.), *A. africanus* (3.0 to 2.0? m.y.a.), *A. garhi* (2.5 m.y.a.), *A. robustus* (2.0? to 1.0? m.y.a.), and *A. boisei* (2.6? to 1.0 m.y.a.). The earliest identifiable hominin remains date to between 7.0 m.y.a. and 5.8 m.y.a. The "Toumai" find from northern Chad is a possible early hominin, as is *Orrorin tugenensis* from Kenya. More generally accepted hominin remains from Ethiopia are classified as *Ardipithecus kadabba* (5.8–5.5 m.y.a.) and *ramidus* (4.4 m.y.a.). Next comes *A. anamensis*, then a group of fossils from Hadar, Ethiopia, and Laetoli, Tanzania, classified as *A. afarensis*.

2. These earliest hominins shared many primitive features, including slashing canines, elongated premolars, a small apelike skull, and marked sexual dimorphism. Still, *A. afarensis* and its recently discovered predecessors were definite hominins. In *A. afarensis* this is confirmed by large molars and, more important, by skeletal evidence (e.g., in Lucy) for upright bipedalism.

3. Remains of two later groups, *A. africanus* (graciles) and *A. robustus* (robusts), were found in South Africa. Both groups show the australopithecine trend toward a powerful chewing apparatus. They had large molars and premolars and large and robust faces, skulls, and muscle markings. All these features are more pronounced in the robusts than they are in the graciles. The basis of the australopithecine diet was savanna vegetation. These early hominins may also have hunted small animals and scavenged the kills of predators.

4. Early *Homo*, *H. habilis* (2.0? to 1.7 m.y.a.), evolved into *H. erectus* (1.7 m.y.a. to 300,000 B.P.). By 2.0 m.y.a. there is ample evidence for two distinct hominin groups: early *Homo* and *A. boisei*, the hyperrobust australopithecines. The latter eventually became extinct around 1.0 m.y.a. *A. boisei* became increasingly specialized, dependent on tough, coarse, gritty, fibrous savanna vegetation. The australopithecine trend toward dental, facial, and cranial robustness continued with *A. boisei*, but these structures were reduced as *H. habilis* evolved into *H. erectus*.

5. Pebble tools dating to between 2.5 and 2.0 m.y.a. have been found in Ethiopia, Congo, and Malawi. Scientists have disagreed about their maker, some arguing that only early *Homo* could have made them. Evidence has been presented that *A. garhi* made pebble tools around 2.5 m.y.a. Cultural abilities developed exponentially with *Homo*'s appearance and evolution.

KEY TERMS

See the flash cards
mhhe.com/kottak

A. afarensis Early form of *Australopithecus*, known from Hadar in Ethiopia ("Lucy") and Laetoli in Tanzania; the Hadar remains date to 3.3–3.0 m.y.a.; the Laetoli remains are older, dating to 3.8–3.6 m.y.a.; despite its many apelike features, *A. afarensis* was an upright biped.

australopithecines Varied group of Pliocene–Pleistocene hominins. The term is derived from their former classification as members of a distinct subfamily, the Australopithecinae; now they are distinguished from *Homo* only at the genus level.

bipedalism Upright two-legged locomotion, the key feature differentiating early hominins from the apes.

gracile Opposite of robust; "gracile" indicates that members of *A. africanus* were smaller and slighter, less robust, than were members of *A. robustus*.

hominid A member of the taxonomic family that includes humans and the African apes and their immediate ancestors.

hominin A member of the human lineage after its split from ancestral chimps; the term *hominin* is used to describe all the human species that ever have existed, including the extinct ones, and excluding chimps and gorillas.

Homo habilis Term coined by L. S. B. and Mary Leakey; immediate ancestor of *H. erectus*; lived from about 2.0 to 1.7 m.y.a.

Oldowan Earliest (2.0 to 2.5 m.y.a.) stone tools; first discovered in 1931 by L. S. B. and Mary Leakey at Olduvai Gorge.

robust Large, strong, sturdy; said of skull, skeleton, muscle, and teeth; opposite of gracile.

CRITICAL THINKING QUESTIONS

For more self-testing, see the self-quizzes
mhhe.com/kottak

1. If you found a new hominid fossil in East Africa, dated to five million years ago, would it most likely be an ape ancestor or a human ancestor? How would you tell the difference?

2. What was the first species of *Australopithecus*? Where and when did it live? What hominins and hominids lived before it?

3. What is the significance of the black skull?

4. Do you think that *Australopithecus* or *Homo* made the first tools? What's the basis of your opinion?

Boaz, N. T.
1999 *Essentials of Biological Anthropology.* Upper Saddle River, NJ: Prentice Hall. Basic text in physical anthropology, with information on paleoanthropology.

Bogin, B.
2001 *The Growth of Humanity.* New York: Wiley. Human growth in relation to human evolution.

Brace, C. L.
1995 *The Stages of Human Evolution,* 5th ed. Englewood Cliffs, NJ: Prentice Hall. Brief introduction to the hominin fossil record.
2000 *Evolution in an Anthropological View.* Walnut Creek, CA: AltaMira. Essays on human evolution.

Calcagno, J. M., ed.
2003 *Biological Anthropology: Historical Perspectives on Current Issues, Disciplinary Connections, and Future Directions.* Special issue of the *American Anthropologist* 101(1). Recent articles on human evolution.

Campbell, B. G.
1998 *Human Evolution: An Introduction to Man's Adaptations,* 4th ed. New York: Aldine de Gruyter. Basic paleoanthropology text.

Campbell, B. G., J. D. Loy, and K. Cruz-Uribe
2006 *Humankind Emerging,* 9th ed. Boston: Pearson Allyn & Bacon. Well-illustrated survey of physical anthropology, particularly the fossil record.

Cole, S.
1975 *Leakey's Luck: The Life of Louis Bazett Leakey, 1903–1972.* New York: Harcourt Brace Jovanovich. The personal and professional life of anthropology's greatest fossil finder, written by an archaeologist.

Johanson, D. C., and B. Edgar
1996 *From Lucy to Language.* New York: Simon & Schuster. Popular account of human evolution by a prominent contributor to understanding the fossil record.

Lewin, R.
2005 *Human Evolution: An Illustrated Introduction,* 5th ed. Malden, MA: Blackwell. Readable and well-illustrated introduction.

McKee, J. K., F. E. Poirier, and W. S. McGraw
2005 *Understanding Human Evolution,* 5th ed. Upper Saddle River, NJ: Prentice Hall. Principles of human evolution.

Park, M. A.
2005 *Biological Anthropology,* 4th ed. Boston: McGraw-Hill. A concise introduction, with a focus on scientific inquiry.

Relethford, J. H.
2005 *The Human Species: An Introduction to Biological Anthropology,* 6th ed. Boston: McGraw-Hill. Up-to-date text in biological anthropology.

Wolpoff, M. H.
1999 *Paleoanthropology,* 2nd ed. Boston: McGraw-Hill. Thorough introduction to the hominin and prehominin fossil record.

SUGGESTED ADDITIONAL READINGS

INTERNET EXERCISES

1. Early Hominin Skulls: Visit Philip L. Walker and Edward H. Hagen's "Human Evolution: The Fossil Evidence in 3D" (**http://www.anth.ucsb.edu/projects/human/#**). Then click the link to enter the gallery.
   a. Click on the human figure labeled "Human origins" and then click on the skull labeled "Australopithecine radiation." You now have a three-dimensional view of an *Australopithecus afarensis* skull, and you can use the mouse to rotate the skull. Compare it with a modern human skull. What are some of the differences you notice? What do these differences mean about diet, environment, and brain size?
   b. Go back and view the *Paranthropus boisei* (equivalent to *Australopithecus boisei* in this text) and *Australopithecus africanus* skulls. What are the major differences between the two, and what do these differences say about diet, environment, and brain size?

2. Paleoanthropologist Fieldwork in Kenya: Go to the Human Origins Field Projects in Kenya page of the Human Origins Program at the Smithsonian, **http://www.mnh.si.edu/anthro/humanorigins/aop/aop_ken.html**. Explore the pages describing the fieldwork and methods (press Continue to Next Page).
   a. The site shows pictures of the modern environment of Kenya. How much has the environment changed since early hominins lived there?
   b. Did the fieldwork just involve excavating fossils? What other types of data are researchers gathering to understand early hominins?
   c. Make sure to read the dispatches from the researchers working at Olorgesailie in 1999 by clicking on "1999 Field Session."
   Read some of the diary entries. What is a day in the field of a paleoanthropologist like?

See Chapter 7 at your McGraw-Hill Online Learning Center for additional review and interactive exercises.

9

The Genus *Homo*

EARLY *HOMO*

As we saw in Chapter 8, at two million years ago, there is East African evidence for two distinct hominin groups: early *Homo* and *A. boisei*, the hyperrobust australopithecines, which became extinct around 1.0 m.y.a. *A. boisei* became increasingly specialized, dependent on tough, coarse, gritty, fibrous savanna vegetation. The australopithecine trend toward dental, facial, and cranial robustness continued with *A. boisei*. However, these structures were reduced as early forms of *Homo* evolved into *H. ergaster* (or early *H. erectus*) by 1.8–1.7 m.y.a. By that date *Homo* had generalized the subsistence

■ *Meet two kinds of early* Homo. *On the left KNM-ER 1813. On the right KNM-ER 1470. The latter (1470) has been classified as H. rudolfensis. What's the classification of 1813?*

quest to the hunting of large animals to supplement the gathering of vegetation and scavenging.

H. rudolfensis and H. habilis

In 1972, in an expedition led by Richard Leakey, Bernard Ngeneo unearthed a skull designated KNM-ER 1470. The name comes from its catalog number in the Kenya National Museum (KNM) and its discovery location (East Rudolph—ER)—east of Lake Rudolph, at a site called Koobi Fora. The 1470 skull attracted immediate attention because of its unusual combination of a large brain (775 cc) and very large molars. Its brain size was more human than that of the australopithecine, but its molars recalled those of the hyperrobust australopithecine. Some paleoanthropologists attributed the large skull and teeth to a very large body, assuming that this had been one *big hominin*. But no postcranial remains were found with 1470, nor have they been found with any later discovery of a 1470-like specimen.

How to interpret KNM-ER 1470? On the basis of its brain size, it seemed to belong in *Homo*. On the basis of its back teeth, it seemed more like *Australopithecus*. There also are problems with dating. The best dating guess is 1.8 m.y.a., but another estimate suggests that 1470 may be as old as 2.4 m.y.a. Originally, some paleoanthropologists assigned 1470 to *H. habilis*, while others saw it as an unusual australopithecine. In 1986, it received its own species name, *Homo rudolfensis*, from the lake near which it was found. This label has stuck—although it isn't accepted by all paleoanthropologists. Those who find *H. rudolfensis* to be a valid species emphasize its contrasts with *H. habilis*. Note the contrasts in the two skulls in the photo above. KNM-ER 1813, on the left, is considered *H. habilis*; KNM-ER 1470, on the right, is *H. rudolfensis*. The *habilis* skull has a more marked brow ridge and a depression behind it, whereas 1470 has a less pronounced brow ridge and a longer, flatter face. Some think that *rudolfensis* lived earlier than and is ancestral to *habilis*. Some think that *rudolfensis* and *habilis* are simply male and female members of the same species—*H. habilis*. Some think they are separate species that coexisted in time and space (from about 2.4 m.y.a. to about 1.7 m.y.a.). Some think that one or the other gave rise to *H. erectus* (also known in Africa

OVERVIEW

This chapter focuses on the genus *Homo,* for which fossil evidence dates back more than 2 million years. The chapter concludes with the much more recent past, when anatomically modern people painted artistic masterpieces on cave walls in France and Spain. We focus here on the biological and cultural changes that eventually led to anatomically modern humans (AMHs).

By about 1.8 million years ago, the earliest member of our genus, *Homo habilis,* had evolved into *Homo erectus,* which extended the hominin range out of Africa. Control of fire permitted expansion into cooler areas, as well as cooking and cave life. *H. erectus* had evolved into archaic *H. sapiens* by 300,000 years ago.

The Neandertals were a form of archaic *H. sapiens* that lived in Western Europe (and elsewhere) early in the last glacial period. Scientists tend to exclude the Neandertals as ancestors of modern humans. The ancestry of modern humans lies among other archaic *H. sapiens* groups, most probably those in Africa. Modern people reached Europe by 50,000 years ago.

Improved Science Puts Modern Humans in Europe Earlier

NEW YORK TIMES NEWS BRIEF

by John Noble Wilford
February 23, 2006

For more than a century anthropologists have known of the overlap between archaic (Neandertal) and anatomically modern humans (AMHs) in Europe. This story reports on the implications of recent revisions and recalibrations in the radiocarbon dating technique that has been applied to Neandertals and AMHs in Europe. Radiocarbon (C^{14}) dating is most useful for remains that are 50,000 years old or less. The revised dating described here suggests that modern humans have been in Europe longer than previously thought—perhaps for 50,000 years—and that their time of overlap with the Neandertals was less than previously thought, perhaps no more than 2,000 years in western Europe.

New advances in radiocarbon dating are threatening to upend old theories about when modern humans migrated to Europe from Africa and how rapidly they advanced. The research casts new light on significant patterns of human migration into Central and Western Europe in the crucial period from 50,000 to 35,000 years ago, scientists say. It suggests that the dispersal of anatomically modern *Homo sapiens* into Europe was more rapid than previously thought.

That, in turn, would mean that their coexistence with Neanderthals was briefer and that their introduction of cave art, symbolic artifacts and personal ornamentation occurred much earlier.

"Evidently the native Neanderthal populations of Europe succumbed much more rapidly to competition from the expanding biologically modern populations than previous estimates have generally assumed," Paul Mellars, an archaeologist at the University of Cambridge in England, wrote in an article appearing today in the journal *Nature*.

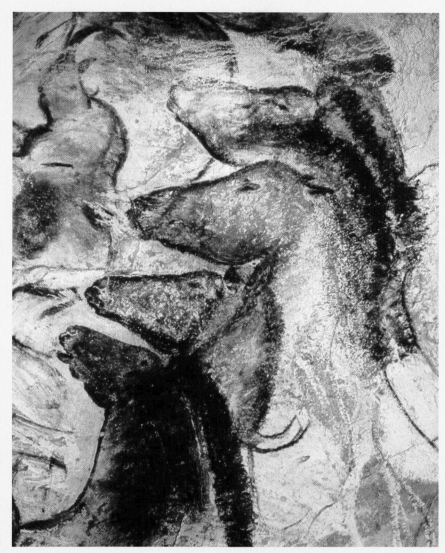

Cave murals recently redated to 36,000 years in Chauvet cave at Vallon-Pont-d'Arc in southern France.

Although other scientists have for several years been pondering the implications of the revised radiocarbon dating for archaeological research throughout the world, Dr. Mellars's description of the new techniques and their significance is the first comprehensive review of the subject in a major journal. The most pronounced discrepancies between radiocarbon and actual ages coincide with the fateful epoch when modern people first made themselves at home in Europe.

For years, it had been thought that modern humans from Africa began arriving in Western Europe at least 40,000 years ago, and so could have competed and mingled with the local population for at least 12,000 years. The revised dating of fossils and artifacts leaves much less time for two species to have been in close contact.

Dr. Mellars concludes from the revised chronology that the overlap between Neanderthals and new arrivals must be shortened to about 6,000 years in Central and Northern Europe, perhaps only 1,000 to 2,000 years in regions like western France.

Katerina Harvati, a paleontologist at the Max-Planck Institute for Evolutionary Anthropology in Leipzig, Germany, said these advances "can potentially lead to a breakthrough in our understanding of this critical time period in European prehistory."

Dr. Harvati agreed that the new chronology suggested "an earlier appearance of early modern human complex behaviors and an earlier Neanderthal extinction and also suggests a shorter coexistence interval of the two species."

Radiocarbon dating, introduced shortly after World War II, has been widely used in measuring time in prehistory, back to the method's effective limit of 50,000 years ago. It assumes that the proportion of radioactively unstable carbon 14 to stable carbon 12 has remained virtually constant in Earth's atmosphere through this time period. It works by measuring the rate of decay of carbon 14 in once living materials, like plant and animal remains.

Although scientists once estimated the dating uncertainty to

be no more than several hundred years, they came to suspect two potential sources of greater error. One was contamination of test samples by intrusions of more recent carbon. The other was fluctuations in proportions of carbon 14 to carbon 12, which scientists came to recognize as a consequence to variations in cosmic radiation reaching the upper atmosphere.

Recent research at the University of Oxford, Dr. Mellars said, has led to a more effective filtration process to reduce contamination in test samples. Other investigations of deep-sea sediments off Venezuela and ice-core records from Greenland yielded evidence of carbon variation problems, which turned out to be especially pronounced between 30,000 and 40,000 years ago. Accordingly, radiocarbon dates were recalibrated.

The revised dates, for example, show that a standard radiocarbon reading of 40,000 years translated into a calendar age of 43,000. Even more consequential, a date of 35,000 years is revised to an actual age of 40,500, Dr. Mellars reported.

If correct, the new chronology means that fossil and archaeological evidence, especially in the crucial 30,000-to-40,000-year period, is much older than once estimated. Modern people may have arrived in Europe slightly earlier, but the extinction of the Neanderthals, pre-

viously thought to have occurred around 30,000 years ago, is now subject to greater revision because the standard dating yielded the most serious underestimates of true ages.

The degree of age discrepancies is also illustrated by the revised date for the splendid wall art in Chauvet cave in southern France. The charcoal used to produce the Chauvet drawings was originally dated around 31,000 to 32,000 years ago. A team of scientists reported in 2004 in the journal *Science* a revised date closer to 36,000.

In previous estimates, the modern human dispersal through Europe occurred 43,000 to 36,000 years ago. The 7,000-year period implies an overall dispersal rate of about 0.3 kilometer a year, less than two-tenths of a mile. Starting somewhat earlier, the faster dispersal over 5,000 years is now clocked at 0.4 kilometer a year.

Dr. Mellars cautioned that the revised dating based on new research must be viewed as provisional, concluding that the implications of the new studies "will need to be kept under active and vigilant review."

SOURCE: John Noble Wilford, "Improved Science Puts Modern Humans in Europe Earlier," *New York Times*, February 23, 2006, p. A10.

as *H. ergaster*). The debate continues. The only sure conclusion is that several different kinds of hominin lived in Africa before and after the advent of *Homo*.

H. habilis and H. ergaster/erectus

L. S. B. and Mary Leakey gave the name *Homo habilis* to the earliest members of our genus, first found at Olduvai Gorge in Tanzania. Olduvai's oldest layer, Bed I, dates to 1.8 m.y.a. This layer has yielded both small-brained *A. boisei* (average 490 cm³) fossils and *H. habilis* skulls, with cranial capacities between 600 and 700 cm³.

Another important *habilis* find was made in 1986 by Tim White of the University of California,

Berkeley. OH62 (Olduvai Hominid 62) is the partial skeleton of a female *H. habilis* from Olduvai Bed I. This was the first find of a *H. habilis* skull with a significant amount of skeletal material. OH62, dating to 1.8 m.y.a., consists of parts of the skull, the right arm, and both legs. This fossil was surprising because of its small size and its apelike limb bones. Scientists had assumed that *H. habilis* would be taller than Lucy (*A. afarensis*), moving gradually in the direction of *H. erectus*. According to expectations, even a female *H. habilis* should have stood somewhere between Lucy's 3 feet (0.9 meter) and the 5 to 6 feet (1.5 to 1.8 meters) of *H. erectus*. However, not only was OH62 just as tiny as Lucy, its arms were longer and more apelike than expected. The limb proportions suggested greater tree-climbing ability than later hominins had. *H. habilis* may still have sought occasional refuge in the trees.

The small size and primitive proportions of *H. habilis* were unexpected given what was already known about early *H. erectus* in East Africa. (Some paleoanthropologists use the term *Homo ergaster* to refer to the earliest *H. erectus* fossils in Africa. Here I follow the more traditional scheme of calling them *Homo erectus*.) In deposits near Lake Turkana, Kenya, Richard Leakey had uncovered two *H. erectus* skulls dating to 1.6 m.y.a. By that date, *H. erectus* had already attained a cranial capacity of 900 cm^3, along with a modern body shape and height. An amazingly complete young male *H. erectus* fossil (WT15,000) found at West Turkana in 1984 by Kimoya Kimeu, a collaborator of the Leakeys, has confirmed this. WT15,000, also known as the Nariokotome boy, was a 12-year-old male who had already reached 5 feet 5 inches (1.67 meters). He might have grown to 6 feet had he lived.

The sharp contrast between the OH62 *H. habilis* (1.8 m.y.a.) and early *H. erectus* (1.7–1.6 m.y.a.) suggests an acceleration in hominin evolution during that 100,000–200,000-year period. This fossil evidence may support a punctuated equilibrium model of the early hominin fossil record. As we saw in Chapter 4, in this view, long periods of equilibrium, during which species change little, are interrupted (punctuated) by sudden changes—evolutionary jumps. Apparently hominins changed very little below the neck between Lucy (*A. afarensis*) and *H. habilis*. Then, between 1.8 and 1.6 m.y.a., a profound change—an evolutionary leap—took place. *H. erectus* looks much more human than *H. habilis* does.

The hominin fossil record exemplifies both gradual and rapid change. Evolution can be slow or fast depending on the rate of environmental change, the speed with which geographic barriers rise or fall, and the effectiveness of the group's adaptive response. There is no doubt that the pace of hominin evolution sped up around 1.8 m.y.a. This spurt resulted in the emergence (in less than 200,000 years) of *H. erectus*. This was followed by a long period of relative stability. One possible key to the rapid emergence of *H. erectus* was a dramatic change in adaptive strategy: greater reliance on hunting through larger body size, along with improved tools and other cultural means of adaptation.

Significant changes in technology occurred during the 200,000-year evolutionary spurt between Bed I (1.8 m.y.a.) and Lower Bed II (1.6 m.y.a) at Olduvai. Tool making got more sophisticated soon after the advent of *H. erectus* in Africa. Out of the crude tools in Bed I evolved better-made and more varied tools. Edges were straighter, for example, and differences in form suggest functional differ-

A. boisei (left) *and* H. habilis (right). *Both* OH5 (L) *and* OH24 (R) *were found in Bed I at Olduvai Gorge, Tanzania, and were probable contemporaries.*

THE FAR SIDE® BY GARY LARSON

© 1983 FarWorks, Inc. All Rights Reserved/Dist. by Creators Syndicate

The Far Side® by Gary Larson © 1983 FarWorks, Inc. All Rights Reserved. The Far Side® and the Larson® signature are registered trademarks of FarWorks, Inc. Used with permission.

"What a find, Williams! The fossilized footprint of a brachiosaurus! ... And a *Homo habilis* thrown in to boot!"

What's wrong with this picture?

entiation—that is, the tools were being made and used for different jobs, such as smashing bones or digging for tubers.

The more sophisticated tools aided in hunting and gathering. With the new tools, *Homo* could obtain meat on a more regular basis and dig and process tubers, roots, nuts, and seeds more efficiently. New tools that could batter,

Headstrong Hominins

In a 2004 article in *Natural History* magazine, Noel Boaz and Russell Ciochon propose that several protective features of the *H. erectus* skull evolved in response to interpersonal violence—fighting among those thick-skulled hominins. Even since the discovery of the first *H. erectus* skull, scholars have been struck by the unusual cranial anatomy. The top and sides of the skull have thick, bony walls (see the photos). The *H. erectus* skullcap resembles a cyclist's helmet—low and streamlined so as to protect the brain, ears, and eyes from impact. "In contrast, we modern humans hold our enormous, easily injured, semiliquid brains in relatively thin-walled bony globes. We have to buy our bicycle helmets" (Boaz and Ciochon 2004, p. 29). In other words, a cultural adaptation (plastic) has replaced a biological one (bone).

Based on these and other cranial features, Boaz and Ciochon speculate that *H. erectus* needed sturdy anatomical headgear to protect against life-threatening breaks. Even today skull fractures can be fatal. An apparently minor fracture can rip blood vessels inside the skull. Blood builds up under the skull. Such a hematoma pushing on the brain can cause a coma and, eventually, death.

For *H. erectus* this bleeding would have been much more problematic than it would be for people with access to modern medicine. The neurological damage caused by such a hematoma can lead to partial paralysis, locomotion problems, poor hand–eye coordination, difficulties in speaking, and cognitive disruptions. Boaz and Ciochon note that "any traits that reduced the chances of cranial fracture would have given a substantial evolutionary advantage to the individuals who possessed them" (Boaz and Ciochon 2004, p. 30)

The authors contend that the blows delivered in a fight are more likely to land at eye level than on the top of the head. Although modern human skulls have some degree of eye-level bony armor, the thicker ring of bone in the *H. erectus* skull would have provided much more protection. The thick brow ridge protected the eye sockets, while bony bulges on each side of the skull shielded the sinus where blood flows into the internal jugular vein. That buttressing also protected the ear region. Finally, the bony ridge at the back of the skull protected several sinuses that carried blood within the rearmost brain lobes.

The thick jaws of *H. erectus* also would have been adaptive. Today, a broken jaw makes it painful, difficult, and sometimes impossible to chew. Surgical wiring of the broken sections is required. For *H. erectus,* such a break could have been life-threatening. There was an inside thickening of the jaw, just behind the chin, to protect against breaks.

Among the several *H. erectus* fossils found near Beijing, China, the anthropologist/anatomist Franz Weidenreich detected several fractures that had healed subsequently. The fact that the trauma victims survived offers confirmation of the protective value of their skulls. Boaz and Ciochon believe that the thick skulls and healed fractures of *H. erectus* provide a record of violence within that species.

This defensive armor—the anatomical headgear—was reduced as *H. sapiens* evolved a larger, more globular, thin-walled skull. Although human violence didn't end, other means of protection, avoidance of conflict, or both, evolved among the descendants of *H. erectus*. Boaz and Ciochon think those new adaptations were probably cultural rather than biological.

■ Homo erectus *skullcaps have been likened to a bicycle helmet because of their protective properties. These three skulls show dramatic similarities despite different ages. The skull shown in the top photo is a cast of skull XII from the "Peking Man" collection, and dates to 670,000 to 410,000 years ago. The two other skulls are much older. Sangiran 2 from Java (middle photo) may be as old as 1.6 m.y.a., while OH9 from Olduvai Gorge, Tanzania (bottom photo), may date back 1.4 million years. What similarities do you note among the three skulls?*

crush, and pulp coarse vegetation also reduced chewing demands.

With changes in the types of foods consumed, the burden on the chewing apparatus eased. Chewing muscles developed less, and supporting structures, such as jaws and cranial crests, also were reduced. With less chewing, jaws developed less, and so there was no place to put large teeth. The size of teeth, which form before they erupt, is under stricter genetic control than jaw size and bone size are. Natural selection began to operate against the genes that caused large teeth. In smaller jaws, large teeth now caused dental crowding, impaction, pain, sickness, fever, and sometimes death (there were no dentists).

Some of the main contrasts between *Australopithecus* and early *Homo* are in dentition. *H. erectus* back teeth are smaller; and the front teeth, relatively larger than australopithecine teeth. *H. erectus* used its front teeth to pull, twist, and grip objects. A massive ridge over the eyebrows (a *superorbital torus*) provided buttressing against the forces exerted in these activities. It also provided protection, as we see in "Interesting Issues" on page 178.

As hunting became more important to *H. erectus,* encounters with large animals increased. Individuals with stronger skulls had better-protected brains and better survival rates. Given the dangers associated with larger prey, and without sophisticated spear or arrow technology, which developed later, natural selection favored the thickening of certain areas for better protection against blows and falls. The base of the skull expanded dramatically, with a ridge of spongy bone (an *occipital bun*) across the back, for the attachment of massive neck muscles. The frontal and parietal (side) areas of the skull also increased, indicating expansion in those areas of the brain. Finally, average cranial capacity expanded from about 500 cm^3 in the australopithecines to 1,000 cm^3 in *H. erectus,* which is within the modern range of variation. Other possible reasons for thick skulls are discussed in "Interesting Issues."

OUT OF AFRICA I: *H. ERECTUS*

Biological and cultural changes enabled *H. erectus* to exploit a new adaptive strategy—gathering and hunting. *H. erectus* pushed the hominin range beyond Africa—to Asia and Europe. Small groups broke off from larger ones and moved a few miles away. They foraged new tracts of edible vegetation and carved out new hunting territories. Through population growth and dispersal, *H. erectus* gradually spread and changed. Hominins were following an essentially human lifestyle based on hunting

This photo shows the early (1.6 m.y.a) Homo erectus WT15,000, or Nariokotome boy, found in 1984 near Lake Turkana, Kenya. This is the most complete Homo erectus *ever found.*

and gathering. This basic pattern survived until recently in marginal areas of the world, although it is now fading rapidly.

This chapter begins around two million years ago, with the transition to *Homo.* It ends in the less distant past, when anatomically modern humans were painting artistic masterpieces on cave walls in France and Spain. We focus in this chapter on the biological and cultural changes that led from early *Homo,* through intermediate forms, to anatomically modern humans—(AMHs).

Paleolithic Tools

The stone-tool-making techniques that evolved out of the Oldowan, or pebble tool, tradition and that lasted until about 15,000 years ago are described by the term **Paleolithic** (from Greek roots meaning "old" and "stone"). The Paleolithic, or Old Stone Age, has three divisions: Lower (early), Middle, and Upper (late). Each part is roughly associated with a particular stage in human evolution. The Lower Paleolithic is roughly associated with *H. erectus;* the Middle Paleolithic with archaic *H. sapiens,* including the Neandertals of Western Europe and the Middle East; and the Upper Paleolithic with anatomically modern humans.

The best stone tools are made from rocks such as flint that fracture sharply and in predictable ways when hammered. Quartz, quartzite, chert,

For more on Oldowan tools see the Virtual Exploration

mhhe.com/kottak

and obsidian are also suitable. Each of the three main divisions of the Paleolithic had its typical *tool-making traditions*—coherent patterns of tool manufacture. The main Lower Paleolithic tool-making tradition used by *H. erectus* was the **Acheulian,** named after the French village of St. Acheul, where it was first identified.

Like Oldowan tools, the characteristic Acheulian tool, the hand ax, consisted of a modified core of rock. Flakes removed from the core when it was struck with a hammerstone also were used as tools. Flakes, smaller tools with finer cutting edges, became progressively more important in human evolution, particularly in Middle and Upper Paleolithic tool making.

Acheulian tools were an advance over pebble tools in several ways. Early hominins had made simple tools by picking up pebbles the size of tennis balls and chipping off a few flakes from one end to form a rough and irregular edge. They used these pebble tools (and some of the flakes as well) for a variety of purposes, such as smashing animal bones to extract marrow. The Acheulian technique involved chipping the core all over rather than at one end only. The core was converted from a round piece of rock into a flattish oval hand ax about 6 inches (15 centimeters) long. Its cutting edge was far superior to that of the pebble tool (see Figure 9.1).

Hand axes, along with digging sticks made of bone, horn, and wood, were used to dig edible roots and other foods from the ground. Hunters made tools with a sharper cutting edge to skin and cut up their prey. Cleavers—core tools with a straight edge at one end—were used for heavy chopping and hacking at the sinews of larger animals. Flakes were used to make incisions and for finer work. The Acheulian tradition illustrates trends in the evolution of technology: greater effi-

ciency, manufacture of tools for specific tasks, and an increasingly complex technology. These trends became even more obvious with the advent of *H. sapiens.*

Adaptive Strategies of *H. erectus*

Interrelated changes in biology and culture have increased human adaptability—the capacity to live in and modify an ever-wider range of environments. Improved tools helped *H. erectus* increase its range. Biological changes also increased hunting efficiency. *H. erectus* had a rugged but essentially modern skeleton that permitted long-distance stalking and endurance during the hunt. The *H. erectus* body was much larger and longer-legged than those of previous hominins, permitting longer-distance hunting of large prey. There is archaeological evidence of *H. erectus*'s success in hunting elephants, horses, rhinos, and giant baboons.

An increase in cranial capacity has been a trend in human evolution. The average *H. erectus* brain (about 1,000 cm³) doubled the australopithecine average. The capacities of *H. erectus* skulls range from 800 to 1,250 cm³, well above the modern minimum.

H. erectus had an essentially modern, though very robust, skeleton with a brain and body closer in size to *H. sapiens* than to *Australopithecus*. Still, several anatomical contrasts, particularly in the cranium, distinguish *H. erectus* from modern humans. Compared with moderns, *H. erectus* had a lower and more sloping forehead accentuated by a large brow ridge above the eyes (see "Interesting Issues"). Skull bones were thicker, and, as noted, average cranial capacity was smaller. The brain case was lower and flatter than in *H. sapiens,* with spongy bone development at the lower rear of the skull. Seen from behind, the *H. erectus* skull has a broad-based angular shape that has been compared to a half-inflated football and a hamburger bun (Figure 9.2). The *H. erectus* face, teeth, and jaws were larger than those in contemporary humans but smaller than those in *Australopithecus*. The front teeth were especially large, but molar size was well below the australopithecine average. Presumably, this reduction reflected changes in diet or food processing.

Taken together, the *H. erectus* skeleton and chewing apparatus provide biological evidence of a fuller commitment to hunting and gathering, which was *Homo*'s only adaptive strategy until plant cultivation and animal domestication emerged some 10,000 to 12,000 years ago. Archaeologists have found and studied several sites of *H. erectus* activity, including cooperative hunting.

Hearths at various sites confirm that fire was part of the human adaptive kit by this time. Even earlier evidence for human control over fire has been found in Israel, dating back to almost

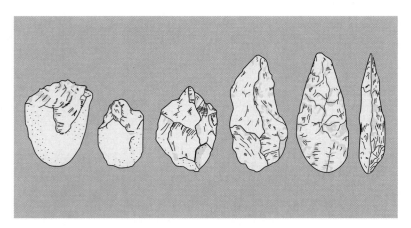

FIGURE 9.1 Evolution in Tool Making.
Finds at Olduvai Gorge and elsewhere show how pebble tools (the first tool at the left) evolved into the Acheulian hand ax of H. erectus. *This drawing begins with an Oldowan pebble tool and moves through crude hand axes to fully developed Acheulian tools associated with* H. erectus.

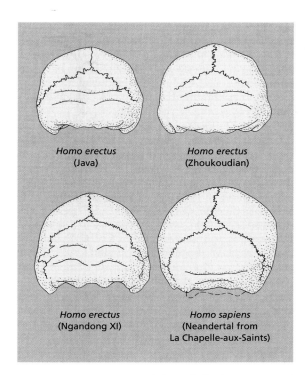

Homo erectus
(Java)

Homo erectus
(Zhoukoudian)

Homo erectus
(Ngandong XI)

Homo sapiens
(Neandertal from
La Chapelle-aux-Saints)

FIGURE 9.2 Rear Views of Three Skulls of *H. erectus* and One of "Archaic" *Homo sapiens* (a Neandertal).
Note the more angular shape of the H. erectus *skulls, with the maximum breadth low down, near the base.* SOURCE: From C. J. Jolly and R. White, *Physical Anthropology and Archaeology,* 5th ed. (New York: McGraw-Hill, 1995), p. 271.

800,000 years ago (Gugliotta 2004), and possibly at Swartkrans, South Africa, dated to 1.6–1.0 m.y.a. Fire provided protection against cave bears and saber-toothed tigers. It permitted *H. erectus* to occupy cave sites, including Zhoukoudian, near Beijing in China, which has yielded the remains of more than 40 specimens of *H. erectus.* Fire widened the range of climates open to human colonization. It may have played a role in the expansion out of Africa. Its warmth enabled people to survive winter cold in temperate regions. Human control over fire offered other advantages, such as cooking, which breaks down vegetable fibers and tenderizes meat. Cooking kills parasites and makes meat more digestible, thus reducing strain on the chewing apparatus.

Could language (fireside chats, perhaps) have been an additional advantage available to *H. erectus?* Archaeological evidence confirms the cooperative hunting of large animals and the manufacture of complicated tools. These activities might have been too complex to have gone on without some kind of language. Speech would have aided coordination, cooperation, and the learning of traditions, including tool making. Words, of course, aren't preserved until the advent of writing. However, given the potential for language-based communication—which even

chimps and gorillas share with *H. sapiens*—and given brain size within the low *H. sapiens* range, it seems plausible to assume that *H. erectus* had rudimentary speech. For contrary views, see Binford (1981), Fisher (1988*b*), and Wade (2002).

The Evolution and Expansion of *H. erectus*

The archaeological record of *H. erectus* activities can be combined with the fossil evidence to provide a more complete picture of our Lower Paleolithic ancestors. We now consider some of the fossil data, whose geographic distribution is shown in Figure 9.3. Early *H. erectus* remains, found by Richard Leakey's team at East and West Turkana, Kenya, and dated to around 1.6 m.y.a., including the Nariokotome boy, were discussed previously.

One fairly complete skull, one large mandible, and two partial skulls—one of a young adult male (780 cm³) and one of an adolescent female (650 cm³)—were found recently at the Dmanisi site in the former Soviet Republic of Georgia. They have been assigned a date of 1.7–1.75 m.y.a. There are notable similarities between the two partial skulls and that of the Nariokotome boy (1.6 m.y.a.). Chopping tools of comparable age associated with the Kenyan and Georgian fossils also are similar. The more recent (2001) skull find is the most primitive, with a stronger resemblance to *H. habilis* than is the case with the other Dmanisi fossils. Primitive characteristics of this skull include its large canine teeth and small cranial capacity (Vekua, Lordkipanidze, and Rightmire 2002). This specimen may be that of a teenage girl whose skull had not yet reached full size, but whose canines had. The

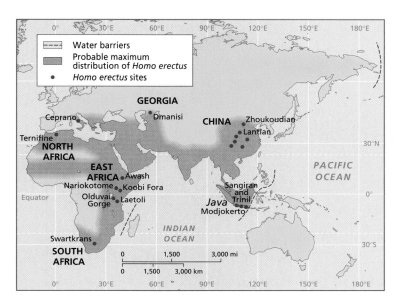

FIGURE 9.3 The Sites of Discovery of *Homo erectus* and Its Probable Maximum Distribution. SOURCE: From C. J. Jolly and R. White, *Physical Anthropology and Archaeology,* 5th ed. (New York: McGraw-Hill, 1995), p. 268.

simplest explanation for the anatomical diversity observed at Dmanisi is that *H. erectus* was at least as variable a species as is *H. sapiens.*

Many paleoanthropologists now assign the Nariokotome and Dmanisi finds to a new species, *Homo ergaster,* intermediate between *H. habilis* and *H. erectus.* Others simply consider all these Dmanisi fossils early *H. erectus.* Whatever their designation, the Dmanisi finds suggest a rapid spread, by 1.7 m.y.a., of early *Homo* out of Africa and into Eurasia (Figure 9.3).

The Dmanisi fossils are the most ancient undisputed human fossils outside Africa. How did those hominins get to Georgia? The most probable answer is meat. As hominins became more carnivorous, they expanded their home ranges in accordance with those of the animals they hunted. The bigger bodies and brains of early *Homo* (compared with the australopithecines) required more energy to run. Meat-rich diets provided higher-quality protein as fuel. The australopithecines had smaller bodies and brains, and so they could live mainly on plants. They probably used a limited range at the edge of forests, not too deep in or too exposed far out on the savanna. Once hominins developed stronger bodies and high-protein meat diets, they could—indeed had to—spread out. They ranged farther to find meat, and this expansion eventually led them out of Africa, into Eurasia (Georgia) and eventually Asia (see Wilford 2000).

In 1891, the Indonesian island of Java yielded the first *H. erectus* fossil find, popularly known as "Java man." Eugene Dubois, a Dutch army surgeon, had gone to Java to discover a transitional form between apes and humans. Of course, we now know that the transition to hominin had taken place much earlier than the *H. erectus* period and occurred in Africa. However, Dubois's good luck did lead him to the most ancient human fossils discovered at that time. Excavating near the village of Trinil, Dubois found parts of a *H. erectus* skull and a thigh bone. During the 1930s and 1940s, excavations in Java uncovered additional remains. The various Indonesian *H. erectus* fossils date back at least 700,000, and perhaps as much as 1.6 million, years. Fragments of a skull and a lower jaw found in northern China at Lantian may be as old as the oldest Indonesian fossils. Other *H. erectus* remains, of uncertain date, have been found in Algeria and Morocco in North Africa.

H. erectus remains also have been found in Upper Bed II at Olduvai, Tanzania, in association with Acheulian tools. In "Interesting Issues" on page 178, you will find a photo of one such find, OH9, which dates back perhaps 1.4 million years, along with a photo of a Javanese find, Sangiran 2, which may be a bit older. African *H. erectus* fossils also have been found in Ethiopia, Eritrea, and South Africa (in addition to Kenya and Tanzania). The time span of *H. erectus* in East Africa was long. *H. erectus* fossils have been found in Bed IV

Map 5 locates these and other sites where fossil representatives of the genus *Homo* have been found.

a

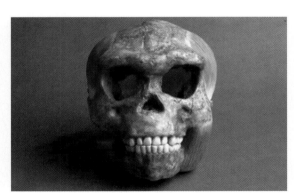

b

c

d

■ *Meet* Homo erectus. *Sangiran 17 is the most complete* H. erectus *skull from Java. In this process of reconstruction, a cast of the fossil (a) was rounded out with teeth, lower jaw, and chewing muscles (b). Additional soft tissues (c) and then the skin (d) were added. Given the robust features of this fossil, it is assumed to be male.*

at Olduvai, dating to 500,000 B.P., about the same age as the Beijing fossils, described below as well as in "Interesting Issues."

The largest group of *H. erectus* fossils was found in the Zhoukoudian cave in China. The Zhoukoudian ("Peking"—now Beijing—"man") site, excavated from the late 1920s to the late 1930s, was a major find for the human fossil record. Zhoukoudian yielded remains of tools, hearths, animal bones, and more than 40 hominins, including five skulls. The analysis of these remains led to the conclusion that the Java and Zhoukoudian fossils were examples of the same broad stage of human evolution. Today they are commonly classified together as *H. erectus.*

A skull of one of these Beijing fossils, Skull XII, is shown in "Interesting Issues" on page 178. The four-stage photo spread (p. 182) shows a reconstruction of *H. erectus* based on the Javanese find Sangiran 17, the most complete *H. erectus* skull found in Indonesia. The Zhoukoudian individuals lived more recently than did the Javanese *H. erectus,* between 670,000 and 410,000 years ago, when the climate in China was colder and moister than it is today. The inference about the climate has been made on the basis of the animal remains found with the human fossils. The people at Zhoukoudian ate venison, and seed and plant remains suggest they were both gatherers and hunters.

What about Europe? A cranial fragment found at Ceprano, Italy, in 1994 has been assigned a date of 800,000 B.P. Other probable *H. erectus* remains have been found in Europe, but their dates are uncertain. All are later than the Ceprano skull, and they usually are classified as late *H. erectus,* or transitional between *H. erectus* and early *H. sapiens.*

ARCHAIC *H. SAPIENS*

Africa, which was center stage during the australopithecine period, is joined by Asia and Europe during the *H. erectus* and *H. sapiens* periods of hominin evolution. European fossils and tools have contributed disproportionately to our knowledge and interpretation of early (archaic) *H. sapiens.* This doesn't mean that *H. sapiens* evolved in Europe or that most early *H. sapiens* lived in Europe. Indeed, the fossil evidence suggests that *H. sapiens,* like *H. erectus* before it, originated in Africa. *H. sapiens* lived in Africa for tens of thousands of years before starting the settlement of Europe around 50,000 B.P. (see the "News Brief" at the beginning of this chapter). There were probably many more humans in the tropics than in Europe during the ice ages. We merely *know more* about recent human evolution in Europe because archaeology and fossil hunting—not human evolution—have been going on longer there than in Africa and Asia.

Recent discoveries, along with reinterpretation of the dating and the anatomical relevance of some earlier finds, are filling in the gap between *H. erectus* and archaic *H. sapiens.* **Archaic *H. sapiens*** (300,000? to 28,000 B.P.) encompasses the earliest members of our species, along with the **Neandertals** (*H. sapiens neanderthalensis*—130,000 to 28,000 B.P.) of Europe and the Middle East and their Neandertal-like contemporaries in Africa and Asia. Brain size in archaic *H. sapiens* was within the modern human range. (The modern average, remember, is about 1,350 cm^3.) (See Table 9.1.) A rounding out of the brain case was associated with the increased brain size. As Jolly and White (1995) put it, evolution was pumping more

See the Internet Exercises at your OLC

mhhe.com/kottak

TABLE 9.1	Summary of Data on *Homo* Fossil Groups

Fossil representatives of the genus *Homo*, compared with modern humans (*Homo sapiens sapiens*) and chimps (*Pan troglodytes*).

Species	Dates	Known Distribution	Important Sites	Brain Size (in cm³)
Anatomically modern humans (AMHs)	130,000 B.P. to present	Worldwide	Beijing, New York, Paris, Nairobi	1,350
Neandertals	130,000 to 28,000 B.P.	Europe, southwestern Asia	La Chapelle-aux-Saints	1,430
Archaic *Homo sapiens*	300,000 to 28,000 B.P.	Africa, Europe, Asia	Kabwe, Arago, Dali, Mount Carmel caves	1,135
Homo erectus	1.7 m.y.a. to 300,000 B.P.	Africa, Asia, Europe	East + West Turkana, Olduvai, Zhoukoudian, Java, Ceprano	900
Pan troglodytes	Modern	Central Africa	Gombe, Mahale	390

brain into the *H. sapiens* cranium—like filling a football with air.

Ice Ages of the Pleistocene

Traditionally and correctly, the geological epoch known as the **Pleistocene** has been considered the epoch of human life. Its subdivisions are the Lower Pleistocene (2 to 1 m.y.a.), the Middle Pleistocene (1 m.y.a. to 130,000 B.P.), and the Upper Pleistocene (130,000 to 10,000 B.P.). These subdivisions refer to the placement of geological strata containing, respectively, older, intermediate, and younger fossils. The Lower Pleistocene extends from the start of the Pleistocene to the advent of the ice ages in the Northern Hemisphere around one million years ago.

Each subdivision of the Pleistocene is associated with a particular group of hominins. Late *Australopithecus* and early *Homo* lived during the Lower Pleistocene. *Homo erectus* spanned most of the Middle Pleistocene. *Homo sapiens* appeared late in the Middle Pleistocene and was the sole hominin of the Upper Pleistocene. The hominins of the Middle and Upper Pleistocene are considered in this chapter and in the "Bringing It All Together" essay that follows it.

During the second million years of the Pleistocene, there were several ice ages, or **glacials,** major advances of continental ice sheets in Europe and North America. These periods were separated by **interglacials,** long warm periods between the major glacials. (Scientists used to think there were four main glacial advances, but the picture has grown more complex.) With each advance, the world climate cooled and continental ice sheets—massive glaciers—covered the northern parts of Europe and North America. Climates that are temperate today were arctic during the glacials.

During the interglacials, the climate warmed up and the *tundra*—the cold, treeless plain—retreated north with the ice sheets. Forests returned to areas, such as southwestern France, that had had tundra vegetation. The ice sheets advanced and receded several times during the last glacial, the *Würm* (75,000 to 12,000 B.P.). Brief periods of relative warmth during the Würm (and other glacials) are called *interstadials,* in contrast to the longer interglacials. Hominin fossils found in association with animals known to occur in cold or warm climates, respectively, permit us to date them to glacial or interglacial (or interstadial) periods.

H. antecessor and *H. heidelbergensis*

In northern Spain's Atapuerca mountains, the site of Gran Dolina has yielded the remains of 780,000-year-old hominins that Spanish researchers call *H. antecessor* and see as a possible common ancestor of the Neandertals and anatomically modern humans. At the nearby cave of Sima dos Huesos a team led by Juan Luis Arsuaga has found thousands of fossils representing at least 33 hominins of all ages. Almost 300,000 years old, they may represent an early stage of Neandertal evolution (Lemonick and Dorfman 1999).

A massive hominin jaw was discovered in 1907 in a gravel pit at Mauer near Heidelberg, Germany. Originally called "Heidelberg man" or *Homo heidelbergensis,* the jaw appears to be around 500,000 years old. The deposits that yielded this jaw also contained fossil remains of several animals, including bear, bison, deer, elephant, horse, and rhinoceros. Recently, some anthropologists have revived the species name *H. heidelbergensis* to refer to a group of fossil hominins that in this text are described as either late *H. erectus* or archaic *H. sapiens.* This group would include hominins (very roughly) dated between 700,000 and 200,000 years ago and found in different parts of the world including Europe, Africa, and Asia. Such fossils, here assigned to either *H. erectus* or archaic *H. sapiens,* would be transitional between *H. erectus* and later hominin forms such as the Neandertals and anatomically modern humans.

Besides the hominin *fossils* found in Europe, there is archaeological—including abundant stone tool—evidence for the presence and behavior of late *H. erectus* and then archaic *H. sapiens* in Europe. A recent chance discovery on England's Suffolk seacoast shows that humans reached northern Europe 700,000 years ago (Gugliotta 2005). Several stone flakes were recovered from seashore sediment bordering the North Sea. These archaic humans crossed the Alps into northern Europe more than 200,000 years earlier than previously imagined—during an interglacial period. At that time, the fertile lowlands they inhabited were part of a land bridge connecting what is now Britain to the rest of Europe. They lived in a large delta with several rivers and a dry, mild Mediterranean climate. Various animals were among its abundant resources. It is not known whether the descendants of these settlers remained in England. The next glacial period may have been too extreme for human habitation so far back. Members of the excavating team, including anthropologist Christopher Stringer, eventually found 32 flakes, made by striking a flint stone core with another stone. One flake had been retouched to sharpen its edges, while another was a sharpened flint stone core. The razor-sharp flakes, 1 to 2 inches long, had probably been used as knife or spear points.

At the site of Terra Amata, which overlooks Nice in southern France, archaeologists have documented human activity dating back some 300,000 years. Small bands of hunters and gatherers consisting of 15 to 25 people made regular visits during the late spring and early summer to Terra Amata, a sandy cove on the coast of the Mediterranean. Archaeologists determined the season of occupation by examining fossilized human excrement, which contained pollen from flowers that are known to bloom in late spring. There is evidence for 21 such visits. Four groups camped on a sand bar, 6 on the beach, and 11 on a sand dune. Archaeologists surmise that the 11 dune sites represent that number of annual visits by the same band (deLumley 1969/1976).

From a camp atop the dune, these people looked down on a river valley where animals were abundant. Bones found at Terra Amata show that their diet included red deer, young elephants, wild boars, wild mountain goats, an extinct variety of rhinoceros, and wild oxen. The Terra Amata people also hunted turtles and birds and collected oysters and mussels. Fish bones also were found at the site. The arrangement of postholes shows that these people used saplings to support temporary huts. There were hearths—sunken pits and piled stone fireplaces—within the shelters. Stone chips inside the borders of the huts show that tools were made from locally available rocks and beach pebbles. Thus, at Terra Amata, hundreds of thousands of years ago, people were already pursuing an essentially human lifestyle, one that survived in certain coastal regions into the 20th century.

Archaic *H. sapiens* lived during the last part of the *Middle Pleistocene*—during the *Mindel* (second) glacial, the interglacial that followed it, and the following *Riss* (third) glacial. The distribution of the fossils and tools of archaic *H. sapiens*, which have been found in Europe, Africa, and Asia, shows that *Homo*'s tolerance of environmental diversity had increased. For example, the Neandertals and their immediate ancestors managed to survive extreme cold in Europe. Archaic *H. sapiens* occupied the Arago cave in southeastern France at a time when Europe was bitterly cold. The only Riss glacial site with facial material, Arago, was excavated in 1971. It produced a partially intact skull, two jaw bones, and teeth from a dozen individuals. With an apparent date of about 200,000 B.P., the Arago fossils have mixed features that seem transitional between *H. erectus* and the Neandertals.

THE NEANDERTALS

Neandertals were first discovered in Western Europe. The first one was found in 1856 in a German valley called Neander Valley—*tal* is the German word for a valley. Scientists had trouble interpreting the discovery. It was clearly human and similar to modern Europeans in many ways, yet different enough to be considered strange

and abnormal. This was, after all, 35 years before Dubois discovered the first *H. erectus* fossils in Java and almost 70 years before the first australopithecine was found in South Africa. Darwin's *On the Origin of Species*, published in 1859, had not yet appeared to offer a theory of evolution through natural selection. There was no framework for understanding human evolution. Over time, the fossil record filled in, along with evolutionary theory. There have been numerous subsequent discoveries of Neandertals in Europe and the Middle East and of archaic human fossils with similar features in Africa and Asia. The similarities and differences between Neandertals and other relatively recent hominins have become clearer.

Fossils that are not Neandertals but that have similar features (such as large faces and brow ridges) have been found in Africa and Asia. The Kabwe skull from Zambia (130,000 B.P.), shown in the photo below, is an archaic *H. sapiens* with a Neandertal-like brow ridge. Archaic Chinese

This 130,000 year-old skull from Kabwe, Zambia, discovered in 1921, is one regional variant of archaic H. sapiens, *also called* H. heidelbergensis.

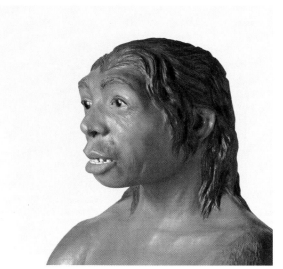

Reconstruction of a Neandertal woman from skull and skeletal evidence found at Tabun in Israel. She lived about 100,000 years ago.

fossils with Neandertal-like features have been found at Maba and Dali. Neandertals have been found in Central Europe and the Middle East. For example, Neandertal fossils found at the Shanidar cave in northern Iraq date to around 60,000 B.P., as does a Neandertal skeleton found at Israel's Kebara cave (Shreeve 1992). At the Israeli site of Tabun on Mount Carmel, a Neandertal female skeleton was excavated in 1932. She was a contemporary of the Shanidar Neandertals, and her brow ridges, face, and teeth show typical Neandertal robustness.

Cold-Adapted Neandertals

By 75,000 B.P., after an interglacial interlude, Western Europe's hominins (Neandertals, by then) again faced extreme cold as the Würm glacial began. To deal with this environment, they wore clothes, made more elaborate tools (see the photo below), and hunted reindeer, mammoths, and woolly rhinos.

The Neandertals were stocky, with large trunks relative to limb length—a phenotype that minimizes surface area and thus conserves heat. Another adaptation to extreme cold was the Neandertal face, which has been likened to a *H. erectus* face that has been pulled forward by the nose. Illustrating Thomson's rule (see Chapter 5), this extension increased the distance between outside air and the arteries that carry blood to the brain and was adaptive in a cold climate. The brain is sensitive to temperature changes and

must be kept warm. The massive nasal cavities of Neandertal fossils suggest long, broad noses. This would expand the area for warming and moistening air.

Neandertal characteristics also include huge front teeth, broad faces, and large brow ridges, and ruggedness of the skeleton and musculature. What activities were associated with these anatomical traits? Neandertal teeth probably did many jobs later done by tools (Brace 1995; Rak 1986). The front teeth show heavy wear, suggesting that they were used for varied purposes, including chewing animal hides to make soft winter clothing out of them. The massive Neandertal face showed the stresses of constantly using the front teeth for holding and pulling.

Comparison of early and later Neandertals shows a trend toward reduction of their robust features. Neandertal technology, a Middle Paleolithic tradition called **Mousterian,** improved considerably during the Würm glacial. Tools assumed many burdens formerly placed on the anatomy. For example, tools took over jobs once done by the front teeth. Through a still imperfectly understood mechanism, facial muscles and supporting structures developed less. Smaller front teeth—perhaps because of dental crowding—were favored. The projecting face reduced, as did the brow ridge, which had provided buttressing against the forces generated when the large front teeth were used for environmental manipulation.

The Neandertals and Modern People

Generations of scientists have debated whether the Neandertals were ancestral to modern Europeans. The current prevailing view, denying this ancestry, proposes that *H. erectus* split into separate groups, one ancestral to the Neandertals, the other ancestral to **anatomically modern humans (AMHs),** who first reached Europe around 50,000 B.P. (Early AMHs in Western Europe often are referred to as *Cro-Magnon*, after the earliest fossil find of an anatomically modern human, in France's Les Eyzies region, Dordogne Valley, in 1868.) The current predominant view is that modern humans evolved in Africa and eventually colonized Europe, displacing the Neandertals there.

Consider the contrasts between the Neandertals and AMHs. Like *H. erectus* before them, the Neandertals had heavy brow ridges and slanting foreheads. However, average Neandertal cranial capacity (more than 1,400 cm^3) exceeded the modern average. Neandertal jaws were large, providing support for huge front teeth, and their faces were massive. The bones and skull were generally more rugged and had greater sexual dimorphism—particularly in the face and skull—than do those of AMHs. In some Western European fossils, these contrasts between Neandertals

■ *Neandertal technology, a Middle Paleolithic tradition called Mousterian, improved considerably during the Würm glacial. These Mousterian flake tools were found at Gorham's Cave, Gibraltar.*

and AMHs are accentuated—giving a stereo-typed, or *classic Neandertal*, appearance. The interpretation of one fossil in particular helped create the popular stereotype of the slouching cave dweller. This was the complete human skeleton discovered in 1908 at La Chapelle-aux-Saints in southwestern France, in a layer containing the characteristic Mousterian tools made by Neandertals. It was the first Neandertal to be discovered with the whole skull, including the face, preserved.

The La Chapelle skeleton was given for study to the French paleontologist Marcellin Boule. His analysis of the fossil helped create an inaccurate stereotype of Neandertals as brutes who had trouble walking upright. Boule argued that La Chapelle's brain, although larger than the modern average, was inferior to modern brains. Further, he suggested that the Neandertal head was slung forward like an ape's. To round out the primitive image, Boule proclaimed that the Neandertals were incapable of straightening their legs for fully erect locomotion. However, later fossil finds show that the La Chapelle fossil wasn't a typical Neandertal but an extreme one. Also, this much-publicized "classic" Neandertal turned out to be an aging man whose skeleton had been distorted by osteoarthritis. Hominins, after all, have been erect bipeds for millions of years. European Neandertals were a variable population. Other Neandertal finds lack La Chapelle's combination of extreme features and are more acceptable ancestors for AMHs.

Those scientists who still believe that Neandertals could have contributed to the ancestry of modern Europeans cite certain fossils to support their view. For example, the Central European site of Mladeč (31,000 to 33,000 B.P.) has yielded remains of several hominins that combine Neandertal robustness with modern features. Wolpoff (1999) also notes modern features in the late Neandertals found at l'Hortus in France and Vindija in Croatia. The fossil remains of a four-year-old boy discovered at Largo Velho in Portugal in 1999 and dated to 24,000 B.P. also shows mixed Neandertal and modern features.

Fossils from Israel's Mount Carmel site of Skhūl also combine archaic and modern features. But most analyses stress the "modernness" of the Skhūl fossils, which date to 100,000 B.P. Another group of modern-looking and similarly dated (92,000 B.P.) skulls comes from the Israeli site of Qafzeh. The Skhūl and Qafzeh fossils cast serious doubt on the Neandertal ancestry of AMHs in Europe and the Middle East. The skulls from Skhūl (Figure 9.4) and Qafzeh have a modern, rather than a Neandertal, shape and are classified as AMHs. Their brain cases are higher, shorter, and rounder than Neandertal skulls. There is a more filled-out forehead region, which rises more vertically above the brows. A marked chin is

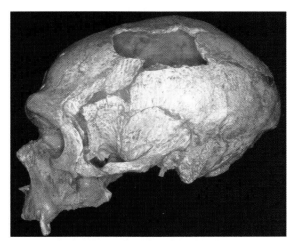

The skull of the classic Neandertal found in 1908 at La Chapelle-aux-Saints. This was the first Neandertal to be discovered with the whole skull, including the face, preserved. Later finds showed that La Chapelle wasn't a typical Neandertal but an extreme form. What was atypical about this fossil?

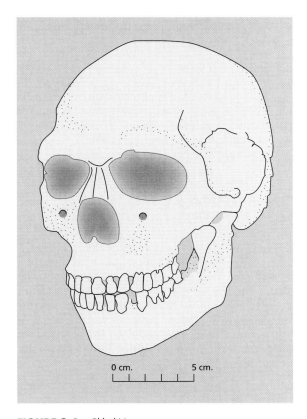

FIGURE 9.4 Skhūl V.
This anatomically modern human with some archaic features dates to 100,000 B.P. This is one of several fossils found at Skhūl, Israel.

another modern feature (see the photo of the original Cro-Magnon find on page 188). Still, Skhūl and Qafzeh, although early AMHs, do retain distinct brow ridges, though reduced from their archaic *H. sapiens* ancestor.

Given these early dates from Israel, AMHs may have inhabited the Middle East before the Neandertals did. Ofer Bar-Yosef (1987) has suggested

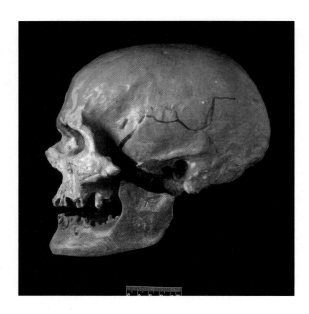

■ *Cro-Magnon I, the skull of a 45 year-old anatomically modern human, discovered in 1868 near Les Eyzies in France's Dordogne region. Note the distinct chin.*

 STUDENT CD-ROM LIVING ANTHROPOLOGY
The First Burials
Track 9

The Israeli site shown in this clip has yielded archaeological evidence of burials from at least two time periods. What time periods are they? French archaeologist Bernard Vandermeersch discusses the significance of the earliest burials at this site, where field workers have uncovered the remains of 25 individuals, including a young woman and a child buried together and an adolescent male. What was buried with the boy, and what is its significance? Why is evidence for intentional burial important? Anatomically modern humans found at Qafzeh in Israel date back some 92,000 years. Read the "Bringing It All Together" essay on pp. 200–203 for more on the origins of behavioral modernity.

that during the last (Würm) glacial period, which began around 75,000 B.P., Western European Neandertals spread east and south (and into the Middle East) as part of a general southward expansion of cold-adapted fauna. AMHs, in turn, followed warmer-climate fauna south into Africa, returning to the Middle East once the Würm ended.

ANATOMICALLY MODERN HUMANS (AMHs)

Most current interpretations of the fossil evidence and dating favor the replacement hypothesis, which denies the Neandertal ancestry of AMHs. Rather, AMHs seem likely to have evolved from an archaic *H. sapiens* African ancestor. Eventually, AMHs spread to other areas, including Western Europe, where they replaced, or interbred with, the Neandertals, whose robust traits eventually disappeared (Figure 9.5).

Out of Africa II

In 1987 a group of molecular geneticists at the University of California at Berkeley offered support for the idea that modern humans (AMHs) arose fairly recently in Africa, then spread out and colonized the world. Rebecca Cann, Mark Stoneking, and Allan C. Wilson (1987) analyzed genetic markers in placentas donated by 147 women whose ancestors came from Africa, Europe, the Middle East, Asia, New Guinea, and Australia.

The researchers focused on mitochondrial DNA (mtDNA). This genetic material is located in the cytoplasm (the outer part of a cell—not the nucleus) of cells. Ordinary DNA, which makes up the genes that determine most physical traits,

is found in the nucleus and comes from both parents. But only the mother contributes mitochondrial DNA to the fertilized egg. The father plays no part in mtDNA transmission, just as the mother has nothing to do with the transmission of the Y chromosome, which comes from the father and determines the sex of the child.

To establish a "genetic clock," the Berkeley researchers measured the variation in mtDNA in their 147 tissue samples. They cut each sample into segments to compare with the others. By estimating the number of mutations that had taken place in each sample since its common origin with the 146 others, the researchers drew an evolutionary tree with the help of a computer.

That tree started in Africa and then branched in two. One group remained in Africa, while the other one split off, carrying its mtDNA to the rest of the world. The variation in mtDNA was greatest among Africans. This suggests they have been evolving the longest. The Berkeley researchers concluded that everyone alive today has mtDNA that descends from a woman (dubbed "Eve") who lived in sub-Saharan Africa around 200,000 years ago. Eve was not the only woman alive then; she was just the only one whose descendants have included a daughter in each generation up to the present. Because mtDNA passes exclusively through females, mtDNA lines disappear whenever a woman has no children or has only sons. The details of the Eve theory suggest that her descendants left Africa no more than 135,000 years ago. They eventually displaced the Neandertals in Europe and went on to colonize the rest of the world.

Recent DNA Evidence

Additional DNA comparisons have been used to support the view that the Neandertals and AMHs were distinct groups, rather than ancestor and descendant. In 1997, ancient DNA was extracted from one of the Neandertal bones originally found in Germany's Neander Valley in 1856. This DNA, from an upper arm bone (humerus), has been compared with the DNA of modern humans. The kinds of matches we would expect in closely related humans did not occur. Thus, there were 27 differences between the Neandertal DNA and a reference sample of modern DNA. By contrast, samples of DNA from modern populations worldwide show only five to eight differences with the reference sample.

This was the first time that DNA of a premodern human had been recovered. The original analysis was done by Svante Pääbo of the University of Munich. The findings then were duplicated by Mark Stoneking and Anne Stone at Pennsylvania State University. The researchers again focused on mitochondrial DNA. Using a "genetic clock" again, these scientists interpreted their results to mean that Neandertals and moderns separated over 550,000 years ago.

The Neandertals may (or may not) have coexisted with modern humans in the Middle East for thousands of years. As reported in this chapter's news story, the overlap in Europe, and especially in Western Europe, appears to have been much shorter. At certain Israeli and African sites, modern humans date back 100,000 years or more. Middle Eastern Neandertals date back 40,000 to 60,000 years. In Western Europe, Neandertals may have survived until about 28,000 years ago.

To what extent did Neandertals and AMHs interact? Did they trade or interbreed (Wilford 2005)? Were the Neandertals outcompeted by modern humans or killed off by them? Were they absorbed into the AMH population and genetically swamped (Rose 1997)? Future discoveries will continue to provide answers to such questions, which have engaged paleoanthropologists for decades.

Recent Fossil and Archaeological Evidence

Besides the DNA dating, fossil and archaeological evidence has been accumulating to support the African origin, perhaps by 150,000 years ago, of AMHs. A major find was announced in 2003: the 1997 discovery in an Ethiopian valley of three anatomically modern skulls—two adults and a child. When found, the fossils had been fragmented so badly that their reconstruction took several years. Tim White and Berhane Asfaw were coleaders of the international team that made the find near the village of Herto, 140 miles northeast of Addis Ababa. All three skulls were missing the lower jaw. The skulls showed evidence of cutting and handling, suggesting they had been detached from their bodies and used—perhaps ritually—after death. A few teeth, but no other bones, were found with the skulls, again

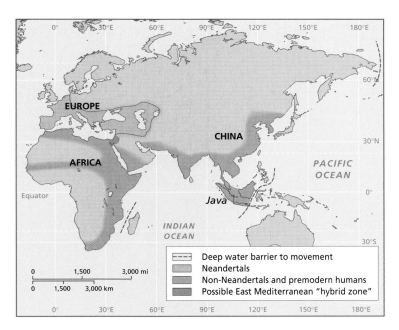

FIGURE 9.5 The Known Distribution of Human Populations Approximately 130,000 to 28,000 B.P.

According to some scholars, Neandertals and moderns may have mixed in the East Mediterranean hybrid zone. In your opinion, would that have been possible?

SOURCE: From C. J. Jolly and R. White, *Physical Anthropology and Archaeology*, 5th ed. (New York: McGraw-Hill, 1995), p. 277.

suggesting their deliberate removal from the body. Layers of volcanic ash allowed geologists to date them to 154,000–160,000 B.P. The people represented by the skulls had lived on the shore of an ancient lake, where they hunted and fished. The skulls were found along with hippopotamus and antelope bones and some 600 tools, including blades and hand axes.

Except for a few archaic characteristics, the Herto skulls are anatomically modern—long with broad midfaces, featuring tall, narrow nasal bones. The cranial vaults are high, falling within modern dimensions. These finds provide additional support for the view that modern humans originated in Africa and then spread into Europe and Asia (Wilford 2003).

From South Africa comes further evidence. At Border Cave, a remote rock shelter, fossil remains dating back perhaps 150,000 years are believed to be those of early modern humans. The remains of at least five AMHs have been discovered, including the nearly complete skeleton of a four- to six-month-old infant buried in a shallow grave. Excavations at Border Cave also have produced some 70,000 stone tools, along with the remains of several mammal species, including elephants, believed to have been hunted by the ancient people who lived there.

A complex of South African caves near the Klasies River Mouth was occupied by a group of

Biocultural Case Study

The "Bringing It All Together" essay that immediately follows Chapter 9 discusses the relation between biological and behavioral modernity—that is, when did people who looked like modern humans start acting like modern humans.

Compare these drawings of H. erectus, archaic H. sapiens, Neandertal, and AMH. What are the main differences you notice? Is the Neandertal more like H. erectus or AMH?

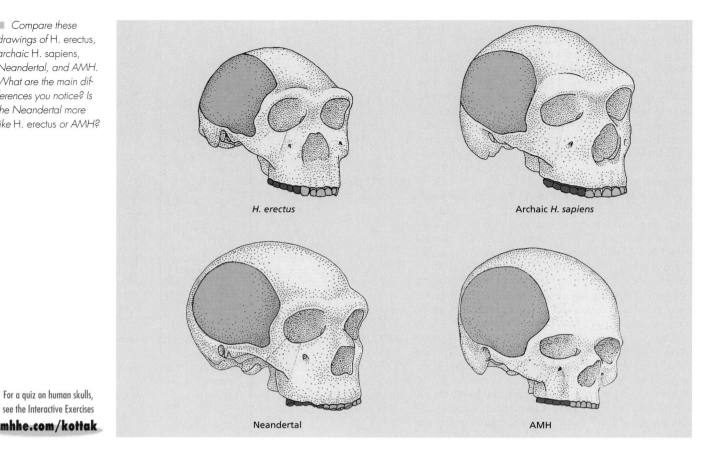

H. erectus

Archaic *H. sapiens*

Neandertal

AMH

For a quiz on human skulls, see the Interactive Exercises

mhhe.com/kottak

hunter-gatherers some 120,000 years ago. Fragmentary bones suggest how those people looked. A forehead fragment has a modern brow ridge. There is a thin-boned cranial fragment and a piece of jaw with a modern chin. The archaeological evidence suggests that these cave dwellers did coastal gathering and used Middle Paleolithic stone tools (see http://www.mc.maricopa.edu/~reffland/anthropology/anthro2003/origins/hominin_journey/modernorigins.html).

If those people were anatomically modern, were they behaviorally modern as well? That question is examined in the "Bringing It All Together" essay that immediately follows this chapter. Several archaeologists believe they've found early evidence for behavioral modernity in Africa. For example, South Africa's Blombos Cave has yielded evidence that apparent AMHs were making bone awls and weapon points more than 70,000 years ago. Earlier excavations in Congo's Katanda region had uncovered barbed bone harpoon points dating back 80,000 to 90,000 years (Yellen, Brooks, and Cornelissen 1995).

Multiregional Evolution

Scientists have defended two competing theories about the origin of anatomically modern humans.

One is the **out of Africa theory** (based on the molecular, fossil, and archaeological evidence discussed in the last section). The other is **multiregional evolution.** According to the first theory, a small group of modern people arose recently in one place (Africa), then spread out and occupied the rest of the world. These AMH colonists eventually replaced the native, and more archaic, populations of all other regions. The multiregional model (Wolpoff 1999; Wolpoff and Caspari 1997) proposes that human evolutionary advances were more widespread. The multiregionalists note that ever since *H. erectus* spread beyond Africa, human bands always have maintained relations with their neighbors, including interbreeding. Linked by gene flow, humans in every region could and would share any beneficial mutation that arose in any one place. If a genetic change conferred a substantial selective advantage, it would spread rapidly from one group to all the others—across the entire human range. In this way human groups in Africa, Asia, and Europe would have come to share the features and behaviors of modern humans.

Advocates of multiregional evolution believe the fossil evidence contradicts the theory of an African Eve who lived as recently as 200,000 B.P. Fossils show that certain physical features have persisted in particular regions for hundreds of thousands of years. For example, there are striking similarities between fossils dating back 750,000 to 500,000 years in Australasia (Indonesia and Australia), China, and Europe and the people who live in each of those regions today. One example is the facial similarity between modern Chinese people and the "vertical flat face" (Fenlason 1990) of *H. erectus* fossils found near Beijing. Another example is the "protruding face with large teeth and heavy brows," which is characteristic of both Indonesian *H. erectus* fossils and modern Native Australians. A third example is the prevalence among both ancient and modern Europeans of "angular faces with large projecting noses."

These unique regional features appeared (in *H. erectus*) long before the proposed migration of Eve's descendants out of Africa. These traits probably arose through the founder effect (random genetic drift) and were neutral with respect to natural selection. By chance, the ancient founders of each regional population happened to have flat, protruding, or angular faces. After the founders settled each region, some of their unique physical features became common among their descendants.

If Eve's descendants arrived later than these fossils lived, and wiped out the previous inhabitants of China, Australasia, and Europe, these specific physical similarities between the fossils and the modern people of each region would not exist. As an alternative to the recent Eve hypothesis, Milford Wolpoff proposes a model of long-term multiregional evolution, in which *H. erectus* evolved into modern *H. sapiens* in each region (Africa, Europe, northern Asia, and Australasia). As the regional populations evolved, gene flow always connected them, so that beneficial mutations would spread rapidly from one group to all the others since they always belonged to the same species. Wolpoff agrees that a mitochondrial Eve might have existed, but much earlier than the Berkeley researchers suggest.

Advances in Technology

In Europe, Upper Paleolithic tool making traditionally is associated with AMHs. In Africa, earlier AMHs made varied tools. The people who lived at the Klasies River Mouth cave sites made Middle Paleolithic tools, as did Neandertals in Europe and the Middle East. However, some of the early African tool finds at Blombos cave and in Katanda are more reminiscent of the European Upper Paleolithic. AMHs in Europe made tools in a variety of traditions, collectively known as **Upper Paleolithic** because of the tools' location in the upper, or more recent, layers of sedimentary deposits. Some cave deposits have Middle Paleolithic Mousterian tools (made by Neander-

The Venus of Brassempouy. This sculpture of a human head was carved in mammoth ivory sometime between 22,000 and 30,000 years ago. Note the distinct hairstyle.

tals) at lower levels and increasing numbers of Upper Paleolithic tools at higher levels.

Although the Neandertals are remembered more for their physiques than for their manufacturing abilities, their tool kits were sophisticated. Mousterian technology included at least 14 categories of tools designed for different jobs. The Neandertals elaborated on a revolutionary technique of flake-tool manufacture (the *Levallois* technique) invented in southern Africa around 200,000 years ago, which spread widely throughout the Old World. Uniform flakes were chipped off a specially prepared core of rock. Additional work on the flakes produced such special-purpose tools as those shown in Figure 9.6. Scrapers were used to prepare animal hides for clothing. And special tools also were designed for sawing, gouging, and piercing (Binford and Binford 1979).

The Upper Paleolithic traditions all emphasized **blade tools.** Blades were hammered off a prepared core, as in Mousterian technology, but a blade is longer than a flake—its length is more than twice its width. Blades were chipped off cores 4 to 6 inches (10 to 15 centimeters) high by hitting a punch made of bone or antler with a hammerstone (Figure 9.7). Blades were then modified to produce a variety of special-purpose implements. Some were composite tools that were made by joining reworked blades to other materials.

The blade-core method was faster than the Mousterian and produced 15 times as much cutting edge from the same amount of material. More

Map Atlas

Map 6 charts migrations of *Homo sapiens* out of Africa to other world areas, including Europe, Asia, Australia, and the Americas. For the peopling of the Americas, see Chapter 10. For the peopling of the Pacific, see the "Bringing It All Together" essay that follows Chapter 11, on pp. 253–257.

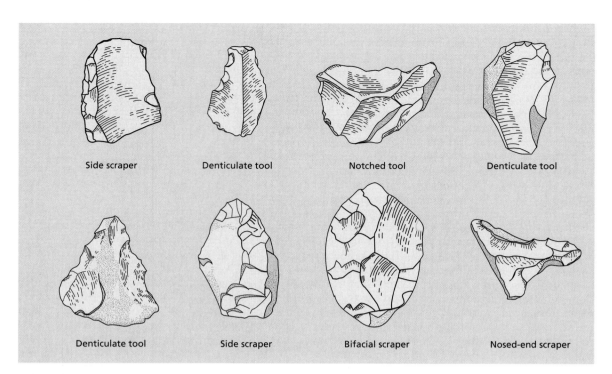

FIGURE 9.6 Middle Paleolithic Tools of the Mousterian Tool-Making Tradition.
The manufacture of diverse tool types for special purposes confirms Neandertal sophistication.

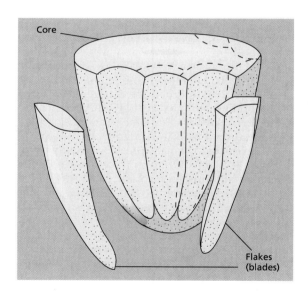

FIGURE 9.7 Upper Paleolithic Blade-Tool Making.
Blades are flakes that are detached from a specially prepared core. A punch (usually a piece of bone or antler) and a hammerstone (not shown here) were used to knock the blade off the core.

efficient tool production might have been especially valued by people whose economy depended on cooperative hunting of mammoths, woolly rhinoceroses, bison, wild horses, bears, wild cattle, wild boars, and—principally—reindeer. It has been estimated that approximately 90 percent of the meat eaten by Western Europeans between 25,000 and 15,000 B.P. came from reindeer.

Trends observable throughout the archaeological record also mark the changeover from the Mousterian to the Upper Paleolithic. First, the number of distinct tool types increased. This trend reflected functional specialization—the manufacture of special tools for particular jobs. A second trend was increasing standardization in tool manufacture. The form and inventory of tools reflect several factors: the jobs tools are intended to perform, the physical properties of the raw materials from which they are made, and distinctive cultural traditions about how to make tools. Furthermore, accidental or random factors also influenced tool forms and the proportions of particular tool types (Isaac 1972). However, Mousterian and Upper Paleolithic tools were more standardized than those of *H. erectus* were.

Other trends include growth in *Homo*'s total population and geographic range and increasing local cultural diversity as people specialized in particular economic activities. Illustrating increasing economic diversity are the varied special-purpose tools made by Upper Paleolithic populations. Scrapers were used to hollow out wood and bone, scrape animal hides, and remove bark from trees. Burins, the first chisels, were used to make slots in bone and wood and to engrave designs on bone. Awls, which were drills with sharp points, were used to make holes in wood, bone, shell, and skin.

Upper Paleolithic bone tools have survived: knives, pins, needles with eyes, and fishhooks. The needles suggest that clothes sewn with thread—made from the sinews of animals—were being worn. Fishhooks and harpoons confirm an increased emphasis on fishing.

Different tool types may represent culturally distinct populations that made their tools differently because of different ancestral traditions. Archaeological sites also may represent different activities carried out at different times of the year by a single population. Some sites, for example, are obviously butchering stations, where prehistoric people hunted, made their kills, and carved them up. Others are residential sites, where a wider range of activities was carried out.

With increasing technological differentiation, specialization, and efficiency, humans have become increasingly adaptable. Through heavy reliance on cultural means of adaptation, *Homo* has become (in numbers and range) the most successful primate by far. The hominin range expanded significantly in Upper Paleolithic times with the colonization of two new continents—North America and South America—a story told in Chapter 10. (Australia was colonized by 60,000 B.P.)

Glacial Retreat

Consider now one regional example, Western Europe, of the consequences of glacial retreat. The Würm glacial ended in Europe between 17,000 and 12,000 years ago, with the melting of the ice sheet in northern Europe (Scotland, Scandinavia, northern Germany, and Russia). As the ice retreated, the tundra and steppe vegetation grazed by reindeer and other large herbivores gradually moved north. Some people moved north, too, following their prey.

Shrubs, forests, and more solitary animals appeared in southwestern Europe. With most of the big-game animals gone, Western Europeans were forced to use a greater variety of foods. To replace specialized economies based on big game, more generalized adaptations developed during the 5,000 years of glacial retreat.

As water flowed from melting glacial ice, sea levels all over the world started rising. Today, off most coasts, there is a shallow-water zone called the *continental shelf*, over which the sea gradually deepens until the abrupt fall to deep water, which is known as the *continental slope*. During the ice ages, so much water was frozen in glaciers that most continental shelves were exposed. Dry land extended right up to the slope's edge. The waters right offshore were deep, cold, and dark. Few species of marine life could thrive in this environment.

How did people adapt to the postglacial environment? As seas rose, conditions more encouraging to marine life developed in the shallower,

warmer offshore waters. The quantity and variety of edible species increased tremendously in waters over the shelf. Furthermore, because rivers now flowed more gently into the oceans, fish such as salmon could ascend rivers to spawn. Flocks of birds that nested in seaside marshes migrated across Europe during the winter. Even inland Europeans could take advantage of new resources, such as migratory birds and springtime fish runs, which filled the rivers of southwestern France.

Although hunting remained important, southwestern European economies became less specialized. A wider range, or broader spectrum, of plant and animal life was being hunted, gathered, collected, caught, and fished. This was the beginning of what anthropologist Kent Flannery (1969) has called the *broad-spectrum revolution*. It was revolutionary because, in the Middle East, it led to food production—human control over the reproduction of plants and animals. In a mere 10,000 years—after more than a million years during which hominins had subsisted by foraging for natural resources—food production based on plant cultivation and animal domestication replaced hunting and gathering in most areas.

Cave Art

It isn't the tools or the skeletons of Upper Paleolithic people but their art that has made them most familiar to us. Most extraordinary are the cave paintings, the earliest of which dates back some 36,000 years. More than a hundred cave painting sites are known, mainly from a limited area of southwestern France and adjacent northeastern Spain. The most famous site is Lascaux, found in 1940 in southwestern France by a dog and his young human companions.

The paintings adorn limestone walls of caves located deep in the earth. Over time, the paintings have been absorbed by the limestone and thus preserved. Prehistoric big-game hunters painted their prey: woolly mammoths, wild cattle and horses, deer, and reindeer. The largest animal image is 18 feet (5.5 meters) long.

Most interpretations associate cave painting with magic and ritual surrounding the hunt. For example, because animals are sometimes depicted with spears in their bodies, the paintings might have been attempts to ensure success in hunting. Artists might have believed that by capturing the animal's image in paint and predicting the kill, they could influence the hunt's outcome.

Another interpretation sees cave painting as a magical human attempt to control animal reproduction. Something analogous was done by Native Australian (Australian aboriginal) hunters and gatherers, who held annual *ceremonies of increase* to honor and to promote, magically, the fertility of the plants and animals that shared their homeland. Australians believed that ceremonies were neces-

BEYOND THE CLASSROOM

Paleolithic Butchering at Verberie

BACKGROUND INFORMATION

STUDENT:
Kelsey Foster

SUPERVISING PROFESSOR:
Dr. James G. Enloe

SCHOOL:
University of Iowa

YEAR IN SCHOOL/MAJOR:
Senior/Anthropology

FUTURE PLANS:
Marine Archaeology Internship/
Graduate School

PROJECT TITLE:
Meat and Marrow:
Paleolithic Butchering at Verberie

How can the analysis of animal bones provide evidence for specific kinds of human activity? What kinds of animals were hunted at this Paleolithic site? What kind of eating behavior went on at the site?

The Paleolithic archaeological site of Verberie le Buisson Campin is located along the banks of the Oise River in Northern France. It was the site of repeated occupation by a small band of Paleolithic hunters to mass-kill reindeer, which make up over 98% of the faunal assemblage. Examinations of the faunal material indicate that the reindeer were killed during the fall of the year, which corresponds with the yearly migration of the reindeer herds.

Dental analysis and postcranial measurements served to determine that the majority of the reindeer remains were from sub-adult males. This shows great selectivity on the part of the Paleolithic hunters for large, healthy prey.

My research focuses on furthering the existing knowledge of Verberie by attempting to determine the butchering pattern used by the Paleolithic hunters at the site. I examined the faunal remains from the entire upper occupation level (Level II1) for any indication of human modification of bone, which is indicated by the presence of stone tool cut marks and/or impact cones. Stone tool cut marks are produced during the filleting of meat from the bones and during the dismemberment of the carcass. The impact cones are the result of the cracking of bones in order to remove the marrow.

During my research I examined 1,133 specimens of reindeer bone fragments to investigate butchering practices at Verberie. Using Lewis Binford's Meat Utility Index and Marrow Utility Index numbers for the nutritive value of reindeer limb elements, I found that the elements with high marrow index values composed a greater percentage of the assemblage, while the elements with high meat index values were much less represented.

I then compared the numbers and degree of human modification between each element and found that the higher marrow utility elements showed a higher degree of exploitation for marrow cracking than did the lower marrow utility elements. This identified the systematic processing of marrow at Ver-

berie. Conversely, the stone tool cut marks present on the assemblage were predominately the result of dismemberment and not the result of meat removal.

I finally compared the percentages of the elements with a similar ethno-archaeologic study performed on the remains from a known marrow processing event at a Nunamuit (Alaskan Eskimos, or Inuit) residential site. The extreme similarity between these two assemblages solidified the claim of extensive marrow processing at Verberie.

When all this information is taken together, the butchering sequence at Verberie becomes clear. The butchering practice of Verberie consisted of primary dismemberment of the carcass into smaller units, with intentional snacking on the high marrow utility elements. The lack of filleting marks indicates that minimal, if any, meat exploitation occurred at the hunting camp. Therefore, if the high meat utility elements were not eaten at Verberie, they were transported to a larger residential camp for later consumption.

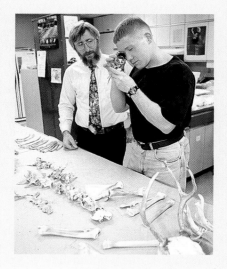

sary to perpetuate the species on which humans depended. Similarly, cave paintings might have been part of annual ceremonies of increase. Some of the animals in the cave murals are pregnant, and some are copulating. Did Upper Paleolithic people believe they could influence the sexual behavior or reproduction of their prey by drawing them? Or did they perhaps think that animals would return

each year to the place where their souls had been captured pictorially?

Paintings often occur in clusters. In some caves, as many as three paintings have been drawn over the original, yet next to these superimposed paintings stand blank walls never used for painting. It seems reasonable to speculate that an event in the outside world sometimes reinforced a painter's choice of a given spot. Perhaps there was an especially successful hunt soon after the painting had been done. Perhaps members of a social subdivision significant in Upper Paleolithic society customarily used a given area of wall for their drawings.

Cave paintings also might have been a kind of pictorial history. Perhaps Upper Paleolithic people, through their drawings, were reenacting the hunt after it took place, as hunters of the Kalahari Desert in southern Africa still do today. Designs and markings on animal bones may indicate that Upper Paleolithic people had developed a calendar based on the phases of the moon (Marshack 1972). If this is so, it seems possible that late Stone Age hunters, who were certainly as intelligent as we are, would have been interested in recording important events in their lives.

It is worth noting that the *late* Upper Paleolithic, when many of the most spectacular multicolored cave paintings were done and Paleolithic artistic techniques were perfected, coincides with the period of glacial retreat. An intensification of cave painting for any of the reasons connected with hunting magic could have been caused by concern about decreases in herds as the open lands of southwestern Europe were being replaced by forests.

The Mesolithic

The broad-spectrum revolution in Europe includes the late Upper Paleolithic and the **Mesolithic,** which followed it. Again, because of the long history of European archaeology, our knowledge of the Mesolithic (particularly in southwestern Europe and the British Isles) is extensive. According to the traditional typology that distinguishes between Old, Middle, and New Stone Ages, the Middle Stone Age, the Mesolithic, had a characteristic tool type—the *microlith* (Greek for "small stone"). Of interest to us is what an abundant inventory of small and delicately shaped stone tools can tell us about the total economy and way of life of the people who made them.

By 12,000 B.P., there were no longer subarctic animals in southwestern Europe. By 10,000 B.P. the glaciers had retreated to such a point that the range of hunting, gathering, and fishing populations in Europe extended to the formerly glaciated British Isles and Scandinavia. The reindeer herds had gradually retreated to the far north, with some human groups following (and ultimately domesticating) them. Europe around 10,000 B.P. was forest rather than treeless steppe and tundra. Europeans were exploiting a wider variety of resources and gearing their lives to the seasonal appearance of particular plants and animals.

People still hunted, but their prey were solitary forest animals, such as the roe deer, the wild ox,

Landscape of the Dordogne region of southwestern France. In this town, Les Eyzies, you can stay at the Cro-Magnon Hotel. You can also visit nearby sites of cave painting. Note the limestone cliffs. What is the significance of this area for prehistory?

and the wild pig, rather than herd species. This led to new hunting techniques: solitary stalking and trapping, similar to more recent practices of many American Indian groups. The coasts and lakes of Europe and the Middle East were fished intensively. Some important Mesolithic sites are Scandinavian shell mounds—the garbage dumps of prehistoric oyster collectors. Microliths were used as fishhooks and in harpoons. Dugout canoes were used for fishing and travel. The process of preserving meat and fish by smoking and salting grew increasingly important. (Meat preservation had been less of a problem in a subarctic environment since winter snow and ice, often on the ground nine months of the year, offered convenient refrigeration.) The bow and arrow became essential for hunting water fowl in swamps and marshes. Dogs were domesticated, as retrievers, by Mesolithic people (Champion and Gamble 1984). Woodworking was important in the forested environment of northern and Western Europe. Tools used by Mesolithic carpenters appear in the archaeological record: new kinds of axes, chisels, and gouges.

Big-game hunting and, thereafter, Mesolithic hunting and fishing were important in Europe, but other foraging strategies were used by prehistoric humans in Africa and Asia. Among contemporary foragers in the tropics, gathering is the dietary mainstay (Lee 1968/1974). Although herds of big-game animals were more abundant in the tropics in prehistory than they are today, gathering probably has always been at least as important as hunting for tropical foragers (Draper 1975).

Generalized, broad-spectrum economies persisted about 5,000 years longer in Europe than in the Middle East. Whereas Middle Easterners had begun to cultivate plants and breed animals by 10,000 B.P., food production came to Western

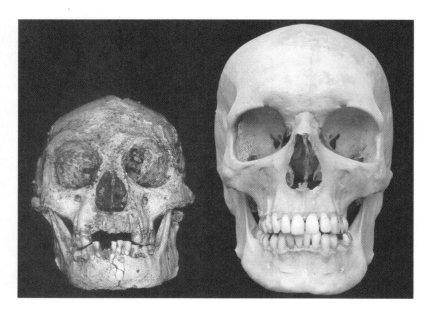

The skull of Homo floresiensis (left; modern human right), a miniature hominid that inhabited Middle Earth, or at least the Indonesian island of Flores, between 95,000 and 13,000 years ago.

Europe only around 5000 B.P. (3000 B.C.E.) and to northern Europe 500 years later. In Chapter 10, we will shift our focus to the Middle East, where the origin of food production took place.

HOMO FLORESIENSIS

In 2004 news reports trumpeted the discovery of bones and tools of a group of tiny humans who inhabited Flores, an Indonesian island 370 miles east of Bali, until fairly recent times (see Wade 2004). Early in hominin evolution, as we saw in the last chapter, it wasn't unusual for different species, even genera, of hominins, to live at the same time. But until the 2003–2004 discoveries on Flores, few scientists imagined that a different human species had survived through 12,000 B.P., and possibly even later. These tiny people lived, hunted, and gathered on Flores from about 95,000 B.P. until at least 13,000 B.P. One of their most surprising features is the very small skull, about 370 cm³—slightly smaller than the chimpanzee average.

A skull and several skeletons of these miniature people were found in a limestone cave on Flores by a team of Australian and Indonesian archaeologists, who assigned them to a new human species, H. floresiensis. (Discovery of additional specimens was announced in 2005; see Gugliotta 2005.) The discovery of H. floresiensis, described as a downsized version of H. erectus, shows that archaic humans survived much later than had been thought. Before modern people reached Flores, which is very isolated, the island was inhabited only by a select group of animals

that had managed to reach it. These animals, including H. floresiensis, faced unusual evolutionary forces that pushed some toward gigantism and some toward dwarfism. The carnivorous lizards that reached Flores, perhaps on natural rafts, became giants. These Komodo dragons now are confined mainly to the nearby island of Komodo. Elephants, which are excellent swimmers, reached Flores, where they evolved to a dwarf form the size of an ox.

Previous excavations by Michael Morwood, one of the discoverers of H. floresiensis, estimated that H. erectus had reached Flores by 840,000 years ago, based on crude stone tools found there. This H. erectus population and its descendants are assumed to have been influenced by the same evolutionary forces that reduced the size of the elephants. The first specimen of H. floresiensis, an adult female, was uncovered in September 2003, from beneath 20 feet (6.1 meters) of silt coating the floor of the Liang Bua cave. Paleoanthropologists identified her as a very small but otherwise normal individual—a diminutive version of H. erectus. Because the downsizing was so extreme, smaller than that in modern human pygmies, she and her fellows were assigned to a new species. Her skeleton is estimated to date back some 18,000 years. Remains of six additional individuals found in the cave date from 95,000 to 13,000 B.P. The cave also has yielded bones of giant lizards, giant rats, pygmy elephants, fish, and birds.

H. floresiensis apparently controlled fire, and the stone tools found with them are more sophisticated than any known to have been made by H. erectus. Among the tools were small blades that might have been mounted on wooden shafts. Hunting elephants—probably cooperatively— and making complex tools, the Floresians may (or may not) have had some form of language. The suggestion of such cultural abilities is surprising for a hominin with a chimplike brain. The small cranium has raised some doubt that H. floresiensis actually made the tools. The ancestors of the anatomically modern people who colonized Australia more than 40,000 years ago may have traveled through this area, and it is possible that they made the stone tools. On the other hand, there is no evidence that modern humans reached Flores prior to 11,000 years ago.

The H. floresiensis population of the Liang Bua cave region appears to have been wiped out by a volcanic eruption around 12,000 B.P., but they may have survived until much later elsewhere on Flores. The Ngadha people of central Flores and the Manggarai people of West Flores still tell stories about little people who lived in caves until the arrival of the Dutch traders in the 16th century (Wade 2004).

1. Dental, facial, and cranial robustness was reduced as *H. habilis* evolved into *H. erectus,* which extended the hominin food quest to the hunting of large animals. *H. erectus,* with a much larger body, had smaller back teeth but larger front teeth and supporting structures, including a massive eyebrow ridge. The Lower Paleolithic Acheulian tradition provided *H. erectus* with better tools. *H. erectus*'s average cranial capacity doubled the australopithecine average. Tool complexity and archaeological evidence for cooperative hunting suggest a long period of enculturation and learning. *H. erectus* extended the hominin range beyond Africa to Asia and Europe.

2. The oldest *H. erectus* skulls yet found come from Kenya and Georgia (in Eurasia) and date back some 1.75–1.6 million years. At Olduvai Gorge, Tanzania, geological strata spanning more than a million years demonstrate a transition from Oldowan tools to the Archeulian implements of *H. erectus. H. erectus* persisted for more than a million years, evolving into archaic *H. sapiens* by the Middle Pleistocene epoch, some 300,000 years ago. Fire allowed *H. erectus* to expand into cooler areas, to cook, and to live in caves.

3. The classic Neandertals, who inhabited Western Europe during the early part of the Würm glacial, were among the first hominin fossils found. With no examples of *Australopithecus* or *H. erectus* yet discovered, the differences between them and modern humans were accentuated. Even today, anthropologists tend to exclude the classic Neandertals from the ancestry of Western Europeans. The ancestors of AMHs (anatomically modern humans) were other archaic *H. sapiens* groups, most probably those in Africa. AMH fossil finds such as Skhūl (100,000 B.P.), Qafzeh (92,000 B.P.), and especially Herto (160,000–154,000 B.P.), and South African sites are cited to support the contention that the Neandertals (130,000 to 28,000 B.P.) and AMHs were contemporaries, rather than ancestor and descendant.

4. The classic Neandertals adapted physically and culturally to bitter cold. Their tool kits were much more complex than those of preceding humans. Their front teeth were among the largest to appear in human evolution. The Neandertals manufactured Mousterian flake tools. AMHs made Upper Paleolithic blade tools. The changeover from Neandertal to modern appears to have occurred in Western Europe by 28,000 B.P.

5. As glacial ice melted, foraging patterns were generalized, adding fish, fowl, and plant foods to the diminishing big-game supply. The beginning of a broad-spectrum economy in Western Europe coincided with an intensification of Upper Paleolithic cave art. On limestone cave walls, prehistoric hunters painted images of animals important in their lives. Explanations of cave paintings link them to hunting magic, ceremonies of increase, and initiation rites.

6. By 10,000 B.P., people were pursuing broad-spectrum economies in the British Isles and Scandinavia. Tool kits adapted to a forested environment included small, delicately shaped stone tools called microliths. The Mesolithic, or Middle Stone Age, had begun. The broad-spectrum revolution, based on a wide variety of dietary resources, began in the Middle East somewhat earlier than in Europe. As we will see in Chapter 10, it culminated in the first food-producing economies in the Middle East around 10,000 B.P.

7. In 2004 and 2005 scientists reported discoveries of bones and tools of a new hominin species they called *H. floresiensis.* This population of tiny humans lived on the isolated island of Flores in Indonesia. A probable descendant of *H. erectus,* which had settled Flores by 840,000 B.P., *H. floresiensis* is marked by the unusually small size of its body and its chimp-sized skull. There is debate about whether *H. floresiensis* was smart enough to have made the stone tools found in association with the skeletal remains, though there is no evidence that AMHs reached Flores before 11,000 B.P. The *H. floresiensis* remains have been assigned dates ranging from 95,000 to 13,000 B.P.

Acheulian Derived from the French village of St. Acheul, where these tools were first identified; Lower Paleolithic tool tradition associated with *H. erectus.*

anatomically modern humans (AMHs) Including the Cro-Magnons of Europe (31,000 B.P.) and the older fossils from Skhūl (100,000), Qafzeh (92,000), Herto, and other sites; continue through the present.

archaic *H. sapiens* Early *H. sapiens,* consisting of the Neandertals of Europe and the Middle East, the Neandertal-like hominins of Africa and Asia, and the immediate ancestors of all these hominins; lived from about 300,000 to 28,000 B.P.

blade tool The basic Upper Paleolithic tool type, hammered off a prepared core.

glacials The four or five major advances of continental ice sheets in northern Europe and North America.

interglacials Extended warm periods between such major glacials as Riss and Würm.

Mesolithic Middle Stone Age, whose characteristic tool type was the microlith; broad-spectrum economy.

Mousterian Middle Paleolithic tool-making tradition associated with Neandertals.

multiregional evolution Theory that *H. erectus* gradually evolved into modern *H. sapiens* in all regions inhabited by humans (Africa, Europe, northern Asia, and Australasia). As the regional populations evolved, gene flow always connected them, and so they always belonged to the same species. This theory opposes replacement models such as the Eve theory.

Neandertals An archaic *H. sapiens* group that lived in Europe and the Middle East between 130,000 and 28,000 B.P.

out of Africa theory Theory that a small group of anatomically modern people arose recently, probably in Africa, from which they spread and replaced the native and more archaic populations of other inhabited areas.

Paleolithic Old Stone Age (from Greek roots meaning "old" and "stone"); divided into Lower (early), Middle, and Upper (late).

Pleistocene Epoch of *Homo's* appearance and evolution; began 1.8 million years ago; divided into Lower, Middle, and Upper.

Upper Paleolithic Blade-tool-making traditions associated with early AMHs; named from their location in upper, or more recent, layers of sedimentary deposits.

CRITICAL THINKING QUESTIONS

For more self-testing, see the self-quizzes

mhhe.com/kottak

1. What were the main differences between *H. habilis* and *H. erectus*? Was *H. habilis* more like *H. erectus*, or more like the australopithecines?

2. How do you evaluate the evidence for a punctuated equilibrium model of hominin evolution?

3. What were the main trends in the evolution of technology during the Paleolithic? Do these trends continue today?

4. How does the geographic distribution of *H. erectus* differ from that of the australopithecines? What did culture have to do with this difference?

5. What cultural changes accompanied glacial retreat in Europe during the late Upper Paleolithic and the Mesolithic? Does anything happening today remind you of the effects of glacial retreat?

SUGGESTED ADDITIONAL READINGS

Boaz, N. T., and R. L. Ciochon
  2004   Headstrong Hominids. *Natural History* 113(1):28–34.

Calcagno, J. M., ed.
  2003   *Biological Anthropology: Historical Perspectives on Current Issues, Disciplinary Connections, and Future Directions.* Special issue of the *American Anthropologist* 101(1). Recent articles on human evolution.

Dibble, H. L., S. P. McPherron, and B. J. Roth
  2003   *Virtual Dig: A Simulated Archaeological Excavation of a Middle Paleolithic Site in France,* 2nd ed. Boston: McGraw-Hill. Interactive computer excavation of a Middle Paleolithic site.

Fagan, B. M.
  2005   *World Prehistory: A Brief Introduction,* 6th ed. New York: Longman. From the Paleolithic to the Neolithic around the world.
  2007   *People of the Earth: A Brief Introduction to World Prehistory,* 12th ed. Upper Saddle River, NJ: Prentice Hall. Prehistoric peoples and civilizations.

Gamble, C.
  1999   *The Palaeolithic Societies of Europe.* New York: Cambridge University Press. Survey mainly of the Middle and Upper Paleolithic in Europe.

Klein, R. G.
  1999   *The Human Career: Human Biological and Cultural Origins,* 2nd ed. Chicago: University of Chicago Press. Hominin fossils, origins, and evolution.

Klein, R. G., with B. Edgar
  2002   *The Dawn of Human Culture.* New York: Wiley. Becoming modern, physically and culturally.

Knecht, H., A. Pike-Tay, and R. White, eds.
  1993   *Before Lascaux: The Complex Record of the Early Upper Paleolithic.* Boca Raton, FL: CRC Press. Before cave art.

Lieberman, P.
  1998   *Eve Spoke: Human Language and Human Evolution.* New York: W. W. Norton. Language and behavior in human evolution.

Oakley, K. P.
  1976   *Man the Tool-Maker,* 6th ed. Chicago: University of Chicago Press. Classic, brief introduction to tool making.

Rightmire, G. P.
  1990   *The Evolution of Homo erectus: Comparative Anatomical Studies of an Extinct Human Species.* New York: Cambridge University Press. Thorough review of the fossil evidence for the *H. erectus* period of human evolution.

Schick, K. D., and N. Toth

1993 *Making Silent Stones Speak: Human Evolution and the Dawn of Technology.* New York: Simon & Schuster. Flint knapping and prehistoric tools.

Shipman, P.

2001 *The Man Who Found the Missing Link.* New York: Simon & Schuster. Eugene Dubois discovers "Java Man" (*H. erectus*).

Tattersall, Ian

1998 *Becoming Human: Evolution and Human Uniqueness.* New York: Harcourt Brace. Human evolution, including primates, fossil hominins, and social evolution.

1999 *The Last Neandertal: The Rise, Success, and Mysterious Extinction of Our Closest Human Relatives,* rev. ed. Boulder, CO: Westview. One view of what happened to the Neandertals.

Ucko, P., and A. Rosenfeld

1967 *Paleolithic Cave Art.* London: Weidenfeld and Nicolson. A survey, including finds and interpretations.

Wenke, R. J., and D. I. Olszewski

2007 *Patterns in Prehistory: Mankind's First Three Million Years,* 5th ed. New York: Oxford University Press. Very thorough survey of fossil and archaeological reconstruction of human evolution.

INTERNET EXERCISES

1. Visit the home page of the Chauvet-Pont-d'Arc cave (**http://www.culture.gouv.fr/culture/arcnat/chauvet/en/index.html**). Read about the discovery and authentication of the cave (under "The Cave Today") and about the archaeological context, dating, and significance of the cave (under "Time and Space").
   a. How was the cave found? How do they know the paintings are as old as they claim?
   b. When was the cave occupied? What kind of hominin was using the cave?
   c. What makes the Chauvet-Pont-d'Arc cave different from other caves used during a similar time period? What do archaeologists know about the people who occupied the cave and made the paintings?

2. Modern Hominin Origins: Visit Philip L. Walker and Edward H. Hagen's "Human Evolution: The Fossil Evidence in 3D" (**http://www.anth.ucsb.edu/projects/human/#**). Then click the link to enter the gallery.
   a. Click on the human figure labeled "Human origins" and then click on the skull labeled "Homo erectus." You now have a three-dimensional view of a *Homo erectus* skull, and you can use the mouse to rotate the skull. Compare it with a modern human skull. What are some of the prominent features that differentiate a *Homo erectus* skull from a modern human skull? From the image, is it clear who has the bigger brain?
   b. Go back and look at the *Homo neanderthalensis* skull. Rotate the skulls to look at a profile or side view. Which skull has a large brow ridge; a low, elongated skull; and a bun on the back of the skull? From the image, is it clear who has the bigger brain? Some people have argued that modern Europeans descended from Neandertals. Based on these skulls, do you think this is possible?

3. Go to the UC Berkeley News website **http://www.berkeley.edu/news/media/hominid/**, for a story titled "Ethiopian Fossil Is Oldest Modern Human." Read the press release, which describes the finds made at Herto. View the short (10 minutes) film by choosing the option "the tape in its entirety."
   a. Describe the fossil evidence shown in the film. How many human skulls were found? What other mammal fossils were excavated at Herto?
   b. According to Dr. Berhane Asfaw, how do the Herto fossils contribute to understanding the relationship between Neandertals and modern humans?
   c. According to Dr. Yonas Beyene, how did these early humans use the large cutting tools (hand axes)?
   d. Besides hand axes, what other tools were found at Herto?

See Chapter 9 at your McGraw-Hill Online Learning Center for additional review and interactive exercises.

When Did Humans Start Acting Like Humans?

See your OLC Bringing
It All Together links
mhhe.com/kottak

Let's summarize what we've learned in the last few chapters and try to bring it all together. As you read this account, note how anthropologists draft hypotheses and use evidence from artifacts, art, language, and other aspects of culture, as well as genetics, anatomy, and animal remains, to reconstruct our past.

Scientists agree that (1) between 7 and 5 million years ago, our hominin ancestors originated in Africa, as apelike creatures became habitual bipeds; (2) by 2.5 million years ago, still in Africa, hominins were making crude stone tools; and (3) by 1.7 million years ago, hominins had spread from Africa into Asia and eventually into Europe.

Most scientists agree on those three points. A smaller majority—but still a majority—of scientists think that anatomically modern humans (AMHs) had evolved by 130,000 years ago from ancestors who had remained in Africa. Like earlier hominins (*H. erectus* or *ergaster*), they too spread out from Africa. Eventually they replaced—perhaps in some cases interbreeding with—nonmodern human types, such as the Neandertals in Europe and parts of Asia and the successors of *H. erectus* in the Far East.

Disagreement remains about when, where, and how these early AMHs achieved *behavioral modernity*—relying on symbolic thought, elaborating cultural creativity, and, as a result, becoming fully human in behavior as well as in anatomy. Was it 90,000 or 40,000 years ago? Was it in Africa, the Middle East, or Europe? Was it population increase, competition with nonmodern humans, or a genetic mutation that triggered the change? The traditional view has been that modern behavior originated fairly recently, around 40,000 years ago, and only after *H. sapiens* had pushed into Europe. This theory of a "creative explosion" is based on evidence such as the impressive cave paintings at Lascaux and Chauvet (Wilford 2002b).

Some researchers think this theory reflects Eurocentrism, in that anthropologists were more likely to believe evidence for early creativity in Western Europe. But when they found signs of early behavioral complexity in Africa or the Middle East, they discounted it. In fact, recent discoveries outside Europe do suggest an older, more gradual evolution of modern behavior, rather than its sudden appearance in Europe.

British archaeologist Clive Gamble observes, "Europe is a little peninsula that happens to have a large amount of spectacular archaeology. But the European grip of having all the evidence is beginning to slip. We're finding wonderful new evidence in Africa and other places. And in the last two or three years, this has changed and widened the debate over modern human behavior" (quoted in Wilford 2002b).

Uncertainty about the origin of modern behavior reflects the long lag between the time when the species first looked modern (150,000–100,000 B.P.) and the time when it started acting modern (90,000–40,000 B.P.) (Wilford 2002b). Did the capacity for behavioral modernity lie latent in early *H. sapiens* until it was needed for survival? According to archaeologist Sally McBrearty of the University of Connecticut, "the earliest *Homo sapiens* probably had the cognitive capability to invent *Sputnik,* but they didn't yet have the history of invention or a need for those things" (quoted in Wilford 2002b). Did the need for behavioral modernity arise gradually, in the context of new social conditions, environmental change, or competition with other early human types? Or did the capacity for modern behavior develop late, reflecting some kind of genetic transformation? Mary Stiner of the University of Arizona reduces the matter to one key question: "Was there some fundamental shift in brain wiring or some change in conditions of life?" (quoted in Wilford 2002b).

According to John Noble Wilford (2002b), Richard G. Klein, a Stanford archaeologist, is the main advocate for the idea that human creativity dawned suddenly, in Europe around 40,000 years ago. Before this "dawn of human culture" (Klein with Edgar 2002), *Homo* had changed very slowly—and more or less simultaneously in anatomy and behavior. After this "dawn of culture," human anatomy changed little, but behavior started changing dramatically. The pace of cultural change has been accelerating ever since 40,000 B.P.

In this traditional view, it was in Europe that modern *H. sapiens* made the first tools that confirm a pattern of abstract and symbolic thought. There, humans who were behaviorally, as well as anatomically, modern also buried their dead with ceremonies, adorned their bodies with pigments and jewelry, and fashioned figurines of fertile females. Their cave paintings expressed images from their minds, as they remembered the hunt and events and symbols associated with it.

To explain such a flowering of creativity, Klein proposes a neurological hypothesis. About 50,000 years ago, he thinks, a genetic mutation acted to rewire the human brain, possibly allowing for an advance in language. Improved communication, in Klein's view, could have given people "the fully modern ability to invent and manipulate culture" (quoted in Wilford 2002b). Klein thinks this genetic change probably happened in Africa and then allowed "human populations to colonize new and challenging environments" (quoted in Wilford 2002b). Reaching Europe, the rewired modern humans, the AMH Cro-Magnons, met and eventually replaced the resident Neandertals.

Klein recognizes that his genetic hypothesis "fails one important measure of a proper scientific hypothesis—it cannot be tested or falsified by experiment or by examination of relevant human fossils" (quoted in Wilford 2002b). AMH skulls from the time period in question show no change in brain size or function. According to Wilford (2002b), Klein's critics object that his concepts of "the dawn of creativity" and of an abrupt "human revolution" are too simplistic, as well as unprovable.

Other archaeologists think it inappropriate and outdated to link the origin of human behavioral modernity so closely to the European evidence. Such thinking was more understandable when few relevant sites were known elsewhere. But in the last 30 years, archaeologists working in Africa and the Middle East have found considerable evidence for early modern behavior, in the form of finely made stone and bone tools, long-distance trade, dietary changes, self-ornamentation, and abstract carvings.

In a survey of African archeological sites dating to between 300,000 and 30,000 years ago, Sally McBrearty and Alison Brooks (2000) conclude that artifacts thought to indicate the "human revolution" of the Upper Paleolithic in Europe—where they appear abruptly about 40,000 years ago—are found in Africa, much earlier but not all at the same time. In other words, what might appear to be a sudden event outside Africa was a slow process of accumulation within Africa. Given the genetic evidence that AMHs came from Africa, this makes good sense. There was a period of gradual cultural development in Africa for thousands of years, followed by migration out of Africa with a fairly developed culture. The implication is that humans were fully "human" long before the Upper Paleolithic and that we do not need to postulate a genetic change 50,000 years ago (e.g., a mutation "for language") to account for the "human revolution."

At South Africa's Blombos Cave, anatomically modern humans were making bone awls and weapon points more than 70,000 years ago. Shown here—some of the more than 100,000 artifacts that have been found in the cave.

At South Africa's Blombos Cave, an archaeological team led by Christopher Henshilwood found evidence that AMHs were making bone awls and weapon points more than 70,000 years ago. Three weapon points had been shaped with a stone blade and then finely polished. Henshilwood thinks these artifacts indicate symbolic behavior and artistic creativity—people trying to make beautiful objects. In January 2002, Henshilwood reported additional evidence from Blombos Cave for early symbolic thought: two small pieces of ocher (a soft red iron oxide stone) with inscribed triangles and horizontal lines, dating back 77,000 years (Wilford 2002b).

Earlier excavations in Congo's Katanda region had uncovered barbed bone harpoon points dating back 80,000 to 90,000 years (Yellen, Brooks, and Cornelissen 1995). Archaeologists Alison Brooks and John Yellen contend that these ancient people "not only possessed considerable technological capabilities at this time, but also incorporated symbolic or stylistic content into their projectile forms" (quoted in Wilford 2002b).

Some scientists still challenge the idea of early behavioral modernity in Africa (Wilford 2002b). The doubters wonder why, if the artifacts are that old and represent a basic change in human behavior, they aren't more common and widespread. John Yellen counters that AMH populations at places such as Blombos Cave and Katanda were probably small and scattered. Low population density would have been a barrier to the spread of ideas and cultural practices between groups (Wilford 2002b).

In Turkey and Lebanon, Steven Kuhn, Mary Stiner, and David Reese (2001) found evidence that, around 43,000 years ago, coastal people

made and wore beads and shell ornaments with repetitive designs (see also Mayell 2004b). Some of the shells were rare varieties, white or brightly colored. The bone of a large bird was incised for use as a pendant. The Mediterranean coastal sites of Ucagizli Cave in Turkey and Ksar Akil in Lebanon are located in a corridor of ancient migrations from Africa into Europe and Asia. There the archaeologists also found remains of animal bones that offered evidence for a dietary change. Over time, the people ate fewer deer, wild cattle, and other large animals. They also hunted fewer of the slower-reproducing, easier-to-catch animals, such as shellfish and tortoises, and more of the more agile animals, such as birds and hares (Kuhn, Stiner, and Reese 2001).

Kuhn, Stiner, and Reese (2001) suggest that population increase could have caused changes in the living conditions of these AMHs—putting pressure on their resources and forcing experimentation with diet and subsistence strategies. Even a modest increase in the population growth rate could double or triple the numbers and populations of small AMH bands, forcing people to vary their subsistence strategies. People would be living nearer to one another, with more opportunities to interact. Body ornaments could have been part of a system of communication, signaling group identity and social status. The archaeologists note

that such standardized ornaments first appeared at about the same time at two other widely separated sites, in Kenya and Bulgaria. Such reliance on communication through ornamentation probably implies "the existence of certain cognitive capacities and that these evolved relatively late in prehistory" (Stiner and Kuhn, quoted in Wilford 2002b; Kuhn, Stiner, and Reese 2001).

Such capacities probably were not the result of a sudden genetic mutation. "The fact that traditions of ornament making emerged almost simultaneously in the earliest Upper Paleolithic/Late Stone Age on three continents argues strongly against their corresponding to a specific event in the cognitive evolution of a single population," according to Stiner and Kuhn (quoted in Wilford 2002b).

Clive Gamble attributes the rise of behavioral modernity more to increasing social competition than to population increase. Competing with neighboring populations, including, in Europe, the Neandertals, could have produced new subsistence strategies, along with new ways of sharing ideas and organizing society. Such innovations would have advantaged AMH bands as they occupied new lands and faced new circumstances, including contact with nonmodern humans.

According to archaeologist Randall White of New York University, an expert on Cro-Magnon creativity, early personal adornment in Africa and the Middle East shows that the human creative capacity was latent in AMHs long before they reached Europe (Wilford 2002*b*). Facing new circumstances, including competition, AMHs honed their cultural abilities, which enabled them to maintain a common identity, communicate ideas, and organize their societies into "stable, enduring regional groups" (quoted in Wilford 2002*b*). Symbolic thought and cultural advances, expressed most enduringly in artifacts, ornamentation, and art, gave them the edge over the Neandertals, with whom they may have interbred, but whom they eventually replaced in Europe.

The origin of behavioral modernity continues to be debated. We see, however, that archaeological work in many world areas suggests strongly that neither anatomical modernity nor behavioral modernity was a European invention. Africa's role in the origin and development of humanity is prominent yet again.

10

The First Farmers

THE NEOLITHIC

In Chapter 9, we considered the economic implications of the end of the Ice Age in Europe. With glacial retreat, foragers pursued a more generalized economy, focusing less on large animals. This was the beginning of what Kent Flannery (1969) has called the **broad-spectrum revolution.** This refers to the period beginning around 15,000 B.P. in the Middle East and 12,000 B.P. in Europe, during which a wider range, or broader spectrum, of plant and animal life was hunted, gathered, collected, caught, and fished. It was revolutionary because, in the Middle East, it led to **food production**—human control over the reproduction of plants and animals.

After 15,000 B.P., throughout the inhabited world, as the big-game supply diminished, foragers had to pursue new resources. Human attention shifted from large-bodied, slow reproducers (such as mammoths) to species such as fish, mollusks, and rabbits that reproduce quickly and prolifically (Hayden 1981).

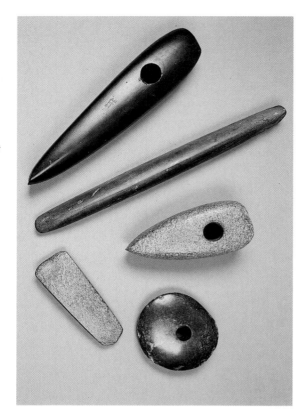

■ Neolithic was coined to refer to techniques of grinding and polishing stone tools, like these axes and hammers from Austria, Hungary, and the Czech Republic. Was the new tool-making style the most significant thing about the Neolithic?

For example, the Japanese site of Nittano (Akazawa 1980), on an inlet near Tokyo, offers evidence of broad-spectrum foraging. Nittano was occupied several times between 6000 and 5000 B.P. by members of the *Jomon* culture, for which 30,000 sites are known in Japan. The Jomon people hunted deer, pigs, bears, and antelope. They also ate fish, shellfish, and plants. Jomon sites have yielded the remains of 300 species of shellfish and 180 species of edible plants (including berries, nuts, and tubers) (Akazawa and Aikens 1986).

Early experiments in food production were the most significant form of broad-spectrum resource use in the post–Ice Age world. By 10,000 B.P., a major economic shift was under way in the Middle East (Turkey, Iraq, Iran, Syria, Jordan, and Israel). People started intervening in the reproductive cycles of plants and animals. Middle Easterners eventually became the world's first farmers and herders (Moore 1985). No longer simply harvesting nature's bounty, they grew their own food and modified the biological characteristics of the plants and animals in their diet. By 10,000 B.P., domesticated plants and animals were part of the broad spectrum of resources used by Middle Easterners. By 7500 B.P., most Middle Easterners were moving away from a broad-spectrum foraging pattern toward more specialized economies based on fewer species, which were domesticates. They were becoming farmers and herders.

Kent Flannery (1969) has proposed a series of eras during which the Middle Eastern transition to farming and herding took place (Table 10.1). The era of seminomadic hunting and gathering (12,000 to 10,000 B.P.) encompasses the last stages of broad-spectrum foraging. This was the period just before the first domesticated plants (wheat and barley) and animals (goats and sheep) were added to the diet. Next came the era of early dry farming (of wheat and barley) and caprine domestication (10,000 to 7500 B.P.). *Dry farming*

OVERVIEW

Food production encompasses the domestication of plants and animals and the farming and herding economies that result. This new economy developed out of foraging, as people added domesticates to the broad spectrum of resources used for subsistence. By 10,000 B.P. ancient Middle Easterners, the first farmers, were cultivating wheat and barley and influencing the reproduction of goats and sheep.

There were at least seven independent inventions of food production: in the Middle East, sub-Saharan Africa, northern and southern China, Mesoamerica, the Andes in South America, and the eastern United States. They occurred at different times and were based on different sets of crops, some more productive and nutritious than others. Domestication spread rapidly—west and east—from the Middle East across Eurasia. The spread of food production was slower in the Americas, where domesticable animals were scarce and played a much less prominent role than they did in Europe, Asia, and Africa.

Food production produced advantages and disadvantages. The advantages included many discoveries and inventions. The disadvantages included harder work, poorer health, crime, war, social inequality, and environmental degradation.

TABLE 10.1 The Transition to Food Production in the Middle East	
Era	**Dates (B.P.)**
Origin of state (Sumer)	5500
Increasing specialization in food production	7500–5500
Early dry farming and caprine domestication	10,000–7500
Seminomadic hunting and gathering (e.g., Natufians)	12,000–10,000

On the Iceman's Trail

ABC NEWS BRIEF

by Amanda Onion
October 31, 2003

Food production refers to the farming and herding economies that resulted from the domestication of plants and animals. Domestication first occurred in the Middle East around 10,000 years ago, as foragers added domesticates, including wheat, barley, sheep, and goats, to the broad spectrum of plants and animals they gathered and hunted. Although domestication first occurred in the Middle East, it happened again in other world areas, at least seven in all. Food production also spread from one area to another, such as from the Middle East into Europe. Neolithic refers to the first cultural period in a given region in which the first signs of domestication are present. Neolithic economies based on food production produced substantial changes in human lifestyles.

This news story describes a late Neolithic Alpine European: the glacially preserved "Iceman" found in the Italian Alps in 1991. This find is significant because of its state of preservation and its combination of a human cadaver with clothing and possessions, including stone and metal (copper) tools. The Iceman probably came from an Alpine farming village, perhaps the archaeological site mentioned here. He was on an autumn hunting trip when he was killed and eventually frozen. DNA analysis of the contents of his stomach has shown that he ate wheat (cultivated) and red deer (hunted) for his last meal (Fountain 2002). The Neolithic, which began some 10,000 years ago in the Middle East, had spread to Western Europe by 6500 B.P. Note that the Iceman died around 5200 B.P.—relatively late in the Neolithic. Although he was a Neolithic man, he lived as close to the present day as he did to the origins of Neolithic farming, which occurred in the Middle East at least 5,200 years before the Iceman's death.

Like a never-ending CSI episode, scientists have been scrutinizing the oldest mummy ever found with nearly all that forensic science has to offer. Over 12 years, they have learned what the man ate, his age, his health and they think they know more about how he died. Now they've answered another question—where he lived.

The latest series of tests on the mysterious, 5,200-year-old Iceman reveal the 46-year-old stuck close to home.

Hikers first found the mummified man frozen in a glacier in the Alps between Italy and Austria in 1991. Researchers have since nicknamed the specimen "Ötzi," after the Ötztal area where he was found.

To trace the ancient man's whereabouts, researchers led by Wolfgang Müller of the Australian National University in Canberra studied the different forms of elements in the Iceman's teeth, bones and intestines and compared them with types found in soil and water in the area.

They found the 5-foot-2-inch-tall man likely spent his entire life within 37 miles mostly south of the location where he was discovered. That would mean the Iceman lived most of his life in what is now Italy. His mummified remains are still in Italy—at a refrigerated museum designed just for him in the northern city of Bolzano . . .

The Iceman has revealed much about the Neolithic Copper Age of Europe. The frozen corpse was still clothed in goatskin leggings and a grass cloak, while a copper-headed ax and a quiver full of arrows were lying nearby. Now researchers say they can confidently link him with an ancient community that once settled in the region.

"I think it is important to know whether the Iceman was a chance wanderer in the Alps or whether he had migrated from farther away—or whether he was living in the local area during most of his life," said Müller. "We can now say that the latter was the case."

To reach that conclusion, Müller turned to chemistry.

Elements such as strontium, oxygen and argon occur in different forms, known as isotopes. Isotopes differ in the number of neutrons

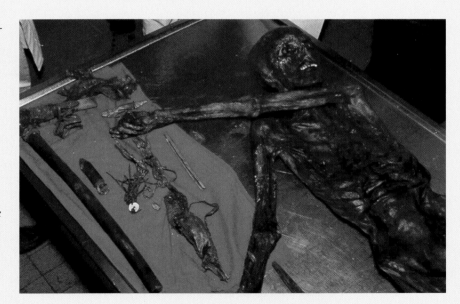

■ *Meet the Iceman. Since his frozen body emerged from a glacier in the Italian Alps in 1991, scientists have come to realize he is the closest we may ever come to meeting a real person from the Stone Age. How would you evaluate his state of preservation?*

they carry in each atom. By comparing the ratio of one isotope found in the water or soil of a region to that found in the body tissue, researchers can locate the source of the Iceman's food or water and link him to that region.

Isotopes in Ötzi's teeth reveal where he spent his youth, since dental enamel is fixed at the time that the tooth is formed. Isotopes in his bones reflect where he spent most of his adult life, since bones are remineralized every 10 to 20 years. And isotopes taken from the mummy's intestine shed light on where he spent his final hours.

Müller and his colleagues also analyzed the chemical makeup of minerals that had been leached into Ötzi's water supplies to try and further narrow down his stomping grounds . . .

Since the Alpine mountains around where the Iceman was found host minerals with a range of distinctive elements and isotopes, it was possible to link Ötzi with very specific locations . . .

Oxygen isotopes from Ötzi's tooth enamel matched those found in valleys just south of where he was found. And in fact, Fricke and Müller suggest that an archaeological site of a small Neolithic village in the nearby Eisack Valley may very well be where Ötzi spent his youth.

Isotopes and minerals from the Iceman's thighbones reflect those found in soil and water between the more northern location where he was found and his childhood one, suggesting he roamed at a slightly higher altitude as an adult.

To determine where the Iceman spent his final days, Müller's team analyzed argon found in white mica from Ötzi's intestines that could have come from a grinding stone used to mash the wheat that he had eaten just hours before his death.

The mica matched pieces found in the Etsch Valley, a region west of the Iceman's assumed childhood home. All locations fall within a 37-mile area. So if Ötzi spent his life close to home, what was he doing in the mountain peaks on that fateful day? . . .

Theories about how the Iceman died have varied wildly since his discovery, but some evidence suggests foul play.

Scientists first believed Ötzi may have been a shepherd who was returning with his flock when he encountered some kind of trouble, hurt his ribs and then fled to the mountains to escape. Then, overtaken by exhaustion, Ötzi propped his copper-headed ax against a rock and lay down or collapsed. Analysis of Ötzi's bones show he suffered from arthritis and so may have needed a rest after scrambling to the alpine ridge where he was discovered.

In 2001, scientists X-rayed the mummy's body and made a shocking discovery: The radiologist noticed what looked like a dense object in the body's shoulder. Further scrutiny showed it was an arrowhead lodged deep inside his shoulder.

One of the first to see the frozen mummy in the alpine glacier later revealed that it appeared Ötzi was clutching a knife in his right hand when he was found. Further analysis showed Ötzi had a deep wound in the same hand and had traces of blood from four different people on his clothes and weapons.

All of these revelations cleared away previous theories that the Iceman might have fallen asleep and died of hypothermia. A new picture emerged suggesting he was attacked and fought back with a hand knife. He eventually fled but was struck by an arrow as he ran away. He reached the top of the mountains, but was exhausted and bleeding and collapsed on the ground, and there he lay for more than 5,000 years.

That's the story for now anyway.

As scientists are learning, the Iceman holds seemingly endless clues, and theories about his life and death could evolve as forensic tools designed to catch new clues improve.

SOURCE: Amanda Onion, "On the Iceman's Trail: Scientists Trace Whereabouts of Man Who Died 5,200 Years Ago," *ABC News*, October 31, 2003. http://www.abcnews.go.com/sections/SciTech/World/iceman031031.html.

---

refers to farming without irrigation; such farming depended on rainfall. *Caprine* (from *capra*, Latin for "goat") refers to goats and sheep, which were domesticated during this era.

During the era of increasing specialization in food production (7500 to 5500 B.P.), new crops were added to the diet, along with more productive varieties of wheat and barley. Cattle and pigs were domesticated. By 5500 B.P., agriculture extended to the alluvial plain of the Tigris and Euphrates rivers (Figure 10.1), where early Mesopotamians lived in walled towns, some of which grew into cities. Metallurgy and the wheel were invented. After two million years of stone-tool making, *H. sapiens* was living in the Bronze Age.

The archaeologist V. Gordon Childe (1951) used the term *Neolithic Revolution* to describe the origin and impact of food production—plant cultivation and animal domestication. **Neolithic**, which means "New Stone Age," was coined to refer to techniques of grinding and polishing stone tools. However, the main significance of the Neolithic was the new total economy rather than just the tool-making techniques. *Neolithic* now refers to the first cultural period in a given region in which the first signs of domestication are present. The Neolithic economy based on food production produced substantial changes in human lifestyles. The pace of social and cultural change increased enormously.

THE FIRST FARMERS AND HERDERS IN THE MIDDLE EAST

Middle Eastern food production arose in the context of four environmental zones. From highest to lowest, they are high plateau (5,000 feet, or 1,500 meters), Hilly Flanks, piedmont steppe (treeless plain), and alluvial desert—the area watered by the Tigris and Euphrates rivers (100 to 500 feet, or 30 to 150 meters). The **Hilly Flanks** is a subtropical woodland zone that flanks those rivers to the north (Figure 10.1).

It was once thought that food production began in oases in the alluvial desert. (*Alluvial* describes rich, fertile soil deposited by rivers and streams.) This arid region was where Mesopotamian civilization arose later. Today, we know that although the world's first civilization (Mesopotamian) did indeed develop in this zone, irrigation, a late (7000 B.P.) invention, was necessary to farm the alluvial desert. Plant cultivation and animal domestication started not in the dry river zone but in areas with reliable rainfall.

The archaeologist Robert J. Braidwood (1975) proposed instead that food production started in the Hilly Flanks, or subtropical woodland, zone, where wild wheat and barley would have been most abundant (see Figure 10.1). In 1948, a team headed by Braidwood started excavations at Jarmo, an early food-producing village inhabited between 9000 and 8500 B.P., located in the Hilly Flanks. We now know, however, that there were farming villages earlier than Jarmo in zones adjacent to the Hilly Flanks. One example is Ali Kosh (Figure 10.1), a village in the foothills (piedmont steppe) of the Zagros mountains. By 9000 B.P., the people of Ali Kosh were herding goats, intensively collecting various wild plants, and harvesting wheat during the late winter and early spring (Hole, Flannery, and Neely 1969).

Climate change played a role in the origin of food production (Smith 1995). The end of the Ice Age brought greater regional and local variation in climatic conditions. Lewis Binford (1968) proposed that in certain areas of the Middle East (such as the Hilly Flanks), local environments were so rich in resources that foragers could adopt **sedentism**—sedentary (settled) life in villages. Binford's prime example is the widespread Natufian culture (12,500 to 10,500 B.P.), based on broad-spectrum foraging. The **Natufians,** who collected wild cereals and hunted gazelles, had year-round villages. They were able to stay in the same place (early villages) because they could harvest nearby wild cereals for six months.

Donald Henry (1989, 1995) documented a climate change toward warmer, more humid conditions just before the Natufian period. This expanded the altitude range of wild wheat and

barley, thus enlarging the available foraging area and allowing a longer harvest season. Wheat and barley ripened in the spring at low altitudes, in the summer at middle altitudes, and in the fall at high altitudes. As locations for their villages, the Natufians chose central places where they could harvest wild cereals in all three zones.

Around 11,000 B.P., this favorable foraging pattern was threatened by a second climate change— to drier conditions. As many wild cereal habitats dried up, the optimal zone for foraging shrank. Natufian villages were now restricted to areas with permanent water. As population continued to grow, some Natufians attempted to maintain productivity by transferring wild cereals to well-watered areas, where they started cultivating.

In the view of many scholars, the people most likely to adopt a new subsistence strategy, such as food production, would be those having the most trouble in following their traditional subsistence strategy (Binford 1968; Flannery 1973; Wenke 1996). Thus, those ancient Middle Easterners living outside the area where wild foods were most abundant would be the most likely to experiment and to adopt new subsistence strategies. This would have been especially true as the climate dried up. Recent archaeological finds support this hypothesis that food production began in *marginal areas*, such as the piedmont steppe, rather than in the optimal zones, such as the Hilly Flanks, where traditional foods were most abundant.

Even today, wild wheat grows so densely in the Hilly Flanks that one person working just an hour with Neolithic tools can easily harvest a kilogram of wheat (Harlan and Zohary 1966). People would have had no reason to invent cultivation when wild grain was ample to feed them. Wild wheat ripens rapidly and can be harvested over a three-week period. According to Flannery, over that time period, a family of experienced

Some 12,000 to 10,000 years ago, ancient Middle Easterners followed the availability of plants and animals, from lower to higher zones. With domestication, this pattern evolved into nomadic herding (pastoralism). Contemporary Middle Eastern herders still take their flocks to grazing areas at different elevations. This 1997 photo shows a Bedouin shepherd in the hills near Bethlehem, West Bank, Israel.

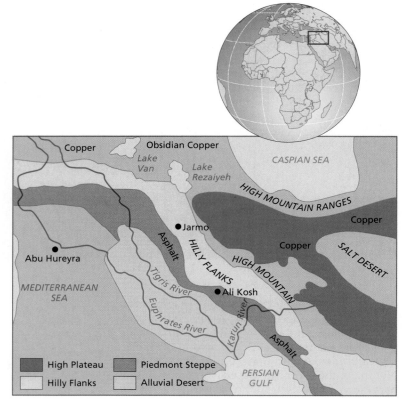

FIGURE 10.1 The Vertical Economy of the Ancient Middle East.
Geographically close but contrasting environments were linked by seasonal movements and trade among broad-spectrum foragers. As people traveled and traded, they removed plants from the zones where they grew wild in the Hilly Flanks into adjacent zones where humans became agents of selection. Food production emerged on the margins of the Hilly Flanks, at places such as Ali Kosh, rather than within that area, at places such as Jarmo.

it was abandoned—to be reoccupied later by food producers, between 9500 and 8000 B.P. From the Natufian period, Abu Hureyra has yielded the remains of grinding stones, wild plants, and 50,000 gazelle bones, which represent 80 percent of all the bones recovered at the site (Jolly and White 1995).

Prior to domestication, the favored Hilly Flanks zone had the densest human population. Eventually, its excess population started to spill over into adjacent areas. Colonists from the Flanks tried to maintain their traditional broad-spectrum foraging in these marginal zones. But with sparser wild foods available, they had to experiment with new subsistence strategies. Eventually, population pressure on more limited resources forced people in the marginal zones to become the first food producers (Binford 1968; Flannery 1969). *Early cultivation began as an attempt to copy, in a less favorable environment, the dense stands of wheat and barley that grew wild in the Hilly Flanks.*

The Middle East, along with certain other world areas where food production originated, is a region that for thousands of years has had a *vertical economy*. (Other examples include Peru and **Mesoamerica**—Middle America, including Mexico, Guatemala, and Belize.) A vertical economy exploits environmental zones that, although close together in space, contrast with one another in altitude, rainfall, overall climate, and vegetation (Figure 10.1). Such a close juxtaposition of varied environments allowed broad-spectrum foragers to use different resources in different seasons.

Early seminomadic foragers in the Middle East had followed game from zone to zone. In winter they hunted in the piedmont steppe region, which had winter rains rather than snow and provided winter pasture for game animals 12,000 years ago. (Indeed it is still used for winter grazing by herders today.) When winter ended, the steppe dried up. Game moved up to the Hilly Flanks and high plateau country as the snow melted. Pasture land became available at higher elevations. Foragers gathered as they climbed, harvesting wild grains that ripened later at higher altitudes. Sheep and goats followed the stubble in the wheat and barley fields after people had harvested the grain.

The four Middle Eastern environmental zones shown in Figure 10.1 also were tied together through trade. Certain resources were confined to specific zones. Asphalt, used as an adhesive in the manufacture of sickles, came from the steppe. Copper and turquoise sources were located in the high plateau. Contrasting environments were linked in two ways: by foragers' seasonal migration and by trade.

The movement of people, animals, and products between zones—plus population increase supported by highly productive broad-spectrum foraging—was a precondition for the emergence of food production. As they traveled between zones, people carried seeds into new habitats.

plant collectors could harvest enough grain— 2,200 pounds (1,000 kilograms)—to feed themselves for a year. But after harvesting all that wheat, they'd need a place to put it. They could no longer maintain a nomadic lifestyle, since they'd need to stay close to their wheat.

Sedentary village life thus developed before farming and herding in the Middle East. The Natufians and other Hilly Flanks foragers had no choice but to build villages near the densest stands of wild grains. They needed a place to keep their grain. Furthermore, sheep and goats came to graze on the stubble that remained after humans had harvested the grain. The fact that basic plants and animals were available in the same area also favored village life. Hilly Flanks foragers built houses, dug storage pits for grain, and made ovens to roast it.

Natufian settlements, occupied year-round, show permanent architectural features and evidence for the processing and storage of wild grains. One such site is Abu Hureyra, Syria (see Figure 10.1), which was initially occupied by Natufian foragers around 11,000 to 10,500 B.P. Then

Mutations, genetic recombinations, and human selection led to new kinds of wheat and barley. Some of the new varieties were better adapted to the steppe and, eventually, the alluvial desert than the wild forms had been.

Genetic Changes and Domestication

What are the main differences between wild and domesticated plants? The seeds of domesticated cereals, and often the entire plant, are larger. Compared with wild plants, crops produce a higher yield per unit of area. Domesticated plants also lose their natural seed dispersal mechanisms. Cultivated beans, for example, have pods that hold together, rather than shattering as they do in the wild. Domesticated cereals have tougher connective tissue holding the seedpods to the stem.

Grains of wheat, barley, and other cereals occur in bunches at the end of a stalk (Figure 10.2). The grains are attached to the stalk by an *axis*, plural *axes*. In wild cereals, this axis is brittle. Sections of the axis break off one by one, and a seed attached to each section falls to the ground. This is how wild cereals spread their seeds and propagate their species. But a brittle axis is a problem for people. Imagine the annoyance experienced by broad-spectrum foragers as they tried to harvest wild wheat, only to have the grain fall off or be blown away.

In very dry weather, wild wheat and barley ripen—their axes totally disintegrating—in just three days (Flannery 1973). The brittle axis must

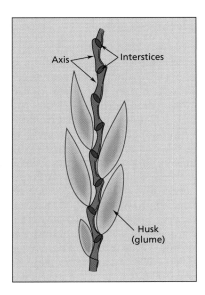

FIGURE 10.2 A Head of Wheat or Barley.
In the wild, the axis comes apart as its parts fall off one by one. The connecting parts (interstices) are tough and don't come apart in domesticated grains. In wild grains, the husks are hard. In domestic plants, they are brittle, which permits easy access to the grain. How did people deal with hard husks before domestication?

have been even more irritating to people who planted the seeds and waited for the harvest. But fortunately, certain stalks of wild wheat and barley happened to have tough axes. These were the ones whose seeds people saved to plant the following year.

Another problem with wild cereals is that the edible portion is enclosed in a tough husk. This husk was too tough to remove with a pounding stone. Foragers had to roast the grain to make the husk brittle enough to come off. However, some wild plants happened to have genes for brittle husks. Humans chose the seeds of these plants (which would have germinated prematurely in nature) because they could be more effectively prepared for eating.

People also selected certain features in animals (Smith 1995). Some time after sheep were domesticated, advantageous new phenotypes arose. Wild sheep aren't woolly; wool coats were products of domestication. Although it's hard to imagine, a wool coat offers protection against extreme heat. Skin temperatures of sheep living in very hot areas are much lower than temperatures on the surface of their wool. Woolly sheep, but not their wild ancestors, could survive in hot, dry alluvial lowlands. Wool had an additional advantage: its use for clothing.

What are some of the differences between wild and domesticated animals? Plants got larger with domestication, while animals got smaller, probably because smaller animals are easier to control. Middle Eastern sites document changes in the horns of domesticated goats. Such change may have been genetically linked to some other desirable trait that has left no skeletal evidence behind.

We've seen that sheep and goats were the first animals to be domesticated in the ancient Middle East, where the domestication of cattle, pigs, and other animals came later. Domestication was an ongoing process, as people kept refining and changing the traits they considered desirable in plants and animals—as they still do today through bioengineering. Different animals were domesticated at different times and in different regions. The factors that govern animal domestication are discussed further in the section "Explaining the Neolithic" later in this chapter.

Food Production and the State

The shift from foraging to food production was gradual. The knowledge of how to grow crops and breed livestock didn't immediately convert Middle Easterners into full-time farmers and herders. Domesticated plants and animals began as minor parts of a broad-spectrum economy. Foraging for fruits, nuts, grasses, grains, snails, and insects continued.

Over time, Middle Eastern economies grew more specialized, geared more exclusively toward

■ *Simple irrigation systems were being used in the Middle East by 7000 B.P. By 6000 B.P., complex irrigation techniques made agriculture possible in the arid lowlands of southern Mesopotamia. Here in Sudan, we see a fairly simple, ox-powered irrigation system.*

between zones, which had developed in the Middle East during the broad-spectrum period. Food production also owed its origin to the need to intensify production to feed an increasing human population—the legacy of thousands of years of productive foraging.

OTHER OLD WORLD FOOD PRODUCERS

The path from foraging to food production was one that people followed independently in at least seven world areas. As we'll see later in this chapter, three were in the Americas. Four were in the Old World, including the very first farmers and herders in the Middle East. In each of these seven centers, people independently invented domestication, although of different sets of crops and animals.

As we'll see in more detail later in this chapter, food production also spread from the Middle East. This happened through trade; through diffusion of plants, animals, products, and information; and through the actual migration of farmers. Middle Eastern domesticates spread westward to northern Africa, including Egypt's Nile Valley, and into Europe (Price 2000). Trade also extended eastward from the Middle East to India and Pakistan. In Egypt, an agricultural economy based on plants and animals originally domesticated in the Middle East led to a pharaonic civilization.

The African Neolithic

Excavations in southern Egypt have revealed considerable complexity in its Neolithic economy and social system, along with very early pottery and cattle, which may have been domesticated locally rather than imported from the Fertile Crescent. Located in the eastern Sahara and southern Egypt, Nabta Playa is a basin that, during prehistoric summers, filled with water. Over several millennia this temporary lake attracted people who used it for social and ceremonial activities (Wendorf and Schild 2000). Nabta Playa was first occupied around 12,000 B.P., as Africa's summer rains moved northward, providing moisture for grasses, trees, bushes, hares, and gazelle, along with humans. The earliest settlements (11,000–9300 B.P.) at Nabta were small seasonal camps of herders of domesticated cattle. (Note the very early, and perhaps independent, domestication of cattle here.) According to Wendorf and Schild (2000), Nabta Playa provides early evidence for what anthropologists have called the "African cattle complex," in which cattle are used economically for their milk and blood, rather than killed for their meat (except on ceremonial occasions). Nabta was occupied only

crops and herds. The former marginal zones became centers of the new economy and of population increase and emigration. Some of the increasing population spilled back into the Hilly Flanks, where people eventually had to intensify production by cultivating. Domesticated crops could now provide a bigger harvest than could the grains that grew wild there. Thus, in the Hilly Flanks, too, farming eventually replaced foraging as the economic mainstay.

Farming colonies spread down into drier areas. By 7000 B.P., simple irrigation systems had developed, tapping springs in the foothills. By 6000 B.P., more complex irrigation techniques made agriculture possible in the arid lowlands of southern Mesopotamia. In the alluvial desert plain of the Tigris and Euphrates rivers, a new economy based on irrigation and trade fueled the growth of an entirely new form of society. This was the *state*, a social and political unit featuring a central government, extreme contrasts of wealth, and social classes. The process of state formation is examined in the next chapter.

We now understand why the first farmers lived neither in the alluvial lowlands, where the Mesopotamian state arose around 5500 B.P., nor in the Hilly Flanks, where wild plants and animals abounded. Food production began in marginal zones, such as the piedmont steppe, where people experimented at reproducing, artificially, the dense grain stands that grew wild in the Hilly Flanks. As seeds were taken to new environments, new phenotypes were favored by a combination of natural and human selection. The spread of cereal grains outside their natural habitats was part of a system of migration and trade

seasonally, as people came over from the Nile, or from better-watered areas to the south. They returned to those areas in the fall.

By 9000 B.P. people were living at Nabta Playa year-round. To survive in the desert, they dug large, deep wells and lived in well-organized villages, with small huts arranged in straight lines. Plant remains show they collected sorghum, millet, legumes (peas and beans), tubers, and fruits. These were wild plants, and so the economy was not fully Neolithic. By 8800 B.P. these people were making their own pottery, possibly the earliest pottery in Egypt. By 8100 B.P., sheep and goats had diffused in from the Middle East.

Around 7500 B.P. new settlers occupied Nabta, whose previous inhabitants had been forced away by a major drought. The newcomers brought a more sophisticated social and ceremonial system. They sacrificed young cattle, which they buried in clay-lined and roofed chambers covered with rough stone slabs. They lined up large, unshaped stones. They also built Egypt's earliest astronomical measuring device: a "calendar circle" used to mark the summer solstice. Nabta Playa had become a regional ceremonial center: a place where various groups gathered seasonally or occasionally to conduct ceremonies and to socialize. The existence of such centers, as well as their religious, political, and social functions, is familiar to ethnographers who have worked in Africa. Nabta seems to have been such a center for prehistoric herders who lived in southern Egypt. It probably began to function as a regional ceremonial center around 8100–7600 B.P., when various groups gathered there for ceremonial and other purposes during the summer wet season.

Gathering on the northwestern shores of the summer lake, those ancient people left debris, including numerous cattle bones. At other African Neolithic sites (Edwards 2004), cattle bones are rarely numerous, which suggests that the cattle were being tapped "on the hoof" for their milk and blood, rather than being slaughtered and eaten. The numerous cattle bones at Nabta Playa, however, suggest that its people killed cattle seasonally for ceremonial purposes. Among modern African herders, cattle, which represent wealth and political power, are rarely killed except on important ceremonial or social occasions.

Nabta's role as a regional ceremonial center is also suggested by an alignment of nine large upright stone slabs near the place where people gathered, along the northwest margin of the seasonal lake. This formation, probably dating between 7500 and 5500 B.P., recalls similarly dated large stone alignments found in Western Europe, which were built during the late Neolithic and early Bronze Age.

Construction of large, complex megalithic structures requires well-organized work parties and a major effort. This suggests that some author-

ity (religious or civil) may have been managing resources and human labor over time. The findings at Nabta Playa represent an elaborate and previously unsuspected ceremonialism, as well as social complexity, during the African Neolithic.

The Neolithic in Europe and Asia

Around 8000 B.P., communities on Europe's Mediterranean shores, in Greece, Italy, and France, started shifting from foraging to farming, using imported species. By 7000 B.P., there were fully sedentary farming villages in Greece and Italy. By 6000 B.P., there were thousands of farming villages as far east as Russia and as far west as northern France (see Bogaard 2004). By chance, we can even meet a man from one of those European Neolithic villages. The "Iceman" discovered in the Italian Alps in 1991 (see the news story at the beginning of this chapter) came from a village of farmers who raised wheat, barley, sheep, and goats.

Domestication and Neolithic economies spread rapidly across Eurasia. Archaeological research confirms the early (8000 B.P.) presence of domesticated goats, sheep, cattle, wheat, and barley in Pakistan (Meadow 1991). In that country's Indus River Valley, ancient cities (Harappa and Mohenjo-daro) emerged slightly later than did the first Mesopotamian city-states. Domestication and state formation in the Indus Valley were influenced by developments in, and trade with, the Middle East.

China was also one of the first world areas to develop farming, based on millet and rice. Millet is a tall, coarse cereal grass still grown in northern China. This grain, which today feeds a third of the world's population, is used in contemporary North America mainly as birdseed. By 7500 B.P., two varieties of millet supported early farming communities in northern China, along the Yellow River. Millet cultivation paved the way for widespread village life and eventually for Shang dynasty civilization, based on irrigated agricul-

Millet, being harvested here on a Chinese plateau, was grown in the Hwang-He (Yellow River) Valley by 7000 B.P. This grain supported early farming communities in northern China. What was being grown in southern China at the same time?

Biocultural Case Study

The "Bringing It All Together" essay on pp. 253–257, right after Chapter 11, surveys the various lines of anthropological evidence for the peopling of the Pacific, which came well after the peopling of the Americas.

both wild and domesticated rice, along with domesticated water buffalo, dogs, and pigs. They also hunted wild game (Jolly and White 1995).

China seems to have been the scene of two independent transitions to food production, based on different crops grown in strikingly different climates. Southern Chinese farming was rice aquaculture in rich subtropical wetlands. Southern winters were mild; and summer rains, reliable. Northern China, by contrast, had harsh winters, with unreliable rainfall during the summer growing season. This was an area of grasslands and temperate forests. Still, in both areas by 7500 B.P., food production supported large and stable villages. Based on the archaeological evidence, early Chinese villagers had architectural expertise. They lived in substantial houses, made elaborate ceramic vessels, and had rich burials.

At Nok Nok Tha in central Thailand, pottery made more than 5,000 years ago has imprints of husks and grains of domesticated rice (Solheim 1972/1976). Animal bones show that the people of Nok Nok Tha also had humped zebu cattle similar to those of contemporary India. Rice might have been cultivated at about the same time in the Indus River Valley of Pakistan and adjacent western India.

It appears that food production arose independently at least seven times in different world areas. Figure 10.3 is a map highlighting those seven areas: the Middle East, north China, south China, sub-Saharan Africa, central Mexico, the south central Andes, and the eastern United States. A different set of major foods was domesticated, at different times, in each area, as we see in Table 10.2. Some grains, such as millet and rice,

ture, between 3600 and 3100 B.P. (See Chapter 11.) The northern Chinese also had domesticated dogs, pigs, and possibly cattle, goats, and sheep by 7000 B.P. (Chang 1977).

Recent discoveries by Chinese archaeologists suggest that rice was domesticated in the Yangtze River corridor of southern China as early as 8400 B.P. (Smith 1995). Other early rice comes from the 7,000-year-old site Hemudu, on Lake Dongting in southern China. The people of Hemudu used

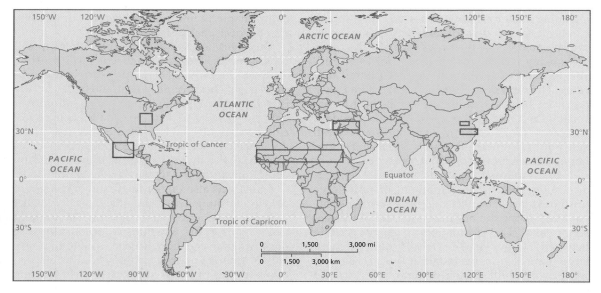

FIGURE 10.3 Seven World Areas Where Food Production Was Independently Invented. *Do any of these areas surprise you?* SOURCE: B. D. Smith, *The Emergence of Agriculture* (New York: Scientific American Library, W. H. Freeman, 1995), p. 12.

TABLE 10.2   Seven World Areas Where Food Production Was Independently Invented

World Area	Major Domesticated Plants/Animals	Earliest Date (B.P.)
Middle East	Wheat, barley Sheep, goats, cattle, pigs	10,000
South China (Yangtze River corridor)	Rice Water buffalo, dogs, pigs	8500–6500
North China (Yellow River)	Millet Dogs, pigs, chickens	7500
Sub-Saharan Africa	Sorghum, pearl millet, African rice	4000
Central Mexico	Maize, beans, squash Dogs, turkeys	4700
South Central Andes	Potato, quinoa, beans Camelids (llama, alpaca), guinea pigs	4500
Eastern United States	Goosefoot, marsh elder, sunflower, squash	4500

SOURCE: Data compiled from B. D. Smith, *The Emergence of Agriculture* (New York: Scientific American Library, W. H. Freeman, 1995).

were domesticated more than once. Millet grows wild in China and Africa, where it became an important food crop, as well as in Mexico, where it did not. Indigenous African rice, grown only in West Africa, belongs to the same genus as Asian rice. Pigs and probably cattle were independently domesticated in the Middle East, China, and sub-Saharan Africa. Independent domestication of the dog was virtually a worldwide phenomenon, including the Western Hemisphere. We turn now to archaeological sequences in the Americas.

THE FIRST AMERICAN FARMERS

Homo did not, of course, originate in the Western Hemisphere. Never have fossils of Neandertals or earlier hominins been found in North or South America. The settlement of the Americas was one of the major achievements of *H. sapiens sapiens.* This colonization continued the trends toward population increase and expansion of geographic range that have marked human evolution generally.

America's First Immigrants

The original settlers of the Americas came from Northeast Asia. They were the ancestors of American Indians. They entered North America via the Bering land bridge, *Beringia,* which connected North America and Siberia several times during the ice ages. Beringia, which today lies under the Bering Sea, was a dry land area several hundred miles wide, exposed during the glacial advances (Figure 10.4).

■	Ice cap
▨	Glaciers
▦	Ice-free corridor
– –	Present-day shore lines
■	Formerly exposed land areas

FIGURE 10.4   The Ancestors of Native Americans Came to North America as Migrants from Asia.

They followed big-game herds across Beringia, an immense stretch of land exposed during the Ice Ages. Was their settlement of the Americas intentional? When did it probably happen? Other migrants reached North America along the shore by boat, fishing and hunting sea animals.

See the Internet Exercise at your OLC

mhhe.com/kottak

Living in Beringia thousands of years ago, the ancestors of Native Americans didn't realize they were embarking on the colonization of a new continent. They were merely big-game hunters who, over the generations, moved gradually eastward as they spread their camps and followed their prey—woolly mammoths and other tundra-adapted herbivores. Other ancient hunters entered North America along the shore by boat, fishing and hunting sea animals.

This was truly a "new world" to its earliest colonists, as it would be to the European voyagers who rediscovered it thousands of years later. Its natural resources, particularly its big game, had never before been exploited by humans. Early bands followed the game south. Although ice sheets covered most of what is now Canada, colonization gradually penetrated the heartland of what is now the United States. Successive generations of hunters followed game through unglaciated corridors, breaks in the continental ice sheets. Others spread by boat down the Pacific coast.

In North America's rolling grasslands, early American Indians, *Paleoindians*, hunted horses, camels, bison, elephants, mammoths, and giant sloths. The **Clovis tradition**—a sophisticated stone technology based on a point that was fastened to the end of a hunting spear (Figure 10.5)—flourished between 12,000 and 11,000 B.P. in the Central Plains, on their western margins, and over a large area of what is now the eastern United States. Indeed, spear points made in the

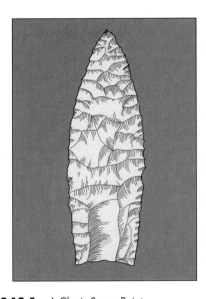

FIGURE 10.5 A Clovis Spear Point.
Such points were attached to spears used by Paleoindians of the North American plains between 12,000 and 11,000 B.P. Are there sites with comparable ages in South America?

Clovis tradition have been found in all 48 of the continental United States (Green 2006).

The Clovis people were not the first settlers of the Americas. The older Monte Verde archaeological site in south central Chile dates to 13,500 B.P. (Green 2006). This evidence for the early occupation of southern South America (along with other

lines of evidence) suggests that the first migration of humans into the Americas may date back 18,000 years. Analysis of DNA—bolstered, some anthropologists believe, by anatomical evidence—suggests that the Americas were settled by more than one *haplogroup:* a lineage marked by one or more specific genetic mutations. The various early colonists (as many as four or five haplogroups, some anthropologists believe) came at different times, perhaps by different routes, and had different physiques and genetic markers, which continue to be discovered and debated (see Bonnichsen and Schneider 2000).

The Foundations of Food Production

As hunters benefiting from the abundance of big game, bands of foragers gradually spread through the Americas. As they moved, these early Americans learned to cope with a great diversity of environments. Thousands of years later, their descendants independently invented food production, paving the way for the emergence of states based on agriculture and trade in Mexico and Peru. New World food production

emerged 3,000 to 4,000 years later than in the Middle East, as did the first states.

The most significant contrast between Old and New World food production involved animal domestication, which was much more important in the Old World than in the New World. The animals that had been hunted during the early American big-game tradition either became extinct before people could domesticate them or were not domesticable. The largest animal ever domesticated in the New World (in Peru, around 4500 B.P.) was the llama. Early Peruvians and Bolivians ate llama meat and used that animal as a beast of burden (Flannery, Marcus, and Reynolds 1989). They bred the llama's relative, the alpaca, for its wool. Peruvians also added animal protein to their diet by raising and eating guinea pigs and ducks.

The turkey was domesticated in Mesoamerica and in the southwestern United States. Lowland South Americans domesticated a type of duck. The dog is the only animal that was domesticated throughout the New World. There were no cattle, sheep, or goats in the areas where food production arose. As a result, neither herding nor the kinds of relationships that developed between

Early Peruvians and Bolivians ate llama meat, harnessed llamas as beasts of burden, and used llama dung to fertilize their fields. What was the largest animal domesticated in the New World?

■ *By diffusion, manioc or cassava, originally domesticated in lowland South America, has become a caloric staple in the tropics worldwide. This young Thai farmer displays his manioc crop.*

Differences in early food production between the Old World and the Americas help us understand their subsequent histories. Domesticable animals were a key ingredient in the origin of food production in the Middle East. Animals and crops thrived together in most regions of early food production in the Old World, including the Middle East, Africa, Europe, and Asia. Not so in the Americas, where wild oxen, horses, pigs, and camels once lived, but went extinct (probably due to a combination of hunting by humans and climatic changes) long before the first crops were cultivated. In the Middle East a mutually supportive relationship could develop between farming and herding. Animals could feed on stubble left in wheat fields after the crops were harvested. Crops could be grown to feed sheep, goats, and eventually cattle, pigs, horses, and donkeys. Animals could be used as beasts of burden, attached to sleds, rollers, and eventually wheeled vehicles.

The widespread use of wheeled vehicles, as diverse as oxcarts, chariots, and carriages, fueled the growth of trade, travel, and transport in the Old World. Advances in transportation led to an eventual "age of discovery" and the European conquest of the Americas. Early farmers in Mesoamerica had no trouble coming up with the idea of the wheel, which they sometimes attached to toys. But how could they have oxcarts or chariots without the appropriate animals to pull them? Dogs do pull sleds in the Arctic (never a center of food production), but dogs and turkeys can't match horses, donkeys, or oxen as beasts of burden. The lack of animal domestication in Mesoamerica is more than a textbook fact to be memorized for a test. It's a key factor in world history, helping us understand the divergent development of societies on different sides of the oceans.

herders and farmers in many parts of the Middle East, Europe, Asia, and Africa emerged in the pre-colonial Americas. The New World crops were different, although staples as nutritious as those of the Old World were domesticated from native wild plants.

Three *caloric staples*, major sources of carbohydrates, were domesticated by Native American farmers. **Maize,** or corn, first domesticated in highland Mexico, became the caloric staple in Mesoamerica and Central America; it eventually spread to coastal Peru. The other two staples were root crops: white ("Irish") potatoes, first domesticated in the Andes, and **manioc,** or cassava, a tuber first cultivated in the South American lowlands. Other crops added variety to New World diets and made them nutritious. Beans and squash, for example, provided essential proteins, vitamins, and minerals. Maize, beans, and squash were the basis of the Mesoamerican diet.

Food production was independently invented in three areas of the Americas: Mesoamerica, the eastern United States, and the south central Andes. Mesoamerica is discussed in detail in the next section. Food plants known as goosefoot and marsh elder, along with the sunflower and a species of squash, were domesticated by Native Americans in the eastern United States by 4500 B.P. These crops supplemented a diet based mainly on hunting and gathering. They never became caloric staples like maize, wheat, rice, millet, manioc, and potatoes. Eventually maize diffused from Mesoamerica into what is now the United States, reaching both the Southwest and the eastern area just mentioned. Maize provided a more reliable caloric staple for Native North American farming. In what is now Peru and Bolivia, six species appear to have been domesticated more or less together in the highland valleys and basins of the south central Andes

between 5000 and 4000 B.P. These domesticates were the potato, quinoa (a cereal grain), beans, llamas, alpacas, and guinea pigs (Smith 1995).

Early Farming in the Mexican Highlands

Long before Mexican highlanders developed a taste for maize, beans, and squash, they hunted as part of a pattern of broad-spectrum foraging. Mammoth remains dated to 11,000 B.P. have been found along with spear points in the basin that surrounds Mexico City. However, small animals were more important than big game, as were the grains, pods, fruits, and leaves of wild plants.

In the *Valley of Oaxaca*, in Mexico's southern highlands, between 10,000 and 4000 B.P., foragers concentrated on certain wild animals—deer and rabbits—and plants—cactus leaves and fruits, and tree pods, especially mesquite (Flannery 1986). Those early Oaxacans dispersed to hunt and gather in fall and winter. But they came together in late spring and summer, forming larger groups to harvest seasonally available plants. Cactus fruits appeared in the spring. Since summer rains would reduce the fruits to mush and since birds, bats, and rodents competed for them, cactus collection required hard work by large groups of people. The edible pods of the mesquite, available in June, also required intensive gathering.

In fall, these early Oaxacan foragers gathered a wild grass known as **teocentli,** or *teosinte*, the wild ancestor of maize. Sometime between 7000 and 4000 B.P., teocentli-maize underwent a series of genetic changes like those described earlier for Middle Eastern wheat and barley. These changes included increases in the number of kernels per cob, cob size, and the number of cobs per stalk (Flannery 1973). Such steps toward domestication made it increasingly profitable to collect wild maize and eventually to plant maize.

Undoubtedly, some of the mutations necessary for domesticated maize had occurred in wild teocentli before people started growing it. However, since teocentli was well adapted to its natural niche, the mutations offered no advantage and didn't spread. But once people started harvesting wild maize intensively, they became selective agents. As foragers wandered during the year, they carried teocentli to environments different from its natural habitat.

Furthermore, as people harvested teocentli, they took back to camp a greater proportion of plants with tough axes and cobs. These were the plants most likely to hold together during harvesting and least likely to disintegrate on the way back home. Now teocentli depended on humans for its survival, since it lacked the natural means of dispersal—a brittle axis or cob. If humans chose plants with tough axes inadvertently, their selection of plants with soft husks must have been intentional. Their selection of corn ears with larger cobs, more kernels per cob, and more cobs per plant was also intentional.

Eventually, people started planting maize in the alluvial soils of valley floors. This was the zone where foragers had traditionally congregated for the annual summer harvest of mesquite pods. By 4000 B.P., a type of maize had been developed that provided more food than the mesquite pods did. Once that happened, people started cutting down mesquite trees and replacing them with corn fields.

As maize cultivation spread, genetic changes led to higher yields and more productive farming. Pressures to intensify cultivation helped improve water-control systems, such as the canal irrigation shown in this mural by Diego Rivera.

Farming triggered a population explosion and *adaptive radiation* throughout Mesoamerica. Yet again, changes were gradual. In the Middle East, thousands of years intervened between the first experiments in domestication and the appearance of the state. The same was true in Mesoamerica.

From Early Farming to the State

Eventually, food production led to the *early village farming community.* Permanent villages sustained by farming were occupied year-round. The earliest such settlements in Mesoamerica developed around 3500 B.P., in two kinds of environment. One was humid lowlands, along the Gulf Coast of Mexico and the Pacific Coast of Mexico and Guatemala. Here, maize farming in rich soils was combined with gathering and hunting of several species of wild plants and animals.

Early village farming communities also emerged in one part of the Mexican highlands. In the Valley of Oaxaca in southern Mexico, winter frosts are absent, and simple irrigation permitted the establishment of early permanent villages based on maize farming. Water close to the surface allowed early farmers to dig wells right in their corn fields. Using pots, they dipped water out of these wells and poured it on their growing plants, a technique known as *pot irrigation.* The earliest year-round Mesoamerican farming depended on reliable rainfall, pot irrigation, or access to humid river bottomlands.

The subsequent spread of maize farming resulted in further genetic changes, higher yields,

See the Internet Exercises at your OLC for information on the domestication of chocolate

mhhe.com/kottak

Along with food plants known as goosefoot and marsh elder and a species of squash, the sunflower had been domesticated by Native Americans in the eastern United States by 4500 B.P. Sunflowers, such as those shown here near Mt. Fuji in Japan, have diffused widely throughout the world.

higher human populations, and more intensive farming. Pressures to intensify cultivation led to improvements in early water-control systems. New varieties of fast-growing maize eventually appeared, expanding the range of areas that could be cultivated. Increasing population and irrigation also helped spread maize farming. The gradual transformation of broad-spectrum foraging into intensive cultivation laid the foundation for the emergence of the state in Mesoamerica— some 3,000 years later than in the Middle East.

EXPLAINING THE NEOLITHIC

This section focuses on the factors that influenced the origin and spread of Neolithic economies in various world areas. (Much of this section is based on observations in Chapters 8 through 10 of Jared Diamond's influential book *Guns, Germs, and Steel: The Fates of Human Societies* [1997]).

The "Bringing It All Together" essay at the end of Chapter 9 discussed various opinions about when human behavioral modernity emerged. Was it 100,000 or more years ago, with the advent of anatomically modern humans? Or was it much later, during or just before the Upper Paleolithic? In either case, it took tens of thousands of additional years for humans to change their basic economy from foraging to food production.

Several factors had to converge to make domestication happen and to promote its spread. Most plants, and especially animals, aren't easy— or particularly valuable—to domesticate. Thus, of some 148 large animal species that seem potentially domesticable, only 14 actually have been

domesticated. And a mere dozen among 200,000 known plant species account for 80 percent of the world's farm production. Those 12 caloric staples are wheat, corn (maize), rice, barley, sorghum (millet), soybeans, potatoes, cassava (manioc), sweet potatoes, sugarcane, sugar beets, and bananas. The first domestication occurred, as we have seen, at a particular place and time—the Fertile Crescent area of the Middle East around 10,000 B.P.

Domestication rested on a combination of conditions and resources that had not come together previously. The development of a full-fledged Neolithic economy required settling down. Sedentism, such as that adopted by ancient Natufian hunter-gatherers, was especially attractive when several species of plants and animals were available locally for foraging and eventual domestication. The Fertile Crescent area of the Middle East had such species, along with a Mediterranean climate favorable to the origin and spread of the Neolithic economy. Among those species were several self-pollinating plants, the easiest wild plants to domesticate, including wheat, which required few genetic changes for domestication. We've seen that the Natufians adopted sedentism prior to farming. They lived off abundant wild grain and the animals attracted to the stubble left after the harvest. Eventually, with climate change, population growth, and the need for people to sustain themselves in the marginal zones, hunter-gatherers started cultivating. (In Mesoamerica, the shift from teocentli to maize required more genetic changes, and so the domestication process took longer. The lack of domesticable animals in Mesoamerica, except for dogs and turkeys, also retarded the emergence of food production, sedentism, and a full-fledged Neolithic economy.)

House Construction and Destruction Patterns of the Early Copper Age on the Great Hungarian Plain

BACKGROUND INFORMATION

STUDENT:
Nisha Kishor Patel

SUPERVISING PROFESSOR:
Dr. Richard Yerkes

SCHOOL:
Ohio State University

YEAR IN SCHOOL/MAJOR:
Senior/Anthropology

FUTURE PLANS:
PhD in Anthropology

PROJECT TITLE:
House Construction
and Destruction Patterns
of the Early Copper Age
on the Great Hungarian Plain

This selection describes excavation and analysis of building remains from a site on the Great Hungarian Plain that is transitional between the Late Neolithic (the time of the Iceman discussed in the news story and the Living Anthropology clip) and the Early Copper Age. Pay attention to the archaeological evidence that marks the site as transitional. What are some possible social implications of the change in house type described in this essay?

The site of Vésztö-Bikeri, Hungary, is the only settlement occupied during the transition from the Late Neolithic to the Early Copper Age on the Great Hungarian Plain that has been systematically excavated. With summer funding from the National Science Foundation Research Experiences for Undergraduates Program (REU-Sites), I participated in the Körös Regional Archaeological Project investigations at this unique site (http://www.anthro.fsu.edu/koros/index.html). In addition to learning field and lab methods in the KRAP field school, I completed an independent research project on prehistoric house construction techniques. I have returned to Hungary in subsequent years to continue my work analyzing the remains of structures at the site and writing a senior honors thesis at Ohio State University.

A great many changes took place ca. 5500 years ago on the Great Hungarian Plain, including settlement patterns, site layout, distribution of culture groups, etc. One of the major changes was that of house form. Prehistoric houses in Southeastern Europe were built of wattle-and-daub. A wooden frame of large posts intertwined with sticks of varying sizes was built, and then clay was applied to the frame. The clay hardened to create the walls. The structures of the Late Neolithic, which have been extensively excavated and studied, were large (6 × 14 meters) multi-roomed (6–8 rooms) longhouses, sometimes two-stories high. The few houses of the Early Copper Age that had been excavated were smaller (6 × 8 meters), one-roomed houses with no internal divisions. These changes suggest a major reworking of social organization, resource acquisition, and household dynamics during this time period. But unlike other Copper Age sites, at Vésztö-Bikeri we found large (6 × 14) structures with a single room. This illustrates the truly transitional nature of the site. Some of the characteristics (e.g., the single room) are typical of the Early Copper Age, others (e.g., house size), of the Late Neolithic.

Another characteristic of these Southeastern European societies is the practice of intentional house burning. Virtually all sites from the Middle Neolithic to the end of the Early Copper Age in the region contain varying amounts of burned daub. During the burning of houses, the clay from the walls hardened into this durable daub material. Often, impressions of sticks and posts from the wooden frame are preserved in the daub. These clues, along with other lines of evidence, help archaeologists reconstruct how a house was built, what materials were used, where the materials came from, the intensity of the fire, and how completely the house was burned. At Vésztö-Bikeri it is clear that some structures were burned more completely than others, though the question of why this is so remains a mystery. In fact, house burning is a mystery that has baffled archaeologists in Southeastern Europe for a long time. Why were so many structures burned over such a long period of time in this part of the world? Were the fires functional (e.g., to destroy vermin) or were they due to other factors such as warfare or ritual? The answers to these questions would help prehistorians learn a great deal about cultures during this time. Warfare says something completely different about prehistoric society than, say, if the houses were burned for ritual purposes. In future years the findings at Vésztö-Bikeri and my analysis of the daub will hopefully help us paint a more complete picture of the vast social changes that were taking place during the Late Neolithic-Early Copper Age transition on the Great Hungarian Plain.

Compared with other world areas, the Fertile Crescent region had the largest area with a Mediterranean climate, with the highest species diversity. As we saw previously, this was an area of vertical economy and closely packed microenvironments. Such diverse terrains and habitats concentrated in a limited area offered a multiplicity of plant species, as well as goats, sheep, pigs, and cattle. The first farmers eventually domesticated several crops: two kinds of wheat, barley, lentils, peas, and chickpeas (garbanzo beans). As in Mesoamerica, where corn (supplying carbohydrate) was supplemented by squash and beans (supplying protein), the Neolithic diet of the Middle East combined caloric staples such as wheat and barley with protein-rich pulses such as lentils, peas, and chickpeas.

Anthropologists once thought, erroneously, that domestication would happen almost automatically once people gained sufficient knowledge of plants and animals and their reproductive habits to figure out how to make domestication work. Anthropologists now realize that foragers have an excellent knowledge of plants, animals, and their reproductive characteristics, and that some other trigger is needed to start and sustain the process of domestication. A full-fledged Neolithic economy requires a minimal set of nutritious domesticates. Some world areas, for example, North America (north of Mesoamerica), managed independently to invent domestication, but the inventory of available plants and animals was too meager to maintain a Neolithic economy. The early domesticates—squash, sunflower, sumpweed, and goosefoot—had to be supplemented by hunting and gathering. A full Neolithic economy and sedentism did not develop in the east, southeast, and southwest of what is now the United States until maize diffused in from Mesoamerica—more than 3,000 years after the first domestication in the eastern United States.

We've seen how the presence or absence of domesticable animals helps explain the divergent trajectories of the eastern and western hemispheres in that the mixed economies that developed in Eurasia and Africa never emerged in Mesoamerica. Of the world's 14 large (over 100 pounds) successful domesticated animal species, 13 are from Eurasia, and only 1 (the llama) is from South America. Ancient Mexicans domesticated dogs and turkeys and created toy wheels, but they lacked sheep, goats, and pigs, as well as the oxen or horses needed to make the wheel a viable transport option. We can only speculate that year-round sedentism and a full-fledged Neolithic economy would have appeared earlier in Mesoamerica if the inventory of Old World plants and animals had been available. Certainly they would have been welcome. Once the big five Eurasian animal domesticates (cow, sheep, goat,

pig, horse) were introduced into Africa and the Americas, they spread rapidly.

We've seen that detailed knowledge of plants and their reproduction is not a sufficient condition for domestication to occur. Similarly, the knowledge that animals can be tamed or kept as pets isn't enough to produce animal domestication, because not all tamed animals can be domesticated. Just as some plants (e.g., self-pollinating annuals) are easier to domesticate than others are, so are some animals. Cattle, dogs, and pigs were so easy to domesticate that they were domesticated independently in multiple world areas.

Consider some reasons why most large animal species (134 out of 148 big species) have not been domesticated. Some are finicky eaters (e.g., koalas). Others have a slow growth rate (e.g., elephants). Yet others refuse to breed in captivity (e.g., vicunas). Some animals are just too nasty to domesticate (e.g., grizzly bears), and others have a tendency to panic (e.g., deer and gazelles).

Perhaps the key factor in domestication is animal social structure. The easiest wild animals to domesticate live in hierarchical herds. Accustomed to dominance relations, they allow humans to assume superior positions in the hierarchy. Herd animals are easier to domesticate than solitary ones are. Among the latter, only cats and ferrets have been domesticated, and there's some question about the completeness of domestication of those animals (hence the expression "It's like herding cats"). A final factor in ease of domestication is whether a wild animal typically shares its range with others. Animals with exclusive territories (e.g., rhinoceros, African antelope) are harder to pen up with others than are animals that share their territories with other species.

Geography and the Spread of Food Production

As Jared Diamond (1997, Chapter 10) observes convincingly, the geography of the Old World facilitated the diffusion of plants, animals, technology (e.g., wheels and vehicles), and information (e.g., writing). Most crops in Eurasia were domesticated just once and spread rapidly in an east–west direction. The first domesticates spread from the Middle East to Egypt, North Africa, Europe, India, and eventually China (which, however, also had its own domesticates, as we have seen). By contrast, there was much less diffusion of American domesticates. Some important crops (e.g., beans and chili peppers) were domesticated twice, in Mesoamerica and again in South America.

Look at Figure 10.6 to see that Eurasia has a much broader east–west spread than does Africa or does either of the Americas, which are arranged north–south. This is important because climates are more likely to be similar moving across thou-

Map Atlas

Map 8 shows major sites of plant and animal domestication, and the spread of domesticates, in the two hemispheres.

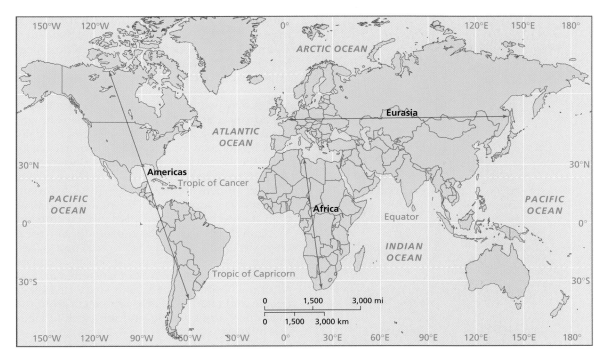

FIGURE 10.6 Major Axes of the Continents.
Note the breadth of the east–west axis in Eurasia, compared with the much narrower east–west spreads in Africa, North America, and South America. Those three continents have north–south as their major axes. SOURCE: J. M. Diamond, *Guns, Germs, and Steel: The Fates of Human Societies* (New York: W. W. Norton 1997), p. 177.

sands of miles east–west than north–south. In Eurasia, plants and animals could spread more easily east–west than north–south because of common day lengths and similar seasonal variations. More radical climatic contrasts have hindered north–south diffusion. In the Americas, for example, although the distance between the cool Mexican highlands and the South American highlands is just 1,200 miles, those two similar zones are separated by a low, hot, tropical region, which supports very different plant species than the highlands. Such environmental barriers to diffusion kept the Neolithic societies (of Mesoamerica and South America) more separate and independent in the Americas than they were in Eurasia. In fact, maize was the only crop that spread in the Americas before Columbus. And it took some 3,000 years for maize to reach what is now the United States, where productive Neolithic economies eventually did develop. They were based on the cultivation of new varieties of maize adapted to a colder climate and different day lengths.

In the Old World, the spread of Middle Eastern crops southward into Africa eventually was halted by climatic contrasts as well. Certain tropical crops did spread west–east in Africa, but they did not reach South Africa because of climatic barriers. Again and again, the geographic and climatic barriers posed by high mountains and broad deserts have slowed the spread of domesticates. In what is now the United States, for example, the east–west spread of farming from the southeast to the southwest was slowed by the dry climates of Texas and the southern great plains.

This section has examined the factors that favored and retarded the origin and spread of Neolithic economies in various world areas. Several factors combined to promote the first domestication in the ancient Middle East. The first domesticates spread rapidly across Eurasia, facilitated by climatic similarities across a broad territorial expanse. In the Americas, food production emerged later and spread less rapidly—and never as successfully—because of north–south contrasts. Another factor that slowed the Neolithic transition in the Americas was the lack of large animals suitable for domestication. Factors that explain the origin and diffusion of food production involve climate, economic adaptation, demography, and the specific attributes of plants and animals.

COSTS AND BENEFITS

Food production brought advantages and disadvantages. Among the advantages were discoveries and inventions. People learned to spin and

■ The labor demands of food production far exceed those associated with foraging. Here, in India's Andra Pradesh, these Banjara women are pounding grain. Such processing of food is just one step in getting the grain from the fields into people's mouths. What are some of the other steps?

palaces. They created sculpture, mural art, writing systems, weights, measures, mathematics, and new forms of political and social organization (Jolly and White 1995).

Because it increased economic production and led to new social, scientific, and creative forms, food production is often considered an evolutionary advance. But the new economy also brought hardships. For example, food producers typically work harder than foragers do—and for a less adequate diet. Because of their extensive leisure time, foragers have been characterized as living in "the original affluent society" (Sahlins 1972). Certain foragers have survived into recent times and have been studied by anthropologists. Among foragers living in the Kalahari Desert of southern Africa, only part of the group needed to hunt and gather, maybe 20 hours a week, to provide an adequate diet for the entire group. Women gathered, and adult men hunted. Their labor supported older people and children. Early retirement from the food quest was possible, and forced child labor was unknown.

With food production, yields are more reliable, but people work much harder. Herds, fields, and irrigation systems need care. Weeding can require hours of arduous bending. No one has to worry about where to keep a giraffe or a gazelle, but pens and corrals are built and maintained for livestock. Trade takes men, and sometimes women, away from home, leaving burdens for those who stay behind. For several reasons, food producers tend to have more children than for-

weave; to make pottery, bricks, and arched masonry; and to smelt and cast metals. They developed trade and commerce by land and sea. By 5500 B.P., Middle Easterners were living in vibrant cities with markets, streets, temples, and

TABLE 10.3 The Benefits and Costs of Food Production (Compared with Foraging)	
Do the costs outweigh the benefits?	
Benefits	**Costs**
Discoveries and inventions	Harder work
New social, political, scientific, and creative forms (e.g., spinning, weaving, pottery, bricks, metallurgy)	Less nutritious diets
	Child labor and child care demands
Monumental architecture, arched masonry, sculpture	Taxes and military drafts
Writing	Public health declines (e.g., more exposure to pathogens, including communicable and epidemic diseases)
Mathematics, weights, and measures	Rise in protein deficiency and dental caries
Trade and markets	Greater stress
Urban life	Social inequality and poverty
Increased economic production	Slavery and other forms of human bondage
More reliable crop yields	Rise in crime, war, and human sacrifice
	Increased environmental degradation (e.g., air and water pollution, deforestation)

agers do. This means greater child care demands, but child labor also tends to be more needed and valued than it is among foragers. Many tasks in farming and herding can be done by children. The division of economic labor grows more complex, so that children and older people have assigned economic roles.

And public health declines. Diets based on crops and dairy products tend to be less varied, less nutritious, and less healthful than foragers' diets, which are usually higher in proteins and lower in fats and carbohydrates. With the shift to food production, the physical well-being of the population often declines. Communicable diseases, protein deficiency, and dental caries increase (Cohen and Armelagos 1984). Greater exposure to pathogens comes with food production.

Compared with a seminomadic foraging band, food producers tend to be sedentary. Their populations are denser, which makes it easier to transmit and maintain diseases. We saw in Chapter 4 that malaria and sickle-cell anemia spread along with food production. Population concentrations, especially cities, are breeding grounds for epidemic diseases. People live nearer to other people and animals and their wastes, which also affect public health (Diamond 1997). Compared with farmers, herders, and city dwellers, foragers were relatively disease-free, stress-free, and well nourished.

Other hardships and stresses accompanied food production and the state. Social inequality and poverty increased. Elaborate systems of social stratification eventually replaced the egalitarianism of the past. Resources were no longer common goods, open to all, as they tend to be among foragers. Property distinctions proliferated. Slavery and other forms of human bondage eventually

were invented. Crime, war, and human sacrifice became widespread.

The rate at which human beings degraded their environments also increased with food production. The environmental degradation in today's world, including air and water pollution and deforestation, is on a much larger scale, compared with early villages and cities, but modern trends are foreshadowed. After food production, population increase and the need to expand farming led to deforestation in the Middle East. Even today, many farmers think of trees as giant weeds to be cut down to make way for productive fields. Previously, we saw how early Mesoamerican farmers cut down mesquite trees for maize cultivation in the Valley of Oaxaca.

Many farmers and herders burn trees, brush, and pasture. Farmers burn to remove weeds; they also use the ashes for fertilizer. Herders burn to promote the growth of new tender shoots for their livestock. But such practices do have environmental costs, including air pollution. Smelting and other chemical processes basic to the manufacture of metal tools also have environmental costs. As modern industrial pollution has harmful effluents, early chemical processes had by-products that polluted air, soils, and waters. Salts, chemicals, and microorganisms accumulate in irrigated fields. These and other pathogens and pollutants, which were by and large nonissues during the Paleolithic, endanger growing human populations. To be sure, food production had benefits. But its costs are just as evident. Table 10.3 summarizes the costs and benefits of food production. We see that progress is much too optimistic a word to describe food production, the state, and many other aspects of the evolution of society.

Biocultural Case Study

For more on deforestation— and on how anthropology's subfields and dimensions unite to study this particular problem— see the "Bringing It All Together" essay on pp. 128–131, which follows Chapter 6.

SUMMARY

1. After 15,000 B.P., as the big-game supply diminished, foragers sought out new foods. By 10,000 B.P., domesticated plants and animals were part of a broad spectrum of resources used by Middle Easterners. By 7500 B.P., most Middle Easterners were moving away from broad-spectrum foraging toward more specialized food-producing economies. *Neolithic* refers to the period when the first signs of domestication appeared.

2. Braidwood proposed that food production started in the Hilly Flanks zone, where wheat and barley grew wild. Others questioned this: The wild grain supply in that zone already provided an excellent diet for the Natufians and other ancient Middle Easterners. There would have been no incentive to domesticate. Other scholars view the origin of food production in the context of increasing population and climate changes.

3. Ancient Middle Eastern foragers migrated seasonally in pursuit of game. They also collected wild plant foods as they ripened at different altitudes. As they moved about, these foragers took grains from the Hilly Flanks zone, where they grew wild, to adjacent areas. Population spilled over from the Hilly Flanks into areas like the piedmont steppe. In such marginal zones people started cultivating plants. They were trying to duplicate the dense wild grains of the Hilly Flanks.

4. After the harvest, sheep and goats fed off the stubble of these wild plants. Animal domestication occurred as people started selecting certain features and behavior and guiding the reproduction of goats, sheep, cattle, and pigs. Gradually, food production spread into the Hilly Flanks. Later, with irrigation it spread down into Mesopotamia's alluvial desert, where the first cities, states, and civilizations developed by 5500 B.P. Food production then spread west from the Middle East into North Africa and Europe and east to India and Pakistan.

5. There were seven independent inventions of food production: in the Middle East, sub-Saharan Africa, northern and southern China, Mesoamerica, the south central Andes, and the eastern United States. Millet was domesticated by 7000 B.P. in northern China; and rice, by 8000 B.P. in southern China.

6. The transition to food production took place thousands of years later in the New World. Humans entered the Americas no more than 20,000 years ago. Pursuing big game or moving by boat along the North Pacific Coast, they gradually moved into North America. Adapting to different environments, Native Americans developed a variety of cultures. Some continued to rely on big game. Others became broad-spectrum foragers.

7. In the New World the most important domesticates were maize, potatoes, and manioc. The llama of the central Andes was the largest animal domesticated in the New World, where herding traditions analogous to those of the Old World did not develop. Economic similarities between the hemispheres must be sought in foraging and farming.

8. The earliest New World farming was in Mesoamerica. At Oaxaca, in Mexico's southern highlands, maize was gradually added to a broad-spectrum diet between 7000 and 4000 B.P. The first permanent villages, supported by maize cultivation, arose in the lowlands and in a few frost-free areas of the highlands. In the Valley of Mexico, quick-growing maize made year-round village life possible and paved the way for the emergence of civilization and city life.

9. Several factors, including a diversity of useful plant and animal species and early sedentism, combined to promote the first domestication in the ancient Middle East. The first domesticates spread rapidly across Eurasia, facilitated by climatic similarities across a broad territorial expanse. In the Americas, food production emerged later and spread less rapidly—and never as successfully—because of north–south contrasts. Another factor that slowed the Neolithic transition in the Americas was the lack of large animals suitable for domestication. Factors that explain the origin and diffusion of food production involve climate, economic adaptation, demography, and the specific attributes of plants and animals.

10. Food production and the social and political system it supported brought advantages and disadvantages. The advantages included discoveries and inventions. The disadvantages included harder work, poorer health, crime, war, social inequality, and environmental degradation.

KEY TERMS

See the flash cards
mhhe.com/kottak

broad-spectrum revolution Period beginning around 15,000 B.P. in the Middle East and 12,000 B.P. in Europe, during which a wider range, or broader spectrum, of plant and animal life was hunted, gathered, collected, caught, and fished; revolutionary because it led to food production.

Clovis tradition Stone technology based on a projectile point that was fastened to the end of a hunting spear; it flourished between 12,000 and 11,000 B.P. in North America.

food production Human control over the reproduction of plants and animals.

Hilly Flanks Woodland zone that flanks the Tigris and Euphrates rivers to the north; zone of wild wheat and barley and of sedentism (settled, non-migratory life) preceding food production.

maize Corn; domesticated in highland Mexico.

manioc Cassava; a tuber domesticated in the South American lowlands.

Mesoamerica Middle America, including Mexico, Guatemala, and Belize.

Natufians Widespread Middle Eastern culture, dated to between 12,500 and 10,500 B.P.; subsisted on intensive wild cereal collecting and gazelle hunting and had year-round villages.

Neolithic "New Stone Age," coined to describe techniques of grinding and polishing stone tools; the first cultural period in a region in which the first signs of domestication are present.

sedentism Settled (sedentary) life; preceded food production in the Old World and followed it in the New World.

teocentli Or *teosinte,* a wild grass; apparent ancestor of maize.

CRITICAL THINKING QUESTIONS

For more self-testing, see the self-quizzes
mhhe.com/kottak

1. What environmental and demographic conditions contributed to the origin of food production in the Middle East? Did they also apply in Mesoamerica?

2. Is your own diet more like that of a forager or that of an early farmer? How so?

3. What were the main similarities and differences between early food production in the Middle East and in Mesoamerica?

4. For the Old World, name four caloric staples. Name three for the New World. Where was each domesticated? For each staple, is it part of your diet? What's the most important caloric staple in your diet?

5. Was the origin of food production good or bad? Why?

Bellwood, P. S.
2004 *The First Farmers: Origins of Agricultural Societies.* Malden, MA: Blackwell. Origins and spread of agriculture in various world areas.

Cohen, M. N., and G. J. Armelagos, eds.
1984 *Paleopathology at the Origins of Agriculture.* New York: Academic Press. Some of the negative consequences of food production for human health.

Diamond, J. M.
1997 *Guns, Germs, and Steel: The Fates of Human Societies.* New York: W. W. Norton. Disease, tools, and environmental forces and effects throughout human history.

Fagan, B. M.
2005 *World Prehistory: A Brief Introduction,* 6th ed. Upper Saddle River, NJ: Pearson/Prentice Hall. Major events in human prehistory, including the emergence of food production and the state in various locales.
2007 *Ancient Lives: An Introduction to Archaeology and Prehistory,* 3rd ed. Upper Saddle River, NJ: Pearson/Prentice Hall. How archaeologists do what they do.

Gamble, C.
2004 *Archaeology, the Basics.* New York: Routledge. The title says it all.

Price, T. D., ed.
2000 *Europe's First Farmers.* New York: Cambridge University Press. The expansion of farming into Europe.

Price, T. D., and A. B. Gebauer, eds.
1995 *Last Hunters, First Farmers: New Perspectives on the Prehistoric Transition to Agriculture.* Santa Fe, NM: School of American Research Press. Recent ideas on the origin of food production.

Price, T. D., and G. M. Feinman
2005 *Images of the Past,* 4th ed. Boston: McGraw-Hill. Introduction to prehistory, including the origin of food production.

Renfrew, C., and P. Bahn
2005 *Archaeology: The Key Concepts.* New York: Routledge. Basic text.

Rindos, D.
1984 *The Origins of Agriculture: An Evolutionary Perspective.* New York: Academic Press. The impact of farming on human social evolution.

Sharer, R., and W. Ashmore
2006 *Discovering Our Past: The Process of Archaeological Research,* 4th ed. Boston: McGraw-Hill.

Smith, B. D.
1995 *Emergence of Agriculture.* New York: Scientific American Library, W. H. Freeman. The first farmers and herders in several world areas.

Wenke, R. J., and D. I. Olszewski
2007 *Patterns in Prehistory: Humankind's First Three Million Years,* 5th ed. New York: Oxford University Press. Rise of food production and the state throughout the world; thorough, useful text.

SUGGESTED ADDITIONAL READINGS

1. Read the article by Jack Challum in *The Nutrition Reporter* titled "Paleolithic Nutrition: Your Future Is in Your Dietary Past" (**http://www.nutrition reporter.com/stone_age_diet.html**).
   a. What kinds of foods typified the Paleolithic diet? What kinds of foods typify the modern American diet?
   b. What changes have occurred to the number and kind of foods consumed by humans? Why are our foods higher in saturated fats? What changes have occurred in vitamin intake?
   c. Despite the fact that humans may not be completely adapted to an agricultural diet, what are the physical and cultural advantages of agriculture?

2. Read the history of maize written by Ricardo J. Salvador (**http://maize.agron.iastate.edu/maizearticle.html**).
   a. When and where was maize domesticated?
   b. Maize is a very important source of carbohydrates and is one of the top three cereal crops in the world (along with rice and wheat). However, what are its nutritional deficiencies? How did Native Americans respond to this deficiency?
   c. When did maize first arrive in Europe? How was it carried there? Where else did it spread?

See Chapter 10 at your McGraw-Hill Online Learning Center for additional review and interactive exercises.

INTERNET EXERCISES

11

The First Cities and States

THE ORIGIN OF THE STATE

As food-producing economies spread and became more productive, chiefdoms, and eventually states, developed in many parts of the world. A **state** is a form of social and political organization that has a formal, central government and a division of society into classes. The first states developed in Mesopotamia by 5500 B.P. and in Mesoamerica some 3,000 years later. Chiefdoms were precursors to states, with privileged and effective leaders—chiefs—but lacking the sharp class divisions that characterize states. By 7000 B.P. in the Middle East and 3200 B.P. in Mesoamerica, there is evidence for what archaeologists call the elite level, indicating a chiefdom or a state.

How and why did chiefdoms and states originate? Compared with foraging, food production could support larger and denser populations. Also, the complexity of the division of social and economic labor tended to grow as food production spread and intensified. Systems of political authority and control typically develop to handle regulatory problems encountered as the population grows and/or the economy increases in scale and diversity. Anthropologists have identified the causes of state formation and reconstructed the rise of several states. A systemic perspective recognizes that multiple factors always contribute to state formation, with the effects of one magnifying those of the others. Although some contributing factors have appeared again and again, no single one is always present. In other words, state formation has generalized rather than universal causes.

Furthermore, because state formation may take centuries, people experiencing the process at any time rarely perceive the significance of the long-term changes. Later generations find themselves dependent on government institutions that took generations to develop.

Hydraulic Systems

One suggested cause of state formation is the need to regulate *hydraulic* (water-based) agricultural economies (Wittfogel 1957). In certain arid areas, such as ancient Egypt and Mesopotamia, states have emerged to manage systems of irrigation, drainage, and flood control. However, hydraulic agriculture is neither a sufficient nor a necessary condition for the rise of the state. That

is, many societies with irrigation never experienced state formation, and states have developed without hydraulic systems.

But hydraulic agriculture does have certain implications for state formation. Water control increases production in arid lands. Because of its labor demands and its ability to feed more people, irrigated agriculture fuels population growth. This in turn leads to enlargement of the system. The expanding hydraulic system supports larger and denser concentrations of people. Interpersonal problems increase, and conflicts over access to water and irrigated land become more frequent. Political authorities may arise to regulate production, as well as interpersonal and intergroup relations.

Large hydraulic works can sustain towns and cities and become essential to their subsistence. Regulators protect the economy by mobilizing crews to maintain and repair the hydraulic system. These life-and-death functions enhance the authority of state officials. Thus, growth in hydraulic systems is often (as in Mesopotamia, Egypt, and the Valley of Mexico), but not always, associated with state formation.

Long-Distance Trade Routes

Another theory is that states arise at strategic locations in regional trade networks. These sites include points of supply or exchange, such as crossroads of caravan routes, and places (e.g., mountain passes and river narrows) situated so as to threaten or halt trade between centers. Here again, however, the cause is generalized but neither necessary nor sufficient. Long-distance trade has been important in the evolution of many states, including those in Mesopotamia and Mesoamerica. Such exchange does eventually develop in all states, but it can follow rather than precede state formation. Furthermore, long-distance trade also occurs in societies such as those of Papua New Guinea, where no states developed.

Population, War, and Circumscription

Robert Carneiro (1970) put forth an influential theory that incorporates three factors working together instead of a single cause of state formation. (We call a theory involving multiple factors or variables a **multivariate** theory.) Wherever and whenever *environmental circumscription (or resource concentration), increasing population, and warfare exist,* suggested Carneiro, state formation will begin. Environmental circumscription may be physical or social. Physically circumscribed environments include small islands and, in arid areas, river plains, oases, and valleys with streams. Social circumscription exists when neighboring

---

OVERVIEW

The spread and intensification of food production fueled processes of state formation in Mesopotamia by 5500 B.P. and in Mesoamerica some 3,000 years later. Chiefdoms were precursors to states, with privileged and effective leaders but lacking the sharp class divisions that characterize states. By 7000 B.P. in the Middle East and 3200 B.P. in Mesoamerica, there is evidence for what archaeologists call the elite level, indicating a chiefdom or a state.

Like food production, states emerged in several world areas. The very first states arose in Mesopotamia (between the Tigris and Euphrates rivers) by 5500 B.P. and in the Nile Valley by 5250 B.P. Another state flourished between 4,600 and 3,900 years ago in the Indus River Valley of Pakistan and western India. The Shang dynasty state arose in the Huang He (Yellow) River valley of northern China around 3,750 years ago. By 2200 B.P., the process of state formation had accelerated in Mesoamerica and the Andes. Early states built on the social, political, and economic hierarchies and flamboyant art styles and architecture of the chiefdoms that preceded them.

With Escorts to the Afterlife, Pharaohs Proved Their Power

NEW YORK TIMES NEWS BRIEF

by John Noble Wilford
March 16, 2004

All states, whether ancient or modern, feature contrasts in wealth, power, prestige, and privilege. The rulers of states have special privileges, ranging from ancient palaces to today's state residences (e.g., the White House) and privileged modes of transportation (e.g., Air Force One). The ideology of some ancient states, such as First Dynasty Egypt, as described in this news story, took the special status of rulers much farther, viewing their rulers as divine and needing companions in the afterlife. As described here, the retinue that accompanied Pharaoh Aha to the afterlife included prominent people. His servants and companions during life became his companions in death. Whether voluntary or involuntary, their deaths appear to have been peaceful, by poison rather than evident trauma.

The Egyptian practice of sending companions to the afterlife along with a deceased pharaoh had long been rumored, but the excavations described here provide the first archaeological evidence. These finds date back to the start of Egypt's first dynasty, around 5,000 years ago (2950 B.C.E.). Also found was evidence for early writing (3200 B.C.E. = 5200 B.P.), one of the hallmarks of ancient states. Fortunately for those who wished to serve later pharaohs, the practice described here did not last through many generations. It was abandoned by the end of the First Dynasty.

When ancient Egypt was on the threshold of greatness, about 5,000 years ago, the rulers were already wielding fateful powers over life and death and obsessing over their own afterlife. The haunting evidence has lain buried for ages in the parched sands of Abydos, resting place of the earliest pharaohs known to history.

In excavations over the last two years, archaeologists have recovered that evidence: the remains of human sacrifices.

The practice of human sacrificial burials in Egypt, presumably to coincide with the pharaoh's own funeral, had long been suspected but never substantiated. Now it has been for the first time, and Dr. David O'Connor of New York University's Institute of Fine Arts said the discovery was "dramatic proof of the great increase in the prestige and power of both kings and the elite" as early as the first dynasty of the Egyptian civilization, beginning about 2950 B.C.

"This was a critical period of transition, when what had been a relatively small-scale civilization before took a gigantic leap under the ruler Aha," said Dr. O'Connor, director of the excavations. "The idea that a king had become so important that you dispatch people to go with him into the afterlife reflected changes in royal power and in religious practice and thinking."

The discovery team, organized by N.Y.U., Yale and the University of Pennsylvania, found six graves next to the ruins of a mortuary ritual site dedicated to the departed Aha, the first pharaoh of the first dynasty, and not far from his tomb. Five of the graves have been excavated, yielding skeletons of court officials, servants and artisans that appear to have been sacrificed to meet the king's needs in the afterlife.

The researchers said this was the first definite archaeological evidence of such human sacrifices. Similar graves previously found closer to Aha's tomb and the more than 200 others associated with Aha's successor, Djer, are now thought to be almost certainly sacrificial burials as well, Dr. O'Connor said . . .

The construction of the graves, the archaeologists said, was the principal clue to the fate of their occupants. A careful study of the graves associated with Djer indicated that they were all contiguous and had been covered with uninterrupted wooden roofing. The excavators said the burials thus had to have been made at the same time.

The excavation at Abydos. The archaeologists are excavating a type of building they call an enclosure. This was an open-air structure with a small building in one corner used to celebrate the funerary cult of the dead king. The enclosures are surrounded by subsidiary graves. The king himself was not buried here, but in a tomb far out in the desert.

Although the graves at the Aha site were separate, their wooden roofs were covered by a continuous mud plaster layer applied at about the same time that the adjacent mortuary ritual structure was erected. "This makes a strong case," Dr. O'Connor said, "that all these people died and were put in the graves at the same time." . . .

"Some of the burials were not just servants of no account but very, very rich people whose names and titles were inscribed on some possessions."

One grave held the bones of donkeys. "The king would need transportation in the afterlife." . . .

Egyptologists said the recent excavations by Dr. O'Connor's team were rewriting the history of the first dynasty, which ruled almost two centuries. They also added to the growing reputation of Abydos as a lode of archaeological riches only now being systematically explored.

At Abydos, 300 miles south of Cairo, British archaeologists led by William Flinders Petrie in the 1890's were among the first to reconnoiter the ruins, including Aha's tomb. Petrie suspected that the many subsidiary graves were sacrificial burials, but found no persuasive proof, and so he turned his attention to more inviting sites. The simple tombs and mud-brick ruins lacked the grandeur of the later temples and palaces, the pyramids at Giza or the huge tombs in the Valley of

the Kings. In recent years, though, German archaeologists have re-examined the royal tombs at Abydos and found, among other things, evidence of early forms of hieroglyphs from about 3200 B.C. If that date is correct, this would seem to show an earlier Egyptian writing than anything previously known, putting its origins at about the same time as that of the Mesopotamian cuneiform.

Four years ago, Dr. O'Connor's group reported finding the buried remains of 14 wooden boats, 5,000-year-old vessels that were part of royal funerary practices related to a pharaoh's eternal journey in the afterlife. Nearby, the archaeologists also uncovered ruins of walled enclosures surrounding small chapels, which appeared to have been erected in the lifetime of a pharaoh and used for rituals venerating him . . .

Of the two ritual enclosures recently uncovered, Dr. O'Connor said, one was positively identified as belonging to Aha, the successor, perhaps son, of the famous king Narmer of predynastic Egypt. Aha's seal and name, written in the image of a falcon, a symbol of royalty, were found in the ruins. The six subsidiary graves were close by.

Dr. O'Connor said the research so far suggested that such human sacrifices in Egypt were a rare custom. No evidence has been found

of the practice before Aha, and it apparently ceased before the end of the first dynasty, even though concepts of the afterlife remained virtually unchanged. For at least that time, the prestige and rewards of serving in the royal household must have been attractive, and members of the court apparently regarded the king as divine, his command not to be denied . . .

The good life of the retainers must have been accompanied by anxiety over the health of their aging monarch. A regime change was not likely to earn them a long retirement, only the ultimate exile.

"We may think of the ritual slaughter of a large number of retainers as a bit barbaric," [said Matthew Adams, a Penn archaeologist], but the ancient Egyptians may have come to look upon the sacrifices as passports to eternal life, a guarantee of immortality accompanying their king into the afterlife . . .

Mr. Adams said the archaeologists found "no trace of any kind of trauma on any of the skeletons." The individuals appeared to have died peacefully, probably by poison.

SOURCE: John Noble Wilford, "With Escorts to the Afterlife, Pharaohs Proved Their Power," *New York Times*, March 16, 2004, late edition, final, Section F, p. 3.

societies block expansion, emigration, or access to resources. When strategic resources are concentrated in limited areas—even when no obstacles to migration exist—the effects are similar to those of circumscription.

Coastal Peru, one of the world's most arid areas, illustrates the interaction of environmental circumscription, warfare, and population increase. The earliest cultivation there was limited to valleys with springs. Each valley was circumscribed by the Andes Mountains to the east, the Pacific Ocean to the west, and desert regions to the north and south. The advent of food production triggered a population increase (Figure 11.1). In each valley,

villages got bigger. Colonists split off from the old villages and founded new ones. With more villages and people, a scarcity of land developed. Rivalries and raiding developed between villages in the same valley.

Population pressure and land shortages were developing in all the valleys. Because the valleys were circumscribed, when one village conquered another, the losers had to submit to the winners—they had nowhere else to go. Conquered villagers could keep their land only if they agreed to pay tribute to their conquerors. To do this, they had to intensify production, using new techniques to produce more food. By working harder, they man-

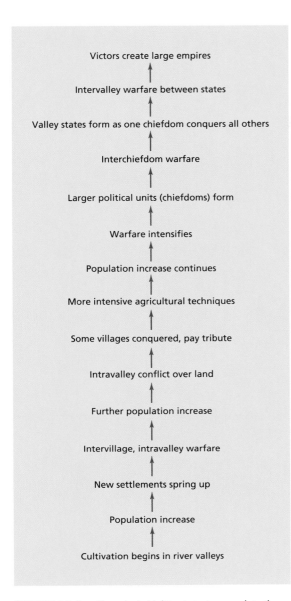

FIGURE 11.1 Carneiro's Multivariate Approach to the Origin of the State as Applied to Coastal Peru.

In this very arid area, food production developed in narrow river valleys where water for cultivation was available (resource concentration). With cultivation, the population increased. Population pressure on land led to warfare, and some villages conquered others. Physical circumscription meant that the losers had no way to escape. The process accelerated as the population grew and as warfare and cultivation intensified. Chiefdoms, states, and empires eventually developed.

aged to pay tribute while meeting their own subsistence needs. Villagers brought new areas under cultivation by means of irrigation and terracing.

Those early inhabitants of the Andes didn't work harder because they chose to do so. They were *forced* to pay tribute, accept political domination, and intensify production by factors beyond their control. Once established, all these trends

accelerated. Population grew, warfare intensified, and villages eventually were united in chiefdoms. The first states developed when one chiefdom in a valley conquered the others (Carneiro 1990). Eventually, different valleys began to fight. The winners brought the losers into growing states and **empires**—mature, territorially larger, and expansive systems—which eventually expanded from the coast to the highlands. By the 16th century, from their capital, Cuzco, in the high Andes, the Inca ruled one of the major empires in the tropics.

Carneiro's theory is very useful, but again, the association between population density and state organization is generalized rather than universal. States do tend to have large and dense populations (Stevenson 1968). However, population increase and warfare within a circumscribed environment did not trigger state formation in highland Papua New Guinea. Certain valleys there are socially or physically circumscribed and have population densities similar to those of many states. Warfare also was present, but no states emerged. Again, we are dealing with an important theory that explains many but not all cases of state formation.

Early states arose in different places, and for many reasons. In each case, interacting causes (often comparable ones) magnified each other's effects. To explain any instance of state formation, we must search for the specific changes in access to resources and in regulatory problems that fostered stratification and state machinery. We also must remember that chiefdoms and states don't inevitably arise from food production. Anthropologists know of, and have studied, many societies that maintained Neolithic economies without ever developing chiefdoms or states. Similarly, there are chiefdoms that never developed into states, just as there are foragers who never adopted food production, even when they knew about it. Recall from the last chapter those early food producers in what is now the eastern United States who had to keep hunting and gathering for the bulk of their subsistence because the foods they had domesticated (e.g., sunflower, marsh elder) could not supply a complete diet.

ATTRIBUTES OF STATES

Certain attributes distinguished states from earlier forms of society:

1. A state controls a specific regional territory, such as the Nile Valley or the Valley of Mexico. The regional expanse of a state contrasts with the much smaller territories controlled by kin groups and villages in prestate societies. Early states were expansionist; they arose from competition among chiefdoms, as the most powerful chiefdom conquered others, extended its rule over a

Early states had hereditary rulers and a military, with the rulers often playing a military role. Rulers stayed in power by combining personal ability, religious authority, economic control, and the privileged use of force. Shown here is a detail from the painted casket of Egypt's Tutankhamun, the famous "King Tut," who ruled between 1347 and 1337 B.C.E.

larger territory, and managed to hold on to, and rule, the land and people acquired through conquest.

2. Early states had productive farming economies, supporting dense populations, often in cities. The agricultural economies of early states usually involved some form of water control or irrigation.

3. Early states used tribute and taxation to accumulate, at a central place, resources needed to support hundreds, or thousands, of specialists. These states had rulers, a military, and control over human labor.

4. States are stratified into social classes. In the first states, the non-food-producing population consisted of a tiny elite, plus artisans, officials, priests, and other specialists. Most people were commoners. Slaves and prisoners constituted the lowest rung of the social ladder. Rulers stayed in power by combining personal ability, religious authority, economic control, and force.

5. Early states had imposing public buildings and monumental architecture, including temples, palaces, and storehouses.

6. Early states developed some form of record-keeping system, usually a written script (Fagan 1996).

STATE FORMATION IN THE MIDDLE EAST

In the last chapter we saw that food production arose in the ancient Middle East around 10,000 B.P. In the ensuing process of change, the center of population growth shifted from the zone where wheat and barley grew wild (Hilly Flanks) to adjacent areas (piedmont steppe) where those grains were first domesticated. By 6000 B.P., population was increasing most rapidly in the alluvial plain of southern Mesopotamia. (**Mesopotamia** refers to the area between the Tigris and Euphrates rivers in what is now southern Iraq and southwestern Iran.) This growing population supported itself through irrigation and intensive river valley agriculture. By 5500 B.P. towns had grown into cities (Gates 2003). The earliest city-states were Sumer (southern Iraq) and Elam (southwestern Iran), with their capitals at Uruk (Warka) and Susa, respectively.

Urban Life

The first towns arose around 10,000 years ago in the Middle East. Over the generations houses of mud brick were built and rebuilt in the same place. Substantial tells or mounds arose from the debris of a succession of such houses. The Middle East and Asia have hundreds or thousands of such mounds, only a few of which have been excavated.

FIGURE 11.2 Sites in Middle Eastern State Formation.

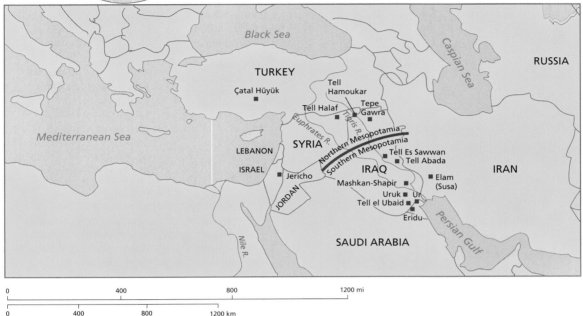

These sites have yielded remains of ancient community life, including streets, buildings, terraces, courtyards, wells, and other artifacts.

The earliest known town was Jericho, located in what is now Israel, below sea level at a well-watered oasis a few miles northwest of the Dead Sea (Figure 11.2). From the lowest (oldest) level, we know that around 11,000 years ago, Jericho was first settled by Natufian foragers. Occupation continued thereafter, through and beyond biblical times, when "Joshua fit the battle of Jericho, and the walls came tumbling down" (Laughlin 2006).

During the phase just after the Natufians, the earliest known town appeared. It was an unplanned, densely populated settlement with round houses and some 2,000 people. At this time, well before the invention of pottery, Jericho was surrounded by a sturdy wall, with a massive tower. The wall may have been built initially as a flood barrier rather than for defense. Around 9000 B.P. Jericho was destroyed, to be rebuilt later. The new occupants lived in square houses with finished plaster floors. They buried their dead beneath their homes, a pattern seen at other sites, such as Çatal Hüyük in Turkey (see below). Pottery reached Jericho around 8000 B.P. (Gowlett 1993).

Long-distance trade, especially of obsidian, a volcanic glass used to make tools and ornaments, became important in the Middle East between 9500 and 7000 B.P. One town that prospered from this trade was Çatal Hüyük in Anatolia, Turkey (DeMarco 1997). A grassy mound 65 feet high holds the remains of this 9,000-year-old town, probably the largest settlement of the Neolithic age. Çatal Hüyük was located on a river, which deposited rich soil for crops, created a lush environment for animals, and was harnessed for irrigation by 7000 B.P. Over the mound's 32 acres (12.9 hectares), up to 10,000 people once lived in crowded mud-brick houses packed so tight that residents entered from their roofs.

Shielded by a defensive wall, Çatal Hüyük flourished between 8000 and 7000 B.P. Its individual mud-brick dwellings, rarely larger than a suburban American bedroom, had separate areas reserved for ritual and secular uses. In a given house, the ritual images (wall paintings) were placed along the walls that faced north, east, or west, but never south. That area was reserved for cooking and other domestic tasks.

The ritual spaces were decorated with wall paintings, sculpted ox heads, bull horns, and

■ The world's earliest known town was Jericho, located in what is now Israel. Jericho was first settled by Natufian foragers around 11,000 B.P. This round tower dates back 8,000 years.

Everyone reading this book lives in a state-organized society. Understanding ourselves means recognizing that our lives are dramatically different from those of our Paleolithic ancestors, or those of more recent foragers, and the state has a lot to do with these differences. In the last chapter we saw that compared with foraging, Neolithic economies posed greater labor demands. The social and political systems associated with states also make significant demands on ordinary people. Museums demonstrate the artistic, architectural, literary, and scientific achievements of early states. Ancient Sumerians (in Mesopotamia), Egyptians, Mexicans, and Peruvians may have had their mathematicians, artists, architects, astronomers, priests, and rulers, as we do, but their ordinary people had to sweat in the fields to grow food for landlords, specialists, and elites. Unlike foragers, people living in states have encounters with bosses and despots. In ancient states, the elites conscripted involuntary labor to build temples and pyramids, to move stone for enduring monuments. In all states, people must pay taxes; in many states, citizens are drafted for work or war.

How does our own state-organized society mirror those of the past? Ordinary people may no longer be drafted for work or war, but we do have to work to pay the taxes that pay for wars and public works. Our society is still stratified. Perks still go with wealth, fame, and power. And most of us still work much harder (usually for bosses) than foragers did. It's a myth that leisure time has increased with civilization. For a few, there is leisure and privilege; for most, there is work and obligation. And that's not because of human nature; it's because of the state.

relief models of bulls and rams. The paintings showed bulls surrounded by stick figures running, dancing, and sometimes throwing stones. Vultures attacked headless humans. One frieze had human hand prints painted below mounted bull horns. These images and their placement are reminiscent of Paleolithic cave art. The dwellings at Çatal Hüyük were entered through the roof, and people had to crawl through holes from room to room, somewhat like moving between chambers in a cave. The deeper down one went, the richer the art became. The town's spiritual life seems to have revolved around a preoccupation with animals, danger, and death, perhaps related to the site's recent hunter-gatherer past.

Two or three generations of a family were buried beneath their homes. In one dwelling, archaeologists found remains of 17 individuals, mostly children. After two or three generations of family burials, the dwelling was burned. The site was then covered with fine dirt, and a floor laid for a new dwelling.

Çatal Hüyük's residents, though living in a town, acted independently in family groups without any apparent control by a priestly or political elite. The town never became a full-fledged city with centralized organization. Just as it lacked priests, Çatal Hüyük never had leaders who controlled or managed trade and production (Fagan

1996). Food was not stored and processed collectively, but on a smaller, domestic scale (DeMarco 1997).

The Elite Level

The first pottery (ceramics) dates back a bit more than 8,000 years, when it first reached Jericho. Before that date, the Neolithic is called the pre-pottery Neolithic. By 7000 B.P., pottery had become widespread in the Middle East. Archaeologists consider pottery shape, finishing, decoration, and type of clay as features used for dating.

The geographic distribution of a given pottery style may indicate trade or alliance spanning a large area at a particular time.

An early and widespread pottery style, the **Halafian,** was first found at Tell Halaf in the mountains of northern Syria. Halafian (7500–6500 B.P.) refers to a delicate ceramic style. It also describes the period during which the elite level and the first chiefdoms emerged. The low number of Halafian ceramics suggests they were luxury goods associated with a social hierarchy.

By 7000 B.P. chiefdoms had emerged in the Middle East. The Ubaid period (7000–6000 B.P.) is named for a southern Mesopotamian pottery type first discovered at a small site, Tell el-Ubaid, located near the major city of Ur in southern Iraq. Similar pottery has been discovered in the deep levels of the Mesopotamian cities of Ur, Uruk, and Eridu. Ubaid pottery is associated with advanced chiefdoms and perhaps the earliest states. It diffused rapidly over a large area, becoming more widespread than earlier ceramic styles such as the Halafian.

Social Ranking and Chiefdoms 🗡

It is easy for archaeologists to identify early states. Evidence for state organization includes monumental architecture, central storehouses, irrigation systems, and written records. In Mesoamerica, even chiefdoms are easy to detect archaeologically. Ancient Mexican chiefdoms left behind stone works, such as temple complexes and the huge carved Olmec heads (see p. 246). Mesoamericans also had a penchant for marking their elites with durable ornaments and prestige goods, including those buried with chiefs and their families. Early Middle Eastern chiefs were less ostentatious in their use of material markers of prestige, making their chiefdoms somewhat harder to detect archaeologically (Flannery 1999).

On the basis of the kinds of status distinctions within society, the anthropologist Morton Fried (1960) divided societies into three types: egalitarian, ranked, and stratified (Table 11.1). An **egalitarian society,** most typically found among foragers, lacks status distinctions except for those based on age, gender, and individual qualities, talents, and achievements. Thus, depending on the society, adult men, elder women, talented musicians, or ritual specialists might receive special respect for their activities or knowledge. In egalitarian societies, status distinctions are not usually inherited. The child of a respected person will not receive special recognition because of his or her parent, but must earn such respect.

Ranked societies, in contrast, do have hereditary inequality. But they lack **stratification** (sharp

Biocultural Case Study

For more on the peopling of the Pacific, where many chiefdoms developed—and on how anthropology's subfields unite to solve a particular problem—see the "Bringing It All Together" essay that immediately follows this chapter.

TABLE 11.1	**Egalitarian, Ranked, and Stratified Societies**			
Kind of Status Distinction	**Nature of Status**	**Common Form of Subsistence Economy**	**Common Forms of Social Organization**	**Examples**
Egalitarian	Status differences are not inherited. All status is based on age, gender, and individual qualities, talents, and achievements.	Foraging	Bands and tribes	Inuit, Ju/'hoansi San, and Yanomami
Ranked	Status differences are inherited and distributed along a continuum from the highest-ranking member (chief) to the lowest without any breaks.	Horticulture, pastoralism, and some foraging groups	Chiefdoms and some tribes	Native American groups of the Pacific Northwest (for example, Salish and Kwakiutl), Natchez, Halaf and Ubaid period polities, Olmec
Stratified	Status differences are inherited and divided sharply between distinct noble and commoner classes.	Agriculture	States	Teotihuacan, Uruk Period states, Inca, Shang dynasty, Rome, U.S., Great Britain

social divisions—*strata*—based on unequal access to wealth and power) into noble and commoner classes. In ranked societies, individuals tend to be ranked in terms of their genealogical distance from the chief. Closer relatives of the chief have higher rank or social status than more distant ones do. But there is a continuum of status, with many individuals and kin groups ranked about equally, which can lead to competition for positions of leadership.

Not all ranked societies are chiefdoms. Robert Carneiro (1991) has distinguished between two kinds of ranked societies, only the second of which is a chiefdom. In the first type, exemplified by some Indians of North America's Pacific Northwest, there were hereditary differences in rank among individuals, but villages were independent of one another and not ranked in relation to each other. Exemplifying the second type were the Cauca of Colombia and the Natchez of the eastern United States. These ranked societies had become **chiefdoms,** societies in which relations among villages as well as among individuals were unequal. The smaller villages had lost their autonomy and were under the authority of leaders who lived at larger villages. According to Kent Flannery (1999), *only those ranked societies with such loss of village autonomy should be called chiefdoms.* In chiefdoms, there is always inequality—differences in rank—among both individuals and communities.

In Mesopotamia, Mesoamerica, and Peru, chiefdoms were precursors to **primary states** (states that arose on their own, not through contact with other state societies—see Wright 1994). Primary states emerged from competition among chiefdoms, as one chiefdom managed to conquer its neighbors and to make them part of a larger political unit (Flannery 1995).

Archaeological evidence for chiefdoms in Mesoamerica dates back more than 3,000 years. Mesoamerican chiefdoms are easy to detect archaeologically because they were flamboyant in the way they marked their aristocracy. High-status families deformed the heads of their infants and buried them with special symbols and grave goods. In burials, prestige goods show a continuum from graves with many, to less, to no precious materials, such as jade and turquoise (Flannery 1999).

The first Middle Eastern states developed between 6000 and 5500 B.P. The first societies based on rank, including the first chiefdoms, emerged during the preceding 1,500 years. In the Middle East, the archaeological record of the period after 7300 B.P. reveals behavior typical of chiefdoms, including exotic goods used as markers of status, along with raiding and political instability. Early Middle Eastern chiefdoms included both the Halafian culture of northern Iraq and the Ubaid culture of southern Iraq, which eventually spread north.

As in Mesoamerica, ancient Middle Eastern chiefdoms had cemeteries where chiefly relatives were buried with distinctive items: vessels, statuettes, necklaces, and high-quality ceramics. Such goods were buried with children too young to have earned prestige on their own, who happened to be born into elite families. In the ancient village of Tell es-Sawwan, infant graves show a continuum of richness from six statuettes, to three statuettes, to one statuette, to none. Such signs of slight gradations in social status are exactly what one expects in ranked societies (Flannery 1999).

Such burials convince Flannery (1999) that hereditary status differences were present in the

Middle East by 7000 B.P. But had the leaders of large villages extended their authority to the smaller villages nearby? Is there evidence for the loss of village autonomy, converting simple ranked societies into chiefdoms? One clue that villages were linked in political units is the use of a common canal to irrigate several villages. This suggests a way of resolving disputes among farmers over access to water, for example, by appeal to a strong leader. By later Halafian times in northern Mesopotamia, there is evidence for such multivillage alliances (Flannery 1999). Another clue to the loss of village autonomy is the emergence of a two-tier settlement hierarchy, with small villages clustering around a large village, especially one with public buildings. There is evidence for this pattern in northern Mesopotamia during the Halafian (Watson 1983).

How Ethnography Helps in Interpreting the Archaeological Record

When they excavate sites, how do archaeologists know whether they've found a chiefdom, or some less complex form of society? Grave goods and settlement hierarchy offer clues. Also, studying ethnography helps archaeologists interpret the past.

Thus, to infer the archaeological characteristics of ancient Middle Eastern chiefdoms, Kent Flannery (1999) looks to recent chiefdoms that have been studied ethnographically in that region. One example is the Basseri, a population of 16,000 migratory herders in Iran (Barth 1964). The Basseri had a large grazing territory, but some of their chiefly families also owned farming villages and city homes. Leading the Basseri was a chief, whose brothers, cousins, uncles, and nephews vied for leadership during "periods of confusion" (Barth 1964). Such political rivalry among close kin is typical of chiefdoms worldwide.

Using the Basseri as an ethnographic analogy, Flannery (1999) suggests likely characteristics of an ancient Middle Eastern chiefdom. Such an ancient confederacy of several thousand people would have had a hereditary aristocracy, but no capital city. There would have been no palace, no temples, no clear territorial boundaries. Its thousands of tents would barely leave a trace archaeologically. But by analogy with the Basseri, we might find remains of a few chiefly houses in mud-walled cities.

According to Barth (1964), a Basseri chief's home was large—to entertain visitors. The chief gave substantial gifts to his prominent subjects, who were expected to reciprocate. The chief's close kinsmen were almost as privileged as he was. By analogy, Flannery (1999) suggests, to identify an ancient Middle Eastern chiefdom, archaeologists should look not for one unique residence but also for the nearby houses of chiefly kin. Such homes would be large enough to entertain many visitors (perhaps with a spacious central court). They might have a large kitchen and storerooms for food staples and craft products used as gifts. Indeed, prehistoric houses fitting this description have been found (Jasim 1985).

According to Robert Carneiro (1991), raiding is especially common in chiefdoms. Illustrating such raiding, early chiefdoms in Mexico and Peru had public art featuring enemy corpses, mutilated prisoners, and trophy heads (Marcus 1992). Middle Eastern chiefdoms lacked this kind of art. But their sites did have defensive walls, ditches, and watchtowers comparable to those of Mesoamerica. Political alliance also offered some protection against raiding.

Despite their defenses and alliances, prehistoric chiefdoms were still raided. There is archaeological evidence that large houses, belonging to community leaders, were sacked and burned during raids in the Halafian and Ubaid periods. Consider Tepe Gawra, a site dating to the late Ubaid period (Tobler 1950). This densely packed town was defended by its position atop a mound, and by a watchtower. Its largest residence had an inner court that illustrates the kind of large, elegant reception space Flannery (1999) expects to find in the home of a chief who hosted many subordinates and visitors. There was also a large kitchen.

On the same street was a slightly less impressive residence, supporting the belief that archaeologists should look for multiple elite houses in chiefly neighborhoods. This town had been raided and partly burned. At least four victims—a baby and three youths—were left unburied in the ruins. The building hardest hit was that with the largest inner court, confirming that, as is usual, the chiefly family was the raid's main target.

This funerary chamber from Sipan, Peru (a Moche site), contains gold jewelry, pottery, and other artifacts. In chiefdoms and states, high-status families often bury their dead with distinctive symbols and grave goods.

Illustrating pictographic writing is this limestone tablet from the proto-urban period of lower Mesopotamia. This Sumerian script records proper names, including that of a landowner—symbolized by the hand—who commissioned the tablet.

From such clues—archaeological and ethnographic—we infer that chiefly families and a pattern of raiding one's rivals were present in the Middle East between 7300 and 5800 B.P.

Advanced Chiefdoms

In northeastern Syria, near the border with Iraq, archaeologists have been excavating an ancient settlement that once lay on a major trade route. This large site, Tell Hamoukar, dates back more than 5,500 years (Wilford 2000). Its remains suggest that advanced chiefdoms arose in northern areas of the Middle East independently of the better-known city-states of southern Mesopotamia, in southern Iraq (Wilford 2000).

The oldest layer yet uncovered at Tell Hamoukar contains traces of villages dating back 6,000 years. By 5700 B.P. the settlement was a prosperous town of 32 acres, enclosed by a defensive wall 10 feet (3 meters) high and 13 feet (3.9 meters) wide. The site had fine pottery and large ovens—evidence of food preparation on an institutional scale. The site has yielded pieces of large cooking pots, animal bones, and traces of wheat, barley, and oats for baking and brewing. The archaeologist McGuire Gibson, one of the excavators, believes that food preparation on this scale is evidence of a ranked society in which elites were organizing people and resources (Wilford 2000). Most likely they were hosting and entertaining in a chiefly manner (as discussed in the preceding section).

Also providing evidence for social ranking are the seals used to mark containers of food and other goods. Some of the seals are small, with only simple incisions or cross-hatching. Others are larger and more elaborate, presumably for higher officials to stamp more valuable goods. Gibson suspects the larger seals with figurative

scenes were held by the few people who had greater authority. The smaller, simply incised seals were used by many more people with less authority (Wilford 2000).

The Rise of the State

In southern Mesopotamia at this time (5700 B.P.), an expanding population and increased food production from irrigation were changing the social landscape even more drastically than in the north. Irrigation had allowed Ubaid communities to spread along the Euphrates River. Travel and trade were expanding, with water serving as the highway system. Such raw materials as hardwood and stone, which southern Mesopotamia lacked, were imported via river routes. Population density increased as new settlements appeared. Social and economic networks now linked communities on the rivers in the south and in the foothills to the north. Settlements spread north into what is now Syria. Social differentials also increased. Priests and political leaders joined expert potters and other specialists. These non-food-producers were supported by the larger population of farmers and herders (Gilmore-Lehne 2000).

Economies were being managed by central leadership. Agricultural villages had grown into cities, some of which were ruled by local kings. The Uruk period (6000–5200 B.P.), which succeeded the Ubaid period, takes its name from a prominent southern city-state located more than 400 miles south of Tell Hamoukar (Table 11.2). The Uruk period established Mesopotamia as "the cradle of civilization" (see Pollock 1999).

There is no evidence of Uruk influence at Tell Hamoukar until 5200 B.P., when some Uruk pottery showed up. When southern Mesopotamians expanded north, they found advanced chiefdoms, which were not yet states. The fact that writing

 STUDENT CD-ROM LIVING ANTHROPOLOGY

The First States
Track 11

The clip offers brief views of Mesopotamia and Egypt, plus commentary by a Canadian professor. The clip poses the contrast between the "city-states" of Mesopotamia and the Egyptian "empire," implying a difference in the scale of political organization, with the Egyptian state controlling a much larger territory than did the rulers of Mesopotamia. What was the key factor in Egyptian territorial expansion? Besides the pharaoh, ancient Egypt had a vizier, who administered state officials and oversaw the royal treasury. What kind of role did rulers and temple officials play, according to the clip and the text, in the Mesopotamian city-states? Based on the clip, the text, and the news story at the beginning of this chapter, what kind of association existed between religion and political control in the two areas?

originated in Sumer, in southern Mesopotamia, indicates a more advanced, state-organized society there. The first writing presumably developed to handle record keeping for a centralized economy.

Writing was initially used to keep accounts, reflecting the needs of trade. Rulers, nobles, priests, and merchants were the first to benefit from it. As we saw in the news brief at the beginning of this chapter, writing had reached Egypt by 5200 B.P., probably from Mesopotamia. The earliest writing was pictographic, for example, with pictorial symbols of horses used to represent them.

Early Mesopotamian scribes used a stylus (writing implement) to scrawl symbols on raw clay. This writing left a wedge-shaped impression on the clay, called **cuneiform** writing, from the Latin word for wedge. Both the Sumerian (southern Mesopotamia) and Akkadian (northern Mesopotamia) languages were written in cuneiform (Gowlett 1993).

Writing and temples played key roles in the Mesopotamian economy. For the historic period after 5600 B.P., when writing was invented, there are temple records of economic activities. States can exist without writing, but literacy facilitates the flow and storage of information. We know that Mesopotamian priests managed herding, farming, manufacture, and trade. Temple officials allotted fodder and pasture land for cattle and donkeys, which were used as plow and cart animals. As the economy expanded, trade, manufacture, and grain storage were centrally managed. Temples collected and distributed meat, dairy products, crops, fish, clothing, tools, and trade items. Potters, metal workers, weavers, sculptors, and other artisans perfected their crafts.

Prior to the invention of **metallurgy** (knowledge of the properties of metals, including their extraction and processing and the manufacture of metal tools), raw copper was shaped by hammer-

Early Mesopotamian scribes used a stylus to scrawl symbols on raw clay. This writing, called cuneiform, left a wedge-shaped impression on the clay. What languages were written in cuneiform?

ing. If copper is hammered too long, it hardens and becomes brittle, with a risk of cracking. But once heated (annealed) in a fire, copper becomes malleable again. Such annealing of copper was an early form of metallurgy. A vital step for metallurgy was the discovery of **smelting,** the high-temperature process by which pure metal is produced from an ore. Ores, including copper ore, have a much wider distribution than does native copper, which was initially traded as a luxury good because of its rarity (Gowlett 1993).

See the Virtual Exploration for information about early writing in the Indus Valley

mhhe.com/kottak

TABLE 11.2	Archaeological Periods in Middle Eastern State Formation	
Dates	Period	Age
3000–2539 B.P.	Neo-Babylonian	Iron Age
3600–3000 B.P.	Kassite	
4000–3600 B.P.	Old Babylonian	Bronze Age
4150–4000 B.P.	Third Dynasty of Ur	
4350–4150 B.P.	Akkadian	
4600–4350 B.P.	Early Dynastic III	
4750–4600 B.P.	Early Dynastic II	
5000–4750 B.P.	Early Dynastic I	
5200–5000 B.P.	Jemdet Nasr	
6000–5200 B.P.	Uruk	Chalcolithic (Copper/Stone)
7500–6000 B.P.	Ubaid (southern Mesopotamia)–Halaf (northern Mesopotamia)	
10,000–7000 B.P.		Neolithic

■ This ziggurat, or temple tower, at Ur, Iraq, dates back to 4100 B.P. (2100 B.C.E.). Temples and their officials played key roles in the Mesopotamian economy. Who handles such duties in our society?

Map Atlas

Maps 9 and 13 locate the archaic states that developed in the Middle East, Asia, Africa, Europe, and the Americas.

royal cemetery, by 4600 B.P. monarchs were being buried with soldiers, charioteers, and ladies in waiting. These subordinates were killed at the time of a royal burial to accompany the monarch to the afterworld.

Agricultural intensification made it possible for the number of people supported by a given area to increase. Population pressure on irrigated fields helped create a stratified society. Land became scarce private property that was bought and sold. Some people amassed large estates, and their wealth set them off from ordinary farmers. These landlords joined the urban elite, while sharecroppers and serfs toiled in the fields. By 4600 B.P., Mesopotamia had a well-defined class structure, with complex stratification into nobles, commoners, and slaves.

When and how smelting was discovered is unknown. But after 5000 B.P., metallurgy evolved rapidly. The Bronze Age began when alloys of arsenic and copper, or tin and copper (in both cases known as **bronze**), became common and greatly extended the use of metals. Bronze flows more easily than copper does when heated to a similar temperature, so bronze was more convenient for metal casting. Early molds were carved in stone, as shaped depressions to be filled with molten metal. A copper ax cast from such a mold has been found in northern Mesopotamia and predates 5000 B.P. Thereafter, other metals came into common use. By 4500 B.P. golden objects were found in royal burials at Ur.

Iron ore is distributed more widely than is copper ore. Iron, when smelted, can be used on its own; there is no need for tin or arsenic to make a metal alloy (bronze). The Iron Age began once high-temperature iron smelting was mastered. In the Old World after 3200 B.P., iron spread rapidly. Formerly valued as highly as gold, iron crashed in value when it became plentiful (Gowlett 1993).

The Mesopotamian economy, based on craft production, trade, and intensive agriculture, spurred population growth and an increase in urbanism. Sumerian cities were protected by a fortress wall and surrounded by a farming area. By 4800 B.P., Uruk, the largest early Mesopotamian city, had a population of 50,000. As irrigation and the population expanded, communities fought over water. People sought protection in the fortified cities (Adams 1981), which defended themselves when neighbors or invaders threatened.

By 4600 B.P., secular authority had replaced temple rule. The office of military coordinator developed into kingship. This change shows up architecturally in palaces and royal tombs. The palace raised armies and supplied them with armor, chariots, and metal armaments. At Ur's

OTHER EARLY STATES

In northwestern India and Pakistan, the Indus River Valley (or *Harappan*) state, with major cities at Harappa and Mohenjo-daro, takes its name from the river valley along which it extended. (Figure 11.3 maps the four great early river valley states of the Old World: Mesopotamia, Egypt, India/Pakistan, and northern China.) Trade and the spread of writing from Mesopotamia may have played a role in the emergence of the Harappan state around 4600 B.P. Located in Pakistan's Punjab Province, the ruins of Harappa were the first to be identified as part of the Indus River Valley civilization. At its peak, the Indus River Valley state incorporated 1,000 cities, towns, and villages, spanning 280,000 square miles (725,000 square kilometers). This state flourished between 4600 and 3900 B.P. It displayed such features of state organization as urban planning, social stratification, and an early writing system, which remains undeciphered. The Harappans maintained a uniform system of weights, and their cites had carefully planned residential areas with wastewater systems. An array of products from sophisticated craft industries included ceramic vessels made on potter's wheels (Meadow and Kenoyer 2000).

The Indus River Valley state collapsed, apparently through warfare, around 3900 B.P. Its cities became largely depopulated. Skeletons of massacre victims have been found in the streets of Mohenjo-daro. Harappa continued to be occupied, but on a much smaller scale than previously (Meadow and Kenoyer 2000). (For more on the ongoing Harappa Archaeological Research Project, visit http://www.harappa.com.)

The first Chinese state, dating to 3750 B.P., was that of the Shang dynasty. It arose in the Huang He (Yellow) River area of northern China, where wheat, rather than rice, was the dietary staple. This state was characterized by urbanism, pala-

242   PART 2   Physical Anthropology and Archaeology

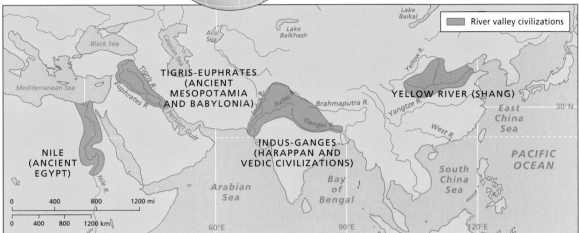

FIGURE 11.3 The Four Great Early River Valley States of the Old World.

By approximately 4000 B.P. urban life had been established along the Tigris and Euphrates rivers in Mesopotamia, the Nile River in Egypt, the Indus and Ganges rivers in India/Pakistan, and the Yellow River in China.
SOURCE: Based on Map 1-1, Chapter 1, "Birth of Civilization." In Albert M. Craig, *The Heritage of World Civilizations, Volume I, to 1650,* 4th ed. Upper Saddle River, NJ: Prentice Hall, 1997.

tial (as well as domestic) architecture, human sacrifice, and a sharp division between social classes. Burials of the aristocracy were marked by ornaments of stone, including jade. The Shang had bronze metallurgy and an elaborate writing system. In warfare they used chariots and took prisoners (Gowlett 1993).

Like Mesopotamia and China, many early civilizations came to rely on metallurgy. At Nok Nok Tha in northern Thailand, metalworking goes back 6,000 years. In Peru's Andes, metalworking appeared around 4000 B.P. The ancient inhabitants of the Andes were skilled workers of bronze, copper, and gold. They are also well known for their techniques of pottery manufacture. Their arts, crafts, and agricultural knowledge compared well with those of Mesoamerica at its height, to which we turn after a discussion of African states. Note that both Mesoamerican and Andean state formation were truncated by Spanish conquest. The Aztecs of Mexico were conquered in A.D. 1519; and the Inca of Peru, in 1532.

African States

Egypt, a major ancient civilization, developed in northern Africa, as one of the world's first states (Morkot 2005). Egyptian influence extended southward along the Nile into what is now Sudan. Sub-Saharan Africa witnessed the emergence of several states (Hooker 1996), only a few of which can be described here.

This bronze vessel was commissioned during China's Shang dynasty. The small elephant on top forms the handle of the lid. Wine was poured through the spout formed by the big elephant's trunk. Three notable features of the Shang dynasty were bronze, writing, and social stratification.

As in the other world areas just discussed, metallurgy (especially iron and gold) played a role in the eventual rise of African states (Connah 2004). About 2,000 years ago, iron smelting began to diffuse rapidly throughout the continent. That spread was aided by the migrations of Bantu speakers. (Bantu is Africa's largest linguistic family.) The Bantu migrations, launched from north central Africa around 2100 B.P., continued for more than a thousand years. Bantu speakers migrated south into the rain forests of the Congo River and east into the African highlands. Along with their language and iron-smelting techniques, they also spread farming, particularly

For more on state formation in Africa, see the Internet Exercises at your OLC
mhhe.com/kottak

The Akhenaten Temple Project

BACKGROUND INFORMATION

STUDENT:
Jerusha Achterberg

SUPERVISING PROFESSOR:
Donald Redford

SCHOOL:
Pennsylvania State University

YEAR IN SCHOOL/MAJOR:
Senior/Anthropology

MINORS:
Mathematics/Education
Policy Studies

FUTURE PLANS:
Graduate school

PROJECT TITLE:
The Akhenaten Temple Project

What is the nature of the student work described here? How independent was this research?

My first archaeological fieldwork experience was in Egypt, where I worked as a site supervisor on the 10th round of excavations at Mendes (Tel er-Rub'a), on Middle Kingdom levels of that site in summer 2000. As a newcomer to the field, many techniques were unfamiliar to me. But the most difficult things for me to adapt to were the working conditions. Egyptian weather in July was not what my body was used to, and I was unprepared for what it would be like to work primarily with a team of native workers with whom I shared very little language. I was assigned a dig site, and a team of Egyptian workers including a Kufdi, who essentially guided the team, two pickmen and four basket-girls who removed the dirt after excavation. Rather than my primary job being the digging, as site supervisor, I recorded, measured, and mapped all our finds and loci. I was also responsible for making on-the-spot decisions about the course of our progress.

Because I had done no hands-on archeology before my arrival in Egypt, I was surprised by how quickly I learned the techniques we used. I kept constant records of every find in my site, as well as of the soil type. For those who have not worked in Egypt, it is hard to imagine the sheer volume of pottery that is found at the sites. Every piece had to be sorted and catalogued following excavation. As a result, after excavating from 6 A.M.–1 P.M., we spent the afternoons sorting and washing pottery. On occasion I was able to participate in the more specialized tasks, such as tracing the stance of representative pottery fragments and sorting through the small finds collection.

One job in which I found particular skill was rebuilding pottery vessels from the excavated fragments. This job is important, although too tedious for most people's patience. I found the repetitiveness of the work relaxing compared to the excavation work of the morning. Also, because of my past work in mathematics I found I was good at profiling the excavation site stratigraphy, and drawing spatial representations of the architecture and finds. This work was usually done with a partner. One person called out measurements from a baseline, while the other plotted the information on a grid. This was later fleshed out with information about the materials involved, orientation, and presence of particular features. Prior to going to Egypt, I was concerned about handling human remains. I had never had a problem considering the idea while sitting in a classroom, but I worried that the hands-on work might be different. Recalling this worry was humorous after several hours of cleaning off a human skull. I had become so involved with the work and the satisfaction of slowly revealing the fragile bone, it hadn't occurred to me to be concerned about handling the remains. In fact, it seemed as though the care I was granting the skull was more respectful than leaving it in the ground to weather further. My reaction, or lack thereof, came as a surprise to me, but a welcome one. Overall, I'm very proud of the work I did in Egypt and the help I provided to the ongoing work at Mendes.

of high-yielding crops such as yams, bananas, and plantains.

One crowning achievement of the Bantu migrations was the Mwenemutapa empire. The southeast-moving ancestors of the Mwenemutapa brought iron smelting and farming to the region called Zimbabwe, south of the Zambezi River and located within the contemporary nation of the same name. This area was rich in gold, which the Mwenemutapa mined and traded with the city of Sofala on the Indian Ocean, starting around 1000 C.E. (1000 B.P.). The Mwenemutapa developed a powerful kingdom based on trade. The first centralized state there was Great Zimbabwe (*zimbabwe* means "stone enclosure"—the capital was protected by huge stone walls), which arose around

1300 C.E. (700 B.P.). By 1500, Great Zimbabwe dominated the Zambezi Valley militarily and commercially as the seat of the Mwenemutapa empire.

Another African region where states arose, also abetted by trade, was the Sahel, the area just south of the Sahara in western Africa. Farming towns started appearing in the Sahel around 2600 B.P. One such town, Kumbi Saleh, eventually became the capital of the ancient kingdom of Ghana. West Africa was rich in gold, precious metals, ivory, and other resources, which after 750 C.E. (1250 B.P.) were traded (thanks to the camel) across the Sahara to North Africa, Egypt, and the Middle East. Cities in the Sahel served as southern terminal points for the trans-Saharan trade (e.g., of gold for salt). Several kingdoms developed in this area: Ghana, Mali, Songhay, and Kanem-Bornu, together known as the Sahelian kingdoms, of which Ghana was the first. By 1000 B.P. Ghana's economic vitality, based on the trans-Saharan trade, was supporting an empire formed through the conquest of local chiefdoms, from which tribute was extracted.

States also arose in the forested region of western Africa south of the Sahel. Between 1000 and 1500 C.E., local farming villages started consolidating into larger units, which eventually became centralized states. The largest and most enduring of these states was Benin, in what is now southern Nigeria. Benin, which thrived in the 15th century C.E. (600–500 B.P.), is known for its artistic creativity, expressed in terracotta, ivory, and brass sculpture. Benin art became one of the most influential African art traditions.

STATE FORMATION IN MESOAMERICA

In the last chapter we examined the independent inventions of farming in the Middle East and Mesoamerica. The processes of state formation that took place in these areas were also comparable, beginning with ranked societies and chiefdoms, and ending with fully formed states and empires.

The first monumental buildings (temple complexes) in the Western Hemisphere were constructed by Mesoamerican chiefdoms in many areas, from the Valley of Mexico to Guatemala. These chiefdoms influenced one another as they traded materials, such as obsidian, shells, jade, and pottery. (Figure 11.4 maps major sites in the emergence of Mesoamerican food production, chiefdoms, and states.)

Early Chiefdoms and Elites

The Olmec built a series of ritual centers on Mexico's southern Gulf Coast between 3,200 and 2,500 years ago. Three of these centers, each from a different century, are known. Earthen mounds were grouped into plaza complexes, presumably for religious use. Such centers show that Olmec chiefs could marshal human labor to construct such mounds. The Olmec were also master sculptors; they carved massive stone heads, perhaps as images of their chiefs or their ancestors.

There is evidence, too, that trade routes linked the Olmec with other parts of Mesoamerica, such as the Valley of Oaxaca in the southern highlands and the Valley of Mexico (see Figure 11.4). By 3000 B.P. a ruling elite had emerged in Oaxaca. The items traded at that time between Oaxaca and the Olmec were for elite consumption. High-status Oaxacans wore ornaments made of mussel shells from the coast. In return, the Olmec elite imported mirrors and jade made by Oaxacan artisans. Chiefdoms in Oaxaca developed canal and well irrigation, exported magnetite mirrors, and were precocious in their use of adobes (mud bricks), stucco, stone masonry, and architecture.

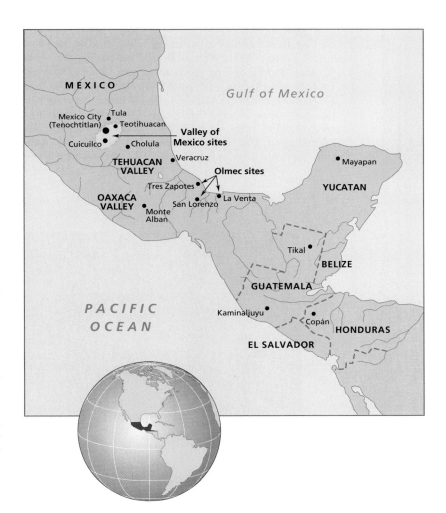

FIGURE 11.4 Major Sites in the Emergence of Food Production and the State in Mesoamerica. SOURCE: From C. J. Jolly and F. Plog, *Physical Anthropology and Archaeology*, 4th ed. (New York: McGraw-Hill, 1986), p. 115.

Pseudo-Archaeology

The study of prehistory has spawned popular-culture creations, including movies, TV programs, and books. In these fictional works, the anthropologists (and the natives as well) usually don't bear much resemblance to their real-life counterparts. Unlike Indiana Jones, normal and reputable archaeologists don't have nonstop adventures—fighting Nazis, lashing whips, or rescuing antiquities. The archaeologist's profession isn't a matter of raiding lost arks or of going on crusades but of reconstructing lifeways through the analysis of material remains, in order to understand culture and human behavior.

Much of the popular nonfiction dealing with prehistory is also suspect. Through books and the mass media, we have been exposed to the ideas of popular writers such as Thor Heyerdahl and Erich von Daniken. Heyerdahl, a well-known diffusionist, believed that developments in one world area were usually based on ideas borrowed from another. Von Daniken carried diffusionism one step further, proposing that major human

achievements had been borrowed from beings from space who visited us at various periods of our past. Heyerdahl and von Daniken seemed to share (with some science-fiction writers) a certain contempt for human inventiveness and originality. They took the position that major changes in ancient human lifestyles were the results of outside instruction or interference rather than the achievements of the natives of the places where the changes took place.

In *The Ra Expeditions* (Heyerdahl 1971), for example, world traveler and adventurer Heyerdahl argued that his voyage in a papyrus boat from the Mediterranean to the Caribbean demonstrated that ancient Egyptians could have navigated to the New World. (The boat was modeled on an ancient Egyptian vessel, but Heyerdahl and his crew took along such modern conveniences as a radio and canned goods.) Heyerdahl maintained that given the possibility of ancient transatlantic voyages, Old World people could have influenced the emergence of civilization in the Americas.

What is the scientific evaluation of Heyerdahl's contention? Even if Old World ancients had reached the New World, they couldn't have done much to propel Native Americans toward state organization because the New World wasn't yet ready for food production and the state. When Egypt became a major power capable of sending scouts across the seas, around 5,000 years ago, Mexicans were broad-spectrum foragers. The gradual nature of the Mesoamerican transition from foraging to food production is clearly demonstrated by archaeological sequences in such sites as Oaxaca and the Valley of Mexico. Had foreign inputs been important, they would have shown up in the material remains that constitute the archaeological record.

Beginning some 2,000 years ago, states comparable to those of Mesopotamia and Egypt began to rise and fall in the Mexican highlands. This occurred more than 1,000 years after the height of ancient Egyptian influence, between 3600 and 3400 B.P. Had Egypt or any other ancient Old World state contributed to the rise

This colossal Olmec head, carved from basalt, is displayed at the La Venta Archaeology Museum in Tabasco state, Mexico, in a setting designed to recall its original site. What is the significance of such a massive artifact?

Chiefdoms in the Olmec area farmed river levees, built mounds of earth, and carved colossal stone heads.

The Olmec are famous for their huge carved stone heads, but other early Mexican chiefdoms also had accomplished artists and builders, using adobes and lime plaster and constructing stone buildings, precisely oriented 8 degrees north of east.

The period between 3200 and 3000 B.P. was one of rapid social change in Mexico. All or almost all of Mesoamerica's chiefdoms were linked by trade and exchange. Many competing chiefly centers were concentrating labor power, intensifying agriculture, exchanging trade goods, and borrowing ideas, including art motifs and styles, from each other. Archaeologists now believe it was the *intensity of competitive interaction*—rather than the supremacy of any one chiefdom—that made social change so rapid. The social and political landscape of Mexico around 3000 B.P. was one in which 25 or so chiefly centers were (1) sufficiently separate and autonomous to adapt to local zones

How much does Indiana Jones tell us about real archaeologists? The photo is from Indiana Jones and the Temple of Doom.

or the fall of Mesoamerican civilization, we would expect this influence to have been exerted during Egypt's heyday as an ancient power—not 1,500 years later.

There is abundant archaeological evidence for the gradual, evolutionary emergence of food production and the state in the Middle East, in Mesoamerica, and in Peru. This evidence effectively counters the diffusionist theories about how and why human achievements, including farming and the state, began. Popular theories to the contrary, changes, advances, and setbacks in ancient American social life were the products of the ideas and activities of the Native Americans themselves.

There is simply no valid evidence for Old World interference before the European Age of Discovery, which began late in the 15th century. Francisco Pizzaro conquered Peru's Inca state in 1532, 11 years after its Mesoamerican counterpart, Tenochtitlan, the Aztec capital, fell to Spanish conquistadores in 1521. (We do have abundant archaeological, as well as written, evidence for this recent, historically known contact between Europeans and Native Americans.)

The archaeological record also casts doubt on contentions that the advances of earthlings came with extraterrestrial help, as Erich von Daniken argued in his book *Chariots of the Gods* (1971), and as Discovery-type TV sometimes suggests. Abundant, well-analyzed archaeological data from the Middle East, Mesoamerica, and Peru tell a clear story. Plant and animal domestication, the state, and city life were not brilliant discoveries, inventions, or secrets that humans needed to borrow from extraterrestrials. They were long-term, gradual processes, developments with down-to-earth causes and effects. They required thousands of years of orderly change, not some chance meeting in the high Andes between an ancient Inca chief and a beneficent Johnny Appleseed from Aldebaran.

This is not to deny, by the way, that intelligent life and civilizations at a variety of technological levels—some more, some less advanced than Earth—may exist throughout the galaxy or even that extraterrestrials may have occasionally ventured into this relatively isolated outer spiral arm of the Milky Way galaxy and even visited Earth itself. However, even if extraterrestrials have been on Earth, archaeological evidence suggests that their starship commanders observed a prime directive of noninterference in the affairs of less-advanced planets. There is no scientifically valid evidence for the rapid kind of change that sustained extraterrestrial intervention would have produced. What would constitute such evidence?

and conditions and (2) sufficiently interacting and competitive to borrow and incorporate new ideas and innovations as they arose in other regions (Flannery and Marcus 2000).

It used to be thought that a single chiefdom could become a state on its own. Archaeologists know now that state formation involves one chiefdom's incorporating several others into the emerging state it controls, and making changes in its own infrastructure as it acquires and holds on to new territories, followers, and goods. Warfare and attracting followers are two key elements in state formation.

Many chiefdoms have dense populations, intensive agriculture, and settlement hierarchies that include hamlets, villages, and perhaps towns. These factors pave the way for greater social and political complexity. Political leaders emerge, and military success (in raiding) often solidifies their position. Such figures attract lots of followers, who are loyal to their leader. Warfare enables leaders to incorporate new lands and people. Success in warfare leads to states' becoming even more densely occupied and in control of new lands. States, in contrast to chiefdoms, can acquire labor and land and hold on to them. States have armies, warfare, developed political hierarchies, law codes, and military force, which can be used in fact or as a threat.

The Olmec and Oaxaca were just two of many flamboyant early Mexican chiefdoms that once thrived in the area from the Valley of Mexico to Guatemala. Oaxaca went on to develop a state as early as the Teotihuacan state in the Valley of Mexico. Oaxaca and other highland areas came to overshadow the Olmec area and the Mesoamerican lowlands in general. By 2500 B.P. the Zapotec state at Oaxaca had developed a distinctive art style, perfected at its capital city of Monte Alban. The Zapotec state lasted almost 2,000 years, until it—along with the rest of Mexico—was conquered by Spain (see Blanton 1999; Marcus and Flannery 1996).

As the Olmec chiefdoms were declining, the elite level was spreading throughout Mesoamerica. By C.E. 1 (2000 B.P.), the Valley of Mexico, located in the highlands where Mexico City now

See the Internet Exercises at your OLC
mhhe.com/kottak

stands, came to prominence in Mesoamerican state formation. In this large valley **Teotihuacan** flourished between 1900 and 1300 B.P. (C.E. 100 and 700).

States in the Valley of Mexico

The Valley of Mexico is a large basin surrounded by mountains. The valley has rich volcanic soils, but rainfall isn't always reliable. The northern part of the valley, where the huge city and state of Teotihuacan eventually arose, is colder and drier than the south. Frosts there limited farming until quick-growing varieties of maize were developed. Until 2500 B.P., most people lived in the

■ *The Pyramid of the Sun, Teotihuacan's largest structure, is shown in the upper part of the photo. At its height around A.D. 500, Teotihuacan was larger than imperial Rome. The mobilization of manual labor to build such structures is one of the costs of state organization.*

■ *The Aztecs played the board game of patolli, as represented here in the Codex Magliabecchiano, housed in the National Library in Florence, Italy.*

warmer and wetter southern part of the valley, where rainfall made farming possible. After 2500 B.P., new maize varieties and small-scale irrigation appeared. Population increased and began to spread north.

By C.E. 1 Teotihuacan was a town of 10,000 people. It governed a territory of a few thousand square kilometers and perhaps 50,000 people (Parsons 1974). Teotihuacan's growth reflected its agricultural potential. Perpetual springs permitted irrigation of a large alluvial plain. Rural farmers supplied food for the growing urban population.

By this time, a clear **settlement hierarchy** had emerged. This is a ranked series of communities that differ in size, function, and building types. The settlements at the top of the hierarchy were political and religious centers. Those at the bottom were rural villages. Such a three-level settlement hierarchy (capital city, smaller urban centers, and rural villages) provides archaeological evidence of state organization (Wright and Johnson 1975).

Along with state organization went large-scale irrigation, status differentiation, and complex architecture. Teotihuacan thrived between C.E. 100 and 700. It grew as a planned city built on a grid pattern, with the Pyramid of the Sun at its center. By C.E. 500 the population of Teotihuacan had reached 130,000, making it larger than imperial Rome. Farmers were one of its diverse specialized groups, along with artisans, merchants, and political, religious, and military personnel.

After 700 C.E. Teotihuacan declined in size and power. By 900 C.E. its population had shrunk to 30,000. Between 900 and 1200 C.E., the Toltec period, the population scattered, and small cities and towns sprang up throughout the valley. People also left the Valley of Mexico to live in larger cities—like Tula, the Toltec capital—on its edge (see Figure 11.4).

Population increase (including immigration by the ancestors of the Aztecs) and urban growth returned to the Valley of Mexico between 1200 and 1520 C.E. During the **Aztec** period (1325 to 1520 C.E.) there were several cities, the largest of which—Tenochtitlan, the capital—may have surpassed Teotihuacan at its height. A dozen Aztec towns had more than 10,000 people. Fueling this population growth was intensification of agriculture, particularly in the southern part of the valley, where the drainage of lake bottoms and swamps added new cultivable land (Parsons 1976).

Another factor in the renaissance of the Valley of Mexico was trade. Local manufacture created products for a series of markets. The major towns and markets were located on the lake shores, with easy access to canoe traffic. The Aztec capital stood on an island in the lake. In Tenochtitlan, the production of luxury goods was more prestigious and more highly organized than that of pottery, basket making, and weaving. Luxury producers, such as stone workers, feather workers, and gold- and silversmiths, occupied a special position in Aztec society. The manufacture of luxury goods for export was an important part of the economy of the Aztec capital (Hassig 1985; Santley 1985).

WHY STATES COLLAPSE

States can be fragile and decomposable, falling apart along the same cleavage lines (e.g., regional political units) that were forged together to form the state originally. Various factors could threaten their economies and political institutions. Invasion, disease, famine, or prolonged drought could upset the balance. A state's citizens might harm the environment, usually with economic costs. For example, farmers and smelters might cut down trees. Such deforestation promotes erosion and leads to a decline in the water supply. Overuse of land may deplete the soil of the nutrients needed to grow crops.

If factors such as irrigation help create states to begin with, does their decline or failure explain the fall of the state? Irrigation does have costs as well as benefits. In ancient Mesopotamia, irrigation water came from the Tigris and Euphrates rivers. Because sediment (silt) had accumulated in those rivers, their beds were higher than the alluvial plain and fields they irrigated. Canals channeled river water as it flowed down into the fields by gravity. As the water evaporated, water-borne mineral salts remained in the fields, eventually creating a poisonous environment for plants.

Mashkan-shapir, for example, was a Mesopotamian city located about 20 miles from the Tigris, to which it was connected by a network of canals. This city was abandoned just 20 years after it was settled. Destruction of its fields by mineral salts seems to have been a prime factor in its collapse (see Annenberg/CPB Exhibits 2000 at http://www.learner.org/exhibits/collapse/mesopotamia.html).

The Mayan Decline

Generations of scholars have debated the decline of classic Mayan civilization around 900 C.E. (1700–1100 B.P.). Classic Mayan culture, featuring several competing states, flourished between 300 and 900 C.E. in parts of what are now Mexico, Honduras, El Salvador, Guatemala, and Belize. The ancient Maya are known for their monuments (temples and pyramids), calendars, mathematics, and hieroglyphic writing.

Archaeological clues to Mayan decline have been found at Copán, in western Honduras. This classic Maya royal center, the largest site in the

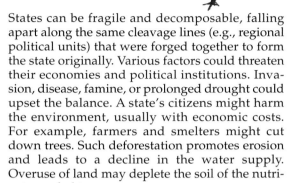

Ruins at Copán, a center of classic Mayan royalty in western Honduras.

southeastern part of the Maya area, covered 29 acres (11.7 hectares). It was built on an artificial terrace overlooking the Copán River. Its rulers inscribed their monuments with accounts of their coronation, their lineage history, and reports of important battles. The Maya dated their monuments with the names of kings and when they reigned. One monument at Copán was intended to be the ruler's throne platform, but only one side had been finished. The monument bears a date, 822 C.E., in a section of unfinished text. Copán has no monuments with later dates. The site probably was abandoned by 830 C.E.

Environmental factors implicated in Copán's demise may have included erosion and soil exhaustion due to overpopulation and overfarming. Overfarming contributes to deforestation and erosion. Hillside farmhouses in particular had debris from erosion—probably caused by overfarming of the hillsides. This erosion began as early as 750 C.E.—until these farm sites were abandoned, with some eventually buried by erosion debris. For the classic Maya in general, William Sanders (1972, 1973) has attributed state decline to overfarming, leading to environmental degradation through grass invasion and erosion.

Food stress and malnutrition were clearly present at Copán, where 80 percent of the buried skeletons display signs of anemia, due to iron deficiency. One skull shows anemia severe enough to have been the cause of death. Even the nobility were malnourished. One noble skull, known to be such from its carved teeth and cosmetic deformation, also has telltale signs of anemia: spongy areas at its rear (Annenberg/CPB Exhibits 2000).

Just as the origins of states, and their causes, are diverse, so are the reasons for state decline. The Mayan state was not as powerful as was once

Biocultural Case Study

For more on deforestation—and on how anthropology's subfields and dimensions unite to study this particular problem—see the "Bringing It All Together" essay on pp, 128–131, which follows Chapter 6.

assumed; it was fragile and vulnerable. Increased warfare and political competition destabilized many of its dynasties and governments. Archaeologists now stress the role of warfare in Mayan state decline. Hieroglyphic texts document increased warfare among many Mayan cities. From the period just before the collapse, there is archaeological evidence for increased concern with fortifications (moats, ditches, walls, and palisades) and moving to defensible locations. Archaeologists have evidence of the burning of structures, the projectile points from spears, and some of the bodies of those killed. Some sites were abandoned, with the people fleeing into the forests to occupy perishable huts. (Copán, as we have seen, was depopulated after 822 C.E.) Archaeologists now believe that social, political, and military upheaval and competition had as much as or more to do with the Mayan decline and abandonment of cities than did natural environmental factors (Marcus, personal communication).

Formerly archaeologists tended to explain state origin and decline mainly in terms of natural environmental factors, such as climate change, habitat destruction, and demographic pressure (see Weiss 2005). Archaeologists now see state origins and declines more fully—in social and political terms—because we can read the texts. And the Mayan texts document competition and warfare between dynasties jockeying for position and power. Warfare was indeed a creator and a destroyer of ancient chiefdoms and states. What's its role in our own?

SUMMARY

1. States develop to handle regulatory problems as the population grows and the economy gets more complex. Multiple factors contribute to state formation. Some appear repeatedly, but no single factor is always present. Among the most important factors are irrigation and long-distance trade. Coastal Peru, a very arid area, illustrates how environmental circumscription, population growth, and warfare may contribute to state formation.

2. A state is a society with a formal, central government and a division of society into classes. The first cities and states, supported by irrigated farming, developed in southern Mesopotamia between 6000 and 5500 B.P. Evidence for early state organization includes monumental architecture, central storehouses, irrigation systems, and written records.

3. Towns predate pottery in the Middle East. The first towns grew up 10,000 to 9,000 years ago. The first pottery dates back just over 8,000 years. Halafian (7500–6500 B.P.) refers to a pottery style and to the period when the first chiefdoms emerged. Ubaid pottery (7000–6000 B.P.) is associated with advanced chiefdoms and perhaps the earliest states. Most state formation occurred during the Uruk period (6100–5100 B.P.).

4. Based on the status distinctions they include, societies may be divided into egalitarian, ranked, and stratified. In egalitarian societies, status distinctions are not usually inherited. Ranked societies have hereditary inequality, but they lack stratification. Stratified societies have sharp social divisions—social classes or *strata*—based on unequal access to wealth and power. Ranked societies with loss of village autonomy are chiefdoms.

5. Mesopotamia's economy was based on craft production, trade, and intensive agriculture. Writing, invented by 5600 B.P., was first used to keep accounts for trade. With the invention of smelting, the Bronze Age began just after 5000 B.P.

6. In northwestern India and Pakistan, the Indus River Valley state flourished from 4600 to 3900 B.P. The first Chinese state, dating to 3750 B.P., was that of the Shang dynasty in northern China. Various states developed in sub-Saharan Africa. The major early states of the Western Hemisphere were in Mesoamerica and Peru.

7. States arose between 2500 and 1600 B.P. (500 B.C.E. and 400 C.E.) in Mesoamerica. Between 3200 and 3000 B.P., intense competitive interaction among the many chiefdoms in Mesoamerica at that time fueled rapid social change. Some chiefdoms would develop into states (e.g., Oaxaca, Valley of Mexico). Others (e.g., Olmec) would not. By 1 C.E. (2000 B.P.), the Valley of Mexico had come to prominence. In this large valley in the highlands, Teotihuacan thrived between 100 and 700 C.E. Tenochtitlan, the capital of the Aztec state (1325 to 1520 C.E.), may have surpassed Teotihuacan at its height.

8. Early states faced various threats: invasion, disease, famine, drought, soil exhaustion, erosion, and the buildup of irrigation salts. States may collapse when they fail to keep social and economic order or to protect themselves against outsiders. The Mayan state fell in the face of increased warfare among competing dynasties.

Aztec Last independent state in the Valley of Mexico; capital was Tenochtitlan. Thrived between 1325 C.E. and the Spanish Conquest in 1520.

bronze An alloy of arsenic and copper or tin and copper.

chiefdom A ranked society in which relations among villages as well as among individuals are unequal, with smaller villages under the authority of leaders in larger villages; has a two-level settlement hierarchy.

cuneiform Early Mesopotamian writing that used a stylus (writing implement) to write wedge-shaped impressions on raw clay; from the Latin word for wedge.

egalitarian society A type of society, most typically found among hunter-gatherers, that lacks status distinctions except for those based on age, gender, and individual qualities, talents, and achievements.

empire A mature, territorially large, and expansive, state; empires are typically multiethnic, multilinguistic, and more militaristic, with a better developed bureaucracy than earlier states.

Halafian An early (7500–6500 B.P.) and widespread pottery style, first found in northern Syria; refers to a delicate ceramic style and to the period when the first chiefdoms emerged.

Mesopotamia The area between the Tigris and Euphrates rivers in what is now southern Iraq and southwestern Iran; location of the first cities and states.

metallurgy Knowledge of the properties of metals, including their extraction and processing and the manufacture of metal tools.

multivariate Involving multiple factors, causes, or variables.

primary states States that arise on their own (through competition among chiefdoms), not through contact with other state societies.

ranked society A type of society with hereditary inequality but not social stratification; individuals are ranked in terms of their genealogical closeness to the chief, but there is a continuum of status, with many individuals and kin groups ranked about equally.

settlement hierarchy A ranked series of communities differing in size, function, and type of building; a three-level settlement hierarchy indicates state organization.

smelting The high-temperature process by which pure metal is produced from an ore.

state A form of social and political organization with a formal, central government and a division of society into classes.

stratification A stratified society has sharp social divisions—*strata*—based on unequal access to wealth and power (e.g., into noble and commoner classes).

Teotihuacan 100 to 700 C.E.; first state in the Valley of Mexico and earliest major Mesoamerican empire.

---

1. Was the origin of the state good or bad? Why?

2. What would be the advantages and disadvantages of being an early chief in the Middle East? Would you rather be the chief or a chief's close relative?

3. Imagine yourself an archaeologist trying to identify ancient chiefdoms in the Middle East after excavating Mesoamerican chiefdom sites. What similar and different lines of evidence for ranking and political alliance might you find in the two hemispheres?

4. What kinds of economic roles were available in early states, as compared with the earliest food-producing societies?

5. Why do you think the earliest states developed about 3,000 years later in Mesoamerica than in the Middle East? Imagine what might have happened if those states had developed at the same time.

Blanton, R. E.
  1999 *Ancient Oaxaca: The Monte Alban State.* New York: Cambridge University Press. The story of an early—and enduring—area of Mesoamerican state formation.

Blanton, R. E., S. A. Kowalewski, G. M. Feinman, and L. M. Finsten, eds.
  1993 *Ancient Mesoamerica: A Comparison of Change in Three Regions,* 2nd ed. New York: Cambridge University Press. This book synthesizes research on three well-studied regions of Mesoamerica: the Valley of Oaxaca, the Valley of Mexico, and the Maya lowlands.

Diamond, J. M.
  1997 *Guns, Germs, and Steel: The Fates of Human Societies.* New York: W. W. Norton. Disease, tools, and environmental forces and effects throughout human history.

Fagan, B. M.
  2005 *World Prehistory: A Brief Introduction,* 6th ed. Upper Saddle River, NJ: Pearson/Prentice Hall. Major events in human prehistory, including the emergence of the state in various locales.

Feinman, G. M., and J. Marcus, eds.
  1998 *Archaic States.* Santa Fe, NM: School of American Research Press. Features of early states, in general and in particular world areas.

Joyce, R. A.
  2000 *Gender and Power in Prehispanic Mesoamerica.* Austin: University of Texas Press. Issues of gender and power in Mesoamerica before the Spanish Conquest.

Pollock, S.
  1999 *Ancient Mesopotamia: The Eden That Never Was.* Cambridge, England: Cambridge University Press. Mesopotamia state formation—a new synthesis.

Trigger, B. G.
  1993 *Early Civilizations: Ancient Egypt in Context.* New York: Columbia University Press. Considers the Incas (Inka); the Shang and western Chou of China; the Aztecs and Mayas of Mesoamerica; the Yoruba and Benin of West Africa; Mesopotamia; and ancient Egypt.
  2003 *Understanding Early Civilizations: A Comparative Study.* Cambridge, England: Cambridge University Press. A comparative study of seven archaic states: ancient Egypt and Mesopotamia, Shang dynasty China, Aztec, Maya, Inca, and Yoruba.

Wenke, R., and D. I. Olszewski
  2007 *Patterns in Prehistory: Humankind's First Three Million Years,* 5th ed. New York: Oxford University Press. Rise of food production and the state throughout the world; thorough, useful text.

INTERNET EXERCISES

1. Early Cities in Mesoamerica: Read *Archaeology* magazine's article on the New Tomb at Teotihuacan, **http://www.archaeology.org/online/features/mexico/index.html**.
   a. Where was the tomb found at Teotihuacan, and how old is it? Was the tomb created early or late in the history of this city? How does the tomb help us understand the history of Teotihuacan?
   b. What was found in the tomb? What do they signify?
   c. As an example of a state, what are some of the institutions that you think may have existed at Teotihuacan? For example, do you think they had military and professional religion practitioners?

2. Indus Valley Civilization: Go to Mark Kenyoyer's "Around the Indus in 90 Slides" presentation, **http://www.harappa.com/indus/indus0.html**, and read his essay about the Indus civilization, **http://www.harappa.com/indus/indus1.html**.
   a. Where is the Indus? When did its first cities arise? What are the names of some of the cities?
   b. What are some of the characteristics of Indus cities? Are they characteristic of a state?
   c. What are some of the common misconceptions about the origins of Indus civilization?
   d. The Indus had a form of writing. What did they write on? What are some of the common images and motifs associated with the inscriptions?

See Chapter 11 at your McGraw-Hill Online Learning Center for additional review and interactive exercises.

The Peopling of the Pacific

On April 28, 1947, the adventurer Thor Heyerdahl and five others set out from Peru, aboard a balsa raft, on a voyage they hoped would end on Polynesia's Easter Island. (They actually reached Raroia, French Polynesia.) Contrary to scientific opinion then and now, Heyerdahl sought to prove that Native South Americans could have rafted to, and then colonized, Polynesia. No scientific evidence has ever been found to support the hypothesis that Polynesia was settled by Native Americans.

Who did settle the vast Pacific? Today, when archaeologists dig in Australia, Papua New Guinea, and the neighboring islands of the southwest Pacific (consult the map on page 254 throughout this discussion), they find traces of humankind more than 30,000 years old. Humans reached northern Australia between 50,000 and 60,000 years ago. People even reached the islands north of Australia, as far as the Solomon Islands, more than 30,000 years ago (Terrell 1998).

And there they stayed. Based on current evidence, people waited thousands of years before they risked sailing farther eastward on the open sea. Until 3000 B.P., the Solomon Islands formed the eastern edge of the inhabited Pacific. The deep-sea crossings and colonization that began around 3000 B.P. were linked to the rapid spread of the earliest pottery found in Oceania, an ornately decorated ware with geometric designs called Lapita.

The first Lapita potsherds were excavated in 1952. The name comes from the discovery site on the Melanesian island of New Caledonia. (Locate New Caledonia the map on page 254. Where does New Caledonia lie in relation to the Solomon Islands, the Bismarck Archipelago, Tonga, and Samoa?) The oldest Lapita artifacts, dating back some 3,500 years, have been found in the Bismarck Archipelago, northeast of New Guinea. Many scholars see this ornate ware as the product of an ethnically distinct people, and think the Lapita "cultural complex" was carried into the Pacific by a migration of racially distinct newcomers from Asia.

No one knows why people with Lapita pottery left home and risked sailing in deeper waters. Was it for reasons of wanderlust, a pioneering spirit, or improvements in canoe building and navigation? Some experts think the domestication of certain plants and animals thought to be of Asian origin—such as dogs, pigs, and chickens—somehow fueled Lapita's expansion (Terrell 1998).

Archaeologist John Terrell has excavated a site dated to 3000 B.P. on the Sepik (midnorthern) coast of Papua New Guinea. At that time, according to Terrell (1998), newly stabilized coastal lagoons were producing an abundance of (mainly wild) foods, fueling human population growth. Like the broad-spectrum economies discussed in Chapter 10, the resource base of the early Lapita pottery makers included diverse foods, some wild and some (e.g., yams, taro, pigs, chickens) domesticated and carefully managed.

Archaeologist David Burley uncovered early Lapita shards (potsherds) at Fanga'uta lagoon on the island of Tongatapu in the Polynesian kingdom of Tonga. Early outrigger canoes reached that lagoon after traveling hundreds, and perhaps more than a thousand, miles from the west. Radiocarbon dating of charcoal among the shards showed that seafarers reached Tonga between 2,950 and 2,850 years ago. *This is the earliest known settlement in Polynesia.* Burley thinks that Tongatapu "probably served as the initial staging point for population expansion" to other islands of Tonga, then to Samoa, and then on to the rest of Polynesia (quoted in Wilford 2002a).

Improvements in their outrigger canoes allowed Lapita navigators to sail across large stretches of open sea, thus propelling the Polynesian diaspora. The larger canoes could have

See your OLC Bringing It All Together links

mhhe.com/kottak

Lapita pottery fragments from the Solomon Islands, dated to 3000 B.P.

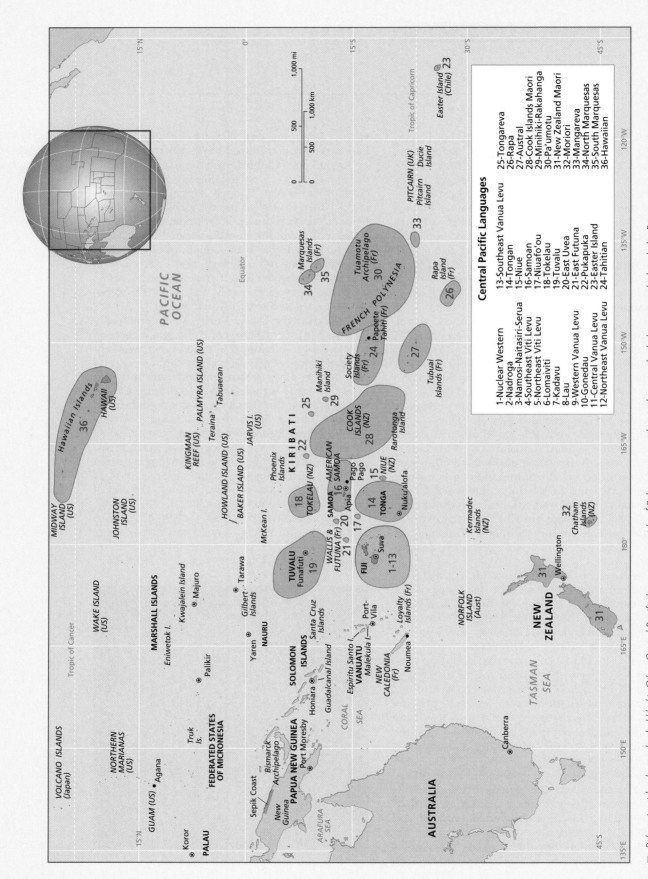

Central Pacific Languages

1-Nuclear Western	13-Southeast Vanua Levu	25-Tongareva
2-Nadroga	14-Tongan	26-Rapa
3-Namosi-Naitasiri-Serua	15-Niue	27-Austral
4-Southeast Viti Levu	16-Samoan	28-Cook Islands Maori
5-Northeast Viti Levu	17-Niuafo'ou	29-Minihiki-Rakahanga
6-Lomaiviti	18-Tokelau	30-Pa'umotu
7-Kadavu	19-Tuvalu	31-New Zealand Maori
8-Lau	20-East Uvea	32-Moriori
9-Western Vanua Levu	21-East Futuna	33-Mangareva
10-Gonedau	22-Pukapuka	34-North Marquesas
11-Central Vanua Levu	23-Easter Island	35-South Marquesas
12-Northeast Vanua Levu	24-Tahitian	36-Hawaiian

■ Polynesian islands are shaded khaki. Other Central Pacific languages are spoken in the area shaded orange, which includes Fiji.

carried dozens of people, plus pigs and other cargo. Polynesian seafarers eventually reached Tahiti to the east, and Hawaii—located more than 2,500 miles northeast of Tonga and Samoa. Later voyages carried the Polynesian diaspora south to New Zealand, and farther east to Easter Island. Covering one-fourth of the Pacific, Polynesia became the last large area of the world to be settled by humans.

The Lapita pottery found at Tongatapu offered clues about where the seafarers originated. Analyzing bits of the shards, William Dickinson, a University of Arizona geologist, found sandy minerals from outside Tonga. Some of the pots had been brought there from elsewhere. It turned out that the artifacts were made of minerals found only on the Santa Cruz Islands in Melanesia, some 1,200 miles to the west of Tonga, and just east of the Solomon Islands (Burley and Dickinson 2001). The shards from Tongatapu provided the first physical evidence linking the voyages of the Lapita people between the western and eastern parts of the Pacific. This evidence may mean that Tonga was first settled by people who came directly from central Melanesia (Wilford 2002a).

Anthropologists from all four subfields—archaeologists and physical, cultural, and linguistic anthropologists—have considered questions about Polynesian origins. Who made Lapita pottery, along with the distinctive stone tools, beads, rings, and shell ornaments often found with it? Were they an ethnically distinct society of new-comers? Or did they consist of several cultural groups that came to share a handicraft style through diffusion or borrowing? How were the Lapita pottery makers linked to earlier settlers of the Pacific—the original colonists of Australia, New Guinea, and nearby islands? Did the Lapita complex originate with indigenous dark-skinned Melanesians, assumed to descend from the first settlers of the Pacific? Or was it introduced by new, lighter-skinned arrivals from Southeast Asia? Did lighter- and darker-skinned groups intermarry in Melanesia, forming a hybrid population that created the Lapita complex and eventually colonized Polynesia?

In the 18th century, the explorer Captain James Cook was struck by how similar were the appearance and customs of light-skinned Polynesians living on islands thousands of miles apart, such as Tonga, Hawaii, New Zealand, and Easter Island. Cook thought that the Polynesians originally had come from Malaysia or Micronesia. French navigators stressed the physical and cultural differences between the Polynesians and the darker-skinned Melanesians who lived near New Guinea, and who resembled the indigenous peoples of Papua New Guinea.

As in the tripartite classification of human races in vogue during the 19th century (see Chapter 5), Europeans grouped Pacific "races" into three: Polynesians ("many islands"), Melanesians ("dark islands"), and Micronesians ("little islands"). Until recently, anthropologists supposed that the ances-

On the left, a Polynesian woman from Tahiti, Society Islands, French Polynesia. On the right, a Melanesian woman from Madang, Papua New Guinea. What differences and similarities do you notice between these two women?

tors of the Polynesians originated in mainland China and/or Taiwan, which they left between 3,600 and 6,000 years ago. They were seen as spreading rapidly through the Pacific, largely bypassing Melanesia. This would explain why the Polynesians are not dark-skinned and why they speak Austronesian languages, rooted in Taiwan, rather than Papuan languages, spoken in parts of Melanesia. This view now seems discredited by the fact that nothing resembling Lapita pottery has ever been found in Taiwan or southern China. Lapita features first show up in Melanesia, on islands of the Bismarck Archipelago. Recent genetic studies also suggest that ancestral Polynesians stopped off in Melanesia. Interbreeding between early Polynesians and Melanesians has left clear genetic markers in today's Polynesians. The debate now focuses on where the interbreeding took place and how extensive it was.

DNA evidence has convinced Mark Stoneking, a molecular anthropologist, that the ancestors of the Polynesians were indeed Austronesians. (The Austronesian, or Malayo-Polynesian, language family covers a large area of the world. Austronesian languages are the main languages of Polynesia [e.g., Hawaiian], Indonesia, and Malaysia, and even of Madagascar, located just off the African coast.) Stoneking thinks that the ancestral Polynesians left Southeast Asia—not necessarily Taiwan—and sailed to, then expanded along, the coast of New Guinea. They intermingled with Melanesians there and then started voyaging eastward into the Pacific. Interacting with other human groups, ancestral Polynesians exchanged genes and cultural traits (Gibbons 2001; Wilford 2002a).

Excavating in Melanesia's Bismarck Archipelago, archaeologist Patrick Kirch found evidence that newcomers from the islands of southeast Asia had reached Melanesia by 3500 B.P. They

built their houses on stilts, as in houses still found in Southeast Asia. They sailed in outrigger canoes and brought agricultural plants along with them. There was mixing between the newcomers and the Melanesians. *Out of their contact and interaction emerged the Lapita pottery style.* Archaeologists aren't sure if Lapita pottery was first developed where the oldest specimens have been found, in the Bismarcks, or if it was introduced there by seafarers from the west (see Kirch 2000).

Why don't Polynesians resemble their presumed Melanesian cousins, or any Asian forebears? Can we explain the physical differences between Polynesians and Melanesians? Might the Polynesian population have originated in what geneticists call a founder event? In such an event, just a few people, whose physical traits do not randomly sample the larger population from which they came, happen to give rise to a very large diaspora. A very small number of people, say, a few canoeloads, reaching Tonga's Fanga'uta lagoon, may have given rise to the entire, geographically dispersed Polynesian population. The physical traits of such a small founding group could not fully represent the population from which they came. Whatever traits the founders happened to have, such as light skin color, would be transmitted to their descendants. This may explain why the Polynesians look so different from Melanesians, even though they have DNA in common.

Whatever their roots, the Lapita people, whose pottery marked their eastward migrations, eventually abandoned the elaborate Lapita style. On Tonga and Samoa, the decorative ceramics soon disappeared in favor of plain, functional bowls, cups, and storage vessels. Nor did the seafarers take Lapita pottery on their later voyages to the rest of Polynesia.

By 2000 B.P., according to Patrick Kirch (2000), the people of Tonga had developed a significant new technology: the double-hull sailing canoe. Even though they could not spot other islands on the distant horizon, as their ancestors had been able to do in the Southwestern Pacific, the notion that the ocean was full of islands endured. Once they could more securely travel long distances—with the new canoe—they set forth. These weren't all accidental voyages and discoveries, as once was thought. These ancient sailors tacked against the prevailing east-to-west winds, knowing that, if necessary, they could ride a following wind back home. Anthropologists have learned from oral tradition that these societies had a social structure with status ranked by birth order. Many of the Polynesian island societies developed into chiefdoms, of the sort discussed in Chapter 11. According to Kirch, the Polynesian islanders "were descendants of settlers who were junior siblings and their own explorations were very often conducted by junior siblings . . . They were the ones with a reason to explore, to find new land and claim that for themselves" (quoted in Wilford 2002*a*). (There was a similar pattern in the early settlement of British North America.)

Long ago, the anthropologist Alexander Lesser disputed what he saw as the "myth of the primitive isolate" (quoted in Terrell 1998)—the idea that ancient peoples lived in closed societies, each one out of contact with others. It is doubtful that the human world has ever been one of distinct societies, sealed cultures, or isolated ethnic groups. Even on the small islands and atolls of the vast Pacific Ocean lived societies that contradicted the "primitive isolate." The adventurous and interconnected peoples of the Pacific and their prehistoric past reveal that human diversity is as much a product of contact as of isolation (Terrell 1998).

12

Methods in Cultural Anthropology

ETHICAL CONSIDERATIONS: NETWORKING AND RECIPROCATION

This chapter, which focuses on methods in cultural anthropology, begins with a brief discussion of some of the ethical considerations that anthropologists face as they plan and conduct their fieldwork. There is further discussion of ethics in Appendix 2, which summarizes the Code of Ethics of the American Anthropological Association (AAA). That code offers guidelines for anthropologists as they plan and conduct research, and as they deal with colleagues at home and abroad. Many ethical issues are common to cultural and linguistic anthropology, to the extent that both work with living people. The discussion of methods in this chapter focuses on cultural anthropology, especially on ethnography. Methods in linguistics and in linguistic anthropology are discussed in the "News Brief" here, but mainly in Chapter 15, "Language and Communication."

Ethnographers (fieldworkers in cultural anthropology) typically have done fieldwork outside their nations of origin. In the host country, the ethnographer seeks permissions, cooperation, and knowledge from government officials, scholars, and many others, most importantly the people of the community being studied. Cultural sensitivity is paramount when the research subjects are living people into whose lives the anthropologist intrudes. Anthropologists need to establish and maintain appropriate, collaborative, and nonexploitative relationships with colleagues and communities in the host country.

To work in a host country and community, researchers must inform officials and colleagues there about the purpose and funding, and the anticipated results and impacts, of the research. Researchers have to gain the informed consent of all affected parties—from the authorities who control access to the field site to the members of the community to be studied. Before the research begins, people should be informed about the purpose, nature, and procedures of the research and its potential costs and benefits to them. *Informed consent* (agreement to take part in the research) should be obtained from anyone who provides information or who might be affected by the research.

A process of culturally appropriate networking, which will vary from country to country, is necessary before fieldwork can begin. As one illustration, consider how I prepared for my first fieldwork in Madagascar, which began in 1966. Before arriving in Madagascar I obtained a visa to do research there from Madagascar's embassy in France, where I spent six months on language preparation. I needed to learn Malagasy, the language of Madagascar, a former colony of France. Once I reached Antananarivo, Madagascar's capital, I visited university anthropologists there to draw on their expertise and get their advice about my plans. Later, when I arrived in the territory of the ethnic group (Betsileo—Figure 12.1) I planned to study, I met with the province chief. Eventually I met with the heads of all the lower-level administrative units where I would be working. Next, I became friendly with knowledgeable people in the small town where I first settled. Townfolk have social networks that extend to rural areas—where I would be doing the bulk of my ethnographic fieldwork. Through personal contacts, I created a network that eventually enabled me to work in several rural villages, one of which was my primary field site. Throughout my stay in Madagascar, I tried to stay in touch with the scholars and officials who had helped me at the outset. When I later applied for grants to return to Madagascar, I included two of those scholars as funded participants in the research. Such networking is an important part of any field research project in cultural or linguistic anthropology.

See the Internet Exercises at your OLC for examples of ethical dilemmas in anthropology

mhhe.com/kottak

OVERVIEW

The anthropologist's deepest ethical commitment is to the people he or she studies. Ethnography refers to the firsthand study of local cultural settings—field sites. Observing and working closely with local people, ethnographers learn the details of their lives. Life histories reveal personal experiences with culture. Genealogical information is important in societies in which kinship, descent, and marriage organize social life. Longitudinal research is the systematic study of an area or field site over time. Multisited ethnography, involving more than one field site, by a team or individual, is increasingly common.

Traditionally, cultural anthropologists worked in small-scale societies; sociologists, in modern nations. How does survey research, which typifies sociology, differ from ethnography? With more literate respondents, survey researchers use questionnaires, which research subjects fill out. Sociologists study samples to make inferences about a larger population. Given the diversity that exists in modern nations, even anthropologists may adopt some survey procedures. However, anthropologists also retain the firsthand investigation characteristic of ethnography.

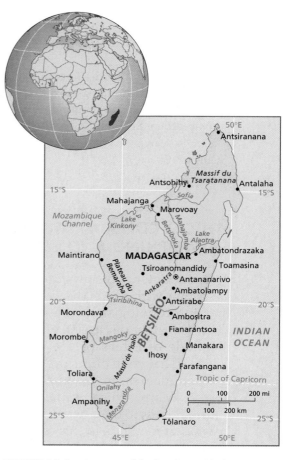

FIGURE 12.1 Location of the Betsileo in Madagascar.

Restoring Lost Languages: A Form of Cultural Heritage Management

NEW YORK TIMES NEWS BRIEF

by John Noble Wilford

March 7, 2006

Language is a key ingredient in being human. Language and culture go together. Cultural transmission depends on language, and language is a vital part of culture. Contemporary Native Americans display a revived pride in cultural heritage, accompanied by an interest in the languages spoken by their ancestors. As we'll see in Chapter 15, "Language and Communication," any language helps organize and express modes of thought, systems of meaning, worldviews, and cultural understandings. When languages die, so do meaning systems; cultural diversity is reduced. This story describes one form of cultural heritage management— the science of reconstructing lost languages, known as language revitalization.

In the new movie about Jamestown, the first permanent English settlement in North America, founded in 1607, the paramount Indian chief Powhatan asks Capt. John Smith where his people came from. The sky?

Responding to the question, translated by an Indian whose smattering of English probably came indirectly from the earlier failed Roanoke colony in North Carolina, Smith replies: "The sky? No. We come from England, an island on the other side of the sea."

The dialogue continues as the interpreter puts Smith's reply in Powhatan's own words, Virginia Algonquian, a language not spoken for more than two centuries. Like most of the 800 or more indigenous languages of North America when Europeans first arrived, Powhatan's became extinct as Indians declined in number, dispersed and lost their cultural identity.

But a small yet growing number of linguists and anthropologists has been busy in recent years recreating such dead or dying Indian speech.

Their field is language revitalization, the science of reconstructing lost languages. One byproduct of the scholarship is the dialogue in Virginia Algonquian for the movie "The New World."

More than moviemaking is behind the research. A revival of ethnic pride and cultural studies among Indians has stimulated Indians' interest in their languages, some long dead. Of the more than 15 original Algonquian languages in eastern North America, the two still spoken are Passamaquoddy-Malecite in Maine and Mikmaq in New Brunswick . . .

The passing of a language diminishes cultural diversity, anthropologists say, and the restoration of at least some part of a language is an act of reclaiming a people's heritage.

Blair A. Rudes, a linguist at the University of North Carolina, Charlotte, who specializes in reconstructing Indian languages, said several Algonquian communities in the East had efforts under way to recover their lost languages and return them to daily use . . .

When the director of "The New World," Terrence Malick, decided that for authenticity Powhatan should speak in his own language, he called in Dr. Rudes, who has worked with Dr. Goddard in reconstructing the defunct Algonquian language of the Pequot of Connecticut. He is also engaged in language restoration for the Catawba of North Carolina and is collaborating with Helen Rountree, emeritus professor of anthropology at Old Dominion University, on a dictionary of Virginia Algonquian.

Dr. Rudes was asked what Powhatan and his daughter Pocahontas would say and how they would say it. It was a daunting assignment.

The related Algonquian languages were among the first in America to die out, and no one is known to have spoken Virginia Algonquian since 1785 . . . Just two contemporary accounts—one by Captain Smith and the other by the Jamestown colony secretary, William Strachey—preserved some Virginia Algonquian words, including ones

■ *In recent years linguists and anthropologists have worked to recreate dead and dying Native American speech. This field is known as language revitalization. One byproduct of the scholarship is the dialogue in Virginia Algonquian for the movie* The New World. *Shown here, from that 2006 film, are Colin Farrell and Q'orianka Kilcher, who play Captain Smith and Pocahontas.*

that have passed into modern English as raccoon, terrapin, moccasins and tomahawk . . .

The first challenge for Dr. Rudes was the limited vocabulary. Smith, the colony leader, set down just 50 Indian words, and Strachey compiled 600. The lists were written phonetically by Englishmen who were not expert in linguistics and whose spelling and pronunciation differed considerably from modern usage, making it difficult to determine the words' actual Indian form.

Dr. Rudes had to apply techniques of historical linguistics to rebuilding a language from these sketchy, unreliable word lists. He compared Strachey's recorded words with vocabularies of related Algonquian languages, especially those spoken from the Carolinas north into Canada that had survived longer and are thus better known.

This family of Indian tongues, in one respect, reminded linguists of the Romance languages. Each was distinctive but as closely related as Spanish is to Italian or Italian to Romanian. Comparisons with related languages revealed the common elements of grammar and sentence structure and many similarities in vocabulary. A translation of the Bible into the language once spoken by Massachusetts Indians offered more insights into the grammar. The Munsee Delaware version spoken by coastal Indians from Delaware to New York . . . may be dead, but its grammar and vocabulary are fairly well known to scholars.

"We have a big fat dictionary of Munsee Delaware," said Dr. Rudes, who adapted some of those words when needed for Virginia Algonquian. Recordings of the last Munsee Delaware speakers, a century ago, were a valuable guide to pronunciations . . .

Pocahontas would not have said to Smith, if she ever actually did, "I love you." She would have used the verb for love, with a prefix meaning you and a suffix for I. "It is one of the few languages that give greater importance to the listener than the speaker," Dr. Rudes said.

Then there was the problem of creating dialogue reflecting what the Indians would have understood in the early 17th century. This also required changing the script for the initial Powhatan-Smith conversation.

In a paper summarizing his methods, Dr. Rudes said the original script had Smith saying: "The sky? No. From England, a land to the east." At the time, though, a land to the east was for the Indians more myth than reality, he noted, but they probably had already heard about "white-skinned people who lived on islands in the Caribbean."

So Smith's reply was changed to "We came from England, an island on the other side of the sea," and the translator then used documented words of Virginia Algonquian for sky, no, island and sea. The spelling was slightly modified to account for Strachey's misspellings and conform to similar words in other Algonquian speech. Because the word signifying a question is not known in Virginia Algonquian, Dr. Rudes borrowed the word . . . from a related language. Of course, Powhatan's interpreter could not be expected to have a word for England. He presumably did his best to reproduce what it sounded like in Algonquian, Inkurent, to which he added the general locational ending -unk, meaning at or in. He also followed the practice of naming the place first and adding the word for "we come from there." . . .

SOURCE: John Noble Wilford, "Linguists Find the Words, and Pocahontas Speaks Again," *New York Times,* March 7, 2006. http://www.nytimes.com/2006/03/07/science/07lang.html.

Anthropologists have a debt to the people they work with in the field, and they should reciprocate in appropriate ways. For example, it is highly appropriate for North American anthropologists working in another country to (1) include host country colleagues in their research plans and funding requests, (2) establish collaborative relationships with those colleagues and their institutions, and (3) include host country colleagues in publication of the research results.

METHODS—ETHNOGRAPHY

Cultural anthropology started to separate from sociology around the turn of the 20th century. Early students of society, such as the French scholar Émile Durkheim, were among the founders of both sociology and anthropology. Theorizing about the organization of simple and complex societies, Durkheim drew on written accounts of the religions of Native Australia (Durkheim 1912/2001) as well as considering mass phenomena (such as suicide rates) in modern nations (Durkheim 1897/1951). Eventually anthropology would specialize in the former, sociology in the latter. (See Appendix 1 for more on Durkheim and early anthropology.)

Anthropology developed into a separate field as early scholars, such as Franz Boas (1940/1966), worked on Indian (Native American) reservations and traveled to distant lands to study small groups of foragers and cultivators. This type of firsthand personal study of local settings is called ethnography. Traditionally, the process of becoming a cultural anthropologist has required field

262 PART 3 *Cultural Diversity*

experience in another society. Early ethnographers lived in small-scale, relatively isolated societies with simple technologies and economies.

Ethnography thus emerged as a research strategy in societies with greater cultural uniformity and less social differentiation than are found in large, modern industrial nations. In such nonindustrial settings, ethnographers have needed to consider fewer paths of enculturation (the process by which one acquires cultural knowledge) to understand social life. Traditionally, ethnographers have tried to understand the whole of a particular culture (or, more realistically, as much as they can, given limitations of time and perception). To pursue this goal, ethnographers adopt a free-ranging strategy for gathering information. In a given society or community, the ethnographer moves from setting to setting, place to place, and subject to subject to discover the totality and interconnectedness of social life.

By expanding our knowledge of the range of human diversity, ethnography provides a foundation for generalizations about human behavior and social life. Chapter 1 pointed out that ethnography involves fieldwork in a particular society, whereas *ethnology* is the comparative aspect of cultural anthropology. The goals of ethnology are to identify, compare, and explain cultural differences and similarities, and to build theory about how social and cultural systems work. You might want to review the section of Chapter 1 titled "Science, Explanation, and Hypothesis Testing." That section discusses how ethnographic data, gathered through the techniques discussed here, can be used to compare and contrast, and to make generalizations about, societies and cultures.

In this chapter we focus on ethnographic field techniques. Ethnographers draw on a variety of techniques to piece together a picture of otherwise alien lifestyles. Anthropologists usually employ several (but rarely all) of the techniques discussed here (see also Bernard 2006; O'Reilly 2004).

ETHNOGRAPHIC TECHNIQUES

The characteristic *field techniques* of the ethnographer include the following:

1. Direct, firsthand observation of daily behavior, including *participant observation.*

2. Conversation with varying degrees of formality, from the daily chitchat that helps maintain rapport and provides knowledge about what is going on to prolonged *interviews*, which can be unstructured or structured. Formal, printed *interview schedules* or questionnaires may be used to ensure that complete, comparable information is available for everyone of interest to the study.

World-famous anthropologist Margaret Mead in the field in Bali, Indonesia, in 1957.

3. The *genealogical method.*

4. Detailed work with *key consultants* about particular areas of community life.

5. In-depth interviewing, often leading to the collection of *life histories* of particular people (narrators).

6. Discovery of local beliefs and perceptions, which may be compared with the ethnographer's own observations and conclusions.

7. Problem-oriented research of many sorts.

8. Longitudinal research—the continuous long-term study of an area or site.

9. Team research—coordinated research by multiple ethnographers.

10. Large-scale approaches that recognize the complexity of modern life.

Observation and Participant Observation

Ethnographers get to know their hosts and usually take an interest in the totality of their lives. Ethnographers must pay attention to hundreds of details of daily life, seasonal events, and unusual happenings. They must observe individual and collective behavior in varied settings. They should record what they see as they see it. Things will never seem quite as strange as they do during the first few days and weeks in the field. The ethnographer eventually gets used to, and accepts as normal, cultural patterns that were initially alien. Ethnographers typically spend more than a year in the field. This permits them to observe the entire annual cycle. Staying a bit more than a year allows the ethnographer to repeat the season of his or her arrival, when certain events and processes may have been missed because of initial unfamiliarity and culture shock.

See the Internet Exercises at your OLC for an ethnographic experience
mhhe.com/kottak

A young interviewer at work on the campus of the University of Southern California (USC). Does this strike you as a formal or an informal interview?

Many ethnographers record their impressions in a personal *diary*, which is kept separate from more formal *field notes*. Later, this record of early impressions will help point out some of the most basic aspects of cultural diversity. Such aspects include distinctive smells, noises people make, how they cover their mouths when they eat, and how they gaze at others. These patterns, which are so basic as to seem almost trivial, are part of what Bronislaw Malinowski called "the imponderabilia of native life and of typical behavior" (Malinowski 1922/1961, p. 20). These features of culture are so fundamental that local people take them for granted. They are too basic even to talk about, but the unaccustomed eye of the fledgling anthropologist picks them up. Thereafter, becoming familiar, they fade to the edge of consciousness. Initial impressions are valuable and should be recorded. First and foremost, ethnographers should try to be accurate observers, recorders, and reporters of what they see in the field.

Ethnographers don't study animals in laboratory cages. The experiments that psychologists do with pigeons, chickens, guinea pigs, and rats are very different from ethnographic procedure. Anthropologists don't systematically control subjects' rewards and punishments or their exposure to certain stimuli. Our subjects are not speechless animals but human beings. It is not part of ethnographic procedure to manipulate them, control their environments, or experimentally induce certain behaviors.

Ethnographers strive to establish *rapport*—a good, friendly working relationship based on personal contact—with our hosts. One of ethnography's most characteristic procedures is *participant observation*, which means that we take part in community life as we study it. As human beings living among others, we cannot be totally impar-

tial and detached observers. We also must take part in many of the events and processes we are observing and trying to comprehend. By participating, we may learn how and why natives find such events meaningful, as well as see how they are organized and conducted.

To exemplify participant observation, let me describe aspects of my own ethnographic fieldwork in Madagascar, a large island off the southeastern coast of Africa, and in Brazil. During the 14 months I lived in Madagascar in 1966–1967, I observed and participated on many occasions in Betsileo life. I helped out at harvest time, joining other people who climbed atop—in order to stomp down on and compact—accumulating stacks of rice stalks. One September, for a reburial ceremony, I bought a silk shroud for a village ancestor. I entered the village tomb and watched people rewrap the bones and decaying flesh of their ancestors. I accompanied Betsileo peasants to town and to market. I observed their dealings with outsiders and sometimes offered help when problems arose.

In Arembepe, Brazil (see Chapter 1, pp. 12–13), I learned about fishing by sailing on the Atlantic in simple boats with local fishermen. I gave Jeep rides into the capital to malnourished babies, to pregnant mothers, and once to a teenage girl possessed by a spirit. All those people needed to consult specialists outside the village. I danced on Arembepe's festive occasions, drank libations commemorating new births, and became a godfather to a village girl. Most anthropologists have similar field experiences. The common humanity of the student and the studied, the ethnographer and the research community, makes participant observation inevitable.

Conversation, Interviewing, and Interview Schedules

Participating in local life means that ethnographers constantly talk to people and ask questions. As their knowledge of the local language and culture increases, they understand more. There are several stages in learning a field language. First is the naming phase—asking name after name of the objects around us. Later we are able to pose more complex questions and understand the replies. We begin to understand simple conversations between two villagers. If our language expertise proceeds far enough, we eventually become able to comprehend rapid-fire public discussions and group conversations.

One data-gathering technique I have used in both Arembepe and Madagascar involves an ethnographic survey that includes an interview schedule. In 1964, my fellow fieldworkers and I attempted to complete an interview schedule in each of Arembepe's 160 households. We entered almost every household (fewer than 5 percent refused to participate) to ask a set of questions on a printed form.

Our results provided us with a census and basic information about the village. We wrote down the name, age, and sex of each household member. We gathered data on family type, political party, religion, present and previous jobs, income, expenditures, diet, possessions, and many other items on our eight-page form.

Although we were doing a survey, our approach differed from the survey research design routinely used by sociologists and other social scientists working in large, industrial nations. That survey research, discussed below, involves *sampling* (choosing a small, manageable study group from a larger population) and impersonal data collection. We did not select a partial sample from the total population. Instead, we tried to interview all households in the community we were studying (that is, to have a total sample). We used an interview schedule rather than a questionnaire. With the **interview schedule,** the ethnographer talks face to face with people, asks the questions, and writes down the answers. **Questionnaire** procedures tend to be more indirect and impersonal; the respondent often fills in the form.

Our goal of getting a total sample allowed us to meet almost everyone in the village and helped us establish rapport. Decades later, Arembepeiros still talk warmly about how we were interested enough in them to visit their homes and ask them questions. We stood in sharp contrast to the other outsiders the villagers had known, who considered them too poor and backward to be taken seriously.

Like other survey research, however, our interview-schedule survey did gather comparable quantifiable information. It gave us a basis for assessing patterns and exceptions in village life. Our schedules included a core set of questions that were posed to everyone. However, some interesting side issues often came up during the interview, which we would pursue then or later.

We followed such leads into many dimensions of village life. One woman, for instance, a midwife, became the key cultural consultant we sought out later when we wanted detailed information about local childbirth. Another woman had done an internship in an Afro-Brazilian cult (*candomblé*) in the city. She still went there regularly to study, dance, and get possessed. She became our *candomblé* expert.

Thus, our interview-schedule survey provided a structure that *directed but did not confine* us as researchers. It enabled our ethnography to be both quantitative and qualitative. The quantitative part consisted of the basic information we gathered and later analyzed statistically. The qualitative dimension came from our follow-up questions, open-ended discussions, pauses for gossip, and work with key consultants.

Anthropologists such as Christie Kiefer typically form personal relationships with their cultural consultants, such as this Guatemalan weaver.

The Genealogical Method

As ordinary people, many of us learn about our own ancestry and relatives by tracing our genealogies. Nowadays various computer programs allow us to trace our "family trees" and degrees of relationship. The **genealogical method** is a well-established ethnographic technique. Early ethnographers developed notation and symbols (see Chapter 18 on "Families, Kinship, and Descent") to deal with kinship, descent, and marriage. Genealogy is a prominent building block in the social organization of nonindustrial societies, where people live and work each day with their close kin. Anthropologists need to collect genealogical data to understand current social relations and to reconstruct history. In many nonindustrial societies, kin links are basic to social life. Anthropologists even call such cultures "kin-based societies." Everyone is related to each other and spends most of his or her time with relatives. Rules of behavior attached to particular kin relations are basic to everyday life (see Carsten 2004). Marriage is also crucial in organizing nonindustrial societies because strategic marriages between villages, tribes, and clans create political alliances.

Key Cultural Consultants

Every community has people who by accident, experience, talent, or training can provide the most complete or useful information about particular aspects of life. These people are **key cultural consultants,** also called *key informants.* In Ivato, the Betsileo village where I spent most of my time, a man named Rakoto was particularly knowledgeable about village history. However, when I asked him to work with me on a genealogy of the 50 to 60 people buried in the village

Kinship and descent are vital social building blocks in nonindustrial cultures. Without writing, genealogical information may be preserved in material culture, such as this totem pole being raised in Metlakatla, Alaska.

tomb, he called in his cousin Tuesdaysfather, who knew more about this subject. Tuesdaysfather had survived an epidemic of influenza that ravaged Madagascar, along with much of the world, around 1919. Immune to the disease himself, Tuesdaysfather had the grim job of burying his kin as they died. He kept track of everyone buried in the tomb. Tuesdaysfather helped me with the tomb genealogy. Rakoto joined him in telling me personal details about the deceased villagers.

Life Histories

In nonindustrial societies as in our own, individual personalities, interests, and abilities vary. Some villagers prove to be more interested in the ethnographer's work and are more helpful, interesting, and pleasant than others. Anthropologists develop likes and dislikes in the field as we do at home. Often, when we find someone unusually interesting, we collect his or her **life history.** This recollection of a lifetime of experiences provides a more intimate and personal cultural portrait than would be possible otherwise. Life histories, which may be recorded or videotaped for later review and analysis, reveal how specific people perceive, react to, and contribute to changes that affect their lives. Such accounts can illustrate diversity, which exists within any community, since the focus is on how different people interpret and deal with some of the same problems. Many ethnographers include the collection of life histories as an important part of their research strategy.

Local Beliefs and Perceptions, and the Ethnographer's

One goal of ethnography is to discover local views, beliefs, and perceptions, which may be compared with the ethnographer's own observations and conclusions. In the field, ethnographers typically combine two research strategies: the emic (local-oriented) and the etic (scientist-oriented). These terms, derived from linguistics, have been applied to ethnography by various anthropologists. Marvin Harris (1968) has popularized the following meanings of the terms. An **emic** approach investigates how local people think. How do they perceive and categorize the world? What are their rules for behavior? What has meaning for them? How do they imagine and explain things? Operating emically, the ethnographer seeks the "local viewpoint," relying on local people to explain things and to say whether something is significant or not. The term **cultural consultant** or *informant* refers to individuals the ethnographer gets to know in the field, the people who teach him or her about their culture, who provide the emic perspective.

The **etic** (scientist-oriented) approach shifts the focus from local categories, expressions, explanations, and interpretations to those of the anthropologist. The etic approach realizes that members of a culture are often too involved in what they are doing to interpret their cultures impartially. Operating etically, the ethnographer emphasizes what he or she (the observer) notices and considers important. As a trained scientist, the ethnographer should try to bring an objective and comprehensive viewpoint to the study of other cultures. Of course, the ethnographer, like any other scientist, is also a human being with cultural blinders that prevent complete objectivity. As in other sciences, proper training can reduce, but not totally eliminate, the observer's bias. But anthropologists do have special training to compare behavior between different societies.

Ethnographers typically combine emic and etic strategies in their fieldwork. Local statements, perceptions, categories, and opinions help ethnographers understand how cultures work. Local beliefs are also interesting and valuable in themselves. However, local people often don't admit, or even recognize, certain causes and consequences of their behavior. This is as true of North Americans as it is of people in other societies. To describe and interpret culture, ethnographers should recognize biases that come from their own culture as well as those of the people being studied.

The Evolution of Ethnography

The Polish anthropologist Bronislaw Malinowski (1884–1942), who spent most of his professional life in England, is generally considered the father of ethnography. Like most anthropologists of his time, Malinowski did *salvage ethnography,* in the belief that the ethnographer's job is to study and record cultural diversity threatened by westernization (see also Boas 1940/1966). Early ethnographic accounts (*ethnographies*), such as Malinowski's

How does the emic–etic distinction help us understand ourselves? To exemplify an emic versus an etic perspective, consider that laypeople (including many Americans) may believe that chills and drafts cause colds, which scientists know are caused by germs. In cultures that lack the germ theory of disease, illnesses are emically explained by various causes, ranging from spirits, to ancestors, to witches. *Illness* refers to a culture's (emic) perception and explanation of bad health, whereas *disease* refers to the scientific—etic—explanation of poor health, involving known pathogens. Like people raised in any culture, we suffer both from illness (what we think we have) and from disease (what we really have), which may not be the same. Bad health has both emic and etic roots.

Another example is the emics and etics of color terminology, to which we return in the chapter on language. In different cultures, people label colors differently. Some cultures have only 2 basic color terms—for light and dark—whereas others have all 11 primary color terms, plus a series of additional ones that recognize finer discriminations of shade and hue. Etically, the color spectrum exists everywhere, but emically, people interpret and classify it differently in different societies.

■ Bronislaw Malinowski (1884–1942), seated with villagers in the Trobriand Islands. A Polish anthropologist who spent most of his professional life in England, Malinowski is generally considered the father of ethnography. Does this photo suggest anything about Malinowski's relationship with the villagers?

classic *Argonauts of the Western Pacific* (1922/1961), were similar to earlier traveler and explorer accounts in describing the writer's discovery of unknown people and places. However, the *scientific* aims of ethnographies set them apart from books by explorers and amateurs.

More recently, the style that dominated "classic" ethnographies has been characterized as *ethnographic realism.* The writer's goal was to present an accurate, objective, scientific account of a different way of life, written by someone who knew it firsthand. This knowledge came from immersion in an alien language and culture. Ethnographers derived their authority—both as scientists and as voices of "the native" or "the other"—from this personal research experience.

Malinowski's ethnographies were guided by the assumption that aspects of culture are linked and intertwined. Beginning by describing a Trobriand sailing expedition, the ethnographer then follows the links between that entry point and other areas of the culture, such as magic, religion, myths, kinship, and trade. Compared with Malinowski, today's ethnographies tend to be less inclusive and holistic, focusing on particular topics, such as kinship or religion.

According to Malinowski, a primary task of the ethnographer is "to grasp the native's point of view, his relation to life, to realize *his* vision of *his* world" (1922/1961, p. 25—Malinowski's italics). This is a good statement of the need for the emic perspective, as was discussed earlier. Since the 1970s, *interpretive anthropology* has considered the task of describing and interpreting that which is meaningful to natives. Interpretivists such as Clifford Geertz (1973) view cultures as meaningful texts that natives constantly "read" and ethnographers must decipher. According to Geertz, anthropologists may choose anything in a culture that interests them, fill in details, and elaborate to inform their readers about meanings in that culture. Meanings are carried by public symbolic forms, including words, rituals, and customs. (For more on Malinowski and Geertz, see Appendix 1.)

One trend in ethnographic writing since the 1980s has been to question traditional goals, methods, and styles, including ethnographic realism and salvage ethnography (Clifford 1982, 1988; Marcus and Cushman 1982). Marcus and Fischer argue that experimentation in ethnographic writing is necessary because all peoples and cultures have already been "discovered" and must now be "*re*discovered . . . in changing historical circumstances" (1986, p. 24).

In general, experimental anthropologists see ethnographies as works of art as well as works of science. Ethnographic texts may be viewed as literary creations in which the ethnographer, as mediator, communicates information from the "natives" to readers. Some experimental ethnographies are "dialogic," presenting ethnography as a dialogue between the anthropologist and one or more native informants (e.g., Behar 1993;

Dwyer 1982). These works draw attention to ways in which ethnographers, and by extension their readers, communicate with other cultures. However, some such ethnographies have been criticized for spending too much time talking about the anthropologist and too little time describing the natives and their culture.

The dialogic ethnography is one genre within a larger experimental category—that is, *reflexive ethnography* (Davies 1999). Here the ethnographer-writer puts his or her personal feelings and reactions to the field situation right in the text. Experimental writing strategies are prominent in reflexive accounts. The ethnographer may adopt some of the conventions of the novel, including first-person narration, conversations, dialogues, and humor. Experimental ethnographies, using new ways of showing what it means to be a Samoan or a Brazilian, may convey to the reader a richer and more complex understanding of human experience.

Linked to salvage ethnography was the idea of the *ethnographic present*—the period before Westernization, when the "true" native culture flourished. This notion often gives classic ethnographies an unrealistic timeless quality. Providing the only jarring note in this idealized picture are occasional comments by the author about traders or missionaries, suggesting that in actuality the natives were already part of the world system. Anthropologists now recognize that the ethnographic present is a rather unrealistic construct. Cultures have been in contact—and have been changing—throughout history (Boas 1940/1966). Most native cultures had at least one major foreign encounter before any anthropologist ever came their way. Most of them had already been incorporated in some fashion into nation-states or colonial systems.

Contemporary ethnographies usually recognize that cultures constantly change and that an ethnographic account applies to a particular moment. A current trend in ethnography is to focus on the ways in which cultural ideas serve political and economic interests. Another trend is to describe how various particular "natives" participate in broader historical, political, and economic processes (Shostak 1981).

Problem-Oriented Ethnography

We see, then, a tendency to move away from holistic accounts toward more problem-focused ethnographies. Although anthropologists are interested in the whole context of human behavior, it is impossible to study everything, and field research usually addresses specific questions. Most ethnographers now enter the field with a specific problem to investigate, and they collect data about variables deemed relevant to that problem. And local people's answers to questions are not the only data source. Anthropologists also

Map Atlas

Map 10 locates classic ethnographic field sites—"cultures" or societies already studied by 1950.

gather information on factors such as population density, environmental quality, climate, physical geography, diet, and land use. Sometimes this involves direct measurement—of rainfall, temperature, fields, yields, dietary quantities, or time allocation (Bailey 1990; Johnson 1978). Often it means that we consult government records or archives.

The information of interest to ethnographers is not limited to what local people can and do tell us. In an increasingly interconnected and complicated world, local people lack knowledge about many factors that affect their lives. Our local consultants may be as mystified as we are by the exercise of power from regional, national, and international centers.

Longitudinal Research

Geography limits anthropologists less now than in the past, when it could take months to reach a field site and return visits were rare. New systems of transportation allow anthropologists to widen the area of their research and to return repeatedly. Ethnographic reports now routinely include data from two or more field stays. **Longitudinal research** is the long-term study of a community, region, society, culture, or other unit, usually based on repeated visits. One example of such research is the longitudinal study of Gwembe District, Zambia (Figure 12.2). This study, planned in 1956 as a longitudinal project by Elizabeth Colson and Thayer Scudder, continues with Colson, Scudder, and their associates of various nationalities. Thus, as is often the case with longitudinal research, the Gwembe study also illustrates team research—coordinated research by multiple ethnographers. The Gwembe research project is both longitudinal (multitime) and *multisited* (considering several field sites) (Colson and Scudder 1975; Scudder and Colson 1980). Four villages, in different areas, have

 STUDENT CD-ROM LIVING ANTHROPOLOGY

Adoption into the Canela
Track 12

The anthropologist Bill Crocker, as shown in this clip, has been studying the Canela Indians of Brazil since 1957. The clip interweaves photos and footage from his various visits to the field. Crocker has been able to make his research longitudinal and ongoing because the limitations on travel and communication are much less severe now than they were in the past. Compare the time it took to reach the field in 1957 with the more recent trip shown in the clip. There is evidence in the clip that the Canela live in a kin-based society. Crocker gained an entry to Canela society by assuming a kinship status. What was it? Did this status turn out to be a good thing? Why did Crocker hesitate when this connection was first proposed?

been followed for five decades. Periodic village censuses provide basic data on population, economy, kinship, and religious behavior. Censused people who have moved are traced and interviewed to see how their lives compare with those of people who have stayed in the villages.

A series of different research questions have emerged, while basic data on communities and individuals continue to be collected. The first focus of study was the impact of a large hydroelectric dam, which subjected the Gwembe people to forced resettlement. The dam also spurred road building and other activities that brought the people of Gwembe more closely in touch with the rest of Zambia (Colson 1971; Scudder 1982; Scudder and Habarad 1991).

Later on, education became the research focus. Scudder and Colson (1980) examined how education provided access to new opportunities as it also widened a social gap between people with different educational levels. A third major study then examined a change in brewing and drinking patterns, including a rise in alcoholism, in relation to changing markets, transportation, and exposure to town values (Colson and Scudder 1988).

Team Research

As mentioned, longitudinal research is often team research. My own field site of Arembepe, Brazil, for example, first entered the world of anthropology as a field-team village in the 1960s. It was one of four sites for the now-defunct Columbia–Cornell–Harvard–Illinois Summer Field Studies Program in Anthropology. For at least three years, that program sent a total of about 20 undergraduates annually, the author included, to do brief summer research abroad. We were stationed in rural communities in four countries: Brazil, Ecuador, Mexico, and Peru. Since my wife, Isabel Wagley Kottak, and I began studying it in 1962, Arembepe has become a longitudinal field site. There generations of researchers have monitored various aspects of change and development. The community has changed from a village into a town. Its economy, religion, and social life have been transformed.

Brazilian and American researchers worked with us on team research projects during the 1980s (on television's impact) and the 1990s (on ecological awareness and environmental risk perception). Graduate students from the University of Michigan have drawn on our baseline information from the 1960s as they have studied various topics in Arembepe. In 1990, Doug Jones, a Michigan student doing biocultural research, used Arembepe as a field site to investigate standards of physical attractiveness. In 1996–1997, Janet Dunn studied family planning and changing female reproductive strategies (Dunn 2000). Chris O'Leary, who first visited Arembepe in summer 1997, has investigated a

See the Virtual Exploration for a discussion of anthropologists' responsibilities to the communities they study

mhhe.com/kottak

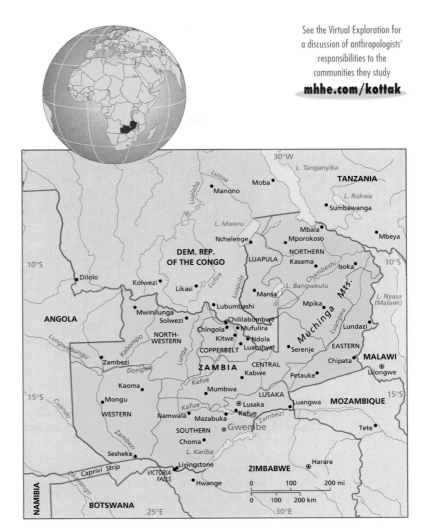

FIGURE 12.2 Location of Gwembe in Zambia.

striking aspect of religious change in Arembepe—the arrival of Protestantism. Later he did a study of changing food preferences (O'Leary 2002).

Arembepe is thus a site where various fieldworkers have worked as members of a longitudinal team. The more recent researchers have built on prior contacts and findings to increase knowledge about how local people meet and manage new circumstances. I think that scholarship should be a community enterprise. The information we gathered in the past is there for new generations to use. To monitor changing attitudes and to understand the relation between television and family planning, Janet Dunn reinterviewed many of the women we had interviewed in the 1980s. Similarly, Chris O'Leary, who compared food habits and nutritional status in Arembepe and another Brazilian town, had access to dietary information from our 1964 interviews.

Contemporary forces of change are too pervasive and complex to be understood fully by a "lone ethnographer"—a researcher who starts

■ Janet Dunn, one of many anthropologists who have worked in Arembepe. Where is Arembepe, and what kinds of research have been done there?

from scratch and works alone, for a limited period of time, and who views his or her field site as relatively discrete and isolated. No longer can any ethnographer imagine that his or her field site represents some sort of pristine or autonomous entity. Nor should the ethnographer assume that he or she has exclusive (owner's) rights to the site, or even to the data gathered there. That information, after all, has been produced in friendship, cooperation, and consultation with local people. More and more anthropological field sites, including Malinowski's Trobriand Islands, have been restudied. Ideally, later ethnographers collaborate with and build on the work of their predecessors. Compared with the lone ethnographer model, team work across time (as in Arembepe) and space (as in our comparative studies in various Brazilian towns) produces better understanding of cultural change and social complexity.

Culture, Space, and Scale

The previous sections on longitudinal and team research illustrate an important shift in cultural anthropology. Traditional ethnographic research focused on a single community or "culture," which was treated as more or less isolated and unique in time and space. The shift has been toward recognition of ongoing and inescapable flows of people, technology, images, and information. The study of such flows and linkages is now part of the anthropological analysis. And, reflecting today's world—in which people, images, and information move about as never before—fieldwork must be more flexible and on a larger scale. Ethnography is increasingly multitimed and multisited. Malinowski could focus on Trobriand culture and spend most of his field time in a particular community. Nowadays we

cannot afford to ignore, as Malinowski did, the "outsiders" who increasingly impinge on the places we study (e.g., migrants, refugees, terrorists, warriors, tourists, developers). Integral to our analyses now are the external organizations and forces (e.g., governments, businesses, nongovernmental organizations) laying claim to land, people, and resources throughout the world. Also important is increased recognition of power differentials and how they affect cultures, and of the importance of diversity within culture and societies.

In two volumes of essays edited by Akhil Gupta and James Ferguson (1997a and 1997b), several anthropologists describe problems in trying to locate cultures in bounded spaces. John Durham Peters (1997), for example, notes that, particularly because of the mass media, contemporary people simultaneously experience the local and the global. He describes those people as culturally "bifocal"—both "near-sighted" (seeing local events) and "far-sighted" (seeing images from far away). Given their "bifocality," their interpretations of the local are always influenced by information from outside. Thus, their attitude about a clear blue sky at home is tinged by their knowledge, through weather reports, that a hurricane may be approaching. The national news may not at all fit opinions voiced in local conversations, but national opinions find their way into local discourse.

The mass media, which anthropologists increasingly study, are oddities in terms of culture and space. Whose image and opinions are these? What culture or community do they represent? They certainly aren't local. Media images and messages flow electronically. TV brings them right to you. The Internet lets you discover new cultural possibilities at the click of a mouse. The Internet takes us to virtual places, but in truth, the electronic mass media are placeless phenomena, which are transnational in scope and play a role in forming and maintaining cultural identities.

Anthropologists increasingly study people in motion. Examples include people living on or near national borders, nomads, seasonal migrants, homeless and displaced people, immigrants, and refugees. Anthropological research today may take us traveling along with the people we study, as they move from village to city, cross the border, or travel internationally on business. As we'll see in Chapter 25 on "Cultural Exchange and Survival," ethnographers increasingly follow the people and images they study. As fieldwork changes, with less and less of a spatially set field, what can we take from traditional ethnography? Gupta and Ferguson correctly cite the "characteristically anthropological emphasis on daily routine and lived experience" (1997a, p. 5). The treatment of communities as discrete entities may be a thing of the past. However, "anthropology's traditional attention to the close observation of particular lives in particular places" (Gupta and Ferguson 1997b, p. 25) has an enduring importance. The method of close observation helps distinguish cultural anthropology from sociology and survey research, to which we now turn.

SURVEY RESEARCH

As anthropologists work increasingly in large-scale societies, they have developed innovative ways of blending ethnography and survey research (Fricke 1994). Before considering such combinations of field methods, I must describe survey research and the main differences between survey research and ethnography as traditionally practiced. Working mainly in large, populous nations, sociologists, political scientists, and economists have developed and refined the **survey research** design, which involves sampling, impersonal data collection, and statistical analysis. Survey research usually draws a **sample** (a manageable study group) from a much larger population. By studying a properly selected and representative sample, social scientists can make accurate inferences about the larger population.

In smaller-scale societies, ethnographers get to know most of the people, but given the greater size and complexity of nations, survey research cannot help being more impersonal. Survey researchers call the people they study *respondents.*

These are people who respond to questions during a survey. Sometimes survey researchers personally interview them. Sometimes, after an initial meeting, they ask respondents to fill out a questionnaire. In other cases, researchers mail printed questionnaires to randomly selected sample members or have graduate students interview or telephone them. (In a **random sample,** all members of the population have an equal statistical chance of being chosen for inclusion. A random sample is selected by randomizing procedures, such as tables of random numbers, which are found in many statistics textbooks.) Table 12.1 summarizes the main differences between ethnography and survey research.

Anyone who has grown up recently in the United States or Canada has heard of sampling. Probably the most familiar example is the polling used to predict political races. The media hire agencies to estimate outcomes and do exit polls to find out what kinds of people voted for which candidates. During sampling, researchers gather information about age, gender, religion, occupation, income, and political party preference. These characteristics (**variables**—attributes that vary among members of a sample or population) are known to influence political decisions.

The number of variables influencing social identity and behavior increases with, and can be considered a measure of, social complexity. Many more variables affect social identities, experiences, and activities in a modern nation than is

Biocultural Case Study

For a more detailed look at the cultural, ethnic, and linguistic aspects of unity and diversity in a contemporary nation-state, see the "Bringing It All Together" essay that immediately follows Chapter 15.

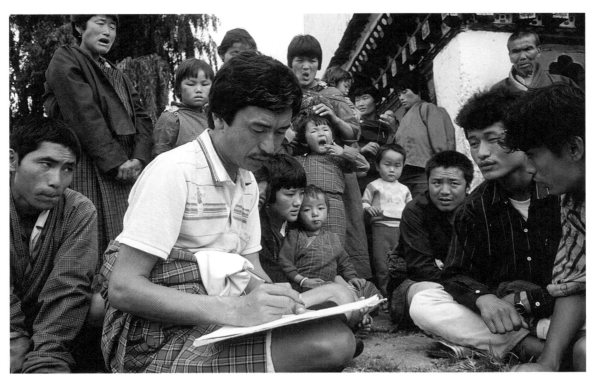

A population census taker surrounded by villagers in Paro, Bhutan. Is the technique of gathering information illustrated here more like ethnography or survey research?

TABLE 12.1   Ethnography and Survey Research Contrasted

Ethnography (Traditional)	Survey Research
Studies whole, functioning communities	Studies a small sample of a larger population
Usually is based on firsthand fieldwork, during which information is collected after rapport, based on personal contact, is established between researcher and hosts	Often is conducted with little or no personal contact between study subjects and researchers, as interviews are frequently conducted by assistants over the phone or in printed form
Traditionally is interested in all aspects of local life (holistic)	Usually focuses on a small number of variables (e.g., factors that influence voting) rather than on the totality of people's lives
Traditionally has been conducted in nonindustrial, small-scale societies, where people often do not read and write	Normally is carried out in modern nations, where most people are literate, permitting respondents to fill in their own questionnaires
Makes little use of statistics, because the communities being studied tend to be small, with little diversity besides that based on age, gender, and individual personality variation	Depends heavily on statistical analyses to make inferences regarding a large and diverse population, based on data collected from a small subset of that population

A Brazilian boy forages for valuables in a sidewalk drain outside a restaurant on Copacabana beach, Rio de Janeiro. Anthropologists have studied street children in Brazil and elsewhere. What techniques do you imagine they use for such studies?

the case in the small communities where ethnography grew up. In contemporary North America, hundreds of factors influence our social behavior and attitudes. These social predictors include our religion; the region of the country in which we grew up; whether we come from a town, suburb, or city; and our parents' professions, ethnic origins, and income levels. Because survey research deals with large and diverse groups and with samples and probability, its results must be analyzed statistically.

Ethnography can be used to supplement and fine-tune survey research. Anthropologists can transfer the personal, firsthand techniques of ethnography to virtually any setting that includes human beings. A combination of survey research and ethnography can provide new perspectives on life in **complex societies** (large and populous societies with social stratification and central governments). Preliminary ethnography also can help develop relevant and culturally appropriate questions for inclusion in surveys.

In my own courses in Ann Arbor, Michigan, undergraduates have done ethnographic research on sororities, fraternities, teams, campus organizations, and the local homeless population. Other students have systematically observed behavior in public places. These include racquetball courts, restaurants, bars, football stadiums, markets, malls, and classrooms. Other "modern anthropology" projects use anthropological techniques to interpret and analyze mass media. Anthropologists have been studying their own cultures for decades, and anthropological research in the United States and Canada is booming today. Wherever there is patterned human behavior, there is grist for the anthropological mill.

In any complex society, many predictor variables (*social indicators*) influence behavior and opinions. Because we must be able to detect, measure, and compare the influence of social indicators, many contemporary anthropological studies have a statistical foundation. Even in rural fieldwork, more anthropologists now draw samples, gather quantitative data, and use statistics to interpret them (see Bernard 2006). Quantifiable information may permit a more precise assessment of similarities and differences between communities. Statisti-

BEYOND THE CLASSROOM

Stories from Women Domestics of the Yucatán

BACKGROUND INFORMATION

STUDENT:
Angela C. Stuesse

SUPERVISING PROFESSOR:
Allan F. Burns

SCHOOL:
University of Florida

YEAR IN SCHOOL/MAJOR:
Senior/Anthropology

FUTURE PLANS:
Master's in Latin American Studies

PROJECT TITLE:
The *Patrona-Empleada**
Relationship Revealed: Stories from
Women Domestics of the Yucatán

*What research techniques are illustrated
in this account of undergraduate research?
Think about this student's approach in
terms of the issues raised in the section
on the evolution of ethnography.*

My fascination with anthropology sprang to life in early 1996, during a semester of study abroad in the Yucatán of Mexico. It was also there that I first came into contact with domestic workers of Latin America. Witness to the daily interactions between my host-family and their servant, I became intrigued by the complex nature of their relationship and decided to return the following year to do research for my honors thesis.

The testimonial of a domestic worker is often the story of both her personal and professional life. This is because she works not in an office, but rather in her *patrona*'s home. Over time, the distinction between employee and family member blurs. The indefinite relationship that results gives rise to many questions: To what extent is the servant influenced by the values and attitudes of her *patrona*? How does the way she perceives her own life compare with the way her *patrona* sees her? Under what conditions does their bond become less work-related and more analogous to family? What causes their association to be hierarchical in nature, and in what ways is this verticality expressed and/or mediated? These themes were the driving force of my investigations.

Through personal contacts, I met four domestic workers who agreed to participate in my research. They ranged in age from 17 to 70 years old, and had between 5 and 50 years of experience. Research methods included auto-photography, unstructured and semi-structured interviews, and participant observation. Our conversations were sometimes light-hearted, sometimes very serious, and always key to a deeper understanding of each individual. Apart from listening and discussing, I also learned from these women by watching and doing. I helped them hang the laundry, set the table, sweep the patio, and fill the swimming pool. I visited their pueblos and met their families. We spent hours exchanging thoughts and discussing life. I laughed along with many and I held a hand as one woman cried. It was by participating in simple events like these that I began to understand the profundity and strength of these unique women. By interviewing and getting to know their *patronas* as well, I was able to analyze the nature of their relationships and place them within the context of existing ethnographic literature and theory.

The resulting thesis gives identity to the faceless numbers common in survey and demographic research. Through my writing I have attempted to let these women speak, to give them decision, control, and value. I also have explored the genre known as "narrative ethnography," which, by including first-person experiences, rejects the idea that a valid, professional study must be "objective" and "scientific." My research adds to the growing body of narrative ethnographic, testimonial, and introspective literature about women domestics and change in the Yucatán and Latin America. With each new study we are a few steps closer to a greater cultural understanding.

*Patrona literally means patron or boss, referring to the female head of the household who oversees the domestic servants.

Empleada literally means employee, here referring to the female domestic servant.

cal analysis can support and round out an ethnographic account of local social life.

However, in the best studies, the hallmark of ethnography remains: Anthropologists enter the community and get to know the people. They participate in local activities, networks, and associations, in the city or in the countryside. They observe and experience social conditions and problems. They watch the effects of national policies and programs on local life. I believe that the ethnographic method and the emphasis on personal relationships in social research are valuable gifts that cultural anthropology brings to the study of a complex society.

1. A code of ethics guides anthropologists' research and other professional activities. Anthropologists need to establish and maintain appropriate, collaborative, and nonexploitative relationships with colleagues and communities in the host country. Researchers must gain the informed consent of all affected parties—from the authorities who control access to the field site to the members of the community being studied.

2. Ethnographic methods include observation, rapport building, participant observation, interviewing, genealogies, work with key consultants, life histories, and longitudinal research. Ethnographers do not systematically manipulate their subjects or conduct experiments. Rather, they work in actual communities and form personal relationships with local people as they study their lives.

3. An interview schedule is a form that an ethnographer completes as he or she visits a series of households. The schedule organizes and guides each interview, ensuring that comparable information is collected from everyone. Key cultural consultants teach about particular areas of local life. Life histories dramatize the fact that culture bearers are individuals. Such case studies document personal experiences with culture and culture change. Genealogical information is particularly useful in societies in which principles of kinship and marriage organize social and political life. Emic approaches focus on native perceptions and explanations. Etic approaches give priority to the ethnographer's own observations and conclusions. Longitudinal research is the systematic study of an area or site over time. Forces of change are often too pervasive and complex to be understood by a lone ethnographer. Anthropological research may be done by teams and at multiple sites. Outsiders, flows, linkages, and people in motion are now included in ethnographic analyses.

4. Traditionally, anthropologists worked in small-scale societies; sociologists, in modern nations. Different techniques were developed to study such different kinds of societies. Social scientists working in complex societies use survey research to sample variation. Anthropologists do their fieldwork in communities and study the totality of social life. Sociologists study samples to make inferences about a larger population. Sociologists often are interested in causal relations among a very small number of variables. Anthropologists more typically are concerned with the interconnectedness of all aspects of social life.

5. The diversity of social life in modern nations and cities requires social survey procedures. However, anthropologists add the intimacy and direct investigation characteristic of ethnography. Anthropologists may use ethnographic procedures to study urban life. But they also make greater use of survey techniques and analysis of the mass media in their research in contemporary nations.

KEY TERMS

See the flash cards
mhhe.com/kottak

complex societies   Nations; large and populous, with social stratification and central governments.

cultural consultants   Subjects in ethnographic research; people the ethnographer gets to know in the field, who teach him or her about their culture.

emic   The research strategy that focuses on local explanations and criteria of significance.

etic   The research strategy that emphasizes the ethnographer's rather than the locals' explanations, categories, and criteria of significance.

genealogical method   Procedures by which ethnographers discover and record connections of kinship, descent, and marriage, using diagrams and symbols.

interview schedule   Ethnographic tool for structuring a formal interview. A prepared form (usually printed or mimeographed) that guides interviews with households or individuals being compared systematically. Contrasts with a *questionnaire* because the researcher has personal contact with the local people and records their answers.

key cultural consultant   Person who is an expert on a particular aspect of local life.

life history   Of a key consultant or narrator; provides a personal cultural portrait of existence or change in a culture.

longitudinal research   Long-term study of a community, region, society, culture, or other unit, usually based on repeated visits.

questionnaire   Form (usually printed) used by sociologists to obtain comparable information from respondents. Often mailed to and filled in by research subjects rather than by the researcher.

random sample   A sample in which all members of the population have an equal statistical chance of being included.

sample   A smaller study group chosen to represent a larger population.

survey research   Characteristic research procedure among social scientists other than anthropologists. Studies society through sampling, statistical analysis, and impersonal data collection.

variables   Attributes (e.g., sex, age, height, weight) that differ from one person or case to the next.

CRITICAL
THINKING
QUESTIONS

For more self-testing,
see the self-quizzes
mhhe.com/kottak

1. How might ethical issues and concerns differently affect cultural, biological, and archaeological anthropologists?

2. If you were an anthropologist planning a field trip, what kinds of preparations would you have to make before and after you planned your research and arranged funding? How would your preparations differ depending on whether you planned to work in an industrial or a nonindustrial society?

3. How might the genealogical method be used in subfields of anthropology other than cultural anthropology?

4. How do you think the subfields of anthropology differ with respect to fieldwork? Are some subfields more likely to use a team approach than others are? What about the equipment needs of the different subfields?

5. What do you see as the strengths and weaknesses of ethnography compared with survey research? Which provides more accurate data? Might one be better for finding questions, while the other is better for finding answers? Or does it depend on the context of the research?

SUGGESTED ADDITIONAL READINGS

Agar, M. H.
  1996 *The Professional Stranger: An Informal Introduction to Ethnography,* 2nd ed. San Diego: Academic Press. Basics of ethnography, illustrated by the author's field experiences in India and among heroin addicts in the United States.

Angrosino, M. V., ed.
  2002 *Doing Cultural Anthropology: Projects for Ethnographic Data Collection.* Prospect Heights, IL: Waveland. How to get ethnographic data.

Berg, B. L.
  2004 *Qualitative Research Methods for the Social Sciences,* 5th ed. Boston: Pearson. How ethnography and other qualitative procedures may be extended across the range of social sciences; very thorough survey of qualitative methods.

Bernard, H. R.
  2006 *Research Methods in Anthropology: Qualitative and Quantitative Methods,* 4th ed. Walnut Creek, CA: AltaMira. Expansion of a classic text on research methods in cultural anthropology.

Bernard, H. R., ed.
  1998 *The Handbook of Methods in Cultural Anthropology.* Walnut Creek, CA: AltaMira. Various authors describe a series of methods in cultural anthropology.

Chiseri-Strater, E., and B. S. Sunstein
  2002 *Fieldworking: Reading and Writing Research,* 2nd ed. Upper Saddle River, NJ: Prentice Hall. Ways of evaluating and presenting research data.

DeVita, P. R., and J. D. Armstrong, eds.
  2002 *Distant Mirrors: America as a Foreign Culture,* 3rd ed. Belmont, CA: Wadsworth. The social life, customs, and popular culture of the United States as viewed and interpreted by outsiders.

Ember, C., and M. Ember
  2001 *Cross-Cultural Research Methods.* Walnut Creek, CA: AltaMira. How to do systematic cross-cultural comparison.

Gupta, A., and J. Ferguson
  1997a *Anthropological Locations: Boundaries and Grounds of a Field Science.* Berkeley: University of California Press. New directions in ethnography.

Kottak, C. P., ed.
  1982 *Researching American Culture: A Guide for Student Anthropologists.* Ann Arbor: University of Michigan Press. Advice for college students doing fieldwork in the United States. Includes papers by undergraduates and anthropologists on contemporary American culture.

Kutsche, P.
  1998 *Field Ethnography: A Manual for Doing Cultural Anthropology.* Upper Saddle River, NJ: Prentice Hall. Useful guide for fledgling ethnographers.

Pelto, P. J., and G. H. Pelto
  1978 *Anthropological Research: The Structure of Inquiry,* 2nd ed. New York: Cambridge University Press. Discusses data collection and analysis, including the relationship between theory and fieldwork, hypothesis construction, sampling, and statistics.

Spradley, J. P.
  1979 *The Ethnographic Interview.* New York: Harcourt Brace Jovanovich. Discussion of the ethnographic method, with emphasis on discovering native viewpoints.

Werner, O., and G. M. Shoepfle
  1987 *Systematic Fieldwork.* Newbury Park, CA: Sage. The first volume focuses on interviewing and other field methods; the second, on data management and analysis.

INTERNET EXERCISES

1. Ethnographic Fieldwork: Look at this collection of papers from the page titled "Papers From the ASU Ethnographic Field School in Southern Appalachia," **http://www.acs.appstate.edu/dept/anthro/ebooks/ethno97/title.html**.
   a. Read the preface. What skills were the students able to develop in the field that cannot be taught in a lecture course?
   b. Go to the paper titled "Women's Work in Allegheny County, NC," **http://www.acs.appstate.edu/dept/anthro/ebooks/ethno97/efird.html**. Skim the paper, paying special attention to the introduction, conclusion, and appendices. What did the student learn? How different are the women portrayed in this article from the women in your own community?
   c. Look specifically at the student's appendices. How did she collect the information she needed to make her conclusions? Are there questions you would have added? Why?
   d. Skim at least one other chapter, focusing on the introduction and conclusion. What are the advantages of doing research as a team? If there were only one person doing work on this project in the Appalachians, how do you think the results might be different? Do you think it is possible for a single ethnographer to understand a community fully?

2. Read the short article by Barbara Schneider titled "The Role of Field Notes in Constructing Ethnographic Knowledge" (**http://www.stthomasu.ca/inkshed/nlett500/schneidr.htm**).
   a. What kind of research methods did the anthropologist employ?
   b. What was the subject of the anthropologist's research? How did the topic of research change over time?
   c. What is the author's concern about how ethnographic material is interpreted? How can anthropologists avoid these problems?

See Chapter 12 at your McGraw-Hill Online Learning Center for additional review and interactive exercises.

LINKAGES

Kottak, *Assault on Paradise*, 4th ed.

Read Chapters 1, 2, and 12–15. Which of the field methods discussed in this text chapter were used in Arembepe? How does the study of Arembepe illustrate the following: (1) longitudinal research, (2) team research, and (3) quantitative and qualitative approaches? How did Malinowski's ethnography, as discussed in the text chapter and in *Assault on Paradise*, influence Kottak's fieldwork in Arembepe?

Peters-Golden, *Culture Sketches*, 4th ed.: Trobriand Islands

The work of Bronislaw Malinowski was highlighted in this chapter's discussion of ethnographic fieldwork. Malinowski's first trip to New Guinea in 1914 helped establish the ethnographic tradition of living among and building rapport with local people, of field work conducted in the local language and situated in a culture's own context. Some 60 years later, anthropologist Annette Weiner did her own fieldwork in the Trobriands. Her findings both added to Malinowski's earlier work and challenged some of its assumptions. In *Culture Sketches,* read Chapter 14, "The Trobriand Islanders." Considering what you have just learned about fieldwork, how did Malinowski's and Weiner's approaches differ? What are some possible reasons for their different perspectives? What are some challenges that ethnographers face in the 21st century? How might modern technology change the way anthropologists do fieldwork?

Knauft, *The Gebusi*, 1st ed.

Read Chapters 2 and 3. Based on chapter 2, what difficulties and challenges are posed by conducting field research among the Gebusi? What are the biggest joys and satisfactions of fieldwork as described by the author?

Based on Chapter 3, list the events that the author "observes" and "participates in" in his "participant observation" concerning Daguwa's death and its aftermath. What events does Knauft describe or discuss in the chapter that he himself does not see or participate in? Describe the process whereby the author turns his observations and conversations with Gebusi into a written ethnographic account.

Based on Chapter 3, what are the biggest moral and ethical challenges that the author and his wife faced during Daguwa's death and its aftermath? Would you have done anything differently?

13

Culture

WHAT IS CULTURE?

The concept of culture has long been basic to anthropology. Well over a century ago, in his book *Primitive Culture,* the British anthropologist Sir Edward Tylor proposed that cultures—systems of human behavior and thought—obey natural laws and therefore can be studied scientifically. Tylor's definition of culture still offers an overview of the subject matter of anthropology and is widely quoted: "Culture . . . is that complex whole which includes knowledge, belief, arts, morals, law, custom, and any other capabilities and habits acquired by man as a member of society" (Tylor 1871/1958, p. 1). The crucial phrase here is "acquired by man as a member of society." Tylor's definition focuses on attributes that people acquire not through biological inheritance but by growing up in a particular society where they are exposed to a specific cultural tradition. **Enculturation** is the process by which a child learns his or her culture.

279

See the Virtual Exploration
for an example of how
cultural values are learned
mhhe.com/kottak

**Bringing It
All Together**

For a more detailed look at the
cultural, ethnic, and linguistic
aspects of unity and diversity in a
contemporary nation-state, see
the "Bringing It All Together"
essay that immediately follows
Chapter 15.

See the Internet Exercises
at your OLC
mhhe.com/kottak

Culture Is Learned

The ease with which children absorb any cultural tradition rests on the uniquely elaborated human capacity to learn. Other animals may learn from experience; for example, they avoid fire after discovering that it hurts. Social animals also learn from other members of their group. Wolves, for instance, learn hunting strategies from other pack members. Such social learning is particularly important among monkeys and apes, our closest biological relatives. But our own *cultural learning* depends on the uniquely developed human capacity to use **symbols,** signs that have no necessary or natural connection to the things they signify or for which they stand.

On the basis of cultural learning, people create, remember, and deal with ideas. They grasp and apply specific systems of symbolic meaning. Anthropologist Clifford Geertz defines culture as ideas based on cultural learning and symbols. Cultures have been characterized as sets of "control mechanisms—plans, recipes, rules, instructions, what computer engineers call programs for the governing of behavior" (Geertz 1973, p. 44). These programs are absorbed by people through enculturation in particular traditions. People gradually internalize a previously established system of meanings and symbols. They use this cultural system to define their world, express their feelings, and make their judgments. This system helps guide their behavior and perceptions throughout their lives.

OVERVIEW

Culture, which is learned, passes from one generation to the next through the process of enculturation. Culture relies on symbols, which have a particular meaning and value for the people who share a culture. Cultural traditions take natural phenomena, including biological urges, and channel them in particular directions. Everyone is cultured, not just people with elite educations. Societies are integrated and patterned through dominant economic forces, social patterns, key symbols, and core values. Cultural means of adaptation have been crucial in human evolution. Cultures constrain individuals, but the actions of individuals can change cultures.

There are different levels of cultural systems. Diffusion and migration carry cultural traits and patterns across social and national boundaries. Also, nations have internal cultural diversity associated with ethnicity, region, and social class. Some aspects of culture are universal. Others are merely widespread or generalized. Still others are unique and distinctive to particular societies. Mechanisms of cultural change include diffusion, acculturation, and independent invention. Globalization describes processes that promote change in a world whose nations and people are increasingly linked.

Every person begins immediately, through a process of conscious and unconscious learning and interaction with others, to internalize, or incorporate, a cultural tradition through the process of enculturation. Sometimes culture is taught directly, as when parents tell their children to say "thank you" when someone gives them something or does them a favor.

Culture also is transmitted through observation. Children pay attention to the things that go on around them. They modify their behavior not just because other people tell them to but as a result of their own observations and growing awareness of what their culture considers right and wrong. Culture also is absorbed unconsciously. North Americans acquire their culture's notions about how far apart people should stand when they talk (see "Interesting Issues" on p. 285) not by being told directly to maintain a certain distance but through a gradual process of observation, experience, and conscious and unconscious behavior modification. No one tells Latins to stand closer together than North Americans do, but they learn to do so anyway as part of their cultural tradition.

Anthropologists agree that cultural learning is uniquely elaborated among humans and that all humans have culture. Anthropologists also accept a doctrine named in the 19th century as "the psychic unity of man." This means that although *individuals* differ in their emotional and intellectual tendencies and capacities, all human *populations* have equivalent capacities for culture. Regardless of their genes or their physical appearance, people can learn *any* cultural tradition.

To understand this point, consider that contemporary Americans and Canadians are the genetically mixed descendants of people from all over the world. Our ancestors were biologically varied, lived in different countries and continents, and participated in hundreds of cultural traditions. However, early colonists, later immigrants, and their descendants have all become active participants in American and Canadian life. All now share a national culture.

Culture Is Shared

Culture is an attribute not of individuals per se but of individuals as members of *groups*. Culture is transmitted in society. Don't we learn our culture by observing, listening, talking, and interacting with many other people? Shared beliefs, values, memories, and expectations link people who grow up in the same culture. Enculturation unifies people by providing us with common experiences.

Today's parents were yesterday's children. If they grew up in North America, they absorbed certain values and beliefs transmitted over the generations. People become agents in the enculturation

Culture Clash: Makah Seek Return to Whaling Past

NEW YORK TIMES NEWS BRIEF

by Sarah Kershaw
September 19, 2005

People do not now, nor have they ever, lived in isolation from other human beings. Links between groups have been provided by cultural practices such as marriage, kinship, religion, trade, travel, exploration, and conquest. For centuries, indigenous peoples have been exposed to a world system. Contemporary forces and events make even the illusion of autonomy hard to maintain. Nowadays, as is described in this news story, members of local cultures and communities must heed not only their own customs but also agencies, laws, and lawsuits operating at the national and international levels. As you read this account and this chapter on culture, pay attention to the various kinds of rights being asserted—animal rights, cultural rights, economic rights, legal rights, and human rights—and how those rights might clash. Also consider the levels of culture and of political regulation (local, regional, national, and global) that determine how contemporary people such as the Makah live their lives and maintain their traditions. Finally, consider the minimal impact on whale populations of the Makah hunt compared with commercial whaling.

The whaling canoes are stored in a wooden shed, idle for the past six years. They were last used when the Makah Indians were allowed to take their harpoons and a .50-caliber rifle and set out on their first whale hunt since the late 1920's.

There were eight young men in a canoe with a red hummingbird, a symbol of speed, painted on the tip. There were motorboats ferrying other hunters, news helicopters, and animal rights activists in speedboats and even a submarine.

On May 17, 1999, a week into the hunt, the Makah killed a 30-ton gray whale, striking it with harpoons and then killing it with a gunshot to the back of the head.

That rainy spring day remains etched in the minds of many Makah as a defining moment in their efforts to reach back to their cultural and historical roots. It was their first kill in seven decades, and it was their last since they were stopped by court rulings. They have asked the federal government for permission to resume hunting, and public meetings on the request are scheduled for October.

The Makah, a tribe of about 1,500 near the mouth of the Strait of Juan de Fuca on the Olympic Peninsula, see themselves as whalers and continue to identify themselves spiritually with whales.

"Everybody felt like it was a part of making history," Micah L. McCarty, a tribal council member, said of the 1999 hunt. "It's inspired a cultural renaissance, so to speak. It inspired a lot of people to learn artwork and become more active in building canoes; the younger generation took a more keen interest in singing and dancing."

The Makah, a tribe of mostly fishermen that faces serious poverty and high unemployment, were guaranteed the right to hunt whales in an 1855 treaty with the United States, the only tribe with such a treaty provision. Whaling had been the tribe's mainstay for thousands of years.

But the tribe decided to stop hunting whales early in the 20th century, when commercial harvesting had depleted the species. Whale hunting was later strictly regulated nationally and internationally, and the United States listed the Northern Pacific gray whale, the one most available to the Makah, as endangered.

The protections helped the whales rebound, and they were taken off the endangered list in 1994. Several years later, the Makah won permission to hunt again, along with a $100,000 federal grant to set up a whaling commission.

By the time they were ready, none of the Makah had witnessed a whale hunt or even tasted the meat, hearing only stories passed down through the generations. They learned that the whale was a touchstone of Makah culture—the tribe's logo today pictures an eagle perched on a whale—and that the tribe's economy was built around the lucrative trade with Europeans in whale oil, used for heating and lighting, during the 18th and early 19th centuries.

For a year before the 1999 hunt, the new Makah whale hunters prepared for their sacramental pursuit, training in canoes on the cold and choppy waters of the Pacific Ocean, praying on the beach in the mornings and at the dock in the evenings.

Animal rights groups were preparing, too. When the hunt began, the small reservation and its surrounding waters were teeming with news helicopters and protest groups. On that May afternoon, when the protesters were somewhere off the reservation,

Makah Indians kill a gray whale in May 1999. More than 500 Makah Indians attended the traditional ceremony of the whale hunt, which was declared illegal in 2002.

the Makah killed their whale. They held a huge celebration on the beach, where 15 men were waiting to butcher the animal, its meat later kippered and stewed.

But the protests and the television cameras "took a lot of the spirituality out of it," said Dave Sones, vice chairman of the tribal council.

Mr. McCarty said, "I equate it with interrupting High Mass."

The Makah went whale hunting, largely unnoticed, again in 2000, paddling out on a 32-foot cedar whaling canoe, but they did not catch anything. Soon after, animal rights groups, including the Humane Society of the United States, sued to stop the hunting. In 2002, an appeals court declared the hunting illegal, saying the National Oceanic and Atmospheric Administration had not adequately studied the impact of Makah hunting on the survival of the whale species.

Despite the strict national and international regulations on whale hunting, several tribes of Alaska Natives, subsistence whale hunters for centuries, are exempt from provisions of the 1972 Marine Mammal Protection Act, allowing them to hunt the bowhead whale. That species, unlike the gray whale, is listed as endangered, said Brian Gorman, a spokesman for the oceanic agency.

Despite their treaty rights, the Makah were not granted an exemption under the 1972 act. Last February, the tribe asked the agency for a waiver that would grant them permanent rights to kill up to 20 gray whales in any five-year period, which they insist they already have under their 1855 treaty.

The Makah's request is "setting a dangerous precedent," said Naomi Rose, a marine mammal scientist for the Humane Society.

The Alaska hunting, Ms. Rose said, "is a true subsistence hunt," whereas the Makah, who view whale hunting mostly as ceremonial, are pursuing "cultural whaling" that is not essential to their diet.

"There are too many other bad actors out there" who might try to apply for waivers too, she said. The Makah "have a treaty right, but we're asking them not to exercise it," she said. But other environmental groups, including Greenpeace, which is adamantly opposed to the commercial harvesting of whales, have remained neutral on the Makah's quest.

"No indigenous hunt has ever destroyed whale populations," said John Hocevar, an oceans specialist with Greenpeace. "And looking at the enormous other threats to whales and putting the Makah whaling in context, it's pretty different."

Mr. Gorman, of the federal fisheries agency, said: "They have a treaty right that the U.S. government signed. It doesn't take an international lawyer to figure out that they do have this treaty."

___

SOURCE: Sarah Kershaw, "In Petition to Government, Tribe Hopes for Return to Whaling Past," *New York Times*, September 19, 2005, p. A16.

of their children, just as their parents were for them. Although a culture constantly changes, certain fundamental beliefs, values, worldviews, and child-rearing practices endure. Consider a simple American example of enduring shared enculturation. As children, when we didn't finish a meal, our parents may have reminded us of starving children in some foreign country, just as our grandparents might have done a generation earlier. The specific country changes (China, India, Bangladesh, Ethiopia, Somalia, Rwanda—what was it in your home?). Still, American culture goes on transmitting the idea that by eating all our brussels sprouts or broccoli, we can justify our own good fortune, compared to a hungry child in an impoverished or war-ravaged country.

Despite characteristic American notions that people should "make up their own minds" and "have a right to their opinion," little of what we think is original or unique. We share our opinions and beliefs with many other people. Illustrating the power of shared cultural background, we are most likely to agree with and feel comfortable with people who are socially, economically, and culturally similar to ourselves. This is one reason why Americans abroad tend to socialize with each other, just as French and British colonials did in their overseas empires. Birds of a feather flock together, but for people, the familiar plumage is culture.

Culture Is Symbolic

Symbolic thought is unique and crucial to humans and to cultural learning. Anthropologist Leslie White defined culture as

> dependent upon symbolling . . . Culture consists of tools, implements, utensils, clothing, ornaments, customs, institutions, beliefs, rituals, games, works of art, language, etc. (White 1959, p. 3)

For White, culture originated when our ancestors acquired the ability to use symbols, that is, to originate and bestow meaning on a thing or event, and, correspondingly, to grasp and appreciate such meanings (White 1959, p. 3).

A symbol is something verbal or nonverbal, within a particular language or culture, that comes to stand for something else. There is no obvious, natural, or necessary connection between the symbol and what it symbolizes. A pet that barks is no more naturally a *dog* than a *chien, Hund,* or *mbwa,* to use the words for the animal we call "dog" in French, German, and Swahili. Language is one of the distinctive possessions of *Homo sapiens.* No other animal has developed anything approaching the complexity of language.

Symbols are usually linguistic. But there are also nonverbal symbols, such as flags, that stand for countries, as arches do for a hamburger chain. Holy water is a potent symbol in Roman Catholicism. As is true of all symbols, the association between a symbol (water) and what is symbolized (holiness) is arbitrary and conventional. Water is not intrinsically holier than milk, blood, or other natural liquids. Nor is holy water chemically different from ordinary water. Holy water is a symbol within Roman Catholicism, which is part of an international cultural system. A natural thing has been arbitrarily associated with a particular meaning for Catholics, who share common beliefs and experiences that are based on learning and that are transmitted across the generations.

For hundreds of thousands of years, humans have shared the abilities on which culture rests.

These abilities are to learn, to think symbolically, to manipulate language, and to use tools and other cultural products in organizing their lives and coping with their environments. Every contemporary human population has the ability to use symbols and thus to create and maintain culture. Our nearest relatives—chimpanzees and gorillas—have rudimentary cultural abilities. However, no other animal has elaborated cultural abilities—to learn, to communicate, and to store, process, and use information—to the extent that *Homo* has.

Culture and Nature

Culture takes the natural biological urges we share with other animals and teaches us how to express them in particular ways. People have to eat, but culture teaches us what, when, and how. In many cultures people have their main meal at noon, but most North Americans prefer a large dinner. English people may eat fish for breakfast, while North Americans may prefer hot cakes and cold cereals. Brazilians put hot milk into strong coffee, whereas North Americans pour cold milk into a weaker brew. Midwesterners dine at 5 or 6 P.M., Spaniards at 10 P.M.

■ *Olympic medalists and their symbols. In Cesana Pariol, Italy, on February 21, 2006, Gold Medal bobsled winners Sandra Kiriasis and Anja Schneiderheinze of Germany* (left) *celebrate with Silver Medal winners Valerie Fleming and Shauna Rohbock of the United States* (right) *on Day 11 of the 2006 Turin Winter Olympics. What are the symbols in this photo and caption?*

People in the United States sometimes have trouble understanding the power of culture because of the value American culture places on the idea of the *individual*. Americans are fond of saying that everyone is unique and special in some way. In American culture, individualism itself is a distinctive *shared* value, a feature of culture. Individualism is transmitted through hundreds of statements and settings in our daily lives. Watch a morning TV show, such as *Today*, for an hour. Count how many stories focus on individuals, especially their achievements. Contrast that with the number of stories that focus on the achievements of communities. From the late Mr. Rogers from daytime TV to "real-life" parents, grandparents, and teachers, our enculturative agents insist we are all "someone special." That is, we are individuals first and members of groups second. This is the opposite of the lesson being taught in this chapter about culture. Without doubt we have distinctive features because we are individuals, but we have other distinct attributes because we are members of groups.

Cultural habits, perceptions, and inventions mold "human nature" in many directions. People have to eliminate wastes from their bodies. But some cultures teach people to defecate squatting, while others tell them to do it sitting down. A generation ago, in Paris and other French cities, it was customary for men to urinate almost publicly, and seemingly without embarrassment, in barely shielded *pissoirs* located on city streets. Our "bathroom" habits, including waste elimination, bathing, and dental care, are parts of cultural traditions that have converted natural acts into cultural customs.

Our culture—and cultural changes—affects the ways in which we perceive nature, human nature, and "the natural." Through science, invention, and discovery, cultural advances have overcome many "natural" limitations. We prevent and cure diseases such as polio and smallpox that felled our ancestors. We use Viagra to restore and enhance sexual potency. Through cloning, scientists have altered the way we think about biological identity and the meaning of life itself. Culture, of course, has not freed us from natural threats. Hurricanes, floods, earthquakes, and other natural forces regularly challenge our wishes to modify the environment through building, development, and expansion. Can you think of other ways in which nature strikes back at people and their products?

 STUDENT CD-ROM LIVING ANTHROPOLOGY

Being Raised Canela
Track 13

This clip focuses on Brazil's Canela Indians, who are also depicted in the clip for Chapter 12. One of the key figures in the clip is the boy Carampei, who was four years old in 1975. Another is the "formal friend" of a small boy whose finger has been burned and who has been disciplined by his mother. The clip depicts enculturation among the Canela—various ways in which children learn their culture. How does the footage of Carampei show his learning of the rhythms of Canela life? The clip shows that children start doing useful work at an early age, but that the playfulness and affection of childhood are prolonged into adulthood. How does the behavior of the formal friend illustrate this playfulness? Notice how Canela culture is integrated in that songs, dances, and tales are interwoven with subsistence activity. From an emic perspective, what is the function of the hunters' dance? Think about how the clip shows the formal and informal, the conscious and unconscious aspects of enculturation.

Culture Is All-Encompassing

For anthropologists, culture includes much more than refinement, taste, sophistication, education, and appreciation of the fine arts. Not only college graduates but all people are "cultured." The most interesting and significant cultural forces are those that affect people every day of their lives, particularly those that influence children during enculturation. *Culture,* as defined anthropologically, encompasses features that are sometimes regarded as trivial or unworthy of serious study, such as "popular" culture (see Appendix 3). To understand contemporary North American culture, we must consider television, fast-food restaurants, sports, and games. As a cultural manifestation, a rock star may be as interesting as a symphony conductor, a comic book as significant as a book-award winner.

Culture Is Integrated

Cultures are not haphazard collections of customs and beliefs. Cultures are integrated, patterned systems. If one part of the system (e.g., the economy) changes, other parts change as well. For example, during the 1950s, most American women planned domestic careers as homemakers and mothers. Most of today's college women, by contrast, expect to get paid jobs when they graduate.

What are some of the social repercussions of the economic change? Attitudes and behavior regarding marriage, family, and children have changed. Late marriage, "living together," and divorce have become more common. The average age at first marriage for American women rose

Bringing It All Together

For a more detailed look at Canadian national and popular culture, see the "Bringing It All Together" essay that immediately follows Chapter 15.

Touching, Affection, Love, and Sex

Comparing the United States to Brazil—or virtually any Latin nation—we can see a striking cultural contrast between a national culture that tends to discourage physical contact and demonstrations of affection and one in which the contrary is true.

"Don't touch me." "Take your hands off me." Such statements are not uncommon in North America, but they are virtually never heard in Brazil, the Western Hemisphere's second most populous country. Brazilians like to be touched (and kissed) more than North Americans do. The world's cultures have strikingly different notions about displays of affection and about matters of personal space. When North Americans talk, walk, and dance, they maintain a certain distance from others—their personal space. Brazilians, who maintain less physical distance, interpret this as a sign of coldness. When conversing with a North American, the Brazilian characteristically moves in as the North American "instinctively" retreats. In these body movements, neither Brazilian nor North American is trying consciously to be especially friendly or unfriendly. Each is merely executing a program written on the self by years of exposure to a particular cultural tradition. Because of different ideas about proper social space, cocktail parties in international meeting places such as the United Nations can resemble an elaborate insect mating ritual as diplomats from different cultures advance, withdraw, and sidestep.

One easily evident difference between Brazil and the United States involves kissing, hugging, and touching. Middle-class Brazilians teach their kids—both boys and girls—to kiss (on the cheek, two or three times, coming and going) every adult relative they ever see. Given the size of Brazilian extended families, this can mean hundreds of people. Females continue kissing throughout their lives. They kiss male and female kin, friends, relatives of friends, friends of relatives, friends of friends, and, when it seems appropriate, more casual acquaintances. Males go on kissing their female relatives and friends. Until they are ado-

lescents, boys also kiss adult male relatives. Brazilian men typically greet each other with hearty handshakes and a traditional male hug (*abraço*). The closer the relationship, the tighter and longer-lasting the embrace. These comments apply to brothers, cousins, uncles, and friends. Many Brazilian men keep on kissing their fathers and uncles throughout their lives. Could it be that homophobia (fear of homosexuality) prevents American men from engaging in such displays of affection with other men? Are American women more likely to show affection with each other than American men are?

Like other North Americans who spend time in a Latin culture, I miss the numerous kisses and handshakes when I get back to the United States. After several months in Brazil, I find North Americans rather cold and impersonal. Many Brazilians share this opinion. I have heard similar feelings expressed by Italian-Americans as they describe North Americans with different ethnic backgrounds.

Question: *Ethnocentrism* is the tendency to view one's own culture as superior and to apply one's own cultural values in judging the behavior and beliefs of people from other cultures (see pp. 288–290). Do you have an ethnocentric position on the matter of displays of affection?

According to clinical psychologist David E. Klimek, who has written about

intimacy and marriage in the United States, "in American society, if we go much beyond simple touching, our behavior takes on a minor sexual twist" (Slade 1984). North Americans define demonstrations of affection between males and females with reference to marriage. Love and affection are supposed to unite the married pair, and they blend into sex. When a wife asks her husband for "a little affection," she may mean, or he may think she means, sex.

A certain lack of clarity in North American definitions of love, affection, and sex is evident on Valentine's Day, which used to be just for lovers. Valentines used to be sent to wives, husbands, girlfriends, and boyfriends. Now, after years of promotion by the greeting card industry, they also go to mothers, fathers, sons, daughters, aunts, and uncles. There is a blurring of sexual and nonsexual affection. In Brazil, Lovers' Day retains its autonomy. Mother, father, and children have their own separate days of recognition.

It's true, of course, that in a good marriage love and affection exist alongside sex. Nevertheless, affection does not necessarily imply sex. The Brazilian culture shows that there can be rampant kissing, hugging, and touching without sex—or fears of improper sexuality. In Brazilian culture, physical demonstrations help cement many kinds of close personal relationships that have no sexual component.

◼ *Cultures have strikingly different standards of personal space, such as how far apart people should stand in normal encounters and interactions. Contrast the distance between the American businessmen and the closeness (including touching) of the two rabbis discussing the Talmud near the Western Wall in Jerusalem. Have you noticed such differences in your own interactions with others?*

from 20 in 1955 to 25 in 2003. The comparable figures for men were 23 and 27 (U.S. Census Bureau 2003). The number of currently divorced Americans more than quadrupled from 4 million in 1970 to about 22 million in 2004 (Statistical Abstract of the United States 2006). Work competes with marriage and family responsibilities and reduces the time available to invest in child care.

Cultures are integrated not simply by their dominant economic activities and related social patterns but also by sets of values, ideas, symbols, and judgments. Cultures train their individual members to share certain personality traits. A set of characteristic central or **core values** (key, basic, or central values) integrates each culture and helps distinguish it from others. For instance, the work ethic and individualism are core values that have integrated American culture for generations. Different sets of dominant values influence the patterns of other cultures.

Culture Can Be Adaptive and Maladaptive

As we saw in Chapter 1, humans have both biological and cultural ways of coping with environmental stresses. Besides our biological means of adaptation, we also use "cultural adaptive kits," which contain customary activities and tools. Although humans continue to adapt biologically, reliance on social and cultural means of adaptation has increased during human evolution.

In this discussion of the adaptive features of our cultural behavior, let's recognize that what's good for the individual isn't necessarily good for the group. Sometimes adaptive behavior that offers short-term benefits to particular individuals may harm the environment and threaten the group's long-term survival. Economic growth may benefit some people while it also depletes resources needed for society at large or for future genera-

tions (Bennett 1969, p. 19). Despite the crucial role of cultural adaptation in human evolution, cultural traits, patterns, and inventions also can be *maladaptive*, threatening the group's continued existence (survival and reproduction). Air conditioners help us deal with heat, as fires and furnaces protect us against the cold. Automobiles permit us to make a living by getting us from home to workplace. But the by-products of such "beneficial" technology often create new problems. Chemical emissions increase air pollution, deplete the ozone layer, and contribute to global warming. Many cultural patterns, such as overconsumption and pollution, appear to be maladaptive in the long run.

CULTURE AND THE INDIVIDUAL: AGENCY AND PRACTICE

Generations of anthropologists have theorized about the relationship between the "system," on the one hand, and the "person" or "individual," on the other. The "system" can refer to various concepts, including culture, society, social relations, and social structure. Individual human beings always make up, or constitute, the system. But, living within that system, humans also are constrained (to some extent, at least) by its rules, and by the actions of other individuals. Cultural rules provide guidance about what to do and how to do it, but people don't always do what the rules say should be done. People use their culture actively and creatively, rather than blindly following its dictates. Humans aren't passive beings who are doomed to follow their cultural traditions like programmed robots. Instead, people learn, interpret, and manipulate the same rules in different ways—or they emphasize different rules that better suit their interests. Culture is *contested:* Different groups in society struggle with one another over whose ideas, values, goals, and beliefs will prevail. Even common symbols may have radically different *meanings* to different individuals and groups in the same culture. Golden arches may cause one person to salivate, while another person plots a vegetarian protest. The same flag may be waved to support or oppose a given war.

Even when they agree about what should and shouldn't be done, people don't always do as their culture directs or as other people expect. Many rules are violated, some very often (e.g., automobile speed limits). Some anthropologists find it useful to distinguish between ideal culture and real culture. The *ideal culture* consists of what people say they should do and what they say they do. *Real culture* refers to their actual behavior as observed by the anthropologist. This contrast is like the emic–etic distinction discussed in the last chapter.

Culture is both public and individual, both in the world and in people's minds. Anthropologists are interested not only in public and collective behavior but also in how *individuals* think, feel, and act. The individual and culture are linked because human social life is a process in which individuals internalize the meanings of *public* (i.e., cultural) messages. Then, alone and in groups, people influence culture by converting their private (and often divergent) understandings into public expressions (D'Andrade 1984).

Conventionally, culture has been seen as social glue transmitted across the generations, binding people through their common past, rather than as something being continually created and reworked in the present. The tendency to view culture as an entity rather than a process is changing. Contemporary anthropologists now emphasize how day-to-day action, practice, or resistance can make and remake culture (Gupta and Ferguson, eds. 1997b). *Agency* refers to the actions that individuals take, both alone and in groups, in forming and transforming cultural identities.

The approach to culture known as *practice theory* (Ortner 1984) recognizes that individuals within a society or culture have diverse motives and intentions and different degrees of power and influence (see also Appendix 1). Such contrasts may be associated with gender, age, ethnicity, class, and other social variables. Practice theory focuses on how such varied individuals—through their ordinary and extraordinary actions and practices—manage to influence, create, and transform the world they live in. Practice theory appropriately recognizes a reciprocal relation between culture (the system—see above) and the individual. The system shapes the way individuals experience and respond to external events, but individuals also play an active role in the way society functions and changes. Practice theory recognizes both constraints on individuals and the flexibility and changeability of cultures and social systems.

Illustrating the international level of culture, Roman Catholics in different nations share knowledge, symbols, beliefs, and values transmitted by their church. Shown here is a Catholic seminary in Xian, China. Besides religious conversion, what other forces work to spread international culture?

Levels of Culture

Of increasing importance in today's world are the distinctions between different levels of culture: national, international, and subcultural. **National culture** refers to those beliefs, learned behavior patterns, values, and institutions that are shared by citizens of the same nation. **International culture** is the term for cultural traditions that extend beyond and across national boundaries. Because culture is transmitted through learning rather than genetically, cultural traits can spread through borrowing or *diffusion* from one group to another.

Because of borrowing, colonialism, migration, and multinational organizations, many cultural traits and patterns have international scope. For example, Roman Catholics in many different countries share beliefs, symbols, experiences, and values transmitted by their church. The contemporary United States, Canada, Great Britain, and Australia share cultural traits they have inherited from their common linguistic and cultural ancestors in Great Britain. The World Cup has become an international cultural event, as people in many countries know the rules of, play, and follow soccer.

Cultures also can be smaller than nations (see Jenks 2004). Although people who live in the same country share a national cultural tradition, all cultures also contain diversity. Individuals, families, communities, regions, classes, and other groups within a culture have different learning experiences as well as shared ones. **Subcultures** are different symbol-based patterns and traditions associated with particular groups in the same complex society. In a large nation like the United States or Canada, subcultures originate in

Bringing It All Together

For a more detailed look at the cultural, ethnic, and linguistic aspects of unity and diversity in a contemporary nation-state, see the "Bringing It All Together" essay that immediately follows Chapter 15.

region, ethnicity, language, class, and religion. The religious backgrounds of Jews, Baptists, and Roman Catholics create subcultural differences between them. While sharing a common national culture, U.S. northerners and southerners also differ in aspects of their beliefs, values, and customary behavior as a result of regional variation. French-speaking Canadians contrast with English-speaking people in the same country. Italian Americans have ethnic traditions different from those of Irish, Polish, and African Americans. Using sports and foods, Table 13.1 gives some examples of international, national, and subculture. Soccer and basketball are played internationally. Monster-truck rallies are held throughout the United States. Bocci is a bowling-like sport from Italy still played in some Italian-American neighborhoods.

Nowadays, many anthropologists are reluctant to use the term *subculture.* They feel that the prefix "sub-" is offensive because it means "below." "Subcultures" may thus be perceived as "less than" or somehow inferior to a dominant, elite, or national culture. In this discussion of levels of culture, I intend no such implication. My point is simply that nations may contain many different culturally defined groups. As mentioned earlier, culture is contested. Various groups may strive to promote the correctness and value of their own practices, values, and beliefs in comparison with those of other groups, or the nation as a whole.

Ethnocentrism, Cultural Relativism, and Human Rights

Ethnocentrism is the tendency to view one's own culture as superior and to apply one's own cultural values in judging the behavior and beliefs of people raised in other cultures. We hear ethnocentric statements all the time. Ethnocentrism is a cultural universal. It contributes to social solidarity, a sense of value and community, among people who share a cultural tradition. People everywhere think that their familiar explanations, opinions, and customs are true, right, proper, and moral. They regard different behavior as strange, immoral, or savage. The tribal names that appear in anthropology books often come from the native word for *people.* "What are you called?" asks the anthropologist. "Mugmug," reply informants. *Mugmug* may turn out to be synonymous with *people,* but it also may be the only word the natives have for themselves. Other tribes are not considered fully human. The not-quite-people in neighboring groups are not classified as *Mugmug.* They are given different names that symbolize their inferior humanity. Neighboring tribes may be ridiculed and insulted because of their customs and preferences. They may be castigated as cannibals, thieves, or people who do not bury their dead.

Opposing ethnocentrism is **cultural relativism,** the argument that behavior in one culture

Level of Culture	Sports Examples	Food Examples
International	Soccer, basketball	Pizza
National	Monster-truck rallies	Apple pie
Subculture	Bocci	Big Joe Pork Barbeque (South Carolina)

TABLE 13.1 Levels of Culture, with Examples from Sports and Foods

should not be judged by the standards of another culture. This position also can present problems. At its most extreme, cultural relativism argues that there is no superior, international, or universal morality, that the moral and ethical rules of all cultures deserve equal respect. In the extreme relativist view, Nazi Germany would be evaluated as nonjudgmentally as Athenian Greece.

In today's world, human rights advocates challenge many of the tenets of cultural relativism. For example, several cultures in Africa and the Middle East have traditions of female genital modification. *Clitoridectomy* is the removal of a girl's clitoris. *Infibulation* involves sewing the lips (labia) of the vagina to constrict the vaginal opening. Both procedures reduce female sexual pleasure and, it is believed in some cultures, the likelihood of adultery. One or both of the procedures have been traditional in several societies, but such practices, characterized as female genital mutilation (FGM), have been opposed by human rights advocates, especially women's rights groups. The idea is that the tradition infringes on a basic human right: disposition over one's body and one's sexuality. Although such practices continue in certain areas, they are fading as a result of worldwide attention to the problem and changing sex-gender roles. Some African countries have banned or otherwise discouraged the procedures, as have Western nations that receive immigration from such cultures. Similar issues arise with circumcision and other male genital operations. Is it right for a baby boy to be circumcised without his permission, as has been routinely done in the United States? Is it proper to require adolescent boys to undergo collective circumcision to fulfill cultural tradition, as is done traditionally in parts of Africa and Australia?

Some would argue that the problems with relativism can be solved by distinguishing between methodological and moral relativism. In anthropology, cultural relativism is not a moral position, but a methodological one. It states: to understand

The notion of indigenous intellectual property rights (IPR) has arisen in an attempt to conserve each society's cultural base, including its medicinal plants, which may have commercial value. Shown here is the hoodia plant, a cactus that grows in the Kalahari Desert of southern Africa. Hoodia, which traditionally is used by the San people to stave off hunger, is used now in diet pills marketed on the Internet.

another culture fully, you must try to see how the people in that culture see things. What motivates them—what are they thinking—when they do those things? Such an approach does not preclude making moral judgments or taking action. When faced with Nazi atrocities, a methodological relativist would have a moral obligation to stop doing anthropology and take action to intervene. In the FGM example, one only can understand the *motivations* for the practice by looking at things from the point of view of those who engage in it. Having done this, one then faces the moral question of whether to intervene to stop it. We should recognize as well that different people and groups living in the same society—for example, women and men, old and young, the more and less powerful—can have widely different views about what is proper, necessary, and moral.

The idea of **human rights** invokes a realm of justice and morality beyond and superior to particular countries, cultures, and religions. Human rights, usually seen as vested in individuals, include the right to speak freely, to hold religious beliefs without persecution, and not to be murdered, injured, enslaved, or imprisoned without charge. These rights are not ordinary laws that particular governments make and enforce. Human rights are seen as *inalienable* (nations cannot abridge or terminate them) and international (larger than and superior to individual nations and cultures). Four United Nations documents describe nearly all the human rights that have

been internationally recognized. Those documents are the UN Charter; the Universal Declaration of Human Rights; the Covenant on Economic, Social and Cultural Rights; and the Covenant on Civil and Political Rights.

Alongside the human rights movement has arisen an awareness of the need to preserve cultural rights. Unlike human rights, **cultural rights** are vested not in individuals but in *groups,* such as religious and ethnic minorities and indigenous societies. Cultural rights include a group's ability to preserve its culture, to raise its children in the ways of its forebears, to continue its language, and not to be deprived of its economic base by the nation in which it is located (Greaves 1995). Many countries have signed pacts endorsing, for cultural minorities within nations, such rights as self-determination; some degree of home rule; and the right to practice the group's religion, culture, and language. The related notion of indigenous intellectual property rights (**IPR**) has arisen in an attempt to conserve each society's cultural base—its core beliefs and principles. IPR are claimed as a cultural right, allowing indigenous groups to control who may know and use their collective knowledge and its applications. Much traditional cultural knowledge has commercial value. Examples include ethnomedicine (traditional medical knowledge and techniques), cosmetics, cultivated plants, foods, folklore, arts, crafts, songs, dances, costumes, and rituals. According to the IPR concept, a particular group may determine how indigenous knowledge

Map 10 locates classic ethnographic field sites— "cultures" or societies already studied by 1950.

and its products may be used and distributed, and the level of compensation required.

The notion of cultural rights is related to the idea of cultural relativism, and the problem discussed previously arises again. What does one do about cultural rights that interfere with human rights? I believe that anthropology's main job is to present accurate accounts and explanations of cultural phenomena. The anthropologist doesn't have to approve customs such as infanticide, cannibalism, and torture to record their existence and determine their causes and the motivations behind them. However, each anthropologist has a choice about where he or she will do field work. Some anthropologists choose not to study a particular culture because they discover in advance or early in field work that behavior they consider morally repugnant is practiced there. Anthropologists respect human diversity. Most ethnographers try to be objective, accurate, and sensitive in their accounts of other cultures. However, objectivity, sensitivity, and a cross-cultural perspective don't mean that anthropologists have to ignore international standards of justice and morality. What do you think?

UNIVERSALITY, GENERALITY, AND PARTICULARITY

In studying human diversity in time and space, anthropologists distinguish among the universal, the generalized, and the particular. Certain biological, psychological, social, and cultural features are **universal**, found in every culture. Others are merely **generalities**, common to several but not all human groups. Still other traits are **particularities**, unique to certain cultural traditions.

Universality

Universal traits are the ones that more or less distinguish *Homo sapiens* from other species (see Brown 1991). Biologically based universals include a long period of infant dependency, year-round (rather than seasonal) sexuality, and a complex brain that enables us to use symbols, languages, and tools. Psychological universals involve common ways in which humans think, feel, and process information. Most such universals probably reflect human biological universals, such as the structure of the human brain or certain physical differences between men and women, or children and adults.

Among the social universals is life in groups and in some kind of family. In all human societies, culture organizes social life and depends on social interactions for its expression and continuation. Family living and food sharing are universals. Among the most significant cultural universals are exogamy and the *incest taboo* (pro-

See the Internet Exercises at your OLC on cultural insults

mhhe.com/kottak

hibition against marrying or mating with a close relative). All cultures consider some people (various cultures differ about *which* people) too closely related to mate or marry. The violation of this taboo is *incest,* which is discouraged and punished in a variety of ways in different cultures. If incest is prohibited, *exogamy*—marriage outside one's group—is inevitable. Because it links human groups together into larger networks, exogamy has been crucial in human evolution. Exogamy elaborates on tendencies observed among other primates. Recent studies of monkeys and apes show that these animals also avoid mating with close kin and often mate outside their native groups.

Generality

Between universals and uniqueness (see the next section) is a middle ground that consists of cultural generalities. These are regularities that occur in different times and places but not in all cultures. One reason for generalities is diffusion. Societies can share the same beliefs and customs because of borrowing or through (cultural) inheritance from a common cultural ancestor. Speaking English is a generality shared by North Americans and Australians because both countries had English settlers. Another reason for generalities is domination, as in colonial rule, when customs and procedures are imposed on one culture by another one that is more powerful. In many countries, use of the English language reflects colonial history. More recently, English has spread through diffusion to many other countries, as it has become the world's foremost language for business and travel.

Cultural generalities also can arise through independent invention of the same cultural trait or pattern in two or more different cultures. For example, farming arose through independent invention in the Eastern (e.g., the Middle East) and Western (e.g., Mexico) Hemispheres. Similar needs and circumstances have led people in different lands to innovate in parallel ways. They have independently come up with the same cultural solution to a common problem.

One cultural generality that is present in many but not all societies is the *nuclear family,* a kinship group consisting of parents and children. Although many middle-class Americans ethnocentrically view the nuclear family as a proper and "natural" group, it is not universal. It is absent, for example, among the Nayars, who live on the Malabar Coast of India. The Nayars live in female-headed households, and husbands and wives do not live together. In many other societies, the nuclear family is submerged in larger kin groups, such as extended families, lineages, and clans. However, the nuclear family is prominent in many of the technologically simple societies that live by hunting and gathering. It is also a significant kin group among contemporary middle-class North Americans and Western Europeans. Later, an explanation of the nuclear family as a basic kinship unit in specific types of society will be given.

Particularity: Patterns of Culture

A cultural particularity is a trait or feature of culture that is not generalized or widespread; rather, it is confined to a single place, culture, or society. Yet because of cultural diffusion, which has accelerated through modern transportation and communication systems, traits that once were limited in their distribution have become more widespread. Traits that are useful, that have the capacity to please large audiences, and that don't clash with the cultural values of potential adopters are more likely to diffuse than others are. Still, certain cultural particularities persist. One example would be a particular food dish (e.g., pork barbeque with a mustard-based sauce available only in South Carolina, or the pastie—beef stew baked in pie dough—characteristic of Michigan's upper peninsula). Besides diffusion, which, for example, has spread McDonald's food outlets, once confined to San Bernadino, California, across the globe, there are other reasons why cultural particularities are increasingly rare. Many cultural traits are shared as cultural universals and as a result of independent invention. Facing similar problems, people in different places have come up with similar solutions. Again and again, similar cultural causes have produced similar cultural results.

At the level of the individual cultural trait or element (e.g., bow and arrow, hot dog, MTV), particularities may be getting rarer. But at a higher level, particularity is more obvious. Different cultures emphasize different things. *Cultures are integrated and patterned differently and display tremendous variation and diversity.* When cultural traits are borrowed, they are modified to fit the culture that adopts them. They are reintegrated— patterned anew—to fit their new setting. MTV in Germany or Brazil isn't at all the same thing as MTV in the United States. As was stated in the earlier section "Culture Is Integrated," patterned beliefs, customs, and practices lend distinctiveness to particular cultural traditions.

Consider universal life-cycle events, such as birth, puberty, marriage, parenthood, and death, which many cultures observe and celebrate. The occasions (e.g., marriage, death) may be the same and universal, but the patterns of ceremonial observance may be dramatically different. Cultures vary in just which events merit special celebration. Americans, for example, regard expensive weddings as more socially appropriate than lavish funerals. However, the Betsileo of Madagascar take the opposite view. The marriage ceremony is a minor event that brings together just the couple and a few close relatives. However, a funeral is a

measure of the deceased person's social position and lifetime achievement, and it may attract a thousand people. Why use money on a house, the Betsileo say, when one can use it on the tomb where one will spend eternity in the company of dead relatives? How unlike contemporary Americans' dreams of home ownership and preference for quick and inexpensive funerals. Cremation, an increasingly common option in the United States, would horrify the Betsileo, for whom ancestral bones and relics are important ritual objects.

Cultures vary tremendously in their beliefs, practices, integration, and patterning. By focusing on and trying to explain alternative customs, anthropology forces us to reappraise our familiar ways of thinking. In a world full of cultural diversity, contemporary American culture is just one cultural variant, more powerful perhaps, but no more natural, than the others.

Cultures use rituals to mark such universal life-cycle events as birth, puberty, marriage, parenthood, and death. But particular cultures differ as to which event merits special celebration and in the emotions expressed during their rituals. Compare the wedding party (top) in Bali, Indonesia, with the funeral (bottom) among the Tanala of eastern Madagascar. How would you describe the emotions suggested by the photos?

■ *Within and between nations, the Internet spreads information about products, rights, and lifestyles. Shown here, a coffee shop in Cairo, Egypt, with men, laptop computer, and hookahs (pipes). For what purposes do you think these men use the computer?*

MECHANISMS OF CULTURAL CHANGE

Why and how do cultures change? One way is **diffusion,** or borrowing of traits between cultures. Such exchange of information and products has gone on throughout human history because cultures have never been truly isolated. Contact between neighboring groups has always existed and has extended over vast areas (Boas 1940/1966). Diffusion is *direct* when two cultures trade, intermarry, or wage war on one another. Diffusion is *forced* when one culture subjugates another and imposes its customs on the dominated group. Diffusion is *indirect* when items move from group A to group C via group B without any firsthand contact between A and C. In this case, group B might consist of traders or merchants who take products from a variety of places to new markets. Or group B might be geographically situated between A and C, so that what it gets from A eventually winds up in C, and vice versa. In today's world, much transnational diffusion is due to the spread of the mass media and advanced information technology.

Acculturation, a second mechanism of cultural change, is the exchange of cultural features that results when groups have continuous firsthand contact. The cultures of either group or both groups may be changed by this contact (Redfield, Linton, and Herskovits 1936). With acculturation, parts of the cultures change, but each group remains distinct. In situations of continuous contact, cultures may exchange and blend foods, recipes, music, dances, clothing, tools, technologies, and languages.

One example of acculturation is a *pidgin*, a mixed language that develops to ease communication between members of different societies in contact. This usually happens in situations of trade or colonialism. Pidgin English, for example, is a simplified form of English. It blends English grammar with the grammar of a native language. Pidgin English was first used for commerce in Chinese ports. Similar pidgins developed later in Papua New Guinea and West Africa.

Independent invention—the process by which humans innovate, creatively finding solutions to problems—is a third mechanism of cultural change. Faced with comparable problems and challenges, people in different societies have innovated and changed in similar ways, which is one reason cultural generalities exist. One example is the independent invention of agriculture in the Middle East and Mexico. Over the course of human history, major innovations have spread at the expense of earlier ones. Often a major invention, such as agriculture, triggers a series of subsequent interrelated changes. These economic revolutions have social and cultural repercussions. Thus, in both Mexico and the Middle East, agriculture led to many social, political, and legal changes, including notions of property and distinctions in wealth, class, and power. (For various theories of culture change see Appendix 1.)

GLOBALIZATION

The term **globalization** encompasses a series of processes, including diffusion and acculturation, working to promote change in a world in which nations and people are increasingly interlinked and mutually dependent. Promoting such linkages are economic and political forces, along with modern systems of transportation and communication. The forces of globalization include international commerce, travel and tourism, transnational migration, the media, and various high-tech information flows (see Appadurai, ed. 2001). During the Cold War, which ended with the fall of the Soviet Union, the basis of international alliance was political, ideological, and military. Thereafter, the focus of international pacts shifted to trade and economic issues. New economic unions have been created through NAFTA (the North American Free Trade Agreement), GATT (the General Agreement on Trade and Tariffs), and the EU (the European Union).

Long-distance communication is easier, faster, and cheaper than ever and extends to remote areas. The mass media help propel a globally spreading culture of consumption, stimulating participation in the world cash economy. Within nations and across their borders, the media spread information about threats, products, services, rights, institu-

Folklore Reveals Ethos of Heating Plant Workers

BACKGROUND INFORMATION

STUDENT:
Mark Dennis

SUPERVISING PROFESSOR:
Usher Fleising

SCHOOL:
University of Calgary

YEAR IN SCHOOL/MAJOR:
Fifth-Year Senior/
Social Anthropology

FUTURE PLANS:
Graduate school, traveling

PROJECT TITLE:
Folklore Reveals Ethos
of Heating Plant Workers

What role does folklore play among the workers described in this account? What functions do common tales serve in enabling workers to adapt to their work setting? What attributes of culture are represented here?

At the periphery of the University of Calgary campus exists a place, ironically called the central heating and cooling plant. Housed within its four walls and three levels are the industrial machinery and a tangle of pipes that snake through an eight-mile tunnel system in the bowels of the earth, bringing heat and cooling to a campus of 21,000.

Folklore is an oral form of knowledge shared by a cultural group. The objective of my research was to reveal the social and cultural manifestations of folklore among the University Central Heating and Cooling Plant (CHCP) employees. In an isolated control room, a fieldworker finds plant employees engaged in a social atmosphere filled with storytelling and humor. Accustomed to the mental and physical distance from the rest of the university, the men of the CHCP were glad to share their knowledge and folklore with me.

In addition to simple observations and document analysis, my research method consisted primarily of unstructured interviews. Using this technique I was able to control the direction of the conversation while still giving the informants (cultural consultants, community members) freedom to express themselves.

Folklore at the CHCP was passed on between employees during their shifts or during shift changes. Most stories were known by all employees. The themes included slapstick humor, disaster stories, tales about eccentric characters, practical jokes, and stories about complaints. The folklore was based entirely on oral history, with no written documentation ever produced.

During the course of fieldwork, I found that folklore functioned as an organic mechanism adapting to the needs of the employees by providing stress relief. Folklore helped them to deal constructively with job frustrations, and it created social cohesion among employees.

The last six years at the CHCP have been turbulent because of a management change. Conflicting working methods and rapid changes in technology made it hard for many employees to adapt. In this context the humor that folklore provided not only lightened the mood, but it also brought back fond memories of the easy-going past.

The CHCP has a unique working environment. At its worst, days can be filled with isolation and mundane activity, leaving the employees feeling that no one cares about the important work they do. Folklore is a healthy way of dealing with the isolation and ignorance of others. Workers share stories of the prestigious visitors, like university presidents, who have visited the plant over the years. By telling these stories the plant workers can see that there is hope for educating people about what they do. Such stories affirm that their jobs are very important.

Finally, folklore is a cohesive force whereby plant workers both old and new can celebrate the shared knowledge and unique work environment that surrounds them, leading to a happier and more productive work environment. Folklore is an interesting starting point from which to analyze subcultures and their social relations. The study of the Central Heating and Cooling Plant at the University of Calgary was one application of folklore as a theoretical basis for social analysis.

tions, and lifestyles. Emigrants transmit information and resources transnationally as they maintain their ties with home (phoning, faxing, e-mailing, making visits, sending money). In a sense, such people live multilocally—in different places and cultures at once. They learn to play various social roles and to change behavior and identity depending on the situation (see Cresswell 2006).

Local people must increasingly cope with forces generated by progressively larger systems— region, nation, and world. An army of alien actors and agents now intrudes on people everywhere. Terrorism is a global threat. Tourism has become the world's number one industry (see Holden 2005). Economic development agents and the media promote the idea that work should be for cash rather than mainly for subsistence. Indigenous peoples and traditional cultures have devised various strategies to deal with threats to their autonomy, identity, and livelihood. New forms of political mobilization and cultural expression are emerging from the interplay of local, regional, national, and international cultural forces (see Ong and Collier, eds. 2005).

SUMMARY

1. Culture, which is distinctive to humanity, refers to customary behavior and beliefs that are passed on through enculturation. Culture rests on the human capacity for cultural learning. Culture encompasses rules for conduct internalized in human beings, which lead them to think and act in characteristic ways.

2. Although other animals learn, only humans have cultural learning, dependent on symbols. Humans think symbolically—arbitrarily bestowing meaning on things and events. By convention, a symbol stands for something with which it has no necessary or natural relation. Symbols have special meaning for people who share memories, values, and beliefs because of common enculturation. People absorb cultural lessons consciously and unconsciously.

3. Cultural traditions mold biologically based desires and needs in particular directions. Everyone is cultured, not just people with elite educations. Cultures may be integrated and patterned through economic and social forces, key symbols, and core values. Cultural rules don't rigidly dictate our behavior. There is room for creativity, flexibility, diversity, and disagreement within societies. Cultural means of adaptation have been crucial in human evolution. Aspects of culture also can be maladaptive.

4. There are levels of culture, which can be larger or smaller than a nation. Diffusion, migration, and colonialism have carried cultural traits and patterns to different areas. Such traits are shared across national boundaries. Nations also include cultural differences associated with ethnicity, region, and social class.

5. Using a comparative perspective, anthropology examines biological, psychological, social, and cultural universals and generalities. There are also unique and distinctive aspects of the human condition. North American cultural traditions are no more natural than any others. Mechanisms of cultural change include diffusion, acculturation, and independent invention. Globalization describes a series of processes that promote change in a world in which nations and people are interlinked and mutually dependent.

KEY TERMS

See the flash cards
mhhe.com/kottak

acculturation   The exchange of cultural features that results when groups come into continuous first-hand contact; the cultural patterns of either or both groups may be changed, but the groups remain distinct.

core values   Key, basic, or central values that integrate a culture and help distinguish it from others.

cultural relativism   The position that the values and standards of cultures differ and deserve respect. Anthropology is characterized by methodological rather than moral relativism: In order to understand another culture fully, anthropologists try to understand its members' beliefs and motivations. Methodological relativism does not preclude making moral judgments or taking action.

cultural rights   Doctrine that certain rights are vested in identifiable groups, such as religious and ethnic minorities and indigenous societies. Cultural rights include a group's ability to preserve its culture, to raise its children in the ways of its forebears, to continue its language, and not to be deprived of its economic base by the nation-state in which it is located.

diffusion   Borrowing of cultural traits between societies, either directly or through intermediaries.

enculturation   The social process by which culture is learned and transmitted across the generations.

ethnocentrism   The tendency to view one's own culture as best and to judge the behavior and beliefs of culturally different people by one's own standards.

generality   Culture pattern or trait that exists in some but not all societies.

globalization   The accelerating interdependence of nations in a world system linked economically and through mass media and modern transportation systems.

human rights   Doctrine that invokes a realm of justice and morality beyond and superior to particular countries, cultures, and religions. Human rights, usually seen as vested in individuals, would include the right to speak freely, to hold religious beliefs without persecution, and not to be murdered, injured, enslaved, or imprisoned without charge.

independent invention   Development of the same cultural trait or pattern in separate cultures as a result of comparable needs, circumstances, and solutions.

international culture   Cultural traditions that extend beyond national boundaries.

IPR   Intellectual property rights, consisting of each society's cultural base—its core beliefs and principles. IPR are claimed as a group right—a cultural right—allowing indigenous groups to control who may know and use their collective knowledge and its applications.

national culture   Cultural experiences, beliefs, learned behavior patterns, and values shared by citizens of the same nation.

particularity   Distinctive or unique culture trait, pattern, or integration.

subcultures   Different cultural traditions associated with subgroups in the same complex society.

symbol   Something, verbal or nonverbal, that arbitrarily and by convention stands for something else, with which it has no necessary or natural connection.

universal   Something that exists in every culture.

---

1. What cultural symbols have the most meaning for you? For your family? For your nation?

2. What are the key symbols and values that work to unite your religious group or another organization to which you belong?

3. Give some examples of cultural practices that are adaptive in the short run but probably maladaptive in the long run.

4. Do you feel you have multiple cultural identities? If so, how do you handle them?

5. What are some issues about which you find it hard to be culturally relativistic?

CRITICAL THINKING QUESTIONS

For more self-testing, see the self-quizzes

mhhe.com/kottak

SUGGESTED ADDITIONAL READINGS

Appadurai, A., ed.
  2001   *Globalization.* Durham, NC: Duke University Press. An anthropological approach to globalization and international relations.

Archer, M. S.
  1996   *Culture and Agency: The Place of Culture in Social Theory,* rev. ed. Cambridge, England: Cambridge University Press. Examines interrelations among individual action, social structure, culture, and social integration.

Bohannan, P.
  1995   *How Culture Works.* New York: Free Press. A consideration of the nature of culture.

Brown, D.
  1991   *Human Universals.* New York: McGraw-Hill. Surveys the evidence for "human nature" and explores the roles of culture and biology in human variation.

Geertz, C.
  1973   *The Interpretation of Cultures.* New York: Basic Books. Essays about culture viewed as a system of symbols and meaning.

Gupta, A., and J. Ferguson, eds.
  1997b   *Culture, Power, Place: Explorations in Critical Anthropology.* Durham, NC: Duke University Press. New ways of conceiving and studying culture.

Hall, E. T.
  1990   *Understanding Cultural Differences.* Yarmouth, ME: Intercultural Press. Focusing on business and industrial management, this book examines the role of national cultural contrasts among France, Germany, and the United States.

Kroeber, A. L., and C. Kluckhohn
  1963   *Culture: A Critical Review of Concepts and Definitions.* New York: Vintage. Discusses and categorizes more than a hundred definitions of culture.

Lindholm, C.
  2001   *Culture and Identity: The History, Theory, and Practice of Psychological Anthropology.* New York: McGraw-Hill. An introduction to psychological anthropology, with special attention to the roles of culture and the individual.

Naylor, L. L.
  1996   *Culture and Change: An Introduction.* Westport, CT: Bergin and Garvey. Anthropology, culture, and change.

Ong, A., and S. J. Collier, eds.
  2005   *Global Assemblages: Technology, Politics, and Ethics as Anthropological Problems.* Malden, MA: Blackwell. This collection examines new ways of doing anthropology in a globalizing world.

Van der Elst, D., and P. Bohannan
  2003   *Culture as Given, Culture as Choice,* 2nd ed. Prospect Heights, IL: Waveland. Culture and individual choices.

Wagner, R.
  1981   *Invention of Culture,* rev. ed. Chicago: University of Chicago Press. Culture, creativity, society, and the self.

Wilson, R., ed.
  1996   *Human Rights: Culture and Context: Anthropological Perspectives.* Chicago: Pluto. Issues of cultural relativism and cross-cultural studies of human rights issues.

INTERNET EXERCISES

1. Acculturation: Go and read Cyndi Patee's article "Pidgins and Creoles," **http://logos.uoregon.edu/explore/socioling/pidgin.html**.
   a. What are pidgins and creoles? How are they examples of acculturation?
   b. What role did colonialism play in the development of pidgins and creoles?
   c. Take the quiz at the end of the page. Which sentences were easiest for you to read? Which were hardest? Look at the answers. Does the substrate language explain your ability or inability to understand?

2. The Kiss: Read Washington State University's page on "The Kiss," **http://www.wsu.edu:8001/vcwsu/commons/topics/culture/behaviors/kissing/kissing-essay.html**.
   a. Is kissing an instinctive human display of affection? Or is it learned?
   b. What is the history of the kiss?
   c. Is there a single, universal meaning for a kiss? How and why can the meanings change by culture and situation?

See Chapter 13 at your McGraw-Hill Online Learning Center for additional review and interactive exercises.

LINKAGES

Kottak, *Assault on Paradise*, 4th ed.

Culture: This text chapter has discussed levels of culture and cultural change. Compare Arembepe of the 1960s and of 2004 in terms of its residents' participation in local, national, and international cultural systems. Based on Chapter 15, would it be accurate to say that Arembepe has been more isolated from the modern world system than has the Betsileo village of Ivato in Madagascar? What were the different processes of cultural change experienced by Ivato and Arembepe?

Peters-Golden, *Culture Sketches*, 4th ed.

Aztec: Most people regard the Aztecs as part of a civilization that was lost long ago. However, in Mexico today there are indigenous social movements that seek to link the present directly with an Aztec past. In *Culture Sketches,* read Chapter 2, "The Aztec: Ancient Legacy, Modern Pride." Think about the uses and meanings of culture you've read about in this textbook. What might motivate contemporary Nahua peoples and others in Mexico to embrace Aztec culture? What is the significance of the ways in which they have chosen to recognize the Aztec heritage? Is this phenomenon something you recognize as happening among other groups? In other nations?

Knauft, *The Gebusi*, 1st ed.

Read Chapters 1 and 7. From Chapter 1, describe the author's description of the key Gebusi concept of "good company" (*kogwayay*) with respect to Kottak's discussion of "culture." Specifically, in what ways is the Gebusi concept of "good company" (a) learned, (b) shared, (c) symbolic, (d) all-encompassing, (e) integrated, (f) adaptive or maladaptive?

In Chapter 7, in what way does the author's description of culture change suggest alterations over time in the central importance of "good company" (*kogwayay*). Discuss how this change relates to issues of diffusion, acculturation, and globalization as described at the end of Kottak's Chapter 4.

14

Ethnicity and Race

CHAPTER OUTLINE

ETHNIC GROUPS AND ETHNICITY

We know from the last chapter that culture is learned, shared, symbolic, integrated, and all-encompassing. Now we consider the relation between culture and ethnicity. Ethnicity is based on cultural similarities and differences in a society or nation. The similarities are with members of the same ethnic group; the differences are between that group and others. Ethnic groups must deal with other such groups in the nation or region they inhabit, so that interethnic relations are important in the study of that nation or region. (Table 14.1 lists American ethnic groups, based on 2004 figures.)

TABLE 14.1 Racial/Ethnic Identification in the United States, 2004
(as Claimed in Census)

Claimed Identity	Millions of People	Percentage
Hispanic	41.3	14.1%
Asian	12.1	4.1
Two or more races	3.9	1.3
Pacific Islander	0.4	0.1
American Indian	2.2	0.8
Black	36.0	12.2
White	197.8	67.4
Total population	293.7	100.0%

SOURCE: U.S. Census Files, 2005.

As with any culture, members of an **ethnic group** *share* certain beliefs, values, habits, customs, and norms because of their common background. They define themselves as different and special because of cultural features. This distinction may arise from language, religion, historical experience, geographic isolation, kinship, or "race" (see Spickard 2004). Markers of an ethnic group may include a collective name, belief in common descent, a sense of solidarity, and an association with a specific territory, which the group may or may not hold (Ryan 1990, pp. xiii, xiv).

OVERVIEW

Ethnicity is based on cultural similarities (among members of the same ethnic group) and differences (between that group and others). Ethnicity is revealed when people claim a certain ethnic identity for themselves and are defined by others as having that identity. A race is an ethnic group that is assumed to have a biological basis.

"Races" are socially constructed, defined in terms of contrasts perceived in particular societies. In the United States children of mixed unions, no matter what they look like, tend to be classified with the minority-group parent. Other cultures have different systems of racial classification.

Environmental variables involving educational, economic, and social backgrounds provide better explanations for performance on intelligence tests by races, classes, and ethnic groups than do genetic differences in learning ability.

Most nation-states are not ethnically homogeneous. Multiculturalism contrasts with assimilation, in which minorities abandon their cultural traditions. Ethnicity can be expressed in peaceful coexistence, or in discrimination or violent confrontation. A dominant group may try to destroy ethnic practices (ethnocide) or force ethnic-group members to adopt the dominant culture (forced assimilation).

According to Fredrik Barth (1969), ethnicity can be said to exist when people claim a certain ethnic identity for themselves and are defined by others as having that identity. **Ethnicity** means identification with, and feeling part of, an ethnic group and exclusion from certain other groups because of this affiliation. But issues of ethnicity can be complex. The "News Brief" describes how African Americans who travel to Ghana to strengthen or reclaim an ethnic heritage are excluded from that heritage by many Ghanaians. Ethnic feelings and associated behavior vary in intensity within ethnic groups and countries and over time. A change in the degree of importance attached to an ethnic identity may reflect political changes (Soviet rule ends—ethnic feeling rises) or individual life-cycle changes (young people relinquish, or old people reclaim, an ethnic background).

We saw in the last chapter that people participate in various levels of culture. Groups within a culture (including ethnic groups in a nation) have different learning experiences as well as shared ones. Cultural differences may be associated with ethnicity, class, region, or religion. Individuals often have more than one group identity. People may be loyal (depending on circumstances) to their neighborhood, school, town, state or province, region, nation, continent, religion, ethnic group, or interest group (Ryan 1990, p. xxii). In a complex society such as the United States or Canada, people constantly negotiate their social identities. All of us "wear different hats," presenting ourselves sometimes as one thing, sometimes as another.

In daily conversation, we hear the term *status* used as a synonym for prestige. In this context, "She's got a lot of status" means she's got a lot of prestige; people look up to her. Among social scientists, that's not the primary meaning of "status." Social scientists use *status* more neutrally—for any position, no matter what the prestige, that someone

Ghana's Uneasy Embrace of Slavery's Diaspora

NEW YORK TIMES NEWS BRIEF

by Lydia Polgreen
December 27, 2005

Consider racial, ethnic, and national identities. This article describes current efforts by Ghana to attract African Americans to that country as tourists, retirees, and permanent residents. It describes how millions of enslaved Africans were exported from Ghana to the Western Hemisphere and how, centuries later, Africans and African Americans shared a common struggle for independence and advancement. Also discussed are identity issues that African Americans face in Ghana, where often they are equated with white foreign tourists. Ghanaians apparently focus more on nationality and class than on skin color in classifying African Americans.

We hear the words ethnicity *and* race *frequently, but American culture doesn't draw a very clear line between them. This chapter argues that, given the lack of a precise distinction between race and ethnicity, it's probably better to use the term* ethnic group *instead of* race *to describe any such social group—for example, African Americans, Asian Americans, Irish Americans, Anglo Americans, or Hispanics.*

CAPE COAST, Ghana—For centuries, Africans walked through the infamous "door of no return" at Cape Coast Castle directly into slave ships, never to set foot in their homelands again. These days, the portal of this massive fort so central to one of history's greatest crimes has a new name, hung on a sign leading back in from the roaring Atlantic Ocean: "The door of return." . . .

Taking Israel as its model, Ghana hopes to persuade the descendants of enslaved Africans to think of Africa as their homeland—to visit, invest, send their children to be educated and even retire here . . .

In many ways it is a quixotic goal. Ghana is doing well by West African standards—with steady economic growth, a stable, democratic government and broad support from the West, making it a favored place for wealthy countries to give aid.

But it remains a very poor, struggling country where a third of the population lives on less than a dollar a day, life expectancy tops out at 59 and basic services like electricity and water are sometimes scarce. Nevertheless, thousands of African-Americans already live here at least part of the year, said Valerie Papaya Mann, president of the African American Association of Ghana.

To encourage still more to come, or at least visit, Ghana plans to offer a special lifetime visa for members of the diaspora and will relax citizenship requirements so that descendants of slaves can receive Ghanaian passports. The government is also starting an advertising campaign to persuade Ghanaians to treat African-Americans more like long-lost relatives than as rich tourists.

That is harder than it sounds. Many African-Americans who visit Africa are unsettled to find that Africans treat them—even refer to them—the same way as white tourists. The term "obruni," or "white foreigner," is applied regardless of skin color.

To African-Americans who come here seeking their roots, the term is a sign of the chasm between Africans and African-Americans. Though they share a legacy, they experience it entirely differently.

"It is a shock for any black person to be called white," said Ms. Mann, who moved here two years ago. "But it is really tough to hear it when you come with your heart to seek your roots in Africa."

The advertising campaign urges Ghanaians to drop "obruni" in favor of "akwaaba anyemi," a slightly awkward phrase fashioned from two tribal languages meaning "welcome, sister or brother." . . .

The government plans to hold a huge event in 2007 to commemorate the 200th anniversary of the end of the trans-Atlantic trade by Britain and the 50th anniversary of Ghana's independence. The ceremonies will include traditional African burial rituals for the millions who died as a result of slavery. Estimates of the trade vary widely. . . .

Some perished on the long march from the inland villages where they were captured to seaports. Others died in the dungeons of slave castles and forts, where they were sometimes kept for months, until enough were gathered to pack the hold of a ship. Still others died in the middle passage, the longest leg of the triangular journey between Europe, Africa and the Americas. Of the estimated 11 million who crossed the sea, most went to South America and the Caribbean. About 500,000 are believed to have ended up in the United States.

The mass deportations and the divisions the slave trade wrought are wounds from which Africa still struggles to recover.

Ghana was the first sub-Saharan African nation to shake off its colonial rulers, winning its independence from Britain in 1957. Its founding father, Kwame Nkrumah, attended Lincoln University, a historically black college in Pennsylvania, and saw in African-Americans a key to developing the new nation. "Nkrumah saw the American Negro as the vanguard of the African people," said Henry Louis Gates Jr., chairman of the African and African-American studies department at Harvard. . . .

To Nkrumah, the struggle for civil rights in the diaspora and the struggles for independence from colonial rule in Africa were inextricably linked, both being expressions of the desire of black people everywhere to regain their freedom.

But Nkrumah was ousted in a coup in 1966, and by then Pan-Africanism had already given way

■ *Ghana's Cape Coast Castle (Fort Carolusborg). For centuries, Africans walked through this castle's infamous "door of no return" directly into slave ships. Today, that door has been renamed "the door of return." Ghana hopes to persuade the descendants of enslaved Africans to visit, invest, send their children to be educated and even retire here.*

to nationalism and cold war politics, sending much of the continent down a trail of autocracy, civil war and heartbreak. Still, African-Americans are drawn to Ghana's rich culture, and the history of slavery.

Ghana still has dozens of slave forts, each a chilling reminder of the brutality of the trade. At Elmina Castle, built by the Portuguese in 1482 and taken over by the Dutch 150 years later, visitors are guided through a Christian chapel built adjacent to the hall where slaves were auctioned, and the balcony over the women's dungeons from which the fort's governor would choose a concubine from the chattel below.

The room through which slaves passed into waiting ships is the emotional climax of the tour, a suffocating dungeon dimly lit by sunlight pouring through a narrow portal leading to the churning sea. . . .

For African-Americans and others in the African diaspora, there is lingering hostility and confusion about the role Africans played in the slave trade.

"The myth was our African ancestors were out on a walk one day and some bad white dude threw a net over them," Mr. Gates said. "But that wasn't the way it happened. It wouldn't have been possible without the help of Africans." Many Africans, meanwhile, often fail to see any connection at all between them and African-Americans, or feel African-Americans are better off for having been taken to the United States. Many Africans strive to emigrate; for the past 15 years, the number of Africans moving to the United States has surpassed estimates of the number forced there during any of the peak years of the slave trade. The number of immigrants from Ghana in the United States is larger than that of any other African country except Nigeria, according to the 2000 census.

"So many Africans want to go to America, so they can't understand why Americans would want to come here," said Philip Amoa-Mensah, a guide at Elmina Castle. . . .

The relationship is clearly a work in progress. Ghanaians are still learning of their ancestors' pivotal

roles in the slave trade, and slave forts on the coast, long used to thousands of foreign visitors, have in recent years become sites for school field trips. . . .

A recent African-American visitor to Cape Coast castle took the emotionally charged step through the door of no return, only to be greeted by a pair of toddlers playing in a fishing boat on the other side, pointing and shouting, "obruni, obruni!"

William Kwaku Moses, 71, a retired security guard who sells shells to tourists on the other side of the door of no return, shushed the children.

"We are trying," he said, with a shrug.

SOURCE: Lydia Polgreen, "Ghana's Uneasy Embrace of Slavery's Diaspora." *New York Times*, December 27, 2005. Retrieved from http://travel2.nytimes.com/2005/12/27/international/africa/27ghana.html?ex=1142312400&en=9830f16f2ed71593&ei=5070.

occupies in society. In this sense, **status** encompasses the various positions that people occupy in society. Parent is a social status. So are professor, student, factory worker, Democrat, shoe salesperson, homeless person, labor leader, ethnic-group member, and thousands of others. People always occupy multiple statuses (e.g., Hispanic, Catholic, infant, brother). Among the statuses we occupy, particular ones dominate in particular settings, such as son or daughter at home and student in the classroom.

Some statuses are **ascribed:** People have little or no choice about occupying them. Age is an ascribed status; we can't choose not to age. Race and gender usually are ascribed; people are born members of a certain group and remain so all their lives. **Achieved statuses,** by contrast, aren't automatic; they come through choices, actions, efforts, talents, or accomplishments, and may be positive or negative (Figure 14.1). Examples of achieved statuses include physician, senator, convicted felon, salesperson, union member, father, and college student.

Status Shifting

Sometimes statuses, particularly ascribed ones, are mutually exclusive. It's hard to bridge the gap between black and white, or male and female. Sometimes, taking a status or joining a group requires a conversion experience, acquiring a new and overwhelming primary identity, such as becoming a "born again" Christian.

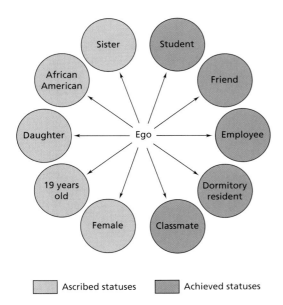

Ascribed statuses | Achieved statuses

FIGURE 14.1 Social Statuses.
The person in this figure—"ego," or "I"—occupies many social statuses. The green circles indicate ascribed statuses; the purple circles represent achieved statuses.

How do we determine who (what kind of a person) we are, and who others are? What kinds of identity cues and clues do people use to figure out who they are dealing with, and how to act in social situations? Part of human adaptive flexibility is our ability to shift statuses, varying our claimed identities in response to context. Many of the social statuses we occupy, the "hats" we wear, depend on the situation. People can be both black and Hispanic, or both a father and a ballplayer. One identity is claimed or perceived in certain settings, another in different ones. Among African Americans a "Hispanic" baseball player might be black; among Hispanics, Hispanic. When claimed or perceived identity varies depending on the audience, this is called the *situational negotiation of social identity.* As an illustration, the same man might declare any of the following, depending on the situation: "I'm Jimmy's father." "I'm your boss." "I'm African American." "I'm your professor."

We'll see in the next chapter that we vary the way we talk, as well as act, depending on our audience. In face-to-face encounters, other people can see who we are. They may expect us to think and act in certain ways based on their visual judgment of our identity, and their stereotypes about how people with that identity act. Although we can't know which aspect of identity they'll focus on (e.g., race, age, or gender), face to face it's hard to be anonymous or to be someone else. That's what masks and costumes are for.

But we don't just interact face to face. We phone, write, and—more than ever—use the Internet. Cyberspace communication is changing notions of identity and the self. Virtual worlds, such as computer role-playing games, are ways of extending ourselves into various forms of cybersocial interaction (Escobar 1994). People choose and vary their identities by using different "handles," multiple names in cyberspace. People may manipulate ("lie about") their ages and genders and create their own cyberfantasies. Of course there are subtle clues, revealed in writing. A greeting of "Dude" suggests a male. Linguistic (e.g., foreign language) background and class (educational) status may be evident in written expression. In psychology, multiple personalities are abnormal, but in anthropology, multiple identities are more and more the norm.

TABLE 14.2 American Hispanics, Latinos, 2002

National Origin	Percentage
Mexican American	66.9%
Puerto Rican	8.6
Cuban	3.7
Central & South American	14.3
Other Hispanic/Latino origin	6.5
Total	100.0%

SOURCE: R. R. Ramirez and G. P. de la Cruz, "The Hispanic Population in the United States," *Current Population Reports*, 2003, P20-545. U.S. Census Bureau.

■ *"Hispanic" and "Latino" are ethnic categories that cross-cut "racial" contrasts such as that between "black" and "white." Note the physical diversity exemplified by these Latina teenagers.*

Some statuses aren't mutually exclusive, but contextual. People can be both black and Hispanic, or both a mother and a senator. One identity is used in certain settings, another in different ones. We call this the *situational negotiation of social identity*. When ethnic identity is flexible and situational, it can become an achieved status (Leman 2001).

Hispanics, for example, may move through levels of culture (shifting ethnic affiliations) as they negotiate their identities. "Hispanic" is an ethnic category based mainly on language. It includes whites, blacks, and "racially" mixed Spanish speakers and their ethnically conscious descendants. (There are also "Native American," and even "Asian," Hispanics.) "Hispanic," representing the fastest growing ethnic group in the United States, lumps together millions of people of diverse geographic origin—Puerto Rico, Mexico, Cuba, El Salvador, Guatemala, the Dominican Republic, and other Spanish-speaking countries of Central and South America and the Caribbean.

"Latino" is a broader category, which can also include Brazilians (who speak Portuguese). The national origins of American Hispanics/Latinos in 2002 were as shown in Table 14.2.

Mexican Americans (Chicanos), Cuban Americans, and Puerto Ricans may mobilize to promote general Hispanic issues (e.g., opposition to "English-only" laws) but act as three separate interest groups in other contexts. Cuban Americans are richer on average than Chicanos and Puerto Ricans are, and their class interests and voting patterns differ. Cubans often vote Republican, but Puerto Ricans and Chicanos are more likely to favor Democrats. Some Mexican Americans whose families have lived in the United States for generations have little in common with new Hispanic immigrants, such as those from Central America. Many Americans (especially those fluent in English) claim Hispanic ethnicity in some contexts but shift to a general "American" identity in others.

In many societies an ascribed status is associated with a position in the social-political hierarchy. Certain groups, called *minority groups,* are subordinate. They have inferior power and less secure access to resources than do *majority groups* (which are superordinate, dominant, or controlling). Often ethnic groups are minorities. When an ethnic group is assumed to have a biological basis (distinctively shared "blood" or genes), it is called a **race**. Discrimination against such a group is called **racism** (Cohen 1998; Kuper 2005; Montagu 1997; Scupin 2003; Shanklin 1995).

RACE

Race, like ethnicity in general, is a cultural category rather than a biological reality. That is, ethnic groups, including "races," derive from contrasts perceived and perpetuated in particular societies, such as Ghana, as described in the "News Brief," rather than from scientific classifications based on common genes (see Wade 2002).

It is not possible to define human races biologically. Only cultural constructions of race are possible—even though the average person conceptualizes "race" in biological terms. The belief that human races exist and are important is much more common among the public than it is among scientists. Most Americans, for example, believe that their population includes biologically based "races" to which various labels have been applied. These labels include "white," "black," "yellow," "red," "Caucasoid," "Negroid," "Mongoloid," "Amerindian," "Euro-American," "African American," "Asian American," and "Native American."

We hear the words *ethnicity* and *race* frequently, but American culture doesn't draw a very clear line between them. As an illustration, consider two articles in the *New York Times* of May 29, 1992. One, discussing the changing ethnic composition of the United States, states (correctly) that Hispanics "can be of any race" (Barringer 1992, p. A12). In other words, "Hispanic" is an ethnic category that cross-cuts "racial" contrasts such as that between "black" and "white." The other article reports that during the Los Angeles riots of spring 1992, "hundreds of Hispanic residents were interrogated about their immigration status on the basis of their *race* alone [emphasis added]" (Mydans 1992a, p. A8). Use of "race" here seems inappropriate because "Hispanic" is usually perceived as referring to a linguistically based (Spanish-speaking) ethnic group, rather than a biologically based race. Since these Los Angeles residents were being interrogated because they were Hispanic, the article is actually reporting on ethnic, not racial, discrimination. However, given the lack of a precise distinction between race and ethnicity, it is probably better to use the term *ethnic group* instead of *race* to describe *any* such social group, for example, African Americans, Asian Americans, Irish Americans, Anglo Americans, or Hispanics.

THE SOCIAL CONSTRUCTION OF RACE

Races are ethnic groups assumed (by members of a particular culture) to have a biological basis, but actually race is socially constructed. The "races" we hear about every day are cultural, or social, rather than biological categories. In Charles Wagley's terms (Wagley 1959/1968), they are **social races** (groups assumed to have a biological basis but actually defined in a culturally arbitrary, rather than a scientific, manner). Many Americans mistakenly assume that "whites" and "blacks," for example, are biologically distinct and that these terms stand for discrete races. But these labels, like racial terms used in other societies, really designate culturally perceived rather than biologically based groups.

Hypodescent: Race in the United States

How is race culturally constructed in the United States? In American culture, one acquires his or her racial identity at birth, but race isn't based on biology or on simple ancestry. Take the case of the child of a "racially mixed" marriage involving one black and one white parent. We know that 50 percent of the child's genes come from one parent and 50 percent from the other. Still, American culture overlooks heredity and classifies this child as black. This rule is arbitrary. From *genotype* (genetic composition), it would be just as logical to classify the child as white.

Tiger Woods in Texas for the EDS Byron Nelson Championship on May 14, 2004. The number of interracial marriages and children is increasing, which has implications for the traditional American system of racial classification. What is Tiger's race?

American rules for assigning racial status can be even more arbitrary. In some states, anyone known to have any black ancestor, no matter how remote, is classified as a member of the black race. This is a rule of **descent** (it assigns social identity on the basis of ancestry), but of a sort that is rare outside the contemporary United States. It is called **hypodescent** (Harris and Kottak 1963) (*hypo* means "lower") because it automatically places the children of a union or mating between members of different groups in the minority group. Hypodescent helps divide American society into groups that have been unequal in their access to wealth, power, and prestige.

The following case from Louisiana is an excellent illustration of the arbitrariness of the hypodescent rule. It also illustrates the role that governments (federal, or state in this case) play in legalizing, inventing, or eradicating race and ethnicity (Williams 1989). Susie Guillory Phipps, a light-skinned woman with "Caucasian" features and straight black hair, discovered as an adult that she was "black." When Phipps ordered a copy of her birth certificate, she found her race listed as "colored." Since she had been "brought up white and married white twice," Phipps challenged a 1970 Louisiana law declaring anyone with at least one-thirty-second "Negro blood" to be legally black. In other words, having 1 "Negro" great-great-great-grandparent out of 32 is sufficient to make one black. Although the state's lawyer

Map Atlas

Map 7 plots the distribution of human skin color in relation to ultraviolet radiation from the sun.

admitted that Phipps "looks like a white person," the state of Louisiana insisted that her racial classification was proper (Yetman 1991, pp. 3–4).

Cases like Phipps's are rare, because "racial" and ethnic identities are usually ascribed at birth and usually don't change. The rule of hypodescent affects blacks, Asians, Native Americans, and Hispanics differently (see Hunter 2005). It's easier to negotiate Indian or Hispanic identity than black identity. The ascription rule isn't as definite, and the assumption of a biological basis isn't as strong.

To be considered "Native American," one ancestor out of eight (great-grandparents) or four (grandparents) may suffice. This depends on whether the assignment is by federal or state law or by an Indian tribal council. The child of a Hispanic may (or may not, depending on context) claim Hispanic identity. Many Americans with an Indian or Latino grandparent consider themselves "white" and lay no claim to minority-group status.

For more about race and the census, see the Virtual Exploration
mhhe.com/kottak

Race in the Census

The U.S. Census Bureau has gathered data by race since 1790. Initially this was done because the Constitution specified that a slave counted as three-fifths of a white person and because Indians were not taxed. The racial categories specified in the U.S. census include White, Black or Negro, Indian (Native American), Eskimo, Aleut or Pacific Islander, and Other. A separate question asks about Spanish-Hispanic heritage. Check out Figure 14.2 for the racial categories in the 2000 census.

An attempt by social scientists and interested citizens to add a "multiracial" census category has been opposed by the National Association for the Advancement of Colored People (NAACP) and the National Council of La Raza (a Hispanic advocacy group). Racial classification is a political issue. It involves access to resources, including jobs, voting districts, and federal funding of programs aimed at minorities. The hypodescent rule results in all the population growth being attributed to the minority category. Minorities fear their political clout will decline if their numbers go down.

But things are changing. Choice of "Some other race" in the U.S. Census more than doubled from 1980 (6.8 million) to 2000 (over 15 million)—suggesting imprecision in and dissatisfaction with the existing categories (Mar 1997). In the year 2000, 274.6 million Americans (out of 281.4 million censused) reported they belonged to just one race, as shown in Table 14.3.

Nearly 48 percent of Hispanics identified as White alone, and about 42 percent as "Some other race" alone. In the 2000 census, 2.4 percent of Americans, or 6.8 million people, chose a first-ever option of identifying themselves as belonging to more than one race. About 6 percent of Hispanics reported two or more races, compared with less than 2 percent of non-Hispanics (http://www.census.gov/Press-Release/www/2001/cb01cn61.html).

The number of interracial marriages and children is increasing, with implications for the traditional system of American racial classification. "Interracial," "biracial," or "multiracial" children who grow up with both parents undoubtedly

→ **NOTE: Please answer BOTH Questions 5 and 6.**

5. Is this person Spanish/Hispanic/Latino? *Mark* ☒ *the* ***"No"*** *box if not Spanish/Hispanic/Latino.*

☐ **No,** not Spanish/Hispanic/Latino
☐ Yes, Puerto Rican
☐ Yes, Mexican, Mexican Am., Chicano
☐ Yes, Cuban
☐ Yes, other Spanish/Hispanic/Latino — *Print group.*

5. What is this person's race? *Mark* ☒ *one or more races to indicate what this person considers himself/herself to be.*

☐ White
☐ Black, African Am., or Negro
☐ American Indian or Alaska Native — *Print name of enrolled or principal tribe.*

☐ Asian Indian
☐ Japanese
☐ Native Hawaiian
☐ Chinese
☐ Korean
☐ Guamanian or Chamorro
☐ Filipino
☐ Vietnamese
☐ Samoan
☐ Other Asian — *Print race.*
☐ Other Pacific Islander — *Print race.*

☐ Some other race — *Print race.*

FIGURE 14.2 Reproduction of Questions on Race and Hispanic Origin from Census 2000.

SOURCE: U.S. Census Bureau, Census 2000 questionnaire.

TABLE 14.3 Americans Reporting They Belonged to Just One Race

White	75.1%
Black or African-American	12.3%
American Indian and Alaska Native	0.9%
Asian	3.6%
Native Hawaiian and Other Pacific Islander	0.1%
Some other race	5.5%

SOURCE: http://www.census.gov/Press-Release/www/2001/cb01cn61.html.

Perceptions of Race and Skin Color on an American College Campus

BACKGROUND INFORMATION

STUDENT:
Gretchen M. Haupt

SUPERVISING PROFESSOR:
Donna Hart

SCHOOL:
University of Missouri–St. Louis

YEAR IN SCHOOL/MAJOR:
Junior/Anthropology

FUTURE PLANS:
Complete a master's in library science and pursue research as a librarian in an academic setting.

PROJECT TITLE:
Perceptions of Race and Skin Color on an American College Campus

For her senior honors thesis, Gretchen Haupt plans to build on the research project described here. To demonstrate that Americans' perceptions of race, in relation to skin color, are arbitrary and socially constructed, Haupt asked a sample of 30 students, Euro-Americans and African Americans, to complete a task: place 30 pigment chips in order from darkest to lightest. Having done so, they were then asked to identify the dividing line between "black" and "white." How much uniformity do you expect she found in their responses? Read the essay to find out.

There is no such biological reality as separate human races. Extensive research conducted on the subject of variation within our species has only served to confirm that the biological definition of race is not applicable to humans. Despite this, people continue to put the global population in neat, concise little groups (or at least they attempt to). Inevitably, the dividing lines between geographic and/or ethnic groups cannot be genetically supported since there are no specific sets of alleles correlated with the common divisions of white, black, red, brown, or however many racial categories are postulated. While *Homo sapiens* manifests variation in physical characteristics related to a population's original geographic environment, the most commonly used method for categorization and race assignment in the United States is skin color. Consequently, I chose to focus my research on the assumptions Americans make about race and skin color.

Through this research project I wanted to test my hypothesis that the point on a continuum at which an individual labels skin color "white" or "black" is arbitrary and subjective, therefore supporting the idea that pigmentation does not translate into perceived races. I collected data from thirty individuals on the University of Missouri–St. Louis campus by means of surveys using thirty skin-tone color chips, from deep brown to pale cream. The chips were paint samples mounted on a white index card, randomly assigned a letter or symbol.

Each participant was asked to place the color chips in order from darkest to lightest and then identify where "black" ended and "white" began. By forcing individuals to choose a dividing point, I was able to evaluate hidden perceptions. They were also asked to select a color they thought most closely matched their own skin tone, where they placed their ancestry geographically, and where they would place their chosen skin color geographically.

Even though a person may intellectually accept that there are no biologically distinct races, it is my opinion that they will still evaluate every other person they encounter and attempt to assign them to one of a minimum of two groups. This illustrates how race is a socially constructed concept rather than one based in scientific fact. For the purpose of my research, I limited the group designations to African descent and European descent.

My research found considerable variability in color placement (no one placed the chips in the same order) and the point of division. My research sub-jects were asked to select the point on their constructed color continuum (the order in which they had placed the color chips) indicating where "white" skin color ended and "black" skin color began. The most commonly chosen division point was between positions 19 and 20 (smaller numbers indicate darker; larger numbers, lighter skin tone). This point was chosen by 9 of the 30 people I surveyed. The choices of the other 21 spanned between positions 15/16 and 26/27.

To prevent bias, I kept track of the colors by means of letters and symbols on the back of each chip. Letters were assigned randomly. On closer examination of the actual color chips chosen by the nine people who selected 19/20, I discovered that they had not chosen the same colors. Where one person had placed chip "Y" as number 19 (indicating s/he felt that was a black skin tone) and chip "X" as 20 (indicating s/he felt that was a white skin tone), the next had chosen different color chips—"J" and "R" (for example) for the same positions. There were even instances where the choices were complete reversals (one person chose "Y" as white and the next chose "Y" as black).

I plan to continue this research as my senior thesis (devoting a total of ten academic credit hours to the project), and expand my data collection to include individuals belonging to other ethnicities (e.g., Native American and Asian) to determine further the degree to which race is socially constructed.

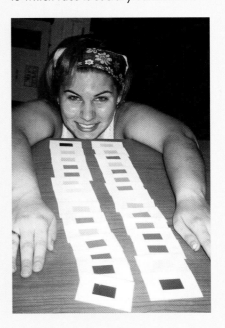

identify with particular qualities of either parent. It is troubling for many of them to have so important an identity as race dictated by the arbitrary rule of hypodescent. It may be especially discordant when racial identity doesn't parallel gender identity, for example, a boy with a white father and a black mother, or a girl with a white mother and a black father.

How does the Canadian census compare with the American census in its treatment of race? Rather than race, the Canadian census asks about "visible minorities." That country's Employment Equity Act defines such groups as "persons, other than Aboriginal peoples [aka First Nations in Canada, Native Americans in the United States], who are non-Caucasian in race or non-white in colour" (Statistics Canada 2001a). Table 14.4 shows that "Chinese" and "South Asian" are Canada's largest visible minorities. Note that Canada's total visible minority population of 13.4 percent (up from 11.2 percent in 1996) contrasts with a figure of about 25 percent for the United States in the 2000 Census. In particular, Canada's black 2.2 percent population contrasts with the American figure of 12.5 percent for African Americans, while Canada's Asian population is significantly higher than the U.S. figure of 3.7 percent on a percentage basis. Only a tiny fraction of the Canadian population (0.2 percent) claimed multiple visible minority affiliation, compared with 2.4 percent claiming "more than one race" in the United States in 2000.

Canada's visible minority population has been increasing steadily. In 1981, 1.1 million visible minorities accounted for 4.7 percent of the total population, versus more than 13.4 percent today. Visible minorities are growing much faster than is Canada's total population. Between 1996 and 2001, the total population increased 4 percent, while visible minorities rose 25 percent. If recent immigration trends continue, by 2016, visible minorities will account for one-fifth of the Canadian population.

Not Us: Race in Japan

American culture ignores considerable diversity in biology, language, and geographic origin as it socially constructs race within the United States. North Americans also overlook diversity by seeing Japan as a nation that is homogeneous in race, ethnicity, language, and culture—an image the Japanese themselves cultivate. Thus in 1986, former Prime Minister Nakasone created an international furor by contrasting his country's supposed homogeneity (responsible, he suggested, for Japan's success in international business) with the ethnically mixed United States. To describe Japanese society, Nakasone used *tan'itsu minzoku,* an expression connoting a single ethnic-racial group (Robertson 1992).

Japan is hardly the uniform entity Nakasone described. Some dialects of the Japanese language are mutually unintelligible. Scholars estimate that

Bringing It All Together

For more on ethnic diversity in Canada, see the "Bringing It All Together" essay that immediately follows Chapter 15.

TABLE 14.4   Visible Minority Population of Canada, 2001 Census

	Number	Percent
Total population	**29,639,030**	**100.0**
Total visible minority population	3,983,845	13.4
Chinese	1,029,395	3.5
South Asian	917,075	3.1
Black	662,210	2.2
Arab/West Asian	303,965	1.0
Filipino	308,575	1.0
Southeast Asian	198,880	0.7
Latin American	216,980	0.7
Korean	100,660	0.3
Japanese	73,315	0.2
Other visible minority	98,915	0.3
Multiple visible minority	73,875	0.2
Nonvisible minority	25,655,185	86.6

SOURCE: From Statistics Canada, 2001a, 2001 Census, http://www40.statcan.ca/101/cst01/demo50a.htm?sdi=visible.

10 percent of Japan's population are minorities of various sorts. These include aboriginal Ainu, annexed Okinawans, outcast *burakumin,* children of mixed marriages, and immigrant nationalities, especially Koreans, who number more than 700,000 (De Vos, Wetherall, and Stearman 1983; Lie 2001).

To describe racial attitudes in Japan, Jennifer Robertson (1992) uses Kwame Anthony Appiah's (1990) term *intrinsic racism*—the belief that a (perceived) racial difference is a sufficient reason to value one person less than another. In Japan, the valued group is majority ("pure") Japanese, who are believed to share "the same blood." Thus, the caption to a printed photo of a Japanese American model reads: "She was born in Japan but raised in Hawaii. Her nationality is American but no foreign blood flows in her veins" (Robertson 1992, p. 5). Something like hypodescent also operates in Japan, but less precisely than in the United States, where mixed offspring automatically become members of the minority group. The children of mixed marriages between majority Japanese and others (including Euro-Americans) may not get the same "racial" label as the minority parent, but they are still stigmatized for their non-Japanese ancestry (De Vos and Wagatsuma 1966).

How is race culturally constructed in Japan? The (majority) Japanese define themselves by opposition to others, whether minority groups in their own nation or outsiders—anyone who is "not us." The "not us" should stay that way; assimilation is generally discouraged. Cultural mechanisms, especially residential segregation and taboos on "interracial" marriage, work to keep minorities "in their place."

In its construction of race, Japanese culture regards certain ethnic groups as having a biological basis, when there is no evidence that they do. The best example is the *burakumin,* a stigmatized group of at least four million outcasts. They are sometimes compared to India's untouchables. The *burakumin* are physically and genetically indistinguishable from other Japanese. Many of them "pass" as (and marry) majority Japanese, but a deceptive marriage can end in divorce if *burakumin* identity is discovered (Aoki and Dardess, eds. 1981).

Burakumin are perceived as standing apart from majority Japanese. Through ancestry and descent (and thus, it is assumed, "blood," or genetics), *burakumin* are "not us." Majority Japanese try to keep their lineage pure by discouraging mixing. The *burakumin* are residentially segregated in neighborhoods (rural or urban) called *buraku,* from which the racial label is derived. Compared with majority Japanese, the *burakumin* are less likely to attend high school and college. When *burakumin* attend the same schools as majority Japanese, they face discrimination. Majority children and teachers may refuse to eat with them because *burakumin* are considered unclean.

■ *Japan's stigmatized* burakumin *are physically and genetically indistinguishable from other Japanese. In response to* burakumin *political mobilization, Japan has dismantled the legal structure of discrimination against* burakumin. *This Sports Day for* burakumin *children is one kind of mobilization.*

In applying for university admission or a job, and in dealing with the government, Japanese must list their address, which becomes part of a household or family registry. This list makes residence in a *buraku,* and likely *burakumin* social status, evident. Schools and companies use this information to discriminate. (The best way to pass is to move so often that the *buraku* address eventually disappears from the registry.) Majority Japanese also limit "race" mixture by hiring marriage mediators to check out the family histories of prospective spouses. They are especially careful to check for *burakumin* ancestry (De Vos et al. 1983).

The origin of the *burakumin* lies in a historic system of stratification (from the Tokugawa period: 1603–1868). The top four ranked categories were warrior-administrators (*samurai*), farmers, artisans, and merchants. The ancestors of the *burakumin* were below this hierarchy. An outcast group, they did unclean jobs, like animal slaughter and disposal of the dead. *Burakumin* still do related jobs, including work with animal products, like leather. The *burakumin* are more likely than majority Japanese to do manual labor (including farm work) and to belong to the national lower class. *Burakumin* and other Japanese minorities are also more likely to have careers in crime, prostitution, entertainment, and sports (De Vos et al. 1983).

Like blacks in the United States, the *burakumin* are class-stratified. Because certain jobs are reserved for the *burakumin,* people who are successful in those occupations (e.g., shoe factory owners) can be wealthy. *Burakumin* also have found jobs as government bureaucrats. Financially successful *burakumin* can temporarily escape their stigmatized status by travel, including foreign travel.

Discrimination against the *burakumin* is strikingly like the discrimination that blacks have faced in the United States. The *burakumin* often live in villages and neighborhoods with poor housing and sanitation. They have limited access to education, jobs, amenities, and health facilities. In response to *burakumin* political mobilization, Japan has dismantled the legal structure of discrimination against *burakumin* and has worked to improve conditions in the *buraku*. Still, Japan has not instituted American-style affirmative action programs for education and jobs. Discrimination against nonmajority Japanese is still the rule in companies. Some employers say that hiring *burakumin* would give their companies an unclean image and thus create a disadvantage in competing with other businesses (De Vos et al. 1983).

Phenotype and Fluidity: Race in Brazil

There are more flexible, less exclusionary ways of constructing social race than those used in the United States and Japan. Along with the rest of Latin America, Brazil has less exclusionary categories, which permit individuals to change their racial classification. Brazil shares a history of slavery with the United States, but it lacks the hypodescent rule. Nor does Brazil have racial aversion of the sort found in Japan.

Brazilians use many more racial labels—over 500 have been reported (Harris 1970)—than Americans or Japanese do. In northeastern Brazil I found 40 different racial terms in use in Arembepe, a village of only 750 people (Kottak 2006). Through their classification system Brazilians recognize and attempt to describe the physical variation that exists in their population. The system used in the United States, by recognizing only three or four races, blinds Americans to an equivalent range of evident physical contrasts. The system Brazilians use to construct social race has other special features. In the United States one's race is an ascribed status; it is assigned automatically by hypodescent and doesn't usually change. In Brazil racial identity is more flexible, more of an achieved status. Brazilian racial classification pays attention to phenotype. **Phenotype** refers to an organism's evident traits, its "manifest biology"—physiology and anatomy, including skin color, hair form, facial features, and eye color. A Brazilian's phenotype and racial label may change because of environmental factors, such as the tanning rays of the sun or the effects of humidity on the hair.

As physical characteristics change (sunlight alters skin color, humidity affects hair form), so do racial terms. Furthermore, racial differences may be so insignificant in structuring community life that people may forget the terms they have applied to others. Sometimes they even forget the ones they've used for themselves. In Arembepe, I made it a habit to ask the same person on different days to tell me the races of others in the village (and my own). In the United States I am always "white" or "Euro-American," but in Arembepe I

got lots of terms besides *branco* ("white"). I could be *claro* ("light"), *louro* ("blond"), *sarará* ("light-skinned redhead"), *mulato claro* ("light mulatto"), or *mulato* ("mulatto"). The racial term used to describe me or anyone else varied from person to person, week to week, even day to day. My best informant, a man with very dark skin color, changed the term he used for himself all the time—from *escuro* ("dark") to *preto* ("black") to *moreno escuro* ("dark brunet").

The American and Japanese racial systems are creations of particular cultures, rather than scientific—or even accurate—descriptions of human biological differences. Brazilian racial classification is also a cultural construction, but Brazilians have developed a way of describing human biological diversity that is more detailed, fluid, and flexible than the systems used in most cultures. Brazil lacks Japan's racial aversion, and it also lacks a rule of descent like that which ascribes racial status in the United States (Degler 1970; Harris 1964).

For centuries the United States and Brazil have had mixed populations, with ancestors from Native America, Europe, Africa, and Asia. Although "races" have mixed in both countries, Brazilian and American cultures have constructed the results differently. The historical reasons for this contrast lie mainly in the different characteristics of the settlers of the two countries. The mainly English early settlers of the United States came as women, men, and families, but Brazil's Portuguese colonizers were mainly men—merchants and adventurers. Many of these Portuguese men married Native American women and recognized their "racially mixed" children as their heirs. Like their North American counterparts, Brazilian plantation owners had sexual relations with their slaves. But the Brazilian landlords more often freed the children that resulted—for demographic and economic reasons. (Sometimes these were their only children.) Freed offspring of master and slave became plantation overseers and foremen and filled many intermediate positions in the emerging Brazilian economy. They were not classed with the slaves, but were allowed to join a new intermediate category. No hypodescent rule developed in Brazil to ensure that whites and blacks remained separate (see Degler 1970; Harris 1964).

STRATIFICATION AND "INTELLIGENCE"

Over the centuries groups with power have used racial ideology to justify, explain, and preserve their privileged social positions. Dominant groups have declared minorities to be *innately,* that is, biologically, inferior. Racial ideas are used

to suggest that social inferiority and presumed shortcomings (in intelligence, ability, character, or attractiveness) are immutable and passed across the generations. This ideology defends stratification as inevitable, enduring, and "natural"—based in biology rather than society. Thus the Nazis argued for the superiority of the "Aryan race," and European colonialists asserted the "white man's burden." South Africa institutionalized *apartheid*. Again and again, to justify exploitation of minorities and native peoples, those in control have proclaimed the innate inferiority of the oppressed. In the United States the supposed superiority of whites was once standard segregationist doctrine. Belief in the biologically based inferiority of Native Americans has been an argument for their slaughter, confinement, and neglect.

However, anthropologists know that most of the behavioral variation among contemporary human groups rests on culture rather than biology. The cultural similarities revealed through thousands of ethnographic studies leave no doubt that capacities for cultural evolution are equal in all human populations. There is also excellent evidence that within any **stratified** (class-based) society, differences in performance between economic, social, and ethnic groups reflect different experiences and opportunities

rather than genetic makeup. (Stratified societies are those with marked differences in wealth, prestige, and power between social classes.)

Stratification, political domination, prejudice, and ignorance continue to exist. They propagate the mistaken belief that misfortune and poverty result from lack of ability. Occasionally doctrines of innate superiority are even set forth by scientists, who, after all, tend to come from the favored stratum of society. One example is Jensenism, named for the educational psychologist Arthur Jensen (Herrnstein 1971; Jensen 1969), its leading proponent. Jensenism is a highly questionable interpretation of the observation that African Americans, on average, perform less well on intelligence tests than Euro-Americans do. Jensenism asserts that blacks are hereditarily incapable of performing as well as whites do. Richard Herrnstein, writing with Charles Murray, makes a similar argument in the 1994 book *The Bell Curve*, to which the following critique also applies.

Environmental explanations for test scores are much more convincing than are the genetic tenets of Jensen, Herrnstein, and Murray (see Montagu, ed. 1999). An environmental explanation does not deny that some people may be smarter than others. In any society, for many reasons, genetic and environmental, the talents of individuals vary. An

These photos, taken in Brazil by the author in 2003 and 2004, give just a glimpse of the spectrum of phenotypical diversity encountered among contemporary Brazilians.

At South Carolina's Clemson University, high school juniors take the SAT as part of a career enrichment program for minority students. How did you prepare for the SAT?

environmental explanation does deny, however, that these differences can be generalized to whole groups. Even when talking about individual intelligence, however, we have to decide which of several abilities is an accurate measure of intelligence.

Most intelligence tests are written by educated people in Europe and North America. They reflect the experiences of the people who devise them. It is not surprising that middle- and upper-class children do better since they are more likely to share the test makers' educational background and standards. Numerous studies have shown that performance on Scholastic Achievement Tests (SATs) can be improved by coaching and preparation. Parents who can afford $500 or more for an SAT preparation course enhance their kids' chances of getting high scores. Standardized college entrance exams are similar to IQ tests in that they purportedly measure intellectual aptitude. They may do this, but they also measure type and quality of high school education, linguistic and cultural background, and parental wealth. No test is free of class, ethnic, and cultural biases.

Tests invariably measure particular learning histories, not the potential for learning. They use middle-class performance as a standard for determining what should be known at a given chronological age. Furthermore, tests are usually administered by middle-class white people who give instructions in a dialect or language that may not be totally familiar to the child being tested. Test performance improves when the subcultural, socioeconomic, and linguistic backgrounds of subjects and test personnel are similar.

Links between social, economic, and educational environment and test performance show up in comparisons of American blacks and whites. At the beginning of World War I, intelligence tests were given to approximately 1 million American army recruits. Blacks from some northern states had higher average scores than did whites from some southern states. At that time northern blacks got a better public education than did many southern whites. Thus, their superior performance is not surprising. On the other hand, southern whites did better than southern blacks. This was also expectable, given the unequal school systems then open to whites and blacks in the South.

Racists tried to dismiss the environmental explanation for the superior performance of northern blacks compared with southern whites by suggesting selective migration—smarter blacks had moved north. However, it was possible to test this hypothesis, which turned out to be false. If smarter blacks had moved north, their superior intelligence should have been evident in their school records while they were still living in the South. It was not. Furthermore, studies in New York, Washington, and Philadelphia showed that as length of residence increased, test scores also rose.

Studies of identical twins raised apart also illustrate the impact of environment on identical heredity. In a study of nineteen pairs of twins, IQ scores varied directly with years in school. The average difference in IQ was only 1.5 points for the eight twin pairs with the same amount of schooling. It was 10 points for the eleven pairs with an average of five years' difference. One subject, with fourteen years more education than his twin, scored 24 points higher (Bronfenbrenner 1975).

These and similar studies provide overwhelming evidence that test performance measures education and social, economic, and cultural background rather than genetically determined intelligence. During the past 500 years Europeans and their descendants extended their political and economic control over most of the world. They colonized and occupied environments that they reached in their ships and conquered with their weapons. Most people in the most powerful contemporary nations—located in North America, Europe, and Asia—have light skin color. Some people in these currently powerful countries may incorrectly assert and believe that their world position has resulted from innate biological superiority. However, all contemporary human populations seem to have comparable learning abilities.

We are living in and interpreting the world at a particular time. In the past there were far different associations between centers of power and human physical characteristics. When Europeans lived in tribes, advanced civilizations thrived in the Middle East. When Europe was in the Dark Ages, there were civilizations in West Africa, on the East African coast, in Mexico, and in Asia. Before the Industrial Revolution, the ancestors of many white Europeans and Americans were living much more like precolonial Africans than like current members of the American middle class. Their average performance on 21st-century IQ tests would have been abominable.

ETHNIC GROUPS, NATIONS, AND NATIONALITIES

The term **nation** was once synonymous with "tribe" or "ethnic group"—what today we might call a cultural community. All these terms have been used to refer to a single ethnic unit, living together or apart, sharing perhaps a common language, religion, history, territory, ancestry, or genealogy. Thus, one could speak interchangeably of the Seneca (American Indian) nation, tribe, or ethnic group. Now, in our everyday language, nation has come to mean a **state**—an independent, centrally organized political unit—a government. Nation and state have become synonymous. Combined in **nation-state,** they refer to an autonomous political entity, a "country"—like the United States, "one nation, indivisible." "Nation" and "state" probably have become synonymous because of the prevalence of the idea of self-determination—that each group of people should have its own state (see Farnan 2004).

Because of migration, conquest, and colonialism, most nation-states are ethnically heterogeneous. Of 132 nation-states existing in 1971, Connor (1972) found only 12 (9 percent) to be ethnically homogeneous. In another 25 countries (19 percent), a single ethnic group accounted for more than 90 percent of the population. Forty percent of the countries had more than 5 significant ethnic groups. In a later study, Nielsson (1985) found that in only 45 of 164 states (27 percent) did a single ethnic group have more than 95 percent of the population.

Nationalities and Imagined Communities

Groups that now have, or wish to have or regain, autonomous political status (their own country) are called **nationalities.** In the words of Benedict Anderson (1991), nationalities are "imagined communities." Their members do not form an actual face-to-face community. They can only imagine that they all belong to and participate in the same group. Even when they become nation-states, they remain imagined communities, because most of their members, though feeling strong comradeship, will never meet (Anderson 1991, pp. 6–10).

Anderson traces Western European nationalism, which arose in imperial powers such as England, France, and Spain, back to the 18th century. He stresses that language and print played a crucial role in the growth of European national consciousness. (See "Interesting Issues" on pp. 314–315 for a modern illustration.) The novel and the newspaper were "two forms of imagining" communities that flowered in the 18th century (Anderson 1991, pp. 24–25). Such communities consisted of people who read the same sources and thus witnessed the same events.

Political upheavals and wars have divided many nationalities. The German and Korean homelands were artificially divided after wars, and according to socialist and capitalist ideologies. World War I split the Kurds, who form a majority in no state. They are a minority group in Turkey, Iran, Iraq, and Syria.

Migration is another reason certain nationally based ethnic groups now live in different nation-states. Massive migration in the decades before and after 1900 brought Germans, Poles, and Italians to Brazil, Canada, and the United States. Chinese, Senegalese, Lebanese, and Jews have spread all over the world. Some such people (e.g., descendants of Germans in Brazil and the United States) have assimilated to their host nations and no longer feel part of the imagined community of their origin. Such dispersed populations, which have spread out, voluntarily or not, from a common center or homeland, are called *diasporas*. The African diaspora, for example, encompasses descendants of Africans worldwide, such as in the United States, the Caribbean, and Brazil.

See the Internet Exercises at your OLC for information on ethnicity in Nigeria

mhhe.com/kottak

Ethnic Nationalism Runs Wild

The Socialist Federal Republic of Yugoslavia was a nonaligned country outside the former Soviet Union (U.S.S.R.). Like the U.S.S.R., Yugoslavia fell apart, mainly along ethnic and religious lines, in the early 1990s. Among Yugoslavia's ethnic groups were Roman Catholic Croats, Eastern Orthodox Serbs, Muslim Slavs, and ethnic Albanians. Citing ethnic and religious differences, several republics broke away from Yugoslavia in 1991–1992. These republics included

For more on Bosnia see the Virtual Exploration and the Internet Exercises at your OLC

mhhe.com/kottak

Slovenia, Croatia, and Bosnia-Herzegovina (see Figure 14.3). Serbia and Montenegro are the two remaining republics within Yugoslavia. In Kosovo, which is a province in Serbia, but one whose population is 90 percent ethnic Albanian, there has been a strong movement for independence, led by the Kosovo Liberation Army.

Much of the ethnic differentiation in Yugoslavia has been based on religion, culture, political and military history, and some differences involving

language. Serbo-Croatian is a Slavic language spoken, with dialect variation, by Serbs, Croats, and Muslim Slavs alike. (Albanian is a separate language.) Croats and Serbs use different alphabets. The Croats have adopted the Roman alphabet, but the Serbs use the Cyrillic alphabet, which they share with Russia and Bulgaria. The two alphabets help promote ethnic differentiation and nationalism. Serbs and Croats, who share speech, are divided by writing—by literature, newsprint, and political manifestos.

The Yugoslav Serbs reacted violently—with military intervention—after a 1992 vote for the independence of Muslim-led Bosnia-Herzegovina, whose population is one-third Serbian. In Bosnia, the Serbs initiated a policy of forced expulsion—"ethnic purification"—against Croats, but mainly against Muslim Slavs. Serbs in Yugoslavia, who controlled the national army, lent their support to the Bosnian Serbs in their "ethnic-cleansing" campaign.

Backed by the Yugoslav army, Bosnian Serb militias rounded up Bosnian Muslims, killed groups of them, and burned and looted their homes. Thousands of Slavs fled. Hundreds of thousands of Muslims became involuntary refugees in tent camps, school gyms, and parks.

The Serbs had no use for the ethnic coexistence that the previous Yugoslav socialist government had encouraged. The Serbs also wished to avenge historic affronts by Muslims and Croats. In the 15th century, Muslim Turks had overthrown a Serbian ruler, persecuted the Serbs, and—eventually—converted

FIGURE 14.3 Former Yugoslavia, with Province and Republics.
The former Yugoslavia, although a socialist nation, was a nonaligned country outside the former Soviet Union. Like the U.S.S.R., Yugoslavia disintegrated in the early 1990s. The breakaway portions included Slovenia, Croatia, and Bosnia-Herzegovina.

In creating multiethnic states, former colonial powers such as France and England often erected boundaries that corresponded poorly with preexisting cultural divisions. But colonial institutions also helped create new "imagined communities" beyond nations. One example is the idea of *négritude* ("black association and

identity"). This concept was developed by dark-skinned intellectuals from the Francophone (French-speaking) colonies of West Africa and the Caribbean. (Günther Schlee, ed. [2002] provides cases illustrating the role of "imagined differences" in ethnic conflict—the dark side of imagining communities.)

Former Yugoslav leader Slobodan Milosevic points across the court as he questions Croatian President Stipe Mesic at Milosevic's genocide trial at The Hague, Netherlands on October 2, 2002. Milosevic was allowed to defend himself during a trial that lasted two and a half years. Milosevic died on March 11, 2006, before his trial could be concluded.

many local people to Islam during their centuries of rule in this area. Bosnian Serbs still resent Muslims—including the descendants of the converts—for the Turkish conquest.

Bosnian Serbs claimed to be fighting to resist the Muslim-dominated government of Bosnia-Herzegovina. They feared that a policy of Islamic fundamentalism might arise and threaten the Serbian Orthodox Church and other expressions of Serbian identity. The Serbs' goal was to carve up Bosnia along ethnic lines, and they wanted two-thirds of it for themselves. A stated aim of Bosnia's ethnic purification was to ensure that the Serbs would never again be dominated by another ethnic group (Burns 1992*a*).

Although the Croats and the Muslim Slavs also carried out forced deportations in other parts of the former Yugoslavia, the Serbian campaign in Bosnia was the widest and the most systematic. More than 200,000 people were killed during the Bosnian conflict (Cohen 1995). With Bosnia's capital,

the multiethnic city of Sarajevo, under siege, the conflict was suspended after a December 1995 peace settlement was signed in Dayton, Ohio.

In spring 1999 NATO began a 78-day bombing campaign against Yugoslavia in retaliation for Serbian atrocities against ethnic Albanians in the separatist province of Kosovo. In May 1999 the then Yugoslav president, Slobodan Milosevic, was indicted for abuses against the Kosovar Albanian population by the war crimes tribunal in the Hague, Netherlands. By June 1999, accords ending 78 days of NATO bombing placed Kosovo under international control, enforced by NATO peacekeepers, who remain there as of this writing. In the year 2000 Yugoslavia itself took several steps toward democracy. In September 2000, Milosevic was voted out of office and replaced by a new president, Vajislav Kostinica. Parliamentary elections in December 2000 removed the last vestiges of power Milosevic had built up during

the previous decade. On June 28, 2001, Milosevic was transferred from a Belgrade jail to a prison cell in the Hague, Netherlands, for trial by the United Nations war crimes tribunal there. Before that trial could end, Milosevic died in his cell in March 2006.

How can we explain Yugoslavia's ethnic conflict? Ethnic distinctions represent people's perceptions of cultural differences, and people may overlook even very strong cultural similarities when circumstances make their differences more important. According to Fredrik Barth (see p. 316), ethnic differences are most secure and enduring in places where the groups occupy different ecological niches: They make their living in different ways or places, don't compete, and are mutually dependent. In Bosnia, the Serbs, the Croats, and the Muslim Slavs were more mixed than they were in any other former Yugoslav republic (Burns 1992*b*). Is it possible that the boundaries among the three groups were not sharp enough to keep them together by keeping them apart?

PEACEFUL COEXISTENCE

Ethnic diversity may be associated with positive group interaction and coexistence or with conflict—which is discussed in the next section. In many nations, multiple cultural groups live together in reasonable harmony. Three ways of realizing such peaceful coexistence are assimilation, the plural society, and multiculturalism.

Assimilation

Assimilation describes the process of change that a minority ethnic group may experience when it moves to a country where another culture dominates. By assimilating, the minority adopts the patterns and norms of its host culture. It is incorporated into the dominant culture to the point that it no longer exists as a separate cultural unit.

This is the "melting pot" model; ethnic groups give up their own cultural traditions as they blend into a common national stew. Some countries, such as Brazil, are more assimilationist than others are. Germans, Italians, Japanese, Middle Easterners, and East Europeans started migrating to Brazil late in the 19th century. These immigrants have assimilated to a common Brazilian culture, which has Portuguese, African, and Native American roots. The descendants of these immigrants speak the national language (Portuguese) and participate in the national culture. (During World War II, Brazil, which was on the Allied side, forced assimilation by banning instruction in any language other than Portuguese—especially in German.)

The Plural Society

Assimilation isn't inevitable, and there can be ethnic harmony without it. Ethnic distinctions can be maintained, rather than assimilated, despite decades, or even generations, of interethnic contact. Through a study of three ethnic groups in Swat, Pakistan, Fredrik Barth (1958/1968) challenged an old idea that interaction always leads to assimilation. He showed that ethnic groups can be in contact for generations without assimilating and that they can live in peaceful coexistence.

German, Italian, Japanese, Middle Eastern, and Eastern European immigrants have assimilated, culturally and linguistically, to a common Brazilian culture. Shown here, a Brazilian farmer of Japanese ancestry in the Amazon. More than 220,000 people of Japanese descent live in Brazil, mostly in and around the southern city of São Paulo, Brazil's largest.

Barth (1958/1968, p. 324) defines a **plural society** as a society combining ethnic contrasts, ecological specialization (that is, use of different environmental resources by each ethnic group), and the economic interdependence of those groups. Consider his description of the Middle East (in the 1950s): "The 'environment' of any one ethnic group is not only defined by natural conditions, but also by the presence and activities of the other ethnic groups on which it depends. Each group exploits only part of the total environment, and leaves large parts of it open for other groups to exploit."

In Barth's view, ethnic boundaries are most stable and enduring when the groups occupy different ecological niches. That is, they make their living in different ways and don't compete. Ideally, they should depend on each other's activities and exchange with one another. Under such conditions, ethnic diversity can be maintained, although the specific cultural features of each group may change. By shifting the analytic focus from specific cultural practices and values to the *relations* between ethnic groups, Barth (1958/1968 and 1969) has made important contributions to ethnic studies.

Multiculturalism and Ethnic Identity

The view of cultural diversity in a country as something good and desirable is called **multiculturalism** (see Kottak and Kozaitis 2003). The multicultural model is the opposite of the assimilationist model, in which minorities are expected to abandon their cultural traditions and values, replacing them with those of the majority population. The multicultural view encourages the practice of cultural-ethnic traditions. A multicultural society socializes individuals not only into the dominant (national) culture but also into an ethnic culture. Thus in the United States millions of people speak both English and another language, eat both "American" (apple pie, steak, hamburgers) and "ethnic" foods, and celebrate both national (July 4, Thanksgiving) and ethnic-religious holidays.

In the United States and Canada multiculturalism is of growing importance. This reflects an awareness that the number and size of ethnic groups have grown dramatically in recent years. If this trend continues, the ethnic composition of the United States will change dramatically (see Figure 14.4).

Because of immigration and differential population growth, whites are now outnumbered by minorities in many urban areas. For example, of the 8,008,278 people living in New York City in 2000, 27 percent were black, 27 percent Hispanic, 10 percent Asian, and 36 percent other—including non-Hispanic whites. The comparable figures for Los Angeles (3,694,820 people) were 11 percent black, 47 percent Hispanic, 9 percent Asian, and 33 percent other—including non-Hispanic whites (Census 2000, www.census.gov; see also Laguerre 2001).

One response to ethnic diversification and awareness has been for many whites to reclaim ethnic identities (Italian, Albanian, Serbian, Lithuanian, etc.) and to join ethnic associations (clubs, gangs). Some such groups are new. Others have existed for decades, although they lost members during the assimilationist years of the 1920s through the 1950s.

Multiculturalism seeks ways for people to understand and interact that don't depend on sameness but rather on respect for differences. Multiculturalism stresses the interaction of ethnic groups and their contribution to the country. It assumes that each group has something to offer and learn from the others.

Several forces have propelled North America away from the assimilationist model toward multiculturalism. First, multiculturalism reflects the fact of recent large-scale migration, particularly from the "less-developed countries" to the "developed" nations of North America and Western Europe. The global scale of modern migration introduces unparalleled ethnic variety to host nations. Multiculturalism is related to globalization: People use modern means of transportation to migrate to nations whose lifestyles they learn about through the media and from tourists who increasingly visit their own countries.

Migration is also fueled by rapid population growth, coupled with insufficient jobs (for both educated and uneducated people), in the less developed countries. As traditional rural economies decline or mechanize, displaced farmers move to cities, where they and their children are often unable to find jobs. As people in the less-developed countries get better educations, they seek more skilled employment. They hope to partake of an international culture of consumption that includes such modern amenities as refrigerators, televisions, and automobiles.

In a world with growing rural-urban and transnational migration, ethnic identities are used increasingly to form self-help organizations focused mainly on enhancing the group's economic competitiveness (Williams 1989). People claim and express ethnic identities for political and economic reasons. Michel Laguerre's (1984, 1998) studies of Haitian immigrants in the United States show that they mobilize to deal with the discriminatory structure (racist in this case, since Haitians tend to be black) of American society. Ethnicity (their common Haitian creole language and cultural background) is an evident basis for their mobilization. Haitian ethnicity then helps distinguish them from African Americans and other ethnic groups who may be competing for the same resources and recognition.

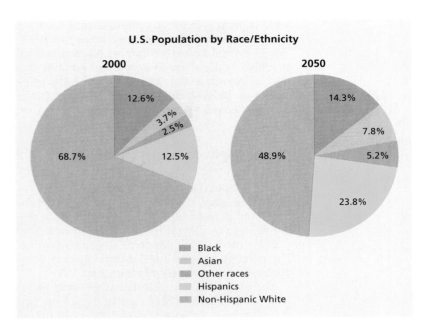

U.S. Population by Race/Ethnicity

- Black
- Asian
- Other races
- Hispanics
- Non-Hispanic White

FIGURE 14.4 Ethnic Composition of the United States.
The proportion of the American population that is white and non-Hispanic is declining. The projection for 2050 shown here comes from a U.S. Census Bureau report issued in March 2004. Note especially the dramatic rise in the Hispanic portion of the American population between 2000 and 2050. SOURCE: Based on data from U.S. Census Bureau, International Data Base, Table 094, http://www.census.gov/ipc/www/idbprint.html.

In the United States and Canada, multiculturalism is of growing importance. Especially in large cities like Toronto (shown here), people of diverse backgrounds attend ethnic fairs and festivals and feast on ethnic foods. What are some other expressions of multiculturalism in your society?

In the face of globalization, much of the world, including the entire "democratic West," is experiencing an "ethnic revival." The new assertiveness of long-resident ethnic groups extends to the Basques and Catalans in Spain, the Bretons and Corsicans in France, and the Welsh and Scots in the United Kingdom. The United States and Canada

Bringing It All Together

For more on Canadian multiculturalism, see the "Bringing It All Together" essay that immediately follows Chapter 15.

are becoming increasingly multicultural, focusing on their internal diversity (see Laguerre 1999). "Melting pots" no longer, they are better described as ethnic "salads" (each ingredient remains distinct, although in the same bowl, with the same dressing). In 1992, then New York mayor David Dinkins called his city a "gorgeous mosaic."

ROOTS OF ETHNIC CONFLICT

Ethnicity, based on perceived cultural similarities and differences in a society or nation, can be expressed in peaceful multiculturalism or in discrimination or violent interethnic confrontation. Culture can be both adaptive and maladaptive. The perception of cultural differences can have disastrous effects on social interaction.

The roots of ethnic differentiation—and therefore, potentially, of ethnic conflict—can be political, economic, religious, linguistic, cultural, or "racial" (see Kuper 2005). Why do ethnic differences often lead to conflict and violence? The causes include a sense of injustice because of resource distribution, economic and/or political competition, and reaction to discrimination, prejudice, and other expressions of threatened or devalued identity (Ryan 1990, p. xxvii).

Prejudice and Discrimination

Ethnic conflict often arises in reaction to prejudice (attitudes and judgments) or discrimination (action). **Prejudice** means devaluing (looking

In New Orleans, Louisiana, four family members wait in a hostile line for buses to take them to the Houston Astrodome on September 1, 2005, days after Hurricane Katrina flooded New Orleans. Discrimination refers to policies and practices that harm a group and its members. Does the fact that African Americans bore the brunt of the devastation caused by Hurricane Katrina in New Orleans constitute discrimination?

 STUDENT CD-ROM LIVING ANTHROPOLOGY

The Return Home
Track 14

This clip focuses on ethnic diversity in Bosnia. The war described in this chapter's "Interesting Issues" box (pp. 314–315) may have ended, but ethnic animosity remains. In discussing the living arrangements of Croats and Muslims, the narrator of the clip describes a "checkerboard" settlement pattern that existed before the war. What does he mean by this? The clip shows that both Muslims and Croats were displaced by the war. Was the village of Bukovica, where the clip is mainly set, originally a Muslim or a Croat village? How is ethnic difference marked in everyday life, in such routine activities as buying things, talking on the phone, and driving an automobile? See "Interesting Issues" for aspects of ethnic diversity in Bosnia not addressed in the clip.

down on) a group because of its assumed behavior, values, capabilities, or attributes. People are prejudiced when they hold stereotypes about groups and apply them to individuals. (*Stereotypes* are fixed ideas—often unfavorable—about what the members of a group are like.) Prejudiced people assume that members of the group will act as they are "supposed to act" (according to the stereotype) and interpret a wide range of individual behaviors as evidence of the stereotype. They use this behavior to confirm their stereotype (and low opinion) of the group.

Discrimination refers to policies and practices that harm a group and its members. Discrimination may be *de facto* (practiced, but not legally sanctioned) or *de jure* (part of the law). An example of de facto discrimination is the harsher treatment that American minorities (compared with other Americans) tend to get from the police and the judicial system. This unequal treatment isn't legal, but it happens anyway. Segregation in the southern United States and *apartheid* in South Africa provide two examples of de jure discrimination, which are no longer in existence. In both systems, by law, blacks and whites had different rights and privileges. Their social interaction ("mixing) was legally curtailed.

Chips in the Mosaic

Although the multicultural model is increasingly prominent in North America, ethnic competition and conflict are just as evident. There is conflict between new arrivals, for instance, Central Americans and Koreans, and long-established ethnic groups, such as African Americans. Ethnic antagonism flared in South-Central Los Angeles in spring 1992 in rioting that followed the acquittal of four white police officers who were tried for the videotaped beating of Rodney King (see Abelmann and Lie 1995).

Angry blacks attacked whites, Koreans, and Latinos. This violence expressed frustration by African Americans about their prospects in an increasingly multicultural society. A *New York Times*/CBS News Poll conducted May 8, 1992, just after the Los Angeles riots, found that blacks had a bleaker outlook than whites about the effects of immigration on their lives. Only 23 percent of the blacks felt they had more opportunities than recent immigrants, compared with twice that many whites (Toner 1992).

Korean stores were hard hit during the 1992 riots, and more than a third of the businesses destroyed were Latino-owned. A third of those who died in the riots were Latinos. These mainly recent migrants lacked deep roots to the neighborhood and, as Spanish speakers, faced language barriers (Newman 1992). Many Koreans also had trouble with English.

Koreans interviewed on ABC's *Nightline* on May 6, 1992, recognized that blacks resented them and considered them unfriendly. One man explained, "It's not part of our culture to smile." African Americans interviewed on the same program did complain about Korean unfriendliness. "They come into our neighborhoods and treat us like dirt." These comments suggest a shortcoming of the multicultural perspective: Ethnic groups (blacks here) expect other ethnic groups in the same nation-state to assimilate to some extent to a shared (national) culture. The African Americans' comments invoked a general American value system that includes friendliness, openness, mutual respect, community participation, and "fair play." Los Angeles blacks wanted their Korean neighbors to act more like generalized Americans—and good neighbors.

Aftermaths of Oppression

Fueling ethnic conflict are such forms of discrimination as genocide, forced assimilation, ethnocide, and cultural colonialism. *Genocide* refers to the physical destruction of an ethnic or religious group (e.g., Jews, Muslims) through mass murder. Examples include the Holocaust of Nazi Germany and "ethnic cleaning" in Bosnia, as described in "Interesting Issues" on pp. 314–315. A dominant group may try to destroy the cultures of certain ethnic groups (*ethnocide*) or force them to adopt the dominant culture (*forced assimilation*). Many countries have penalized or banned the language and customs of an ethnic group (including its religious observances). One example of forced assimilation is the anti-Basque campaign that the dictator Francisco Franco (who ruled between 1939 and 1975) waged in Spain. Franco banned Basque books, journals, newspapers, signs, sermons, and tombstones and imposed fines for using the Basque language in schools. His policies led to the formation of a Basque ter-

A refugee camp in Chad. Arab militias, called the Janjaweed, have forced black Africans off their land in the Darfur region of western Sudan, which borders Chad, through a campaign of killing, rape, and pillage. The Arab militias, equipped by the Sudanese government, are accused of killing up to 30,000 darker-skinned Africans in a campaign that United Nations officials say constitutes ethnic cleansing. Since the violence began in March 2003, more than one million people have fled to refugee camps in Sudan and Chad.

rorist group and spurred strong nationalist sentiment in the Basque region (Ryan 1990).

A policy of *ethnic expulsion* aims at removing groups that are culturally different from a country. There are many examples, including Bosnia-Herzegovina in the 1990s (see "Interesting Issues" on pp. 314–315). Uganda expelled 74,000 Asians in 1972. The neofascist parties of contemporary Western Europe advocate repatriation (expulsion) of immigrant workers (West Indians in England, Algerians in France, and Turks in Germany) (Ryan 1990, p. 9).

A policy of expulsion may create **refugees**—people who have been forced (involuntary refugees) or who have chosen (voluntary refugees) to flee a country, to escape persecution or war.

Colonialism, another form of oppression, refers to the political, social, economic, and cultural domination of a territory and its people by a foreign power for an extended time (Bell 1981). The British and French colonial empires are familiar examples of colonialism, but we can extend the term to the former Soviet empire, formerly known as the "Second World."

Using the labels "First World," "Second World," and "Third World" is a common, although clearly ethnocentric, way of categorizing nations (See Figure 14.5). The First World refers to the "democratic West"—traditionally conceived in opposition to a "Second World" ruled by "communism." The First World includes Canada, the United States, Western

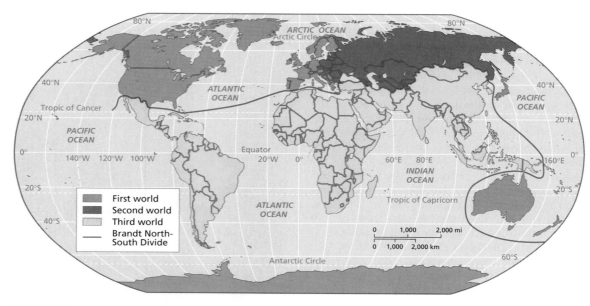

FIGURE 14.5   "First," "Second," and "Third" Worlds.
Use of "First World," "Second World," and "Third World" is a common, albeit ethnocentric, way of categorizing nations. "First World" refers to the "democratic West"—traditionally conceived in opposition to a "Second World" ruled by "communism." The "less-developed countries" or "developing nations" make up the "Third World." Another way of viewing the world in terms of differential economic and political influence is the Brandt North–South divide. This division classifies Australia and New Zealand as northern nations even though they are in the Southern Hemisphere. The map shows both divisions.

Europe, Japan, Australia, and New Zealand. The *Second World* refers to the Warsaw Pact nations, including the former Soviet Union and the Socialist and once-Socialist countries of Eastern Europe and Asia. Proceeding with this classification, the "less-developed countries" or "developing nations" make up the *Third World.*

The frontiers imposed by colonialism weren't usually based on, and often didn't reflect, preex- isting cultural units. In many countries, colonial nation building left ethnic strife in its wake. Thus, over a million Hindus and Muslims were killed in the violence that accompanied the division of the Indian subcontinent into India and Pakistan. Problems between Arabs and Jews in Palestine began during the British mandate period.

Multiculturalism may be growing in the United States and Canada, but the opposite is

Two faces of ethnic difference in the former Soviet empire. A propaganda poster depicts a happy mix of nationalities that make up the population of Kyrgyzstan, Central Asia (left). On September 3, 2004, in Beslan, Russia, two men carry young hostages who managed to escape after Russian special forces entered a school that had been occupied for three days by terrorists, who demanded that Russian troops pull out of Chechnya, a Russian republic with a large Islamic population.

happening in the disintegrating Second World, where ethnic groups (nationalities) want their own nation-states. The flowering of ethnic feeling and conflict as the Soviet empire disintegrated illustrates that years of political repression and ideology provide insufficient common ground for lasting unity.

Cultural colonialism refers to internal domination—by one group and its culture/ideology over others. One example is the domination over the former Soviet empire by Russian people, language, and culture, and by communist ideology. The dominant culture makes itself the official culture. This is reflected in schools, the media, and public interaction. Under Soviet rule ethnic minorities had very limited self-rule in republics and regions controlled by Moscow.

All the republics and their peoples were to be united by the oneness of "socialist internationalism." One common technique in cultural colonialism is to flood ethnic areas with members of the dominant ethnic group. Thus, in the former Soviet Union, ethnic Russian colonists were sent to many areas, to diminish the cohesion and clout of the local people.

"The Commonwealth of Independent States" is all that remains of the Soviet Union (see Yurchak 2005). In this group of new nations, ethnic groups (nationalities) are seeking to establish separate and viable nation-states based on cultural boundaries. This celebration of ethnic autonomy is part of an ethnic florescence that—as surely as globalization and transnationalism—is a trend of the late 20th and early 21st centuries.

SUMMARY

1. An "ethnic group" refers to members of a particular culture in a nation or region that contains others. Ethnicity is based on actual, perceived, or assumed cultural similarities (among members of the same ethnic group) and differences (between that group and others). Ethnic distinctions can be based on language, religion, history, geography, kinship, or "race." A race is an ethnic group assumed to have a biological basis. Usually race and ethnicity are ascribed statuses; people are born members of a group and remain so all their lives.

2. Race is a cultural category, not a biological reality. "Races" derive from contrasts perceived in particular societies, rather than from scientific classifications based on common genes. In the United States "racial" labels such as "white" and "black" designate socially constructed races—categories defined by American culture. American racial classification, governed by the rule of hypodescent, is based neither on phenotype nor on genes. Children of mixed unions, no matter what their appearance, are classified with the minority-group parent.

3. Racial attitudes in Japan illustrate "intrinsic racism"—the belief that a perceived racial difference is a sufficient reason to value one person less than another. The valued group is majority ("pure") Japanese, who are believed to share "the same blood." Majority Japanese define themselves by opposition to others, such as Koreans and *burakumin*. These may be minority groups in Japan or outsiders—anyone who is "not us."

4. Such exclusionary racial systems are not inevitable. Although Brazil shares a history of slavery with the United States, it lacks the hypodescent rule. Brazilian racial identity is more of an achieved status. It can change during someone's lifetime, reflecting phenotypical changes. Given the correlation between poverty and dark skin, the class structure affects Brazilian racial classification. Someone with light skin who is poor will be classified as darker than a comparably colored person who is rich.

5. Some people assert genetic differences in the learning abilities of "races," classes, and ethnic groups. But environmental variables (particularly educational, economic, and social background) provide better explanations for performance on intelligence tests by such groups. Intelligence tests reflect the life experiences of those who develop and administer them. All tests are to some extent culture-bound. Equalized environmental opportunities show up in test scores.

6. The term *nation* was once synonymous with "ethnic group." Now nation has come to mean a state—a centrally organized political unit. Because of migration, conquest, and colonialism, most nation-states are not ethnically homogeneous. Ethnic groups that seek autonomous political status (their own country) are nationalities. Political upheavals, wars, and migrations have divided many imagined national communities.

7. Assimilation describes the process of change an ethnic group may experience when it moves to a country where another culture dominates. By assimilating, the minority adopts the patterns and norms of its host culture. Assimilation isn't inevitable, and there can be ethnic harmony without it. A plural society combines ethnic contrasts and economic interdependence between ethnic groups. The view of cultural diversity in a nation-state as good and desirable is multiculturalism. A multicultural society socializes individuals not only into the dominant (national) culture but also into an ethnic one.

8. Ethnicity can be expressed in peaceful multiculturalism, or in discrimination or violent confrontation. Ethnic conflict often arises in reaction to prejudice (attitudes and judgments) or discrimination (action). The most extreme form of ethnic discrimination is genocide, the deliberate elimination of a group through mass murder. A dominant group may try to destroy certain ethnic practices (ethnocide), or to force ethnic group members to adopt the dominant culture (forced assimilation). A policy of ethnic expulsion may create refugees. Colonialism is the political, social, economic, and cultural domination of a territory and its people by a foreign power for an extended time. Cultural colonialism refers to internal domination—by one group and its culture and/or ideology over others.

KEY TERMS

See the flash cards
mhhe.com/kottak

achieved status   Social status that comes through talents, choices, actions, and accomplishments, rather than ascription.

ascribed status   Social status (e.g., race or gender) that people have little or no choice about occupying.

assimilation   The process of change that a minority group may experience when it moves to a country where another culture dominates; the minority is incorporated into the dominant culture to the point that it no longer exists as a separate cultural unit.

colonialism   The political, social, economic, and cultural domination of a territory and its people by a foreign power for an extended time.

descent   Rule assigning social identity on the basis of some aspect of one's ancestry.

discrimination   Policies and practices that harm a group and its members.

ethnic group   Group distinguished by cultural similarities (shared among members of that group) and differences (between that group and others); ethnic-group members share beliefs, customs, and norms, and, often, a common language, religion, history, geography, and kinship.

ethnicity   Identification with, and feeling part of, an ethnic group, and exclusion from certain other groups because of this affiliation.

hypodescent   Rule that automatically places the children of a union or mating between members of different socioeconomic groups in the less-privileged group.

multiculturalism   The view of cultural diversity in a country as something good and desirable; a multicultural society socializes individuals not only into the dominant (national) culture but also into an ethnic culture.

nation   Once a synonym for "ethnic group," designating a single culture sharing a language, religion, history, territory, ancestry, and kinship; now usually a synonym for *state* or *nation-state*.

nationalities   Ethnic groups that once had, or wish to have or regain, autonomous political status (their own country).

nation-state   An autonomous political entity; a country like the United States or Canada.

phenotype   An organism's evident traits, its "manifest biology"—anatomy and physiology.

plural society   A society that combines ethnic contrasts and economic interdependence of the ethnic groups.

prejudice   Devaluing (looking down on) a group because of its assumed behavior, values, capabilities, attitudes, or other attributes.

race   An ethnic group assumed to have a biological basis.

racism   Discrimination against an ethnic group assumed to have a biological basis.

refugees   People who have been forced (involuntary refugees) or who have chosen (voluntary refugees) to flee a country, to escape persecution or war.

social race   A group assumed to have a biological basis but actually perceived and defined in a social context, by a particular culture rather than by scientific criteria.

state (nation-state)   Complex sociopolitical system that administers a territory and populace with substantial contrasts in occupation, wealth, prestige, and power. An independent, centrally organized political unit; a government. A form of social and political organization with a formal, central government and a division of society into classes.

status   Any position that determines where someone fits in society; may be ascribed or achieved.

stratified   Class-structured; stratified societies have marked differences in wealth, prestige, and power between social classes.

CRITICAL
THINKING
QUESTIONS

For more self-testing,
see the self-quizzes

mhhe.com/kottak

1. What's the difference between a culture and an ethnic group? In what culture(s) do you participate? To what ethnic group(s) do you belong? What is the basis of your primary cultural identity?

2. Name five social statuses you currently occupy. Which of those statuses are ascribed, and which ones are achieved?

3. What kind of racial classification system operates in the community where you grew up or now live? Does it differ from the racial classification system described for American culture in this chapter?

4. If you had to devise an ideal system of racial categories, would it be more like the North American, the Japanese, or the Brazilian system? Why?

5. How does multiculturalism differ from assimilation? Which process do you favor for your country?

SUGGESTED ADDITIONAL READINGS

Abelmann, N., and J. Lie
  1995 *Blue Dreams: Korean Americans and the Los Angeles Riots*. Cambridge, MA: Harvard University Press. Some of the roots of ethnic conflict in Los Angeles today.

Anderson, B.
  1991 *Imagined Communities: Reflections on the Origin and Spread of Nationalism*, rev. ed. London: Verso. The origins of nationalism in Europe and its colonies, with special attention to the role of print, language, and schools.

Barth, F.
  1969 *Ethnic Groups and Boundaries: The Social Organization of Cultural Difference*. London: Allyn and Unwin. Classic discussion of the prominence of differentiation and boundaries (versus cultural features per se) in interethnic relations.

Friedman, J., ed.
  2002 *Globalization, the State, and Violence*. Walnut Creek, CA: AltaMira. Essays by prominent anthropologists focusing on violence in the context of globalization.

Gellner, E.
  1997 *Nationalism*. New York: New York University Press. Up-to-date comments from a long-time anthropological student of nationalism.

Harris, M.
  1964 *Patterns of Race in the Americas*. New York: Walker. Reasons for different racial and ethnic relations in North and South America and the Caribbean.

Hobsbawm, E. J.
  1992 *Nations and Nationalism since 1780: Programme, Myth, Reality*, 2nd ed. New York: Cambridge University Press. The making of modern nation-states.

Kottak, C. P., and K. A. Kozaitis
  2003 *On Being Different: Diversity and Multiculturalism in the North American Mainstream*, 2nd ed. New York: McGraw-Hill. Aspects of diversity in the United States and Canada, plus an original theory of multiculturalism.

Laguerre, M. S.
  1999 *The Global Ethnopolis: Chinatown, Japantown, and Manilatown in American Society*. New York: St. Martin's Press. Asian American urban enclaves, with a focus on San Francisco.

Maybury-Lewis, D.
  2002 *Indigenous Peoples, Ethnic Groups, and the State*, 2nd ed. Boston: Allyn & Bacon. Studies of cultural survival, ethnicity, and social change.

Molnar, S.
  2005 *Human Variation: Races, Types, and Ethnic Groups*, 6th ed. Upper Saddle River, NJ: Prentice Hall. Links between biological and social diversity.

Montagu, A., ed.
  1999 *Race and IQ*, expanded ed. New York: Oxford University Press. Revision of a classic volume of essays.

Ryan, S.
  1995 *Ethnic Conflict and International Relations*, 2nd ed. Brookfield, MA: Dartmouth. Cross-national review of the roots of ethnic conflict.

Schlee, G., ed.
  2002 *Imagined Differences: Hatred and the Construction of Identity*. New York: Palgrave. The dark side of imagining communities.

Scupin, R.
  2003 *Race and Ethnicity: An Anthropological Focus on the United States and the World*. Upper Saddle River, NJ: Prentice Hall. Broad survey of race and ethnic relations.

Spickard, P., ed.
  2004 *Race and Nation: Ethnic Systems in the Modern World*. New York: Routledge. Essays by 19 scholars on ethnic systems in various countries.

Wade, P.

2002 *Race, Nature, and Culture: An Anthropological Perspective.* Sterling, VA: Pluto Press. A processual approach to human biology and race.

Yurchak, A.

2005 *Everything Was Forever Until It Was No More: The Last Soviet Generation.* Princeton, NJ: Princeton University Press. Cultural paradoxes in the fall of the Soviet system.

INTERNET EXERCISES

1. Go to the U.S. Census page titled "Mapping Census 2000: The Geography of US Diversity," pp. 20–23 (**http://www.census.gov/population/cen2000/atlas/censr01-104.pdf**). Examine all four maps showing aspects of racial and ethnic diversity by county in the United States. Try to explain the historic processes that have produced, and are now producing, the patterns of diversity and density of specific groups.

   a. The first map shows the ethnic group with the highest percentage of population for all U.S. counties. What is the closest county to you with a high proportion of Native Americans? How about Hispanics?

   b. Examine Maps 1 and 2 for clusters of African Americans. Why are so many African Americans clustered in the southeastern part of the United States?

   c. Examine Map 2 for clusters of Hispanics. How do you explain high concentrations of Hispanics in the Pacific Northwest, in the Midwest, and on the East Coast?

   d. On Maps 1 and 2 determine where you find the highest concentrations of Asian Americans. Why are the concentrations of Asian Americans so different from those of other ethnic groups?

   e. Examine Map 3 to see which states were the most diverse in 2000. Examine Map 4 to see which states increased most in diversity between 1990 and 2000. Give a brief definition of the diversity index used in the map calculations.

2. Race and the Census: Read Gregory Rodriguez's article in Salon magazine titled "Do the Multiracial Count?" (**http://www.salon.com/news/feature/2000/02/15/census/index.html**).

   a. What was the problem that some people had with the original census? How does this reflect American notions of race as described in this chapter?

   b. What was the compromise that the Clinton administration presented? What are its ramifications?

   c. In this case what role does the federal government play in our society's notions of race? Is the federal government merely responding to changing conceptions of race of the American people, or is it trying to shape the way the American public thinks about race?

   d. Based on this chapter, how do you think this kind of question on the census form would be handled in Brazil? In Japan?

3. Ethnicity on the Border: Read Gregory Rodriguez's article "We're Patriotic Americans Because We're Mexicans" in *Salon* magazine, **http://archive.salon.com/news/feature/2000/ 02/24/laredo**.

   a. Who is participating in the celebration of George Washington's birthday?

   b. How does this celebration reflect the influence of Mexican and American cultures? Since it is a mixture, is this celebration any less "pure"?

   c. Do you think a multiethnic identity is incompatible with a single national identity?

   d. What factors would cause a border community to invest so much energy in recognizing a day such as Washington's birthday that so many other Americans ignore? Do you think it is more important for communities living on the border to assert their nationality than for communities living in the heartland?

See Chapter 14 at your McGraw-Hill Online Learning Center for additional review and interactive exercises.

Kottak, *Assault on Paradise*, 4th ed.

Chapters 1, 3, and 10 contain information on race relations in Arembepe. Read Chapters 1 and 3 to see how Kottak conducted his microproject on racial terminology in 1962. What were his techniques and findings? Read Chapters 3 and 10 to see how race relations changed between the 1960s and the 1980s. What role did ethnicity play in Arembepe in the 1960s, and what role does it play today?

Peters-Golden, *Culture Sketches*, 4th ed.

Read Chapter 5, "Hmong: Struggle and Perseverance." The text chapter you just read discussed ethnic pride, along with ethnic discrimination and violence. The Hmong are a tribal people who traditionally have lived in remote mountain villages throughout China, Laos, Thailand, and Vietnam. Their history is one of struggle, rebellion, and perseverance. For centuries, Hmong have suffered persecution by many groups, while fiercely defending their ethnic heritage. Despite war and resettlement, they continue to strive to maintain their traditions. Hmong in the United States have been criticized as unwilling to assimilate. Why might they be viewed this way? How might their long history of ethnic discrimination influence the way they think about themselves and their cultural heritage? How might you account for the clashes described in their adjustment to life in the United States?

Knauft, *The Gebusi*, 1st ed.

Read Chapter 11. How is the ethnic difference between different peoples reflected in the Independence Day celebrations at Nomad? Describe an activity during the celebrations in which ethnic difference between Gebusi and Bedamini led to opposition and competition. Describe an activity during the celebrations in which ethnic difference led to appreciation and enjoyment between groups. Do you think relations between ethnic groups at Nomad in 1998 were mostly harmonious or mostly based on conflict? Support your answer. In what ways do you think this marks a change from indigenous relations between ethnic groups—for instance, indigenous relations between Gebusi and Bedamini?

15

Language and Communication

WHAT IS LANGUAGE?

Language, which may be spoken (*speech*) or written (*writing*), is our primary means of communication. Writing has existed for about 6,000 years. Language originated thousands of years before that, but no one can say exactly when. Like culture in general, of which language is a part, language is transmitted through learning, as part of enculturation. Language is based on arbitrary, learned associations between words and the things for which they stand. The complexity

■ Apes, such as these Congo chimpanzees, use call systems to communicate in the wild. Their vocal systems consist of a limited number of sounds—calls—that are produced only when particular environmental stimuli are encountered.

OVERVIEW

Linguistic anthropology shares anthropology's overall interest in diversity in time and space. Linguistic anthropology examines language structure and use, linguistic change, and the relations among language, society, and culture.

The call systems of our hominid ancestors eventually grew too complicated for genetic transmission. As hominids relied more and more on learning, their call systems evolved into language. But, like the other primates, humans also continue to use nonverbal communication, such as facial expressions and gestures. No language includes all the sounds the human vocal apparatus can make. Phonology, the study of speech sounds, focuses on sounds that make a difference in a given language.

Sociolinguistics investigates how linguistic variation is associated with social differences. Linguistic diversity reflects region, gender, social class, occupation, ethnicity, and other social variables. Also, people vary their speech on different occasions, shifting styles, dialects, and even languages.

Historical linguistics is useful for anthropologists interested in historical relationships. Linguistic clues can suggest past contacts between cultures. Relationships between languages don't necessarily mean there are biological ties between their speakers, because people can learn new languages.

of language—absent in the communication systems of other animals—allows humans to conjure up elaborate images, to discuss the past and the future, to share our experiences with others, and to benefit from their experiences.

Anthropologists study language in its social and cultural context. Linguistic anthropology illustrates anthropology's characteristic interest in comparison, variation, and change. A key feature of language is that it is always changing. Some linguistic anthropologists reconstruct ancient languages by comparing their contemporary descendants and in so doing make discoveries about history. Others study linguistic differences to discover the varied worldviews and patterns of thought in a multitude of cultures. Sociolinguists examine linguistic diversity in nation-states, ranging from multilingualism (see the "News Brief") to the varied dialects and styles used in a single language, to show how speech reflects social differences (Fasold 1990; Labov 1972a, 1972b). Linguistic anthropologists also explore the role of language in colonization and in the expansion of the world economy (Geis 1987).

NONHUMAN PRIMATE COMMUNICATION

Call Systems

Only humans speak. No other animal has anything approaching the complexity of language. The natural communication systems of other primates (monkeys and apes) are **call systems.** These vocal systems consist of a limited number of sounds—*calls*—that are produced only when particular environmental stimuli are encountered. Such calls may be varied in intensity and duration, but they are much less flexible than language because they are automatic and can't be combined. When primates encounter food and danger simultaneously, they can make only one call. They can't combine the calls for food and danger into a single utterance, indicating that both are present. At some point in human evolution, however, our ancestors began to combine calls and to understand the combinations. The number of calls also expanded, eventually becoming too great to be transmitted even partly through the genes. Communication came to rely almost totally on learning.

Although wild primates use call systems, the vocal tract of apes is not suitable for speech. Until the 1960s, attempts to teach spoken language to apes suggested that they lack linguistic abilities. In the 1950s, a couple raised a chimpanzee, Viki, as a member of their family and systematically tried to teach her to speak. However, Viki learned only four words ("mama," "papa," "up," and "cup").

Spanish At School Translates to Suspension

WASHINGTON POST NEWS BRIEF

by T. R. Reid
December 9, 2005

Linguistic diversity is a fact. Not even identical twins speak just alike. But we do share patterns of speech with other people, such as our parents, our peers, and people with the same ethnic, regional, educational, or occupational background. The United States is not famous for its appreciation of linguistic diversity or for its fostering of foreign language study. Compared with Europeans, Americans have under-developed foreign language skills. Why is that? How many languages do you speak fluently? This article describes a case of blatant sociolinguistic discrimination, in which a boy was suspended from school for speaking Spanish in the hallway. Consider how this account illustrates American atti-tudes about language, ethnicity, and even social class. Do you think the boy would have been suspended for speaking French to a French exchange student? But, then, what are the odds his French is good enough to permit such a conversation? This chapter focuses on how anthropologists and linguists study languages as formal systems, but also in their social and cultural contexts, including sociolinguistic diversity.

On November 27, 2001, several students wait outside their drama classroom at multiethnic Luther Burbank High School in Sacramento, California. Anthropologists and linguists study linguistic diversity—languages and dialects—in its social and cultural context. What languages do you imagine are being spoken in the hallway?

KANSAS CITY, Kan., Dec. 8— Most of the time, 16-year-old Zach Rubio converses in clear, unaccented American teen-speak, a form of English in which the three most common words are "like," "whatever" and "totally." But Zach is also fluent in his dad's native lan-guage, Spanish—and that's what got him suspended from school.

"It was, like, totally not in the classroom," the high school junior said, recalling the infraction. "We were in the, like, hall or whatever, on restroom break. This kid I know, he's like, 'Me prestas un dolar?' ['Will you lend me a dollar?'] Well, he asked in Spanish; it just seemed nat-ural to answer that way. So I'm like, 'No problema.'"

But that conversation turned out to be a big problem for the staff at the Endeavor Alternative School, a small public high school in an ethnically mixed blue-collar neighborhood. A teacher who overheard the two boys sent Zach to the office, where Princi-pal Jennifer Watts ordered him to call his father and leave the school.

Watts, whom students describe as a disciplinarian, said she can't discuss the case. But in a written "discipline referral" explaining her decision to suspend Zach for 1 1/2 days, she noted: "This is not the first time we have [asked] Zach and oth-ers to not speak Spanish at school."

Since then, the suspension of Zach Rubio has become the talk of the town in both English and Span-ish newspapers and radio shows. The school district has officially rescinded his punishment and said that speaking a foreign language is not grounds for suspension. Mean-while, the Rubio family has retained a lawyer, who says a civil rights law-suit may be in the offing.

The tension here surrounding that brief exchange in a high school hall reflects a broader national debate over the language Americans should speak amid a wave of Hispanic immigration.

The National Council of La Raza, a Hispanic advocacy group, says that 20 percent of the U.S. school–age population is Latino. For half of those Latino students, the native language is Spanish.

Conflicts are bursting out nation-wide over bilingual education, "English-only" laws, Spanish-language publications and advertis-ing, and other linguistic collisions. Language concerns have been a key aspect of the growing political movement to reduce immigration.

"There's a lot of backlash against the increasing Hispanic population," said D.C. school board member Victor A. Reinoso. "We've seen some of it in the D.C. schools. You see it in some cities, where people complain that their tax money shouldn't be used to print public notices in Spanish. And there have been cases where schools want to ban foreign languages."

Some advocates of an English-only policy in U.S. schools say that it is particularly important for students from immigrant families to use the nation's dominant language.

California Gov. Arnold Schwarzenegger (R) made that point this summer when he vetoed a bill authorizing various academic subjects to be tested in Spanish in the state's public schools. "As an immigrant," the Austrian-born governor said, "I know the importance of mastering English as quickly and as comprehensively as possible."

Hispanic groups generally agree with that, but they emphasize the value of a multilingual citizenry. "A fully bilingual young man like Zach Rubio should be considered an asset to the community," said Janet Murguia, national president of La Raza.

The influx of immigrants has reached every corner of the country—even here in Kansas City, which is about as far as a U.S. town can be from a border. Along Southwest Boulevard, a main street through some of the older neighborhoods, there are blocks where almost every shop and restaurant has signs written in Spanish.

"Most people, they don't care where you're from," said Zach's father, Lorenzo Rubio, a native of Veracruz, Mexico, who has lived in Kansas City for a quarter-century. "But sometimes, when they hear my accent, I get this, sort of, 'Why don't you go back home?'"

Rubio, a U.S. citizen, credits U.S. immigration law for his decision to fight his son's suspension.

"You can't just walk in and become a citizen," he said. "They make you take this government test. I studied for that test, and I learned that in America, they can't punish you unless you violate a written policy."

Rubio said he remembered that lesson on Nov. 28, when he received a call from Endeavor Alternative saying his son had been suspended.

"So I went to the principal and said, 'My son, he's not suspended for fighting, right? He's not suspended for disrespecting anyone. He's suspended for speaking Spanish in the hall?' So I asked her to show me the written policy about that. But they didn't have one."

Rubio then called the superintendent of the Turner Unified School District, which operates the school. The district immediately rescinded

Zach's suspension, local media reported. The superintendent did not respond to several requests to comment for this article.

Since then, the issue of speaking Spanish in the hall has not been raised at the school, Zach said. "I know it would be, like, disruptive if I answered in Spanish in the classroom. I totally don't do that. But outside of class now, the teachers are like, 'Whatever.'"

For Zach's father, and for the Hispanic organizations that have expressed concern, the suspension is not a closed case. "Obviously they've violated his civil rights," said Chuck Chionuma, a lawyer in Kansas City, Mo., who is representing the Rubio family. "We're studying what form of legal redress will correct the situation."

Said Rubio: "I'm mainly doing this for other Mexican families, where the legal status is kind of shaky and they are afraid to speak up. Punished for speaking Spanish? Somebody has to stand up and say: This is wrong."

_____

SOURCE: T. R. Reid, "Spanish At School Translates to Suspension," *Washington Post*, December 9, 2005, p. A03.

Sign Language

More recent experiments have shown that apes can learn to use, if not speak, true language (Miles 1983). Several apes have learned to converse with people through means other than speech. One such communication system is American Sign Language, or ASL, which is widely used by deaf and mute Americans. ASL employs a limited number of basic gesture units that are analogous to sounds in spoken language. These units combine to form words and larger units of meaning.

The first chimpanzee to learn ASL was Washoe, a female. Captured in West Africa, Washoe was acquired by R. Allen Gardner and Beatrice Gardner, scientists at the University of Nevada in Reno, in 1966, when she was a year old. Four years later, she moved to Norman, Oklahoma, to a converted farm that had become the Institute for Primate Studies. Washoe revolutionized the discussion of

the language-learning abilities of apes. At first she lived in a trailer and heard no spoken language. The researchers always used ASL to communicate with each other in her presence. The chimp gradually acquired a vocabulary of more than 100 signs representing English words (Gardner, Gardner, and Van Cantfort, eds. 1989). At the age of two, Washoe began to combine as many as five signs into rudimentary sentences such as "you, me, go out, hurry."

The second chimp to learn ASL was Lucy, Washoe's junior by one year. Lucy died, or was murdered by poachers, in 1986, after having been introduced to "the wild" in Africa in 1979 (Carter 1988). From her second day of life until her move to Africa, Lucy lived with a family in Norman, Oklahoma. Roger Fouts, a researcher from the nearby Institute for Primate Studies, came two days a week to test and improve Lucy's knowledge of ASL. During the rest of the week, Lucy used ASL to converse with her foster parents. After acquiring language, Washoe and Lucy exhibited several human traits: swearing, joking, telling lies, and trying to teach language to others (Fouts 1997).

When irritated, Washoe called her monkey neighbors at the institute "dirty monkeys." Lucy insulted her "dirty cat." On arrival at Lucy's place, Fouts once found a pile of excrement on the floor. When he asked the chimp what it was, she replied, "dirty, dirty," her expression for feces. Asked whose "dirty, dirty" it was, Lucy named Fouts's coworker, Sue. When Fouts refused to believe her about Sue, the chimp blamed the excrement on Fouts himself.

Cultural transmission of a communication system through learning is a fundamental attribute of language. Washoe, Lucy, and other chimps have tried to teach ASL to other animals, including their own offspring. Washoe has taught gestures to other institute chimps, including her son Sequoia, who died in infancy (Fouts, Fouts, and Van Cantfort 1989).

Because of their size and strength as adults, gorillas are less likely subjects than chimps for such experiments. Lean adult male gorillas in the wild weigh 400 pounds (180 kilograms), and full-grown females can easily reach 250 pounds (110 kilograms). Because of this, psychologist Penny Patterson's work with gorillas at Stanford University seems more daring than the chimp experiments. Patterson raised her now full-grown female gorilla, Koko, in a trailer next to a Stanford museum. Koko's vocabulary surpasses that of any chimp. She regularly employs 400 ASL signs and has used about 700 at least once.

Koko and the chimps also show that apes share still another linguistic ability with humans: **productivity.** Speakers routinely use the rules of their language to produce entirely new expressions that are comprehensible to other native speakers. I can, for example, create "baboonlet" to refer to a baboon infant. I do this by analogy with English words in which the suffix -*let* desig-

At the Language Research Center in Atlanta, Kanzi, the symboling bonobo, signals "Chase Kanzi" to a six-year-old boy. Kanzi points to a lexigram keyboard held by Sue Savage-Rumbaugh.

nates the young of a species. Anyone who speaks English immediately understands the meaning of my new word. Koko, Washoe, Lucy, and others have shown that apes also are able to use language productively. Lucy used gestures she already knew to create "drinkfruit" for watermelon. Washoe, seeing a swan for the first time, coined "waterbird." Koko, who knew the gestures for "finger" and "bracelet," formed "finger bracelet" when she was given a ring.

Chimps and gorillas have a rudimentary capacity for language. They may never have invented a meaningful gesture system in the wild. However, given such a system, they show many humanlike abilities in learning and using it. Of course, language use by apes is a product of human intervention and teaching. The experiments mentioned here do not suggest that apes can invent language (nor are human children ever faced with that task). However, young apes have managed to learn the basics of gestural language. They can employ it productively and creatively, although not with the sophistication of human ASL users.

Apes, like humans, also may try to teach their language to others. Lucy, not fully realizing the difference between primate hands and feline paws, once tried to mold her pet cat's paw into ASL signs. Koko taught gestures to Michael, a male gorilla six years her junior.

Apes also have demonstrated linguistic **displacement.** Absent in call systems, this is a key ingredient in language. Normally, each call is tied to an environmental stimulus such as food. Calls are uttered only when that stimulus is present. Displacement means that humans can talk about things that are not present. We don't have to see the objects before we say the words. Human conversations are not limited by place. We can discuss the past and future, share our experiences with others, and benefit from theirs.

 STUDENT CD-ROM LIVING ANTHROPOLOGY

Bonobos and Language
Track 6

This clip presents the work of Dr. Sue Savage-Rumbaugh of Georgia State University, who has been working with chimpanzees and bonobos for more than 20 years. The clip focuses on her work with Kanzi, a male bonobo, who has learned how to communicate through the manipulation of words and symbols. Like humans, but to a substantially lesser degree, apes can learn from observation, experience, and teaching. What did Kanzi learn that his mother could not learn? Why can't bonobos talk? Based on what you saw in the clip, would you say that Kanzi responds to spoken words or only to symbols?

"He says he wants a lawyer."

Patterson has described several examples of Koko's capacity for displacement (Patterson 1978). The gorilla once expressed sorrow about having bitten Penny three days earlier. Koko has used the sign "later" to postpone doing things she doesn't want to do. Table 15.1 summarizes the contrasts between language, whether sign or spoken, and the call systems that primates use in the wild.

Certain scholars doubt the linguistic abilities of chimps and gorillas (Sebeok and Umiker-Sebeok, eds. 1980; Terrace 1979). These people contend that Koko and the chimps are comparable to trained circus animals and don't really have linguistic ability. However, in defense of Patterson and the other researchers (Hill 1978; Van Cantfort and Rimpau 1982), only one of their critics has worked with an ape. This was Herbert Terrace, whose experience teaching a chimp sign language lacked the continuity and personal involvement that have contributed so much to Patterson's success with Koko.

No one denies the huge difference between human language and gorilla signs. There is a major gap between the ability to write a book or say a prayer and the few hundred gestures employed by

a well-trained chimp. Apes aren't people, but they aren't just animals either. Let Koko express it: When asked by a reporter whether she was a person or an animal, Koko chose neither. Instead, she signed "fine animal gorilla" (Patterson 1978).

The Origin of Language

The capacity to remember and combine linguistic expressions seems to be latent in the apes (Miles 1983). In human evolution, the same ability flowered into language. Language did not appear miraculously at a certain moment in human history. It developed over hundreds of thousands of years, as our ancestors' call systems were gradually transformed. Language offered a tremendous adaptive advantage to *Homo*. Language permits the information stored by a human society to exceed by far that of any nonhuman group. Language is a uniquely effective vehicle for learning. Because we can speak of things we have never experienced, we can anticipate responses before we encounter the stimuli. Adaptation can occur more rapidly in *Homo* than in the other primates because our adaptive means are more flexible.

NONVERBAL COMMUNICATION

Language is our principal means of communicating, but it isn't the only one we use. We communicate when we transmit information about ourselves to others and receive such information from them. Our facial expressions, bodily stances, gestures, and movements, even if unconscious, convey information and are part of our communication styles. Deborah Tannen (1990) discusses differences in the communication styles of American men and women, and her comments go beyond language. She notes that American girls and women tend to look directly at each other when they talk, whereas American boys and men do not. Males are more likely to look straight

See the Internet Exercises at your OLC for more on primate language ability

mhhe.com/kottak

TABLE 15.1 Language Contrasted with Call Systems	
Human Language	**Primate Call Systems**
Has the capacity to speak of things and events that are not present (displacement).	Are stimuli-dependent; the food call will be made only in the presence of food; it cannot be faked.
Has the capacity to generate new expressions by combining other expressions (productivity).	Consist of a limited number of calls that cannot be combined to produce new calls.
Is group specific in that all humans have the capacity for language, but each linguistic community has its own language, which is culturally transmitted.	Tend to be species specific, with little variation among communities of the same species for each call.

Some of our facial expressions reflect our primate heritage. We can see them in monkeys and especially in the apes. How "natural" and universal are the meanings conveyed by facial expressions? Throughout the world, smiles, laughs, frowns, and tears tend to have similar meanings, but culture does intervene. In some cultures, people smile less than in others. In a given culture, men may smile less than women; and adults, less than children. A lifetime of smiling and frowning marks the face, so that smile lines and frown furrows develop. In North America, smile lines may be more marked in women than in men. Margaret Mead focused on kinesics in her studies of infant care in different cultures. She noted differences in mother–child interactions, finding that patterns of holding, releasing, and playing varied from culture to culture. In some cultures, babies were held more securely than in others. Mead thought that patterns of infant and child care played an important role in forming adult personality.

ahead rather than turn and make eye contact with someone, especially another man, seated beside them. Also, in conversational groups, American men tend to relax and sprawl out. American women may adopt a similar relaxed posture in all-female groups, but when they are with men, they tend to draw in their limbs and adopt a tighter stance.

Kinesics is the study of communication through body movements, stances, gestures, and facial expressions. Related to kinesics is the examination of cultural differences in personal space and displays of affection discussed in the chapter "Culture." Linguists pay attention not only to what is said but to how it is said, and to features besides language itself that convey meaning. A speaker's enthusiasm is conveyed not only through words, but also through facial expressions, gestures, and other signs of animation. We use gestures, such as a jab of the hand, for emphasis. We use verbal and nonverbal ways of communicating our moods: enthusiasm, sadness, joy, regret. We vary our intonation and the pitch or loudness of our voices. We communicate through strategic pauses, and even by being silent. An effective communication strategy may be to alter pitch, voice level, and grammatical forms, such as declaratives ("I am . . ."), imperatives ("Go forth . . ."), and questions ("Are you . . . ?"). Culture teaches us that certain manners and styles should accompany certain kinds of speech. Our demeanor, verbal and non-

verbal, when our favorite team is winning would be out of place at a funeral, or when a somber subject is being discussed.

Culture always plays a role in shaping the "natural." Animals communicate through odors, using scent to mark territories, a chemical means of communication. Among modern North Americans, the perfume, mouthwash, and deodorant industries are based on the idea that the sense of smell plays a role in communication and social interaction. But different cultures are more tolerant of "natural" odors than ours is. Cross-culturally, nodding does not always mean affirmative, nor does head shaking from side to side always mean negative. Brazilians wag a finger to mean no. Americans say "uh huh" to affirm, whereas in Madagascar a similar sound is made to deny. Americans point with their fingers; the people of Madagascar point with their lips. Patterns of "lounging around" vary, too. Outside, when resting, some people may sit or lie on the ground; others squat; others lean against a tree.

Body movements communicate social differences. Lower-class Brazilians, especially women, offer limp handshakes to their social superiors. In many cultures, men have firmer handshakes than women do. In Japan, bowing is a regular part of social interaction, but different bows are used depending on the social status of the people who are interacting. In Madagascar and Polynesia, people of lower status should not hold their heads above those of people of higher status. When one approaches someone older or of higher status, one bends one's knees and lowers one's head as a sign of respect. In Madagascar, one always does this, for politeness, when passing between two people. Although our gestures, facial expressions, and body stances have roots in our primate heritage, and can be seen in the monkeys and the apes,

American men and women differ in their phonology, grammar, and vocabulary, and in the body stances and movements that accompany speech. What differences do you note in the communication styles of the two women in the foreground, compared with the several men in the background?

they have not escaped the cultural shaping described in previous chapters. Language, which is so highly dependent on the use of symbols, is the domain of communication, in which culture plays the strongest role.

THE STRUCTURE OF LANGUAGE

The scientific study of a spoken language (*descriptive linguistics*) involves several interrelated areas of analysis: phonology, morphology, lexicon, and syntax. **Phonology,** the study of speech sounds, considers which sounds are present and significant in a given language. **Morphology** studies the forms in which sounds combine to form *morphemes*—words and their meaningful parts. Thus, the word *cats* would be analyzed as containing two morphemes: *cat,* the name for a kind of animal, and *-s,* a morpheme indicating plurality. A language's **lexicon** is a dictionary containing all its morphemes and their meanings. **Syntax** refers to the arrangement and order of words in phrases and sentences. Syntactic questions include whether nouns usually come before or after verbs, or whether adjectives normally precede or follow the nouns they modify.

Speech Sounds

From the movies and TV, and from actually meeting foreigners, we know something about foreign accents and mispronunciations. We know that someone with a marked French accent doesn't pronounce *r* the same way an American does. But at least someone from France can distinguish between "craw" and "claw," which someone from Japan may not be able to do. The difference between *r* and *l* makes a difference in English and in French, but it doesn't in Japanese. In linguistics, we say that the difference between *r* and *l* is *phonemic* in English and French but not in Japanese; that is, *r* and *l* are phonemes in English and French but not in Japanese. A **phoneme** is a sound contrast that makes a difference, that differentiates meaning.

We find the phonemes in a given language by comparing *minimal pairs,* words that resemble each other in all but one sound. The words have totally different meanings, but they differ in just one sound. The contrasting sounds are therefore phonemes in that language. An example in English is the minimal pair *pit/bit*. These two words are distinguished by a single sound contrast between /p/ and /b/ (we enclose phonemes in slashes). Thus /p/ and /b/ are phonemes in English. Another example is the different vowel sound of *bit* and *beat* (see Figure 15.1). This contrast serves to distinguish these two words and the two vowel phonemes written /I/ and /i/ in English.

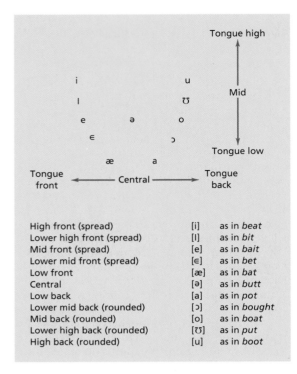

High front (spread)	[i]	as in *beat*
Lower high front (spread)	[I]	as in *bit*
Mid front (spread)	[e]	as in *bait*
Lower mid front (spread)	[ɛ]	as in *bet*
Low front	[æ]	as in *bat*
Central	[ə]	as in *butt*
Low back	[a]	as in *pot*
Lower mid back (rounded)	[ɔ]	as in *bought*
Mid back (rounded)	[o]	as in *boat*
Lower high back (rounded)	[ʊ]	as in *put*
High back (rounded)	[u]	as in *boot*

FIGURE 15.1 Vowel Phonemes in Standard American English.
The phonemes are shown according to height of tongue and tongue position at front, center, or back of mouth. Phonetic symbols are identified by English words that include them; note that most are minimal pairs. SOURCE: Adaptation of excerpt and figure 2–1 from Dwight L. Bolinger and Donald A. Sears, *Aspects of Language,* 3rd ed. (New York: Harcourt Brace Jovanovich, 1981).

Standard (American) English (SE), the "region-free" dialect of TV network newscasters, has about 35 phonemes: at least 11 vowels and 24 consonants. The number of phonemes varies from language to language—from 15 to 60, averaging between 30 and 40. The number of phonemes also varies between dialects of a given language. In American English, for example, vowel phonemes vary noticeably from dialect to dialect (see "Interesting Issues" on page 336). Readers should pronounce the words in Figure 15.1, paying attention to (or asking someone else) whether they distinguish each of the vowel sounds. Most Americans don't pronounce them all.

Phonetics is the study of speech sounds in general, what people actually say in various languages, like the differences in vowel pronunciation described in "Interesting Issues." **Phonemics** studies only the *significant* sound contrasts (phonemes) of a given language. In English, like /r/ and /l/ (remember *craw* and *claw*), /b/ and /v/ are also phonemes, occurring in minimal pairs like *bat* and *vat*. In Spanish, however, the contrast between [b] and [v] doesn't distinguish meaning, and they are therefore not phonemes (we enclose sounds that

Shown here (in 1995) is Leigh Jenkins, who was or is Director of Cultural Preservation for the Hopi tribal council. The Hopi language would not distinguish between was and is in the previous sentence. For the Hopi, present and past are real and are expressed grammatically in the same way while the future remains hypothetical and has a different grammatical expression.

are not phonemic in brackets). Spanish speakers normally use the [b] sound to pronounce words spelled with either *b* or *v*.

In any language, a given phoneme extends over a phonetic range. In English, the phoneme /p/ ignores the phonetic contrast between the [pʰ] in *pin* and the [p] in *spin*. Most English speakers don't even notice that there is a phonetic difference: [pʰ] is aspirated, so that a puff of air follows the [p]; the [p] in *spin* is not. (To see the difference, light a match, hold it in front of your mouth, and watch the flame as you pronounce the two words.) The contrast between [pʰ] and [p] is phonemic in some languages, such as Hindi (spoken in India). That is, there are words whose meaning is distinguished only by the contrast between an aspirated and an unaspirated [p].

Native speakers vary in their pronunciation of certain phonemes, such as the /e/ phoneme discussed in "Interesting Issues." This variation is important in the evolution of language. With no shifts in pronunciation, there can be no linguistic change. The section on sociolinguistics below considers phonetic variation and its relationship to social divisions and the evolution of language.

LANGUAGE, THOUGHT, AND CULTURE

The well-known linguist Noam Chomsky (1955) has argued that the human brain contains a limited set of rules for organizing language, so that all languages have a common structural basis. (Chomsky calls this set of rules *universal grammar*.) The fact that people can learn foreign languages and that words and ideas can be translated from one language into another tends to

support Chomsky's position that all humans have similar linguistic abilities and thought processes. Another line of support comes from creole languages. Such languages develop from pidgins, languages that form in situations of acculturation, when different societies come into contact and must devise a system of communication. As mentioned in the "Culture" chapter, pidgins based on English and native languages developed in the context of trade and colonialism in China, Papua New Guinea, and West Africa. Eventually, after generations of being spoken, pidgins may develop into *creole languages*. These are more mature languages, with developed grammatical rules and native speakers (that is, people who learn the language as their primary means of communication during enculturation). Creoles are spoken in several Caribbean societies. Gullah, which is spoken by African Americans on coastal islands in South Carolina and Georgia, is also a creole language. Supporting the idea that creoles are based on universal grammar is the fact that such languages all share certain features. Syntactically, all use particles (e.g., will, was) to form future and past tenses and multiple negation to deny or negate (e.g., he don't got none). Also, all form questions by changing inflection rather than by changing word order. For example, "You're going home for the holidays?" (with a rising tone at the end) rather than "Are you going home for the holidays?"

The Sapir-Whorf Hypothesis

Other linguists and anthropologists take a different approach to the relation between language and thought. Rather than seeking universal linguistic structures and processes, they believe that different languages produce different ways of

Do Midwesterners Have Accents?

Depending on where we live, Americans have certain stereotypes about how people in other regions talk. Some stereotypes, spread by the mass media, are more generalized than others. Most Americans think they can imitate a "southern accent." We also have nationwide stereotypes about speech in New York City (the pronunciation of *coffee*, for example) and Boston ("I pahked the kah in Hahvahd Yahd").

Many Americans also believe that midwesterners don't have accents. This belief stems from the fact that midwestern dialects don't have many stigmatized linguistic variants—speech patterns that people in other regions recognize and look down on, such as *r*lessness and *dem, dese,* and *dere* (instead of *them, these,* and *there*).

Actually, regional patterns influence the way all Americans speak. Midwesterners do have a variety of detectable accents. College students from out of state easily recognize that their in-state classmates speak differently. In-state students, however, have difficulty hearing their own speech peculiarities, because they are accustomed to them and view them as normal.

Far from having no accents, midwesterners, even in the same high school, exhibit linguistic variation (see Eckert 1989, 2000). Furthermore, dialect differences are immediately obvious to people, like myself, who come from other parts of the country. One of the best examples of variable midwestern pronunciation, involving vowels, is the /e/ phoneme, which occurs in words like *ten, rent, French, section, lecture, effect, best,* and *test.* In southeastern Michigan, where I live and teach, there are four different ways of pronouncing this phoneme. Speakers of Black English and immigrants from Appalachia often pronounce *ten* as *tin,* just as southerners habitually do. Some Michiganders say *ten,* the correct pronunciation in Standard English. However, two other pronunciations are more common. Instead of *ten,* many Michiganders say *tan,* or *tun* (as though they were using the word *ton,* a unit of weight).

My students often astound me with their pronunciation. One day I met one of my Michigan-raised teaching assistants in the hall. She was deliriously happy. When I asked why, she replied, "I've just had the best suction."

"What?" I said.

"I've just had a wonderful suction," she repeated.

"What?" I still wasn't understanding.

She finally spoke more precisely. "I've just had the best saction." She considered this a clearer pronunciation of the word *section.*

Another TA complimented me, "You luctured to great effuct today." After an exam, a student lamented that she hadn't been able to do her "bust on the tust." Once I lectured about uniformity in fast-food restaurant chains. One of my students had just vacationed in Hawaii, where, she told me, hamburger prices were higher than they were on the mainland. It was, she said, because of the runt. Who, I wondered, was this runt? The very puny owner of Honolulu's McDonald's franchise? Perhaps he advertised on television, "Come have a hamburger with the runt." Eventually I figured out that she was talking about the high cost of *rent* on those densely packed islands.

---

thinking. This position is sometimes known as the **Sapir-Whorf hypothesis** after Edward Sapir (1931) and his student Benjamin Lee Whorf (1956), its prominent early advocates. Sapir and Whorf argued that the grammatical categories of different languages lead their speakers to think about things in particular ways. For example, the third-person singular pronouns of English (*he, she; him, her; his, hers*) distinguish gender, whereas those of the Palaung, a small tribe in Burma, do not (Burling 1970). Gender exists in English, although a fully developed noun-gender and adjective-agreement system, as in French and other Romance languages (*la belle fille, le beau fils*), does not. The Sapir-Whorf hypothesis therefore might suggest that English speakers can't help paying more attention to differences between males and females than do the Palaung and less than do French or Spanish speakers.

English divides time into past, present, and future. Hopi, a language of the Pueblo region of the Native American Southwest, does not. Rather, Hopi distinguishes between events that exist or have existed (what we use present and past to discuss) and those that don't or don't yet (our future events, along with imaginary and hypothetical events). Whorf argued that this difference leads Hopi speakers to think about time and reality in different ways than English speakers do. A similar example comes from Portuguese, which employs a future subjunctive verb form, introducing a degree of uncertainty into discussions of the future. In English, we routinely use the future tense to talk about something we think will happen. We don't feel the need to qualify "The sun'll come out tomorrow," by adding "if it doesn't go supernova." We don't hesitate to proclaim "I'll see you next year," even when we can't be absolutely sure we will. The Portuguese future subjunctive qualifies the future event, recognizing that the future can't be certain. Our way of expressing the future as certain is so ingrained that we don't even think about it, just as the Hopi don't see the need to distinguish between present and past, both of which are real, while the future remains hypothetical. It would seem, however, that language does not tightly restrict thought, because cultural changes can produce changes in thought and in language, as we shall see in the next section.

Focal Vocabulary

A **lexicon** (or vocabulary) is a language's dictionary, its set of names for things, events, and ideas. Lexicon influences perception. Thus, Eskimos have several distinct words for different types of snow that in English are all called *snow.* Most English speakers never notice the differences between these types of snow and might have trouble seeing them even if someone pointed them out. Eskimos recognize and think about differences in snow that English speakers don't see because our language provides us with just one word.

Similarly, the Nuer of Sudan have an elaborate vocabulary to describe cattle. Eskimos have several words for snow and Nuer have dozens for cattle because of their particular histories, economies, and environments. When the need arises, English speakers also can elaborate their snow and cattle vocabularies. For example, skiers name varieties of snow with words that are missing from the lexicons of Florida retirees. Similarly, the cattle vocabulary of a Texas rancher is much more ample than that of a salesperson in a New York City department store. Such specialized sets of terms and distinctions that are particularly important to certain groups (those with particular foci of experience or activity) are known as **focal vocabulary.**

Vocabulary is the area of language that changes most readily. New words and distinctions, when needed, appear and spread. For example, who would have "faxed" or e-mailed anything a generation ago? Names for items get simpler as they become common and important. A television has become a *TV,* an automobile a *car,* and a digital video disc a *DVD.*

Olives, but what kinds? Undoubtedly the olive vendor has a more elaborate focal vocabulary for what he sells than you or I do.

Language, culture, and thought are interrelated. However, and in opposition to the Sapir-Whorf hypothesis, it might be more reasonable to say that changes in culture produce changes in language and thought than the reverse. Consider differences between female and male Americans in regard to the color terms they use (Lakoff 2004). Distinctions implied by such terms as *salmon, rust, peach, beige, teal, mauve, cranberry,* and *dusky orange* aren't in the vocabularies of most American men. However, many of them weren't even in American women's lexicons 50 years ago. These changes reflect changes in American economy, society, and culture. Color terms and distinctions have increased with the growth of the fashion and cosmetic industries. A similar contrast (and growth) in Americans' lexicons shows up in football, basketball, and hockey vocabularies. Sports fans, more often males than females, use more terms in reference to, and make more elaborate distinctions between, the games they watch, such as hockey (see Table 15.2). Thus, cultural contrasts and changes affect lexical distinctions (for instance, peach versus salmon) within semantic domains (for instance, color terminology). **Semantics** refers to a language's meaning system.

Meaning

Speakers of particular languages use sets of terms to organize, or categorize, their experiences and perceptions. Linguistic terms and contrasts encode (embody) differences in meaning that people perceive. **Ethnosemantics** studies such classification systems in various languages. Well-studied ethnosemantic *domains* (sets of related things, perceptions, or concepts named in a language) include kinship terminology and color terminology. When we study such domains, we

TABLE 15.2 Focal Vocabulary for Hockey	
Insiders have special terms for the major elements of the game.	
Element of Hockey	**Insiders' Term**
puck	biscuit
goal/net	pipes
penalty box	sin bin
hockey stick	twig
helmet	bucket
space between a goalie's leg pads	five hole

How would a hockey insider use focal vocabulary to describe the items shown in this photo of a Stanley Cup final? How would you describe them?

Bringing It All Together

For a more detailed look at the linguistic, cultural, and ethnic aspects of unity and diversity in a contemporary nation-state (Canada), see the "Bringing It All Together" essay that immediately follows this chapter.

are examining how those people perceive and distinguish between kin relationships or colors. Other such domains include ethnomedicine—the terminology for the causes, symptoms, and cures of disease (Frake 1961); ethnobotany—native classification of plant life (Berlin, Breedlove, and Raven 1974; Carlson and Maffi 2004; Conklin 1954); and ethnoastronomy (Goodenough 1953).

The ways in which people divide up the world—the contrasts they perceive as meaningful or significant—reflect their experiences (see Bicker, Sillitoe, and Pottier, eds. 2004). Anthropologists have discovered that certain lexical domains and vocabulary items evolve in a determined order. For example, after studying color terminology in more than 100 languages, Berlin and Kay (1991, 1999) discovered 10 basic color terms: *white, black, red, yellow, blue, green, brown, pink, orange,* and *purple* (they evolved in more or less that order). The number of terms varied with cultural complexity. Representing one extreme were Papua New Guinea cultivators and Australian hunters and gatherers, who used only two basic terms, which translate as *black* and *white* or *dark* and *light*. At the other end of the continuum were European and Asian languages with all the color terms. Color terminology was most developed in areas with a history of using dyes and artificial coloring.

SOCIOLINGUISTICS

No language is a uniform system in which everyone talks just like everyone else. Linguistic *performance* (what people actually say) is the concern of sociolinguists. The field of **sociolinguistics** investigates relationships between social and linguistic variation, or language in its social context (Eckert and Rickford, eds. 2001). How do different speakers use a given language? How do linguistic features correlate with social stratification, including class, ethnic, and gender differences (Tannen 1990; Tannen, ed. 1993)? How is language used to express, reinforce, or resist power (Geis 1987; Thomas 1999)?

Sociolinguists don't deny that the people who speak a given language share knowledge of its basic rules. Such common knowledge is the basis of mutually intelligible communication. However, sociolinguists focus on features that vary systematically with social position and situation. To study variation, sociolinguists must do fieldwork. They must observe, define, and measure variable use of language in real-world situations. To show that linguistic features correlate with social, economic, and political differences, the social attributes of speakers also must be measured and related to speech (Fasold 1990; Labov 1972a; Trudgill 2000).

Variation within a language at a given time is historic change in progress. The same forces that, working gradually, have produced large-scale linguistic change over the centuries are still at work today. Linguistic change doesn't occur in a vacuum but in society. When new ways of speaking are associated with social factors, they are imitated, and they spread. In this way, a language changes.

Linguistic Diversity

As an illustration of the linguistic variation that is encountered in all nations, consider the contemporary United States. Ethnic diversity is revealed by the fact that millions of Americans learn first languages other than English. Spanish is the most common. Most of those people eventually become bilinguals, adding English as a second language. In many multilingual (including colonized) nations, people use two languages on different occasions: one in the home, for example, and the other on the job or in public.

Whether bilingual or not, we all vary our speech in different contexts; we engage in **style shifts** (see Eckert and Rickford, eds. 2001). In certain parts of Europe, people regularly switch dialects. This phenomenon, known as **diglossia**, applies to "high" and "low" variants of the same language, for example, in German and Flemish (spoken in Belgium). People employ the "high" variant at universities and in writing, professions, and the mass media. They use the "low" variant for ordinary conversation with family members and friends.

Just as social situations influence our speech, so do geographic, cultural, and socioeconomic differences. Many dialects coexist in the United States with Standard (American) English (SE). SE itself is a dialect that differs, say, from "BBC English," which is the preferred dialect in Great Britain. According to the principle of *linguistic relativity*, all dialects are equally effective as systems of communication, which is language's main job. Our tendency to think of particular dialects as cruder or more sophisticated than others is a social rather than a linguistic judgment. We rank certain speech patterns as better or worse because we recognize that they are used by groups that

we also rank. People who say *dese, dem,* and *dere* instead of *these, them,* and *there* communicate perfectly well with anyone who recognizes that the *d* sound systematically replaces the *th* sound in their speech. However, this form of speech has become an indicator of low social rank. We call it, like the use of *ain't,* "uneducated speech." The use of *dem, dese,* and *dere* is one of many phonological differences that Americans recognize and look down on.

Gender Speech Contrasts

Comparing men and women, there are differences in phonology, grammar, and vocabulary, as well as in the body stances and movements that accompany speech (Baron 1986; Eckert and McConnell-Ginet 2003; Lakoff 2004; Tannen 1990). In phonology, American women tend to pronounce their vowels more peripherally ("rant," "rint"), whereas men tend to pronounce theirs more centrally ("runt"—in all cases when saying the word "rent"). In public contexts, Japanese women tend to adopt an artificially high voice, for the sake of politeness, according to their traditional culture. In North America and Great Britain, women's speech tends to be more similar to the standard dialect than men's is. Consider the data in Table 15.3, gathered in Detroit. In all social classes, but particularly in the working class, men were more apt to use double negatives (e.g., "I don't want none"). Women tend to be more careful about "uneducated speech." This trend shows up in both the United States and England. Men may adopt working-class speech because they associate it with masculinity. Perhaps women pay more attention to the media, where standard dialects are employed.

According to Robin Lakoff (2004), the use of certain types of words and expressions has been associated with women's traditional lesser power in American society (see also Coates 1986; Tannen 1990). For example, *Oh dear, Oh fudge,* and *Goodness!* are less forceful than *Hell* and *Damn.* Watch the lips of a disgruntled athlete in a televised competition, such as a football game. What's the likelihood he's saying "Phooey on you"? Women are more likely to use such adjectives as *adorable, charming, sweet, cute, lovely,* and *divine* than men are.

See the Internet Exercises at your OLC for information on the extinction of languages

mhhe.com/kottak

TABLE 15.3 Multiple Negation ("I don't want none") According to Gender and Class (in Percentages)

	Upper Middle Class	Lower Middle Class	Upper Working Class	Lower Working Class
Male	6.3	32.4	40.0	90.1
Female	0.0	1.4	35.6	58.9

SOURCE: Peter Trudgill, *Sociolinguistics: An Introduction to Language and Society* (London: Penguin, 1974, revised edition 1983), p. 85.

■ Certain dialects are stigmatized, not because of actual linguistic deficiencies, but because of a symbolic association between a certain way of talking and low social status. In this scene from My Fair Lady, Professor Henry Higgins (Rex Harrison) encounters Eliza Doolittle (Audrey Hepburn), a Cockney flower girl. Higgins will teach Doolittle how to speak like an English aristocrat.

How does gender help us understand differences in communication styles? Differences in the linguistic strategies and behavior of American men and women are examined in several books by the well-known sociolinguist Deborah Tannen (1990, 1993). Tannen (1990) uses the terms "rapport" and "report" to contrast women's and men's overall linguistic styles. American women, says Tannen, typically use language and the body movements that accompany it to build rapport, social connections with others. American men, on the other hand, tend to make reports, reciting information that serves to establish a place for themselves in a hierarchy, as they also attempt to determine the relative ranks of their conversation mates.

Let's return to the previously discussed domains of sports and color terminology for additional illustration of differences in lexical (vocabulary) distinctions that men and women make. Men typically know more terms related to sports, make more distinctions among them (e.g., runs versus points), and try to use the terms more precisely than women do. Correspondingly, influenced more by the fashion and cosmetics industries than men are, women use more color terms and attempt to use them more specifically than men do. Thus, when I lecture on sociolinguistics, and to make this point, I bring an off-purple shirt to class. Holding it up, I first ask women to say aloud what color the shirt is. The women rarely answer with a uniform voice, as they try to distinguish the actual shade (mauve, lilac, lavender, wisteria, or some other purplish hue). I then ask the men, who consistently answer as one, "PURPLE." Rare is the man who on the spur of the moment can imagine the difference between *fuchsia* and *magenta* or *grape* and *aubergine*.

Language and Status Position

Honorifics are terms used with people, often by being added to their names, to "honor" them. Such terms may convey or imply a status difference between the speaker and the person being referred to ("the good doctor") or addressed ("Professor Dumbledore"). Although Americans tend to be less formal than other nationalities, American English still has its honorifics. They include such terms as "Mr.," "Mrs.," "Ms.," "Dr.," "Professor," "Dean," "Senator," "Reverend," "Honorable," and "Presi-

dent." Often these terms are attached to names, as in "Dr. Wilson," "President Bush," and "Senator Clinton," but some of them can be used to address someone without using his or her name, such as "Dr.," "Mr. President," "Senator," and "Miss." The British have a more developed set of honorifics, corresponding to status distinctions based in class, nobility (e.g., Lord and Lady Trumble), and special recognition (e.g., knighthood—"Sir Elton" or "Dame Maggie").

The Japanese language has several honorifics, some of which convey more respect than others do. The suffix *-sama* (added to a name), showing great respect, is used to address someone of higher social status, such as a lord or a respected teacher. Women can use it to demonstrate love or respect for their husbands. The most common Japanese honorific, *-san*, attached to the last name, is respectful, but less formal than "Mr.," "Mrs.," or "Ms." in American English. Attached to a first name, *-san* denotes more familiarity. The honorific *-dono* shows more respect and is intermediate between *-san* and *-sama*.

Other Japanese honorifics don't necessarily honor the person being addressed. The term *-kun*, for example, conveys familiarity when addressing friends, like using *-san* attached to the first name. The term *-kun* is used also with younger or lower-ranking people. A boss might use *-kun* with employees, especially females. Here the honorific works in reverse; the speaker uses the term (somewhat like "boy" or "girl" in English) to address someone he or she perceives as having lower status. Japanese speakers use the very friendly and familiar term *-chan* with someone of the same age or younger, including close friends, siblings, and children (*Free Dictionary* 2004; Loveday 1986, 2001).

Kin terms also can be associated with gradations in rank and familiarity. "Dad" is a more familiar, less formal kin term than "Father," but it still shows more respect than would using the father's first name. Outranking their children, parents routinely use their kids' first names, nicknames, or baby names, rather than addressing them as "son" and "daughter." American English terms like "bro," "man," "dude," and "girl" (in some contexts) seem similar to the informal/familiar honorifics in Japanese. Southerners up to (and sometimes long past) a certain age routinely use "ma'am" and "sir" for older or higher-status women and men.

Stratification

We use and evaluate speech in the context of *extralinguistic* forces—social, political, and economic. Mainstream Americans evaluate the speech of low-status groups negatively, calling it "uneducated." This is not because these ways of speaking are bad in themselves but because they have come to symbolize low status. Consider variation in the pronunciation of *r*. In some parts of the United States, *r* is regularly pronounced, and in other (*r*less) areas, it is not. Originally, American *r*less speech was modeled on the fashionable speech of England. Because of its prestige, *r*lessness was adopted in many areas and continues as the norm around Boston and in the South.

New Yorkers sought prestige by dropping their *r*'s in the 19th century, after having pronounced them in the 18th. However, contemporary New Yorkers are going back to the 18th-century pattern of pronouncing *r*'s. What matters, and what governs linguistic change, is not the reverberation of a strong midwestern *r* but *social* evaluation, whether *r*'s happen to be "in" or "out."

Studies of *r* pronunciation in New York City have clarified the mechanisms of phonological change. William Labov (1972b) focused on whether *r* was pronounced after vowels in such words as *car, floor, card,* and *fourth*. To get data on how this linguistic variation correlated with social class, he used a series of rapid encounters with employees in three New York City department stores, each of whose prices and locations attracted a different socioeconomic group. Saks Fifth Avenue (68 encounters) catered to the upper middle class, Macy's (125) attracted middle-class shoppers, and S. Klein's (71) had predominantly lower-middle-class and working-class customers. The class origins of store personnel tended to reflect those of their customers.

Having already determined that a certain department was on the fourth floor, Labov approached ground-floor salespeople and asked where that department was. After the salesperson had answered, "Fourth floor," Labov repeated his "Where?" in order to get a second response. The second reply was more formal and emphatic,

My dream was to became a shool teacher. Mrs Stone is rich. I have talents but not opportunity. I am used to standing behind Mrs Stone. I have been a servant for 40 years. Vickie Figueroa.

the salesperson presumably thinking that Labov hadn't heard or understood the first answer. For each salesperson, therefore, Labov had two samples of /r/ pronunciation in two words.

Labov calculated the percentages of workers who pronounced /r/ at least once during the interview. These were 62 percent at Saks, 51 percent at Macy's, but only 20 percent at S. Klein's. He also found that personnel on upper floors, where he asked "What floor is this?" (and where more expensive items were sold), pronounced /r/ more often than ground-floor salespeople did.

In Labov's study, summarized in Table 15.4, /r/ pronunciation was clearly associated with prestige. Certainly the job interviewers who had hired the salespeople never counted *r*'s before offering employment. However, they did use speech evaluations to make judgments about how effective certain people would be in selling particular kinds of merchandise. In other words, they practiced sociolinguistic discrimination, using linguistic features in deciding who got certain jobs.

Our speech habits help determine our access to employment and other material resources. Because of this, "proper language" itself becomes a strategic resource—and a path to wealth, pres-

"Proper language" is a strategic resource, correlated with wealth, prestige, and power. How is linguistic (and social) stratification illustrated in the photo above, including the handwritten comments below it?

TABLE 15.4 Pronunciation of *r* in New York City Department Stores		
Store	Number of Encounters	% *r* Pronunciation
Saks Fifth Avenue	68	62
Macy's	125	51
S. Klein's	71	20

tige, and power (Gal 1989; Thomas and Wareing, eds. 2004). Illustrating this, many ethnographers have described the importance of verbal skill and oratory in politics (Beeman 1986; Bloch, ed. 1975; Brenneis 1988; Geis 1987). Ronald Reagan, known as a "great communicator," dominated American society in the 1980s as a two-term president. Another twice-elected president, Bill Clinton, despite his southern accent, was known for his verbal skills in certain contexts (e.g., televised debates and town-hall meetings). Communications flaws may have helped doom the presidencies of Gerald Ford, Jimmy Carter, and George Bush (the elder) ("Couldn't do that; wouldn't be prudent").

The French anthropologist Pierre Bourdieu views linguistic practices as *symbolic capital* that properly trained people may convert into economic and social capital. The value of a dialect—its standing in a "linguistic market"—depends on the extent to which it provides access to desired positions in the labor market. In turn, this reflects its legitimation by formal institutions: educational institutions, state, church, and prestige media. Even people who don't use the prestige dialect accept its authority and correctness, its "symbolic domination" (Bourdieu 1982, 1984). Thus, linguistic forms, which lack power in themselves, take on the power of the groups they symbolize. The education system, however (defending its own worth), denies linguistic relativity, misrepresenting prestige speech as being inherently better. The linguistic insecurity often felt by lower-class and minority speakers is a result of this symbolic domination.

Black English Vernacular (BEV)

No one pays much attention when someone says "runt" instead of "rent." But some nonstandard speech carries more of a stigma. Sometimes stigmatized speech is linked to region, class, or educational background; sometimes it is associated with ethnicity or "race."

The sociolinguist William Labov and several associates, both white and black, have conducted detailed studies of what they call **Black English**

Vernacular (BEV). (*Vernacular* means ordinary, casual speech.) BEV is the "relatively uniform dialect spoken by the majority of black youth in most parts of the United States today, especially in the inner city areas of New York, Boston, Detroit, Philadelphia, Washington, Cleveland, . . . and other urban centers. It is also spoken in most rural areas and used in the casual, intimate speech of many adults" (Labov 1972a, p. xiii). This does not imply that all, or even most, African Americans speak BEV.

BEV isn't an ungrammatical hodgepodge. Rather, BEV is a complex linguistic system with its own rules, which linguists have described. The phonology and syntax of BEV are similar to those of southern dialects. This reflects generations of contact between southern whites and blacks, with mutual influence on each other's speech patterns. Many features that distinguish BEV from SE (Standard English) also show up in southern white speech, but less frequently than in BEV.

Linguists disagree about exactly how BEV originated (Rickford 1997). Smitherman (1986) calls it an Africanized form of English reflecting both an African heritage and the conditions of servitude, oppression, and life in America. She notes certain structural similarities between West African languages and BEV. African linguistic backgrounds no doubt influenced how early African Americans learned English. Did they restructure English to fit African linguistic patterns? Or did they quickly learn English from whites, with little continuing influence from the African linguistic heritage? Or, possibly, in acquiring English, did African slaves fuse English with African languages to make a pidgin or creole, which influenced the subsequent development of BEV? Creole speech may have been brought to the American colonies by the many slaves who were imported from the Caribbean during the 17th and 18th centuries. Some slaves may even have learned, while still in Africa, the pidgins or creoles spoken in West African trading forts (Rickford 1997).

Origins aside, there are phonological and grammatical differences between BEV and SE. One phonological difference between BEV and SE is that BEV speakers are less likely to pronounce *r* than SE speakers are. Actually, many SE speakers don't pronounce *r*'s that come right before a consonant (ca*r*d) or at the end of a word (ca*r*). But SE speakers do usually pronounce an *r* that comes right before a vowel, either at the end of a word (fou*r* o'clock) or within a word (Ca*r*ol). BEV speakers, by contrast, are much more likely to omit such intervocalic (between vowels) *r*'s. The result is that speakers of the two dialects have different *homonyms* (words that sound the same but have different meanings). BEV speakers who don't pronounce intervocalic *r*'s have the following homonyms: Carol/Cal; Paris/pass.

Observing different phonological rules, BEV speakers pronounce certain words differently than SE speakers do. Particularly in the elementary school context, the homonyms of BEV-speaking students typically differ from those of their SE-speaking teachers. To evaluate reading accuracy, teachers should determine whether students are recognizing the different meanings of such BEV homonyms as *passed, past,* and *pass.* Teachers need to make sure students understand what they are reading, which is probably more important than whether they are pronouncing words correctly according to the SE norm.

The phonological contrasts between BEV and SE speakers often have grammatical consequences. One of these is *copula deletion,* which means the absence of SE forms of the copula—the verb *to be.* For example, SE and BEV may contrast as follows:

SE	SE Contraction	BEV
you are tired	you're tired	you tired
he is tired	he's tired	he tired
we are tired	we're tired	we tired
they are tired	they're tired	they tired

In its deletion of the present tense of the verb *to be,* BEV is similar to many languages, including Russian, Hungarian, and Hebrew. BEV's copula deletion is simply a grammatical result of its phonological rules. Notice that BEV deletes the copula where SE has contractions. BEV's phonological rules dictate that *r*'s (as in *you're, we're,* and *they're*) and word-final *s*'s (as in *he's*) be dropped. However, BEV speakers do pronounce *m,* so that the BEV first-person singular is "I'm tired," just as in SE. Thus, when BEV omits the copula, it merely carries contraction one step further, as a result of its phonological rules.

Also, phonological rules may lead BEV speakers to omit *-ed* as a past-tense marker and *-s* as a marker of plurality. However, other speech contexts demonstrate that BEV speakers do understand the difference between past and present verbs, and between singular and plural nouns. Confirming this are irregular verbs (e.g., *tell, told*) and irregular plurals (e.g., *child, children*), in which BEV works the same as SE.

SE is not superior to BEV as a linguistic system, but it does happen to be the prestige dialect—the one used in the mass media, in writing, and in most public and professional contexts. SE is the dialect that has the most "symbolic capital." In areas of Germany where there is diglossia, speakers of Plattdeusch (Low German) learn the High German dialect to communicate appropriately in the national context. Similarly, upwardly mobile BEV-speaking students learn SE.

HISTORICAL LINGUISTICS

Map Atlas

Map 11 plots the distribution of the world's major language families, including Indo-European, whose languages are spoken now in areas far from its geographic origin.

Sociolinguists study contemporary variation in speech—language change in progress. **Historical linguistics** deals with longer-term change. Historical linguists can reconstruct many features of past languages by studying contemporary **daughter languages.** These are languages that descend from the same parent language and that have been changing separately for hundreds or even thousands of years. We call the original language from which they diverge the **protolanguage.** Romance languages such as French and Spanish, for example, are daughter languages of Latin, their common protolanguage. German, English, Dutch, and the Scandinavian languages are daughter languages of proto-Germanic. Latin and proto-Germanic were both Indo-European languages. Historical linguists classify languages according to their degree of relationship (see Figure 15.2).

Language changes over time. It evolves—varies, spreads, divides into **subgroups** (languages within a taxonomy of related languages that are most closely related). Dialects of a single parent language become distinct daughter languages, especially if they are isolated from one another. Some of them split, and new "granddaughter" languages develop. If people remain in the ancestral homeland, their speech patterns also change. The evolving speech in the ancestral homeland should be considered a daughter language like the others.

FIGURE 15.2 PIE Family Tree.

This is a family tree of the Indo-European languages. All can be traced back to a protolanguage, Proto-Indo-European (PIE), spoken more than 6,000 years ago. PIE split into dialects that eventually evolved into separate languages, which, in turn, evolved into languages such as Latin and proto-Germanic, which are ancestral to dozens of modern daughter languages.

For more on PIE, see the Virtual Exploration

mhhe.com/kottak

Cybercommunication in Collegespace

BACKGROUND INFORMATION

STUDENT:
Jason A. DeCaro

SUPERVISING PROFESSOR:
Robert Herbert

SCHOOL:
State University of New York at Binghamton

YEAR IN SCHOOL/MAJOR:
Senior/Anthropology and Biochemistry dual major

FUTURE PLANS:
Ph.D. in Biological Anthropology; career in academics or public health

PROJECT TITLE:
Cybercommunication in Collegespace: The Electronic/Personal Juncture in a Campus Living Community

How is online communication related to face-to-face communication and to social interaction? On the basis of this research, is electronic communication good or bad for community formation?

Why do people who live in face-to-face proximity communicate using their computers? What is the interaction between their social lives "on-" and "off-line"? How does this affect their sense of community? I conducted research to address these questions through an anthropological case study.

The Internet has been interpreted as personalizing or depersonalizing, as highly democratic or merely chaotic, and as vitalizing or damaging to American "community." Some theorists suppose that electronic communication extends the pool of individuals with whom one maintains contact. However, others suggest that this merely creates an electronic "pseudocommunity" with shifting membership and superficial social ties. If this "pseudo-community" competes for members' time and energy, it may be detrimental to their face-to-face interaction. Despite the active theoretical debate, very few studies have examined the interaction between electronic and face-to-face community in a geographically local group of individuals.

I observed a group of students of mixed gender who live in close proximity on a college campus. These students chose their living arrangement on the basis of common interest in computers, robotics, and engineering. Not all are computer scientists; some pursue majors such as creative writing and chemistry. Roughly a dozen alumni, some of whom no longer live in the local area, remain integral to the organization.

I am an alumnus; thus, I have a personal as well as a professional interest. One of my most challenging jobs was to avoid unintentional manipulation—even distancing myself from the group would have changed it! Yet, by remaining an "insider," I received tremendous access, and had a great deal of fun.

Members maintain face-to-face social activity and a busy electronic mailing list. The "real" and "virtual" communities thus created have overlapping but nonidentical membership. Most members who communicate exclusively within the "virtual" electronic domain are alumni. Students vary with respect to the form of communication that they favor. A few shun the electronic medium entirely and thereby opt out of the "virtual" community.

I distributed questionnaires, analyzed one year's mailing list traffic, and remained a participant in face-to-face social life. I found that conversations sometimes flow on and off the mailing list, and members do organize face-to-face social activities on-line. However, most people segregate the electronic and face-to-face domains, and most messages serve no explicit organizational purpose. Messages in this latter category allow contact between people who are not local, or strengthen bonds between individuals who see each other regularly.

Those who dedicate considerable time and energy to the virtual community put the mailing list to its widest range of uses. However, there is little evidence that electronic communication detracts from face-to-face interaction. Most people who are highly social on-line are highly social off-line as well. I suspect that individuals supplement, rather than replace, their face-to-face social lives with electronic communication. This is particularly valuable to those who do not live locally, or are less than comfortable with face-to-face communication. Thus, on the whole, members are integrated far more than they are alienated by the mailing list.

A close relationship between languages does not necessarily mean that their speakers are closely related biologically or culturally, because people can adopt new languages. In the equatorial forests of Africa, "pygmy" hunters have discarded their ancestral languages and now speak those of the cultivators who have migrated to the area. Immigrants to the United States and Canada spoke many different languages on arrival, but their descendants now speak fluent English.

The Book of Kells, an illustrated manuscript, was created at Kells, an ancient Irish monastery. Shown here is the title page of the book, which now resides in the Trinity College library in Dublin, Ireland. Such documents provide historical linguists with information on how languages change.

Knowledge of linguistic relationships is often valuable to anthropologists interested in history, particularly events during the past 5,000 years. Cultural features may (or may not) correlate with the distribution of language families. Groups that speak related languages may (or may not) be more culturally similar to each other than they are to groups whose speech derives from different linguistic ancestors. Of course, cultural similarities aren't limited to speakers of related languages. Even groups whose members speak unrelated languages have contact through trade, intermarriage, and warfare. Ideas and inventions diffuse widely among human groups. Many items of vocabulary in contemporary English come from French. Even without written documentation of France's influence after the Norman Conquest of England in 1066, linguistic evidence in contemporary English would reveal a long period of important firsthand contact with France. Similarly, linguistic evidence may confirm cultural contact and borrowing when written history is lacking. By considering which words have been borrowed, we also can make inferences about the nature of the contact.

SUMMARY

1. Wild primates use call systems to communicate. Environmental stimuli trigger calls, which cannot be combined when multiple stimuli are present. Contrasts between language and call systems include displacement, productivity, and cultural transmission. Over time, our ancestral call systems grew too complex for genetic transmission, and hominid communication began to rely on learning. Humans still use nonverbal communication, such as facial expressions, gestures, and body stances and movements. But language is the main system humans use to communicate. Chimps and gorillas can understand and manipulate nonverbal symbols based on language.

2. No language uses all the sounds the human vocal tract can make. Phonology—the study of speech sounds—focuses on sound contrasts (phonemes) that distinguish meaning. The grammars and lexicons of particular languages can lead their speakers to perceive and think in certain ways. Studies of domains such as kinship, color terminologies, and pronouns show that speakers of different languages categorize their experiences differently.

3. Linguistic anthropologists share anthropology's general interest in diversity in time and space. Sociolinguistics investigates relationships between social and linguistic variation by focusing on the actual use of language. Only when features of speech acquire social meaning are they imitated. If they are valued, they will spread. People vary their speech, shifting styles, dialects, and languages. As linguistic systems, all languages and dialects are equally complex, rule-governed, and effective for communication. However, speech is used, is evaluated, and changes in the context of political, economic, and social forces. Often the linguistic traits of a low-status group are negatively evaluated. This devaluation is not because of *linguistic* features per se. Rather, it reflects the association of such features with low *social* status. One dialect, supported by the dominant institutions of the state, exercises symbolic domination over the others.

4. Historical linguistics is useful for anthropologists interested in historic relationships among populations. Cultural similarities and differences often correlate with linguistic ones. Linguistic clues can suggest past contacts between cultures. Related languages—members of the same language family—descend from an original protolanguage. Relationships between languages don't necessarily mean that there are biological ties between their speakers, because people can learn new languages.

Black English Vernacular (BEV) A rule-governed dialect of American English with roots in southern English. BEV is spoken by African American youth and by many adults in their casual, intimate speech.

call systems Systems of communication among nonhuman primates, composed of a limited number of sounds that vary in intensity and duration. Tied to environmental stimuli.

cultural transmission A basic feature of language; transmission through learning.

daughter languages Languages developing out of the same parent language; for example, French and Spanish are daughter languages of Latin.

diglossia The existence of "high" (formal) and "low" (informal, familial) dialects of a single language, such as German.

displacement A basic feature of language; the ability to speak of things and events that are not present.

ethnosemantics The study of lexical (vocabulary) contrasts and classifications in various languages.

focal vocabulary A set of words and distinctions that are particularly important to certain groups (those with particular foci of experience or activity), such as types of snow to Eskimos or skiers.

historical linguistics Subdivision of linguistics that studies languages over time.

honorific A term, such as "Mr." or "Lord," used with people, often by being added to their names, to "honor" them.

kinesics The study of communication through body movements, stances, gestures, and facial expressions.

language Human beings' primary means of communication; may be spoken or written; features productivity and displacement and is culturally transmitted.

lexicon Vocabulary; a dictionary containing all the morphemes in a language and their meanings.

morphology The study of form; used in linguistics (the study of morphemes and word construction) and for form in general—for example, biomorphology relates to physical form.

phoneme Significant sound contrast in a language that serves to distinguish meaning, as in minimal pairs.

phonemics The study of the sound contrasts (phonemes) of a particular language.

phonetics The study of speech sounds in general; what people actually say in various languages.

phonology The study of sounds used in speech.

productivity A basic feature of language; the ability to use the rules of one's language to create new expressions comprehensible to other speakers.

protolanguage Language ancestral to several daughter languages.

Sapir-Whorf hypothesis Theory that different languages produce different ways of thinking.

semantics A language's meaning system.

sociolinguistics Study of relationships between social and linguistic variation; study of language (performance) in its social context.

style shifts Variations in speech in different contexts.

subgroups Languages within a taxonomy of related languages that are most closely related.

syntax The arrangement and order of words in phrases and sentences.

KEY TERMS

See the flash cards
mhhe.com/kottak

1. Give some additional examples of nonverbal communication. Check out your classmates during a discussion and see what examples you notice.

2. During a class discussion, what examples do you notice of sociolinguistic variation—say, between men and women, the professor and students, and so forth?

3. List some stereotypes about how different sorts of people speak. Are those real differences, or just stereotypes? Are the stereotypes positive or negative? Why do you think those stereotypes exist?

4. Based on your own experience and observations, list five ways in which men and women differ in their use of language. Now classify these differences as kinesic, phonological, grammatical, lexical—or other.

5. Do you agree with the principle of linguistic relativity? If not, why not? What dialects and languages do you speak? Do you tend to use different dialects, languages, or speech styles in different contexts? Why?

CRITICAL THINKING QUESTIONS

For more self-testing, see the self-quizzes
mhhe.com/kottak

Bonvillain, N.
2003 *Language, Culture, and Communication: The Meaning of Messages,* 4th ed. Upper Saddle River, NJ: Prentice Hall. Up-to-date text on language and communication in cultural context.

Eckert, P.
2000 *Linguistic Variation as Social Practice: The Linguistic Construction of Identity in Belten High.* Malden, MA: Blackwell. How speech correlates with high school social networks and cliques.

SUGGESTED ADDITIONAL READINGS

Eckert, P., and S. McConnell-Ginet
2003 *Language and Gender.* New York: Cambridge University Press. The sociolinguistics of male and female speech.

Eckert, P., and J. R. Rickford, eds.
2001 *Style and Sociolinguistic Variation.* New York: Cambridge University Press. The social context of style shifts.

Foley, W. A.
1997 *Anthroplogical Linguistics: An Introduction.* Cambridge, MA: Blackwell. Language, society, and culture.

Fouts, R.
1997 *Next of Kin: What Chimpanzees Have Taught Me about Who We Are.* New York, William Morrow. A teacher of Washoe, Lucy, and other signing chimps tells what he's learned from them.

Geis, M. L.
1987 *The Language of Politics.* New York: Springer-Verlag. Thorough examination of political uses of speech and oratory and the manipulation of language in power relations.

Lakoff, R. T.
2000 *Language War.* Berkeley: University of California Press. Politics and language in the United States today.
2004 *Language and Woman's Place,* rev. ed. (M. Bucholtz, ed.). New York: Oxford University Press. Influential nontechnical discussion of how women use and are treated in Standard American English.

Rickford, J. R., and R. J. Rickford
2000 *Spoken Soul: The Story of Black English.* New York: Wiley. Readable account of the history and social meaning of BEV.

Romaine, S.
1999 *Communicating Gender.* Mahwah, NJ: Erlbaum. Gender and language.
2000 *Language in Society: An Introduction to Sociolinguistics,* 2nd ed. New York: Oxford University Press. An introduction to sociolinguistics.

Salzmann, Z.
2004 *Language, Culture, and Society: An Introduction to Linguistic Anthropology,* 3rd ed. Boulder, CO: Westview. The function of language in culture and society.

Tannen, D.
1990 *You Just Don't Understand: Women and Men in Conversation.* New York: Ballantine. Popular book on gender differences in speech and conversational styles.

Tannen, D., ed.
1993 *Gender and Conversational Interaction.* New York: Oxford University Press. Twelve papers about conversational interaction illustrate the complexity of the relationship between gender and language use.

Thomas, L., and S. Wareing, eds.
2004 *Language, Society and Power,* 2nd ed. New York: Routledge. Political dimensions and use of language.

Trudgill, P.
2000 *Sociolinguistics: An Introduction to Language and Society,* 4th ed. New York: Penguin. Readable short introduction to the role and use of language in society.

INTERNET EXERCISES

1. Politeness Strategies: Go and read Cyndi Patee's article "Politeness," **http://logos.uoregon.edu/explore/socioling/ politeness.html**.
   a. What kind of strategy do you most often use? Do your strategies change when you are talking to different people (i.e., your friend, your parent, your professor)?
   b. What kind of politeness strategy do you like other people to use with you? Would you prefer people to sacrifice politeness for directness?
   c. Pay attention to what politeness strategies are being used around you in class, at home, and with friends. Can you identify any patterns in the way people select politeness strategies?

2. Urban Legends: Read the Urban Legends and Folklore information page at About.com, **http://urbanlegends.about.com/science/ urbanlegends/library/weekly/aa082497.htm**. Make sure to read some of the examples of urban legends that are provided.
   a. What constitutes an urban legend?
   b. Why are urban legends so popular? Many of them are not true, so why do they continue to be shared?
   c. What role does the Internet play in propagating urban legends?
   d. After reading this page, are you going to be more or less skeptical the next time a friend relates a story to you?

See Chapter 15 at your McGraw-Hill Online Learning Center for additional review and interactive exercises.

Kottak, *Assault on Paradise*, 4th ed.

Read Chapter 7, especially the section "The Hippie Handbook." How did language figure in the way Arembepeiros characterized hippies? Read Chapter 12. How has television affected the way Arembepeiros deal with outsiders? What's your reaction to the stories of Nadia and Olga in relation to the impact of television? Do Brazilian attitudes about reading and print surprise you? Why?

Knauft, *The Gebusi*, 1st ed.

Based on Chapter 1 of Knauft's *The Gebusi,* how *important* was it for the author to learn the Gebusi language during his fieldwork? How easy was it for the author to learn the Gebusi language during his fieldwork? How did the author go about learning the Gebusi language—and how well or poorly did his language abilities develop over time?

Canada: Unity and Diversity in Culture and Language

See your OLC Bringing
It All Together links

mhhe.com/kottak

There are levels of culture, as was pointed out in the chapter titled "Culture." National culture consists of the beliefs, values, behavior patterns, and institutions that people share through growing up in a given nation. Cultures also can be smaller than nations. Such "subcultures" may originate in region, ethnicity, language, class, or religion. Thus, the religious backgrounds of American Jews, Baptists, Roman Catholics, and Muslims create subcultural differences among them. French-speaking Canadians contrast with English-speaking people in the same country.

Studying a modern nation, anthropologists may focus on either unity or diversity—on what is common or what is different. A focus on unity would examine themes, values, behavior, institutions, and experiences that transcend regions and social divisions. A focus on diversity would look at the cultures within the national culture.

The two approaches shouldn't be mutually exclusive. Despite diversity, we can still detect a series of nationally relevant institutions, norms, and expectations. As we saw in the chapter on "Ethnicity and Race," the pressure on members of an ethnic group to observe a set of common national values comes not only from the national culture, but also from other ethnic groups. For example, African Americans in Los Angeles, after that city's 1992 riots, complained about their Korean neighbors. In doing so they referred to such general American values as openness, mutual respect, community participation, and "fair play." They saw their Korean neighbors as deficient in these traits. The Koreans countered by stressing another set of American national

values, involving education, family unity, discipline, hard work, and achievement.

We focus now on unity and diversity in Canada. (American national culture is examined in Appendix 3.) One key feature of Canadian national consciousness is the contrast with the United States. Canadians, when traveling internationally, often are taken for Americans, which emphatically they are not. To be sure, Canada and the United States share many cultural traits. Some reflect the shared English-language heritage of most Canadians and Americans. Some reflect common experiences in the colonization of North America. Still others reflect participation in a global system, or diffusion of products and information across porous borders.

The media, especially television, have helped bring nationalism and its symbols, including cultural contrasts with the United States, to prominence in Canada. In spring 2000, a TV commercial produced in Toronto for Molson Canadian beer gained instantaneous national prominence. The ad featured the character Joe Canadian, delivering what came to be known as The Rant, soon to become a nationalist mantra for 30 million Canadians:

"I'm not a lumberjack or a fur trader; I don't live in an igloo, eat blubber or own a dogsled."

"I have a prime minister, not a president. I speak English and French, not American."

"I can proudly sew my country's flag on my backpack." (This refers to Canada's gender-neutral school curriculum, in which sewing is taught to both boys and girls.)

"I believe in peacekeeping, not policing; diversity, not assimilation."

Images of maple leaves and beavers flashed on the screen as Joe reached his climax:

"Canada is the second-largest land mass, the first nation of hockey and the best part of North America. My name is Joe and I am Canadian" (quoted in Brooke 2000).

The Rant spurred the government of Ontario, Canada's most populous province, to announce that starting in September 2000, each student would start the day by singing "O Canada," and pledging allegiance to the queen (since Canada is a member of the British Commonwealth). Although The Rant was recited by ordinary Canadians from Vancouver to Halifax, one province did not join in this affirmation of national identity. In French-

Jeff Douglas, who plays Joe Canadian, delivers "The Rant" in Ottawa, Ontario, on Canada Day—July 1, 2000.

speaking Quebec, which was governed by the separatist Parti Quebecois between 1994 and 2003, Canadian national symbols such as the flag and the anthem were officially ignored, and Molson Canadian beer was not even marketed (Brooke 2000).

The contrast between Quebec and the rest of Canada is the most dramatic, jarring, and politically problematic in a nation that prides itself on diversity in language and culture. Few countries rival Canada in cultivating a national image of a bilingual, multicultural society. According to a Government of Canada website:

> Canada's experience with diversity distinguishes it from most other countries. Our 30 million inhabitants reflect a cultural, ethnic and linguistic makeup found nowhere else on earth . . . Diversity has been a fundamental characteristic of Canada since its beginnings (http://www.pch.gc.ca/progs/multi/respect_e.cfm).

Unlike the United States, which is suspicious of linguistic difference, bilingualism (with English and French as official languages) lies at the root of the Canadian federation. When the Canadian Confederation was established in 1867, English and French were accorded official, constitutional status. Substantial powers were granted to Canada's constituent provinces. In one of those provinces, Quebec, French-speaking Canadians formed a large majority. They used their constitutional powers to protect and develop a regional culture based on French language and culture and French-Canadian heritage. Elsewhere in Canada, the French language was swamped by immigrants who either were of English origin or were encouraged to speak English. In 2001 86 percent of Canada's native French speakers (Francophones) lived in Quebec, where they made up 82 percent of the population.

The longest-standing test of Canada's capacity to balance unity and diversity is the challenge of linguistic duality. The national dominance of English is troubling to French Canadians. Illustrating a power imbalance that tilts toward English is the fact that there are five times as many bilingual Francophones as Anglophones (native English speakers). Francophones need to learn English more than Anglophones need to learn French.

Because of immigration, linguistic diversity in Canada is increasing. In 2001 (the date of the last census), 5.2 million Canadians, in a population of some 30 million people, reported a mother tongue (language learned in the home in childhood) other than English or French. Anglophone Canadians accounted for 59 percent of the population, versus 23 percent for Francophones. Eighteen percent of Canadians habitually spoke a language other than English or French. Chinese was the third most common, followed by Italian, German, Punjabi, Spanish, Portuguese, Polish, Arabic, Tagalog (Filipino), Ukrainian, Dutch, Vietnamese, Greek, and aboriginal languages.

English-French bilingualism (people speaking both English and French) has increased. In 2001, 18 percent of the population could speak both official languages, compared with 13 percent in 1971. Note that both Canada and Canadians illustrate increased linguistic diversity.

In 1950, 92 percent of Canada's population growth was from births to Canadians. Today, with around 200,000 people moving to Canada each year, immigration accounts for over 55 percent of the overall population growth. Of Canada's population in 2001, 18.4 percent was foreign-born. Canada has been called "the global village in one country." Toronto, Canada's largest city, in its largest province, has become the world's most multicultural city, ahead of New York and London.

Canada has always relied on immigrants to supply settlers and labor. During the late 19th and early 20th centuries, Canada's immigration policy had as its primary objective supplying a labor pool, first for settlement and agriculture and then to support industrialization. In 1960, a Canadian Bill of Rights barred discrimination by federal agencies based on national origin, race, color, religion, or sex. In 1962 a revised Canadian Immigration Act stated that any qualified person from any part of the world could be considered for immigration. The mix of source countries soon shifted from northern Europe to southern Europe, Asia, the West Indies, and the Middle East.

Canada is officially bilingual, but French language and culture dominate in the province of Quebec. Shown here, Quebec Liberal Party leader Jean Charest speaks to supporters during a campaign stop on April 12, 2003. After this successful campaign, Charest became Premier of Quebec in 2003.

Despite its admirable ideology of respect, Canada hasn't totally avoided discrimination. Abuses of the rights of aboriginal peoples, for example, can be traced back to Canada's beginnings. Aboriginal Canadians still have more poverty, poorer health, higher death and suicide rates, and more unemployment than their fellow citizens do. To its credit, the Canadian government has taken many steps to correct past mistakes and to address the needs of aboriginal peoples. For example, in 1973 Canada's Supreme Court recognized land rights based on an aboriginal group's traditional use and occupancy of land. And in 1982, the government affirmed the treaty rights of aboriginal peoples to protect their cultures, customs, traditions and languages.

In 2001 some 975,000 Canadians (3.3 percent of the national population) claimed aboriginal identity as North American Indians (First Nations), métis (mixed), or Inuit. A fifth of the aboriginal population reported an aboriginal language as the mother tongue. At the time of European settlement, Canada had more than 56 aboriginal nations speaking more than 30 languages. Among aboriginal languages reported as mother tongues in 2001, the three largest were Cree (72,690 people), Inuktitut (spoken by Inuit—29,005), and Ojibway (20,890).

The chapter "Ethnicity and Race" discussed the social construction of race in the United States, Japan, and Brazil. Canada constructs race and ethnicity differently from any of those three countries, although there are similarities. For example, the classification of people who claim a métis (mixed) identity as Aboriginal People hints of the American hypodescent rule. Rather than race, the Canadian census asks about "visible minorities." That country's Employment Equity Act defines such groups as "persons, other than Aboriginal peoples, who are non-Caucasian in race or non-white in colour" (Statistics Canada 2001a). Unlike the United States, the Canadian census would seem to assume that racial differences lie in the minds (and eyes) of the beholder rather than being self-identified.

Canada's 1996 census was the first to gather systematic data on visible minorities—for the purpose of assessing employment equity. Like affirmative action in the United States, Canada's Employment Equity Act was a response to evidence of discrimination.

"Chinese" and "South Asian" are Canada's largest visible minorities. Note that Canada's total visible minority population of 13.4 percent contrasts with a comparable figure of about 25 percent for the United States in the 2000 census. In particular, Canada's 2.2 percent black population contrasts with the American figure of 12.5 percent for African Americans. Canada's Asian population is significantly higher than the U.S. figure of 3.7 percent. Only a tiny fraction of the Canadian population (0.2 percent) claimed multiple visible minority affiliations, compared with 2.4 percent claiming "more than one race" in the United States in 2000.

Having read this essay, think about the main similarities and differences between the United States and Canada in terms of racial classification, ethnicity and multiculturalism, and linguistic diversity. What are key symbols of Canadian national culture—and of the national culture of the United States?

16

Making a Living

ADAPTIVE STRATEGIES

Compared with hunting and gathering (foraging), the advent of *food production* (plant cultivation and animal domestication) fueled major changes in human life, such as the formation of larger social and political systems—eventually states. The pace of cultural transformation increased enormously. This chapter provides a framework for understanding a variety of human adaptive strategies and economic systems—ranging from hunting and gathering to farming and herding.

The anthropologist Yehudi Cohen (1974b) used the term *adaptive strategy* to describe a group's system of economic production. Cohen argued that the most important reason for similarities between two (or more) unrelated societies is their possession of a similar adaptive strategy. For example, there are clear similarities among societies that have a foraging (hunting and gathering) strategy. Cohen developed a typology of societies based on correlations between their economies and their social features. His typology includes these five adaptive strategies: foraging, horticulture, agriculture, pastoralism, and industrialism. Industrialism is discussed in the chapter "The Modern World System." The present chapter focuses on the first four adaptive strategies.

FORAGING

Until 10,000 years ago, people everywhere were foragers, also known as hunter-gatherers. However, environmental differences did create substantial contrasts among the world's foragers. Some, such as the people who lived in Europe during the ice ages, were big-game hunters. Today, hunters in the Arctic still focus on large animals and herd animals; they have much less vegetation and variety in their diets than do tropical foragers. In general, as one moves from colder to warmer areas, there is an increase in the

---

OVERVIEW

Nonindustrial adaptive strategies include foraging, horticulture, agriculture, and pastoralism. Ties of kinship and marriage link members of foraging bands, whose men usually hunt and fish, while the women usually gather.

Horticulture and agriculture stand at opposite ends of a continuum based on intensity of land and labor use. Horticulturalists always fallow their land. Agriculturalists farm the same piece of land year after year and use labor intensively, through irrigation, terracing, and caring for domesticated animals. Pastoralists (herders) have mixed economies. Nomadic pastoralists trade with farmers. Among transhumant pastoralists, part of the population farms, while another part pastures the herds.

Economic anthropologists, who study systems of production, distribution, and consumption cross-culturally, counter Western economic assumptions about the universality of scarcity and the profit motive. There are three main forms of exchange. Market exchange is based on purchase and sale, motivated by profit. With redistribution, goods are collected at a central place, with some eventually being given back to the people. Reciprocity governs exchanges between social equals. The primary exchange mode in a society is the one that allocates the means of production.

---

number of species. The tropics contain tremendous biodiversity, a great variety of plant and animal species, many of which have been used by human foragers. Tropical foragers typically hunt and gather a wide range of plant and animal life. The same may be true in temperate areas, such as the North Pacific Coast of North America, where Native American foragers could draw on a rich variety of land and sea resources, including salmon, other fish species, berries, mountain goats, seals, and sea mammals. Nevertheless, despite differences due to environmental variation, all foraging economies have shared one essential feature: People rely on available natural resources for their subsistence, rather than controlling the reproduction of plants and animals.

Such control came with the advent of animal domestication (initially of sheep and goats) and plant cultivation (of wheat and barley), which began 10,000 to 12,000 years ago in the Middle East. Cultivation based on different crops, such as maize, manioc (cassava), and potatoes, arose independently some 3,000 to 4,000 years later in the Americas. In both hemispheres the new economy spread rapidly. Most foragers eventually turned to food production. Today, almost all foragers have at least some dependence on food production or on food producers (Kent 1992).

The foraging way of life survived into modern times in certain environments (see Figure 16.1), including a few islands and forests, along with deserts and very cold areas—places where food production was not practicable with simple technology (see Lee and Daly 1999). In many areas, foragers had been exposed to the "idea" of food production but never adopted it because their own economies provided a perfectly adequate and nutritious diet—with a lot less work. In some areas, people reverted to foraging after trying food production and abandoning it. In most areas where hunter-gatherers did survive, foraging should be described as "recent" rather than "contemporary." All modern foragers live in nation-states, depend to some extent on government assistance, and have contacts with food-producing neighbors, as well as missionaries and other outsiders. We should not view contemporary foragers as isolated or pristine survivors of the Stone Age. Modern foragers are influenced by regional forces (e.g., trade and war), national and international policies, and political and economic events in the world system.

Although foraging is disappearing as a way of life, the outlines of Africa's two broad belts of recent foraging remain evident. One is the Kalahari Desert of southern Africa. This is the home of the *San* ("Bushmen"), who include the *Ju/'hoansi* (see Kent 1996; Lee 2003). The other main African foraging area is the equatorial forest of central and eastern Africa, home of the Mbuti, Efe, and other "pygmies" (Bailey et al. 1989; Turnbull 1965).

Reindeer Herders, at Home on a (Very Cold) Range

NEW YORK TIMES NEWS BRIEF

by Warren Hoge
March 26, 2001

This chapter surveys systems of production and exchange in nonindustrial economies. Some economic roles, such as hunting and herding, have been around for millennia. In Norway, Sweden, and Finland, the Samis (also known as Lapps or Laplanders) domesticated reindeer, which their ancestors used to hunt, in the 16th century. Like other herders, the Samis still follow their animals as they make an annual trek, in this case from the coast to the interior. Their environment may be harsher, but the Samis, like other contemporary herders, live in nation-states. They must deal with outsiders as they make their living through animal husbandry, trade, and sales. The Samis now use modern technology, including snowmobiles and four-wheel-drive vehicles, to follow their herds. In today's world, communities are being incorporated, at an accelerating rate, into larger systems (a trend that began with the advent of food production). The Samis face increased regulation of their economic adaptation—reindeer herding—by the government of Norway. In addition, the reindeer industry has been outflanked by the better organized and far larger commercial beef industry.

K AUTOKEINO, Norway—Johan Martin Eira stepped from his front door into the Arctic dawn and studied the snowbound valley dotted with cozy homes and cabins.

"When the smoke rises straight up from the chimneys like that," he said, "you know it's really cold."

Really cold this February morning meant minus 40 degrees, and presumably even the wind had gone into deep freeze . . .

Mr. Eira, 31, was born and raised in this town, 200 miles north of the Arctic Circle, and has spent his life with creatures who are as comfortable in polar climes as he and his fellow reindeer herders seem to be.

For the indigenous Samis, like Mr. Eira, reindeer can be everything. Samis, also known as Lapps or Laplanders, raise them, sell them, race them, eat them, capture their images in their art, make jewelry from their bones, decorate barn walls with their pelts and use their hides to make coats, boots, leggings, hats and gloves. Economic and cultural activity centers on reindeer . . .

Reindeer husbandry has existed here since the end of the Ice Age. Reindeer followed the ice as it receded, the story goes, and the people followed the reindeer.

These animals are so much a part of the landscape that hundreds huddle silently on a hillside several miles out of town, barely spottable, the pewter color of their skins camouflaging them against the gray sky, white birch and snowy fields. In this cold, they stand unmoving as statues, eager to conserve their energy.

"I can't say they really like it outside in this temperature, but they can survive it," Mr. Eira said. They have a natural interior heating system, warming air in their mouths and lungs and then spreading it through their bodies. Their hairs are hollow, providing insulation . . .

Norway has an estimated 190,000 reindeer, and about 40 percent of the country's land is used for grazing and calving. In the 16th century, there was a gradual transition from hunting wild reindeer to herding, and the Samis became a nomadic people in what is now Europe's last wilderness. Of the 80,000 Samis in Norway, Sweden and Finland, about 10 percent are still reindeer herders. The largest number, about 50,000, live in Norway, where laws passed the last 25 years have given them exclusive right to the trade.

Mr. Eira, his four brothers and their father all mind the family herd of 3,500 animals, and though they have traded in their sleds for snowmobiles, and their wagons for four-wheel-drive vehicles, their lives follow ancient traditions.

Throughout the winter, the herds move across the slopes and valleys,

In northern Norway a Sami herder uses a snow scooter to drive his migrating reindeer.

feeding on moss and lichen the animals dig from beneath the snow and shreds of bark from scrubby trees that poke above the drifts. In the spring they move to milder areas for calving and then to the coast, where they fatten up for the winter on grass, shrubs and mushrooms. They are beasts of rigid habit.

"They're patterned from ancient times," Mr. Eira said, "and when they decide they want to move, they just turn and go . . ." . . .

Each siida, a Sami family cooperative that owns and cares for its herd, has a distinguishing design that is cut into a reindeer's ear at birth to identify it . . .

Predators are by far the greatest worry: bear, wolves, wolverines, lynxes, eagles. An eagle can lift a 40-pound animal and spirit it away for the kill. Losses can approach 40 percent of the herd, and Samis are locked in a dispute over the issue with government conservationists who want to protect large carnivores and see the wolf population grow. When a herder is not there to protect the herd, trained huskies mind the animals, intimidating them into remaining bunched together and trying to scare off tormentors.

In recent years the government has become more active in trying to regulate the reindeer industry, ending traditional slaughtering on the snow and directing it toward large government abattoirs, providing subsidies to herders who will sell at lower prices. The Samis complain that this interference has hurt their business. The quality of the meat has declined with the greater distances the animals have to be trucked to slaughter, prices have dropped by 50 percent and the reindeer folk have been outflanked by the better organized and far larger beef industry.

The supply has also fallen. Reindeer meat is scarce everywhere, from local food stores to Oslo restaurants, where it was long considered a delicacy. In addition, herders must give the entire carcasses to the slaughterhouse and cannot put other parts of the animals to traditional uses, ranging from soup to clothing.

"Agricultural politics have hit the reindeer industry and ruined it," said Erik S. Reinert, an Oslo economist and anthropologist who negotiates for the Samis. "These are the last tribal people of Europe, and they have a unique thing going for them—they have a luxury product." Reindeer meat, aside from being tasty, is fat free.

Mr. Reinert argued that at a time when Europeans are panicked about the quality and safety of their food, meat from reindeer raised in unpolluted surroundings on natural feed ought to command a growing market . . .

SOURCE: Warren Hoge, "Kautokeino Journal; Reindeer Herders, at Home on a (Very Cold) Range," *New York Times*, March 26, 2001, late edition, final, section A, p. 4, col. 3.

People still do subsistence foraging in certain remote forests in Madagascar; in Southeast Asia, including Malaysia and the Philippines; and on certain islands off the Indian coast (Lee and Daly 1999). Some of the best-known recent foragers are the aborigines of Australia. Those Native Australians lived on their island continent for more than 50,000 years without developing food production.

The Western Hemisphere also had recent foragers. The Eskimos, or Inuit, of Alaska and Canada are well-known hunters. Like the Sami herders described in the "News Brief," these (and other) northern foragers now use modern technology, including rifles and snowmobiles, in their subsistence activities (Pelto 1973). The native populations of California, Oregon, Washington, British Columbia, and Alaska all were foragers, as were those of inland subarctic Canada and the Great Lakes. For many Native Americans, fishing, hunting, and gathering remain important subsistence (and sometimes commercial) activities.

Coastal foragers also lived near the southern tip of South America, in Patagonia. On the grassy plains of Argentina, southern Brazil, Uruguay, and Paraguay, there were other hunter-gatherers. The contemporary Aché of Paraguay are usually called "hunter-gatherers" even though they get just a third of their livelihood from foraging. The Aché also grow crops, have domesticated animals, and live in or near mission posts, where they receive food from missionaries (Hawkes, O'Connell, and Hill 1982; Hill et al. 1987).

Throughout the world, foraging survived mainly in environments that posed major obstacles to food production. (Some foragers took refuge in such areas after the rise of food production, the state, colonialism, or the modern world system.) The difficulties of cultivating at the North Pole are obvious. In southern Africa, the Dobe Ju/'hoansi San area studied by Richard Lee is surrounded by a waterless belt 45 to 125 miles (70 to 200 kilometers) in breadth. The Dobe area is hard to reach even today, and there is no archaeological evidence of occupation of this area by food producers before the 20th century (Solway and Lee 1990). However, environmental limits to other adaptive strategies aren't the only reason foragers survived. Their niches have one thing in common: their marginality. Their environments haven't been of immediate interest to groups with other adaptive strategies.

The hunter-gatherer way of life did persist in a few areas that could be cultivated, even after contact with cultivators. Those tenacious foragers, such as indigenous foragers in what is now Cali-

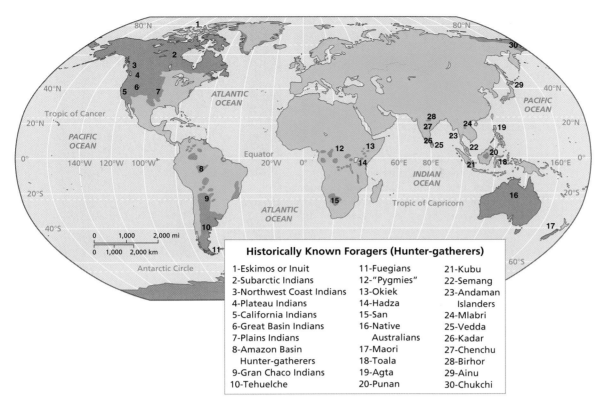

FIGURE 16.1 Worldwide Distribution of Recent Hunter-Gatherers.

SOURCE: Adapted from a map by Ray Sim, in Göran Burenhult, ed., *Encyclopedia of Humankind: People of the Stone Age* (McMahons Point, NSW, Australia: Weldon Owen Pty Ltd., 1993), p. 193.

Historically Known Foragers (Hunter-gatherers)

1-Eskimos or Inuit
2-Subarctic Indians
3-Northwest Coast Indians
4-Plateau Indians
5-California Indians
6-Great Basin Indians
7-Plains Indians
8-Amazon Basin
  Hunter-gatherers
9-Gran Chaco Indians
10-Tehuelche
11-Fuegians
12-"Pygmies"
13-Okiek
14-Hadza
15-San
16-Native
  Australians
17-Maori
18-Toala
19-Agta
20-Punan
21-Kubu
22-Semang
23-Andaman
  Islanders
24-Mlabri
25-Vedda
26-Kadar
27-Chenchu
28-Birhor
29-Ainu
30-Chukchi

fornia, Oregon, Washington, and British Columbia, did not turn to food production because they were supporting themselves very adequately by hunting and gathering (see the section on the potlatch at the end of this chapter). As the modern world system spreads, the number of foragers continues to decline.

Correlates of Foraging

Typologies, such as Cohen's adaptive strategies, are useful because they suggest **correlations**—that is, association or covariation between two or more variables. (Correlated variables are factors that are linked and interrelated, such as food intake and body weight, such that when one increases or decreases, the other tends to change, too.) Ethnographic studies in hundreds of societies have revealed many correlations between the economy and social life. Associated (correlated) with each adaptive strategy is a bundle of particular cultural features. Correlations, however, are rarely perfect. Some foragers lack cultural features usually associated with foraging, and some of those features are found in groups with other adaptive strategies.

What, then, are some correlates of foraging? People who subsist by hunting, gathering, and fishing often live in band-organized societies.

Their basic social unit, the **band,** is a small group of fewer than a hundred people, all related by kinship or marriage. Band size varies between cultures and often from one season to the next in a given culture. In some foraging societies, band size stays about the same year-round. In others, the band splits up for part of the year. Families leave to gather resources that are better exploited by just a few people. Later, they regroup for cooperative work and ceremonies.

Several examples of seasonal splits and reunions are known from ethnography and archaeology. In southern Africa, some San aggregate around waterholes in the dry season and split up in the wet season, whereas other bands disperse in the dry season (Barnard 1979; Kent 1992). This reflects environmental variation. San who lack permanent water must disperse and forage widely for moisture-filled plants. In ancient Oaxaca, Mexico, before the advent of plant cultivation there around 4,000 years ago, foragers assembled in large bands in summer. They collectively harvested tree pods and cactus fruits. Then, in fall, they split into much smaller family groups to hunt deer and gather grasses and plants that were effectively foraged by small teams.

One typical characteristic of the foraging life is mobility. In many San groups, as among the

Integrating Archaeological, Ethnographic, and Analytic Subsistence Data: A Case Study from Patagonia, South America

BACKGROUND INFORMATION

STUDENT:
Jennifer A. Kelly

SUPERVISING PROFESSOR:
Robert Tykot

SCHOOL:
University of South Florida

YEAR IN SCHOOL/MAJOR:
Senior/Archaeology

FUTURE PLANS:
Graduate school in archaeology

In this account, Jennifer Kelly uses various sources to reconstruct the subsistence strategies and diets of the aboriginal inhabitants of Patagonia, located at South America's southern tip. For her senior thesis, Kelly began by reading historic and ethnographic accounts of the region. Then she turned to archaeological data from sites in coastal and inland areas once occupied by different ethnic groups, such as the Ona, the Yamana, and the Tehuelche. Working with samples of human bone and tooth, she did isotope analysis, which demonstrates how specific dietary resources affect the skeleton. From her analysis she concludes there was more variation in subsistence economies and diets than the ethnographic accounts suggested. Classic ethnographies have a tendency to see human groups as culturally programmed to go after certain foods and to ignore others, which may be used by their neighbors. This account suggests that foragers are more opportunistic. Although there are certainly cultural preferences for certain foods and ways of getting them, humans are malleable, pursuing a range of resources as they become available and are needed.

Ethnohistoric, archaeological, and other scientific methods are integrated here to reconstruct prehistoric subsistence adaptations in Patagonia and Tierra del Fuego. Ethnohistoric data from the late 19th and early 20th centuries emphasize discrete dietary practices in coastal, inland, and Fuegan Patagonia. More recent archaeological evidence, however, suggests significant variations in subsistence strategies, each tailored to specific local resources.

At the time of European arrival, several indigenous groups inhabited Patagonia and Tierra del Fuego. The Onas (Haush and Selk'nam) lived in the wooded southern part of Tierra del Fuego. Archaeological evidence suggests that the Ona diet was based mainly on the guanaco (a wild grazing animal related to the llama). Other reports indicate that in some places the Onas did intensive shellfish collection and hunted fish in tidal pools. The Yamana lived along the southern and western coasts and island archipelagos of Tierra del Fuego. Early ethnographies report that they relied on marine mammals. Later accounts suggest a diet based on shellfish and seabirds.

Archaeological evidence indicates that the use of marine resources increased after 6000 B.P., and suggests non-specialized seasonal procurement of shellfish, fish, and mammals using simple hunting and gathering technology.

Carbon and nitrogen isotope analysis of human skeletal remains can differentiate between diets based on land and marine foods, as well as those based on plant foods that use different photosynthetic pathways. Bone collagen (a protein) and bone apatite (the mineral portion of bone) reveal the average diet over the last several years of an individual's life. Tooth enamel reflects diet only at the time of crown formation. As little as one gram of bone and a few milligrams of tooth enamel are sufficient for analysis. Samples of 40 individuals were obtained from coastal sites along the Straits of Magellan, and from sites located well inland. The sites range in age from 7000 B.P. through the early historic period.

For northern Patagonia, the results indicate that the northern Tehuelches who lived on the coast ate a lot of seafood in addition to guanaco. This conclusion is based on positive carbon and nitrogen isotope ratios in their bone collagen and apatite. Inland samples from this region have isotope ratios that suggest consumption of guanaco, which grazed on certain grasses.

Isotope data for coastal areas near the Straits of Magellan, homeland of the southern Tehuelches, also suggest diets dependent on both guanaco and marine resources, although the latter appear more important than in the north. The slightly enriched carbon isotope ratios of individuals from inland sites in this area may reflect their consumption of marine foods on a seasonal basis. In the Selk'nam area of Isla Grande, however, marine foods were less important than the guanaco, even along the coast, thus corroborating ethnohistoric descriptions of this area.

In the Haush region, however, marine foods of high trophic level (e.g. sea lions) accounted for most of the dietary protein. This finding contradicts ethnohistoric accounts, which describe the Haush as intermediate between the Selk'nam and the Yamana in their dependence on marine resources.

In conclusion, isotope analysis confirms some but not all of the ethnohistoric descriptions of subsistence patterns in Patagonia, while providing evidence of significant variation within each cultural group. A larger number of skeletal samples from dated archaeological contexts, and a better sampling of faunal and floral resources in each area, would allow for fuller understanding of dynamic, prehistoric Patagonian subsistence adaptations.

San-speaking "Bushmen" of Botswana's Kalahari Desert use ostrich eggs for drawing and carrying water. In what forms does foraging survive in our own society?

Mbuti of Congo, people shift band membership several times in a lifetime. One may be born, for example, in a band where one's mother has kin. Later, one's family may move to a band where the father has relatives. Because bands are exogamous (people marry outside their own band), one's parents come from two different bands, and one's grandparents may come from four. People may join any band to which they have kinship or marriage links. A couple may live in, or shift between, the husband's band and the wife's band.

One also may affiliate with a band through *fictive kinship*—personal relationships modeled on kinship, such as that between godparents and godchildren. San, for example, have a limited number of personal names. People with the same name have a special relationship; they treat each other like siblings. San expect the same hospitality in bands where they have *namesakes* as they do in a band in which a real sibling lives. Namesakes share a strong identity. They call everyone in a namesake's band by the kin terms the namesake uses. Those people reply as if they were addressing a real relative. Kinship, marriage, and fictive kinship permit San to join several bands, and nomadic (regularly on-the-move) foragers do change bands often. Band membership therefore can change tremendously from year to year.

All human societies have some kind of division of labor based on gender (see the chapter on gender for much more on this). Among foragers, men typically hunt and fish while women gather and collect, but the specific nature of the work varies among cultures. Sometimes women's work contributes most to the diet. Sometimes male hunting and fishing predominate. Among foragers in tropical and semitropical areas, gather-

ing tends to contribute more to the diet than hunting and fishing do—even though the labor costs of gathering tend to be much higher than those of hunting and fishing.

All foragers make social distinctions based on age. Often old people receive great respect as guardians of myths, legends, stories, and traditions. Younger people value the elders' special knowledge of ritual and practical matters. Most foraging societies are *egalitarian*. This means that contrasts in prestige are minor and are based on age and gender.

When considering issues of "human nature," we should remember that the egalitarian band was a basic form of human social life for most of our history. Food production has existed less than 1 percent of the time *Homo* has spent on earth. However, it has produced huge social differences. We now consider the main economic features of food-producing strategies.

CULTIVATION

In Cohen's typology, the three adaptive strategies based on food production in nonindustrial societies are horticulture, agriculture, and pastoralism. In non-Western cultures, as is also true in modern nations, people carry out a variety of economic activities. Each adaptive strategy refers to the main economic activity. Pastoralists (herders), for example, consume milk, butter, blood, and meat from their animals as mainstays of their diet. However, they also add grain to the diet by doing some cultivating or by trading with neighbors. Food producers also may hunt or gather to supplement a diet based on domesticated species.

■ In slash-and-burn horticulture, the land is cleared by cutting down (slashing) and burning trees and bush, using simple technology. After such clearing this woman uses a digging stick to plant mountain rice in Madagascar. What might be the environmental effects of slash-and-burn cultivation?

Horticulture

Horticulture and agriculture are two types of cultivation found in nonindustrial societies. Both differ from the farming systems of industrial nations like the United States and Canada, which use large land areas, machinery, and petrochemicals. According to Cohen, **horticulture** is cultivation that makes intensive use of *none* of the factors of production: land, labor, capital, and machinery. Horticulturalists use simple tools such as hoes and digging sticks to grow their crops. Their fields are not permanently cultivated and lie fallow for varying lengths of time.

Horticulture often involves *slash-and-burn techniques*. Here, horticulturalists clear land by cutting down (slashing) and burning forest or bush or by setting fire to the grass covering a plot. The vegetation is broken down, pests are killed, and the ashes remain to fertilize the soil. Crops are then sown, tended, and harvested. Use of the plot is not continuous. Often it is cultivated for only a year. This depends, however, on soil fertility and weeds, which compete with cultivated plants for nutrients.

When horticulturalists abandon a plot because of soil exhaustion or a thick weed cover, they clear another piece of land, and the original plot reverts to forest. After several years of fallowing (the duration varies in different societies), the cultivator returns to farm the original plot again. Horticulture is also called *shifting cultivation*. Such shifts from plot to plot do not mean that whole villages must move when plots are abandoned. Horticulture can support large permanent villages. Among the Kuikuru of the South American tropical forest, for example, one village of 150 people remained in the same place for 90 years (Carneiro 1956). Kuikuru houses are large and well made. Because the work involved in building them is great, the Kuikuru would rather walk farther to their fields than construct a new village. They shift their plots rather than their settlements. On the other hand, horticulturalists in the montaña (Andean foothills) of Peru live in small villages of about 30 people (Carneiro 1961/1968). Their houses are small and simple. After a few years in one place, these people build new villages near virgin land. Because their houses are so simple, they prefer rebuilding to walking even a half-mile to their fields.

Agriculture

Agriculture is cultivation that requires more labor than horticulture does, because it uses land intensively and continuously. The greater labor demands associated with agriculture reflect its common use of domesticated animals, irrigation, or terracing.

Domesticated Animals

Many agriculturalists use animals as means of production—for transport, as cultivating machines, and for their manure. Asian farmers typically incorporate cattle and/or water buffalo into agricultural economies based on rice production. Rice farmers may use cattle to trample pretilled flooded fields, thus mixing soil and water, prior to transplanting. Many agriculturalists attach animals to plows and harrows for field preparation before planting or transplanting. Also, agriculturalists typically collect manure from their animals, using it to fertilize their plots, thus increasing yields. Animals are attached to carts for transport, as well as to implements of cultivation.

Irrigation

While horticulturalists must await the rainy season, agriculturalists can schedule their planting in advance, because they control water. Like other irrigation experts in the Philippines, the Ifugao (Figure 16.2) irrigate their fields with canals from rivers, streams, springs, and ponds. Irrigation makes it possible to cultivate a plot year after year. Irrigation enriches the soil because the irrigated field is a unique ecosystem with several species of plants and animals, many of them minute organisms, whose wastes fertilize the land.

An irrigated field is a capital investment that usually increases in value. It takes time for a field to start yielding; it reaches full productivity only after several years of cultivation. The Ifugao, like other irrigators, have farmed the same fields for generations. In some agricultural areas, including the Middle East, however, salts carried in the irrigation water can make fields unusable after 50 or 60 years.

Terracing

Terracing is another agricultural technique the Ifugao have mastered. Their homeland has small valleys separated by steep hillsides. Because the population is dense, people need to farm the hills. However, if they simply planted on the steep hillsides, fertile soil and crops would be washed away during the rainy season. To prevent this, the Ifugao cut into the hillside and build stage after stage of terraced fields rising above the valley floor. Springs located above the terraces supply their irrigation water. The labor necessary to build and maintain a system of terraces is great. Terrace walls crumble each year and must be partially rebuilt. The canals that bring water down through the terraces also demand attention.

Costs and Benefits of Agriculture

Agriculture requires human labor to build and maintain irrigation systems, terraces, and other

FIGURE 16.2 Location of the Ifugao.

works. People must feed, water, and care for their animals. Given sufficient labor input and management, agricultural land can yield one or two crops annually for years or even generations. An agricultural field does not necessarily produce a higher single-year yield than does a horticultural plot. The first crop grown by horticulturalists on long-idle land may be larger than that from an agricultural plot of the same size. Furthermore, because agriculturalists work harder than horticulturalists do, agriculture's yield relative to the labor invested is also lower. Agriculture's main advantage is that the long-term yield per area is far greater and more dependable. Because a single field sustains its owners year after year, there is no need to maintain a reserve of uncultivated land as horticulturalists do. This is why agricultural societies tend to be more densely populated than are horticultural ones.

The Cultivation Continuum

Because nonindustrial economies can have features of both horticulture and agriculture, it is useful to discuss cultivators as being arranged along a **cultivation continuum.** Horticultural systems stand at one end—the "low-labor, shifting-plot" end. Agriculturalists are at the other—the "labor-intensive, permanent-plot" end.

We speak of a continuum because there are today intermediate economies, combining horticultural and agricultural features—more intensive than annually shifting horticulture but less

■ *Agriculture requires more labor than horticulture does and uses land intensively and continuously. Labor demands associated with agriculture reflect its use of domesticated animals, irrigation, and terracing. The rice farmers of Luzon in the Philippines, such as the Ifugao, are famous for their irrigated and terraced fields.*

Map Atlas

Map 12 displays the kinds of economies that existed throughout the world at the start of the European age of discovery and conquest—250 years before the Industrial Revolution.

intensive than agriculture. These recall the intermediate economies revealed by archaeological sequences leading from horticulture to agriculture in the Middle East, Mexico, and other areas of early food production. Unlike nonintensive horticulturalists, who farm a plot just once before fallowing it, the South American Kuikuru grow two or three crops of *manioc*, or cassava—an edible tuber—before abandoning their plots. Cultivation is even more intense in certain densely populated areas of Papua New Guinea, where plots are planted for two or three years, allowed to rest for three to five, and then recultivated. After several of these cycles, the plots are abandoned for a longer fallow period. Such a pattern is called *sectorial fallowing* (Wolf 1966). Besides Papua New Guinea, such systems occur in places as distant as West Africa and highland Mexico. Sectorial fallowing is associated with denser populations than is simple horticulture.

The key difference between horticulture and agriculture is that horticulture always uses a fallow period whereas agriculture does not. The earliest cultivators in the Middle East and in Mexico were rainfall-dependent horticulturalists. Until recently, horticulture was the main form of cultivation in several areas, including parts of Africa, Southeast Asia, the Pacific islands, Mexico, Central America, and the South American tropical forest.

Intensification: People and the Environment

The range of environments available for food production has widened as people have increased their control over nature. For example, in arid areas of California, where Native Americans once foraged, modern irrigation technology now sustains rich agricultural estates. Agriculturalists live in many areas that are too arid for nonirrigators or too hilly for nonterracers. Many ancient civilizations in arid lands arose on an agricultural base. Increasing labor intensity and permanent land use have major demographic, social, political, and environmental consequences.

Thus, because of their permanent fields, intensive cultivators are sedentary. People live in larger and more permanent communities located closer to other settlements. Growth in population size and density increases contact between individuals and groups. There is more need to regulate interpersonal relations, including conflicts of interest. Economies that support more people usually require more coordination in the use of land, labor, and other resources.

Intensive agriculture has significant environmental effects. Irrigation ditches and paddies (fields with irrigated rice) become repositories for organic wastes, chemicals (such as salts), and disease microorganisms. Intensive agriculture typically spreads at the expense of trees and forests, which are cut down to be replaced by fields. Accompanying such deforestation is loss of environmental diversity (see Srivastava, Smith, and Forno 1999). Agricultural economies grow increasingly specialized—focusing on one or a few caloric staples, such as rice, and on the animals that are raised and tended to aid the agricultural economy. Because tropical horticulturalists typically cultivate dozens of plant species simultaneously, a horticultural plot tends to mirror the botanical diversity that is found in a tropical forest. Agricultural plots, by contrast, reduce ecological diversity by cutting down trees and concentrating on just a few staple foods. Such crop specialization is true of agriculturalists both in the tropics (e.g., Indonesian paddy farmers) and outside the tropics (e.g., Middle Eastern irrigated farmers).

At least in the tropics, the diets of both foragers and horticulturalists are typically more diverse, although under less secure human control, than the diets of agriculturalists. Agriculturists attempt to reduce risk in production by favoring stability in the form of a reliable annual harvest and long-term production. Tropical foragers and horticulturalists, by contrast, attempt to reduce risk by relying on multiple species and benefiting from ecological diversity. The agricultural strategy is to put all one's eggs in one big and very dependable basket. Of course, even with agriculture, there is a possibility that the single staple crop may fail, and famine may result. The strategy of tropical foragers and horticulturalists is to have several smaller baskets, a few of which may fail without endangering subsistence. The agricultural strategy makes sense when there are lots of children to raise and adults to be fed. Foraging and horticulture, of course, are associated with smaller, sparser, and more mobile populations.

Agricultural economies also pose a series of regulatory problems—which central governments often have arisen to solve. How is water to be managed—along with disputes about access to and distribution of water? With more people living closer together on more valuable land, agriculturalists are more likely to come into conflict than foragers and horticulturalists are. Agriculture paved the way for the origin of the state, and most agriculturalists live in *states:* complex sociopolitical systems that administer a territory and populace with substantial contrasts in occupation, wealth, prestige, and power. In such societies, cultivators play their role as one part of a differentiated, functionally specialized, and tightly integrated sociopolitical system. The social and political implications of food production and intensification are examined more fully in the next chapter, "Political Systems."

PASTORALISM

Pastoralists live in North Africa, the Middle East, Europe, Asia, and sub-Saharan Africa. These herders are people whose activities focus on such domesticated animals as cattle, sheep, goats, camels, and yak. East African pastoralists, like many others, live in symbiosis with their herds. (*Symbiosis* is an obligatory interaction between groups—here humans and animals—that is beneficial to each.) Herders attempt to protect their animals and to ensure their reproduction in return for food and other products, such as leather. Herds provide dairy products, meat, and blood. Animals are killed at ceremonies, which occur throughout the year, and so beef is available regularly.

People use livestock in a variety of ways. Natives of North America's Great Plains, for example, didn't eat, but only rode, their horses. (Europeans reintroduced horses to the Western Hemisphere; the native American horse had become extinct thousands of years earlier.) For Plains Indians, horses served as "tools of the trade," means of production used to hunt buffalo, a main target of their economies. So the Plains Indians were not true pastoralists but *hunters* who used horses—as many agriculturalists use animals—as means of production.

Unlike the use of animals merely as productive machines, pastoralists, including the Samis discussed in the "News Brief" at the beginning of this chapter, typically make direct use of their herds for food. They consume their meat, blood, and milk, from which they make yogurt, butter, and cheese. Although some pastoralists rely on their herds more completely than others do, it is impossible to base subsistence solely on animals.

Most pastoralists therefore supplement their diet by hunting, gathering, fishing, cultivating, or trading. To get crops, pastoralists either trade with cultivators or do some cultivating or gathering themselves.

Unlike foraging and cultivation, which existed throughout the world before the Industrial Revolution, pastoralism was confined almost totally to the Old World. Before European conquest, the only pastoralists in the Americas lived in the Andean region of South America. They used their llamas and alpacas for food and wool and in agriculture and transport. Much more recently, Navajo of the southwestern United States developed a pastoral economy based on sheep, which were brought to North America by Europeans. The populous Navajo are now the major pastoral population in the Western Hemisphere.

■ Pastoralists may be nomadic or transhumant, but they don't typically live off their herds alone. They either trade or cultivate. The photo at the top shows female shepherds in Morocco's Drâa Valley. The photo at the bottom shows a male Alpine shepherd in Germany. This man accompanies his flocks to highland meadows each year.

TABLE 16.1   Yehudi Cohen's Adaptive Strategies (Economic Typology) Summarized

Adaptive Strategy	Also Known As	Key Features/Varieties
Foraging	Hunting-gathering	Mobility, use of nature's resources
Horticulture	Slash-and-burn, shifting cultivation, swiddening, dry farming	Fallow period
Agriculture	Intensive farming	Continuous use of land, intensive use of labor
Pastoralism	Herding	Nomadism and transhumance
Industrialism	Industrial production	Factory production, capitalism, socialist production

For more on pastoralism, see the Internet Exercises at your OLC

mhhe.com/kottak

Two patterns of movement occur with pastoralism: nomadism and transhumance. Both are based on the fact that herds must move to use pasture available in particular places in different seasons. In **pastoral nomadism,** the entire group—women, men, and children—moves with the animals throughout the year. The Middle East and North Africa provide numerous examples of pastoral nomads. In Iran, for example, the Basseri and the Qashqai ethnic groups traditionally followed a nomadic route more than 300 miles (480 kilometers) long. Starting each year near the coast, they took their animals to grazing land 17,000 feet (5,400 meters) above sea level (see Salzman 2004).

With **transhumance,** part of the group moves with the herds, but most people stay in the home village. There are examples from Europe and Africa. In Europe's Alps, it is just the shepherds and goatherds—not the whole village—who accompany the flocks to highland meadows in summer. Among the Turkana of Uganda, men and boys accompany the herds to distant pastures, while much of the village stays put and does some horticultural farming. Villages tend to be located in the best-watered areas, which have the longest pasture season. This permits the village population to stay together during a large chunk of the year.

During their annual trek, pastoral nomads trade for crops and other products with more sedentary people. Transhumants don't have to trade for crops. Because only part of the population accompanies the herds, transhumants can maintain year-round villages and grow their own crops. Table 16.1 summarizes the main features of Cohen's adaptive strategies.

Bringing It All Together

For more on herding in Europe—and the transfer of a herding pattern from Europe to the United States—see the "Bringing It All Together" essay on the Basques that immediately follows the chapter on gender.

MODES OF PRODUCTION

See the Interactive Exercises for a quiz on economics

mhhe.com/kottak

An **economy** is a system of production, distribution, and consumption of resources; *economics* is the study of such systems. Economists tend to

focus on modern nations and capitalist systems, while anthropologists have broadened understanding of economic principles by gathering data on nonindustrial economies. Economic anthropology studies economics in a comparative perspective (see Gudeman, ed. 1998; Plattner, ed. 1989; Sahlins 2004; Wilk 1996).

A **mode of production** is a way of organizing production—"a set of social relations through which labor is deployed to wrest energy from nature by means of tools, skills, organization, and knowledge" (Wolf 1982, p. 75). In the capitalist mode of production, money buys labor power, and there is a social gap between the people (bosses and workers) involved in the production process. By contrast, in nonindustrial societies, labor is not usually bought but is given as a social obligation. In such a *kin-based* mode of production, mutual aid in production is one among many expressions of a larger web of social relations.

Societies representing each of the adaptive strategies just discussed (e.g., foraging) tend to have a similar mode of production. Differences in the mode of production within a given strategy may reflect the differences in environments, target resources, or cultural traditions (Kelly 1995). Thus, a foraging mode of production may be based on individual hunters or teams, depending on whether the game is a solitary or a herd animal. Gathering is usually more individualistic than hunting, although collecting teams may assemble when abundant resources ripen and must be harvested quickly. Fishing may be done alone (as in ice or spear fishing) or in crews (as with open sea fishing and hunting of sea mammals).

Production in Nonindustrial Societies

Although some kind of division of economic labor related to age and gender is a cultural universal, the specific tasks assigned to each sex and to people of different ages vary. Many horticultural societies assign a major productive role to women, but some make men's work primary (see

the chapter on gender for more on this). Similarly, among pastoralists, men generally tend large animals, but in some cultures women do the milking. Jobs accomplished through teamwork in some cultivating societies are done by smaller groups or individuals working over a longer period of time in others.

The Betsileo of Madagascar have two stages of teamwork in rice cultivation: transplanting and harvesting. Team size varies with the size of the field. Both transplanting and harvesting feature a traditional division of labor by age and gender that is well known to all Betsileo and is repeated across the generations. The first job in transplanting is the trampling of a previously tilled flooded field by young men driving cattle, in order to mix earth and water. They bring cattle to trample the fields just before transplanting. The young men yell at and beat the cattle, striving to drive them into a frenzy so that they will trample the fields properly. Trampling breaks up clumps of earth and mixes irrigation water with soil to form a smooth mud into which women transplant seedlings. Once the tramplers leave the field, older men arrive. With their spades, they break up the clumps that the cattle missed. Meanwhile, the owner and other adults uproot rice seedlings and bring them to the field.

At harvest time, four or five months later, young men cut the rice off the stalks. Young women carry it to the clearing above the field. Older women arrange and stack it. The oldest men and women then stand on the stack, stomping and compacting it. Three days later, young men thresh the rice, beating the stalks against a rock to remove the grain. Older men then attack the stalks with sticks to make sure all the grains have fallen off.

Most of the other tasks in Betsileo rice cultivation are done by individual owners and their immediate families. All household members help weed the rice field. It's a man's job to till the fields with a spade or a plow. Individual men repair the irrigation and drainage systems and the earth walls that separate one plot from the next. Among other agriculturalists, however, repairing the irrigation system is a task involving teamwork and communal labor.

Means of Production

In nonindustrial societies, there is a more intimate relationship between the worker and the means of production than there is in industrial nations. **Means, or factors, of production** include land (territory), labor, and technology.

Land

Among foragers, ties between people and land are less permanent than they are among food producers. Although many bands have territories, the boundaries usually are not marked, and there is no way they can be enforced. The hunter's stake in an animal that is being stalked or has been hit with a poisoned arrow is more important than where the animal finally dies. A person acquires the rights to use a band's territory by being born in the band or by joining it through a tie of kinship, marriage, or fictive kinship. In Botswana in southern Africa, Ju/'hoansi San women, whose work provides over half the food, habitually use specific tracts of berry-bearing trees. However, when a woman changes bands, she immediately acquires a new gathering area.

Among food producers, rights to the means of production also come through kinship and marriage. Descent groups (groups whose members claim common ancestry) are common among nonindustrial food producers, and those who descend from the founder share the group's territory and resources. If the adaptive strategy is horticulture, the estate includes garden and fallow land for shifting cultivation. As members of a descent group, pastoralists have access to animals to start their own herds, to grazing land, to garden land, and to other means of production.

Labor, Tools, and Specialization

Like land, labor is a means of production. In nonindustrial societies, access to both land and labor comes through social links such as kinship, marriage, and descent. Mutual aid in production is merely one aspect of ongoing social relations that are expressed on many other occasions.

Nonindustrial societies contrast with industrial nations in regard to another means of production: technology. In bands and tribes, manufacturing is often linked to age and gender. Women may weave and men may make pottery or vice versa. Most people of a particular age and gender share the technical knowledge associated with that age and gender. If married women customarily make baskets, all or most married women know how to make baskets. Neither technology nor technical knowledge is as specialized as it is in states.

However, some tribal societies do promote specialization. Among the Yanomami of Venezuela and Brazil (Figure 16.3), for instance, certain villages manufacture clay pots and others make hammocks. They don't specialize, as one might suppose, because certain raw materials happen to be available near particular villages. Clay suitable for pots is widely available. Everyone knows how to make pots, but not everybody does so. Craft specialization reflects the social and political environment rather than the natural environment. Such specialization promotes trade, which is the first step in creating an alliance with enemy villages (Chagnon 1997). Specialization contributes to keeping the peace, although it has not prevented intervillage warfare.

FIGURE 16.3 Location of the Yanomami.

Alienation in Industrial Economies

There are some significant contrasts between industrial and nonindustrial economies. When factory workers produce for sale and for their employer's profit, rather than for their own use, they may be alienated from the items they make. Such alienation means they don't feel strong pride in or personal identification with their products. They see their product as belonging to someone else, not to the man or woman whose labor actually produced it. In nonindustrial societies, by contrast, people usually see their work through from start to finish and have a sense of accomplishment in the product. The fruits of their labor are their own, rather than someone else's.

In nonindustrial societies, the economic relation between coworkers is just one aspect of a more general social relation. They aren't just coworkers but kin, in-laws, or celebrants in the same ritual. In industrial nations, people don't usually work with relatives and neighbors. If coworkers are friends, the personal relationship usually develops out of their common employment rather than being based on a previous association.

Thus, industrial workers have impersonal relations with their products, coworkers, and employers. People sell their labor for cash, and the economic domain stands apart from ordinary social life. In nonindustrial societies, however, the relations of production, distribution, and consumption are *social relations with economic aspects.*

Economy is not a separate entity but is *embedded* in the society.

A Case of Industrial Alienation

For decades, the government of Malaysia has promoted export-oriented industry, allowing transnational companies to install labor-intensive manufacturing operations in rural Malaysia. The industrialization of Malaysia is part of a global strategy. In search of cheaper labor, corporations headquartered in Japan, Western Europe, and the United States have been moving labor-intensive factories to developing countries. Malaysia has hundreds of Japanese and American subsidiaries, which mainly produce garments, foodstuffs, and electronics components. In electronics plants in rural Malaysia, thousands of young women from peasant families now assemble microchips and microcomponents for transistors and capacitors. Aihwa Ong (1987) did a study of electronics assembly workers in an area where 85 percent of the workers were young unmarried females from nearby villages.

Ong found that, unlike village women, female factory workers had to cope with a rigid work routine and constant supervision by men. The discipline that factories value was being taught in local schools, where uniforms helped prepare girls for the factory dress code. Village women wear loose, flowing tunics, sarongs, and sandals, but factory workers had to don tight overalls and heavy rubber gloves, in which they felt constrained. Assembling electronics components requires precise, concentrated labor. Demanding and depleting, labor in these factories illustrates the separation of intellectual and manual activity—the alienation that Karl Marx considered the defining feature of industrial work. One woman said about her bosses, "They exhaust us very much, as if they do not think that we too are human beings" (Ong 1987, p. 202). Nor does factory work bring women a substantial financial reward, given low wages, job uncertainty, and family claims on wages. Young women typically work just a few years. Production quotas, three daily shifts, overtime, and surveillance take their toll in mental and physical exhaustion.

One response to factory relations of production has been spirit possession (factory women are possessed by spirits). Ong interprets this phenomenon as the women's unconscious protest against labor discipline and male control of the industrial setting. Sometimes possession takes the form of mass hysteria. Spirits have simultaneously invaded as many as 120 factory workers. Weretigers (the Malay equivalent of the werewolf) arrive to avenge the construction of a factory on aboriginal burial grounds. Disturbed earth and grave spirits swarm on the shop floor. First the women see the spirits; then their bodies are invaded. The women become violent and

Employees working in a Celestica factory outside Penang, Malaysia. Celestica, which is based in Toronto, Canada, makes electronics for other companies. In Malaysia, thousands of young women from peasant families now assemble electronic components. Unlike village women, female factory workers often face a rigid work routine and constant supervision by men.

scream abuses. The weretigers send the women into sobbing, laughing, and shrieking fits. To deal with possession, factories employ local medicine men, who sacrifice chickens and goats to fend off the spirits. This solution works only some of the time; possession still goes on. Factory women continue to act as vehicles to express their own frustrations and the anger of avenging ghosts.

Ong argues that spirit possession expresses anguish at, and resistance to, capitalist relations of production. By engaging in this form of rebellion, however, factory women avoid a direct confrontation with the source of their distress. Ong concludes that spirit possession, while expressing repressed resentment, doesn't do much to modify factory conditions. (Other tactics, such as unionization, would do more.) Spirit possession may even help maintain the current system by operating as a safety valve for accumulated tensions.

ECONOMIZING AND MAXIMIZATION

Economic anthropologists have been concerned with two main questions:

1. How are production, distribution, and consumption organized in different societies? This question focuses on *systems* of human behavior and their organization.

2. What motivates people in different cultures to produce, distribute or exchange, and consume? Here the focus is not on systems of behavior but on the motives of the *individuals* who participate in those systems.

Anthropologists view both economic systems and motivations in a cross-cultural perspective. Motivation is a concern of psychologists, but it

Scarcity and the Betsileo

In the late 1960s my wife and I lived among the Betsileo people of Madagascar, studying their economy and social life (Kottak 1980). Soon after our arrival we met two well-educated schoolteachers (first cousins) who were interested in our research. The woman's father was a congressman who became a cabinet minister during our stay. Their family came from a historically important and typical Betsileo village called Ivato, which they invited us to visit with them.

We had traveled to many other Betsileo villages, where we often were displeased with our reception. As we drove up, children would run away screaming. Women would hurry inside. Men would retreat to doorways, where they lurked bashfully. This behavior expressed the Betsileo's great fear of the *mpakafo*. Believed to cut out and devour his victim's heart and liver, the mpakafo is the Malagasy vampire. These cannibals are said to have fair skin and to be very tall. Because I have light skin and stand over six feet tall, I was a natural suspect. The fact that such creatures were not known to travel with their wives helped convince the Betsileo that I wasn't really a mpakafo.

When we visited Ivato, its people were different—friendly and hospitable. Our very first day there we did a brief census and found out who lived in which households. We learned people's names and their relationships to our schoolteacher friends and to each other. We met an excellent informant who knew all about the local history. In a few afternoons I learned much more than I had in the other villages in several sessions.

Ivatans were so willing to talk because we had powerful sponsors, village natives who had made it in the outside world, people the Ivatans knew would protect them. The schoolteachers vouched for us, but even more significant was the cabinet minister, who was like a grandfather and benefactor to everyone in town. The Ivatans had no reason to fear us because their more influential native son had asked them to answer our questions.

Once we moved to Ivato, the elders established a pattern of visiting us every evening. They came to talk, attracted by the inquisitive foreigners but also by the wine, tobacco, and food we offered. I asked questions about their customs and beliefs. I eventually developed interview schedules about various subjects, including rice production. I used these forms in Ivato and in two other villages I was studying less intensively. Never have I interviewed as easily as I did in Ivato.

As our stay neared its end, our Ivatan friends lamented, saying, "We'll miss you. When you leave, there won't be any more cigarettes, any more wine, or any more questions." They wondered what it would be like for us back in the United States. They knew we had an automobile and that we regularly purchased things, including the wine, cigarettes, and food we shared with them. We could afford to buy products they would never have. They commented, "When you go back to your country, you'll need a lot of money for things like cars, clothes, and food. We don't need to buy those things. We make almost everything we use. We don't need as much money as you, because we produce for ourselves."

The Betsileo weren't unusual for nonindustrial people. Strange as it may seem to an American consumer, those rice farmers actually believed *they had all they needed*. The lesson from the Betsileo of the 1960s is that scarcity, which economists view as universal, is variable. Although shortages do arise in nonindustrial societies, the concept of scarcity (insufficient means) is much less developed in stable subsistence-oriented societies than in the societies characterized by industrialism, particularly as the reliance on consumer goods increases.

But, over the past several decades, significant changes have affected the Betsileo—and most nonindustrial peoples. On my last visit to Ivato, in

also has been, implicitly or explicitly, a concern of economists and anthropologists. Economists tend to assume that producers and distributors make decisions rationally by using the *profit motive,* as do consumers when they shop around for the best value. Although anthropologists know that the profit motive is not universal, the assumption that individuals try to maximize profits is basic to the capitalist world economy and to much of Western economic theory. In fact, the subject matter of economics is often defined as **economizing,** or the rational allocation of scarce means (or resources) to alternative ends (or uses).

What does that mean? Classical economic theory assumes that our wants are infinite and that our means are limited. Since means are limited, people must make choices about how to use their scarce resources: their time, labor, money, and capital. (The "Interesting Issues" box "Scarcity and the Betsileo" disputes the idea that people always make economic choices based on scarcity.) Economists assume that when confronted with choices and decisions, people tend to make the one that maximizes profit. This is assumed to be the most rational (reasonable) choice.

The idea that individuals choose to maximize profit was a basic assumption of the classical economists of the 19th century and one that is held by many contemporary economists. However, certain economists now recognize that individuals in Western cultures, as in others, may be motivated by many other goals. Depending on the society and the situation, people may try to maximize profit, wealth, prestige, pleasure, com-

1990, the effects of cash and of rapid population increase were evident there—and throughout Madagascar— where the national growth rate has been about 3 percent per year. Madagascar's population doubled between 1966 and 1991—from 6 to 12 million people. Today it stands near 18 million (Kottak 2004). One result of population pressure has been agricultural intensification. In Ivato, farmers who formerly had grown only rice in their rice fields now were using the same land for commercial crops, such as carrots, after the annual rice harvest. Another change affecting Ivato in 1990 was the breakdown of social and political order, fueled by increasing demand for cash.

Cattle rustling was a growing threat. Cattle thieves (sometimes from neighboring villages) were terrorizing peasants who previously had felt secure in their villages. Some of the rustled cattle were being driven to the coasts for commercial export to nearby islands. Prominent among the rustlers were relatively well-educated young men who had studied long enough to be comfortable negotiating with outsiders, but who had been unable to find formal work, and who were unwilling to work the rice fields like their peasant ancestors. The formal education system had familiarized them with external institutions and norms, including the need for cash. The concepts of scarcity, commerce, and negative reciprocity (see p. 373) now thrived among the Betsileo.

Women hull rice in a Betsileo village. In the village of Ivato, farmers who traditionally grew only rice in their rice fields now use the same land for commercial crops, such as carrots, after the annual rice harvest.

I witnessed other striking evidence of the new addiction to cash during my 1990 visit to Betsileo country. Near Ivato's county seat, we met men selling precious stones—tourmalines, which had been found by chance in a local rice field. Around the corner we saw an amazing site—dozens of villagers destroying an ancestral resource, digging up a large rice field, seeking tourmalines—clear evidence of the encroachment of cash on the local subsistence economy.

Throughout the Betsileo homeland, population growth and density were propelling emigration. Locally, land, jobs, and money were all scarce. One woman with ancestors from Ivato, herself now a resident of the national capital (Antananarivo), remarked that half the children of Ivato now lived in that city. Although she was exaggerating, a census of all the descendants of Ivato would surely reveal a substantial emigrant and urban population.

Ivato's recent history is one of increasing participation in a cash economy. That history, combined with the pressure of a growing population on local resources, has made scarcity not just a concept but a reality for Ivatans and their neighbors.

fort, or social harmony. Individuals may want to realize their personal or family ambitions or those of another group to which they belong (see Sahlins 2004).

Alternative Ends

To what uses do people in various societies put their scarce resources? Throughout the world, people devote some of their time and energy to building up a *subsistence fund* (Wolf 1966). In other words, they have to work to eat, to replace the calories they use in their daily activity. People also must invest in a *replacement fund*. They must maintain their technology and other items essential to production. If a hoe or plow breaks, they must repair or replace it. They also must obtain and

replace items that are essential not to production but to everyday life, such as clothing and shelter.

People also have to invest in a *social fund*. They have to help their friends, relatives, in-laws, and neighbors. It is useful to distinguish between a social fund and a *ceremonial fund*. The latter term refers to expenditures on ceremonies or rituals. To prepare a festival honoring one's ancestors, for example, requires time and the outlay of wealth.

Citizens of nonindustrial states also must allocate scarce resources to a *rent fund*. We think of rent as payment for the use of property. However, rent fund has a wider meaning. It refers to resources that people must render to an individual or agency that is superior politically or economically. Tenant farmers and sharecroppers, for example, either pay rent or give some of

Bringing It All Together

For some effects of marketing and product manipulation on consumption patterns in the United States, see the "Bringing It All Together" essay that immediately follows the last chapter in this book.

What motivates us? Do we have the same motives our parents had? People must choose among alternatives, and economists think such choices are guided mainly by the desire for economic gain. Do you agree? Such an assumption isn't evident among the Betsileo of Madagascar. Is it true of individual Americans? Think about the choices your parents have made. Did they make decisions that maximized their incomes, their lifestyles, their individual happiness, family benefits, or what? What about you? What factors were involved when you chose to apply to and attend a college? Did you want to stay close to home, to attend college with friends, or to maintain a romantic attachment (all social reasons)? Did you seek the lowest tuition and college costs—or get a generous scholarship (economic decisions)? Did you choose prestige, or perhaps the likelihood that one day you would earn more money because of the reputation of your alma mater (maximizing prestige and future wealth)? The profit motive may predominate in contemporary North America, but different individuals, like different cultures, may choose to pursue other goals.

is a profit motive, people are often prevented from rationally maximizing self-interest by factors beyond their control.

DISTRIBUTION, EXCHANGE

The economist Karl Polanyi (1968) stimulated the comparative study of exchange, and several anthropologists followed his lead. To study exchange cross-culturally, Polanyi defined three principles orienting exchanges: the market principle, redistribution, and reciprocity. These principles can all be present in the same society, but in that case they govern different kinds of transactions. In any society, one of them usually dominates. The principle of exchange that dominates in a given society is the one that allocates the means of production.

The Market Principle

In today's world capitalist economy, the **market principle** dominates. It governs the distribution of the means of production: land, labor, natural resources, technology, and capital. "Market exchange refers to the organizational process of purchase and sale at money price" (Dalton, ed. 1967; Madra 2004). With market exchange, items are bought and sold, using money, with an eye to maximizing profit, and value is determined by the *law of supply and demand* (things cost more the scarcer they are and the more people want them).

Bargaining is characteristic of market-principle exchanges. The buyer and seller strive to maximize—to get their "money's worth." In bargaining, buyers and sellers don't need to meet personally. But their offers and counteroffers do need to be open for negotiation over a fairly short time period.

Redistribution

Redistribution operates when goods, services, or their equivalent move from the local level to a center. The center may be a capital, a regional collection point, or a storehouse near a chief's residence. Products often move through a hierarchy of officials for storage at the center. Along the way, officials and their dependents may consume some of them, but the exchange principle here is *re*distribution. The flow of goods eventually reverses direction—out from the center, down through the hierarchy, and back to the common people.

One example of a redistributive system comes from the Cherokee, the original owners of the Tennessee Valley. Productive farmers who subsisted on maize, beans, and squash, supplemented by hunting and fishing, the Cherokee had chiefs. Each of their main villages had a central plaza, where

their produce to their landlords, as peasants did under feudalism.

Peasants are small-scale agriculturalists who live in nonindustrial states and have rent fund obligations (see Kearney 1996). They produce to feed themselves, to sell their produce, and to pay rent. All peasants have two things in common:

1. They live in state-organized societies.

2. They produce food without the elaborate technology—chemical fertilizers, tractors, airplanes to spray crops, and so on—of modern farming or agribusiness.

In addition to paying rent to landlords, peasants must satisfy government obligations, paying taxes in the form of money, produce, or labor. The rent fund is not simply an *additional* obligation for peasants. Often it becomes their foremost and unavoidable duty. Sometimes, to meet the obligation to pay rent, their own diets suffer. The demands of paying rent may divert resources from subsistence, replacement, social, and ceremonial funds.

Motivations vary from society to society, and people often lack freedom of choice in allocating their resources. Because of obligations to pay rent, peasants may allocate their scarce means toward ends that are not their own but those of government officials. Thus, even in societies where there

See the Virtual Exploration for ways in which redistribution and reciprocity can change over time

mhhe.com/kottak

meetings of the chief's council took place, and where redistributive feasts were held. According to Cherokee custom, each family farm had an area where the family could set aside a portion of its annual harvest for the chief. This supply of corn was used to feed the needy, as well as travelers and warriors journeying through friendly territory. This store of food was available to all who needed it, with the understanding that it "belonged" to the chief and was dispersed through his generosity. The chief also hosted the redistributive feasts held in the main settlements (Harris 1978).

Reciprocity

Reciprocity is exchange between social equals, who are normally related by kinship, marriage, or another close personal tie. Because it occurs between social equals, it is dominant in the more egalitarian societies—among foragers, cultivators, and pastoralists. There are three degrees of reciprocity: generalized, balanced, and negative (Sahlins 1968, 2004; Service 1966). These may be imagined as areas of a continuum defined by these questions:

1. How closely related are the parties to the exchange?

2. How quickly and unselfishly are gifts reciprocated?

Generalized reciprocity, the purest form of reciprocity, is characteristic of exchanges between closely related people. In *balanced reciprocity,* social distance increases, as does the need to reciprocate. In *negative reciprocity,* social distance is greatest and reciprocation is most calculated.

With **generalized reciprocity,** someone gives to another person and expects nothing concrete or immediate in return. Such exchanges (including parental gift giving in contemporary North America) are not primarily economic transactions but expressions of personal relationships. Most parents don't keep accounts of every penny they spend on

 STUDENT CD-ROM LIVING ANTHROPOLOGY

Insurance Policies for Hunter-Gatherers?

Track 16

This clip features Polly Wiesnner, an ethnologist (cultural anthropologist) who has worked among the San ("Bushmen") for 25 years. The clip contrasts the foraging way of life with other economies in terms of storage, risk, and insurance against lean times. Industrial nations have banks, refrigerators, and insurance policies. Pastoralists have herds, which store meat and wealth on the hoof. Farmers have larders and granaries. How do the San anticipate and deal with hard times? What form of insurance do they have? What was it, according to Wiesnner, that allowed *Homo sapiens* to "colonize so many niches in this world"?

their children. They merely hope that the children will respect their culture's customs involving love, honor, loyalty, and other obligations to parents.

Among foragers, generalized reciprocity tends to govern exchanges. People routinely share with other band members (Bird-David 1992; Kent 1992). A study of the Ju/'hoansi San (Figure 16.4) found that 40 percent of the population contributed little to the food supply (Lee 1968/1974). Children, teenagers, and people over 60 depended on other people for their food. Despite the high proportion of dependents, the average worker hunted or gathered less than half as much (12 to 19 hours a week) as the average American works. Nonetheless, there was always food because different people worked on different days.

So strong is the ethic of reciprocal sharing that most foragers lack an expression for "thank you." To offer thanks would be impolite because it would imply that a particular act of sharing, which is the keystone of egalitarian society, was unusual. Among the Semai, foragers of central Malaysia (Dentan 1979), to express gratitude would suggest surprise at the hunter's generosity or success (Harris 1974).

Balanced reciprocity applies to exchanges between people who are more distantly related than are members of the same band or household. In a horticultural society, for example, a man presents a gift to someone in another village. The recipient may be a cousin, a trading partner, or a brother's fictive kinsman. The giver expects something in return. This may not come immediately, but the social relationship will be strained if there is no reciprocation.

Exchanges in nonindustrial societies also may illustrate **negative reciprocity,** mainly in dealing with people outside or on the fringes of their social systems. To people who live in a world of close personal relations, exchanges with outsiders are full of ambiguity and distrust. Exchange is one way of establishing friendly rela-

◼ *Sharing the fruits of production, a keystone of many nonindustrial societies, also has been a goal of socialist nations, such as China. These workers in Yunnan province strive for an equal distribution of meat.*

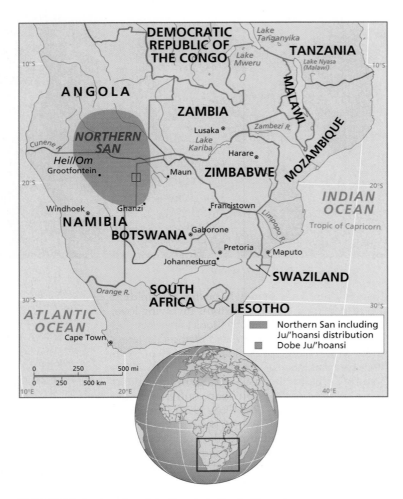

FIGURE 16.4 Location of the San, including Ju/'hoansi.

tions with outsiders, but especially when trade begins, the relationship is still tentative. Often, the initial exchange is close to being purely economic; people want to get something back immediately. Just as in market economies, but without using money, they try to get the best possible immediate return for their investment.

Generalized and balanced reciprocity are based on trust and a social tie. But negative reciprocity involves the attempt to get something for as little as possible, even if it means being cagey or deceitful or cheating. Among the most extreme and "negative" examples of negative reciprocity was 19th-century horse thievery by North American Plains Indians. Men would sneak into camps and villages of neighboring tribes to steal horses. A similar pattern of cattle raiding continues today in East Africa, among tribes like the Kuria (Fleisher 2000). In these cases, the party that starts the raiding can expect reciprocity—a raid on their own village—or worse. The Kuria hunt down cattle thieves and kill them. It's still reciprocity, governed by "Do unto others as they have done unto you."

One way of reducing the tension in situations of potential negative reciprocity is to engage in "silent trade." One example is the silent trade of the Mbuti "pygmy" foragers of the African equatorial forest and their neighboring horticultural villagers. There is no personal contact during their exchanges. A Mbuti hunter leaves game, honey, or another forest product at a customary site. Villagers collect it and leave crops in exchange. Often the parties bargain silently. If one feels the return is insufficient, he or she simply leaves it at the trading site. If the other party wants to continue trade, it will be increased.

Coexistence of Exchange Principles

In today's North America, the market principle governs most exchanges, from the sale of the means of production to the sale of consumer goods. We also have redistribution. Some of our tax money goes to support the government, but some of it also comes back to us in the form of social services, education, health care, and road building. We also have reciprocal exchanges. Generalized reciprocity characterizes the relationship between parents and children. However, even here the dominant market mentality surfaces in comments about the high cost of raising children and in the stereotypical statement of the disappointed parent: "We gave you everything money could buy."

Exchanges of gifts, cards, and invitations exemplify reciprocity, usually balanced. Everyone has heard remarks like "They invited us to their daughter's wedding, so when ours gets married, we'll have to invite them" and "They've been here for dinner three times and haven't invited us yet. I don't think we should ask them back until they do." Such precise balancing of reciprocity would be out of place in a foraging band, where resources are communal (common to all) and daily sharing based on generalized reciprocity is an essential ingredient of social life and survival.

POTLATCHING

One of the most thoroughly studied cultural practices known to ethnography is the **potlatch,** a festive event within a regional exchange system among tribes of the North Pacific Coast of North America, including the Salish and Kwakiutl of Washington and British Columbia and the Tsimshian of Alaska (Figure 16.5). Some tribes still practice the potlatch, sometimes as a memorial to the dead (Kan 1986, 1989). At each such event, assisted by members of their communities, potlatch sponsors traditionally gave away food, blankets, pieces of copper, or other items. In return for this, they got prestige. To give a potlatch enhanced one's reputation. Prestige increased with the lavishness of the potlatch, the value of the goods given away in it.

The potlatching tribes were foragers, but atypical ones. They were sedentary and had chiefs. And unlike the environments of most other recent foragers, theirs was not marginal. They had access to a wide variety of land and sea resources. Among their most important foods were salmon, herring, candlefish, berries, mountain goats, seals, and porpoises (Piddocke 1969).

According to classical economic theory, the profit motive is universal, with the goal of maximizing material benefits. How then does one explain the potlatch, in which substantial wealth is given away (and even destroyed—see below)? Christian missionaries considered potlatching to be wasteful and antithetical to the Protestant work ethic. By 1885, under pressure from Indian Agents, missionaries, and Indian converts to Christianity, both Canada and the United States had outlawed potlatching. Between 1885 and 1951 the custom went underground. By 1951 both countries had discreetly dropped the antipotlatching laws from the books (Miller n.d.).

Some scholars seized on this view of the potlatch as a classic case of economically wasteful behavior. The economist and social commentator Thorstein Veblen cited potlatching as an example of conspicuous consumption in his influential book *The Theory of the Leisure Class* (1934), claiming that potlatching was based on an economically irrational drive for prestige. This interpretation stressed the lavishness and supposed wastefulness, especially of the Kwakiutl displays, to support the contention that in some societies people strive to maximize prestige at the expense of their material well-being. This interpretation has been challenged.

Ecological anthropology, also known as *cultural ecology,* is a theoretical school in anthropology that attempts to interpret cultural practices, such as the potlatch, in terms of their long-term role in helping humans adapt to their environments. A different interpretation of the potlatch has been offered by the ecological anthropologists Wayne Suttles (1960) and Andrew Vayda (1961/1968). These scholars see potlatching not in terms of its apparent wastefulness, but in terms of its long-term role as a cultural adaptive mechanism. This view not only helps us understand potlatching, it also has comparative value because it helps us understand similar patterns of lavish feasting in many other parts of the world. Here is the ecological interpretation: *Customs like the potlatch are cultural adaptations to alternating periods of local abundance and shortage.*

How does this work? The overall natural environment of the North Pacific Coast is favorable, but resources fluctuate from year to year and place to place. Salmon and herring aren't equally abundant every year in a given locality. One vil-

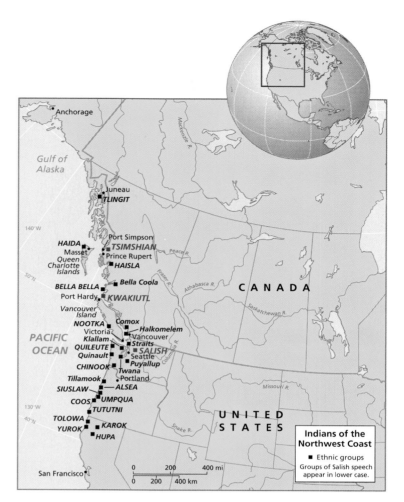

FIGURE 16.5 Location of potlatching groups.

lage can have a good year while another is experiencing a bad one. Later their fortunes reverse. In this context, the potlatch cycle of the Kwakiutl and Salish had adaptive value, and the potlatch was not a competitive display that brought no material benefit.

A village enjoying an especially good year had a surplus of subsistence items, which it could trade for more durable wealth items, like blankets, canoes, or pieces of copper. Wealth, in turn, by being distributed, could be converted into prestige. Members of several villages were invited to any potlatch and got to take home the resources that were given away. In this way, potlatching linked villages together in a regional economy—an exchange system that distributed food and wealth from wealthy to needy communities. In return, the potlatch sponsors and their villages got prestige. The decision to potlatch was determined by the health of the local economy. If there had been subsistence surpluses, and thus a buildup of wealth over several good years, a village could afford a potlatch to convert its food and wealth into prestige.

See the Internet Exercises at your OLC for information about feasting among the Hoploi of Papua New Guinea

mhhe.com/kottak

■ *The historic photo (above) shows the amassing of blankets to be given away at a Kwakiutl potlatch. The man in the foreground is making a speech praising the generosity of the potlatch host. The photo below shows a modern potlatch, lasting four days, celebrated by Alaska's Tsimshian Indians. Nowadays, the gifts to be distributed are piled at the center of the large room where the event is taking place. Have you ever partaken in anything like a potlatch?*

The long-term adaptive value of intercommunity feasting becomes clear when we consider what happened when a formerly prosperous village had a run of bad luck. Its people started accepting invitations to potlatches in villages that were doing better. The tables were turned as the temporarily rich became temporarily poor and vice versa. The newly needy accepted food and wealth items. They were willing to receive rather than bestow gifts and thus to relinquish some of their stored-up prestige. They hoped their luck would eventually improve so that resources could be recouped and prestige regained.

The potlatch linked local groups along the North Pacific Coast into a regional alliance and exchange network. Potlatching and intervillage exchange had adaptive functions, regardless of the motivations of the individual participants. The anthropologists who stressed rivalry for prestige were not wrong. They were merely emphasizing motivations at the expense of an analysis of economic and ecological systems.

The use of feasts to enhance individual and community reputations and to redistribute wealth is not peculiar to populations of the North Pacific Coast. Competitive feasting is widely characteristic of nonindustrial food producers. But among most foragers, who live, remember, in marginal areas, resources are too meager to support feasting on such a level. In such societies, sharing rather than competition prevails.

Like many other cultural practices that have attracted considerable anthropological attention, the potlatch does not, and did not, exist apart from larger world events. For example, within the spreading world capitalist economy of the 19th century, the potlatching tribes, particularly the Kwakiutl, began to trade with Europeans (fur for blankets, for example). Their wealth increased as a result. Simultaneously, a huge proportion of the Kwakiutl population died from previously unknown diseases brought by the Europeans. As a result, the increased wealth from trade flowed into a drastically reduced population. With many of the traditional sponsors dead (such as chiefs and their families), the Kwakiutl extended the right to give a potlatch to the entire population. This stimulated very intense competition for prestige. Given trade, increased wealth, and a decreased population, the Kwakiutl also started converting wealth into prestige by destroying wealth items such as blankets, pieces of copper, and houses (Vayda 1961/1968). Blankets and houses could be burned, and coppers could be buried at sea. Here, with dramatically increased wealth and a drastically reduced population, Kwakiutl potlatching changed its nature. It became much more destructive than it had been previously and than potlatching continued to be among tribes that were less affected by trade and disease.

In any case, note that potlatching also served to prevent the development of socioeconomic stratification, a system of social classes. Wealth relinquished or destroyed was converted into a nonmaterial item: prestige. Under capitalism, we reinvest our profits (rather than burning our cash), with the hope of making an additional profit. However, the potlatching tribes were content to relinquish their surpluses rather than use them to widen the social distance between themselves and their fellow tribe members.

1. Cohen's adaptive strategies include foraging (hunting and gathering), horticulture, agriculture, pastoralism, and industrialism. Foraging was the only human adaptive strategy until the advent of food production (farming and herding) 10,000 years ago. Food production eventually replaced foraging in most places. Almost all modern foragers have at least some dependence on food production or food producers.

2. Horticulture and agriculture stand at opposite ends of a continuum based on labor intensity and continuity and land use. Horticulture doesn't use land or labor intensively. Horticulturalists cultivate a plot for one or two years and then abandon it. Further along the continuum, horticulture becomes more intensive, but there is always a fallow period. Agriculturalists farm the same plot of land continuously and use labor intensively. They use one or more of the following: irrigation, terracing, domesticated animals as means of production and manuring.

3. The pastoral strategy is mixed. Nomadic pastoralists trade with cultivators. Part of a transhumant pastoral population cultivates while another part takes the herds to pasture. Except for some Peruvians and the Navajo, who are recent herders, the New World lacks native pastoralists.

4. Economic anthropology is the cross-cultural study of systems of production, distribution, and consumption. In nonindustrial societies, a kin-based mode of production prevails. One acquires rights to resources and labor through membership in social groups, not impersonally through purchase and sale. Work is just one aspect of social relations expressed in varied contexts.

5. Economics has been defined as the science of allocating scarce means to alternative ends. Western economists assume that the notion of scarcity is universal—which it isn't—and that in making choices, people strive to maximize personal profit. In nonindustrial societies, indeed as in our own, people often maximize values other than individual profit.

6. In nonindustrial societies, people invest in subsistence, replacement, social, and ceremonial funds. States add a rent fund: People must share their output with social superiors. In states, the obligation to pay rent often becomes primary.

7. Besides production, economic anthropologists study and compare exchange systems. The three principles of exchange are the market principle, redistribution, and reciprocity. The market principle, based on supply and demand and the profit motive, dominates in states. With redistribution, goods are collected at a central place, but some of them are eventually given back, or redistributed, to the people. Reciprocity governs exchanges between social equals. It is the characteristic mode of exchange among foragers and horticulturists. Reciprocity, redistribution, and the market principle may coexist in a society, but the primary exchange mode is the one that allocates the means of production.

8. Patterns of feasting and exchanges of wealth among villages are common among nonindustrial food producers, as among the potlatching cultures of North America's North Pacific Coast. Such systems help even out the availability of resources over time.

---

agriculture Nonindustrial systems of plant cultivation characterized by continuous and intensive use of land and labor.

balanced reciprocity See *generalized reciprocity.*

band Basic unit of social organization among foragers. A band includes fewer than 100 people; it often splits up seasonally.

correlation An association between two or more variables such that when one changes (varies), the other also changes (covaries); for example, temperature and sweating.

cultivation continuum A continuum based on the comparative study of nonindustrial cultivating societies in which labor intensity increases and fallowing decreases.

economizing The rational allocation of scarce means (or resources) to alternative ends (or uses); often considered the subject matter of economics.

economy A population's system of production, distribution, and consumption of resources.

generalized reciprocity Principle that characterizes exchanges between closely related individuals. As social distance increases, reciprocity becomes balanced and finally negative.

horticulture Nonindustrial system of plant cultivation in which plots lie fallow for varying lengths of time.

market principle Profit-oriented principle of exchange that dominates in states, particularly industrial states. Goods and services are bought and sold, and values are determined by supply and demand.

means (or factors) of production Land, labor, technology, and capital—major productive resources.

mode of production Way of organizing production—a set of social relations through which labor is deployed to wrest energy from nature by means of tools, skills, and knowledge.

negative reciprocity See *generalized reciprocity.*

nomadism, pastoral Movement throughout the year by the whole pastoral group (men, women, and children) with their animals; more generally, such constant movement in pursuit of strategic resources.

pastoralists People who use a food-producing strategy of adaptation based on care of herds of domesticated animals.

peasant Small-scale agriculturalist living in a state with rent fund obligations.

potlatch Competitive feast among Indians on the North Pacific Coast of North America.

reciprocity One of the three principles of exchange; governs exchange between social equals; major exchange mode in band and tribal societies.

redistribution Major exchange mode of chiefdoms, many archaic states, and some states with managed economies.

transhumance One of two variants of pastoralism; part of the population moves seasonally with the herds while the other part remains in home villages.

CRITICAL THINKING QUESTIONS

For more self-testing, see the self-quizzes

mhhe.com/kottak

1. What are some of the main advantages and disadvantages of living in a foraging society? How about horticulture? Agriculture? Pastoralism? In which one would you want to live, and why?

2. What do you see as the main differences and similarities between ancient and modern hunter-gatherers?

3. What are your scarce means? How do you make decisions about allocating them?

4. What do you attempt to maximize? Does that vary depending on the situation?

5. Give examples from your own exchanges of different degrees of reciprocity.

SUGGESTED ADDITIONAL READINGS

Bates, D. G.
  2005 *Human Adaptive Strategies: Ecology, Culture, and Politics,* 3rd ed. Boston: Pearson/Allyn & Bacon. Recent discussion of the different adaptive strategies and their political correlates.

Cohen, Y.
  1974 *Man in Adaptation: The Cultural Present,* 2nd ed. Chicago: Aldine. Presents Cohen's economic typology of adaptive strategies and uses it to organize a valuable set of essays on culture and adaptation.

Gudeman, S.
  2001 *The Anthropology of Economy: Community, Market, and Culture.* Malden, MA: Blackwell. Economic aspects of globalization in relation to economic anthropology.

Gudeman, S., ed.
  1998 *Economic Anthropology.* Northhampton, MA: E. Elgar. Reference essays in economic anthropology.

Ingold, T., D. Riches, and J. Woodburn
  1991 *Hunters and Gatherers.* New York: Berg (St. Martin's). Volume I examines history and social change among foragers. Volume II looks at their property, ideology, and power relations. These broad regional surveys illuminate current issues and debates.

Kearney, M.
  1996 *Reconceptualizing the Peasantry: Anthropology in Global Perspective.* Boulder, CO: Westview. How peasants live today, in post–Cold War nation-states.

Kelly, R. L.
  1995 *The Foraging Spectrum: Diversity in Hunter-Gatherer Lifeways.* Washington, DC: Smithsonian Institution Press. Survey of foragers in varied environments.

Kent, S.
  1996 *Cultural Diversity among Twentieth-Century Foragers: An African Perspective.* New York: Cambridge University Press. Africa's hunter-gatherers, their adaptations, social life, and variety.

Lee, R. B.
  2003 *The Dobe Ju/'hoansi,* 3rd ed. Belmont, CA: Wadsworth. Account of well-known San foragers, by one of their principal ethnographers.

Lee, R. B., and R. H. Daly
  1999 *The Cambridge Encyclopedia of Hunters and Gatherers.* New York: Cambridge University Press. Indispensable reference work on foragers.

Plattner, S., ed.
  1989 *Economic Anthropology.* Stanford, CA: Stanford University Press. Articles on economic features of foraging, tribal, peasant, state, and industrial societies.

Sahlins, M. D.
  2004 *Stone Age Economics.* New York: Routledge. A reprinted classic, with a new preface.

Salzman, P. C.
  2004 *Pastoralists: Equality, Hierarchy, and the State.* Boulder, CO: Westview. What we can learn from pastoralists about equality, freedom, and democracy.

Salzman, P. C., and J. G. Galaty, eds.
  1990 *Nomads in a Changing World.* Naples: Istituto Universitario Orientale. Pastoral nomads in varied contemporary settings.

Srivastava, J., N. J. H. Smith, and D. A. Forno
  1999 *Integrating Biodiversity in Agricultural Intensification: Toward Sound Practices.* Washington,

DC: World Bank. Environmentally and socially sustainable agriculture in today's world.

Wilk, R. R.
  1996 *Economies and Cultures: An Introduction to Economic Anthropology.* Boulder, CO: Westview. A thorough introduction to economic anthropology.

INTERNET EXERCISES

1. Reciprocity: Go to the Living Link's video collection at Emory University's Center for the Advanced Study of Ape and Human Evolution page, **http://www.emory.edu/LIVING_LINKS/ AV_Library.html**, and watch the Chimpanzee Food Sharing Movie.
   a. What is an example in this film of generalized reciprocity?
   b. What is an example of balanced reciprocity?
   c. What is an example of negative reciprocity?
   d. What inferences can be made from the observation that humans and chimpanzees exhibit similar capacities for reciprocity? Even when humans and chimpanzees enact similar behaviors (i.e., generalized reciprocity), are there important differences?

2. Subsistence and Settlement: Go to the Ethnographic Atlas Cross-tabulations page, **http://lucy. ukc.ac.uk/cgi-bin/uncgi/Ethnoatlas/atlas.vopts**. This site has compiled ethnographic information on many different groups, and you can use the tools provided to cross-tabulate the prevalence of certain traits. Under "Select Row Category" choose "subsistence economy," and under "Select Column Category" select "settlement patterns." Press the Submit Query button. The table that appears shows the frequency with which groups of different subsistence systems use certain mobility strategies.

a. Notice that a high number of groups with agriculture use "Compact and relatively permanent settlements." Is this what you would expect?
b. What kinds of subsistence strategies are used by groups that are the most mobile (have "Migratory or nomadic," "Seminomadic," or "Semisedentary" settlement patterns)?
c. Now let's focus on the groups that are exceptional and do not combine subsistence and settlement strategies in the most usual or common way. There is a single group that uses intensive agriculture and is seminomadic. Click on the number at that location. What is the name of that group, and where are they found?
d. There are a few groups that are in permanent settlements and use hunting, gathering, or fishing. What region of the world are most of these groups from?
e. Feel free to explore many of the other variables listed in the table. We suggest you check "mean size of local communities," "settlement patterns," and "subsistence economy" against each other. What patterns do you see?

See Chapter 16 at your McGraw-Hill Online Learning Center for additional review and interactive exercises.

LINKAGES

Kottak, *Assault on Paradise*, 4th ed.

In Chapter 4, "The Spirit of Fishermen," Arembepe's value system is characterized with reference to two classic formulations in social science: Max Weber's *The Protestant Ethic and the Spirit of Capitalism* (1904/ 1958) and George Foster's "image of limited good." How were Arembepe's fishermen like the early Protestant entrepreneurs described by Weber? Indicate, too, how the image of limited good, which Foster considers characteristic of peasant societies, showed up in Arembepe. What is the "riddle of the spots," and how did it fit within Arembepe's basically egalitarian social structure?

Peters-Golden, *Culture Sketches*, 4th ed.

This text chapter has examined systems of production, distribution, and consumption among societies with various adaptive strategies. In *Culture Sketches*, read the chapter "Basseri: Pastoral Nomads on the il-Rah." What are some ways in which the Basseri's

adaptive strategy—pastoral nomadism—influences their other social institutions and relationships? How might Basseri life change with increasing sedentism?

Knauft, *The Gebusi*, 1st ed.

Based on information in Chapter 2 of *The Gebusi*, what food-related activities of the Gebusi are similar to those of foragers or hunter-gatherers? What food-related activities of Gebusi are similar to those of horticulturalists? List the ways in which Gebusi pigs are domesticated and the ways in which they are still wild. What examples does the author provide concerning the following types of subsistence: (a) intensive foraging that allows for the development of large villages; (b) intensive agriculture paired with intensive animal husbandry? What accounts for such differences in subsistence orientation? Describe some features of Gebusi residence that are "sedentary" and others that are "seminomadic."

17

Political Systems

CHAPTER OUTLINE

WHAT IS "THE POLITICAL"?

Anthropologists and political scientists share an interest in political systems and organization, but the anthropological approach is global and comparative, and includes nonstates as well as the states and nation-states usually studied by political scientists. Anthropological studies have revealed substantial variation in power (formal and informal), authority, and legal systems in different societies and communities. (Power is the ability to exercise one's will over others; authority is the socially approved use of power.) (See Cheater, ed. 1999; Gledhill 2000; Kurtz 2001; Wolf with Silverman 2001.)

■ Citizens routinely use collective action to influence public policy. Shown here, members of Citizens for Responsible Growth in Clemson, South Carolina, have mobilized against the construction of a Wal-Mart Super Center on this 35-acre site. Have your own actions ever influenced public policy?

Recognizing that political organization is sometimes just an aspect of social organization, Morton Fried offered this definition:

Political Organization comprises those portions of social organization that specifically relate to the individuals or groups that manage the affairs of public policy or seek to control the appointment or activities of those individuals or groups. (Fried 1967, pp. 20–21)

OVERVIEW

Politicians lead, manage public policy, make decisions, and try to implement them. Political anthropology is the cross-cultural study of political systems and institutions. Not all societies have had law—in the sense of a formal legal code, judiciary, and enforcement—but all societies have means of social control. Some political systems have informal or temporary leaders with limited local authority. Others have strong and permanent political institutions that prevail over entire regions.

The terms *band, tribe, chiefdom,* and *state* describe forms of social and political organization. Bands are small, mobile, kin-based groups with little differential power. Tribes have villages and/or descent groups but lack a formal government. Chiefdoms, although kin-based, have differential access to resources and a permanent political structure. The state is an autonomous political entity encompassing many communities. Its government can collect taxes, draft people for work or war, and decree and enforce laws. All states have a central government and socioeconomic stratification. The concept of social control is broader than the political and encompasses all beliefs and practices that work to maintain norms, ensure compliance, and regulate conflict.

This definition certainly fits contemporary North America. Under "individuals or groups that manage the affairs of public policy" come federal, state (provincial), and local (municipal) governments. Those who seek to control the activities of the groups that manage public policy include such interest groups as political parties, unions, corporations, consumers, activists, action committees, religious groups, and nongovernmental organizations (NGOs).

Fried's definition is much less applicable to nonstates, where it was often difficult to detect any "public policy." For this reason, I prefer to speak of *socio*political organization in discussing the regulation or management of interrelations among groups and their representatives. In a general sense, regulation is the process that ensures that variables stay within their normal ranges, corrects deviations from the norm, and thus maintains a system's integrity. In the case of political regulation, this includes such things as decision making, social control, and conflict resolution. The study of political regulation draws our attention to those who make decisions and resolve conflicts (are there formal leaders?).

Ethnographic and archaeological studies in hundreds of places have revealed many correlations between economy and social and political organization.

TYPES AND TRENDS

Decades ago, the anthropologist Elman Service (1962) listed four types, or levels, of political organization: band, tribe, chiefdom, and state. Today, none of these political entities (*polities*) can be

Chat Rooms, Bedouin Style

CHRISTIAN SCIENCE MONITOR NEWS BRIEF

by Ilene R. Prusher
April 26, 2000

When we think of politics, we think of government, of federal and state institutions, of Washington, Ottawa, or perhaps our state capital, city hall, or courthouse. We hear discussions of public service, political offices, and elections—and maybe the economic and political power that goes along with holding office, or with influencing those who hold office. Binding decisions are made at the top levels of government. There are also informal political institutions, which aren't part of the governmental apparatus, but which may substantially influence it. Described here are the diwaniyas *of Kuwait—informal, local-level meeting places where informal discussions can have formal consequences. Much of Kuwait's decision making, networking, and influence peddling takes place in these* diwaniyas. *What do you see as the advantages and disadvantages of the* diwaniya *system? Do we have anything like it in our society?*

The process of deliberation and decision making that goes on within—and then beyond—Kuwait's diwaniya *system illustrates a political process. Anthropologists share with political scientists an interest in political processes, systems, and organization, but the anthropological approach is characteristically global and comparative, including nonstates as well as states. Anthropological studies have revealed substantial variation in power, authority, and legal systems among the world's cultures.*

In the historical fabric of Kuwait, *diwaniyas* have been men-only political salons—a local equivalent of neighborhood pub and town-hall meeting combined. They serve not only as parlors for chit-chats, but governance, too. *Diwaniyas* are so integral to Kuwaiti culture that during election season, candidates don't go door to door, but *diwaniya* to *diwaniya*. This is where business deals are made and marriages arranged . . .

Traditionally, most men have an open invitation to attend a *diwaniya* on any given night, and wealthy families have a large, long room adjacent to their homes expressly for their *diwaniya*. Some neighborhoods have a common *diwaniya*, much like a community center.

At a typical men-only *diwaniya* . . . the attendees lounge among the partitions of a never-ending couch that follow the contours of the room in one giant U. They usually gather once a week, starting at 8 in the evening and sometimes going past midnight.

As they discuss issues . . . they twirl smoothly polished beads around their fingers and worry aloud whether change has come to Kuwait too fast. The presence of malls and movies, they fret, is breaking down social norms like the taboo against premarital dating . . .

At the Al-Fanar Center, with its bevy of Body Shops and Benettons, teenage boys say they also have no interest in chattering the night away when they could be flirting. "We like to follow around girls without hijab [veil]," says teenager Abdul Rahman Al-Tarket, roaming the mall with his two friends . . .

Mixed [male and female] *diwaniyas* are still an anomaly. "For me, the *diwaniya* is a very comfortable place to have people come and see me," says artist Thoraya al-Baqsami, who co-hosts one mixed gathering. "I know many people don't like it, but we are in the 21st century now," she says as she gives a tour of her adjacent gallery . . .

Many women here say they're happy to leave the *diwaniya* to the domain of men. But more problematic is that it is the *diwaniya* at which much of the country's decision-making and networking takes place. It is also a forum where a constituent can meet his parliamentary representative and consult him about major problems or minor potholes.

A Kuwaiti diwaniya.

The importance of *diwaniyas* to Kuwaiti society cannot be understated. Kuwait's parliament emerged from a 1921 proposal by *diwaniyas*. And Sheik Jaber al-Sabah, who dissolved the assembly in 1986, restored it in 1992 following pressure from *diwaniyas* . . .

Some here say they wouldn't mind seeing the decline of the *diwaniya*. Says Kuwait University political scientist Shamlan El-Issa: "The positive aspects are that it helps democracy—men meet every day and talk and complain for two or three hours. The negative is that it replaces the family—men go to work and *diwaniya*, and never see their wives."

SOURCE: Excerpted from Ilene R. Prusher, "Chat Rooms, Bedouin Style," *Christian Science Monitor*, April 26, 2000.

studied as a self-contained form of political organization, since all exist within nation-states and are subject to state control. There is archaeological evidence for early bands, tribes, and chiefdoms that existed before the first states appeared. However, since anthropology came into being long after the origin of the state, anthropologists have never been able to observe "in the flesh" a band, tribe, or chiefdom outside the influence of some state. All the bands, tribes, and chiefdoms known to ethnography have been within the borders of a state. There still may be local political leaders (e.g., village heads) and regional figures (e.g., chiefs) of the sort discussed in this chapter, but all exist and function within the context of state organization.

A *band* refers to a small *kin-based* group (all the members are related to each other by kinship or marriage ties) found among foragers. **Tribes** had economies based on nonintensive food production (horticulture and pastoralism). Living in villages and organized into kin groups based on common descent (clans and lineages), tribes lacked a formal government and had no reliable means of enforcing political decisions. **Chiefdom** refers to a form of sociopolitical organization intermediate between the tribe and the state. In chiefdoms, social relations were based mainly on kinship, marriage, descent, age, generation, and gender—just as they were in bands and tribes. Although chiefdoms were kin-based, they featured differential access to resources (some people had more wealth, prestige, and power than others) and a permanent political structure. The **state** is a form of sociopolitical organization based on a formal government structure and socioeconomic stratification.

The four labels in Service's typology are much too simple to account for the full range of political diversity and complexity known to archaeology and ethnography. We'll see, for instance, that tribes have varied widely in their political systems and institutions. Nevertheless, Service's typology does highlight some significant contrasts in political organization, especially those between states and nonstates. For example, in bands and tribes—unlike states, which have clearly visible governments—political organization did not stand out as separate and distinct from the total social order. In bands and tribes, it was difficult to characterize an act or event as political rather than merely social.

Service's labels "band," "tribe," "chiefdom," and "state" are categories or types within a *sociopolitical typology*. These types are correlated with the adaptive strategies (economic typology) discussed in Chapter 16, "Making a Living." Thus, foragers (an economic type) tended to have band organization (a sociopolitical type). Similarly, many horticulturalists and pastoralists lived in tribal societies (or, more simply, tribes). Although most chiefdoms had farming economies, herding was important in some Middle Eastern chiefdoms. Nonindustrial states usually had an agricultural base.

With food production came larger, denser populations and more complex economies than was the case among foragers. These features posed new regulatory problems, which gave rise to more complex relations and linkages. Many sociopolitical trends reflect the increased regulatory demands associated with food production. Archaeologists have studied these trends through time, and cultural anthropologists have observed them among contemporary groups.

BANDS AND TRIBES

This chapter examines a series of societies with different political systems. A common set of questions will be addressed for each one. What kinds of social groups does the society have? How do people affiliate with those groups? How do the groups link up with larger ones? How do the groups represent themselves to each other? How are their internal and external relations regulated? To answer these questions, we begin with bands and tribes and then move on to chiefdoms and states.

Foraging Bands

Modern hunter-gatherers should not be seen as representative of Stone Age peoples, all of whom also were foragers. Anthropologists wonder just how much contemporary foragers can tell us about the economic and social relations that characterized humanity before food production. Modern foragers, after all, live in nation-states and an interlinked world. For generations, the pygmies of Congo have shared a social world with their neighbors who are cultivators. They exchange forest products (e.g., honey and meat) for crops (e.g., bananas and manioc). All foragers now trade with food producers. Most contemporary hunter-gatherers rely on governments and on missionaries for at least part of what they consume.

The San

The San speakers ("Bushmen") of southern Africa have been influenced by Bantu speakers (farmers and herders) for 2,000 years and by Europeans for centuries. Edwin Wilmsen (1989) sees the San as a rural underclass in a larger political and economic system dominated by Europeans and Bantu food producers. Many San now tend cattle for wealthier Bantu rather than foraging independently. Wilmsen also argues that many San descend from herders who were pushed into the desert by poverty or oppression.

Susan Kent (1992, 1996) notes a tendency to stereotype foragers, to treat them all as alike. They used to be stereotyped as isolated, primitive survivors of the Stone Age. A new stereotype sees them as culturally deprived people forced by states, colonialism, or world events into marginal environments. Although this view often is exaggerated, it probably is more accurate than the former one. Modern foragers differ substantially from Stone Age hunter-gatherers.

Kent (1996) stresses variation among foragers, focusing on diversity in time and space among the San. The nature of San life has changed considerably since the 1950s and 1960s, when a series of anthropologists from Harvard University, including Richard Lee, embarked on a systematic study of life in the Kalahari. Lee and others have doc-

■ *Among tropical foragers, women make an important economic contribution through gathering, as is true among the San shown here in Namibia. What evidence do you see in this photo that contemporary foragers participate in the modern world system?*

umented many of the changes in various publications (Lee 1979, 1984, 2003; Silberbauer 1981; Tanaka 1980). Such longitudinal research monitors variation in time, while fieldwork in many San areas has revealed variation in space. One of the most important contrasts is between settled (sedentary) and nomadic groups (Kent and Vierich 1989). Sedentism is increasing, but some San groups (along rivers) have been sedentary for generations. Others, including the Dobe Ju/'hoansi San studied by Lee (1984, 2003) and the Kutse San that Kent studied, have retained more of the hunter-gatherer lifestyle.

Modern foragers are not Stone Age relics, living fossils, lost tribes, or noble savages. Still, to the extent that foraging is the basis of their subsistence, modern hunter-gatherers can illustrate links between a foraging economy and other aspects of society and culture. For example, San groups that still are mobile, or that were so until recently, emphasize social, political, and gender equality. A social system based on kinship, reciprocity, and sharing is appropriate for an economy with few people and limited resources. The nomadic pursuit of wild plants and animals tends to discourage permanent settlement, wealth accumulation, and status distinctions. In this context families and bands are adaptive social units. People have to share meat when they get it; otherwise it rots.

Foraging bands, which were nomadic or semi-nomadic, formed seasonally when component nuclear families got together. The particular families in a band varied from year to year. Marriage and kinship created ties between members of different bands. Because one's parents and grandparents came from different bands, a person had relatives in several of those groups. Trade and visiting also linked local groups, as did fictive kinship, such as the San namesake system described in the last chapter.

 STUDENT CD-ROM LIVING ANTHROPOLOGY

Insurance Policies for Hunter-Gatherers?
Track 16

This clip features Polly Wiessner, an ethnologist (cultural anthropologist) who has studied the San ("Bushmen") for 25 years. As the clip makes clear, Wiessner is well aware that the San are not an isolated people, or a relic population left over from the Stone Age. If there are limitations to what the San can tell us about our past, what, according to Wiessner, is the value of studying them?

For a discussion of relative affluence among foragers, see the Internet Exercises at your OLC

mhhe.com/kottak

Foraging bands tended to be egalitarian in terms of power and authority, although particular talents did lead to special respect. For example, someone could sing or dance well, was an especially good storyteller, or could go into a trance and communicate with spirits. Band leaders were leaders in name only. They were first among equals. Sometimes they gave advice or made decisions, but they had no way to enforce their decisions.

The Inuit

Foragers lacked formal **law** in the sense of a legal code with trial and enforcement, but they did have methods of social control and dispute settlement. The absence of law did not entail total anarchy. The aboriginal Inuit (Hoebel 1954, 1954/ 1968) provide a good example of methods of settling disputes in stateless societies. As described by E. A. Hoebel (1954) in a study of Inuit conflict resolution, a sparse population of some 20,000 Inuit spanned 6,000 miles (9,500 kilometers) of the Arctic region (Figure 17.1). The most significant social groups were the nuclear family and the band. Personal relationships linked the families and bands. Some bands had headmen. There were also shamans (part-time religious specialists). However, these positions conferred little power on those who occupied them.

Hunting and fishing by men were the primary Inuit subsistence activities. The diverse and abundant plant foods available in warmer areas, where female labor in gathering is important, were absent in the Arctic. Traveling on land and sea in a bitter environment, Inuit men faced more dangers than women did. The traditional male role took its toll in lives. Adult women would have outnumbered men substantially without occasional female infanticide (killing of a baby), which Inuit culture permitted.

Despite this crude (and to us unthinkable) means of population regulation, there were still more adult women than men. This permitted some men to have two or three wives. The ability to support more than one wife conferred a certain amount of prestige, but it also encouraged envy. (*Prestige* is esteem, respect, or approval for culturally valued acts or qualities.) If a man seemed to be taking additional wives just to enhance his reputation, a rival was likely to steal one of them. Most disputes were between men and originated over women, caused by wife stealing or adultery. If a man discovered that his wife had been having sexual relations without his permission, he considered himself wronged.

Although public opinion would not let the husband ignore the matter, he had several options. He could try to kill the wife stealer. However, if he succeeded, one of his rival's kinsmen would surely try to kill him in retaliation. One dispute could escalate into several deaths as relatives avenged a succession of murders. No government existed to intervene and stop such a *blood feud* (a murderous feud between families). However, one also could challenge a rival to a song battle. In a public setting, contestants made up insulting songs about each other. At the end of the match, the audience judged one of them the winner. However, if a man whose wife had been stolen won, there was no guarantee she would return. Often she would decide to stay with her abductor.

Thefts are common in societies with marked property differentials, like our own, but thefts are uncommon among foragers. Each Inuit had access to the resources needed to sustain life. Every man could hunt, fish, and make the tools necessary for subsistence. Every woman could obtain the materials needed to make clothing, prepare food, and do domestic work. Inuit men could even hunt and fish in the territories of other local groups. There was no notion of private ownership of territory or animals. However, certain minor personal items were associated with a specific person. In various societies, such items include things such as arrows, a tobacco pouch, clothing, and personal ornaments. One of the most basic Inuit beliefs was that "all natural resources are free or common goods" (Hoebel 1954/1968). Band-organized societies usually lack differential access to strategic resources. If people want something from someone else, they ask for it, and usually it is given.

Tribal Cultivators

As is true with foraging bands, there are no totally autonomous tribes in today's world. Still, there are societies, for example, in Papua New Guinea and in South America's tropical forests, in which tribal principles still operate. Tribes typically have a horticultural or pastoral economy and are organized by village life and/or membership in *descent groups* (kin groups whose members trace descent from a common ancestor). Tribes lack socioeconomic stratification (i.e., a class structure) and a formal government of their own. A few tribes still conduct small-scale warfare, in the form of intervillage raiding. Tribes have more effective regulatory mechanisms than foragers do, but tribal societies have no sure means of enforcing political decisions. The main regulatory officials are village heads, "big men," descent-group leaders, village councils, and leaders of pantribal associations. All these figures and groups have limited authority.

Like foragers, horticulturalists tend to be egalitarian, although some have marked gender stratification: an unequal distribution of resources, power, prestige, and personal freedom between men and women. Horticultural villages are usu-

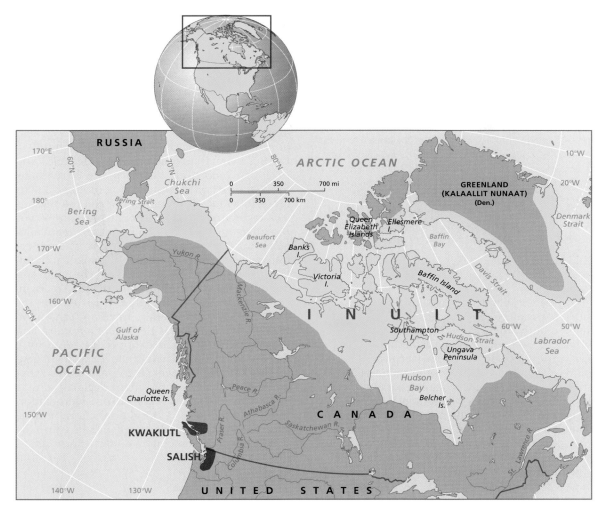

FIGURE 17.1 Location of the Inuit.

ally small, with low population density and open access to strategic resources. Age, gender, and personal traits determine how much respect people receive and how much support they get from others. Egalitarianism diminishes, however, as village size and population density increase. Horticultural villages usually have headmen—rarely, if ever, headwomen.

The Village Head

The Yanomami (Chagnon 1997) are Native Americans who live in southern Venezuela and the adjacent part of Brazil. Their tribal society has about 20,000 people living in 200 to 250 widely scattered villages, each with a population between 40 and 250. The Yanomami are horticulturalists who also hunt and gather. Their staple crops are bananas and plantains (a bananalike crop). There are more significant social groups among the Yanomami than exist in a foraging society. The Yanomami have families, villages, and descent groups. Their descent groups, which span more than one village, are patrilineal (ancestry is traced back through males only) and exogamous (people must marry outside their own descent group). However, local branches of two different descent groups may live in the same village and intermarry.

As has been true in many village-based tribal societies, the only leadership position among the Yanomami is that of **village head** (always a man). His authority, like that of a foraging band's leader, is severely limited. If a headman wants something done, he must lead by example and persuasion. The headman lacks the right to issue orders. He can only persuade, harangue, and try to influence public opinion. For example, if he wants people to clean up the central plaza in preparation for a feast, he must start sweeping it himself, hoping that his covillagers will take the hint and relieve him.

When conflict erupts within the village, the headman may be called on as a mediator who listens to both sides. He will give an opinion and advice. If a disputant is unsatisfied, the headman can do nothing. He has no power to back his decisions and no way to impose punishments. Like the band leader, he is first among equals.

✗ A Yanomami village headman also must lead in generosity. Because he must be more generous than any other villager, he cultivates more land. His garden provides much of the food consumed when his village holds a feast for another village. The headman represents the village in its dealings with outsiders. Sometimes he visits other villages to invite people to a feast. The way a person acts as headman depends on his personal traits and the number of supporters he can muster. One village headman, Kaobawa, intervened in a dispute between a husband and a wife and kept him from killing her (Chagnon 1968). He also guaranteed safety to a delegation from a village with which a covillager of his wanted to start a war. Kaobawa was a particularly effective headman. He had demonstrated his fierceness in battle, but he also knew how to use diplomacy to avoid offending other villagers. No one in the village had a better personality for the headmanship. Nor (because Kaobawa had many brothers) did anyone have more supporters. Among the Yanomami, when a group is dissatisfied with a village headman, its members can leave and found a new village; this is done from time to time.

Yanomami society, with its many villages and descent groups, is more complex than a band-organized society. The Yanomami also face more regulatory problems. A headman sometimes can prevent a specific violent act, but there is no government to maintain order. In fact, intervillage raiding in which men are killed and women are captured has been a feature of some areas of Yanomami territory, particularly those studied by Chagnon (1997).

We also must stress that the Yanomami are not isolated from outside events, including missionization (although there still may be uncontacted villages). The Yanomami live in two nation-states, Venezuela and Brazil, and external warfare waged by Brazilian ranchers and miners increasingly has threatened them (Chagnon 1997; *Cultural Survival Quarterly* 1989; Ferguson 1995). During a Brazilian gold rush between 1987 and 1991, one Yanomami died each day, on average, from external attacks (including biological warfare—introduced diseases to which the Indians lack resistance). By 1991, there were some 40,000 Brazilian miners in the Yanomami homeland. Some Indians were killed outright. The miners introduced new diseases, and the swollen population ensured that old diseases became epidemic. In 1991, a commission of the American Anthropological Association reported on the plight of the Yanomami. Brazilian Yanomami were dying at a rate of 10 percent annually, and their fertility rate had dropped to zero. Since then, both the Brazilian and the Venezuelan governments have intervened to protect the Yanomami. One Brazilian president declared a huge Yanomami territory off-limits to outsiders. Unfortunately, by mid-1992, local politicians, miners, and ranchers were increasingly evading the ban. The future of the Yanomami remains uncertain.

The "Big Man"

In many areas of the South Pacific, particularly the Melanesian Islands and Papua New Guinea, native cultures had a kind of political leader that we call the big man. The **big man** (almost always a male) was an elaborate version of the village head, but with one significant difference. The village head's leadership is within one village; the big man had supporters in several villages. The big man therefore was a regulator of regional political organization. Here we see the trend toward expansion in the scale of sociopolitical regulation—from village to region.

The Kapauku Papuans live in Irian Jaya, Indonesia (which is on the island of New Guinea) (Figure 17.2). Anthropologist Leopold Pospisil (1963) studied the Kapauku (45,000 people), who grow crops (with the sweet potato as their staple) and raise pigs. Their economy is too complex to be described as simple horticulture. The only political figure among the Kapauku was the big man, known as a *tonowi*. A tonowi achieved his status through hard work, amassing wealth in the form of pigs and other native riches. Characteristics that distinguished a big man from his fellows included wealth, generosity, eloquence, physical fitness, bravery, and supernatural powers. Men became big men because they had certain personalities. They had amassed resources during their own lifetimes, as they did not inherit their wealth or position.

A man who was determined enough could become a big man, creating wealth through hard work and good judgment. Wealth resulted from successful pig breeding and trading. As a man's pig herd and prestige grew, he attracted supporters. He sponsored ceremonial pig feasts in which pigs were slaughtered, and their meat distributed to guests.

Unlike the Yanomami village head, a big man's wealth exceeded that of his fellows. His supporters, recognizing his past favors and anticipating future rewards, recognized him as a leader and accepted his decisions as binding. The big man was an important regulator of regional events in Kapauku life. He helped determine the dates for feasts and markets. He persuaded people to sponsor feasts, which distributed pork and wealth. He initiated economic projects requiring the cooperation of a regional community.

The Kapauku big man again exemplifies a generalization about leadership in tribal societies: If someone achieves wealth and widespread respect and support, he or she must be generous. The big man worked hard not to hoard wealth but to be able to give away the fruits of his labor, to convert wealth into prestige and gratitude. A stingy big man would lose his support, his reputation plummeting. The Kapauku might take even more extreme measures against big men who hoarded wealth. Selfish and greedy men sometimes were murdered by their fellows.

Political figures such as the big man emerge as regulators both of demographic growth and of economic complexity. Kapauku cultivation has used varied techniques for specific kinds of land. Labor-intensive cultivation in valleys involves mutual aid in turning the soil before planting. The digging of long drainage ditches is even more complex. Kapauku plant cultivation supports a larger and denser population than does the simpler horticulture of the Yanomami. Kapauku society could not survive in its current form without collective cultivation and political regulation of the more complex economic tasks.

Pantribal Sodalities and Age Grades

Big men could forge regional political organization—albeit temporarily—by mobilizing people from different villages. Other social and political mechanisms in tribal societies, such as a belief in common ancestry, kinship, or descent, could be used to link local groups within a region. The same descent group, for example, might span several villages, and its dispersed members might follow a descent-group leader.

The "big man" persuades people to organize feasts, which distribute pork and wealth. Shown here is such a regional event, drawing on several villages, in Papua New Guinea. Big men owe their status to their individual personalities rather than to inherited wealth or position. Does our society have equivalents of big men?

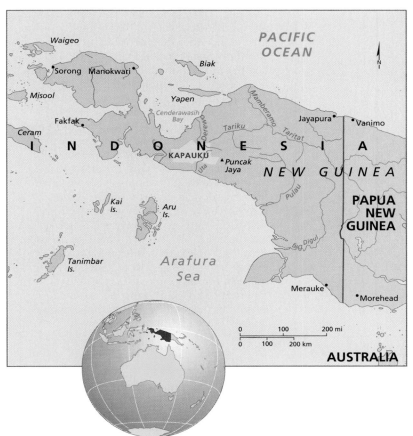

FIGURE 17.2 Location of the Kapauku.

Many factors contribute to political success in a modern nation such as the United States. They include personality, kin connections, and inherited status. Politically valuable attributes of a Melanesian big man included wealth, generosity, eloquence, physical fitness, bravery, and supernatural powers. How do such characteristics influence contemporary political careers? Americans routinely use their own wealth to finance campaigns. Big men get their loyalists to produce and deliver wealth in the form of pigs, just as modern politicians persuade their supporters to make campaign contributions. And, like big men, successful American politicians try to be generous with their supporters. Payback may take the form of a night in the Lincoln bedroom, an invitation to a strategic dinner, an ambassadorship, or largesse to a place that was particularly supportive. Big men amass wealth and then give away pigs. Successful American politicians give away "pork."

As with the big man, eloquence and communication skills contribute to political success (e.g., Bill Clinton and Ronald Reagan), although lack of such skills isn't necessarily fatal (e.g., either President Bush). What about physical fitness? Hair, height, and health are still political advantages. Bravery, for example, as demonstrated through distinguished military service, may help political careers, but it certainly isn't required. Supernatural powers? Candidates who proclaim themselves atheists are as rare as self-identified witches. Almost all political candidates claim to belong to a mainstream religion. Some even present their candidacies as promoting divine wishes. However, contemporary politics isn't just about personality, as it is in big man systems. We live in a state-organized, stratified society with inherited wealth, power, and privilege, all of which have political implications. As is typical of states, inheritance and kin connections play a role in political success. Just think of Kennedys, Bushes, Gores, Clintons, and Doles.

Principles other than kinship also can link local groups. In a modern nation, a labor union, national sorority or fraternity, political party, or religious denomination may provide such a nonkin-based link. In tribes, nonkin groups called associations or sodalities may serve the same linking function. Often, sodalities are based on common age or gender, with all-male sodalities more common than all-female ones.

Pantribal sodalities (those that extend across the whole tribe, spanning several villages) sometimes arose in areas where two or more different cultures came into regular contact. Such sodalities were especially likely to develop in the presence of warfare between tribes. Drawing their membership from different villages of the same tribe, pantribal sodalities could mobilize men in many local groups for attack or retaliation against another tribe.

In the cross-cultural study of nonkin groups, we must distinguish between those that are confined to a single village and those that span several local groups. Only the latter, the pantribal groups, are important in general military mobilization and regional political organization. Localized men's houses and clubs, limited to particular villages, are found in many horticultural societies in tropical South America, Melanesia, and Papua New Guinea. These groups may organize village activities and even intervillage raiding, but their leaders are similar to village heads and their political scope is mainly local. The following discussion, which continues our examination of the growth in scale of regional sociopolitical organization, concerns pantribal groups.

The best examples of pantribal sodalities come from the Central Plains of North America and from tropical Africa. During the 18th and 19th centuries, native populations of the Great Plains of the United States and Canada experienced a rapid growth of pantribal sodalities. This development reflected an economic change that followed the spread of horses, which had been reintroduced to the Americas by the Spanish, to the states between the Rocky Mountains and the Mississippi River. Many Plains Indian societies changed their adaptive strategies because of the horse. At first, they had been foragers who hunted bison (buffalo) on foot. Later, they adopted a mixed economy based on hunting, gathering, and horticulture. Finally, they changed to a much more specialized economy based on horseback hunting of bison (eventually with rifles).

As the Plains tribes were undergoing these changes, other Indians also adopted horseback hunting and moved into the Plains. Attempting to occupy the same area, groups came into conflict. A pattern of warfare developed in which the members of one tribe raided another, usually for horses. The new economy demanded that people follow the movement of the bison herds. During the winter, when the bison dispersed, a tribe fragmented into small bands and families. In the summer, as huge herds assembled on the Plains, members of the tribe reunited. They camped together for social, political, and religious activities, but mainly for communal bison hunting.

Natives of the Great Plains of North America originally hunted bison (buffalo) on foot, using the bow and arrow. The introduction of horses and rifles fueled a pattern of horse raiding and warfare. How far had the change gone, as depicted in this painting?

Only two activities in the new adaptive strategy demanded strong leadership: organizing and carrying out raids on enemy camps (to capture horses) and managing the summer bison hunt. All the Plains cultures developed pantribal sodalities, and leadership roles within them, to police the summer hunt. Leaders coordinated hunting efforts, making sure that people did not cause a stampede with an early shot or an ill-advised action. Leaders imposed severe penalties, including seizure of a culprit's wealth, for disobedience.

Some of the Plains sodalities were **age sets** of increasing rank. Each set included all the men—from that tribe's component bands—born during a certain time span. Each set had its distinctive dance, songs, possessions, and privileges. Members of each set had to pool their wealth to buy admission to the next higher level as they moved up the age hierarchy. Most Plains societies had pantribal warrior associations whose rituals celebrated militarism. As noted previously, the leaders of these associations organized bison hunting and raiding. They also arbitrated disputes during the summer, when large numbers of people came together.

Many of the tribes that adopted this Plains strategy of adaptation had once been foragers for whom hunting and gathering had been individual or small-group affairs. They never had come together previously as a single social unit. Age and gender were available as social principles that could quickly and efficiently forge unrelated people into pantribal groups.

Raiding of one tribe by another, this time for cattle rather than horses, also was common in eastern and southeastern Africa, where pantribal sodalities, including age sets, also developed.

Among the pastoral Masai of Kenya and Tanzania (Figure 17.3), men born during the same four-year period were circumcised together and belonged to the same named group, an age set, throughout their lives. The sets moved through grades, the most important of which was the warrior grade. Members of the set who wished to enter the warrior grade were at first discouraged by its current occupants, who eventually vacated the warrior grade and married. Members of a set felt a strong allegiance to one another and eventually had sexual rights to each other's wives. Masai women lacked comparable set organization, but they also passed through culturally recognized age grades: the initiate, the married woman, and the postmenopausal woman.

To understand the difference between an age set and an age grade, think of a college class, the Class of 2011, for example, and its progress through the university. The age set would be the group of people constituting the Class of 2011, while the first ("freshman"), sophomore, junior, and senior years would represent the age grades.

Not all cultures with age grades also have age sets. When there are no sets, men can enter or leave a particular grade individually or collectively, often by going through a predetermined ritual. The grades most commonly recognized in Africa are these:

1. Recently initiated youths.

2. Warriors.

3. One or more grades of mature men who play important roles in pantribal government.

4. Elders, who may have special ritual responsibilities.

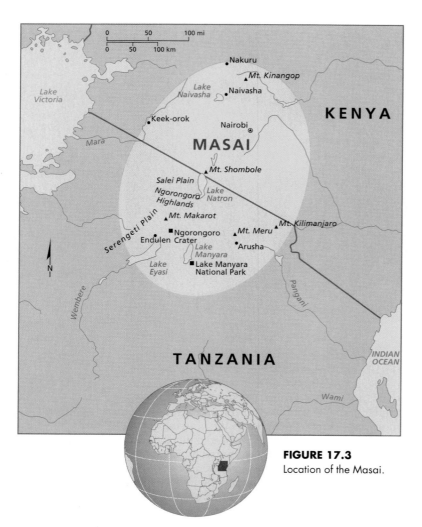

FIGURE 17.3
Location of the Masai.

Among the Masai of Kenya and Tanzania, men born during the same four-year period were circumcised together. They belonged to the same named group, an age set, throughout their lives. The sets moved through grades, of which the most important was the warrior grade. Here we see the warrior (ilmurran) age grade dancing with a group of girls of a lower age grade (intoyie). Do we have any equivalents of age sets or grades in our own society?

In certain parts of West Africa and Central Africa, the pantribal sodalities are *secret societies,* made up exclusively of men or women. Like our college fraternities and sororities, these associations have secret initiation ceremonies. Among the Mende of Sierra Leone, men's and women's secret societies are very influential. The men's group, the Poro, trains boys in social conduct, ethics, and religion and supervises political and economic activities. Leadership roles in the Poro often overshadow village headship and play an important part in social control, dispute management, and tribal political regulation. Like descent, then, age, gender, and ritual can link members of different local groups into a single social collectivity in tribal society and thus create a sense of ethnic identity, of belonging to the same cultural tradition.

Nomadic Politics

Although many pastoralists, such as the Masai, had tribal sociopolitical organization, a range of demographic and sociopolitical diversity occurs with pastoralism. A comparison of pastoralists shows that as regulatory problems increase, political hierarchies become more complex. Political organization becomes less personal, more formal, and less kinship-oriented. The pastoral strategy of adaptation does not dictate any particular political organization. A range of authority structures manage regulatory problems associated with specific environments. Some pastoralists have traditionally existed as well-defined ethnic groups in nation-states. This reflects pastoralists' need to interact with other populations—a need that is less characteristic of the other adaptive strategies.

The scope of political authority among pastoralists expands considerably as regulatory problems increase in densely populated regions. Consider two Iranian pastoral nomadic tribes: the Basseri and the Qashqai (Salzman 1974). Starting each year from a plateau near the coast, these groups took their animals to grazing land 17,000 feet (5,400 meters) above sea level. The Basseri and the Qashqai shared this route with one another and with several other ethnic groups (Figure 17.4).

Use of the same pasture land at different times was carefully scheduled. Ethnic-group movements were tightly coordinated. Expressing this schedule is *il-rah,* a concept common to all Iranian nomads. A group's *il-rah* is its customary path in time and space. It is the schedule, different for each group, of when specific areas can be used in the annual trek.

Each tribe had its own leader, known as the *khan* or *il-khan.* The Basseri *khan,* because he dealt with a smaller population, faced fewer problems in coordinating its movements than did the leaders of the Qashqai. Correspondingly, his rights, privileges, duties, and authority were weaker.

Nevertheless, his authority exceeded that of any political figure we have discussed so far. However, the *khan*'s authority still came from his personal traits rather than from his office. That is, the Basseri followed a particular *khan* not because of a political position he happened to fill but because of their personal allegiance and loyalty to him as a man. The *khan* relied on the support of the heads of the descent groups into which Basseri society was divided.

In Qashqai society, however, allegiance shifts from the person to the office. The Qashqai had multiple levels of authority and more powerful chiefs or *khans*. Managing 400,000 people required a complex hierarchy. Heading it was the *il-khan*, helped by a deputy, under whom were the heads of constituent tribes, under each of whom were descent-group heads.

A case illustrates just how developed the Qashqai authority structure was. A hailstorm prevented some nomads from joining the annual migration at the appointed time. Although everyone recognized that they were not responsible for their delay, the *il-khan* assigned them less favorable grazing land, for that year only, in place of their usual pasture. The tardy herders and other Qashqai considered the judgment fair and didn't question it. Thus, Qashqai authorities regulated the annual migration. They also adjudicated disputes between people, tribes, and descent groups.

These Iranian cases illustrate the fact that pastoralism is often just one among many specialized economic activities within complex nation-states and regional systems. As part of a larger whole, pastoral tribes are constantly pitted against other ethnic groups. In these nations, the state becomes a final authority, a higher-level regulator that attempts to limit conflict between ethnic groups. State organization arose not just to manage agricultural economies but also to regulate the activities of ethnic groups within expanding social and economic systems.

CHIEFDOMS

Having looked at bands and tribes, we turn to more complex forms of sociopolitical organization: chiefdoms and states. The first states emerged in the Old World about 5,500 years ago. The first chiefdoms developed perhaps a thousand years earlier, but few survive today. In many parts of the world the chiefdom was a transitional form of organization that emerged during the evolution of tribes into states. State formation began in Mesopotamia (currently Iran and Iraq). It next occurred in Egypt, the Indus Valley of Pakistan and India, and northern China. A few thousand years later, states also arose in two parts of the Western Hemisphere: Mesoamerica (Mexico, Guatemala,

Political organization is well developed among the Qashqai, who share their nomadic route and strategic resources with several other tribes. Here, Qashqai nomads cross a river in Iran's Fars province.

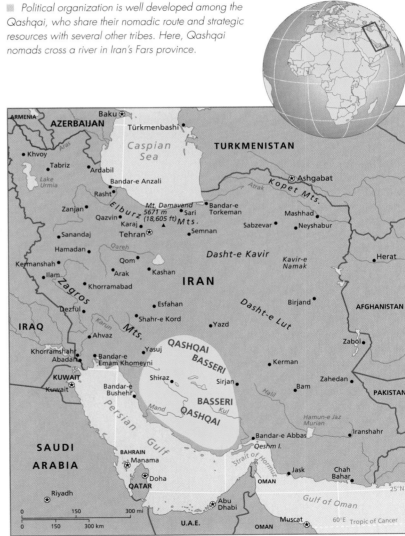

FIGURE 17.4 Location of the Basseri and Qashqai.

Perspectives on Group Membership

BACKGROUND INFORMATION

STUDENT:
Abigail Dreibelbis

SUPERVISING PROFESSOR:
Miriam Chaiken

SCHOOL:
Indiana University of Pennsylvania

YEAR IN SCHOOL/MAJOR:
Senior/Anthropology

FUTURE PLANS:
Seeking positions
in resource management
and environmental protection

PROJECT TITLE:
Delta, Delta, Delta, Can I Help Ya,
Help Ya, Help Ya

This research examines reasons why college women do or don't join sororities. Does the achieved status of sorority membership differ significantly from the mainly ascribed group memberships discussed in this chapter? Do you think that men join fraternities for the same reasons women join sororities? What relation do you see between the Greek system on college campuses and politics?

There is a human need for belonging, for affiliation. Identification with a group that has common norms and roles helps fulfill this need for security and creates social bonds that establish and assure companionship and personal identification.

This understanding has come from the study I did on members and nonmembers of social sororities at Indiana University of Pennsylvania. Since I started college, I had noticed a dichotomy between these two groups. I wanted to find out the real and perceived differences between them. My hypothesis was that there was a higher level of need for group identity and involvement in sorority members, and conversely more independence in nonmembers. I formed a survey for both groups, with questions about demographics and activities and I used open-ended questions to elicit their views and followed up with in-depth interviews to get a more personal response.

I found that participation in high school student government had been three times higher for members of sororities. This showed the great importance of social identity for Greeks, as student government members have prestige as a minority segment of the student body. Membership is competitive and based on peer acceptance. Conversely, activity in the arts was twice as high in the independent (nonsorority) group. This is a more aesthetic, personal activity, done for the act itself (singing or performing) rather than to gain the acceptance of peers.

The affinity for group identity is reflected in the expressed reasons for joining a sorority. Members found a "sense of belonging" and "self-confidence." Independents cited these same as reasons for joining, yet they saw this need as negative, and leading to a "group identity [that] is their identity." They did not like the "controlling" qualities of the sorority. The sorority member acknowledges the search for social and personal identification in a group as well as the resulting gratification in joining.

It has been hypothesized that the eldest child is the most independent. I found that twice as many nonsorority women were the oldest siblings in their family. Independents "just weren't the type" for a sorority. Nonmembers seem to find identity or belonging through other groups (volunteering, sports, honors societies) more for personal interest than social merit. This statistic seemed to support the idea that women who join sororities have a higher value of social involvement and acceptance for security and identity.

Everyone finds support and identity in groups. Groups provide safety along with a sense of personal worth and common identity with at least a few people in this vast world. Through my research I found that this need varies in degree among individuals. Those with a higher level of need find fulfillment in a social group such as a sorority. Non-Greeks do not value and are less dependent on such a social identity. These personality differences may create a sense of separation between the two groups and result in the dichotomy observed on campus.

It was fulfilling to challenge my hypothesis through questions of my own making and to come to an understanding of how and why people function. By gaining these insights on aspects of personality that underlie culture, I have developed a broader view of the intangible differences that affect our daily interactions.

Belize) and the central Andes (Peru and Bolivia). Early states are known as *archaic states,* or nonindustrial states, in contrast to modern industrial nation-states. Robert Carneiro defines the state as "an autonomous political unit encompassing many communities within its territory, having a centralized government with the power to collect taxes, draft men for work or war, and decree and enforce laws" (Carneiro 1970, p. 733).

The chiefdom and the state, like many categories used by social scientists, are *ideal types.* That is, they are labels that make social contrasts seem sharper than they really are. In reality, there is a continuum from tribe to chiefdom to state. Some societies have many attributes of chiefdoms but retain tribal features. Some advanced chiefdoms have many attributes of archaic states and thus are difficult to assign to either category. Recognizing this "continuous change" (Johnson and Earle, eds. 2000), some anthropologists speak of "complex chiefdoms" (Earle 1987), which are almost states.

Political and Economic Systems in Chiefdoms

State formation did not occur, and only chiefdoms emerged in several areas, including the circum-Caribbean (e.g., Caribbean islands, Panama, Colombia), lowland Amazonia, what is now the southeastern United States, and Polynesia. Between the emergence and spread of food production and the expansion of the Roman empire, much of Europe was organized at the chiefdom level, to which it reverted for centuries after the fall of Rome in the fifth century AD. Chiefdoms created the megalithic cultures of Europe, such as the one that built Stonehenge. Bear in mind that chiefdoms and states can fall (disintegrate) as well as rise.

Much of our ethnographic knowledge about chiefdoms comes from Polynesia (Kirch 2000), where they were common at the time of European exploration. In chiefdoms, social relations are mainly based on kinship, marriage, descent, age, generation, and gender—as they are in bands and tribes. This is a basic difference between chiefdoms and states. States bring nonrelatives together and oblige them to pledge allegiance to a government.

Unlike bands and tribes, however, chiefdoms are characterized by *permanent political regulation* of the territory they administer. Chiefdoms might include thousands of people living in many villages and/or hamlets. Regulation was carried out by the chief and his or her assistants, who occupied political offices. An **office** is a permanent position, which must be refilled when it is vacated by death or retirement. Because offices were systematically refilled, the structure of a chiefdom endured across the generations, ensuring permanent political regulation.

Stonehenge, England, and an educational display designed for tourists and visitors. Chiefdoms created the megalithic cultures of Europe, such as the one that built Stonehenge over 5,000 years ago. Between the emergence and spread of food production and the expansion of the Roman empire, much of Europe was organized at the chiefdom level, to which it reverted after the fall of Rome.

In the Polynesian chiefdoms, the chiefs were full-time political specialists in charge of regulating the economy—production, distribution, and consumption. Polynesian chiefs relied on religion to buttress their authority. They regulated production by commanding or prohibiting (using religious taboos) the cultivation of certain lands and crops. Chiefs also regulated distribution and consumption. At certain seasons—often on a ritual occasion such as a first-fruit ceremony—people would offer part of their harvest to the chief through his or her representatives. Products moved up the hierarchy, eventually reaching the chief. Conversely, illustrating obligatory sharing with kin, chiefs sponsored feasts at which they gave back much of what they had received.

Such a flow of resources to and then from a central office is known as *chiefly redistribution.* Redistribution offers economic advantages. If the different areas specialized in particular crops, goods, or services, chiefly redistribution made those products available to the whole society. Chiefly redistribution also played a role in risk management. It stimulated production beyond the immediate subsistence level and provided a central storehouse for goods that might become scarce at times of famine (Earle 1987, 1991). Chiefdoms and archaic states had similar economies, often based on intensive cultivation, and both administered systems of regional trade or exchange.

For more on prehistoric chiefdoms in the southeastern U.S., see the Internet Exercises at your OLC

mhhe.com/kottak

A French Polynesian chief wears a feather headdress at the Pacific Arts festival. How do chiefs differ from ordinary people? What kind of status do you imagine this chief has today?

Social Status in Chiefdoms

Social status in chiefdoms was based on seniority of descent. Because rank, power, prestige, and resources came through kinship and descent, Polynesian chiefs kept extremely long genealogies. Some chiefs (without writing) managed to trace their ancestry back 50 generations. All the people in the chiefdom were thought to be related to each other. Presumably, all were descended from a group of founding ancestors.

The chief (usually a man) had to demonstrate seniority in descent. Degrees of seniority were calculated so intricately on some islands that there were as many ranks as people. For example, the third son would rank below the second, who in turn would rank below the first. The children of an eldest brother, however, would all rank above the children of the next brother, whose children would in turn outrank those of younger brothers. However, even the lowest-ranking person in a chiefdom was still the chief's relative. In such a kin-based context, everyone, even a chief, had to share with his or her relatives.

Because everyone had a slightly different status, it was difficult to draw a line between elites and common people. Although other chiefdoms calculated seniority differently and had shorter genealogies than did those in Polynesia, the concern for genealogy and seniority and the absence of sharp gaps between elites and commoners were features of all chiefdoms.

Status Systems in Chiefdoms and States

The status systems of chiefdoms and states are similar in that both are based on **differential access** to resources. This means that some men and women had privileged access to power, prestige, and wealth. They controlled strategic resources such as land and water. Earle characterizes chiefs as "an incipient aristocracy with advantages in wealth and lifestyle" (1987, p. 290). Nevertheless, differential access in chiefdoms was still very much tied to kinship. The people with privileged access were generally chiefs and their nearest relatives and assistants.

Compared with chiefdoms, archaic states drew a much firmer line between elites and masses, distinguishing at least between nobles and commoners. Kinship ties did not extend from the nobles to the commoners because of *stratum endogamy*—marriage within one's own group. Commoners married commoners; elites married elites.

Such a division of society into socioeconomic strata contrasts strongly with bands and tribes, whose status systems are based on prestige, rather than on differential access to resources. The prestige differentials that do exist in bands reflect special qualities and abilities. Good hunters get respect from their fellows as long as they are generous. So does a skilled curer, dancer, storyteller—or anyone else with a talent or skill that others appreciate.

In tribes, some prestige goes to descent-group leaders, to village heads, and especially to the big man, a regional figure who commands the loyalty and labor of others. However, all these figures must be generous. If they accumulate more resources—that is, property or food—than others in the village, they must share them with the others. Since strategic resources are available to everyone, social classes based on the possession of unequal amounts of resources can never exist.

In many tribes, particularly those with patrilineal descent, men have much greater prestige and power than women do. The gender contrast in rights could diminish in chiefdoms, where prestige and access to resources were based on seniority of descent, so that some women were senior to some men. Unlike big men, chiefs were exempt from ordinary work and had rights and privileges that were unavailable to the masses. However, like big men, they still gave back much of the wealth they took in.

The Emergence of Stratification

The status system in chiefdoms, although based on differential access, differed from the status system in states because the privileged few were always relatives and assistants of the chief. However, this type of status system didn't last very long. Chiefs would start acting like kings and try to erode the kinship basis of the chiefdom. In Madagascar, they would do this by demoting their more distant relatives to commoner status and banning marriage between nobles and commoners (Kottak 1980). Such moves, *if accepted by the society,* created separate social strata—*unrelated* groups that differ in their access to wealth, prestige, and power. (A *stratum* is one of two or more groups that contrast in regard to social status and access to strategic resources. Each stratum includes people of both sexes and all ages.) The creation of separate social strata is called **stratification,** and its emergence signified the transition from chiefdom to state. *The presence and acceptance of stratification is one of the key distinguishing features of a state.*

The influential sociologist Max Weber (1922/ 1968) defined three related dimensions of social stratification: (1) Economic status, or **wealth,** encompasses all a person's material assets, including income, land, and other types of property. (2) **Power,** the ability to exercise one's will over others—to do what one wants—is the basis of political status. (3) **Prestige**—the basis of social status—refers to esteem, respect, or approval for acts, deeds, or qualities considered exemplary. Prestige, or "cultural capital" (Bourdieu 1984), provides people with a sense of worth and respect, which they may often convert into economic and political advantage (Table 17.1).

In archaic states—for the first time in human evolution—there were contrasts in wealth, power, and prestige between entire groups (social strata) of men and women. Each stratum included people of both sexes and all ages. The **superordinate** (the higher or elite) stratum had privileged access to wealth, power, and other valued resources. Access to resources by members of the **subordinate** (lower or underprivileged) stratum was limited by the privileged group.

Socioeconomic stratification continues as a defining feature of all states, archaic or industrial. The elites control a significant part of the means of production, for example, land, herds, water, capital, farms, or factories. Those born at the bottom of the hierarchy have reduced chances of social mobility. Because of elite ownership rights, ordinary people lack free access to resources.

Only in states do the elites get to keep their differential wealth. Unlike big men and chiefs, they don't have to give it back to the people whose labor has built and increased it.

Shown here in Cleveland, Ohio, in January, 2004, Rebecca Jemison meets the media after being announced as the winner of Ohio's first ($162 million) "Mega Millions" lottery. Wealth and prestige are not always correlated. Do you think Jemison's prestige will rise as a result of winning the lottery?

STATES

Table 17.2 summarizes the information presented so far on bands, tribes, chiefdoms, and states. States, remember, are autonomous political units with social classes and a formal government, based on law. States tend to be large and populous, compared to bands, tribes, and chiefdoms. Certain statuses, systems, and subsystems with specialized functions are found in all states. They include the following:

1. *Population control:* fixing of boundaries, establishment of citizenship categories, and the taking of a census.

2. *Judiciary:* laws, legal procedure, and judges.

3. *Enforcement:* permanent military and police forces.

4. *Fiscal:* taxation.

In archaic states, these subsystems were integrated by a ruling system or government composed of civil, military, and religious officials (Fried 1960).

Population Control

To know whom they govern, all states conduct censuses. States demarcate boundaries that separate them from other societies. Customs agents, immigration officers, navies, and coast guards patrol frontiers. Even nonindustrial states have

TABLE 17.1	Max Weber's Three Dimensions of Stratification	
wealth	=>	economic status
power	=>	political status
prestige	=>	social status

TABLE 17.2 Economic Basis of and Political Regulation in Bands, Tribes, Chiefdoms, and States

Sociopolitical Type	Economic Type	Examples	Type of Regulation
Band	Foraging	Inuit, San	Local
Tribe	Horticulture, pastoralism	Yanomami, Kapauku, Masai	Local, temporary regional
Chiefdom	Productive horticulture, pastoral nomadism, agriculture	Qashqai, Polynesia, Cherokee	Permanent regional
State	Agriculture, industrialism	Ancient Mesopotamia, contemporary United States and Canada	Permanent regional

To see how states are created, see the Virtual Exploration

mhhe.com/kottak

boundary-maintenance forces. In Buganda, an archaic state on the shores of Lake Victoria in Uganda, the king rewarded military officers with estates in outlying provinces. They became his guardians against foreign intrusion.

States also control population through administrative subdivision: provinces, districts, "states," counties, subcounties, and parishes. Lower-level officials manage the populations and territories of the subdivisions.

In nonstates, people work and relax with their relatives, in-laws, fictive kin, and agemates—people with whom they have a personal relationship. Such a personal social life existed throughout most of human history, but food production spelled its eventual decline. After millions of years of human evolution, it took a mere 4,000 years for the population increase and regulatory problems spawned by food production to lead from tribe to chiefdom to state. With state organization, kinship's pervasive role diminished. Descent groups may continue as kin groups within states, but their importance in political organization declines.

States foster geographic mobility and resettlement, severing long-standing ties among people, land, and kin. Population displacements have increased in the modern world. War, famine, and job seeking across national boundaries churn up migratory currents. People in states come to identify themselves by new statuses, both ascribed and achieved, including ethnic background, place of birth or residence, occupation, party, religion, and team or club affiliation, rather than only as members of a descent group or extended family.

States also manage their populations by granting different rights and obligations to citizens and noncitizens. Status distinctions among citizens are also common. Many archaic states granted different rights to nobles, commoners, and slaves. Unequal rights within state-organized societies persist in today's world. In recent American history, before the Emancipation Proclamation, there

Map Atlas

Map 13 shows the global distribution of organized states and chiefdoms on the eve of European colonization.

were different laws for slaves and free people. In European colonies, separate courts judged cases involving only natives and those that involved Europeans. In contemporary America, a military code of justice and court system continue to coexist alongside the civil judiciary.

Judiciary

States have *laws* based on precedent and legislative proclamations. Without writing, laws may be preserved in oral tradition, with justices, elders, and other specialists responsible for remembering them. Oral traditions as repositories of legal wisdom have continued in some nations with writing, such as Great Britain. Laws regulate relations between individuals and groups.

Crimes are violations of the legal code, with specified types of punishment. However, a given act, such as killing someone, may be legally defined in different ways (e.g., as manslaughter, justifiable homicide, or first-degree murder). Furthermore, even in contemporary North America, where justice is supposed to be "blind" to social distinctions, the poor are prosecuted more often and more severely than are the rich.

To handle disputes and crimes, all states have courts and judges. Precolonial African states had subcounty, county, and district courts, plus a high court formed by the king or queen and his or her advisers. Most states allow appeals to higher courts, although people are encouraged to solve problems locally.

A striking contrast between states and nonstates is intervention in family affairs. In states, aspects of parenting and marriage enter the domain of public law. Governments step in to halt blood feuds and regulate previously private disputes. States attempt to curb *internal* conflict, but they aren't always successful. About 85 percent of the world's armed conflicts since 1945 have begun within states—in efforts to overthrow a ruling regime or as disputes over tribal, religious, and ethnic minority issues. Only 15 percent have been fights across national borders (Barnaby 1984). Rebellion, resistance, repression, terrorism, and warfare continue. Indeed, recent states have perpetrated some of history's bloodiest deeds.

Enforcement

All states have agents to enforce judicial decisions. Confinement requires jailers, and a death penalty calls for executioners. Agents of the state collect fines and confiscate property. These officials wield real power.

As a relatively new form of sociopolitical organization, states have competed successfully with less-complex societies throughout the world. Military organization helps states subdue neighboring nonstates, but this is not the only reason for the spread of state organization. Although states impose hardships, they also offer advantages. More obviously, they provide protection from outsiders and preserve internal order. By promoting internal peace, states enhance production. Their economies support massive, dense populations, which supply armies and colonists to promote expansion.

Fiscal Systems

A financial or **fiscal** system is needed in states to support rulers, nobles, officials, judges, military personnel, and thousands of other specialists. As in the chiefdom, the state intervenes in production, distribution, and consumption. The state may decree that a certain area will produce certain things or forbid certain activities in particular places. Although, like chiefdoms, states also have redistribution (through taxation), generosity and sharing are played down. A smaller proportion of what comes in flows back to the people.

In nonstates, people customarily share with relatives, but residents of states face added obligations to bureaucrats and officials. Citizens must turn over a substantial portion of what they produce to the state. Of the resources that the state collects, it reallocates part for the general good and uses another part (often larger) for the elite.

The state does not bring more freedom or leisure to the common people, who usually work harder than do the people in nonstates. They may be called on to build monumental public works. Some of these projects, such as dams and irrigation systems, may be economically necessary. However, people also build temples, palaces, and tombs for the elites.

Markets and trade are usually under at least some state control, with officials overseeing distribution and exchange, standardizing weights and measures, and collecting taxes on goods passing into or through the state. Taxes support

government and the ruling class, which is clearly separated from the common people in regard to activities, privileges, rights, and obligations. Taxes also support the many specialists: administrators, tax collectors, judges, lawmakers, generals, scholars, and priests. As the state matures, the segment of the population freed from direct concern with subsistence grows.

The elites of archaic states reveled in the consumption of *sumptuary goods:* jewelry, exotic food and drink, and stylish clothing reserved for, or affordable only by, the rich. Peasants' diets suffered as they struggled to meet government demands. Commoners might perish in territorial wars that had little relevance to their own needs. Are any of these observations true of contemporary states?

To handle disputes and crimes, all states, including Bermuda, shown here, have courts and judges. Does this photo say anything about cultural diffusion and/or colonialism?

SOCIAL CONTROL

Previous sections of this chapter have focused more on formal political organization than on political process. We've considered political regulation in various types of societies, using such convenient labels as *bands, tribes, chiefdoms,* and *states.* We've seen how the scale and strength of political systems have expanded over time and in relation to major economic changes, such as the origin and spread of food production. We've examined reasons why disputes arise and how they are settled in various types of society. We've looked at political decision making, including leaders and their limits. We've also recognized that all contemporary humans have been affected by states, colonialism, and the spread of the modern world system.

In this section we'll see that political systems have their more subtle and informal aspects along with their public and formal dimensions. In

Bringing It All Together

The "Bringing It All Together" essay that immediately follows the chapter on gender discusses the Basques, a minority population and imagined community split between, and subject to the governments of, two nation-states—France and Spain. States have to deal with the conflicting interests of diverse groups within their borders.

studying systems of domination—whether political, economic, religious, or cultural—we must pay attention not only to the formal institutions but to other forms of social control as well. Broader than the political is the concept of **social control,** which refers to "those fields of the social system (beliefs, practices, and institutions) that are most actively involved in the maintenance of any norms and the regulation of any conflict" (N. Kottak 2002, p. 290). (*Norms* are cultural standards or guidelines that enable individuals to distinguish between appropriate and inappropriate behavior.)

Hegemony

Antonio Gramsci (1971) developed the concept of **hegemony** for a stratified social order in which subordinates comply with domination by internalizing their rulers' values and accepting the "naturalness" of domination (this is the way things were meant to be). According to Pierre Bourdieu (1977, p. 164), every social order tries to make its own arbitrariness (including its mechanisms of control and oppression) seem natural. All hegemonic ideologies offer explanations about why the existing order is in everyone's interest. Often promises are made (things will get better if you're patient). Gramsci and others use the idea of hegemony to explain why people conform even when they are not forced to do so.

■ *Because of its costumed anonymity, Carnaval is an excellent arena for expressing normally suppressed speech. Here a man peeks out of the mouth of a giant mask during the parade of the São Clemente Samba school in Rio de Janeiro, Brazil, on March 1, 2003. Is there anything like Carnaval in your society?*

Both Bourdieu (1977) and Michel Foucault (1979) argue that it is easier and more effective to dominate people in their minds than to try to control their bodies. Besides, and often replacing, gross physical violence, industrial societies have devised more insidious forms of social control. These include various techniques of persuading and managing people and of monitoring and recording their beliefs, activities, and contacts. Can you think of some contemporary examples?

Hegemony, the internalization of a dominant ideology, is one way in which elites curb resistance and maintain power. Another way is to make subordinates believe they eventually will gain power—as young people usually foresee when they let their elders dominate them. Another way of curbing resistance is to separate or isolate people while supervising them closely, as is done in prisons. According to Foucault (1979), describing control over prisoners, solitary confinement is one effective way to get them to submit to authority.

Weapons of the Weak

The analysis of political systems also should consider the behavior that lies beneath the surface of evident, public behavior. In public, the oppressed may seem to accept their own domination, even as they question it offstage in private. James Scott (1990) uses **"public transcript"** to describe the open, public interactions between superordinates and subordinates—the outer shell of power relations. He uses **"hidden transcript"** to describe the critique of power that goes on offstage, where the power holders can't see it. In public, the elites and the oppressed observe the etiquette of power relations. The dominants act like haughty masters while their subordinates show humility and defer.

Often, situations that seem to be hegemonic do have active resistance, but it is individual and disguised rather than collective and defiant. James Scott (1985) uses Malay peasants, among whom he did field work, to illustrate small-scale acts of resistance—which he calls "weapons of the weak." The Malay peasants used an indirect strategy to resist an Islamic tithe (religious tax). Peasants were expected to pay the tithe, usually in the form of rice, which was sent to the provincial capital. In theory, the tithe would come back as charity, but it never did. Peasants didn't resist the tithe by rioting, demonstrating, or protesting. Instead they used a "nibbling" strategy, based on small acts of resistance. For example, they failed to declare their land or lied about the amount they farmed. They underpaid or delivered rice contaminated with water, rocks, or mud, to add weight. Because of this resistance, only 15 percent of what was due actually was paid (Scott 1990, p. 89).

Subordinates also use various strategies to resist *publicly,* but, again, usually in disguised form. Discontent may be expressed in public rituals and language, including metaphors, euphemisms, and folk tales. For example, trickster tales (like the Brer Rabbit stories told by slaves in the southern United States) celebrate the wiles of the weak as they triumph over the strong.

Resistance is most likely to be expressed openly when people are allowed to assemble. The hidden transcript may be publicly revealed on such occasions. People see their dreams and anger shared by others with whom they haven't been in direct contact. The oppressed may draw courage from the crowd, from its visual and emotional impact and its anonymity. Sensing danger, the elites discourage such public gatherings. They try to limit and control holidays, funerals, dances, festivals, and other occasions that might unite the oppressed. Thus, in the pre–Civil War era southern United States, gatherings of five or more slaves were forbidden unless a white person was present.

Factors that interfere with community formation—such as geographic, linguistic, and ethnic separation—also work to curb resistance. Consequently, southern U.S. plantation owners sought slaves with diverse cultural and linguistic backgrounds. Despite the measures used to divide them, the slaves resisted, developing their own popular culture, linguistic codes, and religious vision. The masters taught portions of the Bible that stressed compliance, but the slaves seized on the story of Moses, the promised land, and deliverance. The cornerstone of slave religion became the idea of a reversal in the conditions of whites and blacks. Slaves also resisted directly, through sabotage and flight. In many New World areas, slaves managed to establish free communities in the hills and other isolated areas (Price 1973).

Hidden transcripts tend to be expressed publicly at certain times (festivals and *Carnavals*) and in certain places (for example, markets). Because of its costumed anonymity, Carnaval is an excellent arena for expressing normally suppressed speech and aggression—antihegemonic discourse. (*Discourse* includes talk, speeches, gestures, and actions.) Carnavals celebrate freedom through immodesty, dancing, gluttony, and sexuality (DaMatta 1991). Carnaval may begin as a playful outlet for frustrations built up during the year. Over time, it may evolve into a powerful annual critique of stratification and domination and thus a threat to the established order (Gilmore 1987). (Recognizing that ceremonial license could turn into political defiance, the Spanish dictator Francisco Franco outlawed Carnaval.)

Politics, Shame, and Sorcery

We turn now to a case study of sociopolitical process, viewing it as part of a larger system of social control experienced by individuals in their everyday lives. No one today lives in an isolated band, tribe, chiefdom, or state. All groups studied by ethnographers, like the Makua to be discussed below, live in nation-states, where individuals have to deal with various levels and types of political authority, and experience other forms of social control.

Nicholas Kottak (2002) did an ethnographic field study of political systems, and social control more generally, among the rural Makua of northern Mozambique (Figure 17.5). He focused on three fields of social control: political, religious, and reputational systems. (Reputational systems have to do with the way various people are considered in the community—their reputations.) The significance of these fields emerged through conversations about social norms and crimes. Makua revealed their own ideas about social control most clearly in a discussion about stealing a neighbor's chicken.

Most Makua villagers have a makeshift chicken coop in a corner of the home. Chickens leave the coop before sunrise each day and wander in the surrounding area in search of scraps. Chickens usually return to their coop at dusk, but sometimes the chickens, often recently purchased ones, settle in

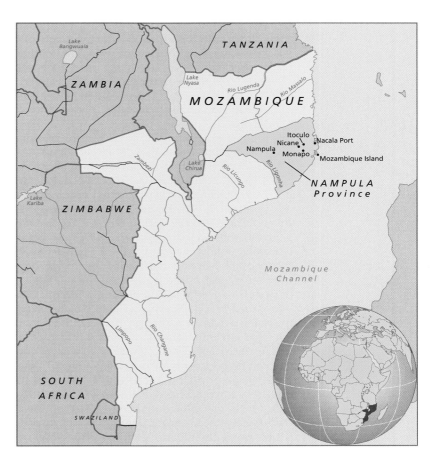

FIGURE 17.5 Location of the Makua and the village of Nicane in northern Mozambique. The province of Nampula shown here is Makua territory.

another villager's coop. Villagers worry about their chickens as mobile assets. Owners can't always be sure where their birds are roaming. Villagers may be tempted to steal a neighbor's chicken when its owner seems oblivious to its whereabouts.

The Makua have few material possessions and a meat-poor diet, making wandering chickens a temptation. As the Makua identified chicken wandering and the occasional chicken theft as community problems, Kottak began to draw out their ideas about social control—about why people did *not* steal their neighbor's chickens. The Makua responses coalesced around three main disincentives or sanctions: *ehaya* (shame), *enretthe* (sorcery attack), and *cadeia* (jail). (As used here, a *sanction* refers to a kind of punishment that follows a norm violation.)

According to Kottak (2002), each of these terms (jail, sorcery, and shame) refers to an imagined "social script," culminating in an undesirable consequence. *Cadeia* (jail), for instance, represents the potential last phase of an extended political and legal process (most violations are resolved before this point). When the Makua responded *enretthe* (sorcery), they were referring to another sequence that might follow the chicken theft. They believed that once the neighbor discovered his chicken had been stolen, he would go to a traditional healer (*mukulukhana*), who would direct a sorcery attack (*opaka enretthe*) on his behalf. The Makua believed that such a punitive sorcery attack would either kill the thief or make him extremely ill.

The third and most popular answer to the chicken theft question was *ehaya* (shame). In the *ehaya* social script, the chicken thief, having been discovered, would have to attend a formal, publicly organized village meeting, where political authorities would meet to determine the appropriate punishment and compensation. Makua were concerned not so much with the fine as with the intense shame or embarrassment they would feel as a confirmed chicken thief in the village

spotlight. The chicken thief also would experience an extended feeling of disgrace, also described as *ehaya*, from his or her knowledge of his or her now spoiled social identity or community reputation.

Living in a nation-state, the Makua have access to several types and levels of potential conflict resolution. A dispute between two people can quickly become a broader conflict between their respective matrilineal descent groups. (In a matrilineal descent group, kinship is calculated through females only—see the next chapter.) The heads of the disputing descent groups meet to resolve the matter. If they can't settle it (e.g., through financial compensation), the conflict moves to a state political authority. Intervention by this official can prevent the individual dispute from escalating into ongoing conflict between the descent groups (e.g., a blood feud, as described earlier in this chapter).

Mozambique has a history of colonialism (under Portugal), independence (achieved late, in 1975), and bloody civil war (1984–1992). Because of this history, its formal authorities have been split into two opposing political fields: the state-appointed and the more "traditional" authorities. Shortly after Mozambique's independence from Portugal, its ruling Marxist political party, *Frelimo*, handpicked a village secretary (*secretário*) for each village. Frelimo had launched a program of villagization, in which rural people were required to move from hamlets dispersed throughout the countryside into nucleated villages. Much of the rural Makua population was upset with both the forced villagization program and the new set of authorities. This resentment helped sustain Mozambique's civil war. After the war, Frelimo made significant efforts to work with the traditional authorities (*regulo, cabo,* and *capitão*)—political leaders whom Frelimo had initially accused of being "colonial collaborators" and alienated. The *regulo* is a territorial chief and succeeds to his political office through matrilineal descent (mother's brother to sister's son). Below him are *cabos*, and below them are *capitães*.

Few village conflicts go beyond the jurisdiction of the locality administrator (*ensatoro*)—an even higher political office that, according to the Makua, originated early in the colonial era. It is this locality administrator (*ensatoro*) who dispatches the police and periodically detains villagers. Thus, he explicitly has control over the state's use of force. Although *regulos* (traditional chiefs) increasingly meet directly with the *ensatoro*, *secretários* (recently appointed state officials) have even better relations with the *ensatoro*. Since access to force strengthens political authority, the *secretário*'s closer link to the *ensatoro* confers a degree of legitimacy. However, most villagers still rank the *regulo* higher in the political hierarchy than the *secretário* and prefer that he handle their conflicts and problems. The *regulo*'s legitimacy derives from the sanctity of the matrilineal principle of descent through which he holds office.

This combination of newer and more traditional offices constitutes the Makua's formal political system. This system, despite its duality, includes legitimate positions and officials and represents formal social control. This "political" part of the Makua social system has been explicitly or "formally" designated to handle conflict and crime. As has been discussed in previous sections of this chapter, anthropologists have tended to focus on the formal aspects of social control (i.e., the political field). But, like the Makua, anthropologists also recognize the importance of other fields of social control. When Nicholas Kottak asked Makua in one rural community about deterrents to theft, only 10 percent mentioned jail (the formal system), compared with the 73 percent who listed *ehaya* (shame) as the reason not to steal a neighbor's chicken.

Shame can be a powerful social sanction. Bronislaw Malinowski (1927) described how Trobriand Islanders might climb to the top of a palm tree and dive to their deaths because they couldn't tolerate the shame associated with public knowledge of some stigmatizing action, especially incest. Makua tell the story of a man rumored to have fathered a child with his stepdaughter. The political authorities imposed no formal sanctions (e.g., a fine or jail time) on this man, but gossip about the affair circulated widely. The gossip crystallized in the lyrics of a song that groups of young women would perform. When the man heard his name and alleged incestuous behavior mentioned in that song, he told a few people he was going to take a trip to the district capital. He was found a few hours later hanging by the neck from a mango tree on the village periphery. The reason for the man's suicide was self-evident to the Makua—"he felt too much *ehaya* (shame)." (Previously we saw the role of song in the social control system of the Inuit.)

Many anthropologists cite the importance of "informal" processes of social control, which include gossip, stigma, and shame, especially in small-scale societies such as the Makua (see Freilich, Raybeck, and Savishinsky 1991). Gossip, which can lead to shame, sometimes is used when a direct or formal sanction is risky or impossible (Herskovits 1937). Margaret Mead (1937) and Ruth Benedict (1946) distinguished between *shame* as an external sanction (i.e., forces set in motion by others) and *guilt* as an internal sanction, psychologically generated by the individual. They regarded shame as a more prominent form of social control in non-Western societies and guilt as a dominant emotional sanction in Western societies.

Of course, to be effective as a sanction, the prospect of being shamed or of shaming oneself must be internalized by the individual. For the Makua, potential shame is a powerful deterrent. Rural Makua tend to remain in or around one community for their entire lives. Such communities usually have fewer than a thousand people, so that residents can keep track of most community members' identities and reputations. According to Kottak (2002), the rural Makua monitor, transmit, and memorize the details of each other's identities with remarkable precision. Tight clustering of homes, markets, and schools facilitates the monitoring process. In this social environment, people try to avoid behavior that might spoil their reputations and alienate them from their native community.

Beliefs in sorcery also facilitate social control. (Religion as social control is discussed further in the chapter on religion.) Although the Makua constantly discuss the existence of sorcerers (*nikwiri*) and sorcery (*opaka enretthe*), they aren't explicit about who the sorcerers are. This identity ambiguity is coupled with a local theory of sorcery that strongly implicates malice, which everyone feels at some point. Having felt malice themselves, individual Makua probably experience moments of self-doubt about their own potential status as a sorcerer. And they recognize that others have similar feelings.

Beliefs in sorcery trigger anxieties about death, since the Makua think that a chicken thief will be the inevitable target of a vengeance sorcery attack. Local theories presume that sickness, social misfortune, and death are directly caused by malicious sorcery. Life expectancy is relatively short and infant mortality very high in a Makua village. Relatives drop dead suddenly from infectious diseases. Health, life, and existence are far more problematic than they are for most Westerners. Such uncertainty heightens the dramatic stakes associated with sorcery. Not just theft, but any conflict, is inherently dangerous because it could trigger a sorcery attack.

The following dialogue reported by Kottak (2002, p. 312) highlights the Makua's recognition of sorcery as a social control process.

Ethnographer: Why don't you steal your neighbor's chicken?

Informant: Huh? My neighbor's not short a chicken.

Ethnographer: No. I know. Your neighbor has a chicken. That chicken is always walking on your land. Sometimes it sleeps in your coop at night. Why don't you just take that chicken? What do you think is stopping you?

Informant: *Enretthe. Akwa.* (Sorcery. Death.)

The efficacy of social control depends on how clearly people envision the sanctions that an antisocial act might trigger. The Makua are well informed about norm violations, conflicts, and the sanctions that follow them. As we have seen, jail (*cadeia*), shame (*ehaya*), and sorcery (*enretthe*) are the main sanctions anticipated by the rural Makua.

This chapter began by quoting Fried's definition of political organization as comprising "those portions of social organization that specifically relate to the individuals or groups that manage the affairs of public policy" (Fried 1967, pp. 20–21). As I noted there, Fried's definition works nicely for nation-states but not so well for nonstate societies, where "public policy" is much harder to detect. For this reason, I claimed it was better to focus on sociopolitical organization in discussing the regulation of interrelations among individuals, groups, and their representatives. (Regulation, remember, is the process that corrects deviations from the norm, and thus maintains a system's integrity.) Such regulation, we have learned, is a process that extends beyond the political to other fields of social control, including religion and reputational systems, which involve an interplay of public opinion with social norms and sanctions internalized by the individual.

SUMMARY

1. One sociopolitical typology classifies societies as bands, tribes, chiefdoms, and states. Foragers tended to live in egalitarian band-organized societies. Personal networks linked individuals, families, and bands. Band leaders were first among equals, with no sure way to enforce decisions. Disputes rarely arose over strategic resources, which were open to all. Political authority and power tend to increase along with population and the scale of regulatory problems. More people mean more relations among individuals and groups to regulate. Increasingly complex economies pose further regulatory problems.

2. Heads of horticultural villages are local leaders with limited authority. They lead by example and persuasion. Big men have support and authority beyond a single village. They are regional regulators, but temporary ones. In organizing a feast, they mobilize labor from several villages. Sponsoring such events leaves them with little wealth but with prestige and a reputation for generosity.

3. Age and gender also can be used for regional political integration. Among North America's Plains Indians, men's associations (pantribal sodalities) organized raiding and buffalo hunting. Such men's associations tend to emphasize the warrior grade. They serve for offense and defense when there is intertribal raiding for animals. Among pastoralists, the degree of authority and political organization reflects population size and density, interethnic relations, and pressure on resources.

4. The state is an autonomous political unit that encompasses many communities. Its government collects taxes, drafts people for work and war, and decrees and enforces laws. The state is defined as a form of sociopolitical organization based on central government and social stratification—a division of society into classes. Early states are known as archaic, or nonindustrial, states, in contrast to modern industrial nation-states.

5. Unlike tribes, but like states, chiefdoms had permanent regional regulation and differential access to resources. But chiefdoms lacked stratification. Unlike states, but like bands and tribes, chiefdoms were organized by kinship, descent, and marriage. State formation did not occur, and only chiefdoms emerged in several areas, including the circum-Caribbean, lowland Amazonia, the southeastern United States, and Polynesia.

6. Weber's three dimensions of stratification are wealth, power, and prestige. In early states—for the first time in human history—contrasts in wealth, power, and prestige between entire groups of men and women came into being. A socioeconomic stratum includes people of both sexes and all ages. The superordinate—higher or elite—stratum enjoys privileged access to resources.

7. Certain systems are found in all states: population control, judiciary, enforcement, and fiscal. These are integrated by a ruling system or government composed of civil, military, and religious officials. States conduct censuses and demarcate boundaries. Laws are based on precedent and legislative

proclamations. Courts and judges handle disputes and crimes. A police force maintains internal order, and a military defends against external threats. A financial or fiscal system supports rulers, officials, judges, and other specialists.

8. *Hegemony* describes a stratified social order in which subordinates comply with domination by internalizing its values and accepting its "naturalness." Often, situations that appear hegemonic have resistance that is individual and disguised rather than collective and defiant. "Public transcript" refers to the open, public interactions between the dominators and the oppressed. "Hidden transcript" describes the critique of power that goes on offstage, where the power holders can't see it. Discontent also may be expressed in public rituals and language.

9. Broader than the political is the concept of social control—those fields of the social system most actively involved in the maintenance of norms and the regulation of conflict. Among the Makua of northern Mozambique, three such fields stand out: the political system (formal authority), religion (mainly involving fear of sorcery), and the reputational system (mainly involving avoidance of shame). Social control works best when people can clearly envision the sanctions that an antisocial act might trigger. The Makua are well informed about norm violations, conflicts, and the sanctions that follow them. Jail, shame, and sorcery attacks are the main sanctions anticipated by the rural Makua.

KEY TERMS

See the flash cards
mhhe.com/kottak

age set   Group uniting all men or women born during a certain time span; this group controls property and often has political and military functions.

big man   Regional figure found among tribal horticulturalists and pastoralists. The big man occupies no office but creates his reputation through entrepreneurship and generosity to others. Neither his wealth nor his position passes to his heirs.

chiefdom   Form of sociopolitical organization intermediate between the tribe and the state; kin-based with differential access to resources and a permanent political structure.

differential access   Unequal access to resources; basic attribute of chiefdoms and states. Superordinates have favored access to such resources, while the access of subordinates is limited by superordinates.

fiscal   Pertaining to finances and taxation.

head, village   A local leader in a tribal society who has limited authority, leads by example and persuasion, and must be generous.

hegemony   As used by Antonio Gramsci, a stratified social order in which subordinates comply with domination by internalizing its values and accepting its "naturalness."

hidden transcript   As used by James Scott, the critique of power by the oppressed that goes on offstage—in private—where the power holders can't see it.

law   A legal code, including trial and enforcement; characteristic of state-organized societies.

office   Permanent political position.

power   The ability to exercise one's will over others—to do what one wants; the basis of political status.

prestige   Esteem, respect, or approval for acts, deeds, or qualities considered exemplary.

public transcript   As used by James Scott, the open, public interactions between dominators and oppressed—the outer shell of power relations.

social control   Those fields of the social system (beliefs, practices, and institutions) that are most actively involved in the maintenance of norms and the regulation of conflict.

sodality, pantribal   A non-kin-based group that exists throughout a tribe, spanning several villages.

state   Sociopolitical organization based on central government and socioeconomic stratification—a division of society into classes.

stratification   Characteristic of a system with socioeconomic strata—groups that contrast in regard to social status and access to strategic resources. Each stratum includes people of both sexes and all ages.

subordinate   The lower, or underprivileged, group in a stratified system.

superordinate   The upper, or privileged, group in a stratified system.

tribe   Form of sociopolitical organization usually based on horticulture or pastoralism. Socioeconomic stratification and centralized rule are absent in tribes, and there is no means of enforcing political decisions.

wealth   All a person's material assets, including income, land, and other types of property; the basis of economic status.

CRITICAL THINKING QUESTIONS

For more self-testing, see the self-quizzes

mhhe.com/kottak

1. What's the rationale for using the term "sociopolitical organization" instead of "political organization"?

2. How do the political roles of village head and big man differ? Does your own society have figures comparable to big men?

3. What are sodalities? Does your society have them? Do you belong to any?

4. What conclusions do you draw from this chapter about the relationship between population density and political hierarchy?

5. What are the advantages and disadvantages of the state from the ordinary citizen's perspective?

SUGGESTED ADDITIONAL READINGS

Arnold, B., and B. Gibson, eds.
1995 *Celtic Chiefdom, Celtic State.* New York: Cambridge University Press. This collection of articles examines the structure and development of Europe's prehistoric Celtic societies and debates whether they were chiefdoms or states.

Borneman, J.
1998 *Subversions of International Order: Studies in the Political Anthropology of Culture.* Albany: State University of New York Press. Political culture, international relations, world politics, and national characteristics.

Chagnon, N. A.
1997 *Yanomamö,* 5th ed. Fort Worth: Harcourt Brace. Most recent revision of a well-known account of the Yanomami, including their social organization, politics, warfare, and cultural change, and the crisis they now confront.

Cheater, A. P., ed.
1999 *The Anthropology of Power: Empowerment and Disempowerment in Changing Structures.* New York: Routledge. Overcoming social marginality through participation and political mobilization in today's world.

Cohen, R., and E. R. Service, eds.
1978 *Origins of the State: The Anthropology of Political Evolution.* Philadelphia: Institute for the Study of Human Issues. Several articles on state formation in many areas.

Earle, T. K.
1997 *How Chiefs Come to Power: The Political Economy in Prehistory.* Stanford, CA: Stanford University Press. Political succession and the economic basis of power in chiefdoms.

Ferguson, R. B.
1995 *Yanomami Warfare: A Political History.* Santa Fe, NM: School of American Research. From village raiding to incursions from nation-states.
2002 *State, Identity, and Violence: Political Disintegration in the Post–Cold War Era.* New York: Routledge. Political relations, the state, ethnic relations, and violence.

Fry, D. P.
2006 *The Human Potential for Peace: An Anthropological Challenge to Assumptions about War and Violence.* New York: Oxford University Press. Is war inevitable?

Gledhill, J.
2000 *Power and Its Disguises: Anthropological Perspectives on Politics.* Sterling, VA: Pluto Press. The anthropology of power.

Heider, K. G.
1997 *Grand Valley Dani: Peaceful Warriors,* 3rd ed. Fort Worth: Harcourt Brace. Comprehensive and readable account of a tribal group on the island of New Guinea, now under Indonesian rule.

Kelly, R. C.
2000 *Warless Societies and the Origin of War.* Ann Arbor, MI: University of Michigan Press. An anthropologist looks at stateless societies in Papua New Guinea to reconstruct the origins of warfare.

Kirch, P. V.
1984 *The Evolution of the Polynesian Chiefdoms.* Cambridge: Cambridge University Press. Diversity and sociopolitical complexity in native Oceania.

Kurtz, D. V.
2001 *Political Anthropology: Power and Paradigms.* Boulder, CO: Westview. Up-to-date treatment of the field of political anthropology.

Otterbein, K.
2005 *How War Began.* College Station: Texas A&M University Press. The origins of war discussed in terms of human evolution, prehistory, and cross-cultural comparison.

Vincent, J., ed.
2002 *The Anthropology of Politics: A Reader in Ethnography, Theory, and Critique.* Malden, MA: Blackwell. Basic and classic articles in political anthropology.

Wolf, E. R., with S. Silverman
2001 *Pathways of Power: Building an Anthropology of the Modern World.* Berkeley: University of California Press. Political and social identity and power in the modern world.

1. Subsistence and Status: Go to the Ethnographic Atlas Cross-tabulations page, **http://lucy.ukc. ac.uk/cgi-bin/uncgi/Ethnoatlas/atlas.vopts**. This site has compiled ethnographic information on many different groups, and you can use the tools provided to cross-tabulate the prevalence of certain traits. Under "Select Row Category" choose "subsistence economy," and under "Select Column Category" select "class stratification, prevailing type." Press the Submit Query button. This table shows the frequency of class stratification among groups with different subsistence strategies.
    a. What kinds of subsistence strategies are most common among groups with "Complex" class stratification? Do any of these groups use hunting, gathering, or fishing as the primary means of feeding themselves?
    b. Is any one subsistence strategy predominant among groups with "Absence among freemen" class stratification (egalitarian)?
    c. Looking at the table, which of the following statements is (are) true: All societies with complex class stratification are agriculturalists. All agriculturalists have complex class stratification. No societies that practice hunting, fishing, and gathering have complex class stratification. All hunting, fishing, and gathering societies have class stratification absent among freemen (egalitarian).

2. Read the Mesa Community College page on "A Look at a Bigman: Bougainville," **http://www. mc.maricopa.edu/dept/d10/asb/anthro2003/ glues/bigman/mumi.html**, and the "35 Key Rules for Bougainville Bigmen," **http://www. mc.maricopa.edu/dept/d10/asb/anthro2003/ glues/bigman/rules.html**.

a. Where is Bougainville? What is the environment like? What are the main sources of food?
b. What is a *mumi*? How does one become a *mumi*? What role do feasts play in determining who is a *mumi*? How important are friends and family for an aspiring *mumi*?
c. What other statuses exist in Bougainville society for men?
d. After reading the rules for a bigman, does the life of a bigman appear to be a life of leisure or does it involve a lot of work?

3. In the year 2000, the field of anthropology was jolted by the announcement of the publication of a book called *Darkness in El Dorado* by the journalist Patrick Tierney (New York: W. W. Norton, 2000). The book contained accusations of inappropriate, unethical, and perhaps even criminal behavior by scientists who had studied the Yanomami Indians of Brazil and Venezuela since the late 1960s.
a. For a brief account of the controversy, check out **dir.salon.com/books/feature/2000/09/ 28/yanomamo/index.html**.
b. Visit the website "The Anthropological Niche of Douglas W. Hume," **http://members.aol. com/archaeodog/darkness_in_el_dorado/ index.htm**. This website is dedicated to providing one place to find all information about Patrick Tierney's *Darkness in El Dorado*. Follow its various links for different accounts of the controversy.
c. What do you make of the controversy? Is it possible to choose sides from the information you have examined?
d. What are the larger ethical issues raised by the furor surrounding Tierney's book?

See Chapter 17 at your McGraw-Hill Online Learning Center for additional review and interactive exercises.

INTERNET EXERCISES

Kottak, *Assault on Paradise*, 4th ed.

Read Chapters 5, 9, and 14 for changes in Arembepe's political organization and orientation from the 1960s through the present. What have been the major changes? Has anything remained the same? Describe Arembepe's patronage system during the 1960s. As discussed in Chapter 5, how does patron-clientship differ from patron-dependency? Have there been leaders in Arembepe? If so, describe their roles and spheres of influence and compare them with the band and tribal leaders discussed in this chapter of the text.

Peters-Golden, *Culture Sketches*, 4th ed.

This text chapter has discussed the formal and informal leadership roles found in various societies, among them that of the "big man." In *Culture Sketches* read Chapter 8, "Kapauku: New Guinea 'Capital-

ists.'" An important role in Kapauku society is that of the *tonowi*, a "big man." How is this leadership role related to the other key features of Kapauku society, such as individualism and economics?

Knauft, *The Gebusi*, 1st ed.

Based on information in Chapter 3 of *The Gebusi*, who was the person most responsible for organizing and orchestrating the community's response to the death of Daguwa? How did this person exert influence or authority, and in what ways did he or did he not serve as a political leader? How does the Gebusi political structure differ from that in societies that have formal leaders, chiefs, and/or class stratification? Although Gebusi politics are decentralized, important status inequalities still remain. What are the greatest social inequalities in Gebusi society? Who has more power, and who has less?

LINKAGES

18

Families, Kinship, and Descent

CHAPTER OUTLINE

FAMILIES

The kinds of societies anthropologists have studied traditionally, such as the Barí discussed in the "News Brief," have stimulated a strong interest in families, along with larger systems of kinship, descent, and marriage. Cross-culturally, the social construction of kinship illustrates considerable diversity. Understanding kinship systems has become an essential part of anthropology because of the importance of those systems to the people we study. We are ready to take a closer look at the systems of kinship and descent that have organized human life during much of our history.

Ethnographers quickly recognize social divisions—groups—within any society they study. During field work, they learn about significant groups by observing their activities and composition. People often live in the same village or neighborhood or work, pray, or celebrate together because they are related in some way. To understand the social structure, an ethnographer must investigate such kin ties. For example, the most significant local groups may consist of descendants of the same grandfather. These people may live in neighboring houses, farm adjoining fields, and help each other in everyday tasks. Other sorts of groups, based on different or more distant kin links, get together less often.

The nuclear family is one kind of kin group that is widespread in human societies. The nuclear family consists of parents and children, normally living together in the same household. Other kin groups include extended families (families consisting of three or more generations) and descent groups—lineages and clans. Such groups are not usually residentially based as the nuclear family is. Extended family members get together from time to time, but they don't necessarily live together. Branches of a given descent group may reside in several villages and rarely assemble for common activity. Descent groups, which are composed of people claiming common ancestry, are basic units in the social organization of nonindustrial food producers.

Nuclear and Extended Families

A nuclear family lasts only as long as the parents and children remain together. Most people belong to at least two nuclear families at different

OVERVIEW

Especially in nonindustrial societies, kinship, descent, and marriage are basic social building blocks, linking individuals and groups in a common social system. Kin groups, such as families and descent groups, are social units whose members can be identified and whose residence patterns and activities can be observed. A nuclear family, for instance, consists of a married couple and their children, living together. Although nuclear families are widespread among the world's societies, other social forms, such as extended families and descent groups, can complement, overshadow, or even replace the nuclear family. Contemporary industrial North America features diverse and changing family, household, and living arrangements, including nuclear families, single-parent households, and expanded family households. Descent groups, typically found among nonindustrial food producers, have perpetuity—they last for generations. Descent groups include lineages and clans, with patrilineal or matrilineal membership rules. Kinship terminologies are ways of classifying one's relatives based on perceived differences and similarities. Worldwide, there are four basic systems for classifying kin on the parental generation.

times in their lives. They are born into a family consisting of their parents and siblings. When they reach adulthood, they may marry and establish a nuclear family that includes the spouse and eventually the children. Since most societies permit divorce, some people establish more than one family through marriage.

Anthropologists distinguish between the **family of orientation** (the family in which one is born and grows up) and the **family of procreation** (formed when one marries and has children). From the individual's point of view, the critical relationships are with parents and siblings in the family of orientation and with spouse and children in the family of procreation.

In most societies, relations with nuclear family members (parents, siblings, and children) take precedence over relations with other kin. Nuclear family organization is very widespread but not universal, and its significance in society differs greatly from one place to another. In a few societies, such as the classic Nayar case described below, nuclear families are rare or nonexistent. In others, the nuclear family plays no special role in social life. The nuclear family is not always the

■ Siblings play a prominent role in child rearing in many societies. Here, in China's Yunnan province, two sisters give their younger brother a drink of water from a folded leaf. Do your siblings belong to your family of orientation or your family of procreation?

When Are Two Dads Better Than One?
When the Women Are in Charge

UNIVERSITY OF EAST LONDON NEWS BRIEF

by Patrick Wilson
June 12, 2002

The kinds of societies that anthropologists have studied traditionally, such as the Barí of Venezuela described in this news story, have stimulated a strong interest in families, along with larger systems of kinship, descent, and marriage. This chapter surveys the varied kinship systems that have organized human life for much of our history. Like race, kinship is socially constructed. Cultures develop their own explanations for biological processes, such as the role of insemination in the creation and growth of a human embryo. Scientifically informed people know that fertilization of an ovum by a single sperm is responsible for conception. But other cultures, including the Barí and their neighbors, hold different views about procreation. In some societies it is believed that spirits, rather than men, place babies in women's wombs. In others it is believed that a fetus must be nourished by continuing insemination during pregnancy. In the societies discussed here people believe that multiple men can create the same fetus. When a baby is born, the Barí mother names the men she recognizes as fathers, and they assist her in raising the child. The realm of cultural diversity contains much more than contemporary North American notions of marriage and the family. In the United States, having two dads may be the result of divorce, remarriage, stepparenthood, or a same-sex union. In the societies discussed here, multiple (partible) paternity is a common and beneficial social fact.

[A mong] the Barí people of Venezuela, . . . multiple paternity is the norm . . . In such societies, children with more than one official father are more likely to survive to adulthood than those with just one Dad . . . The findings have . . . been published in a book, *Cultures of Multiple Fathers: The Theory and Practice of Partible Paternity in Lowland South America* [Beckerman and Valentine 2002], that questions accepted theories about social organization, the balance of power between the sexes and human evolution.

[The book] . . . draws on more than two decades of fieldwork among South American tribal peoples. The central theme . . . is the concept of partible paternity—the widespread belief that fertilization is not a one-time event and that more than one father can contribute to the developing embryo . . .

The authors have discovered a strong correlation between the status of women in the society and the benefits of multiple paternity . . . Among the Barí, 80% of children with two or more official dads survive to adulthood, compared with 64% with one father. This contrasts with male-dominated cultures such as the neighboring Curripaco, where children of doubtful parentage are outcast and frequently die young.

Explaining the significance of this discovery, Paul Valentine said: "The conventional view of the male-

female bargain is that a man will provide food and shelter for a woman and her children if he can be assured that the children are biologically his. Our research turns this idea on its head . . . In societies where women control marriages and other aspects of social life, both men and women have multiple partners and spread the responsibilities of child rearing." It is of course scientifically impossible to have more than one biological father, but aboriginal peoples in South America, Africa and Australasia [Australia and Asia] believe that it takes more than one act of intercourse to make a baby. In some of these societies, nearly all children have multiple fathers. In others, while partible paternity is accepted, socially the child has only one father. However, in the middle are groups where some children do have multiple fathers and some do not. In this case, the children can be compared to see how having more than one father benefits the children—and generational studies show that the children do benefit from the extra care.

When a child is born among the Barí, the mother publicly announces the names of the one or more men she believes to be the fathers, who, if they accept paternity, are expected to provide care for the mother and child . . . "In small egalitarian societies, women's interests are best served if mate choice is a non-binding, female decision; if a network of multiple females to aid or substitute for a woman in her mothering responsibilities exists; if multiple men support a woman and her children; and if a woman is shielded from the effects of male sexual jealousy." . . .

In cultures where women choose their mates, women have broad sexual freedom and partible paternity is accepted, women clearly have the

The Barí of Venezuela believe that a child can have multiple fathers.

upper hand. In Victorian-style societies where women's sexual activity is controlled by men, marriage is exclusive and male sexual jealousy is a constant threat, men have the upper hand. In between is a full range of combinations and options, all represented in the varying South American cultures . . .

Robert Carneiro, curator at the American Museum of Natural History, said: "Rarely does a book thrust open a door, giving us a striking new view. It has long been known that . . . peoples around the world believe that one act of sexual intercourse is not enough for a child to be born. Now for the first time we have a volume that deals with the consequences and ramifications of this belief, and it does so in exhaustive and fascinating detail." . . .

SOURCE: AlphaGalileo: the Internet Press Center for European Science and the Arts. http://www.alphagalileo.org/index.cfm?f useaction=readRelease&Releaseid=9918.

basis of residence or authority organization. Other social units—most notably descent groups and extended families—can assume many of the functions otherwise associated with the nuclear family.

Consider an example from the former Yugoslavia. Traditionally, among the Muslims of western Bosnia (Lockwood 1975), nuclear families lacked autonomy. Several such families were embedded in an extended family household called a *zadruga*. The *zadruga* was headed by a male household head and his wife, the senior woman. It also included married sons and their wives and children, and unmarried sons and daughters. Each nuclear family had a sleeping room, decorated and partly furnished from the bride's trousseau. However, possessions—even clothing items—were freely shared by *zadruga* members. Even trousseau items were appropriated for use elsewhere. Such a residential unit is known as a *patrilocal* extended family, because each couple resides in the husband's father's household after marriage.

The *zadruga* took precedence over its component units. Social interaction was more usual among women, men, or children than between spouses or between parents and children. Larger households ate at three successive settings: for men, women, and children. Traditionally, all children over 12 slept together in boys' or girls' rooms. When a woman wished to visit another village, she sought the permission of the male *zadruga* head. Although men usually felt closer to their own children than to those of their brothers, they were obliged to treat them equally. Children were disciplined by any adult in the household. When a nuclear family broke up, children under seven went with the mother. Older children could choose between their parents. Children were considered part of the household where they were born even if their mother left. One widow who remarried had to leave her five children, all over seven, in their father's *zadruga*, now headed by his brother.

Another example of an alternative to the nuclear family is provided by the Nayars (or Nair), a large and powerful caste on the Malabar

■ This just-married Khasi couple poses (in 1997) in India's northeastern city of Shillong. The Khasis are matrilineal, tracing descent through women and taking their maternal ancestors' surnames. Women choose their husbands; family incomes are pooled, and extended family households are managed by older women.

 STUDENT CD-ROM LIVING ANTHROPOLOGY

Tradition Meets Law: Families of China
Track 18

This clip exposes the conflict between traditional family structures and beliefs in China and the governmental policy allowing only one child per family. The Chinese view that boys are more valuable than girls has led to a widespread pattern of aborting females or abandoning them as infants. This has produced a sharp imbalance in the number of males and females. How large is the imbalance in Hunan province? Why are boys so valuable? What happens to people who choose to have more than one child? Do you think Chinese women will become more valued as the new generation reaches marriageable age?

Coast of southern India (Figure 18.1). Their traditional kinship system was matrilineal (descent traced only through females). Nayar lived in matrilineal extended family compounds called *tarawads*. The *tarawad* was a residential complex with several buildings, its own temple, granary, water well, orchards, gardens, and land holdings. Headed by a senior woman, assisted by her brother, the *tarawad* housed her siblings, sisters' children, and other matrikin—matrilineal relatives (Gough 1959; Shivaram 1996).

Traditional Nayar marriage seems to have been hardly more than a formality—a kind of coming of age ritual. A young woman would go through a marriage ceremony with a man, after which they might spend a few days together at her *tarawad*. Then the man would return to his own *tarawad*, where he lived with his sisters, aunts, and other matrikin. Nayar men belonged to a warrior class, who left home regularly for military expeditions, returning permanently to their *tarawad* on retirement. Nayar women could have multiple sexual partners. Children became members of the mother's *tarawad*; they were not considered to be relatives of their biological father. Indeed, many Nayar children didn't even know who their genitor was. Child care was the responsibility of the *tarawad*. Nayar society therefore reproduced itself biologically without the nuclear family.

Industrialism and Family Organization

For many Americans and Canadians, the nuclear family is the only well-defined kin group. Family isolation arises from geographic mobility, which is associated with industrialism, so that a nuclear family focus is characteristic of many modern nations. Born into a family of orientation, North Americans leave home for work or college, and the break with parents is under way. Eventually most North Americans marry and start a family of procreation. Because less than 3 percent of the U.S. population now farms, most people aren't tied to the land. Selling our labor on the market, we often move to places where jobs are available.

Many married couples live hundreds of miles from their parents. Their jobs have determined where they live. Such a postmarital residence pattern is called **neolocality:** Married couples are expected to establish a new place of residence—a "home of their own." Among middle-class North Americans, neolocal residence is both a cultural preference and a statistical norm. Most middle-class Americans eventually establish households and nuclear families of their own.

Within stratified nations, value systems vary to some extent from class to class, and so does kinship. There are significant differences between middle-class and poorer North Americans. For example, in the lower class the incidence of

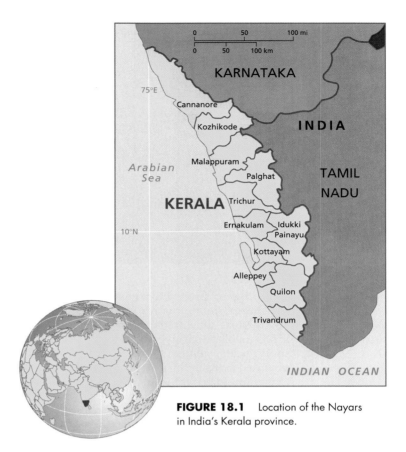

FIGURE 18.1 Location of the Nayars in India's Kerala province.

An extended Navajo family outside a traditional hogan on a Navajo reservation in Arizona.

expanded family households (those that include non-nuclear relatives) is greater than it is in the middle class. When an expanded family household includes three or more generations, it is an **extended family household,** such as the *zadruga*. Another type of expanded family is the *collateral household*, which includes siblings and their spouses and children.

In contemporary North America, single-parent families are increasing at a rapid rate. In 1960, 88 percent of American children lived with both parents, compared with 68 percent today. This divorced mom, Valerie Jones, is enjoying a candlelight dinner with her kids. What do you see as the main differences between nuclear families and single-parent families?

The higher proportion of expanded family households among poorer Americans has been explained as an adaptation to poverty (Stack 1975). Unable to survive economically as nuclear family units, relatives band together in an expanded household and pool their resources. Adaptation to poverty causes kinship values and attitudes to diverge from middle-class norms. Thus, when North Americans raised in poverty achieve financial success, they often feel obligated to provide financial help to a wide circle of less fortunate relatives (see "Interesting Issues" on p. 420).

Changes in North American Kinship

Although the nuclear family remains a cultural ideal for many Americans, Table 18.1 and Figure 18.2 show that nuclear families accounted for just 23 percent of American households in 2003–2004. Other domestic arrangements now outnumber the "traditional" American household more than four to one. There are several reasons for this changing household composition. Women increasingly are joining men in the cash work force. This often removes them from their family of orientation while making it economically feasible to delay marriage. Furthermore, job demands compete with romantic attachments. The median age at first marriage for American women rose from 21 years in 1970 to 25 in 2003. For men the comparable ages were 23 and 27 (Fields 2004).

Also, the U.S. divorce rate has risen, making divorced Americans much more common today than they were in 1970. Between 1970 and 2003 the number of divorced Americans quintupled—some 22 million in 2003 versus 4.3 million in 1970. (Note, however, that each divorce creates two divorced people.) Table 18.2 shows the ratio of divorces to marriages in the United States for selected years between 1950 and 2003. The major jump in the American divorce rate took place between 1960 and 1980. During that period the ratio of divorces to marriage doubled. Since 1980 the ratio has stayed the same, around 50 percent. That is, each year there are about half as many new divorces as there are new marriages.

The rate of growth in single-parent families also has outstripped population growth, quadrupling from fewer than 4 million in 1970 to more than 16 million in 2003. (The overall American population in 2003 was 1.4 times its size in 1970.) The percentage of children living in fatherless (mother-headed, no resident dad) households in 2003 was more than

TABLE 18.1 Changes in Family and Household Organization in the United States: 1970 versus 2004

	1970	2004
Numbers:		
Total number of households	63 million	112 million
Number of people per household	3.1	2.6
Percentages:		
Married couples with children	40%	23%
Family households	81%	68%
Households with five or more people	21%	10%
People living alone	17%	26%
Percentage of single-mother families	5%	12%
Percentage of single-father families	0%	4%
Households with own children under 18	45%	32%

SOURCES: From U.S. Census data in J. M. Fields, "America's Families and Living Arrangements: 2003," *Current Population Reports*, P20-553, November 2004. http://www.census.gov/prod/2004pubs/p20-553.pdf, p. 4; J. M. Fields and L. M. Casper, "America's Families and Living Arrangements: Population Characteristics, 2000," *Current Population Reports*, P20-537, June 2001. http://www.census.gov/prod/2001pubs/p20-537.pdf; U.S. Census Bureau, *Statistical Abstract of the United States 2006*, Tables 55, 56, and 65. http://www.census.gov/prod/www/statistical_abstract.html.

Americans are supposed to love their parents, their siblings, their spouse, and especially their children. Many, perhaps most, of us would agree that "family" is very important, but just how important is kinship in our lives? How might one answer such a question? In nonindustrial societies, people are with their kin *all the time*—at home, at work, at play, in the village, in the fields, with the herds. Contemporary North Americans, by contrast, typically spend our days—weekdays at least—with people we don't love, and may not even like. We have to do balancing acts to be with our families as we also fulfill work demands. How different were TV's leisured Harriet Nelson and Carol Brady from the harried physicians of NBC's medical drama *ER* and all the other TV parents who struggle to maintain family responsibilities even as work demands compete for their time.

How did your parents manage their work/family responsibilities? It's statistically probable that both of your parents worked outside the home at least part of the time you were growing up. It's also likely that your mother, even if she had the higher-paying job, spent more time on child care and home care than your father did. Did your family of orientation illustrate the rule, or was it an exception to it? Do you think it will be different in your household if you form a family of procreation? Why or why not?

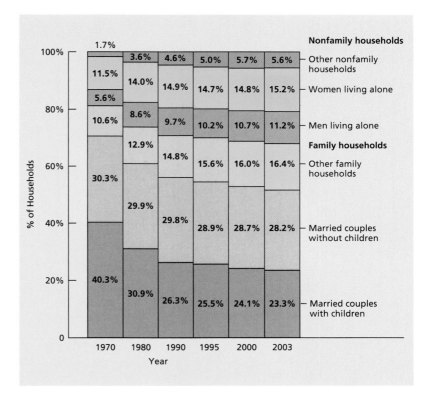

FIGURE 18.2 Households by Type: Selected Years, 1970 to 2003 (percent distribution).

SOURCE: U.S. Census Bureau, *Current Population Survey*, March and Annual Social and Economic Supplements: 1970 to 2003; J. M. Fields, "America's Families and Living Arrangements: 2003," *Current Population Reports*, P20-553, November 2004. http://www.census.gov/prod/2004pubs/p20-553.pdf, p. 4.

TABLE 18.2 Ratio of Divorces to Marriages per 1,000 U.S. Population, Selected Years, 1950–2003

1950	1960	1970	1980	1990	2000	2003
23%	26%	33%	50%	48%	49%	51%

SOURCES: U.S. Census Bureau, *Statistical Abstract of the United States 2006*, Tables 71, p. 64. http://www.census.gov/prod/www/statistical_abstract.html.

twice the 1970 rate, while the percentage in motherless (father-headed, no resident mom) homes increased fivefold. About 57 percent of American women and 60 percent of American men were currently married in 2004, versus 60 and 65 percent, respectively, in 1970 (Fields 2004; Fields and Casper 2001). To be sure, contemporary Americans maintain social lives through work, friendship, sports, clubs, religion, and organized social activities. However, the growing isolation from kin that these figures suggest may well be unprecedented in human history.

Table 18.3 documents similar changes in family and household size in the United States and Canada between 1975 and 2003. Those figures confirm a general trend toward smaller families and living units in North America. This trend is also detectable in Western Europe and other industrial nations.

The entire range of kin attachments is narrower for North Americans, particularly those in the middle class, than it is for nonindustrial peoples. Although we recognize ties to grandparents,

uncles, aunts, and cousins, we have less contact with, and depend less on, those relatives than people in other cultures do. We see this when we answer a few questions: Do we know exactly how we are related to all our cousins? How much do we know about our ancestors, such as their full names and where they lived? How many of the people with whom we associate regularly are our relatives?

Differences in the answers to these questions by people from industrial and those from nonindustrial societies confirm the declining importance of kinship in contemporary nations. Immigrants are often shocked by what they perceive as weak kinship bonds and lack of proper

TABLE 18.3 Household and Family Size in the United States and Canada, 1980 versus 2004		
	1980	**2004**
Average family size:		
United States	3.3	3.1
Canada	3.4	3.0
Average household size:		
United States	2.9	2.6
Canada	2.9	2.6

SOURCES: J. M. Fields, "America's Families and Living Arrangements: 2003," *Current Population Reports*, P20-553, November 2004. http://www.census.gov/prod/2004pubs/p20-553.pdf, pp. 3–4. U.S. Census Bureau, *Statistical Abstract of the United States, 2004–5; Statistics Canada*, 2001 Census. http://www.statcan.ca/english/Pgdb/famil53a.htm, http://www.statcan.ca/english/Pgdb/famil40a.htm.

respect for family in contemporary North America. In fact, most of the people whom middle-class North Americans see every day are either nonrelatives or members of the nuclear family. On the other hand, Stack's (1975) study of welfare-dependent families in a ghetto area of a midwestern city showed that sharing with nonnuclear relatives is an important strategy that the urban poor use to adapt to poverty.

One of the most striking contrasts between the United States and Brazil, the two most populous nations of the Western Hemisphere, is in the meaning and role of the family. Contemporary North American adults usually define their families as consisting of their husbands or wives and their children. However, when middle-class Brazilians talk about their families, they mean their parents, siblings, aunts, uncles, grandparents, and cousins. Later they add their children, but rarely the husband or wife, who has his or her own family. The children are shared by the two families. Because middle-class Americans lack an extended family support system, marriage assumes more importance. The husband–wife relationship is supposed to take precedence over either spouse's relationship with his or her own parents. This places a significant strain on North American marriages.

Living in a less mobile society, Brazilians stay in closer contact with their relatives, including members of the extended family, than North Americans do. Residents of Rio de Janeiro and São Paulo, two of South America's largest cities, are reluctant to leave those urban centers to live away from family and friends. Brazilians find it hard to imagine, and unpleasant to live in, social worlds without relatives. Contrast this with a characteristic American theme: learning to live with strangers.

The Family among Foragers

Populations with foraging economies are far removed from industrial societies in terms of social complexity, but they do feature geographic mobility, which is associated with nomadic or seminomadic hunting and gathering. Here again the nuclear family is often the most significant kin group, although in no foraging society is the nuclear family the only group based on kinship. The two basic social units of traditional foraging societies are the nuclear family and the band.

Unlike middle-class couples in industrial nations, foragers don't usually reside neolocally. Instead, they join a band in which either the husband or the wife has relatives. However, couples and families may move from one band to another several times. Although nuclear families are ultimately as impermanent among foragers as they are in any other society, they are usually more stable than bands are.

Many foraging societies lacked year-round band organization. The Native American Shoshoni of the Great Basin in Utah and Nevada (Figure 18.3) provide an example. The resources available to the Shoshoni were so meager that for most of the year families traveled alone through the countryside hunting and gathering. In certain seasons families assembled to hunt cooperatively as a band; after just a few months together they dispersed.

In neither industrial nor foraging societies are people tied permanently to the land. The mobility and the emphasis on small, economically self-sufficient family units promote the nuclear family as a basic kin group in both types of societies.

DESCENT

We've seen that the nuclear family is important in industrial nations and among foragers. The analogous group among nonindustrial food producers is the descent group. A **descent group** is a permanent social unit whose members say they have ancestors in common. Descent-group members believe they share, and descend from, those common ancestors. The group endures even though its membership changes, as members are born and die, move in and move out. Often, descent-group membership is determined at birth and is lifelong. In this case, it is an ascribed status.

Descent Groups

Descent groups frequently are exogamous (members must seek their mates from other descent groups). Two common rules serve to admit certain people as descent-group members while excluding others. With a rule of **matrilineal descent**, people join the mother's group automatically at birth and stay members throughout life. Matrilineal descent groups therefore include only the children of the group's women. (For a discussion of the prominence of matrilineal descent in early anthropological theory, see Appendix 1.) With **patrilineal descent,** people automatically have lifetime membership in the father's group. The children of all the group's men join the group, but the children of the female members of that group are excluded. (In Figures 18.4 and 18.5, which show matrilineal and patrilineal descent groups, respectively, the triangles stand for males and the circles for females.) Matrilineal and patrilineal descent are types of **unilineal descent.** This means the descent rule uses one line only, either the male or the female line. Patrilineal descent is much more common than is matrilineal descent. In a sample of 564 societies (Murdock 1957), about three times as many were found to be patrilineal (247 to 84).

Descent groups may be **lineages** or **clans.** Common to both is the belief that members descend from the same *apical ancestor.* That person stands at the apex, or top, of the common genealogy. For example, Adam and Eve, according to the Bible, are the apical ancestors of all humanity. Since Eve is said to have come from Adam's rib, Adam stands as the original apical ancestor for the patrilineal genealogies laid out in the Bible.

How do lineages and clans differ? A lineage uses *demonstrated descent.* Members can recite the names of their forebears in each generation from the apical ancestor through the present. (This doesn't mean their recitations are accurate, only that lineage members think they are.) In the Bible the litany of men who "begat" other men is a demonstration of genealogical descent for a large patrilineage that ultimately includes Jews and Arabs (who share Abraham as their last common apical ancestor).

Unlike lineages, clans use *stipulated descent.* Clan members merely say they descend from the apical ancestor. They don't try to trace the actual genealogical links between themselves and that ancestor. The Betsileo of Madagascar have both clans and lineages. Descent may be demonstrated for the most recent 8 to 10 generations, then stipulated for the more remote past—sometimes with mermaids and vaguely defined foreign royalty mentioned among the founders (Kottak 1980). Like the Betsileo, many societies have both lineages and clans. In such a case, clans have more members and cover a larger geographic area than lineages do. Sometimes a clan's apical ancestor is not a human at all but an animal or plant (called a *totem*). Whether human or not, the ancestor symbolizes the social unity and identity of the members, distinguishing them from other groups.

The economic types that usually have descent group organization are horticulture, pastoralism, and agriculture, as discussed in Chapter 16 "Mak-

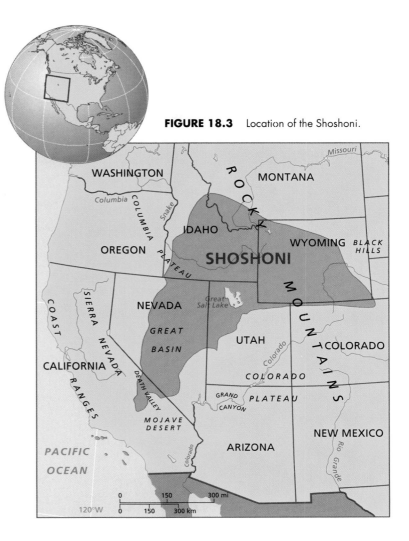

FIGURE 18.3 Location of the Shoshoni.

ing a Living." Such societies tend to have several descent groups. Any one of them may be confined to a single village, but they usually span more than one village. Any branch of a descent group that lives in one place is a *local descent group.* Two or more local branches of different descent groups may live in the same village. Descent groups in the same village or different villages may establish alliances through frequent intermarriage.

Lineages, Clans, and Residence Rules

As we've seen, descent groups, unlike nuclear families, are permanent and enduring units, with new members added in every generation. Members have access to the lineage estate, where some of them must live, in order to benefit from and manage that estate across the generations. To endure, descent groups need to keep at least some of their members at home, on the ancestral estate. An easy way to do this is to have a rule

Bringing It All Together

For information on kinship in a European peasant society, see the "Bringing It All Together" essay on the Basques that immediately follows the chapter on gender.

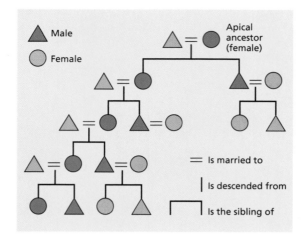

FIGURE 18.4   A Matrilineage Five Generations Deep.
Matrilineages are based on demonstrated descent from a female ancestor. Only the children of the group's women (blue) belong to the matrilineage. The children of the group's men are excluded; they belong to their mother's matrilineage.

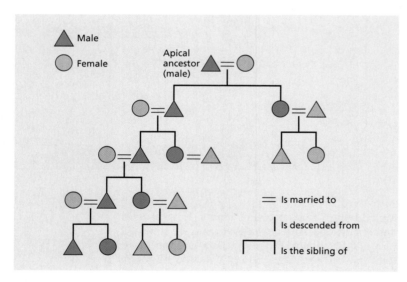

FIGURE 18.5   A Patrilineage Five Generations Deep.
Lineages are based on demonstrated descent from a common ancestor. With patrilineal descent, children of the group's men (blue) are included as descent-group members. Children of the group's female members are excluded; they belong to their father's patrilineage. Also notice lineage exogamy.

about who belongs to the descent group and where they should live after they get married. Patrilineal and matrilineal descent, and the postmarital residence rules that usually accompany them, ensure that about half the people born in each generation will live out their lives on the ancestral estate. Neolocal residence, which is the rule for most middle-class Americans, isn't very common outside modern North America, Western Europe, and the European-derived cultures of Latin America.

Much more common is **patrilocality:** When a couple marries, it moves to the husband's father's community, so that their children will grow up in their father's village. Patrilocality is associated with patrilineal descent. This makes sense. If the group's male members are expected to exercise their rights in the ancestral estate, it's a good idea to raise them on that estate and to keep them there after they marry. This can be done by having wives move to their husband's village, rather than vice versa.

A less common postmarital residence rule, associated with matrilineal descent, is **matrilocality:** Married couples live in the wife's mother's community, and their children grow up in their mother's village. This rule keeps related women together. Together, patrilocality and matrilocality are known as *unilocal* rules of postmarital residence.

Ambilineal Descent

The descent rules examined so far admit certain people as members while excluding others. A unilineal rule uses one line only, either the female or the male. Besides the unilineal rules, there is another descent rule called nonunilineal or **ambilineal** descent. As in any descent group, membership comes through descent from a common ancestor. However, ambilineal groups differ from unilineal groups in that they do not *automatically* exclude either the children of sons or those of daughters. People can choose the descent group they join (for example, that of their father's father, father's mother, mother's father, or mother's mother). People also can change their descent-group membership, or belong to two or more groups at the same time.

Unilineal descent is a matter of ascribed status; ambilineal descent illustrates achieved status. With unilineal descent, membership is automatic; no choice is permitted. People are born members of their father's group in a patrilineal society or of their mother's group in a matrilineal society. They are members of that group for life. Ambilineal descent permits more flexibility in descent-group affiliation.

Before 1950, descent groups were generally described simply as patrilineal or matrilineal. If the society tended toward patrilineality, the anthropologist classified it as a patrilineal rather than an ambilineal group. The treatment of ambilineal descent as a separate category was a formal recognition that many descent systems are flexible—some more so than others.

Family versus Descent

There are rights, duties, and obligations associated with kinship and descent. Many societies have both families and descent groups. Obligations to one may conflict with obligations to the other—more so in matrilineal than in patrilineal societies. In the latter, a woman typically leaves home when she marries and raises her children in her husband's community. After leaving home, she has no primary or substantial obligations to her own descent group. She can invest fully in her children, who will become members of her husband's group. In a matrilineal society things are different. A man has strong obligations both to his family of procreation (his wife and children) and to his closest matrikin (his sisters and their children). The continuity of his descent group depends on his sisters and her children, since descent is carried by females, and he has descent-based obligations to look out for their welfare. He also has obligations to his wife and children. If a man is sure his wife's children are his own, he has more incentive to invest in them than is the case if he has doubts.

Compared with patrilineal systems, matrilineal societies tend to have higher divorce rates and greater female promiscuity (Schneider and Gough, eds. 1961). According to Nicholas Kottak (2002), among the matrilineal Makua of northern Mozambique, a husband is concerned about his wife's potential promiscuity. A man's sister also takes an interest in her brother's wife's fidelity; she doesn't want her brother wasting time on children who may not be his, thus diminishing his investment as an uncle (mother's brother) in her children. A confessional ritual that is part of the Makua birthing process demonstrates the sister's allegiance to her brother. When a wife is deep in labor, the husband's sister, who attends her, must ask, "Who is the real father of this child?" If the wife lies, the Makua believe the birth will be difficult, often ending in the death of the woman and/or the baby. This ritual serves as an important social paternity test. It is in both the husband's and his sister's interest to ensure that his wife's children are indeed his own.

KINSHIP CALCULATION

In addition to studying kin groups, anthropologists are interested in **kinship calculation**: the system by which people in a society reckon kin relationships. To study kinship calculation, an ethnographer must first determine the word or words for different types of "relatives" used in a particular language and then ask questions such as, "Who are your relatives?" Kinship, like race and gender (discussed in other chapters), is culturally constructed. This means that some genealogical kin are considered to be relatives whereas others are not. As we saw in the account of the Barí of Venezuela in the "News Brief" at the beginning of this chapter, even people who aren't genealogical relatives can be constructed socially as kin. The Barí recognize

Most societies have a prevailing opinion about where a couple should live after they marry; this is called a postmarital residence rule. A common rule is patrilocality: the couple lives with the husband's relatives, so that children grow up in their father's community. In the top image, a bride on horseback is escorted to her husband in the Macedonian village of Galicnik in 2004. Her new father-in-law and the marriage witnesses lead the procession. In the bottom image, in Lendak, Slovakia, women transport part of the bride's dowry to the groom's house.

multiple fathers, even though biologically there can be only one actual genitor. Through questioning, the ethnographer discovers the specific genealogical relationships between "relatives" and the person who has named them—the **ego.** *Ego* means *I* (or *me*) in Latin. It's who you, the

Social Security, Kinship Style

My book *Assault on Paradise*, 4th edition (Kottak 2006), describes social relations in Arembepe, the Brazilian fishing community I've studied since the 1960s. When I first studied Arembepe, I was struck by how similar its social relations were to those in the egalitarian, kin-based societies anthropologists have studied traditionally. The twin assertions "We're all equal here" and "We're all relatives here" were offered repeatedly as Arembepeiros' summaries of the nature and basis of local life. Like members of a clan (who claim to share common ancestry, but who can't say exactly how they are related), most villagers couldn't trace precise genealogical links to their distant kin. "What difference does it make, as long as we know we're relatives?"

As in most nonindustrial societies, close personal relations were either based or modeled on kinship. A degree of community solidarity was promoted, for example, by the myth that everyone was kin. However, social solidarity was actually much *less* developed in Arembepe than in societies with clans and lineages—which use genealogy to include some people, and *exclude* others, from membership in a given descent group. Intense social solidarity demands that some people be excluded. By asserting they all were related—that is, by excluding no one—Arembepeiros were actually weakening kinship's potential strength in creating and maintaining group solidarity.

Rights and obligations always are associated with kinship and marriage. In Arembepe, the closer the kin connection and the more formal the marital tie, the greater the rights and obligations. Couples could be married formally or informally. The most common union was a stable common-law marriage. Less common, but with more prestige, was legal (civil) marriage, performed by a justice of the peace and conferring inheritance rights. The union with the most prestige combined legal validity with a church ceremony.

The rights and obligations associated with kinship and marriage constituted the local social security system, but people had to weigh the benefits of the system against its costs. The most obvious cost was this: Villagers had to share in proportion to their success. As ambitious men climbed the local ladder of success, they got more dependents. To maintain their standing in public opinion, and to guarantee that they could depend on others in old age, they had to share. However, sharing was a powerful leveling mechanism. It drained surplus wealth and restricted upward mobility.

How, specifically, did this leveling work? As is often true in stratified nations, Brazilian national cultural norms are set by the upper classes. Middle- and upper-class Brazilians usually marry legally and in church. Even Arembepeiros knew this was the only "proper" way to marry. The most successful and ambitious local men copied the behavior of elite Brazilians. By doing so, they hoped to acquire some of their prestige.

However, legal marriage drained individual wealth, for example, by creating a responsibility to help one's in-laws financially. Such obligations could be regular and costly. Obligations to kids also increased with income, because successful people tended to have more living children. Children were valued as companions and as an eventual economic benefit to their parents. Boys especially were prized because their economic prospects were so much brighter than those of girls.

Children's chances of survival surged dramatically in wealthier households with better diets. The normal household diet included fish—usually in a stew with tomatoes, onions, palm oil, vinegar, and lemon. Dried beef replaced fish once a week. Roasted manioc flour was the main source of calories and was eaten at all meals. Other daily staples included coffee, sugar, and salt. Fruits and vegetables were eaten in season. Diet was one of the main contrasts between households. The poorest people didn't eat fish regularly; often they subsisted on manioc flour, coffee, and sugar. Better-off households supplemented the staples with milk, butter, eggs, rice, beans, and more ample portions of fresh fish, fruits, and vegetables.

Adequate incomes bought improved diets and provided the means and confidence to seek out better medical attention than was locally available. Most of the children born in the wealthier households survived. But this meant more mouths to feed, and (since the heads of such households usually wanted a better education for their children) it meant increased expenditures on schooling. The correlation between economic success and large families was a siphoner of wealth that restricted individual economic advance. Tomé, a fishing entrepreneur, envisioned a life of constant hard work if he was to feed, clothe, and educate his growing family. Tomé and his wife had never lost a child. But he recognized that his growing family would, in the short run, be a drain on his resources. "But in the end, I'll have successful sons to help their mother and me, if we need it, in our old age."

Arembepeiros knew who could afford to share with others; success can't be concealed in a small community. Villagers based their expectations of others on this knowledge. Successful people had to share with more kin and in-laws, and with more distant kin, than did poorer people. Successful captains and boat owners were expected to buy beer for ordinary fishermen; store owners had to sell on credit. As in bands and tribes, any well-off person was expected to exhibit a corresponding generosity. With increasing wealth, people were also asked more frequently to enter ritual kin relationships. Through baptism—which took place twice a year when a priest visited, or which could be done outside—a child acquired two godparents. These people became the coparents (*compadres*) of the baby's parents. The fact that ritual kinship obligations increased with wealth was another factor limiting individual economic advance.

We see that kinship, marriage, and ritual kinship in Arembepe had costs and benefits. The costs were limits on the economic advance of individuals. The primary benefit was social security—guaranteed help from kin, in-laws, and ritual kin in times of need. Benefits, however, came only after costs had been paid—that is, only to those who had lived "proper" lives, not deviating too noticeably from local norms, especially those about sharing.

reader, are in the kin charts that follow. It's your perspective looking out on your kin. By posing the same questions to several local people, the ethnographer learns about the extent and direction of kinship calculation in that society. The ethnographer also begins to understand the relationship between kinship calculation and kin groups: how people use kinship to create and maintain personal ties and to join social groups. In the kinship charts that follow, the black square labeled "ego" identifies the person whose kinship calculation is being examined.

Genealogical Kin Types and Kin Terms

At this point, we may distinguish between *kin terms* (the words used for different relatives in a particular language) and *genealogical kin types.* We designate genealogical kin types with the letters and symbols shown in Figure 18.6. *Genealogical kin type* refers to an actual genealogical relationship (e.g., father's brother) as opposed to a kin term (e.g., *uncle*).

Kin terms reflect the social construction of kinship in a given culture. A kin term may (and usually does) lump together several genealogical relationships. In English, for instance, we use *father* primarily for one kin type: the genealogical father. However, *father* can be extended to an adoptive father or stepfather—and even to a priest. *Grandfather* includes mother's father and father's father. The term *cousin* lumps together several kin types. Even the more specific *first cousin* includes mother's brother's son (MBS), mother's brother's daughter (MBD), mother's sister's son (MZS), mother's sister's daughter (MZD), father's brother's son (FBS), father's brother's daughter (FBD), father's sister's son (FZS), and father's sister's daughter (FZD). *First cousin* thus lumps together at least eight genealogical kin types.

Uncle encompasses mother's and father's brothers, and *aunt* includes mother's and father's sisters. We also used *uncle* and *aunt* for the spouses of our "blood" aunts and uncles. We use the same term for mother's brother and father's brother because we perceive them as being the same sort of relative. Calling them *uncles*, we distinguish between them and another kin type, F, whom we call *Father, Dad,* or *Pop.* In many societies, however, it is common to call a father and a father's brother by the same term. Later we'll see why.

In the United States and Canada, the nuclear family continues to be the most important group based on kinship. This is true despite an increased incidence of single parenthood, divorce, and remarriage. The nuclear family's relative isolation from other kin groups in modern nations reflects geographic mobility within an industrial economy with sale of labor for cash.

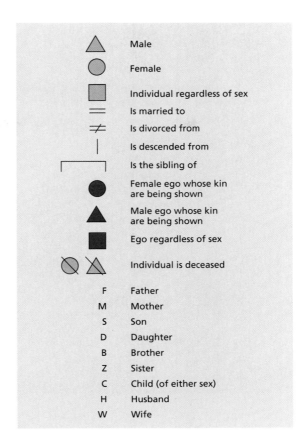

FIGURE 18.6 Kinship Symbols and Genealogical Kin Type Notation.

It's reasonable for North Americans to distinguish between relatives who belong to their nuclear families and those who don't. We are more likely to grow up with our parents than with our aunts and uncles. We tend to see our parents more often than we see our uncles and aunts, who may live in different towns and cities. We often inherit from our parents, but our cousins have first claim to inherit from our aunts and uncles. If our marriage is stable, we see our children daily as long as they remain at home. They are our heirs. We feel closer to them than to our nieces and nephews.

American kinship calculation and kin terminology reflect these social features. Thus, the term *uncle* distinguishes between the kin types MB and FB on the one hand and the kin type F on the other. However, this term also lumps kin types together. We use the same term for MB and FB, two different kin types. We do this because American kinship calculation is **bilateral**—traced equally through males and females, for example, father and mother. Both kinds of uncle are brothers of one of our parents. We think of both as roughly the same kind of relative.

"No," you may object, "I'm closer to my mother's brother than to my father's brother."

That may be. However, in a representative sample of American students, we would find a split, with some favoring one side and some favoring the other. We'd actually expect a bit of *matrilateral skewing*—a preference for relatives on the mother's side. This occurs for many reasons. When contemporary children are raised by just one parent, it's much more likely to be the mother than the father. Also, even with intact marriages, the wife tends to play a more active role in managing family affairs, including family visits, reunions, holidays, and extended family relations, than the husband does. This would tend to reinforce her kin network over his and thus favor matrilateral skewing.

Bilateral kinship means that people tend to perceive kin links through males and females as being similar or equivalent. This bilaterality is expressed in interaction with, living with or near, and rights to inherit from relatives. We don't usually inherit from uncles, but if we do, there's about as much chance that we'll inherit from the father's brother as from the mother's brother. We don't usually live with either aunt, but if we do, the chances are about the same that it will be the father's sister as the mother's sister.

KINSHIP TERMINOLOGY

People perceive and define kin relations differently in different cultures. In any culture, kinship terminology is a classification system, a taxon-omy or typology. It is a *native taxonomy*, developed over generations by the people who live in a particular society. A native classification system is based on how people perceive similarities and differences in the things being classified.

However, anthropologists have discovered that there are a limited number of patterns in which people classify their kin. People who speak very different languages may use exactly the same system of kinship terminology. This section examines the four main ways of classifying kin on the parental generation: lineal, bifurcate merging, generational, and bifurcate collateral. We also consider the social correlates of these classification systems. (Note that each of the systems described here applies to the parental generation. There are also differences in kin terminology on ego's generation. These systems involve the classification of siblings and cousins. There are six such systems, called Eskimo, Iroquois, Hawaiian, Crow, Omaha, and Sudanese cousin terminology, after societies that traditionally used them. You can see them diagrammed and discussed at the following websites: http://anthro.palomar.edu/kinship/kinship_5.htm; http://anthro.palomar.edu/kinship/kinship_6.htm; http://www.umanitoba.ca/anthropology/tutor/kinterms/index.html.)

A **functional explanation** will be offered for each system of kinship terminology, such as lineal, bifurcate merging, and generational terminology. Functional explanations attempt to relate particular customs (such as the use of kin terms) to other features of a society, such as rules of descent and postmarital residence. Certain aspects of a culture are *functions* of others. That is, they are correlated variables, so that when one of them changes, the others inevitably change too. For certain terminologies, the social correlates are very clear.

Kinship terms provide useful information about social patterns. If two relatives are designated by the same term, we can assume that they are perceived as sharing socially significant attributes. Several factors influence the way people interact with, perceive, and classify relatives. For instance, do certain kinds of relatives customarily live together or apart? How far apart? What benefits do they derive from each other, and what are their obligations? Are they members of the same descent group or of different descent groups? With these questions in mind, let's examine systems of kinship terminology.

Lineal Terminology

Our own system of kinship classification is called the *lineal system* (Figure 18.7). The number 3 and the color light blue stand for the term *uncle*, which we apply both to FB and to MB. **Lineal kinship terminology** is found in societies such as the United States and Canada in which the nuclear family is the most important group based on kinship.

Lineal kinship terminology has absolutely nothing to do with lineages, which are found in very different social contexts. (What contexts are those?) Lineal kinship terminology gets its name from the fact that it distinguishes lineal relatives from collateral relatives. What does that mean? A **lineal relative** is an ancestor or descendant, anyone on the direct line of descent that leads to and from ego (Figure 18.8). Thus, lineal relatives are one's parents, grandparents, great-grandparents, and other direct forebears. Lineal relatives also include children, grandchildren, and great-grandchildren. **Collateral relatives** are all other kin. They include siblings, nieces and nephews, aunts and uncles, and cousins (Figure 18.8). **Affinals** are relatives by marriage, whether of lineals (e.g., son's wife) or of collaterals (sister's husband).

Bifurcate Merging Terminology

Bifurcate merging kinship terminology (Figure 18.9) *bifurcates,* or splits, the mother's side and the father's side. But it also *merges* same-sex siblings of each parent. Thus, mother and mother's sister are merged under the same term (1), while father and father's brother also get a common term (2). There are different terms for mother's brother (3) and father's sister (4).

People use this system in societies with unilineal (patrilineal and matrilineal) descent rules and unilocal (patrilocal and matrilocal) postmarital residence rules. When the society is unilineal and unilocal, the logic of bifurcate merging terminol-

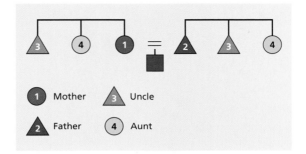

FIGURE 18.7 Lineal Kinship Terminology.

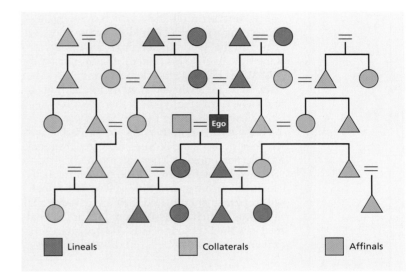

FIGURE 18.8 The Distinctions among Lineals, Collaterals, and Affinals as Perceived by Ego.

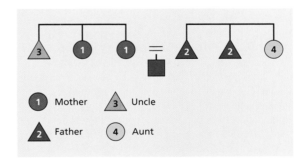

FIGURE 18.9 Bifurcate Merging Kinship Terminology.

ogy is fairly clear. In a patrilineal society, for example, father and father's brother belong to the same descent group, gender, and generation. Since patrilineal societies usually have patrilocal residence, the father and his brother live in the same local group. Because they share so many attributes that are socially relevant, ego regards them as social equivalents and calls them by the same kinship term—2. However, the mother's

The nuclear family still dominates in our society, ideologically if not statistically. Imagine a society where someone doesn't know for sure, and doesn't care much about, who his actual mother was. Consider Joseph Rabe, a Betsileo man who was my field assistant in Madagascar. One of the villages where I worked was his village of origin, where Rabe had been raised by his father's sister. How and why did that happen? I asked him. Rabe told me about two sisters, one of whom was his mother and the other was his mother's sister. He knew their names, but he didn't know which was which. Illustrating a pattern of child fosterage and adoption that is common among the Betsileo, Rabe was given to his father's childless sister to raise when he was a toddler. His mother and her sister lived far away and died in his childhood, and so he didn't really know them. But he was very close to his father's sister, for whom he used the term for mother. Indeed, he had to call her that, because the Betsileo have generational kinship terminology. They call mother, mother's sister, and father's sister by the same term, *reny*. The Betsileo live in an ambilineal society (albeit with a patrilineal tilt), and they use generational kin terms, which are associated with ambilineality. Since the Betsileo socially construct kinship, and encourage fosterage (typically by childless relatives), in these ways, the difference between "real" and socially constructed kinship did not matter to Rabe, or to many others like him.

Contrast the Betsileo case with Americans' attitudes about kinship and adoption. On family-oriented radio talk shows, I've heard hosts who are "helping professionals" distinguish between "birth mothers" and adoptive mothers, and between "sperm daddies" and "daddies of the heart." The latter may be adoptive fathers, or stepfathers who have "been like fathers" to someone. American culture tends to promote the view that kinship is, and should be, biological. Americans have some trouble with the social construction of kinship. Less and less are we warned against searching for our birth parents (which was formerly discouraged as disruptive), even if we've had a perfectly satisfactory upbringing with our adoptive parents. One common reason an adopted person might give for trying to track down his or her birth parents is based in biology—to discover family health history, including inherited diseases. The American emphasis on biology for kinship is also seen in the recent proliferation of DNA testing. Understanding ourselves through cross-cultural comparison helps us see that kinship and biology don't always converge, nor do they need to.

brother belongs to a different descent group, lives elsewhere, and has a different kin term—3.

What about mother and mother's sister in a patrilineal society? They belong to the same descent group, the same gender, and the same generation. Often they marry men from the same village and go to live there. These social similarities help explain the use of the same term—1—for both.

Similar observations apply to matrilineal societies. Consider a society with two matrilineal clans, the Ravens and the Wolves. Ego is a member of his mother's clan, the Raven clan. Ego's father is a member of the Wolf clan. His mother and her sister are female Ravens of the same generation. If there is matrilocal residence, as there often is in matrilineal societies, they will live in the same village. Because they are so similar socially, ego calls them by the same kin term—1.

The father's sister, however, belongs to a different group, the Wolves; lives elsewhere; and has a different kin term—4. Ego's father and father's brother are male Wolves of the same generation. If they marry women of the same clan and live in the same village, this creates additional social similarities that reinforce this usage.

For a quiz on kinship systems, see the Interactive Exercise

mhhe.com/kottak

Generational Terminology

Like bifurcate merging kinship terminology, **generational kinship terminology** uses the same term for parents and their siblings, but the lumping is more complete (Figure 18.10). With generational terminology, there are only two terms for the parental *generation*. We may translate them as "father" and "mother," but more accurate translations would be "male member of the parental generation" and "female member of the parental generation."

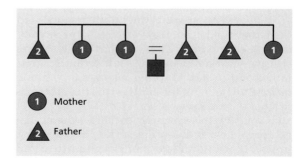

FIGURE 18.10 Generational Kinship Terminology.

TABLE 18.4 The Four Systems of Kinship Terminology, with Their Social and Economic Correlates

Kinship Terminology	Kin Group	Residence Rule	Economy
Lineal	Nuclear family	Neolocal	Industrialism, foraging
Bifurcate merging	Unilineal descent group—patrilineal or matrilineal	Unilocal—patrilocal or matrilocal	Horticulture, pastoralism, agriculture
Generational	Ambilineal descent group, band	Ambilocal	Agriculture, horticulture, foraging
Bifurcate collateral	Varies	Varies	Varies

Generational kinship terminology does not distinguish between the mother's and father's sides. It does not bifurcate, but it certainly does merge. It uses just one term for father, father's brother, and mother's brother. In a unilineal society, these three kin types would never belong to the same descent group. Generational kinship terminology also uses a single term for mother, mother's sister, and father's sister. Nor, in a unilineal society, would these three ever be members of the same group.

Nevertheless, generational terminology suggests closeness between ego and his or her aunts and uncles—much more closeness than exists between Americans and these kin types. How likely would you be to call your uncle "Dad" or your aunt "Mom"? We'd expect to find generational terminology in cultures in which kinship is much more important than it is in our own but in which there is no rigid distinction between the father's side and the mother's side.

It's logical, then, that generational kin terminology is typical of societies with ambilineal descent. In such contexts, descent-group membership is not automatic. People may choose the group they join, change their descent-group membership, or belong to two or more descent groups simultaneously. Generational terminology fits these conditions. The use of intimate kin terms signals that people have close personal relations with all their relatives of the parental generation. People exhibit similar behavior toward their aunts, uncles, and parents. Someday they'll have to choose a descent group to join. Furthermore, in ambilineal societies, postmarital residence is usually ambilocal. This means that the married couple can live with either the husband's or the wife's group.

Significantly, generational terminology also characterizes certain foraging bands, including Kalahari San groups and several native societies of North America. Use of this terminology reflects certain similarities between foraging bands and ambilineal descent groups. In both societies, people have a choice about their kin-group affiliation. Foragers always live with kin, but they often shift band affiliation and so may be members of several different bands during their lifetimes. Just as in food-producing societies with ambilineal descent, generational terminology among foragers helps maintain close personal relationships with several parental-generation relatives whom ego may eventually use as a point of entry into different groups. Table 18.4 summarizes the types of kin group, the postmarital residence rule, and the economy associated with the four types of kinship terminology.

Bifurcate Collateral Terminology

Of the four kin classification systems, **bifurcate collateral kinship terminology** is the most specific. It has separate terms for each of the six kin types of the parental generation (Figure 18.11). Bifurcate collateral terminology isn't as common as the other types. Many of the societies that use it are in North Africa and the Middle East, and many of them are offshoots of the same ancestral group.

Bifurcate collateral terminology also may be used when a child has parents of different ethnic backgrounds and uses terms for aunts and uncles derived from different languages. Thus, if you have a mother who is Latina and a father who is Anglo, you may call your aunts and uncles on your mother's side "tia" and "tio," while calling those on your father's side "aunt" and "uncle." And your mother and father may be "Mom" and "Pop." That's a modern form of bifurcate collateral kinship terminology.

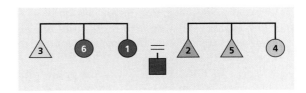

FIGURE 18.11   Bifurcate Collateral Kinship Terminology.

SUMMARY

1. In nonindustrial societies, kinship, descent, and marriage organize social and political life. In studying kinship, we must distinguish between kin groups, whose composition and activities can be observed, and kinship calculation—how people identify and designate their relatives.

2. One widespread kin group is the nuclear family, consisting of a married couple and their children. There are functional alternatives to the nuclear family. That is, other groups may assume functions usually associated with the nuclear family. Nuclear families tend to be especially important in foraging and industrial societies. Among farmers and herders, other kinds of kin groups often overshadow the nuclear family.

3. In contemporary North America, the nuclear family is the characteristic kin group for the middle class. Expanded households and sharing with extended family kin occur more frequently among the poor, who may pool their resources in dealing with poverty. Today, however, even in the American middle class, nuclear family households are declining as single-person households and other domestic arrangements increase.

4. The descent group is a basic kin group among nonindustrial food producers (farmers and herders). Unlike families, descent groups have perpetuity—they last for generations. Descent-group members share and manage a common estate: land, animals, and other resources. There are several kinds of descent groups. Lineages are based on demonstrated descent; clans, on stipulated descent. Descent rules may be unilineal or ambilineal. Unilineal (patrilineal and matrilineal) descent is associated with unilocal (respectively, patrilocal and matrilocal) postmarital residence. Obligations to one's descent group and to one's family of procreation may conflict, especially in matrilineal societies.

5. A kinship terminology is a classification of relatives based on perceived differences and similarities. Comparative research has revealed a limited number of ways of classifying kin. Because there are correlations between kinship terminology and other social practices, we often can predict kinship terminology from other aspects of culture. The four basic kinship terminologies for the parental generation are lineal, bifurcate merging, generational, and bifurcate collateral. Many foraging and industrial societies use lineal terminology, which is associated with nuclear family organization. Cultures with unilocal residence and unilineal descent tend to have bifurcate merging terminology. Generational terminology correlates with ambilineal descent and ambilocal residence.

KEY TERMS

See the flash cards
mhhe.com/kottak

affinals Relatives by marriage, whether of lineals (e.g., son's wife) or collaterals (e.g., sister's husband).

ambilineal Principle of descent that does not automatically exclude the children of either sons or daughters.

bifurcate collateral kinship terminology Kinship terminology employing separate terms for M, F, MB, MZ, FB, and FZ.

bifurcate merging kinship terminology Kinship terminology in which M and MZ are called by the same term, F and FB are called by the same term, and MB and FZ are called by different terms.

bilateral kinship calculation A system in which kinship ties are calculated equally through both sexes: mother and father, sister and brother, daughter and son, and so on.

clan Unilineal descent group based on stipulated descent.

collateral relative A genealogical relative who is not in ego's direct line, such as B, Z, FB, or MZ.

descent group A permanent social unit whose members claim common ancestry; fundamental to tribal society.

ego Latin for *I*. In kinship charts, the point from which one views an egocentric genealogy.

extended family household Expanded household including three or more generations.

family of orientation Nuclear family in which one is born and grows up.

family of procreation Nuclear family established when one marries and has children.

functional explanation Explanation that establishes a correlation or interrelationship between social customs. When customs are functionally interrelated, if one changes, the others also change.

generational kinship terminology Kinship terminology with only two terms for the parental generation, one designating M, MZ, and FZ and the other designating F, FB, and MB.

kinship calculation The system by which people in a particular society reckon kin relationships.

lineage Unilineal descent group based on demonstrated descent.

lineal kinship terminology Parental generation kin terminology with four terms: one for M, one for F, one for FB and MB, and one for MZ and FZ.

lineal relative Any of ego's ancestors or descendants (e.g., parents, grandparents, children, grandchildren) on the direct line of descent that leads to and from ego.

matrilineal descent Unilineal descent rule in which people join the mother's group automatically at birth and stay members throughout life.

matrilocality Customary residence with the wife's relatives after marriage, so that children grow up in their mother's community.

neolocality Postmarital residence pattern in which a couple establishes a new place of residence rather than living with or near either set of parents.

patrilineal descent Unilineal descent rule in which people join the father's group automatically at birth and stay members throughout life.

patrilocality Customary residence with the husband's relatives after marriage, so that children grow up in their father's community.

unilineal descent Matrilineal or patrilineal descent.

---

1. Why is kinship so important to anthropologists? How might the study of kinship be useful for research in fields of anthropology other than cultural anthropology?

2. To what sorts of family or families do you belong? Have you belonged to other kinds of families? When you were growing up, how did you feel about your family compared with those of your friends?

3. Choose two of your friends who have families of orientation that differ from your own. How do they differ?

4. What do "family" and "family values" mean to you?

5. How do the kin terms you use compare with the four classification systems discussed in this chapter? What's the strangest use of kin terms you've ever heard (among your friends or acquaintances)?

CRITICAL THINKING QUESTIONS

For more self-testing, see the self-quizzes
mhhe.com/kottak

SUGGESTED ADDITIONAL READINGS

Carsten, J.
   2004 *After Kinship*. New York: Cambridge University Press. Rethinking anthropological approaches to kinship for the modern world.

Collier, J. F., and S. J. Yanagisako, eds.
   1987 *Gender and Kinship: Essays toward a Unified Analysis*. Stanford, CA: Stanford University Press. Consideration of kinship in the context of gender issues.

Finkler, K.
   2000 *Experiencing the New Genetics: Family and Kinship on the Medical Frontier*. Philadelphia: University of Pennsylvania Press. Examines some medical and genetic aspects of kinship, along with social dimensions of contemporary medical/genetics debates.

Hansen, K. V.
   2004 *Not-So-Nuclear Families: Class, Gender, and Networks of Care*. New Brunswick, NJ: Rutgers University Press. Support networks based in class, gender, and kinship.

Hansen, K. V., and A. I. Garey, eds.
   1998 *Families in the U.S.: Kinship and Domestic Politics*. Philadelphia: Temple University Press. Families, family policy, and diversity in the contemporary United States.

Netting, R. M. C., R. R. Wilk, and E. J. Arnould, eds.
   1984 *Households: Comparative and Historical Studies of the Domestic Groups*. Berkeley: University of California Press. Excellent collection of articles on household research.

O'Dougherty, M.
   2002 *Consumption Intensified: The Politics of Middle-Class Daily Life in Brazil*. Durham, NC: Duke University Press. Families and consumption in contemporary Brazil.

Parkin, R.
   1997 *Kinship: An Introduction to Basic Concepts*. Cambridge, MA: Blackwell. The basics of kinship study.

Parkin, R., and L. Stone, eds.
   2004 *Kinship and Family: An Anthropological Reader*. Malden, MA: Blackwell. Up-to-date reader.

Pasternak, B., C. R. Ember, and M. Ember
   1997 *Sex, Gender, and Kinship: A Cross-Cultural Perspective*. Upper Saddle River, NJ: Prentice Hall. Sex roles, kinship, and marriage in comparative perspective.

Radcliffe-Brown, A. R., and D. Forde, eds.
   1994 *African Systems of Kinship and Marriage*. New York: Columbia University Press. Reissue of a classic work, indispensable to understanding kinship, descent, and marriage.

Stacey, J.
   1998 *Brave New Families: Stories of Domestic Upheaval in Late Twentieth Century America*. Berkeley: University of California Press. Contemporary family life in the United States, based on field work in California's Silicon Valley.

Stone, L.
   2001 *New Directions in Anthropological Kinship*. Lanham, MD: Rowman and Littlefield. How contemporary anthropologists think about kinship.

Willie, C. V.
   2003 *A New Look at Black Families*, 5th ed. Walnut Creek, CA: AltaMira. Family experience in relation to socioeconomic status, presented through case studies.

Yanagisako, S. J.
   2002 *Producing Culture and Capital: Family Firms in Italy*. Princeton, NJ: Princeton University Press. Families making money.

INTERNET EXERCISES

1. Kinship and Conflict: Go to the Yanamamo Interactive: Understanding the Ax Fight page, **http://www.anth.ucsb.edu/projects/axfight/index.html**, and go to the Web version of the CD-ROM, **http://www.anth.ucsb.edu/projects/axfight/prep.html**. View the film of the Ax Fight and read the text titled "Chagnon's Voice-Over Narration from the 1975 *The Ax Fight*." The questions below ask you to interpret the fight, and it may be necessary to view the film or read the text more than once to understand it.
   a. What is the cause of the fight?
   b. Who are the aggressors? Whom are they attacking?
   c. As the fight escalates, more people join in. What is their relationship to the people who start the fight? Why is that important?
   d. How is kinship important for understanding this conflict? Can you think of examples from your own society where kinship served to escalate or diffuse conflict?

2. Descent and Subsistence: Go to the Ethnographic Atlas Cross-tabulations page, **http://lucy.ukc.ac.uk/cgi-bin/uncgi/Ethnoatlas/atlas.vopts**. This site has compiled ethnographic information on many different groups, and you can use the tools provided to cross-tabulate the prevalence of certain traits. Under "Select Row Category" choose "region," and under "Select Column Category" select "descent." Press the Submit Query button. The table that appears shows the frequency of descent patterns from regions around the world.
   a. Look at the total row for descent. Which forms of descent are most common worldwide? What is the *most* common? Is that the system with which you are most familiar in your own society?
   b. Where are most of the patrilineal societies found? Where are most of the bilateral societies found? In the Insular Pacific, is any one descent system predominant?
   c. Now go back to the Ethnographic Atlas Cross-tabulations page and change the "Select Row Category" from "region" to "subsistence economy" and press the Submit Query button. What kind of subsistence economy do most patrilineal societies practice? Are matrilineal societies more likely to use hunting, gathering, or fishing or to use agriculture? Is the pattern as strong as with patrilineal groups? Are there any strong patterns for the type of subsistence economy practiced by bilateral groups?

3. Kinship Terminologies: Go to the website created by Professor Brian Schwimmer of the Department of Anthropology at the University of Manitoba, **http://www.umanitoba.ca/faculties/arts/anthropology/kintitle.html**. Click on "Begin Tutorial." Next click on topic 3—Kinship Terminology. Press "Continue" at the bottom left of the next two pages until you reach a page titled "Systematic Kinship Terminologies." Scroll down the page to the diagram labeled "Eskimo Kin Terms."
   a. To what parental generation kin terminology discussed in the book (lineal, bifurcate merging, generational, or bifurcate collateral) do the Eskimo cousin terms correspond?
   b. Answer the same question for Iroquois, Hawaiian, and Sudanese terms.
   c. Do you see any logic in the relation between the terms used on the parental generation (for parents, aunts, and uncles) and those used on ego's own generation (for siblings and cousins)?
   d. How do these associated sets of kin terms fit with particular kinds of kin groups, for example, the nuclear family, a unilineal descent group, an ambilineal descent group?
   e. At the bottom of the web page, can you see how Omaha kin terms might fit with patrilineal descent, and Crow terms with matrilineal descent?

See Chapter 18 at your McGraw-Hill Online Learning Center for additional review and interactive exercises.

Kottak, *Assault on Paradise,* **4th ed.**

Read Chapters 3 and 11 and comment on the role of kinship and ritual kinship for Dora and Fernando. Why, unlike Alberto and Tomé, did Fernando have to rely so heavily on ritual kinship? To which of her kin did Dora look for present and future support? See Chapter 3 for others like Dora, their status, and how they used the local kinship system.

Peters-Golden, *Culture Sketches,* **4th ed.**

Read Chapter 10, "Nuer: Cattle and Kinship in Sudan." The traditional descent system of the Nuer, called segmentary lineage organization (SLO), offered an effective way of resolving disputes and of mobilizing support among kin groups. In recent years, however, civil war and ethnic clashes in Sudan have led to widespread resettlement and a contemporary refugee crisis. Also, thousands of Nuer have migrated to the United States. This chapter on the Nuer demonstrates the potential political significance of kinship alliances. For Nuer emigrants, what might be some challenges in creating social ties without the political ties and village links that underlie traditional Nuer solidarity?

Knauft, *The Gebusi,* **1st ed.**

Based on information in Chapter 4 of *The Gebusi,* why is kinship important for understanding Gebusi social life? How do Gebusi trace descent? What difference is there in the way Gebusi trace descent in lineages as opposed to in clans? What is Omaha kinship terminology, and how is it important among Gebusi?

19

Marriage

WHAT IS MARRIAGE?

"Love and marriage," "marriage and the family": These familiar phrases show how we link the romantic love of two individuals to marriage and how we link marriage to reproduction and family creation. But marriage is an institution with significant roles and functions in addition to reproduction. What is marriage, anyway?

No definition of marriage is broad enough to apply easily to all societies and situations. A commonly quoted definition comes from *Notes and Queries on Anthropology:*

> Marriage is a union between a man and a woman such that the children born to the woman are recognized as legitimate offspring of both partners. (Royal Anthropological Institute 1951, p. 111)

This definition isn't universally valid for several reasons. In many societies, marriages unite more than two spouses, as we see in the "News Brief" about Kenya. Here we speak of *plural marriages,* as when a man weds two (or more) women, or a woman weds a group of brothers—an arrangement called *fraternal polyandry* that is characteristic of certain Himalayan cultures. In the Brazilian community of Arembepe, people can choose among various forms of marital union. Most people live in long-term "common-law" domestic partnerships that are not legally sanctioned. Some have civil marriages, which are licensed and legalized by a justice of the peace. Still others go through religious ceremonies, so that they are united in "holy matrimony," although not legally. And some have both civil and religious ties. The different forms of union permit someone to have multiple spouses (e.g., one common-law, one civil, one religious) without ever getting divorced.

Some societies recognize various kinds of same-sex marriages. In Sudan, a Nuer woman can marry a woman if her father has only daughters but no male heirs, who are necessary if his patrilineage is to survive. He may ask his daughter to stand as a son in order to take a bride. This daughter will become the socially recognized husband of another woman (the wife). This is a symbolic and social relationship rather than a sexual one. The "wife" has sex with a man or men (whom her female "husband" must approve) until she gets pregnant. The children born to the wife are accepted as the offspring of both the female husband and the wife. Although the female husband is not the actual **genitor,** the biological father, of the children, she is their **pater,** or socially recognized father. What's important in this Nuer case is *social* rather than *biological paternity.* We see again how kinship is socially constructed. The bride's children are considered the legitimate offspring of her female "husband," who is biologically a woman but socially a man, and the descent line continues.

INCEST AND EXOGAMY

In many nonindustrial societies, a person's social world includes two main categories: kin and strangers. Strangers are potential or actual enemies. Marriage is one of the primary ways of converting strangers into kin, of creating and maintaining personal and political alliances, relationships of affinity (*affinal* relationships). **Exogamy,** the practice of seeking a husband or wife outside one's own group, has adaptive value because it links people into a wider social network that nurtures, helps, and protects them in times of need.

Incest refers to sexual relations with someone considered to be a close relative. All cultures have taboos against it. However, although the taboo is a cultural universal, cultures define incest differently. As an illustration, consider some implications of the distinction between two kinds of first cousins: cross cousins and parallel cousins (see Ottenheimer 1996).

The children of two brothers or two sisters are **parallel cousins.** The children of a brother and a sister are **cross cousins.** Your mother's sister's children and your father's brother's children are your parallel cousins. Your father's sister's children and your mother's brother's children are your cross cousins.

The American kin term *cousin* doesn't distinguish between cross and parallel cousins, but in many societies, especially those with unilineal descent, the distinction is essential. As an example, consider a community with only two descent groups. This exemplifies what is known as *moiety* organization—from the French *moitié,* which means "half." Descent bifurcates the community so that everyone belongs to one half or the other. Some societies have patrilineal moieties; others have matrilineal moieties.

In Figures 19.1 and 19.2, notice that cross cousins are always members of the opposite moiety and parallel cousins always belong to your (ego's) own moiety. With patrilineal descent (Figure 19.1), people take the father's descent-group affiliation; in a matrilineal society (Figure 19.2), they take the mother's affiliation. You can see from these diagrams that your mother's sister's children (MZC) and your father's brother's children (FBC) always belong to your group. Your

OVERVIEW

Marriage, which usually involves a domestic partnership, is difficult to define. Marriage establishes the legal parentage of children and gives spouses rights to each other's sexuality, labor, and property. The incest taboo, a cultural universal, promotes exogamy (outmarriage), which widens social networks and builds alliances. Marriages often are relationships between groups as well as between the individual spouses. The groom's relatives may transfer "bridewealth" to the bride and her relatives. As the value of the bridewealth increases, the divorce rate declines. Bridewealth customs show how marriages create and maintain group alliances. So do replacement marriages, for example, when a man marries the sister of his deceased wife, or a woman marries the brother of her deceased husband. The ease and frequency of divorce vary among societies. Many societies permit plural marriages. The two kinds of plural marriage (polygamy) are polygyny and polyandry. The former involves multiple wives; the latter, multiple husbands. Polygyny is much more common than polyandry is.

Nairobi Journal; Is Polygamy Confusing, or Just a Matter of Family Values?

NEW YORK TIMES NEWS BRIEF

by Marc Lacey

December 16, 2003

In nonindustrial societies, marriage is an important means of creating or maintaining alliances beyond one's own kin group. Many societies, such as Kenya, described here, permit plural marriage. This news story reports on polygyny, the form of polygamy (plural marriage) in which a man has more than one wife. Anthropologists also have studied the rarer custom of polyandry, in which a woman has more than one husband. Marriage is usually a domestic partnership, but the secondary wife, who sometimes is chosen by the first wife, may or may not reside near the first wife. In this Kenyan case the president's second wife has her own residence (his ranch) and appears very discreetly at public events that the senior wife also attends. For thousands of years the rich and powerful, especially rulers, have used marriage to build and maintain alliances, to acquire territory, and to guarantee their power base. Monogamy creates an alliance with one group; polygamy, with many.

NAIROBI, Kenya, Dec. 15— When President Mwai Kibaki of Kenya arrived at the White House recently for a state visit, his wife, Lucy Kibaki, was at his side, resplendent in a flowing gown.

Perhaps fortunately for the White House protocol office, which has little experience with polygamous relationships, Mr. Kibaki left his second wife, Wambui Kibaki, back home.

Mr. Kibaki's multiple marriage has been known for decades among close friends and family in his native village of Othaya, near Mount Kenya. But most Kenyan voters first learned of it on Sunday morning, nearly a year into Mr. Kibaki's presidency, when a local newspaper, *The East African Standard*, splashed a profile of Mr. Kibaki's second wife on its front page.

Such a complicated family life is not uncommon here. By no means limited to Muslims, polygamy is widely practiced in Africa, particularly among the well-off members of Mr. Kibaki's generation who can afford multiple dowries [bridewealth] and the expense of keeping more than one home.

But polygamy is also falling from favor, according to social scientists and women's rights advocates, especially among younger Kenyans, and Mr. Kibaki has not sought to publicize his living arrangements. His official campaign Web site, for example, mentioned only one Mrs. Kibaki. "I don't believe in sharing husbands," said Rose Nganga, 20, a Nairobi college student. "If my husband were to bring another wife, he would have to either divorce her or me. Why should I be the second wheel to a man?" For polygamy to work peacefully, the wives must buy into the tradition. Sometimes an older wife will actually assist her husband in choosing a younger bride, typically to provide some assistance with all the work at the homestead. But Kenya's newspapers are rife with stories of disputes between wives of the same husband. They frequently scheme against each other and sometimes come to blows . . .

Mr. Kibaki's home life is, by all accounts, a calm one. Lucy Kibaki, a former schoolteacher whom Mr. Kibaki married in the 1960's, lives with the president. Wambui Kibaki, who was also a schoolteacher before meeting Mr. Kibaki in the 1970's, occupies the presidential ranch.

It is Lucy Kibaki who typically appears at Mr. Kibaki's side at ceremonial functions and acts as first lady. But Wambui Kibaki is often just a few rows behind the first couple, as she was last Friday at a 40th anniversary celebration of Kenya's independence from Britain.

Wambui Kibaki has her own security detail and more access to the presidential office compound than many ministers. Parliament is debating whether the government ought to provide benefits should a retired president have more than one spouse.

■ *Lucy Kibaki, the first lady of Kenya, and her polygynous husband, President Mwai Kibaki, at a state celebration.*

In the only interview she has given since her husband took over the presidency a year ago, Wambui Kibaki said she was comfortable with her arrangement. "I do not feel restricted," she told *The Standard.* "I have my time with him, just as before he became president. I go to State House when I want, and I can't complain. I am his wife, and not being made public does not bother me."

Mr. Kibaki is not the first polygamous politician here. Kenya's first president, Jomo Kenyatta, had several wives, although only one of them took on the official role of first lady.

A recently retired member of Parliament, Dickson Kihaika Kimani, has more than a dozen wives. Last fall he sought to have two of them join him in Parliament, but voters rejected their candidacies—and his as well. Supporters of the practice say that in the AIDS era, polygamy is a far healthier arrangement than another one favored by many men: one wife and one or more mistresses, or even prostitutes . . .

But polygamous relationships, too, are blamed for helping spread AIDS. The more sexual partners involved, critics say, even under the cloak of marriage, the greater risk of

the disease spreading, particularly as some men take on multiple wives and still have affairs on the side. In an advertising campaign aimed at reducing the spread of AIDS, Mr. Kibaki urges Kenyans to "be faithful." He avoids the ticklish question of how much faithfulness he thinks that Kenyan men ought to spread around.

SOURCE: Marc Lacey, "Nairobi Journal; Is Polygamy Confusing, or Just a Matter of Family Values?" *New York Times,* December 16, 2003, late edition, final, section A, p. 4, col. 3.

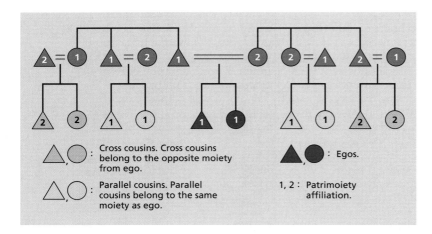

FIGURE 19.1   Parallel and Cross Cousins and Patrilineal Moiety Organization.

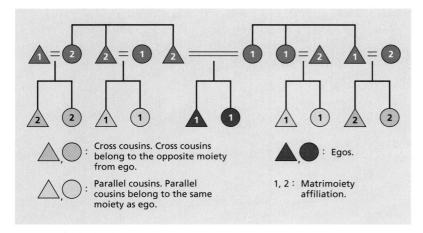

FIGURE 19.2   Matrilineal Moiety Organization.

cross cousins—that is, FZC and MBC—belong to the other moiety.

Parallel cousins belong to the same generation and the same descent group as ego does, and they are like ego's brothers and sisters. They are called by the same kin terms as brother and sister are. Defined as close relatives, parallel cousins are tabooed as sex or marriage partners. They fall within the incest taboo, but cross cousins don't.

In societies with unilineal moieties, cross cousins always belong to the opposite group. Sex with cross cousins isn't incestuous, because they aren't considered relatives. In fact, in many unilineal societies, people must marry either a cross cousin or someone from the same descent group as a cross cousin. A unilineal descent rule ensures that the cross cousin's descent group is never one's own. With moiety exogamy, spouses must belong to different moieties.

Among the Yanomami of Venezuela and Brazil (Chagnon 1997), men anticipate eventual marriage to a cross cousin by calling her "wife." They call their male cross cousins "brother-in-law." Yanomami women call their male cross cousins "husband" and their female cross cousins "sister-in-law." Among the Yanomami, as in many societies with unilineal descent, sex with cross cousins is proper but sex with parallel cousins is considered incestuous.

A custom that is much rarer than cross-cousin marriage also illustrates that people define their kin, and thus incest, differently in different societies. When unilineal descent is very strongly developed, the parent who does not belong to one's own descent group isn't considered a relative. Thus, with strict patrilineality, the mother is not a relative but a kind of in-law who has mar-

ried a member of ego's group—ego's father. With strict matrilineality, the father isn't a relative, because he belongs to a different descent group.

The Lakher of Southeast Asia (Figure 19.3) are strictly patrilineal (Leach 1961). Using the male ego in Figure 19.4, let's suppose that ego's father and mother get divorced. Each remarries and has a daughter by a second marriage. A Lakher always belongs to his or her father's group, all the members of which (one's *agnates*, or patrikin) are considered too closely related to marry because they are members of the same patrilineal descent group. Therefore, ego can't marry his father's daughter by the second marriage, just as in contemporary North America it's illegal for half-siblings to marry.

However, in contrast to our society, where all half-siblings are tabooed, the Lakher permit ego to marry his mother's daughter by a different father. She is not a forbidden relative because she belongs to her own father's descent group rather than ego's. The Lakher illustrate clearly that definitions of forbidden relatives, and therefore of incest, vary from culture to culture.

We can extend these observations to strict matrilineal societies. If a man's parents divorce and his father remarries, ego may marry his pater-

nal half-sister. By contrast, if his mother remarries and has a daughter, the daughter is considered ego's sister, and sex between them is taboo. Cultures therefore have different definitions and expectations of relationships that are biologically or genetically equivalent.

▦ *Among the Yanomami of Brazil and Venezuela (shown here), sex with (and marriage to) cross cousins is proper, but sex with parallel cousins is considered incestuous. With unilineal descent, sex with cross cousins isn't incestuous because cross cousins never belong to ego's descent group.*

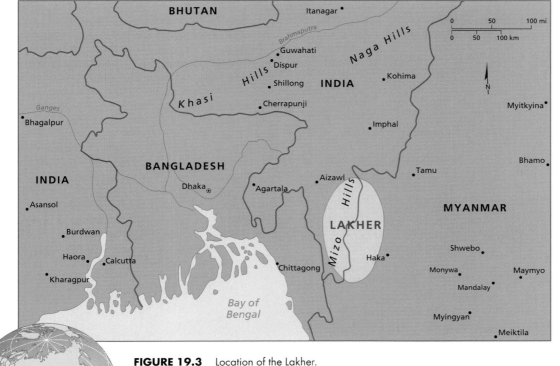

FIGURE 19.3 Location of the Lakher.

For a quiz on marriage patterns, see the Interactive Exercise
mhhe.com/kottak

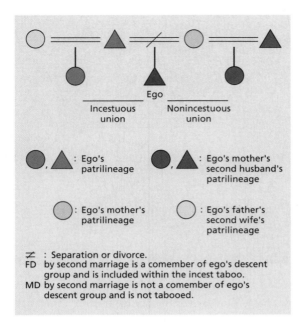

Ego

| Incestuous union | Nonincestuous union |

● , ▲ : Ego's patrilineage

◐ , ◭ : Ego's mother's second husband's patrilineage

◑ : Ego's mother's patrilineage

○ : Ego's father's second wife's patrilineage

≠ : Separation or divorce.
FD by second marriage is a comember of ego's descent group and is included within the incest taboo.
MD by second marriage is not a comember of ego's descent group and is not tabooed.

FIGURE 19.4 Patrilineal Descent-Group Identity and Incest among the Lakher.

EXPLAINING THE TABOO

Although Tabooed, Incest Does Happen

There is no simple or universally accepted explanation for the fact that all cultures ban incest. Do primate studies offer any clues? Research with primates does show that adolescent males (among monkeys) or females (among apes) often move away from the group in which they were born (Rodseth et al. 1991). This emigration reduces the frequency of incestuous unions, but it doesn't eliminate them. DNA testing of wild chimps has confirmed incestuous unions between adult sons and their mothers, who reside in the same group. Human behavior with respect to mating with close relatives may express a generalized primate tendency, in which we see both urges and avoidance.

A cross-cultural study of 87 societies (Meigs and Barlow 2002) revealed that incest did occur in several of them. For example, among the Yanomami, Chagnon reported that "incest, far from being feared, is widely practiced" (1967, p. 66). Meyer Fortes observed about the Ashanti: "In the old days it [incest] was punished by death. Nowadays the culprits are heavily fined" (Fortes 1950, p. 257). Among 24 Ojibwa individuals from whom he obtained information about incest, A. Irving Hallowell found 8 cases of parent–child incest and 10 cases of brother–sister incest (Hallowell 1955, pp. 294–295).

In ancient Egypt, sibling marriage apparently was allowed not just for royalty (see below), but

for commoners as well, in at least some districts. Based on official census records from Roman Egypt (first to third centuries A.D.) preserved on papyrus, 24 percent of all documented marriages in the Arsinoites district were between brothers and sisters. In the second century A.D., the rates were 37 percent for the city of Arsinoe and 19 percent for the surrounding villages. These figures are much higher than any other documented levels of inbreeding among humans (Scheidel 1997).

According to Anna Meigs and Kathleen Barlow (2002), for Western societies with nuclear family organization, statistics show a significant risk of father–daughter incest under certain conditions (Russell 1986). Father–daughter incest is most common with stepfathers and nonbiological male household members, but it also happens with biological fathers, especially those who were absent or did little caretaking of their daughters in childhood (Williams and Finkelhor 1995). In a carefully designed study, Linda M. Williams and David Finkelhor (1995) found father–daughter incest to be least likely when there was substantial paternal parenting of daughters who were four to five years old. This experience enhanced the father's parenting skills and his feelings of nurturance, protectiveness, and identification with his daughter, thus reducing the risk of incest.

Cross-cultural findings show that incest and its avoidance are shaped by kinship structures. Meigs and Barlow (2002) suggest that a cultural focus on risks and avoidance of father–daughter incest correlates with a patriarchal nuclear family structure, whereas the cultural focus is on avoiding brother–sister incest in societies that have such nonnuclear structures as lineages and clans.

■ *Discovered in Egypt's Valley of the Kings, a gold and silver inlaid throne from the tomb of Tutankhamun is now on display in Cairo's Egyptian Museum. Sibling marriage was allowed not only for ancient Egyptian royalty but also for commoners in some regions.*

Instinctive Horror

It has been argued (Hobhouse 1915; Lowie 1920/1961) that the incest taboo is universal because incest horror is instinctive: Humans have a genetically programmed disgust toward incest. Because of this feeling, early humans banned it. However, cultural universality doesn't necessarily entail an instinctual basis. Fire making, for example, is a cultural universal, but it certainly isn't an ability transmitted by the genes. Furthermore, if people really did have an instinctive horror of mating with blood relatives, a formal incest taboo would be unnecessary. No one would do it. However, as we have just seen, and as social workers, judges, psychiatrists, and psychologists know, incest is more common than we might suppose.

A final objection to the instinctive horror theory is that it can't explain why in some societies people can marry their cross cousins but not their parallel cousins. Nor does it tell us why the Lakher can marry their maternal, but not their paternal, half-siblings. No known instinct can distinguish between parallel and cross cousins.

The specific kin types included within the incest taboo—and the taboo itself—have a cultural rather than a biological basis. Even among nonhuman primates, there is no definite evidence for an instinct against incest. Adolescent dispersal does not prevent—but merely limits the frequency of—incestuous unions. Among humans, cultural traditions determine the specific relatives with whom sex is considered incestuous. They also deal with the people who violate prohibited relationships in different ways. Banishment, imprisonment, death, and threats of supernatural retaliation are some of the punishments imposed.

Biological Degeneration

Another theory is that the taboo emerged because early *Homo* noticed that abnormal offspring were born from incestuous unions (Morgan 1877/1963). To prevent this, our ancestors banned incest. The human stock produced after the taboo originated was so successful that it spread everywhere.

What is the evidence for this theory? Laboratory experiments with animals that reproduce faster than humans do (such as mice and fruit flies) have been used to investigate the effects of inbreeding: A decline in survival and fertility does accompany brother–sister mating across several generations. However, despite the potentially harmful biological results of systematic inbreeding, human marriage patterns are based on specific cultural beliefs rather than universal concerns about biological degeneration several generations in the future. Neither instinctive horror nor fear of biological degeneration explains the very widespread custom of marrying cross cousins. Nor can fears about degeneration explain why breeding with parallel cousins but not cross cousins is so often tabooed.

How many fingers do this Indian woman and her child have? Such genetically determined traits as polydactylism (extra fingers) may show up when there is a high incidence of endogamy. Despite the biological effects of inbreeding, marriage preferences and prohibitions are based on specific cultural beliefs rather than universal concerns about future biological degeneration.

Attempt and Contempt

Sigmund Freud is the most famous advocate of the theory that children have sexual feelings toward their parents, which they eventually repress or resolve. Other scholars have looked to the dynamics of growing up for an explanation of the incest taboo. Bronislaw Malinowski believed that children would naturally seek to express their sexual feelings, particularly as they increased in adolescence, with members of their nuclear family, because of preexisting intimacy and affection. Yet, he thought, sex was too powerful a force to unleash in the family. It would threaten existing family roles and ties; it could destroy the family. Malinowski proposed that the incest taboo originated to direct sexual feeling outside—to avoid disruption of—existing family structure and relations.

The opposite theory is that children are not likely to be sexually attracted to those with whom they have grown up (Westermarck 1894). This is related to the idea of instinctive horror, but without assuming a biological (instinctual) basis. The notion here is that a lifetime of living together in particular, nonsexual relationships would make the idea of sex with a family member less desirable. The two opposed theories are sometimes characterized as "familiarity breeds attempt" versus "familiarity breeds contempt." One bit of evidence to support the contempt theory comes from Joseph Shepher's (1983) study of Israeli *kibbutzim*.

He found that unrelated people who had been raised in the same *kibbutz* (domestic community) avoided intermarriage. They tended to choose their mates from outside—not because they were related, but because their prior residential histories and roles made sex and marriage unappealing. Again, there is no final answer to the question of whether people who grow up together, related or unrelated, are likely to be sexually attracted to one another. Usually they aren't; sometimes they are. Incest is universally tabooed, but it does happen.

Marry Out or Die Out

One of the most accepted explanations for the incest taboo is that it arose in order to ensure exogamy, to force people to marry outside their kin groups (Lévi-Strauss 1949/1969; Tylor 1889; White 1959). In this view, the taboo originated early in human evolution because it was adaptively advantageous. Marrying a close relative, with whom one is already on peaceful terms, would be counterproductive. There is more to gain by extending peaceful relations to a wider network of groups. (See Appendix 1 for a discussion of the contributions of Tylor, Malinowski, White, and Lévi-Strauss to the development of anthropological theory.)

This view emphasizes the role of marriage in creating and maintaining alliances. By forcing members to marry out, a group increases its allies. Marriage within the group, by contrast, would isolate that group from its neighbors and their resources and social networks, and might ultimately lead to the group's extinction. Exogamy and the incest taboo that propels it help explain human adaptive success. Besides the sociopolitical function, exogamy ensures genetic mixture between groups and thus maintains a successful human species.

ENDOGAMY

The practice of exogamy pushes social organization outward, establishing and preserving alliances among groups. In contrast, rules of **endogamy** dictate mating or marriage within a group to which one belongs. Formal endogamic rules are less common but are still familiar to anthropologists. Indeed, most societies *are* endogamous units, although they usually do not need a formal rule requiring people to marry someone from their own society. In our own society, classes and ethnic groups are quasi-endogamous groups. Members of an ethnic or religious group often want their children to marry within that group, although many of them do not do so. The outmarriage rate varies among such groups, with some more committed to endogamy than others are.

Homogamy means to marry someone similar, as when members of the same social class intermarry. There's a correlation between socioeconomic status (SES) and education. People with similar SES tend to have similar educational aspirations, to attend similar schools, and to aim at similar careers. For example, people who meet at an elite private university are likely to have similar backgrounds and career prospects. Homogamous marriage may work to concentrate wealth in social classes and to reinforce the system of social stratification. In the United States, for example, the rise in female employment, especially in professional careers, when coupled with homogamy, has dramatically increased household incomes in the upper classes. This pattern has been one factor in sharpening the contrast in household income between the richest and poorest quintiles (top and bottom 20 percent) of Americans.

Caste

An extreme example of endogamy is India's caste system, which was formally abolished in 1949, although its structure and effects linger. Castes are stratified groups in which membership is ascribed at birth and is lifelong. Indian castes are grouped into five major categories, or *varna*. Each is ranked relative to the other four, and these categories extend throughout India. Each *varna* includes a large number of subcastes (*jati*), each of which includes people within a region who may intermarry. All the *jati* in a single *varna* in a given region are ranked, just as the *varna* themselves are ranked.

Occupational specialization often sets off one caste from another. A community may include castes of agricultural workers, merchants, artisans, priests, and sweepers. The untouchable *varna*, found throughout India, includes subcastes whose ancestry, ritual status, and occupations are considered so impure that higher-caste people consider even casual contact with untouchables to be defiling.

The belief that intercaste sexual unions lead to ritual impurity for the higher-caste partner has been important in maintaining endogamy. A man who has sex with a lower-caste woman can restore his purity with a bath and a prayer. However, a woman who has intercourse with a man of a lower caste has no such recourse. Her defilement cannot be undone. Because the women have the babies, these differences protect the purity of the caste line, ensuring the pure ancestry of high-caste children. Although Indian castes are endogamous groups, many of them are internally subdivided into exogamous lineages. Traditionally this meant that Indians had to marry a member of another descent group from the same caste.

Royal Endogamy

Royal endogamy, based in a few societies on brother–sister marriage, is similar to caste endogamy. Inca Peru, ancient Egypt, and traditional Hawaii all allowed royal brother–sister marriages. In ancient Peru and Hawaii, such marriages were permitted despite the sibling incest taboo that applied to commoners in those societies.

Manifest and Latent Functions

To understand royal brother–sister marriage, it is useful to distinguish between the manifest and latent functions of customs and behavior. The *manifest function* of a custom refers to the reasons people in that society give for it. Its *latent function* is an effect the custom has on the society that its members don't mention or may not even recognize. (See Appendix 1 for a discussion of the theoretical school in anthropology known as *functionalism*.)

Royal endogamy illustrates this distinction. Hawaiians and other Polynesians believed in an impersonal force called *mana*. Mana could exist in things or people, in the latter case marking them off from other people and making them sacred. The Hawaiians believed that no one had as much mana as the ruler. Mana depended on genealogy. The person whose own mana was exceeded only by the king's was his sibling. The most appropriate wife for a king was his own full sister. Notice that the brother–sister marriage also meant that royal heirs would be as manaful, or sacred, as possible. The manifest function of royal endogamy in ancient Hawaii was part of that culture's beliefs about mana and sacredness.

Royal endogamy also had latent functions—political repercussions. The ruler and his wife had the same parents. Since mana was believed to be inherited, they were almost equally sacred. When the king and his sister married, their children indisputably had the most mana in the land. No one could question their right to rule. But if the king had taken as a wife someone with less mana than his sister, his sister's children eventually could cause problems. Both sets of children could assert their sacredness and right to rule. Royal sibling marriage therefore limited conflicts about succession by reducing the number of people with claims to rule. The same result would be true in ancient Egypt and Peru.

Other kingdoms, including European royalty, also have practiced endogamy, but based on cousin marriage rather than sibling marriage. In many cases, as in Great Britain, it is specified that the eldest child (usually the son) of the reigning monarch can succeed. This custom is called *primogeniture*. Commonly, rulers have banished or killed claimants who rival the chosen heir.

An extreme example of endogamy is India's caste system, which was formally abolished in 1949, although its structure and effects linger. In Gadwada village, cobblers still make shoes in a traditional style. Here, Devi-Lal sits with his child as his wife looks on. In the traditional caste system, such cobblers had a higher status than did sweepers and tanners, whose work is considered so smelly and dirty that they live at the far end of the village.

Royal endogamy also had a latent economic function. If the king and his sister had rights to inherit the ancestral estate, their marriage to each other, again by limiting the number of heirs, kept it intact. Power often rests on wealth, and royal endogamy tended to ensure that royal wealth remained concentrated in the same line.

MARITAL RIGHTS AND SAME-SEX MARRIAGE

The British anthropologist Edmund Leach (1955) observed that, depending on the society, several different kinds of rights are allocated by marriage. According to Leach, marriage can, but doesn't always, accomplish the following:

1. Establish the legal father of a woman's children and the legal mother of a man's.

2. Give either or both spouses a monopoly in the sexuality of the other.

3. Give either or both spouses rights to the labor of the other.

4. Give either or both spouses rights over the other's property.

On December 21, 2005, Sir Elton John (right) married his long-time domestic partner, David Furnish. The ceremony took place in the town chapel in Windsor, England, where, eight months earlier, Prince Charles had married Camilla Parker-Bowles. The John-Furnish union took place on the first day on which same-sex couples were allowed a legal status comparable to marriage—including the same social security, pension, tax and inheritance rights—in England and Wales. (The law took effect earlier that week in Northern Ireland and Scotland.)

For more on laws affecting same-sex marriage, see the Internet Exercises at your OLC

mhhe.com/kottak

5. Establish a joint fund of property—a partnership—for the benefit of the children.

6. Establish a socially significant "relationship of affinity" between spouses and their relatives.

The discussion of same-sex marriage that follows will serve to illustrate the six rights just listed by seeing what happens in their absence. What if same-sex marriages, which by and large are illegal in the United States, were legal? Could a same-sex marriage establish legal parentage of children born to one or both partners after the partnership is formed? In the case of a different-sex marriage, children born to the wife after the marriage takes place usually are legally defined as her husband's regardless of whether he is the genitor.

Nowadays, of course, DNA testing makes it possible to establish paternity, just as modern reproductive technology makes it possible for a lesbian couple to have one or both partners artificially inseminated. If same-sex marriages were legal, the social construction of kinship could easily make both partners parents. If a Nuer woman married to a woman can be the pater of a child she did not father, why can't two lesbians be the **maters** (socially recognized mothers) of a child one of them did not father? And if a married different-sex couple can adopt a child and have it be theirs through the social and legal construction of kinship, the same logic could be applied to a gay male or lesbian couple.

Continuing with Leach's list of the rights transmitted by marriage, same-sex marriage could certainly give each spouse rights to the sexuality of the other. Unable to marry legally, gay men and lesbians have used various devices, such as mock weddings, to declare their commitment and desire for a monogamous sexual relationship. In April 2000, Vermont passed a bill allowing same-sex

couples to unite legally, with virtually all the benefits of marriage. In June 2003 a court ruling established same-sex marriages as legal in the province of Ontario, Canada. On June 28, 2005, Canada's House of Commons voted to guarantee full marriage rights to same-sex couples throughout that nation. On May 17, 2004, Massachusetts became the first state in the United States to allow same-sex couples to marry. In reaction to same-sex marriage, voters in 18 U.S. states have approved measures in their state constitutions defining marriage as an exclusively heterosexual union.

Legal same-sex marriages could easily give each spouse rights to the other spouse's labor and its products. Some societies have allowed marriage between members of the same biological sex, who may, however, be considered to belong to a different, socially constructed, gender. Several Native American groups had figures known as *berdaches,* representing a third gender (Murray and Roscoe 1998). These were biological men who assumed many of the mannerisms, behavior patterns, and tasks of women. Sometimes *berdaches* married men, who shared the products of their labor from hunting and traditional male roles, as the *berdache* fulfilled the traditional wifely role. Also, in some Native American cultures, a marriage of a "manly-hearted woman" (a third or fourth gender) to another woman brought the traditional male–female division of labor to their household. The manly woman hunted and did other male tasks, while the wife played the traditional female role.

There's no logical reason why same-sex marriage could not give spouses rights over the other's property. But in the United States, the same inheritance rights that apply to male–female couples do not apply to same-sex couples. For instance, even in the absence of a will, property can pass to a widow or a widower without going through probate. The wife or husband pays no inheritance tax. This benefit is not available to gay men and lesbians.

What about Leach's fifth right—to establish a joint fund of property—to benefit the children? Here again, gay and lesbian couples are at a disadvantage. If there are children, property is separately, rather than jointly, transmitted. Some organizations do make staff benefits, such as health and dental insurance, available to same-sex domestic partners.

Finally, there is the matter of establishing a socially significant "relationship of affinity" between spouses and their relatives. In many societies, one of the main roles of marriage is to establish an alliance between groups, in addition to the individual bond. Affinals are relatives through marriage, such as a brother-in-law or mother-in-law. For same-sex couples in contemporary North America, affinal relations are problematic. In an unofficial union, terms like "daughter-in-law"

and "mother-in-law" may sound strange. Many parents are suspicious of their children's sexuality and lifestyle choices and may not recognize a relationship of affinity with a child's partner of the same sex.

This discussion of same-sex marriage has been intended to illustrate the different kinds of rights that typically accompany marriage by seeing what may happen when there is a permanent pair bond without legal sanction. In the United States, with the fleeting exception of Hawaii, which flirted with the legalization of same-sex marriage, Vermont, and Massachusetts, as mentioned previously, such unions are illegal. As we have seen, same-sex marriages have been recognized in different historical and cultural settings. In certain African cultures, including the Igbo of Nigeria and the Lovedu of South Africa, women may marry other women. In situations in which women, such as prominent market women in West Africa, are able to amass property and other forms of wealth, they may take a wife. Such marriage allows the prominent woman to strengthen her social status and the economic importance of her household (Amadiume 1987).

MARRIAGE AS GROUP ALLIANCE

Outside industrial societies, marriage is often more a relationship between groups than one between individuals. We think of marriage as an individual matter. Although the bride and groom usually seek their parents' approval, the final choice (to live together, to marry, to divorce) lies with the couple. The idea of romantic love symbolizes this individual relationship.

In nonindustrial societies, although there can be romantic love, as we see in "Interesting Issues" (on pp. 444–445), marriage is a group concern. People don't just take a spouse; they assume obligations to a group of in-laws. When residence is patrilocal, for example, a woman often must leave the community where she was born. She faces the prospect of spending the rest of her life in her husband's village, with his relatives. She may even have to transfer her major allegiance from her own group to her husband's.

Bridewealth and Dowry

In societies with descent groups, people enter marriage not alone but with the help of the descent group. Descent-group members often have to contribute to the **bridewealth,** a customary gift before, at, or after the marriage from the husband and his kin to the wife and her kin. Another word for bridewealth is *brideprice,* but this term is inaccurate because people with the custom don't usually regard the exchange as a sale. They don't think of marriage as a commercial relationship between a man and an object that can be bought and sold.

Bridewealth compensates the bride's group for the loss of her companionship and labor. More important, it makes the children born to the woman full members of her husband's descent group. For this reason, the institution is also called **progeny price.** Rather than the woman herself, it is her children, or progeny, who are permanently transferred to the husband's group. Whatever we call it, such a transfer of wealth at marriage is common in patrilineal groups. In matrilineal societies, children are members of the mother's group, and there is no reason to pay a progeny price.

For more information about marriage among the Hmong, see the Internet Exercises at your OLC

mhhe.com/kottak

Human Mate Preference in Matrimonial Advertisements from Gujarat, India

BACKGROUND INFORMATION

STUDENT:
Kim Shah

SCHOOL:
Rutgers University

SUPERVISING PROFESSOR:
Lee Kronk

YEAR IN SCHOOL/MAJOR:
Senior/Anthropology

FUTURE PLANS:
Graduate study of nutritional anthropology and public health

This study suggests that Indian marriage customs are changing, and particularly that women may have a stronger role in marital choices than has been thought traditionally (see the section "Bridewealth and Dowry"). It's also true that marriage customs and the roles of men and women vary by region in a country as large and populous as India, which contains considerable cultural diversity. Still, this account also demonstrates that caste still matters and that parents play a significant role in arranging marriages.

Human mate preferences have been studied in many settings, among them newspaper ads, often termed lonely-hearts personal advertisements. In these ads, people describe their own attributes and those they seek in potential mates. The ad might look something like this, "Tall, handsome, intelligent investment banker seeks smart, slim, fun-loving woman."

Most studies of mate preference theory using such advertisements have been done in western settings. My research involved the study of non-western advertisements, specifically from the state of Gujarat in India. These ads were taken from the matrimonial section of a Gujarati newspaper. A typical one looked something like this: "For marriage: vaisshnav, vanik (caste designation) man, 34

years old, owns his own home and car, makes 75,000Rs. per year, (seeks) pretty, smart, lady."

The purpose of my project was to test hypotheses of mate preference based on evolutionary theory. I did this by content analysis focusing on the characteristics sought and offered by advertisers. For this task I took advantage of the cultural diversity of my university (Rutgers) and hired international students from Gujarat to help me in this procedure.

A total of 142 advertisements, 20 seeking wives and 122 seeking husbands, were studied. Under "physical attractiveness" I coded for looks, stature/weight, and fairness. I hypothesized that advertisers seeking wives would look for physical attractiveness more than advertisers seeking husbands would. In turn, women seeking husbands would mention their own physical attractiveness more often than men seeking wives would. These hypotheses were confirmed with the data on good looks and stature/weight.

Yet cultural differences were also apparent. Compared with similar studies done elsewhere, the male preference for good looks was de-emphasized in my results. Only 14% of wife-seeking advertisers requested good looks, significantly fewer than in other studies. An explanation may

be that parental involvement in writing and/or answering these ads affects the male request for good looks. Indeed, on re-analysis, I found that 46% of all advertisers sought responses not from the prospective mate himself or herself, but from the parents of the prospective mate. Thus de-emphasis of the male preference for physical attractiveness may reflect the advertisers' awareness of parental involvement.

Male advertisers were on average 4 years older than female advertisers. The content analysis also revealed that advertisers seeking wives offered information about financial resources more than advertisers seeking husbands did. In other words, prospective husbands were more likely to include information about their salary or possessions than prospective wives were. Logically, advertisers seeking husbands made more inquiries about the prospective mate's financial situation.

Throughout this project it was apparent that cultural and social forces played a significant role. Gujarati society displayed strong adherence to maintaining caste integrity. I also learned that the advertisers had above average educations, so I must view the results of my project as representative of this particular group only. I was able to understand many aspects of Gujarati culture, language, and religion because my own family is from the state of Gujarat. I presented this project at the 14th annual meeting of the Human Evolution and Behavior Society in 2002. Future work on this project will include a study of response rates.

■ Gift-giving customs are associated with marriage throughout the world. In this photo, guests bring presents in baskets to a wedding in Wenjiang, China.

It's hard to make the transition from the family of orientation to the family of procreation. Unlike people in nonindustrial societies, most of us get a head start by "leaving home" long before we marry. We go off to college or find a job that enables us to support ourselves so that we can live independently, or with roommates. In nonindustrial societies people, especially women, may have to leave home abruptly when they marry. In patrilocal societies a woman must leave her home village and her own kin and move in with her husband and his relatives. This can be an unpleasant and alienating transition. Many women complain about feeling isolated when they first arrive in the husband's village. Later they may be mistreated by their husband or in-laws, including the mother-in-law. However, things will be brighter if women from village or descent group A typically marry men from village or descent group B. If this is the case, a woman can be sure to find some of her own relatives, such as her sister or aunt (father's sister), living as wives in her husband's village, and she will feel more at home.

In contemporary North America, neither women nor men typically have to adjust to in-laws living close at hand. But we do have to learn to live with our spouses. Marriage always raises issues of accommodation and adjustment. Initially the married couple is just that, unless there are children from a previous marriage. If there are, adjustment issues will involve stepparenthood—and a prior spouse—as well as the new marital relationship. Once a couple has its own child, the family-of-procreation mentality takes over. In the United States family loyalty shifts, but not completely, from the family of orientation to the family that includes spouse and child(ren). Given our bilateral kinship system, we maintain relations with our sons and daughters after they marry, and grandchildren theoretically are as close to one set of grandparents as to the other. In a patrilineal society there would be a closer bond with the paternal grandparents. What about in a matrilineal society?

Dowry is a marital exchange in which the wife's group provides substantial gifts to the husband's family. Dowry, best known from India, correlates with low female status. Women are perceived as burdens. When husbands and their families take a wife, they expect to be compensated for the added responsibility.

Although India passed a law in 1961 against compulsory dowry, the practice continues. When the dowry is considered insufficient, the bride may be harassed and abused. Domestic violence can escalate to the point where the husband or his family burn the bride, often by pouring kerosene on her and lighting it, usually killing her. It should be pointed out that dowry doesn't necessarily lead to domestic abuse. In fact, Indian dowry murders seem to be a fairly recent phenomenon. It also has been estimated that the rate of spousal murders in the contemporary United States may rival the incidence of India's dowry murders (Narayan 1997).

Sati was the very rare practice through which widows were burned alive, voluntarily or forcibly, on the husband's funeral pyre (Hawley 1994). Although it has become well known, *sati* was mainly practiced in a particular area of northern India by a few small castes. It was banned in 1829. Dowry murders and *sati* are flagrant examples of *patriarchy,* a political system ruled by men in which women have inferior social and political status, including basic human rights.

Bridewealth exists in many more cultures than dowry does, but the nature and quantity of transferred items differ. In many African societies, cattle constitute bridewealth, but the number of cattle given varies from society to society. *As the value of bridewealth increases, marriages become more stable.* Bridewealth is insurance against divorce.

Imagine a patrilineal society in which a marriage requires the transfer of about 25 cattle from the groom's descent group to the bride's. Michael, a member of descent group A, marries Sarah from group B. His relatives help him assemble the bridewealth. He gets the most help from his close agnates (patrilineal relatives): his older brother, father, father's brother, and closest patrilineal cousins.

The distribution of the cattle once they reach Sarah's group mirrors the manner in which they were assembled. Sarah's father, or her oldest

Love and Marriage

Love and marriage, the song says, go together like a horse and carriage. But the link between love and marriage, like the horse–carriage combination, isn't a cultural universal. Described here is a cross-cultural survey, published in the anthropological journal Ethnology, *which found romantic ardor to be widespread, perhaps universal. Previously anthropologists had tended to ignore evidence for romantic love in other cultures, probably because arranged marriages were so common. Today, diffusion, mainly via the mass media, of Western ideas about the importance of love for marriage appears to be influencing marital decisions in other cultures.*

Some influential Western social historians have argued that romance was a product of European medieval culture that spread only recently to other cultures. They dismissed romantic tales from other cultures as representing the behavior of just the elites. Under the sway of this view, Western anthropologists did not even look for romantic love among the peoples they studied. But they are now beginning to think that romantic love is universal . . .

"For decades anthropologists and other scholars have assumed romantic love was unique to the modern West," said Dr. Leonard Plotnicov, an anthropologist at the University of Pittsburgh and editor of the journal *Ethnology.* "Anthropologists came across it in their field work, but they rarely mentioned it because it wasn't supposed to happen."

"Why has something so central to our culture been so ignored by anthropology?" asked Dr. William Jankowiak, an anthropologist at the University of Nevada.

The reason, in the view of Dr. Jankowiak and others, is a scholarly bias throughout the social sciences that viewed romantic love as a luxury in human life, one that could be indulged only by people in Westernized cultures or among the educated elites of other societies. For example it was assumed in societies where life is hard that romantic love has less chance to blossom, because higher economic standards and more leisure time create more opportunity for dalliance. That also contributed to the belief that

romance was for the ruling class, not the peasants.

But, said Dr. Jankowiak, "There is romantic love in cultures around the world." [In 1991] Dr. Jankowiak, with Dr. Edward Fischer, an anthropologist at Tulane University, published in *Ethnology* the first cross-cultural study, systematically comparing romantic love in many cultures.

In the survey of ethnographies from 166 cultures, they found what they considered clear evidence that romantic love was known in 147 of them—89 percent. And in the other 19 cultures, Dr. Jankowiak said, the absence of conclusive evidence seemed due more to anthropologists' oversight than to a lack of romance.

Some of the evidence came from tales about lovers, or folklore that offered love potions or other advice on making someone fall in love.

Another source was accounts by informants to anthropologists. For example, Nisa, a !Kung woman among the Bushmen of the Kalahari, made a clear distinction between the affection she felt for her husband, and that she felt for her lovers, which was "passionate and

brother if the father is dead, receives her bridewealth. He keeps most of the cattle to use as bridewealth for his sons' marriages. However, a share also goes to everyone who will be expected to help when Sarah's brothers marry.

When Sarah's brother David gets married, many of the cattle go to a third group: C, which is David's wife's group. Thereafter, they may serve as bridewealth to still other groups. Men constantly use their sisters' bridewealth cattle to acquire their own wives. In a decade, the cattle given when Michael married Sarah will have been exchanged widely.

In such societies, marriage entails an agreement between descent groups. If Sarah and Michael try to make their marriage succeed but fail to do so, both groups may conclude that the marriage can't last. Here it becomes especially obvious that such marriages are relationships between groups as well as between individuals. If Sarah has a younger sister or niece (her older

brother's daughter, for example), the concerned parties may agree to Sarah's replacement by a kinswoman.

However, incompatibility isn't the main problem that threatens marriage in societies with bridewealth. Infertility is a more important concern. If Sarah has no children, she and her group have not fulfilled their part of the marriage agreement. If the relationship is to endure, Sarah's group must furnish another woman, perhaps her younger sister, who can have children. If this happens, Sarah may choose to stay with her husband. Perhaps she will someday have a child. If she does stay on, her husband will have established a plural marriage.

Most nonindustrial food-producing societies, unlike most foraging societies and industrial nations, allow **plural marriages,** or *polygamy.* There are two varieties; one is common, and the other is very rare. The more common variant is **polygyny,** in which a man has more than one wife. The rare

See the Virtual Exploration for bridewealth traditions of the Nenetsi of Siberia

mhhe.com/kottak

exciting," though fleeting. Of these extramarital affairs, she said: "When two people come together their hearts are on fire and their passion is very great. After a while the fire cools and that's how it stays." . . .

While finding that romantic love appears to be a human universal, Dr. Jankowiak allows that it is still an alien idea in many cultures that such infatuation has anything to do with the choice of a spouse.

"What's new in many cultures is the idea that romantic love should be the reason to marry someone," said Dr. Jankowiak. "Some cultures see being in love as a state to be pitied. One tribe in the mountains of Iran ridicules people who marry for love."

Of course, even in arranged marriages, partners may grow to feel romantic love for each other. For example, among villagers in the Kangra valley of northern India, "people's romantic longings and yearnings ideally would become focused on the person they're matched with by their families," said Dr. Kirin Narayan, an anthropologist at the University of Wisconsin.

But that has begun to change, Dr. Narayan is finding, under the influence of popular songs and movies. "In these villages the elders are worried

that the younger men and women are getting a different idea of romantic love, one where you choose a partner yourself," said Dr. Narayan. "There are starting to be elopements, which are absolutely scandalous."

The same trend toward love matches, rather than arranged marriages, is being noted by anthropologists in many other cultures. Among aborigines in Australia's Outback, for example, marriages had for centuries been arranged when children were very young.

That pattern was disrupted earlier in the last century by missionaries, who urged that marriage not occur until children reached adolescence. Dr. Victoria Burbank, an anthropologist at the University of California at Davis, said that in pre-missionary days, the average age of a girl at marriage was always before menarche, sometimes as young as 9 years. Today the average age at marriage is 17; girls are more independent by the time their parents try to arrange a marriage for them.

"More and more adolescent girls are breaking away from arranged marriages," said Dr. Burbank. "They prefer to go off into the bush for a 'date' with someone they like, get pregnant, and use that pregnancy to get parental approval for the match."

Even so, parents sometimes are adamant that the young people should not get married. They prefer, instead, that the girls follow the traditional pattern of having their mothers choose a husband for them.

"Traditionally among these people, you can't choose just any son-in-law," said Dr. Burbank. "Ideally, the mother wants to find a boy who is her maternal grandmother's brother's son, a pattern that insures partners are in the proper kin group."

Dr. Burbank added: "These groups have critical ritual functions. A marriage based on romantic love, which ignores what's a proper partner, undermines the system of kinship, ritual, and obligation."

Nevertheless, the rules for marriage are weakening. "In the grandmothers' generation, all marriages were arranged. Romantic love had no place, though there were a few stories of a young man and woman in love running off together. But in the group I studied, in only one recent case did the girl marry the man selected for her. All the rest are love matches." . . .

SOURCE: Daniel Goleman, "Anthropology Goes Looking in All the Old Places," *New York Times,* November 24, 1992, p. B1.

variant is **polyandry,** in which a woman has more than one husband. If the infertile wife remains married to her husband after he has taken a substitute wife provided by her descent group, this is polygyny. Reasons for polygyny other than infertility will be discussed shortly.

Durable Alliances

It is possible to exemplify the group-alliance nature of marriage by examining still another common practice: continuation of marital alliances when one spouse dies.

Sororate

What happens if Sarah dies young? Michael's group will ask Sarah's group for a substitute, often her sister. This custom is known as the **sororate** (Figure 19.5). If Sarah has no sister or if all her sisters are already married, another woman

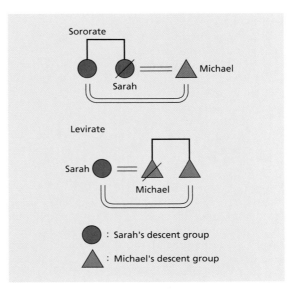

FIGURE 19.5   Sororate and Levirate.

from her group may be available. Michael marries her, there is no need to return the bridewealth, and the alliance continues. The sororate exists in both matrilineal and patrilineal societies. In a matrilineal society with matrilocal postmarital residence, a widower may remain with his wife's group by marrying her sister or another female member of her matrilineage (Figure 19.5).

Levirate

What happens if the husband dies? In many societies, the widow may marry his brother. This custom is known as the **levirate** (Figure 19.5). Like the sororate, it is a continuation marriage that maintains the alliance between descent groups, in this case by replacing the husband with another member of his group. The implications of the levirate vary with age. One study found that in African societies, the levirate, though widely permitted, rarely involves cohabitation of the widow and her new husband. Furthermore, widows don't automatically marry the husband's brother just because they are allowed to. Often, they prefer to make other arrangements (Potash 1986).

DIVORCE

Ease of divorce varies across cultures. What factors work for and against divorce? As we've seen, marriages that are political alliances between groups are more difficult to dissolve than are marriages that are more individual affairs, of concern mainly to the married couple and their children. We've seen that substantial bridewealth may decrease the divorce rate for individuals and that replacement marriages (levirate and sororate) also work to preserve group alliances. Divorce tends to

be more common in matrilineal than in patrilineal societies. When residence is matrilocal (in the wife's place), the wife may simply send off a man with whom she's incompatible.

Among the Hopi of the American Southwest, houses were owned by matrilineal clans, with matrilocal postmarital residence. The household head was the senior woman of that household, which also included her daughters and their husbands and children. A son-in-law had no important role there; he returned to his own mother's home for his clan's social and religious activities. In this matrilineal society, women were socially and economically secure, and the divorce rate was high. Consider the Hopi of Oraibi (Orayvi) pueblo, northeastern Arizona (Levy with Pepper 1992; Titiev 1992). In a study of the marital histories of 423 Oraibi women, Mischa Titiev found that 35 percent had been divorced at least once. Jerome Levy found that 31 percent of 147 adult women had been divorced and remarried at least once. For comparison, of all ever-married women in the United States, only 4 percent had been divorced in 1960, 10.7 percent in 1980, and 11.5 percent in 2004. Titiev characterizes Hopi marriages as unstable. Part of this brittleness was due to conflicting loyalties to matrikin versus spouse. Most Hopi divorces appear to have been matters of personal choice. Levy generalizes that, cross-culturally, high divorce rates are correlated with a secure female economic position. In Hopi society women were secure in their home and land ownership and in the custody of their children. In addition, there were no formal barriers to divorce.

Divorce is harder in a patrilineal society, especially when substantial bridewealth would have to be reassembled and repaid if the marriage failed. A woman residing patrilocally (in her husband's household and community) might be reluctant to leave him. Unlike the Hopi, where the kids stay with the mother, in patrilineal, patrilocal societies, the children of divorce would be expected to remain with their father, as members of his patrilineage. From the women's perspective this is a strong impediment to divorce.

Political and economic factors complicate the divorce process. Among foragers, different factors tend to favor and oppose divorce. What factors work against durable marriages? Since foragers tend to lack descent groups, the political alliance functions of marriage are less important to them than they are to food producers. Foragers also tend to have minimal material possessions. The process of dissolving a joint fund of property is less complicated when spouses do not hold substantial resources in common. What factors favor marital stability among foragers? In societies where the family is an important year-round unit with a gender-based division of labor, ties between spouses tend to be durable. Also, sparse populations mean few alternative spouses if a marriage doesn't work out. But in band-organized societies, foragers can always find a band to join or rejoin if a marriage doesn't work. And food producers can always draw on their descent-group estate if a marriage fails. With patriliny, a woman often can return home, albeit without her children, and with matriliny, a man can do the same. Descent-group estates are not transferred through marriages, although movable resources such as bridewealth cattle certainly are.

In contemporary Western societies, we do stress the idea that romantic love is necessary for a good marriage (see "Interesting Issues," pp. 444–445). When romance fails, so may the marriage. Or it may not fail, if the other rights associated with marriage, as discussed previously in this chapter, are compelling. Economic ties and obligations to kids, along with other factors, such as concern about public opinion, or simple inertia, may keep marriages intact after sex, romance, and/or companionship fade. Also, even in modern societies, royalty, leaders, and other elites may have political marriages similar to the arranged marriages of nonindustrial societies.

In the United States, divorce figures have been kept since 1860. Divorces tend to increase after wars and to decrease when times are bad economically. But with more women working outside the home, economic dependence on the husband as breadwinner is weaker, which no doubt facilitates a decision to divorce when a marriage has major problems.

TABLE 19.1	**Changing Divorce Rates (Number per Year) in the United States, 1940 through 2000**	
Year	Divorce Rate per 1,000 Population	Divorce Rate per 1,000 Women Aged 15 and Older
1940	2.0	8.8
1950	2.6	10.3
1960	2.2	9.2
1970	3.5	14.9
1980	5.2	22.6
1990	4.7	20.9
2000	4.2	19.5
2005	3.6	NA

SOURCES: S. C. Clarke, "Advance Report of Final Divorce Statistics, 1989 and 1990," *Monthly Vital Statistics Report* 43(8, 9). Hyattsville, MD: National Center for Health Statistics; R. Hughes, Jr., "Demographics of Divorce," 1996. http://www.hec.ohio-state.edu/famlife/divorce/demo.htm; *National Vital Statistics Reports* 54(12), 2006. http://www.cdc.gov/nchs/data/nvsr/nvsr54/nvsr54_12.pdf.

Table 19.1 is based on two measures of the divorce rate. The left column shows the rate per 1,000 people per year in the overall population. The right column shows the annual rate per 1,000 married women over the age of 15, which is the best measure of divorce. In either case, comparing 2000 with 1960, the divorce rate more than doubled. Note that the rate rose slightly after World War II (1950), then declined a decade later (1960). The most notable rate rise occurred between 1960 and 1980. The rate actually has been falling since 1980, and continued to fall between 2000 and 2005.

Among nations, the United States has one of the world's highest divorce rates. There are several probable causes: economic, cultural, and religious among them. Economically, the United States has a larger percentage of gainfully employed women than most nations. Work outside the home provides a cash basis for independence, as it also places strains on marriage and social life for both partners. Culturally, Americans tend to value independence and its modern form, self-actualization. Also, Protestantism (in its various guises) is the most common form of religion in the United States. Of the two major religions in the United States and Canada (where Catholicism predominates), Protestantism has been less stringent in denouncing divorce than has Catholicism.

PLURAL MARRIAGES

In contemporary North America, where divorce is fairly easy and common, polygamy (marriage to more than one spouse at the same time) is against the law. Marriage in industrial nations joins individuals, and relationships between individuals can be severed more easily than can those between groups. As divorce grows more common, North Americans practice *serial monogamy*: Individuals have more than one spouse but never, legally, more than one at the same time. As stated earlier, the two forms of polygamy are polygyny and polyandry. Polyandry is practiced in only a few cultures, notably among certain groups in Tibet, Nepal, and India. Polygyny is much more common.

Polygyny

We must distinguish between the social approval of plural marriage and its actual frequency in a particular society. Many cultures approve of a man having more than one wife. However, even when polygyny is encouraged, most men are monogamous, and polygyny characterizes only a fraction of the marriages. Why is this true?

One reason is equal sex ratios. In the United States, about 105 males are born for every 100 females. In adulthood, the ratio of men to women equalizes, and eventually it reverses. The average North American woman outlives the average

Bringing It All Together

For a description of unity and diversity in Canada, see the "Bringing It All Together" essay that immediately follows the chapter "Language and Communication."

■ Members of the Uighur ethnic group, this polygynous family includes two wives, six children, and one husband. They sit in front of their house at the Buzak Commune, near Khotan, Xinjiang Province, People's Republic of China. Would you expect most marriages to be polygynous in a society that allows polygyny?

man. In many nonindustrial societies as well, the male-biased sex ratio among children reverses in adulthood.

The custom of men marrying later than women promotes polygyny. Among the Kanuri people of Bornu, Nigeria (Figure 19.6), men got married between the ages of 18 and 30; women, between 12 and 14 (Cohen 1967). The age difference between spouses meant that there were more widows than widowers. Most of the widows remarried, some in polygynous unions. Among the Kanuri of Bornu and in other polygynous societies, widows made up a large number of the women involved in plural marriages (Hart, Pilling, and Goodale 1988). In many societies, including the Kanuri, the number of wives is an indicator of a man's household productivity, prestige, and social position. The more wives, the more workers. Increased productivity means more wealth. This wealth in turn attracts additional wives to the household. Wealth and wives bring greater prestige to the household and head.

If a plural marriage is to work, there needs to be some agreement among the existing spouses

when another one is to be added, especially if they are to share the same household. In certain societies, the first wife requests a second wife to help with household chores. The second wife's status is lower than that of the first; they are senior and junior wives. The senior wife sometimes chooses the junior one from among her close kinswomen. Among the Betsileo of Madagascar, the different wives always lived in different villages. A man's first and senior wife, called "Big Wife," lived in the village where he cultivated his best rice field and spent most of his time. High-status men with several rice fields and multiple wives had households near each field. They spent most of their time with the senior wife but visited the others throughout the year.

Plural wives can play important political roles in nonindustrial states. The king of the Merina, a society with more than one million people in the highlands of Madagascar, had palaces for each of his 12 wives in different provinces. He stayed with them when he traveled through the kingdom. They were his local agents, overseeing and reporting on provincial matters. The king of

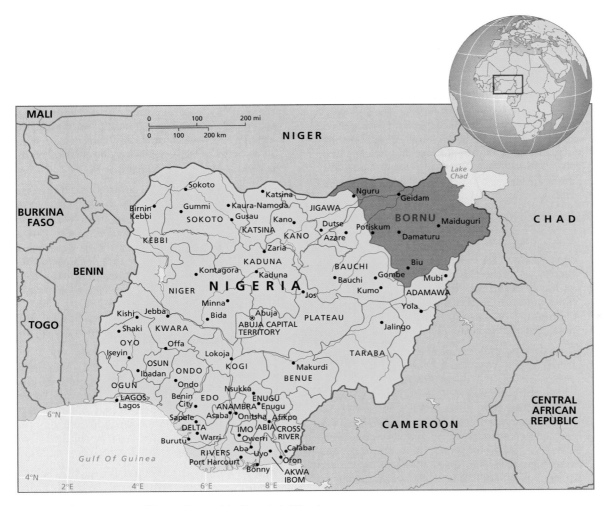

FIGURE 19.6 Location of Bornu, home of the Kanuri, in Nigeria.

Buganda, the major precolonial state of Uganda, took hundreds of wives, representing all the clans in his nation. Everyone in the kingdom became the king's in-law, and all the clans had a chance to provide the next ruler. This was a way of giving the common people a stake in the government.

These examples show that there is no single explanation for polygyny. Its context and function vary from society to society and even within the same society. Some men are polygynous because they have inherited a widow from a brother (the levirate). Others have plural wives because they seek prestige or want to increase household productivity. Still others use marriage as a political tool or a means of economic advancement. Men and women with political and economic ambitions cultivate marital alliances that serve their aims. In many societies, including the Betsileo of Madagascar and the Igbo of Nigeria, women arrange the marriages.

Polyandry

Polyandry is rare and is practiced under very specific conditions. Most of the world's polyandrous peoples live in South Asia—Tibet, Nepal, India, and Sri Lanka. In some of these areas, polyandry seems to be a cultural adaptation to mobility associated with customary male travel for trade, commerce, and military operations. Polyandry ensures there will be at least one man at home to accomplish male activities within a gender-based division of labor. Fraternal polyandry is also an effective strategy when resources are scarce. Brothers with limited resources (in land) pool their resources in expanded (polyandrous) households. They take just one wife. Polyandry restricts the number of wives and heirs. Less competition among heirs means that land can be transmitted with minimal fragmentation.

1. Marriage, which is usually a form of domestic partnership, is hard to define. All societies have some kind of incest taboo. Human behavior with respect to mating with close relatives may express a generalized primate tendency, illustrating both urges and avoidance. But types, risks, and avoidance of incest also reflect specific kinship structures. A cultural focus on father–daughter incest may correlate with a patriarchal nuclear family structure, whereas the cultural focus is on avoiding brother–sister incest in societies with lineages and clans.

2. The following are some of the explanations that have been offered for the incest taboo: (1) It codifies instinctive horror of incest, (2) it expresses concern about the biological effects of incestuous unions, (3) it reflects feelings of attraction or aversion that develop as one grows up in a household, and (4) it has an adaptive advantage because it promotes exogamy, thereby increasing networks of friends and allies.

3. Exogamy extends social and political ties outward. This is confirmed by a consideration of endogamy—marriage within the group. Endogamic rules are common in stratified societies. One extreme example is India, where castes are the endogamous units. Castes are subdivided into exogamous descent groups. The same culture can therefore have both endogamic and exogamic rules. Certain ancient kingdoms encouraged royal incest while condemning incest by commoners.

4. The discussion of same-sex marriage, which, by and large, is illegal in contemporary North America, illustrates the various rights that go along with different-sex marriages. Marriage establishes the legal parents of children. It gives spouses rights to the sexuality, labor, and property of the other. And it establishes a socially significant "relationship of affinity" between spouses and each other's relatives. Some of these rights may be established by same-sex domestic partnerships.

5. In societies with descent groups, marriages are relationships between groups as well as between spouses. With the custom of bridewealth, the groom and his relatives transfer wealth to the bride and her relatives. As the bridewealth's value increases, the divorce rate declines. Bridewealth customs show that marriages among nonindustrial food producers create and maintain group alliances. So do the sororate, by which a man marries the sister of his deceased wife, and the levirate, by which a woman marries the brother of her deceased husband.

6. The ease and frequency of divorce vary across cultures. Political, economic, social, cultural, and religious factors affect the divorce rate. When marriage is a matter of intergroup alliance, as is typically true in societies with descent groups, divorce is less common. A large fund of joint property also complicates divorce.

7. Many societies permit plural marriages. The two kinds of polygamy are polygyny and polyandry. The former involves multiple wives; the latter, multiple husbands. Polygyny is much more common than is polyandry.

KEY TERMS

See the flash cards
mhhe.com/kottak

bridewealth See *progeny price.*

cross cousins Children of a brother and a sister.

dowry A marital exchange in which the wife's group provides substantial gifts to the husband's family.

endogamy Rule or practice of marriage between people of the same social group.

exogamy Rule requiring people to marry outside their own group.

genitor Biological father of a child.

incest Forbidden sexual relations with a close relative.

levirate Custom by which a widow marries the brother of her deceased husband.

mater Socially recognized mother of a child.

parallel cousins Children of two brothers or two sisters.

pater Socially recognized father of a child; not necessarily the genitor.

plural marriage Any marriage with more than two spouses, aka polygamy.

polyandry Variety of plural marriage in which a woman has more than one husband.

polygyny Variety of plural marriage in which a man has more than one wife.

progeny price A gift from the husband and his kin to the wife and her kin before, at, or after marriage; legitimizes children born to the woman as members of the husband's descent group.

sororate Custom by which a widower marries the sister of his deceased wife.

CRITICAL
THINKING
QUESTIONS

For more self-testing,
see the self-quizzes

mhhe.com/kottak

1. Try to come up with a definition of marriage that fits all the cases examined in this chapter. What problems do you encounter in doing this?

2. What is bridewealth? What else is it called, and why? Do we have anything like it in our own society? Why or why not?

3. What is the difference between sororate and levirate? What do they have in common? Do these customs make sense to you?

4. If you had to live in a society with plural marriage, would you prefer polygyny or polyandry? Why?

5. What general conclusions do you draw about the differences between marriage in your society and marriage in nonindustrial societies?

Collier, J. F., ed.
   1988   *Marriage and Inequality in Classless Societies.* Stanford, CA: Stanford University Press. Marriage and issues of gender stratification in bands and tribes.

Goody, J., and S. T. Tambiah
   1973   *Bridewealth and Dowry.* Cambridge, England: Cambridge University Press. Marital exchanges in comparative perspective.

Hart, C. W. M., A. R. Pilling, and J. C. Goodale
   1988   *The Tiwi of North Australia,* 3rd ed. Fort Worth: Harcourt Brace. Latest edition of classic case study of Tiwi marriage arrangements, including polygyny, and social change over 60 years of anthropological study.

Ingraham, C.
   1999   *White Weddings: Romancing Heterosexuality in Popular Culture.* New York: Routledge. Love and marriage, including the ceremony, in today's United States.

Levine, N. E.
   1988   *The Dynamics of Polyandry: Kinship, Domesticity, and Population in the Tibetan Border.* Chicago: University of Chicago Press. Case study of fraternal polyandry and household organization in northwestern Nepal.

Malinowski, B.
   2001   (orig. 1927). *Sex and Repression in Savage Society.* New York: Routledge. Classic study of sex, marriage, and kinship among the matrilineal Trobrianders.

Murray, S. O., and W. Roscoe, eds.
   1998   *Boy-Wives and Female Husbands: Studies in African Homosexualities.* New York: St. Martin's. Same-sex sex and marriage in Africa.

Ottenheimer, M.
   1996   *Forbidden Relatives: The American Myth of Cousin Marriage.* Champaign–Urbana: University of Illinois Press. Incest laws and cousin marriage in the United States and Europe.

Shepher, J.
   1983   *Incest, a Biosocial View.* New York: Academic Press. A view from Israel, based on a case study in the kibbutz.

Simpson, B.
   1998   *Changing Families: An Ethnographic Approach to Divorce and Separation.* New York: Berg. Current marriage and divorce trends in Great Britain.

1. Weddings: Here are some websites that sell wedding supplies for couples from different nationalities and traditions. Pick three of these websites and answer the questions below: Indian, **http://www.weddingsutra.com/**; Jewish, **http://www.mazornet.com/jewishcl/jewishwd.htm**; African American, **http://www.africanweddingguide.com/**; Mormon, **http://www.askginka.com/religions/mormon.htm**; Eastern Orthodox, **http://www.askginka.com/religions/eastern_orthodox.htm**; Muslim, **http://www.askginka.com/religions/muslim.htm**; Roman Catholic, **http://www.askginka.com/religions/catholic.htm**.

a. What kinds of clothes are worn by the bride and the groom? To what degree are the clothes dictated by tradition or modern style? How much choice do the wedding planners have in the clothing that is worn?

b. What kind of locations are popular for the weddings?

c. What aspects of each of these weddings is most different from your own? What aspects are similar?

d. Why do you think wedding traditions vary so much by culture and religion?

2. Descent and Postmarital Residence Rules: Go to the Ethnographic Atlas Cross-Tabulations page, **http://lucy.ukc.ac.uk/cgi-bin/uncgi/Ethnoatlas/atlas.vopts**. This site has compiled ethnographic information on many different groups, and you can use the tools provided to cross-tabulate the prevalence of certain traits. Under "Select Row Category" choose "descent," and under "Select Column Category" select "transfer of residence at marriage: prevalent form." Press the Submit Query button. The table that appears shows the frequency of postmarital residence rules for groups with different descent systems.
   a. What postmarital residence rules are most common for patrilineal groups? For matrilineal groups? Is this what you would expect?
   b. Based on your observations in section a, what postmarital residence practice would you least expect to find in patrilineal societies? How many groups in this chart practice such a pattern? Click on the number at that location to find out which groups those are and where they are located. What postmarital residence pattern would you least expect to find in matrilineal societies? Which groups practice that pattern?
   c. What is the most common form of descent for groups with an "Optional for couple" (ambilocal) postmarital residence pattern? Does this make sense?

See Chapter 19 at your McGraw-Hill Online Learning Center for additional review and interactive exercises.

LINKAGES

Kottak, *Assault on Paradise*, 4th ed.

Chapters 3 and 9 discuss types of marriage and domestic partnership in Arembepe. Chapter 3 describes the arrangements during the 1960s, and Chapter 9 shows how ideas and behavior concerning marriage had changed by the 1980s. What was the main incentive to marry formally in the 1960s? What were the main reasons for the changes described? Have there been significant changes in your own society in ideas about marriage and marital behavior over the last few years?

Peters-Golden, *Culture Sketches*, 4th ed.

In *Culture Sketches,* read Chapter 13, "Tiwi: Tradition in Australia." A tradition, no longer practiced, that all Tiwi females had to be married led to the betrothal of baby girls and the mandatory remarriage of all widows. This practice served several social ends. How do Tiwi marriage customs illustrate the social functions of marriage, as discussed in this text chapter? How do Tiwi customs compare with the rules and functions of marriage in your own society? Have those changed over time? If so, what might be the reason?

Knauft, *The Gebusi*, 1st ed.

Based on information in Chapters 4 and 10 of *The Gebusi*, what is the ideal form of marriage in Gebusi society? How much influence do women have in determining such marriages? Based on Chapter 4, what form of reciprocity do Gebusi practice between the bride's and the groom's groups? What is likely to happen when reciprocity cannot be arranged? What kinds of violence are related to marriage patterns in Gebusi society, and who is most likely to be attacked or killed? Based on Chapter 10 of *The Gebusi,* how did Gebusi marriage patterns change between 1980 and 1998? What benefits and what costs have been experienced by young Gebusi men and women as marriage patterns have changed?

20

Gender

SEX AND GENDER

Because anthropologists study biology, society, and culture, they are in a unique position to comment on nature (biological predispositions) and nurture (environment) as determinants of human behavior. Human attitudes, values, and behavior are limited not only by our genetic predispositions—which are often difficult to identify—but also by our experiences during enculturation. Our attributes as adults are determined both by our genes and by our environment during growth and development.

Questions about nature and nurture emerge in the discussion of human sex-gender roles and sexuality. Men and women differ genetically. Women have two X chromosomes, and men have an X and a Y. The father determines a baby's sex because only he has the Y chromosome to transmit. The mother always provides an X chromosome.

The chromosomal difference is expressed in hormonal and physiological contrasts. Humans are sexually dimorphic, more so than some primates, such as gibbons (small tree-living Asiatic apes), and less so than others, such as gorillas and orangutans. **Sexual dimorphism**

The realm of cultural diversity contains richly different social constructions and expressions of gender roles, as is illustrated by these Wodaabe male celebrants in Niger. (Look closely for suggestions of diffusion.) For what reasons do men decorate their bodies in our society?

Just how far, however, do such genetically and physiologically determined differences go? What effects do they have on the way men and women act and are treated in different societies? Anthropologists have discovered both similarities and differences in the roles of men and women in different cultures. The predominant anthropological position on sex-gender roles and biology may be stated as follows:

> The biological nature of men and women [should be seen] not as a narrow enclosure limiting the human organism, but rather as a broad base upon which a variety of structures can be built. (Friedl 1975, p. 6)

Although in most societies men tend to be somewhat more aggressive than women are, many of the behavioral and attitudinal differences between the sexes emerge from culture rather than biology. Sex differences are biological, but gender encompasses all the traits that a culture assigns to and inculcates in males and females. "Gender," in other words, refers to the cultural construction of male and female characteristics (Rosaldo 1980b).

Given the "rich and various constructions of gender" within the realm of cultural diversity, Susan Bourque and Kay Warren (1987) note that the same images of masculinity and femininity do not always apply. Anthropologists have gathered systematic ethnographic data about similarities and differences involving gender in many cultural settings (Bonvillain 2001; Brettell and Sargent 2005; Gilmore 2001; Mascia-Lees and Black 2000; Nanda 2000; Ward and Edelstein 2006). Anthropologists can detect recurrent themes and patterns involving gender differences. They also can observe that gender roles vary with environment, economy, adaptive strategy, and type of political system. Before we examine the cross-cultural data, some definitions are in order.

Gender roles are the tasks and activities a culture assigns to the sexes. Related to gender roles are **gender stereotypes,** which are oversimplified

refers to differences in male and female biology besides the contrasts in breasts and genitals. Women and men differ not just in primary (genitalia and reproductive organs) and secondary (breasts, voice, hair distribution) sexual characteristics but in average weight, height, strength, and longevity. Women tend to live longer than men and have excellent endurance capabilities. In a given population, men tend to be taller and to weigh more than women do. Of course, there is a considerable overlap between the sexes in terms of height, weight, and physical strength, and there has been a pronounced reduction in sexual dimorphism during human biological evolution.

OVERVIEW

Gender refers to the cultural construction of sexual difference. Male and female are biological sexes that differ in their X and Y chromosomes. Gender roles are the activities a culture assigns to each sex. Gender stratification describes an unequal distribution of rights and resources between the genders. Sometimes a distinction between extradomestic and domestic labor reinforces a contrast between males perceived as being publicly active and females seen as being domestic and less valuable. Patriarchy describes a system in which women have inferior social and political status. Although anthropologists know of no society in which women as a group dominate men as a group, women in many societies wield power and serve as leaders. In North America, female cash labor has increased, promoting greater autonomy for many women. But also increasing, globally, is the feminization of poverty: the rise in poor families headed by women. Despite individual variation in sexual orientation within a society, culture always plays a role in molding individual sexual urges toward a collective norm. Such norms vary widely from culture to culture.

Indonesia's Matriarchal Minangkabau Offer an Alternative Social System

EUREKALERT NEWS BRIEF

by Pam Kosty
May 9, 2002

Cross-culturally, anthropologists have described tremendous variation in the roles of men and women, and the power differentials between them. If a patriarchy is a political system ruled by men, what would a matriarchy be? Would a matriarchy be a political system ruled by women, or a political system in which women play a much more prominent role than men do in social and political organization? This news account reports on Peggy Sanday's conclusion that matriarchies exist, but not as mirror images of patriarchies. The superior power that men typically have in a patriarchy isn't matched by women's equally disproportionate power in a matriarchy. Many societies, like the Minangkabau described here, lack the substantial power

differentials that usually accompany patriarchal systems. In reading this account, pay attention to the centrality of Minangkabau women in social, economic, and ceremonial life and as key symbols. Matrilineality is uncommon as an organizing principle in nation-states, such as Indonesia, where the Minangkabau live. But political systems operate at different levels. We see here that matriliny and matriarchy are expressed locally, at the village level, and regionally, where seniority of matrilineal descent serves as a way to rank villages.

For the last century, . . . scholars have searched both human history and the continents to find a matriarchy—a society where the power was in the hands of women, not men. Most have concluded that a genuine matriarchy does not exist, perhaps may never have existed.

Anthropologist Peggy Reeves Sanday, Consulting Curator, University of Pennsylvania Museum of Archaeology and Anthropology, disagrees. After years of research among the Minangkabau people of West Sumatra, Indonesia, she has accepted that group's own self-labeling, as a "matriarchate," or matriarchy. The problem, she asserts, lies in Western cultural notions of what a matriarchy "should" look like—patriarchy's female-twin.

"Too many anthropologists have been looking for a society where women rule the affairs of everyday life, including government," she said. "That template—and a singular, Western perspective on power—doesn't fit very well when you're looking at non-Western cultures like

A Minangkabau bride and groom in West Sumatra, Indonesia, where anthropologist Peggy Reeves Sanday has conducted several years of ethnographic field work.

the Minangkabau of West Sumatra, Indonesia, where males and females are partners for the common good rather than competitors ruled by self-interest. Social prestige accrues to those who promote good relations by following the dictates of custom and religion."

The four million Minangkabau, one of Indonesia's largest ethnic groups, live in the highlands of the province of West Sumatra. Their society is founded on the coexistence of matrilineal custom and a nature-based philosophy called adat. More recently, Islam has been incorporated into the foundation . . .

The key to Minangkabau matriarchy, according to Sanday, is found in the ever-present adat idea [that] "One must nurture growth in humans, animals, and plants so that society will be strong." . . .

The emphasis on nurturing growth yields a unique emphasis on the maternal in daily life. The Minangkabau glorify their mythical Queen Mother and cooperation. In village social relations senior women are associated with the central pillar of the traditional house, which is the oldest pillar because it is the first erected. The oldest village in a group of villages is referred to as the "mother village." When they stage ceremonies in their full ceremonial regalia, women are addressed by the same term reserved for the mythical Queen. Such practices suggest that matriarchy in this society is about making the maternal the center, origin, and foundation, not just of life but of the social order as well.

The power of Minangkabau women extends to the economic and social realms. Women control land inheritance, and husbands move into the households of their wives . . . During the wedding ceremony the wife collects her husband from his household and, with her female relatives, brings him back to her household to live. In the event of a divorce the husband collects his clothes and leaves. Yet, despite the special position women are accorded in the society, the Minangkabau matriarchy is not the equivalent of female rule.

"Neither male nor female rule is possible because of the Minangkabau belief that decision-making should be by consensus," Dr. Sanday said. "In answer to my persistent questions about 'who rules,' I was often told that I was asking the wrong question. Neither sex rules, it was explained to me, because males and females complement one another."

Today, according to Dr. Sanday, while the Minangkabau matriarchy is based largely on adat, Islam also plays a role. Islam arrived in West Sumatra sometime in the 16th century, long after adat customs and philosophy had been established. At first there was an uneasy relationship between adat and Islam and, in the 19th century, a war between adherents of adat customs and fundamentalist beliefs imported from Mecca. The conflict was resolved by both sides making accommodations. Today, matrilineal adat and Islam are accepted as equally sacred and inviolate.

Resurgent Islamic fundamentalism, nationalism, and expanding capitalism may erode the Minangkabau's nature-based matriarchal culture and the adat that infuses meaning into their lives. [Sanday] remains optimistic that their culture has the innate flexibility to adapt to a changing world. "Had the Minangkabau chosen to fight rather than to accommodate the numerous influences that impinged on their world over the centuries, had they chosen to assert cultural purity, no doubt their 'adat' would have long ago succumbed. The moral of the Minangkabau story is that accommodating differences can preserve a world."

SOURCE: http://www.eurekalert.org/pub_releases/2002-05/uop-imm050902.php.

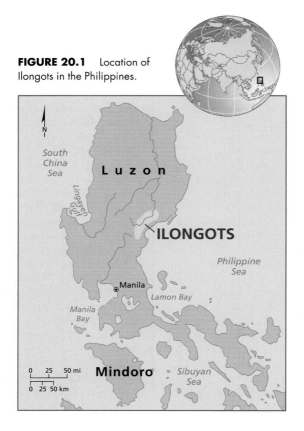

FIGURE 20.1   Location of Ilongots in the Philippines.

but strongly held ideas about the characteristics of males and females. **Gender stratification** describes an unequal distribution of rewards (socially valued resources, power, prestige, human rights, and personal freedom) between men and women, reflecting their different positions in a social hierarchy. According to Ann Stoler (1977), the "economic determinants of gender status" include

freedom or autonomy (in disposing of one's labor and its fruits) and social power (control over the lives, labor, and produce of others).

In stateless societies, gender stratification is often more obvious in regard to prestige than it is in regard to wealth. In her study of the Ilongots of northern Luzon in the Philippines (Figure 20.1), Michelle Rosaldo (1980a) described gender differences related to the positive cultural value placed on adventure, travel, and knowledge of the external world. More often than women, Ilongot men, as headhunters, visited distant places. They acquired knowledge of the external world, amassed experiences there, and returned to express their knowledge, adventures, and feelings in public oratory. They received acclaim as a result. Ilongot women had inferior prestige because they lacked external experiences on which to base knowledge and dramatic expression. On the basis of Rosaldo's study and findings in other stateless societies, Ong (1989) argues that we must distinguish between prestige systems and actual power in a given society. High male prestige may not entail economic or political power held by men over their families.

RECURRENT GENDER PATTERNS

Remember from previous chapters that ethnologists compare ethnographic data from several cultures (i.e., cross-cultural data) to discover and explain differences and similarities. Data relevant to the cross-cultural study of gender can be drawn from the domains of economics, politics, domestic activity, kinship, and marriage. Table 20.1 shows cross-cultural data from 185 randomly selected societies on the division of labor by gender.

For information on multiple genders among Native Americans, see the Internet Exercises at your OLC

mhhe.com/kottak

Remembering the discussion, in Chapter 13 on "Culture," of universals, generalities, and particularities, the findings in Table 20.1 about the division of labor by gender illustrate generalities rather than universals. That is, among the societies known to ethnography, there is a very strong tendency for men to build boats, but there are exceptions. One was the Hidatsa, a Native American group in which the women made the boats used to cross the Missouri River. (Traditionally, the Hidatsa were village farmers and bison hunters on the North American Plains; they now live in North Dakota.) Another exception: Pawnee women worked wood; this is the only Native American group that assigned this activity to women. (The Pawnee, also traditionally Plains farmers and bison hunters, originally lived in what is now central Nebraska and central Kansas; they now live on a reservation in north central Oklahoma.) Among the Mbuti "pygmies" of Africa's Ituri forest, women hunt by catching small, slow animals, using their hands or a net (Murdock and Provost 1973).

Exceptions to cross-cultural generalizations may involve societies or individuals. That is, a society like the Hidatsa can contradict the cross-cultural generalization that men build boats by assigning that task to women. Or, in a society where the cultural expectation is that only men build boats, a particular woman or women can contradict that expectation by doing the male activity. Table 20.1 shows that in a sample of 185 societies, certain activities ("swing activities") are assigned to either or both men and women.

TABLE 20.1 Generalities in the Division of Labor by Gender, Based on Data from 185 Societies

Generally Male Activities	Swing (Male or Female) Activities	Generally Female Activities
Hunting large aquatic animals (e.g., whales, walrus)	Making fire	Gathering fuel (e.g., firewood)
Smelting ores	Body mutilation	Making drinks
Metalworking	Preparing skins	Gathering wild vegetal foods
Lumbering	Gathering small land animals	Dairy production (e.g., churning)
Hunting large land animals	Planting crops	Spinning
Working wood	Making leather products	Doing the laundry
Hunting fowl	Harvesting	Fetching water
Making musical instruments	Tending crops	Cooking
Trapping	Milking	Preparing vegetal food (e.g., processing cereal grains)
Building boats	Making baskets	
Working stone	Carrying burdens	
Working bone, horn, and shell	Making mats	
Mining and quarrying	Caring for small animals	
Setting bones	Preserving meat and fish	
Butchering*	Loom weaving	
Collecting wild honey	Gathering small aquatic animals	
Clearing land	Clothing manufacture	
Fishing	Making pottery	
Tending large herd animals		
Building houses		
Preparing the soil		
Making nets		
Making rope		

*All the activities above "butchering" are almost always done by men; those from "butchering" through "making rope" usually are done by men.

SOURCE: Adapted from G. P. Murdock and C. Provost, "Factors in the Division of Labor by Sex: A Cross-Cultural Analysis," *Ethnology* 12(2):202–225.

In many societies women routinely do hard physical labor, as is illustrated by these women carrying bricks inside a kiln in Adlaj, India in March 2006. Anthropologists have described both commonalities and differences in gender roles and activities among the world's societies.

What's missing from Table 20.1? Notice that there's no mention of trade and market activity, in which either or both men and women are active. Is Table 20.1 somewhat androcentric in detailing more tasks for men than for women? More than men, women do child care, but the study on which Table 20.1 is based (Murdock and Provost 1973) does not break down domestic activities to the same extent that it details extradomestic activities.

Both women and men have to fit their activities into 24-hour days. Based on cross-cultural data, Table 20.2 shows that the time and effort spent in subsistence activities by men and women tend to be about equal. If anything, men do slightly less subsistence work than women do. Think about how female domestic activities could have been specified in greater detail in Table 20.1. The original coding of the data in Table 20.1 probably illustrates a male bias in that extradomestic activities received much more prominence than domestic activities did. For example, is collecting wild honey (listed in Table 20.1) more necessary and/or time-consuming than cleaning a baby's bottom (absent from Table 20.1)? Think about Table 20.1 in terms of today's home and job roles and with respect to the activities done by contemporary women and men. Men still do most of the hunting; either gender can collect the honey from a supermarket, even as most baby bottom wiping continues to be in female hands.

Among the most important of such activities are planting, tending, and harvesting crops. We'll see below that some societies customarily assign more farming chores to women, whereas others call on men to be the main farm laborers. Among the tasks almost always assigned to men (Table 20.1), some (e.g., hunting large animals on land and sea) seem clearly related to the greater average size and strength of males. Others, such as working wood and making musical instruments, seem more culturally arbitrary. And women, of course, are not exempt from arduous and time-consuming physical labor, such as gathering firewood and fetching water. In Arembepe, Bahia, Brazil, women routinely transport water in five-gallon tins, balanced on their heads, from wells and lagoons located at long distances from their homes.

Cross-culturally the subsistence contributions of men and women are roughly equal (Table 20.2). But in domestic activities and child care, female labor predominates, as we see in Tables 20.3 and 20.4. Table 20.3 shows that in about half the societies studied, men did virtually no domestic work. Even in societies where men did

TABLE 20.2 Time and Effort Expended on Subsistence Activities by Men and Women*

More by men	16
Roughly equal	61
More by women	23

*Percentage of 88 randomly selected societies for which information was available on this variable.

SOURCE: M. F. Whyte, "Cross-Cultural Codes Dealing with the Relative Status of Women," *Ethnology* 17(2):211–239.

some domestic chores, the bulk of such work was done by women. Adding together their subsistence activities and their domestic work, women tend to work more hours than men do. Has this changed in the contemporary world?

What about child care? Women tend to be the main caregivers in most societies, but men often play a role. Again there are exceptions, both within and between societies. Table 20.4 uses cross-cultural data to answer the question "Who—men or women—has final authority over the care, handling, and discipline of children younger than four years?" Although women have primary authority over infants in two-thirds of the societies, there are still societies (18 percent of the total) in which men have the major say. In the United States and Canada today, some men are primary child caregivers despite the cultural fact that the female role in child care remains more prominent in both countries. Given the critical role of breast-feeding in ensuring infant survival,

TABLE 20.3 Who Does the Domestic Work?*

Males do virtually none	51
Males do some, but mostly done by females	49

*Percentage of 92 randomly selected societies for which information was available on this variable.

SOURCE: M. F. Whyte, "Cross-Cultural Codes Dealing with the Relative Status of Women," *Ethnology* 17(2):211–239.

TABLE 20.4 Who Has Final Authority over the Care, Handling, and Discipline of Infant Children (under Four Years Old)?*

Males have more say	18
Roughly equal	16
Females have more say	66

*Percentage of 67 randomly selected societies for which information was available on this variable.

SOURCE: M. F. Whyte, "Cross-Cultural Codes Dealing with the Relative Status of Women," *Ethnology* 17(2):211–239.

TABLE 20.5 Does the Society Allow Multiple Spouses?*

Only for males	77
For both, but more commonly for males	4
For neither	16
For both, but more commonly for females	2

*Percentage of 92 randomly selected societies.

SOURCE: M. F. Whyte, "Cross-Cultural Codes Dealing with the Relative Status of Women," *Ethnology* 17(2):211–239.

TABLE 20.6 Is There a Double Standard with Respect to PREMARITAL Sex*

Yes—females are more restricted	44
No—equal restrictions on males and females	56

*Percentage of 73 randomly selected societies for which information was available on this variable.

SOURCE: M. F. Whyte, "Cross-Cultural Codes Dealing with the Relative Status of Women," *Ethnology* 17(2):211–239.

TABLE 20.7 Is There a Double Standard with Respect to EXTRAMARITAL Sex*

Yes—females are more restricted	43
Equal restrictions on males and females	55
Males punished more severely for transgression	3

*Percentage of 75 randomly selected societies for which information was available on this variable.

SOURCE: M. F. Whyte, "Cross-Cultural Codes Dealing with the Relative Status of Women," *Ethnology* 17(2):211–239.

it makes sense, for infants especially, for the mother to be the primary caregiver.

There are differences in male and female reproductive strategies. Women give birth, breast-feed, and assume primary responsibility for infant care. Women ensure that their progeny will survive by establishing a close bond with each baby. It's also advantageous for a woman to have a reliable mate to ease the child-rearing process and ensure the survival of her children. (Again, there are exceptions, for example, the matrilineal Nayars discussed in the chapter "Families, Kinship, and Descent.") Women can have only so many babies during the course of their reproductive years, which begin after menarche (the advent of first menstruation) and end with menopause (cessation of menstruation). Men, in contrast, have a longer reproductive period, which can last into the elder years. If they choose to do so, men can enhance their reproductive success by impregnating several women over a longer time period. Although men do not always have multiple mates, they do have a greater tendency to do so than women do (see Tables 20.5, 20.6, and 20.7). Among the societies known to ethnography, polygyny is much more common than polyandry is (see Table 20.5).

Men mate, within and outside marriage, more than women do. Table 20.6 shows cross-cultural data on premarital sex, and Table 20.7 summarizes the data on extramarital sex. In both cases men are less restricted than women are, although the restrictions are equal in about half the societies studied.

Double standards that restrict women more than men illustrate gender stratification. Several studies have shown that economic roles affect gender stratification. In one cross-cultural study, Sanday (1974) found that gender stratification decreased when men and women made roughly equal contributions to subsistence. She found that gender stratification was greatest when the women contributed either much more or much less than the men did.

■ *Among foragers, gender stratification tends to increase when men contribute much more to the diet than women do—as has been true among the Inuit and other northern hunters and fishers. Shown here, Mikile, an Inuit hunter, opens up a narwhal he hunted and killed near Qeqertat in Northwest Greenland.*

GENDER AMONG FORAGERS

In foraging societies, gender stratification was most marked when men contributed much more to the diet than women did. This was true among the Inuit and other northern hunters and fishers. Among tropical and semitropical foragers, by contrast, gathering usually supplies more food than hunting and fishing do. Gathering is generally women's work. Men usually hunt and fish, but women also do some fishing and may hunt small animals. When gathering is prominent, gender status tends to be more equal than it is when hunting and fishing are the main subsistence activities.

Gender status is also more equal when the domestic and public spheres aren't sharply separated. (*Domestic* means within or pertaining to the home.) Strong differentiation between the home and the outside world is called the **domestic–public dichotomy** or the *private–public contrast.* The outside world can include politics, trade, warfare, or work. Often when domestic and public spheres are clearly separated, public activities have greater prestige than domestic ones do. This can promote gender stratification, because men are more likely to be active in the public domain than women are. Cross-culturally, women's activities tend to be closer to home than men's are. Thus, another reason hunter-gatherers have less gender stratification than food producers do is that the domestic–public dichotomy is less developed among foragers.

We've seen that certain gender roles are more sex-linked than others. Men are the usual hunters and warriors. Given such tools and weapons as spears, knives, and bows, men make better hunters and fighters because they are bigger and stronger on the average than are women in the

same population (Divale and Harris 1976). The male hunter-fighter role also reflects a tendency toward greater male mobility.

In foraging societies, women are either pregnant or lactating during most of their childbearing period. Late in pregnancy and after childbirth, carrying a baby limits a woman's movements, even her gathering. However, among the Agta of the Philippines (Griffin and Estioko-Griffin, eds. 1985) women not only gather, they also hunt with dogs while carrying their babies with them. Still, given the effects of pregnancy and breast-feeding on mobility, it is rarely feasible for women to be the primary hunters (Friedl 1975). Warfare, which also requires mobility, is not found in most foraging societies, nor is interregional trade well developed. Warfare and trade are two public arenas that can contribute to status inequality of males and females among food producers.

The Ju/'hoansi San illustrate the extent to which the activities and spheres of influence of men and women may overlap among foragers (Draper 1975). Traditional Ju/'hoansi gender roles were interdependent. During gathering, women discovered information about game animals, which they passed on to the men. Men and women spent about the same amount of time away from the camp, but neither worked more than three days a week. Between one-third and one-half of the band stayed home while the others worked.

The Ju/'hoansi saw nothing wrong in doing the work of the other gender. Men often gathered food and collected water. A general sharing ethos dictated that men distribute meat and that women share the fruits of gathering. Boys and girls of all ages played together. Fathers took an active role in raising children. Resources were adequate, and competition and aggression were discouraged. Exchangeability and interdependence of roles are adaptive in small groups.

Patricia Draper's field work among the Ju/'hoansi is especially useful in showing the relationships between economy, gender roles, and stratification because she studied both foragers and a group of former foragers who had become sedentary. Just a few thousand Ju/'hoansi continue their culture's traditional foraging pattern. Most are now sedentary, living near food producers or ranchers (see Kent 1992; Solway and Lee 1990; Wilmsen 1989).

Draper studied sedentary Ju/'hoansi at Mahopa, a village where they herded, grew crops, worked for wages, and did a small amount of gathering. Their gender roles were becoming more rigidly defined. A domestic–public dichotomy was developing as men traveled farther than women did. With less gathering, women were confined more to the home. Boys could gain mobility through herding, but girls' movements were more limited. The equal and communal world of the bush was yielding to the social features of sedentary life. A differential ranking of men according to their herds, houses, and sons began to replace sharing. Males came to be seen as more valuable producers.

If there is some degree of male dominance in virtually every contemporary society, it may be because of changes such as those that have drawn the Ju/'hoansi into wage work, market sales, and thus the world capitalist economy. A historic interplay between local, national, and international forces influences systems of gender stratification (Ong 1989). In traditional foraging cultures, however, egalitarianism extended to the relations between the sexes. The social spheres, activities, rights, and obligations of men and women overlapped. Foragers' kinship systems tend to be bilateral (calculated equally through males and females) rather than favoring either the mother's side or the father's side. Foragers may live with either the husband's or the wife's kin and often shift between one group and the other.

One last observation about foragers: It is among them that the public and private spheres are least separate, hierarchy is least marked, aggression and competition are most discouraged, and the rights, activities, and spheres of influence of men and women overlap the most. Our ancestors lived entirely by foraging until 10,000 years ago. If there is any most "natural" form of human society, it is best, although imperfectly, represented by foragers. Despite the popular stereotype of the club-wielding caveman dragging his mate by the hair, relative gender equality is a much more likely ancestral pattern.

GENDER AMONG HORTICULTURALISTS

Gender roles and stratification among cultivators vary widely, depending on specific features of the economy and social structure. Demonstrating this, Martin and Voorhies (1975) studied a sample of 515 horticultural societies, representing all parts of the world. They looked at several variables, including descent and postmarital residence, the percentage of the diet derived from cultivation, and the productivity of men and women.

Women were found to be the main producers in horticultural societies. In 50 percent of those societies, women did most of the cultivating. In 33 percent, contributions to cultivation by men and women were equal. In only 17 percent did men do most of the work. Women tended to do a bit more cultivating in matrilineal compared with patrilineal societies. They dominated horticulture in 64 percent of the matrilineal societies versus 50 percent of the patrilineal ones.

Many jobs that men do in some societies are done by women in others, and vice versa. In West Africa, women play a prominent role in trade and marketing. In Togo, shown here, women dominate textile sales. Is there a textile shop near you? Who runs it?

Women are the main producers in horticultural societies. Women like these South American corn farmers do most of the cultivating in such societies. What kinds of roles do women play in contemporary North American farming?

Reduced Gender Stratification— Matrilineal, Matrilocal Societies

Cross-cultural variation in gender status is related to rules of descent and postmarital residence (Friedl 1975; Martin and Voorhies 1975). Among horticulturalists with matrilineal descent and *matrilocality* (residence after marriage with the

See the Virtual Exploration for more on how gender roles can change
mhhe.com/kottak

societies, including the *Iroquois* (Brown 1975), a confederation of tribes in aboriginal New York, show that women's economic, political, and ritual influence can rival that of men (Figure 20.2).

Iroquois women played a major subsistence role, while men left home for long periods to wage war. As is usual in matrilineal societies, *internal* warfare was uncommon. Iroquois men waged war only on distant groups; this could keep them away for years.

Iroquois men hunted and fished, but women controlled the local economy. Women did some fishing and occasional hunting, but their major productive role was in horticulture. Women owned the land, which they inherited from matrilineal kinswomen. Women controlled the production and distribution of food.

Iroquois women lived with their husbands and children in the family compartments of a communal longhouse. Women born in a longhouse remained there for life. Senior women, or *matrons,* decided which men could join the longhouse as husbands, and they could evict incompatible men. Women therefore controlled alliances between descent groups, an important political job in tribal society.

Iroquois women thus managed production and distribution. Social identity, succession to office and titles, and property all came through the female line, and women were prominent in ritual and politics. Related tribes made up a confederacy, the League of the Iroquois, with chiefs and councils.

A council of male chiefs managed military operations, but chiefly succession was matrilineal. That is, succession went from a man to his brother, his sister's son, or another matrilineal relative. The matrons of each longhouse nominated a man as their representative. If the council rejected their first nominee, the women proposed others until one was accepted. Matrons constantly monitored the chiefs and could impeach them. Women could veto war declarations, withhold provisions for war, and initiate peace efforts. In religion, too, women shared power. Half the tribe's religious practitioners were women, and the matrons helped select the others.

Reduced Gender Stratification— Matrifocal Societies

Nancy Tanner (1974) also found that the combination of male travel and a prominent female economic role reduced gender stratification and promoted high female status. She based this finding on a survey of the **matrifocal** (mother-centered, often with no resident husband-father) organization of certain societies in Indonesia, West Africa, and the Caribbean. Matrifocal societies are not necessarily matrilineal. A few are even patrilineal.

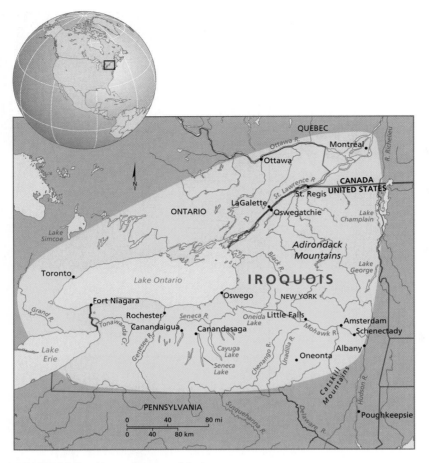

FIGURE 20.2 Historic Territory of the Iroquois.

wife's relatives, so that children grow up in their mother's village), female status tends to be high (see Blackwood 2000). Matriliny and matrilocality disperse related males, rather than consolidating them. By contrast, patriliny and *patrilocality* (residence after marriage with the husband's kin) keep male relatives together, an advantage given warfare. Matrilineal-matrilocal systems tend to occur in societies where population pressure on strategic resources is minimal and warfare is infrequent.

As we saw in the "News Brief" that opened this chapter, women tend to have high status in matrilineal, matrilocal societies for several reasons. Descent-group membership, succession to political positions, allocation of land, and overall social identity all come through female links. In Negeri Sembilan, Malaysia (Peletz 1988), matriliny gave women sole inheritance of ancestral rice fields. Matrilocality created solidarity clusters of female kin. Women had considerable influence beyond the household (Swift 1963). In such matrilineal contexts, women are the basis of the entire social structure. Although public authority may be (or may appear to be) assigned to the men, much of the power and decision making may actually belong to the senior women. Some matrilineal

For example, Tanner (1974) found matrifocality among the Igbo of eastern Nigeria, who are patrilineal, patrilocal, and polygynous (men have multiple wives). Each wife had her own house, where she lived with her children. Women planted crops next to their houses and traded surpluses. Women's associations ran the local markets, while men did the long-distance trading.

In a case study of the Igbo, Ifi Amadiume (1987) noted that either sex could fill male gender roles. Before Christian influence, successful Igbo women used wealth to take titles and acquire wives. Wives freed husbands (male and female) from domestic work and helped them accumulate wealth. Female husbands were not considered masculine but preserved their femininity. Igbo women asserted themselves in women's groups, including those of lineage daughters, lineage wives, and a communitywide women's council led by titled women. The high status and influence of Igbo women rested on the separation of males from local subsistence and on a marketing system that encouraged women to leave home and gain prominence in distribution and—through these accomplishments—in politics.

A significant number of female-centered, or matrifocal, households characterize many Caribbean societies, such as the Bahamas, shown here. As men travel, women pursue such economic activities as handicraft production and sales. This Cat Island beach scene shows a female-run basketry shop.

Increased Gender Stratification— Patrilineal-Patrilocal Societies

The Igbo are unusual among patrilineal-patrilocal societies, many of which have marked gender stratification. Martin and Voorhies (1975) link the decline of matriliny and the spread of the **patrilineal-patrilocal complex** (consisting of patrilineality, patrilocality, warfare, and male supremacy) to pressure on resources. Faced with scarce resources, patrilineal-patrilocal cultivators such as the Yanomami often wage warfare against other villages. This favors patrilocality and patriliny, customs that keep related men together in the same village, where they make strong allies in battle. Such societies tend to have a sharp domestic–public dichotomy, and men tend to dominate the prestige hierarchy. Men may use their public roles in warfare and trade and their greater prestige to symbolize and reinforce the devaluation or oppression of women.

The patrilineal-patrilocal complex characterizes many societies in highland Papua New Guinea. Women work hard growing and processing subsistence crops, raising and tending pigs (the main domesticated animal and a favorite food), and doing domestic cooking, but they are isolated from the public domain, which men control. Men grow and distribute prestige crops, prepare food for feasts, and arrange marriages. The men even get to trade the pigs and control their use in ritual.

In densely populated areas of the Papua New Guinea highlands, male–female avoidance is associated with strong pressure on resources (Lindenbaum 1972). Men fear all female contacts, including

In some parts of Papua New Guinea, the patrilineal-patrilocal complex has extreme social repercussions. Regarding females as dangerous and polluting, men may segregate themselves in men's houses (such as this one, located near the Sepik River), where they hide their precious ritual objects from women. Are there places like this in your society?

sex. They think that sexual contact with women will weaken them. Indeed, men see everything female as dangerous and polluting. They segregate themselves in men's houses and hide their precious ritual objects from women. They delay marriage, and some never marry.

By contrast, the sparsely populated areas of Papua New Guinea, such as recently settled areas, lack taboos on male–female contacts. The image of woman as polluter fades, heterosexual intercourse is valued, men and women live together, and reproductive rates are high.

GENDER AMONG AGRICULTURALISTS

When the economy is based on agriculture, women typically lose their role as primary cultivators. Certain agricultural techniques, particularly plowing, have been assigned to men because of their greater average size and strength (Martin and Voorhies 1975). Except when irrigation is used, plowing eliminates the need for constant weeding, an activity usually done by women.

Cross-cultural data illustrate these contrasts in productive roles. Women were the main workers in 50 percent of the horticultural societies surveyed but in only 15 percent of the agricultural groups. Male subsistence labor dominated 81 percent of the agricultural societies but only 17 percent of the horticultural ones (Martin and Voorhies 1975) (see Table 20.8).

With the advent of agriculture, women were cut off from production for the first time in human history. Perhaps this reflected the need for women to stay closer to home to care for the larger numbers of children that typify agriculture, compared with less labor-intensive economies. Belief systems started contrasting men's valuable extradomestic labor with women's domestic role, now viewed as inferior. (**Extradomestic** means outside the home, within or pertaining to the public domain.) Changes in kinship and postmarital residence patterns also hurt women. Descent groups and polygyny declined with agriculture, and the nuclear family became more common. Living with her husband and children, a woman was isolated from her kinswomen and cowives. Female sexuality is carefully supervised in agricultural economies; men have easier access to divorce and extramarital sex, reflecting a "double standard."

Still, female status in agricultural societies is not inevitably bleak. Gender stratification is asso-

ciated with plow agriculture rather than with intensive cultivation per se. Studies of peasant gender roles and stratification in France and Spain (Harding 1975; Reiter 1975), which have plow agriculture, show that people think of the house as the female sphere and the fields as the male domain. However, such a dichotomy is not inevitable, as my own research among Betsileo agriculturalists in Madagascar shows.

Betsileo women play a prominent role in agriculture, contributing a third of the hours invested in rice production. They have their customary tasks in the division of labor, but their work is more seasonal than men's is. No one has much to do during the ceremonial season, between mid-June and mid-September. Men work in the rice fields almost daily the rest of the year. Women's cooperative work occurs during transplanting (mid-September through November) and harvesting (mid-March through early May). Along with other members of the household, women do daily weeding in December and January. After the harvest, all family members work together winnowing the rice and then transporting it to the granary.

If we consider the strenuous daily task of husking rice by pounding (a part of food preparation rather than production per se), women actually contribute slightly more than 50 percent of the labor devoted to producing and preparing rice before cooking.

Not just women's prominent economic role but traditional social organization enhances female status among the Betsileo. Although postmarital residence is mainly patrilocal, descent rules permit married women to keep membership in and a strong allegiance to their own descent groups. Kinship is broadly and bilaterally calculated (on both sides—as in contemporary North America). The Betsileo exemplify Aihwa Ong's (1989) generalization that bilateral (and matrilineal) kinship systems, combined with subsistence economies in which the sexes have complementary roles in food production and distribution, are characterized by reduced gender stratification. Such societies are common among South Asian peasants (Ong 1989).

Bringing It All Together

See the "Bringing It All Together" essay that immediately follows this chapter.

TABLE 20.8 Male and Female Contributions to Production in Cultivating Societies		
	Horticulture (Percentage of 104 Societies)	Agriculture (Percentage of 93 Societies)
Women are primary cultivators	50	15
Men are primary cultivators	17	81
Equal contributions to cultivation	33	3

SOURCE: K. Martin and B. Voorhies, *Female of the Species* (New York: Columbia University Press, 1975), p. 283.

Traditionally, Betsileo men participate more in politics, but the women also hold political office. Women sell their produce and products in markets, invest in cattle, sponsor ceremonials, and are mentioned during offerings to ancestors. Arranging marriages, an important extradomestic activity, is more women's concern than men's. Sometimes Betsileo women seek their own kinswomen as wives for their sons, reinforcing their own prominence in village life and continuing kin-based female solidarity in the village.

The Betsileo illustrate the idea that intensive cultivation does not necessarily entail sharp gender stratification. We can see that gender roles and stratification reflect not just the type of adaptive strategy but also specific cultural attributes. Betsileo women continue to play a significant role in their society's major economic activity, rice production.

PATRIARCHY AND VIOLENCE

Patriarchy describes a political system ruled by men in which women have inferior social and political status, including basic human rights. Barbara Miller (1997), in a study of systematic neglect of females, describes women in rural northern India as "the endangered sex." Societies that feature a full-fledged patrilineal-patrilocal complex, replete with warfare and intervillage raiding, also typify patriarchy. Such practices as dowry murders, female infanticide, and clitoridectomy exemplify patriarchy, which extends from tribal societies such as the Yanomami to state societies such as India and Pakistan.

Although more prevalent in certain social settings than in others, family violence and domestic abuse of women are worldwide problems. Domestic violence certainly occurs in neolocal–nuclear family settings, such as Canada and the United States. Cities, with their impersonality and isolation from extended kin networks, are breeding grounds for domestic violence.

We've seen that gender stratification is typically reduced in matrilineal, matrifocal, and bilateral societies in which women have prominent roles in the economy and social life. When a woman lives in her own village, she has kin nearby to look after and protect her interests. Even in patrilocal polygynous settings, women often count on the support of their cowives and sons in disputes with potentially abusive husbands. Such settings, which tend to provide a safe haven for women, are retracting rather than expanding in today's world, however. Isolated families and patrilineal social forms have spread at the expense of matrilineality. Many nations have declared polygyny illegal. More and more women, and men, find themselves cut off from extended kin and families of orientation.

With the spread of the women's rights movement and the human rights movement, attention to domestic violence and abuse of women has increased. Laws have been passed, and mediating institutions established. Brazil's female-run police stations for battered women provide an example, as do shelters for victims of domestic abuse in the United States and Canada. But patriarchal institutions do persist in what should be a more enlightened world.

GENDER AND INDUSTRIALISM

The domestic–public dichotomy, which is developed most fully among patrilineal-patrilocal food producers and plow agriculturalists, also has affected gender stratification in industrial societies, including the United States and Canada. However, gender roles have been changing rapidly in North America. The "traditional" idea that "a woman's place is in the home" developed among middle- and upper-class Americans as industrialism spread after 1900. Earlier, pioneer women in the Midwest and West had been recognized as fully productive workers in farming and home industry. Under industrialism, attitudes about gendered work came to vary with class and region. In early industrial Europe, men, women, and children had flocked to factories as wage laborers. Enslaved Americans of both sexes had done grueling work in cotton fields. After abolition, southern African American women continued working as field hands and domestics. Poor white women labored in the South's early cotton mills. In the 1890s, more than one million American women held menial, repetitious, and

Bilateral kinship systems, combined with subsistence economies in which the sexes have complementary roles in food production and distribution, have reduced gender stratification. Such features are common among Asian rice cultivators, such as the Ifugao of the Philippines (shown here).

Sure, ideas about gender are changing along with the employment patterns of men and women. We see this in the media, as shows like *Sex and the City,* featuring characters who display nontraditional gender behavior and sexual behavior, attract significant audiences. But old beliefs, cultural expectations, and gender stereotypes linger. Thus, American culture expects women to be meeker than men. This poses a challenge for women, since our culture also values decisiveness and "standing up for your beliefs." When American men and women display certain behavior—speaking up for their ideas, for example—they are judged differently. A man's assertive behavior may be admired and rewarded, but a women's similar behavior may be labeled "aggressive"—or worse. Women must constantly negotiate this conundrum.

Both men and women are constrained by their cultural training, stereotypes, and expectations. For example, American culture stigmatizes male crying. It's okay for little boys to cry, but becoming a man discourages this natural expression of joy and sadness. Why shouldn't men cry when they feel emotions? American men are trained to make decisions and stick to them. Politicians routinely criticize their opponents for being indecisive, for waffling or flip-flopping on issues. What a strange idea—that people shouldn't change their positions if they've discovered there's a better way. Males, females, and humanity may be equally victimized by aspects of cultural training.

unskilled factory positions (Margolis 1984, 2000; Martin and Voorhies 1975). Poor, immigrant, and African American women continued to work throughout the 20th century.

After 1900, European immigration produced a male labor force willing to work for wages lower than those of American-born men. Those immigrant men moved into factory jobs that previously had gone to women. As machine tools and mass production further reduced the need for female labor, the notion that women were biologically unfit for factory work began to gain ground (Martin and Voorhies 1975).

Maxine Margolis (1984, 2000) has shown how gendered work, attitudes, and beliefs have varied in response to American economic needs. For example, wartime shortages of men have promoted the idea that work outside the home is women's patriotic duty. During the world wars,

the notion that women are biologically unfit for hard physical labor faded. Inflation and the culture of consumption have also spurred female employment. When prices and/or demand rises, multiple paychecks help maintain family living standards.

The steady increase in female paid employment since World War II also reflects the baby boom and industrial expansion. American culture has traditionally defined clerical work, teaching, and nursing as female occupations. With rapid population growth and business expansion after World War II, the demand for women to fill such jobs grew steadily. Employers also found that they could increase their profits by paying women lower wages than they would have to pay returning male war veterans.

Woman's role in the home has been stressed during periods of high unemployment, although when wages fall or inflation occurs simultaneously, female employment may still be accepted. Margolis (1984, 2000) contends that changes in the economy lead to changes in attitudes toward and about women. Economic changes paved the way for the contemporary women's movement, which also was spurred by the publication of Betty Friedan's book *The Feminine Mystique* in 1963 and the founding of NOW, the National Organization of Women, in 1966. The movement in turn promoted expanded work opportunities for women, including the goal of equal pay for equal work. Between 1970 and 2003, the female percentage of the American work force rose from 38 to 47 percent. In other words, almost half of all Americans who work outside the home are women. Over 71 million women now have paid jobs, compared with 80 million men. Women now fill more than half (57 percent) of all professional jobs (*Statistical Abstract of the United States 2006,* p. 429). And it's not mainly single women working, as once was the case. Table 20.9 presents figures on the ever-increasing cash employment of American wives and mothers.

Note in Table 20.9 that the cash employment of American married men has been falling while that of American married women has been rising. There has been a dramatic change in behavior and attitudes since 1960, when 89 percent of all married men worked, compared with just 32 percent of married women. The comparable figures in 2004 were 77 percent and 61 percent. Ideas about the gender roles of males and females have changed. Compare your grandparents and your parents. Chances are you have a working mother, but your grandmother was more likely a stay-at-home mom. Your grandfather is more likely than your father to have worked in manufacturing and to have belonged to a union. Your father is more likely than your grandfather to have shared child care and domestic responsibilities. Age at marriage has been delayed for both men and women.

Bringing It All Together

See the "Bringing It All Together" essay that immediately follows the chapter "Language and Communication" for information on Canada's gender-neutral public school curriculum.

College educations and professional degrees have increased. What other changes do you associate with the increase in female employment outside the home?

Table 20.10 details employment in the United States in 2002 by gender, income, and job type for year-round full-time workers. Overall, the ratio of female to male income rose from 68 percent in 1989 to 76 percent in 2003.

Today's jobs aren't especially demanding in terms of physical labor. With machines to do the heavy work, the smaller average body size and lesser average strength of women are no longer impediments to blue-collar employment. The main reason we don't see more modern-day Rosies working alongside male riveters is that the U.S. work force itself is abandoning heavy-goods manufacture. In the 1950s, two-thirds of American jobs were blue-collar, compared with less than 15 percent today. The location of those jobs has shifted within the world capitalist economy. Third World countries with cheaper labor produce steel, automobiles, and other heavy goods less expensively than the United States can, but the United States excels at services. The American mass education system has many inadequacies, but it does train millions of people for service- and information-oriented jobs, from sales clerks to computer operators.

The Feminization of Poverty

Alongside the economic gains of many American women stands an opposite extreme: the feminization of poverty. This refers to the increasing representation of women (and their children) among America's poorest people. Women head over half of U.S. households with incomes below the poverty line. Feminine poverty has been a trend in the United States since World War II, but it has

During the world wars, the notion that women were biologically unfit for hard physical labor faded. World War II's Rosie the Riveter—a strong, competent woman dressed in overalls and a bandanna—was introduced as a symbol of patriotic womanhood. Is there a comparable poster woman today? What does her image say about modern gender roles?

TABLE 20.9	Cash Employment of American Mothers, Wives, and Husbands, 1960–2002*		
Year	Percentage of Married Women, Husband Present with Children under 6	Percentage of All Married Women[a]	Percentage of All Married Men[b]
1960	19	32	89
1970	30	40	86
1980	45	50	81
1990	59	58	79
2004	59	61	77

*Civilian population 16 years of age and older.
[a]Husband present.
[b]Wife present.
SOURCE: *Statistical Abstract of the United States 2006*, Table 584, p. 392; Table 587, p. 393. http://www.census.gov/prod/www/statistical_abstract.html.

For more on gender differences and poverty, see the Internet Exercises at your OLC

mhhe.com/kottak

accelerated recently. In 1959, female-headed households accounted for just one-fourth of the American poor. Since then, that figure has more than doubled. About half the female poor are "in transition." These are women who are confronting a temporary economic crisis caused by the departure, disability, or death of a husband. The other half are more permanently dependent on the welfare system or on friends or relatives who live nearby. The feminization of poverty and its consequences in regard to living standards and health are widespread even among wage earners. Many American women continue to work part time for low wages and meager benefits.

Married couples are much more secure economically than single mothers are. The data in Table 20.11 demonstrate that the average income for married-couple families is more than twice that of families maintained by a woman. The average one-earner family maintained by a woman had an annual income of $29,307 in 2003. This was less than one-half the mean income ($62,405) of a married-couple household.

The feminization of poverty isn't just a North American trend. The percentage of female-headed households has been increasing worldwide. In Western Europe, for example, it rose from 24 percent in 1980 to 30 percent in 2000. The figure ranges from below 20 percent in certain South Asian and Southeast Asian countries to almost 50 percent in certain African countries and the Caribbean (Buvinic 1995).

Why must so many women be solo household heads? Where are the men going, and why are they leaving? Among the causes are male migration, civil strife (men off fighting), divorce, abandonment, widowhood, unwed adolescent

parenthood, and, more generally, the idea that children are women's responsibility.

Globally, households headed by women tend to be poorer than are those headed by men. In one study, the percentage of single-parent families considered poor was 18 percent in Britain, 20 percent in Italy, 25 percent in Switzerland, 40 percent in Ireland, 52 percent in Canada, and 63 percent in the United States. Poverty, of course, has health consequences. Studies in Brazil, Zambia, and the Philippines show the survival rates of children from female-headed households to be inferior to those of other children (Buvinic 1995).

In the United States, the feminization of poverty is a concern of the National Organization of Women. NOW still exists, alongside many newer women's organizations. The women's movement has become international in scope and membership. And its priorities have shifted from mainly job-oriented to more broadly social issues. These include poverty, homelessness, women's health care, day care, domestic violence, sexual assault, and reproductive rights (Calhoun, Light, and Keller 1997). These issues and others that particularly affect women in the developing countries were addressed at the United Nations' Fourth World Conference on Women held in 1995 in Beijing. In attendance were women's groups from all over the world. Many of these were national and international NGOs (nongovernmental organizations), which work with women at the local level to augment productivity and improve access to credit.

It is widely believed that one way to improve the situation of poor women is to encourage them to organize. New women's groups can in some cases revive or replace traditional forms of social

Map Atlas

Map 14 shows inequalities in cash employment and secondary education among countries of the world.

TABLE 20.11 Median Annual Income of U.S. Households, by Household Type, 2003

	Number of Households (1000s)	Median Annual Income (Dollars)	Percentage of Median Earnings Compared with Married-Couple Households
All households	112,000	$43,318	69
Family households	76,217	53,991	87
Married-couple households	57,719	62,405	100
Male earner, no wife	4,717	41,959	67
Female earner, no husband	13,781	29,307	47
Nonfamily households	35,783	25,741	41
Single male	16,136	31,928	51
Single female	19,647	21,313	34

SOURCE: *Statistical Abstract of the United States 2006,* Table 675, p. 461. http://www.census.gov/prod/www/statistical_abstract.html.

organization that have been disrupted. Membership in a group can help women to mobilize resources, to rationalize production, and to reduce the risks and costs associated with credit. Organization also allows women to develop self-confidence and to decrease dependence on others. Through such organization, poor women throughout the world are working to determine their own needs and priorities, and to change things so as to improve their social and economic situation (Buvinic 1995).

SEXUAL ORIENTATION

Sexual orientation refers to a person's habitual sexual attraction to, and sexual activities with, persons of the opposite sex, *heterosexuality;* the same sex, *homosexuality;* or both sexes, *bisexuality. Asexuality,* indifference toward or lack of attraction to either sex, is also a sexual orientation. All four of these forms are found in contemporary North America, and throughout the world. But each type of desire and experience holds different meanings for individuals and groups. For example, an asexual disposition may be acceptable in some places but may be perceived as a character flaw in others. Male–male sexual activity may be a private affair in Mexico, rather than public, socially sanctioned, and encouraged as it was among the Etoro (see below) of Papua New Guinea (see also Blackwood and Wieringa, eds. 1999; Herdt 1981, Kottak and Kozaitis 2003; Lancaster and Di Leonardo, eds. 1997; Nanda 2000).

Recently in the United States there has been a tendency to see sexual orientation as fixed and biologically based. There is not enough information at this time to determine the extent to which sexual orientation is based on biology. What we can say is that, to some extent at least, all human activities and preferences, including erotic expression, are learned, malleable, and culturally constructed.

In any society, individuals will differ in the nature, range, and intensity of their sexual interests and urges. No one knows for sure why such individual sexual differences exist. Part of the answer may be biological, reflecting genes or hormones. Another part may have to do with experiences during growth and development. But whatever the reasons for individual variation, culture always plays a role in molding individual sexual urges toward a collective norm. And such sexual norms vary from culture to culture.

What do we know about variation in sexual norms from society to society, and over time? A classic cross-cultural study (Ford and Beach 1951) found wide variation in attitudes about masturbation, bestiality (sex with animals), and homosexuality. Even in a single society, such as the United States, attitudes about sex differ over time and with socioeconomic status, region, and rural versus urban residence. However, even in the 1950s, prior to the "age of sexual permissiveness" (the pre-HIV period from the mid-1960s through the 1970s), research showed that almost all American men (92 percent) and more than half of American women (54 percent) admitted to masturbation. In the famous Kinsey report (Kinsey, Pomeroy, and Martin 1948), 37 percent of the men surveyed admitted having had at least one sexual experience leading to orgasm with another male. In a later study of 1,200 unmarried women, 26 percent

[handwritten margin notes: ✓ biological ✓ growth and develop- ✓ culture]

Hidden Women, Public Men—Public Women, Hidden Men

For several years, one of Brazil's top sex symbols was Roberta Close, whom I first saw in a furniture commercial. Roberta ended her pitch with an admonition to prospective furniture buyers to accept no substitute for the advertised product. "Things," she warned, "are not always what they seem."

Nor was Roberta. This petite and incredibly feminine creature was actually a man. Nevertheless, despite the fact that he—or she (speaking as Brazilians do)—is a man posing as a woman, Roberta won a secure place in Brazilian mass culture. Her photos decorated magazines. She was a panelist on a TV variety show and starred in a stage play in Rio with an actor known for his supermacho image. Roberta even inspired a well-known, and apparently heterosexual, pop singer to make a video honoring her. In it, she pranced around Rio's Ipanema Beach in a bikini, showing off her ample hips and buttocks.

The video depicted the widespread male appreciation of Roberta's beauty. As confirmation, one heterosexual man told me he had recently been on the same plane as Roberta and had been struck by her looks. Another man said he wanted to have sex with her. These comments, it seemed to me, illustrated striking cultural contrasts about gender and sexuality. In Brazil, a Latin American country noted for its machismo, heterosexual men did not feel that attraction toward a transvestite blemished their masculine identities.

Roberta Close can be understood in relation to a gender-identity scale that jumps from extreme femininity to extreme masculinity, with little in between. Masculinity is stereotyped as active and public, femininity as passive and domestic. The male–female contrast in rights and behavior is much stronger in Brazil than it is in North America. Brazilians confront a more rigidly defined masculine role than North Americans do.

The active–passive dichotomy also provides a stereotypical model for male–male sexual relations. One man

is supposed to be the active, masculine (inserting) partner, whereas the other is the passive, effeminate one. The latter man is derided as a *bicha* (intestinal worm), but little stigma attaches to the inserter. Indeed, many "active" (and married) Brazilian men like to have sex with transvestite prostitutes, who are biological males.

If a Brazilian man is unhappy pursuing either active masculinity or passive effeminacy, there is one other choice—active femininity. For Roberta Close and others like her, the cultural demand of ultramasculinity has yielded to a performance of ultrafemininity. These men-women form a third gender in relation to Brazil's polarized male–female identity scale.

Transvestites like Roberta are particularly prominent in Rio de Janeiro's annual Carnaval, when an ambience of inversion rules the city. In the culturally accurate words of the American popular novelist Gregory McDonald, who sets one of his books in Brazil at Carnaval time:

> *Everything goes topsy-turvy . . .*
> *Men become women; women*
> *become men; grown-ups become*
> *children; rich people pretend*
> *they're poor; poor people, rich;*
> *sober people become drunkards;*
> *thieves become generous. Very*
> *topsy-turvy. (McDonald 1984,*
> *p. 154)*

Most notable in this costumed inversion (DaMatta 1991), men dress as women. Carnaval reveals and expresses normally hidden tensions and conflicts as social life is turned upside down. Reality is illuminated through a dramatic presentation of its opposite.

This is the final key to Roberta's cultural meaning. She emerged in a setting in which male–female inversion is part of the year's most popular festival. Transvestites are the pièces de résistance at Rio's Carnaval balls, where they dress as scantily as the real women do. They wear postage-stamp bikinis, sometimes with no tops. Photos of real women and transformed

Roberta Close, in her prime.

ones vie for space in the magazines. It is often impossible to tell the born women from the hidden men. Roberta Close is a permanent incarnation of Carnaval—a year-round reminder of the spirit of Carnavals past, present, and yet to come.

Roberta emerged from a Latin culture whose gender roles contrast strongly with those of the United States. From small village to massive city, Brazilian males are public and Brazilian females are private creatures. Streets, beaches, and bars belong to the men. Although bikinis adorn Rio's beaches on weekends and holidays, there are many more men than women there on weekdays. The men revel in their ostentatiously sexual displays. As they sun themselves and play soccer and volleyball, they regularly stroke their genitals to keep them firm. They are living publicly, assertively, and sexually in a world of men.

Brazilian men must work hard at this public image, constantly acting out their culture's definition of masculine behavior. Public life is a play whose strong roles go to men. Roberta Close, of course, was a public figure. Given that Brazilian culture defines the public world as male, we can perhaps better understand now why the nation's number one sex symbol has been a man who excels at performing in public as a woman.

reported same-sex sexual activities. (Because Kinsey's research relied on nonrandom samples, it should be considered merely illustrative, rather than a statistically accurate representation of, sexual behavior at the time.)

Sex acts involving people of the same sex were absent, rare, or secret in only 37 percent of 76 societies for which data were available in the Ford and Beach study (1951). In the others, various forms of same-sex sexual activity were considered normal and acceptable. Sometimes sexual relations between people of the same sex involved transvestism on the part of one of the partners, like the *berdaches* discussed in the last chapter (see "Interesting Issues" on p. 472).

Transvestism did not characterize male–male sex among the Sudanese Azande, who valued the warrior role (Evans-Pritchard 1970). Prospective warriors—young men aged 12 to 20—left their families and shared quarters with adult fighting men, who paid bridewealth for, and had sex with, them. During this apprenticeship, the young men did the domestic duties of women. Upon reaching warrior status, these young men took their own younger male brides. Later, retiring from the

warrior role, Azande men married women. Flexible in their sexual expression, Azande males had no difficulty shifting from sex with older men (as male brides), to sex with younger men (as warriors), to sex with women (as husbands) (see Murray and Roscoe, eds. 1998).

An extreme example of tension involving male–female sexual relations in Papua New Guinea is provided by the Etoro (Kelly 1976), a group of 400 people who subsist by hunting and horticulture in the Trans-Fly region (Figure 20.3). The Etoro illustrate the power of culture in molding human sexuality. The following account, based on ethnographic field work by Raymond C. Kelly in the late 1960s, applies only to Etoro males and their beliefs. Etoro cultural norms prevented the male anthropologist who studied them from gathering comparable information about female attitudes. Note, also, that the activities described have been discouraged by missionaries. Since there has been no restudy of the Etoro specifically focusing on these activities, the extent to which these practices continue today is unknown. For this reason, I'll use the past tense in describing them.

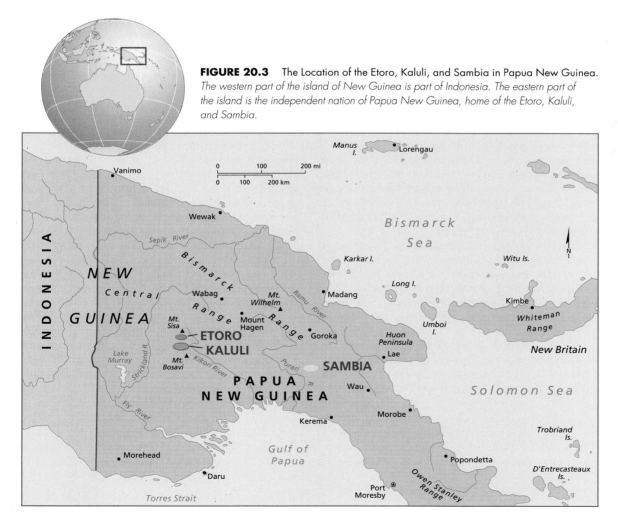

FIGURE 20.3   The Location of the Etoro, Kaluli, and Sambia in Papua New Guinea. *The western part of the island of New Guinea is part of Indonesia. The eastern part of the island is the independent nation of Papua New Guinea, home of the Etoro, Kaluli, and Sambia.*

Do the taboos that have surrounded homosexuality in our own society remind you of Etoro taboos? Homosexual activity has been stigmatized in Western industrial societies. Indeed, sodomy laws continue to make it illegal in many U.S. states. Among the Etoro, male–female sex is banned from the social center and moved to the fringes or margins of society (the woods, filled with dangerous snakes). In our own society, homosexual activity has traditionally been hidden, furtive, and secretive—also moved to the margins of society rather than its valued center. Imagine what our own sex lives would be like if we had been raised with Etoro beliefs and taboos.

Etoro opinions about sexuality were linked to their beliefs about the cycle of birth, physical growth, maturity, old age, and death. Etoro men believed that semen was necessary to give life force to a fetus, which was, they believed, implanted in a woman by an ancestral spirit. Sexual intercourse during pregnancy nourished the growing fetus. The Etoro believed that men had a limited lifetime supply of semen. Any sex act leading to ejaculation was seen as draining that supply, and as sapping a man's virility and vitality. The birth of children, nurtured by semen, symbolized a necessary sacrifice that would lead to the husband's eventual death. Heterosexual intercourse, required only for reproduction, was discouraged. Women who wanted too much sex were viewed as witches, hazardous to their husbands' health. Etoro culture allowed heterosexual intercourse only about 100 days a year. The rest of the time it was tabooed. Seasonal birth clustering shows the taboo was respected.

So objectionable was male–female sex that it was removed from community life. It could occur neither in sleeping quarters nor in the fields. Coitus could happen only in the woods, where it was risky because poisonous snakes, the Etoro claimed, were attracted by the sounds and smells of male–female sex.

Although coitus was discouraged, sex acts between men were viewed as essential. Etoro believed that boys could not produce semen on their own. To grow into men and eventually give life force to their children, boys had to acquire semen orally from older men. From the age of 10 until adulthood, boys were inseminated by older men. No taboos were attached to this. Such oral insemination could proceed in the sleeping area or garden. Every three years, a group of boys around the age of 20 was formally initiated into manhood. They went to a secluded mountain lodge, where they were visited and inseminated by several older men.

Male–male sex among the Etoro was governed by a code of propriety. Although sexual relations between older and younger males were considered culturally essential, those between boys of the same age were discouraged. A boy who took semen from other youths was believed to be sapping their life force and stunting their growth. A boy's rapid physical development might suggest that he was getting semen from other boys. Like a sex-hungry wife, he might be shunned as a witch.

These sexual practices among the Etoro rested not on hormones or genes but on cultural beliefs and traditions. The Etoro were an extreme example of a male–female avoidance pattern that has been widespread in Papua New Guinea and in patrilineal-patrilocal societies. The Etoro shared a cultural pattern, which Gilbert Herdt (1984) calls "ritualized homosexuality," with some 50 other tribes in Papua New Guinea, especially in that country's Trans-Fly region. These societies illustrate one extreme of a male–female avoidance pattern that is widespread in Papua New Guinea and indeed in many patrilineal-patrilocal societies.

Flexibility in sexual expression seems to be an aspect of our primate heritage. Both masturbation and same-sex sexual activity exist among chimpanzees and other primates. Male bonobos (pygmy chimps) regularly engage in a form of mutual masturbation known as "penis fencing." Females get sexual pleasure from rubbing their genitals against those of other females (de Waal 1997). Our primate sexual potential is molded by culture, the environment, and reproductive necessity. Heterosexual coitus is practiced in all human societies—which, after all, must reproduce themselves—but alternatives are also widespread (Rathus, Nevid, and Fichner-Rathus 2005). Like gender roles and attitudes more generally, the sexual component of human personality and identity—just how we express our "natural" sexual urges—is a matter that culture and environment direct and limit.

1. *Gender roles* are the tasks and activities that a culture assigns to each sex. *Gender stereotypes* are oversimplified ideas about attributes of males and females. *Gender stratification* describes an unequal distribution of rewards by gender, reflecting different positions in a social hierarchy. Cross-cultural comparison reveals some recurrent patterns involving the division of labor by gender and gender-based differences in reproductive strategies. Gender roles and gender stratification also vary with environment, economy, adaptive strategy, level of social complexity, and degree of participation in the world economy.

2. When gathering is prominent, gender status is more equal than it is when hunting or fishing dominates the foraging economy. Gender status is more equal when the domestic and public spheres aren't sharply separated. Foragers lack two public arenas that contribute to higher male status among food producers: warfare and organized interregional trade.

3. Gender stratification also is linked to descent and residence. Women's status in matrilineal societies tends to be high because descent-group membership, political succession, land allocation, and overall social identity come through female links. Women in many societies wield power and make decisions. Scarcity of resources promotes intervillage warfare, patriliny, and patrilocality. The localization of related males is adaptive for military solidarity. Men may use their warrior role to symbolize and reinforce the social devaluation and oppression of women.

4. With the advent of plow agriculture, women were removed from production. The distinction between women's domestic work and men's "productive" labor reinforced the contrast between men as public and valuable and women as homebound and inferior. Patriarchy describes a political system ruled by men in which women have inferior social and political status, including basic human rights. Some expressions of patriarchy include female infanticide, dowry murders, domestic abuse, and forced genital operations.

5. Americans' attitudes toward gender vary with class and region. When the need for female labor declines, the idea that women are unfit for many jobs increases, and vice versa. Factors such as war, falling wages, and inflation help explain female cash employment and Americans' attitudes toward it. Countering the economic gains of many American women is the feminization of poverty. This has become a global phenomenon, as impoverished female-headed households have increased worldwide.

6. There has been a recent tendency to see sexual orientation as fixed and biologically based. But to some extent, at least, all human activities and preferences, including erotic expression, are influenced by culture. Sexual orientation stands for a person's habitual sexual attraction to, and activities with, persons of the opposite sex, *heterosexuality*; the same sex, *homosexuality*; or both sexes, *bisexuality*. Sexual norms vary widely from culture to culture.

---

domestic–public dichotomy Contrast between women's role in the home and men's role in public life, with a corresponding social devaluation of women's work and worth.

extradomestic Outside the home; within or pertaining to the public domain.

gender roles The tasks and activities that a culture assigns to each sex.

gender stereotypes Oversimplified but strongly held ideas about the characteristics of males and females.

gender stratification Unequal distribution of rewards (socially valued resources, power, prestige, and personal freedom) between men and women, reflecting their different positions in a social hierarchy.

matrifocal Mother-centered; often refers to a household with no resident husband-father.

patriarchy Political system ruled by men in which women have inferior social and political status, including basic human rights.

patrilineal-patrilocal complex An interrelated constellation of patrilineality, patrilocality, warfare, and male supremacy.

sexual dimorphism Marked differences in male and female biology besides the contrasts in breasts and genitals.

sexual orientation A person's habitual sexual attraction to, and activities with, persons of the opposite sex, heterosexuality; the same sex, homosexuality; or both sexes, bisexuality.

CRITICAL THINKING QUESTIONS

For more self testing, see the self quizzes

mhhe.com/kottak

1. What characteristics of men and women do you see as most directly linked to biological differences between the sexes? What kinds of characteristics are most influenced by culture?

2. Using your own society, give an example of a gender role, a gender stereotype, and gender stratification.

3. What do you see as the main factor that has changed North American gender roles since World War II? How do you expect gender roles to change in the next generation?

4. If you had to pick three factors that play a role in determining cross-cultural variation in gender roles, what would they be?

5. What lessons about human sexuality do you draw from the Etoro? How fixed is human sexual orientation, in your opinion?

SUGGESTED ADDITIONAL READINGS

Behar, R., and D. A. Gordon, eds.
  1995 *Women Writing Culture.* Berkeley: University of California Press. Feminist scholars reflect on identity and difference.

Blackwood, E., and S. Wieringa, eds.
  1999 *Female Desires: Same-Sex Relations and Transgender Practices across Cultures.* New York: Columbia University Press. Lesbianism and male homosexuality in cross-cultural perspective.

Bonvillain, N.
  2001 *Women and Men: Cultural Constructions of Gender,* 3rd ed. Upper Saddle River, NJ: Prentice Hall. A cross-cultural study of gender roles and relationships, from bands to industrial societies.

Brettell, C. B., and C. F. Sargent, eds.
  2005 *Gender in Cross-Cultural Perspective.* Upper Saddle River, NJ: Pearson/Prentice Hall. Articles on variation in gender systems across cultures.

Dahlberg, F., ed.
  1981 *Woman the Gatherer.* New Haven, CT: Yale University Press. Female roles and activities among prehistoric and contemporary foragers.

Kimmel, M., and R. Plante
  2004 *Sexualities: Identities, Behaviors, and Society.* New York: Oxford University Press.

Kimmel, M., J. Hearn, and R. W. Connell
  2005 *Handbook of Studies on Men and Masculinities.* Thousand Oaks, CA: Sage.

Kimmel, M. S., and M. A. Messner, eds.
  2007 *Men's Lives,* 7th ed. Boston: Pearson/Allyn & Bacon. The study of men in society and concepts of masculinity in the United States.

Lamphere, L., H. Ragone, and P. Zavella, eds.
  1997 *Situated Lives: Gender and Culture in Everyday Life.* New York: Routledge. Essays on gender and culture as illustrated by everyday social interaction.

Lancaster, R. N., and M. Di Leonardo, eds.
  1997 *The Gender/Sexuality Reader: Culture, History, Political Economy.* New York: Routledge. Gender and sexuality in history and in the modern social context.

Mascia-Lees, F., and N. J. Black
  2000 *Gender and Anthropology.* Prospect Heights, Il: Waveland. History of gender studies in anthropology.

Nanda, S.
  2000 *Gender Diversity: Crosscultural Variations.* Prospect Heights, Il: Waveland. Sexuality, gender, and genders in various societies.

Nelson, S. N., and M. Rosen-Ayalon, eds.
  2002 *In Pursuit of Gender: Worldwide Archaeological Approaches.* Social archaeology, history of gender roles, and women in prehistory.

Rathus, S. A., J. S. Nevid, and J. Fichner-Rathus
  2005 *Human Sexuality in a World of Diversity,* 6th ed. Boston: Pearson/Allyn & Bacon. Multicultural and ethnic perspectives.

Reiter, R., ed.
  1975 *Toward an Anthropology of Women.* New York: Monthly Review Press. Classic anthology, with a particular focus on peasant societies.

Rosaldo, M. Z., and L. Lamphere, eds.
  1974 *Woman, Culture, and Society.* Stanford, CA: Stanford University Press. Another classic anthology, covering many areas of the world.

Sinnott, M. J.
  2004 *Toms and Dees: Transgender Identity and Female Same-Sex Relationships in Thailand.* Honolulu: University of Hawaii Press. An ethnography about non-Western female same-sex sexuality and transgenderism.

Ward, M. C., and M. Edelstein
  2006 *A World Full of Women,* 4th ed. Boston: Allyn & Bacon. A global and comparative approach to the study of women.

1. Gender in the Classroom: Read the article "Student Ratings of Professors Are Not Gender Blind" by Susan Basow, **http://eserver.org/ feminism/workplace/fces-not-gender-blind.txt**.
   a. How much difference is there between male and female students who are rating a male professor? How much difference is there between male and female students in rating a female professor?
   b. What are the added expectations students have for female professors? What do you think is the source of those expectations? Do you think the expectations discussed in this article hold true for female teachers all over the world?
   c. Do you think the findings of this study are consistent with the way you and your friends rate professors?

2. Gender on the Internet: Read the paper by Amy Bruckman titled "Gender Swapping on the Internet," **http://www.inform.umd.edu/EdRes/ Topic/WomensStudies/Computing/Articles+ ResearchPapers/gender-swapping**.
   a. Do gender roles exist on the Internet, such as in the MUDs described in this article, or in chat rooms, or e-mail? Do gender roles belong on the Internet? Would it be possible for people to remain gender-neutral on the Internet indefinitely?
   b. Imagine you are using a MUD. You encounter a character with a gender-neutral name (like Pat) and description. What clues would you use to identify the gender of Pat and Pat's user? Do you think this detective work would be more or less difficult if Pat's user was also from a different culture than your own?
   c. Do the cases described in this paper say more about the person swapping genders or about the other users?

See Chapter 20 at your McGraw-Hill Online Learning Center for additional review and interactive exercises.

Kottak, *Assault on Paradise,* **4th ed.**

Compare the discussions of gender and female status in Chapters 3 and 9. How did gender issues change over time in Arembepe? How does Dora's case, in Chapter 10, illustrate some of these changes? Chapter 12 considers the impact of television on Arembepeiros. Did it affect gender roles? Pay attention to the description of Nadia in Chapter 12 as you think about this question.

Peters-Golden, *Culture Sketches,* **4th ed.**

Read Chapter 9, "Minangkabau: Merantau and Matriliny." Among the Minangkabau, also discussed in the text chapter, what are some ways in which matrilineality influences, and is reflected in, aspects of their lives other than kinship?

Knauft, *The Gebusi,* **1st ed.**

Read Chapters 1, 5, and 10. Based on Chapter 1, what are the biggest inequalities in Gebusi gender relations? How do Gebusi women seem to view these inequities? Based on Chapter 5, describe sexual relations that traditionally have taken place between Gebusi men. What is the relation between male–male sexuality and the sexual relationship of Gebusi men to Gebusi women, including in marriage? What is the attitude of Gebusi women to the male–male sexual practices, and how does this compare or contrast with attitudes in Western societies? Based on Chapter 10 of *The Gebusi,* described how gender and sex practices among Gebusi have changed over time. What are the primary reasons for these changes? Based on Chapters 5 and 10, what personal tensions do ethnographers face in studying issues of gender and sexuality during fieldwork? Despite these difficulties, why does the cross-cultural study of gender and of sexuality remain important?

The Basques

The Basque people of Spain and France, and their diaspora, including their migration to the United States, have attracted the attention of anthropology's four subfields. Having maintained a strong ethnic identity, perhaps for millennia, the Basques are linguistically unique in that their language is unrelated to any other known language. Genetic differences also set them off from neighboring European populations.

Their homeland lies in the western Pyrenees mountains, straddling the French–Spanish border. Seven traditional provinces within Basque country (three in France and four in Spain) are distinguished by dialect differences. Basques refer to their homeland as Euskal-Herria ("Land of the Basques") or Euskadi ("Country of the Basques"). Although their seven regions have not been unified politically for nearly a millennium, the Basques remain one of Europe's most distinctive ethnic groups.

Romans, Goths, Franks, and Moors all controlled parts of Basque country without ever totally subduing it. For the last thousand years the Basque territory has been influenced by European polities. Yet for much of this time the Basques have managed to retain significant autonomy in their affairs.

The French Revolution of 1789 ended the political autonomy of the three Basque provinces in France. During the 19th century in Spain the Basques fought on the losing side in two internal wars, yielding much of their political autonomy in defeat. When the Spanish Civil War broke out in 1936, the Basques remained loyal to the republic, opposing the eventual Spanish dictator, Francisco Franco, who eventually defeated them. Under Franco's rule (1936–1975), Basques were executed, imprisoned, and exiled, and Basque culture was systematically repressed.

In the late 1950s disaffected Basque youths founded ETA (Euskadi Ta Azkatasuna, or "Basque Country and Freedom"). Its goal was complete independence from Spain (Zulaika 1988). The ETA's opposition to Franco escalated into violence, which continued thereafter, diminishing in recent years. Effective March 24, 2006, the leaders of ETA announced a cease-fire. They planned thereafter to seek full independence from Spain through the political process.

Franco's death in 1975 had ushered in an era of democracy in Spain. Mainline Basque nationalists collaborated in framing a new constitution which gave considerable autonomy to the Basque regions (Trask 1996). Since 1979 the three Spanish Basque

■ The prolific Spanish painter Pablo Picasso portrayed the destruction of a Basque town in his famous painting Guernica (1937).

provinces of Vizcaya, Guipuzcoa, and Alava have been united as the Basque Autonomous Region, which governs the Basque homeland. The Basque language is co-official with Spanish in this territory. Spain's fourth Basque province, Navarra, formed its own autonomous region, where the Basque language has a degree of official standing. In France, Basque, like other regional languages, has been victimized for centuries by laws hostile to languages other than French (Trask 1996).

The ancestral form of the Basque language reached Western Europe thousands—perhaps even tens of thousands—of years ago, from where we cannot say. All the other modern languages of Western Europe arrived much later. Spreading across Europe from the east, the Indo-European languages, such as Latin, Germanic, and Celtic, gradually displaced all but one of the indigenous languages. When the Romans invaded Gaul (France), an early form of Basque, known as Aquitanian, was the only non-Indo-European language that survived there. In Spain, several pre-Indo-European languages were still spoken, including Aquitanian and Iberian. Latin replaced them all, with the sole exception of Aquitanian (ancestral Basque) (Trask 1996).

After generations of decline, the number of Basque speakers is increasing today. Much education, publishing, and broadcasting now proceeds in Basque in the Autonomous Region. Still, Basque faces the same pressures that all other minority languages do: Knowledge of the national language (Spanish or French) is essential, and most education, publishing, and broadcasting is in the national language (Trask 1996).

How long have the Basques been in their homeland? Some scholars believe the Basques may be direct descendants of the Upper Paleolithic cave painters active in southwestern Europe 15,000 years ago. Archaeological evidence suggests that a single group of people lived in the Basque country continuously from late Paleolithic times through the Bronze Age (about 3,000 years ago). There is no evidence to suggest that any new population entered the area after that. However, such an intrusion cannot be ruled out (La Fraugh n.d.).

We've seen that linguistically the Basques are absolutely distinct. To an extent, they also contrast biologically with other Europeans. For example, Basques have the highest proportion of RH-negative blood in Europe (25 percent), and one of the highest percentages of type O blood (55 percent). The geneticist Luigi Cavalli-Sforza (2000), who developed a gene map of Europe, found the Basques to be strikingly different from their neighbors.

However, a recent genetic study involving the Y chromosome, which is passed exclusively from father to son, establishes links between the Basques and the Celts of Wales and Ireland. In

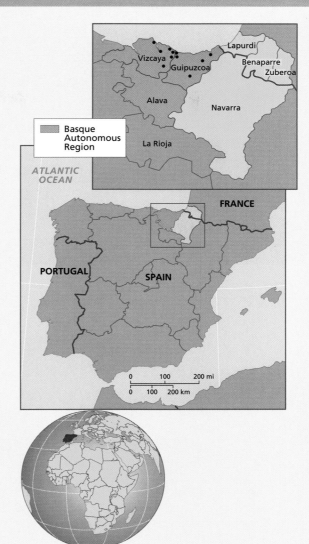

Location of the Basque homeland.

terms of the Y chromosome, the researchers found Celts and Basques to be statistically indistinguishable (Wade 2001).

Historically the Basques have been herders, fishers, and farmers. (Today most of them work in business and industry.) Through the Middle Ages they were mainly herders. As Europe's earliest and most efficient whalers, Basques may have reached North America before Columbus did. There is documentation of Basque whaling and cod fishing along Canada's Labrador coast by 1500. Some Atlantic coastal Native American languages in Canada have Basque loan words. Canadian archivists and archaeologists have discovered a 16th-century Basque whaling station (used seasonally) and a sunken whaling ship at Red Bay, Labrador. Basque activity in Canadian coastal waters lasted into the 19th century (Douglass 1992).

The Basque homeland contains major cities, along with coastal fishing communities and farming (peasant) villages. The typical peasant village

with the production of vegetables, dairy products, and fish aimed at urban markets (Greenwood 1976).

On the family farm, the stem family was the basic social unit. This included an older couple, their heir (usually male), and his wife and children. Unmarried siblings of the heir could reside in their natal households until death, but they had to respect the authority of the male and female heads. The household had to approve the selection of the spouse of the designated heir. Ownership of the farm was transferred to the newlyweds as part of the marital arrangements—to a single heir(ess) in each generation. By custom, male primogeniture was preferred. Siblings who married and moved away received dowries. Because only one child was socialized into the role of the heir(ess), his or her siblings were raised anticipating that they would leave. This system has made the rural Basque country a font of emigration (Douglass 1975, 1992).

BASQUE AMERICANS

Basque immigrants originally entered North America as either Spanish or French nationals. Basque Americans, numbering some 50,000, now invoke Basqueness as their primary ethnic identity. They are concentrated in California, Idaho, and Nevada. First-generation immigrants are usually fluent in Basque. They are more likely to be bilingual in Basque and English than to have their parents' fluency in Spanish or French (Douglass 1992).

Building on a traditional occupation in Basque country, Basques in the United States are notable for their identification with sheep herding (see Ott 1981). Most of them settled and worked in the open-range livestock districts of the 13 states of the American West. Basques first entered the western United States as agents of Spanish colonialism. They numbered among the Spanish soldiers, explorers, missionaries, and administrators in the American Southwest and Spanish California. More Basques came during the California gold rush, many from southern South America, where they were established sheep herders. In the 1870s Basque shepherds spread throughout California's central valleys and expanded into Arizona, New Mexico, and western Nevada (Douglass 1992).

Restrictive immigration laws enacted in the 1920s, which had an anti–southern European bias, limited Basque immigration to the United States. During World War II, with the country in need of shepherds, the U.S. government exempted Basque herders from immigration quotas. Between 1950 and 1975, several thousand Basques entered the United States on three-year

Women unload the catch in Bermeo, a Basque fishing village in Spain. Fishing, farming, and herding are mainstays of the Basque economy.

The herding of sheep, shown here in the Basque homeland (Pyrenees), remained a primary occupation of Basque men who started migrating to the American West in the 19th century.

includes a river valley, where the village is seated, and the surrounding hillsides, which have *baserriak*, or farmsteads. These houses are large stone structures, often three stories tall. The ground floor is for animal stables; the second floor is living space, while the third is used to store hay and other crops (Douglass 1992).

The Basque *basseria* (family farm) once thrived as a mixed-farming unit emphasizing self-sufficiency. The farm family grew wheat, corn, vegetables, fruits, and nuts and raised poultry, rabbits, pigs, cows, and sheep. Subsistence pursuits have become increasingly commercialized,

contracts. Later, the decline of the U.S. sheep industry would slow Basque immigration dramatically (Douglass 1992).

With that decline, many Basque herders returned to Europe; others converted sheep ranches to cattle. Many more moved to nearby small towns where they did construction work or established small businesses (bars, bakeries, motels, gasoline stations). Wherever jai alai (words which mean "happy festival" in Basque) is legal, Basque players are recruited from Europe. They play part of the year in Basque country and the rest in the United States (Douglass 1992).

Catering to Basque sheep herders, most western towns in the open-range country had one or more Basque boardinghouses. The typical one had a bar and a dining room, where meals were served family-style at long tables. A second floor of sleeping rooms was reserved for permanent boarders. Also lodged were herders in town for a brief visit, vacation, or employment layoff or in transit to an employer (Echeverria 1999).

Both traditionally and in the United States, Basque culture has promoted a degree of equality between men and women. In farming, women and men have shared many tasks, including working together in the fields. In Basque cities, where women are increasingly employed in industry and services, there is a income gender gap comparable to the one that exists in the United States. Although domestic tasks remain largely the domain of women, they are not regarded as demeaning for men. Also, whether running a ranching operation, a boardinghouse, or a town business, Basque American women work alongside men and perform virtually any task (Douglass 1992).

The social glue that holds Basque Americans together includes extended bilateral kinship and affinal ties. Basque men recruited their brothers and cousins to herd sheep in the American West. Basque American colonies often included family clusters, with local endogamy increasing the degree of interrelatedness. Even today, extended Basque American families maintain close ties, as they gather for baptisms, graduations, weddings, and funerals (Douglass 1992).

Initially, few Basques came to the United States intending to stay. Most early immigrants were young, unmarried men. The transhumant sheep herding pattern, with solitary summers in the mountains, did not fit well with family life. Eventually, Basque men came with the intent to stay. They either sent back or went back to Europe for brides (few married non-Basques). Many brides, of the "mail order" sort, were sisters or cousins of an acquaintance made in the United States. Basque boardinghouses also became a source of spouses. The boardinghouse owners sent back to Europe for women willing to

Basque-American folk dancers at a Cultural Festival in San Francisco. Basques settled in several western states, including California and Nevada. What was their main occupation?

come to America as domestics. Few remained single for long (Douglass 1992). In these ways Basque Americans drew on their homeland society and culture in establishing the basis of their family and community life in North America.

Among the homeland patterns that the Basques transferred from the Old World to the New were transhumant herding, a blurred division of labor by gender in farming and industry, ethnic endogamy, and strong family ties. Yet another is the role of unrelated neighbors, who traditionally played an important role in rural Basque society (Douglass 1992). After the family, the most important social institution for Basque Americans has been the boardinghouse, where Basques could again draw on the support of their neighbors. The boardinghouse was a multifunctional institution that served as a town address, a bank, an employment agency, an ethnic haven, a source of help and advice, a place to leave one's possessions, a possible source of a bride, and a potential retirement home. For the Basque American, it was a place to recharge ethnic batteries, practice one's rusty Basque, learn something about traditional culture, dance to Basque music, eat Basque cuisine, hire help, and hold baptisms, weddings, and wakes (Douglass 1992; Echeverria 1999).

Basques have not escaped discrimination in the United States. In the American West, sheep herding is an occupation that carries some stigma. Mobile sheep herders competed with settled livestock interests for access to the range. These were some of the sources of anti-Basque sentiment and even legislation. More recently, newspaper coverage of conflict in the Basque country, particularly the activities of the ETA, has made Basque Americans sensitive to the possible charge of being terrorist sympathizers (Douglass 1992; see also Zulaika 1988).

21 Religion

WHAT IS RELIGION?

The anthropologist Anthony F. C. Wallace defined **religion** as "belief and ritual concerned with supernatural beings, powers, and forces" (1966, p. 5). The supernatural is the extraordinary realm outside (but believed to impinge on) the observable world. It is non-empirical and inexplicable in ordinary terms. It must be accepted "on faith." Supernatural beings—gods and goddesses, ghosts, and souls—are not of the material world. Nor are supernatural forces, some of which may be wielded by beings. Other sacred forces are impersonal; they simply exist. In many societies, however, people believe they can benefit from, become imbued with, or manipulate supernatural forces (see Bowie 2006; Crapo 2003).

Another definition of religion (Reese 1999) focuses on bodies of people who gather together regularly for worship. These congregants or adherents subscribe to and internalize a common system of meaning. They accept (adhere to or believe in) a set of doctrines involving the relationship between the individual and divinity, the supernatural, or whatever is taken to be the ultimate nature of reality. Anthropologists have stressed the collective, shared, and enacted nature of religion, the emotions it generates, and the meanings it embodies. Émile Durkheim (1912/ 2001), an early scholar of religion, stressed religious *effervescence,* the bubbling up of collective emotional intensity generated by worship. Victor Turner (1969/1995) updated Durkheim's notion, using the term *communitas,* an intense community spirit, a feeling of great social solidarity, equality, and togetherness. The word *religion* derives from the Latin *religare,* "to tie, to bind," but it is not necessary for all the members of a given religion to meet together as a common body. Subgroups meet regularly at local congregation sites. They may attend occasional meetings with adherents representing a wider region. And they may form an imagined community with people of similar faith throughout the world.

Like ethnicity and language, religion also is associated with social divisions within and between societies and nations, such as those countries into which Islam has diffused, as described in the "News Brief." Religion both unites and divides. Participation in common rites may affirm, and thus maintain, the social solidarity of one religion's adherents. However, as we know from daily headlines, religious difference also may be associated with bitter enmity.

In studying religion cross-culturally, anthropologists pay attention to the social nature and roles of religion as well as to the nature, content, and meaning to people of religious doctrines, acts, events, settings, practitioners, and organizations. We also consider such verbal manifestations of religious beliefs as prayers, chants, myths, texts, and statements about ethics and morality. Religion, by either definition offered here, exists in all human societies. It is a cultural universal. However, we'll see that it isn't always easy to distinguish the supernatural from the natural and that different societies conceptualize divinity, supernatural entities, and ultimate realities very differently.

ORIGINS, FUNCTIONS, AND EXPRESSIONS OF RELIGION

When did religion begin? No one knows for sure. There are suggestions of religion in Neandertal burials and on European cave walls, where painted stick figures may represent shamans, early religious specialists. Nevertheless, any statement about when, where, why, and how religion arose, or any description of its original nature, can only be speculative. However, although such speculations are inconclusive, many have revealed important functions and effects of religious behavior. Several theories will be examined now.

Animism

The founder of the anthropology of religion was the Englishman Sir Edward Burnett Tylor (1871/ 1958). Religion was born, Tylor thought, as people tried to understand conditions and events they could not explain by reference to daily experience. Tylor believed that our ancestors—and contemporary nonindustrial peoples—were particularly intrigued with death, dreaming, and trance. In dreams and trances, people see images they may remember when they wake up or come out of the trance state.

Tylor concluded that attempts to explain dreams and trances led early humans to believe that two entities inhabit the body: one active during the day and the other—a double or soul— active during sleep and trance states. Although they never meet, they are vital to each other.

Islam Expanding Globally, Adapting Locally

NATIONAL GEOGRAPHIC NEWS BRIEF

by Brian Handwerk
October 24, 2003

One well-known anthropological definition of religion stresses beliefs and behavior concerned with supernatural beings, powers, and forces. Another definition focuses on congregants—a body of people who gather together regularly for worship, and who accept a set of doctrines involving the relationship between the individual and divinity. Some religions, and the beliefs, affirmations, and forms of worship they promote, have spread widely. This news brief describes how Islam, the world's fastest-growing religion, has adapted locally to various nations and cultures. In this process, although certain fundamentals endure, there is also room for considerable diversity. Local people always assign their own meanings to the messages and social forms, including religion, they receive from outside. Such meanings reflect their cultural backgrounds and experiences. This news story describes how Islam has adapted successfully to many cultural differences, including linguistic practices, building styles, and the presence of other religions, such as Hinduism, already established in that area.

One in every five people worldwide is a Muslim, some 1.3 billion believers. Islam is the world's fastest growing religion and it has spread across the globe.

Muslims everywhere agree on the Shahadah, the profession of faith: "There is no God but Allah; Mohammed is the prophet of Allah." But Islam is far from homogeneous—the faith reflects the increasingly diverse areas in which it is practiced.

"Islam is a world religion," said Ali Asani, a Harvard professor of Indo-Muslim Languages and Culture. "If you think about doctrine and theology, when these sets of religious ideas and concepts are transferred to different parts of the world—and Muslims live in many cultures and speak many different languages—the expressions of those doctrines and theology will necessarily be influenced by local culture."

Sometimes such regional distinctions are obvious to even casual observers. Mosques, for example, all share common features—they face Mecca and have a mihrab, or niche, that indicates that direction. Yet they also boast unique architectural elements and decor that suggest whether their location is Iran, Africa, or China. The houses of worship provide what Asani calls "a visual reminder of cultural diversity." Other easily grasped regional distinctions have their origins at the level of language. While Arabic is Islam's liturgical language, used for prayer, most Muslims' understanding of their faith occurs in their local language.

"Languages are really windows into culture," Asani explains. "So very often what you find is that theological Islamic concepts get translated into local idioms." . . .

Some Islamic fundamentalists might frown upon the diversity caused by local characteristics, but such are the predominant forms of Islam. "Rather than discussing Islam, we might more accurately talk about 'Islams' in different cultural contexts," Asani said. "We have Muslim literature from China, for example, where Islamic concepts are understood within a Confucian framework."

In the region of Bengal, now part of the nation of Bangladesh and the Indian state of West Bengal, a popular literary tradition created a context for the arrival of Islam. The concept of the avatar is important to the Hindu tradition, in which these deities become incarnate and descend to Earth to guide the righteous and fight evil.

"What you find in 16th century Bengal is the development of what you might call 'folk literature' where the Islamic idea of the prophet becomes understood within the framework of the avatar," Asani said. "So you have bridges being built between religious traditions as concepts resonate against each other."

Muslims before an Islamic mosque in Kano, northern Nigeria.

This example is quite different from conditions in pre-Islam Arabia, at the time of Mohammed, where the poet held a special place in society. "If you consider the Koran, the word means 'recitation' in Arabic, and it's primarily an oral scripture, intended to be recited aloud and heard; to be performed," Asani said. "Viewed from a literary perspective, its form and structure relate very well to the poetic traditions of pre-Islamic Arabia. It's an example where the format of revelation was determined by the culture. In pre-Islamic Arabia the poet was often considered to be inspired in his poetic compositions by jinn from another world. So when the Prophet Muhammed began receiving revelations which were eventually compiled into the Koran, he was accused of being a poet, to which he responded 'I'm not a poet but a prophet.'" . . .

Islam came to Indonesia with merchants who were not theologians but simply practicing Muslims who people looked to as an example. There were also Sufi teachers who were quite willing to create devotional exercises that fit the way people in Sumatra or Java already practiced their faith. The two largest Muslim groups in Indonesia today, and perhaps in the world, are Muhammadyya and Nahdlatul Ulama. Each of them has over 30 million members, and each began as local reform movement rooted in the promotion of a more modern education within the framework of Islam . . .

A large number of Muslims, of course, don't live in Islamic nations at all but as minorities in other countries. The emergence of some minority Muslim communities has been an interesting and important development of the last 25 to 30 years.

Some relatively small communities can have a large impact. The European Muslim populations, for example, have a high component of refugee intellectuals. They've had an effect on their adopted countries, and also on the rest of the Islamic world . . .

In South Africa the Muslim community is less than three percent of the population—but it's highly visible and highly educated. In the days of apartheid they had the advantage of being an intermediary, a community that was neither black nor white. By the 1980s the younger Muslim leadership became very opposed to apartheid on Islamic grounds and on basic human rights grounds. Muslims became quite active in the African National Congress (ANC). Though they were only a small minority when apartheid was destroyed, a number of Muslims became quite visible in the new South African regime—and throughout the larger Muslim world. Encompassing both Islamic states and minority communities, Islam is the world's fastest growing religion and an increasingly common topic of global conversation. Yet much of the discourse paints the faith with a single brush. As more people become familiar with Islam around the world it may be well for them to first ask, as Professor Asani suggests: "Whose Islam? Which Islam?"

SOURCE: Brian Handwerk, "Islam Expanding Globally, Adapting Locally," *National Geographic News*, October 24, 2003. http://news.nationalgeographic.com/news/2003/10/1022_031022_islamdiversity.html.

■ Ancient Greek polytheism is illustrated by this image of Apollo, with a lyre, and Artemis, sacrificing over an altar fire. The red-figured terra-cotta vessel dates to 490–480 B.C.E.

When the double permanently leaves the body, the person dies. Death is departure of the soul. From the Latin for soul, *anima*, Tylor named this belief animism. The soul was one sort of spiritual entity; people remembered various images from their dreams and trances—other spirits. For Tylor, **animism,** the earliest form of religion, was a belief in spiritual beings.

Tylor proposed that religion evolved through stages, beginning with animism. *Polytheism* (the belief in multiple gods) and then *monotheism* (the belief in a single, all-powerful deity) developed later. Because religion originated to explain things people didn't understand, Tylor thought it would decline as science offered better explanations. To an extent, he was right. We now have scientific explanations for many things that religion once elucidated. Nevertheless, because religion persists, it must do something more than explain the mysterious. It must, and does, have other functions and meanings. (For more on Durkheim, Turner, and Tylor, see Appendix 1.)

Mana and Taboo

Besides animism—and sometimes coexisting with it in the same society—is a view of the supernatural as a domain of raw impersonal power, or *force*, that people can control under certain conditions. (You'd be right to think of *Star Wars*.) Such a conception of the supernatural is particularly prominent in Melanesia, the area of the South Pacific that includes Papua New Guinea and adjacent islands. Melanesians believed in **mana**, a sacred impersonal force existing in the universe. Mana can reside in people, animals, plants, and objects.

Melanesian mana was similar to our notion of efficacy or luck. Melanesians attributed success to mana, which people could acquire or manipulate in different ways, such as through magic. Objects with mana could change someone's luck. For example, a charm or amulet belonging to a successful hunter might transmit the hunter's mana to the next person who held or wore it. A woman might put a rock in her garden, see her yields improve dramatically, and attribute the change to the force contained in the rock.

Beliefs in manalike forces are widespread, although the specifics of the religious doctrines vary. Consider the contrast between mana in Melanesia and Polynesia (the islands included in a triangular area marked by Hawaii to the north, Easter Island to the east, and New Zealand to the southwest). In Melanesia, one could acquire mana by chance, or by working hard to get it. In Polynesia, however, mana wasn't potentially available to everyone but was attached to political offices. Chiefs and nobles had more mana than ordinary people did.

So charged with mana were the highest chiefs that contact with them was dangerous to the commoners. The mana of chiefs flowed out of their bodies wherever they went. It could infect the ground, making it dangerous for others to walk in the chief's footsteps. It could permeate the containers and utensils chiefs used in eating. Contact between chief and commoners was dangerous because mana could have an effect like an electric shock. Because high chiefs had so much mana, their bodies and possessions were **taboo** (set apart as sacred and off-limits to ordinary people). Contact between a high chief and commoners was forbidden. Because ordinary people couldn't bear as much sacred current as royalty could, when commoners were accidentally exposed, purification rites were necessary.

One role of religion is to explain (see Horton 1993). A belief in souls explains what happens in sleep, trance, and death. Melanesian mana explains differential success that people can't understand in ordinary, natural terms. People fail at hunting, war, or gardening not because they are lazy, stupid, or inept but because success comes—or doesn't come—from the supernatural world.

The beliefs in spiritual beings (e.g., animism) and supernatural forces (e.g., mana) fit within the definition of religion given at the beginning of this chapter. Most religions include both spirits and impersonal forces. Likewise, the supernatural beliefs of contemporary North Americans include beings (gods, saints, souls, demons) and forces (charms, talismans, crystals, and sacred objects).

Magic and Religion

Magic refers to supernatural techniques intended to accomplish specific aims. These techniques include spells, formulas, and incantations used with deities or with impersonal forces. Magicians use *imitative magic* to produce a desired effect by imitating it. If magicians wish to injure or kill someone, they may imitate that effect on an image of the victim. Sticking pins in "voodoo dolls" is an example. With *contagious magic*, whatever is done to an object is believed to affect a person who once had contact with it. Sometimes practitioners of contagious magic use body products from prospective victims—their nails or hair, for example. The spell performed on the body product is believed to reach the person eventually and work the desired result.

We find magic in cultures with diverse religious beliefs. It can be associated with animism, mana, polytheism, or monotheism. Magic is neither simpler nor more primitive than animism or the belief in mana.

Anxiety, Control, Solace

Religion and magic don't just explain things and help people accomplish goals. They also enter the

Illustrating baseball magic, Los Angeles Dodgers first baseman Nomar Garciaparra goes through his glove adjustment ritual between pitches during the first inning of a spring training game against the New York Mets Sunday, March 5, 2006, in Vero Beach, Florida. Such rituals are most common in batting and pitching.

■ Trobriand Islanders prepare a traditional trading canoe for use in the Kula, which is a regional exchange system. The woman's basket contains trade goods, while the men prepare the long canoe to set sail. Magic is often associated with uncertainty, such as sailing in unpredictable waters.

For information on Ecuadorian curers, see the Internet Exercises at your OLC

mhhe.com/kottak

For information on spiritual beliefs among Native Australians, see the Internet Exercises at your OLC

mhhe.com/kottak

Bringing It All Together

The "Bringing It All Together" essay that follows the last chapter in this book describes ritual behavior in an unlikely setting—a fast-food restaurant.

realm of human feelings. In other words, they serve emotional needs as well as cognitive (e.g., explanatory) ones. For example, supernatural beliefs and practices can help reduce anxiety. Magical techniques can dispel doubts that arise when outcomes are beyond human control. Similarly, religion helps people face death and endure life crises.

Although all societies have techniques to deal with everyday matters, there are certain aspects of people's lives over which they lack control. When people face uncertainty and danger, according to Malinowski, they turn to magic.

> [H]owever much knowledge and science help man in allowing him to obtain what he wants, they are unable completely to control chance, to eliminate accidents, to foresee the unexpected turn of natural events, or to make human handiwork reliable and adequate to all practical requirements. (Malinowski 1931/ 1978, p. 39)

Malinowski found that the Trobriand Islanders used magic when sailing, a hazardous activity. He proposed that because people can't control matters such as wind, weather, and the fish supply, they turn to magic. People may call on magic when they come to a gap in their knowledge or powers of practical control yet have to continue in a pursuit (Malinowski 1931/1978).

Malinowski noted that it was only when confronted by situations they could not control that Trobrianders, out of psychological stress, turned from technology to magic. Despite our improving technical skills, we can't still control every outcome, and magic persists in contemporary societies. Magic is particularly evident in baseball, where George Gmelch (1978, 2001) describes a series of rituals, taboos, and sacred objects. Like Trobriand sailing magic, these behaviors serve to reduce psychological stress, creating an illusion of magical control when real control is lacking. Even

the best pitchers have off days and bad luck. Examples of pitchers' magic include tugging one's cap between pitches, touching the resin bag after each bad pitch, and talking to the ball. Gmelch's conclusions confirm Malinowski's that magic is most prevalent in situations of chance and uncertainty. All sorts of magical behavior surrounded pitching and batting, where uncertainty is rampant, but few rituals involved fielding, where players have much more control. (Batting averages of .350 or higher are very rare after a full season, but a fielding percentage below .900 is a disgrace.)

According to Malinowski, magic is used to establish control, but religion "is born out of . . . the real tragedies of human life" (1931/1978, p. 45). Religion offers emotional comfort, particularly when people face a crisis. Malinowski saw tribal religions as concerned mainly with organizing, commemorating, and helping people get through such life events as birth, puberty, marriage, and death. (For more on Malinowski, see Appendix 1.)

Rituals

Several features distinguish rituals from other kinds of behavior (Rappaport 1974). **Rituals** are formal—stylized, repetitive, and stereotyped. People perform them in special (sacred) places and at set times. Rituals include *liturgical orders*—sequences of words and actions invented prior to the current performance of the ritual in which they occur.

These features link rituals to plays, but there are important differences. Plays have audiences rather than participants. Actors merely *portray* something, but ritual performers—who make up congregations—are in earnest. Rituals convey information about the participants and their traditions. Repeated year after year, generation after generation, rituals translate enduring messages, values, and sentiments into action.

Rituals are *social* acts. Inevitably, some participants are more committed than others are to the beliefs that lie behind the rites. However, just by taking part in a joint public act, the performers signal that they accept a common social and moral order, one that transcends their status as individuals.

Rites of Passage

Magic and religion, as Malinowski noted, can reduce anxiety and allay fears. Ironically, beliefs and rituals also can *create* anxiety and a sense of insecurity and danger (Radcliffe-Brown 1962/ 1965). Anxiety may arise *because* a rite exists. Indeed, participation in a collective ritual may build up stress, whose common reduction, through the completion of the ritual, enhances the solidarity of the participants.

Rites of passage, for example, the collective circumcision of teenagers, can be very stressful. The traditional vision quests of Native Americans, particularly the Plains Indians, illustrate **rites of passage** (customs associated with the transition from one place or stage of life to another), which are found throughout the world. Among the Plains Indians, to move from boyhood to manhood, a youth temporarily separated from his community. After a period of isolation in the wilderness, often featuring fasting and drug consumption, the young man would see a vision, which would become his guardian spirit. He would then return to his community as an adult.

The rites of passage of contemporary cultures include confirmations, baptisms, bar and bat mitzvahs, and fraternity hazing. Passage rites involve changes in social status, such as from boyhood to manhood and from nonmember to sorority sister. There are also rites and rituals in our business and corporate lives. Examples include promotion and retirement parties. More generally, a rite of passage may mark any change in place, condition, social position, or age.

All rites of passage have three phases: separation, liminality, and incorporation. In the first phase, people withdraw from the group and begin moving from one place or status to another. In the third phase, they reenter society, having completed the rite. The *liminal* phase is the most interesting. It is the period between states, the limbo during which people have left one place or state but haven't yet entered or joined the next (Turner 1969/1995).

Liminality always has certain characteristics. Liminal people occupy ambiguous social positions. They exist apart from ordinary distinctions and expectations, living in a time out of time. They are cut off from normal social contacts. A variety of contrasts may demarcate liminality from regular social life. For example, among the Ndembu of Zambia, a chief underwent a rite of passage before taking office. During the liminal period, his past and future positions in society were ignored, even reversed. He was subjected to a variety of insults, orders, and humiliations.

Passage rites are often collective. Several individuals—boys being circumcised, fraternity or sorority initiates, men at military boot camps, football players in summer training camps, women becoming nuns—pass through the rites together as a group. Table 21.1 summarizes the contrasts or oppositions between liminality and normal social life. Most notable is a social aspect of *collective liminality* called **communitas** (Turner 1967), an intense community spirit, a feeling of great social solidarity, equality, and togetherness. People experiencing liminality together form a

TABLE 21.1 Oppositions between Liminality and Normal Social Life

Liminality	Normal Social Structure
Transition	State
Homogeneity	Heterogeneity
Communitas	Structure
Equality	Inequality
Anonymity	Names
Absence of property	Property
Absence of status	Status
Nakedness or uniform dress	Dress distinctions
Sexual continence or excess	Sexuality
Minimization of sex distinctions	Maximization of sex distinctions
Absence of rank	Rank
Humility	Pride
Disregard of personal appearance	Care for personal appearance
Unselfishness	Selfishness
Total obedience	Obedience only to superior rank
Sacredness	Secularity
Sacred instruction	Technical knowledge
Silence	Speech
Simplicity	Complexity
Acceptance of pain and suffering	Avoidance of pain and suffering

SOURCE: Adapted from Victor W. Turner, *The Ritual Process: Structure and Anti-structure* (New York: Aldine de Gruyter, 1969/1995), p. 106.

In a variety of contexts, liminal features signal the sacredness or distinctiveness of groups, persons, settings, and events. Liminal symbols mark entities and circumstances as extraordinary—outside and beyond ordinary social space and routine social events. In the case of cults, group identity typically is expected to transcend individuality. Cult members often wear uniform clothing. They may try to reduce distinctions based on age and gender by using a common hairstyle (shaved head, short hair, or long hair). The Heaven's Gate cult, whose mass suicide garnered headlines in 1997, even used castration to increase androgyny (similarity between males and females). In such cults, the individual, so important in American culture, is submerged in the collective. This is one reason Americans are so fearful and suspicious of "cults." (Note, however, that all the distinction-reducing features of cults described here [uniform clothing, short hair, elimination of sexuality] also are true of the military and of such mainstream religious institutions as monasteries and convents.)

■ *Passage rites are often collective. A group—such as these initiates in Togo or these Navy trainees in San Diego—passes through the rites as a unit. Such liminal people experience the same treatment and conditions and must act alike. They share communitas, an intense community spirit, a feeling of great social solidarity or togetherness.*

community of equals. The social distinctions that have existed before or will exist afterward are temporarily forgotten. Liminal people experience the same treatment and conditions and must act alike. Liminality may be marked ritually and symbolically by reversals of ordinary behavior. For example, sexual taboos may be intensified, or, conversely, sexual excess may be encouraged.

Liminality is a basic part of every passage rite. Furthermore, in certain societies, including our own, liminal symbols may be used to set off one (religious) group from another, and from society as a whole. Such "permanent liminal groups" (e.g., sects, brotherhoods, and cults) are found most characteristically in complex societies—nation-states. Liminal features such as humility, poverty, equality, obedience, sexual abstinence, and silence may be required for all sect or cult

members. Those who join such a group agree to abide by its rules. As if they were undergoing a passage rite—but in this case a never-ending one—they may rid themselves of their previous possessions and cut themselves off from former social links, including those with family members.

Totemism

Rituals serve the social function of creating temporary or permanent solidarity among people—forming a social community. We see this also in practices known as totemism. Totemism has been important in the religions of Native Australians. *Totems* can be animals, plants, or geographic features. In each tribe, groups of people have particular totems. Members of each totemic group believe themselves to be descendants of their totem. Traditionally they customarily neither killed nor ate a totemic animal, but this taboo was lifted once a year, when people assembled for ceremonies dedicated to the totem. These annual rites were believed to be necessary for the totem's survival and reproduction.

Totemism uses nature as a model for society. The totems are usually animals and plants, which are part of nature. People relate to nature through their totemic association with natural species. Because each group has a different totem, social differences mirror natural contrasts. Diversity in the natural order becomes a model for diversity in the social order. However, although totemic plants and animals occupy different niches in nature, on another level they are united because they all are part of nature. The unity of the human social order is enhanced by symbolic association with and imitation of the natural order (Durkheim 1912/2001; Lévi-Strauss 1963; Radcliffe-Brown 1962/1965).

One role of religious rites and beliefs is to affirm, and thus maintain, the solidarity of a religion's adherents. Totems are sacred emblems symbolizing common identity. This is true not just among Native Australians, but also among Native American groups of the North Pacific coast of North America, whose totem poles are well known. Their totemic carvings, which commemorate, and tell visual stories about, ancestors, animals, and spirits, also are associated with ceremonies. In totemic rites, people gather together to honor their totem. In so doing, they use ritual to maintain the social oneness that the totem symbolizes.

In contemporary nations, too, totems continue to mark groups, such as states and universities (e.g., Badgers, Buckeyes, and Wolverines), professional teams (Lions, Tigers, and Bears), and political parties (donkeys and elephants). Although the modern context is more secular, one can still witness, in intense college football rivalries, some of the effervescence Durkheim noted in Australian totemic religion.

RELIGION AND CULTURAL ECOLOGY

Another domain in which religion plays a prominent role is cultural ecology. Behavior motivated by beliefs in supernatural beings, powers, and forces may help people survive in their material environment. In this section, we will see how beliefs and rituals may function as part of a group's cultural adaptation to its environment.

Sacred Cattle in India

The people of India revere zebu cattle, which are protected by the Hindu doctrine of *ahimsa,* a principle of nonviolence that forbids the killing of animals generally. Western economic development experts occasionally (and erroneously) cite the Hindu cattle taboo to illustrate the idea that religious beliefs can stand in the way of rational economic decisions. Hindus might seem to be irrationally ignoring a valuable food (beef) because of their cultural or religious traditions. The economic developers also comment that Indians don't know how to raise proper cattle. They point to the scraggly zebus that wander about town and country. Western techniques of animal

India's zebu cattle are protected by the doctrine of ahimsa, a principle of nonviolence that forbids the killing of animals generally. This Hindu doctrine puts the full power of organized religion behind the command not to destroy a valuable resource even in times of extreme need. What kinds of animal avoidance taboos do you observe? Is their origin religious or secular?

husbandry grow bigger cattle that produce more beef and milk. Western planners lament that Hindus are set in their ways. Bound by culture and tradition, they refuse to develop rationally.

However, these assumptions are both ethnocentric and wrong. Sacred cattle actually play an important adaptive role in an Indian ecosystem that has evolved over thousands of years (Harris 1974, 1978). Peasants' use of cattle to pull plows and carts is part of the technology of Indian agriculture. Indian peasants have no need for large, hungry cattle of the sort that economic developers, beef marketers, and North American cattle ranchers prefer. Scrawny animals pull plows and carts well enough but don't eat their owners out of house and home. How could peasants with limited land and marginal diets feed supersteers without taking food away from themselves?

Indians use cattle manure to fertilize their fields. Not all the manure is collected, because peasants don't spend much time watching their cattle, which wander and graze at will during certain seasons. In the rainy season, some of the manure that cattle deposit on the hillsides washes down to the fields. In this way, cattle also fertilize the fields indirectly. Furthermore, in a country where fossil fuels are scarce, dry cattle dung, which burns slowly and evenly, is a basic cooking fuel.

Far from being useless, as the development experts contend, sacred cattle are essential to Indian cultural adaptation. Biologically adapted to poor pasture land and a marginal environment, the scraggly zebu provides fertilizer and fuel, is indispensable in farming, and is affordable for peasants. The Hindu doctrine of *ahimsa* puts the full power of organized religion behind the command not to destroy a valuable resource even in times of extreme need.

Ewe Traditional and Biomedical Healing Practices in Ghana's Volta Region

BACKGROUND INFORMATION

STUDENT:
(Lauren) Charlie Graham

SUPERVISING PROFESSOR:
Kara Hoover

SCHOOL:
Georgia State University

YEAR IN SCHOOL/MAJOR:
Fourth year/Anthropology (Medical)

FUTURE PLANS:
Internship/Graduate School

PROJECT TITLE:
Ewe Traditional and Biomedical
Healing Practices in Ghana's
Volta Region

In summer 2004 Charlie Graham initiated a preliminary study of traditional and biomedical healing among the Ewe of Ghana's Volta region. She plans to continue this work as a graduate student in medical anthropology. Unlike our own society, where medicine is a separate and distinct field, it is common in nonindustrial societies for medicine to be intertwined with religion. The Ewe, like the Makua discussed in Chapter 17 on "Political Systems," and many other cultures believe that sorcery can cause mental and physical unrest, which traditional healers can treat.*

In summer 2004 I began fieldwork in Ghana which I plan on continuing in graduate school. Ghana's Volta Region is home to the Ewe, a historically migrant tribe who also reside in Togo and Benin. My research compares and contrasts traditional herbal healing with biomedical treatment methods among the Ewe. The cultural synthesis of traditional and British/Western imposed customs makes for a particularly interesting perspective.

Ghana gained independence from British rule in 1957, making it the first self-governing country in Africa. Since then, it has remained a democratic nation, enjoying peaceful relations with neighboring countries and among its several tribes. Divided into 10 regions, Ghana's tribal leaders share political power with elected officials. Ghanaians practice traditional religions, although Islam and Christianity dominate the North and South respectively, due in large part to missionary influence.

For nine weeks I lived in Ho, the Volta Region's capital, volunteering part time at the Ho District Hospital. I observed various units, including Psychiatric, Maternity, Diabetic, Family Planning, Children's, Male and Female wards. I shadowed the doctor on her rounds and learned alongside third-year nursing students in the midst of their residencies. I also worked with and learned from local medicine men. I traveled to different areas of Volta Region to visit high priests, observing and surveying their medicinal diversity. I conducted extensive formal and informal interviews of patients, healers, and third parties; observed diagnostic and treatment procedures; and even served as the patient, receiving assorted treatments from both doctors and traditional healers.

Although Ghana's biomedical system bears a fundamental likeness to Britain's, I routinely encountered disparities in medical practices. From doctor-patient relations to disease etiologies to administrative protocol, the differences stood out as opportunities

SOCIAL CONTROL

Religion has meaning for people. It helps men and women cope with adversity and tragedy. It offers hope that things will get better. Lives can be transformed through spiritual healing or rebirth. Sinners can repent and be saved—or they can go on sinning and be damned. If the faithful truly internalize a system of religious rewards and punishments, their religion becomes a powerful means of controlling their beliefs, their behavior, and what they teach their children.

Many people engage in religious activity because it seems to work. Prayers get answered. Faith healers heal. Sometimes it doesn't take much to convince the faithful that religious actions are efficacious. Many American Indian people in southwestern Oklahoma use faith healers at high monetary costs, not just because it makes them feel better about the uncertain but because it works (Lassiter 1998). Each year legions of Brazilians visit a church, Nosso Senhor do Bomfim, in the city of Salvador, Bahia. They vow to repay "Our Lord" (Nosso Senhor) if healing happens. Showing that the vows work, and are repaid, are the thousands of ex votos, plastic impressions of every conceivable body part, that adorn the church, along with photos of people who have been cured.

Religion can work by getting inside people and mobilizing their emotions—their joy, their wrath, their righteousness. We've seen how Émile Durkheim (1912/2001), a prominent French social theorist and scholar of religion (see Appendix 1), described the collective "effervescence" that can develop in religious contexts. Intense emotion bubbles up. People feel a deep sense of shared joy, meaning, experience, communion, belonging, and commitment to their religion.

The power of religion affects action. When religions meet, they can coexist peacefully, or their differences can be a basis for enmity and dishar-

for cultural exchange and theoretical application. One unique aspect of my research was the incorporation of traditional etiological beliefs, like *juju*, into biomedical practice. *Juju* refers to interpersonally imposed evil forces that create physical and mental unrest (sorcery). Although the majority of Southern Ghanaians practice Christianity, they incorporate traditional beliefs such as this.

In the hospital, language barriers caused miscommunication. Because many Ghanaian doctors leave the country to work in private or better-paying hospitals, many government hospitals employ Spanish-speaking doctors from Cuba who speak basic English and little Ewe. Moreover, although English is Ghana's official language, most patients speak only Ewe. Thus as a Spanish speaker, I often served as a translator. Nurses interviewed patients in Ewe, roughly conveyed the information to me in English, and in Spanish, I reported to the doctor. Due to this linguistic disparity, the healthcare system is inefficient, and patient recovery is often stunted.

My background in medical anthropology and the research I conducted prior to arrival enabled me to recognise the traditional healing practices I encountered. Medicine men train for three years and rank from herbalist to

Charlie Graham with village children in Ghana.

high priest or sorcerer. I encountered practitioners in each year of study during my time in Ghana. Treatment ranges from preventative to curative, and revolves around belief in patients' physical or spiritual unrest. Relief comes from spiritual penitence via the healer. I sat in on sessions with first-time and regular clients with complaints of behavioral to epidermal abnormalities. Some sorcerers performed ceremonies specifically for me,

communicating with their spirits on my behalf. All communication was in Ewe, for which I had a translator.

It was an honor to learn first-hand from healers on both ends of the medical spectrum, and my fieldwork thrived with rich and intricate data collection. I had the unique opportunity to engage in and scrutinize two different medical realms, struggling to find and maintain their complementary balance in a developing country.

---

mony, even battle. Religious fervor has inspired Christians on crusades against the infidel and has led Muslims to wage holy wars against non-Islamic peoples. Throughout history, political leaders have used religion to promote and justify their views and policies.

By late September 1996, the Taliban movement had firmly imposed an extreme form of social control in the name of religion on Afghanistan (Figure 21.1) and its people. Led by Muslim clerics, the Taliban attempted to create their version of an Islamic society modeled on the teachings of the Koran (Burns 1997). Various repressive measures were instituted. The Taliban barred women from work and girls from school. Females past puberty were prohibited from talking to unrelated men. Women needed an approved reason, such as shopping for food, to leave their homes. Men, who were required to grow bushy beards, also faced an array of bans—against playing cards, listening to music, keeping pigeons, and flying kites.

To enforce their decrees, the Taliban sent armed enforcers throughout the country. Those agents took charge of "beard checks" and other forms of scrutiny on behalf of a religious police force known as the General Department for the Preservation of Virtue and the Elimination of Vice (Burns 1997). By late fall 2001 the Taliban had been overthrown, with a new interim government established in Kabul, the Afghani capital, on December 22. The collapse of the Taliban followed American bombing of Afghanistan in response to the September 11, 2001, attacks on New York's World Trade Center and Washington's Pentagon. As the Taliban yielded Kabul to victorious Northern Alliance forces, local men flocked to barbershops to have their beards trimmed or shaved. They were using a key Taliban symbol to celebrate the end of religious repression.

Note that in the case of the Taliban, forms of social control were used to support a strict religious orthodoxy. This wasn't repression in

Kite flying, traditionally a popular sport in Afghanistan, was banned by the Taliban. Shown here, on Fridays, after prayers, hundreds of men and boys come to a hilltop overlooking Kabul to fly kites in the windy skies. A kite flyer's goal is to maneuver his kite so as to cut the strings of other kite flyers around him, causing their kites to fall from the sky. The fallen kite belongs to the boy who runs for and finds it first.

religion's name, but repressive religion. In other countries, secular leaders use religion to justify social control. Seeking power, they use religious rhetoric to get it. The Saudi Arabian government, for example, can be seen as using religion to divert attention from a repressive social policy.

How may leaders mobilize communities and, in so doing, gain support for their own policies? One way is by persuasion; another is by instilling hatred or fear. As we saw in the chapter "Political Systems," fears about and accusations of witchcraft and sorcery can be powerful means of social control by creating a climate of danger and insecurity that affects everyone.

Witchcraft accusations often are directed at socially marginal or anomalous individuals. Among the Betsileo of Madagascar, for example, who prefer patrilocal postmarital residence, men living in the wife's or the mother's village violate a

FIGURE 21.1 Location of Afghanistan.

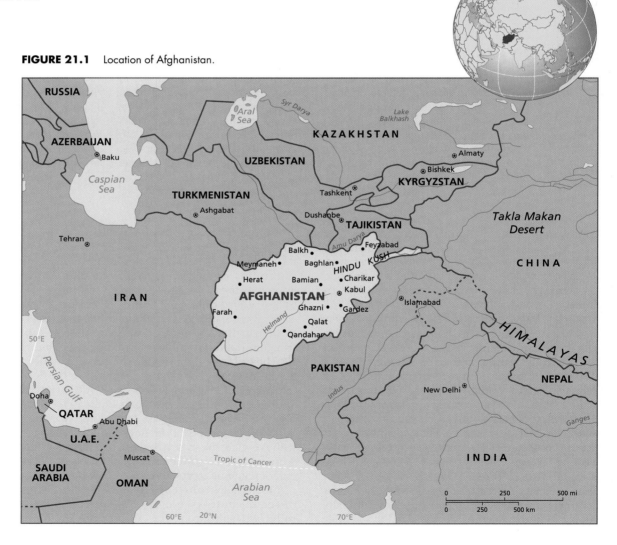

cultural norm. Linked to their anomalous social position, just a bit of unusual behavior (e.g., staying up late at night) on their part is sufficient for them to be called witches and avoided as a result. In tribes and peasant communities, people who stand out economically, especially if they seem to be benefiting at the expense of others, often face accusations of witchcraft, leading to social ostracism or punishment. In this case witchcraft accusation becomes a **leveling mechanism,** a custom or social action that operates to reduce differences in wealth and thus to bring standouts in line with community norms—another form of social control.

To ensure proper behavior, religions offer rewards, such as the fellowship of the religious community, and punishments, such as the threat of being cast out or excommunicated. Many religions promise rewards for the good life and punishment for the bad. Your physical, mental, moral, and spiritual health, now and forever, may depend on your beliefs and behavior. For example, if you don't pay enough attention to the ancestors, they may snatch your kids from you.

Religions, especially the formal organized ones typically found in state societies, often prescribe a code of ethics and morality to guide behavior. The Judaic Ten Commandants lay down a set of prohibitions against killing, stealing, adultery, and other misdeeds. Crimes are breaches of secular laws, just as sins are breaches of religious strictures. Some rules (e.g., the Ten Commandments) proscribe or prohibit behavior; others prescribe behavior. The Golden Rule, for instance, is a religious guide to do unto others as you would have them do unto you. Moral codes are ways of maintaining order and stability. Codes of morality and ethics are repeated constantly in religious sermons, catechisms, and the like. They become internalized psychologically. They guide behavior and produce regret, guilt, shame, and the need for forgiveness, expiation, and absolution when they are not followed.

Religions also maintain social control by stressing the temporary and fleeting nature of this life. They promise rewards (and/or punishment) in an afterlife (Christianity) or reincarnation (Hinduism and Buddhism). Such beliefs serve to reinforce the status quo. People accept what they have now, knowing they can expect something better in the afterlife or the next life if they follow religious guidelines. Under slavery in the American South, the masters taught portions of the Bible, such as the story of Job, that stressed compliance. The slaves, however, seized on the story of Moses, the promised land, and deliverance.

KINDS OF RELIGION

Religion is a cultural universal. But religions are parts of particular cultures, and cultural differences show up systematically in religious beliefs and practices. For example, the religions of stratified, state societies differ from those of cultures with less marked social contrasts and power differentials.

Considering several cultures, Wallace (1966) identified four types of religion: shamanic, communal, Olympian, and monotheistic (Table 21.2). Unlike priests, the **shamans** of a shamanic religion aren't full-time religious officials but part-time religious figures who mediate between people and supernatural beings and forces. All cultures have medico-magico-religious specialists. *Shaman* is the general term encompassing curers ("witch doctors"), mediums, spiritualists, astrologers, palm readers, and other diviners. Wallace found shamanic religions to be most characteristic of foraging societies, particularly those found in the northern latitudes, such as the Inuit and the native peoples of Siberia.

Although they are only part-time specialists, shamans often set themselves off symbolically

For more on shamans, see the Virtual Exploration
mhhe.com/kottak

TABLE 21.2	Anthony F. C. Wallace's Typology of Religions		
Type of Religion (Wallace)	**Type of Practitioner**	**Conception of Supernatural**	**Type of Society**
Monotheistic	Priests, ministers, etc.	Supreme being	States
Olympian	Priesthood	Hierarchical pantheon with powerful deities	Chiefdoms and archaic states
Communal	Part-time specialists; occasional community-sponsored events, including rites of passage	Several deities with some control over nature	Food-producing tribes
Shamanic	Shaman = part-time	Zoomorphic practitioner	Foraging bands (plants and animals)

For a quiz on types of religion, see the Interactive Exercise
mhhe.com/kottak

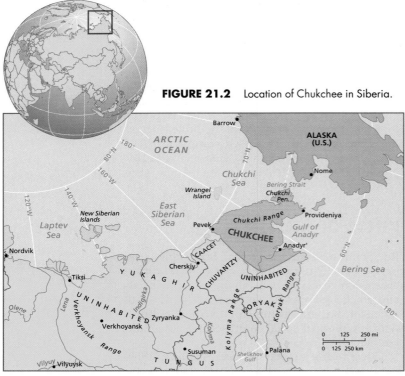

FIGURE 21.2 Location of Chukchee in Siberia.

■ *We'wha, a Zuni berdache, in 1885. In some Native American societies, certain ritual duties were reserved for* berdaches, *men who rejected the male role and joined a third gender.*

from ordinary people by assuming a different or ambiguous sex or gender role. (In nation-states, priests, nuns, and vestal virgins do something similar by taking vows of celibacy and chastity.) Transvestism is one way of being sexually ambiguous. Among the Chukchee of Siberia (Figure 21.2), where coastal populations fished and interior groups hunted, male shamans copied the dress, speech, hair arrangements, and life styles of women (Bogoras 1904). These shamans took other men as husbands and sex partners and received respect for their supernatural and curative expertise. Female shamans could join a fourth gender, copying men and taking wives.

Among the Crow of the North American Plains, certain ritual duties were reserved for *berdaches,* men who rejected the male role of bison hunter, raider, and warrior and joined a third gender. The fact that certain key rituals could be conducted only by *berdaches* indicates their regular and normal place in Crow social life (Lowie 1935).

Communal religions have, in addition to shamans, community rituals such as harvest ceremonies and rites of passage. Although communal religions lack *full-time* religious specialists, they believe in several deities (**polytheism**) who control aspects of nature. Although some hunter-gatherers, including Australian totemites, have communal religions, these religions are more typical of farming societies.

Olympian religions, which arose with state organization and marked social stratification, add full-time religious specialists—professional *priesthoods.* Like the state itself, the priesthood is hierarchically and bureaucratically organized. The term *Olympian* comes from Mount Olympus, home of the classical Greek gods. Olympian religions are polytheistic. They include powerful anthropomorphic gods with specialized functions, for example, gods of love, war, the sea, and death. Olympian *pantheons* (collections of supernatural beings) were prominent in the religions of many nonindustrial nation-states, including the Aztecs of Mexico, several African and Asian kingdoms, and classical Greece and Rome. Wallace's fourth type—**monotheism**—also has priesthoods and notions of divine power, but it views the supernatural differently. In monotheism, all supernatural phenomena are manifestations of, or are under the control of, a single eternal, omniscient, omnipotent, and omnipresent supreme being.

RELIGION IN STATES

Robert Bellah (1978) coined the term "world-rejecting religion" to describe most forms of Christianity, including Protestantism. World-rejecting religions arose in ancient civilizations, along with literacy and a specialized priesthood. These religions are so named because of their tendency to reject the natural (mundane, ordinary, material, secular) world and to focus instead on a higher (sacred, transcendent) realm of reality. The divine is a domain of exalted morality to which humans can only aspire. Salvation through fusion with the supernatural is the main goal of such religions.

Protestant Values and the Rise of Capitalism

Notions of salvation and the afterlife dominate Christian ideologies. However, most varieties of Protestantism lack the hierarchical structure of earlier monotheistic religions, including Roman Catholicism. With a diminished role for the priest (minister), salvation is directly available to individuals. Regardless of their social status, Protestants have unmediated access to the supernatural. The individualistic focus of Protestantism offers a close fit with capitalism and with American culture.

In his influential book *The Protestant Ethic and the Spirit of Capitalism* (1904/1958), the social theorist Max Weber linked the spread of capitalism to the values preached by early Protestant leaders. Weber saw European Protestants (and eventually their American descendants) as more successful financially than Catholics. He attributed this difference to the values stressed by their religions. Weber saw Catholics as more concerned with immediate happiness and security. Protestants were more ascetic, entrepreneurial, and future-oriented, he thought.

Capitalism, said Weber, required that the traditional attitudes of Catholic peasants be replaced by values fitting an industrial economy based on capital accumulation. Protestantism placed a premium on hard work, an ascetic life, and profit seeking. Early Protestants saw success on earth as a sign of divine favor and probable salvation. According to some Protestant credos, individuals could gain favor with God through good works. Other sects stressed predestination, the idea that only a few mortals have been selected for eternal life and that people cannot change their fates. However, material success, achieved through hard work, could be a strong clue that someone was predestined to be saved.

Weber also argued that rational business organization required the removal of industrial production from the home, its setting in peasant societies. Protestantism made such a separation possible by emphasizing individualism: individuals, not families or households, would be saved or not. Interestingly, given the connection that is usually made with morality and religion in contemporary American discourse about family values, the family was a secondary matter for Weber's early Protestants. God and the individual reigned supreme.

Today, of course, in North America as throughout the world, people of many religions and with diverse worldviews are successful capitalists. Furthermore, traditional Protestant values often have little to do with today's economic maneuvering. Still, there is no denying that the individualistic focus of Protestantism was compatible with the severance of ties to land and kin that industrialism demanded. These values remain prominent in the religious background of many of the people of the United States.

WORLD RELIGIONS

Information on the world's major religions is provided in Table 21.3 (number of adherents) and Figure 21.3 (percentage of world population). Based on people's claimed religions, Christianity is the world's largest, with some 2.1 billion adherents. Islam, with some 1.3 billion practitioners, is next, followed by Hinduism, then Chinese traditional religion (also known as Chinese folk religion or Confucianism), and Buddhism. More than a billion people claim no official religion, but only about a fifth of them are self-proclaimed atheists. Worldwide, Islam is growing at a rate of about 2.9 percent annually, versus 2.3 percent for Christianity, whose overall growth rate is the same as the rate of world population increase (Adherents.com 2002; Ontario Consultants 2001).

Within Christianity, there is variation in the growth rate. There were an estimated 680 million "born-again" Christians (e.g., Pentecostals and Evangelicals) in the world in 2001, with an annual worldwide growth rate of 7 percent, versus just 2.3 percent for Christianity overall. (This would translate into 954 million Pentecostals and Evangelicals in 2006.) The global growth rate of

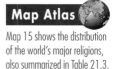

Map 15 shows the distribution of the world's major religions, also summarized in Table 21.3.

TABLE 21.3 Religions of the World, by Estimated Number of Adherents, 2005

Christianity	2.1 billion
Islam	1.3 billion
Secular/Nonreligious/Agnostic/Atheist	1.1 billion
Hinduism	900 million
Chinese traditional religion	394 million
Buddhism	376 million
Primal-indigenous	300 million
African traditional and diasporic	100 million
Sikhism	23 million
Juche	19 million
Spiritism	15 million
Judaism	14 million
Baha'i	7 million
Jainism	4.2 million
Shinto	4 million
Cao Dai	4 million
Zoroastrianism	2.6 million
Tenrikyo	2 million
Neo-Paganism	1 million
Unitarian-Universalism	800 thousand
Rastafarianism	600 thousand
Scientology	500 thousand

SOURCE: Adherents.com. 2005. http//www.adherents.com/Religions_By_Adherents.html.

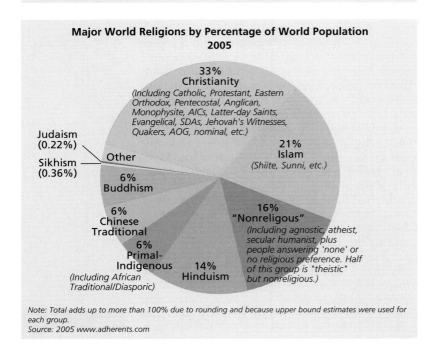

Major World Religions by Percentage of World Population 2005

Note: Total adds up to more than 100% due to rounding and because upper bound estimates were used for each group.
Source: 2005 www.adherents.com

FIGURE 21.3 Major World Religions by Percentage of World Population, 2005.
SOURCE: Adherents.com. 2005. http//www.adherents.com/Religions_By_Adherents.html.

Roman Catholics has been estimated at only 1.3 percent, compared with a Protestant growth rate of 3.3 percent per year (Winter 2001). Much of this explosive growth, especially in Africa, is of a type of Protestantism that would be scarcely recognizable to most Americans, given its incorporation of many animistic elements.

Table 21.4 classifies 11 world religions according to their degree of internal unity and diversity. Listed first are the most cohesive/unified groups. Listed last are the religions with the most internal diversity. The list is based mainly on the degree of doctrinal similarity among the various subgroups. To a lesser extent it reflects diversity in practice, ritual, and organization. (The list includes the majority manifestations of each religion, as well as subgroups that the larger branches may label "heterodox.") How would you decide whether a value judgment is implied by this list? Is it better for a religion to be highly unified, cohesive, monolithic, and lacking in internal diversity, or to be fragmented, schismatic, multifaceted, and abounding in variations on the same theme? Over time such diversity can give birth to new religions; for example, Christianity arose from Judaism, Buddhism from Hinduism, Baha'i from Islam, and Sikhism from Hinduism. Within Christianity, Protestantism developed out of Roman Catholicism.

RELIGION AND CHANGE

Fundamentalists seek order based on strict adherence to purportedly traditional standards, beliefs, rules, and customs. Christian and Islamic fundamentalists recognize, decry, and attempt to redress change, yet they also contribute to change. In a worldwide process, new religions challenge established churches. In the United States, conservative Christian TV hosts have become influential broadcasters and opinion shapers. In Latin America, evangelical Protestantism is winning millions of converts from Roman Catholicism.

Like political organization, religion helps maintain social order. And, like political mobilization, religious energy can be harnessed not just for change, but also for revolution. Reacting to conquest or to actual or perceived foreign domination, for instance, religious leaders may seek to alter or revitalize their society. In an "Islamic Revolution," for example, Iranian ayatollahs marshaled religious fervor to create national solidarity and radical change. We call such movements nativistic movements (Linton 1943) or revitalization movements (Wallace 1956).

Revitalization Movements

Revitalization movements are social movements that occur in times of change, in which religious leaders emerge and undertake to alter or revital-

TABLE 21.4   Classical World Religions Ranked by Internal Religious Similarity

Most unified

Baha'i

Zoroastrianism

Sikhism

Islam

Jainism

Judaism

Taoism

Shinto

Christianity

Buddhism

Hinduism

Most diverse

SOURCE: Adherents.com. 2001. http//www.adherents.com/Religions_By_Adherents.html.

ize a society. Christianity originated as a revitalization movement. Jesus was one of several prophets who preached new religious doctrines while the Middle East was under Roman rule. It was a time of social unrest, when a foreign power ruled the land. Jesus inspired a new, enduring, and major religion. His contemporaries were not so successful.

The Handsome Lake religion arose around 1800 among the Iroquois of New York State (Wallace 1970). Handsome Lake, the founder of this revitalization movement, was a leader of one of the Iroquois tribes. The Iroquois had suffered because of their support of the British against the American colonials (and for other reasons). After the colonial victory and a wave of immigration to their homeland, the Iroquois were dispersed on small reservations. Unable to pursue traditional horticulture and hunting in their homeland, they became heavy drinkers and quarreled among themselves.

Handsome Lake was a heavy drinker who started having visions from heavenly messengers. The spirits warned him that unless the Iroquois changed their ways, they would be destroyed. His visions offered a plan for coping with the new order. Witchcraft, quarreling, and drinking would end. The Iroquois would copy European farming techniques, which, unlike traditional Iroquois horticulture, stressed male rather than female labor. Handsome Lake preached that the Iroquois should also abandon their communal longhouses and matrilineal descent groups for more permanent marriages and individual family households. The teachings of Handsome Lake produced a new

church and religion, one that still has members in New York and Ontario. This revitalization movement helped the Iroquois adapt to and survive in a modified environment. They eventually gained a reputation among their non-Indian neighbors as sober family farmers.

Syncretisms

Especially in today's world, religious expressions emerge from the interplay of local, regional, national, and international cultural forces. **Syncretisms** are cultural mixes, including religious blends, that emerge from acculturation—the exchange of cultural features when cultures come into continuous firsthand contact. One example of religious syncretism is the mixture of African, Native American, and Roman Catholic saints and deities in Caribbean *vodun,* or "voodoo," cults. This blend also is present in Cuban *santeria* and in *candomblé,* an "Afro-Brazilian" cult. Another syncretism is the blend of Melanesian and Christian beliefs in cargo cults.

Like the Handsome Lake religion just discussed, cargo cults are revitalization movements. Such movements may emerge when natives have regular contact with industrial societies but lack their wealth, technology, and living standards. Some such movements attempt to explain European domination and wealth and to achieve similar success magically by mimicking European behavior and manipulating symbols of the desired lifestyle. The syncretic **cargo cults** of Melanesia and Papua New Guinea weave Christian doctrine with aboriginal beliefs (Figure 21.4). They take their name from their focus on cargo: European goods of the sort natives have seen unloaded from the cargo holds of ships and airplanes.

In one early cult, members believed that the spirits of the dead would arrive in a ship. These ghosts would bring manufactured goods for the natives and would kill all the whites. More recent cults replaced ships with airplanes (Worsley 1959/1985). Many cults have used elements of European culture as sacred objects. The rationale is that Europeans use these objects, have wealth, and therefore must know the "secret of cargo." By mimicking how Europeans use or treat objects, natives hope also to come upon the secret knowledge needed to gain cargo.

For example, having seen Europeans' reverent treatment of flags and flagpoles, the members of one cult began to worship flagpoles. They believed the flagpoles were sacred towers that could transmit messages between the living and the dead. Other natives built airstrips to entice planes bearing canned goods, portable radios, clothing, wristwatches, and motorcycles. Near the airstrips they made effigies of towers, airplanes, and radios. They talked into the cans in a magical attempt to establish radio contact with the gods.

FIGURE 21.4 Location of Melanesia.

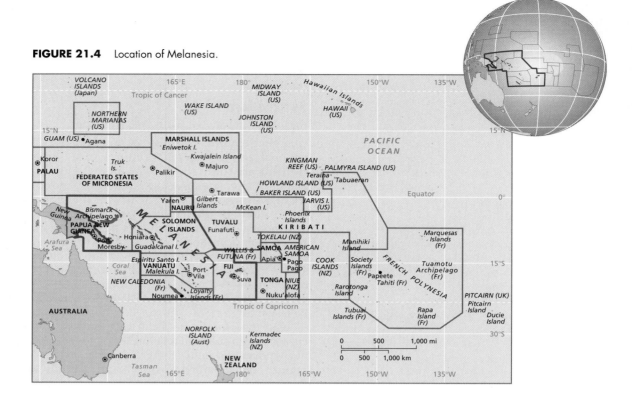

A cargo cult in Vanuatu. Boys and men march with spears, imitating British colonial soldiers. Does anything in your own society remind you of a cargo cult?

Some cargo cult prophets proclaimed that success would come through a reversal of European domination and native subjugation. The day was near, they preached, when natives, aided by God, Jesus, or native ancestors, would turn the tables. Native skins would turn white, and those of Europeans would turn brown; Europeans would die or be killed.

As syncretisms, cargo cults blend aboriginal and Christian beliefs. Melanesian myths told of ancestors shedding their skins and changing into powerful beings and of dead people returning to life. Christian missionaries, who had been in Melanesia since the late 19th century, also spoke of resurrection. The cults' preoccupation with cargo is related to traditional Melanesian big-man systems. In the chapter "Political Systems," we saw that a Melanesian big man had to be generous. People worked for the big man, helping him amass wealth, but eventually he had to give a feast and give away all that wealth.

Because of their experience with big-man systems, Melanesians believed that all wealthy people eventually had to give their wealth away. For decades, they had attended Christian missions and worked on plantations. All the while they expected Europeans to return the fruits of their labor as their own big men did. When the Europeans refused to distribute the wealth or even to let natives know the secret of its production and distribution, cargo cults developed.

Like arrogant big men, Europeans would be leveled, by death if necessary. However, natives lacked the physical means of doing what their traditions said they should do. Thwarted by well-armed colonial forces, natives resorted to magical leveling. They called on supernatural beings to intercede, to kill or otherwise deflate the European big men and redistribute their wealth.

Cargo cults are religious responses to the expansion of the world capitalist economy. However, this religious mobilization had political and economic results. Cult participation gave Melanesians a basis for common interests and activities and thus helped pave the way for political parties and economic interest organizations. Previously separated by geography, language, and customs, Melanesians started forming larger groups as members of the same cults and followers of the same prophets. The cargo cults paved the way for political action through which the indigenous peoples eventually regained their autonomy.

Antimodernism and Fundamentalism

Antimodernism describes the rejection of the modern in favor of what is perceived as an earlier, purer, and better way of life. This viewpoint grew out of disillusionment with Europe's Industrial Revolution and subsequent developments in science, technology, and consumption patterns. Antimodernists typically consider technology's use today to be misguided, or think technology should have a lower priority than religious and cultural values.

The modern and the antimodern are key ingredients in Benjamin R. Barber's (1992, 1995) contention that tribalism and globalism are the two key—and opposed—principles of our age. Tribalism, which Barber sums up with the term "Jihad" (borrowed loosely from Islam, where it means quest or struggle), is an antimodern force pitting culture against culture, tribe against tribe, and religion against religion. For Jihad's enemy, Barber coins the term "McWorld," which subsumes the modern forces that promote global integration and uniformity, including the diffusion of music, computers, and fast food—MTV, Macintosh, and McDonald's. Barber argues that Jihad and McWorld operate today with equal force in opposite directions. Jihad is driven by parochial hatreds; McWorld, by universalizing markets.

Jihad resists McWorld, which spans nations, cultures, and ideologies. Groups like Al Qaeda exist in perpetual rebellion against McWorld and its perceived values and consumption patterns. To its warriors and adherents, Jihad offers an identity and a sense of community. But that social solidarity is grounded in exclusion, separation, opposition, and anger. Solidarity is achieved through war against outsiders. In places like Afghanistan under Taliban rule, solidarity might entail submission to an arbitrary hierarchy, fanaticism in beliefs, and the absorption or destruction of the individual self for the goals of the group.

Religious fundamentalism, a form of contemporary antimodernism, can be compared to the revitalization movements discussed previously. **Fundamentalism** describes antimodernist movements in various religions. Ironically, religious fun-

damentalism is itself a modern phenomenon, based on a strong feeling among its adherents of alienation from the surrounding (modern) culture. Fundamentalists assert an identity separate from the larger religious group from which they arose. Their separation reflects their belief that the founding principles on which the larger religion is based have been corrupted, neglected, compromised, forgotten, or replaced with other principles. Fundamentalists advocate strict fidelity to the "true" religious principles of the larger religion.

Fundamentalists also seek to rescue religion from absorption into modern, Western culture, which they see as already having corrupted the mainstream version of their religion—and others. Fundamentalists establish a "wall of virtue" against alien religions, as well as against the modernized, compromised version of their own religion. In Christianity, fundamentalists are "born again," as opposed to "mainline," "liberal," or "modernist" Protestants. In Islam they are *jama'at* (in Arabic, enclaves based on close fellowship) engaged in *jihad* (struggle) against a Western culture hostile to Islam and the God-given (*shariah*) way of life. In Judaism they are *Haredi*, "Torah-true" Jews. All such groups see a sharp divide between themselves and other religions, and between a "sacred" view of life and the "secular" world and "nominal religion" (see Antoun 2001).

Fundamentalists strive to protect a distinctive doctrine and way of life and of salvation. A strong sense of community is created, focused on a clearly defined religious way of life. The prospect of joining such a community may appeal to people who find little that is distinctive or vital in their previous religious identity. Fundamentalists get their converts, mainly from their larger religion, by convincing them of its inauthenticity.

Many fundamentalists are politically aware citizens of nation-states. Often they believe that government processes and policies must recognize

A Pentecostal church service in Brooklyn, New York. Pentecostalism is a rapidly expanding Christian religious movement that emphasizes the "gifts of the Holy Spirit," traditionally first bestowed on the day of Pentecost (50 days after Easter). There is considerable diversity among Pentecostals, who are not necessarily fundamentalists.

TABLE 21.5 Religious Composition (in Percentages) of the Populations of the United States, 1990 and 2001, and Canada, 1991 and 2001

	United States		Canada	
	1990	2001	1991	2001
Protestant	60%	52%	36%	29%
Catholic	26	24	46	44
Jewish	2	1	1	1
Other	5	10	4	9
None given	7	13	12	17

SOURCE: *Statistical Abstract of the United States 2003*, Table 79, p. 67. http://www.census.gov/statab/www/; *Census of Canada*, 2001. http://www40.statcan.ca/l01/cst01/demo30a.htm?sdi=religion.

the way of life set forth in scripture. In their eyes, the state should be subservient to God. The governments of many Muslim countries, such as Afghanistan, Iran, and Saudi Arabia, are Islamic, and include people with fundamentalist beliefs, as is also true of many countries where Christians predominate.

A New Age

Fundamentalists may or may not be correct in seeing a rise in secularism in contemporary North America. Between 1990 and 2001, the number of Americans giving no religious preference grew from 7 to 13 percent. In Canada the comparable figure rose from 12 to 17 percent in that period (Table 21.5). Of course, people who lack a religious preference aren't necessarily atheists. Many of them are believers who don't belong to a church. According to U.S. Census Bureau figures for 2001, about two million Americans (just 1 percent of the population) self-identified as atheists or agnostics. Even fewer (less than 100,000 in 2001) called themselves "secular" or "humanists." Still, atheists and secular humanists do exist, and they, too, are organized.

Like members of religious groups, they use varied media, including print and the Internet, to communicate among themselves. Just as Buddhists can peruse *Tricycle: The Buddhist Review*, secular humanists can find their views validated in *Free Inquiry*, a quarterly identifying itself as "the international secular humanist magazine." Secular humanists speak out against organized religion and its "dogmatic pronouncements" and "supernatural or spiritual agendas" and the "obscurantist views" of religious leaders who presume "to inform us of God's views" by appealing to sacred texts (Steinfels 1997).

Is American society really growing more secular? A considerable body of sociological research

suggests that levels of American religiosity haven't changed much over the past century (see Finke and Stark 2005). To be sure, there are new religious trends and forms of spiritualism. Some Americans have turned to charismatic Christianity. In the United States and Australia, respectively, some people who are not Native Americans or Native Australians have appropriated the symbols, settings, and purported religious practices of Native Americans and Native Australians, for New Age religions. Many natives have strongly protested the use of their sacred symbols and places by such groups.

New religious movements have varied origins. Some have been influenced by Christianity, others by Eastern (Asian) religions, still others by mysticism and spiritualism. Religion also evolves in tandem with science and technology. For example, the Raelian Movement, a religious group centered in Switzerland and Montreal, promotes cloning as a way of achieving "eternal life." Raelians believe that extraterrestrials called "Elohim" artificially created all life on earth. The group has established a company called Valiant Venture Ltd., which offers infertile and homosexual couples the opportunity to have a child cloned from one of the spouses (Ontario Consultants 1996).

In the United States, the official recognition of a religion entitles it to a modicum of respect, and certain benefits, such as exemption from taxation on its income and property (as long as it does not engage in political activity). Not all would-be religions receive official recognition. For example, Scientology is recognized as a church in the United States but not in Germany. In 1997, United States government officials spoke out against Germany's persecution of Scientologists as a form of "human rights abuse." Germans protested vehemently, calling Scientology a dangerous nonreligious political movement, with between 30,000 and 70,000 German members.

SECULAR RITUALS

In concluding this discussion of religion, we may recognize some problems with the definition of religion given at the beginning of this chapter. The first problem: If we define religion with reference to supernatural beings, powers, and forces, how do we classify ritual-like behavior that occurs in secular contexts? Some anthropologists believe there are both sacred and secular rituals. Secular rituals include formal, invariant, stereotyped, earnest, repetitive behavior and rites of passage that take place in nonreligious settings.

A second problem: If the distinction between the supernatural and the natural is not consistently made in a society, how can we tell what is religion and what isn't? The Betsileo of Madagascar, for example, view witches and dead ancestors as real people who play roles in ordinary life. However, their occult powers are not empirically demonstrable.

A third problem: The behavior considered appropriate for religious occasions varies tremendously from culture to culture. One society may consider drunken frenzy the surest sign of faith, whereas another may inculcate quiet reverence. Who is to say which is "more religious"?

Many Americans believe that recreation and religion are separate domains. From my field work in Brazil and Madagascar and my reading about other societies, I believe that this separation is both ethnocentric and false. Madagascar's tomb-centered ceremonies are times when the living and the dead are joyously reunited, when people get drunk, gorge themselves, and enjoy sexual license. Perhaps the gray, sober, ascetic, and moralistic aspects of many religious events in the United States, in taking the "fun" out of religion, force us to find our religion in fun. Many Americans seek in such apparently secular contexts as amusement parks, rock concerts, and sporting events what other people find in religious rites, beliefs, and ceremonies (see Appendix 3).

SUMMARY

1. Religion, a cultural universal, consists of belief and behavior concerned with supernatural beings, powers, and forces. Religion also encompasses the feelings, meanings, and congregations associated with such beliefs and behavior. Anthropological studies have revealed many aspects and functions of religion.

2. Tylor considered animism—the belief in spirits or souls—to be religion's earliest and most basic form. He focused on religion's explanatory role, arguing that religion would eventually disappear as science provided better explanations. Besides animism, yet another view of the supernatural also occurs in nonindustrial societies. This sees the supernatural as a domain of raw, impersonal power or force (called mana in Polynesia and Melanesia). People can manipulate and control mana under certain conditions.

3. When ordinary technical and rational means of doing things fail, people may turn to magic. Often they use magic when they lack control over outcomes. Religion offers comfort and psychological security at times of crisis. However, rites also can create anxiety. Rituals are formal, invariant, stylized, earnest acts in which people subordinate their particular beliefs to a social collectivity. Rites of passage have three stages: separation, liminality, and incorporation. Such rites can mark any change in social status, age, place, or social condition. Collective rites often are cemented by communitas, a feeling of intense solidarity.

4. Besides their psychological and social functions, religious beliefs and practices play a role in the adaptation of human populations to their environments. The Hindu doctrine of *ahimsa*, which prohibits harm to living things, makes cattle sacred and beef a tabooed food. The taboo's force stops peasants from killing their draft cattle even in times of extreme need.

5. Religion establishes and maintains social control through a series of moral and ethical beliefs, and real and imagined rewards and punishments, internalized in individuals. Religion also achieves social control by mobilizing its members for collective action.

6. Wallace defines four types of religion: shamanic, communal, Olympian, and monotheistic. Each has its characteristic ceremonies and practitioners. Religion helps maintain social order, but it also can promote change. Revitalization movements blend old and new beliefs and have helped people adapt to changing conditions.

7. Protestant values have been important in the United States, as they were in the rise and spread of capitalism in Europe. The world's major religions vary in their growth rates, with Islam expanding more rapidly than Christianity. There is growing religious diversity in the United States and Canada. Fundamentalists are antimodernists who claim an identity separate from the larger religious group from which they arose; they advocate strict fidelity to the "true" religious principles on which the larger religion was founded. Religious trends in contemporary North America include rising secularism and new religions, some inspired by science and technology, some by spiritism. There are secular as well as religious rituals.

KEY TERMS

See the flash cards
mhhe.com/kottak

animism   Belief in souls or doubles.

antimodernism   The rejection of the modern in favor of what is perceived as an earlier, purer, and better way of life.

cargo cults   Postcolonial, acculturative religious movements, common in Melanesia, that attempt to explain European domination and wealth and to achieve similar success magically by mimicking European behavior.

communal religions   In Wallace's typology, these religions have, in addition to shamanic cults, communal cults in which people organize community rituals such as harvest ceremonies and rites of passage.

communitas   Intense community spirit, a feeling of great social solidarity, equality, and togetherness; characteristic of people experiencing liminality together.

fundamentalism   Describes antimodernist movements in various religions. Fundamentalists assert an identity separate from the larger religious group from which they arose; they advocate strict fidelity to the "true" religious principles on which the larger religion was founded.

leveling mechanism   A custom or social action that operates to reduce differences in wealth and thus to bring standouts in line with community norms.

liminality   The critically important marginal or in-between phase of a rite of passage.

magic   Use of supernatural techniques to accomplish specific aims.

mana   Sacred impersonal force in Melanesian and Polynesian religions.

monotheism   Worship of an eternal, omniscient, omnipotent, and omnipresent supreme being.

Olympian religions   In Wallace's typology, develop with state organization; have full-time religious specialists—professional priesthoods.

polytheism   Belief in several deities who control aspects of nature.

religion   Belief and ritual concerned with supernatural beings, powers, and forces.

revitalization movements   Movements that occur in times of change, in which religious leaders emerge and undertake to alter or revitalize a society.

rites of passage   Culturally defined activities associated with the transition from one place or stage of life to another.

ritual   Behavior that is formal, stylized, repetitive, and stereotyped, performed earnestly as a social act; rituals are held at set times and places and have liturgical orders.

shaman   A part-time religious practitioner who mediates between ordinary people and supernatural beings and forces.

syncretisms   Cultural mixes, including religious blends, that emerge from acculturation—the exchange of cultural features when cultures come into continuous firsthand contact.

taboo   Set apart as sacred and off-limits to ordinary people; prohibition backed by supernatural sanctions.

CRITICAL THINKING QUESTIONS

For more self-testing, see the self-quizzes

mhhe.com/kottak

1. Do you see any problem in talking about religion in terms of its functions?

2. What's an example of a religious ritual in which you've engaged? How about a nonreligious ritual?

3. Describe a rite of passage you, or a friend, have been through. How did it fit the three-stage model given in the text?

4. From the news or your own knowledge, can you provide additional examples of revitalization movements, new religions, or liminal cults?

5. How are shamans similar to and different from priests? Are there shamans in your society? Who are they?

SUGGESTED ADDITIONAL READINGS

Bowie, F.
   2006   *The Anthropology of Religion: An Introduction.* Malden, MA: Blackwell. Surveys classic and recent work in the anthropology of religion, including the politics of religious identity.

Brown, K. M.
   2001   *Mama Lola: A Vodou Priestess in Brooklyn,* rev. ed. Berkeley: University of California Press. Ethnographic study of a religious community and its leader.

Child, A. B., and I. L. Child
   1993   *Religion and Magic in the Life of Traditional Peoples.* Englewood Cliffs, NJ: Prentice Hall. A cross-cultural study.

Crapo, R. H.
   2003   *Anthropology of Religion: The Unity and Diversity of Religions.* Boston: McGraw-Hill. Examines religious universals and variation.

Cunningham, G.
   1999   *Religion and Magic: Approaches and Theories.* New York: New York University Press. A survey of approaches to magic and religion, ancient and modern.

Durkheim, E.
   2001   (orig. 1912). *The Elementary Forms of the Religious Life.* Translated by Carol Cosman. Abridged with an introduction and notes by Mark S. Cladis. New York: Oxford University Press. Shortened edition of a classic work.

Hicks, D., ed.
   2001   *Ritual and Belief: Readings in the Anthropology of Religion,* 2nd ed. Boston: McGraw-Hill. Up-to-date reader, with useful annotation.

Klass, M.
   1995   *Ordered Universes: Approaches to the Anthropology of Religion.* Boulder, CO: Westview. Wide-ranging overview of key issues in the anthropology of religion.
   2003   *Mind over Mind: The Anthropology and Psychology of Spirit Possession.* Lanham, MD: Rowman and Littlefield. Understanding a mysterious process.

Klass, M., and M. Weisgrau, eds.
   1999   *Across the Boundaries of Belief: Contemporary Issues in the Anthropology of Religion.* Boulder, CO: Westview. Up-to-date collection of articles.

Lehmann, A. C., J. E. Meyers, and P. A. Moro, eds.
   2005 *Magic, Witchcraft, and Religion: An Anthropological Study of the Supernatural*, 6th ed. Boston: McGraw-Hill. A comparative reader covering Western and non-Western cultures.

Lessa, W. A., and E. Z. Vogt, eds.
   1979 *Reader in Comparative Religion: An Anthropological Approach*, 4th ed. New York: Harper & Row. Excellent collection of major articles on the origins, functions, and expressions of religion in comparative perspective.

Rappaport, R. A.
   1999 *Holiness and Humanity: Ritual in the Making of Religious Life*. New York: Cambridge University Press. The nature, meaning, and functions of ritual in religion.

Stein, R. L., and P. L. Stein
   2005 *The Anthropology of Religion, Magic, and Witchcraft*. Boston: Pearson/Allyn & Bacon. Religion and culture.

Turner, V. W.
   1995 (orig. 1969). *The Ritual Process*. Hawthorne, NY: Aldine de Gruyter. Liminality among the Ndembu discussed in a comparative perspective.

INTERNET EXERCISES

1. Go to the anthropology tutorials at Palomar College in San Marcos, California, at the website **http://anthro.palomar.edu/religion/rel_2.htm**, and read the section titled "Common Elements of Religion."
   a. What's the difference between animatism and animism? Which is related to the idea of mana discussed in this chapter?
   b. How do European and Chinese cultures differ in their attitudes about ancestral spirits?
   c. What is an otiose god, and does your religion have one?
   d. Bugs Bunny is likened here to what kind of minor spiritual being?

2. Read the article by Robert Hefner titled "September 11 and the Struggle for Islam," **http://www.ssrc.org/sept11/essays/hefner.htm**.
   a. How might the rise of "hardline" Islam be viewed as a revitalization movement? How is it different?
   b. Where is the "real struggle," according to this author? Do you agree? Why or why not?
   c. How can anthropology contribute to an understanding of September 11 and its aftermath? What questions should anthropologists now look at to achieve this understanding?

See Chapter 21 at your McGraw-Hill Online Learning Center for additional review and interactive exercises.

LINKAGES

Kottak, *Assault on Paradise*, 4th ed.

Chapter 4 discusses the rise and role of *candomblé*, Afro-Brazilian religion, in Arembepe between the 1960s and 1973. In Chapter 10, the section "The Birth of Religion" describes an increase in *candomblé* activity and other religious changes in Arembepe from the 1960s to the 1980s. Chapter 13 reports on further changes, including the growing importance of evangelical Protestantism. What kinds of people were initially attracted to *candomblé*? How had religious activity become a social role in Arembepe by the 1980s? Why were Carolina, as described in Chapter 4, and Fernando, as described in Chapter 11, attracted to *candomblé*?

Peters-Golden, *Culture Sketches*, 4th ed.

This text chapter has discussed ways in which religious beliefs may serve to establish social control and to provide comfort and answers in times of crisis. Read Chapter 1, "Azande: Witchcraft and Oracles in Africa." Witchcraft among the Azande traditionally served as an effective means of social control. What are the major institutions and beliefs in your own culture that function similarly? Think about the ways in which members of your society are compelled to behave in socially acceptable ways. Is religion among them? There is a "logic" to the Azande belief in witchcraft and the causality of

misfortune. Do you employ logic that is similar or different when explaining negative events? Are there several different "systems of logic" that may be invoked, depending on the circumstances?

Knauft, *The Gebusi*, 1st ed.

Read Chapters 3, 5–6, and 8. Based on Chapter 3, describe how Gebusi have contacted traditional spirits and how spiritual communications have influenced Gebusi actions. Describe how spiritual beliefs relate to Gebusi practices concerning death and violence. Based on Chapters 5 and 6, describe how spiritual influence is related to growth and maturity in Gebusi society. In Gebusi initiation rituals, what in-between stages and traumas are initiates subjected to? What values of Gebusi culture are emphasized to the initiates, and how does their costuming and etiquette reflect these spiritual and social values? Based on Chapter 8, describe the biggest changes that have taken place in Gebusi religion. Why did Yuway decide to change his religion, and what wider forces and changes are reflected in his religious conversion? How does contemporary Christianity among Gebusi compare to and contrast with what you know of Christianity in North America? How would you assess the costs and benefits of Gebusi conversions to Christianity?

22

The Arts

WHAT IS ART?

The **arts** include music, theater arts, visual arts, and storytelling and literature (oral and written). These manifestations of human creativity sometimes are called **expressive culture.** People express themselves in dance, music, song, painting, sculpture, pottery, cloth, storytelling, verse, prose, drama, and comedy. Many cultures lack terms that can be translated easily as "art" or "the arts." Yet even without a word for art, people everywhere do associate an aesthetic experience—a sense of beauty, appreciation, harmony, pleasure—with sounds, patterns, objects, and events that have certain qualities. The Bamana people of Mali have a word (like "art") for something that attracts your attention and directs your thoughts (Ezra 1986). Among the Yoruba of Nigeria, the word for art, *ona*, encompasses the designs made on objects, the art objects themselves, and the profession of the creators of such patterns and works. For two Yoruba lineages of leather workers, Otunisona and Osiisona, the suffix *-ona* in their names denotes art (Adepegba 1991).

A dictionary defines **art** as "the quality, production, expression, or realm of what is beautiful or of more than ordinary significance; the

For cross-cultural meanings of art, see the Virtual Exploration **mhhe.com/kottak**

507

■ Art serving religion. This photo was taken in Phnom Penh, Cambodia, in 1988. On the grounds of a Buddhist temple, artisans make religious artifacts. We see a young man carving a Buddha, along with several completed Buddha statues.

class of objects subject to aesthetic criteria" (*The Random House College Dictionary* 1982, p. 76). Drawing on the same dictionary, **aesthetics** involves "the qualities perceived in works of art . . .; the . . . mind and emotions in relation to the sense of beauty" (p. 22). However, it is possible for a work of art to attract our attention, direct our thoughts, and have more than ordinary significance without being judged as beautiful by most people who experience that work. Pablo Picasso's *Guernica*, a famous

OVERVIEW

People everywhere associate an aesthetic experience—a sense of beauty, appreciation, harmony, pleasure—with certain sounds, patterns, objects, and events. The arts are part of culture, and aesthetic judgments reflect cultural background. Experiencing art involves feelings as well as appreciation of form. The arts, sometimes called "expressive culture," include the visual arts, literature, music, and theater arts. Students of non-Western art have been criticized for ignoring individual artists, and for focusing too much on the social nature and context of art. Many non-Western societies do recognize the achievements of individual artists. Folk art, music, and lore refer to the expressive culture of ordinary people. Myths, legends, tales, and storytelling play important roles in transmitting culture and preserving traditions. The arts go on changing, although certain art forms have survived for thousands of years. In today's world, a huge "arts and leisure" industry links Western and non-Western art forms in an international network with both aesthetic and commercial dimensions.

painting of the Spanish Civil War (see p. 478), comes to mind as a scene that, while not beautiful, is indisputably moving, and thus is a work of art.

George Mills (1971) notes that in many cultures, the role of art lover lacks definition because art isn't viewed as a separate activity. But this doesn't stop individuals from being moved by sounds, patterns, objects, and events in a way that we would call aesthetic. Our own society does provide a fairly well-defined role for the connoisseur of the arts, as well as sanctuaries—concert halls, theaters, museums—where people can retreat to be aesthetically pleased and emotionally moved by objects and performances.

This chapter will not attempt to do a systematic survey of all the arts, or even their major subdivisions. Rather, the general approach will be to examine topics and issues that apply to expressive culture generally. "Art" will be used to encompass all the arts, including the print and film narratives discussed in the "News Brief," not just the visual ones. In other words, the observations to be made about "art" are intended to apply to music, theater, film, television, books, stories, and lore, as well as to painting and sculpture.

That which is aesthetically pleasing is perceived with the senses. Usually, when we think of art, we have in mind something that can be seen or heard. But others might define art more broadly to include things that can be smelled (scents, fragrances), tasted (recipes), or touched (cloth textures). How enduring must art be? Visual works and written works, including musical compositions, may last for centuries. Can a single noteworthy event, such as a feast, which is not in the least eternal, except in memory, be a work of art?

Art and Religion

Some of the issues raised in the discussion of religion also apply to art. Definitions of both art and religion mention the "more than ordinary" or the "extraordinary." Religious scholars may distinguish between the sacred (religious) and the profane (secular). Similarly, art scholars may distinguish between the artistic and the ordinary.

If we adopt a special attitude or demeanor when confronting a sacred object, do we display something similar when experiencing a work of art? According to the anthropologist Jacques Maquet (1986), an artwork is something that stimulates and sustains contemplation. It compels attention and reflection. Maquet stresses the importance of the object's form in producing such artistic contemplation. But other scholars stress feeling and meaning in addition to form. The experience of art involves feeling, such as being moved, as well as appreciation of form, such as balance or harmony.

Narratives of Social Class and the Social Gap

NEW YORK TIMES NEWS BRIEF

by Charles McGrath
June 8, 2005

All cultures express imagination—in dreams, fantasies, songs, myths, and stories. The arts allow us to imagine a set of possible lives beyond our own. One very important source for this imagining has been the mass media, including television, movies, and the popular press. In this news story we see how American popular culture has moved from a preoccupation with class differences to a tendency to deny or ignore their existence. Although the media continue to celebrate the lifestyles of the rich and famous, what is gone is the preoccupation with difference. The narratives we see on screen and in print today often present a homogenized upper-middle-class lifestyle in which social differences are minimized and the economic underpinnings of class are ignored. An anthropological approach to the arts recognizes that they exist in society and can be understood in relation to sociocultural change.

On television and in the movies now, and even in the pages of novels, people tend to dwell in a classless, homogenized American Never-Never Land. This place is an upgrade, but not a drastic one, from the old neighborhood where Beaver, Ozzie and Harriet, and Donna Reed used to live; it's those yuppified city blocks where the friends on "Friends" and the "Seinfeld" gang had their apartments, or in the now more fashionable version, it's part of the same exurb as One Tree Hill and Wisteria Lane—those airbrushed suburbs where all the cool young people hang out and where the pecking order of sex and looks has replaced the old hierarchy of jobs and money . . .

In the years before World War II, you couldn't go to the movies or get very far in a novel without being reminded that ours was a society where some were much better off than others, and where the class

divide—especially the gap separating middle from upper—was an inescapable fact of life. The yearning to bridge this gap is most persistently and most romantically evoked in [F. Scott] Fitzgerald, of course, in characters like the former Jay Gatz of Nowhere, N.D. (*The Great Gatsby*), staring across Long Island Sound at that distant green light, and all those moony young men standing in the stag line at the country club, hoping to be noticed by the rich girls.

But there is also a darker version, the one that turns up in Dreiser's "American Tragedy" (1925), for example, where class envy . . . causes Clyde Griffiths to drown his hopelessly proletarian sweetheart, and where the impossibility of transcending his lot leads him inevitably to the electric chair. (In the upstate New York town of Lycurgus, where the story takes place, Dreiser reminds us that "the line of demarcation and stratification between the rich and the poor was as sharp as though cut by a knife or divided by a high wall.")

Some novels trade on class anxiety to evoke not the dream of betterment but the great American nightmare: the dread of waking up one day and finding yourself at the bottom. Frank Norris's "McTeague" is about a San Francisco dentist who, unmasked as a fraud, sinks to a life of crime and degradation . . . These books . . . suggested that the worst thing that could possibly happen to an American was to topple from his perch on the class ladder . . .

The poor are noticeably absent, however, in the great artistic flowering of the American novel at the turn of the 19th century, in the work of writers like Henry James, William Dean Howells and Edith Wharton, who are almost exclusively concerned with the rich or the aspiring middle classes: their marriages, their houses, their money and their stuff. Not accidentally, these novels coincided with America's Gilded Age, the era of overnight fortunes and conspicuous spending that followed in the wake of the Civil War . . .

One of the messages of the novel is that in America new money very

■ *What's the class status of these "Desperate Housewives," who reside on TV's Wisteria Lane? From what do they derive this class status?*

quickly, in a generation or less, takes on the patina of old; another is that the class structure is necessarily propped up by deceit and double standards . . .

What was the appeal? Vouyerism, in part . . . Fiction back then had a kind of documentary function; it was one of the places Americans went to learn about how other Americans lived. In time novels ceased to be so reportorial . . .

Novels these days take place in a kind of all-purpose middle-class America, in neighborhoods that could be almost anyplace, and where the burdens are more psychic than economic, with people too busy tending to their faltering relationships to pay much attention to keeping up with the neighbors.

It's a place where everyone fits in, more or less, but where, if you look hard enough, nobody feels really at home.

Novel reading is a middle-class pastime, which is another reason that novels have so often focused on the middle and upper classes. Mass entertainment is another matter, and when Hollywood took up the class theme, which it did in the 1930's, it made a crucial adjustment. During the Depression, the studios, which were mostly run by immigrant Jews, turned out a string of formulaic fantasies about life among the Gentile upper crust.

These movies were essentially twin variations on a single theme: either a rich young man falls for a working girl . . . or an heiress takes up with a young man who has to work for a living . . .

The upper-class person is thawed and humanized by the poorer one, but in every case the exchange is seen as fair and equitable, with the lower-class character giving as much as he or she gets in return. Unlike the novels of class, with their anxieties and sense of unbridgeable gaps, these are stories of harmony and inclusion, and they added what proved to be an enduring twist on the American view of class: the notion that wealth and privilege are somewhat crippling conditions . . .

Television used to be fascinated with blue-collar life, in shows like "The Honeymooners," "All in the Family," "Sanford and Son" and "Roseanne," but lately it too has turned its attention elsewhere. The only people who work on televison now are cops, doctors and lawyers, and they're so busy they seldom get to go home. The one vestige of the old curiosity about how other people live is in so-called reality television, when Paris Hilton and Nicole Richie drop in on rubes in "The Simple Life," or when upper- and middle-class families trade moms on "Wife Swap" and experience a week of culture shock.

But most reality television trades in a fantasy of sorts, based on the old game-show formula: the idea that you can be plucked out of ordinary life and anointed the new super-model, the new diva, the new survivor, the new assistant to Donald Trump. You get an instant infusion of wealth and are simultaneously vested with something far more valuable: celebrity, which has become a kind of super-class in America, and one that renders all the old categories irrelevant.

Celebrities, in fact, have inherited much of the glamour and sexiness that used to attach itself to the aristocracy. If Gatsby were to come back today, he would come back as Donald Trump and would want a date not with Daisy [Buchanan] but with Britney Spears.

But if the margins have shifted, and if fame, for example, now counts for more than breeding, what persists is the great American theme of longing, of wanting something more, or other, than what you were born with—the wish not to rise in class so much as merely to become classy. If you believe the novels of Dickens or Thackeray, say, the people who feel most at home in Britain are those who know their place, and that has seldom been the case in this country, where the boundaries of class seem just elusive and permeable enough to sustain both the fear of falling and the dream of escape.

SOURCE: Charles McGrath, "In Fiction, a Long History of Fixation on the Social Gap," *New York Times*, June 8, 2005, final, Section E, p. 1.

Bringing It All Together

See the "Bringing It All Together" essay that immediately follows the chapter "Gender" for *Guernica* and its political context.

Such an artistic attitude can be combined with and used to bolster a religious attitude. Much art has been done in association with religion. Many of the high points of Western art and music had religious inspiration, or were done in the service of religion, as a visit to a church or a large museum will surely illustrate. Bach and Handel are as well known for their church music as Michelangelo is for his religious painting and sculpture. The buildings (churches and cathedrals) in which religious music is played and in which visual art is displayed may themselves be works of art. Some of the major architectural achievements of Western art are religious structures. Examples include the Amiens, Chartres, and Notre Dame cathedrals in France.

Art may be created, performed, or displayed outdoors in public, or in special indoor settings, such as a theater, concert hall, or museum. Just as churches demarcate religion, museums and theaters set art off from the ordinary world, making it special, while inviting spectators in. Buildings dedicated to the arts help create the artistic atmosphere. Architecture may accentuate the setting as a place for works of art to be presented.

The settings of rites and ceremonies, and of art, may be temporary or permanent. State societies have permanent religious structures: churches and temples. So, too, may state societies have buildings and structures dedicated to the arts. Nonstate societies tend to lack such permanently demarcated settings. Both art and religion are more "out there" in society. Still, in bands and tribes, religious settings can be created without churches. Similarly, an artistic atmosphere can be created without museums. At particular times of the year, ordinary space can be set aside for a visual art display or a musical performance. Such special occasions parallel the times set aside for religious ceremonies. In fact, in tribal performances, the arts and religion often mix. For example, masked and costumed performers may imitate spirits. Rites of passage often feature special music, dance, song, bodily adornment, and other manifestations of expressive culture.

In the chapter "Making a Living," we looked at the potlatching tribes of the North Pacific Coast of North America. Erna Gunther (1971) shows how various art forms combined among those tribes to create the visual aspects of ceremonialism. During the winter, spirits were believed to pervade the atmosphere. Masked and costumed dancers represented the spirits. They dramatically reenacted spirit encounters with human beings, which are part of the origin myths of villages, clans, and lineages. In some areas, dancers devised intricate patterns of choreography. Their esteem was measured by the number of people who followed them when they danced.

In any society, art is produced for its aesthetic value as well as for religious purposes. According to Schildkrout and Keim (1990), non-Western art is usually, but wrongly, assumed to have some kind of connection to ritual. Non-Western art may be, but isn't always, linked with religion. Westerners have trouble accepting the idea that non-Western societies have art for art's sake just as Western societies do. There has been a tendency for Westerners to ignore the individuality of non-Western artists and their interest in creative expression. According to Isidore Okpewho (1977), an oral literature specialist, scholars have tended to see religion in all traditional African arts. Even when acting in the service of religion, there is room for individual creative expression. In the oral arts, for example, the audience is much more interested in the delivery and performance of the artist than in the particular god for whom the performer may be speaking.

Locating Art

Aesthetic value is one way of distinguishing art. Another way is to consider placement. The special places where we find art include museums, concert halls, opera houses, and theaters. If something is displayed in a museum, or in another socially accepted artistic setting, someone at least

■ Space transformed into art. "The Gates," by the experimental artist Christo and his wife, Jeanne-Claude, was unveiled in 2005 in New York City's Central Park. Long, billowy saffron ribbons meandered through the park. An army of paid helpers gradually released the panels of colored fabric from atop 7,500 gates standing 16-feet tall.

must think it's art. Although tribal societies typically lack museums, they may maintain special areas where artistic expression takes place. One example, discussed below, is the separate space in which ornamental burial poles are manufactured among the Tiwi of North Australia.

Will we know art if we see it? Art has been defined as involving that which is beautiful and of more than ordinary significance. But isn't beauty in the eye of the beholder? Don't reactions to art differ among spectators? And, if there can be secular ritual, can there also be ordinary art? The boundary between what's art and what's not is blurred. The American artist Andy Warhol is famous for transforming Campbell's soup cans, Brillo pads, and images of Marilyn Monroe into art. Many recent artists, such as Christo (see the photo above) have tried to erase the distinction between art and ordinary life by converting the everyday into a work of art.

If something is mass produced or industrially modified, can it be art? Prints made as part of a series certainly may be considered art. Sculptures that are created in clay, then fired with molten metal, such as bronze, at a foundry, also are art. But how does one know if a film is art? Is *Star Wars* art? How about *Citizen Kane?* When a book wins a National Book Award, is it immediately elevated to the status of art? What kinds of prizes make art? Objects never intended as art, such as an Olivetti typewriter, may be transformed into art by being placed in a museum, such as New York's Museum of Modern Art. Jacques Maquet (1986) distinguishes such "art by transformation" from art created and intended to be art, which he calls "art by destination."

In state societies, we have come to rely on critics, judges, and experts to tell us what's art and what isn't. A play titled *Art* is about conflict that arises among three friends when one of them buys an all-white painting. They disagree, as people often do, about the definition and value of a work of art. Such variation in art appreciation is especially common in contemporary society, with its professional artists and critics and great cultural diversity. We'd expect more uniform standards and agreement in less-diverse, less-stratified societies.

To be culturally relativistic, we need to avoid applying our own standards about what art is to the products of other cultures. Sculpture is art, right? Not necessarily. Previously, we challenged the view that non-Western art always has some kind of connection to religion. The Kalabari case to be discussed now makes the opposite point: that religious sculpture is not always art.

See the Internet Exercises at your OLC for Kalabari masks
mhhe.com/kottak

Among the Kalabari of southern Nigeria (Figure 22.1), wooden sculptures are not carved for aesthetic reasons, but to serve as "houses" for spirits (Horton 1963). These sculptures are used to control the spirits of Kalabari religion. The Kalabari place such a carving, and thus localize a spirit, in a cult house into which the spirit is invited. Here, sculpture is done not for art's sake but as a means of manipulating spiritual forces. The Kalabari do have standards for the carvings, but beauty isn't one of them. A sculpture must be sufficiently complete to represent its spirit. Carvings judged too crude are rejected by cult members. Also, carvers must base their work on past models. Particular spirits have particular images associated with them. It's considered dangerous to produce a carving that deviates too much from a previous image of the spirit or that resembles another spirit. Offended spirits may retaliate. As long as they observe these standards of com-

pleteness and established images, carvers are free to express themselves. But these images are considered repulsive rather than beautiful. And they are not manufactured for artistic but for religious reasons.

Art and Individuality

Those who work with non-Western art have been criticized for ignoring the individual and focusing too much on the social nature and context of art. When art objects from Africa or Papua New Guinea are displayed in museums, generally only the name of the tribe and of the Western donor are given, rather than that of the individual artist. It's as though skilled individuals don't exist in non-Western societies. The impression is that art is collectively produced. Sometimes it is; sometimes it isn't.

To some extent, there *is* more collective production of art in non-Western societies than in the United States and Canada. According to Hackett (1996), African artworks (sculpted figures, textiles, paintings, or pots) generally are enjoyed, critiqued, and used by communities or groups, rather than being the prerogative of the individual alone. The artist may receive more feedback during the creative process than the individual artist typically encounters in our own society. Here, the feedback often comes too late, after the product is complete, rather than during production, when it can still be changed.

During his field work among Nigeria's Tiv people, Paul Bohannan (1971) concluded that the

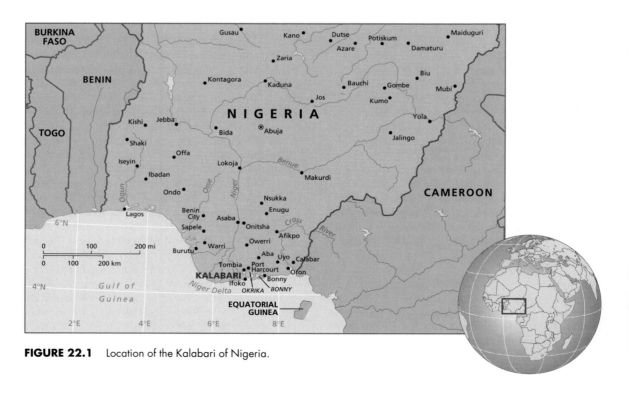

FIGURE 22.1 Location of the Kalabari of Nigeria.

proper study of art there should pay less attention to artists and more attention to art critics and products. There were few skilled Tiv artists, and such people avoided doing their art publicly. However, mediocre artists would work in public, where they routinely got comments from onlookers (critics). Based on critical suggestions, an artist often changed a design, such as a carving, in progress. There was yet another way in which Tiv artists worked socially rather than individually. Sometimes, when an artist put his work aside, someone else would pick it up and start working on it. The Tiv clearly didn't recognize the same kind of connection between individuals and their art that we do. According to Bohannan, every Tiv was free to know what he liked and to try to make it if he could. If not, one or more of his fellows might help him out.

In Western societies, artists of many sorts (e.g., writers, painters, sculptors, actors, classical and rock musicians) have reputations for being iconoclastic and antisocial. Social acceptance may be more important in the societies anthropologists have traditionally studied. Still, there are well-known individual artists in non-Western societies. They are recognized as such by other community members and perhaps by outsiders as well. Their artistic labor may even be conscripted for special displays and performances, including ceremonies, or palace arts and events.

To what extent can a work of art stand apart from its artist? Philosophers of art commonly regard works of art as autonomous entities, independent of their creators (Haapala 1998). Haapala argues the contrary, that artists and their works are inseparable. "By creating works of art a person creates an artistic identity for himself. He creates himself quite literally into the pieces he puts into his art. He exists in the works he has created." In this view, Picasso created many Picassos, and exists in and through those works of art.

Sometimes little is known or recognized about the individual artist responsible for an enduring art work. We are more likely to know the name of the recording artist than that of the writer of the songs we most commonly remember and perhaps sing. Sometimes we fail to acknowledge art individually because the artwork was collectively created. To whom should we attribute a pyramid or a cathedral? Should it be the architect, the ruler or leader who commissioned the work, or the master builder who implemented the design? A thing of beauty may be a joy forever even if and when we do not credit its creator(s).

The Work of Art

Some may see art as a form of expressive freedom, as giving free range to the imagination and the human need to create or to be playful. But consider the word *opera*. It is the plural of *opus*, which means a work. For the artist, at least, art is work, albeit creative work. In nonstate societies, artists may have to hunt, gather, herd, fish, or farm in order to eat, but they still manage to find time to work on their art. In state societies, at least, artists have been defined as specialists—professionals who have chosen careers as artists, musicians, writers, or actors. If they manage to support themselves from their art, they may be full-time professionals. If not, they do their art part time, while earning a living from another activity. Sometimes artists associate in professional groups such as medieval guilds or contemporary unions. Actors Equity in New York, a labor union, is a modern guild, designed to protect the interests of its artist members.

Just how much work is needed to make a work of art? In the early days of French impressionism, many experts viewed the paintings of Claude Monet and his colleagues as too sketchy and spontaneous to be true art. Established artists and critics were accustomed to more formal and classic studio styles. The French impressionists got their name from their sketches—*impressions* in French—of natural and social settings. They took advantage of technological innovations, particularly the availability of oil paints in tubes, to take their palettes, easels, and canvases into the field. There they captured the images of changing light and color that hang today in so many museums, where they are now fully recognized as art. But before impressionism became an officially recognized "school" of art, its works were perceived by its critics as crude and unfinished. In terms of community standards, the first impressionist paintings were evaluated as harshly as were the overly crude and incomplete Kalabari wood carvings of spirits, as discussed previously.

To what extent does the artist—or society—make the decision about completeness? For familiar genres, such as painting or music, societies tend to have standards by which they judge whether an art work is complete or fully realized. Most people would doubt, for instance, that an all-white painting could be a work of art. Standards may be maintained informally in society, or by specialists, such as art critics. It may be difficult for unorthodox or renegade artists to innovate. But, like the impressionists, they may eventually succeed. Some societies tend to reward conformity, an artist's skill with traditional models and techniques. Others encourage breaks with the past, innovation.

ART, SOCIETY, AND CULTURE

More than 70,000 years ago, some of the world's first artists occupied Blombos Cave, located in a high cliff facing the Indian Ocean at the tip of what is now South Africa. They hunted game and ate

■ *This musician living in the Central African Republic carved this instrument himself.*

also confirm artistic expression throughout the Upper Paleolithic.

Art usually is more public than the cave paintings. Typically, it is exhibited, evaluated, performed, and appreciated in society. It has spectators or audiences. It isn't just for the artist.

Ethnomusicology

Ethnomusicology is the comparative study of the musics of the world and of music as an aspect of culture and society. The field of ethnomusicology thus unites music and anthropology. The music side involves the study and analysis of the music itself and the instruments used to create it. The anthropology side views music as a way to explore a culture, to determine the role—historic and contemporary—that music plays in that society, and the specific social and cultural features that influence how music is created and performed.

Ethnomusicology studies non-Western music, traditional and folk music, even contemporary popular music from a cultural perspective. To do this there has to be field work—firsthand study of particular forms of music, their social functions and cultural meanings, within particular societies. Ethnomusicologists talk with local musicians, make recordings in the field, and learn about the place of musical instruments, performances, and performers in a given society (Kirman 1997). Nowadays, given globalization, diverse cultures and musical styles easily meet and mix. Music that draws on a wide range of cultural instruments and styles is called World Fusion, World Beat, or World Music—another topic within contemporary ethnomusicology

Because music is a cultural universal, and because musical abilities seem to run in families, it has been suggested that a predisposition for music may have a genetic basis (Crenson 2000). Could a "music gene" that arose tens, or hundreds, of thousands of years ago have conferred an evolutionary advantage on those early humans who possessed it? The fact that music has existed in all known cultures suggests that it arose early in human history. Providing direct evidence for music's antiquity is an ancient carved bone flute from a cave in Slovenia. This "Divje babe flute," the world's oldest known musical instrument, dates back more than 43,000 years.

Exploring the possible biological roots of music, Sandra Trehub (2001) notes striking similarities in the way mothers worldwide sing to their children—with a high pitch, a slow tempo, and a distinctive tone. All cultures have lullabies, which sound so much alike they cannot be mistaken for anything else (Crenson 2000). Trehub speculates that music might have been adaptive in human evolution because musically talented

fish from the waters below them. In terms of body and brain size, these ancient Africans were anatomically modern humans. They also were turning animal bones into finely worked tools and weapon points. Furthermore, they were engraving artifacts with symbolic marks—manifestations of abstract and creative thought and, presumably, communication through language (Wilford 2002*b*).

A group led by Christopher Henshilwood of South Africa has analyzed 28 bone tools and other artifacts from Blombos Cave, along with the mineral ocher, which may have been used for body painting. The most impressive bone tools are three sharp instruments. The bone appears first to have been shaped with a stone blade, then finished into a symmetrical shape and polished for hours. According to Henshilwood (quoted in Wilford 2002*b*), "It's actually unnecessary for projectile points to be so carefully made. It suggests to us that this is an expression of symbolic thinking. The people said, 'Let's make a really beautiful object . . .' Symbolic thinking means that people are using something to mean something else. The tools do not have to have only a practical purpose. And the ocher might be used to decorate their equipment, perhaps themselves."

In Europe, art goes back more than 30,000 years, to the Upper Paleolithic period in Western Europe (see Conkey et al. 1997). The earliest musical instrument, the "Divje babe flute," was made more than 43,000 years ago. Cave paintings, the best-known examples of Upper Paleolithic art, were separated from ordinary life and everyday social space. Those images were painted in true caves, located deep in the bowels of the earth. They may have been painted as part of some kind of rite of passage involving retreat from society. Portable art objects carved in bone and ivory, along with musical whistles and flutes,

mothers had an easier time calming their babies. Calm babies who fell asleep easily and rarely made a fuss might well have been more likely to survive to adulthood. Their cries would not attract predators; they and their mothers would get more rest; and they would be less likely to be mistreated. If a gene conferring musical ability appeared early in human evolution, given a selective advantage, musical adults would pass their genes to their children.

Music would seem to be among the most social of the arts. Usually it unites people in groups. Indeed, music is all about groups—choirs, symphonies, ensembles, and bands. Could it be that early humans with a biological penchant for music were able to live more effectively in social groups—another possible adaptive advantage? Even master pianists and violinists are frequently accompanied by orchestras or singers. Alan Merriam (1971) describes how the Basongye people of the Kasai province of Congo (Figure 22.2) use three features to distinguish between music and other sounds, which are classified as "noise." First, music always involves humans. Sounds emanating from nonhuman creatures, such as birds and animals, are not music. Second, musical sounds must be organized. A single tap on the drum isn't music, but drummers playing together in a pattern is. Third, music must continue. Even if several drums are struck together simultaneously, it isn't music. They must go on playing to establish some kind of sound pattern. For the Basongye, then, music is inherently cultural (distinctly human) and social (dependent on cooperation).

Originally coined for European peasants, **"folk"** art, music, and lore refer to the expressive culture of ordinary people, as contrasted with the "high" art or "classic" art of the European elites. When European folk music is performed (see photo on p. 516), the combination of costumes, music, and often song and dance is supposed to say something about local culture and about tradition. Tourists and other outsiders often perceive rural and folk life mainly in terms of such performances. Community residents themselves often use such performances to display and enact their local culture and traditions for outsiders.

In Planinica, a Muslim village in (prewar) Bosnia, Yvonne Lockwood (1983) studied folksong, which could be heard there day or night. The most active singers were unmarried females age 16 to 26 (maidens). Lead singers, those who customarily began and led songs, had strong, full, clear voices with a high range. Like some of their counterparts in contemporary North America (but in a much milder fashion), some lead singers acted unconventionally. One was regarded as immodest because of her risqué lyrics. Another

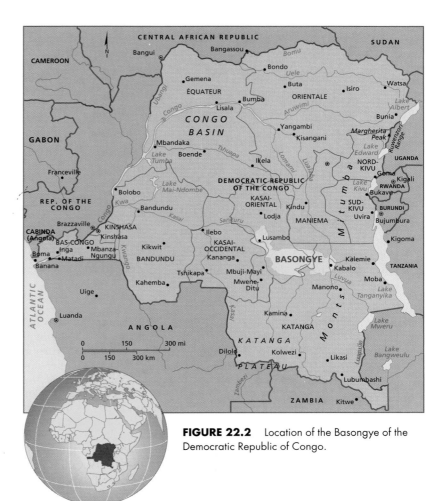

FIGURE 22.2 Location of the Basongye of the Democratic Republic of Congo.

smoked (usually a man's habit) and liked to wear men's trousers. Local criticism aside, she was thought to be witty and to improvise songs better than others did.

The social transition from girl to maiden (marriageable female) was signaled by active participation in public song and dance. Adolescent girls were urged to join in by women and performing maidens. This was part of a rite of passage by which a little girl (*dite*) became a maiden (*cura*). Marriage, in contrast, moved most women from the public to the private sphere; public singing generally stopped. Married women sang in their own homes or among other women. Only occasionally would they join maidens in public song, but they never called attention to themselves by taking the lead. After age 50 wives tended to stop singing, even in private.

For women, singing thus signaled a series of transitions between age grades: girl to maiden (public singing), maiden to wife (private singing), and wife to elder (no more singing). Lockwood describes how one recently married woman

■ *Musicians in folk outfits play violins in a town square in Ljubljana, Slovenia. For whose pleasure do you suppose this performance is being given? Nowadays, such performances attract tourists as well as local people.*

made her ritual first visit after marriage to her family of origin. (Postmarital residence was patrilocal.) Then, as she was leaving to return to her husband's village, for "old times' sake" she led the village maidens in song. She used her native daughter status to behave like a maiden this one last time. Lockwood calls it a nostalgic and emotional performance for all who attended.

Singing and dancing were common at *prelos* attended by males and females. In Planinica the Serbo-Croatian word *prelo*, usually defined as "spinning bee," meant any occasion for visiting. *Prelos* were especially common in winter. During the summer, villagers worked long hours, and *prelos* were few. The *prelo* offered a context for play, relaxation, song, and dance. All gatherings of maidens, especially *prelos*, were occasions for song. Married women encouraged them to sing, often suggesting specific songs. If males were also present, a singing duel might occur, in which maidens and young men teased each other. A successful *prelo* was well attended, with much singing and dancing.

Public singing was traditional in many other contexts among prewar Bosnian Muslims. After a day of cutting hay on mountain slopes, parties of village men would congregate at a specific place on the trail above the village. They formed lines according to their singing ability, with the best singers in front and the less talented ones behind. They proceeded to stroll down to the village together, singing as they went, until they reached the village center, where they dispersed. According to Lockwood, whenever an activity of work or leisure brought together a group of maidens or young men, it rarely ended without public song. It would not be wrong to trace the inspiration for parts of *Snow White* and *Shrek* (the movies) back to the European countryside.

Representations of Art and Culture

Art can stand for tradition, even when traditional art is removed from its original (rural) context. As will be seen in Chapter 25 titled "Cultural Exchange and Survival," the creative products and images of folk, rural, and non-Western cultures are increasingly spread—and commercialized—by the media and tourism. A result is that many Westerners have come to think of "culture" in terms of colorful customs, music, dancing, and adornments: clothing, jewelry, and hairstyles.

A bias toward the arts and religion, rather than more mundane, less photogenic, economic and social tasks, shows up on TV's Discovery Channel, and even in many anthropological films. Many ethnographic films start off with music, often drum beats: "Bonga, bonga, bonga, bonga. Here in (supply place name), the people are very religious." We see in such presentations the previously critiqued assumption that the arts of nonindustrial societies usually have a link with religion. The (usually unintended) message is that non-Western peoples spend much of their time wearing colorful clothes, singing, dancing, and practicing religious rituals. Taken to an extreme, such images portray culture as recreational and ultimately unserious, rather than as something that ordinary people live every day of their lives—not just when they have festivals.

Art and Communication

Art also functions in society as a form of communication between artist and community or audience. Sometimes, however, there are intermediaries between the artist and the audience. Actors, for example, are artists who translate the works and ideas of other artists (writers and directors) into the performances that audiences see and appreciate. Musicians play and sing compositions of other people along with music they themselves have composed. Using music written by others, choreographers plan and direct patterns of dance, which dancers then execute for audiences.

How does art communicate? We need to know what the artist intends to communicate and how the audience reacts. Often, the audience communicates right back to the artist. Live performers, for instance, get immediate feedback, as may writers and directors by viewing a performance of their own work. Artists expect at least some variation in reception. In contemporary societies, with increasing diversity in the audience, uniform reactions are rare. Contemporary artists, like businesspeople, are well aware that they have target audiences. Certain segments of the population are more likely to appreciate certain forms of art than other segments are.

One key development in North American culture since the 1970s, especially evident in the media, is a general shift from "massification" to "segmental appeal." An increasingly differentiated nation celebrates diversity. The mass media—print and electronic—join the trend, measuring various "demographics." The media aim their products and messages at particular segments—*target audiences*—rather than at an undifferentiated mass audience. Television, films, radio, music, magazines, and Internet forums all gear their topics, formats, and styles toward particular homogeneous segments of the population. In particular, cable and satellite TV, along with VCR and DVD players, have helped direct television, the most important mass medium, away from the networks' cherished mass audiences of the 1950s and 1960s and toward particular viewing segments. Special-interest audiences can now choose from a multiplicity of targeted channels. Those channels specialize in music (country, pop, rock, Latin, or Black Entertainment), sports, news (financial, weather, headline), comedy, science fiction, gossip, movies (commercial, foreign, "art," "classic"), cartoons, old TV sitcoms, Spanish language, nature, travel, adventure, history, biography, and home shopping. The Super Bowl, Academy Awards, and Olympics still manage to capture large national and international audiences. But in 1998, the final episode of *Seinfeld,* though hugely popular, could not rival the mass audience shares of *Roots,* Lucy Ricardo's childbirth, or the final episode of *M*A*S*H.*

Art can transmit several kinds of messages. It can convey a moral lesson or tell a cautionary tale. It can teach lessons the artist, or society, wants told. Like the rites that induce, then dispel, anxiety, the tension and resolution of drama can lead to **catharsis,** intense emotional release, in the audience. Art can move emotions, make us laugh, cry, feel up or down. Art appeals to the intellect as well as to the emotions. We may delight in a well-constructed, nicely balanced, well-realized work of art.

Often, art is meant to commemorate and to last, to carry an enduring message. Like a ceremony, art may serve a mnemonic function, making people remember. Art may be designed to make people remember either individuals or events, such as the AIDS epidemic that has proved so lethal in many world areas, or the cataclysmic events of September 11, 2001.

Art and Politics

What is art's social role? To what extent should art serve society? Art can be self-consciously prosocial. It can be used either to express or challenge community sentiment and standards. Art enters the political arena. Decisions about what counts as a work of art, or about how to display art, may be political and controversial. Museums have to balance concern over community standards with a wish to be as creative and innovative as the artists and works they display.

Much art that is valued today was received with revulsion in its own time. New York's Brooklyn Museum of Art has documented how art that shocks or offends when it is new becomes accepted and valued over time. Children were prohibited from seeing paintings by Matisse, Braque, and Picasso when those works first were displayed in New York in the Armory Show of 1913. The *New York Times* called that Armory Show "pathological." Almost a century later, the City of New York and then Mayor Rudolph Giuliani took the Brooklyn Museum to court over its 1999–2000 "Sensation" show. After religious groups protested Chris Ofili's *Holy Virgin Mary,* a collage that included elephant dung, Giuliani deemed the work sacrilegious. The ensuing court trial prompted anticensorship groups and art advocates to speak out against the mayor's actions. The museum won the case, but Ofili's work again came under attack when a man smuggled paint inside the Brooklyn exhibition and tried to smear it on the *Virgin* (University of Virginia, n.d.). According to art professor Michael Davis, Ofili's collage is "shocking" because it

Appreciation for the arts must be learned. Here, three American boys seem intrigued by the painting Paris on a Rainy Day at the Chicago Art Institute. How does the placement of art in museums affect art appreciation?

deliberately provokes and intends to jolt viewers into an expanded frame of reference. The mayor's reactions may have been based on the narrow definition that art must be beautiful and an equally limited vision of a Virgin Mary as depicted in Italian Renaissance paintings (Mount Holyoke College 1999).

Today, no museum director can mount an exhibit without worrying that it will offend some politically organized segment of society. In the United States there has been an ongoing battle between liberals and conservatives involving the National Endowment for the Arts. Artists have been criticized as aloof from society, as creating only for themselves and for elites, as out of touch with conventional and traditional aesthetic values, even as mocking the values of ordinary people.

The Cultural Transmission of the Arts

Because art is part of culture, appreciation of the arts depends on cultural background. Watch Japanese tourists in a Western art museum trying to interpret what they are seeing. Conversely, the form and meaning of a Japanese tea ceremony, or a demonstration of origami (Japanese paper folding), will be alien to a foreign observer. Appreciation for the arts must be learned. It is part of

enculturation, as well as of more formal education. Robert Layton (1991) suggests that whatever universal principles of artistic expression may exist, they have been put into effect in a diversity of ways in different cultures.

What is aesthetically pleasing depends to some extent on culture. Based on familiarity, music with certain tonalities and rhythm patterns will please some people and alienate others. In a study of Navajo music, McAllester (1954) found that it reflected the overall culture of that time in three main ways: First, individualism is a key Navajo cultural value. Thus, it's up to the individual to decide what to do with his or her property—whether it be physical property, knowledge, ideas, or songs. Second, McAllester found that a general Navajo conservatism also extended to music. The Navajo saw foreign music as dangerous and rejected it as not part of their culture. (This second point is no longer true; there are now Navajo rock bands.) Third, a general stress on proper form applied to music. There is, in Navajo belief, a right way to sing every kind of song (see Figure 22.3 for the location of the Navajo).

People learn to listen to certain kinds of music and to appreciate particular art forms, just as they learn to hear and decipher a foreign language. Unlike Londoners and New Yorkers, Parisians don't flock to musicals. Despite its multiple French origins, even the musical *Les Miserables,* a huge hit in London, New York, and dozens of cities worldwide, bombed in Paris. Humor, too, a form of verbal art, depends on cultural background and setting. What's funny in one culture may not translate as funny in another. When a joke doesn't

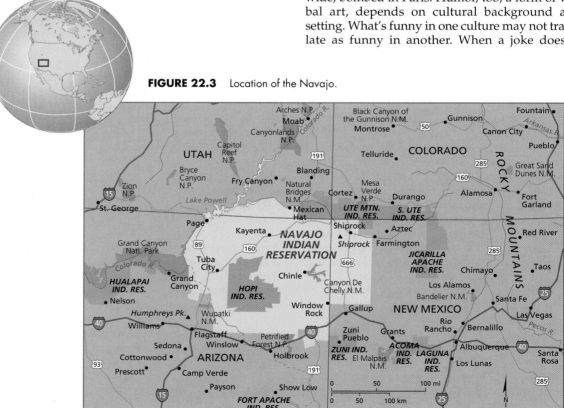

FIGURE 22.3 Location of the Navajo.

STUDENT CD-ROM LIVING ANTHROPOLOGY

Art of the Aborigines
Track 22

This clip focuses on an aboriginal artist in the community of Galiwinku in northern Australia. The clip provides an excellent illustration of how aspects of culture (art, religion, kinship, economics, law) that stand apart in our own society are so closely related as to be inseparable in others. The artist makes a string bag, based on a pattern her father originated. She uses knowledge taught to her by her mother, grandmother, and grandfather. According to the narrator, the artist weaves a story of the dreamtime—the mythical past when the world as we know it was created—into the bag, which thus has spiritual as well as artistic and functional significance. How widespread is this art in the community shown here? How was the bag used during gathering? How does the creative act here depict enculturation?

■ *A violin class for a large group of four-year-old children at a Korean music school.*

■ *This photo was taken on St. Paul Island, on the Bering Sea coast of Alaska. A traditional Aleut storyteller uses a drum to tell his tale to young Aleut people. Who are the storytellers of your society? How do their narrative techniques and styles differ from the one shown here?*

work, an American may say, "Well, you had to be there at the time." Jokes, like aesthetic judgments, depend on context.

At a smaller level of culture, certain artistic traditions may be transmitted in families. In Bali, for example, there are families of carvers, musicians, dancers, and mask makers. Among the Yoruba of Nigeria, two lineages of leatherworkers are entrusted with important bead embroidery works, such as for the king's crown and the bags and bracelets of priests. The arts, like other professions, often "run" in families. The Bachs, for example, produced not only Johann Sebastian, but several other noted composers and musicians.

In Chapter 1, anthropology's approach to the arts was contrasted with a traditional humanities focus on "fine arts" and elite expressions. Anthropology has extended the definition of "cultured" well beyond the elitist meaning of "high" art and culture. For anthropologists, everyone acquires culture through enculturation. In academia, growing acceptance of the anthropological definition of culture has helped broaden the study of the humanities from fine art and elite art to popular and folk art and the creative expressions of the masses and of many cultures.

In many societies, myths, legends, tales, and the art of storytelling play important roles in the transmission of culture and the preservation of tradition. In the absence of writing, oral traditions may preserve details of history and genealogy, as in many parts of West Africa. Art forms often go together. For example, music and storytelling may be combined for drama and emphasis (see the lower photo), much as they are in films and theater.

At what age do children start learning the arts? In some cultures, they start early. Contrast the photo of the Korean violin class above right with the photo of the Aleut gathering below. The Korean scene shows formal instruction. The teachers take the lead in showing the kids how to play the violin. The Aleut photo shows a more informal local scene in which children are learning about the arts as part of their overall enculturation. Presumably, the Korean children are learning the arts because their parents want them to, not necessarily because they have an artistic temperament that they need or wish to express. Sometimes children's participation in arts or performance, including sports, exemplifies forced enculturation. It may be pushed by parents rather than by kids themselves. In the United States, performance, usually associated with schools, has a strong social, and usually competitive, component. Kids perform with their peers.

I'll Get You, My Pretty, and Your Little R2

Techniques that anthropologists have used to analyze myths and folktales can be extended to two fantasy films that most of you have seen. *The Wizard of Oz* has been telecast annually for decades. The original *Star Wars* remains one of the most popular films of all time. Both are familiar and significant cultural products with obvious mythic qualities. The contributions of the French structuralist anthropologist Claude Lévi-Strauss (1967) and the neo-Freudian psychoanalyst Bruno Bettelheim (1975) to the study of myths and fairy tales permit the following analysis of visual fairy tales that contemporary Americans know well.

Examining the myths and tales of different cultures, Lévi-Strauss determined that one tale could be converted into another through a series of simple operations, for example, by doing the following:

1. Converting the positive element of a myth into its negative.
2. Reversing the order of the elements.
3. Replacing a male hero with a female hero.
4. Preserving or repeating certain key elements.

Through such operations, two apparently dissimilar myths can be shown to be variations on a common structure, that is, to be transformations of each other.

We'll see now that *Star Wars* is a systematic structural transformation of *The Wizard of Oz.* We may speculate about how many of the resemblances were conscious and how many simply reflect a process of enculturation that *Star Wars* writer and director George Lucas shares with other Americans.

The Wizard of Oz and *Star Wars* both begin in arid country, the first in Kansas and the second on the desert planet Tatooine (Table 22.1). *Star Wars* converts *The Wizard*'s female hero into a boy, Luke Skywalker. Fairy-tale heroes usually have short, common first names and second names that describe their origin or activity. Thus Luke, who travels aboard spaceships, is a Skywalker, while Dorothy Gale is swept off to Oz by a cyclone (a gale of wind). Dorothy leaves home with her dog, Toto, who is pursued by and has managed to escape from a woman who in Oz becomes the Wicked Witch of the West. Luke follows his "Two-Two" (R2D2), who is fleeing Darth Vader, the witch's structural equivalent.

Dorothy and Luke each start out living with an uncle and an aunt. However, because of the gender change of the hero, the primary relationship is reversed and inverted. Thus, Dorothy's relationship with her aunt is primary, warm, and loving, whereas Luke's relationship with his uncle, though primary, is strained and distant. Aunt and uncle are in the tales for the same reason. They represent home (the nuclear family of orientation), which children (according to American culture norms) must eventually leave to make it on their own. As Bettelheim (1975) points out, fairy tales often disguise parents as uncle and aunt, and this establishes social distance. The child can deal with the hero's separation (in *The Wizard of Oz*) or the aunt's and uncle's deaths (in *Star Wars*) more easily than with the death of or separation from real parents. Furthermore, this permits the child's strong feelings toward his or her real parents to be represented in different, more central characters, such as the Wicked Witch of the West and Darth Vader.

Both films focus on the child's relationship with the parent of the same sex, dividing that parent into three parts. In *The Wizard,* the mother is split into two parts bad and one part good.

They are the Wicked Witch of the East, dead at the beginning of the movie; the Wicked Witch of the West, dead at the end; and Glinda, the good mother, who survives. The original *Star Wars* reversed the proportion of good and bad, giving Luke a good father (his own), the Jedi knight who is proclaimed dead at the film's beginning. There is another good father, Ben Kenobi, who is ambiguously dead when the movie ends. Third is the evil father figure, Darth Vader. As the good-mother third survives *The Wizard of Oz,* the bad-father third lives on after *Star Wars,* to strike back in the sequel.

The child's relationship with the parent of the opposite sex also is represented in the two films. Dorothy's father figure is the Wizard of Oz, an initially terrifying figure who later is proved to be a fake. Bettelheim notes that the typical fairy-tale father is disguised as a monster or giant. Or else, when preserved as a human, he is weak, distant, or ineffective. Dorothy counts on the wizard to save her but finds that he makes seemingly impossible demands and in the end is just an ordinary man. She succeeds on her own, no longer relying on a father who offers no more than she herself possesses.

In *Star Wars* (although emphatically not in the later films), Luke's mother figure is Princess Leia. Bettelheim notes that boys commonly fantasize their mothers to be unwilling captives of their fathers. Fairy tales often disguise mothers as princesses whose freedom the boy-hero must obtain. In graphic Freudian imagery, Darth Vader threatens Princess Leia with a needle the size of the witch's broomstick. By the end of the film, Luke has freed Leia and defeated Vader.

There are other striking parallels in the structure of the two films. Fairy-tale heroes often are accompanied on their adventures by secondary characters who personify the virtues needed in a successful quest. Such characters often come in threes. Dorothy takes along wisdom (the Scarecrow), love (the Tin Woodman), and courage (the Lion). *Star Wars* includes a structurally equivalent trio—Han Solo, C3PO, and Chewbacca—but their association with particular qualities isn't as precise. The minor characters are also structurally parallel: Munchkins and Jawas, Apple Trees and Sand People, Flying Monkeys and Stormtroopers. And compare settings—the witch's castle and the Death Star, the Emerald City and the rebel base. The endings are also parallel. Luke accomplishes his objective on his own, using the Force (mana, magical power). Dorothy's goal is to return to Kansas. She does that by tapping her shoes together and drawing on the Force in her ruby slippers.

All successful cultural products blend old and new, drawing on familiar themes. They may rearrange them in novel ways and thus win a lasting place in the imaginations of the culture that creates or accepts them. *Star Wars* successfully used old cultural themes in novel ways. It did that by drawing on *the* American fairy tale, one that had been available in book form since the turn of the 20th century.

TABLE 22.1   *Star Wars* **as a Structural Transformation of** *The Wizard of Oz*

Star Wars	*The Wizard of Oz*
Male hero (Luke Skywalker)	Female hero (Dorothy Gale)
Arid Tatooine	Arid Kansas

Luke follows R2D2:
    R2D2 flees Vader
	Dorothy follows Toto:
	    Toto flees witch

Luke lives with uncle and aunt:
    Primary relationship with uncle
    (same sex as hero)
    Strained, distant relationship with uncle
	Dorothy lives with uncle and aunt:
	    Primary relationship with aunt
	    (same sex as hero)
	    Warm, close relationship with aunt

Tripartite division of same-sex parent:
    2 parts good, 1 part bad father
    Good father dead at beginning
    Good father dead (?) at end
    Bad father survives
	Tripartite division of same-sex parent:
	    2 parts bad, 1 part good mother
	    Bad mother dead at beginning
	    Bad mother dead at end
	    Good mother survives

Relationship with parent of opposite sex
    (Princess Leia Organa):
    Princess is unwilling captive
    Needle
    Princess is freed
	Relationship with parent of opposite sex
	    (Wizard of Oz):
	    Wizard makes impossible demands
	    Broomstick
	    Wizard turns out to be sham

Trio of companions:
    Han Solo, C3PO, Chewbacca
	Trio of companions:
	    Scarecrow, Tin Woodman, Cowardly Lion

Minor characters:
    Jawas
    Sand People
    Stormtroopers
	Minor characters:
	    Munchkins
	    Apple Trees
	    Flying Monkeys

Settings:
    Death Star
    Verdant Tikal (rebel base)
	Settings:
	    Witch's castle
	    Emerald City

Conclusion:
    Luke uses magic to accomplish goal
    (destroy Death Star)
	Conclusion:
	    Dorothy uses magic to accomplish goal
	    (return to Kansas)

In the process, they learn to compete, whether for a first place finish in a sports event or a first chair in the school orchestra or band.

The Artistic Career

In nonindustrial societies, artists tend to be part-time specialists. In states, there are more ways for artists to practice their craft full time. The number of positions in "arts and leisure" has mushroomed in contemporary societies, especially in North America. Many non-Western societies also offer career tracks in the arts: For example, a child born into a particular family or lineage may discover that he or she is destined for a career in leather working or weaving. Some societies are noted for particular arts, such as dance, wood carving, or weaving.

An artistic career also may involve some kind of a calling. Individuals may discover they have a particular talent and find an environment in which that talent is nourished. Separate career paths for artists usually involve special training and apprenticeship. Such paths are more likely in a complex society, where there are many separate career tracks, than in band or tribal societies, where expressive culture is less formally separated from daily life.

Artists need support if they are to devote full time to creative activity. They find support in their families or lineages if there is specialization in the arts involving kin groups. State societies often have patrons of the arts. Usually members of the elite class, patrons offer various kinds of support to aspiring and talented artists, such as court and palace painters, musicians, or sculptors. In some cases, an artistic career may entail a lifetime of dedication to religious art.

Goodale and Koss (1971) describe the manufacture of ornamental burial poles among the Tiwi of North Australia. Temporary separation and detachment from other social roles allowed burial pole artists to devote themselves to their work. The pole artists were ceremonially commissioned as such after a death. They were granted temporary freedom from the daily food quest. Other community members agreed to serve as their patrons. They supplied the artists with hard-to-get materials needed for their work. The burial pole artists were sequestered in a work area near the grave. That area was taboo to everyone else.

The arts usually are defined as neither practical nor ordinary. They rely on talent, which is individual, but which must be channeled and shaped in socially approved directions. Inevitably, artistic talent and production pull the artist away from the practical need to make a living. The issue of how to support artists and the arts arises again and again. We've all heard the phrase "struggling artist." But how should society support the arts? If there is state or religious support, something is typically expected in return. There is inevitably some limitation of the artist's "free" expression. Patronage and sponsorship also may result in the creation of art works that are removed from public display. Art commissioned for elites often is displayed only in their homes, perhaps finding its way into museums after their deaths. Church-commissioned art may be closer to the people. Artistic expressions of popular culture, intended for public rather than elite consumption, are discussed further in the chapter "Cultural Exchange and Survival."

Continuity and Change

The arts go on changing, although certain art forms have survived for thousands of years. The Upper Paleolithic cave art that has survived for more than 30,000 years was itself a highly developed manifestation of human creativity and symbolism, with an undoubtedly long evolutionary history. Monumental architecture, along with sculpture, reliefs, ornamental pottery, and written music, literature, and drama, have survived from early civilizations.

Countries and cultures are known for particular contributions, including art. The Balinese are known for dance; the Navajo for sand paintings, jewelry, and weaving; and the French for making cuisine an art form. We still read Greek tragedies and comedies in college, as we also read Shakespeare and Milton, and view the works of Michelangelo. Greek theater is among the most enduring of the arts. The words of Aeschylus,

■ In Athens, Greece, ancient Greek theater is being staged for a contemporary audience. Theater is typically a multimedia experience, with visual, aural, and often musical attributes.

Capoeira: The Afro-Brazilian Art of Unity and Survival

BACKGROUND INFORMATION

STUDENT:
Anne Haggerson

SUPERVISING PROFESSOR:
Rudi Colloredo-Mansfeld

SCHOOL:
University of Iowa

YEAR IN SCHOOL/MAJOR:
Senior/Anthropology and Spanish

FUTURE PLANS:
Internship in Washington, D.C.;
Ph.D.

PROJECT TITLE:
Capoeira: The Afro-Brazilian
Art of Unity and Survival

Which of the features and functions of art are illustrated by this account? Can you think of parallels to capoeira in form and/or function in your own society?

For two months, I lived in a small, concrete apartment in Mangueira, an inner-city shantytown constructed over trash and swamps in Salvador, Bahia. I was doing a fieldwork project for my senior thesis while working as an English teacher for GRUCON (Grupo de União e Consciência Negra), the local black consciousness movement that had been actively involved in community mobilization and youth-based consciousness raising projects for 30 years. My research focused on institutions that helped children and families overcome the forces of poverty, unemployment, racism, and failing schools.

Thus, I set out to investigate capoeira, an Afro-Brazilian martial art that assumes metaphors of slavery, liberation, and survival. The capoeira academy in the neighborhood was a subset of GRUCON and was grounded in a shared historical identity, fighting against economic oppression and political exclusion through music, dance, and African pride.

To prepare for this work, I researched problems of street children, took advanced Portuguese language courses, and worked out a research design that included interviews and participant observation. I trained formally with a local capoeira group for five months before going to Brazil, familiarizing myself with the key movements and game etiquette. Joining a capoeira academy in Brazil was one of the most challenging aspects of my research since I was a white, American woman participating in an activity dominated by Afro-Brazilian men. However, my active participation in the art was a crucial part of my fieldwork, allowing me to enter into the physical and psychological space of my informants, experience the power of symbolic movement, and access the sense of friendship, unity, and commitment among the players.

The practices were held in a small, humble concrete room and were administered with a high level of discipline and seriousness. The mestre served as the teacher, role model, and mediator of the 40 team members and created meaning and stability in their lives, encouraging them to pass physical limits, harness leadership roles on the team, proudly display their skills in the roda or performance circle, and

research the history of capoeira in their free time.

Beyond participant observation, I also recorded important events and interviewed participants. I witnessed a spectacular annual community event called a batizado or baptism, where the students graduate to a higher-level capoeira belt. By observing and photographing this yearly initiation, it became clear that capoeira was much more than a pastime; it was a survival strategy, an educational tool, and a microcosmic social hierarchy that was maintained by a complex web of community political leaders and organizers.

Associated with rich memories of embarrassment and accomplishment, I proudly wear the capoeira warrior name the mestre gave me, "Serpente" or Snake, which, to me, is a symbolic tattoo that represents the dynamic beauty of doing anthropological fieldwork at the base level of urban society and thereby unleashing important insight on the resilient spirit of a vital civil society and the importance of building robust community institutions that spark political change and cultural solidarity.

A Brazilian capoeira *dancer.*

Sophocles, Euripides, and Aristophanes have been captured in writing and live on. Who knows how many great preliterate creations and performances have been lost?

Classic Greek theater survives throughout the world. It is read in college courses, seen in the

movies, and performed live on stages from Athens to New York. In today's world, the dramatic arts are part of a huge "arts and leisure" industry, which links Western and non-Western art forms in an international network that has both aesthetic and commercial dimensions (see

■ *A synthesis of new and old theater techniques, including puppetry, is used in the Broadway production of Disney's* The Lion King. *What artistic influences have inspired the images shown in this photo?*

Marcus and Myers, eds. 1995; Root 1996). For example, non-Western musical traditions and instruments have joined the modern world system. We've seen that local musicians perform for outsiders, including tourists who increasingly visit their villages. And "tribal" instruments such as the Native Australian didgeridoo, a very long wooden wind instrument, are now exported worldwide. At least one store in Amsterdam, the Netherlands, specializes in didgeridoos, the only item it carries. Dozens of stores in any world capital hawk "traditional" arts, including musical instruments, from a hundred Third World countries. The commodification of non-Western art and the contemporary use of the arts to forge and redefine group identities are discussed further in the last chapter in this book.

We've seen that the arts typically draw in multiple media. Given the richness of today's media world, multimedia are even more marked. As ingredients and flavors from all over the world are combined in modern cuisine, so, too, are elements from many cultures and epochs woven into contemporary art and performance.

Our culture values change, experimentation, innovation, and novelty. But creativity also may be based on tradition. The Navajo, remember, can be at once individualistic, conservative, and attentive to proper form. In some cases and cultures, it's not necessary for artists to be innovative as they are being creative. Creativity can be expressed in variations on a traditional form. We see an example of this in "Interesting Issues" on pages 520–521, in which *Star Wars*, despite its specific story and innovative special effects, is shown to share its narrative structure with a previous film and fairy tale. It isn't always necessary for artists, in their work, to make a statement separating themselves from the past. Often, artists pay fealty to the past, associating with and building on, rather than rejecting, the work of their predecessors.

SUMMARY

1. Even if they lack a word for "art," people everywhere do associate an aesthetic experience with objects and events having certain qualities. The arts, sometimes called "expressive culture," include the visual arts, literature (written and oral), music, and theater arts. Some issues raised about religion also apply to art. If we adopt a special attitude or demeanor when confronting a sacred object, do we display something similar with art? Much art has been done in association with religion. In tribal performances, the arts and religion often mix. But non-Western art isn't always linked to religion.

2. The special places where we find art include museums, concert halls, opera houses, and theaters. However, the boundary between what's art and what's not may be blurred. Variation in art appreciation is especially common in contemporary society, with its professional artists and critics and great cultural diversity.

3. Those who work with non-Western art have been criticized for ignoring individual artists and for focusing too much on the social context and collective artistic production. Art is work, albeit creative work. In state societies, some people manage to support themselves as full-time artists. In nonstates artists are normally part time. Community standards judge the mastery and completion displayed in a work of art. Typically, the arts are exhibited, evaluated, performed, and appreciated in society. Music, which is often performed in groups, is among the most social of the arts. "Folk" art, music, and lore refer to the expressive culture of ordinary, usually rural, people.

4. Art can stand for tradition, even when traditional art is removed from its original context. Art can express community sentiment, with political goals, used to call attention to social issues. Often, art is meant to commemorate and to last. Growing acceptance of the anthropological definition of culture has guided the humanities beyond fine art,

elite art, and Western art to the creative expressions of the masses and of many cultures. Myths, legends, tales, and the art of storytelling often play important roles in the transmission of culture. Many societies offer career tracks in the arts; a child born into a particular family or lineage may discover that he or she is destined for a career in leatherworking or weaving.

5. The arts go on changing, although certain art forms have survived for thousands of years. Countries and cultures are known for particular contributions. Today, a huge "arts and leisure" industry links Western and non-Western art forms in an international network with both aesthetic and commercial dimensions.

aesthetics Appreciation of the qualities perceived in works of art; the mind and emotions in relation to a sense of beauty.

art An object or event that evokes an aesthetic reaction—a sense of beauty, appreciation, harmony, and/or pleasure; the quality, production, expression, or realm of what is beautiful or of more than ordinary significance; the class of objects subject to aesthetic criteria.

arts The arts include the visual arts, literature (written and oral), music, and theater arts.

catharsis Intense emotional release.

ethnomusicology The comparative study of the musics of the world and of music as an aspect of culture and society.

expressive culture The arts; people express themselves creatively in dance, music, song, painting, sculpture, pottery, cloth, storytelling, verse, prose, drama, and comedy.

folk Of the people; originally coined for European peasants; refers to the art, music, and lore of ordinary people, as contrasted with the "high" art or "classic" art of the European elites.

CRITICAL THINKING QUESTIONS

1. Think of something visual that you consider to be art, but whose status as art is debatable. How would you convince someone else that it is art? What kinds of arguments against your position would you expect to hear?

2. Think of a musical composition or performance you consider to be art, but whose status as such is debatable. How would you convince someone else that it is art? What kinds of arguments against your position would you expect to hear?

3. Where did you last witness art? In what kind of a setting was it? Did people go there to appreciate the arts, or for some other reason?

4. Based on your own experience, how may the arts be used to buttress religion?

5. Can you think of a political dispute involving art or the arts? What were the different positions being debated?

SUGGESTED ADDITIONAL READINGS

Anderson, R.
  1989 *Art in Small-Scale Societies.* Upper Saddle River, NJ: Prentice Hall. Introduction to non-Western art, with a focus on the visual arts.
  2004 *Calliope's Sisters: A Comparative Study of Philosophies of Art,* 2nd ed. Upper Saddle River, NJ: Prentice Hall. A comparative study of aesthetics in 10 cultures.

Anderson, R., and K. Field, eds.
  1993 *Art in Small-Scale Societies: Contemporary Readings.* Upper Saddle River, NJ: Prentice Hall. An anthology of studies of non-Western art, with a focus on the visual arts.

Askew, K. M.
  2001 *Performing the Nation: Swahili Music and Cultural Politics in Tanzania.* Chicago: University of Chicago Press. Field-based study of music and politics in Tanzania.

Conkey, M., O. Soffer, D. Stratmann, and N. Jablonski
  1997 *Beyond Art: Pleistocene Image and Symbol.* San Francisco: Memoirs of the California Academy of Sciences, no. 23. A consideration of the symbolic basis and nature of prehistoric art.

Coote, J., and A. Shelton, eds.
  1992 *Anthropology, Art, and Aesthetics.* New York: Oxford University Press. Useful collection of essays.

Dublin, M.
  2001 *Native America Collected: The Culture of an Art World.* Albuquerque: University of New Mexico Press. Indians in art, tourism, and popular culture.

Hatcher, E. P.
  1999 *Art as Culture: An Introduction to the Anthropology of Art,* 2nd ed. Westport, CT: Bergin & Garvey. Up-to-date introduction.

Layton, R.

    1991   *The Anthropology of Art,* 2nd ed. New York: Cambridge University Press. Survey of the major issues, with a focus on visual art.

Marcus, G. E., and F. R. Myers, eds.

    1995   *The Traffic in Culture: Refiguring Art and Anthropology.* Berkeley: University of California Press. Art, society, and the marketing of culture in global perspective.

Moisala, P., and B. Diamond, eds.

    2000   *Music and Gender.* Champaign–Urbana: University of Illinois Press. Studies of the musical roles and performances of men and women in several societies.

Myers, F. R.

    2002   *Painting Culture: The Making of an Aboriginal High Art.* Durham, NC: Duke University Press. Artistic transformation in Australia's western desert.

Napier, A. D.

    1992   *Foreign Bodies: Performance, Art, and Symbolic Anthropology.* Berkeley: University of California Press. Focuses on the performing arts and symbols of society.

Root, D.

    1996   *Cannibal Culture: Art, Appropriation, and the Commodification of Difference.* Boulder, CO: Westview. How Western art and commerce classify, co-opt, and commodify "native" experiences, creations, and products.

Urban, Greg

    2001   *Metaculture: How Culture Moves through the World.* Minneapolis: University of Minnesota Press. Patterns, images, and cultural evaluation, with contemporary examples.

INTERNET EXERCISES

1. Body Art: Visit the National Museum of Natural History's online exhibit of "Canela body adornment," **http://www.nmnh.si.edu/naa/canela/canela1.htm**. Read all three pages of the exhibit and answer the questions below:

   a. In this example, how interrelated are art and worldview? How is art being used by the Canela?

   b. What individuals among the Canela get their ears pierced, and what does it signify? Who participates in the piercing? How does this practice compare to ear piercing in Western society?

   c. Cultures can change through time. What kinds of changes have occurred in the Canela practices of ear piercing since the 1950s? In the same way, what kinds of changes have occurred in ear piercing practices in Western society? What do these changes signify?

2. Comparing Art: Go to the Metropolitan Museum of Art's Collections page, **http://www.metmuseum.org/collections/index.asp** and browse the collections of Egyptian Art, **http://www.metmuseum.org/collections/department.asp?dep=10**, European Paintings, **http://www.metmuseum.org/collections/department.asp?dep=11**, and Modern Art, **http://www.metmuseum.org/Works_Of_Art/department.asp?dep=21**. For each of these collections, address the following questions:

   a. By whom is this art produced, and for whom is it produced?

   b. For what purpose is this art being produced (e.g., religious, aesthetic, political, monetary)?

   c. What themes and subjects are portrayed in the art?

   d. By just looking at the art, what can you learn about the culture that produced it?

See Chapter 22 at your McGraw-Hill Online Learning Center for additional review and interactive exercises.

Kottak, *Assault on Paradise,* **4th ed.**

Read Chapter 12, which discusses, among other aspects of globalization, television and its impact on Arembepe and Arembepeiros. What kind of TV programs do Arembepeiros habitually watch? What influence has television had on how Arembepeiros stage their festivals and performances?

Peters-Golden, *Culture Sketches,* **4th ed.**

This chapter has discussed the uses and places of arts in social life, describing music as one of the most social forms of expressive culture. In *Culture Sketches,* read Chapter 7, "Kaluli: Story, Song, and Ceremony." How does Kaluli music reflect central cultural ideas? What aspects of Kaluli life and society are represented in their music? How is the Kaluli relationship to music similar to, or different from, your own society's relationship to music? Several American and European musicians have joined to produce a recording of Bosavi music, *Voices of the Rainforest* (see "Interesting Issues" on pages 576–577). Profits from its sale benefit the Bosavi People's Fund, set up to provide financial aid to maintain Kaluli cultural survival in the face of threats to their rainforest environment. Why might it be that music, in particular, was chosen to raise money for the Kaluli?

Knauft, *The Gebusi,* **1st ed.**

Read Chapters 5, 6, and 11. Based on Chapters 5 and 6, what forms of artistic display and colorful performance are most developed among Gebusi? What symbols are reflected and encoded in Gebusi dance and initiation costuming? How does the art of Gebusi initiation costuming reflect social relations on the bodies of the initiates? Based on Chapter 11, what are the biggest changes in Gebusi artistic performances between 1980 and 1998? During Independence Day celebrations, are Gebusi exposed to more or to less artistic variety than they used to be? What do bodily art and performance during Independence Day celebrations reflect about changing social relations between Gebusi and other people?

23

The Modern World System

CHAPTER OUTLINE

THE EMERGENCE OF THE WORLD SYSTEM

Travel, trade, and murder may be as old as humanity. However, there is no doubt, as the "News Brief" confirms, that contact with Europe increased the scale of trade, interethnic contact, and violence in the Americas—and throughout the world. These trends continue today. Thus, although field work in small communities is anthropology's hallmark, isolated groups are impossible to find today and probably never have existed. For thousands of years, human groups have been in contact with one another. Local societies always have participated in a larger system, which today has global dimensions. We call it the *modern world system*, by which we mean a world in which nations are economically and politically interdependent. (Some earlier systems that controlled and blended large areas included the Roman empire, imperial China, and the spice trade.)

   City, nation, and world increasingly invade local communities. Today, if anthropologists want to study a fairly isolated society, they must journey to the highlands of Papua New Guinea or the tropical forests of South America. Even in those places, they probably will encounter missionaries, prospectors, and tourists. In contemporary Australia, sheep owned by people who speak English graze where totemic ceremonies once were held. Farther in the outback, some descendants of those totemites may be working for a TV crew filming

529

■ December 26, 2003: Illustrating a process of indigenizing offerings of the modern world system, children dress as Colonel Sanders to promote egg tarts (a local dish now offered by an international restaurant chain) at a KFC store in Shanghai, China.

interrelated parts assembled into a system. Societies are subsystems of bigger systems, with the world system as the largest.

As Europeans took to ships, developing a transoceanic trade-oriented economy, people throughout the world entered Europe's sphere of influence. In the 15th century, Europe established regular contact with Asia, Africa, and eventually the New World (the Caribbean and the Americas). Christopher Columbus's first voyage from Spain to the Bahamas and the Caribbean in 1492 was soon followed by additional voyages. These journeys opened the way for a major exchange of people, resources, diseases, and ideas, as the Old and New Worlds were forever linked (Crosby 1986, 2003; Diamond 1997; Viola and Margolis 1991). Led by Spain and Portugal, Europeans extracted silver and gold, conquered the natives (taking some as slaves), and colonized their lands.

a new *Survivor* program. A Hilton hotel stands in the capital of faraway Madagascar, and a paved highway now has an exit for Arembepe, the Brazilian fishing village I have been studying since 1962. When and how did the modern world system begin?

The world system and the relations among the countries within that system are shaped by the world capitalist economy. World-system theory can be traced to the French social historian Fernand Braudel. In his three-volume work *Civilization and Capitalism, 15th–18th Century* (1981, 1982, 1992), Braudel argued that society consists of

Previously in Europe as throughout the world, rural people had produced mainly for their own needs, growing their own food and making clothing, furniture, and tools from local products. Production beyond immediate needs was undertaken to pay taxes and purchase trade items such as salt and iron. As late as 1650, the English diet, like diets in most of the world today, was based on locally grown starches (Mintz 1985). However, in the 200 years that followed, the English became extraordinary consumers of imported goods. One of the earliest and most popular of those goods was sugar (Mintz 1985).

Sugarcane was originally domesticated in Papua New Guinea, and sugar was first processed in India. Reaching Europe via the Middle East and the eastern Mediterranean, it was carried to the New World by Columbus (Mintz 1985). The climate of Brazil and the Caribbean proved ideal for growing sugarcane, and Europeans built plantations there to supply the growing demand for sugar. This led to the development in the 17th century of a plantation economy based on a single cash crop—a system known as monocrop production.

The demand for sugar in a growing international market spurred the development of the transatlantic slave trade and New World plantation economies based on slave labor. By the 18th century, an increased English demand for raw cotton led to rapid settlement of what is now the southeastern United States and the emergence there of another slave-based monocrop production system. Like sugar, cotton was a key trade item that fueled the growth of the world system.

The increasing dominance of trade led to the **capitalist world economy** (Wallerstein 1982, 2004*b*), a single world system committed to production for sale or exchange, with the object of maximizing profits rather than supplying domestic needs. **Capital** refers to wealth or resources invested in business, with the intent of using the means of production to produce a profit.

OVERVIEW

The modern world system refers to a global system in which nations are economically and politically interdependent. The world economy is based on production for sale, guided by the profit motive. This capitalist world economy has political and economic specialization based on three positions: core, semiperiphery, and periphery. These positions have existed since the 16th century, although the particular countries filling them have changed.

Starting around 1750, industrialization increased production in farming and manufacturing. Workers moved from homes to factories, from rural areas to industrial cities. Today's world system maintains the distinction between those who own the means of production and those who don't. But the division is now worldwide. A middle class of skilled and professional workers has been added to the class structure. There is a marked contrast between capitalists and workers in the core nations and workers on the periphery. One effect of industrial expansion has been the destruction of indigenous peoples, cultures, and resources. For the last 500 years, the main forces influencing cultural interaction have been commercial expansion and the differential power of core nations.

Bones Reveal Some Truth in "Noble Savage Myth"

WASHINGTON POST NEWS BRIEF

by Jack Lucentini
April 15, 2002

This "News Brief" reports on research demonstrating how contact with Europe increased the scale of trade, interethnic contact, and violence in the Americas. The research brings into focus an anthropological debate about the origin and nature of warfare and the role of European contact in fostering conflicts among indigenous peoples. The study shows that violence among Native Americans increased after contact. As the article begins, it suggests, mistakenly, that Native Americans lived in prehistory and lacked "civilization." In fact, Native Americans developed states and "civilizations" (e.g., Aztec, Maya, Inca) comparable to those of the Old World (e.g., ancient Mesopotamia and Egypt). Native Americans, most notably the Maya, also developed writing, which they used to

◼ *The encounter between Hernán Cortés (1485–1547) and Montezuma II (1466–1520) was the subject of this 1820 painting by Gallo Gallina of Milan, Italy. Cortés went on to conquer Montezuma's Aztec empire.*

record their history—rendering the label prehistory *inaccurate. As you read, to understand why violence increased after contact, pay attention to the role of trade, disease, and slave raiding.*

A romantic-sounding notion dating back more than 200 years has it that people in prehistory, such as Native Americans, lived in peace and harmony.

Then "civilization" showed up, sowing violence and discord. Some see this claim as naive. It even has a derisive nickname, the "noble savage myth." But new research seems to suggest the "myth" contains at least some truth. Researchers examined thousands of Native American skeletons and found that those from after Christopher Columbus landed in the New World showed a rate of traumatic injuries more than 50 percent higher than those from before the Europeans arrived.

"Traumatic injuries do increase really significantly," said Philip L. Walker, an anthropology professor at the University of California at Santa Barbara, who conducted the study with Richard H. Steckel of Ohio State University.

The findings suggest "Native Americans were involved in more violence after the Europeans arrived than before," Walker said. But he emphasized there was also widespread violence before the Europeans came. Nevertheless, he said, "probably we're just seeing the tip of the iceberg" as far as the difference between violence levels before and after. That's because as many as half of bullet wounds miss the skeleton. Thus, the study couldn't detect much firearm violence, though some tribes wiped each other out using European-supplied guns.

The findings shed light on a controversy that has stirred not only living room discussions, but also an intense, sometimes ugly debate among anthropologists.

It involves two opposing views of human nature: Are we hard-wired for violence, or pushed into it?

Anthropologists who believe the latter seized on the findings as evidence for their view. "What it all says to me is that humans aren't demonic. Human males don't have an ingrained propensity for war . . . They can learn to be very peaceful, or terribly violent," said R. Brian Ferguson, a professor of anthropology at Rutgers University in Newark. Ferguson contends that before about 10,000 years ago, war was virtually nonexistent. But experts on the opposing side also said the findings fit their views.

"A 50 percent increase is the equivalent of moving from a suburb to the city, in terms of violence," said Charles Stanish, a professor of anthropology at the University of California at Los Angeles. "This shows the Native Americans were like us. Under stress, they fought more." Both sides called the study, which was presented Friday at the annual meeting of the American Association of Physical Anthropologists in Buffalo, a valuable contribution . . .

Walker and colleagues examined the skeletons of 3,375 pre-Columbian and 1,165 post-Columbian Native Americans, from archaeological sites throughout North and Central America.

The North Americans came mostly from the coasts and the Great Lakes region, Walker said.

Pre-Columbian skeletons showed an 11 percent incidence of traumatic injuries, he said, compared with almost 17 percent for the post-Columbians.

Walker said his findings surprised him. "I wasn't really expecting it," he said. Yet it undeniably suggests violence, he added. Most of the increase consisted of head injuries in young males, "which conforms pretty closely to the pattern you see today in homicides."

The researchers defined "traumatic injury" as anything leaving a mark on the skeleton, such as a skull fracture, a healed broken arm, or an embedded arrow point or bullet.

Walker said that although part of the increased injury rate doubtless stems from violence by whites themselves, it probably reflects mostly native-on-native violence. "In a lot of cases, such as in California, there weren't that many Europeans around—just a few priests, and thousands of Indians," he said.

Walker said the higher injury rate could have many explanations. Increased violence is normally associated with more densely populated, settled life, which Native Americans experienced in modernity, he said. Disease could also touch off war, he said.

"Here in California, there was a lot of inter-village warfare associated with the introduction of European diseases. People would attribute the disease to evil shamanic activity in another village," he said. Ferguson cited other factors. The Europeans often drew natives into their imperial wars, he said.

"Sometimes, the Europeans would enable someone to pursue a preexisting fight more aggressively, by backing one side," he added. Other times, he said, Europeans got natives to conduct slave raids on one another. Natives also fought over control of areas around trading outposts, to become middlemen, he said. "Sometimes that was a life-or-death matter, since it meant the difference between who would get guns or not." Stanish agreed. "Obviously, having an expanding imperial power coming at you is going to exacerbate tensions," he said . . . They're going to push you somewhere—into other groups."

"You're also going to get competition over access to the Europeans, who are a form of wealth," he added. Native Americans fought over areas rich in fur, which the whites would buy.

Yet Native American warfare was widespread long before that, Stanish said . . .

Keith F. Otterbein, an anthropology professor at the State University of New York at Buffalo, said the skeleton findings contribute to a balanced, middle-of-the-road view.

"The folks who are saying there was no early warfare—they're wrong, too. There is, in fact, a myth of the peaceful savage," he said. Otterbein said the controversy won't end here; both sides are too ideologically entrenched.

"Underlying the 'noble savage' myth," Stanish said, "is a political agenda by both the far right and far left. The right tries to turn the 'savages' into our little brown brothers, who need to be pulled up . . . On the left, they have another agenda, that the Western world is bad."

SOURCE: http://www.washingtonpost.com/ac2/wp-dyn?pagename=article&node=&contentId=A48 202-2002Apr14; in newspaper on p. A09.

The key claim of world-system theory is that an identifiable social system, based on wealth and power differentials, extends beyond individual states and nations. That system is formed by a set of economic and political relations that have characterized much of the globe since the 16th century, when the Old World established regular contact with the New World.

According to Wallerstein (1982, 2004b), the nations within the world system occupy three different positions of economic and political power: core, periphery, and semiperiphery. There is a geographic center or **core,** the dominant position in the world system, consisting of the strongest and most powerful nations. In core nations, "the complexity of economic activities and the level of capital accumulation is [sic] the greatest" (Thompson 1983, p. 12). With its sophisticated technologies and mechanized means of production, the core produces capital-intensive high-technology goods. Most of those products flow to other core nations, but some also go to the periphery and semiperiphery. According to Arrighi (1994), the core monopolizes the most profitable activities, especially the control of world finance.

Semiperiphery and **periphery** nations have less power, wealth, and influence. The semiperiphery is intermediate between the core and the periphery. Contemporary nations of the semiperiphery are industrialized. Like core nations, they export both industrial goods and commodities, but they lack the power and economic dominance of core nations. Thus Brazil, a semiperiphery nation, exports automobiles to Nigeria (a periphery nation) and auto engines, orange juice extract, coffee, and shrimp to the United States (a core nation).

Economic activities in the periphery are less mechanized than are those in the semiperiphery. The periphery produces raw materials, agricultural commodities, and, increasingly, human labor for export to the core and the semiperiphery. Today, although some degree of industrialization has reached even peripheral nations, the relationship between the core and the periphery remains fundamentally exploitative. Trade and other economic relations between core and periphery disproportionately benefit capitalists in the core (Shannon 1996).

In the United States and Western Europe today, immigrants, legal and illegal, supply cheap labor for agriculture in core countries. U.S. states as far-flung as California, Michigan, and South Carolina make significant use of farm labor from Mexico. The availability of relatively cheap workers from noncore nations such as Mexico (in the United States) and Turkey (in Germany) benefits farmers and business owners in core countries, while also supplying remittances to families in the semiperiphery and periphery. As a result of 21st-century telecommunications technology, cheap labor doesn't even need to migrate to the United States. Thousands of families in India are being supported as American companies "outsource" jobs—from telephone assistance to software engineering—to nations outside the core.

Consider recent moves by IBM, the world's largest information technology company. On June 24, 2005, the *New York Times* reported that IBM was planning to hire more than 14,000 additional workers in India, while laying off some 13,000 workers in Europe and the United States (Lohr 2005). These figures illustrate the ongoing globalization of work and the migration of even skilled jobs to low-wage countries. Its critics accuse IBM of shopping the globe for the cheapest labor to enhance corporate profits at the expense of wages, benefits, and job security in the United States and other developed countries. In explaining the hiring in India, an IBM senior vice president (quoted in Lohr 2005) cited a surging demand for technology services in India's thriving economy and the opportunity to tap the many skilled Indian software engineers to work on projects around the world. Skilled Western workers must compete now against well-educated workers in such low-wage countries as India, where an experienced software programmer earns one-fifth the average salary of a comparable American worker ($15,000 versus $75,000) (Lohr 2005).

INDUSTRIALIZATION

By the 18th century, the stage had been set for the **Industrial Revolution**—the historic transformation (in Europe, after 1750) of "traditional" into "modern" societies through industrialization of the economy. Industrialization required capital for investment. The established system of transoceanic trade and commerce supplied this capital from the enormous profits it generated. Wealthy people sought investment opportunities and eventually found them in machines and engines to drive machines. Industrialization increased production in both farming and manufacturing, as capital and scientific innovation fueled invention.

European industrialization developed from (and eventually replaced) the domestic system (cottage industry or home-handicraft system)

of manufacture. In this system, an organizer-entrepreneur supplied the raw materials to workers in their homes and collected the finished products from them. The entrepreneur, whose sphere of operations might span several villages, owned the materials, paid for the work, and arranged the marketing.

Causes of the Industrial Revolution

The Industrial Revolution began in the cotton products, iron, and pottery trades. These were widely used goods whose manufacture could be broken down into simple routine motions that machines could perform. When manufacturing moved from home to factory, where machinery replaced handwork, agrarian societies evolved into industrial ones. As factories produced cheap staple goods, the Industrial Revolution led to a dramatic increase in production. Industrialization

▒ From producer to consumer, in the modern world system. The top photo, taken in the Caribbean nation of Dominica, shows the hard labor required to extract sugar using a manual press. In the bottom photo, an English middle-class family enjoys afternoon tea, sweetened with imported sugar. Which of the ingredients in your breakfast today were imported?

FIGURE 23.1 Location of England (United Kingdom) and France.

fueled urban growth and created a new kind of city, with factories crowded together in places where coal and labor were cheap.

The Industrial Revolution began in England rather than in France (Figure 23.1). Why? Unlike the English, the French didn't have to transform their domestic manufacturing system by industrializing. Faced with an increased need for products, with a late-18th-century population twice that of Great Britain, France could simply extend its domestic system of production by drawing in new homes. The French were able to increase production without innovating—they could enlarge the existing system rather than adopt a new one. However, to meet mounting demand for staples—at home and in its colonies—England, with fewer workers, had to industrialize.

As its industrialization proceeded, Britain's population began to increase dramatically. It doubled during the 18th century (especially after 1750) and did so again between 1800 and 1850. This demographic explosion fueled consumption, but British entrepreneurs couldn't meet the increased demand with the traditional production methods. This spurred experimentation, innovation, and rapid technological change.

English industrialization drew on national advantages in natural resources. Great Britain was rich in coal and iron ore and had navigable waterways and easily negotiated coasts. It was a seafaring island-nation located at the crossroads of international trade. These features gave Britain a favored position for importing raw materials and exporting manufactured goods. Another factor in England's industrial growth was the fact that much of its 18th-century colonial empire was occupied by English settler families who looked to the mother country as they tried to replicate European civilization in the New World. These colonies bought large quantities of English staples.

It also has been argued that particular cultural values and religion contributed to industrialization. Thus, many members of the emerging English middle class were Protestant nonconformists. Their beliefs and values encouraged industry, thrift, the dissemination of new knowledge, inventiveness, and willingness to accept change (Weber 1904/1958). Weber's ideas about Protestant values and capitalism were discussed in the chapter on "Religion."

STRATIFICATION

The socioeconomic effects of industrialization were mixed. English national income tripled between 1700 and 1815 and increased 30 times more by 1939. Standards of comfort rose, but prosperity was uneven. At first, factory workers got wages higher than those available in the domestic system. Later, owners started recruiting labor in places where living standards were low and labor (including that of women and children) was cheap.

Social ills increased with the growth of factory towns and industrial cities, with conditions like those Charles Dickens described in *Hard Times.* Filth and smoke polluted the 19th-century cities. Housing was crowded and unsanitary, with insufficient water and sewage disposal facilities and rising disease and death rates. This was the world of Ebenezer Scrooge, Bob Cratchit, Tiny Tim—and Karl Marx.

Industrial Stratification

The social theorists Karl Marx and Max Weber focused on the stratification systems associated with industrialization. From his observations in England and his analysis of 19th-century industrial capitalism, Marx (Marx and Engels 1848/1976) saw socioeconomic stratification as a sharp and simple division between two opposed classes: the bourgeoisie (capitalists) and the proletariat (property-less workers). The bourgeoisie traced its origins to overseas ventures and the world capitalist economy, which had transformed the social structure of northwestern Europe, creating a wealthy commercial class.

Industrialization shifted production from farms and cottages to mills and factories, where mechanical power was available and where workers could be assembled to operate heavy machinery. The **bourgeoisie** were the owners of the factories, mines, large farms, and other means of production. The **working class,** or proletariat, was made up of people who had to sell their labor to survive. With the decline of subsistence production and with the rise of urban migration and the possibility

The Art of STOCKING-FRAME-WORK-KNITTING.

Engrav'd for the Universal Magazine 1750 for J. Hinton at the Kings Arms in St Pauls Church Yard LONDON.

In the home-handicraft, or domestic, system of production, an organizer supplied raw materials to workers in their homes and collected their products. Family life and work were intertwined, as in this English scene. Is there a modern equivalent to the domestic system of production?

of unemployment, the bourgeoisie came to stand between workers and the means of production.

Industrialization hastened the process of *proletarianization*—the separation of workers from the means of production. The bourgeoisie also came to dominate the means of communication, the schools, and other key institutions. Marx viewed the nation-state as an instrument of oppression and religion as a method of diverting and controlling the masses.

Class consciousness (recognition of collective interests and personal identification with one's economic group) was a vital part of Marx's view of class. He saw bourgeoisie and proletariat as socioeconomic divisions with radically opposed interests. Marx viewed classes as powerful collective forces that could mobilize human energies to influence the course of history. On the basis of their common experience, workers would develop class consciousness, which could lead to revolutionary change. Although no proletarian revolution was to occur in England, workers did develop organizations to protect their interests and increase their share of industrial profits. During the 19th century, trade unions and socialist parties emerged to express a rising anticapitalist spirit.

The concerns of the English labor movement were to remove young children from factories and limit the hours during which women and children could work. The profile of stratification in industrial core nations gradually took shape. Capitalists controlled production, but labor was organizing for better wages and working conditions. By 1900, many governments had factory legislation and social-welfare programs. Mass living standards in core nations rose as population grew.

Large paintings of Karl Marx (1818–1883) on display in Tiananmen Square, Beijing, China.

Max Weber (1864–1920). Did Weber improve on Marx's view of stratification?

In today's capitalist world system the class division between owners and workers is now worldwide. However, publicly traded companies complicate the division between capitalists and workers in industrial nations. Through pension plans and personal investments, many American workers now have some proprietary interest in the means of production. They are part-owners rather than propertyless workers. The key difference is that the wealthy have *control* over these means. The key capitalist now is not the factory owner, who may have been replaced by thousands of stockholders, but the CEO or the chair of the board of directors, neither of whom may actually own the corporation.

Modern stratification systems aren't simple and dichotomous. They include (particularly in core and semiperiphery nations) a middle class of skilled and professional workers. Gerhard Lenski (1966) argues that social equality tends to increase in advanced industrial societies. The masses improve their access to economic benefits and political power. In Lenski's scheme, the shift of political power to the masses reflects the growth of the middle class, which reduces the polarization between owning and working classes. The proliferation of middle-class occupations creates opportunities for social mobility. The stratification system grows more complex (Giddens 1973).

Faulting Marx for an overly simple and exclusively economic view of stratification, Weber (1922/1968) defined three dimensions of social stratification: wealth (economic status), power (political status), and prestige (social status). Although, as Weber showed, wealth, power, and prestige are separate components of social ranking, they do tend to be correlated. Weber also believed that social identities based on ethnicity, religion, race, nationality, and other attributes could take priority over class (social identity based on economic status). In addition to class contrasts, the modern world system is cross-cut by status groups, such as ethnic and religious groups and nations (Shannon 1996). Class conflicts tend to occur within nations, and nationalism has prevented global class solidarity, particularly of proletarians.

Although the capitalist class dominates politically in most countries, growing wealth has made it easier for core nations to grant higher wages to their own citizens (Hopkins and Wallerstein 1982). However, the improvement in core workers' living standards wouldn't have occurred without the world system. The added surplus and cheaper labor that come from the semiperiphery and the periphery allow core capitalists to maintain their profits while satisfying the demands of core workers. In the periphery, wages and living standards are much lower. The current *world stratification system* features a substantial contrast between both capitalists and workers in the core nations and workers on the periphery.

Asian Factory Women

Nike, the world's leading manufacturer of athletic shoes, has relied heavily on Asian labor in shoe manufacture, which Nike subcontracts to factories in Vietnam, Indonesia, China, Thailand, and Pakistan. Most of the factory workers are women between the ages of 15 and 28. The practices of Nike's Asian subcontractors, and of Nike itself, have been questioned by international media, labor, and human rights groups. Publicity centered on the fact that the shoes were being produced by very cheap Asian labor, then being sold in North America for up to $100 a pair. A group of Vietnamese Americans organized to form a new NGO (nongovernmental organization), Vietnam Labor Watch. With Nike's cooperation, this group carried out a study of Nike's Vietnamese operations—eventually suggesting changes, which Nike and its subcontractors agreed to implement (see Figure 23.2).

FIGURE 23.2 Location of Vietnam and Malaysia.

BEYOND THE CLASSROOM

The Residue of Apartheid in Southern Africa

BACKGROUND INFORMATION

STUDENT:
Chanelle Mac Nab

SUPERVISING PROFESSOR:
Les Field

SCHOOL:
University of New Mexico

YEAR IN SCHOOL/MAJOR:
Senior/Anthropology (Ethnology)

FUTURE PLANS:
Graduate or medical school

PROJECT TITLE:
The Residue of Apartheid
in Southern Africa

Pay attention to the author's use of a personal perspective and personal vignettes in describing an experience abroad. How would you react in the author's situation? Are you surprised that the legacy of apartheid lingers in Southern Africa?

I spent six months in Botswana, Africa, on an international youth exchange program. I lived in six different villages and gained insight into the rural life of these pastoral people. During this time, I traveled to South Africa, Namibia, and Zimbabwe and witnessed varying degrees of racism. The color of my skin as a Caucasian allowed me to review both the white and black perspectives on racism.

Apartheid, which is an Afrikaans word that literally means "separateness," was a policy of racial segregation that was implemented in South Africa in 1948 when the Nationalist Party came to power. Apartheid resulted in one of the most unabashed forms of racism in the world.

Prior to going to southern Africa, like most of my American counterparts, I could see little good in the Afrikaners because of all the hate and violence they have bred. However, once I had lived in southern Africa, I realized that I too was passing judgment. In my own personal experience with Afrikaners, I found them to be quite opposite than their stereotypes had described them. To me they were a kindly and humane people, often giving me a ride, a meal, and a free place to stay. It is unfortunate that their view on race has separated them from the world. I had to stop blaming the whites for one moment and realize that the whites, like the blacks, are a product of their own cultural conditioning. They are victims of their own cultural constructions. Yes, the whites are capable of taking a new stance on racism. South Africa must move beyond their issues of race and strive for cohesion if they wish to build an equitable future for both whites and blacks in all of Africa.

Why did the supposed nonracial governments of the neighboring South African countries such as Botswana and Namibia also allow whites to come in and implement their racist laws? This answer lies in the history of Africa. Colonial powers drew lines across the African continent and divided it into pieces. With colonial rule controlling Africa throughout most of the 20th century, I assume that racism was adopted and implemented in all countries where whites were the minority in an effort to maintain power.

The greatest obstacle during my stay in Africa was overcoming the numerous confrontations I had with the whites in regards to race. Every day my own beliefs and cultural norms were being challenged by this unfamiliar culture. I had extensive conversations with whites and blacks about race. Here is a brief description of one of my journal entries.

August 14—Tonight I went with Rey (the Afrikaner who drove me from Namibia to Botswana) to the opening of the annual Agricultural Trade Fair . . . I am aware that apartheid ended only in 1994, and that, although apartheid is physically gone, it is latently present, but never did those words seem more real than tonight . . . As we drove into the fair grounds,

Vietnam Labor Watch confirmed that wages and working conditions were problematic. Across Asia, the wages paid to Nike workers averaged $1.84 per day. In Vietnam's Ho Chi Minh City, where the cost of three simple meals was $2.10 per day, Nike factory workers made only $1.60 per day. Health was also a concern, as was factory safety. Workers had to endure overheated factories with bad air filled with chemical smells of paint and glue.

Nike's young female workers, like those in the Malaysian electronics factories discussed in the chapter "Making a Living," had to wear uniforms. Adding to their regimentation was a military boot camp atmosphere. Workers were bullied, insulted, and subjected to harsh discipline. Workers were allowed only one toilet break and two chances to drink per eight hours. There were complaints of physical abuse and sexual harassment by male supervisors and insults by foreign supervisors (Koreans).

The Malaysian factory women previously described used spirit possession to vent their frustration over working conditions. Nike's Vietnamese workers did something more effective. They adopted labor union tactics, including strikes, work stoppages, and slowdowns. The Vietnamese workers also enlisted the support of NGOs, international labor organizations, and concerned Vietnamese Americans. Through such

they did not know who I was on the inside. Yes, I was white but I was not one of them . . . I felt guilty, as if I were betraying all of my black friends and my black host family . . . As hard as it was, I kept my calm and I told Rey I would never be able to see it the way he does because of my different upbringing. Rey admitted that perhaps his children's children would one day see it the way I do. As Rey and I left the party to go home, I dared him to go with me to the "other side" so that we could dance. He responded with two words: "I cannot." Our conversation ended and we drove home in silence.

Today, the ideology of racism has seeped across borders and across imaginary lines like an oil spill and is ever present throughout the world's social, political, and economic systems. It is important to understand that apartheid is not isolated in South Africa. Apartheid has permeated all of the borders of southern Africa. Hence, racism is not exclusively a South African problem.

This research has attempted to shed light on the serious issue of racism, with its emphasis on the continuing effects of the apartheid regime in southern Africa. I hope that more people will come to understand apartheid and use this knowledge to understand why racism denies and oppresses people all around the world.

South Africa's segregationist policy known as apartheid lasted from 1948 until 1994. This historical image shows a train station with separate windows for parcels and refreshments for white and nonwhite people.

I could see the silhouettes of hundreds of black people dancing against the dimness of the lantern lights. The loud African music was familiar to me . . . [I]nstead of continuing forward to where the blacks were, we took a sharp left turn to the white sector of the fair. The whites were standing around a fire drinking while their black servants stoked the fire and prepared the food. I was stunned to be standing on segregated soil. I could not believe that I was in Botswana and not in South Africa. Every moment that I was with the whites I felt uncomfortable . . . I could not identify with these people . . . I was furious underneath my skin because

efforts and actions they managed to improve their working conditions and salaries.

Open and Closed Class Systems

Inequalities, which are built into the structure of state societies, tend to persist across the generations. The extent to which they do or don't is a measure of the openness of the stratification system, the ease of social mobility it permits. Within the world capitalist economy, stratification has taken many forms, including caste, slavery, and class systems.

Caste systems are closed, hereditary systems of stratification that often are dictated by religion.

Hierarchical social status is ascribed at birth, so that people are locked into their parents' social position. Caste lines are clearly defined, and legal and religious sanctions are applied against those who seek to cross them.

The world's best-known caste system is associated with Hinduism in traditional India. As described by Gargan (1992), despite the formal abolition of the caste system in 1949, caste-based stratification remains important in modern India. An estimated 5 million adults and 10 million children are bonded laborers. These people live in complete servitude, working to repay real or imagined debts. Most of them are untouchables, impoverished and powerless people at the bottom of the

Slavery is the most extreme, coercive, and abusive form of legalized inequality. Although proletarians, such as these "white slaves of England," also lacked control over the means of production, they did have some control over where they worked. In what other ways do proletarians differ from slaves?

See your OLC Internet Exercises
mhhe.com/kottak

 STUDENT CD-ROM LIVING ANTHROPOLOGY

Globalization
Track 23

This clip draws parallels between the 1890s and today, mentioning advances in technology that took place through the discoveries and efforts of Bell, Edison, Carnegie, and Morgan. A century ago, laissez-faire economic policies allowed the barons of industry to increase profits and grow wealthy. The United States moved from semiperiphery to core. The clip mentions sweatshops, child labor, and low wages as the downside of capitalism. Today, transnational corporations increasingly operate internationally, beyond the boundaries of uniform national laws. This creates new business opportunities but also new legal, ethical, and moral challenges. What's the technological basis of the global village described in the clip? Because the world is so tightly integrated, the clip suggests that events in Asia can have immediate ripple effects in the West. Can you think of any examples?

caste hierarchy. Some families have been bonded for generations; people are born into servitude because their parents or grandparents were sold previously. Bonded workers toil unpaid in stone quarries, brick kilns, and rice paddies.

Another castelike system, *apartheid*, existed until recently in South Africa (see "Beyond the Classroom"). In that legally maintained hierarchy, blacks, whites, and Asians had their own separate (and unequal) neighborhoods, schools, laws, and punishments.

In **slavery,** the most inhumane and degrading form of stratification, people are treated as property. In the Atlantic slave trade, millions of human beings were treated as commodities. The plantation systems of the Caribbean, the southeastern United States, and Brazil were based on forced slave labor. Slaves lacked control over the means of production. They were like proletarians in this respect. But proletarians at least are legally free. Unlike slaves, they have some control over where they work, how much they work, for whom they work, and what they do with their wages. Slaves, in contrast, were forced to live and work at their master's whim. Defined as lesser human beings, slaves lacked legal rights. They could be sold and resold; their families, split apart. Slaves had nothing to sell—not even their own labor (Mintz 1985).

Slavery is the most extreme, coercive, and abusive form of legalized inequality.

Vertical mobility is an upward or downward change in a person's social status. A truly **open class system** would facilitate mobility. Individual achievement and personal merit would determine social rank. Hierarchical social statuses would be achieved on the basis of people's efforts. Ascribed statuses (family background, ethnicity, gender, religion) would be less important. Open class systems would have blurred class lines and a wide range of status positions.

Compared with nonindustrial states and contemporary peripheral and semiperipheral nations, core industrial nations tend to have more open class systems. Under industrialism, wealth is based to some extent on **income**—earnings from wages and salaries. Economists contrast such a return on labor with interest, dividends, rent, and profits, which are *returns on property* or capital.

THE WORLD SYSTEM TODAY

We will see in "Interesting Issues: The American Periphery" (pp. 542–543) that the world economy also can create peripheral regions within core nations, such as rural areas of the American South. World-system theory stresses the existence of a global culture. It emphasizes historic contacts, linkages, and power differentials between local people and international forces. The major forces influencing cultural interaction during the past 500 years have been commercial expansion, industrial capitalism, and the differential power of colonial and core nations (Wallerstein 1982, 2004b; Wolf 1982). As state formation had done

540 PART 4 The Changing World

Most Americans think they belong to, and claim identity with, the middle class, which they tend to perceive as a vast undifferentiated group. However, the American class system isn't as open or undifferentiated as most Americans assume it to be. There are substantial differences in income and wealth between the richest and the poorest Americans, and the gap is widening. According to U.S. Census data, from 1967 to 2000 the top (richest) fifth, or quintile, of American households increased their share of national income by 13.5 percent, while the shares of all the other quintiles fell. The percentage share of the lowest fifth fell most dramatically—17.6 percent. In 2003 the highest fifth of American households got about 48 percent of all national income, while the share of the lowest fifth was 4 percent. The richest fifth of American households, with a mean annual income of $141,621, had become 14 times wealthier than the poorest fifth, with a mean annual income of $10,188 (U.S. Census Bureau 2004), and the trend continues today. When we consider wealth (investments, property, possessions, etc.) rather than income, the contrast is even more striking: 1 percent of American families hold one-third of the nation's wealth (Calhoun, Light, and Keller 1997). Understanding ourselves means recognizing that our ideology about class doesn't accord with socioeconomic reality.

duce and in which market exchanges occur with profit as the primary motive (Bodley 2001).

After 1870, European business initiated a concerted search for markets in Asia, Africa, and other less-developed areas. This process led to European imperialism in Africa, Asia, and Oceania. **Imperialism** refers to a policy of extending the rule of a nation or empire, such as the British empire, over foreign nations and of taking and holding foreign colonies. *Colonialism* refers to the political, social, economic, and cultural domination of a territory and its people by a foreign power for an extended time. European imperial expansion was aided by improved transportation, which brought huge new areas within easy reach. Europeans also colonized vast areas of previously unsettled or sparsely settled lands in the interior of North and South America and Australia. The new colonies purchased masses of goods from the industrial centers and shipped back wheat, cotton, wool, mutton, beef, and leather. Thus began the second phase of colonialism (the first had been in the New World after Columbus) as European nations competed for colonies between 1875 and 1914, a process that helped cause World War I.

Industrialization spread to many other nations in a process that continues today (Table 23.1). By 1900, the United States had become a core nation within the world system. It had overtaken Great Britain in iron, coal, and cotton production. In a few decades (1868–1900), Japan changed from a medieval handicraft country to an industrial one, joining the semiperiphery by 1900 and moving to the core between 1945 and 1970. Figure 23.4 is a map showing the modern world system.

Twentieth-century industrialization added hundreds of new industries and millions of new jobs. Production increased, often beyond immediate demand. This spurred strategies such as advertising to sell everything that industry could churn out. Mass production gave rise to a culture of overconsumption, which valued acquisitiveness and conspicuous consumption (Veblen 1934). Industrialization entailed a shift from reliance on renewable resources to the use of fossil fuels, such

previously, industrialization accelerated local participation in larger networks. According to Bodley (2001), perpetual expansion (whether in population or consumption) is the distinguishing feature of industrial economic systems. Bands and tribes are small, self-sufficient, subsistence-based systems. Industrial economies, by contrast, are large, highly specialized systems in which local areas don't consume the products they pro-

TABLE 23.1 Ascent and Decline of Nations within the World System		
Periphery to Semiperiphery	**Semiperiphery to Core**	**Core to Semiperiphery**
United States (1800–1860)	United States (1860–1900)	Spain (1620–1700)
Japan (1868–1900)	Japan (1945–1970)	
Taiwan (1949–1980)	Germany (1870–1900)	
S. Korea (1953–1980)		

SOURCE: Thomas Richard Shannon, *An Introduction to the World-System Perspective,* 2nd ed. (Boulder, CO: Westview Press, 1996), p. 147.

The American Periphery

The effects of the world economy also can create peripheral regions within core nations, such as areas of the rural South in the United States. In a comparative study of two counties at opposite ends of Tennessee (Figure 23.3), Thomas Collins (1989) reviewed the effects of industrialization on poverty and unemployment. Hill County, with an Appalachian white population, is on the Cumberland Plateau in eastern Tennessee. Delta County, which is predominantly African American, is 60 miles from Memphis in western Tennessee's lower Mississippi region. Both counties once had economies based on agriculture and timber, but jobs in those sectors declined sharply with the advent of mechanization. Both counties have unemployment rates more than twice that of Tennessee as a whole. More than a third of the people in each county live below the poverty level. Such poverty pockets represent a slice of the world periphery within modern America. Given very restricted job opportunities, the best-educated local youths have migrated to northern cities for three generations.

To increase jobs, local officials and business leaders have tried to attract industries from outside. Their efforts exemplify a more general rural southern strategy, which began during the 1950s, of courting industry by advertising "a good business climate"—which means low rents, cheap utilities, and a nonunion labor pool. However, few firms are attracted to an impoverished and poorly educated work force. All the industries that have come to such areas have very limited market power and a narrow profit margin. Such firms

FIGURE 23.3 Location of Cumberland Plateau and Memphis Vicinity (Delta County) in Tennessee.

survive by offering low wages and minimal benefits, with frequent layoffs. These industries tend to emphasize traditional female skills such as sewing and mostly attract women.

The garment industry, which is highly mobile, is Hill County's main employer. The knowledge that a garment plant can be moved to another locale very rapidly tends to reduce employee demands. Management can be as arbitrary and authoritarian as it

wishes. The unemployment rate and low educational level ensure that many women will accept sewing jobs for a bit more than the minimum wage.

In neither county has new industry brought many jobs for men, who have a higher unemployment rate than do women (as do blacks, compared with whites). Collins found that many men in Hill County had never been permanently employed; they had just done temporary jobs, always for cash.

as oil. Energy from fossil fuels, which have been stored over millions of years, is being depleted rapidly to support a previously unknown and probably unsustainable level of consumption (Bodley 2001).

Table 23.2 compares energy consumption in various types of cultures. Americans are the world's foremost consumers of nonrenewable resources. In terms of energy consumption, the average American is about 35 times more expensive than the average forager or tribesperson. Since 1900, the United States has tripled its per capita energy use. It also has increased its total energy consumption 30-fold.

Table 23.3 compares energy consumption, per capita and total, in the United States and selected other countries. The United States represents 23.7 percent of the world's annual energy consumption, compared with China's 10.5 percent, but the average American consumes 10 times the energy

The effects of industrialization in Delta County have been similar. That county's recruitment efforts also have drawn only marginal industries. The largest is a bicycle seat and toy manufacturer, which employs 60 percent women. Three other large plants, which make clothing and auto seat covers, employ 95 percent women. Egg production was once significant in Delta County but folded when the market for eggs fell in response to rising national concern over the effects of cholesterol.

In both counties, the men, ignored by industrialization, maintain an informal economy. They sell and trade used goods through personal networks. They take casual jobs, such as operating farm equipment on a daily or seasonal basis. Collins found that maintaining an automobile was the most important and prestigious contribution these men made to their families. Neither county has public transportation; Hill County even lacks school buses. Families need cars to get women to work and kids to school. Men who keep an old car running longest get special respect.

Reduced opportunities for men to do well at work—to which American culture attributes great importance—lead to a feeling of lowered self-worth, which is expressed in physical violence. The rate of domestic violence in Hill County exceeds the state average. Spousal abuse arises from men's demands to control women's paychecks. (Men regard the cash they earn themselves as their own, to spend on male activities.)

One important difference between the two counties involves unionization. In Delta County, organizers have waged successful campaigns for unionization. Attitudes toward workers' rights in Tennessee correlate with race.

Poverty pockets of the rural South, illustrated by this scene from the Mississippi delta region, represent a slice of the world periphery within modern America. Through mechanization, industrialization, and other changes promoted by larger systems, local people have been deprived of land and jobs. Emigration of educated and talented locals continues as the opportunities shrink.

Rural southern whites usually don't vote for unions when they have a chance to do so, whereas African Americans are more likely to challenge management about pay and work rules. Local blacks view their work situation in terms of black against white rather than from a position of working-class solidarity. They are attracted to unions because they see only whites in managerial positions and resent differential advancement of white factory workers. One manager expressed to Collins that "once the work force of a plant becomes more than one-third black, you can expect to have union representation within a year" (Collins 1989, p. 10). Responding to this probability of unionization, core capitalists from Japan don't build plants in the primarily African American counties of the lower Mississippi. The state's Japanese

factories cluster in eastern and central Tennessee.

Poverty pockets of the rural South (and other regions) represent a slice of the world periphery within modern America. Through mechanization, industrialization, and the other changes promoted by larger systems, local people have been deprived of land and jobs. After years of industrial development, a third of the people of Hill and Delta counties remain below the poverty level. Emigration of educated and talented locals continues as the opportunities shrink. Collins concluded that rural poverty would not be reduced by attracting additional peripheral industries because these firms lack the market power to improve wages and benefits. Different development schemes are needed for these counties and the rural South generally.

used by the average Chinese, and 26 times the energy used by the average inhabitant of India.

Industrial Degradation

Industrialization and factory labor now characterize many societies in Latin America, Africa, the Pacific, and Asia. One effect of the spread of industrialization has been the destruction of indigenous economies, ecologies, and populations.

Two centuries ago, as industrialization was developing, 50 million people still lived beyond the periphery in politically independent bands, tribes, and chiefdoms. Occupying vast areas, those nonstate societies, although not totally isolated, were only marginally affected by nation-states and the world capitalist economy. In 1800 bands, tribes, and chiefdoms controlled half the globe and 20 percent of its population (Bodley, ed. 1988). Industrialization tipped the balance in favor of states.

Map Atlas

Map 16 shows the annual consumption of commercial energy per capita by country.

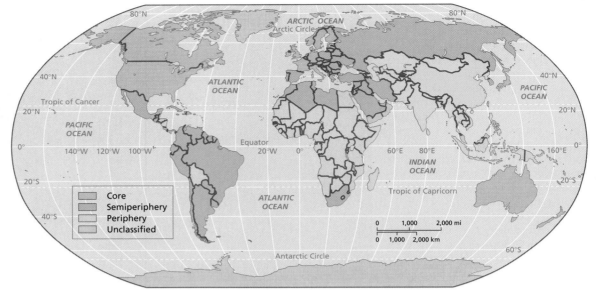

See the Interactive Exercise for a quiz on the world system in the past

mhhe.com/kottak

FIGURE 23.4 The World System in 2000.

TABLE 23.2 Energy Consumption in Various Contexts	
Type of Society	**Daily Kilocalories per Person**
Bands and tribes	4,000–12,000
Preindustrial states	26,000 (maximum)
Early industrial states	70,000
Americans in 1970	230,000
Americans in 1990	275,000

SOURCE: John H. Bodley, *Anthropology and Contemporary Human Problems* (Mountain View, CA: Mayfield, 1985).

TABLE 23.3 Energy Consumption in Selected Countries, 2002		
	Total	**Per capita**
World	411.2*	66**
United States	97.6	342
China	43.2	33
Russia	27.5	191
Germany	14.3	173
India	14.0	13
Canada	13.1	418
France	11.0	184
United Kingdom	9.6	162

*411.2 quadrillion (411,200,000,000,000,000) Btu.

**66 million Btu.

SOURCE: Based on data in *Statistical Abstract of the United States, 2004–2005* (Table 1367), and *Statistical Abstract of the United States, 2003* (Table 1365).

◼ *Copsa Mica, Romania, may well be the world's most polluted city. A factory belches out smoke that leaves its mark on these boys' faces, food, and lungs. What's the term for such environmental devastation?*

As industrial states have conquered, annexed, and "developed" nonstates, there has been genocide on a grand scale. *Genocide* refers to a deliberate policy of exterminating a group through warfare or murder. Examples include the Holocaust, Rwanda in 1994, and Bosnia, as discussed in the chapter "Ethnicity and Race." Bodley (1988) estimates that an average of 250,000 indigenous people perished annually between 1800 and 1950. Besides warfare, the causes included foreign diseases (to which natives lacked resistance), slavery, land grabbing, and other forms of dispossession and impoverishment.

Many native groups have been incorporated within nation-states, in which they have become ethnic minorities. Some such groups have been able to recoup their population. Many indigenous peoples survive and maintain their ethnic identity despite having lost their ancestral cultures to varying degrees (partial ethnocide). And many descendants of tribespeople live on as culturally distinct and self-conscious colonized peoples, many of whom aspire to autonomy. As the original inhabitants of their territories, they are called **indigenous peoples** (see Maybury-Lewis 2002).

Around the world many contemporary nations are repeating—at an accelerated rate—the process of resource depletion that started in Europe and the United States during the Industrial Revolution. Fortunately, however, today's world has some environmental watchdogs that did not exist during the first centuries of the Industrial Revolution. Given national and international cooperation and sanctions, the modern world may benefit from the lessons of the past.

See your OLC Internet Exercises for more on indigenous peoples
mhhe.com/kottak

SUMMARY

1. Local societies increasingly participate in wider systems—regional, national, and global. Columbus's voyages opened the way for a major and continuing exchange between the Old and New Worlds. Seventeenth-century plantation economies in the Caribbean and Brazil were based on sugar. In the 18th century, plantation economies based on cotton arose in the southeastern United States.

2. The capitalist world economy is based on production for sale, with the goal of maximizing profits. World capitalism has political and economic specialization based on three positions. Core, semiperiphery, and periphery have existed since the 16th century, although the particular countries filling these niches have changed.

3. The Industrial Revolution began around 1750. Transoceanic trade and commerce supplied capital for industrial investment. Industrialism began in England rather than in France because French industry could grow through expansion of the domestic system. England, with fewer people, had to industrialize.

4. Industrialization hastened the separation of workers from the means of production. Marx saw stratification as a sharp division between the bourgeoisie (capitalists) and the proletariat (propertyless workers). Class consciousness was a key part of Marx's view of class. Weber believed that social solidarity based on ethnicity, religion, race, or nationality could take priority over class.

Today's capitalist world system maintains the contrast between those who own the means of production and those who don't, but the division is now worldwide. Modern stratification systems also include a middle class of skilled and professional workers.

5. Nationalism has prevented global class solidarity. There is a substantial contrast between capitalists and workers in the core nations and workers on the periphery. The extent to which inequalities persist across the generations is a measure of the openness of the class system, the ease of social mobility it permits. Under world capitalism, stratification has taken many forms, including caste, slavery, and class systems.

6. The major forces influencing cultural interaction during the past 500 years have been commercial expansion and industrial capitalism. In the 19th century, industrialization spread to Belgium, France, Germany, and the United States. After 1870, businesses began a concerted search for more secure markets. This process led to European imperialism in Africa, Asia, and Oceania.

7. By 1900 the United States had become a core nation. Mass production gave rise to a culture that valued acquisitiveness and conspicuous consumption. One effect of industrialization has been the destruction of indigenous economies, ecologies, and populations. Two centuries ago, 50 million people lived in independent bands, tribes, and chiefdoms. Industrialization tipped the balance in favor of states.

KEY TERMS

bourgeoisie One of Marx's opposed classes; owners of the means of production (factories, mines, large farms, and other sources of subsistence).

capital Wealth or resources invested in business, with the intent of producing a profit.

capitalist world economy The single world system, which emerged in the 16th century, committed to production for sale, with the object of maximizing profits rather than supplying domestic needs.

caste system Closed, hereditary system of stratification, often dictated by religion; hierarchical social status is ascribed at birth, so that people are locked into their parents' social position.

core Dominant structural position in the world system; consists of the strongest and most powerful states with advanced systems of production.

imperialism A policy of extending the rule of a nation or empire over foreign nations or of taking and holding foreign colonies.

See the flash cards
mhhe.com/kottak

income   Earnings from wages and salaries.

indigenous peoples   The original inhabitants of particular territories; often descendants of tribespeople who live on as culturally distinct colonized peoples, many of whom aspire to autonomy.

Industrial Revolution   The historic transformation (in Europe, after 1750) of "traditional" into "modern" societies through industrialization of the economy.

open class system   Stratification system that facilitates social mobility, with individual achievement and personal merit determining social rank.

periphery   Weakest structural position in the world system.

semiperiphery   Structural position in the world system intermediate between core and periphery.

slavery   The most extreme, coercive, abusive, and inhumane form of legalized inequality; people are treated as property.

vertical mobility   Upward or downward change in a person's social status.

working class   Or proletariat; those who must sell their labor to survive; the antithesis of the bourgeoisie in Marx's class analysis.

CRITICAL THINKING QUESTIONS

For more self-testing, see the self-quizzes

mhhe.com/kottak

1. According to world-system theory, societies are subsystems of bigger systems, with the world system as the largest. What are the various systems, at different levels, in which you participate?

2. Give two examples each of core, semiperiphery, and periphery nations. Does any nation seem poised to move from one slot to another, such as semiperiphery to core, or vice versa? What's the last nation to make such a move?

3. How has social stratification in industrial societies changed over time? Think of comparing London of the 1850s (the era of Dickens and Marx) and today.

4. How did the views of Marx and Weber on stratification differ? Which approach makes the most sense to you? Why?

5. How open is the class system of your society? Describe what's open and what's closed about it.

SUGGESTED ADDITIONAL READINGS

Abu-Lughod, J. L.
   1989   *Before European Hegemony: The World System A. D. 1250–1350.* New York: Oxford University Press. Regional economies and politics before the age of European exploration and the capitalist world economy.

Arrighi, G.
   1994   *The Long Twentieth Century: Money, Power, and the Origins of Our Times.* New York: Verso. How core nations control finance and power in the modern world system.

Braudel, F.
   1973   *Capitalism and Material Life: 1400–1800.* London: Fontana. The role of the masses in the history of capitalism.
   1992   *Civilization and Capitalism, 15th–18th Century.* Volume III: The Perspective of the World. Berkeley: University of California Press. On the emergence of the world capitalist economy; case histories of European countries and various areas of the rest of the world.

Crosby, A. W., Jr.
   2003   *The Columbian Exchange: Biological and Cultural Consequences of 1492.* Westport, CT: Praeger. Describes how Columbus's voyages opened the way for a major exchange of people, resources, and ideas as the Old and New Worlds were forever joined together.

Diamond, J. M.
   1997   *Guns, Germs, and Steel: The Fates of Human Societies.* New York: W. W. Norton. An ecological approach to expansion and conquest in world history.

Fagan, B. M.
   1998   *Clash of Cultures,* 2nd ed. Walnut Creek, CA: AltaMira. Culture conflicts during European territorial expansion.

Kardulias, P. N.
   1999   *World-Systems Theory in Practice: Leadership, Production, and Exchange.* Lanham, MD: Rowman and Littlefield. Social systems, social change, and economic history in the context of world-system theory.

Kearney, M.
   2004   *Changing Fields of Anthropology: From Local to Global.* Lanham, MD: Rowman and Littlefield. Globalization from a Mexican perspective.

Mintz, S. W.
   1985   *Sweetness and Power: The Place of Sugar in Modern History.* New York: Viking Penguin. The place of sugar in the formation of the modern world system.

Shannon, T. R.
   1996   *An Introduction to the World-System Perspective,* 2nd ed. Boulder, CO: Westview Press. Useful review of world-system theory and developments.

Wallerstein, I. M.
   2004a   *The Decline of American Power: The U.S. in a Chaotic World.* New York: New Press. The reasons behind what Wallerstein sees as a coming U.S. decline within the world system of the 21st century.
   2004b   *World-Systems Analysis: An Introduction.* Durham, NC: Duke University Press. Basics of world-system theory from the master of that approach.

Wolf, E. R.

   1982 *Europe and the People without History.* Berkeley: University of California Press. An anthropologist examines the effects of European expansion on tribal peoples and sets forth a world-system approach to anthropology.

Wolf, E. R., with S. Silverman

   2001 *Pathways of Power: Building an Anthropology of the Modern World.* Berkeley: University of California Press. Political anthropology for the modern world, a comparative approach.

INTERNET EXERCISES

1. Read the page titled "Life of the Industrial Workers in Nineteenth-Century Britain" by Laura Del Col (**http://www.victorianweb.org/history/workers2.html**). The page contains excerpts from a report generated by a parliamentary panel charged with investigating conditions in British factories.
   a. What were conditions like for workers? What were their lives like? Their work? What were their expectations?
   b. What were the conditions like for children?
   c. In what way are these life stories different from those which might have been told 100 or 200 years earlier in preindustrial Britain?
   d. How are these conditions different from today's Britain? Are there areas of the world where workers might identify with these accounts?
2. Go to the United Nation's Human Development Report (HDR) website: **http://hdr.undp.org/statistics/data/**. At this site you have access to all sorts of data on the countries of the world, which you can retrieve by country, by indicator, or by data tables in the order they were published in the printed version of the HDR. Click on "Data by indicator." Click on "GDP per capita, in US$."

   a. View the countries in terms of their per capita GDP (gross domestic product) in 2002 (right-hand column). Which country has the highest GDP per capita? How do the Arab States compare with the least-developed countries in terms of GDP per capita (see bottom of table)? How about with the United States?
   b. Go back to the home site and click on the "Human Development and Income Growth" animation. Click on "next" at the bottom and view the three dimensions on which the Human Development Index (HDI) is based. What are they?
   c. Go back to the home site and click on "Data by country." Click on "Malaysia, data." How does Malaysia rank on the human poverty index (HPI)? Has Malaysia's Human Development Index been rising or falling since 1975?
   d. Go back to the home site and view data on three countries and indicators of your choice. Compare the three countries in terms of three key indicators.

See Chapter 23 at your McGraw-Hill Online Learning Center for additional review and interactive exercises.

LINKAGES

Kottak, *Assault on Paradise*, 4th ed.

When Conrad Kottak revisited Arembepe in 1980, major and dramatic transformations were evident. Three economic changes had enmeshed Arembepe much more strongly in the Brazilian nation and the world capitalist economy: (1) changes in the fishing industry, from wind power to motors, (2) the opening of a paved highway and the rise of tourism, attracting people from all over the world, (3) the construction of a nearby factory and the resulting chemical pollution of Arembepe's waters. Read Chapter 8 and describe how these changes influenced Arembepe's economy and its pattern of socioeconomic stratification.

Peters-Golden, *Culture Sketches*, 4th ed.

This text chapter has discussed consequences of the spread of the industrial world system. Many foraging societies find their ways of life threatened. Two or three decades ago, the Ju/'hoansi maintained much more traditional lifestyles. They now find themselves fully drawn into a market economy, affected not only by institutions like schools and hospitals, but also by militarization, civil war, sedentism, resettlement, and governmental control. In *Culture Sketches* read Chapter 6, "Ju/'hoansi: Reciprocity and Sharing." Which effects of the modern world system are demonstrated in contemporary Ju/'hoansi life? The Ju/'hoansi tradition is one of egalitarianism and reciprocity. It is reported that the Dobe Ju/'hoansi still hold those values above all else. Do you think they can integrate their belief that no one should be denied the necessities of life with the demands of their modern situation? Why or why not?

Knauft, *The Gebusi*, 1st ed.

Read Chapter 7 and the conclusion. Based on Chapter 7, what influences of the modern world system had impacted Gebusi by 1998? How have these changes influenced Gebusi material aspirations? How have they influenced patterns of dominance between outsiders and Gebusi? Based on the conclusion, do you think the Gebusi's history of interaction with the modern world system has been fortunate or not compared with most other non-Western peoples? Why or why not?

24

Colonialism and Development

COLONIALISM

In the last chapter, we saw that after 1870, Europe began a concerted search for markets in Asia and Africa. That process led to European imperialism in Africa, Asia, and Oceania. Imperialism refers to a policy of extending the rule of a nation or empire, such as the British empire, over foreign nations and of taking and holding foreign colonies. **Colonialism** refers to the political, social, economic, and cultural domination of a territory and its people by a foreign power for an extended period of time. The influence of colonialism doesn't disappear just because formal independence has been granted.

OVERVIEW

Imperialism is the policy of extending the rule of a nation or empire over other nations. Colonialism is the long-term domination of a territory and its people by a foreign power. European colonialism had two broad phases. The first spanned the period from 1492 to 1825. The second, more imperialistic, phase ran from 1850 to just after the end of World War II. The British and French colonial empires reached their height around 1914.

Like colonialism, economic development has an intervention philosophy—an ideological justification for outsiders to lead—usually based on the assumption that particular social or economic models are beneficial and universally applicable. Development anthropology focuses on social issues in, and the cultural dimension of, economic development. Culturally compatible and successful development projects try to change just enough, not too much. Motives to change come from people's traditional culture and the small concerns of everyday life. The most productive strategy for change is to base the social design for innovation on traditional social forms in each affected area.

Imperialism

Imperialism goes back to early states, including Egypt in the Old World and the Incas in the New. A Greek empire was forged by Alexander the Great, and Julius Caesar and his successors spread the Roman empire. The term also has been used for more recent examples, including the British, French, and Soviet empires (Scheinman 1980).

If imperialism is almost as old as the state itself, colonialism can be traced back to the ancient Phoenicians, who established colonies along the eastern Mediterranean by 3,000 years

For a quiz on colonies throughout history, see the Interactive Exercise

mhhe.com/kottak

ago. The ancient Greeks and Romans were avid colonizers, as well as empire builders. Modern colonialism began with the European "Age of Discovery"—of the Americas and of a sea route to the Far East. After 1492, European states started founding colonies abroad. In South America, Portugal gained rule over Brazil. The Spanish, the original conquerors of the Aztecs and the Incas, explored the New World widely. They looked to the Caribbean, Mexico, and the southern portions of what was to become the United States, as well as colonizing in Central and South America. In what is now Latin America, especially in areas that had indigenous chiefdoms (e.g., Colombia and Venezuela) and states (e.g., Mexico, Guatemala, Peru, and Bolivia), native populations were large and dense. Today's Latin American population still reflects the intermingling of peoples and cultures during the first phase of colonialism. North of Mexico, indigenous populations were smaller and sparser. Such intermingling is less marked in the United States and Canada than in Latin America.

Rebellions and wars aimed at independence for American nations ended the first phase of European colonialism by the early 19th century. Brazil's independence from Portugal was declared in 1822. By 1825, most of Spain's colonies were politically independent. Spain held on to Cuba and the Philippines until 1898, but otherwise withdrew from the colonial field.

British Colonialism

At its peak about 1914, the British empire covered a fifth of the world's land surface and ruled a fourth of its population (see Figure 24.1). Like several other European nations, Britain had two

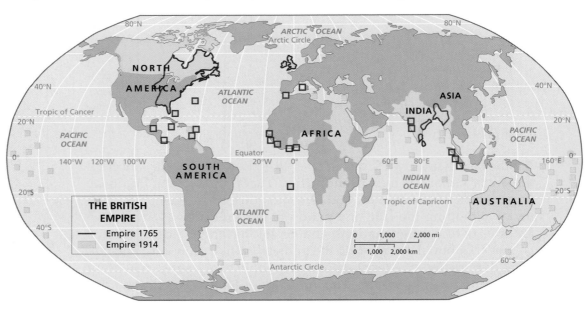

FIGURE 24.1 Map of the British Empire in 1765 and 1914. SOURCE: *Academic American Encyclopedia*, Vol. 3 (Danbury, CT: Grolier, 1998), p. 496.

See your OLC Internet Exercises for more on the British colonization of the Americas

mhhe.com/kottak

Prediction Tool Puts Development in Hands of Locals

NATIONAL GEOGRAPHIC NEWS BRIEF

by John Roach
March 24, 2004

For Indonesia's poorest province, Papua, on the island of New Guinea, conservationists have introduced an innovative software program designed to assist local people in guiding their homeland toward sustainable development. The program allows local people to make informed judgments, based on anticipation and discussion of the likely effects of their decisions on their communities. Development anthropologists assume that motives to change come from people's traditional culture and the small concerns of everyday life. The software discussed here inputs cultural, social, and environmental, as well as economic, data in modeling potential development. This approach is unlike traditional economic development, which, like colonialism, has typically tried to impose an outsider's vision or blueprint, based on a particular intervention philosophy, on local people.

Indonesia's poorest province, Papua, is a natural-resource trove that is both awaiting exploitation and begging for protection. Conservationists hope an innovative software program will help

residents guide the province to sustainable development. The program essentially allows local people to predict the effects of their civic decisions . . . on their communities.

"Papua significantly contributes to Indonesia's status as one of the biologically richest countries in the world," said Dessy Anggraeni, a resource economist in Indonesia with the Washington, D.C.-based environmental organization Conservation International (CI). "But its people are also among the poorest in Indonesia." . . .

To many people, Papua's lush forests of old-growth timber, latent precious metals, and untapped reserves of oil and natural gas are the answer to the province's poverty woes. But environmentalists have long argued against large-scale resource extraction, saying it benefits big, multinational corporations and leaves locals impoverished.

To determine if there is a way to alleviate the poverty of Papuans without irreparably harming the environment, CI has brought a planning tool, called Threshold 21, to Papua. The tool is a computerized development model that helps stakeholders and decision makers create and analyze strategies for the future.

"It won't predict the future, but it's the best way of getting a consistent idea of where things will lead," said John Shilling, a senior advisor with the Millennium Institute in Arlington, Virginia. With his colleagues, Shilling has worked over the past 20 years to develop the model.

Already customized for more than 15 different countries and regions around the world, CI recently asked the Millennium Institute to develop a version of Threshold 21 for Papua. Ultimately, CI hopes that Papuans will take control of the model and use it to chart their own course . . .

A deciding factor in CI's choice of Threshold 21 was the model's embrace of environmental and social factors in addition to economic factors as it analyzes any given strategy for the future.

The result of this integrated, three-pillar approach creates what the Millennium Institute says is a more "comprehensive" picture of what happens when one path is chosen over another. And that picture comes with all the details of how it was put together, a concept referred to as transparency.

For example, a local group in Bangladesh wanted to limit education to only men. So, using Threshold 21, they theoretically took women out of the schools and ran the computer program to find out what would happen. Shilling said that some things, like a reduction in gross domestic product and higher fertility rates, were predictable outcomes. But the local group was surprised to learn that by taking women out of the schools, male life expectancy went down. Since the model is transparent, they tracked back to find out why.

■ *Of various development scenarios, an urban development plan did the most to reduce poverty while also protecting the environment. These Papuan women are returning from a market town.*

"It turns out that women are significant health care providers," Shilling said. "If they are not educated, the health of the whole family declines." . . .

In the case of the model being developed for Papua, CI has a vision of poverty reduction and economic development for the local people. At the same time, they want to protect the environment, a goal the organization says is consistent with the challenges faced by the province's decentralized government . . .

The modelers solicit information from as many local everyday people and decision-makers as possible—specific data on the economy, the social structure, and the environment. With the data, the modelers prep the computer program to model the impact of strategies for future development.

"It is using the best information available," Shilling said. "It lays out a range of plausible scenarios

and their implications so decision-makers have the best estimates on which to make their decisions. And it is transparent about the assumptions and the positive and negative outcomes." . . .

CI chose four widely discussed development strategies for Papua to run through the model as a means to demonstrate the model's effectiveness: keeping the status quo, a major roadbuilding and logging initiative, a major dambuilding and mining initiative, and a locally focused urban development initiative.

According to CI's analysis of the outcomes, the urban development initiative proved the best at providing poverty alleviation as well as protecting the environment, whereas the other scenarios led to greater environmental degradation with most of the money from resource extraction going to foreign investors and foreign workers.

Anggraeni said the goal of running the scenarios was not meant to dictate specific development paths. The goal was to impart this approach and method to local planners and other residents. Then they could use the approach to analyze the effects of several widely discussed scenarios and come up with their own agreed strategy. Feedback from the two workshops held so far suggests CI's plan is working.

"Indeed, most of the participants are really enthusiastic to discuss the results of the model and the model itself," Anggraeni said.

___

SOURCE: John Roach, "Prediction Tool Puts Development in Hands of Locals," *National Geographic News,* March 24, 2004. National Geographic Society. http://news.nationalgeographic.com/news/2004/03/0324_040324_indonesia.html.

---

stages of colonialism. The first began with the Elizabethan voyages of the 16th century. During the seventeenth century, Britain acquired most of the eastern coast of North America, Canada's St. Lawrence basin, islands in the Caribbean, slave stations in Africa, and interests in India.

The British shared the exploration of the New World with the Spanish, Portuguese, French, and Dutch. The British by and large left Mexico, along with Central and South America, to the Spanish and the Portuguese. The end of the Seven Years' War in 1763 forced a French retreat from most of Canada and India, where France had previously competed with Britain (Cody 1998; Farr 1980).

The American revolution ended the first stage of British colonialism. A second colonial empire, on which the "sun never set," rose from the ashes of the first. Beginning in 1788, but intensifying after 1815, the British settled Australia. Britain had acquired Dutch South Africa by 1815. The establishment of Singapore in 1819 provided a base for a British trade network that extended to much of South Asia and along the coast of China. By this time, the empires of Britain's traditional rivals, particularly Spain, had been severely diminished in scope. Britain's position as imperial power and the world's leading industrial nation was unchallenged (Cody 1998; Farr 1980).

During the Victorian era (1837–1901), as Britain's acquisition of territory and of further trading concessions continued, Prime Minister Benjamin Disraeli implemented a foreign policy justified by a view of imperialism as shouldering "the white man's burden"—a phrase coined by the poet Rudyard Kipling. People in the empire were seen as unable to govern themselves, so that British guidance was needed to civilize and Christianize them. This paternalistic and racist doctrine served to legitimize Britain's acquisition and control of parts of central Africa and Asia (Cody 1998).

After World War II, the British empire began to fall apart, with nationalist movements for independence. India became independent in 1947, as did Ireland in 1949. Decolonization in Africa and Asia accelerated during the late 1950s. Today, the ties that remain between Britain and its former colonies are mainly linguistic or cultural rather than political (Cody 1998).

French Colonialism

French colonialism also had two phases. The first began in the early 1600s. The second came late in the 19th century. This was the French manifestation of a more general European imperialism that

Bringing It All Together

See the "Bringing It All Together" essay that immediately follows the chapter "Language and Communication" for information on Canada's Anglo-French heritage.

followed the spread of industrialization and the search for new markets, raw materials, and cheap labor. However, compared with Great Britain, where the drive for profit led expansion, French colonialism was spurred more by the state, church, and armed forces than by business interests. Prior to the French Revolution, in 1789, missionaries, explorers, and traders had led French expansion. They carved niches for France in Canada, the Louisiana territory, and several Caribbean islands, along with parts of India, which were lost, along with Canada (New France), to Great Britain in 1763. By 1815, only West Indian sugar islands and scattered African and Asian posts remained under French control (Harvey 1980).

The foundations of the second French empire were established between 1830 and 1870. France acquired Algeria and part of what eventually became Indochina. Like Britain, France rode a post-1870 wave of new imperialism. By 1914, the French empire covered 4 million square miles and included some 60 million people (see Figure 24.2). By 1893, French rule had been fully established in Indochina, and Tunisia and Morocco became French protectorates (Harvey 1980).

To be sure, the French, like the British, had substantial business interests in their colonies. But they also sought, again like the British, international glory and prestige. The French intervention philosophy was that of a *mission civilisatrice*, their equivalent of Britain's "white man's burden." The goal was to implant French culture, language, and religion—in the form of Roman Catholicism—throughout the colonies (Harvey 1980).

The French used two forms of colonial rule. They used *indirect rule*, governing through native leaders and established political structures, in

areas with long histories of state organization, such as Morocco and Tunisia. They brought *direct rule* by French officials to many areas of Africa. Here, the French imposed new government structures to control diverse tribes and cultures, many of them previously stateless. Like the British empire, the French empire began to disintegrate after World War II. France fought long—and ultimately futile—wars to keep its empire intact in Indochina and Algeria (Harvey 1980).

On January 1, 1900 a British officer in India receives a pedicure from a servant. What does this photo say to you about colonialism? Who gives pedicures in your society?

Colonialism and Identity

Many geopolitical labels in the news today had no equivalent meaning before colonialism. Whole countries, along with social groups and divisions

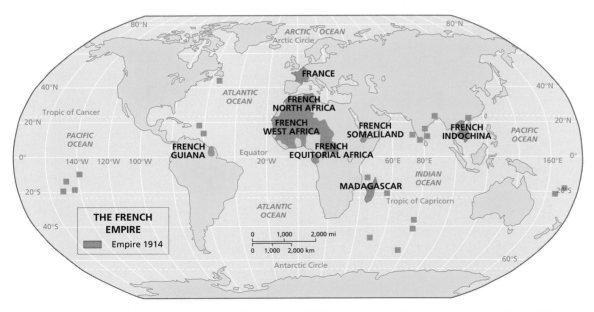

FIGURE 24.2 Map of the French Empire at Its Height around 1914. SOURCE: *Academic American Encyclopedia*, Vol. 8 (Danbury, CT: Grolier, 1998), p. 309.

within them, were colonial inventions. In West Africa, for example, by geographic logic, several adjacent countries could be one (Togo, Ghana, Côte d'Ivoire, Guinea, Guinea-Bissau, Sierra Leone, Liberia) (Figure 24.3). Instead, they are ✗ separated by linguistic, political, and economic contrasts promoted under colonialism.

Hundreds of ethnic groups and "tribes" are colonial constructions (see Ranger 1996). The Sukuma of Tanzania, for instance, were first registered as a single tribe by the colonial administration. Then missionaries standardized a series of dialects into a single Sukuma language as they translated the Bible and other religious texts. Thereafter, those texts were taught in missionary schools, and to European foreigners and other non-Sukuma speakers. Over time, this standardized the Sukuma language and ethnicity (Finnstrom 1997).

As in much of East Africa, in Rwanda and Burundi, farmers and herders live in the same areas and speak the same language. Historically, they have shared the same social world, although their social organization is "extremely hierarchical," almost "castelike" (Malkki 1995, p. 24). There has been a tendency to see the pastoral Tutsis as superior to the agricultural Hutus. Tutsis have been presented as nobles, Hutus as commoners. Yet when distributing identity cards in Rwanda, the Belgian colonizers simply identified all people with more than 10 head of cattle as Tutsi. Owners of fewer cattle were registered as Hutus (Bjuremalm 1997). Years later, these arbitrary colonial registers were used systematically for "ethnic" identification during the mass killings (genocide) that took place in Rwanda in 1994.

Postcolonial Studies

In anthropology, history, and literature, the field of postcolonial studies has gained prominence since the 1970s (see Ashcroft, Griffiths, and Tiffin 1989; Cooper and Stoler, eds. 1997). **Postcolonial** refers to the study of the interactions between European nations and the societies they colonized (mainly after 1800). In 1914, European empires, which broke up after World War II, ruled more than 85 percent of the world (Petraglia-Bahri 1996). The term *postcolonial* also has been used to describe the second half of the 20th century in general, the period succeeding colonialism. Even more generically, "postcolonial" may be used to signify a position against imperialism and Eurocentrism (Petraglia-Bahri 1996).

The former colonies (*postcolonies*) can be divided into settler, nonsettler, and mixed (Petraglia-Bahri 1996). The settler countries, with large numbers of European colonists and sparser native populations, include Australia and Canada. Examples of nonsettler countries include India, Pakistan, Bangladash, Sri Lanka, Malaysia, Indonesia, Nigeria, Senegal, Madagascar, and Jamaica. All these had substantial native populations and relatively few European settlers. Mixed countries include South Africa, Zimbabwe, Kenya (photo on page 555), and Algeria. Such countries had significant European settlement despite having sizable native populations.

FIGURE 24.3 Small West African Nations Created by Colonialism.

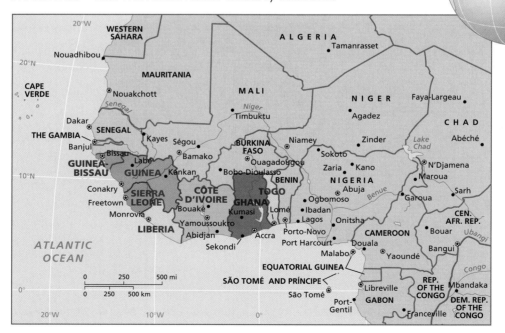

Given the varied experiences of such countries, "postcolonial" has to be a loose term. The United States, for instance, was colonized by Europeans and fought a war for independence from Britain. Is the United States a postcolony? It isn't usually perceived as such, given its current world power position, its treatment of native Americans (sometimes called internal colonization), and its annexation of other parts of the world (Petraglia-Bahri 1996). Research in postcolonial studies is growing, permitting a wide-ranging investigation of power relations in varied contexts. Broad topics in the field include the formation of an empire, the impact of colonization, and the state of the post-colony today (Petraglia-Bahri 1996).

Here are some common questions addressed in postcolonial studies: How did colonization affect colonized people—and their colonizers? How did colonial powers manage to subjugate so much of the world? How did people in the colonies resist colonial control? How have cultures and identities been affected by colonization? How do gender, race, and class function in colonial and postcolonial settings? How have colonial education systems influenced the postcolonies? With regard to literature, should postcolonial writers use a colonial language, like English or French, to reach a wider audience? Or should they write in their native language, to reach others in the postcolony? Finally, are new forms of imperialism, such as development and globalization, replacing old ones? (Petraglia-Bahri 1996).

DEVELOPMENT

During the Industrial Revolution, a strong current of thought viewed industrialization as a beneficial process of organic development and progress. Many economists still assume that industrialization increases production and income. They seek to create in Third World ("developing") countries a process—*economic development*—like the one that first occurred spontaneously in 18th-century Great Britain. Economic development generally aims at getting people to convert from subsistence to cash economies and thus to increase local participation in the world capitalist economy.

We just saw that Great Britain used the "white man's burden" to justify its imperialist expansion. Similarly, France claimed to be involved in a *mission civilisatrice*, a civilizing mission, in its colonies. Both of these ideas illustrate an **intervention philosophy,** an ideological justification for outsiders to guide in specific directions. Economic development plans also have intervention philosophies. John Bodley (1988) argues that the basic belief behind interventions—whether by colonialists, missionaries, governments, or development planners—has been the same for more

What traces of colonialism do you detect in this photo, taken recently at the Jockey Club in Nairobi, Kenya? What story is the photo telling you?

than 100 years. This belief is that industrialization, modernization, westernization, and individualism are desirable evolutionary advances and that development schemes that promote them will bring long-term benefits to local people. In a more extreme form, intervention philosophy may pit the assumed wisdom of enlightened colonial or other First World planners against the purported conservatism, ignorance, or "obsolescence" of "inferior" local people.

Neoliberalism

A recent and dominant intervention philosophy is neoliberalism. The term encompasses a set of assumptions and economic policies that have become widespread during the last 25 to 30 years and that are being implemented in capitalist and developing nations, including postsocialist societies. Neoliberalism is a new form of the old economic liberalism laid out in Adam Smith's famous capitalist manifesto, *The Wealth of Nations,* published in 1776, soon after the Industrial Revolution. Smith advocated laissez-faire economics as the basis of capitalism: The government should stay out of its nation's economic affairs. Free trade, Smith thought, was the best way for a nation's economy to develop. There should be no restrictions on manufacturing, no barriers to commerce, and no tariffs. Such ideas were "liberal" in the sense of advocating no controls. Economic liberalism encouraged "free" enterprise and competition, with the goal of generating profits. (Note the difference between this meaning of *liberal* and the one that has been popularized on American talk radio, in which "liberal" is used—usually as a derogatory term—as the opposite of "conservative." Ironically, Adam Smith's liberalism is today's capitalist "conservatism.")

For more on development efforts, see the Virtual Exploration

mhhe.com/kottak

Economic liberalism prevailed in the United States until President Franklin Roosevelt's New Deal during the 1930s. The Great Depression produced a turn to Keynesian economics, which challenged liberalism. John Maynard Keynes (1927, 1936) insisted that full employment was necessary for capitalism to grow, that governments and central banks should intervene to increase employment, and that government should promote the common good.

Especially since the fall of Communism (1989–1991), there has been a revival of economic liberalism, now known as neoliberalism, which has been spreading globally. Around the world, neoliberal policies have been imposed by powerful financial institutions such as the International Monetary Fund (IMF), the World Bank, and the Inter-American Development Bank (see Edelman and Haugerud 2004). In many developing countries, corruption in state-controlled industries has been an overwhelming problem, and free markets have been seen as a way out.

Neoliberalism differs little from Adam Smith's original idea that governments should not regulate private enterprise and market forces. Neoliberalism entails open (tariff and barrier free) international trade and investment. Profits are sought through lowering of costs, whether through improved productivity, laying off workers, or seeking workers who accept lower wages. To obtain loans, the governments of postsocialist and developing nations have been required to accept the neoliberal premise that deregulation leads to economic growth, which eventually will benefit everyone through a process sometimes called "trickle down." Accompanying the belief in free markets and the idea of cutting costs is a tendency to impose austerity measures that cut government expenses. This means reduced public spending on education, health care, and other social services (Martinez and Garcia 2000). Throughout the world, neoliberal policies have promoted deregulation and privatization—the sale to private investors of state-owned enterprises, such as banks, key industries, railroads, toll highways, utilities, schools, hospitals, and even fresh water. With its characteristic capitalist focus on individualism, neoliberalism places more emphasis on "individual responsibility" than on "the common good." The effects of neoliberal policies vary among countries. In some nations, social programs are negligible to begin with, and health care benefits go mainly to the elites.

THE SECOND WORLD

Remember from the chapter "Ethnicity and Race" that the labels "First World," "Second World," and "Third World" represent a com-

mon, although ethnocentric, way of categorizing nations. *First World* refers to the "democratic West"—traditionally conceived as being in opposition to a "Second World" ruled by "communism." *Second World* refers to the Warsaw Pact nations, including the former Soviet Union and the socialist and once-socialist countries of Eastern Europe and Asia. Proceeding with this classification, the "less-developed countries" or "developing nations" make up the *Third World*, to which we turn after a discussion of Communism and its fall.

Communism

The two meanings of communism involve how it is written, whether with a lowercase (small) or a capital (large) *c*. Small-*c* **communism** describes a social system in which property is owned by the community and in which people work for the common good. Large-*C* **Communism** was a political movement and doctrine seeking to overthrow capitalism and establish a form of communism such as that which prevailed in the Soviet Union (USSR) from 1917 to 1991. The heyday of Communism was a 40-year period from 1949 to 1989 when more Communist regimes existed than at any time before or after. By the year 2000, there were only five Communist states left, including China, Cuba, Laos, North Korea, and Vietnam, compared with 23 in 1985. For Communists the term *Communism* has meant both an international movement dedicated to the overthrow of capitalism and a classless future society. What Americans called Communist systems were called socialist by the Communists themselves, as in the Union of Soviet Socialist Republics. (*Socialism* is a political-economic theory advocating that land, natural resources, and major industries should be owned by society as a whole. Social democratic parties in many nations have sought to achieve this goal through democratic elections.)

Communism, which originated with Russia's Bolshevik Revolution in 1917, and took its inspiration from Karl Marx and Friedrich Engels, was not uniform over time or among countries. All Communist systems were authoritarian (promoting obedience to authority rather than individual freedom). Many were totalitarian (banning rival parties and demanding total submission of the individual to the state.) Several features distinguished Communist societies from other authoritarian regimes (e.g., Spain under Franco) and from socialism of a social democratic type. First, the Communist party monopolized power in every Communist state. Second, relations within the party were highly centralized and strictly disciplined. Third, Communist nations had state ownership, rather than private ownership, of the means of production. Finally, all Communist regimes, with the goal of advancing communism,

Before and after communism. Above: on May Day (May 1, 1975), large photos of Politburo members (Communist party leaders) adorn buildings in Moscow. Below: on January 31, 2006 in a Moscow electronics store, a potential customer considers a display of TV sets, broadcasting live the annual press conference of Russian President Vladimir Putin.

cultivated a sense of belonging to an international movement (Brown 2001).

Social scientists have tended to refer to such societies as socialist rather than Communist. Today there is a great deal of research by anthropologists and others on postsocialist societies—those that once emphasized bureaucratic redistribution of wealth according to a central plan (Verdery 2001). In the postsocialist period, states that once had planned economies have been following the neoliberal agenda by divesting themselves of state-owned resources in favor of privatization. These societies in transition are undergoing democratization and marketization. Some common problems of the transition have included (1) the rise of nationalism, in the form of ethnic-religious minorities, (2) corruption, (3) unemployment and poverty, and (4) difficulties in establishing new values, social relations, and groups. Some of these societies have moved toward formal liberal democracy, with political parties, elections, and a balance of powers (Grekova 2001).

Postsocialist Transitions

Neoliberal economists assumed that dismantling the Soviet Union's planned economy would raise GDP (gross domestic product) and living standards. The goal was to enhance production by substituting a decentralized market system and providing incentives through privatization. In October 1991, Boris Yeltsin, who had been elected president of Russia that June, announced a program of radical market-oriented reform, pursuing a changeover to capitalism. Yeltsin's program of "shock therapy" cut subsidies to farms and industries and ended price controls. Since then, postsocialist Russia has faced many problems. The anticipated gains in productivity did not materialize. After the fall of the Soviet Union, Russia's GDP fell by half. Poverty increased, with a quarter of the population now living below the poverty line. Life expectancy and the birth rate also declined. Let's look more closely at two problems mentioned above as common to postsocialist transitions: ethnic/religious nationalism and corruption.

Ethnic/Religious Nationalism

In the chapter "Ethnicity and Race" we saw how Russians dominated the former Soviet Union. Ethnic minorities had only limited self-rule in republics and regions controlled by Moscow. To cement Soviet rule Russian colonists were sent to many areas, such as Tajikistan (see Figure 24.4), to diminish the cohesion and clout of the local people. Tajikistan is a small, poor state (and former Soviet republic) in central Asia, bordering Afghanistan. In Tajikistan, as in central Asia generally, most people are Muslims. Since the fall of the Soviet empire, Islam, as an alternative way of ordering spiritual and social life, has been replacing socialist ideology. This follows more than 70 years of official atheism and suppression of religion. Although the Soviets destroyed mosques and discouraged religious practice, Islam survived in homes, around the kitchen table, and so it has been called "kitchen Islam." When the Russians left Tajikistan, the force of Russian culture and language receded. Islamic influence has grown, with more and more people speaking and praying in Tajik, a language related to Persian (which is spoken in Iran) (Erlanger 1992).

Compared with Tajikistan, the postsocialist transition was much more violent in Yugoslavia, whose breakup was examined in the chapter "Ethnicity and Race." The Socialist Federal Republic of Yugoslavia was a nonaligned country outside the USSR. Yugoslavia's disintegration took place in the wake of the dramatic collapse of Communism throughout Eastern Europe in fall 1989. The spirit of change spread rapidly in Yugoslavia, offering the prospect of democracy and freedom. In Bosnia, one of Yugoslavia's republics, the fall of Communism seemed to herald the free expression of religion without the fear of accusations of Muslim nationalism or "fundamentalism." Under Communism it had been difficult for Bosnian Muslims to combine their duties as workers in a factory or shop with those of devout Muslims. Having a job and working for the state kept Muslims from performing their ritual obligations. There were no officially recognized times or places for prayer and rituals (Bringa 1995).

In 1989 few Yugoslavs foresaw that the end of Communism would also mean the end of their country. Well into 1990, Yugoslavia's federal government continued to enjoy widespread support. After Yugoslavia's Communist party disbanded in January 1990, the opening toward political pluralism proceeded rapidly. During the first months of 1990, dozens of new political parties were formed. The scheduling of elections for April and May in the republics of Slovenia and Croatia provided less than four months to select the first post-Communist governments. By the end of 1990, nationalist parties had won elections in the republics. A series of secessions began, and the federal government lost its electoral base. Just two years separated the end of 1989, with its expectation of democratic change, and the end of 1991, when the European Community decided to recognize the seceded republics as independent states. An ethnic war that began in Croatia shortly thereafter then engulfed Bosnia (Bower 2000).

This first war in Europe in almost 50 years generated tremendous interest in the region. Media coverage took two approaches. The first assumed the various ethnic groups in Bosnia had always hated each other. Whatever tolerance and coexistence had existed there previously had been imposed by the Communist regime. The second was an idealized view that Bosnia previously had been a harmonious multicultural society. Its problems originated mainly with the fall of Communism and the collapse of the federal government, due in part to the imposition of neoliberal austerity measures (Bringa 1995).

Corruption

Corruption has been mentioned as a second common problem in postsocialist nations. Since 1996, the World Bank and other international organiza-

FIGURE 24.4 Former Soviet Socialist Republics of Central Asia, Including Tajikistan.

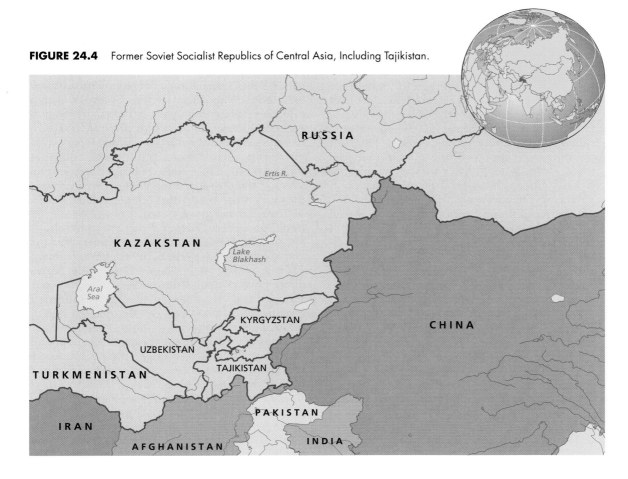

tions have launched anticorruption programs worldwide. *Corruption* is defined as the abuse of public office for private gain. The World Bank's approach to corruption assumes, erroneously, that the state (public)–private dichotomy is universal and takes a similar form in all societies. (This illustrates the fallacy of underdifferentiation, as discussed later in this chapter.)

According to Janine Wedel (2002), postsocialist states, which now, guided by neoliberalism, are divesting themselves of state-owned resources, provide rich contexts in which to explore diversity and flux in state–private relationships. The societies feature competition for influence at the intersection of the public and private spheres. For example, in Poland there are informal circles of people (dubbed "institutional nomads") whose primary loyalty is to their circle rather than to the formal positions they occupy (in government, business, or wherever). The Russian "clan," as Olga Kryshtanovskaya (1997) describes it, is a similar informal group of elites whose members promote their mutual interests. These informal groups place their members in formal positions in order to advantage their "clan." They maximize their influence by bridging and blending the spheres of public and private.

The anthropologist Alexei Yurchak (2002) describes two spheres within the contemporary Russian state. We'll call them the official-public and the personal-public. They refer to different systems that coexist and sometimes overlap. State officials may respect the law (official-public), while also working with informal or even criminal groups (personal-public). Officials switch from official-public to personal-public behavior all the time, in order to accomplish specific tasks.

Consider an illustrative case from Poland. A man selling an apartment he had inherited was to pay a huge sum in taxes. He visited the state tax office, where a bureaucrat informed him of how much he was being assessed (official-public). She also told him how to avoid paying it (personal-public). He followed her advice and saved a lot of money. The man did not know the bureaucrat personally. She didn't expect anything in return, and he didn't offer anything. She said she routinely offers such help.

What is legal (official-public) and what is considered morally correct don't necessarily correspond. The bureaucrat just described seemed still to be operating under the old communist notion that state property (tax dollars in this case) belongs both to everyone and to no one. For a further illustration of this view of state property, imagine two people working in the same state-owned construction enterprise. To take home for private use materials belonging to the enterprise (that is, to everyone and no one) is morally acceptable. No one will fault you for it, because "everyone does it." However, if a fellow worker comes along and takes materials someone else had planned to take home, that is considered stealing, and morally wrong (Wedel 2002). In evaluating charges of corruption, anthropologists such as Janine Wedel (2002) are well aware that property notions and spheres of official action in postsocialist societies are in transition.

In postsocialist and developing nations, as well as in contemporary North America, the neoliberal agenda has included the promotion of **civil society.** This concept refers to voluntary collective action around shared interests, goals, and values. Civil society encompasses such organizations as NGOs (nongovernmental organizations), registered charities, community groups, women's organizations, faith-based and professional groups, trade unions, self-help groups, social movements, business associations, coalitions, and advocacy groups. In theory, civil society is distinct from the state, family, and market. In practice, those boundaries are often complex, blurred, and negotiated, as we just saw in the discussion of institutional nomads and Russian "clans" in postsocialist societies (London School of Economics 2004).

DEVELOPMENT ANTHROPOLOGY

Applied anthropology, already examined in Chapter 2, refers to the application of anthropological perspectives, theory, methods, and data to identify, assess, and solve social problems. **Development anthropology** is the branch of applied anthropology that focuses on social issues in, and the cultural dimension of, economic development. Development anthropologists do not just carry out development policies planned by others; they also plan and guide policy. (For more detailed discussions of issues in development anthropology, see Escobar [1995], Ferguson [1994], and Robertson [1995].)

However, ethical dilemmas often confront development anthropologists (Escobar 1991, 1995). Our respect for cultural diversity is often offended because efforts to extend industry and technology may entail profound cultural changes. Foreign aid doesn't usually go where need and suffering are greatest. It is spent on political, economic, and strategic priorities as international donors, political leaders, and powerful interest groups perceive them. Planners' interests don't always coincide with the best interests of the local people.

Although the aim of most development projects is to enhance the quality of life, living standards often decline in the target area (Bodley, ed. 1988).

Studying people at the local level, enthnographers have a unique view of the impact of national and international development planning on intended "beneficiaries." Local-level research often reveals inadequacies in the measures that economists use to assess development and a nation's economic health. For example, per capita income and gross national product don't measure the distribution of wealth. Because the first is an average and the second is a total, they may rise as the rich get richer and the poor get poorer.

Today, many government agencies, international groups, NGOs, and private foundations encourage attention to local-level social factors and the cultural dimension of economic development, as we saw in the "News Brief" at the beginning of this chapter. Anthropological expertise in economic development planning is important because social problems can doom even potentially beneficial projects to failure. A study of 50 economic development projects (Lance and McKenna 1975) judged only 21 to be successes. Social and cultural incompatabilities had doomed most of the failed projects.

For example, a 1981 anthropological study of a multimillion-dollar development project in Madagascar uncovered several reasons for its failure. The project had been planned and funded by the World Bank in the late 1960s. The planners (no anthropologists among them) anticipated none of the problems that emerged. The project was aimed at draining and irrigating a large plain to increase rice production. Its goal was to raise production through machinery and double cropping—growing two crops annually on the same plot. However, the planners disregarded several things, including the unavailability of spare parts and fuel for the machines. The designers also ignored the fact, well known to anthropologists, that cross-culturally, intensive cultivation is associated with dense populations. If there are no machines to do the work, there have to be people around to do it. However, population densities in the project area were much too low to support intensive cultivation without modern machinery.

The planners should have known that labor and machinery for the project were unavailable. Furthermore, many local people were understandably hostile toward the project because it gave their ancestral land away to outsiders. (Unfortunately, this is a common occurrence in development projects.) Many land-grant recipients were members of regional and national elites. They used their influence to get fields that were intended for poor farmers. The project also suffered from technical problems. The foreign firm hired to dig the irrigation canals dug them lower than the land they had to irrigate. The water couldn't flow up into the fields.

Millions of development dollars could have been spent more wisely if anthropologists, consulting with local farmers, had helped plan, implement, and monitor the project. It stands to reason that experts, such as anthropologists, who are familiar with the language and customs of a country can better evaluate prospects of project success than can those who are not. Accordingly, anthropologists increasingly work in organizations that promote, manage, and assess programs that influence human life in the United States and abroad.

The Greening of Java

Anthropologist Richard Franke (1977) conducted a classic study of discrepancies between goals and results in a scheme to promote social and economic change in Java, Indonesia (Figure 24.5). Experts and planners in the 1960s and 1970s assumed that as small-scale farmers got modern technology and more productive crop varieties,

An anthropological study of an irrigated rice project in Madagascar found several reasons why it failed. If there are no machines to do the work, there have to be people around to do it—like these Betsileo women who are transplanting rice in the traditional manner.

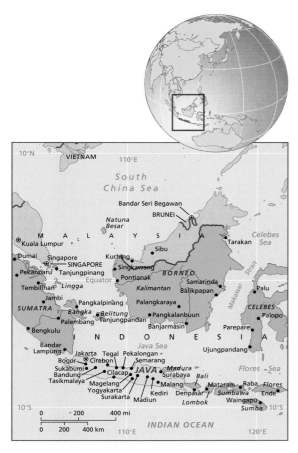

FIGURE 24.5 Location of Java (yellow) in Indonesia (orange).

their lives would improve. The media publicized new, high-yielding varieties of wheat, maize, and rice. These new crops, along with chemical fertilizers, pesticides, and new cultivation techniques, were hailed as the basis of a **green revolution.** This "revolution" was expected to increase the world's food supply and thus improve the diets and living conditions of victims of poverty, particularly in land-scarce, overcrowded regions.

The green revolution was an economic success. It did increase the global food supply. New strains of wheat and rice doubled or tripled farm supplies in many Third World countries. Thanks to the green revolution, world food prices declined by more than 20 percent during the 1980s (Stevens 1992). But its social effects were not what its advocates had intended, as we learn from Javanese experience.

Java received a genetic cross between rice strains from Taiwan and Indonesia—a high-yielding "miracle" rice known as IR-8. This hybrid could raise the productivity of a given plot by at least half. Governments throughout southern Asia, including Indonesia, encouraged the cultivation of IR-8, along with the use of chemical fertilizers and pesticides.

The Indonesian island of Java, one of the most densely populated places in the world (over 2,000 people per square mile), was a prime target for the green revolution. Java's total crop was insufficient to supply its people with minimal daily requirements of calories (2,150) and protein (55 grams). In 1960, Javanese agriculture supplied 1,950 calories and 38 grams of protein per capita. By 1967, these already inadequate figures had fallen to 1,750 calories and 33 grams. Could miracle rice, by increasing crop yields 50 percent, reverse the trend?

Many Asian governments have promoted the cultivation of new rice varieties, along with the use of chemical fertilizers and pesticides. What costs and benefits may accompany such changes? Shown here is Vietnam's Can Tho Rice Research Institute.

Java shares with many other underdeveloped nations a history of socioeconomic stratification and colonialism. Indigenous contrasts in wealth and power were intensified by Dutch colonialism. Although Indonesia gained political independence from the Netherlands in 1949, internal stratification continued. Today, contrasts between the wealthy (government employees, businesspeople, large landowners) and the poor (small-scale peasants) exist even in small farming communities. Stratification led to problems during Java's green revolution.

In 1963, the University of Indonesia's College of Agriculture launched a program in which students went to live in villages. They worked with peasants in the fields and shared their knowledge of new agricultural techniques while learning from the peasants. The program was a success. Yields in the affected villages increased by half. The program, directed by the Department of Agriculture, was expanded in 1964; nine universities and 400 students joined. These intervention programs succeeded where others had failed because the outside agents recognized that economic development rests not only on technological change but on political change as well. Students could observe firsthand how interest groups resisted attempts by peasants to improve their lot. Once, when local officials stole fertilizer destined for peasant fields, students got it back

by threatening in a letter to turn evidence of the crime over to higher-level officials.

The combination of new work patterns and political action was achieving promising results when, in 1965–1966, there was an insurrection against the government. In the eventual military takeover, Indonesia's President Sukarno was ousted and replaced by President Suharto, who ruled Indonesia until 1998. Efforts to increase agricultural production resumed soon after Suharto took control. However, the new government assigned the task to multinational corporations based in Japan, West Germany, and Switzerland rather than to students and peasants. These industrial firms were to supply miracle rice and other high-yielding seeds, fertilizers, and pesticides. Peasants adopting the whole green revolution kit were eligible for loans that would allow them to buy food and other essentials in the lean period just before harvesting.

Java's green revolution soon encountered problems. One pesticide, which had never been tested in Java, killed the fish in the irrigation canals and thus destroyed an important protein resource. Java's green revolution also encountered problems at the village level because of entrenched interests. Traditionally, peasants had fed their families by taking temporary jobs, or borrowing, from wealthier villagers before the harvest. However, having accepted loans, the peasants were obliged to work for wages lower than those paid on the open market. Low-interest loans would have made peasants less dependent on wealthy villagers, thus depriving local patrons of cheap labor.

Local officials were put in charge of spreading information about how the program worked. Instead, they limited peasant participation by withholding information. Wealthy villagers also discouraged peasant participation more subtly: They raised doubts about the effectiveness of the new techniques and about the wisdom of taking government loans when familiar patrons were nearby. Faced with the thought that starvation might follow if innovation failed, peasants were reluctant to take risks—an understandable reaction.

Production increased, but wealthy villagers rather than small-scale farmers reaped the benefits of the green revolution. Just 20 percent of one village's 151 households participated in the program. However, because they were the wealthiest households, headed by people who owned the most land, 40 percent of the land was being cultivated by means of the new system. Some large-scale landowners used their green revolution profits at the peasants' expense. They bought up peasants' small plots and purchased labor-saving machinery, including rice-milling machines and tractors. As a result, the poorest peasants lost both their means of subsistence—land—and local work opportunities. Their only recourse was to move to cities, where a growing pool of unskilled laborers depressed already low wages.

In a complementary view of the green revolution's social effects, Ann Stoler (1977) focused on gender and stratification. She took issue with Esther Boserup's (1970) contention that colonialism and development inevitably hurt Third World women more than men by favoring commercial agriculture and excluding women from farming. Stoler found that the green revolution had permitted some women to gain power over other women and men. Javanese women were not a homogeneous group but varied by class. Stoler found that whether the green revolution helped or harmed Javanese women depended on their position in the class structure. The status of landholding women rose as they gained control over more land and the labor of more poor women. The new economy offered wealthier women higher profits, which they used in trading. However, poor women suffered along with poor men as traditional economic opportunities declined. Nevertheless, the poor women fared better than did the poor men, who had no access at all to off-farm work.

These studies of the local effects of the green revolution reveal results different from those foreseen by policy makers, planners, and the media. We see the unintended and undesirable effects of development programs that ignore traditional social, political, and economic divisions. New technology, no matter how promising, does not inevitably help the intended beneficiaries. It may very well hurt them if vested interests interfere. The Javanese student–peasant projects of the 1960s worked because peasants need not just technology but also political clout. This ambitious development program in Java, although designed to alleviate poverty, actually increased it. Peasants stopped relying on their own subsistence production and started depending on a more volatile pursuit—cash sale of labor. Agricultural production became profit-oriented, machine-based, and chemical-dependent. Local autonomy diminished as linkages with the world system increased. Production rose, as the rich got richer and poverty increased.

Equity

A commonly stated goal of recent development policy is to promote equity. **Increased equity** means reduced poverty and a more even distribution of wealth. However, if projects are to increase equity, they must have the support of reform-minded governments. Wealthy and powerful people typically resist projects that threaten their vested interests.

Some types of development projects, particularly irrigation schemes, are more likely than others to widen wealth disparities, that is, to have a negative equity impact. An initial uneven distribu-

A mix of boats harbored at Dai-Lanh fishing village in Vietnam. A boat owner gets a loan to buy a motor. To repay it, he increases the share of the catch he takes from his crew. Later, he uses his rising profits to buy a more expensive boat, and takes even more from his crew. Can a more equitable solution be found?

tion of resources (particularly land) often becomes the basis for greater skewing after the project. The social impact of new technology tends to be more severe, contributing negatively to quality of life and to equity, when inputs are channeled to or through the rich, as in Java's green revolution.

Many fisheries projects also have had negative equity results. In Bahia, Brazil (Kottak 2006), sailboat owners (but not nonowners) got loans to buy motors for their boats. To repay the loans, the owners increased the percentage of the catch they took from the men who fished in their boats. Over the years, they used their rising profits to buy larger and more expensive boats. The result was stratification—the creation of a group of wealthy people within a formerly egalitarian community. These events hampered individual initiative and interfered with further development of the fishing industry. With new boats so expensive, ambitious young men who once would have sought careers in fishing no longer had any way to obtain their own boats. They sought wage labor on land instead. To avoid such results, credit-granting agencies must seek out enterprising young fishers rather than giving loans only to owners and established businesspeople.

STRATEGIES FOR INNOVATION

Development anthropologists, who are concerned with social issues in, and the cultural dimension of, economic development, must work closely with local people to assess and help realize their own wishes and needs for change. Too many true local needs cry out for a solution to waste money funding development projects that are inappropriate in area A but needed in area B, or unnecessary anywhere. Development anthropology can

This long and interesting clip describes the development process as a series of changes among Quichua Indians living near a national park created at Guagua Sumaco in Ecuador's Amazonian rain forest. It describes the supportive role of a German development agency (GTZ) in assisting (rather than imposing) development projects. Local people are interviewed about their development goals and the pluses and minuses of change. One of the main changes has been the arrival of electricity, from which the community derives part of its income. The clip describes how development has shifted the Quichua way of life from foraging to farming and work for cash. Yet aspects of their social organization—such as the clan system—remain and have been incorporated in the development process. Which changes would you regard as positive, and which as negative? The clip offers a good definition of sustainable development. What is it? After viewing the entire clip, do you agree with the narrator that development among the Quichua is sustainable?

help sort out the A's and B's and fit projects accordingly. Projects that put people first by consulting with them, and responding to their expressed needs, must be identified (Cernea 1991). Thereafter, development anthropologists can work to ensure socially compatible ways of implementing the project.

In a comparative study of 68 rural development projects from all around the world, I found the *culturally compatible* economic development projects to be twice as successful financially as the incompatible ones (Kottak 1990b, 1991). This finding shows that using applied anthropological expertise in planning, to ensure cultural compatibility, is cost-effective. To maximize social and economic benefits, projects must (1) be culturally compatible, (2) respond to locally perceived needs, (3) involve men and women in planning and carrying out the changes that affect them, (4) harness traditional organizations, and (5) be flexible.

Overinnovation

In my comparative study, the compatible and successful projects avoided the fallacy of **overinnovation** (too much change). We would expect people to resist development projects that require major changes in their daily lives, especially ones that interfere with subsistence pursuits. People usually want to change just enough to keep what they have. Motives for modifying behavior come from the traditional culture and the small concerns of ordinary life. Peasants' values are not such abstract ones as "learning a better way," "progressing," "increasing technical know-how,"

Change, we think, is good. Leaders are expected to offer "visions" of change. Few politicians get elected by promising, "I'm going to keep things just as they are." The assumption usually is that change is better—but what kind of change? From this discussion of the fallacy of overinnovation there are lessons to be learned and applied in our own lives.

Like most people, contemporary North Americans generally seek changes that will enable them to maintain or improve their lifestyles—not to revise them radically. Imagine someone chosen to lead an organization, someone from outside who is unfamiliar with the culture of that organization. He or she should follow the anthropologist's example and study the local culture before trying to change it. The leader should try to determine what works and what doesn't and what the natives (i.e., the men and women within the organization) want and really need. After local perceptions and needs have been assessed, if change seems in order, the leader must determine how to plan and implement change in the least disruptive way. Again, he or she should follow the applied anthropologist's strategy of consulting with and enlisting the help and support of local people throughout the process of change. To be an effective "change agent" requires listening and trying to tailor innovation to fit the local culture.

This process of study and collaboration illustrates participatory change—change from the "bottom up." By contrast, top-down change is often problematic. A top-down leader typically draws on an organizational blueprint—perhaps one he or she has brought from another organization. Unmodified blueprints usually don't work. Just as the linguistic blueprint in our brain is modified to fit a particular language, an organizational blueprint must be flexible enough to be modified to fit a specific organization. If it is not, that blueprint should be discarded. The fallacies of blueprint planning and overinnovation aren't just obscure lessons from failed development projects. They are vital considerations for any leader who wishes to run, or change, an organization.

"improving efficiency," or "adopting modern techniques." (Those phrases exemplify intervention philosophy.) Instead, their objectives are down-to-earth and specific ones. People want to improve yields in a rice field, amass resources for a ceremony, get a child through school, or have enough cash to pay the tax bill on time. The goals and values of subsistence producers differ from those of people who produce for cash, just as they differ from the intervention philosophies of development planners. Different value systems must be considered during planning.

In the comparative study, the projects that failed were usually both economically and culturally incompatible. For example, one South Asian project promoted the cultivation of onions and peppers, expecting this practice to fit into a preexisting labor-intensive system of rice growing. Cultivation of these cash crops wasn't traditional in the area. It conflicted with existing crop priorities and other interests of farmers. Also, the labor peaks for pepper and onion production coincided with those for rice, to which the farmers naturally gave priority.

Throughout the world, project problems have arisen from inadequate attention to, and consequent lack of fit with, local culture. Another naive and incompatible project was an overinnovative scheme in Ethiopia. Its major fallacy was to try to convert nomadic herders into sedentary cultivators. It ignored traditional land rights. Outsiders—commercial farmers—were to get much of the herders' territory. The pastoralists were expected to settle down and start farming. This project helped wealthy outsiders instead of the natives. The planners naively expected free-ranging herders to give up a generations-old way of life to work three times harder growing rice and picking cotton.

Underdifferentiation

The fallacy of **underdifferentiation** is the tendency to view "the less-developed countries" as more alike than they are. Development agencies often have ignored cultural diversity (e.g., between Brazil and Burundi) and adopted a uniform approach to deal with very different sets of people. Neglecting cultural diversity, many projects also have tried to impose incompatible property notions and social units. Most often, the faulty social design assumes either (1) individualistic productive units that are privately owned by an individual or couple and worked by a nuclear family or (2) cooperatives that are at least partially based on models from the former Eastern bloc and socialist countries.

Often, development aims at generating *individual* cash wealth through exports. This goal contrasts with the tendency of bands and tribes to share resources and to depend on local ecosystems and renewable resources (Bodley, ed. 1988). Development planners commonly emphasize benefits that will accrue to individuals. More concern with the effects on communities is needed (Bodley, ed. 1988).

One example of faulty Euro-American models (the individual and the nuclear family) was a West

In Bangladesh, women count money at a weekly meeting where loans from the female-run Grameen Credit Bank are repaid. Groups promoting development can be particularly effective when they are based on traditional social organization or on a socioeconomic similarity among members.

African project designed for an area where the extended family was the basic social unit. The project succeeded despite its faulty social design because the participants used their traditional extended family networks to attract additional settlers. Eventually, twice as many people as planned benefited as extended family members flocked to the project area. Here, settlers modified the project design that had been imposed on them by following the principles of their traditional society.

The second dubious foreign social model that is common in development strategy is the cooperative. In the comparative study of rural development projects, new cooperatives fared badly. Cooperatives succeeded only when they harnessed preexisting local-level communal institutions. This is a corollary of a more general rule: Participants' groups are most effective when they are based on traditional social organization or on a socioeconomic similarity among members.

Neither foreign social model—the nuclear family farm nor the cooperative—has an unblemished record in development. An alternative is needed: greater use of Third World social models for Third World development. These are traditional social units, such as the clans, lineages, and other extended kinship groups of Africa, Oceania, and many other areas, with their communally held estates and resources. The most humane and productive strategy for change is to base the social design for innovation on traditional social forms in each target area.

Third World Models

Many governments are not genuinely, or realistically committed to improving the lives of their citizens. Interference by major powers also has kept governments from enacting needed reforms. In highly stratified societies, the class structure is very rigid. Movement of individuals into the

■ *An effective social design for innovation may incorporate existing groups and institutions, such as descent groups in Africa and Oceania. Here, in Bali, Indonesia, a traditional system of planning and management by Hindu temples and priests has been harnessed for culturally appropriate agricultural development (see Lansing 1991).*

middle class is difficult. It is equally hard to raise the living standards of the lower class as a whole. Many nations have a long history of government control by antidemocratic leaders and powerful interest groups, which tend to oppose reform.

In some nations, however, the government acts more as an agent of the people. Madagascar provides an example. As in many areas of Africa, precolonial states had developed in Madagascar before its conquest by the French in 1895. The people of Madagascar, the Malagasy, had been organized into descent groups before the origin of the state. The Merina, creators of the major precolonial state of Madagascar, wove descent groups into its structure, making members of important groups advisers to the king and thus giving them authority in government. The Merina state made provisions for the people it ruled. It collected taxes and organized labor for public works projects. In return, it redistributed resources to peasants in need. It also granted them some protection against war and slave raids and allowed them to cultivate their rice fields in peace. The government maintained the water works for rice cultivation. It opened to ambitious peasant boys the chance of becoming, through hard work and study, state bureaucrats.

Throughout the history of the Merina state—and continuing in modern Madagascar—there have been strong relationships between the individual, the descent group, and the state. Local Malagasy communities, where residence is based on descent, are more cohesive and homogeneous than are communities in Java or Latin America. Madagascar gained political independence from France in 1960. Although it was still economically dependent on France when I first did research there in 1966–1967, the new government was committed to a form of economic development designed to increase the ability of the Malagasy to feed themselves. Government policy emphasized increased production of rice, a subsistence crop, rather than cash crops. Furthermore, local communities, with their traditional cooperative patterns and solidarity based on kinship and descent, were treated as partners in, not obstacles to, the development process.

In a sense, the descent group is preadapted to equitable national development. In Madagascar, members of local descent groups have customarily pooled their resources to educate their ambitious members. Once educated, these men and women gain economically secure positions in the nation. They then share the advantages of their new positions with their kin. For example, they give room and board to rural cousins attending school and help them find jobs.

Malagasy administrations appear generally to have shared a commitment to democratic economic development. Perhaps this is because government officials are of the peasantry or have strong personal ties to it. By contrast, in Latin American countries, the elites and the lower class typically have different origins and no strong connections through kinship, descent, or marriage.

Furthermore, societies with descent-group organization contradict an assumption that many social scientists and economists seem to make. It is not inevitable that as nations become more tied to the world capitalist economy, native forms of social organization will break down into nuclear family organization, impersonality, and alienation. Descent groups, with their traditional communalism and corporate solidarity, have important roles to play in economic development.

Realistic development promotes change but not overinnovation. Many changes are possible if the aim is to preserve local systems while making them work better. Successful economic development projects respect, or at least don't attack, local cultural patterns. Effective development draws on indigenous cultural practices and social structures.

1. Imperialism is the policy of extending the rule of a nation or empire over other nations and of taking and holding foreign colonies. Colonialism is the domination of a territory and its people by a foreign power for an extended time. European colonialism has had two main phases. The first started in 1492 and lasted through 1825. For Britain this phase ended with the American Revolution. For France it ended when Britain won the Seven Years' War, forcing the French to abandon Canada and India. For Spain, it ended with Latin American independence. The second phase of European colonialism extended approximately from 1850 to 1950. The British and French empires were at their height around 1914, when European empires controlled 85 percent of the world. Britain and France had colonies in Africa, Asia, Oceania, and the New World.

2. Political, ethnic, and tribal labels and identities were created under colonialism. Postcolonial studies is a growing academic field. It studies the interactions between European nations and the societies they colonized (mainly after 1800). Its topics include the impact of colonization and the state of postcolonies today.

3. Like colonialism, economic development has an intervention philosophy. This provides a justification for outsiders to guide native peoples toward particular goals. Development is usually justified by the idea that industrialization and modernization are desirable evolutionary advances. Yet many problems faced by Third World peoples have been caused by their incorporation in the world cash economy. Roads, mining, hydroelectric projects, ranching, lumbering, and agribusiness threaten indigenous peoples and their ecosystems. Neoliberalism revives and extends classic economic liberalism: the idea that governments should not regulate private enterprise and that free market forces should rule. This intervention philosophy currently dominates aid agreements with postsocialist and developing nations.

4. Spelled with a lowercase *c*, communism describes a social system in which property is owned by the community and in which people work for the common good. Spelled with a capital *C*, Communism indicates a political movement and doctrine seeking to overthrow capitalism and to establish a form of communism such as that which prevailed in the Soviet Union from 1917 to 1991. The heyday of Communism was between 1949 and 1989. The fall of Communism can be traced to 1989–1990 in eastern Europe and 1991 in the Soviet Union. Postsocialist states have followed the neoliberal agenda, through privatization, deregulation, and democratization. Common problems of the postsocialist transition include the rise of nationalism, in the form of ethnic-religious minorities, and corruption. Civil society encompasses NGOs, charities, community groups, women's organizations, faith-based and professional groups, unions, self-help groups, social movements, business associations, coalitions, and advocacy groups.

5. Development anthropology focuses on social issues in, and the cultural dimension of, economic development. Development projects typically promote cash employment and new technology at the expense of subsistence economies. Research in Java found that the green revolution was failing. The reason: It promoted only new technology, rather than a combination of technology and peasant political organization.

6. Not all governments seek to increase equality and end poverty. Resistance by elites to reform is typical—and hard to combat. Local people rarely cooperate with projects requiring major changes in their daily lives, especially ones that interfere with customary subsistence pursuits. Many projects seek to impose inappropriate property notions and incompatible social units on their intended beneficiaries. The best strategy for change is to base the social design for innovation on traditional social forms in each target area.

civil society Voluntary collective action around shared interests, goals, and values. Encompasses such organizations as NGOs, registered charities, community groups, women's organizations, faith-based and professional groups, trade unions, self-help groups, social movements, business associations, coalitions, and advocacy groups.

colonialism The political, social, economic, and cultural domination of a territory and its people by a foreign power for an extended time.

communism Spelled with a lowercase *c*, describes a social system in which property is owned by the community and in which people work for the common good.

Communism Spelled with a capital *C*, a political movement and doctrine seeking to overthrow capitalism and to establish a form of communism such as that which prevailed in the Soviet Union from 1917 to 1991.

development anthropology The branch of applied anthropology that focuses on social issues in, and the cultural dimension of, economic development.

equity, increased A reduction in absolute poverty and a fairer (more even) distribution of wealth.

green revolution Agricultural development based on chemical fertilizers, pesticides, 20th-century cultivation techniques, and new crop varieties such as IR-8 ("miracle rice").

intervention philosophy Guiding principle of colonialism, conquest, missionization, or development; an ideological justification for outsiders to guide native peoples in specific directions.

neoliberalism Revival of Adam Smith's classic economic liberalism, the idea that governments should not regulate private enterprise and that free market forces should rule; a currently dominant intervention philosophy.

overinnovation Characteristic of projects that require major changes in natives' daily lives, especially ones that interfere with customary subsistence pursuits.

postcolonial Referring to interactions between European nations and the societies they colonized (mainly after 1800); more generally, "postcolonial" may be used to signify a position against imperialism and Eurocentrism.

underdifferentiation Planning fallacy of viewing less-developed countries as an undifferentiated group; ignoring cultural diversity and adopting a uniform approach (often ethnocentric) for very different types of project beneficiaries.

CRITICAL THINKING QUESTIONS

For more self-testing, see the self-quizzes

mhhe.com/kottak

1. How is the diversity you see in your classroom related to the colonies and empires discussed in this chapter?

2. Think of a recent case in which a core nation, such as the United States, has intervened in the affairs of another nation. What was the intervention philosophy used to justify the action?

3. Devise a plan to equalize the distribution of computers in your public school system. What kind of opposition would you expect? Who would your supporters be?

4. Thinking of your own society and recent history, give an example of a proposal or policy that failed because it was overinnovative.

5. Think of a change you'd like to see happen. What groups would you enlist to make it happen? What would their roles be, from start to finish?

SUGGESTED ADDITIONAL READINGS

Arce, A., and N. Long, eds.
  2000 *Anthropology, Development, and Modernities: Exploring Discourses, Counter-Tendencies, and Violence.* New York: Routledge. Applied anthropology, rural development, social change, violence, and social and economic policy in developing countries.

Bodley, J. H.
  2001 *Anthropology and Contemporary Human Problems,* 4th ed. Boston: McGraw-Hill. Overview of major problems of today's industrial world: overconsumption, the environment, resource depletion, hunger, overpopulation, violence, and war.
  2003 *The Power of Scale: A Global History Approach.* Armonk, NY: M. E. Sharpe. Capitalism and geopolitics in world history.

Bodley, J. H., ed.
  1988 *Tribal Peoples and Development Issues: A Global Overview.* Mountain View, CA: Mayfield. An overview of case studies, policies, assessments, and recommendations concerning tribal peoples and development.

Bremen, J. V., and A. Shimizu, eds.
  1999 *Anthropology and Colonialism in Asia and Oceania.* London: Curzon. One in a series on the anthropology of Asia.

Cernea, M. M., ed.
  1991 *Putting People First: Sociological Variables in Rural Development,* 2nd ed. New York: Oxford University Press (published for the World Bank). First collection of articles by social scientists based on World Bank files and project experiences. Examines development successes and failures and the social and cultural reasons for them.

Cooper, F., and A. L. Stoler, eds.
  1997 *Tensions of Empire: Colonial Cultures in a Bourgeois World.* Berkeley: University of California Press. The social complexity of colonial encounters is explored in several articles.

Edelman, M., and A. Haugerud
  2004 *The Anthropology of Development and Globalization: From Classical Political Economy to Contemporary Neoliberalism.* Malden, MA: Blackwell. Surveys theories and approaches to development and the global.

Escobar, A.
  1995 *Encountering Development: The Making and Unmaking of the Third World.* Princeton, NJ: Princeton University Press. A critique of economic development and development anthropology.

Lansing, J. S.
  1991 *Priests and Programmers: Technologies of Power in the Engineered Landscape of Bali.* Princeton, NJ: Princeton University Press. The role of a traditional priesthood in managing irrigation and culturally appropriate economic development in Bali, Indonesia.

Nolan, R. W.

2002 *Development Anthropology: Encounters in the Real World.* Boulder, CO: Westview Press. Cases in development anthropology.

2003 *Anthropology in Practice.* Boulder, CO: Lynne Reiner. Putting anthropology to work for change.

Nussbaum, M. C.

2000 *Women and Human Development: The Capabilities Approach.* New York: Cambridge University Press. The untapped power of women in developing countries.

1. Colonialism in California: Go to the Original Voices website, **http://originalvoices.org/Homepage.htm**, and read the chapters on Precontact Culture and Economy, Human Price of Gold Rush, and U.S. Government Roles.
   a. What cultures lived in Northern California before the gold rush? What were their lifestyles like?
   b. What were the gold miners' attitudes toward the indigenous people? What actions did they take that reflected those attitudes? Would you characterize these actions as ethnocide or genocide?
   c. What role did the U.S. government play in the gold rush? Did it just tolerate the actions of the miners or did it encourage them?
   d. Some names of professional sports teams have been in the news recently because some Native Americans consider them offensive (e.g., Washington Redskins, Atlanta Braves, Cleveland Indians). After reading this page, what do you think native groups from Northern California might feel about the name of the San Francisco 49ers (named after the gold rushers of 1849)?

2. Human Rights: Read the preamble and skim the articles of the United Nations Universal Declaration of Human Rights, **http://www.un.org/Overview/rights.html**.
   a. What are the central points of the declaration?
   b. Do you agree with them? Do you find them all reasonable? Is anything missing?
   c. How do colonial strategies and development projects threaten human rights as spelled out in this declaration?
   d. How would you suggest the U.N. enforce these rights?

See Chapter 24 at your McGraw-Hill Online Learning Center for additional review and interactive exercises.

INTERNET EXERCISES

Kottak, *Assault on Paradise*, 4th ed.

Read Chapters 4 and 8 and describe the main changes affecting Arembepe's fishing industry during the period of study. How does Arembepe's experience illustrate this text chapter's point (in the section "Equity") about appropriate strategies for developing a local fishing industry?

Peters-Golden, *Culture Sketches*, 4th ed.

This text chapter has discussed the far-reaching and long-lasting results of colonialism. In *Culture Sketches*, read Chapter 4, "Haiti: A Nation in Turmoil." How do you think Haiti's colonial past has contributed to its contemporary situation? What sorts of problems does Haiti face owing to development, or lack thereof? How does Haiti compare to some other examples mentioned in the text chapter?

Knauft, *The Gebusi*, 1st ed.

Read Chapters 7, 9, and the conclusion. Based on Chapter 7 and the conclusion, how benign or brutal do you think the Gebusi's experience with colonialism has been? What evidence would you use to support your opinion? Based on Chapter 9, why do you think economic development is so relatively undeveloped among Gebusi—despite their strong desire for it? In an attempt to gain access to money, what kinds of economic activity are pursued by Gebusi women, and how successful are these activities?

LINKAGES

25

Cultural Exchange
and Survival

ACCULTURATION

Since at least the 1920s anthropologists have investigated the changes—on both sides—that arise from contact between industrial and nonindustrial societies. Studies of "social change" and "acculturation" are abundant. British and American ethnographers, respectively, have used these terms to describe the same process. *Acculturation* refers to changes that result when groups come into continuous firsthand contact—changes in the cultural patterns of either or both groups (Redfield, Linton, and Herskovits 1936, p. 149).

Acculturation differs from diffusion, or cultural borrowing, which can occur without firsthand contact. For example, most North Americans who eat hot dogs ("frankfurters") have never been to Frankfurt, Germany, nor have most North American Toyota owners or sushi

■ *This photo, taken on April 16, 1945, shows Holocaust survivors at the Buchenwald (Germany) Concentration Camp, which had just been liberated by U.S. troops. Genocidal policies, such as the Nazis' campaign against the Jews, aim at the physical extinction of a people.*

CONTACT AND DOMINATION

Different degrees of destruction, domination, resistance, survival, adaptation, and modification of native cultures may follow interethnic contact. In the most destructive encounters, native and subordinate cultures face obliteration. In cases where contact between the indigenous societies and more powerful outsiders leads to destruction—a situation that is particularly characteristic of colonialist and expansionist eras—a "shock phase" often follows the initial encounter (Bodley, ed. 1988). Outsiders may attack or exploit the native people. Such exploitation may increase mortality, disrupt subsistence, fragment kin groups, damage social support systems, and inspire new religious movements, such as the cargo cults examined in the chapter "Religion" (Bodley, ed. 1988). During the shock phase, there may be civil repression backed by military force. Such factors may lead to the group's cultural collapse (*ethnocide*) or physical extinction (*genocide*).

Outsiders often attempt to remake native landscapes and cultures in their own image. Political and economic colonialists have tried to redesign conquered and dependent lands, peoples, and cultures, imposing their cultural standards on others. The aim of many agricultural development projects, for example, seems to have been to make the world as much like Iowa as possible, complete with mechanized farming and nuclear family ownership—despite the fact that these models may be inappropriate for settings outside the North American heartland.

eaters ever visited Japan. Although *acculturation* can be applied to any case of cultural contact and change, the term most often has described **westernization**—the influence of Western expansion on indigenous peoples and their cultures. Thus, local people who wear store-bought clothes, learn Indo-European languages, and otherwise adopt Western customs are called acculturated. Acculturation may be voluntary or forced, and there may be considerable resistance to the process.

Development and Environmentalism

Today it is often multinational corporations, usually based in core nations, rather than the governments of those nations, that are changing the nature of Third World economies. However, nations do tend to support the predatory enterprises that seek cheap labor and raw materials in countries outside the core, such as Brazil, where economic development has contributed to ecological devastation.

Simultaneously, environmentalists from core nations increasingly state their case, promoting conservation, to the rest of the world. The ecological devastation of the Amazon has become a focus of international environmentalist attention. Yet many Brazilians complain that northerners talk about global needs and saving the Amazon after having destroyed their own forests for First World economic growth. Akbar Ahmed (1992, 2004) concludes that non-Westerners tend to be cynical about Western ecological morality, seeing it as yet another imperialist message. "The Chinese have cause to snigger at the Western suggestion that they forgo the convenience of the fridge to save the ozone layer" (Ahmed 1992, p. 120).

> ### OVERVIEW
>
> In our world in flux, new identities emerge, while others disappear. In worse cases, a culture may collapse or be absorbed (ethnocide). Its people may die off or be exterminated (genocide). Cultural imperialism refers to one culture's spread at the expense of others. A text, such as a media-born image, is interpreted by each person exposed to it. People may accept, resist, or oppose a text's established meaning. When outside forces enter new settings, they typically are indigenized—modified to fit the local culture. Mass media can diffuse the culture of a country within its borders, thus enhancing national identity. The mass media also play a role in preserving ethnic identities among people who lead transnational lives. Today's global culture is driven by flows of people, technology, finance, and information. Business and the media have stoked a global culture of consumption. Governments and international organizations have adopted policies, including constitutional reforms, designed to recognize and benefit indigenous peoples. Identity is a fluid, dynamic process, and there are multiple ways of being indigenous. No social movement exists apart from the nation and world that includes it.

Cultural Diversity Highest in Resource-Rich Areas, Study Says

NATIONAL GEOGRAPHIC NEWS BRIEF

by Stefan Lovgren
March 17, 2004

This chapter focuses on challenges to cultural diversity and cultural survival, and the resilience of people and cultures in the face of those challenges. This news story reports on a recent study of the origins and survival of cultural diversity. The point is made that people tend to move for economic reasons and that if resources are ample at home, people tend to stay put and continue doing what they have always done. This reinforces the point made in the last chapter that motives for modifying behavior come from the traditional culture and the small concerns of ordinary life.

An intriguing argument in this study is that patterns of cultural and biological diversity are similar, with diversity greatest in equatorial regions and least near the poles. Abundant resources in the tropics have allowed diverse societies to survive. When resources are less concentrated and abundant, people have to range widely to meet their daily needs. This movement works to homogenize cultures, as people constantly come into contact with others. This study also draws attention to a tendency for cultures to maintain themselves, even in the face of migration to new areas, such as North American cities, so that ethnic and other cultural distinctions remain important in a globalizing world.

We may rightfully beat our drums and toot our horns: No species come close to the wealth of culture that humans boast. We have different religions, marriage systems, languages, and dances.

"Humans are a very young species with very little genetic diversity, yet we've got enormous cultural diversity that other species really don't have," said Mark Pagel, a professor of evolutionary biology . . . at the University of Reading in England. But what explains our extreme cultural diversity?

In an article in this week's issue of the science journal *Nature*, Pagel and

Ruth Mace, an anthropologist at the University College London, argue that our cultural evolution is driven in large part by a desire to control resources.

"Humans have a proclivity for drawing a ring around themselves and say[ing], 'This is my territory and I'm going to exclude others from occupying it,'" Pagel said. "That leads to different cultures arising through the usual processes of diversification and drifting apart when they're isolated from each other."

It may seem strange to talk about our great cultural diversity at a time when many of us fear that a cultural homogenization is sweeping the world . . .

Pagel doesn't deny that a cultural erosion is taking place. But, he says, it's happened far less than it appears. In fact, unless they're tempted financially to move and assimilate into a new culture, most people prefer to stay where they are and continue doing what they have always done. "What's remarkable is how little movement we have seen in people, given the ability we have to move

Linguistic and cultural diversity characterizes Papua New Guinea, where this man lives. Body decoration is one way of marking cultural differences.

people," he said. "It's the natural tendency for cultures to be quite cohesive and exclusive that we want to draw attention to."

The study found that human cultures distribute themselves around the world in patterns similar to animal species. In animals, a trend known as Rapaport's rule holds that the density of species is highest in the equatorial regions and declines steadily toward the poles. Different languages—the standard by which the study differentiates cultures—are spoken every few square miles in some equatorial areas, while less climatologically hospitable regions have few languages.

Some 700 to 1,000 different languages, about 15 percent of the total on Earth, are spoken in Papua New Guinea. By comparison, only 90 languages are spoken in China.

"When resources are abundant, it is possible for a small group of humans to survive, while in areas where resources are not very abundant people have to range over large areas to meet their daily needs, and that seems to homogenize cultures, because they're constantly coming into contact with other people," Pagel said.

But how come humans don't form one large and homogenous cultural group in ecologically rich areas like Papua New Guinea?

Pagel says that's because humans display forms of social behavior that favor living in small groups, such as rewarding cooperation, punishing those who deviate from the norms, and being wary of outsiders. "In trying to control resources and excluding others from using them, we have developed [sophisticated group behaviors such as] hunting and warfare," he said. "These things require enormous amounts of cooperation, coherence, and communication among individuals."

It may also be a matter of choice. While our genes are transmitted vertically and can't be chosen, cultural traits can be accepted or rejected. However, most people still get their traits from their ancestors rather than other cultures.

"People tend to speak the same language as their parents, and have the same political and religious beliefs," Pagel said.

Although our cultural diversity is still strong, it is perhaps only a fraction of what it was, say, 10,000 years ago, when agriculturists moved out of Mesopotamia and replaced hunter-gatherer cultures in Europe and elsewhere, wiping out languages in the process.

"There are only about 50 languages spoken in Europe today," Pagel said. "If it hadn't been for the advance of the agriculturists, we would probably have greater linguistic diversity in Europe, and probably greater cultural diversity too."

We may be in another state of transition now. While some experts suggest that mass migrations of people moving from poor regions to rich areas will dent our cultural diversity, Pagel is not so sure. "Whether things will change in the next hundred years and we'll have one big homogenous world, we can't really say," he said . . .

After all, Pagel says, you can walk down a street in Manhattan and find three generations of Italian speakers. Walk a few blocks more, and people are speaking Chinese. "The cultural differences in Manhattan still remain," he said.

SOURCE: Stefan Lovgren, "Cultural Diversity Highest in Resource-Rich Areas, Study Says," *National Geographic News,* March 17, 2004. National Geographic Society. http://news.nationalgeographic.com/news/2004/03/0317_040317_cultures.html.

■ *At a mall in Poodong district, China, consumers can shop in one of Asia's biggest supermarkets. What would be the environmental effects if China had a level of consumption paralleling that of the United States?*

In the last chapter, we saw that development projects usually fail if they try to replace native forms with culturally alien property concepts and productive units. A strategy that incorporates the native forms is more effective than the fallacies of overinnovation and underdifferentiation. The same caveats would seem to apply to an intervention philosophy that seeks to impose global ecological morality without due attention to cultural variation and autonomy. Countries and cultures may resist interventionist philosophies aimed at either development or globally justified environmentalism.

A clash of cultures related to environmental change may occur when *development threatens indigenous peoples and their environments.* Hundreds of native groups throughout the world, including the Kayapó Indians of Brazil (Turner 1993) and the Kaluli of Papua New Guinea (see "Interesting Issues" on pp. 576–577), have been threatened by plans and forces, such as dam construction or commercially driven deforestation, that would destroy their homelands.

A second clash of cultures related to environmental change occurs when *external regulation threatens indigenous peoples.* Native groups may actually be threatened by environmental plans that seek to *save* their homelands. Sometimes outsiders expect local people to give up many of their customary economic and cultural activities without clear substitutes, alternatives, or incentives in order to conserve endangered species. The traditional approach to conservation has been to restrict access to protected areas, hire guards, and punish violators.

Problems often arise when external regulation replaces the native system. Like development projects, conservation schemes may ask people to change the way they have been doing things for generations to satisfy planners' goals rather than local goals. Ironically, well-meaning conservation efforts can be as insensitive as development schemes that promote radical changes without involving local people in planning and carrying out the policies that affect them. When people are asked to give up the basis of their livelihood, they usually resist.

Consider the case of a Tanosy man who lives on the edge of the Andohahela forest reserve of southeastern Madagascar. For years he has relied on rice fields and grazing land inside that reserve. Now external agencies are trying to get him to abandon this land for the sake of conservation. This man is a wealthy *ombiasa* (traditional sorcerer-healer). With four wives, a dozen children, and 20 head of cattle, he is an ambitious, hardworking, and productive peasant. With money, social support, and supernatural authority, he is mounting effective resistance against the park ranger who has been trying to get him to abandon his fields. The *ombiasa* claims he has already relinquished some of his land, but he is waiting for compensatory fields. His most effective resistance has been supernatural. The death of the ranger's son was attributed to the *ombiasa's* magical power. Since then, the ranger has been less vigilant in his enforcement efforts.

Given the threat that deforestation poses to global biodiversity, it is vitally important to devise conservation strategies that will work. Laws and enforcement may help stem the tide of commercially driven deforestation, which takes the form of burning and clear-cutting. However, local people also use and abuse forested lands. A challenge for the environmentally oriented applied anthropologist is to make forest preservation attractive to people like the Tanosy of Madagascar. Like development plans, effective conservation strategies must pay attention to the customs, needs, and incentives of the people living in the affected area. Conservation depends on local cooperation. In the Tanosy case, the guardians of the reserve must do more to satisfy the *ombiasa* and other affected people, through boundary adjustments, negotiation, and compensation. For effective conservation (as for development), the task is to devise culturally appropriate strategies. Neither development agencies nor NGOs (nongovernmental organizations) will succeed if they try to impose their goals without considering the practices, customs, rules, laws, beliefs, and values of the people to be affected (see Johansen 2003; Reed 1997).

Religious Change

Religious proselytizing can promote ethnocide, as native beliefs and practices are replaced by Western ones. Sometimes a religion and associated customs are replaced by ideology and behavior more compatible with Western culture. One example is the Handsome Lake religion (as described in the chapter on religion), which led the Iroquois to copy European farming techniques, stressing male rather than female labor. The Iroquois also gave up their communal longhouses and matrilineal descent groups for nuclear family households. The teachings of

Handsome Lake led to a new church and religion. This revitalization movement helped the Iroquois survive in a drastically modified environment, but much ethnocide was involved.

Handsome Lake was a native who created a new religion, drawing on Western models. More commonly, missionaries and proselytizers representing the major world religions, especially Christianity and Islam, are the proponents of religious change. Protestant and Catholic missionization continues even in remote corners of the world. Evangelical Protestantism, for example, is advancing in Peru, Brazil, and other parts of Latin America. It challenges an often jaded Catholicism that has too few priests and that is sometimes seen mainly as women's religion.

Sometimes the political ideology of a nation-state is pitted against traditional religion. Officials of the former Soviet empire discouraged Catholicism, Judaism, and Islam. In Central Asia, Soviet dominators destroyed Muslim mosques and discouraged religious practice. On the other hand, governments often use their power to advance a religion, such as Islam in Iran or Sudan (see Figure 25.1).

A military government seized power in Sudan in 1989. It immediately launched a campaign to change that country of more than 35 million people, where one-quarter were not Muslims, into an Islamic nation. Sudan adopted a policy of religious, linguistic, and cultural imperialism. The government sought to extend Islam and the Arabic language to the non-Muslim south. This was

For information on Sarawak cultural survival, see your OLC Internet Exercises

mhhe.com/kottak

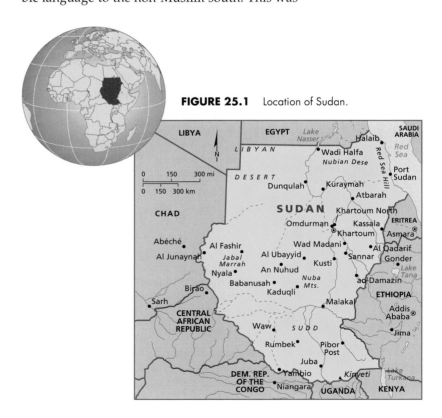

FIGURE 25.1 Location of Sudan.

Voices of the Rainforest

The government of Papua New Guinea has approved oil exploration by American, British, Australian, and Japanese companies in the rainforest habitat of the Kaluli (Figure 25.2) and other indigenous peoples. The forest degradation that usually accompanies logging, ranching, road building, and drilling endangers plants, animals, peoples, and cultures. Lost along with trees are songs, myths, words, ideas, artifacts, and techniques—the cultural knowledge and practices of rainforest people like the Kaluli, whom the anthropologist and ethnomusicologist Steven Feld has been studying for more than 20 years.

Feld teamed up with Mickey Hart of the Grateful Dead in a project designed to promote the cultural survival of the Kaluli through their music. For years, Hart has worked to preserve musical diversity through educational funding, concert promotion, and recording, including a successful series called "The World" on the Rykodisc label. *Voices of the Rainforest* was the first CD completely devoted to indigenous music from Papua New Guinea. In 1 hour, it encapsulates 24 hours of a day in Kaluli life in Bosavi village. The recording permits a form of cultural survival and diffusion in a high-quality commercial product. Bosavi is presented as a "soundscape" of blended music and natural environmental sounds. Kaluli weave the natural sounds of birds, frogs, rivers, and streams into their texts, melodies, and rhythms. They sing and whistle with birds and waterfalls. They compose instrumental duets with birds and cicadas.

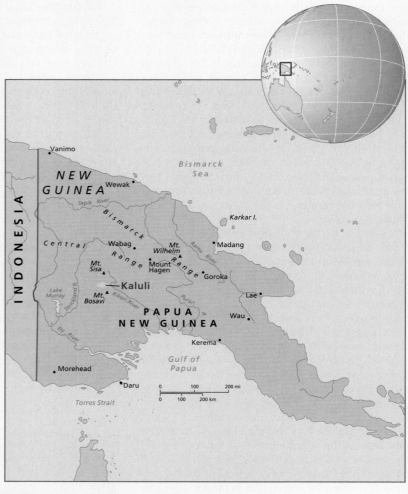

FIGURE 25.2   Location of the Kaluli in Papua New Guinea.

The Kaluli project was launched on Earth Day 1991 at *Star Wars* creator George Lucas's Skywalker Ranch. There, Randy Hayes, the executive director of the Rainforest Action Network, and musician Mickey Hart spoke about the linked issues of rainforest destruction and musical survival.

---

an area of Christianity and tribal religions that had resisted the central government for a decade (Hedges 1992*a*). Resistance continues.

Cultural Imperialism

Cultural imperialism refers to the spread or advance of one culture at the expense of others, or its imposition on other cultures, which it modifies, replaces, or destroys—usually because of dif-ferential economic or political influence. Thus, children in the French colonial empire learned French history, language, and culture from standard textbooks also used in France. Tahitians, Malagasy, Vietnamese, and Senegalese learned the French language by reciting from books about "our ancestors the Gauls."

To what extent is modern technology, especially the mass media, an agent of cultural imperialism? Some commentators see modern technology as

the voices of teachers and students at an English-only school.

Initially, Feld anticipated criticism for attempting to create an idealized Kaluli "soundscape" insulated from invasive forces and sounds. Among the Kaluli, he expected varied opinions about the value of his project:

> *It is a soundscape world that some Kaluli care little about, a world that other Kaluli momentarily choose to forget, a world that some Kaluli are increasingly nostalgic and uneasy about, a world that other Kaluli are still living and creating and listening to. It is a sound world that increasingly fewer Kaluli will actively know about and value, but one that increasingly more Kaluli will only hear on cassette and sentimentally wonder about. (Feld 1991, p. 137)*

Despite these concerns, Feld was met with an overwhelmingly positive response when he returned to Papua New Guinea in 1992 armed with a boombox and the recording. The people of Bosavi reacted very favorably. Not only did they appreciate the recording, they also have been able to build a much-needed community school with the *Voices of the Rainforest* royalties that have been donated to the Bosavi People's Fund.

SOURCE: Based on Steven Feld, "Voices of the Rainforest," *Public Culture* 4(1): 131–140 (1991).

Next came a San Francisco benefit dinner for the Bosavi People's Fund. This is the trust established to receive royalties from the Kaluli recording—a financial prong in Steven Feld's strategy to foster Kaluli cultural survival.

Voices of the Rainforest has been marketed as "world music." This term is intended to point up musical diversity, the fact that musics originate from all world regions and all cultures. "Tribal" music joins Western music as a form of artistic expression worth performing, hearing, and preserving. Hart's series offers musics of non-Western origin as well as those of ethnically dominated groups of the Western world.

Hart's record series aims at preserving "endangered music" against the artistic loss suffered by indigenous peoples. Its intent is to give a "world voice" to people who are being silenced by the dominant world system. In 1993, Hart launched a new series, the Library of Congress Endangered Music Project, which includes digitally remastered field recordings collected by the American Folklife Center. The first of this series, *The Spirit Cries*, concentrated on music from a broad range of cultures in South and Central America and the Caribbean. Proceeds from this project were used to support the performers and their cultural traditions.

In *Voices of the Rainforest*, Feld and Hart excised all "modern" and "dominant" sounds from their recording. Gone are the world-system sounds that Kaluli villagers now hear every day. The recording temporarily silences the "machine voices": the tractor that cuts the grass on the local airstrip, the gas generator, the sawmill, the helicopters, and light planes buzzing to and from the oil-drilling areas. Gone, too, are the village church bells, Bible readings, evangelical prayers and hymns, and

erasing cultural differences, as homogeneous products reach more people worldwide. But others see a role for modern technology in allowing social groups (local cultures) to express themselves and to survive (Marcus and Fischer 1999) (see "Interesting Issues" on p. 580). Modern radio and TV, for example, constantly bring local happenings (for example, a "chicken festival" in Iowa) to the attention of a larger public. The North American media play a role in stimulating local activities of many sorts. Similarly, in Brazil, local practices, celebrations, and performances are changing in the context of outside forces, including the mass media and tourism.

In the town of Arembepe Brazil (Kottak 1999*a*), TV coverage has stimulated participation in a traditional annual performance, the *Chegança*. This is a fishermen's danceplay that reenacts the Portuguese discovery of Brazil. Arembepeiros have traveled to the state capital to perform the

Chegança before television cameras, for a TV program featuring traditional performances from many rural communities.

One national Brazilian Sunday-night variety program (*Fantástico*) is especially popular in rural areas because it shows such local events. In several towns along the Amazon River, annual folk ceremonies are now staged more lavishly for TV cameras. In the Amazon town of Parantíns, for example, boatloads of tourists arriving any time of year are shown a videotape of the town's annual Bumba Meu Boi festival. This is a costumed performance mimicking bullfighting, parts of which have been shown on *Fantástico*. This pattern, in which local communities preserve, revive, and intensify the scale of traditional ceremonies to perform for TV and tourists, is expanding.

Brazilian television also has played a "top-down" role, by spreading the popularity of holidays like Carnaval and Christmas (Kottak 1990*a*). TV has aided the national spread of Carnaval beyond its traditional urban centers. Still, local reactions to the nationwide broadcasting of Carnaval and its trappings (elaborate parades, costumes, and frenzied dancing) are not simple or uniform responses to external stimuli.

Rather than direct adoption of Carnaval, local Brazilians respond in various ways. Often they don't take up Carnaval itself but modify their local festivities to fit Carnaval images. Others actively spurn Carnaval. One example is Arembepe, where Carnaval has never been important, probably because of its calendrical closeness to the main local festival, which is held in February to honor Saint Francis of Assisi. In the past, villagers couldn't afford to celebrate both occasions. Now, not only do the people of Arembepe reject Carnaval, they are also increasingly hostile to their own main festival. Arembepeiros resent the

For more on strategies of cultural survival, see your OLC Internet Exercises

mhhe.com/kottak

fact that Saint Francis has become "an outsiders' event," because it draws thousands of tourists to Arembepe each February. The villagers think that commercial interests and outsiders have appropriated Saint Francis.

In opposition to these trends, many Arembepeiros now say they like and participate more in the traditional June festivals honoring Saint John, Saint Peter, and Saint Anthony. In the past, these were observed on a much smaller scale than was the festival honoring Saint Francis. Arembepeiros celebrate them now with a new vigor and enthusiasm, as they react to outsiders and their celebrations, real and televised.

MAKING AND REMAKING CULTURE

Any media-borne image, such as that of Carnaval, can be analyzed in terms of its nature and effects. It also can be analyzed as a **text.** We usually think of a text as a textbook, like this one. But the term has a more general meaning. Anthropologists use text to refer to anything that may be "read," interpreted, and assigned meaning by anyone exposed to it. In this sense, a text doesn't have to be written. The term may refer to a film, an image, or an event, such as Carnaval. As Brazilians participate in Carnaval, they "read" it as a text. These "readers" derive their own meanings and feelings from Carnaval events, images, and activities. Such meanings may be very different from what the creators of the text, such as official sponsors, imagined. (The "reading" or meaning that the creators intended—or the one that the elites consider to be the intended or correct meaning—can be called the *hegemonic reading*.)

"Readers" of media messages constantly produce their own meanings. They may resist or oppose the hegemonic meanings of a text, or they may seize on the antihegemonic aspects of a text. Previously, we saw this process when American slaves preferred the biblical story of Moses and deliverance to the hegemonic lessons of acceptance and obedience that their masters taught.

Popular Culture

In his book *Understanding Popular Culture* (1989), John Fiske views each individual's use of popular culture as a creative act (an original "reading" of a text). (For example, Madonna, the Rolling Stones, and *The Lord of the Rings* mean something different to each of their fans.) As Fiske puts it, "the meanings I make from a text are pleasurable when I feel that they are *my* meanings and that they relate to *my* everyday life in a practical, direct way" (1989, p. 57). All of us can creatively "read" magazines, books, music, television, films, celebrities, and other popular culture products (see Fiske and Hartley 2003).

Individuals also draw on popular culture to express resistance. Through their use of popular culture, people can symbolically resist the unequal power relations they face each day—in the family, at work, and in the classroom. Popular culture (from hip-hop music to comedy) can be used to express discontent and resistance by groups that are or feel powerless or oppressed.

Indigenizing Popular Culture

To understand culture change, it is important to recognize that meaning may be locally manufactured. People assign their own meanings and value to the texts, messages, and products they receive. Those meanings reflect their cultural backgrounds and experiences. When forces from world centers enter new societies, they are **indigenized**—modified to fit the local culture. This is true of cultural forces as different as fast food, music, housing styles, science, terrorism, celebrations, and political ideas and institutions (Appadurai 1990).

Consider the reception of the movie *Rambo* in Australia as an example of how popular culture may be indigenized. Michaels (1986) found *Rambo* to be very popular among aborigines in the deserts of central Australia, who had manufactured their own meanings from the film. Their "reading" was very different from the one imagined by the movie's creators, and by most North Americans. The Native Australians saw Rambo as a representative of the Third World who was engaged in a battle with the white officer class. This reading expressed their negative feelings about white paternalism and about existing race relations. The Native Australians also imagined that there were tribal ties and kin links between Rambo and the prisoners he was rescuing. All this made sense, based on their experience. Native Australians are disproportionately represented in Australian jails. Their most likely liberator would be someone with a personal link to them. These readings of *Rambo* were relevant meanings produced *from* the text, not *by* it (Fiske 1989).

A World System of Images

All cultures express imagination—in dreams, fantasies, songs, myths, and stories. Today, however, more people in many more places imagine "a wider set of 'possible' lives than they ever did before. One important source of this change is the mass media, which present a rich, ever-changing store of possible lives" (Appadurai 1991, p. 197). The United States as a media center has been joined by Canada, Japan, Western Europe, Brazil, Mexico, Nigeria, Egypt, India, and Hong Kong.

As print has done for centuries (Anderson 1991), the electronic mass media also can spread, even help create, national and ethnic identities. Like print, television and radio can diffuse the cultures of different countries within their own boundaries, thus enhancing national cultural identity. For example, millions of Brazilians who were formerly cut off (by geographic isolation or illiteracy) from urban and national events and information now participate in a national communication system, through TV networks (Kottak 1990a).

Cross-cultural studies of television contradict a belief Americans ethnocentrically hold about televiewing in other countries. This misconception is that American programs inevitably triumph over local products. This doesn't happen when there is appealing local competition. In Brazil, for example, the most popular network (TV Globo) relies heavily on native productions. TV Globo's most popular programs are *telenovelas*, locally made serials that are similar to American soap operas. Globo plays each night to the world's largest and most devoted audience (60 to 80 million viewers throughout the nation). The programs that attract this horde are made by Brazilians, for Brazilians. Thus, it is not North American culture but a new pan-Brazilian national culture that Brazilian TV is propagating. Brazilian productions also compete internationally. They are exported to over 100 countries, spanning Latin America, Europe, Asia, and Africa.

We may generalize that programming that is culturally alien won't do very well anywhere when a quality local choice is available. Confirmation comes from many countries. National productions are highly popular in Japan, Mexico, India, Egypt, and Nigeria. In a survey during the mid-1980s, 75 percent of Nigerian viewers preferred local productions. Only 10 percent favored

Native children throughout the French colonial empire learned the French language by reciting from books about "our ancestors the Gauls." More recently, French citizens have criticized or resisted what they see as American "cultural imperialism"—one prominent symbol of which has been Euro Disneyland. Has there also been resistance to the expansion of Disney enterprises in the United States?

Using Modern Technology to Preserve Linguistic and Cultural Diversity

Although some see modern technology as a threat to cultural diversity, others see a role for this technology in allowing social groups to express themselves. The anthropologist H. Russell Bernard has been a pioneer in teaching speakers of endangered languages how to write their language using a computer. Bernard's work permits the preservation of languages and cultural memories. Native peoples from Mexico to Cameroon are using their mother tongue to express themselves as individuals and to provide insiders' accounts of different cultures.

Jesús Salinas Pedraza, a rural schoolteacher in the Mexican state of Hidalgo, sat down to a word processor a few years back and produced a monumental book, a 250,000-word description of his own Indian culture written in the Nähñu language. Nothing seems to be left out: folktales and traditional religious beliefs, the practical uses of plants and minerals and the daily flow of life in field and village . . .

Mr. Salinas is neither a professional anthropologist nor a literary stylist. He is, though, the first person to write a book in Nähñu (NYAW-hnyu), the native tongue of several hundred thousand Indians but a previously unwritten language.

Such a use of microcomputers and desktop publishing for languages with no literary tradition is now being encouraged by anthropologists for recording ethnographies from an insider's perspective. They see this as a means of preserving cultural diversity and a wealth of human knowledge.

With even greater urgency, linguists are promoting the techniques as a way of saving some of the world's languages from imminent extinction.

Half of the world's 6,000 languages are considered by linguists to be endangered. These are the languages spoken by small societies that are dwindling with the encroachment of larger, more dynamic cultures. Young people feel economic pressure to learn only the language of the dominant culture, and as the older people die, the non-written language vanishes, unlike languages with a history of writing, like Latin.

Dr. H. Russell Bernard, the anthropologist at the University of Florida at Gainesville who taught Mr. Salinas to read and write his native language, said: "Languages have always come and gone . . . But languages seem to be disappearing faster than ever before." . . .

Dr. Michael E. Krauss, the director of the Alaska Native Language Center at the University of Alaska in Fairbanks, estimates that 300 of the 900 indigenous languages in the Americas are moribund. That is, they are no longer being spoken by children, and so could disappear in a generation or two. Only two of the 20 native languages in Alaska are still being learned by children . . .

In an effort to preserve language diversity in Mexico, Dr. Bernard and Mr. Salinas decided in 1987 on a plan to teach the Indian people to read and write their own language using microcomputers. They established a native literacy center in Oaxaca, Mexico, where others could follow in the footsteps of Mr. Salinas and write books in other Indian languages.

The Oaxaca center goes beyond most bilingual education programs, which concentrate on teaching people to speak and read their native languages. Instead, it operates on the premise that, as Dr. Bernard decided, what most native languages lack is native authors who write books in their own languages . . .

The Oaxaca project's influence is spreading. Impressed by the work of Mr. Salinas and others, Dr. Norman Whitten, an anthropologist at the University of Illinois, arranged for schoolteachers from Ecuador to visit Oaxaca and learn the techniques.

Now Ecuadorian Indians have begun writing about their cultures in the Quechua and Shwara languages. Others from Bolivia and Peru are learning to use the computers to write their languages, including Quechua, the tongue of the ancient Incas, still spoken by about 12 million Andean Indians . . .

Dr. Bernard emphasized that these native literacy programs are not intended to discourage people from learning the dominant language of their country as well. "I see nothing useful or charming about remaining monolingual in any Indian language if that results in being shut out of the national economy," he said.

SOURCE: Excerpted from John Noble Wilford, "In a Publishing Coup, Books in 'Unwritten' Languages," *New York Times,* December 31, 1991, pp. B5, B6.

imports, and the remaining 15 percent liked the two options equally. Local productions are successful in Nigeria because "they are filled with everyday moments that audiences can identify with. These shows are locally produced by Nigerians" (Gray 1986). Thirty million people watched one of the most popular series, *The Village Headmaster,* each week. That program brought rural values to the screens of urbanites who had lost touch with their rural roots (Gray 1986).

The mass media also can play a role in maintaining ethnic and national identities among people who lead transnational lives. Arabic-speaking Muslims, including migrants, in several countries follow the TV network Al Jazeera, based in Qatar, which helps reinforce ethnic and religious identities. As groups move, they can stay linked to each other and to their homeland through the media. Diasporas (people who have spread out from an original, ancestral homeland) have enlarged the markets for media, communication, and travel services targeted at specific ethnic, national, or religious audiences. For a fee, a PBS station in Fairfax, Virginia, offers more than 30 hours a week to immigrant groups in the D.C. area, to make programs in their own languages.

A Transnational Culture of Consumption

Besides the electronic media, another key transnational force is finance. Multinational corporations and other business interests look beyond national boundaries for places to invest and draw profits. As Arjun Appadurai (1991, p. 194) puts it, "money, commodities, and persons unendingly chase each other around the world." Residents of many Latin American communities now depend on outside cash, remitted from international labor migration. Also, the economy of the United States is increasingly influenced by foreign investment, especially from Britain, Canada, Germany, the Netherlands, and Japan (Rouse 1991). The American economy also has increased its dependence on foreign labor—through both the immigration of laborers and the export of jobs.

Contemporary global culture is driven by flows of people, technology, finance, information, images, and ideology (Appadurai 1990, 2001). Business, technology, and the media have increased the craving for commodities and images throughout the world (Gottdiener 2000). This has forced nation-states to open to a global culture of consumption. Almost everyone today participates in this culture. Few people have never seen a T-shirt advertising a Western product. American and English rock stars' recordings blast through the streets of Rio de Janeiro, while taxi drivers from Toronto to Madagascar play Brazilian music tapes. Peasants and tribal people participate in the modern world system not only because they have been hooked on cash, but also because their products and images are appropriated by world capitalism (Root 1996). They are commercialized by others (like the San in the movie *The Gods Must Be Crazy*). Furthermore, indigenous peoples also market their own images and products, through outlets like Cultural Survival (see Mathews 2000).

PEOPLE IN MOTION

The linkages in the modern world system have both enlarged and erased old boundaries and distinctions. Arjun Appadurai (1990, p. 1) characterizes today's world as a "translocal" "interactive system" that is "strikingly new." Whether as refugees, migrants, tourists, pilgrims, proselytizers, laborers, businesspeople, development workers, employees of nongovernmental organizations, politicians, terrorists, soldiers, sports figures, or media-borne images, people appear to travel more than ever.

In previous chapters, we saw that foragers and herders are typically seminomadic or nomadic. Today, however, the scale of human movement has expanded dramatically. So important is transnational migration that many Mexican villagers find "their most important kin and friends are as likely to be living hundreds or thousands of miles away as immediately around them" (Rouse 1991). Most migrants maintain their ties with their native land (phoning, e-mailing, visiting, sending money, watching "ethnic TV"). In a sense, they live multilocally—in different places at once. Dominicans in New York City, for example, have been characterized as living "between two islands": Manhattan and the Dominican Republic (Grasmuck and Pessar 1991). Many Dominicans—like migrants from other countries—migrate to the United States temporarily, seeking cash to transform their lifestyles when they return to the Caribbean.

With so many people "in motion," the unit of anthropological study expands from the local community to the **diaspora**—the offspring of an area who have spread to many lands. Anthropologists increasingly follow descendants of the villages we have studied as they move from rural to urban areas and across national boundaries. For the 1991 annual meeting of the American Anthropological Association in Chicago, the anthropologist Robert Kemper organized a session of presentations about long-term ethnographic field work. Kemper's own longtime research focus has been the Mexican village of Tzintzuntzan, which,

When products and images enter new settings, they are typically indigenized—modified to fit the local culture. Jeans Street, in Bandung, Indonesia, is a strip of stores, vendors, and restaurants catering to young people interested in Western pop culture. How is the poster of Batman and Robin *indigenized*?

Business and the media have increased the craving for products throughout the world. Barbie dolls and Pocahontas videos are sold in China, as is Häagen-Dazs ice cream in the Middle East.

Biocultural Case Study

See the "Bringing It All Together" essay that immediately follows this chapter for some of the causes and effects of, and international resistance to, the spread of the fast-food industry.

with his mentor George Foster, he has studied for decades. However, their database now includes not just Tzintzuntzan, but its descendants all over the world. Given the Tzintzuntzan diaspora, Kemper was even able to use some of his time in Chicago to visit people from Tzintzuntzan who had established a colony there. In today's world, as people move, they take their traditions and their anthropologists along with them.

Postmodernity describes our time and situation: today's world in flux, these people on the move who have learned to manage multiple identities depending on place and context. In its most general sense, **postmodern** refers to the blurring and breakdown of established canons (rules or standards), categories, distinctions, and boundaries. The word is taken from **postmodernism**—a style and movement in architecture that succeeded modernism, beginning in the 1970s. Postmodern architecture rejected the rules, geometric order, and austerity of modernism. Modernist buildings were expected to have a clear and functional design. Postmodern design is "messier" and more playful. It draws on a diversity of styles from different times and places—including popular, ethnic, and non-Western cultures. Postmodernism extends "value" well beyond classic, elite, and Western cultural forms. *Postmodern* is now used to describe comparable developments in music, literature, and visual art. From this origin, *postmodernity* describes a world in which traditional standards, contrasts, groups, boundaries, and identities are opening up, reaching out, and breaking down.

Globalization promotes intercultural communication, including travel and migration, which bring people from different societies into direct contact. The world is more integrated than ever. Yet *dis*integration also surrounds us. Nations dissolve (Yugoslavia, the Soviet Union), as do political blocs (the Warsaw Pact nations) and ideologies ("Communism"). The notion of a "Free World" collapses because it existed mainly in opposition to a group of "Captive Nations"—a label once applied by the United States and its allies to the former Soviet empire that has lost much of its meaning today.

Simultaneously, new kinds of political and ethnic units are emerging. In some cases, cultures and ethnic groups have banded together in larger associations. There is a growing pan-Indian identity (Nagel 1996) and an international pantribal movement as well. Thus, in June 1992, the World Conference of Indigenous Peoples met in Rio de Janeiro concurrently with UNCED (the United Nations Conference on the Environment and Development). Along with diplomats, journalists, and environmentalists came 300 representatives of the tribal diversity that survives in the modern world—from Lapland to Mali (Brooke 1992; see also Maybury-Lewis 2002).

INDIGENOUS PEOPLES

The term and concept *indigenous people* gained legitimacy within international law with the creation in 1982 of the United Nations Working Group on Indigenous Populations (WGIP). This group, which meets annually, has representation from all six continents. The draft of the Declaration of Indigenous Rights, produced by the WGIP in 1989, was accepted by the U.N. for discussion in 1993. Convention 169, an ILO (International Labor Organization) document that supports cul-

There's a difference between being a member of a diaspora and having a diasporic identity, such as a pan-Indian or pan-African identity. Diasporic identities, which have been abetted by the media and by various political and cultural organizations devoted to spreading or reinforcing such identities, are increasingly important in today's world. As for being a member of some diaspora, all humans are. All Americans, including Native Americans, originated somewhere else. Several groups, including English, French, Spanish, Portuguese, Dutch, Italians, Poles, Jews, Muslims, Lebanese, Africans, and Chinese, have migrated widely and settled in many countries. But there were older migrations, such as the one the led to the settling of the Polynesian islands—the Polynesian diaspora—starting around 3,000 years ago. Diasporas of ancestral Native Americans spread throughout North and South America. Australia was first settled, probably from Indonesia, between 50,000 and 60,000 years ago, and was "resettled" much later as part of the British colonial diaspora.

Once hunting was incorporated into the human adaptive strategy, *Homo erectus* extended the human range out of Africa and into Eurasia and beyond. Migrating bands of *Homo erectus* were part of a highly significant diaspora, but they certainly lacked a diasporic identity. There would be later diasporas out of Africa, including the migration that took ancient anatomically modern humans to Europe, Asia, and eventually the Americas. The forced migration out of Africa that occurred under slavery was responsible for a more recent African diaspora, contributing to the settlement of the United States, the Caribbean, Brazil, and many other countries in the Western Hemisphere. Although many of us lack any conscious diasporic identity, exposure to anthropology should certainly convince us that we all have the right to such an identity. Few, if any, of us can claim to belong to a lineage that has lived eternally in its homeland.

■ *With so many people on the move, the unit of anthropological study has expanded from the local community to the diaspora. This refers to the offspring of an area (e.g., Africa) who have spread to many lands, such as these Afro-Caribbean pub owners in West Broomwich, England. Do you belong to a diaspora?*

"indigenous people" as a self-identifying and political label based on past oppression but now legitimizing a search for social, cultural, and political rights (de la Peña 2005).

In Spanish-speaking Latin America, social scientists and politicians favor the term *indígena* (indigenous person) over *indio* (Indian)—the colonial term that the Spanish and Portuguese conquerors used to refer to the native inhabitants of the Americas. With the national independence movements that ended Latin American colonialism, the situation of indigenous peoples did not necessarily improve. For the white and *mestizo* (mixed) elites of the new nations, *indios* and their lifestyle were perceived as alien to (European) civilization. But Indians also were seen as redeemable by intellectuals, who argued for social policies to improve their welfare (de la Peña 2005).

Until the mid- to late 1980s, Latin American public discourse and state policies emphasized assimilation and discouraged indigenous identification and mobilization. Indians were associated with a romanticized past, but marginalized in the present, except for museums, tourism, and folkloric events. Argentina's Indians were all but invisible. Indigenous Bolivians and Peruvians were encouraged to self-identify as *campesinos* (peasants). The past 30 years have seen a dramatic shift. The emphasis has shifted from biological and cultural assimilation—*mestizaje*—to identities that value difference, especially Indianness. In Ecuador groups seen previously as Quichua-speaking peasants are classified now as indigenous communities with assigned territories. Other Andean "peasants" have experienced reindigenization as well. Brazil has recognized 30

tural diversity and indigenous empowerment, was approved in 1989. Such declarations and documents, along with the work of the WGIP, have influenced governments, NGOs, and international agencies, including the World Bank, to express greater concern for, and to adopt policies designed to benefit, indigenous peoples. Social movements worldwide have adopted the term

new indigenous communities in the northeast, a region previously seen as having lost its indigenous population (see "Beyond the Classroom"). In Guatemala, Nicaragua, Brazil, Colombia, Mexico, Paraguay, Ecuador, Argentina, Bolivia, Peru, and Venezuela, constitutional reforms have recognized those nations as multicultural (Jackson and Warren 2005). Several national constitutions now recognize the rights of indigenous peoples to cultural distinctiveness, sustainable development, political representation, and limited self-government. In Colombia, for example, indigenous communities have been confirmed as rightful owners of large territories. Their leaders and councils have the same benefits as any local government. Two seats in the Colombian senate are reserved for Indian representatives (de la Peña 2005).

In Latin America, the drive by indigenous peoples for self-determination has emphasized (1) their cultural distinctiveness; (2) political reforms involving a restructuring of the state; (3) territorial rights and access to natural resources, including control over economic development; and (4) reforms of military and police powers over indigenous peoples (Jackson and Warren 2005).

The indigenous rights movement, and government responses to it, take place in the context of globalization, including transnational social movements focusing on such issues as human rights, women's rights, and environmentalism. Transnational organizations have helped indigenous peoples influence national legislative agendas. NGOs specializing in development and human rights have come to see indigenous peoples as clients. Many Latin American countries

have signed international human rights treaties and covenants.

Although Latin America has experienced a general shift from authoritarian to democratic rule since the 1980s, ethnic and racial discrimination and inequality haven't disappeared. We should recognize as well that indigenous organizing has a high toll, including assassinations of indigenous leaders and their supporters. Especially in Guatemala, Peru, and Colombia there has been severe political repression, along with thousands of indigenous deaths, indigenous refugees, and internally displaced persons (Jackson and Warren 2005).

Ceuppens and Geschiere (2005) explore a recent upsurge of the notion of *autochthony* (being native to, or formed in, the place where found)—with an implicit call for excluding strangers—in different parts of the world. The terms *autochthony* and *indigenous* both go back to classical Greek history, with similar implications. *Autochthony* refers to self and soil. *Indigenous* literally means born inside, with the connotation in classical Greek of being born "inside the house." Both notions stress the need to safeguard ancestral lands (patrimony) from strangers, along with the rights of first-comers to special rights and protection versus later immigrants—legal or illegal (Ceuppens and Geschiere 2005).

During the 1990s, autochthony became an issue in many parts of Africa, inspiring violent efforts to exclude "strangers"—especially in Francophone (French-speaking) areas, but spilling over into Anglophone (English-speaking) countries as well. Simultaneously, autochthony became

Urban Indigenous Identity in Salvador, Bahia, Brazil

BACKGROUND INFORMATION

STUDENT:
Jessica F. Nelson

SUPERVISING PROFESSOR:
Conrad P. Kottak

SCHOOL:
University of Michigan

YEAR IN SCHOOL/MAJOR:
Senior/Cultural Anthropology

FUTURE PLANS:
Graduate School
in Cultural Anthropology

PROJECT TITLE:
Urban Indigenous Identity
in Salvador, Bahia, Brazil

As an exchange student in Brazil, I recall walking along *Baixa dos Sapateiros,* the street known as "Shoemakers' Hollow," as it curved its way through the hills of the historic district of Salvador, the capital city of Bahia state. I had heard that this street was once a river, the boundary between Portuguese and Indian territories, and the scene of the first of their battles. I wondered about the stories such places held. This inspired me to design an independent study through which I planned to discover the stories of the indigenous people of Salvador.

My intent was to identify the concepts of identity held by indigenous people and their descendants living in Salvador, as well as the general public. I hoped also to learn how those who claim to be indigenous construct such an identity. Though aware of entering a cultural context in which indigenous identity might be considered irrelevant, I was unprepared to be confronted with statements that indigenous people do not exist in Salvador. Many residents of that city, Brazil's third largest, warned me that I would "be disappointed." Yet nearly every neighborhood had at least one person whose nickname was *índio,* or "Indian." "Why?" I asked. "Oh, because he or she *is* Indian," would be the response.

This contradiction gave new purpose to my research. Why, despite so many signs of indigenous people living in Salvador, do people believe they have disappeared? How could concepts of both identity and disappearance exist simultaneously?

For six months, I compiled information through participant observation, literary research, and taped interviews with indigenous people and their descendants, representing three generations. During these interviews, which were informal, I gathered quantifiable information, such as the names, ages, and birthplaces of family members. I also asked open-ended questions designed to lead into stories of personal experiences and perspectives. I worked with a list of questions, so as to facilitate later comparisons of information, although our conversations often drifted from those topics. Unforeseen information surfaced as we talked, joked, and spent time together. Interviewing allowed me to get to know people I otherwise never would have met, some of whom became good friends. At times

intensely personal, their stories were candid testimonies of struggle and inner strength. No less moving perhaps were stories I could not collect: those of people who might have claimed, but who chose to deny, indigenous identity. I learned of such people through my own observation, and at times from their own family members who did claim indigenous identity.

Through the interviews, I discovered that many people construct their indigenous identity by using elements and symbols of popular culture, such as stereotypical clothing, ornaments, and body decorations associated with Indians in the media—though with sharply contrasting intent and message. After decades of virtual silence, when it was physically and socially dangerous to be *índio,* many ethnic groups have "emerged," or officially reclaimed their existence within the eyes of the law. Others, who have had this recognition, though often left unnoticed on the margins of society, are becoming increasingly vocal about their rights. Many people in Salvador now are claiming indigenous identity on a personal level. This is happening within a cultural context that has assumed indigenous people to have been assimilated; either entirely, or by occupying a *caboclo,* or mixed racial and cultural, status. Like many others in Latin America, indigenous people and their descendants in Salvador are challenging their "disappearance," and redefining what it means to be Indian.

■ La Paz, Bolivia, May 23, 2005: Bolivians claiming an Indian (indigenous) identity rally for indigenous rights and the nationalization of that country's gas resources. In December 2005, Bolivians elected as their president Evo Morales, the candidate of the Indigenous Movement toward Socialism party. The party made further gains in 2006 parliamentary elections.

a key notion in debates about immigration and multiculturalism in Europe. Unlike "indigenous peoples," the label *autochthon* has been claimed by majority groups in Europe. This term highlights the prominence that the exclusion of strangers has assumed in day-to-day politics worldwide (Ceuppens and Geschiere 2005). One familiar example is the United States, as represented in the congressional debate that broke out, beginning in spring 2006, over illegal immigration.

Identity in Indigenous Politics

Essentialism describes the process of viewing an identity as established, real, and frozen, to hide the historical processes and politics within which that identity developed. One example would be the ethnic labels "Hutu" and "Tutsi" in Rwanda, as discussed in the chapter "Colonialism and Development." Those labels actually had nothing to do with ethnicity when they were created. Nation-states have used essentializing strategies (e.g., the Tutsi–Hutu distinction) to perpetuate hierarchies and to justify violence against categories seen as less than fully human.

Identities, emphatically, are not fixed. We saw in the chapter "Ethnicity and Race" that identities are fluid and multiple. People seize on particular, sometimes competing, self-labels and identities. Some Peruvian groups, for instance, self-identify as *mestizos* but still see themselves as indigenous. Identity is a fluid, dynamic process, and there are multiple ways of being indigenous. Neither speaking an indigenous language nor wearing "native" clothing is required. Identities are asserted at particular times and places by particular individuals and groups, and after various kinds of negotiations. Indigenous identity co-exists with, and must

be managed in the context of, other identity components, including religion, race, and gender. Identities always must be seen as (1) potentially plural, (2) emerging through a specific process, and (3) ways of being someone or something in particular times and places (Jackson and Warren 2005).

Indigenous Peoples and Ethnography

How have indigenous movements, political mobilization, and identity politics affected ethnography? Pauline Turner Strong (2005) answers this question through an extensive review of recent ethnographic research among Native Americans in North America. The hallmark of traditional ethnographic research has been intensive, long-term participant observation in a local community. Such research continues among North American Indians today, but often it takes place in institutional settings such as tribal schools, museums, cultural centers, casinos, and tourist complexes. This shift in part reflects indigenous preferences: These institutions mediate between indigenous communities and the outside world. At such sites anthropologists can contribute to community-based research without intruding on private life. Also, these settings are ideal for the study of self-representation, self-determination, repatriation, and economic development. Museum studies, for example, have generated new ethnographies on tribal cultural centers (Strong 2005). One of these is a collaborative ethnography on the Cultural and Research Center of the Makah, whose whale hunt was described in the "News Brief" for the chapter "Culture" (Erickson, Ward, and Wachendorf 2002).

Increasingly as well, ethnographic research with Native Americans is situated in governmental institutions, including tribal offices, courts, and social service agencies. Such research may rely as much on formal interviews and archival research as it does on participant observation. Topics of such studies include (1) the articulation of tribal politics with the regional, national, and global political economy; (2) political divisions within, and alliances between, indigenous communities; (3) racial politics within indigenous communities and between them and surrounding non-Indian communities; and (4) governing and judicial bodies in tribal communities (Strong 2005). Sovereignty and the politics of identity have emerged as central themes, and anthropologists have worked as researchers for tribes in their efforts aimed at recognition, acknowledgment, and repatriation.

Compared with research in North America and Latin America since the 1990s, anthropological studies of social movements and identity politics have been less characteristic of Australia, whose indigenous peoples comprise about 2 percent of the national population. In Australia, the 1990s were a decade of reconciliation, with the aim of creating a new relationship between settler Australia and its indigenous peoples. The Council for Aboriginal Reconciliation (CAR) situated itself within a people's movement. On May 28, 2000, in the People's Walk for Reconciliation, a quarter of a million people crossed Sydney's Harbor Bridge on foot, following a major public event called Corroboree 2000. CAR produced its final report in December 2002. Although Aboriginal and other Australians have been working together to recognize and help heal the wounds of the past, the federal government has not yet officially recognized the 2002 CAR report (Merlan 2005).

Francesca Merlan (2005) writes that until fairly recently, views of Australian indigenous peoples and their cultures tended to overlook their responses to colonization and settlement by Europeans. Indigenous societies were seen either as having been crushed by colonial impact (in areas of major European settlement), or, in more remote areas, as unchanging. Anthropologists valued Australia's indigenous cultures to the extent that they could be viewed as traditional and distinct from the dominant society. With the focus on the "traditional" life and institutions, interactions of indigenous peoples and outsiders were neglected.

One exception was Ronald Berndt (1969), who described what he saw as a gradual and late emergence of indigenous protest in Australia. Berndt found outside agents to be behind most of the protests. He saw activist Aborigines as "for all practical purposes Australian-Europeans," seeking common identity in the Aboriginal past, this trend itself a "kind of social movement" (p. 41). He concluded that once people "see themselves in relation to others, once they are in a position to compare, the way becomes wide open for . . . protest" (p. 42). In other words, although the protests reflected marginalization and oppression, the ideas and styles of activism that have guided Native Australian protest have arisen in interaction with Australian national culture (Merlan 2005). This is not unusual. No social movement exists apart from the nation that includes it. Nor is any contemporary nation isolated from the world system, globalization, and transnational organization.

THE CONTINUANCE OF DIVERSITY

Anthropology has a crucial role to play in promoting a more humanistic vision of social change, one that respects the value of human biological and cultural diversity. The existence of anthropology is itself a tribute to the continuing need to understand similarities and differences among human beings throughout the world. Anthropology teaches us that the adaptive responses of humans can be more flexible than can those of other species because our main adaptive means are sociocultural. However, the cultural forms, institutions, values, and customs of the past always influence subsequent adaptation, producing continued diversity and giving a certain uniqueness to the actions and reactions of different groups. With our knowledge and our awareness of our professional responsibilities, let us work to keep anthropology, the study of humankind, the most humanistic of all the sciences.

1. Different degrees of destruction, domination, resistance, survival, and modification of native cultures may follow interethnic contact. This may lead to a tribe's cultural collapse (ethnocide) or its physical extinction (genocide). Multinational corporations have fueled economic development and ecological devastation. Either development or external regulation may pose a threat to indigenous peoples, their cultures, or their environments. The most effective conservation strategies pay attention to the needs, incentives, and customs of people living in the affected area.

2. *Cultural imperialism* refers to the spread of one culture and its imposition on other cultures, which it modifies, replaces, or destroys—usually because of differential economic or political influence. Some worry that modern technology, including the mass media, is destroying traditional cultures. But others see an important role for new technology in allowing local cultures to express themselves.

3. The term *text* is used here to describe anything that can be creatively "read," interpreted, and assigned meaning by someone who receives it. People may resist the hegemonic meaning of a text. Or they may seize on its antihegemonic aspects. When forces from world centers enter new societies, they are *indigenized.* Like print, the electronic mass media can help diffuse a national culture within its own boundaries. The media also play a role in preserving ethnic and national identities among people who lead transnational lives. Business, technology, and the media have increased the craving for commodities and images throughout the world, creating a global culture of consumption.

SUMMARY

4. People travel more than ever. But migrants also maintain ties with home, so they live multi-locally. With so many people "in motion," the unit of anthropological study expands from the local community to the diaspora. *Postmodernity* describes this world in flux, such people on the move who manage multiple social identities depending on place and context. New kinds of political and ethnic units are emerging as others break down or disappear.

5. The term and concept *indigenous people* has gained legitimacy within international law. Governments, NGOs, and international agencies have adopted policies designed to recognize and benefit indigenous peoples. Social movements worldwide have adopted this term as a self-identifying and political label based on past oppression but now signaling a search for social, cultural, and political rights. In Latin America, emphasis has shifted from biological and cultural assimilation to identities that value difference. Several national constitutions now recognize the rights of indige-

nous peoples. Transnational organizations have helped indigenous peoples influence national legislative agendas. Recent use of the notion of *autochthony* (being native to, or formed in, the place where found) includes a call to exclude strangers, such as recent and illegal immigrants. Identity is a fluid, dynamic process, and there are multiple ways of being indigenous.

6. Indigenous movements and identity politics have affected anthropology. Ethnographic research among North American Indians today often takes place in institutional and government settings. Topics of such studies include the articulation of tribal politics with the regional, national, and global political economy and political divisions within, and alliances between, indigenous communities. In Australia, where native resistance has been downplayed by anthropologists, the ideas and styles of activism that have guided indigenous protest have arisen in interaction with Australian national culture. No social movement exists apart from the nation and world that includes it.

KEY TERMS

See the flash cards
mhhe.com/kottak

cultural imperialism   The rapid spread or advance of one culture at the expense of others, or its imposition on other cultures, which it modifies, replaces, or destroys—usually because of differential economic or political influence.

diaspora   The offspring of an area who have spread to many lands.

essentialism   The process of viewing an identity as established, real, and frozen, to hide the historical processes and politics within which that identity developed.

indigenized   Modified to fit the local culture.

postmodern   In its most general sense, describes the blurring and breakdown of established canons (rules, standards), categories, distinctions, and boundaries.

postmodernism   A style and movement in architecture that succeeded modernism. Compared with modernism, postmodernism is less geometric, less functional, less austere, more playful, and more willing to include elements from diverse times and cultures; postmodern now describes comparable developments in music, literature, visual art, and anthropology.

postmodernity   Condition of a world in flux, with people on the move, in which established groups, boundaries, identities, contrasts, and standards are reaching out and breaking down.

text   Something that is creatively "read," interpreted, and assigned meaning by each person who receives it; includes any media-borne image, such as Carnaval.

westernization   The acculturative influence of Western expansion on native cultures.

CRITICAL THINKING QUESTIONS

For more self-testing, see the self-quizzes
mhhe.com/kottak

1. Are you a conservationist? What do you see as the pros and cons of forcing people, businesses, or communities to conserve when such conservation conflicts with cultural patterns or economic interests? Revisit the "News Brief" in the chapter "Culture" on Makah whale hunting. What's your opinion about cultural rights in the context of conservationist initiatives?

2. Consider majority and minority rights in the context of contemporary events involving religion, politics, and law. Should religion be an ascribed or an achieved status? Should someone in a Muslim nation be allowed to convert to a

different religion? In your country, how much influence should majority and minority religions be allowed to have on politics and the law?

3. How do you participate in a world system of images? Are the images to which you relate mainly national, or foreign/international as well?

4. How do you use the media? Is there a program or group that has special meaning for you? Are you personally irritated when someone questions your meaning?

5. Do you now live, or have you ever lived, multi-locally? How so?

Ahmed, A. S.

2004 *Postmodernism and Islam: Predicament and Promise,* rev. ed. New York: Routledge. Clear presentation of postmodernism in relation to the media and to images of Islam.

Appadurai, A. , ed.

2001 *Globalization.* Durham, NC: Duke University Press. The flows that create today's world system.

Bodley, J. H.

1999 *Victims of Progress,* 4th ed. Mountain View, CA: Mayfield. Social change, acculturation, and culture conflict involving indigenous peoples.

Cultural Survival Inc.

1992 *At the Threshold.* Cambridge, MA: Author. Originally published as the Spring 1992 issue of *Cultural Survival Quarterly.* Manual for the promotion of the rights of indigenous peoples. Highlights activist successes, gives instructions for affecting policy, working in schools and communities, directly helping native societies, and using the media as a human rights ally.

Feld, S.

1990 *Sound and Sentiment: Birds, Weeping, Poetics, and Song in Kaluli Expression,* 2nd ed. Philadelphia: University of Pennsylvania Press. Ethnographic study of sound as a cultural system among the Kaluli people of Papua New Guinea.

Fiske, J., and J. Hartley

2003 *Reading Television,* 2nd ed. New York: Routledge. Interpreting television and its content as a text.

Gottdiener, M., ed.

2000 *New Forms of Consumption: Consumers, Culture, and Commodification.* Lanham, MD: Rowman and Littlefield. Cultural consumption, diversity, and market segmentation in today's global economy.

Johansen, B. E.

2003 *Indigenous Peoples and Environmental Issues: An Encyclopedia.* Westport, CT: Greenwood. A compendium of knowledge about environmental issues as they affect and reflect local communities.

Laird, S. A.

2002 *Biodiversity and Traditional Knowledge: Equitable Partnerships in Practice.* Sterling, VA: Earthscan. What local people and scientists have to offer each other in regard to biodiversity.

Lutz, C., and J. L. Collins

1993 *Reading National Geographic.* Chicago: University of Chicago Press. How the cultural narratives of the magazine are received and interpreted; the relation between images of other peoples, cultures, and lifestyles and middle-class North American values.

Marcus, G. E., and M. M. J. Fischer

1999 *Anthropology as Cultural Critique: An Experimental Moment in the Human Sciences,* 2nd ed. Chicago: University of Chicago Press. New edition of an influential book on modern and postmodern anthropology.

Maybury-Lewis, D.

2002 *Indigenous Peoples, Ethnic Groups, and the State,* 2nd ed. Boston: Allyn & Bacon. Indigenous peoples and ethnicity in the contemporary world.

Nagel, J.

1996 *American Indian Ethnic Renewal: Red Power and the Resurgence of Identity and Culture.* New York: Oxford University Press. The meaning of activism for Native American individual ethnic identification; the role of federal, tribal, and personal politics in the growth of American Indian identity.

Reed, R.

1997 *Forest Dwellers, Forest Protectors: Indigenous Models for International Development.* Boston: Allyn & Bacon. Applying indigenous knowledge and practices to economic development.

Robbins, R.

2005 *Global Problems and the Culture of Capitalism,* 3rd ed. Boston: Pearson/Allyn & Bacon. Examines issues of domination, resistance, and social and economic problems in today's world.

Root, D.

1996 *Cannibal Culture: Art, Appropriation, and the Commodification of Difference.* Boulder, CO: Westview Press. How Western art and commerce classify, co-opt, and commodify "native" experiences, creations, and products.

Scott, J. C.

1990 *Domination and the Arts of Resistance.* New Haven, CT: Yale University Press. A study of institutionalized forms of domination, such as colonialism, slavery, serfdom, racism, caste, concentration camps, prisons, and old-age homes—and the forms of resistance that oppose them.

SUGGESTED ADDITIONAL READINGS

1. Peacemaking among the Nuer and Dinka: Read the *Washington Post* article about the recent history of these groups, **http://www.washingtonpost. com/wp-srv/inatl/daily/july99/sudan7.htm**.

   a. Anthropologists in the middle of the 20th century recorded conflict between the Nuer and the Dinka. In this article, they became allies against what opponent? How did conflict reemerge between the Nuer and the Dinka?

   b. What were the traditional views of warfare and death among the Nuer and the Dinka? How did these change with the introduction of modern machine guns?

   c. What impact did these new views have on the recent Nuer–Dinka conflicts?

   d. Despite the cultural changes brought about by the pressures of modern nations and the introduction of machine guns, the Nuer and the Dinka used traditional cultural symbols to help bring about peace. What are some examples?

   e. Do you think this peace will be short-lived? What needs to take place in order to maintain peace?

2. Ishi and Cultural Survival: Visit the website **http://www.mohicanpress.com/mo08019.html** and read about Ishi.

   a. Who was Ishi? To what tribe did he belong, and what happened to it?

   b. In what way was Ishi successful in preserving native culture and educating people about it? Who was Alfred Kroeber, and what role did he play in Ishi's life?

   c. How did Ishi's family perish? Where did he live after he was rescued?

   d. The website draws parallels between Ishi and James Fennimore Cooper's *The Last of the Mohicans.* Do you think those parallels are apt?

See Chapter 25 at your McGraw-Hill Online Learning Center for additional review and interactive exercises.

Kottak, *Assault on Paradise*, 4th ed.

Read the section of Chapter 6 titled "The Magic of Success and the Growth of Religion." How was the increase in *candomblé* activity related to new economic opportunities in Arembepe? Both the textbook and *Assault on Paradise* (Chapter 12) have discussed how Arembepeiros resisted outsiders' appropriation of their traditional February festival. Having finished *AOP,* provide three other examples of resistance by Arembepeiros to the ideas or actions of outsiders, such as people claiming higher status, hippies, or fish buyers.

Peters-Golden, *Culture Sketches*, 4th ed.

This text chapter discusses the potentially grave consequences of economic development and environmental degradation. Outside exploitation poses a threat to indigenous peoples. In *Culture Sketches,* read Chapter 15, "The Yanomamo: Challenges in the Rainforest." What are some challenges faced by the Yanomamo (aka Yanomami)? What is the anthropologist's role in conflicts between indigenous peoples and the governments of the countries in which they live? Should an anthropologist be an objective observer, an advocate, or neither of these things? What are some difficulties involved in choosing a position?

Knauft, *The Gebusi*, 1st ed.

Read Chapter 11 and the conclusion. Based on Chapter 11, what features of Gebusi culture are preserved, transformed, or made fun of at Independence Day celebrations? What extra-local images, activities, and social relations are evident in the celebrations? In what ways is Gebusi culture becoming blurred with regional or national culture? Based on the conclusion, do you think Gebusi culture has changed more than it has stayed the same? What evidence can be used to support your opinion? In what ways have Gebusi become modern in a unique cultural fashion?

The Biology and Culture of Overconsumption

In the chapter "The Modern World System," we learned that Americans are the world's foremost consumers. Using some 275,000 calories of energy per day, the average American is 35 times more expensive than the average forager or tribesperson, who uses just 8,000 calories. Since 1900, the United States has increased its total energy consumption 30-fold. And in the last two decades, Americans have increased their *food* consumption by an average of 200 calories per day. American agribusiness now produces 500 food calories more per person per day than it did 30 years ago, which is about 1,000 more calories per day than most people need (Pollan 2003). This provides a dramatic contrast with the food scarcity that accompanies poverty in the less-developed countries. In the chapter "Colonialism and Development," for example, we saw that in Java, daily food calories available per capita had dropped from 1,950 to 1,750, less than half the current American figure of 3,800 (Pollan 2003).

In his book *Fat Land: Supersizing America* (2003), Greg Critser examines how Americans rapidly are becoming the fattest people on earth. Sixty percent of all Americans, and 25 percent of American children, are now overweight. Since 1970, the percentage of American children who are overweight has doubled. Food companies have fueled this epidemic of obesity as they have attempted to maintain their profitability—by getting people to eat more—at a time when the American food supply has been growing much faster than the American population has. A key ingredient in the fattening of America has been the rise and spread of "supersizing."

Critser (2003) traces how David Wallerstein— an executive at McDonald's—invented supersizing. In the 1960s, Wallerstein, then working for a movie theater chain, was looking for ways to expand sales of soda pop and popcorn. He discovered that although the typical moviegoer was reluctant to buy more than one drink or bag of popcorn, people would consume more drink and popcorn if they came in a single large serving. Such supersizing is an effective business strategy because the raw materials for soda, popcorn, fries, and burgers make up only a small fraction of their price—compared with the costs of labor, packaging, and advertising. Expanding the size of portions allowed businesses to raise prices and increase sales without adding much to costs.

Ray Kroc, the founder of McDonald's, adopted Wallerstein's strategy of supersizing. In McDonald's advertising, Big Macs and large fries replaced "regular" (i.e., small) hamburgers and fries. Dave Thomas offered "biggie" fries and drinks at Wendy's. All the fast-food chains started hawking combos (for breakfast, lunch, or later). This greatly enhanced the American (and worldwide) consumption of that old Peruvian domesticate, the "Irish" potato, in the form of "French" fries. (Talk about a world system!)

When people are offered larger portions, studies show they will eat up to 30 percent more than they otherwise would. (Think about our holiday feasts.) For human hunger to be elastic like this makes evolutionary sense. By feasting whenever they had the chance, our hunter-gatherer ancestors could store fat to use later when they were confronted with food scarcity or famine. We've seen that in Papua New Guinea and Melanesia, "big men" and their followers work hard to organize feasts at which pigs are killed and cooked and pork is widely distributed and eaten. In those societies it's a rare and welcome treat to "pig out." In the contemporary United States it's easy to "pig out" any day of the year. If a "thrifty

See your OLC Bringing It All Together links
mhhe.com/kottak

Fast food leaves its imprint on the body. The 4-year-old Russian boy on the right weighs 123 pounds. The Georgian boy on the left has just turned 5 and weighs 112 pounds. After a wrestling match in which they tied, they went off to enjoy a meal in Tbilisi, Georgia, on July 9, 2003.

Whether in North America or in Denmark, as shown here on May 13, 2002, McDonald's presents itself as a place where families can eat comfortably.

gene" facilitating fat storage was adaptive for our hunter-gatherer ancestors, it has become maladaptive today given the food surplus just described (see Brown and Bentley-Condit 1996; Farb and Armelagos 1980).

The American epidemic of obesity is a consequence of cheap and abundant food. As applied anthropologists know, changes take place as part of systems: One change leads to other changes, which are related and compensatory. Thus, as Critser (2003) notes, to accommodate fatter customers, restaurants have increased the size of their seats. American government agencies have relaxed their weight, fitness, and dietary guidelines. Named diets and fitness centers have proliferated, and clothing sizes have been recalibrated to make fatter people feel thinner. "It runs large" and "it runs small" are common phrases in the linguistic strategies of garment salespeople.

Overeating has clear health consequences. The new American diet has ushered in an epidemic of Type 2 diabetes, formerly known as "adult-onset diabetes," which, however, now afflicts millions of children. The cost of overconsumption to the American health system runs to billions of dollars annually. According to Pollan (2003), the fattening of America may be emerging as a political issue. A grassroots parents' movement seeks to remove fast food and vending machines from schools. Obese customers have filed lawsuits against fast-food chains, seeking to hold those companies liable for health problems, as tobacco companies have been held liable through legal action. Questions have been raised about the ethics of marketing unhealthy products to children.

We've seen how the business strategy of supersizing fueled the expansion of fast food and overeating. An anthropological perspective can reveal more subtle cultural factors within the culture of overconsumption, which characterizes not only the United States but also the consuming (middle and upper) classes of nations around the world.

The sun, it was said, never set on the British empire. We could make the same observation about the global presence of McDonald's in the 21st century. The number of McDonald's outlets today far surpasses the total number of fast-food restaurants in the United States in 1945. McDonald's has grown from a single hamburger stand in San Bernardino, California, into today's international web of thousands of outlets.

The success of McDonald's is founded on modern technology, particularly automobiles, television, work away from home, and the short lunch break (see Brown and Krick 2001). Several years ago, I began to notice certain ritual-like aspects of Americans' behavior at fast-food restaurants, especially at McDonald's. Tell your fellow Americans that going to a fast-food restaurant is similar in some ways to going to church and their bias as natives will reveal itself in laughter, denial, or questions about your sanity. McDonald's, for natives, is just a place to eat. However, an analysis of what natives do there will reveal a very high degree of formal, uniform behavior by staff members and customers alike. It is particularly interesting that this invariance in word and deed has developed without any theological doctrine. It is striking that a commercial organization should be so successful in producing behavioral invariance. Factors other than low cost, fast service, and the taste of the food—all of which are approximated by other chains—have contributed to our acceptance of McDonald's and adherence to its rules.

Remarkably, when Americans travel abroad, even in countries noted for good food, many go to the local McDonald's outlet. The same factors that lead us to visit McDonald's at home are responsible. Because Americans are thoroughly familiar with how to eat and more or less what they will pay at McDonald's, in its outlets overseas they have a home away from home. In Paris, whose people aren't known for making tourists, particularly Americans, feel at home, McDonald's offers sanctuary (along with relatively clean, free rest rooms). It is, after all, an originally American institution where natives, programmed by years of prior experience, can feel completely at home.

This devotion to McDonald's rests in part on uniformities associated with its outlets: food, setting, architecture, ambience, acts, and utterances. The McDonald's symbol, the golden arches, is an almost universal symbol, as familiar to Americans as Mickey Mouse, Oprah, and the flag. A McDonald's (now closed) near my university was a brick structure whose stained-glass windows had golden arches as their central theme. Sunlight flooded in through a skylight that was like the clerestory of a church.

Americans enter a McDonald's restaurant for an ordinary, secular act—eating. However, the surroundings tell us we are somehow apart from the variability of the world outside. We know what we are going to see, what we are going to say, and what will be said to us. We know what we will eat, how it will taste, and how much it will cost. Behind the counter, agents wear similar attire. Permissible utterances by customer and worker are written above the counter. Throughout the United States, with only minor variations, the menu is in the same place, contains the same items, and has the same prices. The food, again with only minor variation, is prepared according to plan and varies little in taste. Obviously, customers are limited in what they can choose. Less obviously, they are limited linguistically—in terms of what they can say. Each item has its appropriate designation: "large fry," "quarter pounder with cheese." The novice who innocently asks, "What kind of hamburgers do you have?" or "What's a Big Mac?" is out of place.

A linguistic anthropologist would notice that other ritual phrases are uttered by the person behind the counter. After the customer has completed an order, if no potatoes are requested, the agent ritually asks, "You want the combo?" Once food is presented and picked up, the agent conventionally says, "Have a nice day." (McDonald's has surely played a strong role in the diffusion of this linguistic cliché into every corner of contemporary American life.)

Understandably, as the world's number one fast-food chain, McDonald's evokes hostility. The Ann Arbor campus McDonald's once was the scene of a ritual rebellion—desecration by the Radical Vegetarian League, which held a "puke-in." Standing on the second-story balcony just below the clerestory, a dozen vegetarians gorged themselves on mustard and water and vomited down on the customer waiting area. McDonald's, defiled, lost many customers that day. Worldwide, McDonald's has become one of the most potent symbols of globalization and perceived American cultural and economic imperialism. McDonald's has felt the brunt of cultural, including religious, opposition to its meals, meats, and mission.

Eating at McDonald's and religious feasts are in complementary distribution in American life. That is, when one occurs, the other doesn't. Most Americans would consider it inappropriate to eat at a fast-food restaurant on Christmas, Thanksgiving, Easter, or Passover. Our culture regards these as family days, occasions when relatives and close friends get together. However, although Americans neglect McDonald's on holidays, television reminds us that McDonald's still endures, that it will welcome us back once our holiday is over. The television presence of McDonald's is particularly evident on such occasions—whether through a float in the Macy's Thanksgiving Day

On April 18, 2002, students hold a sit-in at a McDonald's outlet in Beirut, Lebanon, as part of a campaign to boycott American products. McDonald's international success has made it a target of protests against perceived American cultural imperialism.

parade or through sponsorship of special programs, particularly "family entertainment."

Although Burger King, Wendy's, and Arby's compete with McDonald's for the fast-food business, none has equaled the success of McDonald's. The explanation may lie in the particularly skillful ways in which McDonald's advertising plays up the features just discussed. On Saturday morning television, with its steady stream of cartoons, McDonald's has been a ubiquitous sponsor. Breakfast at McDonald's has been promoted by a fresh-faced, sincere, happy, clean-cut young woman. Actors gambol on ski slopes or in mountain pastures. The single theme that for years has run through the commercials is personalism. McDonald's, the commercials drone on, is something other than a fast-food restaurant. It's a warm, friendly place where you are graciously welcomed and feel at home, where your children won't get into trouble. McDonald's commercials tell you that you aren't simply an anonymous face in an amorphous crowd. You find respite from a hectic and impersonal society, the break you deserve. Your individuality and dignity are respected at McDonald's. And "I'm lovin it."

McDonald's advertising tries to deemphasize the fact that the chain is a commercial organization. One jingle proclaimed, "You, you're the one; we're fixin' breakfast for ya"—not "We're making millions off ya." "Family" television entertainment often is "brought to you by McDonald's."

McDonald's commercials regularly tell us that it supports and works to maintain the values of American family life.

I am not arguing here that McDonald's has become a religion. I merely am suggesting that specific ways in which Americans participate in McDonald's bear analogies to religious systems involving myth, symbol, and ritual. Just as in rituals, participation in McDonald's requires temporary subordination of individual differences in a social and cultural collectivity. In a land of ethnic, social, economic, and religious diversity, we demonstrate that we share something with millions of others. Furthermore, as in rituals, participation in McDonald's is linked to a cultural system that transcends the chain itself. By eating there, we say something about ourselves as Americans, about our acceptance of certain collective values, customs, and ways of living.

Such widespread learned behavior patterns, fueled in this case by a savvy business model, also have biological—weight and health—consequences, as we saw at the beginning of this essay. Consider finally the explosion of paper, plastic, and Styrofoam associated with the fast-food industry. Such material remains, along with distinctive arches and architecture, offer evidence that contemporary garbologists, or future archaeologists, might use to reconstruct the culture of consumption in the early 21st century.

Appendix 1

A History of Theories in Anthropology

Anthropology has various fathers and mothers. The fathers include Lewis Henry Morgan, Sir Edward Burnett Tylor, Franz Boas, and Bronislaw Malinowski. The mothers include Ruth Benedict and especially Margaret Mead. Some of the fathers might be classified better as grandfathers, since one, Franz Boas, was the intellectual father of Mead and Benedict, and since what is known now as Boasian anthropology arose mainly in opposition to the 19th-century evolutionism of Morgan and Tylor.

My goal here is to survey the major theoretical perspectives that have characterized anthropology since its emergence in the second half of the nineteenth century. Evolutionary perspectives, especially those associated with Morgan and Tylor, dominated early anthropology. The early 20th century witnessed various reactions to 19th-century evolutionism. In Great Britain, functionalists such as Malinowski and Alfred Reginald Radcliffe-Brown abandoned the speculative historicism of the evolutionists in favor of studies of present-day living societies. In the United States, Boas and his followers rejected the search for evolutionary stages in favor of a historical approach that traced borrowing between cultures and the spread of culture traits across geographic areas. Functionalists and Boasians alike saw cultures as integrated and patterned. The functionalists especially viewed societies as systems in which various parts worked together to maintain the whole.

By the mid-20th century, following World War II and the collapse of colonialism, there was a revived interest in change, including new evolutionary approaches. Other anthropologists concentrated on the symbolic basis and nature of culture, using symbolic and interpretive approaches to uncover patterned symbols and meanings. By the 1980s anthropologists had grown more interested in the relation between culture and the individual, and the role of human action (agency) in transforming culture. There was also a resurgence of historical approaches, including those that viewed local cultures in relation to colonialism and the world system. Contemporary anthropology is marked by increasing specialization, based on special topics and identities. Reflecting this specialization, some universities have moved away from the holistic, biocultural view of anthropology that is reflected in this book. However, the Boasian view of anthropology as a four-subfield discipline—including biological, archaeological, cultural, and linguistic anthropology—continues to thrive at many universities as well.

EVOLUTIONISM

Both Tylor and Morgan wrote classic books during the 19th century. Tylor (1871/1958) offered a classic definition of culture and proposed it as a topic that could be studied scientifically. Morgan's influential books included *Ancient Society* (1877/1963), *The League of the Ho-dé-no-sau-nee or Iroquois* (1851/1966), and *Systems of Consanguinity and Affinity of the Human Family* (1870/1997). The first was a key work in cultural evolution. The second was an early ethnography. The third was the first systematic compendium of cross-cultural data on systems of kinship terminology.

Ancient Society is a key example of 19th-century evolutionism applied to society. Morgan assumed that human society had evolved through a series of stages, which he called savagery, barbarism, and civilization. He subdivided savagery and barbarism into three substages each: lower, middle, and upper savagery and lower, middle, and upper barbarism. In Morgan's scheme, the earliest

A1

humans lived in lower savagery, with a subsistence based on fruits and nuts. In middle savagery people started fishing and gained control over fire. The invention of the bow and arrow ushered in upper savagery. Lower barbarism began when humans started making pottery. Middle barbarism in the Old World depended on the domestication of plants and animals, and in the Americas on irrigated agriculture. Iron smelting and the use of iron tools ushered in upper barbarism. Civilization, finally, came about with the invention of writing.

Morgan's brand of evolutionism is known as *unilinear evolutionism*, because he assumed there was one line or path through which all societies had to evolve. Any society in upper barbarism, for example, had to include in its history, in order, periods of lower, middle, and upper savagery, and then lower and middle barbarism. Stages could not be skipped. Furthermore, Morgan believed that the societies of his time could be placed in the various stages. Some had not advanced beyond upper savagery. Others had made it to middle barbarism, while others had attained civilization.

Critics of Morgan disputed various elements of his scheme, particularly the criteria he used for progress. Thus, because Polynesians never developed pottery, they were frozen, in Morgan's scheme, in upper savagery. In fact, in sociopolitical terms, Polynesia was an advanced region, with many chiefdoms and at least one state—ancient Hawaii. We know now, too, that Morgan was wrong in assuming that societies pursued only one evolutionary path. Societies (e.g., Maya versus Mesopotamia) followed different paths to civilization, based on very different economies.

In his book *Primitive Culture* (1871/1958), Tylor developed his own evolutionary approach to the anthropology of religion, as was discussed in the chapter "Religion." Like Morgan, Tylor proposed a unilinear path—from animism to polytheism, then monotheism, and finally science. Religion would end, Tylor thought, when it lost its primary function—to explain the unexplainable. In Tylor's view, religion would retreat as science provided better and better explanations. Both Tylor and Morgan were interested in *survivals*, practices that survived in contemporary society form earlier evolutionary stages. The belief in ghosts today, for example, would represent a survival from the stage of animism—the belief in spiritual beings. Survivals were taken as evidence that a particular society had passed through earlier evolutionary stages.

Morgan is well known also for *The League of the Iroquois*, anthropology's earliest ethnography. It was based on occasional rather than protracted fieldwork. Morgan, although one of anthropology's founders, was not himself a professionally trained anthropologist. He was a lawyer in upper New York state, who was fond of visiting a nearby Seneca reservation and learning about their history and customs. The Seneca were one of six Iroquois tribes. Through his field work, and his friendship with Ely Parker (see Chapter 1), an educated Iroquois man, Morgan was able to describe the social, political, religious, and economic principles of Iroquois life, including the history of their confederation. He laid out the structural principles on which Iroquois society was based. Morgan also used his skills as a lawyer to help the Iroquois in their fight with the Ogden Land Company, which was attempting to seize their lands.

Although Morgan was a strong advocate for the Iroquois, his work contains some assumptions that would be considered racist today. There are statements in *The League* and elsewhere suggesting, erroneously, that cultural traits, such as hunting and a type of kinship terminology, have a biological basis. Morgan assumed that the desire to hunt was intrinsic to being Indian, transmitted "in the blood" rather than through enculturation. It was up to Franz Boas, writing decades later, to show that cultural traits are transmitted culturally rather than genetically, and to show the malleability of human biology and its openness to variable enculturation.

THE BOASIANS

Four-Field Anthropology

Indisputably, Boas is the father of four-field American anthropology. His book *Race, Language, and Culture* (1940/1966) is a collection of essays on those key topics. Boas contributed to cultural, biological, and linguistic anthropology. His biological studies of European immigrants to the United States revealed and measured phenotypical plasticity. The children of immigrants differed physically from their parents not because of genetic change but because they had grown up in a different environment. Boas showed that human biology was plastic. It could be changed by the environment, including cultural forces. Boas and his students worked hard to demonstrate that biology (including race) did not determine culture. In an important book, Ruth Benedict (1940) stressed the idea that people of many races have contributed to major historical advances and that civilization is the achievement of no single race.

As was mentioned in Chapter 1, the four subfields of anthropology initially formed around interests in Native Americans—their cultures, histories, languages, and physical characteristics. Boas himself studied language and culture among Native Americans, most notably the Kwakiutl of the North Pacific coast of the United States and Canada.

Historical Particularism

Boas and his many influential followers, who studied with him at Columbia University in New York City, took issue with Morgan on many counts. They disputed the criteria he used to define his stages. They disputed the idea of one evolutionary path. They argued that the same cultural result, for example, totemism, could not have a single explanation, because there were many paths to totemism. Their position was one of *historical particularism.* Because the particular histories of totemism in societies A, B, and C had all been different, those forms of totemism had different causes, which made them incomparable. They might seem to be the same, but they were really different because they had different histories. Any cultural form, from totemism to clans, could develop, they believed, for all sorts of reasons. Boasian historical particularism rejected what those scholars called the *comparative method,* which was associated not only with Morgan and Tylor, but with any anthropologist interested in cross-cultural comparison. The evolutionists had compared societies in attempting to reconstruct the evolutionary history of *Homo sapiens.* Later anthropologists, such as Émile Durkheim and Claude Lévi-Strauss (see below), also compared societies in attempting to explain cultural phenomena such as totemism. As we have seen throughout this text, cross-cultural comparison is alive and well in contemporary anthropology.

Independent Invention versus Diffusion

Remember from the chapter "Culture" that *cultural generalities* are shared by some but not all societies. To explain cultural generalities, such as totemism and the clan, the evolutionists had stressed independent invention: Eventually people in many areas (as they evolved along a preordained evolutionary path) had come up with the same cultural solution to a common problem. Agriculture, for example, was invented several times. The Boasians, while not denying independent invention, stressed the importance of diffusion, or borrowing, from other cultures. The analytic units they used to study diffusion were the culture trait, the trait complex, and the culture area. A culture trait was something like a bow and arrow. A trait complex was the hunting pattern that went along with it. A culture area was based on the diffusion of traits and trait complexes across a particular geographic area, such as the Plains, the Southwest, or the North Pacific coast of North America. Such areas usually had environmental boundaries that could limit the spread of culture traits outside that area. For the Boasians historical particularism and diffusion were complementary. As culture traits diffused, they developed their particular histories as they entered and moved through particular societies. Boasians such as Alfred Kroeber, Clark Wissler, and Melville Herskovits studied the distribution of traits and developed culture area classifications for Native North America (Wissler and Kroeber) and Africa (Herskovits).

Historical particularism was based on the idea that each element of culture, such as the culture trait or trait complex, had its own distinctive history, and that social forms (such as totemism in different societies) that might look similar were far from identical because of their different histories. Historical particularism rejected comparison and generalization in favor of an individuating historical approach. In this rejection, historical particularism stands in contrast to most of the approaches that have followed it.

FUNCTIONALISM

Another challenge to evolutionism (and to historical particularism) came from Great Britain. *Functionalism* postponed the search for origins (through evolution or diffusion) and instead focused on the role of culture traits and practices in contemporary society. The two main strands of functionalism are associated with Alfred Reginald Radcliffe-Brown and Bronislaw Malinowski, a Polish anthropologist who taught mainly in Great Britain.

Malinowski

Both Malinowski and Radcliffe-Brown focused on the present rather than on historical reconstruction. Malinowski did pioneering field work among living people. Usually considered the father of ethnography by virtue of his years of field work in the Trobriand Islands, Malinowski was a functionalist in two senses. In the first, rooted in his ethnography, he believed that all customs and institutions in society were integrated and interrelated, so that if one changed, others would change as well. Each, then, was a function of the others. A corollary of this belief was that the ethnography could begin anywhere and eventually get at the rest of the culture. Thus, a study of Trobriand fishing eventually would lead the ethnographer to study the entire economic system, the role of magic and religion, myth, trade, and kinship. The second strand of Malinowski's functionalism is known as *needs functionalism.* Malinowski (1944) believed that humans had a set of universal biological needs, and that customs developed to fulfill those needs. The function of any practice was the role it played in satisfying those universal biological needs, such as the need for food, sex, shelter, and so on.

Conjectural History

According to Radcliffe-Brown (1962/1965), although history is important, social anthropology could never hope to discover the histories of people without writing. (*Social anthropology* is what cultural anthropology is called in Great Britain.) He trusted neither evolutionary nor diffusionist reconstructions. Since all history was conjectural, Radcliffe-Brown urged social anthropologists to focus on the role that particular practices play in the life of societies today. In a famous essay Radcliffe-Brown (1962/1965) examined the prominent role of the mother's brother among the Ba Thonga of Mozambique. An evolutionist priest working in Mozambique previously had explained the special role of the mother's brother in this patrilineal society as a survival from a time when the descent rule had been matrilineal. (The unilinear evolutionists believed all human societies had passed through a matrilineal stage.) Since Radcliffe-Brown believed that the history of Ba Thonga society could only be conjectural, he explained the special role of the mother's brother with reference to the institutions of present rather than past Ba Thonga society. Radcliffe-Brown advocated that social anthropology be a *synchronic* rather than a *diachronic* science, that is, that it study societies as they exist today (synchronic, at one time) rather than across time (diachronic).

Structural Functionalism

The term *structural functionalism* is associated with Radcliffe-Brown and Edward Evan Evans-Pritchard, another prominent British social anthropologist. The latter is famous for many books, including *The Nuer* (1940), an ethnographic classic that laid out very clearly the structural principles that organized Nuer society in Sudan. According to functionalism and structural functionalism, customs (social practices) function to preserve the social structure. In Radcliffe-Brown's view, the *function* of any practice is what it does to maintain the system of which it is a part. That system has a structure whose parts work or function to maintain the whole. Radcliffe-Brown saw social systems as comparable to anatomical and physiological systems. The function of organs and physiological processes is their role in keeping the body running smoothly. So, too, he thought, did customs, practices, social roles, and behavior function to keep the social system running smoothly.

Dr. Pangloss versus Conflict

Given this suggestion of harmony, some functionalist models have been criticized as Panglossian, after Dr. Pangloss, a character in Voltaire's *Candide* who was fond of proclaiming this "the best of all possible worlds." Panglossian functionalism means a tendency to see things as functioning not just to maintain the system but to do so in the most optimal way possible, so that any deviation from the norm would only damage the system. A group of British social anthropologists working at the University of Manchester, dubbed the Manchester school, are well known for their research in African societies and their departure from a Panglossian view of social harmony. Manchester anthropologists Max Gluckman and Victor Turner made conflict an important part of their analysis, such as when Gluckman wrote about rituals of rebellion. However, the Manchester school did not abandon functionalism totally. Its members examined how rebellion and conflict were regulated and dissipated, thus maintaining the system.

Functionalism Persists

A form of functionalism persists in the widely accepted view that there are social and cultural systems and that their elements, or constituent parts, are functionally related (are functions of each other) so that they covary: when one part changes, others also change. Also enduring is the idea that some elements—often the economic ones—are more important than others are. Few would deny, for example, that significant economic changes, such as the increasing cash employment of women, have led to changes in family and household organization, and in related variables such as age at marriage and frequency of divorce. Changes in work and family arrangements then affect other variables, such as frequency of church attendance, which has declined in the United States and Canada.

CONFIGURATIONALISM

Two of Boas's students, Benedict and Mead, developed an approach to culture that has been called *configurationalism*. This is related to functionalism in the sense that culture is seen as integrated. We've seen that the Boasians traced the geographic distribution of culture traits. But Boas recognized that diffusion wasn't automatic. Traits might not spread if they met environmental barriers, or if they were not accepted by a particular culture. There had to be a fit between the culture and the trait diffusing in, and borrowed traits would be reworked to fit the culture adopting them. This process recalls the discussion, in the chapter "Cultural Exchange and Survival," of how borrowed traits are indigenized—modified to fit the existing culture. Although traits may diffuse in from various directions, Benedict stressed that culture traits—indeed, whole cultures—are uniquely patterned or integrated. Her best-selling book *Patterns of Culture* (1934/1959) described such culture patterns.

Mead also found patterns in the cultures she studied, including Samoa, Bali, and Papua New Guinea. Mead was particularly interested in how cultures varied in their patterns of enculturation. Stressing the plasticity of human nature, she saw culture as a powerful force that created almost endless possibilities. Even among neighboring societies, different enculturation patterns could produce very different personality types and cultural configurations. Mead's best-known—albeit controversial—book is *Coming of Age in Samoa* (1928/1961). Mead traveled to Samoa to study female adolescence there in order to compare it with the same period of life in the United States. Suspicious of biologically determined universals, she assumed that Samoan adolescence would differ from the same period in the United States and that this would affect adult personality. Using her Samoan ethnographic findings, Mead contrasted the apparent sexual freedom and experimentation there with the repression of adolescent sexuality in the United States. Her findings supported the Boasian view that culture, not biology or race, determines variation in human behavior and personality. Mead's later field work among the Arapesh, Mundugumor, and Tchambuli of New Guinea resulted in *Sex and Temperament in Three Primitive Societies* (1935/1950). That book documented variation in male and female personality traits and behavior across cultures. She offered it as further support for cultural determinism. Like Benedict, Mead was more interested in describing how cultures were uniquely patterned or configured than in explaining how they got to be that way.

NEOEVOLUTIONISM

Around 1950, with the end of World War II and a growing anticolonial movement, anthropologists renewed their interest in culture change and even evolution. The American anthropologists Leslie White and Julian Steward complained that the Boasians had thrown the baby (evolution) out with the bath water (the particular flaws of 19th-century evolutionary schemes). There was a need, the neoevolutionists contended, to reintroduce within the study of culture a powerful concept—evolution itself. This concept, after all, remains basic to biology. Why should it not apply to culture as well?

In his book *The Evolution of Culture* (1959), White claimed to be returning to the same concept of cultural evolution used by Tylor and Morgan, but now informed by a century of archaeological

discoveries and a much larger ethnographic record. White's approach has been called *general evolution,* the idea that over time and through the archaeological, historical, and ethnographic records, we can see the evolution of culture as a whole. For example, human economies have evolved from Paleolithic foraging, through early farming and herding, to intensive forms of agriculture, and to industrialism. Sociopolitically, too, there has been evolution, from bands and tribes to chiefdoms and states. There can be no doubt, White argued, that culture has evolved. But unlike the unilinear evolutionists of the 19th century, White realized that particular cultures might not evolve in the same direction.

Julian Steward, in his influential book *Theory of Culture Change* (1955), proposed a different evolutionary model, which he called *multilinear evolution.* He showed how cultures had evolved along several different lines. For example, he recognized different paths to statehood (e.g., those followed by irrigated versus nonirrigated societies). Steward was also a pioneer in a field of anthropology he called *cultural ecology,* today generally known as *ecological anthropology,* which considers the relationships between cultures and environmental variables.

Unlike Mead and Benedict, who were not interested in causes, White and Steward were. For White, energy capture was the main measure and cause of cultural advance: Cultures advanced in proportion to the amount of energy harnessed per capita per year. In this view, the United States is one of the world's most advanced societies because of all the energy it harnesses and uses. White's formulation is ironic in viewing societies that deplete nature's bounty as being more advanced than those that conserve it.

Steward was equally interested in causality, and he looked to technology and the environment as the main causes of culture change. The environment and the technology available to exploit it were seen as part of what he called the *culture core*—the combination of subsistence and economic activities that determined the social order and the configuration of that culture in general.

CULTURAL MATERIALISM

In proposing *cultural materialism* as a theoretical paradigm, Marvin Harris adapted multilayered models of determinism associated with White and Steward. For Harris (1979/2001) all societies had an *infrastructure,* corresponding to Steward's culture core, consisting of technology, economics, and demography—the systems of production and reproduction without which societies could not survive. Growing out of infrastructure was *structure*—social relations, forms of kinship and descent, patterns of distribution and consumption. The third layer was *superstructure*: religion, ideology, play—aspects of culture furthest away from the meat and bones that enable cultures to survive. Harris's key belief, shared with White, Steward, and Karl Marx, was that in the final analysis infrastructure determines structure and superstructure.

Harris therefore took issue with theorists (he called them "idealists") such as Max Weber who argued for a prominent role of religion (the Protestant ethic, as discussed in the chapter "Religion") in changing society. Weber didn't argue that Protestantism had caused capitalism. He merely contended that the individualism and other traits associated with early Protestantism were especially compatible with capitalism and therefore aided its spread. One could infer from Weber's argument that without Protestantism, the rise and spread of capitalism would have been much slower. Harris probably would counter that given the change in economy, some new religion compatible with the new economy would appear and spread with that economy, since infrastructure (what Karl Marx called the base) always determines in the final analysis.

SCIENCE AND DETERMINISM

Harris's influential books include *The Rise of Anthropological Theory* (1968/2001) and *Cultural Materialism: The Struggle for a Science of Culture* (1979/2001). Like most of the anthropologists discussed so far, Harris insisted that anthropology is a *science*; that science is based on explanation, which uncovers relations of cause and effect; and that the role of science is to discover causes, to find determinants. One of White's two influential books was *The Science of Culture* (1949). Malinowski set forth his theory of needs functionalism in a book titled *A Scientific Theory of Culture, and Other Essays* (1944). Mead viewed anthropology as a humanistic science of unique value in understanding and improving the human condition.

Like Harris, White, and Steward, all of whom looked to infrastructural factors as determinants, Mead was a determinist, but of a very different sort. Mead's cultural determinism viewed human nature as more or less a blank slate on which culture could write almost any lesson. Culture was so powerful that it could change drastically the expression of adolescence in Samoa and the United States. Mead stressed the role of culture rather than economy, environment, or material factors in this difference.

CULTURE AND THE INDIVIDUAL

Culturology

Interestingly, Leslie White, the avowed evolutionist and champion of energy as a measure of cultural progress, was, like Mead, a strong advocate of the importance of culture. White saw cultural anthropology as a science, and he named that science *culturology*. Cultural forces, which rested on the unique human capacity for symbolic thought, were so powerful, White believed, that individuals made little difference. White disputed what was then called the "great man theory of history," the idea that particular individuals were responsible for great discoveries and epochal changes. White looked instead to the constellation of cultural forces that produced great individuals. During certain historical periods, such as the Renaissance, conditions were right for the expression of creativity and greatness, and individual genius blossomed. At other times and places, there may have been just as many great minds, but the culture did not encourage their expression. As proof of this theory, White pointed to the simultaneity of discovery. Several times in human history, when culture was ready, people working independently in different places have come up with the same revolutionary idea or achievement. Examples include the formulation of the theory of evolution through natural selection by Charles Darwin and Alfred Russel Wallace, the independent rediscovery of Mendelian genetics by three separate scientists in 1917, and the independent invention of flight by the Wright brothers in the United States and Santos Dumont in Brazil.

The Superorganic

Much of the history of anthropology has been about the roles and relative prominence of culture and the individual. Like White, the prolific Boasian anthropologist Alfred Kroeber stressed the power of culture. Kroeber (1952/1987) called the cultural realm, whose origin converted an ape into an early hominid, the *superorganic*. The superorganic opened up a new domain of analysis separable from, but comparable in importance to, the organic (life—without which there could be no superorganic) and the inorganic (chemistry and physics—the basis of the organic). Like White (and long before him Tylor, who first proposed a science of culture), Kroeber saw culture as the basis of a new science, which became cultural anthropology. Kroeber (1923) laid out the basis of this science in anthropology's first textbook. He attempted to demonstrate the power of culture over the individual by focusing on particular styles and fashions, such as those involving women's hem lengths. According to Kroeber (1944), hordes of individuals were carried along helplessly by the alternating trends of various times, swept up in the undulation of styles. Unlike White, Steward, and Harris, Kroeber did not attempt to explain such shifts; he simply used them to show the power of culture over the individual. Like Mead, he was a cultural determinist.

Durkheim

In France, Émile Durkheim had taken a similar approach, calling for a new social science to be based in what he called, in French, the *conscience collectif*. The usual translation of this as "collective consciousness" does not convey adequately the similarity of this notion to Kroeber's superorganic and White's culturology. This new science, Durkheim proposed, would be based on the study of *social facts,* analytically distinct from the individuals from whose behavior those facts were inferred. Many anthropologists agree with the central promise that the role of the anthropologist is to study something larger than the individual. Psychologists study individuals; anthropologists study individuals as representative of something more. It is those larger systems, which consist of social positions—statuses and roles—and which are perpetuated across the generations through enculturation, that anthropologists should study.

Of course sociologists also study such social systems, and Durkheim, as was discussed in the chapter "Culture," is a common father of anthropology and sociology. Durkheim wrote of religion in Native Australia as readily as of suicide rates in modern societies. As analyzed by Durkheim, suicide rates (1897/1951) and religion (1912/2001) are collective phenomena. Individuals commit suicide for all sorts of reasons, but the variation in rates (which apply only to collectivities) can and should be linked to social phenomena, such as a sense of anomie, malaise, or alienation at particular times and in particular places.

SYMBOLIC AND INTERPRETIVE ANTHROPOLOGY

Victor Turner was a colleague of Max Gluckman in the Department of Social Anthropology at the University of Manchester, and thus a member of the Manchester school, previously described, before moving to the United States, where he taught at the University of Chicago and the University of Virginia. Turner wrote several important books and essays on ritual and symbols. His monograph *Schism and Continuity in an African Society* (1957/1996) illustrates the interest in conflict and its resolution previously mentioned as characteristic of the Manchester school. *The Forest of Symbols* (1967) is a collection of essays about symbols and rituals among the Nbembu of Zambia, where Turner did his major field work. In *The Forest of Symbols* Turner examines how symbols and rituals are used to redress, regulate, anticipate, and avoid conflict. He also examines a hierarchy of meanings of symbols, from their social meanings and functions to their internalization within individuals.

Turner recognized links between *symbolic anthropology* (the study of symbols in their social and cultural context), a school he pioneered, and such other fields as social psychology, psychology, and psychoanalysis. The study of symbols is all important in psychoanalysis, whose founder, Sigmund Freud, also recognized a hierarchy of symbols, from potentially universal ones to those that had meaning for particular individuals and emerged during the analysis and interpretation of their dreams. Turner's symbolic anthropology flourished at the University of Chicago, where another major advocate, David Schneider (1968), developed a symbolic approach to American culture in his book *American Kinship: A Cultural Account* (1968).

Related to symbolic anthropology, and also associated with the University of Chicago (and later with Princeton University), is *interpretive anthropology,* whose main advocate is Clifford Geertz. As mentioned in the chapter "Culture," Geertz defines culture as ideas based on cultural learning and symbols. During enculturation, individuals internalize a previously established system of meanings and symbols. They use this cultural system to define their world, express their feelings, and make their judgments.

Interpretive anthropology (Geertz 1973, 1983) approaches cultures as texts whose forms and, especially, meanings must be deciphered in particular cultural and historical contexts. Geertz's approach recalls Malinowski's belief that the ethnographer's primary task is "to grasp the native's point of view, his relation to life, to realize *his* vision of *his* world" (1922/1961, p. 25—Malinowski's italics). Since the 1970s, interpretive anthropology has considered the task of describing and interpreting that which is meaningful to natives. Cultures are texts that natives constantly "read" and ethnographers must decipher. According to Geertz (1973), anthropologists may choose anything in a culture that interests or engages them (such as a Balinese cockfight he interprets in a famous essay), fill in details, and elaborate to inform their readers about meanings in that culture. Meanings are carried by public symbolic forms, including words, rituals, and customs.

STRUCTURALISM

In anthropology structuralism mainly is associated with Claude Lévi-Strauss, a prolific and long-lived French anthropologist. Lévi-Strauss's structuralism evolved over time, from his early interest in the structures of kinship and marriage systems to his later interest in the structure of the human mind. In this latter sense, Lévi-Straussian structuralism (1967) aims not at explaining relations, themes, and connections among aspects of culture but at discovering them.

Structuralism rests on Lévi-Strauss's belief that human minds have certain universal characteristics which originate in common features of the *Homo sapiens* brain. These common mental structures lead people everywhere to think similarly regardless of their society or cultural background. Among these universal mental characteristics are the need to classify: to impose order on aspects of nature, on people's relation to nature, and on relations between people.

According to Lévi-Strauss, a universal aspect of classification is opposition, or contrast. Although many phenomena are continuous rather than discrete, the mind, because of its need to impose order, treats them as being more different than they are. One of the most common means of classifying is by using binary opposition. Good and evil, white and black, old and young, high and low are oppositions that, according to Lévi-Strauss, reflect the universal human need to convert differences of degree into differences of kind.

Lévi-Strauss applied his assumptions about classification and binary opposition to myths and folk tales. He showed that these narratives have simple building blocks—elementary structures or "mythemes." Examining the myths of different cultures, Lévi-Strauss shows that one tale can be converted into another through a series of simple operations, for example, by doing the following:

1. Converting the positive element of a myth into its negative

2. Reversing the order of the elements

3. Replacing a male hero with a female hero

4. Preserving or repeating certain key elements

Through such operations, two apparently dissimilar myths can be shown to be variations on a common structure, that is, to be transformations of each other. One example is Lévi-Strauss's (1967) analysis of "Cinderella," a widespread tale whose elements vary between neighboring cultures. Through reversals, oppositions, and negations, as the tale is told, retold, diffused, and incorporated within the traditions of successive societies, "Cinderella" becomes "Ash Boy," along with a series of other oppositions (e.g., stepfather versus stepmother) related to the change in gender from female to male.

PROCESSUAL APPROACHES: PRACTICE THEORY

Agency

Structuralism has been faulted for being overly formal and for ignoring social process. We saw in the chapter "Culture" that culture conventionally has been seen as social glue transmitted across the generations, binding people through their common past. More recently, anthropologists have come to see culture as something continually created and reworked in the present. The tendency to view culture as an entity rather than a process is changing. Contemporary anthropologists now emphasize how day-to-day action, practice, or resistance can make and remake culture (Gupta and Ferguson, eds. 1997*b*). *Agency* refers to the actions that individuals take, both alone and in groups, in forming and transforming cultural identities.

Practice Theory

The approach to culture known as *practice theory* (Ortner 1984) recognizes that individuals within a society or culture have diverse motives and intentions and different degrees of power and influence. Such contrasts may be associated with gender, age, ethnicity, class, and other social variables. Practice theory focuses on how such varied individuals—through their actions and practices—influence and transform the world they live in. Practice theory appropriately recognizes a reciprocal relation between culture and the individual. Culture shapes how individuals experience and respond to external events, but individuals also play an active role in how society functions and changes. Practice theory recognizes both constraints on individuals and the flexibility and changeability of cultures and social systems. Well-known practice theorists include Sherry Ortner, an American anthropologist, and Pierre Bourdieu and Anthony Giddens, French and British social theorists, respectively.

Leach

Some of the germs of practice theory, sometimes also called action theory (Vincent 1990), can be traced to the British anthropologist Edmund Leach, who wrote the influential book *Political Systems of Highland Burma* (1954/1970). Influenced by the Italian social theorist Vilfredo Pareto, Leach focused on how individuals work to achieve power and how their actions can transform society. In the Kachin Hills of Burma, now Myanmar, Leach described three forms of sociopolitical organization, which he called *gumlao, gumsa,* and Shan. Greatly oversimplifying, these three forms in that order suggest tribal, chiefdom, and state organization as discussed in previous chapters. But Leach made a tremendously important point by taking a regional rather than a local perspective. The Kachins participated in a regional system that included all three forms of organization. Traditional typologies suggest that tribes, chiefdoms, and states are separate units. Leach showed how they coexist and interact, as forms and possibilities known to everyone, in the same region. He also showed how Kachins creatively use power struggles, for example, to convert *gumlao* into *gumsa* organization, and how they negotiate their own identities within the regional system. Leach brought process to the formal models of structural functionalism. By focusing on power and how individuals get and use it, he showed the creative role of the individual in transforming culture.

WORLD-SYSTEM THEORY AND POLITICAL ECONOMY

Leach's regional perspective was not all that different from another development at the same time. Julian Steward, discussed previously as a neoevolutionist, joined the faculty of Columbia University in 1946, where he worked with several graduate students, including Eric Wolf and Sidney Mintz. Steward, Mintz, Wolf, and others planned and conducted a team research project in Puerto Rico, described in Steward's volume *The People of Puerto Rico* (1956). This project exemplified a post–World War II turn of anthropology away from "primitive" and nonindustrial societies, assumed to be somewhat isolated and autonomous, to contemporary societies recognized as forged by colonialism and participating fully in the modern world system. The team studied communities in different parts of Puerto Rico. The field sites were chosen to sample major events and adaptations, such as the sugar plantation, in the island's history. The approach emphasized economics, politics, and history.

Wolf and Mintz retained their interest in history throughout their careers. Wolf wrote the modern classic *Europe and the People without History* (1982), which viewed local people, such as Native Americans, in the context of world system events, such as the fur trade in North America. Wolf focused on how such "people without history"—that is, nonliterate people, those who lacked written histories of their own—participated in and were transformed by the world system and the spread of capitalism. Mintz's *Sweetness and Power* (1985) is another example of historical anthropology focusing on *political economy* (the web of interrelated economic and power relations). Mintz traces the domestication and spread of sugar, its transformative role in England, and its impact on the New World, where it became the basis for slave-based plantation economies in the Caribbean and Brazil. Such works in political economy illustrate a movement of anthropology toward interdisciplinarity, drawing on other academic fields, such as history and sociology. Any world-system approach in anthropology would have to pay attention to sociologist Immanuel Wallerstein's writing on world-system theory, including his model of core, periphery, and semiperiphery, as discussed in the chapter "The Modern World System." World-system approaches in anthropology have been criticized for overstressing the influence of outsiders, and for paying insufficient attention to the transformative actions of "the people without history" themselves.

CULTURE, HISTORY, POWER

More recent approaches in historical anthropology, while sharing an interest in power with the world system theorists, have focused more on local agency, the transformative actions of individuals and groups within colonized societies. Archival work has been prominent in recent historical anthropology, particularly on areas, such as Indonesia, for which colonial and postcolonial archives contain valuable information on relations between colonizers and colonized and the actions of various actors in the colonial context. Studies of culture, history, and power have drawn heavily on the work of European social theorists such as Antonio Gramsci and Michel Foucault.

As we saw in the chapter "Political Systems," Gramsci (1971) developed the concept of *hegemony* for a stratified social order in which subordinates comply with domination by internalizing their rulers' values and accepting domination as "natural." Both Pierre Bourdieu (1977) and Foucault (1979) contend that it is easier to dominate people in their minds than to try to control their bodies. Contemporary societies have devised various forms of social control in addition to physical violence. These include techniques of persuading, coercing, and managing people and of monitoring and recording their beliefs, behavior, movements, and contacts. Anthropologists interested in culture, history and power, such as Ann Stoler (1995, 2002), have examined systems of power, domination, accommodation, and resistance in various contexts, including colonies, postcolonies, and other stratified contexts.

ANTHROPOLOGY TODAY

Early American anthropologists, such as Morgan, Boas, and Kroeber, were interested in, and made contributions to, more than a single subfield. If there has been a single dominant trend in anthropology since the 1960s, it has been one of increasing specialization. During the 1960s, when this author attended graduate school at Columbia University, I had to study and take qualifying exams in all four subfields. This has changed. There are still strong four-field anthropology departments, but many excellent departments lack one or more of the subfields. Four-field departments such as the University of Michigan's still require courses and teaching expertise across the subfields, but graduate students must choose to specialize in a particular subfield, and take qualifying exams only in that subfield. In Boasian anthropology, all four subfields shared a single theoretical assumption about human plasticity. Today, following specialization, the theories that guide the subfields differ. Evolutionary paradigms of various sorts still dominate biological anthropology and remain strong in archaeology as well. Within cultural anthropology, it has been decades since evolutionary approaches thrived.

Ethnography, too, has grown more specialized. Cultural anthropologists now head for the field with a specific problem in mind, rather than with the goal of producing a holistic ethnography—a complete account of a given culture—as Morgan and Malinowski intended when they studied, respectively, the Iroquois and the people of the Trobriand Islands. We've seen, too, in previous chapters that "the field" has become more amorphous over time. Boas, Malinowski, and Mead went somewhere and stayed there for a while, studying the local culture. Today the field has expanded to include regional and national systems and the movement of people, such as immigrants and diasporas, across national boundaries. Many anthropologists now follow the flows of people, information, finance, and media to multiple sites. Such movement has been made possible by advances in transportation and communication. However, with so much time in motion and with the need to adjust to various field sites and contexts, the richness of traditional ethnography may diminish.

Anthropology also has witnessed a crisis in representation—questions about the role of the ethnographer and the nature of ethnographic authority. What right do ethnographers have to represent a people or culture to which they don't belong? Some argue that insiders' accounts are more valuable and appropriate than are studies by outsiders, because native anthropologists not only know the culture better, they also should be in charge of representing their culture to the public. Reflecting the trends just described, the AAA (American Anthropological Association) now has all sorts of subgroups. In its beginning, there were just anthropologists within the AAA. Now there are groups representing biological anthropology, archaeology, and linguistic, cultural, and applied anthropology, as well as dozens of groups formed around particular interests and identities. These groups represent psychological anthropology, urban anthropology, culture and agriculture, anthropologists in small colleges, midwestern anthropologists, senior anthropologists, lesbian and gay anthropologists, Latino/a anthropologists, and so on. Many of the identity-based groups accept the premise that group members are better qualified to study issues and topics involving that group than outsiders are.

The chapter "Cultural Exchange and Survival" described *postmodernity*—our world in flux, where mobile people manage multiple identities depending on place and context. The term *postmodern* refers to the blurring and breakdown of established canons, categories, distinctions, and boundaries. Postmodernity has influenced anthropology in many ways. It has changed our units of analysis. Postmodernism is like anthropology itself in extending value beyond high culture to the culture of ordinary people from all over the world. Yet postmodern approaches in anthropology also question established assumptions, such as the outside ethnographer's right to represent. Science itself is challenged. Doubters argue that science can't be trusted because it is carried out by scientists. All scientists, the doubters contend, come from particular individual or cultural backgrounds that prevent objectivity, leading to artificial and biased accounts that have no more value than do those of insiders who are nonscientists.

What are we to do if we, as I do, continue to share Mead's view of anthropology as a humanistic science of unique value in understanding and improving the human condition? We must try to stay aware of our biases and our inability totally to escape them. The best scientific choice would seem to be to combine the perpetual goal of objectivity with skepticism about achieving it. Kluckhohn's statement (1944, p. 9) of the need for anthropology's scientific objectivity still stands: "Anthropology provides a scientific basis for dealing with the crucial dilemma of the world today: how can peoples of different appearance, mutually unintelligible languages, and dissimilar ways of life get along peaceably together?" In this world of failed states, terrorism, and preemptive war, most anthropologists never would have chosen their profession had they doubted that anthropology could play a significant role in answering such questions.

Appendix 2
Ethics and Anthropology

As the main organization representing the breadth of anthropology (all four subfields, academic and applied dimensions), the American Anthropological Association believes that generating and appropriately using knowledge of the peoples of the world, past and present, is a worthy goal. The production of anthropological knowledge is a dynamic process involving different and ever-evolving approaches. The mission of the AAA is to advance anthropological research and encourage the spread of anthropological knowledge through publications, teaching, public education, and application. Part of that mission is to help educate AAA members about ethical obligations and challenges (http://www.aaanet.org).

As anthropologists conduct research and engage in other professional activities, ethical issues inevitably arise. Anthropologists have typically worked abroad, outside their own society. In the context of international contacts and cultural diversity, different value systems will meet, and often compete. To guide its members in making decisions involving ethics and values, the AAA offers a Code of Ethics. The most recent Code was approved in June 1998 and updated on March 31, 1999. The Code's preamble states that anthropologists have obligations to their scholarly field, to the wider society and culture, and to the human species, other species, and the environment. This Code's aim is to offer guidelines and to promote discussion and education. Although the AAA has investigated allegations of misconduct by anthropologists, it does not adjudicate such claims. The AAA also recognizes that anthropologists belong to multiple groups—including, perhaps, a family, a community, a religion, and other organizations—each of which may have its own ethical and moral rules. Because anthropologists can find themselves in complex situations and subject to more than one ethical code, the AAA Code provides a framework, not an ironclad formula, for making decisions.

The AAA wants its members to be attentive to ethical issues, and it urges anthropology departments to include ethical training in their curricula. The AAA Code addresses several contexts in which anthropologists work. Its main points about the ethical dimensions of research may be summarized.

Anthropologists should be open and honest about all dimensions of their research projects with funding agencies, colleagues, and all parties affected by the research. These parties should be informed about the purpose(s), potential impacts, and source(s) of support for the research. Anthropologists should disseminate the results of their research in an appropriate and timely way.

Researchers should not compromise anthropological ethics in order to conduct research. They should also pay attention to proper relations between themselves as guests and the host nations and communities where they work. The AAA does not advise anthropologists to avoid taking stands on issues. Indeed, the Code states that leadership in seeking to shape actions and policies may be as ethically justifiable as inaction.

Here are some of the headings and subheadings of the Code:

A. RESPONSIBILITY TO PEOPLE AND ANIMALS

1. The primary ethical obligation of the anthropologist is to the people, species, and materials they study. This obligation takes precedence over the goal of seeking new knowledge. It can also lead to the decision not to undertake, or to discontinue, research when ethical conflicts arise. This primary

ethical obligation—anthropology's "prime directive"—entails:

Avoiding harm or wrong.

Understanding that the production of knowledge can have positive or negative effects on the people or animals worked with or studied.

Respecting the well-being of humans and non-human primates.

Working for the long-term conservation of the archaeological, fossil, and historical records.

Consulting actively with the affected individuals or group(s), with the goal of establishing a working relationship that will benefit all parties.

2. Researchers must do all they can to preserve the safety, dignity, and privacy of the people with whom they work. Anthropologists working with animals should not endanger their safety, psychological well-being, or survival.

3. Anthropologists should determine whether their hosts wish to remain anonymous or to receive recognition, and should try to comply with those wishes. Researchers should make clear to research participants that, despite the best efforts of the anthropologist, anonymity may be compromised or recognition fail to materialize.

4. Researchers must obtain the *informed consent* of affected parties. That is, prior to their agreement to participate, people should be told about the purpose, nature, and procedures of the research and its potential impact on them. Informed consent (agreement to take part in the research) should be obtained from anyone providing information, owning materials being studied, or otherwise having an interest that might be impacted by the research. Informed consent does not necessarily imply or require a written or signed form.

5. Researchers who develop ongoing relationships with individuals providing information or with hosts must continue to respect the obligations of openness and informed consent.

6. Anthropologists may gain personally from their work, but they should not exploit individuals, groups, animals, or cultural or biological materials. They should recognize their debt to the communities and societies in which they work and to the people with whom they work. They should reciprocate in appropriate ways.

B. RESPONSIBILITY TO SCHOLARSHIP AND SCIENCE

1. Anthropologists should attempt to identify potential ethical conflicts and dilemmas when preparing proposals, and as projects proceed.

2. Anthropologists are responsible for the integrity and reputation of their field, of scholarship, and of science. They are subject to the general moral rules of scientific and scholarly conflict. They should not deceive or knowingly misrepresent (i.e., fabricate evidence, falsify, plagiarize). They should not attempt to prevent reporting of misconduct, or obstruct the scholarly research of others.

3. Anthropologists should do all they can to preserve opportunities for future researchers to follow them to the field.

4. To the extent possible, anthropologists should disseminate their findings to the scientific and scholarly community.

5. Anthropologists should consider all reasonable requests for access to their data and materials for purposes of research. They should preserve their data for use by posterity.

C. RESPONSIBILITY TO THE PUBLIC

1. Anthropologists should strive to ensure that their findings are contextualized properly and used responsibly. Anthropologists should also consider the social and political implications of their conclusions. They should be honest about their qualifications and philosophical and political biases. They must be alert to possible harm their information might cause people with whom they work, or colleagues.

2. Anthropologists may move beyond disseminating research results to a position of advocacy. This is an individual decision, but not an ethical responsibility.

D. ETHICS PERTAINING TO APPLIED ANTHROPOLOGY

1. The same ethical guidelines apply to all anthropological work—academic and applied. Applied anthropologists should use their results appropriately (i.e., publi-

cation, teaching, program and policy development) within a reasonable time. Applied anthropologists should be honest about their skills and intentions. They should monitor the effects of their work on everyone affected.

2. In dealings with employers, applied anthropologists should be honest about their qualifications, abilities, and goals. The applied anthropologist should review the aims and interests of the prospective employer, taking into consideration the employer's past activities and future goals. Applied anthropologists should not accept conditions contrary to professional ethics.

The full Code of Ethics, which is abbreviated and paraphrased here, is available at the AAA website (http://www.aaanet.org).

Appendix 3
American Popular Culture

Culture is shared. But all cultures have divisive as well as unifying forces. Tribes are divided by residence in different villages and membership in different descent groups. Nations, though united by government, are divided by class, region, ethnicity, religion, and political party. Unifying forces in tribal cultures include marriage, trade, and a belief in common descent. In any society, of course, a common cultural tradition also may provide a basis for uniformity.

Whatever unity contemporary American culture has doesn't rest on a particularly strong central government. Nor is national unity based on a belief in common descent or marital exchange networks. In fact, many of the commonalities of experience, belief, behavior, and activity that enable us to speak of "contemporary American culture" are relatively new. Like the globalizing forces discussed in the chapter "Cultural Exchange and Survival," they are founded on and perpetuated by recent developments, particularly in business, transportation, and the mass media.

ANTHROPOLOGISTS AND AMERICAN CULTURE

When anthropologists study urban ethnic groups or relationships between class and household organization, they focus on variation, a very important topic. When we look at the creative use that each individual makes of popular culture, as we did in the chapter "Cultural Exchange and Survival," we are also considering variation. However, anthropology traditionally has been concerned as much with uniformity as with variation. "National character" studies of the 1940s and 1950s foreshadowed anthropology's interest in unifying themes in modern nations. Unfortunately, those studies, of such countries as Japan and Russia, focused too much on the psychological characteristics of individuals.

Contemporary anthropologists interested in national culture realize that culture is an attribute of groups. Despite increasing ethnic diversity, we can still talk about an "American national cul-

ture." Through common experiences in their enculturation, especially through the media, most Americans do come to share certain knowledge, beliefs, values, and ways of thinking and acting (as was discussed in the chapter "Culture"). The shared aspects of national culture override differences among individuals, genders, regions, or ethnic groups.

The chapter "Cultural Exchange and Survival" examined the creative use that individuals and cultures make of introduced cultural forces, including media images. That chapter discussed how, through different "readings" of the same media "text," individuals and cultures constantly make and remake popular culture. Here we take a different approach. We focus on a few texts that have diffused most successfully in a given national (i.e., American) culture. Other such texts examined in previous chapters include *Star Wars* and *The Wizard of Oz*. These texts have spread because they are culturally appropriate. For various reasons, they are able to carry some sort of meaning to millions of people. Previous chapters focused on variation and diversity, but this appendix stresses unifying factors: common experiences, actions, and beliefs in American culture.

Anthropologists *should* study American society and culture. Anthropology, after all, deals with universals, generalities, and uniqueness. A national culture is a particular cultural variant, as interesting as any other. Although survey research traditionally is used to study modern nations, techniques developed to interpret and analyze smaller-scale societies, where sociocultural uniformity is more marked, also can contribute to an understanding of American life.

Native anthropologists are those who study their own cultures, for example, American anthropologists working in the United States, Canadian anthropologists working in Canada, or Nigerians working in Nigeria. Anthropological training and fieldwork abroad provide an anthropologist with a certain degree of detachment and objectivity that most natives lack. However, life experience as a native gives an advantage to anthropologists who wish to study their own cultures. Nevertheless, more than when working abroad, the native anthropologist is both participant and observer, often emotionally and intellectually involved in the events and beliefs being studied. Native anthropologists must be particularly careful to resist their own biases and prejudices as natives. They must strive to be as objective in describing their own cultures as they are in analyzing others.

Natives often see and explain their behavior very differently than anthropologists do. For example, most Americans have probably never considered the possibility that apparently secular, commercial, and recreational institutions such as sports, movies, and fast-food restaurants have things in common with myths, religious beliefs, symbols, and behavior. However, these similarities do exist. A key theme of this book has been that *anthropology helps us understand ourselves.* By studying other cultures, we learn both to appreciate and to question aspects of our own culture. Furthermore, the same techniques that anthropologists use in describing and analyzing other cultures can be applied to American culture.

American readers may not find the analyses that follow convincing. In part, this is because you are natives, who know much more about your own culture than you do about any other. Also, as we saw in the chapter "Cultural Exchange and Survival," people in a culture may "read" that culture differently. Furthermore, American culture assigns a high value to differences in individual opinion—and to the belief that one opinion is as good as another. Here I am trying to extract *culture* (widely shared aspects of behavior) from diverse *individual* opinions, actions, and experiences.

The following analyses depart from areas that can be easily quantified, such as demography and economics. We are entering a more impressionistic domain, where cultural analysis sometimes seems much more like literary analysis than like science. You will be right in questioning some of the conclusions that follow. Some are surely debatable; some may be plain wrong. However, if they illustrate how anthropology can be used to shed light on aspects of your own life and experience and to revise and broaden your understanding of your own culture, they will have served a worthwhile function.

A reminder (from the chapter "Culture") about culture, ethnocentrism, and native anthropologists is needed here. For anthropologists, *culture* means much more than refinement, cultivation, education, and appreciation of "classics" and "fine arts"—its popular usage. Curiously, however, when some anthropologists confront their own culture, they seem to forget this. Like other academics and intellectuals, they may regard American "pop" culture as trivial and unworthy of serious study. In doing so, they demonstrate ethnocentrism and reveal a bias that comes with being members of an academic-intellectual subculture.

In examining American culture, native anthropologists must be careful to overcome the bias associated with the academic subculture. Although some academics discourage their children from watching television, the fact that TVs outnumber toilets in American households is a significant cultural datum that anthropologists can't afford to ignore. My own research on Michigan college students may be generalizable to other young Americans. They visit fast-food restaurants more often than they visit houses of worship. I found that almost all had seen a Walt Disney movie and had attended rock concerts or football games. Such shared experiences are major features of American enculturation patterns. As we saw in the last "Bringing It All Together" essay, they affect our bodies as well as our minds. Certainly, any extraterrestrial anthropologist doing field work in the United States would stress such aspects of mass culture. Within the United States, the mass media and the culture of consumption have created major themes in contemporary national culture. These themes merit study.

From the popular domains of sports, TV, and movies I have chosen certain very popular texts to discuss here. (Other features of popular culture, such as fast food, have been discussed previously.) I could have used other texts (for example, blue jeans, baseball, or pizza) to make the same points: that there are powerful shared aspects of contemporary American national culture and that anthropological techniques can be used to interpret them.

FOOTBALL

Football, we say, is only a game, yet it has become a popular spectator sport. On fall Saturdays, millions of people travel to and from college football games. Smaller congregations meet in high school stadiums. Millions of Americans watch televised football. Indeed, nearly half the adult population of the United States watches the Super Bowl. Because football is of general interest to Americans, it is a unifying cultural institution that merits attention. Our most popular sports manage to attract fans of diverse ethnic backgrounds, regions, religions, political parties, jobs, social statuses, levels of wealth, and even genders.

The popularity of football, particularly professional football, depends directly on the mass media, especially television. Is football, with its territorial incursion, hard hitting, and violence—occasionally resulting in injury—popular because Americans are violent people? Are football spectators vicariously realizing their own hostile and aggressive tendencies? The anthropologist W. Arens (1981) discounts this interpretation. He points out that football is a peculiarly American pastime. Although a similar game is played in Canada, it is less popular there. Baseball has become a popular sport in the Caribbean, parts of Latin America, and Japan. Basketball and volleyball also are spreading. However, throughout most of the world, soccer is the most popular sport. Arens argues that if football were a particularly effective channel for expressing aggression, it would have spread (like soccer and baseball) to many other countries, where people have as many aggressive tendencies and hostile feelings as Americans do. Furthermore, he suggests that if a sport's popularity rested simply on a bloodthirsty temperament, boxing, a far bloodier sport, would be America's national pastime. Arens concludes that the explanation for the sport's popularity lies elsewhere, and I agree.

He contends that football is popular because it symbolizes certain key features of American life. In particular, it is characterized by teamwork based on specialization and division of labor, which are pervasive features of modern life. Susan Montague and Robert Morais (1981) take the analysis a step further. They argue that Americans appreciate football because it presents a miniaturized and simplified version of modern organizations. People have trouble understanding organizational bureaucracies, whether in business, universities, or government. Football, the anthropologists argue, helps us understand how decisions are made and rewards are allocated in organizations.

Montague and Morais link football's values, particularly teamwork, to those associated with business. Like corporate workers, the ideal players are diligent and dedicated to the team. Within corporations, however, decision making is complicated, and workers aren't always rewarded for their dedication and good job performance. Decisions are simpler and rewards are more consistent in football, these anthropologists contend, and this helps explain its popularity. Even if we can't figure out how General Motors and Microsoft run, any fan can become an expert on football's rules, teams, scores, statistics, and patterns of play. Even more important, football suggests that the values stressed by business really do pay off. Teams whose members work the hardest, show the most spirit, and best develop and coordinate their talents can be expected to win more often than other teams do.

STAR TREK*

Star Trek, a familiar, powerful, and enduring force in American popular culture, can be used to illustrate the idea that popular media content often is derived from prominent values expressed in many other domains of culture. Americans first encountered the Starship *Enterprise* on NBC in 1966. *Star Trek* was shown in prime time for just three seasons. However, the series not only survives but thrives today in syndication, reruns, books, websites, cassettes, and theatrical films. Revived as a regular weekly series with an entirely new cast in 1987, *Star Trek: The Next Generation* became the third most popular syndicated program in the United States (after *Wheel of Fortune* and *Jeopardy*). *Deep Space Nine, Voyager,* and *Enterprise* have been somewhat less popular successors in the *Star Trek* family.

What does the enduring mass appeal of *Star Trek* tell us about American culture? I believe the answer to be this: *Star Trek* is a transformation of a fundamental American origin myth. The same myth shows up in the image and celebration of Thanksgiving, a distinctively American holiday. Thanksgiving sets the myth in the past, and *Star Trek* sets it in the future.

The myths of contemporary America are drawn from a variety of sources, including such popular-culture fantasies as *Star Wars, The Wizard of Oz* (see the chapter on the arts), and *Star Trek.*

*This section is adapted from Conrad Phillip Kottak, *Prime-Time Society: An Anthropological Analysis of Television and Culture* (Belmont, CA: Wadsworth, 1990).

Our myths also include real people, particularly national ancestors, whose lives have been reinterpreted and endowed with special meaning over the generations. The media, schools, churches, communities, and parents teach the national origin myths to American children. The story of Thanksgiving, for example, continues to be important. It recounts the origin of a national holiday celebrated by Protestants, Catholics, and Jews. All those denominations share a belief in the Old Testament God, and they find it appropriate to thank God for their blessings.

Again and again, Americans have heard idealized retellings of that epochal early harvest. We have learned how Indians taught the Pilgrims to farm in the New World. Grateful Pilgrims then invited the Indians to share their first Thanksgiving. Native American and European labor, techniques, and customs thus blended in that initial biethnic celebration. Annually reenacting the origin myth, the American public schools commemorate "the first Thanksgiving" as children dress up as Pilgrims, Indians, and pumpkins.

More rapidly and pervasively as the mass media grow, each generation of Americans writes its own revisionist history. Our culture constantly reinterprets the origin, nature, and meaning of national holidays. The collective consciousness of contemporary Americans includes TV-saturated memories of "the first Thanksgiving" and "the first Christmas." Our mass culture has instilled the widely shared images of a *Peanuts*-peopled Pilgrim-and-Indian "love-in."

We also conjure up a fictionalized Nativity with Mary, Joseph, Jesus, manger animals, shepherds, three eastern kings, a little drummer boy, and, in some versions, Rudolph the Red-Nosed Reindeer. Note that the interpretation of the Nativity that American culture perpetuates is yet another variation on the same dominant myth. We remember the Nativity as a Thanksgiving involving interethnic contacts (e.g., the three kings) and gift giving. It is set in Bethlehem rather than Massachusetts.

We impose our present on the past as we reinterpret quasi-historic and actual events. For the future, we do it in our science-fiction and fantasy creations. *Star Trek* places in the future what the Thanksgiving story locates in the past: *the myth of the assimilationist, incorporating, melting-pot society.* The myth says that America is distinctive not just because it is assimilationist but because it is *founded* on unity in diversity. (Our *origin* is unity in diversity. After all, we call ourselves "the United States.") Thanksgiving and *Star Trek* illustrate the credo that unity through diversity is essential for survival (whether of a harsh winter or of the perils of outer space). Americans survive by sharing the fruits of specialization.

Star Trek proclaims that the sacred principles that validate American society, because they lie at its foundation, will endure across the generations and even the centuries. The Starship *Enterprise* crew is a melting pot. Captain James Tiberius Kirk is symbolic of real history. His clearest historic prototype is Captain James Cook, whose ship, the *Endeavor,* also sought out new life and civilizations. Kirk's infrequently mentioned middle name, from the Roman general and eventual emperor, links the captain to the earth's imperial history. Kirk is also symbolic of the original Anglo American. He runs the *Enterprise* (America is founded on free enterprise), just as laws, values, and institutions derived from England continue to guide the United States.

McCoy's Irish (or at least Gaelic) name represents the next wave, the established immigrant. Sulu is the successfully assimilated Asian American. The African American female character Uhura, "whose name means freedom," indicates that blacks will become full partners with all other Americans. However, Uhura was the only major female character in the original crew. Female extradomestic employment was less characteristic of American society in 1966 than it is now.

One of *Star Trek*'s constant messages is that strangers, even enemies, can become friends. Less obviously, this message is about cultural imperialism, the assumed irresistibility of American culture and institutions. Russian nationals (Chekhov) could be seduced and captured by an expansive American culture. Spock, although from Vulcan, is half human, with human qualities. We learn, therefore, that our assimilationist values eventually will not just rule the earth but extend to other planets as well. By "the next generation," Klingons, even more alien than Vulcans, and personified by Bridge Officer Worf, had joined the melting pot.

Even God was harnessed to serve American culture, in the person of Scotty. His role was that of the ancient Greek *deus ex machina.* He was a stage controller who "beamed" people up and down, back and forth, from earth to the heavens. Scotty, who kept society going, was also a servant-employee who did his engineering for management—illustrating loyalty and technical skill.

The Next Generation contained many analogues of the original characters. Several "partial people" were single-character personifications of particular human qualities represented in more complex form by the original *Star Trek* crew members. Kirk, Spock, and McCoy were split into multiple characters. Captain Jean-Luc Picard possessed the intellectual and managerial attributes of James T. Kirk. With his English accent and

French name, Picard, like Kirk, drew his legitimacy from symbolic association with historic Western European empires. First Officer Riker replaced Kirk as a romantic man of action.

Spock, an alien (strange ears) who represented science, reason, and intellect, was split in two. One half was Worf, a Klingon bridge officer whose cranial protuberances were analogous to Spock's ears. The other was Data, an android whose brain contained the sum of human knowledge. Two female characters, an empath and the ship's doctor, replaced Dr. McCoy as the repository of healing, emotion, and feeling.

Mirroring contemporaneous American culture, *The Next Generation* featured prominent black, female, and physically challenged characters. An African American actor played the Klingon Mr. Worf. Another, LeVar Burton, appeared as Geordi La Forge. Although blind, Geordi managed, through a vision-enhancing visor, to see things that other people could not. His mechanical vision expressed the characteristic and enduring American faith in technology. So did the android, Data.

During its first year, *The Next Generation* had three prominent female characters. One was the ship's doctor, a working professional with a teenage son. Another was an empath, the ultimate "helping professional." The third was the ship's security officer.

America had become more specialized, differentiated, and professional than it was in the 1960s. The greater role specificity and diversity of *Next Generation* characters reflected this. Nevertheless, both series convey the central *Star Trek* message, one that dominates the culture that created them: Americans are diverse. Individual qualities, talents, and specialties divide us. However, we make our livings and survive as members of cohesive, efficient groups. We explore and advance as members of a crew, a team, an enterprise, or, most generally, a society. Our nation is founded on and endures through assimilation—effective subordination of individual differences within a smoothly functioning multiethnic team. The team is American culture. It worked in the past. It works today.

It will go on working across the generations. Orderly and progressive democracy based on mutual respect is best. Inevitably, American culture will triumph over all others—by convincing and assimilating rather than conquering them. Unity in diversity guarantees human survival.

ANTHROPOLOGY AND "POP" CULTURE

The examples of mass or popular culture considered in this appendix and elsewhere in this book are shared cultural forms that have appeared and spread rapidly because of major changes in the material conditions of American life—particularly work organization, communication, and transportation. Most contemporary Americans deem at least one automobile a necessity. Televisions outnumber toilets in our households. Through the mass media, institutions such as sports, movies, TV shows, amusement parks, and fast-food restaurants have become powerful elements of national culture. They provide a framework of common expectations, experiences, and behavior overriding differences in region, class, formal religious affiliation, political sentiments, gender, ethnic group, and place of residence. Although some of us may not like these changes, it's difficult to deny their significance.

The rise of these institutions is linked not just to the mass media but also to decreasing American participation in traditional religion and the weakening of ties based on kinship, marriage, and community within industrial society. Neither a single church, a strong central government, nor a belief in common descent unites most Americans.

These dimensions of contemporary culture are dismissed as passing, trivial, or "pop" by some. However, because millions of people share them, they deserve and are receiving scholarly attention. Such studies help fulfill the promise that by studying anthropology, we can better understand ourselves.

Bibliography

Abelmann, N., and J. Lie
  1995   *Blue Dreams: Korean Americans and the Los Angeles Riots.* Cambridge, MA: Harvard University Press.

Abiodun, R.
  1996   Foreword. In *Art and Religion in Africa,* by R. I. J. Hackett, pp. viii–ix. London: Cassell.

Abu-Lughod, J. L.
  1989   *Before European Hegemony: The World System a.d. 1250–1350.* New York: Oxford University Press.

Adams, R. M.
  1981   *Heartland of Cities.* Chicago: Aldine.

Adepegba, C. O.
  1991   The Yoruba Concept of Art and Its Significance in the Holistic View of Art as Applied to African Art. *African Notes* 15: 1–6.

Adherents.com
  2002   Major Religions of the World Ranked by Number of Adherents. http://www.adherents.com/Religions_By_Adherents.html.

Agar, M. H.
  1980   *The Professional Stranger: An Informal Introduction to Ethnography.* New York: Academic Press.

Ahmed, A. S.
  1992   *Postmodernism and Islam: Predicament and Promise.* New York: Routledge.
  2004   *Postmodernism and Islam: Predicament and Promise,* rev. ed. New York: Routledge.

Aiello, L., and M. Collard
  2001   Our Newest Oldest Ancestor? *Nature* 410: 526–527.

Akazawa, T.
  1980   *The Japanese Paleolithic: A Techno-Typological Study.* Tokyo: Rippo Shobo.

Akazawa, T., and C. M. Aikens, eds.
  1986   *Prehistoric Hunter-Gatherers in Japan: New Research Methods.* Tokyo: University of Tokyo Press.

Albert, B.
  1989   Yanomami "Violence": Inclusive Fitness or Ethnographer's Representation? *Current Anthropology* 30: 637–640.

Altman, D.
  2001   *Global Sex.* Chicago: University of Chicago Press.

Amadiume, I.
  1987   *Male Daughters, Female Husbands.* Atlantic Highlands, NJ: Zed.
  1997   *Reinventing Africa: Matriarchy, Religion, and Culture.* New York: Zed.

American Almanac 1994–1995
  1994   *Statistical Abstract of the United States,* 114th ed. Austin, TX: Reference Press.

American Almanac 1996–1997
  1996   *Statistical Abstract of the United States,* 116th ed. Austin, TX: Reference Press.

American Anthropological Association
  AAA Guide: A Guide to Departments, a Directory of Members. (Formerly *Guide to Departments of Anthropology.*) Published annually by the American Anthropological Association, Washington, DC.
  Anthropology Newsletter. Published nine times annually by the American Anthropological Association, Washington, DC.
  General Anthropology: Bulletin of the Council for General Anthropology.

Amick III, B., S. Levine, A. R. Tarlov, and D. C. Walsh, eds.
  1995   *Society and Health.* New York: Oxford University Press.

Anderson, B.
  1991   *Imagined Communities: Reflections on the Origin and Spread of Nationalism,* rev. ed. London: Verso.
  1998   *The Spectre of Comparisons: Nationalism, Southeast Asia, and the World.* New York: Verso.

Anderson, R.
1989 *Art in Small Scale Societies.* Upper
Saddle River, NJ: Prentice Hall.
1996 *Magic, Science, and Health: The Aims and
Achievements of Medical Anthropology.* Fort
Worth: Harcourt Brace.
2000 *American Muse: Anthropological
Excursions into Art and Aesthetics.* Upper
Saddle River, NJ: Prentice Hall.
2004 *Calliope's Sisters: A Comparative Study
of Philosophy of Art,* 2nd ed. Upper Saddle
River, NJ: Prentice Hall.

Anderson, R., and K. Field, eds.
1993 *Art in Small-Scale Societies: Contemporary
Readings.* Upper Saddle River, NJ: Prentice
Hall.

Angier, N.
1998 When Nature Discovers the Same
Design Over and Over, Lookalike Creatures
Spark Evolutionary Debate. *New York Times,*
December 15, pp. D1, D6.
2002 Why We're So Nice: We're Wired to
Cooperate. *New York Times,* July 23.
http://www.nytimes.com/2002/07/23/
health/psychology/23COOP.html.

Angrosino, M. V., ed.
2002 *Doing Cultural Anthropology: Projects for
Ethnographic Data Collection.* Prospect
Heights, IL: Waveland.

Annenberg/CPB Exhibits
2000 "Collapse, Why Do Civilizations Fall?"
http://www.learner.org/exhibits/collapse/.

Antoun, R. T.
2001 *Understanding Fundamentalism: Christian,
Islamic, and Jewish Movements.* Walnut Creek,
CA: AltaMira.

Aoki, M. Y., and M. B. Dardess, eds.
1981 *As the Japanese See It: Past and Present.*
Honolulu: University Press of Hawaii.

Aoyagi, K., P. J. M. Nas, and J. Traphagan, eds.
1998 *Toward Sustainable Cities: Readings in the
Anthropology of Urban Environments.* Leiden,
Netherlands: Leiden Development Studies,
Institute of Cultural and Social Studies, Uni-
versity of Leiden.

Apostolopoulos, Y., S. Sönmez, and D. J. Timothy
2001 *Women as Producers and Consumers of
Tourism in Developing Regions.* Westport, CT:
Praeger.

Appadurai, A.
1990 Disjuncture and Difference in the Global
Cultural Economy. *Public Culture* 2(2): 1–24.
1991 Global Ethnoscapes: Notes and
Queries for a Transnational Anthropology.
In *Recapturing Anthropology: Working in the
Present,* ed. R. G. Fox, pp. 191–210. Santa Fe:
School of American Research Advanced
Seminar Series.

Appadurai, A., ed.
2001 *Globalization.* Durham, NC: Duke
University Press.

Appel, R., and P. Muysken
1987 *Language Contact and Bilingualism.*
London: Edward Arnold.

Appell, G. N.
1978 *Ethical Dilemmas in Anthropological
Inquiry: A Case Book.* Waltham, MA:
Crossroads Press.

Appiah, K. A.
1990 Racisms. In *Anatomy of Racism,* ed.
David Theo Goldberg, pp. 3–17. Minneapolis:
University of Minnesota Press.

Applebome, P.
1996 English Unique to Blacks Is Officially
Recognized. *New York Times,* December 20.
http://www.nytimes.com.
1997 Dispute over Ebonics Reflects a
Volatile Mix. *New York Times,* March 1.
http://www.nytimes.com.

Arce, A., and N. Long, eds.
2000 *Anthropology, Development, and Modernities: Exploring Discourses, Counter-Tendencies,
and Violence.* New York: Routledge.

Archer, M. S.
1996 *Culture and Agency: The Place of Culture
in Social Theory,* rev ed. Cambridge, UK:
Cambridge University Press.

Arens, W.
1981 Professional Football: An American
Symbol and Ritual. In *The American
Dimension: Cultural Myths and Social Realities,*
2nd ed., ed. W. Arens and S. P. Montague,
pp. 1–10. Sherman Oaks, CA: Alfred.

Arens, W., and S. P. Montague
1981 *The American Dimension: Cultural Myths
and Social Realities,* 2nd ed. Sherman Oaks,
CA: Alfred.

Arensberg, C.
1987 Theoretical Contributions of Industrial
and Development Studies. In *Applied Anthropology in America,* ed. E. M. Eddy and W. L.
Partridge. New York: Columbia University
Press.

Arnold, B., and B. Gibson, eds.
1995 *Celtic Chiefdom, Celtic State.* New York:
Cambridge University Press.

Arrighi, G.
1994 *The Long Twentieth Century: Money,
Power, and the Origins of Our Times.* New York:
Verso.

Asfaw, B., T. White, and O. Lovejoy
1999 *Australopithecus garhi:* A New Species
of Early Hominid from Ethiopia. *Science*
284: 629.

Ashcroft, B., G. Griffiths, and H. Tiffin
 1989   *The Empire Writes Back: Theory and Practice in Post-Colonial Literatures.* New York: Routledge.

Ashmore, W., and R. Sharer
 2000   *Discovering Our Past: A Brief Introduction to Archaeology,* 3rd ed. Boston: McGraw-Hill.

Askew, K. M.
 2001   *Performing the Nation: Swahili Music and Cultural Politics in Tanzania.* Chicago: University of Chicago Press.

Auman-Bauer, K.
 2006   Penn State Part of International Malaria Research, Education Partnership, February 9. http://live.psu.edu/story/16002.

Baer, H. A., M. Singer, and I. Susser
 2003   *Medical Anthropology and the World System.* Westport, CT: Praeger.

Bailey, E. J.
 2000   *Medical Anthropology and African American Health.* Westport, CT: Bergin and Garvey.

Bailey, R. C.
 1990   *The Behavioral Ecology of Efe Pygmy Men in the Ituri Forest, Zaire.* Ann Arbor: Anthropological Papers, Museum of Anthropology, University of Michigan, no. 86.

Bailey, R. C., G. Head, M. Jenike, B. Owen, R. Rechtman, and E. Zechenter
 1989   Hunting and Gathering in Tropical Rain Forests: Is It Possible? *American Anthropologist* 91: 59–82.

Baker, P. T.
 1978   *The Biology of High Altitude Peoples.* New York: Cambridge University Press.

Baker, P. T., and J. S. Weiner, eds.
 1966   *The Biology of Human Adaptability.* Oxford: Oxford University Press.

Bakhtin, M.
 1984   *Rabelais and His World.* Translated by Helen Iswolksy. Bloomington: Indiana University Press.

Balick, M. J., and P. A. Cox
 1996   *Plants, People, and Culture: The Science of Ethnobotany.* New York: Scientific American Library.

Balick, M. J., E. Elisabetsky, and S. A. Laird
 1995   *Medicinal Resources of the Tropical Forest: Biodiversity and Its Importance to Human Health.* New York: Columbia University Press.

Banton, M.
 1957   *West African City: A Study in Tribal Life in Freetown.* London: Oxford University Press.

Barash, D. P.
 1982   *Sociobiology and Behavior,* 2nd ed. Amsterdam: Elsevier.

Barber, B. R.
 1992   Jihad vs. McWorld. *Atlantic Monthly* 269(3): 53–65, March 1992.
 1995   *Jihad vs. McWorld.* New York: Times Books.

Barlett, P. F., ed.
 1980   *Agricultural Decision Making: Anthropological Contribution to Rural Development.* New York: Academic Press.

Barnaby, F., ed.
 1984   *Future War: Armed Conflict in the Next Decade.* London: M. Joseph.

Barnard, A.
 1979   Kalahari Settlement Patterns. In *Social and Ecological Systems,* ed. P. Burnham and R. Ellen, pp. 131–144. New York: Academic Press.

Barnouw, V.
 1985   *Culture and Personality,* 4th ed. Belmont, CA: Wadsworth.

Baron, D.
 1986   *Grammar and Gender.* New Haven, CT: Yale University Press.

Barringer, F.
 1989   32 Million Lived in Poverty in '88, a Figure Unchanged. *New York Times,* October 19, p. 18.
 1992   New Census Data Show More Children Living in Poverty. *New York Times,* May 29, pp. A1, A12, A13.

Barry, H., M. K. Bacon, and I. L. Child
 1959   Relation of Child Training to Subsistence Economy. *American Anthropologist* 61: 51–63.

Barth, F.
 1964   *Nomads of South Persia: The Basseri Tribe of the Khamseh Confederacy.* London: Allen and Unwin.
 1968   (orig. 1958). Ecologic Relations of Ethnic Groups in Swat, North Pakistan. In *Man in Adaptation: The Cultural Present,* ed. Yehudi Cohen, pp. 324–331. Chicago: Aldine.
 1969   *Ethnic Groups and Boundaries: The Social Organization of Cultural Difference.* London: Allen and Unwin.

Bar-Yosef, O.
 1987   Pleistocene Connections between Africa and Southwest Asia: An Archaeological Perspective. *African Archaeological Review* 5: 29–38.

Batalla, G. B.
 1966   Conservative Thought in Applied Anthropology: A Critique. *Human Organization* 25: 89–92.

Bates, D. G.
 2005   *Human Adaptive Strategies: Ecology, Culture, and Politics,* 3rd ed. Boston: Allyn & Bacon.

Bateson, M. C.
   1984   *With a Daughter's Eye: A Memoir of Margaret Mead and Gregory Bateson.* New York: William Morrow.

Beall, C. M.
   2001   Tibetan and Andean Patterns of Adaptation to High-Altitude Hypoxia. *Human Biology* 72: 201–228.

Beckerman, S., and P. Valentine
   2002   *Cultures of Multiple Fathers: The Theory and Practice of Partible Paternity in Lowland South America.* Gainesville: University of Florida Press.

Beeman, W.
   1986   *Language, Status, and Power in Iran.* Bloomington: Indiana University Press.

Begun, D. R.
   2003   Planet of the Apes. *Scientific American* 289(2): 74–83.

Begun, D. R., C. V. Ward, and M. D. Rose
   1997   *Description: Function, Phylogeny, and Fossils: Miocene Hominoid Evolution and Adaptations.* New York: Plenum Press.

Behar, R.
   1993   *Translated Woman: Crossing the Border with Esperanza's Story.* Boston: Beacon Press.

Behar, R., and D. A. Gordon, eds.
   1995   *Women Writing Culture.* Berkeley: University of California Press.

Bell, W.
   1981   Neocolonialism. In *Encyclopedia of Sociology,* p. 193. Guilford, CT: DPG Publishing.

Bellah, R. N.
   1978   Religious Evolution. In *Reader in Comparative Religion: An Anthropological Approach,* 4th ed., ed. W. A. Lessa and E. Z. Vogt, pp. 36–50. New York: Harper & Row.

Bellwood, P. S.
   2004   *The First Farmers: Origins of Agricultural Societies.* Malden, MA: Blackwell.

Benedict, B.
   1970   Pluralism and Stratification. In *Essays in Comparative Social Stratification,* ed. L. Plotnicov and A. Tuden, pp. 29–41. Pittsburgh: University of Pittsburgh Press.

Benedict, R.
   1940   *Race, Science and Politics.* New York: Modern Age Books.
   1946   *The Chrysanthemum and the Sword.* Boston: Houghton Mifflin.
   1959   (orig. 1934). *Patterns of Culture.* New York: New American Library.

Bennett, J. W.
   1969   *Northern Plainsmen: Adaptive Strategy and Agrarian Life.* Chicago: Aldine.

Bennett, J. W., and J. R. Bowen, eds.
   1988   *Production and Autonomy: Anthropological Studies and Critiques of Development.* Monographs in Economic Anthropology, no. 5, Society for Economic Anthropology. New York: University Press of America.

Berg, B. L.
   2004   *Qualitative Research Methods for the Social Sciences,* 5th ed. Boston: Pearson.

Berkeleyan
   1999   Berkeley Researchers Head Team That Discovers New Species of Human Ancestor: Earliest Evidence of Meat-Eating, Early Beings Has Been Unearthed in Ethiopia. April 28–May 4, pp. 27, 32. http://www.berkeley.edu/news/berkeleyan/1999/0428/species.html.

Berlin, B. D., E. Breedlove, and P. H. Raven
   1974   *Principles of Tzeltal Plant Classification: An Introduction to the Botanical Ethnography of a Mayan-Speaking People of Highland Chiapas.* New York: Academic Press.

Berlin, B. D., and P. Kay
   1969   *Basic Color Terms: Their Universality and Evolution.* Berkeley: University of California Press.
   1991   *Basic Color Terms: Their Universality and Evolution,* 2nd ed. Berkeley: University of California Press.
   1999   *Basic Color Terms: Their Universality and Evolution.* Stanford, CA: Center for the Study of Language and Information.

Bernard, H. R.
   1994   *Research Methods in Cultural Anthropology,* 2nd ed. Thousand Oaks, CA: Sage.
   2006   *Research Methods in Anthropology: Qualitative and Quantitative Methods,* 4th ed. Walnut Creek, CA: AltaMira.

Bernard, H. R., ed.
   1998   *Handbook of Methods in Cultural Anthropology.* Walnut Creek, CA: AltaMira.

Berndt, R. M.
   1969   The Concept of Protest within an Australian Aboriginal Context. In *A Question of Choice: An Australian Aboriginal Dilemma,* ed. R. M. Berndt, pp. 25–43. Nedlands: University of West Australia Press.

Berreman, G. D.
   1962   Pahari Polyandry: A Comparison. *American Anthropologist* 64: 60–75.
   1975   Himalayan Polyandry and the Domestic Cycle. *American Ethnologist* 2: 127–138.

Besteman, C. L., and H. Gusterson
   2005   *Why America's Top Pundits Are Wrong: Anthropologists Talk Back.* Berkeley: University of California Press.

Bettelheim, B.
   1975   *The Uses of Enchantment: The Meaning and Importance of Fairy Tales.* New York: Vintage.

Bicker, A., P. Sillitoe, and J. Pottier, eds.
   2004   *Investigating Local Knowledge: New Directions, New Approaches.* Burlington, VT: Ashgate.

Binford, L. R.
   1968   Post-Pleistocene Adaptations. In *New Perspectives in Archeology*, ed. S. R. Binford and L. R. Binford, pp. 313–341. Chicago: Aldine.
   1981   *Bones: Ancient Men and Modern Myths.* New York: Academic Press.

Binford, L. R., and S. R. Binford
   1979   Stone Tools and Human Behavior. In *Human Ancestors, Readings from Scientific American*, ed. G. L. Isaac and R. E. F. Leakey, pp. 92–101. San Francisco: W. H. Freeman.

Biology-Online.org
   2005   Natural selection in action: Industrial melanism. http://www.biology-online.org/2/11_natural_selection.htm.

Bird-David, N.
   1992   Beyond "The Original Affluent Society": A Culturalist Reformulation. *Current Anthropology* 33(1): 25–47.

Birdsell, J. B.
   1981   *Human Evolution: An Introduction to the New Physical Anthropology*, 3rd ed. Boston: Houghton Mifflin.

Bjuremalm, H.
   1997   Rättvisa kan skipas i Rwanda: Folkmordet 1994 går att förklara och analysera på samma sätt som förintelsen av judarna. *Dagens Nyheter* [06-03-1997, p. B3].

Blackwood, E.
   2000   *Webs of Power: Women, Kin, and Community in a Sumatran Village.* Lanham, MD: Rowman and Littlefield.

Blackwood, E., and S. Wieringa, eds.
   1999   *Female Desires: Same-Sex Relations and Transgender Practices across Cultures.* New York: Columbia University Press.

Blanton, R. E.
   1999   *Ancient Oaxaca: The Monte Alban State.* New York: Cambridge University Press.

Blanton, R. E., S. A. Kowalewski, G. M. Feinman, and L. M. Finsten, eds.
   1993   *Ancient Mesoamerica: A Comparison of Change in Three Regions*, 2nd ed. New York: Cambridge University Press.

Bloch, M., ed.
   1975   *Political Language and Oratory in Traditional Societies.* London: Academic.

Blum, H. F.
   1961   Does the Melanin Pigment of Human Skin Have Adaptive Value? *Quarterly Review of Biology* 36: 50–63.

Boas, F.
   1966   (orig. 1940). *Race, Language, and Culture.* New York: Free Press.

Boaz, N. T.
   1993   *Quarry: Closing in on the Missing Link.* New York: Free Press.
   1997   *Eco Homo: How the Human Being Emerged from the Cataclysmic History of the Earth.* New York: Basic Books.
   1999   *Essentials of Biological Anthropology.* Upper Saddle River, NJ: Prentice Hall.

Boaz, N. T., and A. J. Almquist
   2002   *Biological Anthropology: A Synthetic Approach to Human Evolution*, 2nd ed. Upper Saddle River, NJ: Prentice Hall.

Boaz, N. T., and R. L. Ciochon
   2004   Headstrong Hominids. *Natural History* 113(1): 28–34.

Bock, P. K.
   1980   *Continuities in Psychological Anthropology.* San Francisco: W. H. Freeman.

Bodley, J. H.
   1985   *Anthropology and Contemporary Human Problems*, 2nd ed. Mountain View, CA: Mayfield.
   1995   *Anthropology and Contemporary Human Problems*, 3rd ed. Mountain View, CA: Mayfield.
   1999   *Victims of Progress*, 4th ed. Mountain View, CA: Mayfield.
   2001   *Anthropology and Contemporary Human Problems*, 4th ed. Boston: McGraw-Hill.
   2003   *The Power of Scale: A Global History Approach.* Armonk, NY: M. E. Sharpe.

Bodley, J. H., ed.
   1988   *Tribal Peoples and Development Issues: A Global Overview.* Mountain View, CA: Mayfield.

Bogaard, A.
   2004   *Neolithic Farming in Central Europe: An Archaeobotanical Study of Crop Husbandry Practices.* New York: Routledge.

Bogin, B.
   1999   *Patterns of Human Growth*, 2nd ed. New York: Cambridge University Press.
   2001   *The Growth of Humanity.* New York: Wiley-Liss.

Bogoras, W.
   1904   The Chukchee. In *The Jesup North Pacific Expedition*, ed. F. Boas. New York: Memoir of the American Museum of Natural History.

Bogucki, P. I.
   1988   *Forest Farmers and Stockherders: Early Agriculture and Its Consequences in North-Central Europe.* New York: Cambridge University Press.

Bohannan, P.
   1955   Some Principles of Exchange and Investment among the Tiv. *American Anthropologist* 57: 60–70.
   1971   Artist and Critic in an African Society. In *Anthropology and Art: Readings in Cross-Cultural Aesthetics,* ed. C. Otten, pp. 172–181. Austin: University of Texas Press.
   1995   *How Culture Works.* New York: Free Press.

Bohannan, P., and J. Middleton, eds.
   1968   *Marriage, Family, and Residence.* Garden City, NY: Natural History Press.

Bolton, R.
   1981   Susto, Hostility, and Hypoglycemia. *Ethnology* 20(4): 227–258.

Bond, G. C., J. Kreniske, I. Susser, and J. Vincent, eds.
   1996   *AIDS in Africa and the Caribbean.* Boulder, CO: Westview Press.

Bonnichsen, R., and A. L. Schneider
   2000   *Battle of the Bones.* New York Academy of Sciences, *The Sciences,* July/August. http://www.friendsofpast.org/forum/battle.html.

Bonvillain, N.
   2001   *Women and Men: Cultural Constructions of Gender,* 3rd ed. Upper Saddle River, NJ: Prentice Hall.
   2003   *Language, Culture, and Communication: The Meaning of Messages,* 4th ed. Upper Saddle River, NJ: Prentice Hall.

Borneman, J.
   1998   *Subversions of International Order: Studies in the Political Anthropology of Culture.* Albany: State University of New York Press.

Boserup, E.
   1965   *The Conditions of Agricultural Growth.* Chicago: Aldine.
   1970   *Women's Role in Economic Development.* London: Allen and Unwin.

Bourdieu, P.
   1977   *Outline of a Theory of Practice.* Translated by Richard Nice. Cambridge, UK: Cambridge University Press.
   1982   *Ce Que Parler Veut Dire.* Paris: Fayard.
   1984   *Distinction: A Social Critique of the Judgment of Taste.* Translated by R. Nice. Cambridge, MA: Harvard University Press.

Bourguignon, E.
   1979   *Psychological Anthropology: An Introduction to Human Nature and Cultural Differences.* New York: Harcourt Brace Jovanovich.

Bourque, S. C., and K. B. Warren
   1981   *Women of the Andes: Patriarchy and Social Change in Two Peruvian Villages.* Ann Arbor: University of Michigan Press.
   1987   Technology, Gender and Development. *Daedalus* 116(4): 173–197.

Bower, B.
   2000   Inside Violent Worlds—Social Scientists Study Social Consequences of Violent Conflicts. *Science News Online,* August 5. http://www.sciencenews.org/articles/20000805/bob8ref.asp.

Bower, J., and D. Lubell, eds.
   1988   *Prehistoric Cultures and Environments in the Late Quaternary of Africa.* Cambridge Monographs in African Archaeology, 26. Oxford, UK: B.A.R.

Bowie, F.
   2006   *The Anthropology of Religion: An Introduction.* Malden, MA: Blackwell.

Brace, C. L.
   1964   A Nonracial Approach towards the Understanding of Human Diversity. In *The Concept of Race,* ed. A. Montagu, pp. 103–152. New York: Free Press.
   1995   *The Stages of Human Evolution,* 5th ed. Englewood Cliffs, NJ: Prentice Hall.
   2000   *Evolution in an Anthropological View.* Walnut Creek, CA: AltaMira.

Brace, C. L., and F. B. Livingstone
   1971   On Creeping Jensenism. In *Race and Intelligence,* ed. C. L. Brace, G. R. Gamble, and J. T. Bond, pp. 64–75. Anthropological Studies, no. 8. Washington, DC: American Anthropological Association.

Bradley, B. J., D. M. Doran-Sheehy, D. Lukas, C. Boesch, and L. Vigilant
   2004   Dispersed Male Networks in Western Gorillas. *Current Biology* 14: 510–513.

Bradley, C., C. Moore, M. Burton, and D. White
   1990   A Cross-Cultural Historical Analysis of Subsistence Change. *American Anthropologist* 92(2): 447–457.

Brady, I., ed.
   1983   Special Section: Speaking in the Name of the Real: Freeman and Mead on Samoa. *American Anthropologist* 85: 908–947.

Braidwood, R. J.
   1975   *Prehistoric Men,* 8th ed. Glenview, IL: Scott, Foresman.

Braudel, F.
   1973   *Capitalism and Material Life: 1400–1800.* Translated by M. Kochan. London: Weidenfeld and Nicolson.
   1981   *Civilization and Capitalism, 15th–18th Century.* Volume I: *The Structure of Everyday Life: The Limits.* Translated by S. Reynolds. New York: Harper & Row.

1982   *Civilization and Capitalism, 15th–18th Century.* Volume II: *The Wheels of Commerce.* New York: HarperCollins.

1984   *Civilization and Capitalism, 15th–18th Century.* Volume III: *The Perspective of the World.* New York: HarperCollins.

1992   *Civilization and Capitalism, 15th–18th Century.* Volume III: *The Perspective of the World.* Berkeley: University of California Press.

Bremen, J. V., and A. Shimizu, eds.
1999   *Anthropology and Colonialism in Asia and Oceania.* London: Curzon.

Brenneis, D.
1988   Language and Disputing. *Annual Review of Anthropology* 17: 221–237.

Brettell, C. B., and C. F. Sargent, eds.
2005   *Gender in Cross-Cultural Perspective.* Upper Saddle River, NJ: Pearson/Prentice Hall.

Brim, J. A., and D. H. Spain
1974   *Research Design in Anthropology.* New York: Harcourt Brace Jovanovich.

Bringa, T.
1995   *Being Muslim the Bosnian Way: Identity and Community in a Central Bosnian Village.* Princeton, NJ: Princeton University Press.

Brogger, J.
1992   *Nazaré: Women and Men in a Prebureaucratic Portuguese Fishing Village.* Fort Worth: Harcourt Brace.

Bronfenbrenner, U.
1975   Nature with Nurture: A Reinterpretation of the Evidence. In *Race and IQ,* ed. A. Montagu, pp. 114–144. New York: Oxford University Press.

Brooke, J.
1992   Rio's New Day in Sun Leaves Laplander Limp. *New York Times,* June 1, p. A7.
2000   A Commercial Makes Canadian Self-Esteem Bubble to the Surface. *New York Times,* May 29, late edition, final, section A, p. 6, column 1.

Brown, A.
2001   Communism. *International Encyclopedia of the Social & Behavioral Sciences,* pp. 2323–2326. New York: Elsevier.

Brown, D.
1991   *Human Universals.* New York: McGraw-Hill.

Brown, J. K.
1975   Iroquois Women: An Ethnohistoric Note. In *Toward an Anthropology of Women,* ed. R. Reiter, pp. 235–251. New York: Monthly Review Press.

Brown, K. M.
2001   *Mama Lola: A Vodou Priestess in Brooklyn,* rev. ed. Berkeley: University of California Press.

Brown, P. J.
1998   *Understanding and Applying Medical Anthropology.* Boston: McGraw-Hill.

Brown, P. J., and V. Bentley-Condit
1996   Culture, Evolution, and Obesity. In *Obesity: Its Causes and Management,* eds. A. J. Stunkard and T. Wadden. New York: Raven Press.

Brown, P. J., and S. V. Krick
2001   Culture and Economy in the Etiology of Obesity: Diet, Television and the Illusions of Personal Choice. Atlanta, GA: Emory University MARIAL Center, Working Paper 003-01.

Brown, R. W.
1958   *Words and Things.* Glencoe, IL: Free Press.

Brumfiel, E. M.
1980   Specialization, Market Exchange, and the Aztec State: A View from Huexotla. *Current Anthropology* 21(4): 459–478.

Bryant, B., and P. Mohai
1991   Race, Class, and Environmental Quality in the Detroit Area. In *Environmental Racism: Issues and Dilemmas,* ed. B. P. Bryant and Mohai. Ann Arbor: University of Michigan Office of Minority Affairs.

Bryson, K.
1996   Household and Family Characteristics: March 1995, P20-488, November 26, 1996. United States Department of Commerce, Bureau of Census, Public Information Office, CB96-195.

Buchler, I. R., and H. A. Selby
1968   *Kinship and Social Organization: An Introduction to Theory and Method.* New York: Macmillan.

Burke, P., and R. Porter
1987   *The Social History of Language.* Cambridge, UK: Cambridge University Press.

Burley, D. V., and W. R. Dickinson
2001   Origin and Significance of a Founding Settlement in Polynesia. *Proceedings of the National Academy of Sciences* 98: 11829–11831.

Burling, R.
1970   *Man's Many Voices: Language in Its Cultural Context.* New York: Harcourt Brace Jovanovich.

Burns, J. F.
1992*a*   Bosnian Strife Cuts Old Bridges of Trust. *New York Times,* May 22, pp. A1, A6.
1992*b*   A Serb, Fighting Serbs, Defends Sarajevo. *New York Times,* July 12, section 4, p. E3.
1997   A Year of Harsh Islamic Rule Weighs Heavily for Afghans. *New York Times,* September 24, late edition, final, section A, p. 6, column 1.

Burton, F. D., and M. Eaton
  1995a *The Multimedia Guide to Non-Human Primates.* Upper Saddle River, NJ: Prentice Hall. A CD-ROM combining photos, illustrations, video, sound, and text—presenting over 200 species of nonhuman primates.
  1995b *The Guide to Non-Human Primates.* Englewood Cliffs, NJ: Prentice Hall. The print version of the above.

Buvinic, M.
  1995 The Feminization of Poverty? Research and Policy Needs. In *Reducing Poverty through Labour Market Policies.* Geneva: International Institute for Labour Studies.

Calcagno, J. M., ed.
  2003 *Biological Anthropology: Historical Perspectives on Current Issues, Disciplinary Connections, and Future Directions.* Special issue of the *American Anthropologist* 101(1).

Caldeira, T. P. R.
  1996 Fortified Enclaves: The New Urban Segregation. *Public Culture* 8(2): 303–328.

Calhoun, C., D. Light, and S. Keller
  1997 *Sociology,* 7th ed. New York: McGraw-Hill.

Campbell, B. G.
  1998 *Human Evolution: An Introduction to Man's Adaptations,* 4th ed. New York: Aldine.

Campbell, B. G., J. D. Loy, and K. Cruz-Uribe eds.
  2006 *Humankind Emerging,* 9th ed. Boston: Pearson Allyn & Bacon.

Cann, R. L., M. Stoneking, and A. C. Wilson
  1987 Mitochondrial DNA and Human Evolution. *Nature* 325: 31–36.

Carlson, T. J. S., and L. Maffi
  2004 *Ethnobotany and Conservation of Biocultural Diversity.* Bronx: New York Botanical Garden Press.

Carneiro, R. L.
  1956 Slash-and-Burn Agriculture: A Closer Look at Its Implications for Settlement Patterns. In *Men and Cultures,* Selected Papers of the Fifth International Congress of Anthropological and Ethnological Sciences, pp. 229–234. Philadelphia: University of Pennsylvania Press.
  1968 (orig. 1961). Slash-and-Burn Cultivation among the Kuikuru and Its Implications for Cultural Development in the Amazon Basin. In *Man in Adaptation: The Cultural Present,* ed. Y. A. Cohen, pp. 131–145. Chicago: Aldine.
  1970 A Theory of the Origin of the State. *Science* 69: 733–738.
  1990 Chiefdom-Level Warfare as Exemplified in Fiji and the Cauca Valley. In *The Anthropology of War,* ed. J. Haas, pp. 190–211. Cambridge, UK: Cambridge University Press.
  1991 The Nature of the Chiefdom as Revealed by Evidence from the Cauca Valley of Colombia. In *Profiles in Cultural Evolution,* ed. A. T. Rambo and K. Gillogly, *Anthropological Papers* 85, pp. 167–190. Ann Arbor: University of Michigan Museum of Anthropology.

Carrier, J.
  1995 *De Los Otros: Intimacy and Homosexuality among Mexican Men: Hidden in the Blood.* New York: Columbia University Press.

Carsten, J.
  2004 *After Kinship.* New York: Cambridge University Press.

Carter, J.
  1988 Freed from Keepers and Cages, Chimps Come of Age on Baboon Island. *Smithsonian,* June, pp. 36–48.

Cartmill, M.
  1974 Rethinking Primate Origins. *Science* (April 26): 436–437.
  1992 New Views on Primate Origins. *Evolutionary Anthropology* 1: 105–111.

Carver, T.
  1996 *Gender Is Not a Synonym for Women.* Boulder, CO: Lynne Rienner.

Casper, L., and K. Bryson
  1998 Growth in Single Fathers Outpaces Growth in Single Mothers, Census Bureau Reports. http://www.census.gov/Press-Release/cb98-228.html.

Casson, R.
  1983 Schemata in Cognitive Anthropology. *Annual Review of Anthropology* 12: 429–462.

Cavalli-Sforza, L. L.
  1977 *Elements of Human Genetics,* 2nd ed. Menlo Park, CA: W. A. Benjamin.
  2000 *Genes, Peoples, and Languages.* Translated from the Italian by M. Seielstad. New York: North Point.

Cavalli-Sforza, L. L., and W. F. Bodmer
  1994 *The History and Geography of Human Genes.* Princeton, NJ: Princeton University Press.
  1999 *The Genetics of Human Populations.* Mineola, NY: Dover.

Centers for Disease Control and Prevention (CDC)
  2006 *National Vital Statistics Report,* v. 54, no. 12, March 3, 2006. http://www.cdc.gov/nchs/products/pubs/pubd/nvsr/54/54-pre.htm.

Cernea, M. M., ed.
  1991 *Putting People First: Sociological Variables in Rural Development,* 2nd ed. New York: Oxford University Press (published for the World Bank).

Cernea, M. M., and C. McDowell, eds.
  2000 *Risks and Reconstruction: Experiences of Resettlers and Refugees.* Washington, DC: World Bank.

Chagnon, N. A.
  1967 *Yanomamo Warfare: Social Organization and Marriage Alliances.* Ann Arbor, MI: University Microfilms.
  1968 *Yanomamo: The Fierce People.* New York: Holt, Rinehart and Winston.
  1997 *Yanomamö,* 5th ed. Fort Worth: Harcourt Brace.

Chagnon, N. A., and W. Irons, eds.
  1979 *Evolutionary Biology and Human Social Behavior: An Anthropological Perspective.* North Scituate, MA: Duxbury.

Chambers, E.
  1985 *Applied Anthropology: A Practical Guide.* Englewood Cliffs, NJ: Prentice Hall.
  1987 Applied Anthropology in the Post-Vietnam Era: Anticipations and Ironies. *Annual Review of Anthropology* 16: 309–337.
  2000 *Native Tours: The Anthropology of Travel and Tourism.* Prospect Heights, IL: Waveland.

Chambers, E., ed.
  1997 *Tourism and Culture: An Applied Perspective.* Albany: State University of New York Press.

Champion, T., and C. Gamble, eds.
  1984 *Prehistoric Europe.* New York: Academic Press.

Chang, K. C.
  1977 *The Archaeology of Ancient China.* New Haven, CT: Yale University Press.

Chatty, D.
  1996 *Mobile Pastoralists: Development Planning and Social Change in Oman.* New York: Columbia University Press.

Cheater, A. P., ed.
  1999 *The Anthropology of Power: Empowerment and Disempowerment in Changing Structures.* New York: Routledge.

Cheney, D. L., and R. M. Seyfarth
  1990 In the Minds of Monkeys: What Do They Know and How Do They Know It? *Natural History,* September, pp. 38–46.

Cheney, D. L., R. M. Seyfarth, B. B. Smuts, and R. W. Wrangham
  1987 The Study of Primate Societies. In *Primate Societies,* ed. B. B. Smuts, D. L. Cheney, R. M. Seyfarth, R. W. Wrangham, and T. T. Struhsaker, pp. 1–8. Chicago: University of Chicago Press.

Cherlin, A. J.
  1992 *Marriage, Divorce, Remarriage.* Cambridge, MA: Harvard University Press.

Child, A. B., and I. L. Child
  1993 *Religion and Magic in the Life of Traditional Peoples.* Englewood Cliffs, NJ: Prentice Hall.

Childe, V. G.
  1951 *Man Makes Himself.* New York: New American Library.

Chiseri-Strater, E., and B. S. Sunstein
  2002 *Fieldworking: Reading and Writing Research,* 2nd ed. Upper Saddle River, NJ: Prentice Hall.

Chomsky, N.
  1955 *Syntactic Structures.* The Hague: Mouton.

Cigno, A.
  1994 *Economics of the Family.* New York: Oxford University Press.

Ciochon, R. L.
  1983 Hominoid Cladistics and the Ancestry of Modern Apes and Humans. In *New Interpretations of Ape and Human Ancestry,* ed. R. L. Ciochon and R. S. Corruccini, pp. 783–843. New York: Plenum Press.

Ciochon, R. L., J. Olsen, and J. James
  1990 *Other Origins: The Search for the Giant Ape in Human Prehistory.* New York: Bantam Books.

Clammer, J., ed.
  1976 *The New Economic Anthropology.* New York: St. Martin's Press.

Clark, J. D., and S. A. Brandt
  1984 *From Hunters to Farmers: The Causes and Consequences of Food Production in Africa.* Berkeley: University of California Press.

Clarke, S. C.
  1995 Advance Report of Final Divorce Statistics, 1989 and 1990. *Monthly Vital Statistics Report,* v. 43, nos. 8, 9. Hyattsville, MD: National Center for Health Statistics.

Clifford, J.
  1982 *Person and Myth: Maurice Leenhardt in the Melanesian World.* Berkeley: University of California Press.
  1988 *The Predicament of Culture: Twentieth-Century Ethnography, Literature, and Art.* Cambridge, MA: Harvard University Press.

Clifton, J. A., ed.
  1970 *Applied Anthropology: Readings in the Uses of the Science of Man.* Boston: Houghton Mifflin.

Coates, J.
  1986 *Women, Men, and Language.* London: Longman.

Cody, D.
  1998 British Empire. http://www.victorianweb.org/.

Coe, M. D., and K. Flannery
  1964   Microenvironments and Mesoamerican Prehistory. *Science* 143: 650–654.

Cohen, M.
  1998   *Culture of Intolerance: Chauvinism, Class, and Racism.* New Haven, CT: Yale University Press.

Cohen, M. N., and G. J. Armelagos, eds.
  1984   *Paleopathology at the Origins of Agriculture.* New York: Academic Press.

Cohen, Roger
  1995   Serbs Shift Opens a Chance for Peace, a U.S. Envoy Says. *New York Times,* September 1, pp. A1, A6.

Cohen, Ronald
  1967   *The Kanuri of Bornu.* New York: Harcourt Brace Jovanovich.

Cohen, Ronald, and E. R. Service, eds.
  1978   *Origins of the State: The Anthropology of Political Evolution.* Philadelphia: Institute for the Study of Human Issues.

Cohen, Y. A.
  1974a *Man in Adaptation: The Cultural Present,* 2nd ed. Chicago: Aldine.
  1974b Culture as Adaptation. In *Man in Adaptation: The Cultural Present,* 2nd ed., ed. Y. A. Cohen, pp. 45–68. Chicago: Aldine.

Cole, S.
  1975   *Leakey's Luck: The Life of Louis Bazett Leakey, 1903–1972.* New York: Harcourt Brace Jovanovich.

Collier, J. F.
  1997   *From Duty to Desire: Remaking Families in a Spanish Village.* Princeton, NJ: Princeton University Press.

Collier, J. F., ed.
  1988   *Marriage and Inequality in Classless Societies.* Stanford, CA: Stanford University Press.

Collier, J. F., and S. J. Yanagisako, eds.
  1987   *Gender and Kinship: Essays toward a Unified Analysis.* Stanford, CA: Stanford University Press.

Collins, T. W.
  1989   Rural Economic Development in Two Tennessee Counties: A Racial Dimension. Paper presented at the annual meetings of the American Anthropological Association, Washington, DC.

Colson, E.
  1971   *The Social Consequences of Resettlement: The Impact of the Kariba Resettlement on the Gwembe Tonga.* Manchester, UK: Manchester University Press.

Colson, E., and T. Scudder
  1975   New Economic Relationships between the Gwembe Valley and the Line of Rail. In *Town and Country in Central and Eastern Africa,* ed. David Parkin, pp. 190–210. London: Oxford University Press.
  1988   *For Prayer and Profit: The Ritual, Economic, and Social Importance of Beer in Gwembe District, Zambia, 1950–1982.* Stanford, CA: Stanford University Press.

Comaroff, J.
  1982   Dialectical Systems, History and Anthropology: Units of Study and Questions of Theory. *Journal of Southern African Studies* 8: 143–172.

Combs-Schilling, E.
  1989   *Sacred Performances: Islam, Sexuality, and Sacrifice.* New York: Columbia University Press.

Conkey, M., O. Soffer, D. Stratmann, and N. Jablonski
  1997   *Beyond Art: Pleistocene Image and Symbol.* San Francisco: Memoirs of the California Academy of Sciences, no. 23.

Conklin, H. C.
  1954   *The Relation of Hanunóo Culture to the Plant World.* Unpublished Ph.D. dissertation, Yale University.

Connah, G.
  1987   *African Civilizations.* New York: Cambridge University Press.
  2004   *Forgotten Africa: An Introduction to Its Archaeology.* New York: Routledge.

Connell, R. W.
  1995   *Masculinities.* Berkeley: University of California Press.
  2002   *Gender.* Malden, MA: Blackwell.

Conner, J. K., and D. L. Hartl
  2004   *A Primer of Population Genetics.* Sunderland, MA: Sinauer.

Connor, W.
  1972   Nation-Building or Nation Destroying. *World Politics* 24(3): 319–355.

Cook-Gumperz, J.
  1986   *The Social Construction of Literacy.* Cambridge, UK: Cambridge University Press.

Cooper, F., and A. L. Stoler
  1989   Introduction, Tensions of Empire: Colonial Control and Visions of Rule. *American Ethnologist* 16: 609–621.

Cooper, F., and A. L. Stoler, eds.
  1997   *Tensions of Empire: Colonial Cultures in a Bourgeois World.* Berkeley: University of California Press.

Coote, J., and A. Shelton, eds.
  1992   *Anthropology, Art, and Aesthetics.* New York: Oxford University Press.

Crane, J. G., and M. V. Angrosino
  1992   *Field Projects in Anthropology: A Student Handbook,* 3rd ed. Prospect Heights, IL: Waveland.

Crapo, R. H.
  2006   *Anthropology of Religion: The Unity and Diversity of Religions.* Boston: McGraw-Hill.

Cresswell, T.
  2006   *On the Move: Mobility in the Modern West.* New York: Routledge.

Crick, F. H. C.
  1968   (orig. 1962). The Genetic Code. In *The Molecular Basis of Life: An Introduction to Molecular Biology, Readings from Scientific American,* pp. 198–205. San Francisco: W. H. Freeman.

Critser, G.
  2003   *Fat Land: How Americans Became the Fattest People in the World.* Boston: Houghton Mifflin.

Crosby, A. W., Jr.
  1986   *Ecological Imperialism: The Biological Expansion of Europe, 900–1900.* New York: Cambridge University Press.
  1994   *Germs, Seeds & Animals: Studies in Ecological History.* Armonk, NY: M.E. Sharpe.
  2003   *The Columbian Exchange: Biological and Cultural Consequences of 1492.* Westport, CT: Praeger.

Cueppens, B., and P. Geschiere
  2005   Autocthony: Local or Global? New Modes in the Struggle over Citizenship and Belonging in Africa and Europe. *Annual Review of Anthropology* 34: 385–407.

Cultural Survival Inc.
  1992   *At the Threshold.* Cambridge, MA: Cultural Survival. Originally published as the Spring 1992 issue of *Cultural Survival Quarterly.*

Cultural Survival Quarterly
  Quarterly journal. Cambridge, MA: Cultural Survival.

Cunningham, G.
  1999   *Religion and Magic: Approaches and Theories.* New York: New York University Press.

Dahlberg, F., ed.
  1981   *Woman the Gatherer.* New Haven, CT: Yale University Press.

Dalton, G., ed.
  1967   *Tribal and Peasant Economies.* Garden City, NY: Natural History Press.

Dalton, R.
  2006   Ethiopia: Awash with Fossils. http://www.nature.com/news/2006/060102/full/439014a.html.

DaMatta, R.
  1991   *Carnivals, Rogues, and Heroes: An Interpretation of the Brazilian Dilemma.* Translated from the Portuguese by John Drury. Notre Dame, IN: University of Notre Dame Press.

D'Andrade, R.
  1984   Cultural Meaning Systems. In *Culture Theory: Essays on Mind, Self, and Emotion,* ed. R. A. Shweder and R. A. Levine, pp. 88–119. Cambridge, UK: Cambridge University Press.
  1995   *The Development of Cognitive Anthropology.* New York: Cambridge University Press.

Darwin, C.
  1958   (orig. 1859). *On the Origin of Species.* New York: Dutton.

Darwin, E.
  1796   (orig. 1794). *Zoonomia, Or the Laws of Organic Life,* 2nd ed. London: J. Johnson.

Das, V.
  1995   *Critical Events: An Anthropological Perspective on Contemporary India.* New York: Oxford University Press.

Davies, C. A.
  1999   *Reflexive Ethnography: Guide to Researching Selves and Others.* New York: Routledge.

Davis, D. L., and R. G. Whitten
  1987   The Cross-Cultural Study of Human Sexuality. *Annual Review of Anthropology* 16: 69–98.

Degler, C.
  1970   *Neither Black nor White: Slavery and Race Relations in Brazil and the United States.* New York: Macmillan.

Delamont, S.
  1995   *Appetites and Identities: An Introduction to the Social Anthropology of Western Europe.* London: Routledge.

de la Peña, G.
  2005   Social and Cultural Policies toward Indigenous Peoples: Perspectives from Latin America. *Annual Review of Anthropology* 34: 717–739.

Delson, E., ed.
  1985   *Ancestors: The Hard Evidence.* New York: Alan R. Liss.

DeLumley, H.
  1976   (orig. 1969). A Paleolithic Camp at Nice. In *Avenues to Antiquity, Readings from Scientific American,* ed. B. M. Fagan, pp. 36–44. San Francisco: W. H. Freeman.

DeMarco, E.
  1997   New Dig at 9,000-Year-Old City Is Changing Views on Ancient Life. *New York Times,* November 11. http://www.nytimes.com.

Dembski, W. A.
  2004   *The Design Revolution: Answering the Toughest Questions about Intelligent Design.* Downers Grove, IL: InterVarsity Press.

Dentan, R. K.
  1979   *The Semai: A Nonviolent People of Malaya,* fieldwork edition. New York: Harcourt Brace.

Desjarlais, R., L. Eisenberg, B. Good,
and A. Kleinman, eds.
    1995   *World Mental Health: Problems and Priorities in Low-Income Countries.* New York: Oxford University Press.

Despres, L., ed.
    1975   *Ethnicity and Resource Competition.* The Hague: Mouton.

DeVita, P. R.
    1992   *The Naked Anthropologist: Tales from around the World.* Belmont, CA: Wadsworth.

DeVita, P. R., and J. D. Armstrong, eds.
    2002   *Distant Mirrors: America as a Foreign Culture,* 3rd ed. Belmont, CA: Wadsworth.

De Vos, G. A.
    1971   *Japan's Outcastes: The Problem of the Burakumin.* London: Minority Rights Group.

De Vos, G. A., and H. Wagatsuma
    1966   *Japan's Invisible Race: Caste in Culture and Personality.* Berkeley: University of California Press.

De Vos, G. A., W. O. Wetherall, and K. Stearman
    1983   *Japan's Minorities: Burakumin, Koreans, Ainu and Okinawans.* Report no. 3. London: Minority Rights Group.

De Waal, F. B. M.
    1995   Bonobo Sex and Society: The Behavior of a Close Relative Challenges Assumptions about Male Supremacy in Human Evolution. *Scientific American,* March, pp. 82–88.
    1997   *Bonobo: The Forgotten Ape.* Berkeley: University of California Press.
    2000   *Chimpanzee Politics: Power and Sex among Apes,* rev. ed. Baltimore: Johns Hopkins University Press.
    2001   *The Ape and the Sushi Master: Cultural Reflections by a Primatologist.* New York: Basic Books.

Diamond, J. M.
    1989   Blood, Genes, and Malaria. *Natural History,* February, pp. 8–18.
    1990   A Pox upon Our Genes. *Natural History,* February, pp. 26–30.
    1997   *Guns, Germs, and Steel: The Fates of Human Societies.* New York: W. W. Norton.

Dibble, H. L., S. P. McPherron, and B. J. Roth
    2003   *Virtual Dig: A Simulated Archaeological Excavation of a Middle Paleolithic Site in France,* 2nd ed. Boston: McGraw-Hill.

Di Leonardo, M., ed.
    1991   *Gender at the Crossroads of Knowledge: Feminist Anthropology in the Postmodern Era.* Berkeley: University of California Press.

Divale, W. T., and M. Harris
    1976   Population, Warfare, and the Male Supremacist Complex. *American Anthropologist* 78: 521–538.

Dobzhansky, T., F. J. Ayala, G. L. Stebbins,
and J. W. Valentine
    1977   *Evolution.* San Francisco: W. H. Freeman.

Dolhinow, P., and A. Fuentes, eds.
    1999   *The Nonhuman Primates.* Mountain View, CA: Mayfield.

Douglass, W. A.
    1969   *Death in Murelaga: Funerary Ritual in a Spanish Basque Village.* Seattle: University of Washington Press.
    1975   *Echalar and Murelaga: Opportunity and Rural Exodus in Two Spanish Basque Villages.* London: C. Hurst
    1992   Basques. *Encyclopedia of World Cultures,* ed. L. Bennett, vol. 4. Boston: GK Hall. http://ets.umdl.umich.edu/cgi/e/ehraf/ehraf-idx?c=ehrafe&view=owc&owc=EX08.

Downes, W.
    1998   *Language and Society,* 2nd ed. New York: Cambridge University Press.

Draper, P.
    1975   !Kung Women: Contrasts in Sexual Egalitarianism in Foraging and Sedentary Contexts. In *Toward an Anthropology of Women,* ed. R. Reiter, pp. 77–109. New York: Monthly Review Press.

Dreifus, C.
    2000   Saving the Orangutan: Preserving Paradise. *New York Times,* March 21. http://www.nytimes.com/library/national/science/032100sci-animal-orangutan.html.

Drennan, R. D., and C. A. Uribe, eds.
    1987   *Chiefdoms in the Americas.* Landon, MD: University Press of America.

Dublin, M.
    2001   *Native America Collected: The Culture of an Art World.* Albuquerque: University of New Mexico Press.

Dunn, J. S.
    2000   *The Impact of Media on Reproductive Behavior in Northeastern Brazil.* Ph.D. dissertation, Department of Anthropology, University of Michigan, Ann Arbor.

Durkheim, E.
    1951   (orig. 1897). *Suicide: A Study in Sociology.* Glencoe, IL: Free Press.
    2001   (orig. 1912). *The Elementary Forms of the Religious Life.* Translated by Carol Cosman. Abridged with an introduction and notes by Mark S. Cladis. New York: Oxford University Press.

Dwyer, K.
    1982   *Moroccan Dialogues: Anthropology in Question.* Baltimore: Johns Hopkins University Press.

Eagleton, T.
    1983   *Literary Theory: An Introduction.* Minneapolis: University of Minnesota Press.

Earle, T. K.
1987   Chiefdoms in Archaeological and Ethnohistorical Perspective. *Annual Review of Anthropology* 16: 279–308.
1991   *Chiefdoms: Power, Economy, and Ideology.* New York: Cambridge University Press.
1997   *How Chiefs Come to Power: The Political Economy in Prehistory.* Stanford, CA: Stanford University Press.

Eastman, C. M.
1975   *Aspects of Language and Culture.* San Francisco: Chandler and Sharp.

Echeverria, J.
1999   *Home away from Home: A History of Basque Boardinghouses.* Reno: University of Nevada Press.

Eckert, P.
1989   *Jocks and Burnouts: Social Categories and Identity in the High School.* New York: Teachers College Press, Columbia University.
2000   *Linguistic Variation as Social Practice: The Linguistic Construction of Identity in Belten High.* Malden, MA: Blackwell.

Eckert, P., and S. McConnell-Ginet
2003   *Language and Gender.* New York: Cambridge University Press.

Eckert, P., and J. R. Rickford, eds.
2001   *Style and Sociolinguistic Variation.* New York: Cambridge University Press.

Eddy, E. M., and W. L. Partridge, eds.
1987   *Applied Anthropology in America,* 2nd ed. New York: Columbia University Press.

Edelman, M., and A. Haugerud
2004   *The Anthropology of Development and Globalization: From Classical Political Economy to Contemporary Neoliberalism.* Malden, MA: Blackwell.

Eder, J.
1987   *On the Road to Tribal Extinction: Depopulation, Deculturation, and Adaptive Well-Being among the Batak of the Philippines.* Berkeley: University of California Press.

Edgerton, R.
1965   "Cultural" versus "Ecological" Factors in the Expression of Values, Attitudes and Personality Characteristics. *American Anthropologist* 67: 442–447.

Edwards, D. N.
2004   *The Nubian Past: An Archaeology of Sudan.* New York: Routledge.

Eggert, K.
1988   Malafaly as Misnomer. In *Madagascar: Society and History,* ed. C. P. Kottak, J. A. Rakotoarisoa, A. Southall, and P. Verin, pp. 321–336. Durham, NC: Carolina Academic Press.

Eiseley, L.
1961   *Darwin's Century.* Garden City, NY: Doubleday, Anchor Books.

Eldredge, N.
1985   *Time Frames: The Rethinking of Darwinian Evolution and the Theory of Punctuated Equilibria.* New York: Simon & Schuster.
1997   *Fossils: The Evolution and Extinction of Species.* Princeton, NJ: Princeton University Press.

Ellen, R., P. Parkes, and A. Bicker, eds.
2000   *Indigenous Environmental Knowledge and its Transformations.* Amsterdam: Harwood Academic.

Ember, C., and Ember, M.
2001   *Cross-Cultural Research Methods.* Walnut Creek, CA: AltaMira.

Ember, M., and C. R. Ember
1997   Science in Anthropology. In *The Teaching of Anthropology: Problems, Issues, and Decisions,* ed. C. P. Kottak, J. J. White, R. H. Furlow, and P. C. Rice, pp. 29–33. Mountain View, CA: Mayfield.

Endicott, K. M., and R. Welsch
2001   *Taking Sides: Clashing Views on Controversial Issues in Anthropology.* Guilford, CT: McGraw-Hill/Dushkin.

Erickson P., H. Ward, and K. Wachendorf
2002   *Voices of a Thousand People: The Makah Cultural and Research Center.* Lincoln/London: University of Nebraska Press.

Erlanger, S.
1992   An Islamic Awakening in Central Asian Lands. *New York Times,* June 9, pp. A1, A7.

Errington, F., and D. Gewertz
1987   *Cultural Alternatives and a Feminist Anthropology: An Analysis of Culturally Constructed Gender Interests in Papua New Guinea.* New York: Cambridge University Press.

Ervin, A. M.
2005   *Applied Anthropology: Tools and Perspectives for Contemporary Practice.* 2nd ed. Boston: Pearson/Allyn & Bacon.

Escobar, A.
1991   Anthropology and the Development Encounter: The Making and Marketing of Development Anthropology. *American Ethnologist* 18: 658–682.
1994   Welcome to Cyberia: Notes on the Anthropology of Cyberculture. *Current Anthropology* 35(3): 211–231.
1995   *Encountering Development: The Making and Unmaking of the Third World.* Princeton, NJ: Princeton University Press.

Eskridge, W. N., Jr.
1996   *The Case for Same-Sex Marriage: From Sexual Liberty to Civilized Commitment.* New York: Free Press.

Evans-Pritchard, E. E.
    1940   *The Nuer: A Description of the Modes of Livelihood and Political Institutions of a Nilotic People.* Oxford: Clarendon Press.
    1970   Sexual Inversion among the Azande. *American Anthropologist* 72: 1428–1433.

Ezra, K.
    1986   *A Human Ideal in African Art: Bamana Figurative Sculpture.* Washington, DC: Smithsonian Institution Press for the National Museum of African Art.

Fagan, B. M.
    1987   *The Great Journey: The Peopling of Ancient America.* London: Thames and Hudson.
    1996   *World Prehistory: A Brief Introduction.* New York: HarperCollins.
    1998   *Clash of Cultures,* 2nd ed. Walnut Creek, CA: AltaMira.
    2000   *Ancient Lives: An Introduction to Method and Theory in Archaeology.* Upper Saddle River, NJ: Prentice Hall.
    2005   *World Prehistory: A Brief Introduction,* 6th ed. Upper Saddle River, NJ: Prentice Hall.
    2006   *Archaeology: A Brief Introduction,* 9th ed. Upper Saddle River, NJ: Prentice Hall.
    2007   *People of the Earth: A Brief Introduction to World Prehistory,* 12th ed. Upper Saddle River, NJ: Prentice Hall.

Falk, D.
    2000   *Primate Diversity.* New York: W. W. Norton.

Farb, P., and G. Armelagos.
    1980   *Consuming Passions: The Anthropology of Eating.* Boston: Literary Guild.

Farner, R. F., ed.
    2004   *Nationalism, Ethnicity, and Identity: Cross-National and Comparative Perspectives.* New Brunswick, NJ: Transaction.

Farnsworth, C. H.
    1992   Canada to Divide Its Northern Land. *New York Times,* May 6, p. A7.

Farooq, M.
    1966   Importance of Determining Transmission Sites in Planning Bilharziasis Control: Field Observations from the Egypt-49 Project Area. *American Journal of Epidemiology* 83: 603–612.

Farr, D. M. L.
    1980   British Empire. *Academic American Encyclopedia,* vol. 3, pp. 495–496. Princeton, NJ: Arete.

Fasold, R. W.
    1990   *The Sociolinguistics of Language.* Oxford: Blackwell.

Feder, K. L.
    2004   *Linking to the Past: A Brief Introduction to Archaeology.* New York: Oxford University Press.

Fedigan, L. M.
    1992   *Primate Paradigms: Sex Roles and Social Bonds.* Chicago: University of Chicago Press.

Feinman, G. M., and J. Marcus, eds.
    1998   *Archaic States.* Santa Fe, NM: School of American Research Press.

Feinman, G. M., and T. D. Price
    2001   *Archaeology at the Millennium: A Sourcebook.* New York: Kluwer Academic/Plenum Press.

Feld, S.
    1990   *Sound and Sentiment: Birds, Weeping, Poetics, and Song in Kaluli Expression,* 2nd ed. Philadelphia: University of Pennsylvania Press.
    1991   Voices of the Rainforest. *Public Culture* 4(1): 131–140.

Fenlason, L.
    1990   Wolpoff Questions "Eve's" Origin Date, Says It Ignores Contradictory Fossil Data. *University Record* (University of Michigan, Ann Arbor) 45(21): 12.

Ferguson, J.
    1994   *The Anti-Politics Machine: "Development," Depoliticization, and Bureaucratic Power in Lesotho.* Minneapolis: University of Minnesota Press.

Ferguson, R. B.
    1995   *Yanomami Warfare: A Political History.* Santa Fe, NM: School of American Research.
    2002   *The State, Identity, and Violence: Political Disintegration in the Post-Cold War Era.* New York: Routledge.

Ferguson, R. B., and N. L. Whitehead
    1991   *War in the Tribal Zone: Expanding States and Indigenous Warfare.* Santa Fe, NM: School of American Research Press.

Ferraro, G. P.
    2006   *The Cultural Dimension of International Business,* 5th ed. Upper Saddle River, NJ: Prentice Hall.

Fields, J. M., and L. M. Casper
    2001   America's Families and Living Arrangements: Population Characteristics, 2000. U.S. Census Bureau. *Current Population Reports,* P20-537, June 2001. http://www.census.gov/prod/2001pubs/p20-537.pdf.

Finke, R., and R. Stark
    2005   *The Churching of America, 1776–2005: Winners and Losers in Our Religious Economy.* New Brunswick, NJ: Rutgers University Press.

Finkler, K.
    1985   *Spiritualist Healers in Mexico: Successes and Failures of Alternative Therapeutics.* South Hadley, MA: Bergin and Garvey.
    2000   *Experiencing the New Genetics: Family and Kinship on the Medical Frontier.* Philadelphia: University of Pennsylvania Press.

Finnstrom, S.
 1997   Postcoloniality and the Postcolony:
    Theories of the Global and the Local.
    http://www.postcolonialweb.org/.

Fisher, A.
 1988a   The More Things Change. *MOSAIC*
    19(1): 22–33.
 1988b   On the Emergence of Humanness.
    MOSAIC 19(1): 34–45.

Fiske, J.
 1989   *Understanding Popular Culture.* Boston:
    Unwin Hyman.

Fiske, J., and J. Hartley
 2003   *Reading Television,* 2nd ed. New York:
    Routledge.

Flannery, K. V.
 1969   Origins and Ecological Effects of Early
    Domestication in Iran and the Near East. In
    *The Domestication and Exploitation of Plants
    and Animals,* ed. P. J. Ucko and G. W.
    Dimbleby, pp. 73–100. Chicago: Aldine.
 1972   The Cultural Evolution of Civilizations.
    Annual Review of Ecology and Systematics 3:
    399–426.
 1973   The Origins of Agriculture. *Annual
    Review of Anthropology* 2: 271–310.
 1995   Prehistoric Social Evolution. In *Research
    Frontiers in Anthropology,* ed. C. R. Ember and
    M. Ember, pp. 1–26. Englewood Cliffs, NJ:
    Prentice Hall.
 1999   Chiefdoms in the Early Near East: Why
    It's So Hard to Identify Them. In *The Iranian
    World: Essays on Iranian Art and Archaeology,*
    ed. A. Alizadeh, Y. Majidzadeh, and S. M.
    Shahmirzadi. Tehran: Iran University Press.

Flannery, K. V., ed.
 1986   *Guila Naquitz: Archaic Foraging and Early
    Agriculture in Oaxaca, Mexico.* Orlando, FL:
    Academic Press.

Flannery, K. V., and J. Marcus
 2000   Formative Mexican Chiefdoms and the
    Myth of the "Mother Culture." *Journal of
    Anthropological Archaeology* 19: 1–37.

Flannery, K. V., J. Marcus, and R. G. Reynolds
 1989   *The Flocks of the Wamani: A Study of
    Llama Herders on the Punas of Ayacucho, Peru.*
    San Diego: Academic Press.

Fleagle, J. G.
 1999   *Primate Adaptation and Evolution,* 2nd
    ed. San Diego: Academic Press.

Fleagle, J. G., C. H. Janson, and K. E. Reed, eds.
 1999   *Primate Communities.* New York: Cam-
    bridge University Press.

Fleisher, M. L.
 1998   Cattle Raiding and Its Correlates: The
    Cultural-Ecological Consequences of Market-
    Oriented Cattle Raiding among the Kuria of
    Tanzania. *Human Ecology* 26(4): 547–572.

 2000   *Kuria Cattle Raiders: Violence and Vigilan-
    tism on the Tanzania/Kenya Frontier.* Ann
    Arbor: University of Michigan Press.

Foley, W. A.
 1997   *Anthropological Linguistics: An Introduc-
    tion.* Cambridge, MA: Blackwell.

Ford, C. S., and F. A. Beach
 1951   *Patterns of Sexual Behavior.* New York:
    Harper Torchbooks.

Forman, S., ed.
 1994   *Diagnosing America: Anthropology and
    Public Engagement.* Ann Arbor: University of
    Michigan Press.

Fortes, M.
 1950   Kinship and Marriage among the
    Ashanti. In *African Systems of Kinship and
    Marriage,* ed. A. R. Radcliffe-Brown and
    D. Forde, pp. 252–284. London: Oxford
    University Press.

Fossey, D.
 1981   The Imperiled Mountain Gorilla.
    National Geographic 159: 501–523.
 1983   *Gorillas in the Mist.* Boston: Houghton
    Mifflin.

Foster, G. M.
 1965   Peasant Society and the Image of Limited
    Good. *American Anthropologist* 67: 293–315.

Foster, G. M., and B. G. Anderson
 1978   *Medical Anthropology.* New York:
    McGraw-Hill.

Foucault, M.
 1979   *Discipline and Punish: The Birth of the
    Prison.* Translated by Alan Sheridan. New
    York: Vintage Books, University Press.

Fountain, H.
 2002   Iceman's Last Meal. *New York Times,*
    September 17. http://www.nytimes.com/
    2002/09/17/science/17OBSE.html.

Fouts, R.
 1997   *Next of Kin: What Chimpanzees Have
    Taught Me about Who We Are.* New York:
    William Morrow.

Fouts, R. S., D. H. Fouts, and T. E. Van Cantfort
 1989   The Infant Loulis Learns Signs from
    Cross-Fostered Chimpanzees. In *Teaching
    Sign Language to Chimpanzees,* ed. R. A. Gard-
    ner, B. T. Gardner, and T. E. Van Cantfort,
    pp. 280–292. Albany: State University of New
    York Press.

Fox, J. W.
 1987   *Maya Postclassic State Formation.*
    Cambridge, UK: Cambridge University Press.

Fox, Richard. G., ed.
 1990   Nationalist Ideologies and the Produc-
    tion of National Cultures. American
    Ethnological Society Monograph Series, no.
    2. Washington, DC: American Anthropologi-
    cal Association.

Fox, Robin
  1985   *Kinship and Marriage.* New York: Viking Penguin.
Frake, C. O.
  1961   The Diagnosis of Disease among the Subanun of Mindanao. *American Anthropologist* 63: 113–132.
Franke, R.
  1977   Miracle Seeds and Shattered Dreams in Java. In *Readings in Anthropology,* pp. 197–201. Guilford, CT: Dushkin.
Free Dictionary
  2004   Honorific. http://encyclopedia.thefreedictionary.com/Honorific.
Freeman, D.
  1983   *Margaret Mead and Samoa: The Making and Unmaking of an Anthropological Myth.* Cambridge, MA: Harvard University Press.
Freilich, M., D. Raybeck, and J. Savishinsky
  1991   *Deviance: Anthropological Perspectives.* Westport, CT: Bergin and Garvey.
French, H. W.
  1992   Unending Exodus from the Caribbean, with the U.S. a Constant Magnet. *New York Times,* May 6, pp. A1, A8.
  2002   Whistling Past the Global Graveyard. *New York Times,* July 14. http://www.nytimes.com/2002/07/14/weekinreview/14FREN.html.
Freud, S.
  1950   (orig. 1918). *Totem and Taboo.* Translated by J. Strachey. New York: W. W. Norton.
Fricke, T.
  1994   *Himalayan Households: Tamang Demography and Domestic Processes,* 2nd ed. New York: Columbia University Press.
Fried, M. H.
  1960   On the Evolution of Social Stratification and the State. In *Culture in History,* ed. S. Diamond, pp. 713–731. New York: Columbia University Press.
  1967   *The Evolution of Political Society: An Essay in Political Anthropology.* New York: McGraw-Hill.
Friedan, B.
  1963   *The Feminine Mystique.* New York: W. W. Norton.
Friedl, E.
  1975   *Women and Men: An Anthropologist's View.* New York: Harcourt Brace Jovanovich.
Friedman, J.
  1994   *Cultural Identity and Global Process.* Thousand Oaks, CA: Sage.
Friedman, J., ed.
  2002   *Globalization, the State, and Violence.* Walnut Creek, CA: AltaMira.

Friedman, J., and M. J. Rowlands, eds.
  1978   *The Evolution of Social Systems.* Pittsburgh: University of Pittsburgh Press.
Frisancho, A. R.
  1975   Functional Adaptation to High Altitude Hypoxia. *Science* 187: 313–319.
  1990   *Anthropometric Standards for the Evaluation of Growth and Nutritional Status.* Ann Arbor: University of Michigan Press.
  1993   *Human Adaptation and Accommodation.* Ann Arbor: University of Michigan Press.
Fry, D. P.
  2006   *The Human Potential for Peace: An Anthropological Challenge to Assumptions about War and Violence.* New York: Oxford University Press.
Fry, D. P., and K. Bjorkqvist, eds.
  1997   *Cultural Variation in Conflict Resolution: Alternatives to Violence.* Mahwah, NJ: Lawrence Erlbaum.
Futuyma, D. J.
  1995   *Science on Trial,* updated ed. New York: Pantheon.
  1998   *Evolutionary Biology.* Sunderland, MA: Sinauer Associates.
Gal, S.
  1989   Language and Political Economy. *Annual Review of Anthropology* 18: 345–367.
Gamble, C.
  1999   *The Palaeolithic Societies of Europe.* New York: Cambridge University Press.
  2004   *Archaeology, the Basics.* New York: Routledge.
Garbarino, M. S., and R. F. Sasso
  1994   *Native American Heritage,* 3rd ed. Prospect Heights, IL: Waveland.
Gardner, R. A., B. T. Gardner, and T. E. Van Cantfort, eds.
  1989   *Teaching Sign Language to Chimpanzees.* Albany: State University of New York Press.
Gargan, E. A.
  1992   A Single-Minded Man Battles to Free Slaves. *New York Times,* June 4, p. A7.
Gates, C.
  2003   *Ancient Cities: The Archaeology of Urban Life in the Ancient Near East and Egypt, Greece, and Rome.* New York: Routledge.
Geertz, C.
  1973   *The Interpretation of Cultures.* New York: Basic Books.
  1980   Blurred Genres: The Refiguration of Social Thought. *American Scholar* 29(2): 165–179.
  1983   *Local Knowledge.* New York: Basic Books.
  1995   *After the Fact: Two Countries, Four Decades, One Anthropologist.* Cambridge, MA: Harvard University Press.

Geis, M. L.
 1987   *The Language of Politics.* New York:
  Springer-Verlag.

Gellner, E.
 1983   *Nations and Nationalism.* Ithaca, NY:
  Cornell University Press.
 1997   *Nationalism.* New York: New York
  University Press.

*General Anthropology: Bulletin of the Council
for General Anthropology*

Gibbons, A.
 2001   The Peopling of the Pacific. *Science* 291:
  1735. http://www.familytreedna.com/pdf/
  Gibbons_Science2001.pdf.

Gibbs, N.
 1989   How America Has Run Out of Time.
  Time, April 24, pp. 59–67.

Giddens, A.
 1973   *The Class Structure of the Advanced Societies.* New York: Cambridge University Press.

Gilad, Y., V. Wiebe, M. Przeworski, D. Lancet,
and S. Pääbo
 2004   Loss of Olfactory Receptor Genes
  Coincides with the Acquisition of Full
  Trichomatic Vision in Primates.
  http://www.pubmedcentral.nih.gov/
  articlerender.fcgi?artid=314465.

Gilchrist, R.
 1999   *Gender and Archaeology: Contesting the
  Past.* New York: Routledge.

Gillespie, J. H.
 2004   *Population Genetics: A Concise Guide,* 2nd
  ed. Baltimore: Johns Hopkins University Press.

Gilmore, D. D.
 1987   *Aggression and Community: Paradoxes of
  Andalusian Culture.* New Haven, CT: Yale
  University Press.
 1991   *Manhood in the Making: Cultural Concepts
  of Masculinity.* New Haven, CT: Yale University
  Press.
 2001   *Misogyny: The Male Malady.* Philadelphia:
  University of Pennsylvania Press.

Gilmore-Lehne, W. J.
 2000   Pre-Sumerian Cultures: Natufian
  through Ubaid Eras: 10,500–3500 B.C.E.
  http://loki.stockton.edu/~gilmorew/
  consorti/1bnear.htm.

Gledhill, J.
 2000   *Power and Its Disguises: Anthropological
  Perspectives on Politics.* Sterling, VA: Pluto
  Press.

Glick-Schiller, N., and G. Fouron
 1990   "Everywhere We Go, We Are in Danger":
  Ti Manno and the Emergence of Haitian
  Transnational Identity. *American Ethnologist*
  17(2): 327–347.

Gmelch, G.
 1978   Baseball Magic. *Human Nature* 1(8): 32–40.
 2001   *Inside Pitch: Life in Professional Baseball.*
  Washington, DC: Smithsonian Institution Press.

Gmelch, G., and W. Zenner
 2002   *Urban Life: Readings in the Anthropology
  of the City.* Prospect Heights, IL: Waveland.

Goldberg, D. T.
 1997   *Racial Subjects: Writing on Race in America.* New York: Routledge.

Goldberg, D. T., ed.
 1990   *Anatomy of Racism.* Minneapolis:
  University of Minnesota Press.

Goldberg, P., V. T. Holliday, and C. R. Ferring
 2000   *Earth Sciences and Archaeology.* New
  York: Kluwer Academic/Plenum Press.

Golden, T.
 1997   Oakland Revamps Plan to Teach Black
  English. *New York Times,* January 14. http://
  www.nytimes.com.

Goldschmidt, W.
 1965   Theory and Strategy in the Study
  of Cultural Adaptability. *American
  Anthropologist* 67: 402–407.

Goodale, J., and J. D. Koss
 1971   The Cultural Context of Creativity
  among Tiwi. In *Anthropology and Art:
  Readings in Cross-Cultural Aesthetics,* ed.
  C. Otten, pp. 182–203. Austin: University
  of Texas Press.

Goodall, J.
 1968   A Preliminary Report on Expressive
  Movements and Communication in Gombe
  Stream Chimpanzees. In *Primates: Studies
  in Adaptation and Variability,* ed. P. C. Jay,
  pp. 313–374. New York: Harcourt Brace
  Jovanovich.
 1986   *The Chimpanzees of Gombe: Patterns of
  Behavior.* Cambridge, MA: Belknap Press of
  Harvard University Press.
 1988   *In the Shadow of Man,* rev. ed. Boston:
  Houghton Mifflin.
 1996   *My Life with the Chimpanzees.* New York:
  Pocket Books.

Goodenough, W. H.
 1953   *Native Astronomy in the Central
  Carolines.* Philadelphia: University of
  Pennsylvania Press.

Goodman, J., P. E. Lovejoy, and A. Sherratt
 1995   *Consuming Habits: Drugs in History and
  Anthropology.* London: Routledge.

Goodman, M., M. L. Baba, and L. L. Darga
 1983   The Bearings of Molecular Data on the
  Cladograms and Times of Divergence of
  Hominoid Lineages. In *New Interpretations of
  Ape and Human Ancestry,* ed. R. L. Ciochon
  and R. S. Corruccini, pp. 67–87. New York:
  Plenum Press.

Goody, J.
    1977   *Production and Reproduction: A Comparative Study of the Domestic Domain.* New York: Cambridge University Press.

Goody, J., and S. T. Tambiah
    1973   *Bridewealth and Dowry.* Cambridge, UK: Cambridge University Press.

Gordon, A. A.
    1996   *Transforming Capitalism and Patriarchy: Gender and Development in Africa.* Boulder, CO: Lynne Rienner.

Gorer, G.
    1943   Themes in Japanese Culture. *Transactions of the New York Academy of Sciences* (Series II) 5: 106–124.

Gorman, C. F.
    1969   Hoabinhian: A Pebble-Tool Complex with Early Plant Associations in Southeast Asia. *Science* 163: 671–673.

Gottdiener, M., ed.
    2000   *New Forms of Consumption: Consumers, Culture, and Commodification.* Lanham, MD: Rowman and Littlefield.

Gough, E. K.
    1959   The Nayars and the Definition of Marriage. *Journal of Royal Anthropological Institute* 89: 23–34.

Gould, S. J.
    1996   *The Mismeasure of Man.* New York: W. W. Norton.
    1999   *Rock of Ages: Science and Religion in the Fullness of Life.* New York: Ballantine Books.
    2002   *The Structure of Evolutionary Theory.* Cambridge, MA: Belknap Press of Harvard University Press.

Gowlett, J. A. J.
    1993   *Ascent to Civilization: The Archaeology of Early Humans.* New York: McGraw-Hill.

Graburn, N.
    1976   *Ethnic and Tourist Arts: Cultural Expressions from the Fourth World.* Berkeley: University of California Press.

Graburn, N., ed.
    1971   *Readings in Kinship and Social Structure.* New York: Harper & Row.

Gramsci, A.
    1971   *Selections from the Prison Notebooks.* Edited and translated by Quenten Hoare and Geoffrey Nowell Smith. London: Wishart.

Grasmuck, S., and P. Pessar
    1991   *Between Two Islands: Dominican International Migration.* Berkeley: University of California Press.

Grassmuck, K.
    1985   Local Educators Join Push for "A Computer in Every Classroom." *Ann Arbor News,* February 10, p. A11. (Quotes testimony of Linda Tarr-Whelan of the National Education Association to the House Committee on Science, Research and Technology.)

Gray, J.
    1986   With a Few Exceptions, Television in Africa Fails to Educate and Enlighten. *Ann Arbor News,* December 8.

Gray, J. P.
    1985   *Primate Sociobiology.* New Haven, CT: HRAF Press.

Greaves, T. C.
    1995   Problems Facing Anthropologists: Cultural Rights and Ethnography. *General Anthropology* 1(2): 1, 3–6.

Green, E. C.
    1992   (orig. 1987). The Integration of Modern and Traditional Health Sectors in Swaziland. In *Applying Anthropology,* ed. A. Podolefsky and P. J. Brown, pp. 246–251. Mountain View, CA: Mayfield.

Green, G. M., and R. W. Sussman
    1990   Deforestation History of the Eastern Rain Forests of Madagascar from Satellite Images. *Science* 248: 212–215.

Green, T.
    2006   Archaeologist Makes the Case for Burying Dominant Theory of First Americans. Austin: University of Texas Research. http://www.utexas.edu/research/impact/collins.html.

Greenwood, Davydd J.
    1976   *Unrewarding Wealth: The Commercialization and Collapse of Agriculture in a Spanish Basque Town.* Cambridge, UK: Cambridge University Press.

Greiner, T. M.
    2003   What Is the Difference between Hominin and Hominid When Classifying Humans? MadSci Network: Evolution. http://www.madsci.org/posts/archives/Apr2003/1050350684.Ev.r.html.

Grekova, M.
    2001   Postsocialist Societies. *International Encyclopedia of the Social and Behavioral Sciences,* pp. 11877–11881. New York: Elsevier.

Griffin, P. B., and A. Estioko-Griffin, eds.
    1985   *The Agta of Northeastern Luzon: Recent Studies.* Cebu City, Philippines: University of San Carlos.

Gross, D.
    1971   The Great Sisal Scheme. *Natural History,* March, pp. 49–55.

Gross, D., and B. Underwood
    1971   Technological Change and Caloric Costs: Sisal Agriculture in Northeastern Brazil. *American Anthropologist* 73: 725–740.

Gudeman, S.
2001 *The Anthropology of Economy: Community, Market, and Culture.* Malden, MA: Blackwell.

Gudeman, S., ed.
1998 *Economic Anthropology.* Northhampton, MA: E. Elgar.

Gugliotta, G.
2002 Earliest Human Ancestor? Skull Dates to When Apes, Humans Split. *Washington Post,* July 11, p. A01.
2004 New Evidence of Controlled Fire Is Unearthed: Israeli Team's Finds at Ancient Campsite Near Jordan River Suggest Humans Harnessed Blazes 790,000 Years Ago. *Washington Post,* May 10, p. A-10.
2005a More Fossil Evidence from 'Hobbit' Island. *Washington Post,* October 12, p. A-03.
2005b Tools Found in Britain Show Much Earlier Human Existence. *Washington Post,* December 15, p. A-24.

Gulliver, P. H.
1974 (orig. 1965). The Jie of Uganda. In *Man in Adaptation: The Cultural Present,* 2nd ed., ed. Y. A. Cohen, pp. 323–345. Chicago: Aldine.

Gumperz, J. J.
1982 *Language and Social Identity.* Cambridge, UK: Cambridge University Press.

Gumperz, J. J., and S. C. Levinson, eds.
1996 *Rethinking Linguistic Relativity.* New York: Cambridge University Press.

Gunther, E.
1971 Northwest Coast Indian Art. In *Anthropology and Art: Readings in Cross-Cultural Aesthetics,* ed. C. Otten, pp. 318–340. Austin: University of Texas Press.

Gupta, A., and J. Ferguson
1997a Culture, Power, Place: Ethnography at the End of an Era. In *Culture, Power, Place: Explorations in Critical Anthropology,* ed. A. Gupta and J. Ferguson, pp. 1–29. Durham, NC: Duke University Press.
1997b Beyond "Culture": Space, Identity, and the Politics of Difference. In *Culture, Power, Place: Explorations in Critical Anthropology,* ed. A. Gupta and J. Ferguson, pp. 33–51. Durham, NC: Duke University Press.

Gupta, A., and J. Ferguson, eds.
1997a *Anthropological Locations: Boundaries and Grounds of a Field Science.* Berkeley: University of California Press.
1997b *Culture, Power, Place: Explorations in Critical Anthropology.* Durham, NC: Duke University Press.

Guthrie, S.
1995 *Faces in the Clouds: A New Theory of Religion.* New York: Oxford University Press.

Gwynne, M. A.
2003 *Applied Anthropology: A Career-Oriented Approach.* Boston: Allyn & Bacon.

Haapala, A.
1998 Literature: Invention of the Self. *Canadian Aesthetics Journal* 2. http://www.uqtr.ca/AE/vol_2/haapala.html.

Hackett, R. I. J.
1996 *Art and Religion in Africa.* London: Cassell.

Hall, E. T.
1990 *Understanding Cultural Differences.* Yarmouth, ME: Intercultural Press.
1992 *An Anthropology of Everyday Life: An Autobiography.* New York: Doubleday.

Hall, T. D., ed.
1999 *A World-System Reader: New Perspectives on Gender, Urbanism, Cultures, Indigenous Peoples, and Ecology.* Lanham, MD: Rowman and Littlefield.

Hallowell, A. I.
1955 *Culture and Experience.* Philadelphia: University of Pennsylvania Press.

Hamburg, D. A., and E. R. McCown, eds.
1979 *The Great Apes.* Menlo Park, CA: Benjamin Cummings.

Hamilton, M. B.
1995 *The Sociology of Religion: Theoretical and Comparative Perspectives.* London: Routledge.

Hanks, W. F.
1995 *Language and Communicative Practices.* Boulder, CO: Westview Press.

Hansen, K. V.
2004 *Not-So-Nuclear Families: Class, Gender, and Networks of Care.* New Brunswick, NJ: Rutgers University Press.

Hansen, K. V., and A. I. Garey, eds.
1998 *Families in the U.S.: Kinship and Domestic Politics.* Philadelphia: Temple University Press.

Harcourt, A. H., D. Fossey, and J. Sabater-Pi
1981 Demography of *Gorilla gorilla. Journal of Zoology* 195: 215–233.

Harding, S.
1975 Women and Words in a Spanish Village. In *Toward an Anthropology of Women,* ed. R. Reiter, pp. 283–308. New York: Monthly Review Press.

Hargrove, E. C.
1986 *Religion and Environmental Crisis.* Athens: University of Georgia Press.

Harlan, J. R., and D. Zohary
1966 Distribution of Wild Wheats and Barley. *Science* 153: 1074–1080.

Harlow, H.
1966 Development of Patterns of Affection in Macaques. *Yearbook of Physical Anthropology* 14: 1–7.

Harris, M.
 1964   *Patterns of Race in the Americas*. New York: Walker.
 1970   Referential Ambiguity in the Calculus of Brazilian Racial Identity. *Southwestern Journal of Anthropology* 26(1): 1–14.
 1974   *Cows, Pigs, Wars, and Witches: The Riddles of Culture*. New York: Random House.
 1978   *Cannibals and Kings*. New York: Vintage.
 1989   *Our Kind: Who We Are, Where We Came from, Where We Are Going*. New York: Harper & Row.
 2001   (orig. 1979). *Cultural Materialism: The Struggle for a Science of Culture*. Walnut Creek, CA: AltaMira.
 2001   (orig. 1968). *The Rise of Anthropological Theory*. Walnut Creek, CA: AltaMira.

Harris, M., and C. P. Kottak
 1963   The Structural Significance of Brazilian Racial Categories. *Sociologia* 25: 203–209.

Harris, N. M., and G. Hillman
 1989   *Foraging and Farming: The Evolution of Plant Exploitation*. London: Unwin Hyman.

Harrison, G. G., W. L. Rathje, and W. W. Hughes
 1994   Food Waste Behavior in an Urban Population. In *Applying Anthropology: An Introductory Reader*, 3rd ed., ed. A. Podolefsky and P. J. Brown, pp. 107–112. Mountain View, CA: Mayfield.

Hart, C. W. M., A. R. Pilling, and J. C. Goodale
 1988   *The Tiwi of North Australia*, 3rd ed. Fort Worth: Harcourt Brace.

Hart, D., and R. W. Sussman
 2005   *Man the Hunted: Primates, Predators, and Human Evolution*. Boulder, CO: Westview Press.

Hartl, D. L.
 1997   *Principles of Population Genetics*, 3rd ed. Sunderland, MA: Sinauer.

Hartl, D. L., and E. W. Jones
 2006   *Essential Genetics*, 4th ed. Boston: Jones and Bartlett.

Harvey, D. J.
 1980   French Empire. *Academic American Encyclopedia*, vol. 8, pp. 309–310. Princeton, NJ: Arete.

Harvey, K.
 1996   Online for the Ancestors: The Importance of Anthropological Sensibility in Information Superhighway Design. *Social Science Computing Review* 14(1): 65–68.

Hassig, R.
 1985   *Trade, Tribute, and Transportation: The Sixteenth-Century Political Economy of the Valley of Mexico*. Norman: University of Oklahoma Press.

Hastings, A.
 1997   *The Construction of Nationhood: Ethnicity, Religion, and Nationalism*. New York: Cambridge University Press.

Hatcher, E. P.
 1999   *Art as Culture: An Introduction to the Anthropology of Art*, 2nd ed. Westport, CT: Bergin & Garvey.

Hatfield, E., and R. L. Rapson
 1996   *Love and Sex: Cross-Cultural Perspectives*. Needham Heights, MA: Allyn & Bacon.

Hausfater, G., and S. Hrdy, eds.
 1984   *Infanticide: Comparative and Evolutionary Perspectives*. Hawthorne, NY: Aldine.

Hawkes, K., J. O'Connell, and K. Hill
 1982   Why Hunters Gather: Optimal Foraging and the Aché of Eastern Paraguay. *American Ethnologist* 9: 379–398.

Hawks, J., and M. Wolpoff
 2003   Sixty Years of Modern Human Origins in the American Anthropological Association. *American Anthropologist* 105(1): 89–100.

Hawley, J. S,. ed.
 1994   *Sati, the Blessing and the Curse: The Burning of Wives in India*. New York: Oxford University Press.

Hayden, B.
 1981   Subsistence and Ecological Adaptations of Modern Hunter/Gatherers. In *Omnivorous Primates: Gathering and Hunting in Human Evolution*, ed. R. S. Harding and G. Teleki, pp. 344–421. New York: Columbia University Press.

Headland, T. N., ed.
 1992   *The Tasaday Controversy: Assessing the Evidence*. Washington, DC: American Anthropological Association.

Headland, T. N., and L. A. Reid
 1989   Hunter-Gatherers and Their Neighbors from Prehistory to the Present. *Current Anthropology* 30: 43–66.

Heath, D. B., ed.
 1995   *International Handbook on Alcohol and Culture*. Westport, CT: Greenwood Press.

Hedges, C.
 1992*a*   Sudan Presses Its Campaign to Impose Islamic Law on Non-Muslims. *New York Times*, June 1, p. A7.
 1992*b*   Sudan Gives Its Refugees a Desert to Contemplate. *New York Times*, June 3, p. A4.

Heider, K. G.
 1988   The Rashomon Effect: When Ethnographers Disagree. *American Anthropologist* 90: 73–81.
 1997   *Grand Valley Dani: Peaceful Warriors*, 3rd ed. Fort Worth: Harcourt Brace.

Heller, M.
    1988   *Codeswitching: Anthropological and Soci-olinguistic Perspectives.* Berlin: Mouton de Gruyter.
Helman, C.
    2001   *Culture, Health, and Illness: An Introduction for Health Professionals,* 4th ed. Boston: Butterworth-Heinemann.
Henry, D. O.
    1989   *From Foraging to Agriculture: The Levant at the End of the Ice Age.* Philadelphia: University of Pennsylvania Press.
    1995   *Prehistoric Cultural Ecology and Evolution: Insights from Southern Jordan.* New York: Plenum Press.
Henry, J.
    1955   Docility, or Giving Teacher What She Wants. *Journal of Social Issues* 2: 33–41.
Herdt, G.
    1981   *Guardians of the Flutes.* New York: McGraw-Hill.
    1986   *The Sambia: Ritual and Gender in New Guinea.* Fort Worth: Harcourt Brace.
Herdt, G. H., ed.
    1984   *Ritualized Homosexuality in Melanesia.* Berkeley: University of California Press.
Herrnstein, R. J.
    1971   I.Q. *Atlantic* 228(3): 43–64.
Herrnstein, R. J., and C. Murray
    1994   *The Bell Curve: Intelligence and Class Structure in American Life.* New York: Free Press.
Herskovits, M.
    1937   *Life in a Haitian Valley.* New York: Knopf.
Hess, D. J.
    1995   A Democratic Research Agenda in the Social Studies of the National Information Infrastructure. Paper prepared for the National Science Foundation Workshop on Culture, Society, and Advanced Information Technology. Washington, DC: May 31–June 1, 1995.
Hess, D. J., and R. A. DaMatta, eds.
    1995   *The Brazilian Puzzle: Culture on the Borderlands of the Western World.* New York: Columbia University Press.
Hewitt, R.
    1986   *White Talk, Black Talk.* Cambridge, UK: Cambridge University Press.
Heyerdahl, T.
    1971   *The Ra Expeditions.* Translated by P. Crampton. Garden City, NY: Doubleday.
Heyneman, D.
    1984   Development and Disease: A Dual Dilemma. *Journal of Parasitology* 70: 3–17.
Hicks, D., ed.
    2001   *Ritual and Belief: Readings in the Anthropology of Religion,* 2nd ed. Boston: McGraw-Hill.

Hill, C. E., ed.
    1986   Current Health Policy Issues and Alternatives: An Applied Social Science Perspective. *Southern Anthropological Society Proceedings.* Athens: University of Georgia Press.
Hill, J. H.
    1978   Apes and Language. *Annual Review of Anthropology* 7: 89–112.
Hill, K., H. Kaplan, K. Hawkes, and A. Hurtado
    1987   Foraging Decisions among Aché Hunter-Gatherers: New Data and Implications for Optimal Foraging Models. *Ethology and Sociobiology* 8: 1–36.
Hill-Burnett, J.
    1978   Developing Anthropological Knowledge through Application. In *Applied Anthropology in America,* ed. E. M. Eddy and W. L. Partridge, pp. 112–128. New York: Columbia University Press.
Hinde, R. A., ed.
    1983   *Primate Social Relationships: An Integrated Approach.* Sunderland, MA: Sinauer.
Hobhouse, L. T.
    1915   *Morals in Evolution,* rev. ed. New York: Holt.
Hobsbawm, E. J.
    1992   *Nations and Nationalism since 1780: Programme, Myth, Reality,* 2nd ed. New York: Cambridge University Press.
Hoebel, E. A.
    1954   *The Law of Primitive Man.* Cambridge, MA: Harvard University Press.
    1968   (orig. 1954). The Eskimo: Rudimentary Law in a Primitive Anarchy. In *Studies in Social and Cultural Anthropology,* ed. J. Middleton, pp. 93–127. New York: Crowell.
Holden, A.
    2005   *Tourism Studies and the Social Sciences.* New York: Routledge.
Hole, F., K. V. Flannery, and J. A. Neely
    1969   *The Prehistory and Human Ecology of the Deh Luran Plain.* Memoir no. 1. Ann Arbor: University of Michigan Museum of Anthropology.
Holland, D., and N. Quinn, eds.
    1987   *Cultural Models in Language and Thought.* Cambridge, UK: Cambridge University Press.
Holloway, R. L.
    1975   (orig. 1974). The Casts of Fossil Hominid Brains. In *Biological Anthropology, Readings from Scientific American,* ed. S. H. Katz, pp. 69–78. San Francisco: W. H. Freeman.
Holmes, L. D.
    1987   *Quest for the Real Samoa: The Mead/Freeman Controversy and Beyond.* South Hadley, MA: Bergin and Garvey.

Holtzman, J.
2000   *Nuer Journeys, Nuer Lives.* Boston: Allyn & Bacon.

Hooker, R.
1996   Civilizations in Africa. http://www.wsu.edu:8080/~dee/CIVAFRCA/CONTENTS.HTM.

Hopkins, T., and I. Wallerstein
1982   Patterns of Development of the Modern World System. In *World System Analysis: Theory and Methodology,* by T. Hopkins, I. Wallerstein, R. Bach, C. Chase-Dunn, and R. Mukherjee, pp. 121–141. Thousand Oaks, CA: Sage.

Hopkins, T. K.
1996   *The Age of Transition: Trajectory of the World-System 1945–2025.* Atlantic Highlands, NJ: Zed.

Horton, R.
1963   The Kalabari Ekine Society: A Borderland of Religion and Art. *Africa* 33: 94–113.
1993   *Patterns of Thought in Africa and the West: Essays on Magic, Religion, and Science.* New York: Cambridge University Press.

Hostetler, J., and G. E. Huntington
1992   *Amish Children: Education in the Family,* 2nd ed. Fort Worth: Harcourt Brace.
1996   *The Hutterites in North America,* 3rd ed. Fort Worth: Harcourt Brace.

Howells, W. W.
1976   Explaining Modern Man: Evolutionists versus Migrationists. *Journal of Human Evolution* 5: 477–496.

Hrdy, S. B.
1999   *The Woman That Never Evolved,* rev. ed. Cambridge, MA: Harvard University Press.

Hughes, R., Jr.
1996   Demographics of Divorce. http://missourifamilies.org/features/divorcearticles/divorcefeature17.htm.

Human Organization
Quarterly journal. Oklahoma City: Society for Applied Anthropology.

Hunter, M. L.
2005   *Race, Gender, and the Politics of Skin Tone.* New York: Routledge.

Hutchinson, S.E.
1996   *Nuer Dilemmas: Coping with Money, War, and the State.* Berkeley: University of California Press.

Ingold, T., D. Riches, and J. Woodburn
1991   *Hunters and Gatherers.* New York: Berg (St. Martin's Press).

Ingraham, C.
1999   *White Weddings: Romancing Heterosexuality in Popular Culture.* New York: Routledge.

Inhorn, M. C., and P. J. Brown
1990   The Anthropology of Infectious Disease. *Annual Review of Anthropology* 19: 89–117.

Irving, W. N.
1985   Context and Chronology of Early Man in the Americas. *Annual Review of Anthropology* 14: 529–555.

Isaac, G. L.
1972   Early Phases of Human Behavior: Models in Lower Paleolithic Archaeology. In *Models in Archaeology,* ed. D. L. Clarke, pp. 167–199. London: Methuen.
1978   Food Sharing and Human Evolution: Archaeological Evidence from the Plio-Pleistocene of East Africa. *Journal of Anthropological Research* 34: 311–325.

Ives, E. D.
1995   *The Tape-Recorded Interview: A Manual for Fieldworkers in Folklore and Oral History,* 2nd ed. Knoxville: University of Tennessee Press.

Jackson, B.
1987   *Fieldwork.* Champaign–Urbana: University of Illinois Press.

Jackson, J., and K. B. Warren
2005   Indigenous Movements in Latin America, 1992–2004: Controversies, Ironies, New Directions. *Annual Review of Anthropology* 34: 549–573.

Jacoby, R., and N. Glauberman, eds.
1995   *The Bell Curve Debate: History, Documents, Opinions.* New York: Free Press. New York: Random House/Times Books.

Jameson, F.
1984   Postmodernism, or the Cultural Logic of Late Capitalism. *New Left Review* 146: 53–93.
1988   *The Ideologies of Theory: Essays 1971–1986.* Minneapolis: University of Minnesota Press.

Jankowiak, W. R., and E. F. Fischer
1992   A Cross-Cultural Perspective on Romantic Love. *Ethnology* 31(2): 149–156.

Janson, C. H.
1986   Capuchin Counterpoint: Divergent Mating and Feeding Habits Distinguish Two Closely Related Monkey Species of the Peruvian Forest. *Natural History* 95: 44–52.

Jasim, S. A.
1985   The Ubaid Period in Iraq: Recent Excavations in the Hamrin Region. *BAR International Series* 267 (Oxford).

Jenks, C.
2004   *Culture,* 2nd ed. New York: Routledge.

Jensen, A.
1969   How Much Can We Boost I.Q. and Scholastic Achievement? *Harvard Educational Review* 29: 1–123.

Jodelet, D.
1991   *Madness and Social Representations: Living with the Mad in One French Community.* Translated from the French by Gerard Duveen. Berkeley: University of California Press.

Johansen, B. E.
2003   *Indigenous Peoples and Environmental Issues: An Encyclopedia.* Westport, CT: Greenwood Press.

Johanson, D. C., and M. Edey
1981   *Lucy: The Origins of Humankind.* New York: Simon & Schuster.

Johanson, D. C., and B. Edgar
1996   *From Lucy to Language.* New York: Simon & Schuster.

Johanson, D. C., and T. D. White
1979   A Systematic Assessment of Early African Hominids. *Science* 203: 321–330.

Johnson, A. W.
1978   *Quantification in Cultural Anthropology: An Introduction to Research Design.* Stanford, CA: Stanford University Press.

Johnson, A. W., and T. Earle, eds.
1987   *The Evolution of Human Societies: From Foraging Group to Agrarian State.* Stanford, CA: Stanford University Press.
2000   *The Evolution of Human Societies: From Foraging Group to Agrarian State,* 2nd ed. Stanford, CA: Stanford University Press.

Johnson, G. A.
1987   The Changing Organization of Uruk Administration in the Susiana Plain. In *The Archaeology of Western Iran,* ed. F. Hole, pp. 107–139. Washington, DC: Smithsonian Institution Press.

Johnson, T. J., and C. F. Sargent, eds.
1990   *Medical Anthropology: A Handbook of Theory and Method.* New York: Greenwood Press.

Johnston, F. E., and S. Low
1994   *Children of the Urban Poor: The Sociocultural Environment of Growth, Development, and Malnutrition in Guatemala City.* Boulder, CO: Westview Press.

Jolly, A.
1985   *The Evolution of Primate Behavior,* 2nd ed. New York: Macmillan.

Jolly, C. J., and F. Plog
1986   *Physical Anthropology and Archaeology,* 4th ed. New York: McGraw-Hill.

Jolly, C. J., and R. White
1995   *Physical Anthropology and Archaeology,* 5th ed. New York: McGraw-Hill.

Jones, D.
1999   Hot Asset in Corporate: Anthropology Degrees. *USA Today,* February 18, p. B1.

Jones, G., and R. Krautz
1981   *The Transition to Statehood in the New World.* Cambridge, UK: Cambridge University Press.

Joralemon, D.
1999   *Exploring Medical Anthropology.* Boston: Allyn & Bacon.

Jordan, A.
2003   *Business Anthropology.* Prospect Heights, IL: Waveland.

Joyce, R. A.
2000   *Gender and Power in Prehispanic Mesoamerica.* Austin: University of Texas Press.

Jurmain, R.
1997   *Introduction to Physical Anthropology,* 7th ed. Belmont, CA: Wadsworth.

Kan, S.
1986   The 19th-Century Tlingit Potlatch: A New Perspective. *American Ethnologist* 13: 191–212.
1989   *Symbolic Immortality: The Tlingit Potlatch of the Nineteenth Century.* Washington, DC: Smithsonian Institution Press.

Kantor, P.
1996   Domestic Violence against Women: A Global Issue. http://www.ucis.unc.edu/resources/pubs/carolina/Abuse/Abuse.html.

Kaplan, R. D.
1994   The Coming Anarchy: How Scarcity, Crime, Overpopulation, and Disease Are Rapidly Destroying the Social Fabric of Our Planet. *Atlantic Monthly,* February, pp. 44–76.

Kardiner, A., ed.
1939   *The Individual and His Society.* New York: Columbia University Press.

Kardulias, P. N.
1999   *World-Systems Theory in Practice: Leadership, Production, and Exchange.* Lanham, MD: Rowman and Littlefield.

Katzenberg, M.A., and S. R. Saunders, eds.
2000   *Biological Anthropology of the Human Skeleton.* New York: Wiley.

Kearney, M.
1996   *Reconceptualizing the Peasantry: Anthropology in Global Perspective.* Boulder, CO: Westview Press.
2004   *Changing Fields of Anthropology: From Local to Global.* Lanham, MD: Rowman and Littlefield.

Kehoe, A. B.
1989   *The Ghost Dance Religion: Ethnohistory and Revitalization.* Fort Worth: Harcourt Brace.

Keiser, L.
1991   *Friend by Day, Enemy by Night: Organized Vengeance in a Kohistani Community.* Fort Worth: Harcourt Brace.

Kelly, R. C.

1976 Witchcraft and Sexual Relations: An Exploration in the Social and Semantic Implications of the Structure of Belief. In *Man and Woman in the New Guinea Highlands,* ed. P. Brown and G. Buchbinder, pp. 36–53. Special Publication, no. 8. Washington, DC: American Anthropological Association.

1985 *The Nuer Conquest: The Structure and Development of an Expansionist System.* Ann Arbor: University of Michigan Press.

2000 *Warless Societies and the Origin of War.* Ann Arbor: University of Michigan Press.

Kelly, R. L.

1995 *The Foraging Spectrum: Diversity in Hunter-Gatherer Lifeways.* Washington, DC: Smithsonian Institution Press.

Kemp, T. S.

1999 *Fossils and Evolution.* New York: Oxford University Press.

Kennedy, R. G.

1994 *Hidden Cities: The Discovery and Loss of Ancient North American Civilization.* New York: Free Press.

Kent, S.

1992 The Current Forager Controversy: Real versus Ideal Views of Hunter-Gatherers. *Man* 27: 45–70.

1996 *Cultural Diversity among Twentieth-Century Foragers: An African Perspective.* New York: Cambridge University Press.

1998 *Gender in African Prehistory.* Walnut Creek, CA: AltaMira.

Kent, S., and H. Vierich

1989 The Myth of Ecological Determinism: Anticipated Mobility and Site Organization of Space. In *Farmers as Hunters: The Implications of Sedentism,* ed. S. Kent, pp. 96–130. New York: Cambridge University Press.

Kerr, R. A.

1998 Sea-Floor Dust Shows Drought Felled Akkadian Empire. *Science* 279 (5349—January 16): 325–326.

Keynes, J. M.

1927 *The End of Laissez-Faire.* London: L. and Virginia Woolf.

1936 *General Theory of Employment, Interest, and Money.* New York: Harcourt Brace.

Kimbel, W. H., and L. B. Martin, eds.

1993 *Species, Species Concepts, and Primate Evolution.* New York: Plenum Press.

Kimmel, M. S.

2004 *The Gendered Society,* 2nd ed. New York: Oxford University Press.

Kimmel, M. S., J. Hearn, and R. W. Connell

2005 *Handbook of Studies on Men and Masculinities.* Thousand Oaks, CA: Sage.

Kimmel, M. S., and M. A. Messner, eds.

2007 *Men's Lives,* 7th ed. Boston: Allyn & Bacon.

Kimmel, M. S., and R. Plante

2004 *Sexualities: Identities, Behaviors, and Society.* New York: Oxford University Press.

King, B. J., ed.

1994 *The Information Continuum: Evolution of Social Information Transfer in Monkeys, Apes, and Hominids.* Santa Fe: School of American Research Press.

Kinsey, A. C., W. B. Pomeroy, and C. E. Martin

1948 *Sexual Behavior in the Human Male.* Philadelphia: W. B. Saunders.

Kirch, P. V.

1984 *The Evolution of the Polynesian Chiefdoms.* Cambridge, UK: Cambridge University Press.

2000 *On the Road of the Winds: An Archaeological History of the Pacific Islands before European Contact.* Berkeley: University of California Press.

Kirman, P.

1997 An Introduction to Ethnomusicology. http://www.insideworldmusic.com/library/weekly/aa101797.htm.

Klass, M.

1995 *Ordered Universes: Approaches to the Anthropology of Religion.* Boulder, CO: Westview Press.

2003 *Mind over Mind: The Anthropology and Psychology of Spirit Possession.* Lanham, MA: Rowman and Littlefield.

Klass, M., and M. Weisgrau, eds.

1999 *Across the Boundaries of Belief: Contemporary Issues in the Anthropology of Religion.* Boulder, CO: Westview Press.

Klein, R. G.

1999 *The Human Career: Human Biological and Cultural Origins,* 2nd ed. Chicago: University of Chicago Press.

Klein, R. G., with B. Edgar

2002 *The Dawn of Human Culture.* New York: Wiley.

Kleinfeld, J.

1975 Positive Stereotyping: The Cultural Relativist in the Classroom. *Human Organization* 34: 269–274.

Kleymeyer, C. D., ed.

1994 *Cultural Expression and Grassroots Development: Cases from Latin America and the Caribbean.* Boulder, CO: Lynne Rienner.

Klineberg, O.

1951 Race and Psychology. In *The Race Question in Modern Science.* Paris: UNESCO.

Kling, R.

1996 Synergies and Competition between Life in Cyberspace and Face-to-Face Communities. *Social Science Computing Review* 14(1): 50–54.

Kluckhohn, C.
1944 *Mirror for Man: A Survey of Human Behavior and Social Attitudes.* Greenwich, CT: Fawcett.

Kluge, A. G.
1983 Cladistics and the Classification of the Great Apes. In *New Interpretations of Ape and Human Ancestry,* ed. R. L. Ciochon and R. S. Corruccini, pp. 151–177. New York: Plenum Press.

Knecht, H., A. Pike-Tay, and R. White, eds.
1993 *Before Lascaux: The Complex Record of the Early Upper Paleolithic.* Boca Raton, FL: CRC Press.

Kohler, M., and S. Moyá-Solá
1997 Ape-Like or Hominid-Like? The Positional Behavior of *Oreopithecus bambolii* Reconsidered. *Proceedings of the National Academy of Sciences* 94 (October 14):11, 747.

Kolata, G.
1997 On Cloning Humans, "Never" Turns Swiftly into "Why Not." *New York Times,* December 2, late edition, final, section A, p. 1.

Kopytoff, V. G.
1995 Meat Viewed as Staple of Chimp Diet and Mores. *New York Times,* June 27, pp. B5–B6.

Korten, D. C.
1980 Community Organization and Rural Development: A Learning Process Approach. *Public Administration Review,* September–October, pp. 480–512.

Kosty, P.
2002 Indonesia's Matriarchal Minangkabau Offer an Alternative Social System, EurekAlert.org May 9. http://www.eurekalert.org/pub_releases/2002-05/uop-imm050902.php.

Kottak, C. P.
1980 *The Past in the Present: History, Ecology, and Social Organization in Highland Madagascar.* Ann Arbor: University of Michigan Press.
1990a *Prime-Time Society: An Anthropological Analysis of Television and Culture.* Belmont, CA: Wadsworth.
1990b Culture and Economic Development. *American Anthropologist* 92(3): 723–731.
1991 When People Don't Come First: Some Lessons from Completed Projects. In *Putting People First: Sociological Variables in Rural Development,* 2nd ed., ed. M. Cernea, pp. 429–464. New York: Oxford University Press.
1999a *Assault on Paradise: Social Change in a Brazilian Village,* 3rd ed. New York: McGraw-Hill.
1999b The New Ecological Anthropology. *American Anthropologist* 101(1): 23–35.
2004 An Anthropological Take on Sustainable Development: A Comparative Study of Change. *Human Organization* 63(4): 501–510.

2006 *Assault on Paradise: The Globalization of a Little Community in Brazil,* 4th ed. New York: McGraw-Hill.

Kottak, C. P., ed.
1982 *Researching American Culture: A Guide for Student Anthropologists.* Ann Arbor: University of Michigan Press.

Kottak, C. P., and A. C. G. Costa
1993 Ecological Awareness, Environmentalist Action, and International Conservation Strategy. *Human Organization* 52(4): 335–343.

Kottak, C. P., L. L. Gezon, and G. Green
1994 Deforestation and Biodiversity Preservation in Madagascar: The View from Above and Below. CIESIN Human Dimensions Kiosk. http://www.ciesin.com.

Kottak, C. P., and K. A. Kozaitis
2003 *On Being Different: Diversity and Multiculturalism in the North American Mainstream,* 2nd ed. Boston: McGraw-Hill.

Kottak, N. C.
2002 *Stealing the Neighbor's Chicken: Social Control in Northern Mozambique.* Ph.D. dissertation. Department of Anthropology, Emory University, Atlanta, GA.

Kramarae, R., M. Shulz, and M. O'Barr, eds.
1984 *Language and Power.* Thousand Oaks, CA: Sage.

Kreider, R. M., and J. M. Fields
2002 Number, Timing and Duration of Marriages and Divorces: 1996. U.S. Census Bureau. *Current Population Reports,* P70–80, February, 2002. http://www.census.gov/prod/2002pubs/p70-80.pdf.

Kretchmer, N.
1975 (orig. 1972). Lactose and Lactase. In *Biological Anthropology, Readings from Scientific American,* ed. S. H. Katz, pp. 310–318. San Francisco: W. H. Freeman.

Kristof, N. D.
1995 Japan's Feminine Falsetto Falls Right out of Favor. *New York Times,* December 13, pp. A1, A4.

Kroeber, A. L.
1923 *Anthropology.* New York: Harcourt, Brace.
1944 *Configurations of Cultural Growth.* Berkeley: University of California Press.
1987 (orig. 1952). *The Nature of Culture.* Chicago: University of Chicago Press.

Kroeber, A. L., and C. Kluckhohn
1963 *Culture: A Critical Review of Concepts and Definitions.* New York: Vintage.

Kryshtanovskaya, O.
1997 Illegal Structures in Russia. *Trends in Organized Crime* 3(1): 14–17.

Kuhn, S. L., M. C. Stiner, and D. S. Reese
  2001   Ornaments of the Earliest Upper
         Paleolithic: New Insights from the Levant.
         *Proceedings of the National Academy of Sciences
         of the United States of America* 98(13):
         7641–7646.

Kulick, D.
  1998   *Travesti: Sex, Gender, and Culture among
         Brazilian Transgendered Prostitutes.* Chicago:
         University of Chicago Press.

Kuniholm, P. I.
  1995   Dendrochronology, in Science in
         Archaeology: A Review. *American Journal of
         Archaeology* 99: 79–142.
  2004   Home page of the Malcolm and Carolyn
         Wiener Laboratory for Aegean and Near East-
         ern Dendrochronology at Cornell University.
         http://www.arts.cornell.edu/dendro/.

Kunitz, S. J.
  1994   *Disease and Social Diversity: The
         European Impact on the Health of Non-
         Europeans.* New York: Oxford University
         Press.

Kuper, L.
  2006   *Race, Class, and Power: Ideology and Revo-
         lutionary Change in Plural Societies.* New
         Brunswick, NJ: Transaction.

Kurtz, D. V.
  2001   *Political Anthropology: Power and
         Paradigms.* Boulder, CO: Westview Press.

Kutsche, P.
  1998   *Field Ethnography: A Manual for Doing
         Cultural Anthropology.* Upper Saddle River,
         NJ: Prentice Hall.

LaBarre, W.
  1945   Some Observations of Character Struc-
         ture in the Orient: The Japanese. *Psychiatry* 8:
         326–342.

Labov, W.
  1972a *Language in the Inner City: Studies in the
         Black English Vernacular.* Philadelphia:
         University of Pennsylvania Press.
  1972b *Sociolinguistic Patterns.* Philadelphia:
         University of Pennsylvania Press.

La Fraugh, R. J.
  n.d.   Euskara: The History, a True Mystery. The
         La Fraugh Name History. http://planetrjl.
         tripod.com/LaFraughName/id5.html.

Laguerre, M. S.
  1984   *American Odyssey: Haitians in New York.*
         Ithaca, NY: Cornell University Press.
  1998   *Diasporic Citizenship: Haitian Americans
         in Transnational America.* New York: St. Mar-
         tin's Press.
  1999   *The Global Ethnopolis: Chinatown, Japan-
         town, and Manilatown in American Society.*
         New York: St. Martin's Press.

  2001   *Urban Multiculturalism and Globalization
         in New York City.* New York: Palgrave
         Macmillan.

Laird, S. A.
  2002   *Biodiversity and Traditional Knowledge:
         Equitable Partnerships in Practice.* Sterling, VA:
         Earthscan.

Lakoff, R. T.
  2000   *Language War.* Berkeley: University of
         California Press.
  2004   *Language and Woman's Place.* New York:
         Harper & Row.

Lamberg-Karlovsky, C. C., and J. A. Sabloff
  1995   *Ancient Civilizations: The Near East and
         Mesoamerica.* Prospect Heights, IL: Waveland.

Lamphere, L., H. Ragone, and P. Zavella, eds.
  1997   *Situated Lives: Gender and Culture in
         Everyday Life.* New York: Routledge.

Lancaster, R. N., and M. Di Leonardo, eds.
  1997   *The Gender/Sexuality Reader: Culture,
         History, Political Economy.* New York:
         Routledge.

Lance, L. M., and E. E. McKenna
  1975   Analysis of Cases Pertaining to the
         Impact of Western Technology on the Non-
         Western World. *Human Organization* 34: 87–94.

Lansing, J. S.
  1991   *Priests and Programmers: Technologies of
         Power in the Engineered Landscape of Bali.*
         Princeton, NJ: Princeton University Press.

Larsen, C. S.
  2000   *Skeletons in Our Closet: Revealing Our
         Past through Bioarchaeology.* Princeton, NJ:
         Princeton University Press.

Larson, A.
  1989   Social Context of Human Immunodefi-
         ciency Virus Transmission in Africa: Histori-
         cal and Cultural Bases of East and Central
         African Sexual Relations. *Review of Infectious
         Diseases* 11: 716–731.

Lassiter, L. E.
  1998   *The Power of Kiowa Song: A Collaborative
         Ethnography.* Tucson: University of Arizona
         Press.

Laughlin, J. C. H.
  2003   *Fifty Major Cities of the Bible.* New York:
         Routledge.

Layton, R.
  1991   *The Anthropology of Art,* 2nd ed. New
         York: Cambridge University Press.

Leach, E. R.
  1955   Polyandry, Inheritance and the Defini-
         tion of Marriage. *Man* 55: 182–186.
  1961   *Rethinking Anthropology.* London:
         Athlone Press.
  1970   (orig. 1954). *Political Systems of Highland
         Burma: A Study of Kachin Social Structure.*
         London: Athlone Press.

1985   *Social Anthropology*. New York: Oxford University Press.

Leakey, M. G., C. S. Feibel, I. McDougall, and A. Walker
1995   New Four-Million-Year-Old Hominid Species from Kanapoi and Allia Bay, Kenya. *Nature* 376: 565–571.

Leakey, R. E., M. G. Leakey, and A. C. Walker
1988   Morphology of *Afropithecus turkanensis* from Kenya. *American Journal of Physical Anthropology* 76: 289–307.

LeClair, E. E., and H. K. Schneider, eds.
1968   (orig. 1961). *Economic Anthropology: Readings in Theory and Analysis*. New York: Holt, Rinehart and Winston.

Lee, R. B.
1974   (orig. 1968). What Hunters Do for a Living, or, How to Make Out on Scarce Resources. In *Man in Adaptation: The Cultural Present*, 2nd ed., ed. Y. A. Cohen, pp. 87–100. Chicago: Aldine.
1979   *The !Kung San: Men, Women, and Work in a Foraging Society*. New York: Cambridge University Press.
1984   *The Dobe !Kung*. New York: Holt, Rinehart and Winston.
2003   *The Dobe Ju/'hoansi*, 3rd ed. Belmont, CA: Wadsworth.

Lee, R. B., and R. H. Daly
1999   *The Cambridge Encyclopedia of Hunters and Gatherers*. New York: Cambridge University Press.

Lee, R. B., and I. DeVore, eds.
1977   *Kalahari Hunter-Gatherers: Studies of the !Kung San and Their Neighbors*. Cambridge, MA: Harvard University Press.

Lehmann, A. C., J. E. Meyers, and P. A. Moro, eds.
2005   *Magic, Witchcraft, and Religion: An Anthropological Study of the Supernatural*, 6th ed. Mountain View, CA: Mayfield.

Leman, J.
2001   *The Dynamics of Emerging Ethnicities: Immigrant and Indigenous Ethnogenesis in Confrontation*. New York: Peter Lang.

Lemonick, M. D., and A. Dorfman
1999   Up from the Apes: Remarkable New Evidence Is Filling in the Story of How We Became Human. *Time* 154(8): 5–58.

Lenski, G.
1966   *Power and Privilege: A Theory of Social Stratification*. New York: McGraw-Hill.

Lessa, W. A., and E. Z. Vogt, eds.
1979   *Reader in Comparative Religion: An Anthropological Approach*, 4th ed. New York: Harper & Row.

Lévi-Strauss, C.
1963   *Totemism*. Translated by R. Needham. Boston: Beacon Press.

1967   *Structural Anthropology*. New York: Doubleday.
1969   (orig. 1949). *The Elementary Structures of Kinship*. Boston: Beacon Press.

Levine, L., ed.
1995   *Genetics of Natural Populations: The Continuing Importance of Theodosius Dobzhansky*. New York: Columbia University Press.

Levine, N. E.
1988   *The Dynamics of Polyandry: Kinship, Domesticity, and Population on the Tibetan Border*. Chicago: University of Chicago Press.

Levine, R. A.
1982   *Culture, Behavior, and Personality: An Introduction to the Comparative Study of Psychosocial Adaptation*, 2nd ed. Chicago: Aldine.

Levine, R. A., ed.
1974   *Culture and Personality: Contemporary Readings*. Chicago: Aldine.

Levy, J. E., with B. Pepper
1992   *Orayvi Revisited: Social Stratification in an "Egalitarian" Society*. Santa Fe, NM: School of American Research Press, and Seattle: University of Washington Press.

Lewin, R.
1998   *Principles of Human Evolution: A Core Textbook*. Malden, MA: Blackwell Science.
2005   *Human Evolution: An Illustrated Introduction*, 5th ed. Malden, MA: Blackwell.

Lewis, H. S.
1989   *After the Eagles Landed: The Yemenites of Israel*. Boulder, CO: Westview Press.

Lewis, O.
1959   *Five Families*. New York: Basic Books.

Lewis, P.
1992   U.N. Sees a Crisis in Overpopulation. *New York Times*, April 30, p. A6.

Lewontin, R.
2000   *It Ain't Necessarily So: The Dream of the Human Genome and Other Illusions*. New York: New York Review of Books.

Lie, J.
2001   *Multiethnic Japan*. Cambridge, MA: Harvard University Press.

Lieban, R. W.
1977   The Field of Medical Anthropology. In *Culture, Disease, and Healing: Studies in Medical Anthropology*, ed. D. Landy, pp. 13–31. New York: Macmillan.

Lieberman, P.
1998   *Eve Spoke: Human Language and Human Evolution*. New York: W. W. Norton.

Light, D., S. Keller, and C. Calhoun
1994   *Sociology*, 6th ed. New York: McGraw-Hill.

Linden, E.
1986   *Silent Partners: The Legacy of the Ape Language Experiments*. New York: Times Books.

Lindenbaum, S.
   1972   Sorcerers, Ghosts, and Polluting
          Women: An Analysis of Religious Belief and
          Population Control. *Ethnology* 11: 241–253.

Lindholm, C.
   2001   *Culture and Identity: The History, Theory,
          and Practice of Psychological Anthropology.*
          Boston: McGraw-Hill.

Linton, R.
   1927   Report on Work of Field Museum
          Expedition in Madagascar. *American Anthro-
          pologist* 29: 292–307.
   1943   Nativistic Movements. *American
          Anthropologist* 45: 230–240.

Lipke, D. J.
   2000   Dead End Ahead? Income May Be the
          Real Barrier to the Internet On-Ramp. *Ameri-
          can Demographics,* August. http://www.
          demographics.com/publications/ad/
          00_ad/ad000805c.htm.

Little, K.
   1965   *West African Urbanization: A Study of
          Voluntary Associations in Social Change.* Cam-
          bridge, UK: Cambridge University Press.
   1971   *Some Aspects of African Urbanization
          South of the Sahara. McCaleb Modules in
          Anthropology.* Reading, MA: Addison-Wesley.

Livingstone, F. B.
   1958   Anthropological Implications of Sickle
          Cell Gene Distribution in West Africa. *Ameri-
          can Anthropologist* 60: 533–562.
   1969   Gene Frequency Clines of the *b* Hemo-
          globin Locus in Various Human Populations
          and Their Similarities by Models Involving
          Differential Selection. *Human Biology* 41:
          223–236.

Lizot, J.
   1985   *Tales of the Yanomami: Daily Life in the
          Venezuelan Forest.* New York: Cambridge
          University Press.

Lockwood, W. G.
   1975   *European Moslems: Economy and Ethnic-
          ity in Western Bosnia.* New York: Academic
          Press.

Lockwood, Y. R.
   1983   *Text and Context: Folksong in a Bosnian
          Muslim Village.* Columbus, OH: Slavica.

Lohr, S.
   2005   Cutting Here, but Hiring Over There.
          New York Times, June 24. http://www.
          nytimes.com/2005/06/24/technology/
          24blue.html?pagewanted=print.

Loomis, W. F.
   1967   Skin-Pigmented Regulation of Vitamin-
          D Biosynthesis in Man. *Science* 157: 501–506.

London School of Economics
   2004   Definition of Civil Society. LSE Centre
          for Civil Society, March 22. http://www.lse.
          ac.uk/collections/CCS/introduction.htm.

Lordkipanidze, D., et al.
   2005   The Earliest Toothless Hominin Skull.
          Nature 434: 717–718.

Loveday, L.
   1986   Japanese Sociolinguistics: An Introduc-
          tory Survey. *Journal of Pragmatics* 10: 287–326.
   2001   *Explorations in Japanese Sociolinguistics.*
          Philadelphia: J. Benjamins.

Lowie, R. H.
   1935   *The Crow Indians.* New York: Farrar and
          Rinehart.
   1961   (orig. 1920). *Primitive Society.* New York:
          Harper & Brothers.

Lugaila, T.
   1998a Numbers of Divorced and Never-
          Married Adults Increasing, Says Census
          Bureau Report. http://www.census.gov/
          Press-Release/cb98-56.html.
   1998b Marital Status and Living
          Arrangements, March 1998 (Update).
          http://www.census.gov/prod/99pubs/
          p20-514.pdf.
   1999   Married Adults Still in the Majority,
          Census Bureau Reports. http://www.
          census.gov/Press-Release/www/1999/
          cb99-03.html.

Lutz, C., and J. L. Collins
   1993   *Reading National Geographic.* Chicago:
          University of Chicago Press.

Lyell, C.
   1969   (orig. 1830–37). *Principles of Geology.*
          New York: Johnson.

Lyotard, J. F.
   1993   *The Postmodern Explained.* Translated
          by J. Pefanis, M. Thomas, and D. Barry.
          Minneapolis: University of Minnesota Press.

MacKinnon, J.
   1974   *In Search of the Red Ape.* New York:
          Ballantine.

Madra, Y. M.
   2004   Karl Polanyi: Freedom in a Complex
          Society. *Econ-Atrocity Bulletin: In the History
          of Thought.* http://www.fguide.org/Bulletin/
          polanyi.htm.

Maher, J. C., and G. MacDonald, eds.
   1995   *Diversity and Language in Japanese
          Culture.* New York: Columbia University
          Press.

Mair, L.
   1969   *Witchcraft.* New York: McGraw-Hill.

Malinowski, B.
   1926   *Crime and Custom in Savage Society.*
          London: Routledge and Kegan Paul.
   1927   *Sex and Repression in Savage Society.*
          London and New York: International Library
          of Psychology, Philosophy and Scientific
          Method.
   1929a Practical Anthropology. *Africa* 2: 23–38.

1929b *The Sexual Life of Savages in North-Western Melanesia.* New York: Harcourt, Brace, and World.

1944 *A Scientific Theory of Culture, and Other Essays.* Chapel Hill: University of North Carolina Press.

1961 (orig. 1922). *Argonauts of the Western Pacific.* New York: Dutton.

1978 (orig. 1931). The Role of Magic and Religion. In *Reader in Comparative Religion: An Anthropological Approach,* 4th ed., ed. W. A. Lessa and E. Z. Vogt, pp. 37–46. New York: Harper & Row.

2001 (orig. 1927). *Sex and Repression in Savage Society.* Chicago: University of Chicago Press.

Malkin, C.
2004 Earliest Primate Discovered in China. *Science Now,* January 5. American Association for the Advancement of Science. http://cmbi.bjmu.edu.cn/news/0401/13.htm.

Malkki, L. H.
1995 *Purity and Exile: Violence, Memory, and National Cosmology among Hutu Refugees in Tanzania.* Chicago: University of Chicago Press.

Mann, A.
1975 *Paleodemographic Aspects of the South African Australopithecines.* Publications in Anthropology, no. 1. Philadelphia: University of Pennsylvania.

Manners, R.
1973 (orig. 1956). Functionalism, Realpolitik and Anthropology in Underdeveloped Areas. *America Indigena* 16. Also in *To See Ourselves: Anthropology and Modern Social Issues,* gen. ed. T. Weaver, pp. 113–126. Glenview, IL: Scott, Foresman.

Maquet, J.
1964 Objectivity in Anthropology. *Current Anthropology* 5: 47–55 (also in Clifton, ed., 1970).

1986 *The Aesthetic Experience: An Anthropologist Looks at the Visual Arts.* New Haven, CT: Yale University Press.

Mar, M. E.
1997 Secondary Colors: The Multiracial Option. *Harvard Magazine,* May–June 1997, pp. 19–20.

Marcus, G. E., and D. Cushman
1982 Ethnographies as Texts. *Annual Review of Anthropology* 11: 25–69.

Marcus, G. E., and M. M. J. Fischer
1986 *Anthropology as Cultural Critique: An Experimental Moment in the Human Sciences.* Chicago: University of Chicago Press.

1999 *Anthropology as Cultural Critique: An Experimental Moment in the Human Sciences,* 2nd ed. Chicago: University of Chicago Press.

Marcus, G. E., and F. R. Myers, eds.
1995 *The Traffic in Culture: Refiguring Art and Anthropology.* Berkeley: University of California Press.

Marcus, J.
1992 *Mesoamerican Writing Systems: Propaganda, Myth, and History in Four Ancient Civilizations.* Princeton, NJ: Princeton University Press.

Marcus, J., and K. V. Flannery
1996 *Zapotec Civilization: How Urban Society Evolved in Mexico's Oaxaca Valley.* New York: Thames and Hudson.

Margolis, M.
1984 *Mothers and Such: American Views of Women and How They Changed.* Berkeley: University of California Press.

1994 *Little Brazil: An Ethnography of Brazilian Immigrants in New York City.* Princeton, NJ: Princeton University Press.

2000 *True to Her Nature: Changing Advice to American Women.* Prospect Heights, IL: Waveland.

Marks, J. M.
1995 *Human Biodiversity: Genes, Race, and History.* New York: Aldine.

Marshack, A.
1972 *Roots of Civilization.* New York: McGraw-Hill.

Martin, E.
1987 *The Woman in the Body: A Cultural Analysis of Reproduction.* Boston: Beacon Press.

Martin, J.
1992 *Cultures in Organizations: Three Perspectives.* New York: Oxford University Press.

Martin, K., and B. Voorhies
1975 *Female of the Species.* New York: Columbia University Press.

Martin, P., and E. Midgley
1994 Immigration to the United States: Journey to an Uncertain Destination. *Population Bulletin* 49(3): 1–47.

Martinez, E., and A. Garcia
2000 What Is Neo-Liberalism: A Brief Definition. Updated February 26, 2000. http://www.globalexchange.org/campaigns/econ101/neoliberalDefined.html.

Marx, K., and F. Engels
1976 (orig. 1848). *Communist Manifesto.* New York: Pantheon.

Mascia-Lees, F., and N. J. Black
2000 *Gender and Anthropology.* Prospect Heights, IL: Waveland.

Mathews, G.
2000 *Global Culture/Individual Identity: Searching for Home in the Cultural Supermarket.* New York: Routledge.

Maybury-Lewis, D.
    2002   *Indigenous Peoples, Ethnic Groups, and the State,* 2nd ed. Boston: Allyn & Bacon.

Mayell, H.
    2003   Orangutans Show Signs of Culture, Study Says. *National Geographic News,* January 3. http://news.nationalgeographic.com/news/2002/12/1220_021226_orangutan.html.
    2004*a*   Wild Orangs, Extinct by 2023? *National Geographic News,* March 9. http://news.nationalgeographic.com/news/2003/09/0930_030930_orangutanthreat.html.
    2004*b*   Is Bead Find Proof Modern Thought Began in Africa? *National Geographic News,* March 31. http://news.nationalgeographic.com/news/2004/03/0331_040331_ostrichman.html.

Mayr, E.
    1970   *Population, Species, and Evolution.* Cambridge, MA: Harvard University Press.
    2001   *What Evolution Is.* New York: Basic Books.

McAllester, D. P.
    1954   *Enemy Way Music: A Study of Social and Esthetic Values as Seen in Navaho Music.* Cambridge, MA: Peabody Museum of American Archaeology and Ethnology, Papers 41(3).

McBrearty, S., and A. S. Brooks
    2000   The Revolution That Wasn't: A New Interpretation of the Origin of Modern Human Behavior. *Journal of Human Evolution* 39: 453–563.

McBrearty, S., and N. G. Jablonski
    2005   First Fossil Chimpanzee. *Nature* 437: 105–108.

McCaskie, T. C.
    1995   *State and Society in Pre-Colonial Asante.* New York: Cambridge University Press.

McDonald, G.
    1984   *Carioca Fletch.* New York: Warner Books.

McDonald, J. H., ed.
    2002   *The Applied Anthropology Reader.* Boston: Allyn & Bacon.

McElroy, A., and P. K. Townsend
    1996   *Medical Anthropology in Ecological Perspective,* 3rd ed. Boulder, CO: Westview Press.

McGraw, T. K., ed.
    1986   *America versus Japan.* Boston: Harvard Business School Press.

McGrew, W. C.
    1979   Evolutionary Implications of Sex Differences in Chimpanzee Predation and Tool Use. In *The Great Apes,* ed. D. A. Hamburg and E. R. McCown, pp. 441–463. Menlo Park, CA: Benjamin Cummings.

McGrew, W., L. Marchant, and T. Nishida
    1996   *Great Ape Societies.* Cambridge, UK: Cambridge University Press.

McKee, J. K., F. E. Poirier, and W. S. McGraw
    2005   *Understanding Human Evolution,* 5th ed. Upper Saddle River, NJ: Prentice Hall.

McKinley, J.
    1996   Board's Decision on Black English Stirs Debate. *New York Times,* December 21. http://www.nytimes.com.

McKusick, V.
    1966   *Mendelian Inheritance in Man.* Baltimore: Johns Hopkins University Press.
    1990   *Mendelian Inheritance in Man: Catalogs of Autosomal Dominant, Autosomal Recessive, and X-Linked Phenotypes,* 9th ed. Baltimore: Johns Hopkins University Press.

Mead, M.
    1930   *Growing Up in New Guinea.* New York: Blue Ribbon.
    1937   *Cooperation and Competition among Primitive Peoples.* New York: McGraw-Hill.
    1950   (orig. 1935). *Sex and Temperament in Three Primitive Societies.* New York: New American Library.
    1961   (orig. 1928). *Coming of Age in Samoa.* New York: Morrow Quill.
    1972   *Blackberry Winter: My Earlier Years.* New York: Simon & Schuster.

Meadow, R., ed.
    1991   *Harappa Excavations 1986–1990: A Multi-disciplinary Approach to Third Millennium Urbanism.* Monographs in World Archeology, no. 3. Madison, WI: Prehistory Press.

Meadow, R. H., and J. M. Kenoyer
    2000   The Indus Valley Mystery: One of the World's First Great Civilizations Is Still a Puzzle. *Discovering Archaeology,* April, pp. 38–43.

Meigs, A., and K. Barlow
    2002   Beyond the Taboo: Imagining Incest. *American Anthropologist* 104(1): 38–49.

Mercader, J., M. Panger, and C. Boesch
    2002   Excavation of a Chimpanzee Stone Tool Site in the African Rainforest. *Science* 296: 1452–1455.

Merlan, F.
    2005   Indigenous Movements in Australia. *Annual Review of Anthropology* 34: 473–494.

Merriam, A.
    1971   The Arts and Anthropology. In *Anthropology and Art: Readings in Cross-Cultural Aesthetics,* ed. C. Otten, pp. 93–105. Austin: University of Texas Press.

Michaels, E.
    1986   Aboriginal Content. Paper presented at the meeting of the Australian Screen Studies Association, December, Sydney.

Michaelson, K.
  1996 Information, Community, and Access. *Social Science Computing Review* 14(1): 57–59.

Michrina, B. P., and C. Richards
  1996 *Person to Person: Fieldwork, Dialogue, and the Hermeneutic Method.* Albany: State University of New York Press.

Middleton, J.
  1967 Introduction. *In Myth and Cosmos: Readings in Mythology and Symbolism,* ed. John Middleton, pp. ix–xi. Garden City, NY: Natural History Press.
  1993 *The Lugbara of Uganda,* 2nd ed. Fort Worth: Harcourt Brace.

Middleton, J., ed.
  1967 *Gods and Rituals.* Garden City, NY: Natural History Press.

Miles, H. L.
  1983 Apes and Language: The Search for Communicative Competence. *In Language in Primates,* ed. J. de Luce and H. T. Wilder, pp. 43–62. New York: Springer-Verlag.

Miller, B. D.
  1997 *The Endangered Sex: Neglect of Female Children in Rural North India.* New York: Oxford University Press.

Miller, B. D., ed.
  1993 *Sex and Gender Hierarchies.* New York: Cambridge University Press.

Miller, J.
  n.d. Alaskan Tlingit and Tsimtsian. Seattle: University of Washington Libraries, Digital Collections. http://content.lib.washington.edu/aipnw/miller1.html.

Miller, L.
  2004 The Ancient Bristlecone Pine, Dendrochronology. http://www.sonic.net/bristlecone/dendro.html.

Miller, N., and R. C. Rockwell, eds.
  1988 *AIDS in Africa: The Social and Policy Impact.* Lewiston, ME: Edwin Mellen.

Mills, G.
  1971 Art: An Introduction to Qualitative Anthropology. *In Anthropology and Art: Readings in Cross-Cultural Aesthetics,* ed. C. Otten, pp. 66–92. Austin: University of Texas Press.

Mintz, S. W.
  1985 *Sweetness and Power: The Place of Sugar in Modern History.* New York: Viking Penguin.

Mirzoeff, N.
  1999 *An Introduction to Visual Culture.* New York: Routledge.

Mishler, E. G.
  1991 *Research Interviewing: Context and Narrative.* Cambridge, MA: Harvard University Press.

Mitani, J. C., and D. P. Watts
  1999 Demographic Influences on the Hunting Behavior of Chimpanzees. *American Journal of Physical Anthropology* 109: 439–454.

Mitchell, J. C.
  1966 Theoretical Orientations in African Urban Studies. *In The Social Anthropology of Complex Societies,* ed. M. Banton, pp. 37–68. London: Tavistock.

Moerman, M.
  1965 Ethnic Identification in a Complex Civilization: Who Are the Lue? *American Anthropologist* 67(5 Part I): 1215–1230.

Moisala, P., and B. Diamond, eds.
  2000 *Music and Gender.* Champaign–Urbana: University of Illinois Press.

Molnar, S.
  2005 *Human Variation: Races, Types, and Ethnic Groups,* 6th ed. Upper Saddle River, NJ: Prentice Hall.

Moncure, S.
  1998 Anthropologist Assists in Police Investigations. *University of Delaware Update* 17, no. 39, August 20. http://www.udel.edu/PR/UpDate/98/39/anthrop.html.

Montagu, A.
  1975 *The Nature of Human Aggression.* New York: Oxford University Press.
  1981 *Statement on Race: An Annotated Elaboration and Exposition of the Four Statements on Race Issued by the United Nations Educational, Scientific, and Cultural Organization.* Westport, CT: Greenwood Press.

Montagu, A., ed.
  1996 *Race and IQ,* expanded ed. New York: Oxford University Press.
  1997 *Man's Most Dangerous Myth: The Fallacy of Race,* 6th ed. Walnut Creek, CA: AltaMira.
  1999 *Race and IQ,* expanded ed. New York: Oxford University Press.

Montague, S., and R. Morais
  1981 Football Games and Rock Concerts: The Ritual Enactment. *In The American Dimension: Cultural Myths and Social Realities,* 2nd ed., ed. W. Arens and S. B. Montague, pp. 33–52. Sherman Oaks, CA: Alfred.

Montgomery, S.
  1991 *Walking with the Great Apes: Jane Goodall, Dian Fossey, Biruté Galdikas.* Boston: Houghton Mifflin.

Moore, A. D.
  1985 The Development of Neolithic Societies in the Near East. *Advances in World Archaeology* 4:1–69.

Moore, S. F.
  1986 *Social Facts and Fabrications.* Cambridge, UK: Cambridge University Press.

Moran, E. F.
1982   *Human Adaptability: An Introduction to Ecological Anthropology*. Boulder, CO: Westview Press.

Moran, L.
1993   Evolution Is a Fact and a Theory. The Talk Origins Archive. http://www.talkorigins.org/faqs/evolution-fact.html.

Morbeck, M. E., A. Galloway, and A. L. Zihlman, eds.
1997   *The Evolving Female: A Life-History Perspective*. Princeton, NJ: Princeton University Press.

Morgan, L. H.
1963   (orig. 1877). *Ancient Society*. Cleveland: World Publishing.
1966   (orig. 1851). *League of the Ho-dé-no-sau-nee or Iroquois*. New York: B. Franklin.
1997   (orig. 1870). *Systems of Consanguinity and Affinity of the Human Family*. Lincoln: University of Nebraska Press.

Morgen, S., ed.
1989   *Gender and Anthropology: Critical Reviews for Research and Teaching*. Washington, DC: American Anthropological Association.

Morkot, R.
2005   *The Egyptians: An Introduction*. New York: Routledge.

Morris, B.
1987   *Anthropological Studies of Religion: An Introductory Text*. New York: Cambridge University Press.

Mount Holyoke College
1999   Dung-Covered Madonna Sparks Controversy; Art Professor Michael Davis Takes a Look. *College Street Journal* 13(6), October 8. http://www.mtholyoke.edu/offices/comm/csj/991008/madonna.html.

Mowat, F.
1987   *Woman in the Mists: The Story of Dian Fossey and the Mountain Gorillas of Africa*. New York: Warner Books.

Moyá-Solá, S., et al.
2004   *Pierolapithecus catalaunicus*: A New Middle Miocene Great Ape from Spain. *Science* 306(5700): 1339–1344.

Muhlhausler, P.
1986   *Pidgin and Creole Linguistics*. London: Blackwell.

Mukhopadhyay, C., and P. Higgins
1988   Anthropological Studies of Women's Status Revisited: 1977–1987. *Annual Review of Anthropology* 17: 461–495.

Mullings, L., ed.
1987   *Cities of the United States: Studies in Urban Anthropology*. New York: Columbia University Press.

Murdock, G. P.
1934   *Our Primitive Contemporaries*. New York: Macmillan.
1957   World Ethnographic Sample. *American Anthropologist* 59: 664–687.

Murdock, G. P., and C. Provost
1973   Factors in the Division of Labor by Sex: A Cross-Cultural Analysis. *Ethnology* XII(2): 203–225.

Murphy, R. F.
1990   *The Body Silent*. New York: W. W. Norton.

Murphy, R. F., and L. Kasdan
1959   The Structure of Parallel Cousin Marriage. *American Anthropologist* 61: 17–29.

Murray, S. O., and W. Roscoe, eds.
1998   *Boy-Wives and Female Husbands: Studies in African Homosexualities*. New York: St. Martin's Press.

Mydans, S.
1992*a*   Criticism Grows over Aliens Seized during Riots. *New York Times*, May 29, p. A8.
1992*b*   Judge Dismisses Case in Shooting by Officer. *New York Times*, June 4, p. A8.

Myers, F. R.
2002   *Painting Culture: The Making of an Aboriginal High Art*. Durham, NC: Duke University Press.

Nafte, M.
2000   *Flesh and Bone: An Introduction to Forensic Anthropology*. Durham, NC: Carolina Academic Press.

Nagel, J.
1996   *American Indian Ethnic Renewal: Red Power and the Resurgence of Identity and Culture*. New York: Oxford University Press.

Nanda, S.
2000   *Gender Diversity: Crosscultural Variations*. Prospect Heights, IL: Waveland.

Napier, A. D.
1992   *Foreign Bodies: Performance, Art, and Symbolic Anthropology*. Berkeley: University of California Press.

Narayan, U.
1997   *Dislocating Cultures: Identities, Traditions, and Third World Feminisms*. New York: Routledge.

Nash, D.
1999   *A Little Anthropology*, 3rd ed. Upper Saddle River, NJ: Prentice Hall.

Nash, J., and H. Safa, eds.
1986   *Women and Change in Latin America*. South Hadley, MA: Bergin and Garvey.

National Association for the Practice of Anthropology
1991   *NAPA Directory of Practicing Anthropologists*. Washington, DC: American Anthropological Association.

National Vital Statistics Reports
   2000   Births, Marriages, Divorces, and Deaths: Provisional Data for November 1999. October 31, 2000. Hyattsville, MD: U.S. Department of Health and Human Services, Center for Disease Control and Prevention, National Center for Health Statistics.
   2001   *National Vital Statistics Reports*, vol. 46, no. 6. http://www.cdc.gov/nchs/data/nvsr/nvsr49/nvsr49_06.pdf.

Naylor, L. L.
   1996   *Culture and Change: An Introduction.* Westport, CT: Bergin and Garvey.

Nelson, H., and R. Jurmain
   1991   *Introduction to Physical Anthropology,* 5th ed. St. Paul, MN: West.

Nelson, S. N., and M. Rosen-Ayalon, eds.
   2002   *In Pursuit of Gender: Worldwide Archaeological Approaches.* Walnut Creek, CA: AltaMira.

Netting, R. M. C., R. R. Wilk, and E. J. Arnould, eds.
   1984   *Households: Comparative and Historical Studies of the Domestic Group.* Berkeley: University of California Press.

Nevid, J. S., and Rathus, S. A.
   1995   *Human Sexuality in a World of Diversity,* 2nd ed. Needham Heights, MA: Allyn & Bacon.

New York Times
   1990   Tropical Diseases on March, Hitting 1 in 10. March 28, p. A3.
   1992a   Alexandria Journal: TV Program for Somalis Is a Rare Unifying Force. December 18.
   1992b   Married with Children: The Waning Icon. August 23, p. E2.
   2005   Intelligent Design Derailed. Editorial Desk, December 22. http://www.nytimes.com/2005/12/22/opinion/22thur1.html?ex=1292907600&en=af56b21719a9dd8f&ei=5090&partner=rssuserland&emc=rss.

Newman, M.
   1992   Riots Bring Attention to Growing Hispanic Presence in South-Central Area. *New York Times,* May 11, p. A10.

Ni, X., W. Wang, Y. Hu, and C. Li
   2004   A Euprimate Skull from the Early Eocene of China. *Nature* 427: 65–68.

Nielsson, G. P.
   1985   States and Nation-Groups: A Global Taxonomy. In *New Nationalisms of the Developed World,* ed. E. A. Tiryakian and R. Rogowski, pp. 27–56. Boston: Allen and Unwin.

Nolan, R. W.
   2002   *Development Anthropology: Encounters in the Real World.* Boulder, CO: Westview Press.
   2003   *Anthropology in Practice.* Boulder, CO: Lynne Rienner.

Nowak, R. M.
   1999   *Walker's Primates of the World.* Baltimore: Johns Hopkins University Press.

Nussbaum, M. C.
   2000   *Women and Human Development: The Capabilities Approach.* New York: Cambridge University Press.

Nussbaum, M., and J. Glover, eds.
   1995   *Women, Culture, and Development: A Study of Human Capabilities.* New York: Oxford University Press.

Oakley, K. P.
   1976   *Man the Tool-Maker,* 6th ed. Chicago: University of Chicago Press.

O'Dougherty, M.
   2002   *Consumption Intensified: The Politics of Middle-Class Daily Life in Brazil.* Durham, NC: Duke University Press.

Okpewho, I.
   1977   Principles of Traditional African Art. *Journal of Aesthetics and Art Criticism* 35(3): 301–314.

O'Leary, C. M.
   2002   *Class Formation, Diet and Economic Transformation in Two Brazilian Fishing Communities.* Ph.D. Dissertation, Department of Anthropology, University of Michigan, Ann Arbor.

Omohundro, J. T.
   2001   *Careers in Anthropology,* 2nd ed. Boston: McGraw-Hill.

Ong, A.
   1987   *Spirits of Resistance and Capitalist Discipline: Factory Women in Malaysia.* Albany: State University of New York Press.
   1989   Center, Periphery, and Hierarchy: Gender in Southeast Asia. In *Gender and Anthropology: Critical Reviews for Research and Teaching,* ed. S. Morgen, pp. 294–312. Washington, DC: American Anthropological Association.
   2006   *Neoliberalism as Exception: Mutations in Citizenship and Sovereignty.* Durham, NC: Duke University Press.

Ong, A., and S. J. Collier, eds.
   2005   *Global Assemblages: Technology, Politics, and Ethics as Anthropological Problems.* Malden, MA: Blackwell.

Ong, A., and M. G. Peletz, eds.
   1995   *Bewitching Women, Pious Men: Gender and Body Politics in Southeast Asia.* Berkeley: University of California Press.

Ontario Consultants on Religious Tolerance
   1996   Religious Access Dispute Resolved. Internet Mailing List, April 12.
   1997   Swiss Cult Promotes Cloning.
   2001   Religions of the World: Number of Adherents; Rates of growth. http://www.religioustolerance.org/worldrel.htm.

O'Reilly, K.
 2004 *Ethnographic Methods.* New York: Routledge.

O'Rourke, D. H.
 2003 Anthropological Genetics in the Genomic Era: A Look Back and Ahead. *American Anthropologist* 105(1): 101–109.

Ortner, S. B.
 1984 Theory of Anthropology Since the Sixties. *Comparative Studies in Society and History* 126(1): 126–166.

Ott, S.
 1981 *The Circle of Mountains: A Basque Shepherding Community.* Oxford, UK: Clarendon Press.

Otten, C. M., ed.
 1971 *Anthropology and Art; Readings in Cross-Cultural Aesthetics.* Garden City, NY: American Museum of Natural History.

Ottenheimer, M.
 1996 *Forbidden Relatives: The American Myth of Cousin Marriage.* Champaign–Urbana: University of Illinois Press.

Otterbein, K. F.
 1968 (orig. 1963). Marquesan Polyandry. In *Marriage, Family and Residence,* ed. P. Bohannan and J. Middleton, pp. 287–296. Garden City, NY: Natural History Press.
 2004 *How War Began.* College Station: Texas A&M University Press.

Palmer, S.
 2001 The Rael Deal. *Religion in the News* 4:2. Hartford, CT: Trinity College, The Leonard E. Greenberg Center for the Study of Religion in Public Life. http://www.trincoll.edu/depts/csrpl/RINVol4No2/Rael.htm.

Park, M. A.
 2005 *Biological Anthropology,* 4th ed. Boston: McGraw-Hill.

Parker, S., and R. Kleiner
 1970 The Culture of Poverty: An Adjustive Dimension. *American Anthropologist* 72: 516–527.

Parkin, R.
 1997 *Kinship: An Introduction to Basic Concepts.* Cambridge, MA: Blackwell.

Parkin, R., and L. Stone, eds.
 2004 *Kinship and Family: An Anthropological Reader.* Malden, MA: Blackwell.

Parsons, J. R.
 1974 The Development of a Prehistoric Complex Society: A Regional Perspective from the Valley of Mexico. *Journal of Field Archaeology* 1: 81–108.
 1976 The Role of Chinampa Agriculture in the Food Supply of Aztec Tenochtitlan. In *Cultural Change and Continuity: Essays in Honor of James Bennett Griffin,* ed. C. E. Cleland, pp. 233–262. New York: Academic Press.

Pasternak, B., C. R. Ember, and M. Ember
 1997 *Sex, Gender, and Kinship: A Cross-Cultural Perspective.* Upper Saddle River, NJ: Prentice Hall.

Patterson, F.
 1978 Conversations with a Gorilla. *National Geographic,* October, pp. 438–465.

Patterson, T. C.
 1993 *Archaeology: The Historical Development of Civilizations,* 2nd ed. Englewood Cliffs, NJ: Prentice Hall.

Paul, R.
 1989 Psychoanalytic Anthropology. *Annual Review of Anthropology* 18: 177–202.

Pear, R.
 1992 Ranks of U.S. Poor Reach 35.7 Million, the Most Since '64. *New York Times,* September 3, pp. A1, A12.

Peletz, M.
 1988 *A Share of the Harvest: Kinship, Property, and Social History among the Malays of Rembau.* Berkeley: University of California Press.

Pelto, P.
 1973 *The Snowmobile Revolution: Technology and Social Change in the Arctic.* Menlo Park, CA: Cummings.

Pelto, P. J., and G. H. Pelto
 1978 *Anthropological Research: The Structure of Inquiry,* 2nd ed. New York: Cambridge University Press.

Peplau, L. A., ed.
 1999 *Gender, Culture, and Ethnicity: Current Research about Women and Men.* Mountain View, CA: Mayfield.

Perlman, D.
 2004 Fossil Find May Be the Father of Us All: It's Hailed as Last Common Kin of the Great Apes and Humans. *San Francisco Chronicle,* November 22, p. A-4.

Peters, J. D.
 1997 Seeing Bifocally: Media, Place, Culture. In *Culture, Power, Place: Explorations in Critical Anthropology,* ed. A. Gupta and J. Ferguson, pp. 75–92. Durham, NC: Duke University Press.

Peters-Golden, H.
 2006 *Culture Sketches,* 4th ed. Boston: McGraw-Hill.

Petraglia-Bahri, D.
 1996 Introduction to Postcolonial Studies. http://www.emory.edu/ENGLISH/Bahri/.

Pettifor, E.
 1995 From the Teeth of the Dragon— *Gigantopithecus blacki.* http://www.wynja.com/arch/gigantopithecus.html.

Pfeiffer, J.
    1985   *The Emergence of Humankind,* 4th ed.
        New York: HarperCollins.

Phillipson, D. W.
    1993   *African Archaeology,* 2nd ed. New York:
        Cambridge University Press.

Pickrell, J.
    2004   Gorilla Mafia? Groups Ruled by Related
        Males, Study Says. *National Geographic News,*
        March 31. http://news.nationalgeographic.
        com/news/2004/03/0331_040331_
        westerngorillas.html.

Piddington, R.
    1970   Action Anthropology. In *Applied
        Anthropology: Readings in the Uses of the
        Science of Man,* ed. James Clifton, pp. 127–143.
        Boston: Houghton Mifflin.

Piddocke, S.
    1969   The Potlatch System of the Southern
        Kwakiutl: A New Perspective. In *Environment
        and Cultural Behavior,* ed. A. P. Vayda,
        pp. 130–156. Garden City, NY: Natural
        History Press.

Plattner, S., ed.
    1989   *Economic Anthropology.* Stanford, CA:
        Stanford University Press.

Podolefsky, A.
    1992   *Simbu Law: Conflict Management in the
        New Guinea Highlands.* Fort Worth: Harcourt
        Brace.

Podolefsky, A., and P. J. Brown, eds.
    1992   *Applying Anthropology: An Introductory
        Reader,* 2nd ed. Mountain View, CA: Mayfield.
    2007   *Applying Anthropology: An Introductory
        Reader,* 8th ed. Boston: McGraw-Hill.

Polanyi, K.
    1968   *Primitive, Archaic and Modern Economies:
        Essays of Karl Polanyi.* Edited by G. Dalton.
        Garden City, NY: Anchor Books.

Pollan, M.
    2003   You Want Fries with That? *New York
        Times Book Review,* January 12, p. 6.

Pollard, T. M., and S. B. Hyatt
    1999   *Sex, Gender, and Health.* New York:
        Cambridge University Press.

Pollock, S.
    1999   *Ancient Mesopotamia: The Eden That
        Never Was.* Cambridge, UK: Cambridge
        University Press.

Pospisil, L.
    1963   *The Kapauku Papuans of West New
        Guinea.* New York: Harcourt Brace
        Jovanovich.

Potash, B., ed.
    1986   *Widows in African Societies: Choices
        and Constraints.* Stanford, CA: Stanford
        University Press.

Potts, D. T.
    1997   *Mesopotamian Civilization: The Material
        Foundations.* Ithaca, NY: Cornell University
        Press.

Prag, J., and R. Neave
    1997   *Making Faces: Using Forensic and Archae-
        ological Evidence.* College Station: Texas A&M
        University Press.

Price, R., ed.
    1973   *Maroon Societies.* New York: Anchor
        Press, Doubleday.

Price, T. D., ed.
    2000   *Europe's First Farmers.* New York:
        Cambridge University Press.

Price, T. D., and G. M. Feinman
    2005   *Images of the Past,* 4th ed. Boston:
        McGraw-Hill.

Price, T. D. and A. B. Gebauer, eds.
    1995   *Last Hunters, First Farmers: New Perspec-
        tives on the Prehistoric Transition to Agriculture.*
        Santa Fe, NM: School of American Research
        Press.

Public Culture
    Journal published by the University of
        Chicago.

Punch, M.
    1985   *The Politics and Ethics of Fieldwork.*
        Beverly Hills, CA: Sage.

Quiatt, D., and V. Reynolds
    1995   *Primate Behavior: Information, Social
        Knowledge, and the Evolution of Culture.* New
        York: Cambridge University Press.

Quinn, N., and C. Strauss
    1989   A Cognitive Cultural Anthropology.
        Paper presented at the Invited Session
        "Assessing Developments in Anthropology,"
        American Anthropological Association 88th
        Annual Meeting, November 15–19, 1989,
        Washington, DC.
    1994   A Cognitive Cultural Anthropology.
        In Assessing Cultural Anthropology, ed.
        R. Borofsky. New York: McGraw-Hill.

Radcliffe-Brown, A. R.
    1965   (orig. 1962). *Structure and Function in
        Primitive Society.* New York: Free Press.

Radcliffe-Brown, A. R., and D. Forde, eds.
    1994   *African Systems of Kinship and Marriage.*
        New York: Columbia University Press.

Rak, Y.
    1986   The Neandertal: A New Look at an Old
        Face. *Journal of Human Evolution* 15(3): 151–164.

Random House College Dictionary
    1982   Revised ed. New York: Random House.

Ranger, T. O.
    1996   Postscript. In *Postcolonial Identities,* ed.
        R. Werbner and T. O. Ranger. London: Zed.

Rappaport, R. A.
　　1974　Obvious Aspects of Ritual. *Cambridge Anthropology* 2: 2–60.
　　1979　*Ecology, Meaning, and Religion.* Richmond, CA: North Atlantic Books.
　　1999　*Holiness and Humanity: Ritual in the Making of Religious Life.* New York: Cambridge University Press.

Rathje, W. L.
　　2001　*Rubbish!: The Archaeology of Garbage.* Tucson: University of Arizona Press.

Rathus, S. A., J. S. Nevid, and J. Fichner-Rathus
　　1997　*Human Sexuality in a World of Diversity,* 3rd ed. Boston: Allyn & Bacon.
　　2005　*Human Sexuality in a World of Diversity,* 6th ed. Boston: Allyn & Bacon.

Read-Martin, C. E., and D. W. Read
　　1975　Australopithecine Scavenging and Human Evolution: An Approach from Faunal Analysis. *Current Anthropology* 16: 359–368.

Reade, J.
　　1991　*Mesopotamia.* Cambridge, MA: Harvard University Press.

Redfield, R.
　　1941　*The Folk Culture of Yucatan.* Chicago: University of Chicago Press.

Redfield, R., R. Linton, and M. Herskovits
　　1936　Memorandum on the Study of Acculturation. *American Anthropologist* 38: 149–152.

Redmond, E. M.
　　1994　Tribal and Chiefly Warfare in South America. *Museum of Anthropology Memoir* 28, University of Michigan (Ann Arbor).

Redmond, E. M., ed.
　　1998　*Chiefdoms and Chieftaincy in the Americas.* Gainesville: University of Florida Press.

Reed, R.
　　1997　*Forest Dwellers, Forest Protectors: Indigenous Models for International Development.* Boston: Allyn & Bacon.

Reese, W. L.
　　1999　*Dictionary of Philosophy and Religion: Eastern and Western Thought.* Amherst, NY: Humanities Books.

Reiter, R.
　　1975　Men and Women in the South of France: Public and Private Domains. In *Toward an Anthropology of Women,* ed. R. Reiter, pp. 252–282. New York: Monthly Review Press.

Reiter, R., ed.
　　1975　*Toward an Anthropology of Women.* New York: Monthly Review Press.

Relethford, J. H.
　　2005　*The Human Species: An Introduction to Biological Anthropology,* 6th ed. Boston: McGraw-Hill.

Renfrew, C., and P. Bahn
　　1996　*Archaeology: Theories, Methods, and Practice,* 2nd ed. London: Thames and Hudson.
　　2004　*Archaeology: Theories, Methods, and Practices,* 4th ed. New York: Thames and Hudson.
　　2005　*Archaeology: The Key Concepts,* New York: Routledge.

Reynolds, V.
　　1971　*The Apes.* New York: Harper Colophon.

Rice, P.
　　2002　Paleoanthropology 2001—Part II. *General Anthropology.* 8(2): 11–14.

Richards, D.
　　1994　*Masks of Difference: Cultural Representations in Literature, Anthropology, and Art.* New York: Cambridge University Press.

Richards, P.
　　1973　The Tropical Rain Forest. *Scientific American* 229(6): 58–67.

Rickford, J. R.
　　1997　Suite for Ebony and Phonics. http:// www.stanford.edu/~rickford/papers/ SuiteForEbonyandPhonics.html (also published in *Discover,* December 1997).
　　1999　*African American Vernacular English: Features, Evolution, Educational Implications.* Malden, MA: Blackwell.

Rickford, J. R., and Rickford, R. J.
　　2000　*Spoken Soul: The Story of Black English.* New York: Wiley.

Ricoeur, P.
　　1971　The Model of the Text: Meaningful Action Considered as a Text. *Social Research* 38: 529–562.

Rightmire, G. P.
　　1990　*The Evolution of* Homo erectus: *Comparative Anatomical Studies of an Extinct Human Species.* New York: Cambridge University Press.

Rilling, J. K., D. A. Gutman, T. R. Zeh, G. Pagnoni, G. S. Berns, and C. D. Kilts
　　2002　A Neural Basis for Social Cooperation. *Neuron* 35: 395–405.

Rindos, D.
　　1984　*The Origins of Agriculture: An Evolutionary Perspective.* New York: Academic Press.

Robbins, R.
　　2005　*Global Problems and the Culture of Capitalism,* 3rd ed. Boston: Pearson/Allyn & Bacon.

Roberts, D. F.
　　1953　Body Weight, Race and Climate. *American Journal of Physical Anthropology* 11: 533–558.
　　1986　*Genetic Variation and Its Maintenance: With Particular Reference to Tropical Populations.* New York: Cambridge University Press.

Roberts, J.
　　1995　*Dian Fossey.* San Diego: Lucent Books.

Roberts, S.
1979 *Order and Dispute: An Introduction to Legal Anthropology.* New York: Penguin.

Robertson, A. F.
1995 *The Big Catch: A Practical Introduction to Development.* Boulder, CO: Westview Press.

Robertson, J.
1992 Koreans in Japan. Paper presented at the University of Michigan Department of Anthropology, Martin Luther King Jr. Day Panel, January 1992. Ann Arbor: University of Michigan Department of Anthropology (unpublished).

Rodseth, L., R. W. Wrangham, A. M. Harrigan, and B. Smuts
1991 The Human Community as a Primate Society. *Current Anthropology* 32: 221–254.

Rogers, C.
2005 A Conversation with Carel van Schaik; Revealing Behavior in 'Orangutan Heaven and Human Hell.' *New York Times,* November 15, late edition, final, p. F2.

Romaine, S.
1994 *Language in Society: An Introduction to Sociolinguistics.* New York: Oxford University Press.
1999 *Communicating Gender.* Mahwah, NJ: Erlbaum.

Romer, A. S.
1960 *Man and the Vertebrates,* 3rd ed., Vol. 1. Harmondsworth, UK: Penguin.

Root, D.
1996 *Cannibal Culture: Art, Appropriation, and the Commodification of Difference.* Boulder, CO: Westview Press.

Rosaldo, M. Z.
1980a *Knowledge and Passion: Notions of Self and Social Life.* Stanford, CA: Stanford University Press.
1980b The Use and Abuse of Anthropology: Reflections on Feminism and Cross-Cultural Understanding. *Signs* 5(3): 389–417.

Rosaldo, M. Z., and L. Lamphere, eds.
1974 *Woman, Culture, and Society.* Stanford, CA: Stanford University Press.

Rose, M.
1997 Neandertal DNA. Newsbriefs. *Archaeology* 50 (September/October): 5. http://www.archaeology.org/9709/newsbriefs/dna.html.

Roseberry, W.
1988 Political Economy. *Annual Review of Anthropology* 17: 161–185.

Rosenberg, K.R., and W.R. Trevathan
2001 The Evolution of Human Birth. *Scientific American* 285(5): 60–65.

Rouse, R.
1991 Mexican Migration and the Social Space of Postmodernism. *Diaspora* 1(1): 8–23.

Royal Anthropological Institute
1951 *Notes and Queries on Anthropology,* 6th ed. London: Routledge and Kegan Paul.

Rushing, W. A.
1995 *The AIDS Epidemic: Social Dimension of an Infectious Disease.* Boulder, CO: Westview Press.

Rushing, W. Jackson, ed.
1999 *Native American Art in the Twentieth Century.* New York: Routledge.

Russell, D.
1986 *The Secret Trauma: Incest in the Lives of Girls and Women.* New York: Basic Books.

Russon, A. E., K. A. Bard, and S. Taylor Parker, eds.
1996 *Reaching into Thought: The Minds of the Great Apes.* New York: Cambridge University Press.

Ryan, S.
1990 *Ethnic Conflict and International Relations.* Brookfield, MA: Dartmouth.
1995 *Ethnic Conflict and International Relations,* 2nd ed. Brookfield, MA: Dartmouth.

Sachs, C. E.
1996 *Gendered Fields: Rural Women, Agriculture, and Environment.* Boulder, CO: Westview Press.

Sade, D.
1972 A Longitudinal Study of Social Behavior of Rhesus Monkeys. In *The Functional and Evolutionary Biology of Primates,* ed. R. Tuttle, pp. 378–398. Chicago: University of Chicago Press.

Saggs, H.
1989 *Civilization before Greece and Rome.* New Haven, CT: Yale University Press.

Sahlins, M. D.
1961 The Segmentary Lineage: An Organization of Predatory Expansion. *American Anthropologist* 63: 322–345.
1968 *Tribesmen.* Englewood Cliffs, NJ: Prentice Hall.
1981 *Historical Metaphors and Mythical Realities: Structure in the Early History of the Sandwich Islands Kingdom.* Ann Arbor: University of Michigan Press.
2004 (orig. 1974). *Stone Age Economics.* New York: Routledge.

Saitoti, T. O.
1988 *The Worlds of a Maasai Warrior: An Autobiography.* Berkeley: University of California Press.

Saluter, A.
1995 Household and Family Characteristics: March 1994, P20-483, Press release, October 16, CB95-186, Single-Parent Growth Rate Stabilized; 2-parent Family Growth Renewed, Census Bureau Reports. United States Department of Commerce, Bureau of Census, Public Information Office.

1996   Marital Status and Living Arrangements: March 1994, P20-484, U.S. Census Bureau, Press release, March 13, 1996, CB96-33. United States Department of Commerce, Bureau of Census, Public Information Office, http://www.census.gov/prod/www/titles.html#popspec.

Salzman, P. C.
1974   Political Organization among Nomadic Peoples. In *Man in Adaptation: The Cultural Present*, 2nd ed., ed. Y. A. Cohen, pp. 267–284. Chicago: Aldine.
2004   *Pastoralists: Equality, Hierarchy, and the State.* Boulder, CO: Westview Press.

Salzman, P. C., and J. G. Galaty, eds.
1990   *Nomads in a Changing World.* Naples: Istituto Universitario Orientale.

Salzmann, Z.
2004   *Language, Culture, and Society: An Introduction to Linguistic Anthropology,* 3rd ed. Boulder, CO: Westview Press.

Sanday, P. R.
1974   Female Status in the Public Domain. In *Woman, Culture, and Society,* ed. M. Z. Rosaldo and L. Lamphere, pp. 189–206. Stanford, CA: Stanford University Press.
2002   *Women at the Center: Life in a Modern Matriarchy.* Ithaca, NY: Cornell University Press.

Sanders, W. T.
1972   Population, Agricultural History, and Societal Evolution in Mesoamerica. In *Population Growth: Anthropological Implications,* ed. B. Spooner, pp. 101–153. Cambridge, MA: MIT Press.
1973   The Cultural Ecology of the Lowland Maya: A Reevaluation. In *The Classic Maya Collapse,* ed. T. P. Culbert, pp. 325–366. Albuquerque: University of New Mexico Press.

Sanders, W. T., J. R. Parsons, and R. S. Santley
1979   *The Basin of Mexico: Ecological Processes in the Evolution of a Civilization.* New York: Academic Press.

Sankoff, G.
1980   *The Social Life of Language.* Philadelphia: University of Pennsylvania Press.

Santino, J.
1983   Night of the Wandering Souls. *Natural History* 92(10): 42.

Santley, R. S.
1984   Obsidian Exchange, Economic Stratification, and the Evolution of Complex Society in the Basin of Mexico. In *Trade and Exchange in Early Mesoamerica,* ed. K. G. Hirth, pp. 43–86. Albuquerque: University of New Mexico Press.
1985   The Political Economy of the Aztec Empire. *Journal of Anthropological Research* 41(3): 327–337.

Sapir, E.
1931   Conceptual Categories in Primitive Languages. *Science* 74: 578–584.

Sargent, C. F., and C. B. Brettell
1996   *Gender and Health: An International Perspective.* Upper Saddle River, NJ: Prentice Hall.

Schaefer, R.
1989   *Sociology,* 3rd ed. New York: McGraw-Hill.

Schaik, C. V.
2004   *Among Orangutans: Red Apes and the Rise of Human Culture.* Tucson: University of Arizona Press.

Schaller, G.
1963   *The Mountain Gorilla: Ecology and Behavior.* Chicago: University of Chicago Press.

Scheffler, H. W.
2001   *Filiation and Affiliation.* Boulder, CO: Westview Press.

Scheidel, W.
1997   Brother-Sister Marriage in Roman Egypt. *Journal of Biosocial Science* 29(3): 361–371.

Scheinman, M.
1980   Imperialism. *Academic American Encyclopedia,* vol. 11, pp. 61–62. Princeton, NJ: Arete.

Scheper-Hughes, N.
1987   Culture, Scarcity, and Maternal Thinking: Mother Love and Child Death in Northeast Brazil. In *Child Survival,* ed. N. Scheper-Hughes, pp. 187–208. Boston: D. Reidel.
1992   *Death without Weeping: The Violence of Everyday Life in Brazil.* Berkeley: University of California Press.

Schick, K. D., and N. Toth
1993   *Making Silent Stones Speak: Human Evolution and the Dawn of Technology.* New York: Simon & Schuster.

Schieffelin, E.
1976   *The Sorrow of the Lonely and the Burning of the Dancers.* New York: St. Martin's Press.

Schildkrout, E., and C. A. Keim
1990   *African Reflections: Art from Northeastern Zaire.* Seattle: University of Washington Press.

Schlee, G., ed.
2002   *Imagined Differences: Hatred and the Construction of Identity.* New York: Palgrave.

Schneider, D. M.
1968   *American Kinship: A Cultural Account.* Englewood Cliffs, NJ: Prentice Hall.

Schneider, D. M., and K. Gough, eds.
1961   *Matrilineal Kinship.* Berkeley: University of California Press.

Scholte, J. A.
2000   *Globalization: A Critical Introduction.* New York: St. Martin's Press.

Schweingruber, F. H.
   1988   *Tree Rings: Basics and Applications of Dendrochronology.* Hingham, MA: Kluwer Academic.

Scott, J.
   2002   Prehistoric Human Footpaths Lure Archaeologists Back to Costa Rica. University of Colorado Press Release, May 20. http://www.eurekalert.org/pub_releases/2002-05/uoca-phf052002.php.

Scott, J. C.
   1985   *Weapons of the Weak.* New Haven, CT: Yale University Press.
   1990   *Domination and the Arts of Resistance.* New Haven, CT: Yale University Press.
   1998   *Seeing Like a State: How Certain Schemes to Improve the Human Condition Have Failed.* New Haven, CT: Yale University Press.

Scudder, T.
   1982   The Impact of Big Dam-building on the Zambezi River Basin. In *The Careless Technology: Ecology and International Development,* eds. M. T. Farvar and J. P. Milton, pp. 206–235. New York: Natural History Press.

Scudder, T., and E. Colson
   1980   *Secondary Education and the Formation of an Elite: The Impact of Education on Gwembe District, Zambia.* London: Academic Press.

Scudder, T., and J. Habarad
   1991   Local Responses to Involuntary Relocation and Development in the Zambian Portion of the Middle Zambezi Valley. In *Migrants in Agricultural Development,* ed. J. A. Mollett, pp. 178–205. New York: New York University Press.

Scupin, R.
   2003   *Race and Ethnicity: An Anthropological Focus on the United States and the World.* Upper Saddle River, NJ: Prentice Hall.

Sebeok, T. A., and J. Umiker-Sebeok, eds.
   1980   *Speaking of Apes: A Critical Anthropology of Two-Way Communication with Man.* New York: Plenum Press.

Seligson, M. A.
   1984   *The Gap between Rich and Poor: Contending Perspectives on the Political Economy of Development.* Boulder, CO: Westview Press.

Sengupta, S.
   2004   Kinshasa Journal: The Gentlest of Beasts, Making Love, Ravaged by War. *New York Times,* May 3, 2004, late edition, final, section A, p. 4, column 3.

Senut, B., M. Pickford, D. Gommery, P. Mein, K. Cheboi, and Y. Coppens
   2001   First Hominid from the Miocene (Lukeino Formation, Kenya). *Comptes Rendus de l'Academie des Sciences, Series IIA—Earth and Planetary Science* 332. 2(30): 137–144.

Sered, S. S.
   1996   *Priestess, Mother, Sacred Sister: Religions Dominated by Women.* New York: Oxford University Press.

Service, E. R.
   1962   *Primitive Social Organization: An Evolutionary Perspective.* New York: McGraw-Hill.
   1966   *The Hunters.* Englewood Cliffs, NJ: Prentice Hall.
   1975   *Origins of the State and Civilization: The Process of Cultural Evolution.* New York: W. W. Norton.

Shabecoff, P.
   1989*a*   Ivory Imports Banned to Aid Elephant. *New York Times,* June 7, p. 15.
   1989*b*   New Lobby Is Helping Wildlife of Africa. *New York Times,* June 9, p. 14.

Shanklin, E.
   1995   *Anthropology and Race.* Belmont, CA: Wadsworth.

Shannon, T. R.
   1989   *An Introduction to the World-System Perspective.* Boulder, CO: Westview Press.
   1996   *An Introduction to the World-System Perspective,* 2nd ed. Boulder, CO: Westview Press.

Sharer, R., and W. Ashmore
   2003   *Discovering Our Past: The Process of Archaeological Research.* 3rd. ed. Boston: McGraw-Hill.

Shepher, J.
   1983   *Incest, a Biosocial View.* New York: Academic Press.

Shermer, M.
   2002   *In Darwin's Shadow: The Life and Science of Alfred Russel Wallace.* New York: Oxford University Press.

Shigeru, K.
   1994   *Our Land Was a Forest: An Ainu Memoir.* Boulder, CO: Westview Press.

Shipman, P.
   2001   *The Man Who Found the Missing Link.* New York: Simon & Schuster.

Shivaram, C.
   1996   Where Women Wore the Crown: Kerala's Dissolving Matriarchies Leave a Rich Legacy of Compassionate Family Culture. *Hinduism Today* 96(02). http://www.hinduism-today.com/archives/1996/2/1996-2-03.shtml.

Shore, B.
   1996   *Culture in Mind: Meaning, Construction, and Cultural Cognition.* New York: Oxford University Press.

Shostak, M.
   1981   *Nisa, the Life and Words of a !Kung Woman.* New York: Vintage Books.
   2000   *Return to Nisa.* Cambridge, MA: Harvard University Press.

Shreeve, J.
    1992   The Dating Game: How Old Is the
            Human Race? *Discover* 13(9): 76–83.
Shweder, R., and H. Levine, eds.
    1984   *Culture Theory: Essays on Mind, Self,
            and Emotion.* Cambridge, UK: Cambridge
            University Press.
Sibley, C. G., and J. E. Ahlquist
    1984   The Phylogeny of the Hominoid
            Primates, as Indicated by DNA-DNA
            Hybridization. *Journal of Molecular Evolution*
            20: 2–15.
Signo, A.
    1994   *Economics of the Family.* New York:
            Oxford University Press.
Silberbauer, G.
    1981   *Hunter and Habitat in the Central Kalahari
            Desert.* New York: Cambridge University
            Press.
Silverberg, J., and J. P. Gray, eds.
    1992   *Aggression and Peacefulness in Humans
            and Other Primates.* New York: Oxford
            University Press.
Simons, A.
    1995   *Networks of Dissolution: Somalia Undone.*
            Boulder, CO: Westview Press.
Simons, E. L., and P. C. Ettel
    1970   *Gigantopithecus. Scientific American,*
            January, pp. 77–85.
Simpson, B.
    1998   *Changing Families: An Ethnographic
            Approach to Divorce and Separation.* New York:
            Berg.
Sinnott, M. J.
    2004   *Toms and Dees: Transgender Identity and
            Female Same-Sex Relationships in Thailand.*
            Honolulu: University of Hawaii Press.
Slade, M. F.
    1984   Displaying Affection in Public. *New
            York Times,* December 17, p. B14.
Small, M. F.
    1993   *Female Choices: Sexual Behavior of Female
            Primates.* Ithaca, NY: Cornell University Press.
Smith, B. D.
    1995   *The Emergence of Agriculture.* New York:
            Scientific American Library, W. H. Freeman.
Smith, C. A.
    1990   The Militarization of Civil Society in
            Guatemala: Economic Reorganization as a
            Continuation of War. *Latin American Perspec-
            tives* 17: 8–41.
Smith, M. E., and M. A. Masson, eds.
    2000   *The Ancient Civilizations of Mesoamerica:
            A Reader.* Malpen, MA: Blackwell.
Smith, M. G.
    1965   *The Plural Society in the British West
            Indies.* Berkeley: University of California Press.

Smitherman, G.
    1986   *Talkin and Testifyin: The Language of Black
            America.* Detroit: Wayne State University
            Press.
Smuts, B. B.
    1999   (orig. 1985) *Sex and Friendship in
            Baboons.* Cambridge, MA: Harvard University
            Press.
Solheim, W. G., II
    1976   (orig. 1972). An Earlier Agricultural
            Revolution. In *Avenues to Antiquity: Readings
            from Scientific American,* ed. B. M. Fagan,
            pp. 160–168. San Francisco: W. H. Freeman.
Solway, J., and R. Lee
    1990   Foragers, Genuine and Spurious: Situat-
            ing the Kalahari San in History (with CA treat-
            ment). *Current Anthropology* 31(2): 109–146.
Sonneville-Bordes, D. de
    1963   Upper Paleolithic Cultures in Western
            Europe. *Science* 142: 347–355.
Spickard, P., ed.
    2004   *Race and Nation: Ethnic Systems in the
            Modern World.* New York: Routledge.
Spindler, G. D., ed.
    1978   *The Making of Psychological Anthropology.*
            Berkeley: University of California Press.
    1982   *Doing the Ethnography of Schooling: Edu-
            cational Anthropology in Action.* New York:
            Holt, Rinehart and Winston.
    2000   *Fifty Years of Anthropology and Education,
            1950–2000: A Spindler Anthology.* Mahwah,
            NJ: Erlbaum.
    2005   *New Horizons in the Anthropology of
            Education.* Mahwah, NJ: Erlbaum.
Spiro, M. E.
    1993   *Oedipus in the Trobriands.* New
            Brunswick, NJ: Transaction.
Sponsel, L. E., and T. Gregor, eds.
    1994   *The Anthropology of Peace and
            Nonviolence.* Boulder, CO: Lynne Rienner.
Spradley, J. P.
    1979   *The Ethnographic Interview.* New York:
            Harcourt Brace Jovanovich.
Srivastava, J., N. J. H. Smith, and D. A. Forno
    1999   *Integrating Biodiversity in Agricultural
            Intensification: Toward Sound Practices.* Wash-
            ington, DC: World Bank.
Stacey, J.
    1996   *In the Name of the Family: Rethinking
            Family Values in the Postmodern Age.* Boston:
            Beacon Press.
    1998   *Brave New Families: Stories of Domestic
            Upheaval in Late Twentieth Century America.*
            Berkeley: University of California Press.
Stack, C. B.
    1975   *All Our Kin: Strategies for Survival in a
            Black Community.* New York: Harper
            Torchbooks.

Staeck, J.
    2002   *Back to the Earth: An Introduction to Archaeology.* Boston: McGraw-Hill.

Stanford, C. B.
    1999   *The Hunting Apes: Meat Eating and the Origins of Human Behavior.* Princeton, NJ: Princeton University Press.

Stanford, C. B., and H. T. Bunn, eds.
    2001   *Meat-Eating and Human Evolution.* New York: Oxford University Press.

Statistical Abstract of the United States
    1991   111th ed. Washington, DC: U.S. Bureau of the Census, U.S. Government Printing Office.
    1996   116th ed. Washington, DC: U.S. Bureau of the Census, U.S. Government Printing Office.
    2003   *Statistical Abstract of the United States, 2003.* http://www.census.gov/statab/www/.

Statistics Canada
    1998   1996 Census: Ethnic Origin, Visible Minorities. *The Daily,* February 17. http://www.statcan.ca/Daily/English/980217/d980217.htm.
    2001*a*   1996 Census. Nation Tables. http://www.statcan.ca/english/census96/nation.htm.
    2001*b*   Selected Religions, Provinces and Territories. http://www40.statcan.ca/101/cst01/demo30a.htm.

Staub, S.
    1989   *Yemenis in New York City: The Folklore of Ethnicity.* Philadelphia: Balch Institute Press.

Steegman, A. T., Jr.
    1975   Human Adaptation to Cold. *In Physiological Anthropology,* ed. A. Damon, pp. 130–166. New York: Oxford University Press.

Stein, R. L., and P. L. Stein
    2005   *The Anthropology of Religion, Magic, and Witchcraft.* Boston: Pearson/Allyn & Bacon.

Steinfels, P.
    1997   Beliefs: Cloning, as Seen by Buddhists and Humanists. *New York Times,* July 12. http://www.nytimes.com.

Stephens, S., ed.
    1996   *Children and the Politics of Culture.* Princeton, NJ: Princeton University Press.

Stephens, W. R.
    2002   *Careers in Anthropology: What an Anthropology Degree Can Do for You.* Boston: Allyn & Bacon.

Steponaitis, V.
    1986   Prehistoric Archaeology in the Southeastern United States. *Annual Review of Anthropology* 15: 363–404.

Stern, A.
    2000   Experts Say 138 World Primate Species Endangered. Reuters. http://www.forests.org/archive/general/exsay138.htm.

Stevens, W. K.
    1992   Humanity Confronts Its Handiwork: An Altered Planet. *New York Times,* May 5, pp. B5–B7.

Stevenson, D.
    2003   *Cities and Urban Cultures.* Philadelphia: Open University Press.

Stevenson, R. F.
    1968   *Population and Political Systems in Tropical Africa.* New York: Columbia University Press.

Steward, J. H.
    1955   *Theory of Culture Change.* Urbana: University of Illinois Press.
    1956   *The People of Puerto Rico: A Study in Social Anthropology.* Urbana: University of Illinois Press.

Stocking, G. W., ed.
    1986   *Malinowski, Rivers, Benedict and Others: Essays on Culture and Personality.* Madison: University of Wisconsin Press.

Stoler, A.
    1977   Class Structure and Female Autonomy in Rural Java. *Signs* 3: 74–89.

Stoler, A. L.
    1995   *Race and the Education of Desire: Foucault's History of Sexuality and the Colonial Order of Things.* Durham, NC: Duke University Press.
    2002   *Carnal Knowledge and Imperial Power: Race and the Intimate in Colonial Rule.* Berkeley: University of California Press.

Stone, L.
    2000   *Kinship and Gender: An Introduction,* 2nd ed. Boulder, CO: Westview.
    2001   *New Directions in Anthropological Kinship.* Lanham, MD: Rowman and Littlefield.

Stoneman, B.
    1997   Income Is Rising, So Is Poverty. *American Demographics,* Forecast, November 1997, http://www.demographics.com/publications/fc/97_fc/9711_fc/fc97111.htm.

Strachan, T., and A. P. Read
    2004   *Human Molecular Genetics,* 3rd ed. New York: Garland Press.

Strathern, A., and P. J. Stewart
    1999   *Curing and Healing: Medical Anthropology in Global Perspective.* Durham, NC: Carolina Academic Press.

Strathern, M.
    1988   *The Gender of the Gift: Problems with Women and Problems with Society in Melanesia.* Berkeley: University of California Press.

Strier, K. B.
    2003   Primate Behavioral Ecology: From Ethnography to Ethology and Back. *American Anthropologist* 105(1): 16–27.
    2007   *Primate Behavioral Ecology,* 3rd ed. Boston: Allyn & Bacon.

Strong, P. T.
    2005   Recent Ethnographic Research on North American Indigenous Peoples. *Annual Review of Anthropology* 34: 253–268.

Strum, S. C., and L. M. Fedigan, eds.
    2000   *Primate Encounters: Models of Science, Gender, and Society.* Chicago: University of Chicago Press.

Suarez-Orozco, M. M., G. Spindler, and L. Spindler, eds.
    1994   *The Making of Psychological Anthropology II.* Fort Worth: Harcourt Brace.

Susman, R. L.
    1987   Pygmy Chimpanzees and Common Chimpanzees: Models for the Behavioral Ecology of the Earliest Hominids. In *The Evolution of Human Behavior: Primate Models*, ed. W. G. Kinzey, pp. 72–86. Albany: State University of New York Press.

Susser, I., and T. C. Patterson, eds.
    2000   *Cultural Diversity in the United States: A Critical Reader.* Malden, MA: Blackwell.

Sussman, R. W.
    2004   Flowering Plants and the Origins of Primates: A New Theory. In *Encyclopedia of Animal Behavior*, ed. M. Bekoff, pp. 967–969. Portsmouth, NH: Greenwood Press.

Suttles, W.
    1960   Affinal Ties, Subsistence, and Prestige among the Coast Salish. *American Anthropologist* 62: 296–395.

Swift, M.
    1963   Men and Women in Malay Society. In *Women in the New Asia*, ed. B. Ward, pp. 268–286. Paris: UNESCO.

Swindler, D. R.
    1998   *Introduction to the Primates.* Seattle: University of Washington Press.

Tague, R. G., and C. O. Lovejoy
    1986   The Obstetric Pelvis of A. L. 288-1 (Lucy). *Journal of Human Evolution* 15: 237–255.

Tainter, J.
    1987   *The Collapse of Complex Societies.* New York: Cambridge University Press.

Tanaka, J.
    1980   *The San Hunter-Gatherers of the Kalahari.* Tokyo: University of Tokyo Press.

Tannen, D.
    1990   *You Just Don't Understand: Women and Men in Conversation.* New York: Ballantine.

Tannen, D., ed.
    1993   *Gender and Conversational Interaction.* New York: Oxford University Press.

Tanner, N.
    1974   Matrifocality in Indonesia and Africa and among Black Americans. In *Women, Culture, and Society*, ed. M. Z. Rosaldo and L. Lamphere, pp. 127–156. Stanford, CA: Stanford University Press.

Tattersall, I.
    1995*a*   *The Fossil Trail: How We Know What We Think We Know about Human Evolution.* New York: Oxford University Press.
    1995*b*   *The Last Neanderthal: The Rise, Success, and Mysterious Extinction of Our Closest Human Relatives.* New York: Macmillan.
    1998   *Becoming Human: Evolution and Human Uniqueness.* New York: Harcourt Brace.

Taylor, A.
    1993   *Women Drug Users: An Ethnography of a Female Injecting Community.* New York: Oxford University Press.

Taylor, C.
    1987   Anthropologist-in-Residence. In *Applied Anthropology in America*, 2nd ed., ed. E. M. Eddy and W. L. Partridge. New York: Columbia University Press.
    1996   *The Black Churches of Brooklyn.* New York: Columbia University Press.

Teleki, G.
    1973   *The Predatory Behavior of Wild Chimpanzees.* Lewisburg, PA: Bucknell University Press.

Terrace, H. S.
    1979   *Nim.* New York: Knopf.

Terrell, J. E.
    1998   The Prehistoric Pacific. *Archaeology*, vol. 51, no. 6. Archaeological Institute of America. http://www.archaeology.org/9811/abstracts/pacific.html.

Thomas, L., and S. Wareing, eds.
    2004   *Language, Society and Power.* New York: Routledge.

Thomason, S. G., and T. Kaufman
    1988   *Language Contact, Creolization and Genetic Linguistics.* Berkeley: University of California Press.

Thompson, W.
    1983   Introduction: World System with and without the Hyphen. In *Contending Approaches to World System Analysis*, ed. W. Thompson, pp. 7–26. Thousand Oaks, CA: Sage.

Thomson, A., and L. H. D. Buxton
    1923   Man's Nasal Index in Relation to Certain Climatic Conditions. *Journal of the Royal Anthropological Institute* 53: 92–112.

Tice, K.
    1997   Reflections on Teaching Anthropology for Use in the Public and Private Sector. In *The Teaching of Anthropology: Problems, Issues, and Decisions*, ed. C. P. Kottak, J. J. White, R. H. Furlow, and P. C. Rice, pp. 273–284. Mountain View, CA: Mayfield.

Titiev, M.
1992   *Old Oraibi: A Study of the Hopi Indians of Third Mesa.* Albuquerque: University of New Mexico Press.

Tobler, A. J.
1950   *Excavations at Tepe Gawra,* vol. 2. Philadelphia: University of Pennsylvania Museum.

Todt, R.
2000   Western Hemisphere Inhabited at Least 15,000 Years Ago. ABCNews.Go.com News Briefs, April 7. http://abcnews.go.com/sections/science/DailyNews/first_americans000407.html.

Toner, R.
1992   Los Angeles Riots Are a Warning, Americans Fear. *New York Times,* May 11, pp. A1, A11.

Toth, N., and Schick, K.
1986   The First Million Years: The Archaeology of Protohuman Culture. *Advances in Archaeological Method and Theory,* pp. 1–96.

Trask, L.
1996   FAQs about Basque and the Basques. http://www.cogs.susx.ac.uk/users/larryt/basque.faqs.html.

Trehub, S. E.
2001   Musical Predispositions in Infancy. *Annals of the New York Academy of Sciences* 930(1): 1–16.

Trigger, B. G.
1993   *Early Civilizations: Ancient Egypt in Context.* New York: Columbia University Press.
2003   *Understanding Early Civilizations: A Comparative Study.* Cambridge, UK: Cambridge University Press.

Trudgill, P.
1983   *Sociolinguistics: An Introduction to Language and Society,* rev. ed. Baltimore: Penguin.
2000   *Sociolinguistics: An Introduction to Language and Society,* 4th ed. New York: Penguin.

Turnbaugh, W. A., R. Jurmain, L. Kilgore, and H. Nelson
2002   *Understanding Physical Anthropology and Archaeology,* 8th ed. Belmont, CA: Wadsworth.

Turnbull, C.
1965   *Wayward Servants: The Two Worlds of the African Pygmies.* Garden City, NY: Natural History Press.

Turner, B. S.
1998   *Readings in the Anthropology and Sociology of Family and Kinship.* London: Routledge/Thoemmes.

Turner, T.
1993   The Role of Indigenous Peoples in the Environmental Crisis: The Example of the Kayapo of the Brazilian Amazon. *Perspectives in Biology and Medicine* 36: 526–545.

Turner, V. W.
1967   *The Forest of Symbols: Aspects of Ndembu Ritual.* Ithaca, NY: Cornell University Press.
1995   (orig. 1969). *The Ritual Process.* Hawthorne, NY: Aldine.
1996   (orig. 1957). *Schism and Continuity in an African Society: A Study of Ndembu Village Life.* Washington, DC: Berg.

Tylor, E. B.
1889   On a Method of Investigating the Development of Institutions: Applied to Laws of Marriage and Descent. *Journal of the Royal Anthropological Institute* 18: 245–269.
1958   (orig. 1871). *Primitive Culture.* New York: Harper Torchbooks.

Ucko, P. J., and G. W. Dimbleby, eds.
1969   *The Domestication and Exploitation of Plants and Animals.* Chicago: Aldine.

Ucko, P., and A. Rosenfeld
1967   *Paleolithic Cave Art.* London: Weidenfeld and Nicolson.

University of Virginia
n.d.   American Studies Program, Armory Show of 1913. http://xroads.virginia.edu/~MUSEUM/Armory/ofili.html.

Urban, Greg
2001   *Metaculture: How Culture Moves through the World.* Minneapolis: University of Minnesota Press.

U.S. Census Bureau
1998   Unpublished Tables—Marital Status and Living Arrangements, March 1998 (Update). http://www.census.gov/prod/99pubs/p20-514u.pdf.
1999   *Statisical Abstract of the United States.* http://www.census.gov/prod/99pubs/99statab/sec01.pdf and http://www.census.gov/prod/99pubs/99statab/sec02.pdf.
2004   *Statistical Abstract of the United States, 2003.* Table 688, p. 459. http://www.census.gov/prod/2004pubs/03statab/income.pdf.
2005   *Statistical Abstract of the United States, 2004.* http://www.census.gov/prod/2004pubs/04statab/labor.pdf.
2006   *Statistical Abstract of the United States, 2006.* http://www.census.gov/prod/www/statistical-abstract.html.

Valentine, C.
1968   *Culture and Poverty.* Chicago: University of Chicago Press.

Valladas, H., J. L. Reyss, J. L. Joron, G. Valladas, O. Bar-Joseph, and B. Vandermeersch
1988   Thermoluminescence Dating of Mousterian "Proto-Cro-Magnon" Remains from Israel and the Origin of Modern Man. *Nature* 331: 614–616.

Van Cantfort, T. E., and J. B. Rimpau
1982 Sign Language Studies with Children and Chimpanzees. *Sign Language Studies* 34: 15–72.

Van der Elst, D., and P. Bohannan
2003 *Culture as Given, Culture as Choice.* 2nd ed. Prospect Heights, IL: Waveland.

Van Schaik, C. P., and J. A. R. A. M. van Hooff
1983 On the Ultimate Causes of Primate Social Systems. *Behaviour* 85: 91–117.

Van Willingen, J.
1987 *Becoming a Practicing Anthropologist: A Guide to Careers and Training Programs in Applied Anthropology.* NAPA Bulletin 3. Washington, DC: American Anthropological Association/National Association for the Practice of Anthropology.
2002 *Applied Anthropology: An Introduction,* 3rd ed. Westport CT: Bergin and Garvey.

Vayda, A. P.
1968 (orig. 1961). Economic Systems in Ecological Perspective: The Case of the Northwest Coast. In *Readings in Anthropology,* 2nd ed., vol. 2, ed. M. H. Fried, pp. 172–178. New York: Crowell.

Veblen, T.
1934 *The Theory of the Leisure Class: An Economic Study of Institutions.* New York: The Modern Library.

Vekua, A., D. Lordkipanidze, and G. P. Rightmire
2002 A Skull of Early Homo from Dmanisi, Georgia. *Science,* July 5, pp. 85–89.

Verdery, K.
2001 Socialist Societies: Anthropological Aspects. *International Encyclopedia of the Social & Behavioral Sciences,* pp. 14496–14500. New York: Elsevier.

Verlinden, C.
1980 Colonialism. *Academic American Encyclopedia,* vol. 5, pp. 111–112. Princeton, NJ: Arete.

Vidal, J.
2003 Every Third Person Will be a Slum Dweller within 30 Years, UN Agency Warns: Biggest Study of World's Cities Finds 940 Million Already Living in Squalor. *The Guardian,* October 4. http://www.guardian.co./uk/international/story/0,3604,1055785,00.html.

Viegas, J.
2000 Planet of the Dying Apes: Conference Reveals Steep Decline in Primate Populations. http://abcnews.go.com/sections/science/DailyNews/apeconference000512.html.

Vietnam Labor Watch
1997 Nike Labor Practices in Vietnam, March 20. http://www.saigon.com/~nike/reports/report1.html.

Vincent, J.
1990 *Anthropology and Politics: Visions, Traditions, and Trends.* Tucson: University of Arizona Press.

Vincent, J., ed.
2002 *The Anthropology of Politics: A Reader in Ethnography, Theory, and Critique.* Malden, MA: Blackwell.

Viola, H. J., and C. Margolis
1991 *Seeds of Change: Five Hundred Years Since Columbus, a Quincentennial Commemoration.* Washington, DC: Smithsonian Institution Press.

Von Daniken, E.
1971 *Chariots of the Gods: Unsolved Mysteries of the Past.* New York: Bantam.

Wade, N.
1997 Testing Genes to Save a Life without Costing You a Job. *New York Times.* September 14. http://www.nytimes.com.
2001 Gene Study Shows Ties Long Veiled in Europe. *New York Times,* April 10. http://www.angelfire.com/nt/dragon9/BASQUES2.html.
2003 A Course in Evolution, Taught by Chimps. *New York Times,* November 25, late edition, final, section F, p. 1, column 1.
2004 New Species Revealed: Tiny Cousins of Humans. *New York Times,* October 28, 2004, national edition, pp. A1, A6.

Wade, N., ed.
2001 *The New York Times Book of Fossils and Evolution,* rev. ed. New York: Lyons Press.

Wade, P.
2002 *Race, Nature, and Culture: An Anthropological Perspective.* Sterling, VA: Pluto Press.

Wagley, C. W.
1968 (orig. 1959). The Concept of Social Race in the Americas. In *The Latin American Tradition,* ed. C. Wagley, pp. 155–174. New York: Columbia University Press.

Wagner, R.
1981 *The Invention of Culture,* rev. ed. Chicago: University of Chicago Press.

Wallace, A. F. C.
1956 Revitalization Movements. *American Anthropologist* 58: 264–281.
1966 *Religion: An Anthropological View.* New York: McGraw-Hill.
1970 *The Death and Rebirth of the Seneca.* New York: Knopf.

Wallerstein, I. M.
1974 *The Modern World-System: Capitalist Agriculture and the Origins of the European World-Economy in the Sixteenth Century.* New York: Academic Press.

1980 *The Modern World System II: Mercantilism and the Consolidation of the European World-Economy, 1600–1750.* New York: Academic Press.

1982 The Rise and Future Demise of the World Capitalist System: Concepts for Comparative Analysis. In *Introduction to the Sociology of "Developing Societies,"* ed. H. Alavi and T. Shanin, pp. 29–53. New York: Monthly Review Press.

2000 *The Essential Wallerstein.* New York: New Press, W. W. Norton.

2004*a* *The Decline of American Power: The U.S. in a Chaotic World.* New York: New Press.

2004*b* *World-Systems Analysis: An Introduction.* Durham, NC: Duke University Press.

Wallman, S., ed.
    1977 *Perceptions of Development.* New York: Cambridge University Press.

Ward, C.
    2003 The Evolution of Human Origins. *American Anthropologist* 105(1): 77–88.

Ward, C. V., M. G. Leakey, and A. Walker
    2001 Morphology of Australopithecus anamensis from Kanapoi and Allia Bay, Kenya. *Journal of Human Evolution* 40–41: 253–368.

Ward, M. C., and M. Edelstein
    2006 *A World Full of Women*, 4th ed. Needham Heights, MA: Allyn & Bacon.

Ward, S., B. Brown, A. Hill, J. Kelley, and W. Downs
    1999 Equatorius: A New Hominoid Genus from the Middle Miocene of Kenya. *Science EurekAlert!* August 27. http://www.eurekalert.org.

Warren, K. B.
    1998 *Indigenous Movements and Their Critics: Pan-Maya Activism in Guatemala.* Princeton, NJ: Princeton University Press.

Washburn, S. L., and R. Moore
    1980 *Ape into Human: A Study of Human Evolution*, 2nd ed. Boston: Little, Brown.

Watson, J. D.
    1970 *Molecular Biology of the Gene.* New York: Benjamin.

Watson, P.
    1972 *Can Racial Discrimination Affect IQ?* In *Race and Intelligence; The Fallacies behind the Race-IQ Controversy,* ed. K. Richardson and D. Spears, pp. 56–67. Baltimore: Penguin.

Watson, P. J.
    1983 The Halafian Culture: A Review and Synthesis. In *The Hilly Flanks and Beyond: Essays on the Prehistory of Southwestern Asia,* ed. T. C. Young, Jr., P. E. L. Smith, and P. Mortensen. *Studies in Ancient Oriental Civilization* 36: 231–250. Oriental Institute, University of Chicago.

Watzman, H.
    2006 The Echoes of Ancient Humans. *Chronicle of Higher Education,* January 27. http://chronicle.com/weekly/v52/i21/21a01601.htm.

Weaver, T., gen. ed.
    1973 *To See Ourselves: Anthropology and Modern Social Issues.* Glenview, IL: Scott, Foresman.

Weber, M.
    1958 (orig. 1904). *The Protestant Ethic and the Spirit of Capitalism.* New York: Scribner.
    1968 (orig. 1922). *Economy and Society.* Translated by E. Fischoff et al. New York: Bedminster Press.

Webster's New World Encyclopedia
    1993 College Edition. Englewood Cliffs, NJ: Prentice Hall.

Wedel, J.
    2002 Blurring the Boundaries of the State-Private Divide: Implications for Corruption. Paper presented at the European Association of Social Anthropologists (EASA) Conference in Copenhagen, August 14–17. http://www.anthrobase.com/Txt/W/Wedel_J_01.htm.

Weiner, A.
    1988 *The Trobrianders of Papua New Guinea.* New York: Holt, Rinehart and Winston.

Weiner, J.
    1994 *Beak of the Finch: A Story of Evolution in Our Time.* New York: Knopf.

Weiner, J. S.
    1954 Nose Shape and Climate. *American Journal of Physical Anthropology* 12: 1–4.

Weise, E.
    1999 Anthropologists Adapt Technology to World's Cultures. *USA Today,* May 26. http://eclectic.ss.uci.edu/~drwhite/center/news/USAToday5-25-99.htm.

Weiss, H.
    2005 *Collapse.* New York: Routledge.

Weiss, K. M.
    1993 *Genetic Variation and Human Disease: Principles and Evolutionary Approaches.* New York: Cambridge University Press.

Weiss, M. L., And A. E. Mann
    1990 *Human Biology and Behavior: An Anthropological Perspective,* 5th ed. Glenview, IL: Scott, Foresman.

Wendorf, F., and R. Schild
    2000 Late Neolithic Megalithic Structures at Nabta Playa (Sahara), Southwestern Egypt. http://www.comp-archaeology.org/WendorfSAA98.html.

Wenke, R. J.
    1996 *Patterns in Prehistory: Mankind's First Three Million Years,* 4th ed. New York: Oxford University Press.

Wenke, R. J., and D. I. Olszewski
2007 *Patterns in Prehistory: Mankind's First Three Million Years,* 5th ed. New York: Oxford University Press.

Werner, O., and G. M. Shoepfle
1987 *Systematic Fieldwork.* Newbury Park, CA: Sage.

Westermarck, E.
1894 *The History of Human Marriage.* London: Macmillan.

Weston, K.
1991 *Families We Choose: Lesbians, Gays, Kinship.* New York: Columbia University Press.

White, L. A.
1949 *The Science of Culture: A Study of Man and Civilization.* New York: Farrar, Strauss.
1959 *The Evolution of Culture: The Development of Civilization to the Fall of Rome.* New York: McGraw-Hill.

White, T. D., and P. A. Folkens
2000 *Human Osteology,* 2nd ed. San Diego: Academic Press.

Whiting, B. E., ed.
1963 *Six Cultures: Studies of Child Rearing.* New York: Wiley.

Whiting, J. M.
1964 Effects of Climate on Certain Cultural Practices. In *Explorations in Cultural Anthropology: Essays in Honor of George Peter Murdock,* ed. W. H. Goodenough, pp. 511–544. New York: McGraw-Hill.

Whorf, B. L.
1956 A Linguistic Consideration of Thinking in Primitive Communities. In *Language, Thought, and Reality: Selected Writings of Benjamin Lee Whorf,* ed. J. B. Carroll, pp. 65–86. Cambridge, MA: MIT Press.

Whyte, M. F.
1978 Cross-Cultural Codes Dealing with the Relative Status of Women. *Ethnology* 17(2): 211–239.

Wikipedia
2004 Fundamentalism, in *Wikipedia, the Free Encyclopedia.* http://en.wikipedia.org/wiki/Fundamentalism.

Wilford, J. N.
1995 The Transforming Leap, from 4 Legs to 2. *New York Times,* September 5, pp. B5(N), C1(L).
2000 Ruins Alter Ideas of How Civilization Spread. *New York Times,* May 23. http://www.nytimes.com.
2001a Skull May Alter Experts' View of Human Descent's Branches. *New York Times,* March 22, late edition, final, section A, p. 1, column 1. http://www.nytimes.com.

2001b African Artifacts Suggest an Earlier Modern Human. *New York Times,* December 2, late edition, final, section 1A, p. 1, column 5. http://www.nytimes.com.
2002a Seeking Polynesia's Beginnings in an Archipelago of Shards. *New York Times,* January 8, Science Desk.
2002b When Humans Became Human. *New York Times,* February 26, late edition, final, section F, p. 1, column 1. http://www.nytimes.com.
2003 Big Teeth in Ancient Jaw Offer Clues about Our Ancestors. *New York Times* September 30, late edition, final, section F, p. 4, column 2.
2005a For Neandertals and *Homo Sapiens,* Was It De-Lovely? *New York Times,* February 15. http://www.nytimes.com/2005/02/15/science/15nean.html?ex=1147492800&en=7d5fadb91364f1d5&ei=5070.
2005b Fossils of Apelike Creature Still Stir Lineage Debate. *New York Times,* April 12, late edition, final, p. F4.

Wilk, R. R.
1996 *Economies and Cultures: An Introduction to Economic Anthropology.* Boulder, CO: Westview Press.

Williams, B.
1989 A Class Act: Anthropology and the Race to Nation across Ethnic Terrain. *Annual Review of Anthropology* 18: 401–444.

Williams, L. M., and D. Finkelhor
1995 Paternal Caregiving and Incest: Test of a Biosocial Model. *American Journal of Orthopsychiatry* 65(1): 101–113.

Willie, C. V.
2003 *A New Look at Black Families.* Walnut Creek, CA: AltaMira.

Wilmsen, E. N.
1989 *Land Filled with Flies: A Political Economy of the Kalahari.* Chicago: University of Chicago Press.

Wilmsen, E. N., and P. McAllister, eds.
1996 *The Politics of Difference: Ethnic Premises in a World of Power.* Chicago: University of Chicago Press.

Wilson, C.
1995 *Hidden in the Blood: A Personal Investigation of AIDS in the Yucatan.* New York: Columbia University Press.

Wilson, D. S.
2002 *Darwin's Cathedral: Evolution, Religion, and the Nature of Society.* Chicago: University of Chicago Press.

Wilson, M. L., and R. W. Wrangham
2003 Intergroup Relations in Chimpanzees. *Annual Review of Anthropology* 32:363–392.

Wilson, R., ed.
1996   *Human Rights: Culture and Context: Anthropological Perspectives.* Chicago: Pluto Press.

Winslow, J. H., and A. Meyer
1983   The Perpetrator at Piltdown. *Science 83* (September): 33–43.

Winter, R.
2001   Religions of the World: Number of Adherents; Names of Houses of Worship; Names of Leaders; Rates of Growth. http://www.religioustolerance.org/worldrel.htm.

Winzeler, R. L.
1995   *Latah in Southeast Asia: The Ethnography and History of a Culture-Bound Syndrome.* New York: Cambridge University Press.

Wittfogel, K. A.
1957   *Oriental Despotism: A Comparative Study of Total Power.* New Haven, CT: Yale University Press.

Wolf, E. R.
1966   *Peasants.* Englewood Cliffs, NJ: Prentice Hall.
1982   *Europe and the People without History.* Berkeley: University of California Press.
1999   *Envisioning Power: Ideologies of Dominance and Crisis.* Berkeley: University of California Press.

Wolf, E. R., with S. Silverman
2001   *Pathways of Power: Building an Anthropology of the Modern World.* Berkeley: University of California Press.

Wolpoff, M., B. Senut, M. Pickford, and J. Hawks
2002   Sahelanthropus or "Sahelpithecus"? *Nature* 419: 581–582.

Wolpoff, M. H.
1980*a*   *Paleoanthropology.* Boston: McGraw-Hill.
1980*b*   Cranial Remains of Middle Pleistocene Hominids. *Journal of Human Evolution* 9: 339–358.
1999   *Paleoanthropology,* 2nd ed. New York: McGraw-Hill.

Wolpoff, M. H., And R. Caspari
1997   *Race and Human Evolution.* New York: Simon & Schuster.

Woolard, K. A.
1989   *Double Talk: Bilingualism and the Politics of Ethnicity in Catalonia.* Stanford, CA: Stanford University Press.

World Almanac & Book of Facts
Published annually. New York: Newspaper Enterprise Association.

World Health Organization
1997   *World Health Report.* Geneva: World Health Organization.

World Malaria Report 2005
2005   Roll Back Malaria. World Health Organization, UNICEF. http://rbm.who.int/wmr2005/pdf/WMReport_lr.pdf.

Worsley, P.
1984   *The Three Worlds: Culture and World Development.* Chicago: University of Chicago Press.
1985   (orig. 1959). Cargo Cults. In *Readings in Anthropology 85/86.* Guilford, CT: Dushkin.

Wrangham, R. W.
1980   An Ecological Model of Female-Bonded Primate Groups. *Behavior* 75: 262–300.
1987   The Significance of African Apes for Reconstructing Human Social Evolution. In *The Evolution of Human Behavior: Primate Models,* ed. W. G. Kinzey, pp. 51–71. Albany: State University of New York Press.

Wrangham, R. W., ed.
1994   *Chimpanzee Cultures.* Cambridge, MA: Harvard University Press.

Wrangham, R., W. McGrew, F. de Waal, and P. Heltne, eds.
1994   *Chimpanzee Cultures.* Cambridge, MA: Harvard University Press.

Wrangham, R. W., and D. Peterson
1996   *Demonic Males: Apes and the Origins of Human Violence.* Boston: Houghton Mifflin.

Wright, H. T., and G. A. Johnson
1975   Population, Exchange, and Early State Formation in Southwestern Iran. *American Anthropologist* 77: 267–289.
1994   Prestate Political Formations. In *Chiefdoms and Early States in the Near East: The Organizational Dynamics of Complexity,* ed. G. Stein and M. S. Rothman, *Monographs in World Archaeology* 18: 67–84. Madison, WI: Prehistory Press.

Wright, S., ed.
1994   *Anthropology of Organizations.* London: Routledge.

Wulff, R. M., and S. J. Fiske, eds.
1987   *Anthropological Praxis: Translating Knowledge into Action.* Boulder, CO: Westview Press.

Yanagisako, S. J.
2002   *Producing Culture and Capital: Family Firms in Italy.* Princeton, NJ: Princeton University Press.

Yellen, J. E., A. S. Brooks, and E. Cornelissen.
1995   A Middle Stone Age Worked Bone Industry from Katanda, Upper Semliki Valley, Zaire. *Science* 268: 553–556.

Yetman, N., ed.
1991   *Majority and Minority: The Dynamics of Race and Ethnicity in American Life,* 5th ed. Boston: Allyn & Bacon.

1999 *Majority and Minority: The Dynamics of Race and Ethnicity in American Life,* 6th ed. Boston: Allyn & Bacon.

Young, W. C.
1996 *The Rashaayada Bedouin: Arab Pastoralists of Eastern Sudan.* Fort Worth: Harcourt Brace.

Yurchak, A.
2002 Entrepreneurial Governmentality in Postsocialist Russia. In *The New Entrepreneurs of Europe and Asia,* ed. V. Bonnell and T. Gold, p. 301. Armonk, NY: M.E. Sharpe.
2005 *Everything Was Forever Until It Was No More: The Last Soviet Generation.* Princeton, NJ: Princeton University Press.

Zeder, Melinda A.
1997 The American Archaeologist: Results of the 1994 SAA Census. *SAA Bulletin* 15(2): 12–17.

Zou, Y., and E. T. Trueba
2002 *Ethnography and Schools: Qualitative Approaches to the Study of Education.* Lanham, MD: Rowman and Littlefield.

Zulaika, J.
1988 *Basque Violence: Metaphor and Sacrament.* Reno: University of Nevada Press.

Glossary

Audible pronunciations for many of the following terms are provided in the electronic Glossary at the Online Learning Center for this book.

A. afarensis Early forms of *Australopithecus,* known from Hadar in Ethiopia ("Lucy") and Laetoli in Tanzania; the Hadar remains date to 3.3–3.0 m.y.a.; the Laetoli remains are older, dating to 3.8–3.6 m.y.a.; despite its many apelike features, *A. afarensis* was an upright biped.

absolute dating Dating techniques that establish dates in numbers or ranges of numbers; examples include the radiometric methods of ^{14}C, K/A, ^{238}U, TL, and ESR dating.

acculturation The exchange of cultural features that results when groups come into continuous firsthand contact; the cultural patterns of either or both groups may be changed, but the groups remain distinct.

Acheulian Derived from the French village of St. Acheul, where these tools were first identified; Lower Paleolithic tool tradition associated with *H. erectus.*

achieved status Social status that comes through talents, choices, actions, and accomplishments, rather than ascription.

adapids Early (Eocene) primate family ancestral to lemurs and lorises.

adaptive Favored by natural selection in a particular environment.

aesthetics Appreciation of the qualities perceived in works of art; the mind and emotions in relation to a sense of beauty.

affinals Relatives by marriage, whether of lineals (e.g., son's wife) or collaterals (e.g., sister's husband).

age set Group uniting all men or women born during a certain time span; this group controls property and often has political and military functions.

agriculture Nonindustrial systems of plant cultivation characterized by continuous and intensive use of land and labor.

allele A biochemical variant of a particular gene.

Allen's rule Rule stating that the relative size of protruding body parts (such as ears, tails, bills, fingers, toes, and limbs) tends to increase in warmer climates.

ambilineal Principle of descent that does not automatically exclude the children of either sons or daughters.

analogies Similarities arising as a result of similar selective forces; traits produced by convergent evolution.

anatomically modern humans (AMHs) Including the Cro-Magnons of Europe (31,000 B.P.) and the older fossils from Skhūl (100,000), Qafzeh (92,000), Herto, and other sites; continue through the present; also known as *H. sapiens sapiens.*

animism Belief in souls or doubles.

anthropoids Members of Anthropoidea, one of the two suborders of primates; monkeys, apes, and humans are anthropoids.

anthropology The study of the human species and its immediate ancestors.

anthropology and education Anthropological research in classrooms, homes, and neighborhoods, viewing students as total cultural creatures whose enculturation and attitudes toward education belong to a larger context that includes family, peers, and society.

anthropometry The measurement of human body parts and dimensions, including skeletal parts (*osteometry*).

antimodernism The rejection of the modern in favor of what is perceived as an earlier, purer, and better way of life.

applied anthropology The application of anthropological data, perspectives, theory, and methods to identify, assess, and solve contemporary social problems.

arboreal Tree-dwelling; arboreal primates include gibbons, New World monkeys, and many Old World monkeys.

arboreal hypothesis Idea that the primates evolved by adapting to life high up in the trees, where visual abilities would have been favored over the sense of smell, and grasping hands and feet would have been used for movement along branches.

archaeological anthropology The study of human behavior and cultural patterns and processes through the culture's material remains.

archaic *H. sapiens* Early *H. sapiens,* consisting of the Neandertals of Europe and the Middle East, the Neandertal-like hominids of Africa and Asia, and the immediate ancestors of all these hominids; lived from about 300,000 to 28,000 B.P.

art An object or event that evokes an aesthetic reaction—a sense of beauty, appreciation, harmony, and/or pleasure; the quality, production, expression, or realm of what is beautiful or of more than ordinary significance; the class of objects subject to aesthetic criteria.

arts The arts include the visual arts, literature (written and oral), music, and theater arts.

ascribed status Social status (e.g., race or gender) that people have little or no choice about occupying.

assimilation The process of change that a minority group may experience when it moves to a country where another culture dominates; the minority is incorporated into the dominant culture to the point that it no longer exists as a separate cultural unit.

australopithecines Varied group of Pliocene–Pleistocene hominids. The term is derived from their former classification as members of a distinct subfamily, the Australopithecinae; now they are distinguished from *Homo* only at the genus level.

Aztec Last independent state in the Valley of Mexico; capital was Tenochtitlan. Thrived between A.D. 1325 and the Spanish Conquest in 1520.

balanced polymorphism Two or more forms, such as alleles of the same gene, that maintain a constant frequency in a population from generation to generation.

balanced reciprocity See *generalized reciprocity.*

band Basic unit of social organization among foragers. A band includes fewer than 100 people; it often splits up seasonally.

behavioral ecology Study of the evolutionary basis of social behavior.

Bergmann's rule Rule stating that the smaller of two bodies similar in shape has more surface area per unit of weight and therefore can dissipate heat more efficiently; hence, large bodies tend to be found in colder areas and small bodies in warmer ones.

bifurcate collateral kinship terminology Kinship terminology employing separate terms for M, F, MB, MZ, FB, and FZ.

bifurcate merging kinship terminology Kinship terminology in which M and MZ are called by the same term, F and FB are called by the same term, and MB and FZ are called by different terms.

big man Regional figure found among tribal horticulturalists and pastoralists. The big man occupies no office but creates his reputation through entrepreneurship and generosity to others. Neither his wealth nor his position passes to his heirs.

bilateral kinship calculation A system in which kinship ties are calculated equally through both sexes: mother and father, sister and brother, daughter and son, and so on.

biochemical genetics Field that studies structure, function, and changes in genetic material—aka molecular genetics.

biocultural Referring to the inclusion and combination (to solve a common problem) of both biological and cultural approaches—one of anthropology's hallmarks.

biological anthropology The study of human biological variation in time and space; includes evolution, genetics, growth and development, and primatology.

bipedalism Upright two-legged locomotion, the key feature distinguishing early hominins from the apes.

Black English Vernacular (BEV) A rule-governed dialect of American English with roots in southern English. BEV is spoken by African American youth and by many adults in their casual, intimate speech—sometimes called "ebonics."

blade tool The basic Upper Paleolithic tool type, hammered off a prepared core.

bone biology The study of bone as a biological tissue, including its genetics; cell structure; growth, development, and decay; and patterns of movement (*biomechanics*).

bourgeoisie One of Marx's opposed classes; owners of the means of production (factories, mines, large farms, and other sources of subsistence).

brachiation Under-the-branch swinging; characteristic of gibbons, siamangs, and some New World monkeys.

bridewealth See *progeny price.*

broad-spectrum revolution Period beginning around 15,000 B.P. in the Middle East and 12,000 B.P. in Europe, during which a wider range, or broader spectrum, of plant and animal life was hunted, gathered, collected, caught, and fished; revolutionary because it led to food production.

bronze An alloy of arsenic and copper or tin and copper.

call systems Systems of communication among nonhuman primates, composed of a limited number of sounds that vary in intensity and duration. Tied to environmental stimuli.

capital Wealth or resources invested in business, with the intent of producing a profit.

capitalist world economy The single world system, which emerged in the 16th century, committed to production for sale, with the object of maximizing profits rather than supplying domestic needs.

cargo cults Postcolonial, acculturative religious movements, common in Melanesia, that attempt to explain European domination and wealth and to achieve similar success magically by mimicking European behavior.

caste system Closed, hereditary system of stratification, often dictated by religion; hierarchical social status is ascribed at birth, so that people are locked into their parents' social position.

catastrophism View that extinct species were destroyed by fires, floods, and other catastrophes. After each destructive event, God created again, leading to contemporary species.

catharsis Intense emotional release.

chiefdom A ranked society in which relations among villages as well as among individuals are unequal, with smaller villages under the authority of leaders in larger villages; has a two-level settlement hierarchy.

chiefdom Form of sociopolitical organization intermediate between the tribe and the state; kin-based with differential access to resources and a permanent political structure.

chromosomes Basic genetic units, occurring in matching (homologous) pairs; lengths of DNA made up of multiple genes.

civil society Voluntary collective action around shared interests, goals, and values. Encompasses such organizations as NGOs, registered charities, community groups, women's organizations, faith-based and professional groups, trade unions, self-help groups, social movements, business associations, coalitions, and advocacy groups.

clan Unilineal descent group based on stipulated descent.

cline A gradual shift in gene frequencies between neighboring populations.

Clovis tradition Stone technology based on a projectile point that was fastened to the end of a hunting spear; it flourished between 12,000 and 11,000 B.P. in North America.

collateral relative A genealogical relative who is not in ego's direct line, such as B, Z, FB, or MZ.

colonialism The political, social, economic, and cultural domination of a territory and its people by a foreign power for an extended time.

communal religions In Wallace's typology, these religions have, in addition to shamanic cults, communal cults in which people organize community rituals such as harvest ceremonies and rites of passage.

Communism Spelled with a capital C, a political movement and doctrine seeking to overthrow capitalism and to establish a form of communism such as that which prevailed in the Soviet Union from 1917 to 1991.

communism Spelled with a lowercase *c*, describes a social system in which property is owned by the community and in which people work for the common good.

communitas Intense community spirit, a feeling of great social solidarity, equality, and togetherness; characteristic of people experiencing liminality together.

complex societies Nations; large and populous, with social stratification and central governments.

convergent evolution Independent operation of similar selective forces; the process by which analogies are produced.

core Dominant structural position in the world system; consists of the strongest and most powerful states with advanced systems of production.

core values Key, basic, or central values that integrate a culture and help distinguish it from others.

correlation An association between two or more variables such that when one changes (varies), the other(s) also change(s) (covaries); for example, temperature and sweating.

creationism Explanation for the origin of species given in Genesis: God created the species during the original six days of Creation.

cross cousins Children of a brother and a sister.

crossing over   During meiosis, the process by which homologous chromosomes intertwine and exchange segments of their DNA.

cultivation continuum   A continuum based on the comparative study of nonindustrial cultivating societies in which labor intensity increases and fallowing decreases.

cultural anthropology   The study of human society and culture; describes, analyzes, interprets, and explains social and cultural similarities and differences.

cultural consultants   Subjects in ethnographic research; people the ethnographer gets to know in the field, who teach him or her about their culture.

cultural imperialism   The rapid spread or advance of one culture at the expense of others, or its imposition on other cultures, which it modifies, replaces, or destroys—usually because of differential economic or political influence.

cultural relativism   The position that the values and standards of cultures differ and deserve respect. Anthropology is characterized by methodological rather than moral relativism: In order to understand another culture fully, anthropologists try to understand its members' beliefs and motivations. Methodological relativism does not preclude making moral judgments or taking action.

cultural resource management (CRM)   The branch of applied archaeology aimed at preserving sites threatened by dams, highways, and other projects.

cultural rights   Doctrine that certain rights are vested in identifiable groups, such as religious and ethnic minorities and indigenous societies. Cultural rights include a group's ability to preserve its culture, to raise its children in the ways of its forebears, to continue its language, and not to be deprived of its economic base by the nation-state in which it is located.

cultural transmission   A basic feature of language; transmission through learning.

culture   Distinctly human; transmitted through learning; traditions and customs that govern behavior and beliefs.

cuneiform   Early Mesopotamian writing that used a stylus (writing implement) to write wedge-shaped impressions on raw clay; from the Latin word for "wedge."

curer   Specialized role acquired through a culturally appropriate process of selection, training, certification, and acquisition of a professional image; the curer is consulted by patients, who believe in his or her special powers, and receives some form of special consideration; a cultural universal.

daughter languages   Languages developing out of the same parent language; for example, French and Spanish are daughter languages of Latin.

dendrochronology   Or tree-ring dating: a method of absolute dating based on the study and comparison of patterns of tree-ring growth.

descent   Rule assigning social identity on the basis of some aspect of one's ancestry.

descent group   A permanent social unit whose members claim common ancestry; fundamental to tribal society.

development anthropology   The branch of applied anthropology that focuses on social issues in—and the cultural dimension of—economic development.

diaspora   The offspring of an area who have spread to many lands.

differential access   Unequal access to resources; basic attribute of chiefdoms and states. Superordinates have favored access to such resources, while the access of subordinates is limited by superordinates.

diffusion   Borrowing of cultural traits between societies, either directly or through intermediaries.

diglossia   The existence of "high" (formal) and "low" (informal, familial) dialects of a single language, such as German.

discrimination   Policies and practices that harm a group and its members.

disease   A scientifically identified health threat caused by a bacterium, virus, fungus, parasite, or other pathogen.

displacement   A basic feature of language; the ability to speak of things and events that are not present.

domestic–public dichotomy   Contrast between women's role in the home and men's role in public life, with a corresponding social devaluation of women's work and worth.

dominant   Allele that masks another allele in a heterozygote.

dowry   A marital exchange in which the wife's group provides substantial gifts to the husband's family.

Dryopithecus   Zoological ape family living in Europe during the middle and late Miocene; probably includes the common ancestor of the lesser apes (gibbons and siamangs) and the great apes.

economizing   The rational allocation of scarce means (or resources) to alternative ends (or uses); often considered the subject matter of economics.

economy   A population's system of production, distribution, and consumption of resources.

egalitarian society A type of society, most typically found among hunter-gatherers, that lacks status distinctions except for those based on age, gender, and individual qualities, talents, and achievements.

ego Latin for *I*. In kinship charts, the point from which one views an egocentric genealogy.

emic The research strategy that focuses on local explanations and criteria of significance.

empire A mature, territorially large, and expansive, state; empires are typically multiethnic, multilinguistic, and more militaristic, with a better developed bureaucracy than earlier states.

enculturation The social process by which culture is learned and transmitted across the generations.

endogamy Rule or practice of marriage between people of the same social group.

equity, increased A reduction in absolute poverty and a fairer (more even) distribution of wealth.

essentialism The process of viewing an identity as established, real, and frozen to hide the historical processes and politics within which that identity developed.

estrus Period of maximum sexual receptivity in female baboons, chimpanzees, and other primates, signaled by vaginal area swelling and coloration.

ethnic group Group distinguished by cultural similarities (shared among members of that group) and differences (between that group and others); ethnic-group members share beliefs, customs, and norms, and, often, a common language, religion, history, geography, and kinship.

ethnicity Identification with, and feeling part of, an ethnic group, and exclusion from certain other groups because of this affiliation.

ethnocentrism The tendency to view one's own culture as best and to judge the behavior and beliefs of culturally different people by one's own standards.

ethnography Field work in a particular culture.

ethnology Cross-cultural comparison; the comparative study of ethnographic data, society, and culture.

ethnomusicology The comparative study of the musics of the world and of music as an aspect of culture and society.

ethnosemantics The study of lexical (vocabulary) contrasts and classifications in various languages.

etic The research strategy that emphasizes the ethnographer's rather than the locals' explanations, categories, and criteria of significance.

evolution Belief that species arose from others through a long and gradual process of transformation, or descent with modification.

excavation Digging through the layers of deposits that make up an archaeological or fossil site.

exogamy Rule requiring people to marry outside their own group.

expressive culture The arts; people express themselves creatively in dance, music, song, painting, sculpture, pottery, cloth, storytelling, verse, prose, drama, and comedy.

extended family household Expanded household including three or more generations.

extradomestic Outside the home; within or pertaining to the public domain.

family of orientation Nuclear family in which one is born and grows up.

family of procreation Nuclear family established when one marries and has children.

fiscal Pertaining to finances and taxation.

focal vocabulary A set of words and distinctions that are particularly important to certain groups (those with particular foci of experience or activity), such as types of snow to Eskimos or skiers.

folk Of the people; originally coined for European peasants; refers to the art, music, and lore of ordinary people, as contrasted with the "high" art or "classic" art of the European elites.

food production Cultivation of plants and domestication (stockbreeding) of animals; first developed 10,000 to 12,000 years ago.

fossils Remains (e.g., bones), traces, or impressions (e.g., footprints) of ancient life.

functional explanation Explanation that establishes a correlation or interrelationship between social customs. When customs are functionally interrelated, if one changes, the others also change.

fundamentalism Describes antimodernist movements in various religions. Fundamentalists assert an identity separate from the larger religious group from which they arose; they advocate strict fidelity to the "true" religious principles on which the larger religion was founded.

gender roles The tasks and activities that a culture assigns to each sex.

gender stereotypes Oversimplified but strongly held ideas about the characteristics of males and females.

gender stratification Unequal distribution of rewards (socially valued resources, power, prestige, and personal freedom) between men and women, reflecting their different positions in a social hierarchy.

gene Area in a chromosome pair that determines, wholly or partially, a particular biological trait, such as whether one's blood type is A, B, or O.

gene flow Exchange of genetic material between populations of the same species through direct or indirect interbreeding.

gene pool All the alleles, genes, chromosomes, and genotypes within a breeding population—the "pool" of genetic material available.

genealogical method Procedures by which ethnographers discover and record connections of kinship, descent, and marriage, using diagrams and symbols.

general anthropology The field of anthropology as a whole, consisting of cultural, archaeological, biological, and linguistic anthropology.

generality Culture pattern or trait that exists in some but not all societies.

generalized reciprocity Principle that characterizes exchanges between closely related individuals. As social distance increases, reciprocity becomes balanced and finally negative.

generational kinship terminology Kinship terminology with only two terms for the parental generation, one designating M, MZ, and FZ and the other designating F, FB, and MB.

genetic evolution Change in gene frequency within a breeding population.

genitor Biological father of a child.

genotype An organism's hereditary makeup.

gibbons The smallest apes, natives of Asia; arboreal.

glacials The four or five major advances of continental ice sheets in northern Europe and North America.

globalization The accelerating interdependence of nations in a world system linked economically and through mass media and modern transportation systems.

gracile Opposite of robust; "gracile" indicates that members of *A. africanus* were a bit smaller and slighter, less robust, than were members of *A. robustus*.

green revolution Agricultural development based on chemical fertilizers, pesticides, 20th-century cultivation techniques, and new crop varieties such as IR-8 ("miracle rice").

Halafian An early (7500–6500 B.P.) and widespread pottery style, first found in northern Syria; refers to a delicate ceramic style and to the period when the first chiefdoms emerged.

head, village A local leader in a tribal society who has limited authority, leads by example and persuasion, and must be generous.

health-care systems Beliefs, customs, and specialists concerned with ensuring health and preventing and curing illness; a cultural universal.

hegemony As used by Antonio Gramsci, a stratified social order in which subordinates comply with domination by internalizing its values and accepting its "naturalness."

heterozygous Having dissimilar alleles of a given gene.

hidden transcript As used by James Scott, the critique of power by the oppressed that goes on offstage—in private—where the power holders can't see it.

Hilly Flanks Woodland zone that flanks the Tigris and Euphrates rivers to the north; zone of wild wheat and barley and of sedentism (settled, nonmigratory life) preceding food production.

historical linguistics Subdivision of linguistics that studies languages over time.

holistic Interested in the whole of the human condition: past, present, and future; biology, society, language, and culture.

hominid A member of the taxonomic family that includes humans and the African apes and their immediate ancestors.

hominin A member of the human lineage after its split from ancestral chimps; the term *hominin* is used to describe all the human species that ever have existed, including the extinct ones, and excluding chimps and gorillas.

hominoids Members of the superfamily including humans and all the apes.

Homo habilis Term coined by L. S. B. and Mary Leakey; immediate ancestor of *H. erectus;* lived from about 2.0 to 1.7 m.y.a.

homologies Traits that organisms have jointly inherited from a common ancestor.

homozygous Possessing identical alleles of a particular gene.

honorific A term, such as "Mr." or "Lord," used with people, often by being added to their names, to "honor" them.

horticulture Nonindustrial system of plant cultivation in which plots lie fallow for varying lengths of time.

human rights Doctrine that invokes a realm of justice and morality beyond and superior to particular countries, cultures, and religions. Human rights, usually seen as vested in individuals, would include the right to speak freely, to hold religious beliefs without persecution, and not to be murdered, injured, enslaved, or imprisoned without charge.

hypervitaminosis D Condition caused by an excess of vitamin D; calcium deposits build up in the body's soft tissues, and the kidneys may fail; symptoms include gallstones and joint and circulation problems; may affect unprotected light-skinned individuals in the tropics.

hypodescent Rule that automatically places the children of a union or mating between members of different socioeconomic groups in the less-privileged group.

illness A condition of poor health perceived or felt by an individual.

imperialism A policy of extending the rule of a nation or empire over foreign nations or of taking and holding foreign colonies.

incest Forbidden sexual relations with a close relative.

income Earnings from wages and salaries.

independent assortment Mendel's law of; chromosomes are inherited independently of one another.

independent invention Development of the same cultural trait or pattern in separate cultures as a result of comparable needs, circumstances, and solutions.

indigenized Modified to fit the local culture.

indigenous peoples The original inhabitants of particular territories; often descendants of tribespeople who live on as culturally distinct colonized peoples, many of whom aspire to autonomy.

Industrial Revolution The historic transformation (in Europe, after 1750) of "traditional" into "modern" societies through industrialization of the economy.

informed consent Agreement to take part in research, after the people being studied have been told about that research's purpose, nature, procedures, and potential impact on them.

interglacials Extended warm periods between such major glacials as Riss and Würm.

international culture Cultural traditions that extend beyond national boundaries.

intervention philosophy Guiding principle of colonialism, conquest, missionization, or development; an ideological justification for outsiders to guide native peoples in specific directions.

interview schedule Ethnographic tool for structuring a formal interview. A prepared form (usually printed or mimeographed) that guides interviews with households or individuals being compared systematically. Contrasts with a *questionnaire* because the researcher has personal contact with the local people and records their answers.

IPR Intellectual property rights, consisting of each society's cultural base—its core beliefs and principles. IPR are claimed as a group right—a cultural right—allowing indigenous groups to control who may know and use their collective knowledge and its applications.

key cultural consultant Person who is an expert on a particular aspect of local life.

kinesics The study of communication through body movements, stances, gestures, and facial expressions.

kinship calculation The system by which people in a particular society reckon kin relationships.

language Human beings' primary means of communication; may be spoken or written; features productivity and displacement and is culturally transmitted.

law A legal code, including trial and enforcement; characteristic of state-organized societies.

leveling mechanism A custom or social action that operates to reduce differences in wealth and thus to bring standouts in line with community norms.

levirate Custom by which a widow marries the brother of her deceased husband.

lexicon Vocabulary; a dictionary containing all the morphemes in a language and their meanings.

life history Of a key consultant or narrator; provides a personal cultural portrait of existence or change in a culture.

liminality The critically important marginal or in-between phase of a rite of passage.

lineage Unilineal descent group based on demonstrated descent.

lineal kinship terminology Parental generation kin terminology with four terms: one for M, one for F, one for FB and MB, and one for MZ and FZ.

lineal relative Any of ego's ancestors or descendants (e.g., parents, grandparents, children, grandchildren) on the direct line of descent that leads to and from ego.

linguistic anthropology The descriptive, comparative, and historical study of language and of linguistic similarities and differences in time, space, and society.

longitudinal research Long-term study of a community, region, society, culture, or other unit, usually based on repeated visits.

macroevolution Large-scale changes in allele frequencies in a population over a longer time period (than microevolution)—changes that culminate in the evolution of new species.

magic Use of supernatural techniques to accomplish specific aims.

maize Corn; domesticated in highland Mexico.

mana Sacred impersonal force in Melanesian and Polynesian religions.

manioc Cassava; a tuber domesticated in the South American lowlands.

market principle Profit-oriented principle of exchange that dominates in states, particularly industrial states. Goods and services are bought and sold, and values are determined by supply and demand.

mater Socially recognized mother of a child.

matrifocal Mother-centered; often refers to a household with no resident husband-father.

matrilineal descent Unilineal descent rule in which people join the mother's group automatically at birth and stay members throughout life.

matrilocality Customary residence with the wife's relatives after marriage, so that children grow up in their mother's community.

means (or factors) of production Land, labor, technology, and capital—major productive resources.

medical anthropology Unites biological and cultural anthropologists in the study of disease, health problems, health-care systems, and theories about illness in different cultures and ethnic groups.

meiosis Special process by which sex cells are produced; four cells are produced from one, each with half the genetic material of the original cell.

melanin Substance manufactured in specialized cells in the lower layers of the epidermis (outer skin layer); melanin cells in dark skin produce more melanin than do those in light skin.

Mendelian genetics Studies ways in which chromosomes transmit genes across the generations.

Mesoamerica Middle America, including Mexico, Guatemala, and Belize.

Mesolithic Middle Stone Age, whose characteristic tool type was the microlith; broad-spectrum economy.

Mesopotamia The area between the Tigris and Euphrates rivers in what is now southern Iraq and southwestern Iran; location of the first cities and states.

metallurgy Knowledge of the properties of metals, including their extraction and processing and the manufacture of metal tools.

microevolution Small-scale changes in allele frequencies over generations without speciation.

m.y.a. Million years ago.

mitosis Ordinary cell division; DNA molecules copy themselves, creating two identical cells out of one.

mixed diet hypothesis The idea that increased use of angiosperms (flowering plants) led to modern primate characteristics. Early primates would have relied on vision as they sought fruits, seeds, and flowers as well as insects.

mode of production Way of organizing production—a set of social relations through which labor is deployed to wrest energy from nature by means of tools, skills, and knowledge.

molecular anthropology Genetic analysis, involving comparison of DNA sequences, to determine evolutionary links and distances among species and among ancient and modern populations.

monotheism Worship of an eternal, omniscient, omnipotent, and omnipresent supreme being.

morphology The study of form; used in linguistics (the study of morphemes and word construction) and for form in general—for example, biomorphology relates to physical form.

Mousterian Middle Paleolithic tool-making tradition associated with Neandertals.

multiculturalism The view of cultural diversity in a country as something good and desirable; a multicultural society socializes individuals not only into the dominant (national) culture but also into an ethnic culture.

multiregional evolution Theory that *H. erectus* gradually evolved into modern *H. sapiens* in all regions inhabited by humans (Africa, Europe, northern Asia, and Australasia). As the regional populations evolved, gene flow always connected them, and so they always belonged to the same species. This theory opposes replacement models such as the Eve theory.

multivariate Involving multiple factors, causes, or variables.

mutation Change in the DNA molecules of which genes and chromosomes are built.

nation Once a synonym for "ethnic group," designating a single culture sharing a language, religion, history, territory, ancestry, and kinship; now usually a synonym for state or *nation-state*.

national culture Cultural experiences, beliefs, learned behavior patterns, and values shared by citizens of the same nation.

nationalities Ethnic groups that once had, or wish to have or regain, autonomous political status (their own country).

nation-state An autonomous political entity; a country like the United States or Canada.

Natufians Widespread Middle Eastern culture, dated to between 12,500 and 10,500 B.P.; subsisted on intensive wild cereal collecting and gazelle hunting and had year-round villages.

natural selection The process by which the forms most fit to survive and reproduce in a given environment do so in greater numbers than others in the same population; more than survival of the fittest, natural selection is differential reproductive success.

Neandertals *H. sapiens neanderthalensis*, representing an archaic *H. sapiens* subspecies, lived in Europe and the Middle East between 130,000 and 28,000 B.P.

negative reciprocity See *generalized reciprocity.*

neoliberalism Revival of Adam Smith's classic economic liberalism, the idea that governments should not regulate private enterprise and that free market forces should rule; a currently dominant intervention philosophy.

Neolithic "New Stone Age," coined to describe techniques of grinding and polishing stone tools; the first cultural period in a region in which the first signs of domestication are present.

neolocality Postmarital residence pattern in which a couple establishes a new place of residence rather than living with or near either set of parents.

nomadism, pastoral Movement throughout the year by the whole pastoral group (men, women, and children) with their animals; more generally, such constant movement in pursuit of strategic resources.

office Permanent political position.

Oldowan Earliest (2.5 to 2.0 m.y.a.) stone tools; first discovered in 1931 by L. S. B. and Mary Leakey at Olduvai Gorge.

Olympian religions In Wallace's typology, develop with state organization; have full-time religious specialists—professional priesthoods.

omomyids Early (Eocene) primate family found in North America, Europe, and Asia; early omomyids may be ancestral to all anthropoids; later ones may be ancestral to tarsiers.

open class system Stratification system that facilitates social mobility, with individual achievement and personal merit determining social rank.

opposable thumb A thumb that can touch all the other fingers.

out of Africa theory Theory that a small group of anatomically modern people arose recently, probably in Africa, from which they spread and replaced the native and more archaic populations of other inhabited areas.

overinnovation Characteristic of projects that require major changes in natives' daily lives, especially ones that interfere with customary subsistence pursuits.

paleoanthropology Study of hominid and human life through the fossil record.

Paleolithic Old Stone Age (from Greek roots meaning "old" and "stone"); divided into Lower (early), Middle, and Upper (late).

paleontology Study of ancient life through the fossil record.

paleopathology Study of disease and injury in skeletons from archaeological sites.

palynology Study of ancient plants through pollen samples from archaeological or fossil sites in order to determine a site's environment at the time of occupation.

parallel cousins Children of two brothers or two sisters.

particularity Distinctive or unique culture trait, pattern, or integration.

pastoralists People who use a food-producing strategy of adaptation based on care of herds of domesticated animals.

pater Socially recognized father of a child; not necessarily the genitor.

patriarchy Political system ruled by men in which women have inferior social and political status, including basic human rights.

patrilineal descent Unilineal descent rule in which people join the father's group automatically at birth and stay members throughout life.

patrilineal-patrilocal complex An interrelated constellation of patrilineality, patrilocality, warfare, and male supremacy.

patrilocality Customary residence with the husband's relatives after marriage, so that children grow up in their father's community.

peasant Small-scale agriculturalist living in a state with rent fund obligations.

periphery Weakest structural position in the world system.

phenotype An organism's evident traits, its "manifest biology"—anatomy and physiology.

phenotypical adaptation Adaptive biological changes that occur during the individual's lifetime, made possible by biological plasticity.

phoneme Significant sound contrast in a language that serves to distinguish meaning, as in minimal pairs.

phonemics The study of the sound contrasts (phonemes) of a particular language.

phonetics The study of speech sounds in general; what people actually say in various languages.

phonology The study of sounds used in speech.

physical anthropology See *biological anthropology.*

Pleistocene Epoch of *Homo*'s appearance and evolution; began 1.8 million years ago; divided into Lower, Middle, and Upper.

plural marriage Any marriage with more than two spouses, aka polygamy.

plural society A society that combines ethnic contrasts and economic interdependence of the ethnic groups.

polyandry Variety of plural marriage in which a woman has more than one husband.

polygyny Variety of plural marriage in which a man has more than one wife.

polytheism Belief in several deities who control aspects of nature.

population genetics Field that studies causes of genetic variation, maintenance, and change in breeding populations.

postcolonial Referring to interactions between European nations and the societies they colonized (mainly after 1800); more generally, "postcolonial" may be used to signify a position against imperialism and Eurocentrism.

postcranium The area behind or below the head; the skeleton.

postmodern In its most general sense, describes the blurring and breakdown of established canons (rules, standards), categories, distinctions, and boundaries.

postmodernism A style and movement in architecture that succeeded modernism. Compared with modernism, postmodernism is less geometric, less functional, less austere, more playful, and more willing to include elements from diverse times and cultures; postmodern now describes comparable developments in music, literature, visual art, and anthropology.

postmodernity Condition of a world in flux, with people on the move, in which established groups, boundaries, identities, contrasts, and standards are reaching out and breaking down.

potlatch Competitive feast among Indians on the North Pacific Coast of North America.

power The ability to exercise one's will over others—to do what one wants; the basis of political status.

practicing anthropologists Used as a synonym for applied anthropology; anthropologists who practice their profession outside academia.

prejudice Devaluing (looking down on) a group because of its assumed behavior, values, capabilities, attitudes, or other attributes.

prestige Esteem, respect, or approval for acts, deeds, or qualities considered exemplary.

primary states States that arise on their own (through competition among chiefdoms), not through contact with other state societies.

primatology The study of fossil and living apes, monkeys, and prosimians, including their behavior and social life.

Proconsul Early Miocene genus of the pliopithecoid superfamily; the most abundant and successful anthropoids of the early Miocene; the last common ancestor shared by the Old World monkeys and the apes.

productivity A basic feature of language; the ability to use the rules of one's language to create new expressions comprehensible to other speakers.

progeny price A gift from the husband and his kin to the wife and her kin before, at, or after marriage; legitimizes children born to the woman as members of the husband's descent group.

prosimians The primate suborder that includes lemurs, lorises, and tarsiers.

protolanguage Language ancestral to several daughter languages.

public transcript As used by James Scott, the open, public interactions between dominators and oppressed—the outer shell of power relations.

punctuated equilibrium Evolutionary theory that long periods of stasis (stability), during which species change little, are interrupted (punctuated) by evolutionary leaps.

questionnaire Form (usually printed) used by sociologists to obtain comparable information from respondents. Often mailed to and filled in by research subjects rather than by the researcher.

race An ethnic group assumed to have a biological basis.

racial classification The attempt to assign humans to discrete categories (purportedly) based on common ancestry.

racism Discrimination against an ethnic group assumed to have a biological basis.

random genetic drift Change in gene frequency that results not from natural selection but from chance; most evident in small populations.

random sample A sample in which all members of the population have an equal statistical chance of being included.

ranked society A type of society with hereditary inequality but not social stratification; individuals are ranked in terms of their genealogical closeness to the chief, but there is a continuum of status, with many individuals and kin groups ranked about equally.

recessive Genetic trait masked by a dominant trait.

reciprocity   One of the three principles of exchange; governs exchange between social equals; major exchange mode in band and tribal societies.

recombination   Following independent assortment of chromosomes, new arrangements of hereditary units produced through bisexual reproduction.

redistribution   Major exchange mode of chiefdoms, many archaic states, and some states with managed economies.

refugees   People who have been forced (involuntary refugees) or who have chosen (voluntary refugees) to flee a country, to escape persecution or war.

relative dating   Dating technique, for example, stratigraphy, that establishes a time frame in relation to other strata or materials, rather than absolute dates in numbers.

religion   Belief and ritual concerned with supernatural beings, powers, and forces.

remote sensing   Use of aerial photos and satellite images to locate sites on the ground.

revitalization movements   Movements that occur in times of change, in which religious leaders emerge and undertake to alter or revitalize a society.

rickets   Nutritional disease caused by a shortage of vitamin D; interferes with the absorption of calcium and causes softening and deformation of the bones.

rites of passage   Culturally defined activities associated with the transition from one place or stage of life to another.

ritual   Behavior that is formal, stylized, repetitive, and stereotyped, performed earnestly as a social act; rituals are held at set times and places and have liturgical orders.

robust   Large, strong, sturdy; said of skull, skeleton, muscle, and teeth; opposite of gracile.

sample   A smaller study group chosen to represent a larger population.

Sapir-Whorf hypothesis   Theory that different languages produce different ways of thinking.

science   A systematic field of study or body of knowledge that aims, through experiment, observation, and deduction, to produce reliable explanations of phenomena, with reference to the material and physical world.

scientific medicine   As distinguished from Western medicine, a health-care system based on scientific knowledge and procedures, encompassing such fields as pathology, microbiology, biochemistry, surgery, diagnostic technology, and applications.

sedentism   Settled (sedentary) life; preceded food production in the Old World and followed it in the New World.

semantics   A language's meaning system.

semiperiphery   Structural position in the world system intermediate between core and periphery.

settlement hierarchy   A ranked series of communities differing in size, function, and type of building; a three-level settlement hierarchy indicates state organization.

sexual dimorphism   Marked differences in male and female biology besides the contrasts in breasts and genitals.

sexual orientation   A person's habitual sexual attraction to, and activities with, persons of the opposite sex, heterosexuality; the same sex, homosexuality; or both sexes, bisexuality.

sexual selection   Based on differential success in mating, the process in which certain traits of one sex (e.g., color in male birds) are selected because of advantages they confer in winning mates.

shaman   A part-time religious practitioner who mediates between ordinary people and supernatural beings and forces.

Sivapithecus   Widespread fossil group first found in Pakistan; includes specimens formerly called *"Ramapithecus"* and fossil apes from Turkey, China, and Kenya; early *Sivapithecus* may contain the common ancestor of the orangutan and the African apes; late *Sivapithecus* is now seen as ancestral to the modern orang.

slavery   The most extreme, coercive, abusive, and inhumane form of legalized inequality; people are treated as property.

smelting   The high-temperature process by which pure metal is produced from an ore.

social control   Those fields of the social system (beliefs, practices, and institutions) that are most actively involved in the maintenance of norms and the regulation of conflict.

social race   A group assumed to have a biological basis but actually perceived and defined in a social context, by a particular culture rather than by scientific criteria.

sociolinguistics   Investigates relationships between social and linguistic variations.

sodality, pantribal   A non-kin-based group that exists throughout a tribe, spanning several villages.

sororate   Custom by which a widower marries the sister of his deceased wife.

speciation   Formation of new species; occurs when subgroups of the same species are separated for a sufficient length of time.

species Population whose members can interbreed to produce offspring that can live and reproduce.

state (nation-state) Complex sociopolitical system that administers a territory and populace with substantial contrasts in occupation, wealth, prestige, and power. An independent, centrally organized political unit; a government. A form of social and political organization with a formal, central government and a division of society into classes.

state Sociopolitical organization based on central government and socioeconomic stratification—a division of society into classes.

status Any position that determines where someone fits in society; may be ascribed or achieved.

stratification A stratified society has sharp social divisions—*strata*—based on unequal access to wealth and power (e.g., into noble and commoner classes).

stratification Characteristic of a system with socioeconomic strata—groups that contrast in regard to social status and access to strategic resources. Each stratum includes people of both sexes and all ages.

stratified Class-structured; stratified societies have marked differences in wealth, prestige, and power between social classes.

stratigraphy Science that examines the ways in which earth sediments are deposited in demarcated layers known as *strata* (singular, *stratum*).

style shifts Variations in speech in different contexts.

subcultures Different cultural traditions associated with subgroups in the same complex society.

subgroups Languages within a taxonomy of related languages that are most closely related.

subordinate The lower, or underprivileged, group in a stratified system.

superordinate The upper, or privileged, group in a stratified system.

survey research Characteristic research procedure among social scientists other than anthropologists. Studies society through sampling, statistical analysis, and impersonal data collection.

symbol Something, verbal or nonverbal, that arbitrarily and by convention stands for something else, with which it has no necessary or natural connection.

syncretisms Cultural mixes, including religious blends, that emerge from acculturation—the exchange of cultural features when cultures come into continuous firsthand contact.

syntax The arrangement and order of words in phrases and sentences.

systematic survey Information gathered on patterns of settlement over a large area; provides a regional perspective on the archaeological record.

taboo Set apart as sacred and off-limits to ordinary people; prohibition backed by supernatural sanctions.

taphonomy The study of the processes that affect the remains of dead animals, such as their scattering by carnivores and scavengers, their distortion by various forces, and their possible fossilization.

taxonomy Classification scheme; assignment to categories (*taxa;* singular, *taxon*).

teocentli Or teosinte, a wild grass; apparent ancestor of maize.

Teotihuacan A.D. 100 to 700; first state in the Valley of Mexico and earliest major Mesoamerican empire.

terrestrial Ground-dwelling; baboons, macaques, and humans are terrestrial primates; gorillas spend most of their time on the ground.

text Something that is creatively "read," interpreted, and assigned meaning by each person who receives it; includes any media-borne image, such as Carnaval.

theory A set of ideas formulated (by reasoning from known facts) to explain something. The main value of a theory is to promote new understanding. A theory suggests patterns, connections, and relationships that may be confirmed by new research.

Thomson's nose rule Rule stating that the average nose tends to be longer in areas with lower mean annual temperatures; based on the geographic distribution of nose length among human populations.

transhumance One of two variants of pastoralism; part of the population moves seasonally with the herds while the other part remains in home villages.

tribe Form of sociopolitical organization usually based on horticulture or pastoralism. Socioeconomic stratification and centralized rule are absent in tribes, and there is no means of enforcing political decisions.

tropics Geographic belt extending about 23 degrees north and south of the equator, between the Tropic of Cancer (north) and the Tropic of Capricorn (south).

underdifferentiation Planning fallacy of viewing less developed countries as an undifferentiated group; ignoring cultural diversity and adopting a uniform approach (often ethnocentric) for very different types of project beneficiaries.

uniformitarianism Belief that explanations for past events should be sought in ordinary forces that continue to work today.

unilineal descent   Matrilineal or patrilineal descent.

universal   Something that exists in every culture.

Upper Paleolithic   Blade-tool-making traditions associated with early *H. sapiens sapiens*; named from their location in upper, or more recent, layers of sedimentary deposits.

variables   Attributes (e.g., sex, age, height, weight) that differ from one person or case to the next.

vertical mobility   Upward or downward change in a person's social status.

visual predation hypothesis   Idea that the primates evolved in lower branches and undergrowth by developing visual and tactile abilities to aid in hunting and snaring insects.

wealth   All a person's material assets, including income, land, and other types of property; the basis of economic status.

westernization   The acculturative influence of Western expansion on native cultures.

working class   Or proletariat; those who must sell their labor to survive; the antithesis of the bourgeoisie in Marx's class analysis.

Credits

Photo Credits

CHAPTER 1
2: © Jean-Leo Dugast/Peter Arnold; 5: © Francesco Broli/The New York Times; 8: © Smithsonian Institution; 9: © Lauren Greenfield/VII; 11: © Randy Olson/Aurora Photos; 14: Courtesy Alicia Wilbur; 17: © Bruce Avera Hunter/National Geographic Image Collection; 18: © William Campbell/Homefire Productions/Corbis Images

CHAPTER 2
22: © Mark Edwards/Peter Arnold; 25: © Ozier Muhammad/The New York Times; 27: © Mike Yamashita/Woodfin Camp & Associates; 28: © Will & Deni McIntyre/Corbis Images; 30: © Paul Conklin/Photo Edit, Inc.; 31: © Charles Harbutt/Actuality, Inc.; 32: © Hahn/Laif/Aurora Photos; 33: © Ron Giling/Peter Arnold; 34: © Erich Lessing/Magnum Photos; 35: © UNEP/Peter Arnold; 36: Courtesy, Ann L. Bretnall; 37: Professor Marietta Baba, Michigan State University

CHAPTER 3
42: © Douglas Mason/Woodfin Camp & Associates; 45: © Moises Castill/AP/Wide World Photos; 47: Payson Sheets, University of Colorado, Boulder; 48: © Payson Sheets, University of Colorado, Boulder; 49: © Richard T. Nowitz/Corbis; 51: © Peter Turnley/Corbis Images; 52: © Dr. Jerome Rose, University of Arkansas; 54: © Kenneth Garrett/National Geographic Image Collection; 55: © Jonathan Blair/Corbis; 56: © Mary Rhodes/Earth Scenes/Animals Animals; 57: © Topham/The Image Works; 58: © Jim Sugar/Corbis Images

CHAPTER 4
62: © Mary Altaffer/AP/WideWorld Photos; 64: © Noah's Ark by Edward Hicks, 1846, 261/2 x 301/2, Oil on canvas, Philadelphia Museum of Art, Bequest of Lisa Norris Elkins [1950-92-7]; 67: © English Heritage/Topham-HIP/Image Works; 69: © Michael Willmer Forbes Tweedie/Photo Researchers, Inc.; 70: © National Library of Medicine; 73: © Dr. Gopal Mujrti/PhotoTake; 75: © Paul Hunter/Toronto Star/ZUMA Press; 76: © Clayton Sharrard/Photo Edit, Inc.; 77: © Alfred Pasieka/Peter Arnold; 79: © Michael Newman/PhotoEdit

CHAPTER 5
84: © Catherine Karnow; 86: © Paul Grebliunas/Getty Images; 87: © Alison Wright/Corbis Images; 89 (top): © Sabine Vielmo/Argus Fotoarchiv/Peter Arnold; 89 (center): © Darrell Gulin/Corbis; 89 (bottom): © Penny Tweedie/Woodfin Camp & Associates; 91: © Gueorgui Plnkhassov/Magnum Photos; 92: © Steve McCurry/Magnum Photos; 93 (top): © Jan Spieczny/Peter Arnold; 93 (bottom): © Hartmut Schwarzbach/Argus Fotoarchiv/Peter Arnold; 94: Courtesy, Heather Norton; 96 (top): © Tony Camerano/AP/Wide World Photos; 96 (bottom): © National Library of Medicine; 98: © Robert Caputo/Stock Boston; 99: © David Hiser/Getty Images

CHAPTER 6
102: © Tom Brakefield/Corbis Images; 104: © Mike Nichols/Magnum Photos; 109: © Kenneth Garrett/National Geographic Image Collection; 110: © Topham/The Image Works; 111: Courtesy Stephen Ham; 113 (top): © David Haring/Animals Animals; 113 (bottom): © Frans Lanting/Corbis; 114: © Manoj Shah/Animals Animals; 115: © Karen Kasmauski/National Geographic Society; 116 (top): © Sandra Dawes/Image Works; 116 (bottom): © Mack Henley/Visuals Unlimited; 118: © Gallo Images/Corbis; 120: © M. Gunther/BIOS/Peter Arnold; 122: © Osf/Clive Bromhall/Animals Animals; 123: © D. Novellino/Still Pictures/Peter Arnold; 128: © Ed Parker/Photographers Direct/Chris Fairclough Worldwide Ltd.; 129: © Olivier Langrand/BIOS/Peter Arnold; 130: © Nigel Dickinson/Still Pictures/Peter Arnold

CHAPTER 7
132: © M. Harvey/Peter Arnold; 136: © L. & D. Klein/Photo Researchers; 137: Ni, X, Wang, Y, Hu, Y, Li ,C. A euprimate skull from the early Eocene of China. Nature. 2004 Jan 1; 427 (6969):22-3. Courtesy, X. Ni, W. Wang, C. Li; 139 (left): © n/a/Denver Museum of Nature and Science; 139 (right): © Tom McHugh/Photo Researchers; 140 (left): © Tom McHugh/Photo Researchers; 140 (right): © Roland Seitre/Peter Arnold; 141: Courtesy, Jennifer Burns; 143 (left): © Science VU/Visuals Unlimited; 143 (right): © Manoj Shah/Animals Animals; 144: © Russell L. Ciochon, University of Iowa; 145: From Rhetorica Christiana, by Didacus Valades, 1579; 147: © Lluis Gene/AFP/Getty Images; 148: © AFP/Getty Images

CHAPTER 8

152: National History Museum, London; **154:** National History Museum, London; **155:** © Tim D. White/Brill Atlanta; **158:** © Kenneth Garrett; **160:** © John Reader/SPL/Photo Researchers; **161:** © Kenneth Garrett/National Geographic Society; **162:** National History Museum, London; **165** (*both*): National History Museum, London; **166** (*all*): © Luba Dmytryk/National Geographic Image Collection; **167:** © Des Bartlett/Photo Researchers; **168** (*both*): © Peter Bostrom; **169:** Courtesy, Josh Trapani

CHAPTER 9

172: © AAAC/Topham/The Image Works; **174:** © Kenneth Garrett; **175:** © French Ministry of Culture and Communication, Regional Direction for Cultural Affairs, Rhône-Alpes region, Regional department of archaeology; **177:** The Natural History Museum, London; **178** (*top*): © David Brill ; **178** (*center*): © John Reader/Photo Researchers; **178** (*bottom*): © Natural History Museum, London; **179:** © Kenneth Garrett/National Geographic Image Collection; **182** (*all*): © Hisao Baba; **185** (*both*): The Natural History Museum, London; **187** (*top*): Courtesy, Milford H. Wolpoff; **188:** The Natural History Museum, London; **190** (*all*): © Luba Dmytryk/National Geographic Image Collection; **191:** The Natural History Museum, London; **194:** Courtesy, Kelsey Foster; **195:** © Kenneth Garrett/National Geographic Image Collection; **196:** © Dr. Peter Brown; **201:** © Kenneth Garrett/National Geographic Image Collection; **202** (*left*): © Lindsay Hebberd/Woodfin Camp & Associates; **202** (*right*): © Toby Canham/Pressnet/Topham/Image Works

CHAPTER 10

204: © Frank Lukasseck/Zefa /Corbis; **206:** © Erich Lessing/Art Resource; **207:** © Gerhard Hinterleitner/Gamma Press; **209:** © Will Yurman/Image Works; **212:** © Mike Yamashita/Woodfin Camp & Associates; **214:** © Michael Andrews/Earth Scenes/Animals Animals; **216:** © Robert Frerck/Odyssey Productions; **217:** © Craig Lovell/Corbis Images; **218:** © Ron Giling/Lineair/Peter Arnold; **219:** © 2006 Banco de Mexico Diego Rivera & Frida Kahlo Museums Trust. Av. Cinco de Mayo No. 2, Col. Centro, Del. Cuauhtemoc 06059, Mexico, D.F. Photo: Schalkwijk/Art Resource; **220:** © Karen Kasmauski/National Geographic Society; **221:** Courtesy, Richard Yerkes and Nisha Patel; **224:** © John Isaac/Still Pictures/Peter Arnold

CHAPTER 11

228: © Michael Freeman/IPN Stock; **231:** Courtesy, PYIFA Expedition, University of Pennsylvania, Yale University, Institute of Fine Arts, New York University; **234:** © Roger Wood/Corbis; **236:** © Ancient Art and Architecture Collection Ltd./Bridgeman Art Library; **238:** © Robert Grossman; **239:** © Heinz Plenge/Peter Arnold; **240:** © Erich Lessing/Art Resource; **241:** © Barry Iverson/Woodfin Camp & Associates; **242:** © Georg Gerster/Photo Researchers; **243:** © Freer Gallery of Art/Arthur M. Sackler Gallery, Smithsonian Institution; **244:** Achterberg, JT (2002) "The Akhenaten Temple Project." In Kottak, Conrad Phillip, *Anthropology: The Exploration of Human Diversity*, 9th ed., 260. Boston : McGraw Hill.; **246:** © Robert Frerck/Odyssey Productions; **247:** © PhotoFest; **248** (*top*): © Jacques Jangoux/Peter Arnold; **248** (**bottom**): © Scala/Art Resource; **249:** © F. Stuart Westmorland/Photo Researchers; **253:** © Roger Green, Anthropology Photo-graphic Archive, University of Auckand; **255:** © Gianni Dagli Orti/Corbis; **256** (*left*): © Gonzalez/laif/Aurora Photos; **256** (*right*): © Albrecht G. Schaefer/Corbis Images

CHAPTER 12

258: © Michael Doolittle/The Image Works; **261:** © Photos 12/Polaris; **263:** © AP/Wide World Photos; **264:** © Michael Newman/PhotoEdit; **265:** © Peggy & Yoran Kahana/Peter Arnold; **266:** © Lawrence Migdale/Photo Researchers; **267:** © British Library of Political & Economics Science/London School of Economics and Political Science; **270:** © Christopher M. O'Leary; **271:** © Mark Edwards/Still Pictures/Peter Arnold; **272:** © John Maier/Peter Arnold; **273:** Courtesy, Angela C. Stuesse

CHAPTER 13

278: Courtesy, Kenneth Garrett; **281:** © Bolante Anthony/Corbis Images; **283:** © Jed Jacobsohn/Getty Images; **285** (*left*): © Jason Homa/Getty Images; **285** (*right*): © Ted Spiegel/Corbis Images; **286** (*left*): © William Gottlieb/Corbis; **286** (*right*): © Jamie Rose/Aurora; **287:** © Sean Sprague/Image Works; **289:** © Joao Silva/PIcturenet Africa; **291** (*top*): © Hideo Haga/Image Works; **291** (*bottom*): © Carl D. Walsh/Aurora Photos; **292:** © Barry Iverson; **293:** Courtesy, Mark Dennis

CHAPTER 14

298: © Sidali Djenidi/Gamma Presse; **302:** © Werner Forman/Corbis; **304:** © T. Arruza/Image Works; **305:** © Ronald Martinez/Getty Images; **307:** Gretchen M. Haupt; **309:** © PJ. Griffiths/Magnum Photos; **311** (*all*): Conrad P. Kottak; **312:** © Mary Ann Chatain/AP/Wide World Photos; **315:** ICTY, Via APTN (Television)/AP Photo; **316:** © Mark Edwards/Peter Arnold; **317:** © Alain Buu/Gamma Presse; **318:** © Michael Ainsworth/Dallas Morning News/Corbis; **319:** © Thomas Grabka/Laif/Redux; **320** (*left*): © Bradley Mayhew/Lonely Planet Images; **320** (*right*): © Yuri Kochetkov/Epa/Corbis

CHAPTER 15

326: © Stuart Franklin/Magnum Photos; **328:** © Michael Nichols/Magnum Photos; **329:** © Hector Amezcua/The Sacramento Bee/ZUMA Press; **331:** © Michael Nichols/National Geographic Society; **333:** © David William Hamilton; **335:** © Lonny Shavelson; **337:** © Ira Block/National Geographic Image Collection; **338:** © Vincent Laforet/New York Times Pictures; **340:** © PhotoFest; **341:** © Jim Goldberg/Magnum Photos; **343:** Gary Hershorn/Reuters/Corbis; **345:** Courtesy, Jason A. DeCaro; **346:** © Photos 12/Polaris; **350:** © Rod Macivor/AP/Wide World Photos; **351:** © Reuters/Corbis; **352:** © Andre Forget/AP/Wide World Photos

CHAPTER 16

354: © Max Galli/laif/Redux; **357:** © B.C. Alexander/Photo Researchers; **360:** Courtesy, Jennifer A. Kelly; **361:** © Georg Gerster/Photo Researchers; **362:** © D. Halleux/BIOS/Peter Arnold; **364:** © Paul Chesley/Getty Images; **365** (*top*): © Bruno Barbey/Magnum Photos; **365** (*center*): © H. Schwarzbach/Argus Fotoarchiv/Peter Arnold; **367:** © David Austen/Woodfin Camp & Associates; **369:** © Darcy Padilla/Redux; **371:** © Carl D. Walsh/Aurora; **373:** © John Eastcott/Yva Momatiuk/Woodfin Camp & Associates; **376** (*top*): © American Museum of Natural History, Neg# 336116; **376** (*center*): © Lawrence Migdale/Stock Boston

CHAPTER 17

380: © Christain Hartmann/Epa/Corbis; **382:** © Sarah Leen/National Geographic Image Collection; **383:** © Abbas/Magnum Photos; **385:** © Joy Tessman/National Geographic Society; **389:** © Burt Glinn/Magnum Photos; **391:** © Library of Congress (LC-USZC2-3231); **393:** © Douglas Kirkland; **394:** Courtesy, Abrigail Dreibelbis; **395:** Michael Schneps; **396:** © John A. Novak/Animals Animals; **397** (top): © James Davis/Eye Ubiquitous/Corbis Images; **397** (bottom): © Greg Ruffing/Getty Images; **399:** © Catherine Karnow/Woodfin Camp & Associates; **400:** © Renzo Gostoli/AP/Wide World Photos; **402:** © Nicholas C. Kottak

CHAPTER 18

408: © Julio Donoso/Woodfin Camp & Associates; **410:** © Eastcott-Momatiuk/The Image Works; **411:** © Stephen Beckerman/Pennsylvania State University; **412:** © Reuters/Str Old; **413:** © Caleb Kenna/IPN Stock; **414:** © Najlah Feanny/Stock Boston; **419** (top): © Ognen Teofilovski/Reuters; **419** (bottom): © D.H. Hessell/Stock Boston; **422:** © Larry Williams/Corbis Images

CHAPTER 19

430: © Danny Zhan/AP/WideWorld Photos; **433:** © AFP/Getty Images; **435:** © Mark Edwards/Still Photos/Peter Arnold; **436:** Kenneth Garrett; **437:** © DPA/Image Works; **439:** © Pablo Bartholomew/Getty Images; **440:** © National Pictures/Topham/The Image Works; **441:** © James Marshall/Image Works; **442:** Courtesy, Kim Shah; **443:** © Cary Wolinsky/Stock Boston; **448:** © Earl & Nazima Kowall/Corbis Images

CHAPTER 20

454: © Jodi Cobb/National Geographic Image Collection; **456:** Ziva Santop; **457:** © Lindsay Hebberd/Corbis Images; **460:** © Amit Dave/Reuters/Corbis; **462:** © Bryan & Cherry Alexander/Arctic Photo; **463** (top): © Wendy Stone; **463** (bottom): © Stuart Franklin/Magnum Photos; **465** (top): © David Allan Harvey/Magnum Photos; **465** (bottom): © George Holton/Photo Researchers; **467:** © Martha Cooper/Peter Arnold; **469:** © National Archives; **472:** "Memories of Rio de Janeiro"; **478:** © John Bigelow Taylor/Art Resource; **478:** John Bigelow Taylor/Art Resource and ARS, NY; **480** (top): © David Alan Harvey/Magnum Photos; **480** (bottom): © Mountain Light Photography/Odyssey/Chicago; **481:** © Stephen Saks/Lonely Planet

CHAPTER 21

482: © R. Giling/Peter Arnold; **485:** © M. and E. Bernheim/Woodfin Camp & Associates; **486:** © Erich Lessing/Art Resource; **487:** © Rick Silva/AP/Wide World Photos; **488:** © Peter Essick/Aurora Photos; **490** (top): © Thierry Secretan/COSMOS/Woodfin Camp & Associates; **490** (bottom): © Joe McNally/IPNstock.com; **491:** © Michele Burgess; **493:** Courtesy, Charlie Graham; **494:** © Sara Terry/Polaris; **496:** © National Anthropological Archives. Neg.#85-8666; **500:** © Kal Muller/Woodfin Camp & Associates; **501:** © Robert Nickelsberg/Getty Images

CHAPTER 22

506: © Robert Fried Photography; **508:** © Gilles Peress/Magnum Photos; **509:** © The Kobal Collection/ABC-TV/Getty Images; **511:** © David Berkwitz/Polaris; **514:** © John Moss/Photo Researchers; **516:** © James P. Blair/National Geographic Image Collection; **517:** © Robert Frerck; **519** (top): © Stephanie Maze/Woodfin Camp & Associates; **519** (bottom): © Yva Momatiuk & John Eastcott/Woodfin Camp & Associates; **522:** © James P. Blair/National Geographic Image Collection; **523:** © Inge Yspeert/Corbis Images; **524:** © Joan Marcus

CHAPTER 23

528: © Chris Stowers/Panos; **530:** © Hu Sheng/epa/Corbis; **531:** © Archives Charmet/Bridgeman Art Library; **533** (top): © Bruce Dale/National Geographic Image Collection; **533** (bottom): © David Reed; **535:** © ARPL/Topham/Image Works; **536** (top): © Michael Nichols/National Geographic Image Collection; **536** (bottom): © Culver Pictures; **539:** MinBuZa/Peter Arnold; **540:** © The New York Public Library/Art Resource, NY; **543:** Robin Nelson/PhotoEdit, Inc.; **544:** © V. Leloup/Gamma Press

CHAPTER 24

548: © Mark Edwards/Still Pictures/Peter Arnold; **551:** © Rob Huibers/Panos Pictures; **553:** © Hulton Archive/Getty Images; **555:** © Stuart Franklin/Magnum Photos; **557** (top): © Bettmann/Corbis Images; **557** (bottom): © Denis Sinyakov/AFP/Getty Images; **561:** © Alexander Low/Woodfin Camp & Associates; **562:** © Jorgen Schytte/Still Pictures/Peter Arnold; **563:** © J.L. Dugast/Lineair/Peter Arnold; **565:** © Noorani/Still Pictures/Peter Arnold; **566:** © Dr. Steven Lansing

CHAPTER 25

570: © S. Nagendra/Photo Researchers; **572:** United States Holocaust Memorial Museum, Courtesy of National Archives; **573:** © Jodi Cobbs/National Geographic Image Collection; **574:** © Gueorgui Pinkhassov/Magnum Photos; **577:** © Steven Feld; **579:** © Buu Deville Turpin/Gamma Presse; **581:** © Andres Hernandez/Getty Images; **582** (top): © Julio Etchart/Peter Arnold; **582** (bottom): © Christopher Morris; **583:** © Peter Marlow/Magnum Photos; **584:** © Ricardo Funari; **586:** © Jose Luis Quintana/Reuters/Corbis; **587:** Jessica Nelson; **591:** © AP/Wide World Photos; **592:** © Francis Dean/Image Works; **593:** © Mohamed Azakir/Reuters/Landov

Text and Illustration Credits

FRONT MATTER

xl-xli: From *Student Atlas of World Geography*, Third Edition, by John L. Allen. Copyright © 2003 by The McGraw-Hill Companies, Inc. Reprinted by permission of McGraw-Hill/Dushkin, a division of The McGraw-Hill Companies, Guilford, CT 06437.

CHAPTER 1

5-6: Excerpts from Marc Lacey, "Remote and Poked, Anthropology's Dream Tribe," *New York Times*, December 18, 2005, section 1, p. 1. Copyright © 2005 by The New York Times Co. Reprinted with permission.

CHAPTER 2

25-26: Excerpts from John Schwartz, "Archaeologist in New Orleans Finds a Way to Help the Living," *New York Times*, January 3, 2006, pp. F1, F4. Copyright © 2006 by The New York Times Co. Reprinted with permission. **38:** Del Jones, "Hot Asset in Corporate: Anthropology Degrees," *USA Today*, February 18, 1999, p. B1. Copyright © 1999 USA TODAY. Reprinted with permission.

CHAPTER 14

301-2: Excerpts from Lydia Polgreen, "Ghana's Uneasy Embrace of Slavery's Diaspora," *New York Times*, December 27, 2005. Copyright © 2005 by The New York Times Co. Reprinted with permission.

CHAPTER 15

329-30: T. R. Reid, "Spanish at School Translates to Suspension," *Washington Post*, December 9, 2005, p. A03. © 2005, The Washington Post, reprinted with permission. **334:** Figure 15.1, from *Aspects of Language*, 3rd edition by Dwight Bolinger and Donald A. Sears. © 1981. Reprinted with permission of Heinle, a division of Thomson Learning: www.thomsonrights.com. Fax 800 730-2215. **339:** Table 15.3, from *Sociolinguistics: An Introduction to Language and Society* by Peter Trudgill (Penguin Books, 1974. Revised Edition 1983). Copyright © Peter Trudgill 1974, 1983. Reproduced by permission of Penguin Books Ltd.

CHAPTER 16

357-58: Excerpts from Warren Hoge, "Kautokeino Journal; Reindeer Herders, at Home on a (Very Cold) Range," *New York Times*, March 26, 2001, section A, p. 4. Copyright © 2001 by The New York Times Co. Reprinted with permission. **359:** Figure 16.1, adaptation of key and map by Ray Sim from *Encyclopedia of Humankind: People of the Stone Age.* © Weldon Owen Pty Ltd. Used with permission.

CHAPTER 17

383-84: Ilene R. Prusher, "Chat Rooms, Bedouin Style." Excerpted with permission from the April 26, 2000 issue of *The Christian Science Monitor* (www.csmonitor.com). © 2000 The Christian Science Monitor. All rights reserved.

CHAPTER 18

411-12: Excerpts from Patrick Wilson, "When Are Two Dads Better Than One? When the Women Are in Charge," http://alphagalileo.org (June 12, 2002). Reprinted by permission of the University of East London, UK.

CHAPTER 19

433-34: Excerpts from Marc Lacey, "Nairobi Journal; Is Polygamy Confusing, or Just a Matter of Family Values?" *New York Times*, December 16, 2003, section A, p. 4. Copyright © 2003 by The New York Times Co. Reprinted with permission. **444-45:** Excerpts from Daniel Goleman, "Anthropology Goes Looking in All the Old Places," *New York Times*, November 24, 1992, p. B1. Copyright © 1992 by The New York Times Co. Reprinted with permission.

CHAPTER 20

457-58: Excerpts from Pam Kosty, "Indonesia's Matriarchal Minangkabau Offer an Alternative Social System," http://www.eurekalert.org (May 9, 2002). Reprinted by permission of the University of Pennsylvania Museum of Archaeology and Anthropology.

CHAPTER 21

485-86: Excerpts from Brian Handwerk, "Islam Expanding Globally, Adapting Locally," *National Geographic News*, October 24, 2003. http://news.nationalgeographic.com. © 2003 National Geographic Society. Reprinted with permis-sion. **489:** Table 21.1, reprinted with permission from Victor W. Turner, *The Ritual Process: Structure and Anti-Structure* (New York: Aldine de Gruyter). Copyright © 1995 by Walter de Gruyter, Inc. **498:** Table 21.3, reprinted by permission of Preston Hunter, www.adherents.com. **498:** Figure 21.3, reprinted by permission of Preston Hunter, www.adherents.com. **499:** Table 21.4, reprinted by permission of Preston Hunter, www.adherents.com.

CHAPTER 22

509-10: Excerpts from Charles McGrath, "In Fiction, a Long History of Fixation on the Social Gap," *New York Times*, June 8, 2005, Final, Section E, p. 1. Copyright © 2005 by The New York Times Co. Reprinted with permission.

CHAPTER 23

531-32: Excerpts from Jack Lucentini, "Bones Reveal Some Truth in 'Noble Savage Myth'," *Washington Post*, April 15, 2002, p. A09. Reprinted by permission of Jack Lucentini. **541:** Table 23.1, from *An Introduction to the World-System Perspective*, 2nd ed. by Thomas Shannon. Copyright © 1989, 1996 by Westview Press. Reprinted by permission of Westview Press, a member of Perseus Books, L.L.C. **544:** Table 23.2, from John H. Bodley, *Anthropology and Contemporary Human Problems*. Mayfield Publishing. Copyright © 1985 by The McGraw-Hill Companies, Inc. Reprinted with permission.

CHAPTER 24

550: Figure 24.1, from the *Academic American Encyclopedia*, Vol. 3, p. 496. 1998 Edition. Copyright © 1998 by Grolier Incorporated. Reprinted with permission. **551-52:** Excerpts from John Roach, "Prediction Tool Puts Development in Hands of Locals," *National Geographic News*, March 24, 2004. http://news.nationalgeographic.com. © 2004 National Geographic Society. Reprinted with permission. **553:** Figure 24.2, from the *Academic American Encyclopedia*, Vol. 8, p. 309. 1998 Edition. Copyright © 1998 by Grolier Incorporated. Reprinted with permission.

CHAPTER 25

573-74: Excerpts from Stefan Lovgren, "Cultural Diversity Highest in Resource-Rich Areas, Study Says," *National Geographic News*, March 17, 2004. http://news.nationalgeographic.com. © 2004 National Geographic Society. Reprinted with permission. **580:** Excerpts from John Noble Wilford, "In a Publishing Coup, Books in 'Unwritten' Languages," *New York Times*, December 31, 1991, pp. B5, B6. Copyright © 1991 by The New York Times Co. Reprinted with permission.

APPENDIX 2

A11-A13: AAA Code of Ethics. Adapted from http://www.aaanet.org/committees/ethics/ethcode.htm. With permission of the American Anthropological Association.

APPENDIX 3

A16-A18: Adapted from *Prime-Time Society: An Anthropological Analysis of Television and Culture*, 1st edition, by Conrad Phillip Kottak. © 1990. Reprinted with permission of Wadsworth, a division of Thomson Learning: www.thomsonrights.com. Fax 800 730-2215.

Name Index

Gamble, C., 195, 198, 227
Garawale, K., 5
Garcia, A., 556
Garciaparra, N., 487
Gardner, B., 330
Gardner, R. A., 330
Garey, A. J., 427
Gargan, E. A., 539
Gates, C., 234
Gates, H. L. Jr., 301–302
Gebauer, A. B., 227
Geertz, C., 20, 267, 280, 295
Geis, M. L., 328, 338, 342, 348
Gellner, E., 323
Geschiere, 584, 585
Gezon, L. L., 48
Gibbons, A., 256
Gibson, B., 406
Gibson, M., 240
Giddens, A., 536
Gilad, Y., 114
Gillespie, J. H., 74, 82
Gilmore, D. D., 401, 456
Gilmore-Lehne, W. J., 240
Giuliani, R., 517
Gledhill, J., 381, 406
Gmelch, G., 31, 40, 488
Goddard, Dr., 261
Goldberg, P., 60
Goodale, J. C., 451, 522
Goodall, J., 111, 118, 121, 123, 126
Goody, J., 451
Gordon, D. A., 476
Gorman, C. F., 282
Gottdiener, M., 589
Gough, E. K., 413
Gough, K., 419
Gould, S. J., 67, 79, 82
Gowlett, J. A. J., 235, 241, 242, 243
Graham, L. C., 491–493
Gramsci, A., 400, 405
Grasmuck, S., 581
Gray, J., 580
Gray, J. P., 123
Greaves, T. C., 289
Green, E. C., 216
Green, G., 35, 48, 129
Greenwood, D. J., 480
Grekova, M., 558
Griffin, P. B., 462
Griffiths, J., 554
Gudeman, S., 378
Gugliotta, G., 137, 147, 148, 181, 184, 196
Gupta, A., 270, 275, 287, 295
Gwynne, M. A., 40

H

Haapala, A., 513
Hackett, R. I. J., 512
Hagen, E. H., 171
Haggerson, A., 523
Haile-Selassie, Y., 155
Hall, E. T., 295
Hallowell, I., 436
Ham, S., 111
Handel, G. F., 510
Handwerk, B., 485–486
Hannenhalli, S., 65
Hansen, K. V., 427
Harcourt, A. H., 117
Harder, 144
Harding, S., 466
Harlan, J. R., 209

Harris, M., 20, 305, 310, 323, 373, 462, 491
Harrison, G. G., 11
Hart, C. W. M., 448
Hart, D., 307
Hart, M., 576–577
Hartl, D. L., 74, 82
Hartley, J., 579, 589
Harvati, K., 176
Harvey, D. J., 553
Hassig, R., 249
Hatcher, E. P., 525
Haugerud, A., 556
Haupt, G. M., 307
Haussler, D., 66
Hauter, 306
Hawkes, K., 358
Hawks, J., 148
Hawley, J. S., 443
Hayden, B., 205
Hayes, R., 576
Hearn, J., 476
Hedges, C., 576
Heider, K. G., 406
Helman, C., 32
Henry, D., 209
Henry, J., 29
Henshilwood, C., 514
Herbert, R., 345
Herdt, G., 471, 474
Herrnstein, R., 311
Herskovits, M., 292, 571
Heyerdahl, T., 246, 253
Heyneman, D., 33
Hicks, D., 504
Hill, C. E., 332
Hill, K., 358
Hill-Burnett, J., 29
Hilton, P., 510
Himmelgreen, D., 36
Hinde, R. A., 115
Hitler, A., 91
Hobhouse, L. T., 437
Hobwbawm, E. J., 323
Hocevar, J., 282
Hoebel, E. A., 386
Hoge, W., 357
Hole, F., 209
Holland, D., 111
Holliday, V. T., 60
Holtzman, J., 32, 40
Hooker, R., 243
Hoover, K., 492
Hopkins, T. K., 537
Horton, R., 487, 512
Howard, C., 141
Hrdy, S. B., 150
Hughes, W. W., 11

I

Ingold, T., 378
Ingraham, C., 451
Inhorn, M. C., 33
Isaac, G. L., 192

J

Jablonski, N., 525
Jackson, J., 584, 586
James, J., 144
Jankowiak, W., 444
Jasim, S. A., 239
Jeanne-Claude, 511
Jenkins, L., 335
Jenks, C., 287

Jensen, A., 311
Jesus, 499
Johansen, B. E., 589
Johanson, D., 158, 159, 166–167, 171
John, E., 440
John, Saint, 578
Johnson, A. W., 268, 393
Johnson, G. A., 248
Jolly, C. J., 134, 167, 183, 210, 214, 224
Jones, D., 38, 269
Jones, E. W., 82
Jones, V., 414
Joralemon, D., 32, 41
Jordan, A., 35
Joyce, R. A., 252
Julius Caesar, 550
Jurmain, R., 60, 136

K

Kan, S., 374
Kaobawa, 388
Kardulias, P. N., 546
Katzenberg, M. A., 49
Kearney, M., 372, 378, 546
Keim, C. A., 511
Keller, S., 470
Kelly, J. A., 360
Kelly, R. C., 406, 473
Kelly, R. L., 366, 378
Kemp, T. S., 150
Kent, S., 356, 359, 373, 378, 385
Kenyatta, J., 434
Kershaw, S., 281–282
Keynes, J.M., 556
Kibaki, L., 433
Kibaki, M., 433–434
Kibaki, W., 433–434
Kilcher, G., 261
Kilgore, L., 60
Kimani, D.K., 434
Kimbel, W. H., 150
Kimeu, K., 177
Kimmel, M., 476
King, R., 318
Kinsey, A. C., 471
Kipling, R., 552
Kirch, P., 256, 395, 406
Kirman, P., 514
Klass, M., 504
Klein, R. G., 198
Kleinfeld, J., 29
Klimek, D. E., 285
Kluckhohn, C., 15, 295
Knecht, H. A., 198
Kohler, M., 145, 150
Kopytoff, V. G., 122
Koss, D., 522
Koss, M., 38
Kostinica, V., 315
Kottak, I. W., 269
Kottak, N., 399, 403, 419
Kowalewski, S. A., 251
Kozaitis, K. A., 316, 471
Krauss, M. E., 580
Kretchmer, N., 99
Krick, S. V., 592
Kroc, R., 591
Kroeber, A. L., 295
Kronk, L., 442
Kryshtanovskaya, O., 559
Kuniholm, P., 58
Kuper, L., 304, 318
Kurtz, D. V., 381, 406
Kutsche, P., 275

Peletz, M., 464
Pelto, G. H., 275
Pelto, P. J., 275, 358
Pepper, B., 446
Perlman, D., 150
Pessar, P., 581
Peter, Saint, 578
Peters, J. D., 270
Peterson, C., 123
Petraglia-Bahri, D.,554, 555
Petrie, W. F., 232
Pettifor, E., 144
Pevzner, Dr., 65, 66
Phipps, S. G., 305
Piazza, A., 82
Picasso, P., 508, 513, 517
Pickford, M., 148
Pickrell, J., 117, 118
Piddocke, S., 375
Pike-Tay, A., 198
Pilling, A. R., 451
Pizzaro, F., 247
Plante, R., 476
Plattner, S., 378
Plotnicov, L., 444
Pocahontas, 262
Podolefsky, A., 11, 20
Poirier, F. E., 171
Polanyi, K., 372
Polgreen, L., 301
Pollan, M., 591, 592
Pollock, S., 252
Pomeroy, W. B., 471
Pospisil, L., 388
Potash, B., 446
Powhatan, 261
Prag, J., 50, 60
Price, T. D., 212, 227
Provost, C., 459, 460
Prusher, I. R., 383–384

R

Rabe, J., 424
Radcliffe-Brown, A. R., 427, 488, 491
Ragone, H., 476
Rakoto, 265
Random House College Dictionary, 508
Rappaport, R. A., 488, 505
Rathje, W. L., 11
Rathus, S. A., 474, 476
Raybeck, D., 403
Read, A. P., 74
Reagan, R., 342
Redfield, R., 31, 292, 571
Redford, D., 244
Reed, R., 589
Reichs, K., 28, 45–46
Reid, T. R., 329–330
Reinoso, V.A., 329
Reiter, R., 466, 476
Relethford, J. H., 171
Renfrew, C., 60, 227
Reynolds, R. G., 217
Riches, D., 378
Richie, N., 510
Rickford, J. R., 338, 339, 342, 348
Rickford, R.J., 348
Rightmire, G. P., 181, 198
Rilling, J., 50
Rimpau, J. B., 332
Rindos, D., 227
Roach, J., 551–552
Robbins, R., 589
Roberts, D. F., 98, 101, 120

Robertson, 560
Robertson, J., 308, 309
Rockwell, R. C., 34
Rodseth, L., 115, 436
Roeper, T., 335
Rogers, C., 105–106
Romaine, S., 348
Roosevelt, F. D., 556
Root, D., 526, 581, 589
Rosaldo, M., 456, 458, 476
Roscoe, W., 451, 473
Rose, K., 137–138
Rose, M. D., 146, 150
Rose, N., 282
Rosen-Ayalon, M., 476
Rosenberg, K., 50, 51
Roth, B. J., 198
Rouse, R., 581
Roxo, G., 13
Rubio, L., 330
Rubio, Z., 329
Rudes, B. A., 261–262
Russell, D., 436
Russon, A. E., 127
Ryan, S., 300, 318, 319, 323

S

Sabater-Pi, J., 117
Sahlins, M. D., 224, 373, 378
Salvador, R. J., 227
Salzman, P. C., 366, 378, 379, 392
Salzmann, Z., 348
Sanday, P. R., 457–458, 461
Sanders, W., 249
Santley, R. S., 249
Sapir, E., 336
Sargent, C. F., 41, 456, 476
Saunders, S. R., 49, 60
Savage-Rumbaugh, S., 121
Saveri, A., 37
Savishinsky, J., 403
Schaik, C. von, 105–106, 117
Schaller, G., 117
Scheidel, W., 436
Scheinman, 550
Schild, R., 212
Schildkrout, E., 511
Schlee, G., 314, 323
Schneider, A. L., 217
Schneider, B., 276
Schneider, D. M., 419
Schwartz, J., 25
Schwarzenegger, A., 330
Schweingruber, F. H., 58
Scott, J., 47, 48, 400, 405, 589
Scudder, T., 268
Scupin, R., 304, 323
Sebeok, T. A., 332
Selassie, H., 6
Sengupta, S., 129
Senut, B., 148
Service, E., 373, 382–383
Service, E. R., 406
Seyfarth, R. M., 115
Shah, A. K., 442
Shakespeare, W., 522
Shanklin, E., 101, 304
Shannon, T. R., 537, 546
Sharer, R., 227
Sheets, P., 47, 48
Shelton, A., 525
Shepher, J., 437, 451
Shermer, M., 67, 82
Shilling, J., 551–552

Shimizu, A., 568
Shivaram, C., 413
Shoepfle, G. M., 275
Shore, B., 16
Shostak, M., 268
Shreeve, J., 57, 186
Shriver, M., 94
Silberbauer, G., 385
Silverberg, J., 123
Silverman, S., 381, 406, 547
Simons, E. L., 144
Simpson, B., 451
Singer, M., 33, 34
Sinnott, M. J., 476
Slade, M. F., 285
Small, M. F., 127
Smith, A., 555, 556
Smith, B. D., 209, 211, 214, 215, 218, 227
Smith, H. J. H., 364, 379
Smith, J., 261
Smitherman, G., 342
Smuts, B. B., 127
Snow, C., 46
Soffer, O., 525
Solheim, W. G., II, 214
Solway, J., 358, 461
Sones, D., 282
Sophocles, 523
Spears, B., 510
Spindler, G. D., 29, 41
Spindler, L., 41
Spiro, M., 16
Spradley, J. P., 275
Srivastava, J., 364, 379
Stacey, J., 427
Stack, C. B., 414, 416
Stahl, P., 169
Stanford, C., 122, 127
Stanish, C., 531
Stark, R., 502
Statistical Abstract of the United
    States, 468
Statistics Canada, 308, 352
Stearman, K., 309
Steckel, R. H., 531
Steegman, A. T., Jr., 98
Stein, P. L., 505
Stein, R. L., 505
Steinfels, P., 502
Stephens, W. R., 41
Stevens, W. K., 31, 561
Stevenson, D., 41, 233
Stewart, P. J., 32, 41
Stoler, A., 458, 563, 564
Stone, A., 189
Stone, L., 427
Stoneking, M., 58, 188, 189, 256
Strachan, T., 74
Strachey, W., 261
Strathern, A., 32, 41
Stratmann, D., 525
Strier, K. B., 127
Stringer, C., 55, 184
Strong, P. T., 586
Strum, S. C., 127
Stuesse, A. C., 273
Suchman, L., 37
Suharto, President of Indonesia, 562
Sukarno, President of Indonesia, 562
Sunstein, B. S., 275
Susman, R. L., 118
Susser, I., 33, 34
Sussman, R., 129, 136
Sussman, R. W., 48

Subject Index

American Association of Physical
    Anthropologists, 531
"American Tragedy" (Dreiser), 509
Analogies, 106–107, 126
Anatomically modern humans
    (AMHs)
    African origin of, 188–190
    art and, 514
    body ornamentation and, 201–203
    body weight, 162
    brain size, 162, 201
    cave art, 193–195
    dating of, 58, 162, 175
    description of, 197
    Homo floresiensis, 196
    mitochondrial DNA (mtDNA), 188
    multiregional evolution of, 190–191,
        198, 200
    Neandertals and, 186–189
    symbolic thought and, 200, 203
    tools and, 191–193
ANC. *See* African National Congress
    (ANC)
Anemia, 129, 249
Angiosperms, 136
Animal domestication, *See also* Food
    production; specific animals
    as adaptive strategy, 363
    broad-spectrum revolution and,
        195–196
    climate and, 209
    difficulty of, 222
    disease and, 95–97
    ease of, 222
    factors in, 220
    food production and, 217
    genetic changes and, 211
Animism, 484, 486, 503
ANNA-T. *See* "Acculturation and
    Nutritional Needs Assessment of
    Tampa" (ANNA–T)
Anosmia, 110
Anthropoids, 108, 110, 112, 126,
    139–140
Anthropology, *See also* specific
    subfields of anthropology
    anthropology and education,
        29–31, 39
    business and, 35, 37
    careers and, 37–39
    as comparative field, 4
    definition of, 3–4, 19
    development of, 262
    dimensions of, 23–27
    and education, 29–31, 39
    general anthropology, 7–9
    as holistic science, 4
    interdisciplinary studies and, 15–16
    psychology and, 16
    as science, 15, 16–17
Anthropometry, 49, 59
Antimodernism, 501, 503
Anxiety control, 487–488
Apartheid, 311, 318, 338–339, 486,
    538–540
Apes, 13, 118–119, *See also* Primates
Apical ancestors, 417
Applied anthropology
    applications of, 27–28
    definition of, 39, 560
    deforestation and, 131
    ethnography and, 29
    growth of, 28–29
    organizational societies for, 27

overview of, 23–27
public policy and, 27–28
Arboreal hypothesis, 135–136, 149
Arboreal primates, 48, 108, 113–118, 126
Arby's, 593
Archaean era, 134
Archaic *H. sapiens*, 183, 197
Archeological anthropology
    applications of, 27
    definition of, 19
    ethics and, 44
    excavation and, 53–54, 59
    kinds of archaeology, 54
    methods and, 46–52
    overview of, 10–11
    pseudo-archaeology, 246–247
    as subfield of anthropology, 5
    systematic survey and, 52–53
    teams and, 52
Ardipithecus, 162
Ardipithecus kadabba, 148, 155, 158
Ardipithecus ramidus, dating of, 135, 158
Arenal volcano, 47
Argentina, 45, 358, 583, 584
Argonauts of the Western Pacific
    (Malinowski), 267
Ariaal people, 5
Aristocracy, 396
Armory Show, 517
Art, 511–512
Art
    body ornamentation, 201–202
    careers in, 522
    catharsis and, 517
    cave art, 176, 179, 193–195, 200–201,
        513–514
    change and, 522–523
    communal art, 512–513
    communication and, 516–517
    culture and, 513–519, 522–524
    definition of, 507, 508, 525
    ethnomusicology, 514–516
    folk art, 514–515
    Greek theater, 523
    impressionism, 513
    individuality and, 512–513, 518
    Olmec art, 246
    overview of, 507–508
    placement of, 511
    politics and, 517–518
    religion and, 508, 510–511, 516
    tradition and, 516
    war art, 239
    Zapotec style, 247
Arts, definition of, 507, 525
Ascribed status, 303, 322
Asexuality, 471
Ashanti people, 436
Asian people, 300
Asphalt, 210
Assault on Paradise (Kottak), 420
Assimilation, 315–316, 319, 322
Attractiveness standards, 8
Australia, 8, 358, 511, 522, 529–530, 586
Australian National University of
    Canberra, 207
Australopithecines, 154, 158, 164–165, 170
Australopithecus, 154, 156, 157
Authority, definition of, 381
Autochthony, 584–585
Awls, 192, 201
Axes, 211
Azande people, 473
Aztecs, 247, 248, 251, 550

B
Baboons, 114–115, 120, 122
Baganda people, 99
Baha'i, 498, 499
Balanced reciprocity, definition of,
    373, 377
Balanced polymorphism, definition
    of, 76, 81
Bali, 519, 522
Bamana people, 507
Bananas, 220, 244
Bands
    definition of, 359, 377, 382
    energy consumption and, 544
    foraging and, 359, 385, 398
    industrialization and, 543
    kinship and, 384, 385
    land and, 368
    manufacturing and, 368
    marriage and, 385
    overview of, 384
Bangladesh, 485, 551
Bantu speakers, 243–245
Barí people, 411
Barley, 211, 213, 215, 220, 222, 240
Bart, 419
Baseball, 487, 488
Basongye people, 515
Basques, 319, 478–481
Basseri people, 239, 366, 392
"BBC English," 339
Beagle, 67
Beans, 215, 218, 222
Bedouins, 5, 383–384
Behavioral ecology, 124, 126, 141
Bell Curve (Murray), 311
Beloit College, 38
Benin, 245
Berdaches, 440, 473, 496
Bergmann's rule, 98, 100
Beringia, 215
Betsileo people
    burial ceremonies, 291
    child fosterage, 424
    descent and, 417
    division of labor and, 466
    ethnographic field work with, 260
    plural marriage and, 448–449
    rice cultivation, 367
    scarcity and, 370–371
    witchcraft and, 494–495
BEV. *See* Black English Vernacular
    (BEV)
Bias, 18
Bible, 64
Bifurcate collateral kinship
    terminology, 425, 426
Bifurcate merging kinship
    terminology, 423–426
"Big men," 386, 388–389, 405, 500, 591
Bigfoot (Sasquatch), 144–145
Bilateral kinship calculation, 421, 426
Bioarchaeology, 47
Biochemical genetics, 70, 72–73, 81
Biocultural, definition of, 8, 19
Biological adaptation, 4, 6–7
Biological anthropology
    applications of, 27
    bone biology and, 49–50, 59
    culture and, 4, 8–9
    definition of, 19
    methods and, 46–52
    overview of, 11–13
    primatology and, 13

Biomechanics, definition of, 49
Biomedical research, 120
Biomedicine, 34
Bipedalism
    A. afarensis and, 160
    definition of, 126, 170
    hominins and, 160–162, 187
    overview of, 154, 165
Birth control, 18
Birthing process, 51, 93, 163, 419
Bisexuality, 471
Bison, 216, 390
Black English Vernacular (BEV),
    30–31, 336, 342–343, 347
"Black skull," 167
Blade tools, 191, 197
Blindness. *See* Sight
Blombos Cave, 201, 513–514
Blondism, 95
Blood, 87–88, 96–99
Blood feuds, 386
Body mass index, 49
Body ornamentation, 201–203
Body size and build, 98
Bolivia, 217, 218, 583, 584
Bone biology, 49–50, 59
Bone tools, 514
Bones, 45
Bonobos, 118, 119, 129
Book of Kells, 346
Borneo, 119, 123
Bosavi People's Fund, 577
Bosnia, 45, 46, 319, 515, 544, 558
Bosnia-Herzegovina, 314–315, 319
Boston University, 6
Botswana, 538–539
Bougainvillians, 95
Bourgeoisie, definition of, 535, 545
Brachiation, 113–116, 126, 140–142
Brain, *See also* Skull
    brain size, 49, 112, 166, 201
    brain-to-body size, 112
    chimpanzee brain size, 162
    cognitive ability and, 200–201
    early hominins and, 156, 162
    H. erectus, 180
    poverty in, 470
    symbolic thought and, 200, 203
    temperature control and, 154–155
Brain complexity, 109
Brazil
    AIDS and, 97
    anthropological studies in, 12
    assimilation in, 316
    author's ethnographic fieldwork
        in, 264
    capoeira and, 523
    Chegança performance and, 577
    deforestation in, 129
    development and, 572, 574
    division of labor in, 460
    environmentalism and, 572
    faith healers in, 492
    family and, 416
    female body perspectives, 8, 9
    foraging and, 358
    indigenous population, 584–586
    kinship in, 420
    malaria spread in, 94
    marriage in, 432
    nonverbal communication in, 333
    Portugal and, 550, 577–578
    race and, 310
    as semiperiphery nation, 532

slavery and, 540, 583
team research in, 269
television in, 291
touching and, 285
transvestitism in, 472
Bridewealth, 433, 441, 443–446, 450
Broad-spectrum revolution, 193, 195,
    205, 206, 210, 226
Bronx Zoo, 48
Bronze, 242, 251
Bronze Age, 208, 241, 242
Brooklyn College, 46
Brooklyn Museum of Art, 517
Bubonic plague, 97
Buddhism, 497, 498, 499, 508
Buganda, 397, 449
Bulgaria, 58, 314
Burakumin, 309–310
Burger King, 593
Burial practices
    burial ceremonies, 291
    burial poles, 522
    cemeteries, 238
    early Middle Eastern states and, 235
    Pharaohs and, 231–232
    religious artifacts and, 25
    socioeconomic hierarchy and,
        231–232, 243
Burins, 192
Burma, 336
Burundi, 99
Business, anthropology applications,
    35, 37
Butchery, 168, 193, 194

C

Caboclo, 585
Cactus fruit, 219
Calendars, 195, 213, 249
Call systems, 328, 330–332, 347
Calorimeter, 49
Cambrian period, 134
Camels, 216, 365
Cameroon, 117, 118
Campesinos, 583
Canada
    Basques and, 479
    Canadian Immigration Act, 351
    childcare and, 460–461
    diversity in culture and language
        in, 350–352
    domestic violence and, 467
    early colonization of, 216
    Employment Equity Act, 308, 352
    energy consumption in, 544
    family and, 415, 421
    female swimmers and, 8
    foraging and, 358
    French colonization of, 553
    pantribal societies in, 390
    race and, 308
    same-sex marriage and, 440
    subcultures and, 287–288
Cancer, 49, 66, 74, 92
Candomblé, 265, 499
Cannibals, 370
Cao Dai, 498
Capital, definition of, 530, 545
Capitalism, 366, 368–371, 372, 497, 558
Capitalist world economy, definition
    of, 530, 545
Capoeira, 523
Caprine farming, 206, 208
Carbon-14 technique, 56, 57

Carboniferous period, 134
Cargo cults, 499–501, 503
Carnaval, 472, 578
Carnegie Museum of Natural
    History, 137
Carnivora, 106
Case Western Reserve University, 87
Cash crops, 530
Cash economies, 368–371
Cassava, 218, 220, 226, 356, 364
Caste systems, 539–540, 545
Castration, 490
Çatal Hüyük, 58, 235–236
Catarrhines, 108, 112–114, 140
Catastrophism, 65, 81
Catharsis, definition of, 517, 525
Cathedrals, 510
Catopithecus, 139
Cats, 222
Cattle
    as bridewealth, 443–444
    cattle rustling, 371, 374, 391
    domestication of, 208, 211–215, 222
    food production and, 363, 365, 367
    as sacred, 491
    temple records and, 241
Cave art, 193–195, 200–201, 513–514
Celebrity, 510
Cell division, 73
Cemeteries, 238
Cenozoic era, 134–135
Center for Ethnographic Research, 38
Central African Republic, 117
Central Park Zoo, 48
Ceremonial funds, 371
Chad, 147, 155
Chalcolithic Age, 241
Chariots of the Gods (von Daniken), 247
Chat rooms, 383–384
Chauvet cave, 176, 200
Chegança performance, 577
Cherokee, 372–373
Chicano, 304
Chickpeas, 222
Chiefdoms
    advanced chiefdoms, 240
    definition of, 251, 382, 384, 405
    development of, 393
    economic systems in, 395, 398
    emergence of, 237, 245–248
    ethnography and, 239–240
    hosting and entertaining in, 240
    industrialization and, 543
    political systems in, 395
    redistribution and, 395
    social ranking, 237–239, 245–248,
        395–397
    states and, 229, 230, 233, 238
Chiefly redistribution, 395
Chile, 216
Chimfunshi Wildlife Orphanage, 111
Chimpanzees
    body weight, 162
    brain size, 162, 166
    as great apes, 115
    as homonids, 107
    incest and, 436
    as meat eaters, 122, 146
    overview of, 118–119
    tools and, 121
China
    anthropoid discoveries in, 139
    Asian factory women, 537
    energy consumption in, 542–544

China (continued)
food production in, 213–214
fossils sold in, 144
H. erectus and, 182
human sacrifice and, 243
Islam and, 485
languages spoken in, 573
Neandertals and, 185–186
primate species discoveries in, 136
Sivapithecus discovered in, 143
states and, 242–243, 393
Zhoukoudian cave site, 181, 183
Chinese traditional religion, 497, 498
Cholera, 97
Choppers, 167
Christianity, 68, 375, 495–499, 501, 575
Chromosomal rearrangement, 74
Chromosomes
definition of, 81
disease and, 66
fusion of, 74
as hereditary unit, 64
history of, 65–66
Chukchee people, 496
CI. *See* Conservation International (CI)
Circumcision, 288, 391
Citicorp, 38
Civil rights, 301
Civil society, 560, 567
Civilization, first civilization, 209
Civilization and Capitalism, 15th–18th Century (Braudel), 530
Clans, 417–418, 426, 559, 560
Class consciousness, definition of, 535
Classical archaeology, 54
Cleveland Museum of Natural History, 155
Climate, 58, 209, 223
Climatologists, 88
Clines, 86, 100
Clitoridectomy, 288
Closed class systems, 539–540
Clothing, 211
Clovis tradition, 216, 226
Codominance, 71
Cold War, 292
Collateral households, 413
Collateral relatives, definition of, 423, 426
Collective liminality, 489–490
College of William & Mary, 26
Colombia, 584
Colonial anthropology, 28
Colonial archaeology, 54
Colonialism
British colonialism, 550, 552
cultural colonialism, 321
definition of, 319, 322, 541, 549, 567
French colonialism, 552–553
identity and, 553–554
imperialism and, 541, 549–550
Indonesia and, 562
overview of, 550
postcolonial, 554–555
race and, 88, 90
Color blindness, 93, 112
Columbia University, 12
Columbia-Cornell-Harvard-Illinois Summer Field Studies Program in Anthropology, 269
Communal religions, 495, 496, 503
Communication and language, *See also* specific languages
accents and, 336

Algonquin language, 261
art and, 516–517
Bantu speakers, 243–245
Basque language, 479
Creole languages, 292, 335, 342
cultural diversity and, 573
culture and, 91
cybercommunication, 345
daughter languages, 344, 347
diglossia and, 339, 347
displacement and, 331, 347
education and, 29–31
focal vocabulary, 337, 347
global communications, 7
historical linguistics, 328, 344–347
kinesics, 333, 347
language defined, 347
language subgroups, 344, 347
linguistic anthropology, 13, 15
lost languages, 261
meaning and, 337–338
missionaries and, 554
nationalities and, 313
nonhuman primate communication, 328, 330–332
nonverbal communication, 328, 332–334, 339
origin of language, 332
overview of, 327–328
pidgin languages, 292, 335
preservations of languages, 580
primates and, 13, 48
productivity and, 331, 347
protolanguages, 344
Sapir-Whorf hypothesis, 335–337, 347
sign language, 330–332
social stratification and, 583
sociolinguistics, 338–343, 347
speech sounds, 334
status position and, 340–342
structure of language, 334–335
symbols and, 283
thought and culture and, 335–338
universal grammar, 335
writing and literacy and, 224, 240–241, 243, 249, 251
Communism, 556–558, 567
Communitas, 489–490, 504
Complex societies, 272, 274
Confessional rituals, 419
Conflict. *See* War and conflict
Confucianism, 497
Congo, 117, 118, 201, 515
Consent, 44, 59, 260
Conservation International (CI), 551
Consumption activities, 10
Contagious magic, 487
Continental drift, 137, 143
Continental shelf, 193
Continental slope, 193
Contract archaeologists, 54
Convention on International Trade in Endangered Species, 119
Convergent evolution, 107, 126
Conversation and ethnography, 264–265
CONVIGUA. *See* National Coordination of Guatemalan Widows (CONVIGUA)
Cooking, 181, 240
Cooperation, 50, 51
Cooperative hunting, 180–181
Cooperatives, 565

Copán, 129, 249, 250
Copper, 210, 221, 241
Copper Age, 221
Copula deletion, 343
Core nations, 532, 537, 541, 545, 572
Core values, definition of, 286, 294
Corn. *See* Maize
Cornell University, 58
Correlation, 359, 361–362, 377
Corruption, 558–560
Costa Rica, 52, 57
Cotton, 530, 533
Cousins, 432, 434
Covenant on Civil and Political Rights (UN), 289
Covenant on Economic, Social and Cultural Rights (UN), 289
Creationism, 64, 68, 81
Creative explosion, 200
Creole languages, 292, 335, 342
Cretaceous period, 134
Crime, 224, 225, 443
Cro-Magnon, 187, 201, 202–203
Croatia, 187, 314, 558
Cross cousins, 432, 437, 450
Crossdating, 58
Crossing over, 73, 81
Crow Indians, 422, 496
Cuba, 550, 556
Cult houses, 512
Cultivation, 362–365, 377
Cultivation continuum, 363–364, 377
Cults, 490, 499–501, 512
Cultural anthropology
applications of, 27
definition of, 7, 19
deforestation and, 128
educational research and, 29–30
overview of, 9–10
sociology and, 15–16
studies focus of, 7–8
Cultural colonialism, 321
Cultural consultants, 265–266, 274
Cultural exchange
acculturation and, 571–572
contact and domination and, 572, 574–578
indigenous peoples and, 582–587
popular culture and, 578–579
religious change and, 575–576
remaking culture, 578–581
text and, 578, 588
Cultural imperialism, 576–578, 588
Cultural relativism, 288, 294
Cultural resource management (CRM), 28, 39, 53, 54
Cultural rights, definition of, 289, 294
Cultural transmission, 331, 347
Culture
acculturation, 292, 294, 499, 571–572
adaptation and, 4, 7, 286
as all-encompassing, 284
art and, 513–519, 522–524
attractiveness standards and, 8
biology and, 4, 8–9
body effected by, 8
concept of, 279–280, 282–283, 286
consumption activities, 10
cultural change mechanisms, 292
cultural relativism, 288, 294
cultural transmission, 331, 347
culture clashes, 281–282
definition of, 4, 19
diffusion, 287, 290, 291, 292, 294

enculturation, 279, 280, 282, 294
ethnocentrism and, 27, 285, 288, 294
ethnography and, 270–271
expressive culture, 507, 525
folklore and, 293
generality and, 290–291, 294
globalization and, 292–294
independent invention and, 292, 294
individuality and, 284, 286–287
as integrated, 284, 286
international culture, 287, 295
language and, 91
as learned, 280
levels of, 287–288
as maladaptive, 286
national culture, 287, 295
nature and, 283–284
overview of, 280
particularity and, 291, 295
personal space and, 280, 285
popular culture, 509–510, 578–579, 585
propriety and, 8
race and, 7
as shared, 280, 282
subcultures, 287–288, 295, 350
symbols and, 280, 282–283, 287, 295
text and, 578, 588
universal traits and, 290, 295
Cultures of Multiple Fathers: The Theory and Practice of Partible Paternity in Lowland South America (Beckerman and Valentine), 411
Cuneiform writing, 241, 251
Curers, 34–35, 39
Cybercommunication, 345
Cyprus, 58
Cyrillic alphabet, 314
Cytoplasm, 72

D

Dance, 516, 522, 523
Dating techniques
  absolute dating, 56–57, 59
  carbon-14 technique, 56, 57
  fluorine absorption analysis, 56
  "genetic clock" and, 52, 58
  multidisciplinary approaches, 47
  overview of, 55
  radiocarbon dating, 175
  relative dating, 55–56, 59
  stratigraphy and, 55
Daughter languages, 344, 347
Death. *See* Afterlife; Burial
Deer, 219
Deforestation
  conservation strategies and, 575
  endangered species and, 48–49, 119–120
  food production and, 128–131, 225, 364
  state collapse and, 249
Democratic Republic of Congo (DRC), 118, 119, 129
Demonstrated descent, 417
Dendrochronology, 57–58, 59
Dentition
  of *A. afarensis,* 160
  of *A. robustus,* 154
  comparisons of ape, human, and *A. afarensis,* 161
  dental comb, 139
  diet and, 136, 143, 165, 173

early hominins and, 156–157, 164, 166–167
food production and, 224, 225
of *Homo,* 165
isotopes and, 208
KNM-ER 1470 teeth, 174
lophs and, 142
monkeys and, 114
natural selection and, 179
of, *A. africanus,* 154
of oligocene anthropoids, 140
primate evolution and, 139, 142, 143, 148
Proconsul group and, 141
Depth perception, 110, 112
Derived traits, 142
Descent
  ambilineal descent, 418, 426
  clans and, 417–418
  definition of, 322
  demonstrated descent, 417
  development and, 566
  descent groups, 416–417, 426
  ego and, 419, 421, 422, 426, 434
  family versus, 417–418
  lineages and, 417–418
  local descent groups, 417
  matrilineal descent, 402, 416–417, 426
  moiety and, 432, 434
  patrilineal descent, 417, 427
  race and, 305
  stipulated descent, 417
  unilineal descent, 417, 427, 434
Descent groups, 386, 416–417, 426
Descriptive linguistics, 334
Development
  civil society and, 560
  communism and, 556–558
  corruption and, 558–560
  descent-groups and, 566
  developmental anthropology and, 560–563, 567
  environmentalism and, 561–563, 572, 574–575
  equity and, 563, 567
  greening of Java, 561–563
  innovation strategies, 563–566
  intervention philosophy and, 555, 568
  neoliberalism and, 555–556, 568
  overinnovation, 564–565, 568
  overview of, 555
  privatization, 557
  Second World and, 556–560
  Third World models, 565–566
  underdifferentiation, 565, 568
Developmental anthropology, 560–563, 567
Devonian period, 134
Diabetes, 93
Diaries, 264
Diaspora
  African diaspora, 301, 313, 583
  Basque diaspora, 478
  definition of, 581, 588
  media and, 581
  slavery and, 301
Didgeridoo, 524
Diet and nutrition, *See also* Disease; Health
  of *A. afarensis,* 160
  of ancient apes, 140
  Ariaal and, 5
  body affected by, 8

dentition and, 136, 143, 165, 173
of early hominins, 160, 164–167
education about, 36
evolution and, 135–136
food habits, 269
food production and, 206, 208
of foragers, 364
health and, 249, 420
hunting and, 180–181
mixed diet hypothesis, 136, 149
of Old World monkeys, 114
population density and, 202
poverty and, 9
of primates, 107, 114, 116–117, 122–123, 135–136, 144–146
religion and, 120
sedentism and, 202
sexual behavior and, 17–18
social status and, 47
Differential access, definition of, 396, 405
Differential reproduction, 124
Diffusion, 287, 290, 291, 292, 294, 571, 572
Diglossia, 339, 347
Dinosaurs, 134, 135, 216
Direct diffusion, 292
Direct rule, 553
Directional selection, 75
Disaster Mortuary Operational Response Teams (Dmort), 25
Discourse, definition of, 401
Discovery Channel, 516
Discrimination, 309–310, 318, 322
Disease, *See also* Diet and nutrition; Health
  AIDS/HIV, 33–34, 97
  biological adaptation and, 93
  blood groups and, 96–97
  bubonic plague, 97
  cholera, 97
  curers and, 34–35, 39
  definition of, 32–33, 39
  dentition and, 179
  disease-theory systems, 34
  domesticated animals and, 95–97
  food production and, 95, 225
  genetics and, 66, 73–74, 94–97
  health-care systems and, 34–35, 39
  illness differentiated from, 33
  infectious disease, 95
  rickets, 93, 100
  schistosomiasis (liver flukes), 33
  sexually transmitted diseases, 33–34, 97
  sickle-cell anemia, 69
  smallpox, 95–97
  state collapse and, 249
  syphilis, 97
  taboos and, 17–18
Displacement, 331, 347
Diurnal animals, 48, 110, 139
Diversity, 287, 329–330, 339, 350–352, 573–574
"Divje babe flute," 514
Divorce, 286, 410, 414, 446–447
Diwaniya, 383
Dmort. *See* Disaster Mortuary Operational Response Teams (Dmort)
DNA (deoxyribonucleic acid), *See also* Genetics
  biological anthropology and, 14
  crossing over and, 73, 81

overview of, 63
punctuated equilibrium and, 79–80
school courses and, 68
theory and fact and, 64, 67–69
Evolution Highway, 65
Evolutionary leaps, 177
Ewe people, 492–493
Excavations, 53–54, 59
Exogamy
  bands and, 361
  definition of, 290, 450
  descent groups and, 416–417
  incest and, 432, 434–435
Experimental anthropology, 267–268
Experimental archaeology, 54
Expressive culture, definition of, 507, 525
Extended family households, 410, 412–413, 426
Extinction, 79–80
Extradomestic, 466, 475

F

Facial features, 97–98
Faith healers, 492
Falsification, 18, 68
Family, *See also* Kinship; Marriage
  Ariaal people, 5
  bands and, 384, 385
  chiefdoms and, 384
  child fosterage, 424
  cultural transmission and, 519
  descent groups and, 386, 417–418
  divorce, 286, 410, 414
  education and, 29–30
  extended family households, 410, 412–413, 426
  family of orientation, 410, 426
  family of procreation, 410, 426
  fictive kinship, 361
  foragers and, 416
  industrialization and, 413–414
  kin-based modes of production, 366
  lineal relatives, 423, 426
  matrilineal descent group, 402, 416–417, 426
  matrilineal families, 413
  matrilineal kinship, 16
  matrilocality and, 419, 427
  neolocality and, 413, 417, 427
  in North America, 413–416, 421
  nuclear families, 290–291, 410, 412–413, 421
  overview of, 409–410
  parental investment, 109
  paternity, 411, 419
  patrilocality and, 412, 418
  post-marital resident rules, 412, 417–418, 427, 463–464
  primates and, 124
  reproduction and, 124
  single-parent families, 414–415
  tribes and, 384
Family of orientation, 410, 426
Family of procreation, 410, 426
Famine, 364
Fantástico, 578
Farming. *See* Cultivation; Food production; Horticulture
Fat Land: Supersizing America (Critser), 591
Federal Emergency Management Agency (FEMA), 25

FEMA. *See* Federal Emergency Management Agency (FEMA)
Female genital mutilation (FGM), 288
Female husbands, 465
Feminine Mystique (Freidan), 468
Ferrets, 222
Fertile crescent, 220, 222
FGM. *See* Female genital mutilation (FGM)
Field Museum of Chicago, 137
Field notes, 264
Filariasis, 94
Fire, 180–181, 196
First World, 319–320, 556
Fiscal, 399, 405
Fishing tools, 193, 195
Fixation, 77
Flakes, 167
Florida State University, 55
Flotation, definition of, 54
Fluorine absorption analysis, 56
Focal vocabulary, 337, 347
Folk, 514–515, 525, 578
Folklore, 293
Food production, *See also* Animal domestication; Plant domestication
  as adaptive strategy, 355–356
  advantages of, 206
  areas of development of, 206, 215, 222–223
  benefits of, 223–225
  broad-spectrum revolution and, 193, 195, 205
  butchery and, 168, 193, 194
  caprine farming, 206, 208
  ceremonies of increase and, 193–194
  costs of, 223–225
  cultivation, 362–365, 377
  cultural adaptation and, 7
  definition of, 19, 205, 226
  deforestation and, 128–131, 225
  disadvantages of, 206
  disease and, 95, 225
  dry farming, 206–208
  environmental impact of, 129
  first American farmers, 215–220
  first farmers in Middle East, 209–212
  geographical spread of, 222–223
  health decline and, 224, 225
  hydraulic agriculture and, 230
  irrigation and, 212, 219, 230, 234, 240
  Neolithic, 205–214
  overview of, 206
  population growth and, 224–225, 230, 242, 248
  poverty and, 224, 225, 591
  property distinctions and, 225
  settlement patterns, 53
  slavery and, 224
  state and, 211–212, 219–220, 398
  transition to agriculture, 135
Foraging
  compared with other adaptive strategies, 366
  correlates of, 359, 361–362
  cultural adaptation and, 7
  diet of, 364
  divorce and, 446–447
  egalitarian societies and, 361–362
  environmental impact of, 129
  family and, 416
  gender and, 361

overview of, 356, 358–359, 361–362
religion and, 495
Foramen magnum, 162
Forced assimilation, 319
Forced diffusion, 292
Forensic anthropology
  application of, 45–46
  methods of, 49–50
  race identification and, 50
  relevance of, 14
  skeletal identification and, 45
Fossils
  creationism and, 64
  dating techniques and, 55–58
  definition of, 59
  environment and, 55
  fossil record, 55, 56
Founder effect, 191
France
  AIDS and, 97
  cave painting and, 176, 179, 200
  Chauvet cave, 176, 200
  Dryopithecus and, 143
  early humans in, 184–185
  energy consumption in, 544
  French colonialism, 552–553
  Industrial Revolution and, 534
  Neandertals in, 187
  Neolithic and, 213
Fraternal polyandry, 432
Free Inquiry, 502
French language, 336
Frontal sinus cavity, 146
Fruit flies, 12
Fulani people, 99
Functional explanation, definition of, 422–423, 426
Functionalism, definition of, 439
Fundamentalism, 498, 501–502, 504

G

G. Blacki, 145
Gabon, 117, 118
Gambia, 118
Gamets, 72
Garbanzo beans, 222
Garbology, 11
GATT (General Agreement on Trade and Tariffs), 292
Gazelles, 209, 210, 212
GDP (Gross domestic product), 558
Gender
  agriculturalists and, 466–467
  cooperation and, 50
  division of labor and, 361, 367, 368, 458–461, 481
  female genital mutilation (FGM) and, 288
  foragers and, 462–463
  gender roles, 456, 458, 475
  gender speech contrasts, 339–340
  gender stereotypes, 456, 458, 475
  gender stratification, 458, 464–466, 475
  horticulturalists and, 463–466
  industrialism and, 467–471
  political systems and, 383–384
  sex and, 455, 456–458
  sexual orientation and, 471–474, 475
Gender roles, 456, 458, 475
Gender stereotypes, 456, 458, 475
Gender stratification, 454–466, 458, 475
Gene flow, 77–78, 81

Knuckle walking, 140
Kosovo Liberation Army, 314
Koss, 38
Kuikuru people, 362, 364
!Kung people, 444
Kuria, 374
Kuwait, 383–384
Kwakiutl, 374, 376
Kwashiorkor, 17

L

Labor
  adaptive strategies and, 355–356
  careers in anthropology, 37–38
  cash employment statistics, 469
  child labor, 535
  division of labor and, 361, 367, 368, 458–461, 466, 481
  domestic workers, 273
  immigrants and, 532–533
  marriage affected by, 286
  median annual income in U.S., 471
  women and, 5, 414
Lactose intolerance, 99
Laissez–faire economics, 555
Lakher people, 435
Land resources, 367–368
Language. See Communication and language
Laos, 556
Laplanders, 357–358
Lascaux cave art, 193, 200
Latent function, definition of, 439
Latino, 304
Law, 398, 405
Learning, 121
Lebanon, 201–202
Lemurs, 108, 110, 129–130, 138, 139, 141
Lentils, 222
Les Miserables, 518
Levallois tool making, 191
Leveling mechanisms, definition of, 495, 504
Levirate, 446, 450
Lexicon, definition of, 334, 347
Liberia, 118
Library of Congress Endangered Music Project, 577
Life histories, 266, 274
Liminality, definition of, 489, 504
Lincoln University, 301
Lineages, 417–418, 426
Lineal kinship terminology, 423, 425, 426
Lineal relatives, 423, 426
Linguistic anthropology
  definition of, 19
  deforestation and, 128
  education and, 27
  McDonald's ritual phrases and, 593
  overview of, 13, 15, 328
Linguistic relativity, 339
Linnaean Society, 67
Literacy. See Writing and literacy
Liver flukes. See Schistosomiasis (liver flukes)
Llamas, 215, 217, 222, 365
Llongot, 458
Local beliefs and perceptions, 266
Local descent groups, 417
Locomotion
  bipedalism, 154, 156, 160, 161–162, 170, 187
  four-footed locomotion, 161

primate evolution and, 140–141
quadrupedalism, 154–155
Logging, 129–130
Long-term physiological adaptation, 6–7
Longitudinal research, 268–269, 274
Lophs, 142
Lorises, 108, 139
Louisiania territory, 553
Love, 444–445
Lovedu, 441
Lucy skeleton, 158–161, 176

M

Macaques, 114–115, 120
McDonald's Corporation, 591–594
McGill University, 6
Macroevolution, 78–79, 81
"McTeague" (Norris), 509
McWorld, 501
Madagascar
  author's field work in, 260, 264
  burial ceremonies in, 291
  deforestation in, 129–130
  descent and, 417, 566
  development and, 560
  foraging and, 358
  nonverbal communication in, 333
  plural marriage and, 448–449
  primates in, 48, 110, 141
  rice cultivation, 367
  witchcraft and, 494–495
Magic, 193–194, 213, 487–488, 504
Magico-religious specialists, 34–35
Maize, 215, 218, 219, 220, 226, 248
Makah Indians, 281–282, 401–402, 419, 586
Malagasy people, 141
Malaria, 76, 86, 94, 225
Malaysia, 35, 110, 358, 369, 373
Male sexual jealousy, 411–412
Male-female avoidance, 465–466, 474
Mali, 507
Malnutrition, 249
Mammoths, 216, 218–219
Mana, 487, 504
Manggarai people, 196
Manifest function, definition of, 439
Manioc, 218, 220, 226, 356, 363
Manon Lescaut, 26
Marine Mammal Protection Act, 282
Market principle, 372, 377
Marmosets, 139
Marriage, See also Family; Kinship
  adultery, 288, 386, 461
  age at first marriage, 284, 286, 414, 468
  Ariaal people and, 5
  bands and, 385
  bridewealth and, 433, 441, 443–445, 446, 450
  "common law" marriage, 432
  cousins and, 432, 434, 437
  culture and, 284, 286
  divorce and, 286, 446–447
  dowries and, 433, 441, 443–445, 450
  endogamy and, 438–439
  exogamy and, 290, 361, 416–417, 432, 434–435, 450
  female husbands, 465
  fertility and, 444, 445
  as group alliance, 441, 443–446
  human/ape differences and, 124
  incest taboo and, 290, 432, 434–439

levirate, 446, 450
love and, 444–445
marriage rites, 130
matrimonial advertisements, 442
moiety and, 432, 434
music and, 515–516
overview of, 431–432
plural marriage, 432, 433–434, 444–445, 447–450
post-marital resident rules, 412, 417–418, 427, 463–464
race and, 309
rights and obligations and, 420, 439–441
same–sex marriage, 432, 439–441, 465
sororate, 445–446, 450
wife stealing, 386
Marrow Utility Index, 194
Marsh elder, 215, 218
Masai, 5, 391, 392
Matai system, 32
Maters, 440, 450
Mathematics, 224
Matriarchy, 457–458
Matrifocal societies, 464–465, 475
Matrilineal descent, 402, 416–417, 426
Matrilineal families, 413, 419
Matrilineal kinship, 16
Matrilocality, 419, 427, 463–464
Max-Planck Institute for Evolutionary Anthropology, 176
Maximization, 369–372
Mayan civilization, 129, 249–250
Mayan hieroglyphic writing, 249
Mbuti people, 356, 361, 374, 459
Meaning in language, 337–338
Means of production, 367–368, 377
Meat Utility Index, 194
Medical anthropology, 32–35, 40
Meiosis, 73, 81
Melanasia, 390, 487, 499–500, 591
Melanin, 92, 100
Mende, 392
Mendelian genetics, 70–71, 81
Men's Health, 6
Mesoamerica
  broad-spectrum foraging and, 210
  cemeteries and, 238
  definition of, 210, 226
  early farming and, 218–220
  state emergence and, 229–230
  state formation in, 245–249, 393
Mesolithic, 195–196, 198
Mesopotamia, 229–230, 234, 240, 251
Mesoproterozoic period, 134
Mesozoic era, 79–80, 134
Mesquite, 219
Mestizos, 583, 586
Metallurgy, 208, 224, 241, 243, 251
Methods
  anthropometry and, 49
  bone biology, 49–50
  dating techniques and, 47, 55–58
  ethical considerations, 259–260, 262–263
  ethnographic techniques, 263–271
  molecular anthropology and, 51–52
  multidisiplinary approaches to, 47–48
  overview of, 46
  paleoanthropology, 52
  primatology and, 48–49
  survey research, 271–273

Mexico
  cheap labor and, 533
  colonialism and, 550
  domestic workers in, 273
  endangered languages and, 580
  food production in, 214, 217, 218–219
  foraging and, 359
  pyramids, 11
  Spanish conquer of, 247
  state and, 219
  television and, 579–580
  transnational migration and, 581
  urban versus rural societies and, 31
  Valley of Mexico, 247–249
  violent art and, 239
Michigan State University, 37
Microenculturation, definition of, 35
Microevolution, definition of, 78, 81
Middle East, *See also* specific countries
  AMHs and, 200
  domestication and, 356
  first civilization, 209
  first farmers and, 206, 209–212
  states and, 211–212, 229, 234–242
Migrations, 85, 92, 94, 179–183
Mikmaq language, 261
Millennium Institute, 551
Millet, 200, 213, 215, 218
Minangkabau, 457–458
Mindel glacial, 185
Minority groups, 304
Miocene epoch, 134–135, 157, 158
Missing link, 145–148
Mission Civilisatrice, 553, 555
Missionaries, 388, 445, 473, 553, 554
Mitochondrial DNA (mtDNA), 58, 94–95, 188
Mitosis, 73, 81
Mixed diet hypothesis, 136, 149
Modern world system. *See* World system
Modes of production, 366–369, 377
Moiety, 432, 434
Molecular anthropology, 51–52, 59, 137
Molecular clock, 137
Molson Canadian beer, 350–351
Monkeys
  brachiation and, 113, 114, 126, 142
  communication systems and, 13
  New World monkeys, 108, 112–114
  Old World monkeys, 114–115
  terrestrial monkeys, 104, 126
  types of monkeys, 112–114
Monocrop production, 530
Monotheistic religion, 495, 496, 504
Morocco, 182, 553
Morphology, definition of, 334, 347
Motivation, 369–370
Motorola, 38
Mousterian, 186, 191–192, 198
Movement. *See* Locomotion
Mozambique, 401–402, 419
MtDNA. *See* Mitochondrial DNA (mtDNA)
Multiculturalism, 316–318, 322
Multiregional evolution, 190–191, 198
Multisited research, 268
Multivariate, 230, 251
Munsee Delaware language, 262
Museum of Modern Art in New York, 511
Music, 508, 510, 511, 514, 514–519, 524
Mutation, 66, 70, 72, 73–74, 79, 81
M.y.a. (million years ago), 133

N
NAACP. *See* National Association for the Advancement of Colored People (NAACP)
NAFTA (North American Free Trade Agreement), 292
Nähñu language, 580
Namibia, 538–539
NAPA. *See* National Association for the Practice of Anthropology (NAPA).
Nariokotome boy, 177, 181–182
NASA. *See* National Aeronautics and Space Administration (NASA)
Nation, definition of, 313, 322
Nation–states and, definition of, 313, 322
National Aeronautics and Space Administration (NASA), 47
National Association for the Advancement of Colored People (NAACP), 306
National Association for the Practice of Anthropology (NAPA)., 27
National Cancer Institute, 65
National Coordination of Guatemalan Widows (CONVIGUA), 45
National Council of La Raza, 306, 329–330
National culture, 287, 295
National Endowment for the Arts, 518
National Geographic, 5
National Oceanic and Atmospheric Administration, 282
National Organization of Women (NOW), 468, 470
National Science Foundation Research Experiences for Undergraduates Program (REU–Sites), 221
Nationalities, definition of, 313–314, 322
Native Americans, *See also* specific tribes
  anthropological studies of, 7, 14
  berdaches and, 440, 473, 496
  biological anthropology and, 14
  division of labor and, 459
  family and, 416
  foraging and, 358
  haplogroups and, 51, 217
  immigration of, 85
  intelligence and, 311
  languages of, 261
  livestock and, 365
  migration of ancestors, 215–217
  "noble savage myth," 531–532
  ranked societies and, 237
  religion and, 489, 492–495
  rites of passage and, 489, 515–516
  tree-ring dating and, 58
Nativist movements, 498
Natufians, 209–210, 220, 226, 235
Natural History magazine, 178
Natural History Museum of Switzerland, 145
Natural selection, *See also* DNA (deoxyribonucleic acid); Genetics
  adaptation and, 75–77
  blood types and, 96–97
  definition of, 67, 81
  dentition and, 179
  directional selection, 75
  disease and, 66, 73–74, 94–97
  environmental change and, 64
  facial features and, 97–98
  food production and, 212
  gene flow and, 77–78
  genetic evolution and, 75
  genetic mutation and, 66, 72, 73–74, 81
  genotypes and, 75
  industrial melanism, 69
  overview of, 75
  peppered moth and, 69
  phenotypes and, 71, 75, 81, 86–89, 97–98
  race and, 86
  random genetic drift, 77, 81
  reproduction and, 124
  sexual selection, 75–76, 81
  skin color and, 92–93
  stabilizing selection, 76–77
  variety and, 67, 69–70
Naturalistic disease theories, 34
Nature, 137, 175
Navajo Indians, 365, 518, 522, 524
Nayars, 290, 412–413
Nazis, 91, 319
Ndembu, 489
Neanderthals
  AMHs and, 186–189
  Archaic *H. sapiens*, 183, 197
  cold-adapted Neandertals, 186
  dating of, 51, 175
  description of, 198
  Middle Paleolithic and, 179
  overview of, 185–186
  sexual dimorphism and, 186–187
Needles, 193
Negative reciprocity, 373–374, 377
Négritude, 314
Neo-Paganism, 498
Neoliberalism, 555–556, 568
Neolithic
  definition of, 226
  explanation for, 220, 222
  food production and, 205–214
  house construction and, 221
  state formation and, 241
Neolocality, 413, 417, 427
Neoproterozoic period, 134
Nepal, 87, 143, 449
Netherlands, 8, 562
New age, 502
New Deal, 556
New Orleans, 25–26
New Stone Age. *See* Neolithic
New World monkeys, 108, 112–114
New York Times, 305, 517, 533
New York University, 202, 231
New Zealand, 89
Ngadha people, 196
NGOs
  applied anthropology and, 27
  Asian factory women and, 537–539
  development and, 560
  ethics and, 44
  indigenous people and, 584
Nicaragua, 584
Nigeria
  art and, 507, 512, 519
  gorillas in, 117
  immigration to U.S. and, 302
  lactose tolerance and, 99
  marriage in, 441, 448–449, 465
  as periphery nation, 532
  religion and, 512–513
  state formation and, 245
  television and, 579–580

Posture, 140–141
Pot irrigation, 219
Potassium–argon (K/A) technique,
    56–57
Potato, 215, 218, 220, 356
Potlatching, 374–376, 378
Potsherds, 10
Pottery
    Akhenaten Temple project and, 244
    early Middle Eastern states and, 235
    food production and, 213, 214
    Halafian pottery, 237, 251
    socioeconomic hierarchy and,
        236–237
    Ubaid period pottery, 237
Poverty
    African Americans and, 467–468
    feminization of, 469–471
    food production and, 224, 225, 591
    health and, 35, 420
    kinship and, 414, 416
    nutrition and, 9
    in Papua New Guinea, 551
    in Russia, 558
    urbanization and, 31
Power, definition of, 381, 396, 405, 536
Practice theory, definition of, 287
Practicing anthropology. See Applied
    anthropology
Prejudice, 318, 322
Prelos, 516
Prestige, See also Status
    definition of, 386, 396, 405
    plural marriage and, 448
    public activities and, 462
    as social stratification
        dimension, 536
    women and, 458
Preventive health care, 35
Primary states, 238, 251
Primate evolution
    Afropithecus, 142–143
    arboreal hypothesis, 135–136, 149
    derived traits, 142
    diet and, 135–136
    Dryopithecus, 143, 145, 149
    early cenozoic primates, 136, 138–139
    early miocene hominoids, 140–142
    early primates, 135–140
    Eurasian apes, 142–145
    fossil record, 133–135
    Gigantopithecus, 144–145
    grasping and, 135
    Heliopithecus, 142–143
    missing link, 145–148
    mixed diet hypothesis, 136
    oligocene anthropoids, 139–140
    Oreopithecus, 145
    Orrorin tugenensis, 148
    Pierolapithecus catalaunicus, 146–147
    primitive traits, 142
    Proconsul, 141–142, 149
    sight over smell, 109, 135, 139
    Sivapithecus, 143–144, 149
    "Toumai," 147–148
    visual adaptation, 135, 136, 149
Primates (nonhuman primates), See
    also specific types of primates
    aggression and, 123
    analogies and, 106–107, 126
    anthropoids, 108, 110, 112, 126
    arboreal primates, 48, 108,
        113–118, 126

    brachiation and, 113–116, 126,
        140–142
    brain complexity, 109
    communication systems and, 13,
        48, 328
    cooperation and, 51, 123–124
    definition of, 129
    deforestation and, 48–49, 119–120,
        128–131
    diet of, 107, 116–117, 122–123
    as endangered species, 48–49,
        119–120
    grasping and, 108–109, 135
    homologies and, 106–107, 126
    human/ape differences, 123–124
    human/ape similarities, 51, 65,
        103–107, 120–124
    hunting and poaching of, 120
    knuckle walking, 140
    learning and, 121
    molecular anthropology and,
        51–52
    nose to hand shift, 109
    opposable thumbs and,
        108–109, 126
    parental investment, 109
    as predators, 122–123
    primate tendencies, 107–109
    prosimians, 110
    sexual behavior, 119, 122–125
    sexual dimorphism and, 114–115,
        117, 118, 126, 141
    smell to sight shift, 109, 135, 139
    social nature of, 105, 109, 117, 119,
        124–125
    terrestrial primates, 104, 126
    tools and, 105–106, 121
Primatology
    definition of, 13, 103, 126
    ethics and, 44
    methods and, 48–49
    overview of, 103–107, 105
Primitive Culture (Tylor), 279
Primitive traits, 142
Primogeniture, definition of, 439
Principles of Geology (Lyell), 67
Privatization, 557
Proconsul, 141–142, 149
Productivity in language, definition
    of, 331, 347
Profit motives, 370
Progeny price, definition of, 441, 450
Project New Life–good Health (Nueva
    Vida–Buena Salud), 36
Proletarianization, definition of, 535
Promiscuity, 419
Property distinctions, 225
Propliopithecid family, 140
Propriety, 8
Prosimians, 108, 110, 126, 138
Proterozoic era, 134
Protestant Ethic and the Spirit of
    Capitalism (Weber), 497
Proto–apes, 140, 142
Protolanguages, 344
Pseudo–archaeology, 246–247
"Psychic unity of man," 280
Psychology, 16
Public policy, 27–28
Public transcript, 400, 405
Punctuated equilibrium, 79–80, 81
Pygmies, 98, 345, 356
Pyramids, 248

Q
Qashqai, 366, 392
Quadrupedalism, 154–155
Quarternary period, 134–135
Questionnaires, 265, 274
Quichua language, 583
Quinoa, 215, 218

R
Ra Expeditions (Heyerdahl), 246
Rabbits, 219
Race
    biological distinctiveness and,
        89–91, 97–98
    census and, 306, 308
    colonialism and, 88
    concept of, 85–93
    culture and, 7
    definition of, 304, 322
    discrimination and, 309–310
    facial features, 97–98
    forensic identification and, 50
    hypodescent, 305–306
    intelligence and, 310–313
    natural selection and, 86
    overview of, 304–305
    perceptions of, 307
    phenotypes and, 86, 88–89
    racial classification, 86, 90–91, 100
    skin color and, 86, 88–89, 92–93
    social construction of, 305–306,
        308–310
Racial classification, 86, 90–91, 100
Racism
    Apartheid, 311, 318, 338–339, 486,
        538–540
    definition of, 304, 309, 322
    "white man's burden" and, 552, 555
Radical Vegetarian League, 593
Radiocarbon dating, 175
Raelian Movement, 502
Rain forest, 129, 141, 154
Rainforest, 576–577
Rainforest Action Network, 576–577
Rambo, 579
Random genetic drift, 77, 81, 191
Random sample, 271, 274
Ranked societies, 237–239, 251
Ranomafana National Park, 141
Rapaport's rule, 573
Rapport, 264
Rastafarianism, 498
Real culture, definition of, 287
Recessive, 70, 81
Reciprocity, 373–374, 378
Recombination, 72, 81
Redistribution, 372–373, 378, 395
Refugees, 319, 322
Reindeer, 357–358
Relative dating, 55–56, 59
Religion, See also specific religions
    of American slaves, 401
    animism, 484, 486, 503
    anxiety control and, 487–488
    art and, 508, 510–511, 516
    capitalism and, 497
    cargo cults, 499–501, 503
    change and, 498–502
    colonialism and, 269
    cults, 490, 499–501
    cultural ecology and, 491
    cultural exchange and, 575–576
    definition of, 483–484, 504

Smelting, 225, 241, 243, 251
Smilodectes, 139
Smith College, 5
Smithsonian Institution, 3, 6
Social adaptation, 7
Social capital, 342
Social control, 399–404, 405, 492–495
Social funds, 371
Social indicators, 272
Social races, 305, 322
Social status, diet and, 47
Socialism, definition of, 556
Society, definition of, 4
Society of American Archaeology, 54
Society for Applied Anthropology
    (SfAA), 27
Sociocultural anthropology. *See*
    Cultural anthropology
Socioeconomic hierarchy
    Olmecs and, 245–248
    Pharaohs and, 231–232
    pottery and, 236–237
    ranked societies, 237–239, 251
    stratification, 237–239
Socioeconomic status (SES), 438
Sociolinguistics
    definition of, 15, 19, 328, 347
    educational research and, 29–30
    gender speech contrasts, 339–340
    linguistic diversity, 339
    overview of, 338–343
Sociology, 15–16
Sodality, pantribal, 389–392, 405
Sorcery, 401–402, 403, 575
Sorghum, 200, 215
Sororate, 445–446, 450
Sororities, 394
South Africa, 164, 189–190, 201,
    311, 441, 486, 513–514, 538–539,
    558–559
South Korea, 541
Soybeans, 220
Spain, 143, 146–147, 179, 530, 541,
    550, 556
Speciation
    definition of, 78, 81, 106
    evolution and, 78–79
    taxonomy and, 106, 107
Species
    definition of, 78, 81
    evolution and, 78–79
    punctuated equilibrium and,
        79–80, 81
    taxonomy and, 104, 107
Speech. *See* Communication and
    language
Spinning, 223–224
Spirit Cries, 577
Spirit possession, 369
Spiritism, 498
Squash, 215, 218, 222, 372
Sri Lanka, 449
Standard English (SE), 30, 334, 336, 339
Stanford University, 200, 331
Star Wars, 520–521
Starship Enterprise, 3
State University of New York, 169, 345
States, *See also* Political systems
    attributes of, 233–234
    definition of, 229, 251, 313, 322, 382,
        393, 405
    emergence of, 135, 240, 393

empires, 233, 251
enforcement and, 398–399
fiscal systems, 399
food production and, 211–212,
    219–220, 365
hegemony and, 400
irrigation and, 212, 219
judiciary and, 398
Middle East and, 234–242
multivariate theory and, 230, 232
origin of, 229–230
overview of, 397
population control and, 397–398
population growth and, 230, 232
primary states, 238, 251
ranked societies, 237–239, 251
reasons for collapse of, 249–250
religion and, 496–497
resource circumscription and,
    230, 232
social control and, 399–404
trade and, 212, 230, 235
tribute and, 232–234
war and, 230, 232, 247
Status, *See also* Prestige
    chiefdoms and, 395–397
    definition of, 300, 303, 311, 322
    language and, 340–342
    potlatching and, 374–376
    women and, 463–464
Status shifting, 303
stipulated descent, 417
Stone tools, 167, 194, 196
Storytelling, 519
Stratification
    Asian factory women and, 537–539
    definition of, 237–238, 251, 322, 405
    emergence of, 237–239, 396–397
    gender stratification, 458,
        464–466, 475
    industrial stratification, 535–537
    language and, 341–342, 583
    social stratification dimensions, 536
Stratified, definition of, 311
Stratigraphy, 47, 54, 55, 59
Style shifts in language, 339, 347
Subcultures, 287–288, 295, 350
Subgroups in language, 344, 347
Subordinate, definition of, 397, 405
Subsistence funds, 371
Subspecies, 104, 106
Substance abuse, 35
Sudan, 90, 243, 337, 422, 432, 575–576
Sugar beets, 220
Sugarcane, 220, 530
Suicide, 403, 490
Sukuma tribe, 554
Sumatra, 105, 119, 123
Sumer, 234
Sumpweed, 222
Sun Pyramid, 248
Sunburn, 92
Sunflower, 215, 218, 222
Superordinate, definition of, 397, 405
Superposition, 53
Supersizing, 591–592
Supply and demand, 372
Survey research, 271–274
Susto (soul loss), 34
Sweet potato, 220
Switzerland, 145, 470, 502
Symbolic capital, 342

Symbols
    art and, 514
    brain and symbolic thought,
        200, 203
    cultural symbols, 280, 282–283,
        287, 295
    ritual and, 592–594
Syncretisms, 499–501, 504
Syntax, 334, 342, 347
Syphilis, 49, 97
Syria, 206, 237, 240
Systematic surveys, 52–53

T
Taboo
    incest taboo, 290, 432, 434–439, 450
    postpartum sex taboo, 17–18
    religion and, 487, 490–491, 504
Taiwan, 541
Tajik language, 558
Tajikistan, 558
Taliban, 493, 501
Tamarins, 139
Tanosy people, 575
Tanzania
    A. afarensis and, 159, 160
    chimpanzees and, 118, 122
    colonialism and, 554
    H. habilis and, 176
    Oldowan tools and, 167
    pantribal sodalities in, 391
    Rift Valley and, 154
Taoism, 499
Taphonomy, definition of, 55, 169
Tarsiers, 108, 110
Taxes, 224
Taxonomy, 64, 104, 106, 126
Team research, 268–270
Technological adaptation, 7
Teeth. *See* Dentition
Teilhardina asiatica, 136, 138
Telenovelas, 579
Television, 45, 350, 417, 578–581
Tell Hamoukar site, 240
Temple University, 94
Tenochtitlan, 247, 248–249
Tenrikyo, 498
Teocentli, 219, 220, 226
Teotihuacan, 248, 251
Terracing, 363
Terrestrial primates, 104, 126
Tertiary period, 134–135
Texas A&M University, 55, 65
Text, definition of, 578, 588
Thailand, 214, 243, 537
Theory
    definition of, 17, 19, 67, 81
    disease-theory systems, 34
    evolution and, 64, 67–69
    falsification of, 18, 68
    overview of, 17–18
    theory and fact, 64, 67–69
Theory of the Leisure Class (Veblen), 375
Thermoluminescene (TL), 57
Third World, 320, 556, 565–566, 572
Thomson's nose rule, 97, 100
Threshold 21, 551
Thumb opposability, 11, 108–109, 126
Tibet, 6, 87, 98, 449
Tierra del Fuego, 360
Titanic, 54
Tiv people, 512–513

Tiwi people, 511, 522
TL. *See* Thermoluminescene (TL)
Tools
    Acheulian tools, 180, 197
    awls, 192, 201
    axes, 211
    blade tools, 191, 197
    bone tools, 514
    burins, 192
    choppers, 167
    early hominins and, 156
    fishing tools, 193, 195
    flakes, 167, 191
    hominids and, 52
    Mousterian tools, 186, 191–192, 198
    needles, 193
    Oldowan tools, 167–168, 170,
        179–180
    Paleolithic and, 179–180, 198
    primates and, 105–106
    scrapers, 192
    sewing tools, 88
    stone tools, 167, 194, 196
    symbolic thought and, 200
Totemism, 417, 490–491, 522, 529–530
Touching, 280, 285
"Toumai," 147–148, 155
Trade, *See also* Economics
    as adaptive strategy, 372, 374
    balance reciprocity, 374
    emergence of, 210
    expansion of, 212, 224, 240
    fiscal systems and, 399
    long-distance trade routes, 230, 235
    settlement patterns and, 53
    State emergence and, 212, 245
    world system and, 530
Training anthropology teams, 44, 46
Transformism. *See* Evolution
Transhumance, 366, 378
Transvestism, 472, 473, 496
Tree-ring dating, 57–58
Triassic period, 134
Tribes
    age sets and, 391–392
    "big men" and, 386, 388–389,
        405, 500
    colonial construction of, 554
    definition of, 382, 405
    economy of, 384, 386, 398
    energy consumption and, 544
    industrialization and, 543
    manufacturing and, 368
    overview of, 386–387
    pantribal societies, 389–392
    as taxonomic level, 107
    village head and, 387–388, 405
Tribute, 232–234
Trichromatic color vision, 114
Tricycle: The Buddhist Review, 502
Trobriand Islanders, 16, 267, 270
Troops, 117
Tropics, 92, 100
Tsimshian, 374
Tuaregs, 5
Tuberculosis, 49
Tulane University, 444
Tundra, 184
Tunisia, 553
Turkana, 366
Turkey, 58, 143, 201–202, 206, 222,
    235, 533
Turkeys, 215

Turquoise, 210
Tutsis, 99, 554
Twins, 312–313

U
Ubaid culture, 237, 238, 240
Ucagizli Cave, 202
Uganda
    boundary control and, 397
    chimpanzees and, 111, 118, 122
    endangered species in, 119
    ethnic expulsion and, 319
    gorilla studies in, 117
    lactose tolerance and, 99
    plural marriage and, 449
    population control and, 397
    racial classification and, 90
    transhumance and, 366
UNCED, 582
Underdifferentiation, 565, 568
Underwater archaeology, 54, 55
Uniformitarianism, definition of,
    67, 81
Unilineal descent, 417, 427, 434
Unilocality, 418
Union of Soviet Socialist Republics
    (USSR), 556
Unitarian-Universalism, 498
United Nations (UN)
    Conference on the Environment
        and Development (UNCED), 582
    forensic anthropology supported
        by, 46
    Fourth World Conference on
        Women, 470
    human rights and, 289
    UN Charter, 289
    urban slums and, 31
    Working Group on Indigenous
        Populations (WGIP), 582
United States
    accents and, 336
    Basque Americans, 480–481
    childcare and, 460–461
    as core nation, 541
    cremation and, 291
    creole languages in, 335
    divorce and, 447
    domestic violence and, 467
    energy consumption in,
        542–544, 591
    family organization in, 413–416, 421
    food production in, 214
    foreign investment and, 581
    immigrants and, 532–533
    immigration and, 330
    international economics and, 369
    linguistic diversity in, 329–330, 339
    pantribal societies in, 390
    periphery in, 542
    poverty in, 470
    racial/ethnic identification in, 300
    same-sex marriage and, 440
    sexual orientation and, 471
    slavery and, 540, 583
    socioeconomic status (SES) and, 438
    Spanish colonialism and, 550
    subcultures and, 287–288
United States Agency for
    International Development
    (USAID), 24
Universal Declaration of Human
    Rights (UN), 289

Universal grammar, 335
Universal traits, 290, 295
University of Alaska, 580
University of Arizona, 57–58, 200
University of Calgary, 293
University of California, 58, 66, 87,
    155, 188, 445, 531
University of Cambridge, 175
University of Chicago, 25, 26
University College London, 573
University of Colorado, 47
University of Connecticut, 200
University of East London, 411
University of Florida, 273, 580
University of Illinois, 65
University of Indonesia, 562
University of Iowa, 194, 523
University of London, 6
University of Michigan, 26, 37, 94,
    269, 585
University of Missouri, 307
University of Munich, 189
University of Nevada, 330
University of New Mexico, 38, 338
University of New Orleans, 26
University of New York, 532
University of North Carolina, 111, 261
University of Oxford, 176
University of Pennsylvania, 65, 231,
    232, 457–458
University of Pittsburgh, 444
University of Reading, 573–574
University of South Florida, 36,
    38, 360
University of Southern California, 122
University of Toronto, 156
University of Virginia, 517
University of Washington, 66
University of Wisconsin, 445
Uranium series dating, 57
Urban anthropology, 31–32
Urbanization, 31–32
Uruguay, 358
U.S. Census Bureau, 36
U.S. Constitution, 68
U.S. Justice Department, 32
USAID. *See* United States Agency for
    International Development
    (USAID)
USSR, 556

V
Valiant Venture Ltd., 502
Valley of Mexico, 247–249
Valley of Oaxaca, 219
Variables, 271
Variety
    body size and build and, 98
    crossing over, 73
    facial features, 97–98
    genes and disease, 94–97
    genetics and, 12–13
    linguistic variety, 15
    natural selection, 67, 69–70
    race concept and, 85–93
Venezuela, 176, 237, 368, 387–388, 411,
    584
Verberie le Buisson Campin site, 194
Vertical economy, 210, 222
Vertical mobility, definition of, 540, 546
Vietnam, 28, 144, 537, 556
Vietnam Labor Watch, 537–539
Vietnam War, 28

MAP ATLAS

CONTENTS

MAP 1

Annual Percent of World Forest Loss, 1990–2000

Deforestation is a major environmental problem. In the tropics, large corporations clear forests seeking hardwoods for the global market in furniture and fine woods. As well, the agriculturally driven clearing of the great rain forests of the Amazon Basin, west and central Africa, Middle America, and Southeast Asia has drawn public attention. Reduced forest cover means the world's vegetation system will absorb less carbon dioxide, resulting in global warming. Of concern, too, is the loss of biodiversity (large numbers of plants and animals), the destruction of soil systems, and disruptions in water supply that accompany clearing.

QUESTIONS

Look at Map 1, "Annual Percent of World Forest Loss, 1990–2000."

1. On what continents do you find stable or increased forest cover?

2. Are there areas of Africa with stable or increased forest cover? Where are they? What might the reasons be for this lack of deforestation?

3. How does deforestation in India compare with the area to its east, which includes mainland and insular Southeast Asia?

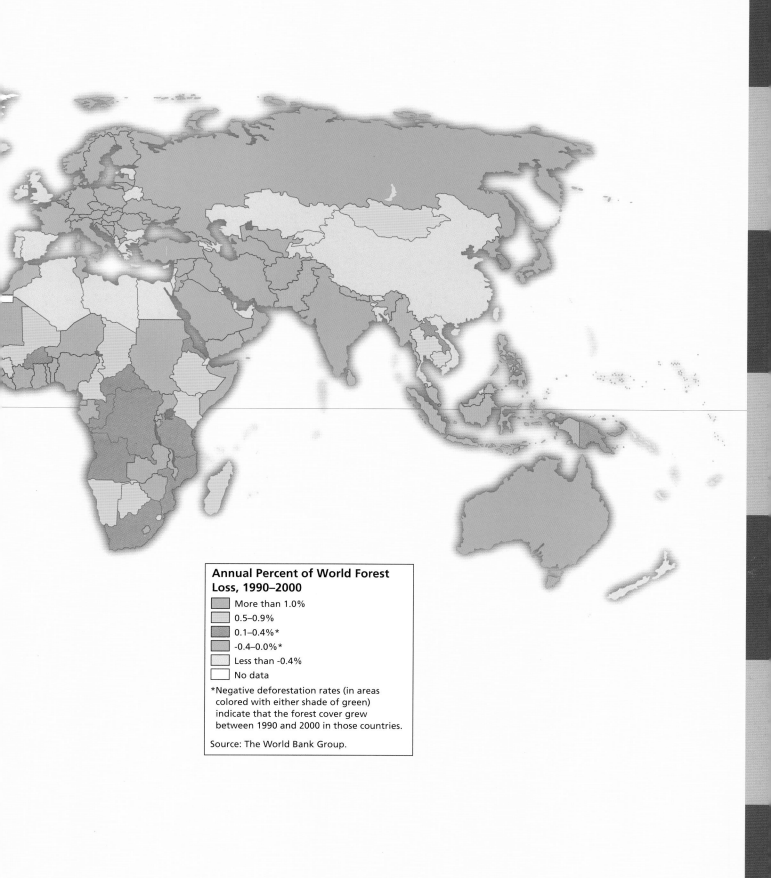

**Annual Percent of World Forest
Loss, 1990–2000**

More than 1.0%

0.5–0.9%

0.1–0.4%*

-0.4–0.0%*

Less than -0.4%

No data

*Negative deforestation rates (in areas
 colored with either shade of green)
 indicate that the forest cover grew
 between 1990 and 2000 in those countries.

Source: The World Bank Group.

MAP 2
Major Primate Groups

The primate zoological order includes prosimians (lemurs, lorises, and tarsiers), monkeys, apes, and humans. Except for humans, contemporary primates live mainly in the tropics. As the map shows, primates used to have a wider distribution. Fossils of ancient primates have been found outside the tropics, including North America and Europe.

QUESTIONS

Look at Map 2, "Major Primate Groups."

1. On what continents are there nonhuman primates today? How does this differ from the past? What primate thrives today in North America?

2. What nonhuman primates live on the island of Madagascar? Are they monkeys or what? Where do other members of their suborder live?

3. On what continents can you find apes in the wild today? What continent that used to have apes lacks them today (except, of course, in zoos).

Major Primate Groups

- New World Monkeys (living)
- Old World Monkeys (living)
- Prosimians (living)
- Apes (living)
- Fossil only

MAP 3
Evolution of the Primates

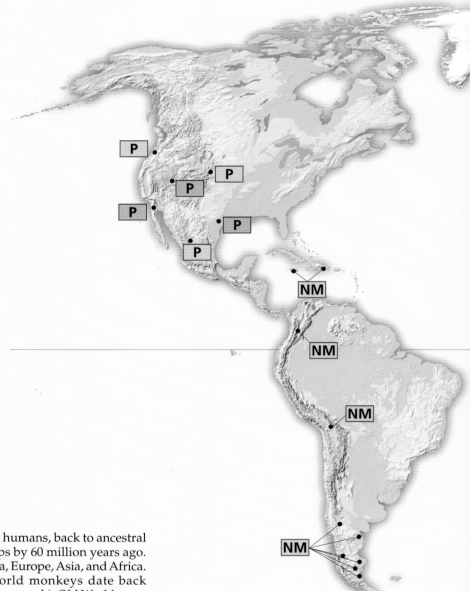

Scientists trace modern primates, including humans, back to ancestral forms. Prosimians evolved earliest, perhaps by 60 million years ago. Their fossils have been found in North America, Europe, Asia, and Africa. Fossil sites with the ancestors of New World monkeys date back between 37 and 23 million years (to the Oligocene epoch). Old World monkeys and apes evolved at about the same time, but Old World monkeys spread into many parts of the Old World only in the last 5 million years. Apes lived in Africa, Europe, and Asia during the Miocene (23–5 million years ago).

QUESTIONS

Look at Map 3, "Evolution of the Primates."

1. What continent(s) had the first primates? What kinds of primates were those?

2. On what continent has the evolution of primates been most continuous? Does this have implications for human evolution?

3. Which continent with several of the earliest primates has the fewest nonhuman primates today?

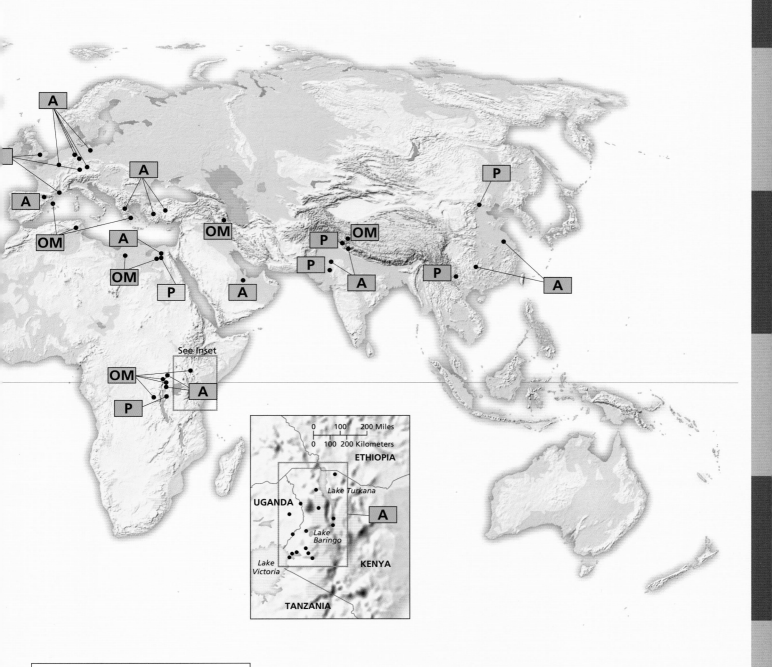

Evolution of the Primates

Eocene: 57–37 million years ago
Oligocene: 37–23 million years ago
Miocene: 23–5 million years ago

OM Old World monkeys
NM New World monkeys
 P Prosimians
 A Apes

A
A
OM
OM
A
A
A
OM
P
OM
A
P
P
P
OM
P
A
P
A
A
OM
A
P

See Inset

0   100   200 Miles
0 100 200 Kilometers

ETHIOPIA
Lake Turkana
UGANDA
A
Lake
Baringo
Lake
Victoria
KENYA
TANZANIA

MAP 4
Early Hominids: Origins and Diffusion

The earliest hominids, which included the ancestors of modern humans, evolved in Africa around 6 million years ago. There are many sites dating to the late Miocene (8-5 million years ago) when the lines leading to modern humans, chimps, and gorillas may have separated. Some sites dating to the end of the Pliocene epoch (5-1.8 million years ago) contain fossil remains of human ancestors, *Homo*. During the Pleistocene Era (1.8 million–11,000 years ago), humans spread all over the world.

QUESTIONS

Look at Map 4, "Early Hominids: Origins and Diffusion."

1. How many African countries have hominid sites? How many have sites from the Miocene? From the Pliocene? And from the Pleistocene?

2. Compare the African distribution of nonhuman primate fossils in Map 3 with the distribution of early hominids in Map 4. Which fossil record is better—the one for nonhuman primates or the one for hominids?

3. Compare the distribution of contemporary African apes, as shown in Map 2, with the distribution of early hominid sites in Map 4. Also look at the distribution of extinct African apes in Map 3. What patterns do you notice? Where did early hominids overlap with the African apes (extinct and contemporary)? Where were there apes but no known early hominids, and vice versa?

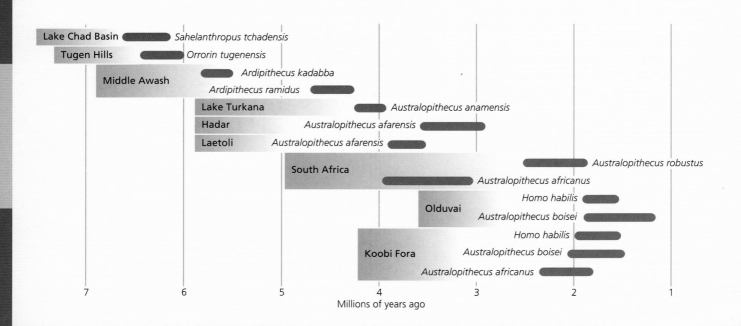

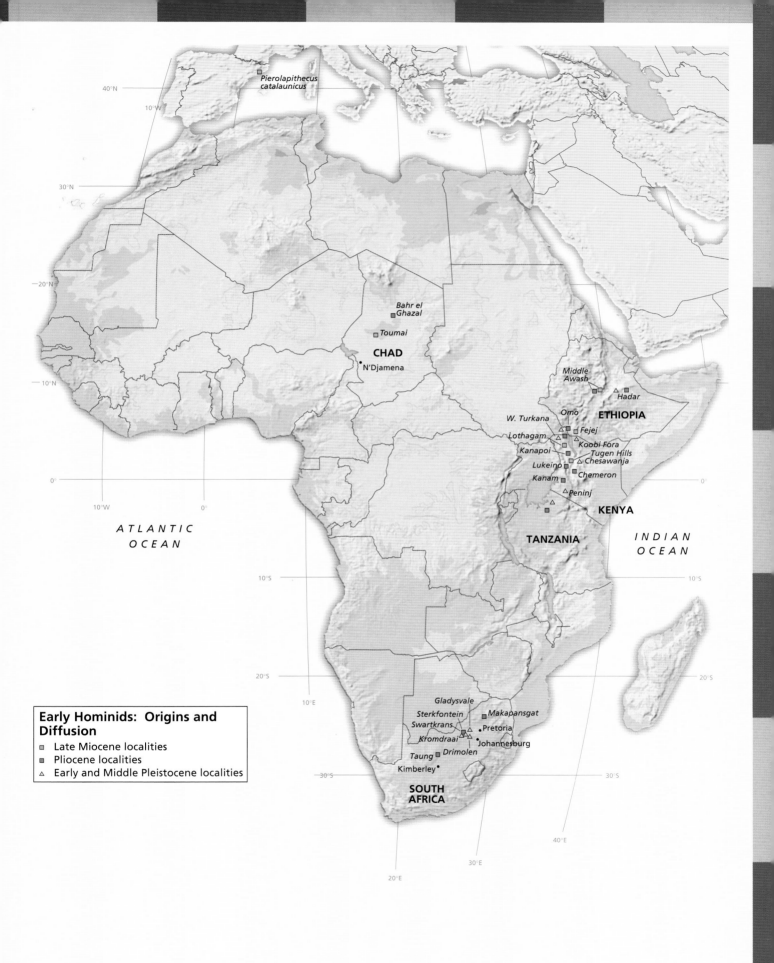

Early Hominids: Origins and Diffusion

- ◻ Late Miocene localities
- ◼ Pliocene localities
- △ Early and Middle Pleistocene localities

Pierolapithecus catalaunicus

40°N

10°W

30°N

20°N

Bahr el Ghazal

Toumai

CHAD

N'Djamena •

10°N

Middle Awash

Hadar △

Omo

ETHIOPIA

W. Turkana

Fejej

Lothagam

Koobi Fora

Kanapoi

Tugen Hills

Lukeino

△ *Chesawanja*

Kanam

Chemeron

△ *Peninj*

KENYA

0°

10°W

0°

ATLANTIC OCEAN

10°E

10°S

TANZANIA

INDIAN OCEAN

10°S

20°S

Gladysvale

Sterkfontein

◼ *Makapansgat*

Swartkrans

• *Pretoria*

Kromdraai

Drimolen

• *Johannesburg*

Taung

30°S

Kimberley •

SOUTH AFRICA

30°S

40°E

30°E

20°E

MAP 5
The Emergence of Modern Humans

Early forms of *Homo (H.) erectus,* sometimes called *H. ergaster,* have been found in East Africa and the former Soviet Georgia. By 1.7 million years ago, *H. erectus* had spread from Africa into Asia, including Indonesia, and eventually Europe. The *H. erectus* period may have lasted until 300,000 years ago. Other archaic forms of *Homo,* including fossils sometimes called *H. antecessor* and *H. heidelbergensis,* have been found in various parts of the Old World.

QUESTIONS

Look at Map 5, "The Emergence of Modern Humans."

1. Locate the site of Dmanisi (Georgia). Locate the site of Nariokotome (East Turkana, Kenya). These are sites where similarly dated early remains of *Homo erectus* (or *Homo ergaster*) have been found. Find two additional sites where hominins with similar dates (1.8–1.6 m.y.a.) have been found.

2. Considering Africa and Asia, name five sites (other than Dmanisi and Nariokotome) where *Homo erectus* fossils have been found.

3. Locate Heidelberg and Ceprano. What kinds of hominin fossils have been found there?

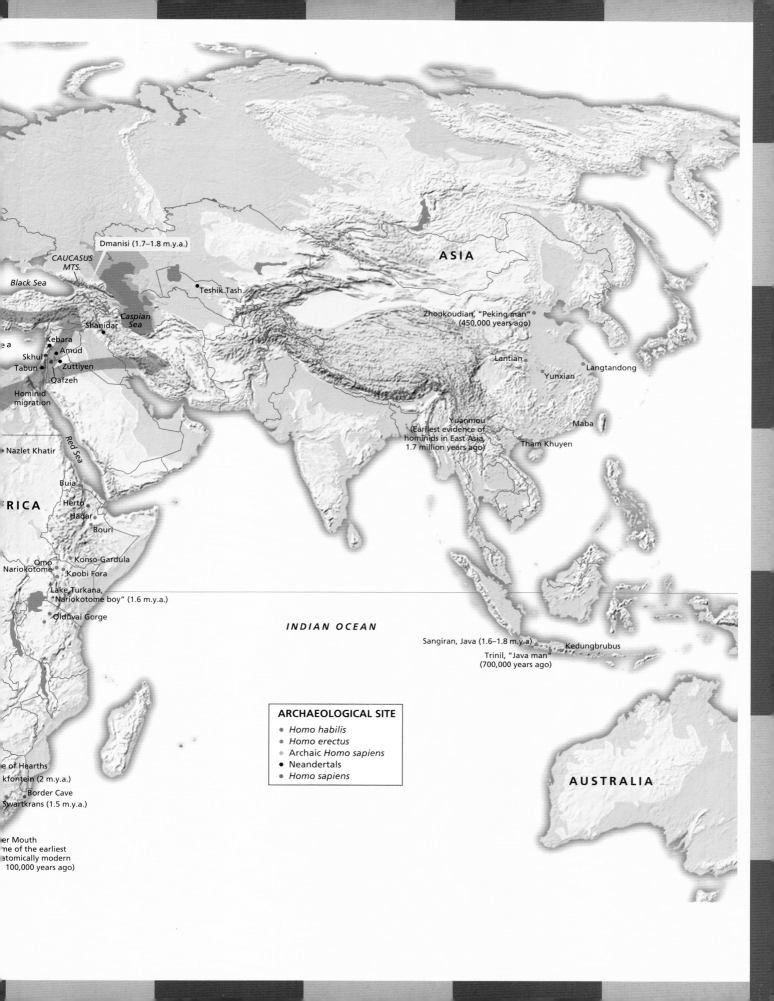

Dmanisi (1.7–1.8 m.y.a.)

CAUCASUS
MTS.

Black Sea

ASIA

Teshik Tash

*Caspian
Sea*

Shanidar

Kebara
Amud
Skhul
Tabun
Zuttiyen
Qafzeh

Hominid
migration

Zhoukoudian, "Peking man"
(450,000 years ago)

Lantian

Langtandong

Yunxian

Red Sea

Nazlet Khatir

Yuanmou
(Earliest evidence of
hominids in East Asia,
1.7 million years ago)

Maba

Tham Khuyen

Buia

RICA

Herto
Hadar

Bouri

Omo
Nariokotome

Konso-Gardula

Koobi Fora

Lake Turkana,
"Nariokotome boy" (1.6 m.y.a.)

Olduvai Gorge

INDIAN OCEAN

Sangiran, Java (1.6–1.8 m.y.a)

Kedungbrubus

Trinil, "Java man"
(700,000 years ago)

ARCHAEOLOGICAL SITE

- ● *Homo habilis*
- ● *Homo erectus*
- ● Archaic *Homo sapiens*
- ● Neandertals
- ● *Homo sapiens*

AUSTRALIA

e of Hearths
kfontein (2 m.y.a.)

Border Cave
Swartkrans (1.5 m.y.a.)

er Mouth
me of the earliest
atomically modern
100,000 years ago)

MAP 6
Origins and Distribution of Modern Humans

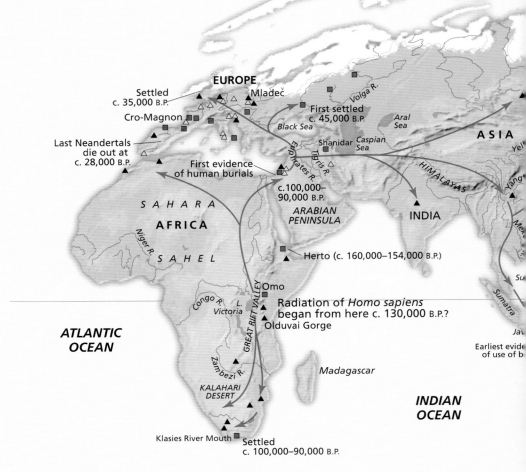

Homo sapiens sapiens, aka anatomically modern humans (AMHs), appeared earliest in Africa (at Herto) and spread into the rest of the Old World after 130,000 years ago. Whether these early modern humans interbred with archaic humans, such as Neandertals, outside of Africa is still debated. Sometime between 25,000 and 9,000 years ago, humans colonized the New World.

QUESTIONS

Look at Map 6, "Origins and Distribution of Modern Humans."

1. When and from where was Australia first settled?

2. When and from where was North America first settled? How many migrations are shown as figuring in the settlement of North America? How were these migrations related to the glacial ice cover? Did they all follow the same route?

3. Locate three sites providing early evidence of AMHs in Africa. How do their dates compare with those of AMHs in Europe?

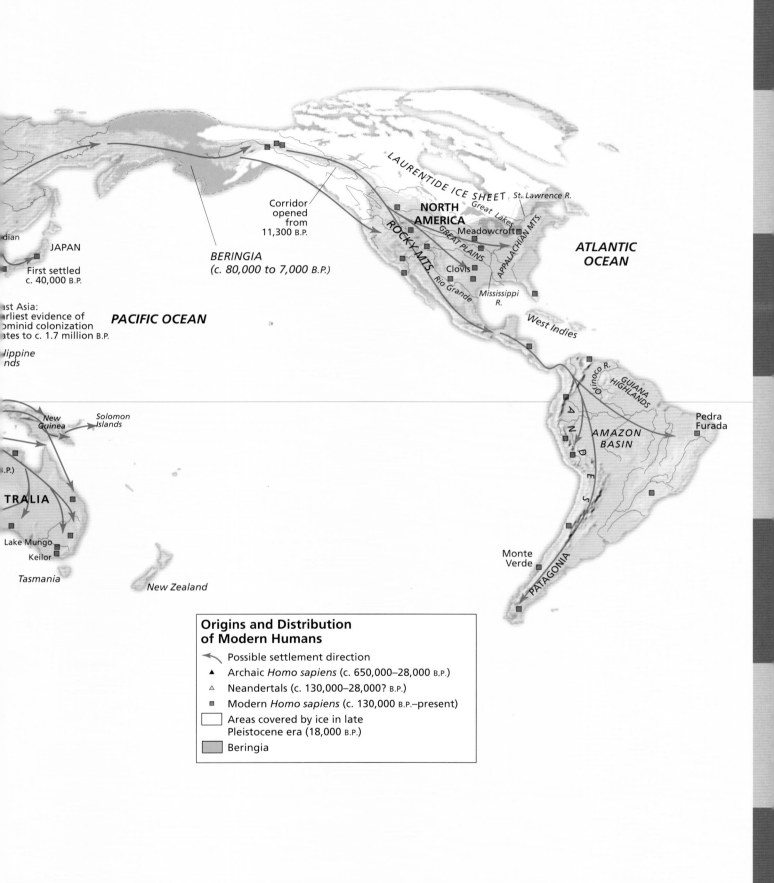

dian

JAPAN
First settled
c. 40,000 B.P.

ast Asia:
arliest evidence of
ominid colonization
ates to c. 1.7 million B.P.

lippine
nds

PACIFIC OCEAN

New
Guinea

Solomon
Islands

.P.)

TRALIA

Lake Mungo
Keilor

Tasmania

New Zealand

Corridor
opened
from
11,300 B.P.

BERINGIA
(c. 80,000 to 7,000 B.P.)

LAURENTIDE ICE SHEET

St. Lawrence R.

Great Lakes

NORTH
AMERICA

ROCKY MTS.

GREAT PLAINS

Meadowcroft

APPALACHIAN MTS.

ATLANTIC
OCEAN

Clovis

Rio Grande

Mississippi
R.

West Indies

Orinoco R.

GUIANA
HIGHLANDS

A
N
D
E
S

AMAZON
BASIN

Pedra
Furada

Monte
Verde

PATAGONIA

Origins and Distribution
of Modern Humans

↖ Possible settlement direction

▲ Archaic *Homo sapiens* (c. 650,000–28,000 B.P.)

△ Neandertals (c. 130,000–28,000? B.P.)

■ Modern *Homo sapiens* (c. 130,000 B.P.–present)

☐ Areas covered by ice in late
Pleistocene era (18,000 B.P.)

☐ Beringia

MAP 7

The Distribution of Human Skin Color (Before A.D. 1400)

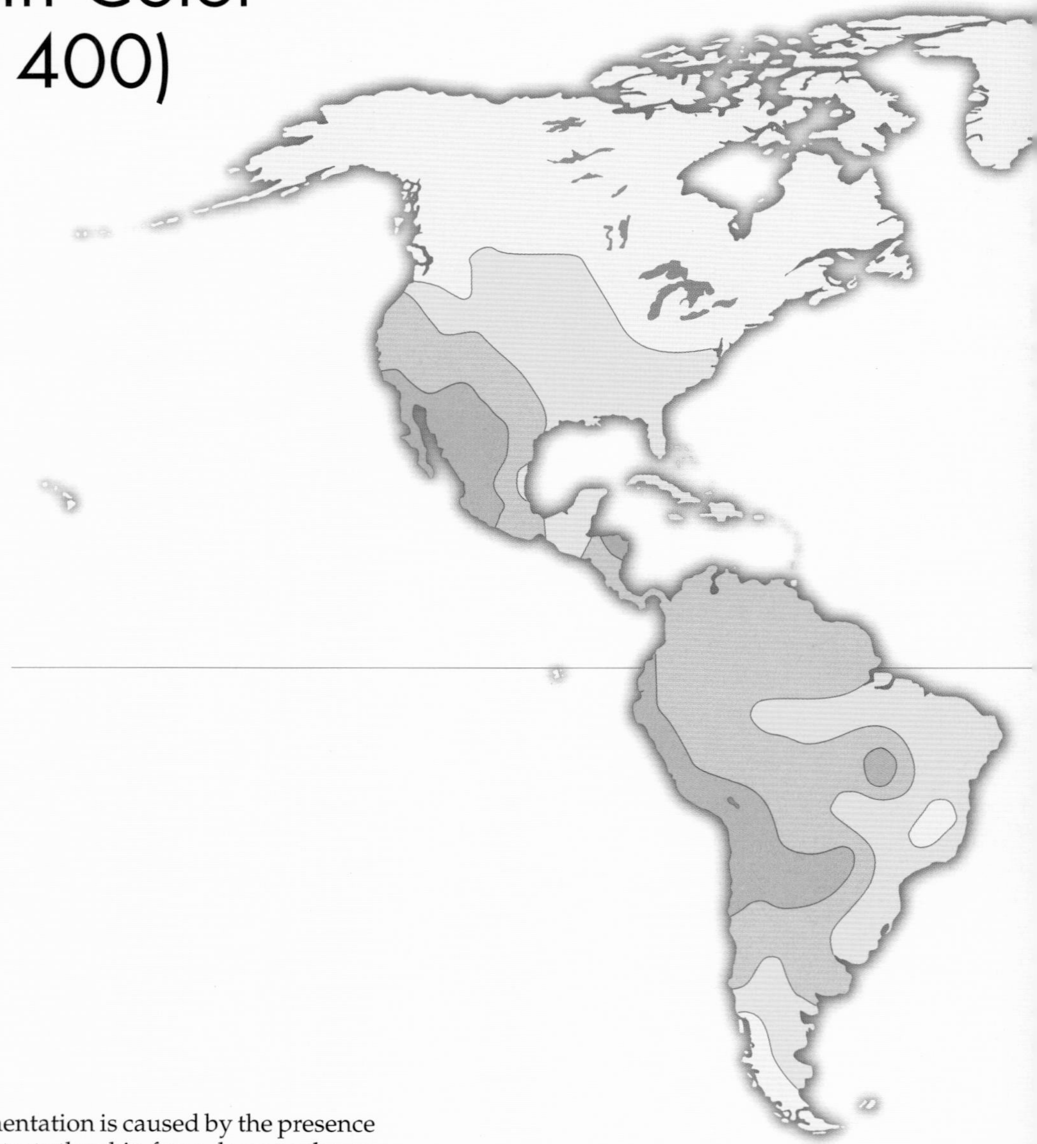

Human skin color varies. The pigmentation is caused by the presence of melanin in the skin, which protects the skin from damage due to ultraviolet radiation. In areas with much UV radiation, people biologically adapted to their environments by increased melanin production.

QUESTIONS

Look at Map 7, "The Distribution of Human Skin Color (Before A.D. 1400)."

1. Where are the Native Americans with the darkest skin color located? What factors help explain this distribution?

2. In both western and eastern hemispheres, is the lightest skin color found in the north or the south? Outside Asia, where do you find skin color closest to northern Asian skin color? Is this surprising given what you have read about migrations and settlement history?

3. Where are skin colors darkest? How might you explain this distribution?

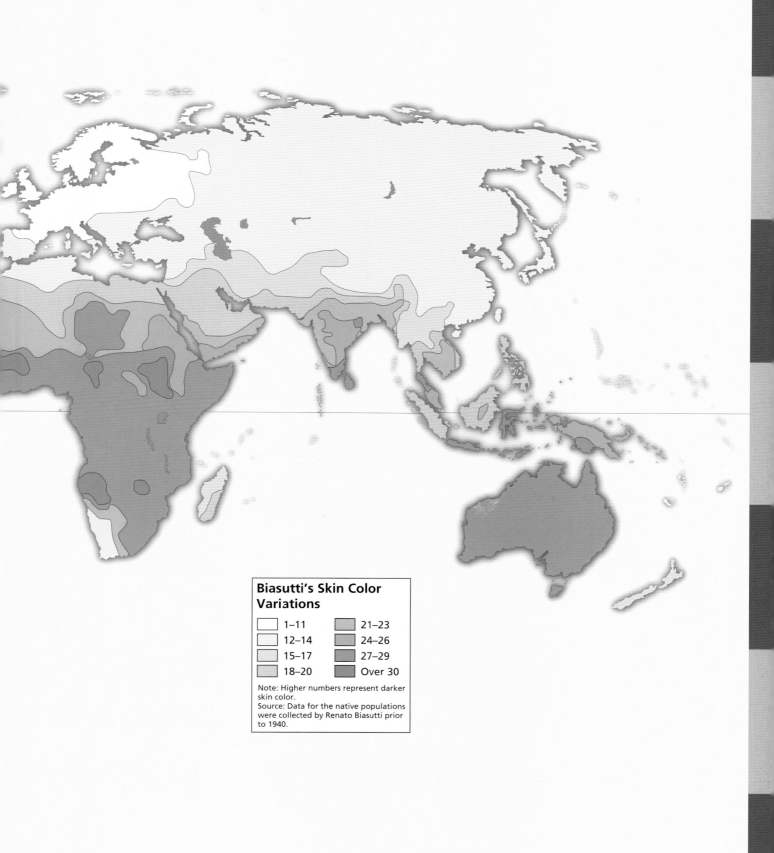

Biasutti's Skin Color Variations

☐ 1–11	☐ 21–23
☐ 12–14	☐ 24–26
☐ 15–17	☐ 27–29
☐ 18–20	☐ Over 30

Note: Higher numbers represent darker skin color.
Source: Data for the native populations were collected by Renato Biasutti prior to 1940.

MAP 8
The Origin and Spread of Food Production

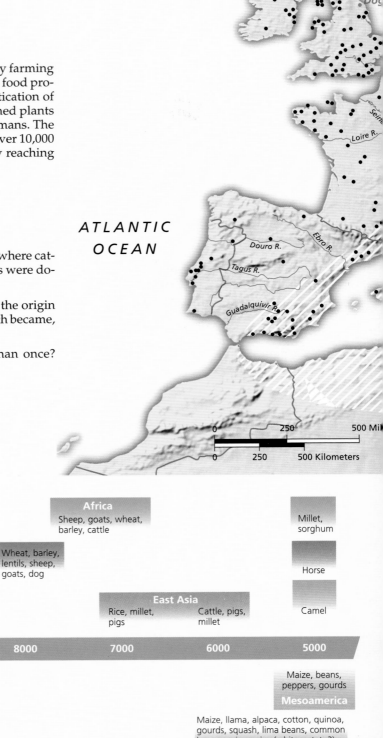

The Neolithic, or New Stone Age, refers to the period of early farming settlements when people who had been foragers shifted to food production. This pattern of subsistence was based on the domestication of plants and animals. Through domestication, people transformed plants and animals from their wild state to a form more useful to humans. The Neolithic began in the fertile crescent area of the Middle East over 10,000 years ago. It spread to the Levant and Mediterranean, finally reaching Britain and Scandinavia around 5,000 years ago.

QUESTIONS

Look at Map 8, "The Origin and Spread of Food Production."

1. Considering the map and the timeline, name three regions where cattle were domesticated. Based on the timeline, what animals were domesticated in North America?

2. Did Ireland receive Middle Eastern domesticates? What is the origin of the "Irish potato," or white potato (see the timeline), which became, much later, the caloric basis of Irish subsistence?

3. Besides cattle, what animals were domesticated more than once? Where were those areas of domestication?

ATLANTIC
OCEAN

Douro R.
Tagus R.
Ebro R.
Guadalquivir R.
Loire R.
Seine
Dog

0   250   500 Mil
0   250   500 Kilometers

		Africa		
		Sheep, goats, wheat, barley, cattle		Millet, sorghum

	Southern Europe			
Dog	Cattle	Wheat, barley, lentils, sheep, goats, dog		Horse

Middle East/SW Asia					East Asia		
Dog	Sheep	Goats, wheat barley, dog, cattle, lentils	Dog		Rice, millet, pigs	Cattle, pigs, millet	Camel

11,000 Years Ago	10,000	9000	8000	7000	6000	5000

Dog		Squash				Maize, beans, peppers, gourds
						Mesoamerica

Maize, llama, alpaca, cotton, quinoa, gourds, squash, lima beans, common beans, guinea pigs (white potato?)
South America (Andes)

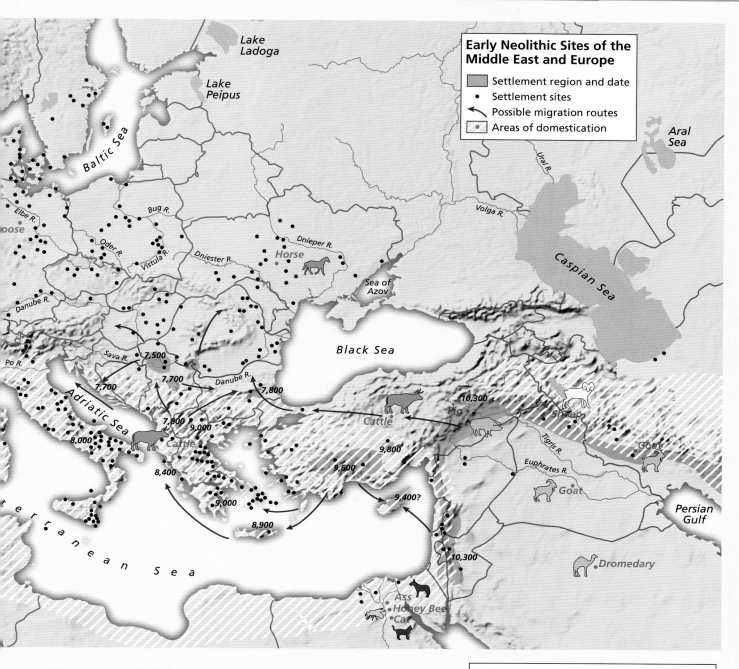

Early Neolithic Sites of the Middle East and Europe

- Settlement region and date
- • Settlement sites
- ← Possible migration routes
- Areas of domestication

Lake Ladoga

Lake Peipus

Baltic Sea

Aral Sea

Elbe R.

oose

Bug R.

Oder R.

Vistula R.

Dniester R.

Dnieper R.

Horse

Sea of Azov

Volga R.

Ural R.

Caspian Sea

Danube R.

Po R.

Sava R.

7,500

7,700

7,700

Danube R.

7,800

Black Sea

Adriatic Sea

7,800

9,000

8,000

Cattle

8,400

9,000

8,900

9,600

9,800

9,400?

Cattle

Pig

10,300

Sheep

Goat

Tigris R.

Euphrates R.

Goat

Goat

Persian Gulf

Dromedary

10,300

Ass

Honey Bee

Cat

terranean Sea

Mediterranean Domestication

Barley	Dates	Grapes
Cattle	Garlic	Lentils
Celery	Goat	Lettuce
		Olives

Southwest Asia Domestication

Barley	Duck	Melons
Beans	Fruits (seed	Oats
Beets	and stone)	Oil seeds
Camel (Bactrian)	Goat	Onions
Carrots	Grapes	Rye
Cattle	Hemp	Sheep
Dog	Horse	Wheat

Yam, oil palm

Cat (Egypt)

Chickens (south-central Asia)

4000	3000	2000	1000 Years Ago

Marsh elder
Sunflower
Squash

Lamb's quarters

Maize

North America

White potato

MAP 9

Ancient Civilizations of the Old World

A rchaic states developed in many parts of the Old World at different periods. The earliest civilizations, such as Mesopotamia, Egypt, and the Indus Valley, are generally placed at about 5500 B.P. States developed later in Asia, Africa, and the Americas (see Map 13).

QUESTIONS

Look at Map 9, "Ancient Civilizations of the Old World."

1. What contemporary nations would you have to visit if you wanted to see all the places where ancient civilizations developed in the Old World? Would some countries be off limits for political reasons? How do you think such limitations have affected the archaeological record?

2. Of the ancient states shown on Map 9, which developed latest? Why do you think the first states developed when and where they did?

3. In which of the ancient states shown on Map 9 were Middle Eastern domesticates basic to the economy? In which states shown on Map 9 were other domesticates basic to the economy?

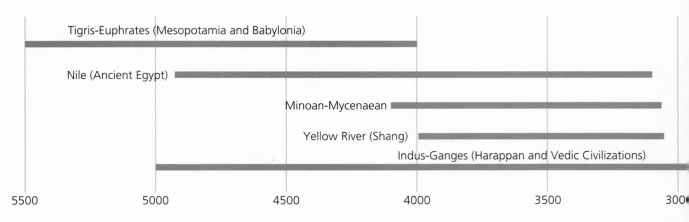

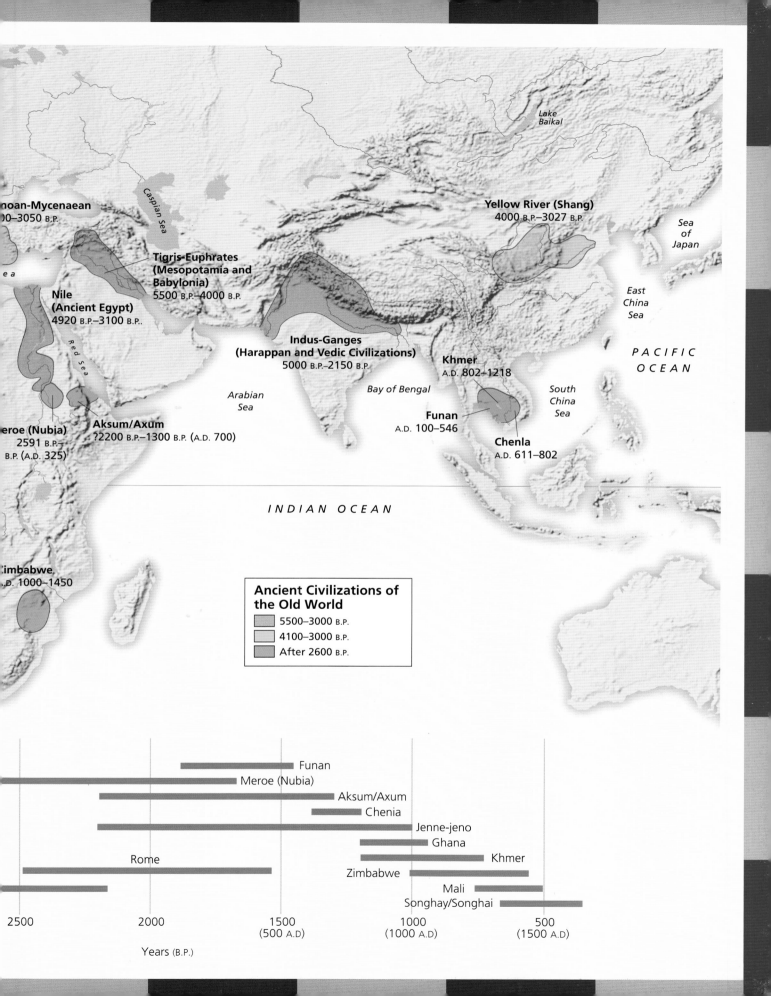

noan-Mycenaean
00–3050 B.P.

Yellow River (Shang)
4000 B.P.–3027 B.P.

*Lake
Baikal*

Caspian Sea

Tigris-Euphrates
(Mesopotamia and
Babylonia)
5500 B.P.–4000 B.P.

Nile
(Ancient Egypt)
4920 B.P.–3100 B.P.

Red Sea

Indus-Ganges
(Harappan and Vedic Civilizations)
5000 B.P.–2150 B.P.

*Sea
of
Japan*

*East
China
Sea*

Khmer
A.D. 802–1218

*Arabian
Sea*

Bay of Bengal

*South
China
Sea*

*PACIFIC
OCEAN*

Funan
A.D. 100–546

eroe (Nubia)
2591 B.P.–
B.P. (A.D. 325)

Aksum/Axum
?2200 B.P.–1300 B.P. (A.D. 700)

Chenla
A.D. 611–802

INDIAN OCEAN

imbabwe,
.D. 1000–1450

**Ancient Civilizations of
the Old World**
5500–3000 B.P.
4100–3000 B.P.
After 2600 B.P.

Funan
Meroe (Nubia)
Aksum/Axum
Chenia
Jenne-jeno
Ghana
Khmer
Rome
Zimbabwe
Mali
Songhay/Songhai

2500   2000   1500   1000   500
                      (500 A.D)   (1000 A.D)   (1500 A.D)

Years (B.P.)

MAP 10
Ethnographic Study Sites Prior to 1950

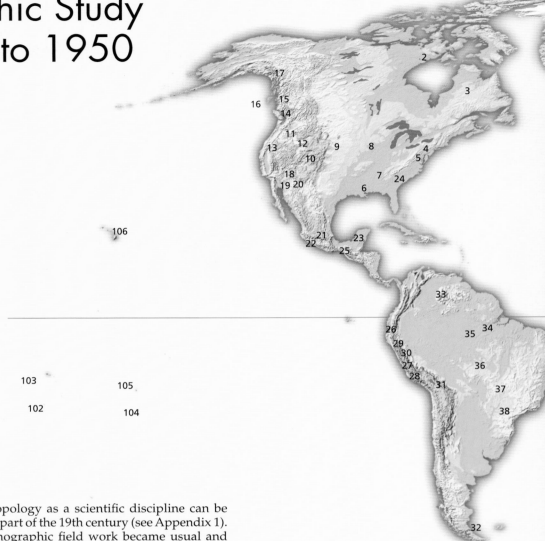

The development of anthropology as a scientific discipline can be traced to the middle to late part of the 19th century (see Appendix 1). In cultural anthropology, ethnographic field work became usual and common during the early 20th century. American ethnographers turned to the study of Native Americans, while European anthropologists often studied people living in world areas, such as Africa, which had been conquered and/or colonized by the anthropologist's nation of origin.

QUESTIONS

Look at Map 10, "Ethnographic Study Sites Prior to 1950."

1. Anthropology originated as the scientific study of nonwestern peoples and cultures. Yet Map 10 shows that many anthropological studies conducted prior to 1950 were done in North America. What societies were being studied in North America? Were they considered western or nonwestern? What does this tell us about the concept of "western"?

2. How would you describe the range of ethnographic sites prior to 1950? Were some world areas being neglected, such as the Middle East or mainland Asia? What might be the reasons for such omissions?

3. Think about how changes in transportation and communication have affected the way anthropologists do their research. How might a list of contemporary ethnographic sites contrast with the distribution shown in Map 10. How has longitudinal research been affected by changes in transportation and communication?

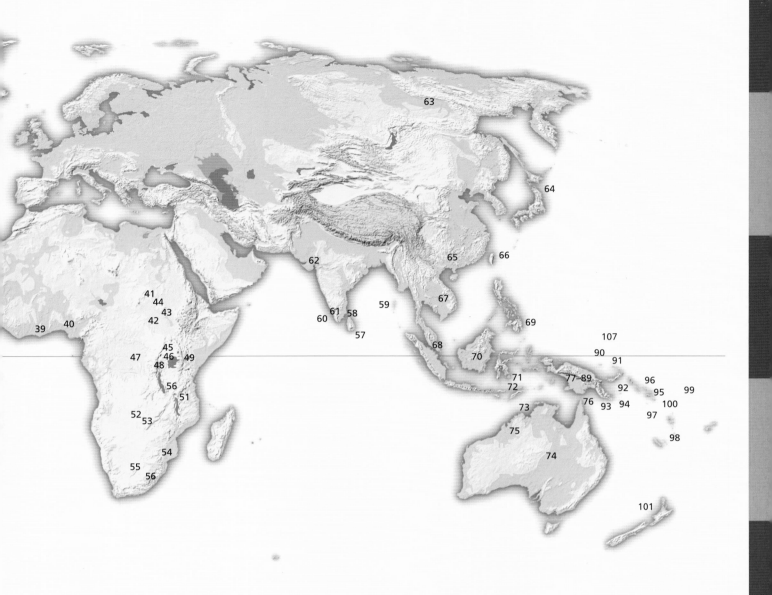

Ethnographic Study Sites Prior to 1950

North America
1. Eastern Eskimo
2. Central Eskimo
3. Naskapi
4. Iroquois
5. Delaware
6. Natchez
7. Shawnee
8. Kickapoo
9. Sioux
10. Crow
11. Nez Percé
12. Shoshone
13. Paviotso
14. Kwakiutl
15. Tsimshian
16. Haida
17. Tlingit
18. Navajo
19. Hopi
20. Zuñi
21. Aztec
22. Tzintzuntzan and Cuanajo
23. Maya
24. Cherokee
25. San Pedro

South America
Ecuador
26. Jívaro
Peru
27. Inca
28. Machiguenga
29. Achuara
30. Campa
Bolivia
31. Aymara
Chile
32. Yahgan
Venezuela
33. Yanomamö
Brazil
34. Tapirapé
35. Mundurucu
36. Mehinacu
37. Kuikuru
38. Caingang

Africa
Ghana
39. Ashanti
Nigeria
40. Kadar

Sudan
41. Fur
42. Dinka
43. Nuer
44. Azande
Uganda
45. Bunyoro
46. Ganda
Dem. Rep. of Congo
47. Mbuti
Rwanda
48. Watusi
Kenya
49. Masai
Tanzania
50. Nyakyusa
51. Lovedu
Zambia
52. Ndembu
53. Barotse
Mozambique
54. Bathonga
South Africa
55. !Kung Bushmen
56. Zulu

Asia
Sri Lanka
57. Vedda
58. Sinhalese
India
59. Andaman
60. Nayar
61. Tamil
62. Rajput
Siberia
63. Tungus
Japan
64. Ainu
China
65. Luts'un village
Taiwan
66. Taiwan Chinese
Vietnam
67. Mnong-Gar
Malaya
68. Semai

Pacific
Philippines
69. Tasaday
Indonesia Area
70. Dyaks
71. Alorese
72. Tetum
Australia
73. Tiwi
74. Arunta
75. Murngin
76. Saibai Islanders
New Guinea
77. Arapesh
78. Dani
79. Gururumba
80. Kai
81. Kapauku
82. Mae Enga
83. Kuma
84. Mundugumor
85. Tchambuli
86. Tsembaga Maring
87. Tavade
88. Foré
89. Etoro

Melanesian Islands
90. Manus Islanders
91. New Hanover Islanders
92. Trobriand Islanders
93. Dobuans
94. Rossel Islanders
95. Kaoka
96. Malaita Islanders
97. Espiritu Santo Islanders
98. Tana Islanders
99. Tikopia
100. Sivai
Polynesian Islands
101. Maori
102. Tongans
103. Samoans
104. Mangians
105. Tahitians
106. Hawaiians
Micronesian Islands
107. Truk

MAP 11
Major Families of World Languages

Language, like religion, is an important identifying and distinguishing characteristic of culture. Knowing the distribution of the major world languages and language families helps us understand some of the reasons behind important current events. In areas that have emerged from recent colonial rule, for example, the participants in conflicts over territory and power are often defined in terms of linguistic groups. Language distributions also help us understand our past by providing clues that enable us to chart the course of human migrations, as is suggested by the distribution of Indo-European, Austronesian, and Hamito-Semitic languages.

QUESTIONS

Look at Map 11, "Major Families of World Languages."

1. Name three language families or subfamilies that are spoken on more than one continent. How do you explain this distribution?

2. Where are the Austronesian languages spoken? How might one explain this distribution?

3. What language families are spoken on the African continent? Locate the Niger-Congo language family, of which the Bantu languages comprise a subfamily.

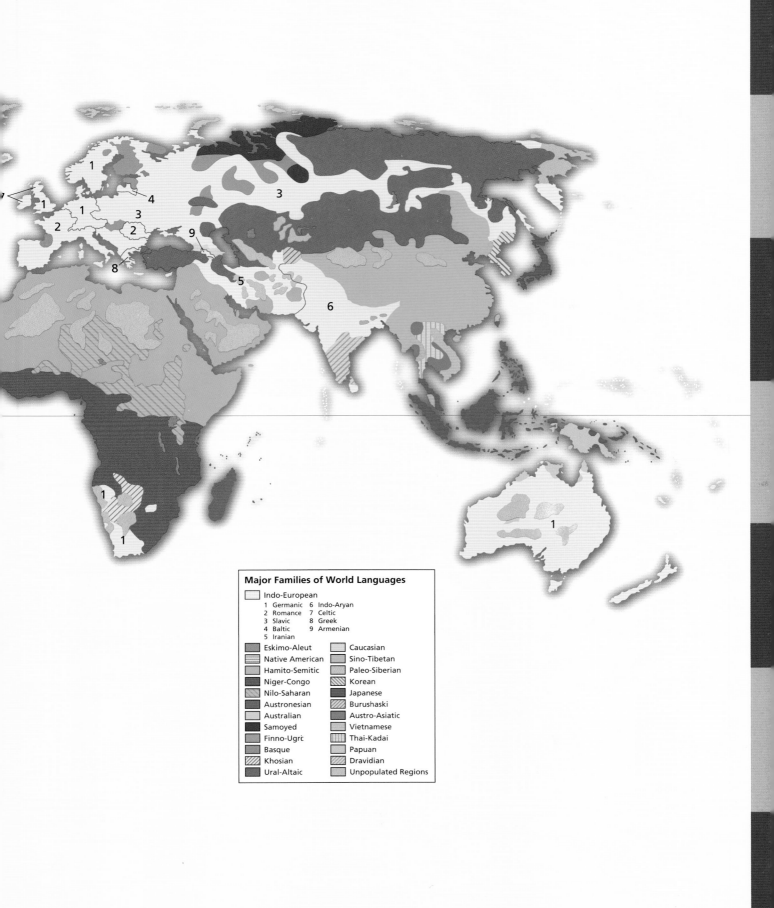

Major Families of World Languages

Indo-European
1 Germanic 6 Indo-Aryan
2 Romance 7 Celtic
3 Slavic 8 Greek
4 Baltic 9 Armenian
5 Iranian

Eskimo-Aleut
Native American
Hamito-Semitic
Niger-Congo
Nilo-Saharan
Austronesian
Australian
Samoyed
Finno-Ugric
Basque
Khosian
Ural-Altaic

Caucasian
Sino-Tibetan
Paleo-Siberian
Korean
Japanese
Burushaski
Austro-Asiatic
Vietnamese
Thai-Kadai
Papuan
Dravidian
Unpopulated Regions

MAP 12
World Land Use,
A.D. 1500

In the late 1400s there were a variety of self-sustaining economies in the world. Foragers hunted and gathered wild forms of animals and plants. Horticulturalists practiced a simple form of cultivation, using hoes or digging sticks as their basic tools. They sometimes cleared their land by burning, and then planted crops. Pastoralists herded animals as their basic subsistence pattern. Some state-level societies, such as the Mongols, had pastoralism as their economic base. Intensive agriculturalists based their subsistence economies on complicated irrigation systems and/or the plow and draft animals. Wheat and rice were two kinds of crops that supported large populations

QUESTIONS

Look at Map 12, "World Land Use, A.D. 1500."

1. Name three continents with significant herding economies. On which continents was pastoralism absent?

2. How do the various types of agriculture vary among the continents? Which continent had the largest area under intensive cultivation? Which continent or continents had the least amount of intensive cultivation?

3. What were the main uses of land in Europe when the European age of discovery and conquest began?

World Land Use, A.D. 1500

- Foraging
- Pastoralism
- Horticulture
- Intensive agriculture

MAP 13

Organized States and Chiefdoms, A.D. 1500

TARASCA

PACIFIC
OCEAN

AZTEC STATE

OTHER MEXICAN STATES

CHIBCHA

INCA STATE

ATLANTIC
OCEAN

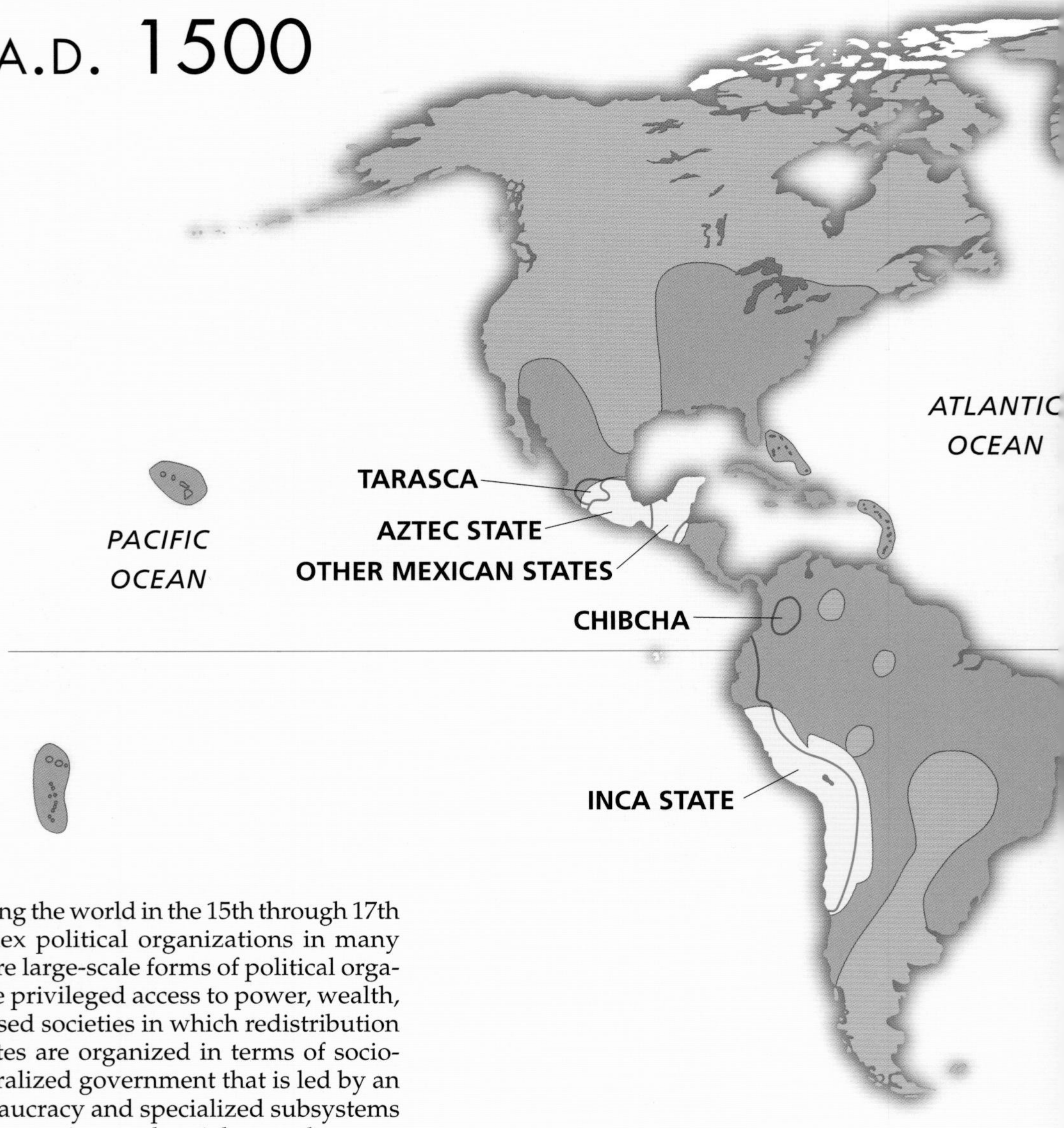

When Europeans started exploring the world in the 15th through 17th centuries, they found complex political organizations in many places. Both chiefdoms and states are large-scale forms of political organization in which some people have privileged access to power, wealth, and prestige. Chiefdoms are kin-based societies in which redistribution is the major economic pattern. States are organized in terms of socioeconomic classes, headed by a centralized government that is led by an elite. States include a full-time bureaucracy and specialized subsystems for such activities as military action, taxation, and social control.

QUESTIONS

Look at Map 13, "Organized States and Chiefdoms, A.D. 1500."

1. Locate and name the states that existed in the Western Hemisphere in A.D. 1500. Compare Map 12, "World Land Use: A.D. 1500," with Map 13. Looking at the Western Hemisphere, can you detect a correlation between land use (and economy) and the existence of states? What's the nature of that correlation? Does that correlation also characterize other parts of the world?

2. Locate three regions of the world where chiefdoms existed in A.D. 1500. Compare Map 12, "World Land Use: A.D. 1500," with Map 13. Can you detect a correlation between land use (and economy) and the existence of chiefdoms? What's the nature of that correlation?

3. Some parts of the world lacked either chiefdoms or states in A.D. 1500. What are some of those areas? What kinds of political systems did they probably have?

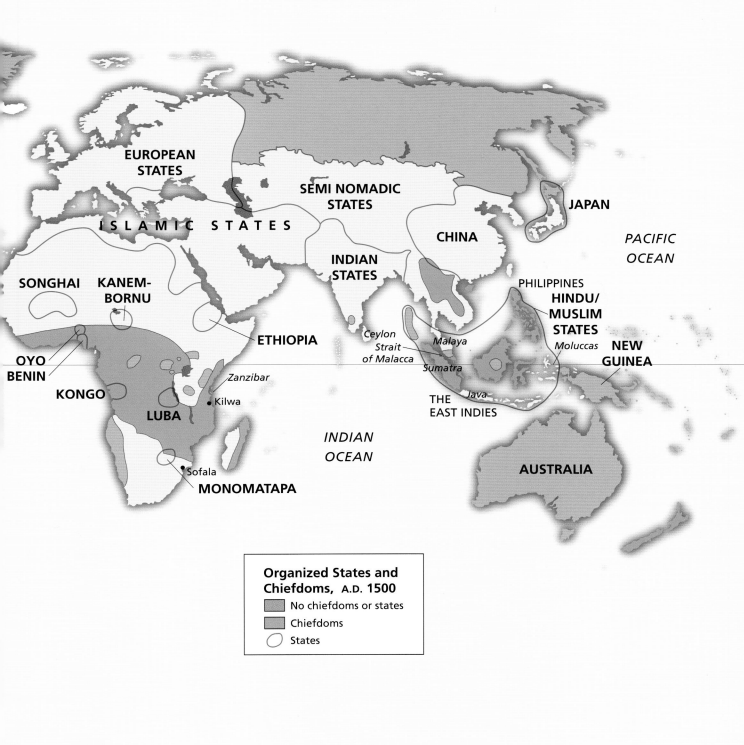

EUROPEAN
STATES

SEMI NOMADIC
STATES

JAPAN

PACIFIC
OCEAN

ISLAMIC STATES

CHINA

INDIAN
STATES

SONGHAI

KANEM-
BORNU

ETHIOPIA

PHILIPPINES

HINDU/
MUSLIM
STATES

OYO
BENIN

Ceylon
Strait
of Malacca

Malaya

Moluccas

NEW
GUINEA

KONGO

Zanzibar

Sumatra

Kilwa

LUBA

Java

THE
EAST INDIES

INDIAN
OCEAN

Sofala

AUSTRALIA

MONOMATAPA

**Organized States and
Chiefdoms,** A.D. **1500**

No chiefdoms or states

Chiefdoms

States

MAP 14

Female/Male Inequality in Education and Employment

Women in developed countries have made significant advances in socioeconomic status in recent years. In most of the world, however, females suffer from significant inequality when compared with their male counterparts. Although women can vote in most countries, in over 90 percent of those countries that right was granted only during the last 50 years. In most regions, literacy rates for women still fall far short of those for men. In Africa and Asia, for example, only about half as many women are as literate as men. Inequalities in education and employment are perhaps the most telling indicators of the unequal status of women in most of the world. Even where women are employed in positions similar to those held by men, they tend to receive less compensation. The gap between rich and poor involves not only a clear geographic differentiation, but a clear gender differentiation as well.

QUESTIONS

Look at Map 14 "Female/Male Inequality in Education and Employment."

1. Locate and name three Third World countries with the same degree of gender-based inequality as the United States and Canada.

2. Two of the world's largest developing nations are coded as having "less inequality." What are they?

3. Most European countries are coded as having "least inequality." Which western European countries are exceptions?

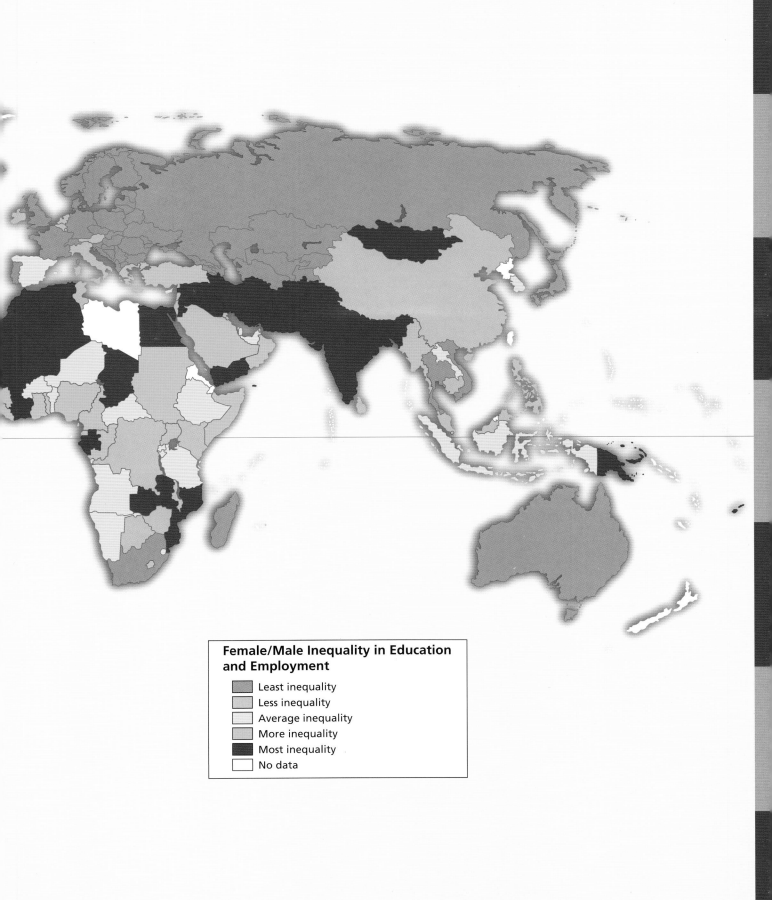

Female/Male Inequality in Education and Employment

- Least inequality
- Less inequality
- Average inequality
- More inequality
- Most inequality
- No data

MAP 15
World Religions

Because religion is a fundamental characteristic of human culture, a depiction of the spatial distribution of religions comes close to a map of cultural patterns. More than just a set of behavior patterns having to do with worship and ceremony, religion influences the ways in which people deal with one another, with their institutions, and with their environments. An examination of this map in the context of conflict within and among nations also shows that the tension between countries and the internal stability of states are also functions of the spatial distribution of religion.

QUESTIONS

Look at Map 15, "World Religions."

1. Which continent has the most diversity with respect to the major religions?

2. Which continent is most Protestant? Why do you think that is the case?

3. Where in the world are "tribal" religions still practiced?

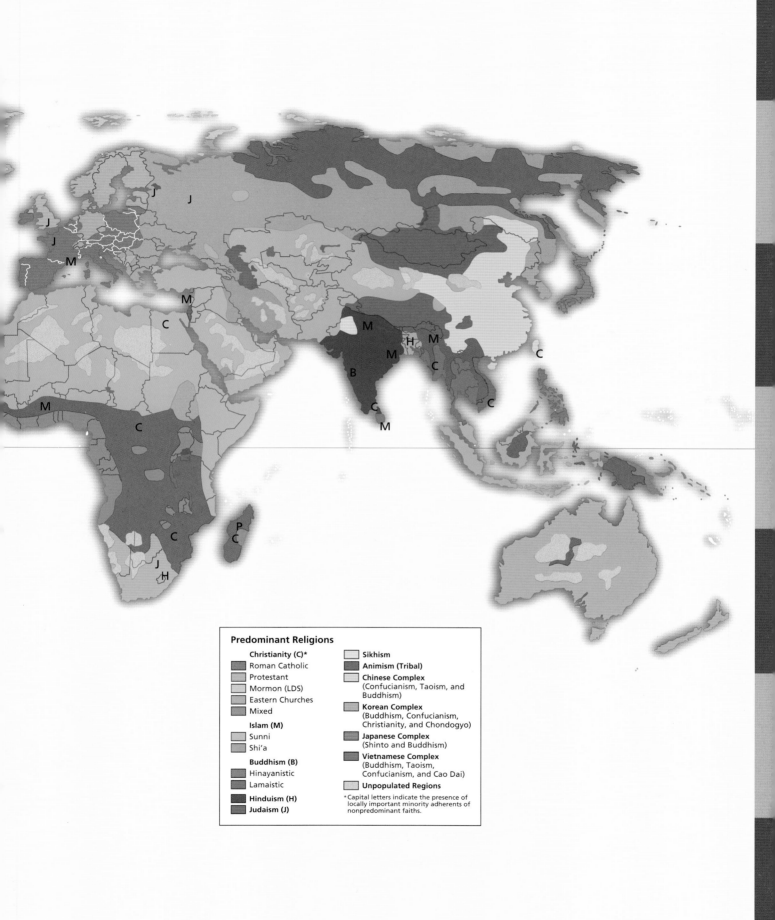

Predominant Religions

Christianity (C)*
- Roman Catholic
- Protestant
- Mormon (LDS)
- Eastern Churches
- Mixed

Islam (M)
- Sunni
- Shi'a

Buddhism (B)
- Hinayanistic
- Lamaistic

Hinduism (H)

Judaism (J)

- Sikhism
- **Animism (Tribal)**
- **Chinese Complex** (Confucianism, Taoism, and Buddhism)
- **Korean Complex** (Buddhism, Confucianism, Christianity, and Chondogyo)
- **Japanese Complex** (Shinto and Buddhism)
- **Vietnamese Complex** (Buddhism, Taoism, Confucianism, and Cao Dai)
- **Unpopulated Regions**

*Capital letters indicate the presence of locally important minority adherents of nonpredominant faiths.

MAP 16

Annual Energy Consumption per Capita

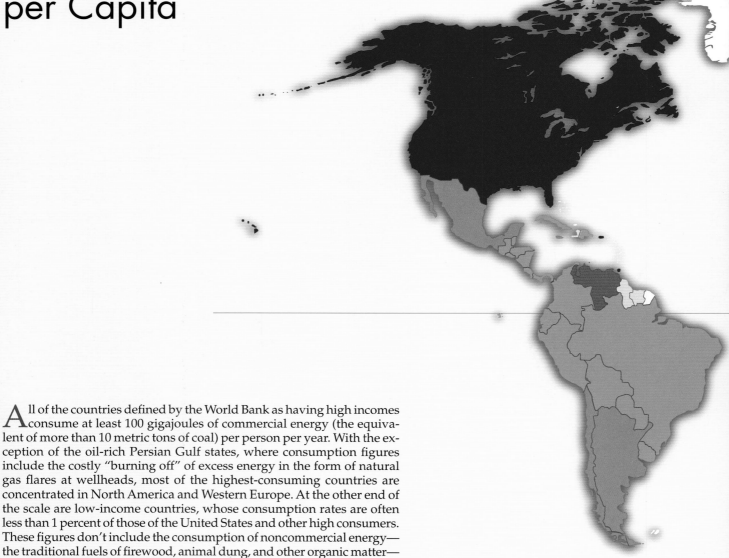

All of the countries defined by the World Bank as having high incomes consume at least 100 gigajoules of commercial energy (the equivalent of more than 10 metric tons of coal) per person per year. With the exception of the oil-rich Persian Gulf states, where consumption figures include the costly "burning off" of excess energy in the form of natural gas flares at wellheads, most of the highest-consuming countries are concentrated in North America and Western Europe. At the other end of the scale are low-income countries, whose consumption rates are often less than 1 percent of those of the United States and other high consumers. These figures don't include the consumption of noncommercial energy—the traditional fuels of firewood, animal dung, and other organic matter—widely used in the less developed parts of the world.

QUESTIONS

Look at Map 16, "Annual Energy Consumption Per Capita."

1. Compare energy consumption in Europe and North America. Do all European countries consume energy at the same rate as the United States and Canada?

2. What are some exceptions to the generalization that the highest rates of energy consumption are in core countries, with the lowest rates on the periphery.

3. How is energy consumption related to measures of the quality of life, as shown in Map 17?

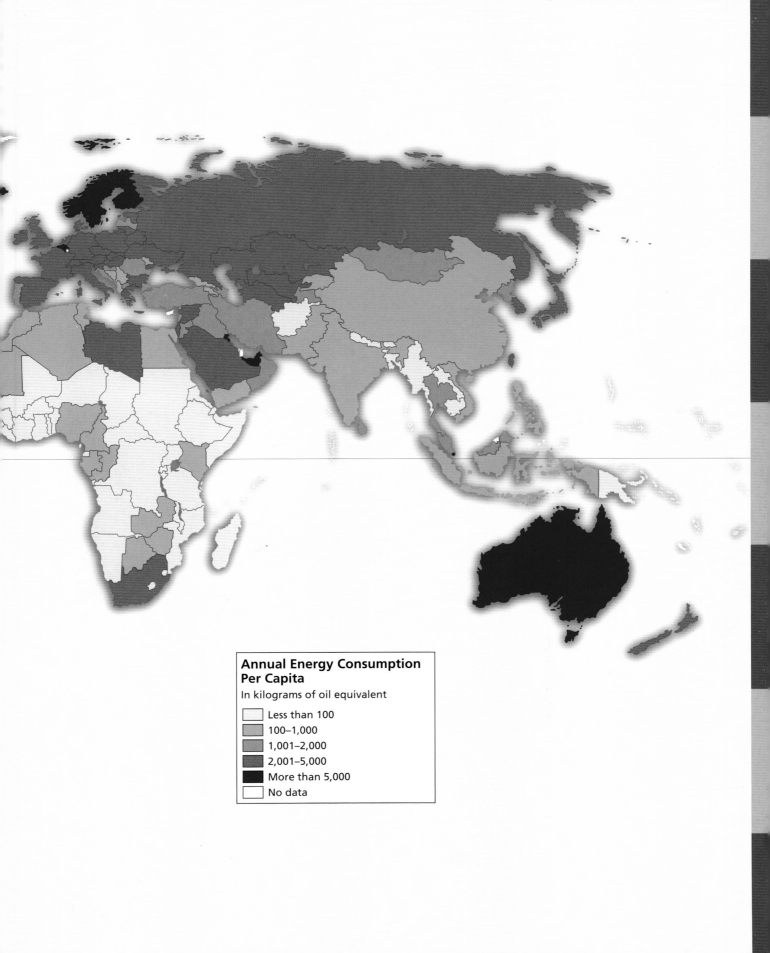

Annual Energy Consumption Per Capita

In kilograms of oil equivalent

- Less than 100
- 100–1,000
- 1,001–2,000
- 2,001–5,000
- More than 5,000
- No data

MAP 17

The Quality of Life: The Index of Human Development

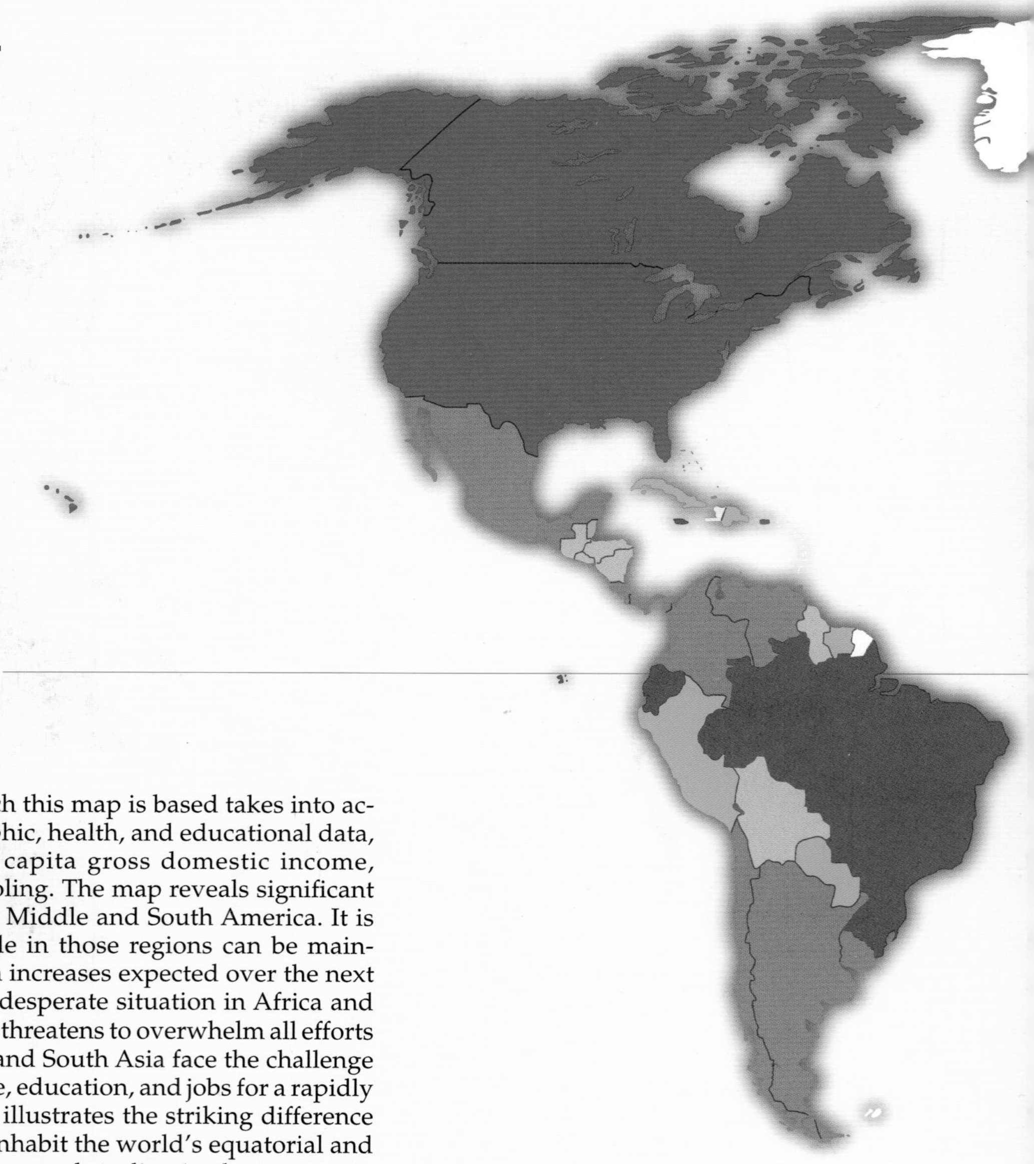

The development index upon which this map is based takes into account a wide variety of demographic, health, and educational data, including population growth, per capita gross domestic income, longevity, literacy, and years of schooling. The map reveals significant improvement in the quality of life in Middle and South America. It is questionable whether the gains made in those regions can be maintained given the dramatic population increases expected over the next 30 years. This map illustrates a near desperate situation in Africa and South Asia, where population growth threatens to overwhelm all efforts to improve the quality of life. Africa and South Asia face the challenge of providing basic access to health care, education, and jobs for a rapidly increasing population. The map also illustrates the striking difference in quality of life between those who inhabit the world's equatorial and tropical regions and those fortunate enough to live in the temperate zones, where the quality of life is significantly higher.

QUESTIONS

Look at Map 17, "The Quality of Life: The Index of Human Development."

1. What countries in central and South America have Human Development Index (HDI) scores comparable to those of some European nations? Does this surprise you?

2. Given that Brazil has one of the world's top 10 economies, does its HDI score surprise you? How do Brazil, Mexico, and Venezuela compare in terms of the HDI?

3. Do you notice a correlation between deforestation (Map 1) and quality of life? Does India fit this correlation?